A SELECT LIBRARY

OF THE

NICENE AND POST-NICENE FATHERS

OF

THE CHRISTIAN CHURCH

EDITED BY

PHILIP SCHAFF, D.D., LL.D.,

PROFESSOR IN THE UNION THEOLOGICAL SEMINARY, NEW YORK,

IN CONNECTION WITH A NUMBER OF PATRISTIC SCHOLARS OF EUROPE
AND AMERICA.

VOLUME III

ST. AUGUSTIN:

ON THE HOLY TRINITY
DOCTRINAL TREATISES
MORAL TREATISES

WM. B. EERDMANS PUBLISHING COMPANY
GRAND RAPIDS   MICHIGAN

ISBN 0-8028-8100

Reprinted, September 1980

PHOTOLITHOPRINTED BY CUSHING - MALLOY, INC.
ANN ARBOR, MICHIGAN, UNITED STATES OF AMERICA

PREFACE.

THIS third volume contains the most important doctrinal and moral treatises of St. Augustin, and presents a pretty complete view of his dogmatics and ethics.

The most weighty of the doctrinal treatises is that on the *Holy Trinity*. The Latin original (*De Trinitate contra Arianos libri quindecim*), is contained in the 8th volume of the Benedictine edition. It is the most elaborate, and probably also the ablest and profoundest patristic discussion of this central doctrine of the Christian religion, unless we except the *Orations against the Arians*, by Athanasius, "the Father of Orthodoxy," who devoted his life to the defense of the Divinity of Christ. Augustin, owing to his defective knowledge of Greek, wrote his work independently of the previous treatises of the Eastern Church on that subject. He bestowed more time and care upon it than on any other book, except the *City of God*.

The value of the present translation, which first appeared in Mr. Clark's edition, 1873, has been much increased by the revision, the introductory essay, and the critical notes of a distinguished American divine, who is in full sympathy with St. Augustin, and thoroughly at home in the history of this dogma. I could not have intrusted it to abler hands than those of my friend and colleague, Dr. Shedd.

The moral treatises (contained in the 6th volume of the Benedictine edition) were first translated for the Oxford Library of the Fathers (1847). They contain much that will instruct and interest the reader; while some views will appear strange to those who fail to distinguish between different ages and different types of virtue and piety. Augustin shared with the Greek and Latin fathers the ascetic preference for voluntary celibacy and poverty. He accepted the distinction which dates from the second century, between two kinds of morality: a lower morality of the common people, which consists in keeping the ten commandments; and a higher sanctity of the elect few, which observes, in addition, the evangelical counsels, so called, or the monastic virtues. He practiced this doctrine after his conversion. He ought to have married the mother of his son; but in devoting himself to the priesthood, he felt it his duty to remain unmarried, according to the prevailing spirit of the church in his age. His teacher, Ambrose, and his older contemporary, Jerome, went still further in the enthusiastic praise of single life. We must admire their power of self-denial and undivided consecration, though we may dissent from their theory.[1]

---

[1] On the ascetic tendencies of the second and third centuries, and the gradual introduction of clerical celibacy (which began with a decree of Bishop Siricius of Rome, 385), see Schaff, *Church Hist.*, vol. ii. 367-414, and vol. iii. 242-250.

The asceticism of the early church was a reaction against the awful sexual corruption of surrounding heathenism, and with all its excesses it accomplished a great deal of good. It prepared the way for Christian family life. The fathers appealed to the example of Christ, who in this respect, as the Son of God, stood above ordinary human relations, and the advice of St. Paul, which was given in view of "the present distress," in times of persecution. They deemed single life better adapted to the undivided service of Christ and his church than the married state with its unavoidable secular cares (1 Cor. vii. 25 sqq.). Augustin expresses this view when he says, on *Virginity*, § 27 :

"Therefore go on, Saints of God. boys and girls, males and females, unmarried men and women ; go on and persevere unto the end. Praise more sweetly the Lord, whom ye think on more richly ; hope more happily in Him, whom ye serve more earnestly ; love more ardently Him, whom ye please more attentively. With loins girded, and lamps burning, wait for the Lord, when He returns from the marriage. Ye shall bring unto the marriage of the Lamb a new song, which ye shall sing on your harps."

The Reformation has abolished the system of monasticism and clerical celibacy, and substituted for it, as the normal condition for the clergy as well as the laity, the purity, chastity and beauty of family life, instituted by God in Paradise and sanctioned by our Saviour's presence at the wedding at Cana.

New York, March, 1887

CONTENTS.

ST. AUGUSTIN:

ON THE TRINITY

[DE TRINITATE, LIBRI XV.]

TRANSLATED BY THE

REV. ARTHUR WEST HADDAN, B.D.,

HON. CANON OF WORCESTER, AND RECTOR OF BARTON-ON-THE-HEATH, WARWICKSHIRE.

REVISED AND ANNOTATED, WITH AN INTRODUCTORY ESSAY,

BY

WILLIAM G. T. SHEDD, D.D.,

ROOSEVELT PROFESSOR OF SYSTEMATIC THEOLOGY IN UNION THEOLOGICAL
SEMINARY, NEW YORK.

INTRODUCTORY ESSAY.

By William G. T. Shedd, D.D.

The doctrine of the Divine Unity is a truth of natural religion; the doctrine of the Trinity is a truth of revealed religion. The various systems of natural theism present arguments for the Divine existence, unity, and attributes, but proceed no further. They do not assert and endeavor to demonstrate that the Supreme Being is three persons in one essence. It is because this doctrine is not discoverable by human reason, that the Christian church has been somewhat shy of attempts to construct it analytically; or even to defend it upon grounds of reason. The keen Dr. South expresses the common sentiment, when he remarks that " as he that denies this fundamental article of the Christian religion may lose his soul, so he that much strives to understand it may lose his wits." Yet all the truths of revelation, like those of natural religion, have in them the element of reason, and are capable of a rational defense. At the very least their self-consistence can be shown, and objections to them can be answered. And this is a rational process. For one of the surest characteristics of reason is, freedom from self contradiction, and consonance with acknowledged truths in other provinces of human inquiry and belief.

It is a remarkable fact, that the earlier forms of Trinitarianism are among the most metaphysical and speculative of any in dogmatic history. The controversy with the Arian and the Semi-Arian, brought out a statement and defense of the truth, not only upon scriptural but ontological grounds. Such a powerful dialectician as Athanasius, while thoroughly and intensely scriptural—while starting from the text of scripture, and subjecting it to a rigorous exegesis—did not hesitate to pursue the Arian and Semi-Arian dialectics to its most recondite fallacy in its subtlest recesses. If any one doubts this, let him read the four Orations of Athanasius, and his defence of the Nicene Decrees. In some sections of Christendom, it has been contended that the doctrine of the Trinity should be received without any attempt at all to establish its rationality and intrinsic necessity. In this case, the tenets of eternal generation and procession have been regarded as going beyond the Scripture data, and if not positively rejected, have been thought to hinder rather than assist faith in three divine persons and one God. But the history of opinions shows that such sections of the church have not proved to be the strongest defenders of the Scripture statement, nor the most successful in keeping clear of the Sabellian, Arian, or even Socinian departure from it.

Those churches which have followed Scripture most implicitly, and have most feared human speculation, are the very churches which have inserted into their creeds the most highly analytic statement that has yet been made of the doctrine of the Trinity. The Nicene Trinitarianism is incorporated into nearly all the symbols of modern Christendom; and this specifies, particularly, the tenets of eternal generation and procession with their corollaries. The English Church, to whose great divines, Hooker, Bull, Waterland, and Pearson, scientific Trinitarianism owes a very lucid and careful statement, has added the Athanasian creed to the Nicene. The Presbyterian churches, distinguished for the closeness of their adherence to the simple Scripture, yet call upon their membership to confess, that " in the unity of the Godhead there be three persons, of one substance, power, and eternity; God the Father, God the Son, and God the Holy Ghost. The Father is of none, neither begotten nor proceeding; the Son is eternally begotten of the Father; the Holy Ghost eternally proceeding from the Father and the Son." [1]

The treatise of Augustin upon the Trinity, which is here made accessible to the English reader, is one of the ablest produced in the patristic age. The author devoted nearly thirty years of his matured life to its composition (A. D. 400 to 428). He was continually touching and retouching it, and would have delayed its publication longer than he did, had a copy not been obtained surreptitiously and published. He seems to have derived little assistance from others; for although the great Greek Trinitarians—Athanasius, the two Gregories, and Basil—had published their treatises, yet he informs us that his knowledge of Greek, though sufficient for understanding the exegetical and practical writings of his brethren of the Greek Church, was not adequate to the best use of their dialectical and metaphysical compositions. [2] Accordingly, there is no trace in this work of the writings of the Greek Trinitarians, though a substantial agreement with them. The only Trinitarian author to whom he alludes is Hilary—a highly acute and abstruse Trinitarian.

In his general position, Augustin agrees with the Nicene creed; but laying more emphasis upon the consubstantiality of the persons, and definitely asserting the procession of the Spirit from the Father and Son. Some dogmatic historians seem to imply that he differed materially from the Nicene doctrine on the point of *subordination*. Hagenbach (Smith's Ed. § 95) asserts that " Augustin completely purified the dogma of the Trinity from the older vestiges of subordination;" and adds that " such vestiges are unquestionably to be found in the most orthodox Fathers, not only in the East but also in the West." He cites Hilary and Athanasius as examples, and quotes the remark of Gieseler, that " the idea of a subordination lies at the basis of such declarations." Neander (II. 470, Note 2) says that Augustin " kept at a distance everything that bordered on subordinationism." These statements are certainly too sweeping and unqualified. There are three kinds of subordination: the filial or trinitarian; the theanthropic; and the Arian. The first is taught, and the second implied, in the Nicene creed. The last is denied and excluded. Accordingly, dogmatic historians like Petavius, Bull, Waterland, and Pearson, contend that the Nicene creed, in affirming the filial, but denying the Arian subordination; in teaching subordination as to person and relationship, but denying it as to essence; enunciates a revealed truth, and that this is endorsed by all the Trinitarian fathers, Eastern and Western. And there certainly can be no doubt that Augustin held this view. He maintains, over and over again, that Sonship as a relationship is second and subordinate to Fatherhood; that while a Divine Father and a Divine Son must necessarily be of the very same nature and grade of being, like a human father and a human son, yet the latter issues from the former, not the former from the latter. Augustin's phraseology on this point is as positive as that of Athanasius, and in some respects even more bold and capable of misinterpretation. He denominates the Father the " beginning " (principium) of the Son, and the Father and Son the " beginning " (principium) of the Holy Spirit. " The Father is the beginning of the whole divinity, or if it is better so expressed, deity." IV. xx. 29. " In their mutual relation to one another in the Trinity itself, if the begetter is a beginning (principium) in rela-

---

[1] Westminster Confession, II. iii.

[2] That Augustin had considerable acquaintance with Greek is proved by his many references and citations throughout his writings. In this work, see XII. vii. 11; XII. xiv. 22; XIII. x. 14; XIV. i. 1; XV. ix. 15. His statement in III. i. 1, is, that he was " not *so* familiar with the Greek tongue (*Græca lingua non sit nobis tantus habitus*), as to be able to read and understand the books that treat of such [metaphysical] topics." In V. viii. 10, he remarks that he does not comprehend the distinction which the Greek Trinitarians make between οὐσία and ὑπόστασις; which shows that he had not read the work of Gregory of Nyssa, in which it is defined with great clearness. One may have a good knowledge of a language for general purposes, and yet be unfamiliar with its philosophical nomenclature.

tion to that which he begets, the Father is a beginning in relation to the Son, because he begets Him." V. xiv. 15. Since the Holy Spirit proceeds from both Father and Son, "the Father and Son are a beginning (principium) of the Holy Spirit, not two beginnings." V. xiv. 15. Compare also V. xiii.; X. iv.; and annotations pp.   Augustin employs this term "beginning" only in relation to the person, not to the essence. There is no "beginning," or source, when the essence itself is spoken of. Consequently, the "subordination" (implied in a "beginning" by generation and spiration) is not the Arian subordination, as to essence, but the trinitarian subordination, as to person and relation.[1]

Augustin starts with the assumption that man was made in the image of the *triune* God, the God of revelation; not in the image of the God of natural religion, or the untriune deity of the nations. Consequently, it is to be expected that a trinitarian analogue can be found in his mental constitution. If man is God's image, he will show traces of it in every respect. All acknowledge that the Divine unity, and all the communicable attributes, have their finite correspondants in the unity and attributes of the human mind. But the Latin father goes further than this. This, in his view, is not the whole of the Divine image. When God says, "Let *us* make man in *our* image, after *our* likeness" (Gen. i. 26), Augustin understands these words to be spoken *by* the Trinity, and *of* the Trinity—by and of the true God, the God of revelation: the Father, Son, and Holy Spirit, one God. He denies that this is merely the *pluralis excellentiæ*, and that the meaning of these words would be expressed by a change of the plural to the singular, and to the reading, "Let *me* make man in *my* image, after *my* likeness." "For if the Father alone had made man without the Son, it would not have been written, 'Let us make man in our image, after our likeness.'" City of God XVI. vi.; Trinity I. vii. 14. In Augustin's opinion, the Old Testament declaration that God is a unity, does not exclude the New Testament declaration that he is a trinity. "For" says he, "that which is written, 'Hear O Israel: the Lord our God is one Lord' ought certainly not to be understood as if the Son were excepted, or the Holy Spirit were excepted; which one Lord our God we rightly call our Father, as regenerating us by his grace." Trinity V. xi. 12. How far Moses *understood* the full meaning of the Divine communication and instruction, is one thing. *Who* it really and actually was that made the communication to him, is another. Even if we assume, though with insufficient reason for so doing, that Moses himself had no intimation of the Trinity, it does not follow that it was not the Trinity that inspired him, and all the Hebrew prophets. The apostle Peter teaches that the Old Testament inspiration was a Trinitarian inspiration, when he says that "the prophets who prophesied of the grace that should come, searched what the Spirit of *Christ* which was in them did signify, when it testified beforehand of the sufferings of Christ, and the glory that should follow." (1 Pet. i. 10, 11).

In asserting, however, that an image of the Trinity exists in man's nature, Augustin is careful to observe that it is utterly imperfect and inadequate. He has no thought or expectation of clearing up the mystery by any analogy whatever. He often gives expression to his sense of the inscrutability and incomprehensibility of the Supreme Being, in language of the most lowly and awe-struck adoration. "I pray to our Lord God himself, of whom we ought always to think, and yet of whom we are not able to think worthily, and whom no speech is sufficient to declare, that He will grant me both help for understanding and explaining that which I design, and pardon if in anything I offend." V. i. 1. "O Lord the one God, God the Trinity, whatever I have said in these books that is of Thine, may they acknowledge who are Thine; if anything of my own, may it be pardoned both by Thee and by those who are Thine. Amen." XV. xxviii.

---

[1] For an analysis of Augustin's Trinitarianism, see Bauv: *Dreieinigkeitslehre* I. 828-885 ; Gangauf : *Des Augustinus speculative Lehre von Gott dem Dreieinigen;* Schaff: *History*, iii. 684 sq.

Augustin's method in this work is (1.) The exegetical; (2.) The rational. He first deduces the doctrine of the Trinity from Scripture, by a careful collation and combination of the texts, and then defends it against objections, and illustrates it by the analogies which he finds in nature generally, and in the human mind particularly. The Scripture argument is contained in the first seven books; the rational in the last eight. The first part is, of course, the most valuable of the two. Though the reader may not be able to agree with Augustin in his interpretation of some Scripture passages, particularly some which he cites from the Old Testament, he will certainly be impressed by the depth, acumen, and accuracy with which the Latin father reaches and exhausts the meaning of the acknowledged trinitarian texts. Augustin lived in an age when the Scriptures and the Greek and Roman classics were nearly all that the student had, upon which to expend his intellectual force. There was considerable metaphysics, it is true, but no physics, and little mathematics. There was consequently a more undivided and exclusive attention bestowed upon revealed religion as embodied in the Scriptures, and upon ethics and natural religion as contained in the classics, than has ever been bestowed by any subsequent period in Christendom. One result was that scripture was expounded by scripture; things spiritual by things spiritual. This appears in the exegetical part of this treatise. Augustin reasons out of the Scriptures; not out of metaphysics or physics.

The second, or speculative division of the work, is that which will be most foreign to the thinking of some trinitarians. In it they will find what seems to them to be a philosophy, rather than an interpretation of the word of God. We shall, therefore, in this introductory essay, specify some of the advantages, as it seems to us, of the general method of defending and illustrating the doctrine of the Trinity employed by Augustin and the patristic Trinitarians.

1. Fuller justice is done to Scripture by this method. Revelation denominates the first trinitarian person the Father, the second the Son, the third the Spirit. These terms are literal, not metaphorical; because the relations denoted by them are eternally in the essence. Scripture clearly teaches that the Father is such from eternity. Consequently, " paternity " (implied in the name Father) can no more be ascribed to the first person of the Godhead in a figurative sense, than eternity can be. For a person that is a father must be so in relation to a son. No son, no father. Consequently, an *eternal* Father implies an eternal Son. And the same reasoning holds true of the relation of the Father and Son to the Spirit. The terms Father, Son, and Spirit, in the baptismal formula and the apostolic benediction, must designate primary and eternal distinctions. The rite that initiates into the kingdom of God, certainly would not be administered in three names that denote only assumed and temporal relations of God; nor would blessings for time and eternity be invoked from God under such secondary names.

Hence, these trinal names given to God in the baptismal formula and the apostolic benediction, actually *force* upon the trinitarian theologian, the ideas of paternity, generation, filiation, spiration, and procession. He cannot reflect upon the implication of these names without forming these ideas, and finding himself necessitated to concede their literal validity and objective reality. He cannot say that the first person is the Father, and then deny that he "begets." He cannot say that the second person is the Son, and then deny that he is "begotten." He cannot say that the third person is the Spirit, and then deny that he "proceeds" by "spiration" (*spiritus quia spiratus*) from the Father and Son. When therefore Augustin, like the primitive fathers generally, endeavors to illustrate this eternal, necessary, and constitutional energizing and activity (*opera ad intra*) in the Divine Essence, whereby the Son issues from the Father and the Spirit from Father and Son, by the emanation of sunbeam from sun, light from light, river from fountain, thought from mind, word

from thought—when the ternaries from nature and the human mind are introduced to eluci-
date the Trinity—nothing more is done than when by other well-known and commonly
adopted analogies the Divine unity, or omniscience, or omnipresence, is sought to be illus-
trated.   There is no analogy taken from the finite that will clear up the mystery of the infinite—whether it be the mystery of the eternity of God, or that of his trinity.   But, at the
same time, by the use of these analogies the mind is kept close up to the Biblical term or
statement, and is not allowed to content itself with only a half-way understanding of it.   Such
a method brings thoroughness and clearness into the interpretation of the Word of God.

2. A second advantage in this method is, that it shows the doctrine of the Trinity to be
inseparable from that of the Unity of God.   The Deistical conception of the Divine unity
is wholly different from the Christian.   The former is that of natural religion, formed by
the unassisted human mind in its reflection upon the Supreme Being.   The latter is that of
revealed religion, given to the human mind by inspiration.   The Deistical unity is mere
singleness.   The Christian unity is a trinality.   The former is a unit.   The latter a true
unity, and union.   The former is meagre, having few contents.   The latter is a pleni-
tude—what St. Paul denominates "the fullness of the Godhead" ($\pi\lambda\acute{\eta}\rho\omega\mu\alpha\,\tau\tilde{\eta}\varsigma\,\theta\varepsilon\acute{o}\tau\eta\tau o\varsigma$).
Coloss. i. 9.

It follows, consequently, that the Divine unity cannot be discussed by itself without
reference to trinality, as the Deist and the Socinian endeavor to do.[1]   Trinality belongs as
necessarily and intrinsically to the Divine unity as eternity does to the Divine essence.
"If," says Athanasius (Oration I. 17) "there was not a Blessed Trinity from eternity, but
only a unity existed first, which at length became a Trinity, it follows that the Holy Trinity
must have been at one time imperfect, and at another time entire: imperfect until the Son
came to be created, as the Arians maintain, and then entire afterwards."   If we follow the
teachings of Revelation, and adopt the revealed idea of God, we may not discuss mere and
simple unity, nor mere and simple trinality; but we must discuss unity *in* trinality, and
trinality *in* unity.   We may not think of a monad which originally, and in the order either
of nature or of time, is not trinal, but becomes so.   The instant there is a monad, there
is a triad; the instant there is a unity, there are Father, Son, and Holy Spirit.   The
Christian Trinity is not that of Sabellius: namely, an original untrinal monad that subsequently, in the order of nature if not of time, becomes a triad; whereby four factors are
introduced into the problem.   God is not one *and* three, but one *in* three.   There is no primary monad, as such, and without trinality, to which the three distinctions are secondary
adjuncts.   The monad, or essence, never exists in and by itself as untrinalized, as in the
Sabellian scheme.   It exists only as in the three Persons; only as trinalized.   The Essence,
consequently, is not prior to the Persons, either in the order of nature or of time, nor subsequent to them, but simultaneously and eternally in and with them.

The Primitive church took this ground with confidence.   Unity and trinality were inseparable in their view.   The term God meant for them the Trinity.   A "theologian," in
their nomenclature, was a trinitarian.   They called the Apostle John $\delta\ \theta\varepsilon\acute{o}\lambda o\gamma o\varsigma$, because
he was enlightened by the Holy Spirit to make fuller disclosures, in the preface to his Gos-
pel, concerning the deity of the Logos and the doctrine of the Trinity, than were the other
evangelists.   And they gave the same epithet to Gregory Nazianzum, because of the acumen
and insight of his trinitarian treatises.   This work of Augustin adopts the same position,
and defends it with an ability second to none.

3. A third advantage of this method of illustrating the doctrine of the Trinity is, that
it goes to show that the personality of God depends upon the trinality of the Divine Essence

---

[1] The Mohammedan conception of the Divine Unity, also, is deistic.   In energetically rejecting the doctrine of the Trinity, the Mohammedan is the Oriental Unitarian.

—that if there are no interior distinctions in the Infinite Being, he cannot be self-contemplative, self-cognitive, or self-communing.

This is an important and valuable feature of the method in question, when viewed in its bearing upon the modern assertion that an Infinite Being cannot be personal. This treatise of Augustin does not develope the problem upon this point, but it leads to it. In illustrating the Trinity by the ternaries in nature, and especially in the human mind, he aims only to show that trinality of a certain kind does not conflict with *unity* of a certain kind. Memory, understanding, and will are three faculties, yet one soul. Augustin is content with elucidating the Divine unity by such illustrations. The elucidation of the Divine *personality* by them, was not attempted in his day nor in the Mediæval and Reformation churches. The conflict with pantheism forced this point upon the attention of the Modern church.

At the same time, these Christian fathers who took the problem of the Trinity into the centre of the Divine essence, and endeavored to show its necessary grounds there, prepared the way for showing, by the same method, that trinality is not only consistent with personality, but is actually indispensable to it. In a brief essay like this, only the briefest hints can be indicated.

If God is personal, he is self-conscious. Self-consciousness is, (1), the power which a rational spirit, or mind, has of making itself its own object; and, (2), of knowing that it has done so. If the first step is taken, and not the second, there is no self-consciousness. For the subject would not know that the object is the *self*. And the second step cannot be taken, if the first has not been. These two acts of a rational spirit, or mind, involve three distinctions in it, or three modes of it. The whole mind as a subject contemplates the very same whole mind as an object. Here are two distinctions, or modes of one mind. And the very same whole mind perceives that the contemplating subject and the contemplated object are one and the same essence or being. Here are three modes of one mind, each distinct from the others, yet all three going to make up the one self-conscious spirit. Unless there were these three distinctions, there would be no self-knowledge. Mere singleness, a mere subject without an object, is incompatible with self-consciousness.

In denying distinctions in the Divine Essence, while asserting its personality, Deism, with Socinianism and Mohammedanism, contends that God can be self-knowing and self-communing as a single subject without an object. The controversy, consequently, is as much between the deist and the psychologist, as it is between him and the trinitarian. It is as much a question whether his view of personality and self-consciousness is correct, as whether his interpretation of Scripture is. For the dispute involves the necessary conditions of personality. If a true psychology does not require trinality in a spiritual essence in order to its own self-contemplation, and self-knowledge, and self-communion, then the deist is correct; but if it does, then he is in error. That the study of self-consciousness in modern metaphysics has favored trinitarianism, is unquestionable. Even the spurious trinitarianism which has grown up in the schools of the later pantheism goes to show, that a trinal constitution is requisite in an essence, in order to explain self-consciousness, and that absolute singleness, or the absence of all interior distinctions, renders the problem insoluble.[1]

But the authority of Scripture is higher than that of psychology, and settles the matter. Revelation unquestionably discloses a deity who is "blessed forever;" whose blessedness is *independent* of the universe which he has made from nonentity, and who must therefore find all the conditions of blessedness within himself alone. He is blessed from eternity, in his own self-contemplation and self-communion. He does not need the universe in order

---

[1] "That view of the divine nature which makes it inconsistent with the Incarnation and Trinity is *philosophically* imperfect, as well as scripturally incorrect." H. B. Smith: *Faith and Philosophy*, p. 191.

that he may have an object which he can know, which he can love, and over which he can rejoice. "The Father knoweth the Son," from all eternity (Matt. xi. 27); and "loveth the Son," from all eternity (John iii. 35); and "glorifieth the Son," from all eternity (John xvii. 5). Prior to creation, the Eternal Wisdom "was by Him as one brought up with Him, and was daily His delight, rejoicing always before Him" (Prov. viii. 30); and the Eternal Word "was in the beginning with God" (John i. 2); and "the Only Begotten Son (or God Only Begotten, as the uncials read) was eternally in the bosom of the Father" (John i. 18).

Here is society within the Essence, and wholly independent of the universe; and communion and blessedness resulting therefrom. But this is impossible to an essence without personal distinctions. Not the singular Unit of the deist, but the plural Unity of the trinitarian, explains this. A subject without an object could not know. What is there to be known? Could not love. What is there to be loved? Could not rejoice. What is there to rejoice over? And the object cannot be the universe. The *infinite* and *eternal* object of God's infinite and eternal knowledge, love, and joy, cannot be his creation: because this is neither eternal, nor infinite. There was a time when the universe was not; and if God's self-consciousness and blessedness depends upon the universe, there was a time when God was neither self-conscious nor blessed. The objective God for the subjective God must, therefore, be very God of very God, begotten not made, the eternal Son of the eternal Father.

The same line of reasoning applies to the third trinitarian person, but there is no need of going through with it. The history of opinion shows, that if the first two eternal distinctions are conceded, there is no denial of the reality and eternity of the third. [1]

The analogue derived from the nature of finite personality and self-consciousness has one great advantage—namely, that it illustrates the independence of the Divine personality and self-consciousness. The later pantheism (not the earlier of Spinoza) constructs a kind of trinity, but it is dependent upon the universe. God distinguishes Himself from the *world*, and thereby finds the object required for the subject. But this implies either that the world is eternal, or else, that God is not eternally self-conscious. The Christian trinitarianism, on the contrary, finds all the media and conditions of self-consciousness within the Divine Essence. God distinguishes himself from *himself*, not from the universe. The eternal Father beholds himself in the eternal Son, his *alter ego*, the "express image of his own person" (Heb. i. 3). God does not struggle gradually into self-consciousness, as in the Hegelian scheme, by the help of the universe. Before that universe was in existence, and in the solitude of his own eternity and self-sufficiency, he had within his own essence all the media and conditions of self-consciousness. And after the worlds were called into being, the Divine personality remained the same immutable and infinite self-knowledge, unaffected by anything in his handiwork.

> "O Light Eterne, sole in thyself that dwellest,
> Sole knowest thyself, and known unto thyself,
> And knowing, lovest and smilest on thyself!"—DANTE: *Paradise* xxxiii. 125.

While, however, this analogue from the conditions of finite personality approaches nearer to the eternal distinctions in the Godhead than does that ternary which Augustin employs—namely, memory, understanding, and will—yet like all finite analogies to the Infinite it is inadequate. For the subject-ego, object-ego, and ego-percipient, are not so essentially distinct and completely objective to each other, as are the Father, Son, and Holy Spirit. They cannot employ the personal pronouns in reference to each other. They cannot reciprocally perform acts and discharge functions towards each other, like the

---

[1] Upon the necessary conditions of self consciousness in God, see Müller: *On Sin*, II. 136 sq. (Urwick's Trans.); Dorner: *Christian Doctrine*, I. 412-465; Christlieb: *Modern Doubt*, Lecture III.; Kurtz: *Sacred History*, § 2; Billroth: *Religions Philosophie*, § 89, 90; Wilberforce: *Incarnation*, Chapter III; Kidd: *On the Trinity*, with Candlish's *Introduction*; Shedd: *History of Doctrine*, I. 365-368.

Divine Three.   Revelation is explicit upon this point.   It specifies at least the following twelve actions and relations, that incontestably prove the conscious distinctness and mutual objectivity of the persons of the Trinity.   One divine person loves another (John iii. 35); dwells in another (John xiv. 10, 11); knows another (Matt. xi. 27); sends another (Gen. xvi. 7); suffers from another (Zech. xiii. 7–13); addresses another (Heb. i. 8); is the way to another (John xiv. 6); speaks of another (Luke iii. 22;) glorifies another (John xvii. 5); confers with another (Gen. i. 26; xi. 7); plans with another (Is. ix. 6): rewards another (Phil. ii. 5–11; Heb. ii. 9).

Such are some of the salient features of this important treatise upon the Trinity.   It has its defects; but they pertain to the form more than to the matter; to arrangement and style more than to dogma.   Literary excellence is no the forte of the patristic writers. Hardly any of them are literary artists.   Lactantius among the Latins, and Chrysostom among the Greeks, are almost the only fathers that have rhetorical grace.   And none of them approach the beauty of the classic writers, as seen in the harmonious flow and diction of Plato, and the exquisite finish of Horace and Catullus.

Augustin is prolix, repetitious, and sometimes leaves his theme to discuss cognate but distantly related subjects.   This appears more in the last eight chapters, which are speculative, than in the first seven, which are scriptural.   The material in this second division is capable of considerable compression.   The author frequently employs two illustrations when one would suffice, and three or more when two are enough.   He discusses many themes which are not strictly trinitarian.

Yet the patient student will derive some benefit from this discursiveness.   He will find, for example, in this treatise on the Trinity, an able examination of the subject of miracles (Book III); of creation *ex nihilo* (III. ix); of vicarious atonement (IV. vii–xiv); of the faculty of memory (XI. x); and, incidentally, many other high themes are touched upon.   Before such a contemplative intellect as that of Augustin, all truth lay spread out like the ocean, with no limits and no separating chasms.   Everything is connected and fluid.   Consequently, one doctrine inevitably leads to and merges in another, and the eager and intense inquirer rushes forward, and outward, and upward, and downward, in every direction. The only aim is to see all that can be seen, and state all that can be stated.   The neglect of the form, and the anxiety after the substance, contribute to the discursiveness.   Caring little for proportion in method, and nothing for elegance in diction, the writer, though bringing forth a vast amount of truth, does it at the expense of clearness, conciseness, and grace.   Such is the case with the North African father—one of the most voluminous and prolix of authors, yet one of the most original, suggestive, and fertilizing of any.

And this particular treatise is perhaps as pregnant and suggestive as any that Augustin, or any other theologian, ever composed.   The doctrine of the Trinity is the most *immense* of all the doctrines of religion.   It is the foundation of theology.   Christianity, in the last analysis, is Trinitarianism.   Take out of the New Testament the persons of the Father, the Son, and the Holy Spirit, and there is no God left.   Take out of the Christian consciousness the thoughts and affections that relate to the Father, the Son, and the Holy Spirit, and there is no Christian consciousness left.   The Trinity is the constitutive idea of the evangelical theology, and the formative idea of the evangelical experience.   The immensity of the doctrine makes it of necessity a mystery; but a mystery which like night enfolds in its unfathomed depths the bright stars—points of light, compared with which there is no light so keen and so glittering.   Mysterious as it is, the Trinity of Divine Revelation is the doctrine that holds in it all the hope of man; for it holds within it the infinite pity of the Incarnation and the infinite mercy of the Redemption.

And it shares its mysteriousness with the doctrine of the Divine Eternity.   It is difficult to say which is most baffling to human comprehension, the all-comprehending, simultaneous, successionless consciousness of the Infinite One, or his trinal personality. Yet no theist rejects the doctrine of the Divine eternity because of its mystery. The two doctrines are antithetic and correlative. On one of the Northern rivers that flows through a narrow chasm whose depth no plummet has sounded, there stand two cliffs fronting each other, shooting their pinnacles into the blue ether, and sending their roots down to the foundations of the earth. They have named them Trinity and Eternity. So stand, antithetic and confronting, in the Christian scheme, the trinity and eternity of God.

The translation of this treatise is the work of the Rev. Arthur West Haddan, Hon. Canon of Worcester, who, according to a note of the publisher, died while it was passing through the press. It has been compared with the original, and a considerable number of alterations made. The treatise is exceedingly difficult to render into English—probably the most so of any in the author's writings. The changes in some instances were necessary from a misconception of the original; but more often for the purpose of making the meaning of the translator himself more clear. It is believed that a comparison between the original and revised translation will show that the latter is the more intelligible. At the same time, the reviser would not be too confident that in every instance the exact meaning of Augustin has been expressed, by either the translator or reviser.

The annotations of the reviser upon important points in the treatise, it is hoped, will assist the reader in understanding Augustin's reasoning, and also throw some light upon the doctrine of the Trinity.

WILLIAM G. T. SHEDD.

NEW YORK, *Feb.* 1, 1887.

TRANSLATOR'S PREFACE.

THE history of St. Augustin's treatise on the Trinity, as gathered by Tillemont and others from his own allusions to it, may be briefly given. It is placed by him in his *Retractations* among the works written (which in the present case, it appears, must mean begun) in A.D. 400. In letters of A.D. 410, 414, and at the end of A.D. 415 (*Ad Consentium*, Ep. 120, and two *Ad Evodium*, Epp. 162, 169), it is referred to as still unfinished and unpublished. But a letter of A.D. 412 (*Ad Marcellinum*, Ep. 143) intimates that friends were at that time importuning him, although without success, to complete and publish it. And the letter to Aurelius, which was sent to that bishop with the treatise itself when actually completed, informs us that a portion of it, while it was still unrevised and incomplete, was in fact surreptitiously made public,—a proceeding which the letters above cited postpone apparently until at least after A.D. 415. It was certainly still in hand in A.D. 416, inasmuch as in Book XIII. a quotation occurs from the 12th Book of the *De Civitate Dei;* and another quotation in Book XV., from the 90th lecture on St. John, indicates most probably a date of at least a year later, *viz.* A.D. 417. The *Retractations*, which refer to it, are usually dated not later than A.D. 428. The letter to Bishop Aurelius also informs us that the work was many years in progress, and was begun in St. Augustin's early manhood, and finished in his old age. We may infer from this evidence that it was written by him between A.D. 400, when he was forty-six years old, and had been Bishop of Hippo about four years, and A.D. 428 at the latest; but probably it was published ten or twelve years before this date. He writes of it, indeed, himself, as if the "*nonum prematur in annum*" very inadequately represented the amount of deliberate and patient thought which a subject so profound and so sacred demanded, and which he had striven to give to it; and as if, even at the very last, he shrank from publishing his work, and was only driven to do so in order to remedy the mischief of its partial and unauthorized publication.

His motive for writing on the subject may be learned from the treatise itself. It was not directed against any individual antagonist, or occasioned by any particular controversial emergency. In fact, his labors upon it were, he says, continually interrupted by the distraction of such controversies. Certain ingenious and subtle theories respecting types or resemblances of the Holy Trinity, traceable in human nature as being the image of God, seemed to him to supply, not indeed a logical proof, but a strong rational presumption, of the truth of the doctrine itself; and thus to make it incumbent upon him to expound and unfold them in order to meet rationalizing objectors upon (so to say) their own ground. He is careful not to deal with these analogies or images as if they either constituted a purely argumentative proof or exhausted the full meaning of the doctrine, upon both which assumptions such speculations have at all times been the fruitful parent both of presumptious theorizing and of grievous heresy. But he nevertheless employs them more affirmatively than would perhaps have been the case. While modern theologians would argue negatively, from the triplicity of independent faculties,—united, nevertheless, in the unity of a single human person,—that any presumption of reason against the Trinity of persons in the Godhead is thereby, if not removed, at least materially and enormously lessened, St. Augustin seems to argue positively from analogous grounds, as though they constituted a direct intimation of the doctrine itself. But he takes especial pains, at the same time, to dwell upon the incapacity of human thought to fathom the depths of the nature of God; and he carefully prefaces his reasonings by a statement of the Scripture evidence of the catholic doctrine as a matter of faith and not of reason, and by an explanation of difficult texts upon the subject. One of the most valuable portions, indeed, of the treatise is the eloquent and profound exposition given in this part of it of the rule of interpretation to be applied to Scripture language respecting the person of our Lord. It should be noticed, however, that a large proportion of St. Augustin's scriptural exegesis is founded upon a close verbal exposition of the old Latin version, and is frequently not borne out by the original text. And the rule followed in rendering Scripture texts in the present translation has been, accordingly, wherever the argument in the context rests upon the variations of the old Latin, there to translate the words as St. Augustin gives them, while adhering otherwise to the language of the authorized English version. The reader's attention may allowably be drawn to the language of Book V. c.x., and to its close resemblance to some of the most remarkable phrases of the Athanasian Creed, and again to the striking passage respecting miracles in Book III. c.v., and to that upon the nature of God at the beginning of Book V.; the last named of which seems to have suggested one of the profoundest passages in the profoundest of Dr. Newman's *University Sermons* (p. 353, ed. 1843). It may be added, that the writings of the Greek Fathers on the subject were, if not wholly unknown, yet unfamiliar to Augustin, who quotes directly only the Latin work of Hilary of Poictiers.

It remains to say, that the translation here printed was made about four years since by a friend of the writer of this preface, and that the latter's share in the work has been that of thoroughly revising and correcting it, and of seeing it through the press. He is therefore answerable for the work as now published.

                                                                        A. W. HADDAN.

Nov. 5, 1872.

In the *Retractations* (ii. 15) Augustin speaks of this work in the following terms:—

" I spent some years in writing fifteen books concerning the Trinity, which is God. When, however, I had not yet finished the thirteenth Book, and some who were exceedingly anxious to have the work were kept waiting longer than they could bear, it was stolen from me in a less correct state than it either could or would have been had it appeared when I intended. And as soon as I discovered this, having other copies of it, I had determined at first not to publish it myself, but to mention what had happened in the matter in some other work; but at the urgent request of brethren, whom I could not refuse, I corrected it as much as I thought fit, and finished and published it, with the addition, at the beginning, of a letter that I had written to the venerable Aurelius, Bishop of Carthage, in which I set forth, in the way of prologue, what had happened, what I had intended to do of myself, and what love of my brethren had forced me to do."

The letter to which he here alludes is the following :—

" To the most blessed Lord, whom he reveres with most sincere love, to his holy brother and fellow-priest, Pope Aurelius, Augustin sends health in the Lord.

" I began as a very young man, and have published in my old age, some books concerning the Trinity, who is the supreme and true God. I had in truth laid the work aside, upon discovering that it had been prematurely, or rather surreptitiously, stolen from me before I had completed it, and before I had revised and put the finishing touches to it, as had been my intention. For I had not designed to publish the Books one by one, but all together, inasmuch as the progress of the inquiry led me to add the later ones to those which precede them. When, therefore, these people had hindered the fulfillment of my purpose (in that some of them had obtained access to the work before I intended), I had given over dictating it, with the idea of making my complaint public in some other work that I might write, in order that whoso could might know that the Books had not been published by myself, but had been taken away from my possession before they were in my own judgment fit for publication. Compelled, however, by the eager demands of many of my brethren, and above all by your command, I have taken the pains, by God's help, to complete the work, laborious as it is; and as now corrected (not as I wished, but as I could, lest the Books should differ very widely from those which had surreptitiously got into people's hands), I have sent them to your Reverence by my very dear son and fellow-deacon, and have allowed them to be heard, copied, and read by every one that pleases. Doubtless, if I could ha fulfilled my original intention, although they would have contained the same sentiments, they would have been worked out much more thoroughly and clearly, so far as the difficulty of unfolding so profound a subject, and so far, too, as my own powers, might have allowed. There are some persons, however, who have the first four, or rather five, Books without the prefaces, and the twelfth with no small part of its later chapters omitted. But these, if they please and can, will amend the whole, if they become acquainted with the present edition. At any rate, I have to request that you will order this letter to be prefixed separately, but at the beginning of the Books. Farewell. Pray for me."

CONTENTS OF THE TRINITY.

THE

FIFTEEN BOOKS OF AURELIUS AUGUSTINUS,

BISHOP OF HIPPO,

ON THE TRINITY

BOOK I.

IN WHICH THE UNITY AND EQUALITY OF THE SUPREME TRINITY IS ESTABLISHED FROM THE SA-
CRED SCRIPTURES, AND SOME TEXTS ALLEGED AGAINST THE EQUALITY OF THE SON ARE EX-
PLAINED.

CHAP. I.—THIS WORK IS WRITTEN AGAINST THOSE WHO SOPHISTICALLY ASSAIL THE FAITH OF THE TRINITY, THROUGH MISUSE OF REASON. THEY WHO DISPUTE CONCERNING GOD ERR FROM A THREEFOLD CAUSE. HOLY SCRIPTURE, REMOVING WHAT IS FALSE, LEADS US ON BY DEGREES TO THINGS DIVINE. WHAT TRUE IMMORTALITY IS. WE ARE NOURISHED BY FAITH, THAT WE MAY BE ENABLED TO APPREHEND THINGS DIVINE.

1. THE following dissertation concerning the Trinity, as the reader ought to be informed, has been written in order to guard against the sophistries of those who disdain to begin with faith, and are deceived by a crude and perverse love of reason. Now one class of such men endeavor to transfer to things incorporeal and spiritual the ideas they have formed, whether through experience of the bodily senses, or by natural human wit and diligent quickness, or by the aid of art, from things corporeal; so as to seek to measure and conceive of the former by the latter. Others, again, frame whatever sentiments they may have concerning God according to the nature or affections of the human mind; and through this error they govern their discourse, in disputing concerning God, by distorted and fallacious rules. While yet a third class strive indeed to transcend the whole creation, which doubtless is changeable, in order to raise their thought to the unchangeable substance, which is God; but being weighed down by the burden of mortality, whilst they both would seem to know what they do not, and cannot know what they would, preclude themselves from entering the very path of understanding, by an over-bold affirmation of their own presumptuous judgments; choosing rather not to correct their own opinion when it is perverse, than to change that which they have once defended. And, indeed, this is the common disease of all the three classes which I have mentioned,—viz., both of those who frame their thoughts of God according to things corporeal, and of those who do so according to the spiritual creature, such as is the soul; and of those who neither regard the body nor the spiritual creature, and yet think falsely about God; and are indeed so much the further from the truth, that nothing can be found answering to their conceptions, either in the body, or in the made or created spirit, or in the Creator Himself. For he who thinks, for instance, that God is white or red, is in error; and yet these things are found in the body. Again, he who thinks of God as now forgetting and now remembering, or anything of the same kind, is none the less in error; and yet these things are found in the mind. But he who thinks that God is of such power as to have generated Himself, is so much the

more in error, because not only does God not so exist, but neither does the spiritual nor the bodily creature; for there is nothing whatever that generates its own existence.[1]

2. In order, therefore, that the human mind might be purged from falsities of this kind, Holy Scripture, which suits itself to babes, has not avoided words drawn from any class of things really existing, through which, as by nourishment, our understanding might rise gradually to things divine and transcendent. For, in speaking of God, it has both used words taken from things corporeal, as when it says, "Hide me under the shadow of Thy wings;"[2] and it has borrowed many things from the spiritual creature, whereby to signify that which indeed is not so, but must needs so be said: as, for instance, "I the Lord thy God am a jealous God;"[3] and, "It repenteth me that I have made man."[4] But it has drawn no words whatever, whereby to frame either figures of speech or enigmatic sayings, from things which do not exist at all. And hence it is that they who are shut out from the truth by that third kind of error are more mischievously and emptily vain than their fellows; in that they surmise respecting God, what can neither be found in Himself nor in any creature. For divine Scripture is wont to frame, as it were, allurements for children from the things which are found in the creature; whereby, according to their measure, and as it were by steps, the affections of the weak may be moved to seek those things that are above, and to leave those things that are below. But the same Scripture rarely employs those things which are spoken properly of God, and are not found in any creature; as, for instance, that which was said to Moses, "I am that I am;" and, "I Am hath sent me to you."[5] For since both body and soul also are said in some sense to *be*, Holy Scripture certainly would not so express itself unless it meant to be understood in some special sense of the term. So, too, that which the Apostle says, "Who only hath immortality."[6] Since the soul also both is said to be, and is, in a certain manner immortal, Scripture would not say "only hath," unless because true immortality is unchangeableness; which no creature can possess, since it belongs to the creator alone.[7]

So also James says, "Every good gift and every perfect gift is from above, and cometh down from the Father of Lights, with whom is no variableness, neither shadow of turning."[8] So also David, "Thou shalt change them, and they shall be changed; but Thou art the same."[9]

3. Further, it is difficult to contemplate and fully know the substance of God; who fashions things changeable, yet without any change in Himself, and creates things temporal, yet without any temporal movement in Himself. And it is necessary, therefore, to purge our minds, in order to be able to see ineffably that which is ineffable; whereto not having yet attained, we are to be nourished by faith, and led by such ways as are more suited to our capacity, that we may be rendered apt and able to comprehend it. And hence the Apostle says, that "in Christ indeed are hid all the treasures of wisdom and knowledge;"[10] and yet has commended Him to us, as to babes in Christ, who, although already born again by His grace, yet are still carnal and psychical, not by that divine virtue wherein He is equal to the Father, but by that human infirmity whereby He was crucified. For he says, "I determined not to know anything among you, save Jesus Christ and Him crucified;"[11] and then he continues, "And I was with you in weakness, and in fear, and in much trembling." And a little after he says to them, "And I, brethren, could not speak unto you as unto spiritual, but as unto carnal,[12] even as unto babes in Christ. I have fed you with milk, and not with meat: for hitherto ye were not able to bear it, neither yet now are ye able."[13] There are some who are angry at language of this kind, and think it is used in slight to themselves, and for the most part prefer rather to believe that they who so speak to them have nothing to say, than that they themselves cannot understand what they have said. And sometimes, indeed, we do allege to them, not certainly that account of the case which they seek in their inquiries about God,—because neither can they themselves receive it, nor can we perhaps either apprehend or express it,—but such an account of it as to demonstrate to them how incapable and utterly unfit they are to understand that which they require of us. But they, on their parts, because

---

[1] [Augustin here puts *generare* for *creare*—which is rarely the case with him, since the distinction between generation and creation is of the highest importance in discussing the doctrine of the Trinity. His thought here is, that God does not bring himself into being, because he always is. Some have defined God as the Self-caused: *causa sui*. But the category of cause and effect is inapplicable to the Infinite Being.—W. G. T. S.]

[2] Ps. xvii. 8. [3] Ex. xx. 5. [4] Gen. vi. 7.
[5] Ex. iii. 14. [6] 1 Tim. vi. 16.

[7] [God's being is necessary; that of the creature is contingent. Hence the name I Am, or Jehovah,—which denotes this difference. God alone has immortality *a parte ante*, as well as *a parte post*.—W. G. T. S.]

[8] Jas. i. 17. [9] Ps. cii. 26, 27.
[10] Col. ii. 3. [11] 1 Cor. ii. 2, 3.
[12] [St. Paul, in this place, denominates imperfect but true believers "carnal," in a relative sense, only. They are comparatively carnal, when contrasted with the law of God, which is absolutely and perfectly spiritual. (Rom. vii. 14.) They do not, however, belong to the *class* of carnal or natural men, in distinction from spiritual. The persons whom the Apostle here denominates "carnal," are "babes in Christ."—W. G. T. S.]
[13] 1 Cor. iii. 1, 2.

they do not hear what they desire, think that we are either playing them false in order to conceal our own ignorance, or speaking in malice because we grudge them knowledge; and so go away indignant and perturbed.

CHAP. 2.—IN WHAT MANNER THIS WORK PRO-
POSES TO DISCOURSE CONCERNING THE TRIN-
ITY.

4. Wherefore, our Lord God helping, we will undertake to render, as far as we are able, that very account which they so importunately demand: viz., that the Trinity is the one and only and true God, and also how the Father, the Son, and the Holy Spirit are rightly said, believed, understood, to be of one and the same substance or essence; in such wise that they may not fancy themselves mocked by excuses on our part, but may find by actual trial, both that the highest good is that which is discerned by the most purified minds, and that for this reason it cannot be discerned or understood by themselves, because the eye of the human mind, being weak, is dazzled in that so transcendent light, unless it be invigorated by the nourishment of the righteousness of faith. First, however, we must demonstrate, according to the authority of the Holy Scriptures, whether the faith be so. Then, if God be willing and aid us, we may perhaps at least so far serve these talkative arguers—more puffed up than capable, and therefore laboring under the more dangerous disease—as to enable them to find something which they are not able to doubt, that so, in that case where they cannot find the like, they may be led to lay the fault to their own minds, rather than to the truth itself or to our reasonings; and thus, if there be anything in them of either love or fear towards God, they may return and begin from faith in due order: perceiving at length how healthful a medicine has been provided for the faithful in the holy Church, whereby a heedful piety, healing the feebleness of the mind, may render it able to perceive the unchangeable truth, and hinder it from falling headlong, through disorderly rashness, into pestilent and false opinion. Neither will I myself shrink from inquiry, if I am anywhere in doubt; nor ashamed to learn, if I am anywhere in error.

CHAP. 3.—WHAT AUGUSTIN REQUESTS FROM
HIS READERS.   THE ERRORS OF READERS DULL
OF COMPREHENSION NOT TO BE ASCRIBED TO
THE AUTHOR.

5. Further let me ask of my reader, wher-

ever, alike with myself, he is certain, there to go on with me; wherever, alike with myself, he hesitates, there to join with me in inquiring; wherever he recognizes himself to be in error, there to return to me ; wherever he recognizes me to be so, there to call me back: so that we may enter together upon the path of charity, and advance towards Him of whom it is said, "Seek His face evermore."[1] And I would make this pious and safe agreement, in the presence of our Lord God, with all who read my writings, as well in all other cases as, above all, in the case of those which inquire into the unity of the Trinity, of the Father and the Son and·the Holy Spirit; because in no other subject is error more dangerous, or inquiry more laborious, or the discovery of truth more profitable.   If, then, any reader shall say, This is not well said, because I do not understand it; such an one finds fault with my language, not with my faith: and it might perhaps in very truth have been put more clearly; yet no man ever so spoke as to be understood in all things by all men.   Let him, therefore, who finds this fault with my discourse, see whether he can understand other men who have handled similar subjects and questions, when he does not understand me: and if he can, let him put down my book, or even, if he pleases, throw it away; and let him spend labor and time rather on those whom he understands.[2]   Yet let him not think on that account that I ought to have been silent, because I have not been able to express myself so smoothly and clearly to him as those do whom he understands. For neither do all things, which all men have written, come into the hands of all.   And possibly some, who are capable of understanding even these our writings, may not find those more lucid works, and may meet with ours only.   And therefore it is useful that many persons should write many books, differing in style but not in faith, concerning even the same questions, that the matter itself may reach the greatest number—some in one way, some in another.   But if he who complains that he has not understood these things has never been able to comprehend any careful and exact reasonings at all upon such subjects, let him in that case deal with himself by resolution and study, that he may

---

[1] Ps. cv. 4.
[2] [This request of Augustin to his reader, involves an admirable rule for authorship generally—the desire, namely, that truth be attained, be it through himself or through others. Milton teaches the same, when he says that the author must "study and love learning for itself, not for lucre, or any other end, but the service of God and of truth, and perhaps that lasting fame and perpetuity of praise, which God and good men have consented shall be the reward of those whose published labors advance the good of mankind."—W. G. T. S.]

know better; not with me by quarrellings and wranglings, that I may hold my peace. Let him, again, who says, when he reads my book, Certainly I understand what is said, but it is not true, assert, if he pleases, his own opinion, and refute mine if he is able. And if he do this with charity and truth, and take the pains to make it known to me (if I am still alive), I shall then receive the most abundant fruit of this my labor. And if he cannot inform myself, most willing and glad should I be that he should inform those whom he can. Yet, for my part, "I meditate in the law of the Lord,"[1] if not "day and night," at least such short times as I can; and I commit my meditations to writing, lest· they should escape me through forgetfulness; hoping by the mercy of God that He will make me hold steadfastly all truths of which I feel certain; "but if in anything I be otherwise minded, that He will himself reveal even this to me,"[2] whether through secret inspiration and admonition, or through His own plain utterances, or through the reasonings of my brethren. This I pray for, and this my trust and desire I commit to Him, who is sufficiently able to keep those things which He has given me, and to render those which He has promised.

6. I expect, indeed, that some, who are more dull of understanding, will imagine that in some parts of my books I have held sentiments which I have not held, or have not held those which I have. But their error, as none can be ignorant, ought not to be attributed to me, if they have deviated into false doctrine through following my steps without apprehending me, whilst I am compelled to pick my way through a hard and obscure subject: seeing that neither can any one, in any way, rightly ascribe tne numerous and various errors of heretics to the holy testimonies themselves of the divine books; although all of them endeavor to defend out of those same Scriptures their own false and erroneous opinions. The law of Christ, that is, charity, admonishes me clearly, and commands me with a sweet constraint, that when men think that I have held in my books something false which I have not held, and that same falsehood displeases one and pleases another, I should prefer to be blamed by him who reprehends the falsehood, rather than praised by him who praises it. For although I, who never held the error, am not rightly blamed by the former, yet the error itself is rightly censured; whilst by the latter neither am I rightly praised, who am thought to have held

that which the truth censures, nor the sentiment itself, which the truth also censures. Let us therefore essay the work which we have undertaken in the name of the Lord.

CHAP. 4.—WHAT THE DOCTRINE OF THE CATHOLIC FAITH IS CONCERNING THE TRINITY.

7. All those Catholic expounders of the divine Scriptures, both Old and New, whom I have been able to read, who have written before me concerning the Trinity, Who is God, have purposed to teach, according to the Scriptures, this doctrine, that the Father, and the Son, and the Holy Spirit intimate a divine unity of one and the same substance in an indivisible equality;[3] and therefore that they are not three Gods, but one God: although the Father hath begotten the Son, and so He who is the Father is not the Son; and the Son is begotten by the Father, and so He who is the Son is not the Father; and the Holy Spirit is neither the Father nor the Son, but only the Spirit of the Father and of the Son, Himself also co-equal with the Father and the Son, and pertaining to the unity of the Trinity. Yet not that this Trinity was born of the Virgin Mary, and crucified under Pontius Pilate, and buried, and rose again the third day, and ascended into heaven, but only the Son. Nor, again, that this Trinity descended in the form of a dove upon Jesus when He was baptized;[4] nor that, on the day of Pentecost, after the ascension of the Lord, when "there came a sound from heaven, as of a rushing mighty wind,"[5] the same Trinity "sat upon each of them with cloven tongues like as of fire," but only the Holy Spirit. Nor yet that this Trinity said from heaven, "Thou art my Son,"[6] whether when He was baptized by John, or when the three disciples were with Him in the mount,[7] or when the voice sounded, saying, "I have both glorified it, and will glorify it again;"[8] but that it was a word of the Father only, spoken to the Son; although the Father, and the Son, and the Holy Spirit, as they are indivisible, so work indivisibly.[9] This is also my faith, since it is the Catholic faith.

---

3 [Augustin teaches the Nicene doctrine of a numerical unity of essence in distinction from a specific unity. The latter is that of mankind. In this case there is *division* of substance—part after part of the specific nature being separated and formed, by propagation, into individuals. No human individual contains the whole specific nature. But in the case of the numerical unity of the Trinity, there is no division of essence. The whole divine nature is in each divine person. The three divine persons do not constitute a species—that is, three divine individuals made by the division and distribution of one common divine nature—but are three modes or "forms" (Phil. ii. 6) of one undivided substance, numerically and identically the same in each.— W. G. T. S.]

4 Matt. iii. 16.   5 Acts. ii. 2, 4.   6 Mark i. 11.
7 Matt. xvii. 5.   8 John xii. 28.

9 [The term Trinity denotes the Divine essence in all three modes. The term Father (or Son, or Spirit) denotes the essence in only one mode. Consequently, there is something in the

---

CHAP. 5.—OF DIFFICULTIES CONCERNING THE
TRINITY : IN WHAT MANNER THREE ARE ONE
GOD, AND HOW, WORKING INDIVISIBLY, THEY
YET PERFORM SOME THINGS SEVERALLY.

8. Some persons, however, find a difficulty
in this faith; when they hear that the Father
is God, and the Son God, and the Holy
Spirit God, and yet that this Trinity is
not three Gods, but one God; and they
ask how they are to understand this :
especially when it is said that the Trinity
works indivisibly in everything that God
works, and yet that a certain voice of the
Father spoke, which is not the voice of the
Son; and that none except the Son was born
in the flesh, and suffered, and rose again, and
ascended into heaven; and that none except
the Holy Spirit came in the form of a dove.
They wish to understand how the Trinity
uttered that voice which was only of the
Father; and how the same Trinity created
that flesh in which the Son only was born of
the Virgin; and how the very same Trinity
itself wrought that form of a dove, in which
the Holy Spirit only appeared. Yet, otherwise, the Trinity does not work indivisibly,
but the Father does some things, the Son
other things, and the Holy Spirit yet others:
or else, if they do some things together, some
severally, then the Trinity is not indivisible.
It is a difficulty, too, to them, in what manner the Holy Spirit is in the Trinity, whom
neither the Father nor the Son, nor both,
have begotten, although He is the Spirit both
of the Father and of the Son. Since, then,
men weary us with asking such questions, let
us unfold to them, as we are able, whatever
wisdom God's gift has bestowed upon our
weakness on this subject; neither "let us go
on our way with consuming envy."[1] Should
we say that we are not accustomed to think
about such things, it would not be true; yet
if we acknowledge that such subjects commonly dwell in our thoughts, carried away as
we are by the love of investigating the truth,
then they require of us, by the law of charity,
to make known to them what we have herein
been able to find out. "Not as though I had
already attained, either were already perfect"
(for, if the Apostle Paul, how much more
must I, who lie far beneath his feet, count
myself not to have apprehended!); but, according to my measure, "if I forget those
things that are behind, and reach forth unto
those things which are before, and press to-

wards the mark for the prize of the high calling,"[2] I am requested to disclose so much of
the road as I have already passed, and the
point to which I have reached, whence the
course yet remains to bring me to the end.
And those make the request, whom a gener-
ous charity compels me to serve. Needs
must too, and God will grant that, in supplying them with matter to read, I shall profit
myself also; and that, in seeking to reply to
their inquiries, I shall myself likewise find
that for which I was inquiring. Accordingly
I have undertaken the task, by the bidding
and help of the Lord my God, not so much
of discoursing with authority respecting things
I know already, as of learning those things
by piously discoursing of them.

CHAP. 6.—THAT THE SON IS VERY GOD, OF THE
SAME SUBSTANCE WITH THE FATHER. NOT
ONLY THE FATHER, BUT THE TRINITY, IS
AFFIRMED TO BE IMMORTAL. ALL THINGS
ARE NOT FROM THE FATHER ALONE, BUT ALSO
FROM THE SON. THAT THE HOLY SPIRIT IS
VERY GOD, EQUAL WITH THE FATHER AND
THE SON.

9. They who have said that our Lord Jesus
Christ is not God, or not very God, or not
with the Father the One and only God, or not
truly immortal because changeable, are proved
wrong by the most plain and unanimous voice
of divine testimonies; as, for instance, " In
the beginning was the Word, and the Word
was with God, and the Word was God." For
it is plain that we are to take the Word of God
to be the only Son of God, of whom it is afterwards said, "And the Word was made flesh,
and dwelt among us," on account of that birth
of His incarnation, which was wrought in time
of the Virgin. But herein is declared, not
only that He is God, but also that He is of
the same substance with the Father; because,
after saying, "And the Word was God," it is
said also, "The same was in the beginning
with God: all things were made by Him, and
without Him was not anything made."[3] Not
simply "all things;" but only all things that
were *made*, that is; the whole creature. From
which it appears clearly, that He Himself was
not made, by whom all things were made.
And if He was not made, then He is not a
creature; but if He is not a creature, then He
is of the same substance with the Father. For
all substance that is not God is creature; and
all that is not creature is God.[4] And if the

Trinity that cannot be attributed to any one of the Persons, as
such; and something in a Person that cannot be attributed to
the Trinity, as such. Trinality cannot be ascribed to the first
Person; paternity cannot be ascribed to the Trinity.—W. G. T. S.]
    [1] Wisd. vi. 23.

    [2] Phil. iii. 12-14.   [3] John i. 1, 14, 2, 3.
    [4] [Augustin here postulates the theistic doctrines of two sub-
stances—infinite and finite; in contradiction to the postulate of pantheism, that there is only one substance—the infinite.—W. G. T. S.]

Son is not of the same substance with the Father, then He is a substance that was made: and if He is a substance that was made, then all things were not made by Him; but "all things were made by Him," therefore He is of one and the same substance with the Father. And so He is not only God, but also very God. And the same John most expressly affirms this in his epistle: "For we know that the Son of God is come, and hath given us an understanding, that we may know the true God, and that we may be in His true Son Jesus Christ. This is the true God, and eternal life." [1]

10. Hence also it follows by consequence, that the Apostle Paul did not say, "Who alone has immortality," of the Father merely; but of the One and only God, which is the Trinity itself. For that which is itself eternal life is not mortal according to any changeableness; and hence the Son of God, because "He is Eternal Life," is also Himself understood with the Father, where it is said, "Who only hath immortality." For we, too, are made partakers of this eternal life, and become, in our own measure, immortal. But the eternal life itself, of which we are made partakers, is one thing; we ourselves, who, by partaking of it, shall live eternally, are another. For if He had said, "Whom in His own time the Father will show, who is the blessed and only Potentate, the King of kings, and Lord of lords; who only hath immortality;" not even so would it be necessarily understood that the Son is excluded. For neither has the Son separated the Father from Himself, because He Himself, speaking elsewhere with the voice of wisdom (for He Himself is the Wisdom of God),[2] says, "I alone compassed the circuit of heaven."[3] And therefore so much the more is it not necessary that the words, "Who hath immortality," should be understood of the Father alone, omitting the Son; when they are said thus: "That thou keep this commandment without spot, unrebukeable, until the appearing of our Lord Jesus Christ: whom in His own time He will show, who is the blessed and only Potentate, the King of kings, and Lord of lords; who only hath immortality, dwelling in the light which no man can approach unto; whom no man hath seen, nor can see: to whom be honor and power everlasting. Amen."[4] In which words neither is the Father specially named, nor the Son, nor the Holy Spirit; but the blessed and only Potentate, the King of kings, and

Lord of lords; that is, the One and only and true God, the Trinity itself.

11. But perhaps what follows may interfere with this meaning; because it is said, "Whom no man hath seen, nor can see:" although this may also be taken as belonging to Christ according to His divinity, which the Jews did not see, who yet saw and crucified Him in the flesh; whereas His divinity can in no wise be seen by human sight, but is seen with that sight with which they who see are no longer men, but beyond men. Rightly, therefore, is God Himself, the Trinity, understood to be the "blessed and only Potentate," who "shows the coming of our Lord Jesus Christ in His own time." For the words, "Who only hath immortality," are said in the same way as it is said, "Who only doeth wondrous things."[5] And I should be glad to know of whom they take these words to be said. If only of the Father, how then is that true which the Son Himself says, "For what things soever the Father doeth, these also doeth the Son likewise?" Is there any, among wonderful works, more wonderful than to raise up and quicken the dead? Yet the same Son saith, "As the Father raiseth up the dead, and quickeneth them, even so the Son quickeneth whom He will."[6] How, then, does the Father alone "do wondrous things," when these words allow us to understand neither the Father only, nor the Son only, but assuredly the one only true God, that is, the Father, and the Son, and the Holy Spirit?[7]

12. Also, when the same apostle says, "But to us there is but one God, the Father, of whom are all things, and we in Him; and one Lord Jesus Christ, by whom are all things, and we by Him,"[8] who can doubt that he speaks of all things which are created; as does John, when he says, "All things were made by Him"? I ask, therefore, of whom he speaks in another place: "For of Him, and through Him, and in Him, are all things: to whom be glory for ever. Amen."[9] For if of the Father, and the Son, and the Holy Spirit, so as to assign each clause severally to each person: of Him, that is to say, of the Father; through Him, that is to say, through the Son; in Him, that is to say, in the Holy Spirit,—it is manifest that the Father, and the Son, and the Holy Spirit is one God, inasmuch as the words continue in the singular number, "To whom[10] be glory for ever."

---

[1] 1 John v. 20.   [2] 1 Cor. i. 24.
[3] Ecclus. xxiv. 5.   [4] 1 Tim. vi. 14-16.

[5] Ps. lxxii. 18.   [6] John v. 19, 21.
[7] [Nothing is more important, in order to a correct interpretation of the New Testament, than a correct explanation of the term God. Sometimes it denotes the Trinity, and sometimes a person of the Trinity. The context always shows which it is. The examples given here by Augustin are only a few out of many.—W. G. T. S.]   [8] 1 Cor. viii. 6.   [9] Rom. xi. 36.   [10] Ipsi.

For at the beginning of the passage he does not say, "O the depth of the riches both of the wisdom and knowledge" of the Father, or of the Son, or of the Holy Spirit, but "of the wisdom and knowledge of God!" "How unsearchable are His judgments, and His ways past finding out! For who hath known the mind of the Lord? or who hath been His counsellor? Or who hath first given to Him and it shall be recompensed unto him again? For of Him, and through Him, and in Him, are all things: to whom be glory for ever. Amen."[1] But if they will have this to be understood only of the Father, then in what way are all things by the Father, as is said here; and all things by the Son, as where it is said to the Corinthians, "And one Lord Jesus Christ, by whom are all things,"[2] and as in the Gospel of John, "All things were made by Him?" For if some things were made by the Father, and some by the Son, then all things were not made by the Father, nor all things by the Son; but if all things were made by the Father, and all things by the Son, then the same things were made by the Father and by the Son. The Son, therefore, is equal with the Father, and the working of the Father and the Son is indivisible. Because if the Father made even the Son, whom certainly the Son Himself did not make, then all things were not made by the Son; but all things *were* made by the Son: therefore He Himself was not made, that with the Father He might make all things that were made. And the apostle has not refrained from using the very word itself, but has said most expressly, "Who, being in the form of God, thought it not robbery to be equal with God;"[3] using here the name of God specially of the Father;[4] as elsewhere, "But the head of Christ is God."[5]

---

[1] Rom. xi. 33-36.   [2] 1 Cor. viii. 6.   [3] Phil. ii. 6.

[4] [It is not generally safe to differ from Augustin in trinitarian exegesis. But in Phil. ii. 6 "God" must surely denote the Divine Essence, not the first Person of the Essence. St. Paul describes "Christ Jesus" as "subsisting" (ὑπάρχων) originally, that is prior to incarnation, "in a form of God" (ἐν μορφῇ θεοῦ), and because he so subsisted, as being "equal with God." The word μορφή is anarthrous in the text: *a* form, not *the* form; as the A.V. and R.V. render. St. Paul refers to one of three "forms" of God—namely, that particular form of Sonship, which is peculiar to the second person of the Godhead. Had the apostle employed the article with μορφή, the implication would be that there is only one "form of God"—that is, only one person in the Divine Essence.

If then θεοῦ, in this place, denotes the Father, as Augustin says, St. Paul would teach that the Logos subsisted "in a form of the *Father*," which would imply that the Father had more than one "form," or else (if μορφῇ be rendered with the article) that the Logos subsisted in the "form" of the Father, neither of which is true. But if "God," in this place, denotes the Divine Essence, then St. Paul teaches that the unincarnate Logos subsisted in a particular "form" of the Essence—the Father and Spirit subsisting in other "forms" of it.

The student will observe that Augustin is careful to teach that the Logos, when he took on him "a form of a servant," did not *lay aside* "a form of God." He understands the kenosis (ἐκένωσε) to be, the humbling of the divinity by its *union* with the humanity; not the exinanition of it in the extremest sense of entirely divesting himself of the divinity, nor the less extreme sense of a *total* non-use of it during the humiliation.—W.G.T.S.].

[5] 1 Cor. xi. 3.

---

13. Similar evidence has been collected also concerning the Holy Spirit, of which those who have discussed the subject before ourselves have most fully availed themselves, that He too is God, and not a creature. But if not a creature, then not only God (for men likewise are called gods[6]), but also very God; and therefore absolutely equal with the Father and the Son, and in the unity of the Trinity consubstantial and co-eternal. But that the Holy Spirit is not a creature is made quite plain by that passage above all others, where we are commanded not to serve the creature, but the Creator;[7] not in the sense in which we are commanded to "serve" one another by love,[8] which is in Greek δουλεύειν, but in that in which God alone is served, which is in Greek λατρεύειν. From whence they are called idolaters who tender that service to images which is due to God. For it is this service concerning which it is said, "Thou shalt worship the Lord thy God, and Him only shalt thou serve."[9] For this is found also more distinctly in the Greek Scriptures, which have λατρεύσεις. Now if we are forbidden to serve the creature with such a service, seeing that it is written, "Thou shalt worship the Lord thy God, and Him only shalt thou serve" (and hence, too, the apostle repudiates those who worship and serve the creature more than the Creator), then assuredly the Holy Spirit is not a creature, to whom such a service is paid by all the saints; as says the apostle, "For we are the circumcision, which serve the Spirit of God,"[10] which is in the Greek λατρεύοντες. For even most Latin copies also have it thus, "We who serve the Spirit of God;" but all Greek ones, or almost all, have it so. Although in some Latin copies we find, not "We worship the Spirit of God," but, "We worship God in the Spirit." But let those who err in this case, and refuse to give up to the more weighty authority, tell us whether they find this text also varied in the MSS.: "Know ye not that your body is the temple of the Holy Ghost, which is in you, which ye have of God?" Yet what can be more senseless or more profane, than that any one should dare to say that the members of Christ are the temple of one who, in their opinion, is a creature inferior to Christ? For the apostle says in another place, "Your bodies are members of Christ." But if the members of Christ are also the temple of the Holy Spirit, then the Holy Spirit is not a creature; because we must needs owe to Him, of whom our body is the

---

[6] Ps. lxxxii. 6.   [7] Rom. i. 25.
[8] Gal. v. 13.   [9] Deut. vi. 13.
[10] Phil. iii. 3 (Vulgate, etc.).

temple, that service wherewith God only is to be served, which in Greek is called λατρεία. And accordingly the apostle says, "Therefore glorify God in your body."[1]

CHAP. 7.—IN WHAT MANNER THE SON IS LESS THAN THE FATHER, AND THAN HIMSELF.

14. In these and like testimonies of the divine Scriptures, by free use of which, as I have said, our predecessors exploded such sophistries or errors of the heretics, the unity and equality of the Trinity are intimated to our faith. But because, on account of the incarnation of the Word of God for the working out of our salvation, that the man Christ Jesus might be the Mediator between God and men,[2] many things are so said in the sacred books as to signify, or even most expressly declare, the Father to be greater than the Son; men have erred through a want of careful examination or consideration of the whole tenor of the Scriptures, and have endeavored to transfer those things which are said of Jesus Christ according to the flesh, to that substance of His which was eternal before the incarnation, and is eternal. They say, for instance, that the Son is less than the Father, because it is written that the Lord Himself said, "My Father is greater than I."[3] But the truth shows that after the same sense the Son is less also than Himself; for how was He not made less also than Himself, who "emptied[4] Himself, and took upon Him the form of a servant?" For He did not so take the form of a servant as that He should lose the form of God, in which He was equal to the Father. If, then, the form of a servant was so taken that the form of God was not lost, since both in the form of a servant and in the form of God He Himself is the same only-begotten Son of God the Father, in the form of God equal to the Father, in the form of a servant the Mediator between God and men, the man Christ Jesus; is there any one who cannot perceive that He Himself in the form of God is also greater than Himself, but yet likewise in the form of a servant less than Himself? And not, therefore, without cause the Scripture says both the one and the other, both that the Son is equal to the Father, and that the Father is greater than the Son. For there is no confusion when the former is understood as on account of the form of God, and the latter as on account of the form of a servant. And, in truth, this rule for clearing the question through all the sacred Scriptures is set forth in one chapter of an epistle of the

Apostle Paul, where this distinction is commended to us plainly enough. For he says, "Who, being in the form of God, thought it not robbery to be equal with God; but emptied Himself, and took upon Him the form of a servant, and was made in the likeness of men: and was found in fashion[5] as a man."[6] The Son of God, then, is equal to God the Father in nature, but less in "fashion."[7] For in the form of a servant which He took He is less than the Father; but in the form of God, in which also He was before He took the form of a servant, He is equal to the Father. In the form of God He is the Word, "by whom all things are made;"[8] but in the form of a servant He was "made of a woman, made under the law, to redeem them that were under the law."[9] In like manner, in the form of God He made man; in the form of a servant He was made man. For if the Father alone had made man without the Son, it would not have been written, "Let us make man in *our* image, after *our* likeness."[10] Therefore, because the form of God took the form of a servant, both is God and both is man; but both God, on account of God who takes; and both man, on account of man who is taken. For neither by that taking is the one of them turned and changed into the other: the Divinity is not changed into the creature, so as to cease to be Divinity; nor the creature into Divinity, so as to cease to be creature.

CHAP. 8.—THE TEXTS OF SCRIPTURE EXPLAINED RESPECTING THE SUBJECTION OF THE SON TO THE FATHER, WHICH HAVE BEEN MISUNDERSTOOD. CHRIST WILL NOT SO GIVE UP THE KINGDOM TO THE FATHER, AS TO TAKE IT AWAY FROM HIMSELF. THE BEHOLDING HIM IS THE PROMISED END OF ALL ACTIONS. THE HOLY SPIRIT IS SUFFICIENT TO OUR BLESSEDNESS EQUALLY WITH THE FATHER.

15. As for that which the apostle says, "And when all things shall be subdued unto Him, then shall the Son also Himself be subject unto Him that put all things under Him:" either the text has been so turned, lest any one should think that the "fashion"[11] of Christ, which He took according to the human creature, was to be transformed hereafter into the Divinity, or (to express it more precisely) the Godhead itself, who is not a creature, but is the unity of the Trinity,—a nature incorporeal, and unchangeable, and consubstantial, and co-eternal with itself; or if

---

[1] 1 Cor. vi. 19, 15, 20.   [2] 1 Tim. ii. 5.
[3] John xiv. 28.   [4] *Exinanivit.*
[5] *Habitu.*   [6] Phil. ii. 6, 7.   [7] *Habitu.*
[8] John i. 3.   [9] Gal. iv. 4, 5.   [10] Gen. i. 26.
[11] *Habitum.*

any one contends, as some have thought, that the text, "Then shall the Son also Himself be subject unto Him that put all things under Him," is so turned in order that one may believe that very "subjection" to be a change and conversion hereafter of the creature into the substance or essence itself of the Creator, that is, that that which had been the substance of a creature shall become the substance of the Creator;—such an one at any rate admits this, of which in truth there is no possible doubt, that this had not yet taken place, when the Lord said, "My Father is greater than I." For He said this not only before He ascended into heaven, but also before He had suffered, and had risen from the dead. But they who think that the human nature in Him is to be changed and converted into the substance of the Godhead, and that it was so said, "Then shall the Son also Himself be subject unto Him that put all things under Him,"—as if to say, Then also the Son of man Himself, and the human nature taken by the Word of God, shall be changed into the nature of Him who put all things under Him,—must also think that this will then take place, when, after the day of judgment, "He shall have delivered up the kingdom to God, even the Father." And hence even still, according to this opinion, the Father is greater than that form of a servant which was taken of the Virgin. But if some affirm even further, that the man Christ Jesus has already been changed into the substance of God, at least they cannot deny that the human nature still remained, when He said before His passion, "For my Father is greater than I;" whence there is no question that it was said in this sense, that the Father is greater than the form of a servant, to whom in the form of God the Son is equal. Nor let any one, hearing what the apostle says, "But when He saith all things are put under Him, it is manifest that He is excepted which did put all things under Him,"[1] think the words, that He hath put all things under the Son, to be so understood of the Father, as that He should not think that the Son Himself put all things under Himself. For this the apostle plainly declares, when he says to the Philippians, "For our conversation is in heaven; from whence also we look for the Saviour, the Lord Jesus Christ: who shall change our vile body, that it may be fashioned like unto His glorious body, according to the working whereby He is able even to subdue[2] all things unto Himself."[3] For the working of the Father and of the Son is indivisible. Otherwise, neither

hath the Father Himself put all things under Himself, but the Son hath put all things under Him, who delivers the kingdom to Him, and puts down all rule and all authority and power. For these words are spoken of the Son: "When He shall have delivered up," says the apostle, "the kingdom to God, even the Father; when He shall have put down[4] all rule, and all authority, and all power." For the same that puts down, also makes subject.

16. Neither may we think that Christ shall so give up the kingdom to God, even the Father, as that He shall take it away from Himself. For some vain talkers have thought even this. For when it is said, "He shall have delivered up the kingdom to God, even the Father," He Himself is not excluded; because He is one God together with the Father. But that word "until" deceives those who are careless readers of the divine Scriptures, but eager for controversies. For the text continues, "For He must reign, until He hath put all enemies under His feet;"[5] as though, when He had so put them, He would no more reign. Neither do they perceive that this is said in the same way as that other text, "His heart is established: He shall not be afraid, until He see His desire upon His enemies."[6] For He will not then be afraid when He has seen it. What then means, "When He shall have delivered up the kingdom to God, even the Father," as though God and the Father has not the kingdom now? But because He is hereafter to bring all the just, over whom now, living by faith, the Mediator between God and men, the man Christ Jesus, reigns, to that sight which the same apostle calls "face to face;"[7] therefore the words, "When He shall have delivered up the kingdom to God, even the Father," are as much as to say, When He shall have brought believers to the contemplation of God, even the Father. For He says, "All things are delivered unto me of my Father: and no man knoweth the Son, but the Father; neither knoweth any man the Father, save the Son, and he to whomsoever the Son will reveal Him."[8] The Father will then be revealed by the Son, "when He shall have put down all rule, and all authority, and all power;" that is, in such wise that there shall be no more need of any economy of similitudes, by means of angelic rulers, and authorities, and powers. Of whom that is not unfitly understood, which is said in the Song of Songs to the bride, "We will make thee borders[9] of gold, with studs of silver, while the King sitteth at His

---

[1] 1 Cor. xv. 28, 24, 27.
[2] *Subjicere.*
[3] Phil. iii. 20, 21.

[4] *Evacuaverit.*
[5] 1 Cor. xv. 24, 25.
[6] Ps. cxii. 8.
[7] 1 Cor. xiii. 12.
[8] Matt. xi. 27.
[9] *Similitudines.*

table;"[1] that is, as long as Christ is in His secret place: since "your life is hid with Christ in God; when Christ, who is our[2] life, shall appear, then shall ye also appear with Him in glory."[3] Before which time, "we see now through a glass, in an enigma," that is, in similitudes, "but then face to face."[4]

17. For this contemplation is held forth to us as the end of all actions, and the everlasting fullness of joy. For "we are the sons of God; and it doth not yet appear what we shall be: but we know that, when He shall appear, we shall be like Him; for we shall see Him as He is."[5] For that which He said to His servant Moses, "I am that I am; thus shalt thou say to the children of Israel, I Am hath sent me to you;"[6] this it is which we shall contemplate when we shall live in eternity. For so it is said, "And this is life eternal, that they might know Thee, the only true God, and Jesus Christ, whom Thou hast sent.'"[7] This shall be when the Lord shall have come, and "shall have brought to light the hidden things of darkness;"[8] when the darkness of this present mortality and corruption shall have passed away. Then will be our morning, which is spoken of in the Psalm, "In the morning will I direct my prayer unto Thee, and will contemplate Thee."[9] Of this contemplation I understand it to be said, "When He shall have delivered up the kingdom to God, even the Father;" that is, when He shall have brought the just, over whom now, living by faith, the Mediator between God and man, the man Christ Jesus, reigns, to the contemplation of God, even the Father. If herein I am foolish, let him who knows better correct me; to me at least the case seems as I have said.[10] For we shall not seek anything else, when we shall have come to the contemplation of Him. But that contemplation is not yet, so long as our joy is in hope. For "hope that is seen is not hope: for what a man seeth, why doth he yet hope for? But if we hope for that we see not, then do we with patience wait for it,"[11] viz. "as long as the King sitteth at His table."[12] Then will take place that which is written, "In Thy presence is fullness of joy."[13] Nothing more than that joy will be required; because there

will be nothing more than can be required. For the Father will be manifested to us, and that will suffice for us. And this much Philip had well understood, so that he said to the Lord, "Show us the Father, and it sufficeth us." But he had not yet understood that he himself was able to say this very same thing in this way also: Lord, show Thyself to us, and it sufficeth us. For, that he might understand this, the Lord replied to him, "Have I been so long time with you, and yet hast thou not known me, Philip? he that hath seen me hath seen the Father." But because He intended him, before he could see this, to live by faith, He went on to say, "Believest thou not that I am in the Father, and the Father in me?"[14] For "while we are at home in the body, we are absent from the Lord: for we walk by faith, not by sight."[15] For contemplation is the recompense of faith, for which recompense our hearts are purified by faith; as it is written, "Purifying their hearts by faith."[16] And that our hearts are to be purified for this contemplation, is proved above all by this text, "Blessed are the pure in heart, for they shall see God."[17] And that this is life eternal, God says in the Psalm, "With long life will I satisfy him, and show him my salvation."[18] Whether, therefore, we hear, Show us the Son; or whether we hear, Show us the Father; it is even all one, since neither can be manifested without the other. For they are one, as He also Himself says, "My Father and I are one."[19] Finally, on account of this very indivisibility, it suffices that sometimes the Father alone, or the Son alone, should be named, as hereafter to fill us with the joy of His countenance.

18. Neither is the Spirit of either thence excluded, that is, the Spirit of the Father and of the Son; which Holy Spirit is specially called "the Spirit of truth, whom the world cannot receive."[20] For to have the fruition of God the Trinity, after whose image we are made, is indeed the fullness of our joy, than which there is no greater. On this account the Holy Spirit is sometimes spoken of as if He alone sufficed to our blessedness: and He does alone so suffice, because He cannot be divided from the Father and the Son; as the Father alone is sufficient, because He cannot be divided from the Son and the Holy Spirit; and the Son alone is sufficient because He cannot be divided from the Father and the Holy Spirit. For what does He mean by saying, "If ye love me, keep my commandments; and I will pray the Father, and He shall give

---

[1] In recubitu. Cant. i. 11; see LXX.
[2] Vestra.   [3] Col. iii. 3, 4.   [4] 1 Cor. xiii. 12.
[5] 1 John iii. 2.   [6] Ex. iii. 14.   [7] John xvii. 3.
[8] 1 Cor. iv. 5.   [9] Ps. v. 5.
[10] [The common explanation is better, which regards the "kingdom" that is to be delivered up, to be the mediatorial commission. When Christ shall have finished his work of redeeming men, he no longer discharges the office of a mediator. It seems incongruous to denominate the beatific vision of God by the redeemed, a surrender of a kingdom. In I. x. 21, Augustin says that when the Redeemer brings the redeemed from faith to sight, "He is said to 'deliver up the kingdom to God, even the Father.'" —W.G.T.S.]
[11] Rom. viii. 24, 25.   [12] Cant. i. 12.   [13] Ps. xvi. 11.

[14] John xiv. 8, 10.   [15] 2 Cor. v. 6, 7.   [16] Acts xv. 9.
[17] Matt. v. 8.   [18] Ps. xci. 16.   [19] John x. 30.
[20] John xiv. 17.

you another Comforter, that He may abide with you for ever; even the Spirit of truth, whom the world cannot receive,"[1] that is, the lovers of the world? For "the natural man receiveth not the things of the Spirit of God."[2] But it may perhaps seem, further, as if the words, "And I will pray the Father, and He shall give you another Comforter," were so said as if the Son alone were not sufficient. And that place so speaks of the Spirit, as if He alone were altogether sufficient: "When He, the Spirit of truth, is come, He will guide you into all truth."[3] Pray, therefore, is the Son here excluded, as if He did not teach all truth, or as if the Holy Spirit were to fill up that which the Son could not fully teach? Let them say then, if it pleases them, that the Holy Spirit is greater than the Son, whom they are wont to call less. Or is it, forsooth, because it is not said, He alone,—or, No one else except Himself—will guide you into all truth, that they allow that the Son also may be believed to teach together with Him? In that case the apostle has excluded the Son from knowing those things which are of God, where he says, "Even so the things of God knoweth no one, but the Spirit of God:"[4] so that these perverse men might, upon this ground, go on to say that none but the Holy Spirit teaches even the Son the things of God, as the greater teaches the less; to whom the Son Himself ascribes so much as to say, "But because I have said these things unto you, sorrow hath filled your heart. Nevertheless I tell you the truth; it is expedient for you that I go away: for if I go not away, the Comforter will not come unto you."[5]

CHAP. 9.—ALL ARE SOMETIMES UNDERSTOOD IN ONE PERSON.

But this is said, not on account of any inequality of the Word of God and of the Holy Spirit, but as though the presence of the Son of man with them would be a hindrance to the coming of Him, who was not less, because He did not "empty Himself, taking upon Him the form of a servant,"[6] as the Son did. It was necessary, then, that the form of a servant should be taken away from their eyes, because, through gazing upon it, they thought that alone which they saw to be Christ. Hence also is that which is said, "If ye loved me, ye would rejoice because I said, 'I go unto the Father; for my Father is greater than I:'"[7] that is, on that account it is necessary for me to go to the Father, be-

cause, whilst you see me thus, you hold me to be less than the Father through that which you see; and so, being taken up with the creature and the "fashion" which I have taken upon me, you do not perceive the equality which I have with the Father. Hence, too, is this: "Touch me not; for I am not yet ascended to my Father."[8] For touch, as it were, puts a limit to their conception, and He therefore would not have the thought of the heart, directed towards Himself, to be so limited as that He should be held to be only that which He seemed to be. But the "ascension to the Father" meant, so to appear as He is equal to the Father, that the limit of the sight which sufficeth us might be attained there. Sometimes also it is said of the Son alone, that He himself sufficeth, and the whole reward of our love and longing is held forth as in the sight of Him. For so it is said, "He that hath my commandments, and keepeth them, he it is that loveth me; and he that loveth me shall be loved of my Father; and I will love him, and will manifest myself to him."[9] Pray, because He has not here said, And I will show the Father also to him, has He therefore excluded the Father? On the contrary, because it is true, "I and my Father are one," when the Father is manifested, the Son also, who is in Him, is manifested; and when the Son is manifested, the Father also, who is in Him, is manifested. As, therefore, when it is said, "And I will manifest myself to him," it is understood that He manifests also the Father; so likewise in that which is said, "When He shall have delivered up the kingdom to God, even the Father," it is understood that He does not take it away from Himself; since, when He shall bring believers to the contemplation of God, even the Father, doubtless He will bring them to the contemplation of Himself, who has said, "And I will manifest myself to him." And so, consequently, when Judas had said to Him, "Lord, how is it that Thou wilt manifest Thyself unto us, and not unto the world?" Jesus answered and said to him, "If a man love me, he will keep my words: and my Father will love him, and we will come unto him, and make our abode with him."[10] Behold, that He manifests not only Himself to him by whom He is loved, because He comes to him together with the Father, and abides with him.

19. Will it perhaps be thought, that when the Father and the Son make their abode with him who loves them, the Holy Spirit

[1] John xiv. 15-17.   [2] 1 Cor. ii. 14.   [3] John xvi. 13.
[4] 1 Cor. ii. 11.   [5] John xvi. 6, 7.   [6] Phil. ii. 7.
[7] John xiv. 28.

[8] John xx. 17.   [9] John xiv. 21.
[10] John xiv. 22, 23.

is excluded from that abode? What, then, is that which is said above of the Holy Spirit: "Whom the world cannot receive, because it seeth Him not: but ye know Him; for He abideth with you, and is in you"? He, therefore, is not excluded from that abode, of whom it is said, "He abideth with you, and is in you;" unless, perhaps, any one be so senseless as to think, that when the Father and the Son have come that they may make their abode with him who loves them, the Holy Spirit will depart thence, and (as it were) give place to those who are greater. But the Scripture itself meets this carnal idea; for it says a little above: "I will pray the Father, and He shall give you another Comforter, that He may abide with you for ever." [1] He will not therefore depart when the Father and the Son come, but will be in the same abode with them eternally; because neither will He come without them, nor they without Him. But in order to intimate the Trinity, some things are separately affirmed, the Persons being also each severally named; and yet are not to be understood as though the other Persons were excluded, on account of the unity of the same Trinity and the One substance and Godhead of the Father and of the Son and of the Holy Spirit. [2]

CHAP. 10.—IN WHAT MANNER CHRIST SHALL DELIVER UP THE KINGDOM TO GOD, EVEN THE FATHER. THE KINGDOM HAVING BEEN DELIVERED TO GOD, EVEN THE FATHER, CHRIST WILL NOT THEN MAKE INTERCESSION FOR US.

20. Our Lord Jesus Christ, therefore, will so deliver up the kingdom to God, even the Father, Himself not being thence excluded, nor the Holy Spirit, when He shall bring believers to the contemplation of God, wherein is the end of all good actions, and everlasting rest, and joy which never will be taken from us. For He signifies this in that which He says: "I will see you again, and your heart shall rejoice; and your joy no man taketh from you." [3] Mary, sitting at the feet of the Lord, and earnestly listening to His word, foreshowed a similitude of this joy; resting

as she did from all business, and intent upon the truth, according to that manner of which this life is capable, by which, however, to prefigure that which shall be for eternity. For while Martha, her sister, was cumbered about necessary business, which, although good and useful, yet, when rest shall have succeeded, is to pass away, she herself was resting in the word of the Lord. And so the Lord replied to Martha, when she complained that her sister did not help her: "Mary hath chosen the best part, which shall not be taken away from her." [4] He did not say that Martha was acting a bad part; but that "best part that shall not be taken away." For that part which is occupied in the ministering to a need shall be "taken away" when the need itself has passed away. Since the reward of a good work that will pass away is rest that will not pass away. In that contemplation, therefore, God will be all in all; because nothing else but Himself will be required, but it will be sufficient to be enlightened by and to enjoy Him alone. And so he in whom "the Spirit maketh intercession with groanings which cannot be uttered," [5] says, "One thing have I desired of the Lord, that I will seek after; that I may dwell in the house of the Lord all the days of my life, to contemplate the beauty of the Lord." [6] For we shall then contemplate God, the Father and the Son and the Holy Spirit, when the Mediator between God and men, the man Christ Jesus, shall have delivered up the kingdom to God, even the Father, so as no longer to make intercession for us, as our Mediator and Priest, Son of God and Son of man; [7] but that He Himself too, in so far as He is a Priest that has taken the form of a servant for us, shall be put under Him who has put all things under Him, and under whom He has put all things: so that, in so far as He is God, He with Him will have put us under Himself; in so far as He is a Priest, He with us will be put under Him. [8] And therefore as the [incarnate] Son is both God and man, it is rather to be said that the manhood in the Son is another substance [from the Son], than that the Son in the Father [is another substance from the Father]; just as

---

[1] John xiv. 16-23.
[2] [An act belonging eminently and officially to a particular trinitarian person is not performed to the total *exclusion* of the other persons, because of the numerical unity of essence. The whole undivided essence is in each person; consequently, what the essence in one of its personal modes, or forms, does officially and eminently, is participated in by the essence in its other modes or forms. Hence the interchange of persons in Scripture. Though creation is officially the Father's work, yet the Son creates (Col. i. 16; Heb. i. 3). The name Saviour is given to the Father (1 Tim. i. 1). Judgment belongs officially to the Son (John v. 22; Matt. xxv. 31); yet the Father judgeth (1 Pet. i. 17). The Father raises Christ (Acts xiii. 30); yet Christ raises himself (John x. 18; Acts x. 41; Rom. xiv. 9).—W. G. T. S.]
[3] John xvi. 22.

[4] Luke x. 30-42.   [5] Rom. viii. 26.   [6] Ps. xxvii. 4.
[7] [The redeemed must forever stand in the relation of redeemed sinners to their Redeemer. Thus standing, they will forever need Christ's sacrifice and intercession in respect to their *past* sins in this earthly state. But as in the heavenly state they are sinless, and are incurring no new guilt, it is true that they do not require the fresh application of atoning blood for new sins, nor Christ's intercession for such. This is probably what Augustin means by saying that Christ "no longer makes intercession for us," when he has delivered up the kingdom to God. When the Mediator has surrendered his commission, he ceases to redeem sinners from death, while yet he continues forever to be the Head of those whom he has redeemed, and their High Priest forever, after the order of Melchizedek (Heb. vii. 1; .)—W. G. T. S.]   [8] 1 Cor. xv. 24-28.

the carnal nature of my soul is more another substance in relation to my soul itself, although in one and the same man, than the soul of another man is in relation to my soul. [1]

21. When, therefore, He "shall have delivered up the kingdom to God, even the Father,"—that is, when He shall have brought those who believe and live by faith, for whom now as Mediator He maketh intercession, to that contemplation, for the obtaining of which we sigh and groan, and when labor and groaning shall have passed away,—then, since the kingdom will have been delivered up to God, even the Father, He will no more make intercession for us. And this He signifies, when He says: "These things have I spoken unto you in similitudes; [2] but the time cometh when I shall no more speak unto you in similitudes, [2] but I shall declare [3] to you plainly of the Father:" that is, they will not then be "similitudes," when the sight shall be "face to face." For this it is which He says, "But I will declare to you plainly of the Father;" as if He said, I will plainly show you the Father. For He says, I will "declare" to you, because He is His word. For He goes on to say, "At that day ye shall ask in my name; and I say not unto you, that I will pray the Father for you: for the Father Himself loveth you, because ye have loved me, and have believed that I came out from God. I came forth from the Father, and am come into the world: again, I leave the world, and go to the Father." [4] What is meant by "I came forth from the Father," unless this, that I have not appeared in that form in which I am equal to the Father, but otherwise, that is, as less than the Father, in the creature which I have taken upon me? And what is meant by "I am come into the world," unless this, that I have manifested to the eyes even of sinners who love this world, the form of a servant which I took, making myself of no reputation? And what is meant by "Again, I leave the world," unless this, that I take away from the sight of the lovers of this world that which they have seen? And what is meant by "I go to the Father," unless this, that I teach those who are my faithful ones to understand me in that being in which I am equal to the Father? Those who be-

lieve this will be thought worthy of being brought by faith to sight, that is, to that very sight, in bringing them to which He is said to "deliver up the kingdom to God, even the Father." For His faithful ones, whom He has redeemed with His blood, are called His kingdom, for whom He now intercedes; but then, making them to abide in Himself there, where He is equal to the Father, He will no longer pray the Father for them. "For," He says, "the Father Himself loveth you." For indeed He "prays," in so far as He is less than the Father; but as He is equal with the Father, He with the Father grants. Wherefore He certainly does not exclude Himself from that which He says, "The Father Himself loveth you;" but He means it to be understood after that manner which I have above spoken of, and sufficiently intimated,—namely, that for the most part each Person of the Trinity is so named, that the other Persons also may be understood. Accordingly, "For the Father Himself loveth you," is so said that by consequence both the Son and the Holy Spirit also may be understood: not that He does not now love us, who spared not His own Son, but delivered Him up for us all; [5] but God loves us, such as we shall be, not such as we are, For such as they are whom He loves, such are they whom He keeps eternally; which shall then be, when He who now maketh intercession for us shall have "delivered up the kingdom to God, even the Father," so as no longer to ask the Father, because the Father Himself loveth us. But for what deserving, except of faith, by which we believe before we see that which is promised? For by this faith we shall arrive at sight; so that He may love us, being such, as He loves us in order that we may become; and not such, as He hates us because we are, and exhorts and enables us to wish not to be always.

CHAP. 11 —BY WHAT RULE IN THE SCRIPTURES IT IS UNDERSTOOD THAT THE SON IS NOW EQUAL AND NOW LESS.

22. Wherefore, having mastered this rule for interpreting the Scriptures concerning the Son of God, that we are to distinguish in them what relates to the form of God, in which He is equal to the Father, and what to the form of a servant which He took, in which He is less than the Father; we shall not be disquieted by apparently contrary and mutually repugnant sayings of the sacred books. For both the Son and the Holy Spirit, according to the form of God, are equal to the Father,

---

[1] [The animal soul is different in kind from the rational soul, though both constitute one person; while the rational soul of a man is the same in kind with that of another man. Similarly, says Augustin, there is a difference in kind between the human nature and the divine nature of Christ, though constituting one theanthropic person, while the divine nature of the Son is the same in substance with that of the Father, though constituting two different persons, the Father and Son.—W. G. T. S.]

[2] Proverbs—A. V.   [3] Show--A.V.   [4] John xvi. 25-28.   [5] Rom. viii. 32.

because neither of them is a creature, as we have already shown: but according to the form of a servant He is less than the Father, because He Himself has said, "My Father is greater than I;"[1] and He is less than Himself, because it is said of Him, He emptied Himself;"[2] and He is less than the Holy Spirit, because He Himself says, "Whosoever speaketh a word against the Son of man, it shall be forgiven him; but whosoever speaketh against the Holy Ghost, it shall not be forgiven Him."[3] And in the Spirit too He wrought miracles, saying: "But if I with the Spirit of God cast out devils, no doubt the kingdom of God is come upon you."[4] And in Isaiah He says,—in the lesson which He Himself read in the synagogue, and showed without a scruple of doubt to be fulfilled concerning Himself,—"The Spirit of the Lord God," He says, "is upon me: because He hath anointed me to preach good tidings unto the meek He hath sent me to proclaim liberty to the captives,"[5] etc.: for the doing of which things He therefore declares Himself to be "sent," because the Spirit of God is upon Him. According to the form of God, all things were made by Him;[6] according to the form of a servant, He was Himself made of a woman, made under the law.[7] According to the form of God, He and the Father are one;[8] according to the form of a servant, He came not to do His own will, but the will of Him that sent Him.[9] According to the form of God, "As the Father hath life in Himself, so hath He given to the Son to have life in Himself;"[10] according to the form of a servant, His "soul is sorrowful even unto death;" and, "O my Father," He says, "if it be possible, let this cup pass from me."[11] According to the form of God, "He is the True God, and eternal life;"[12] according to the form of a servant, "He became obedient unto death, even the death of the cross."[13]—23. According to the form of God, all things that the Father hath are His,[14] and "All mine," He says, "are Thine, and Thine are mine;"[15] according to the form of a servant, the doctrine is not His own, but His that sent Him.[16]

CHAP. 12.—IN WHAT MANNER THE SON IS SAID NOT TO KNOW THE DAY AND THE HOUR WHICH THE FATHER KNOWS. SOME THINGS SAID OF CHRIST ACCORDING TO THE FORM OF GOD, OTHER THINGS ACCORDING TO THE FORM OF A SERVANT. IN WHAT WAY IT IS OF CHRIST TO GIVE THE KINGDOM, IN WHAT NOT OF CHRIST. CHRIST WILL BOTH JUDGE AND NOT JUDGE.

Again, "Of that day and that hour knoweth no man, no, not the angels which are in heaven; neither the Son, but the Father."[17] For He is ignorant of this, as *making others ignorant;* that is, in that He did not so know as at that time to show His disciples:[18] as it was said to Abraham, "Now I know that thou fearest God,"[19] that is, now I have caused thee to know it; because he himself, being tried in that temptation, became known to himself. For He was certainly going to tell this same thing to His disciples at the fitting time; speaking of which yet future as if past, He says, "Henceforth I call you not servants, but friends; for the servant knoweth not what his Lord doeth: but I have called you friends; for all things that I have heard of my Father I have made known unto you;"[20] which He had not yet done, but spoke as though He had already done it, because He certainly would do it. For He says to the disciples themselves, "I have yet many things to say unto you; but ye cannot bear them now."[21] Among which is to be understood also, "Of the day and hour." For the apostle also says, "I determined not to know anything among you, save Jesus Christ, and Him crucified;"[22] because he was speaking to those who were not able to receive higher things concerning the Godhead of Christ. To whom also a little while after he says, "I could not speak unto you as unto spiritual, but as unto carnal."[23] He was "ignorant," therefore, among them of that which they were not able to know from him. And that only he said that he knew, which it was fitting that they should know from him. In short, he knew among the perfect what he knew not among babes; for he there says: "We speak wisdom among them that are perfect."[24] For a man is said

---

[1] John xiv. 28.
[2] Phil. ii. 7.
[3] Matt. xii. 32.
[4] Matt. xii. 28.
[5] Isa lxi. 1; Luke iv. 18, 19.
[6] John i. 3.
[7] Gal. iv. 4.
[8] John. x. 30.
[9] John vi. 38.
[10] John v. 26. [In communicating the Divine Essence to the Son, in eternal generation, the essence is communicated with all its attributes. Self existence is one of these attributes. In this way, the Father " gives to the Son to have life in himself." when he makes common (κοινωνεῖν), between Himself and the Son, the one Divine Essence.—W. G. T. S.]
[11] Matt. xxvi. 38, 39.
[12] 1 John v. 20.
[13] Phil. ii. 8.
[14] John xvii. 15.
[15] John xvii. 10.
[16] John vii. 16.

[17] Mark xiii. 32.
[18] [The more common explanation of this text in modern exegesis makes the ignorance to be literal, and referable solely to the human nature of our Lord, not to his person as a whole. Augustin's explanation, which Bengel, on Mark xiii. 32, is inclined to favor, escapes the difficulty that arises from a seeming division of the one theanthopic person into two portions, one of which knows, and the other does not. Yet this same difficulty besets the fact of a *growth* in knowledge, which is plainly taught in Luke i. 80. In this case, the increase in wisdom must relate to the humanity alone.—W.G.T.S.]
[19] Gen. xxii. 12.
[20] John xv. 15.
[21] John xvi. 12.
[22] 1 Cor. ii. 2.
[23] 1 Cor. iii. 1.
[24] 1 Cor. ii. 6.

not to know what he hides, after that kind of speech, after which a ditch is called blind which is hidden. For the Scriptures do not use any other kind of speech than may be found in use among men, because they speak to men.

24. According to the form of God, it is said, "Before all the hills He begat me,"[1] that is, before all the loftinesses of things created; and, "Before the dawn I begat Thee,"[2] that is, before all times and temporal things: but according to the form of a servant, it is said, "The Lord created me in the beginning of His ways."[3] Because, according to the form of God, He said, "I am the truth;" and according to the form of a servant, "I am the way."[4] For, because He Himself, being the first-begotten of the dead,[5] made a passage to the kingdom of God to life eternal for His Church, to which He is so the Head as to make the body also immortal, therefore He was "created in the beginning of the ways" of God in His work. For, according to the form of God, He is the beginning,[6] that also speaketh unto us, in which "beginning" God created the heaven and the earth;[7] but according to the form of a servant, "He is a bridegroom coming out of His chamber."[8] According to the form of God, "He is the first-born of every creature, and He is before all things and by him all things consist;" according to the form of a servant, "He is the head of the body, the Church."[9] According to the form of ·God, "He is the Lord of glory."[10] From which it is evident that He Himself glorifies His saints: for, "Whom He did predestinate, them He also called; and whom He called, them He also justified; and whom He justified, them He also glorified."[11] Of Him accordingly it is said, that He justifieth the ungodly;[12] of Him it is said, that He is just and a justifier.[13] If, therefore, He has also glorified those whom He has justified, He who justifies, Himself also glorifies; who is, as I have said, the Lord of glory. Yet, according to the form of a servant, He replied to His disciples, when inquiring about their own glorification: "To sit on my right hand and on my left is not mine to give, but [it shall be given to them] for whom it is prepared by my Father."[14]

25. But that which is prepared by His Father is prepared also by the Son Himself, because He and the Father are one.[15] For we have already shown, by many modes of speech in the divine Scriptures, that, in this Trinity, what is said of each is also said of all, on account of the indivisible working of the one and same substance. As He also says of the Holy Spirit, "If I depart, I will send Him unto you."[16] He did not say, *We* will send; but in such way as if the Son only should send Him, and not the Father; while yet He says in another place, "These things have I spoken unto you, being yet present with you; but the Comforter, which is the Holy Ghost, whom the Father will send in my name, He shall teach you all things."[17] Here again it is so said as if the Son also would not send Him, but the Father only. As therefore in these texts, so also where He says, "But for them for whom it is prepared by my Father," He meant it to be understood that He Himself, with the Father, prepares seats of glory for those for whom He will. But some one may say: There, when He spoke of the Holy Spirit, He so says that He Himself will send Him, as not to deny that the Father will send Him; and in the other place, He so says that the Father will send Him, as not to deny that He will do so Himself; but here He expressly says, 'It is not mine to give," and so goes on to say that these things are prepared by the Father. But this is the very thing which we have already laid down to be said according to the form of a servant: *viz.*, that we are so to understand "It is not mine to give," as if it were said, This is not in the power of man to give; that so He may be understood to give it through that wherein He is God equal to the Father. "It is not mine," He says, "to give;" that is, I do not give these things by human power, but "to those for whom it is prepared by my Father;" but then take care you understand also, that if "all things which the Father hath are mine,"[18] then this certainly is mine also, and I with the Father have prepared these things.

26. For I ask again, in what manner this is said, "If any man hear not my words, I will not judge him?"[19] For perhaps He has said here, "I will not judge him," in the same sense as there, "It is not mine to give." But what follows here? "I came not," He says, "to judge the world, but to save the world;" and then He adds, "He that rejecteth me, and receiveth not my words, hath one that judgeth him." Now here we should understand the Father, unless He had added, "The word that I have spoken, the same shall judge him in the last day." Well, then, will neither the Son judge, because He says, "I will not judge him," nor the Father, but the word which the Son hath spoken? Nay,

---

[1] Prov. viii. 25.　　[2] Ps. cx. 3, *Vulgate.*
[3] Prov. viii. 22.　　[4] John xiv. 6.　　[5] Apoc. i. 5.
[6] John viii. 25.　　[7] Gen. i. 1.　　[8] Ps. xix. 5.
[9] Col. i. 15, 17, 18.　[10] 1 Cor. ii. 8.　[11] Rom. viii. 30.
[12] Rom. iv. 5.　　[13] Rom. iii. 26.　[14] Matt. xx. 23.
[15] John x. 30.

[16] John xvi. 7.　　　　　[17] John xiv. 25, 26.
[18] John xvi 15.　　　　　[19] John xii. 47-50.

but hear what yet follows: "For I," He says, "have not spoken of myself; but the Father which sent me, He gave me a commandment, what I should say, and what I should speak; and I know that His commandment is life everlasting: whatsoever I speak therefore, even as the Father said unto me, so I speak." If therefore the Son judges not, but "the word which the Son hath spoken;" and the word which the Son hath spoken therefore judges, because the Son "hath not spoken of Himself, but the Father who sent Him gave Him a commandment what He should say, and what He should speak:" then the Father assuredly judges, whose word it is which the Son hath spoken; and the same Son Himself is the very Word of the Father. For the commandment of the Father is not one thing, and the word of the Father another; for He hath called it both a word and a commandment. Let us see, therefore, whether perchance, when He says, "I have not spoken of myself," He meant to be understood thus, —I am not born of myself. For if He speaks the word of the Father, then He speaks Himself,[1] because He is Himself the Word of the Father. For ordinarily He says, "The Father gave to me;" by which He means it to be understood that the Father begat Him: not that He gave anything to Him, already existing and not possessing it; but that the very meaning of, To have given that He might have, is, To have begotten that He might be. For it is not, as with the creature, so with the Son of God before the incarnation and before He took upon Him our flesh, the Only-begotten by whom all things were made; that He *is* one thing, and *has* another: but He *is* in such way as to *be* what He *has*. And this is said more plainly, if any one is fit to receive it, in that place where He says: "For as the Father hath life in Himself, so hath He given to the Son to have life in Himself."[2] For He did not give to Him, already existing and not having life, that He should have life in Himself; inasmuch as, in that He *is*, He is life. Therefore "He gave to the Son to have life in Himself" means, He begat the Son to be unchangeable life, which is life eternal. Since, therefore, the Word of God is the Son of God, and the Son of God is "the true God and eternal life,"[3] as John says in his Epistle; so here, what else are we to acknowledge when the Lord says, "The word which I have spoken, the same shall judge him at the last day,"[4] and calls that very word the word of the Father and the commandment of the Father, and that very

commandment everlasting life?" "And I know," He says, "that His commandment is life everlasting."

27. I ask, therefore, how we are to understand, "I will not judge him; but the Word which I have spoken shall judge him:" which appears from what follows to be so said, as if He would say, I will not judge; but the Word of the Father will judge. But the Word of the Father is the Son of God Himself. Is it to be so understood: I will not judge, but I will judge? How can this be true, unless in this way: *viz.*, I will not judge by human power, because I am the Son of man; but I will judge by the power of the Word, because I am the Son of God? Or if it still seems contradictory and inconsistent to say, I will not judge, but I will judge; what shall we say of that place where He says, "My doctrine is not mine?" How "mine," when "not mine?" For He did not say, *This* doctrine is not mine, but "*My* doctrine is not mine:" that which He called His own, the same He called not His own. How can this be true, unless He has called it His own in one relation; not His own, in another? According to the form of God, His own; according to the form of a servant, not His own. For when He says, "It is not mine, but His that sent me,"[5] He makes us recur to the Word itself. For the doctrine of the Father is the Word of the Father, which is the Only Son. And what, too, does that mean, "He that believeth on me, believeth not on me?"[6] How believe on Him, yet not believe on Him? How can so opposite and inconsistent a thing be understood—"Whoso believeth on me," He says, "believeth not on me, but on Him that sent me;"—unless you so understand it, Whoso believeth on me believeth not on that which he sees, lest our hope should be in the creature; but on Him who took the creature, whereby He might appear to human eyes, and so might cleanse our hearts by faith, to contemplate Himself as equal to the Father? So that in turning the attention of believers to the Father, and saying, "Believeth not on me, but on Him that sent me," He certainly did not mean Himself to be separated from the Father, that is, from Him that sent Him; but that men might so believe on Himself, as they believe on the Father, to whom He is equal. And this He says in express terms in another place, "Ye believe in God, believe also in me:"[7] that is, in the same way as you believe in God, so also believe in me; because I and the Father are One God. As therefore, here, He has as it were withdrawn

[1] *Seipsum loquitur.*   [2] John v. 26.
[3] 1 John v. 20   [4] John xii. 48.   [5] John vii. 16.   [6] John xii. 44.   [7] John xiv. 1.

the faith of men from Himself, and transferred it to the Father, by saying, " Believeth not on me, but on Him that sent me," from whom nevertheless He certainly did not separate Himself; so also, when He says, " It is not mine to give, but [it shall be given to them] for whom it is prepared by my Father," it is I think plain in what relation both are to be taken. For that other also is of the same kind, "I will not judge;" whereas He Himself shall judge the quick and dead.[1] But because He will not do so by human power, therefore, reverting to the Godhead, He raises the hearts of men upwards; which to lift up, He Himself came down.

CHAP. 13.—DIVERSE THINGS ARE SPOKEN CONCERNING THE SAME CHRIST, ON ACCOUNT OF THE DIVERSE NATURES OF THE ONE HYPOSTASIS [THEANTHROPIC PERSON]. WHY IT IS SAID THAT THE FATHER WILL NOT JUDGE, BUT HAS GIVEN JUDGMENT TO THE SON.

28. Yet unless the very same were the Son of man on account of the form of a servant which He took, who is the Son of God on account of the form of God in which He is; Paul the apostle would not say of the princes of this world, " For had they known it, they would not have crucified the Lord of glory."[2] For He was crucified after the form of a servant, and yet " the Lord of glory " was crucified. For that " taking " was such as to make God man, and man God. Yet what is said on account of what, and what according to what, the thoughtful, diligent, and pious reader discerns for himself, the Lord being his helper. For instance, we have said that He glorifies His own, as being God, and certainly then as being the Lord of glory; and yet the Lord of glory was crucified, because even God is rightly said to have been crucified, not after the power of the divinity, but after the weakness of the flesh:[3] just as we say, that He judges as God, that is, by divine power, not by human; and yet the man Himself will judge, just as the Lord of glory was crucified: for so He expressly says, " When the Son of man shall come in His glory, and all the holy angels with Him, and before Him shall be gathered all nations;"[4] and the rest that is foretold of the future judgment in that place even to the last sentence. And the Jews, inasmuch as they will be punished in that judgment for persisting in their wickedness, as it is elsewhere written, " shall look upon Him whom they have pierced."[5] For whereas both good and bad shall see the Judge of the

quick and dead, without doubt the bad will not be able to see Him, except after the form in which He is the Son of man; but yet in the glory wherein He will judge, not in the lowliness wherein He was judged. But the ungodly without doubt will not see that form of God in which He is equal to the Father. For they are not pure in heart; and " Blessed are the pure in heart: for they shall see God."[6] And that sight is face to face,[7] the very sight that is promised as the highest reward to the just, and which will then take place when He " shall have delivered up the kingdom to God, even the Father;" and in this " kingdom " He means the sight of His own form also to be understood, the whole creature being made subject to God, including that wherein the Son of God was made the Son of man. Because, according to this creature, " The Son also Himself shall be subject unto Him, that put all things under Him, that God may be all in all."[8] Otherwise if the Son of God, judging in the form in which He is equal to the Father, shall appear when He judges to the ungodly also; what becomes of that which He promises, as some great thing, to him who loves Him, saying, "And I will love him, and will manifest myself to him?"[9] Wherefore He will judge as the Son of man, yet not by human power, but by that whereby He is the Son of God; and on the other hand, He will judge as the Son of God, yet not appearing in that [unincarnate] form in which He is God equal to the Father, but in that [incarnate form] in which He is the Son of man.[10]

29. Therefore both ways of speaking may be used; the Son of man will judge, and, the Son of man will not judge: since the Son of man will judge, that the text may be true which says, " When the Son of man shall come, then before Him shall be gathered all nations;" and the Son of man will not judge, that the text may be true which says, " I will not judge him;"[11] and, " I seek not mine own glory: there is One that seeketh and judgeth."[12] For in respect to this, that in the judgment, not the form of God, but the form of the Son of man will appear, the Father Himself will not judge; for according to this

---

[1] 2 Tim. iv. 1. [2] 1 Cor. ii. 8. [3] 2 Cor. xiii. 4.
[4] Matt. xxv. 31, 32. [5] Zech. xii. 10.

[6] Matt. v. 8. [7] 1 Cor. xiii. 12.
[8] 1 Cor. xv. 24-28. [9] John xiv. 21.
[10] [Augustin, in this discussion, sometimes employs the phrase " Son of man " to denote the human nature of Christ, in distinction from the divine. But in Scripture and in trinitarian theology generally, this phrase properly denotes the whole theanthropic *person* under a human title—just as " man," (1 Tim. ii. 5),"last Adam" (1 Cor. xv. 45), and " second man " (1 Cor. xv. 47), denote not the human nature, but the whole divine-human person under a human title. Strictly used, the phrase " Son of man " does not designate the difference between the divine and human natures in the theanthropos, but between the person of the *un*-incarnate and that of the incarnate Logos. Augustin's meaning is, that the Son of God will judge men at the last day, not in his original " form of God," but as this is united with human nature—as the Son of man.—W. G. T. S.] [11] John xii. 47. [12] John viii. 50.

it is said, "For the Father judgeth no man, but hath committed all judgment unto the Son." Whether this is said after that mode of speech which we have mentioned above, where it is said, "So hath He given to the Son to have life in Himself,"[1] that it should signify that so He begat the Son; or, whether after that of which the apostle speaks, saying, "Wherefore God also hath highly exalted Him, and given Him a name which is above every name:"—(For this is said of the Son of man, in respect to whom the Son of God was raised from the dead; since He, being in the form of God equal to the Father, wherefrom He "emptied" Himself by taking the form of a servant, both acts and suffers, and receives, in that same form of a servant, what the apostle goes on to mention: "He humbled Himself, and became obedient unto death, even the death of the cross; wherefore God also hath highly exalted Him, and given Him a name which is above every name; that at the name of Jesus every knee should bow, of things in heaven, and things in earth, and things under the earth; and that every tongue should confess that Jesus Christ is Lord, in the Glory of God the Father:"[2])—whether then the words, "He hath committed all judgment unto the Son," are said according to this or that mode of speech; it sufficiently appears from this place, that if they were said according to that sense in which it is said, "He hath given to the Son to have life in Himself," it certainly would not be said, "The Father judgeth no man." For in respect to this, that the Father hath begotten the Son equal to Himself, He judges with Him. Therefore it is in respect to this that it is said, that in the judgment, not the form of God, but the form of the Son of man will appear. Not that He will not judge, who hath committed all judgment unto the Son, since the Son saith of Him, "There is One that seeketh and judgeth:" but it is so said, "The Father judgeth no man, but hath committed all judgment unto the Son;" as if it were said, No one will see the Father in the judgment of the quick and the dead, but all will see the Son: because He is also the Son of man, so that He can be seen even by the ungodly, since they too shall see Him whom they have pierced.

30. Lest, however, we may seem to conjecture this rather than to prove it clearly, let us produce a certain and plain sentence of the Lord Himself, by which we may show that this was the cause why He said, "The Father judgeth no man, but hath committed all judg-

ment unto the Son," *viz.* because He will appear as Judge in the form of the Son of man, which is not the form of the Father, but of the Son; nor yet that form of the Son in which He is equal to the Father, but that in which He is less than the Father; in order that, in the judgment, He may be visible both to the good and to the bad. For a little while after He says, "Verily, verily, I say unto you, He that heareth my word, and believeth on Him that sent me, hath everlasting life, and shall not come into condemnation; but shall pass[3] from death unto life." Now this life eternal is that sight which does not belong to the bad. Then follows, "Verily, verily, I say unto you, The hour is coming, and now is, when the dead shall hear the voice of the Son of God, and they that hear shall live."[4] And this is proper to the godly, who so hear of His incarnation, as to believe that He is the Son of God, that is, who so receive Him, as made for their sakes less than the Father, in the form of a servant, that they believe Him equal to the Father, in the form of God. And thereupon He continues, enforcing this very point, "For as the Father hath life in Himself, so hath He given to the Son to have life in Himself." And then He comes to the sight of His own glory, in which He shall come to judgment; which sight will be common to the ungodly and to the just. For He goes on to say, "And hath given Him authority to execute judgment also, because He is the Son of man."[5] I think nothing can be more clear. For inasmuch as the Son of God is equal to the Father, He does not receive this power of executing judgment, but He has it with the Father in secret; but He receives it, so that the good and the bad may see Him judging, inasmuch as He is the Son of man. Since the sight of the Son of man will be shown to the bad also: for the sight of the form of God will not be shown except to the pure in heart, for they shall see God; that is, to the godly only, to whose love He promises this very thing, that He will show Himself to them. And see, accordingly, what follows: "Marvel not at this," He says. Why does He forbid us to marvel, unless it be that, in truth, every one marvels who does not understand, that therefore He said the Father gave Him power also to execute judgment, because He is the Son of man; whereas, it might rather have been anticipated that He would say, since He is the Son of God? But because the wicked are not able to see the Son of God as He is in the form of God equal to the Father,

---

[1] John v. 22, 26.   [2] Phil. ii. 8-11.

[3] Trans*it* in Vulg.; and so in the Greek.
[4] John v. 24, 25.   [5] John v. 25, 26.

but yet it is necessary that both the just and the wicked should see the Judge of the quick and dead, when they will be judged in His presence; "Marvel not at this," He says, "for the hour is coming, in the which all that are in the graves shall hear His voice, and shall come forth; they that have done good, unto the resurrection of life; and they that have done evil, unto the resurrection of damnation."[1] For this purpose, then, it was necessary that He should therefore receive that power, because He is the Son of man, in order that all in rising again might see Him in the form in which He can be seen by all, but by some to damnation, by others to life eternal. And what is life eternal, unless that sight which is not granted to the ungodly? "That they might know Thee," He says, "the One true God, and Jesus Christ, whom Thou hast sent."[2] And how are they to know Jesus Christ Himself also, unless as the One true God, who will show Himself to them; not as He will show Himself, in the form of the Son of man, to those also that shall be punished?[3]

31. He is "good," according to that sight, according to which God appears to the pure in heart; for "truly God is good unto Israel, even to such as are of a clean heart."[4] But when the wicked shall see the Judge, He will not seem good to them; because they will not rejoice in their heart to see Him, but all "kindreds of the earth shall then wail because of Him,"[5] namely, as being reckoned in the number of all the wicked and unbelievers. On this account also He replied to him, who had called Him Good Master, when seeking advice of Him how he might attain eternal life, "Why askest thou me about good?[6] there is none good but One, that is, God."[7] And yet the Lord Himself, in another place, calls man good: "A good man," He says, "out of the good treasure of his heart, bringeth forth good things: and an evil man, out of the evil treasure of his heart, bringeth forth evil things."[8] But because that man was seeking eternal life, and eternal life consists in that contemplation in which God is seen, not for punishment, but for everlasting joy; and because he did not under-

stand with whom he was speaking, and thought Him to be only the Son of man:[9] Why, He says, askest thou me about good? that is, with respect to that form which thou seest, why askest thou about good, and callest me, according to what thou seest, Good Master? This is the form of the Son of man, the form which has been taken, the form that will appear in judgment, not only to the righteous, but also to the ungodly; and the sight of this form will not be for good to those who are wicked. But there is a sight of that form of mine, in which when I was, I thought it not robbery to be equal with God: but in order to take this form I emptied myself.[10] That one God, therefore, the Father and the Son and the Holy Spirit, who will not appear, except for joy which cannot be taken away from the just; for which future joy he sighs, who says, "One thing have I desired of the Lord, that will I seek after; that I may dwell in the house of the Lord all the days of my life, to behold the beauty of the Lord:"[11] that one God, therefore, Himself, I say, is alone good, for this reason, that no one sees Him for sorrow and wailing, but only for salvation and true joy. If you understand me after this latter form, then I am good; but if according to that former only, then why askest thou me about good? If thou art among those who "shall look upon Him whom they have pierced,"[12] that very sight itself will be evil to them, because it will be penal. That after this meaning, then, the Lord said, "Why askest thou me about good? there is none good but One, that is, God," is probable upon those proofs which I have alleged, because that sight of God, whereby we shall contemplate the substance of God unchangeable and invisible to human eyes (which is promised to the saints alone; which the Apostle Paul speaks of, as "face to face;"[13] and of which the Apostle John says, "We shall be like Him, for we shall see Him as He is;"[14] and of which it is said, "One thing have I desired of the Lord, that I may behold the beauty of the Lord," and of which the Lord Himself says, "I will both love him, and will manifest myself to him;"[15] and on account of which alone we cleanse our hearts by faith, that we may be those "pure in heart who are blessed for they shall see God:"[16] and what-

---

[1] John v. 22-29. [2] John xvii. 3.
[3] [Augustin here seems to teach that the phenomenal appearance of Christ to the redeemed in heaven will be different from that to all men in the day of judgment. He says that he will show himself to the former "in the form of God;" to the latter, "in the form of the Son of man." But, surely, it is one and the same Godman who sits on the judgment throne, and the heavenly throne. His appearance must be the same in both instances: namely, that of God incarnate. The *effect* of his phenomenal appearance upon the believer will, indeed, be very different from that upon the unbeliever. For the wicked, this vision of God incarnate will be one of terror; for the redeemed one of joy.—W. G. T. S.]
[4] Ps. lxxiii. 1. [5] Apoc. i. 7.
[6] [Augustin's reading of this text is that of the uncials; and in that form which omits the article with ἀγαθοῦ.—W. G. T. S.]
[7] Matt. xix. 17. [8] Matt. xii. 35.

[9] [That is, a mere man. Augustin here, as in some other places, employs the phrase "Son of man" to denote the human nature by itself—not the divine and human natures united in one person, and designated by this human title. The latter is the Scripture usage. As "Immanuel" does not properly denote the divine nature, but the union of divinity and humanity, so "Son of man" does not properly denote the human nature, but the union of divinity and humanity.—W. G. T. S.]
[10] Phil. ii. 6, 7. [11] Ps. xxvii. 4. [12] Zech. xii. 10.
[13] 1 Cor. xiii. 12. [14] 1 John iii. 2. [15] John xiv. 21.
[16] Matt. v. 8.

ever else is spoken of that sight: which whosoever turns the eye of love to seek it, may find most copiously scattered through all the Scriptures),—that sight alone, I say, is our chief good, for the attaining of which we are directed to do whatever we do aright. But that sight of the Son of man which is foretold, when all nations shall be gathered before Him, and shall say to Him, "Lord, when saw we Thee an hungered, or thirsty, etc.?" will neither be a good to the ungodly, who shall be sent into everlasting fire, nor the chief good to the righteous. For He still goes on to call these to the kingdom which has been prepared for them from the foundation of the world. For, as He will say to those, "Depart into everlasting fire;" so to these, "Come, ye blessed of my Father, inherit the kingdom prepared for you." And as those will go into everlasting burning; so the righteous will go into life eternal. But what is life eternal, except "that they may know Thee," He says, "the One true God, and Jesus Christ, whom Thou hast sent?"[1] but know Him now in that glory of which He says to the Father, "Which I had with Thee before the world was."[2] For then He will deliver up the kingdom to God, even the Father,[3] that the good servant may enter into the joy of his Lord,[4] and that He may hide those whom God keeps in the hiding of His countenance from the confusion of men, namely, of those men who shall then be confounded by hearing this sentence; of which evil hearing "the righteous man shall not be afraid"[5] if only he be kept in "the tabernacle," that is, in the true faith of the Catholic Church, from "the strife of tongues,"[6] that is, from the sophistries of heretics. But if there is any other explanation of the words of the Lord, where He says, "Why asketh thou me about good? there is none good, but One, that is, God;" provided only that the substance of the Father be not therefore believed to be of greater goodness than that of the Son, according to which He is the Word by whom all things were made; and if there is nothing in it abhorrent from sound doctrine; let us securely use it, and not one explanation only, but as many as we are able to find. For so much the more powerfully are the heretics proved wrong, the more outlets are open for avoiding their snares. But let us now start afresh, and address ourselves to the consideration of that which still remains.

---

[1] Matt. xxv. 37, 41, 34.   [2] John xvii. 3-5.

[3] 1 Cor. xv. 24.   [4] Matt. xxv. 21, 23.
[5] Ps. cxii. 7.   [6] Ps. xxxi. 21.

BOOK II.

AUGUSTIN PURSUES HIS DEFENSE OF THE EQUALITY OF THE TRINITY; AND IN TREATING OF THE SENDING OF THE SON AND OF THE HOLY SPIRIT, AND OF THE VARIOUS APPEARANCES OF GOD, DEMONSTRATES THAT HE WHO IS SENT IS NOT THEREFORE LESS THAN HE WHO SENDS, BECAUSE THE ONE HAS SENT, THE OTHER HAS BEEN SENT; BUT THAT THE TRINITY, BEING IN ALL THINGS EQUAL, AND ALIKE IN ITS OWN NATURE UNCHANGEABLE AND INVISIBLE AND OMNIPRESENT, WORKS INDIVISIBLY IN EACH SENDING OR APPEARANCE.

PREFACE.

WHEN men seek to know God, and bend their minds according to the capacity of human weakness to the understanding of the Trinity; learning, as they must, by experience, the wearisome difficulties of the task, whether from the sight itself of the mind striving to gaze upon light unapproachable, or, indeed, from the manifold and various modes of speech employed in the sacred writings (wherein, as it seems to me, the mind is nothing else but roughly exercised, in order that it may find sweetness when glorified by the grace of Christ);—such men, I say, when they have dispelled every ambiguity, and arrived at something certain, ought of all others most easily to make allowance for those who err in the investigation of so deep a secret. But there are two things most hard to bear with, in the case of those who are in error: hasty assumption before the truth is made plain; and, when it has been made plain, defence of the falsehood thus hastily assumed. From which two faults, inimical as they are to the finding out of the truth, and to the handling of the divine and sacred books, should God, as I pray and hope, defend and protect me with the shield of His good will,[1] and with the grace of His mercy, I will not be slow to search out the substance of God, whether through His Scripture or through the creature. For both of these are set forth for our contemplation to this end, that He may Himself be sought, and Himself be loved, who inspired the one, and

created the other. Nor shall I be afraid of giving my opinion, in which I shall more desire to be examined by the upright, than fear to be carped at by the perverse. For charity, most excellent and unassuming, gratefully accepts the dovelike eye; but for the dog's tooth nothing remains, save either to shun it by the most cautious humility, or to blunt it by the most solid truth; and far rather would I be censured by any one whatsoever, than be praised by either the erring or the flatterer. For the lover of truth need fear no one's censure. For he that censures, must needs be either enemy or friend. And if an enemy reviles, he must be borne with: but a friend, if he errs, must be taught; if he teaches, listened to. But if one who errs praises you, he confirms your error; if one who flatters, he seduces you into error. "Let the righteous," therefore, "smite me, it shall be a kindness; and let him reprove me; but the oil of the sinner shall not anoint my head."[2]

CHAP. I.—THERE IS A DOUBLE RULE FOR UNDERSTANDING THE SCRIPTURAL MODES OF SPEECH CONCERNING THE SON OF GOD. THESE MODES OF SPEECH ARE OF A THREEFOLD KIND.

2. Wherefore, although we hold most firmly, concerning our Lord Jesus Christ, what may be called the canonical rule, as it is both disseminated through the Scriptures, and has been demonstrated by learned and Catholic handlers of the same Scriptures, namely, that the Son of God is both under-

---

[1] Ps. v. 12.

[2] Ps. cxli. 5.

stood to be equal to the Father according to the form of God in which He is, and less than the Father according to the form of a servant which He took;[1] in which form He was found to be not only less than the Father, but also less than the Holy Spirit; and not only so, but less even than Himself,—not than Himself who was, but than Himself who is; because, by taking the form of a servant, He did not lose the form of God, as the testimonies of the Scriptures taught us, to which we have referred in the former book: yet there are some things in the sacred text so put as to leave it ambiguous to which rule they are rather to be referred; whether to that by which we understand the Son as less, in that He has taken upon Him the creature, or to that by which we understand that the Son is not indeed less than, but equal to the Father, but yet that He is from Him, God of God, Light of light. For we call the Son God *of* God; but the Father, God only; not *of* God. Whence it is plain that the Son has another *of* whom He is, and to whom He is Son; but that the Father has not a Son *of* whom He is, but only to whom He is father. For every son is what he is, *of* his father, and is son to his father; but no father is what he is, *of* his son, but is father to his son.[2]

3. Some things, then, are so put in the Scriptures concerning the Father and the Son, as to intimate the unity and equality of their substance; as, for instance, "I and the Father are one;"[3] and, "Who, being in the form of God, thought it not robbery to be equal with God;"[4] and whatever other texts there are of the kind. And some, again, are so put that they show the Son as less on account of the form of a servant, that is, of His having taken upon Him the creature of a changeable and human substance; as, for instance, that which says, "For my Father is greater than I;"[5] and, "The Father judgeth no man, but hath committed all judgment unto the Son." For a little after he goes on to say, "And hath given Him authority to execute judgment also, because He is the Son of man." And further, some are so put, as to show Him at that time neither as less

nor as equal, but only to intimate that He is of the Father; as, for instance, that which says, "For as the Father hath life in Himself, so hath He given to the Son to have life in Himself;" and that other: "The Son can do nothing of Himself, but what He seeth the Father do."[6] For if we shall take this to be therefore so said, because the Son is less in the form taken from the creature, it will follow that the Father must have walked on the water, or opened the eyes with clay and spittle of some other one born blind, and have done the other things which the Son appearing in the flesh did among men, before the Son did them;[7] in order that He might be able to do those things, who said that the Son was not able to do anything of Himself, except what He hath seen the Father do. Yet who, even though he were mad, would think this? It remains, therefore, that these texts are so expressed, because the life of the Son is unchangeable as that of the Father is, and yet He is of the Father; and the working of the Father and of the Son is indivisible, and yet so to work is given to the Son from Him of whom He Himself is, that is, from the Father; and the Son so sees the Father, as that He is the Son in the very seeing Him. For to be of the Father, that is, to be born of the Father, is to Him nothing else than to see the Father; and to see Him working, is nothing else than to work with Him: but therefore not from Himself, because He is not from Himself. And, therefore, those things which "He sees the Father do, these also doeth the Son likewise," because He is of the Father. For He neither does other things in like manner, as a painter paints other pictures, in the same way as he sees others to have been painted by another man; nor the same things in a different manner, as the body expresses the same letters, which the mind has thought; but "whatsoever things," saith He, "the Father doeth, these same things also doeth the Son likewise."[8] He has said both "these same things," and "likewise;" and hence the working of both the Father and the Son is indivisible and equal, but it is from the Father to the Son. Therefore the Son cannot do anything of Himself, except what He seeth the Father do. From this rule, then, whereby the Scriptures so speak as to mean, not to set forth one as less than another, but only to show which is of which, some have drawn this meaning, as if the Son were said to be less. And some among ourselves who are more unlearned and least instructed in these things,

---

[1] Phil. ii. 6, 7.
[2] [Augustin here brings to view both the trinitarian and the theanthropic or mediatorial subordination. The former is the status of Sonship. God the Son is God *of* God. Sonship as a *relation* is subordinate to paternity. But a son must be of the same grade of being, and of the same nature with his father. A human son and a human father are alike and equally *human*. And a Divine Son and a Divine Father are alike and equally *divine*. The theanthropic or mediatorial subordination is the status of humiliation, by reason of the incarnation. In the words of Augustin, it is "that by which we understand the Son as less, in that he has taken upon Him the creature." The subordination in this case is that of voluntary condescension, for the purpose of redeeming sinful man.—W.G.T.S.]
[3] John x. 30.   [4] Phil. ii. 6.   [5] John xiv. 28.
[6] John v. 22, 27, 26, 19.   [7] Matt. xiv. 26. and John ix. 6, 7.
[8] John v. 19.

endeavoring to take these texts according to the form of a servant, and so mis-interpreting them, are troubled. And to prevent this, the rule in question is to be observed, whereby the Son is not less, but it is simply intimated that He is of the Father, in which words not His inequality but His birth is declared.

CHAP. 2.—THAT SOME WAYS OF SPEAKING CONCERNING THE SON ARE TO BE UNDERSTOOD ACCORDING TO EITHER RULE.

4. There are, then, some things in the sacred books, as I began by saying, so put, that it is doubtful to which they are to be referred: whether to that rule whereby the Son is less on account of His having taken the creature; or whether to that whereby it is intimated that although equal, yet He is of the Father. And in my opinion, if this is in such way doubtful, that which it really is can neither be explained nor discerned, then such passages may without danger be understood according to either rule, as that, for instance, "My doctrine is not mine, but His that sent me."[1] For this may both be taken according to the form of a servant, as we have already treated it in the former book;[2] or according to the form of God, in which He is in such way equal to the Father, that He is yet of the Father. For according to the form of God, as the Son is not one and His life another, but the life itself is the Son; so the Son is not one and His doctrine another, but the doctrine itself is the Son. And hence, as the text, "He hath given life to the Son," is no otherwise to be understood than, He hath begotten the Son, who is life; so also when it is said, He hath given doctrine to the Son, it may be rightly understood to mean, He hath begotten the Son, who is doctrine; so that, when it is said, "My doctrine is not mine, but His who sent me," it is so to be understood as if it were, I am not from myself, but from Him who sent me.

CHAP. 3.—SOME THINGS CONCERNING THE HOLY SPIRIT ARE TO BE UNDERSTOOD ACCORDING TO THE ONE RULE ONLY.

5. For even of the Holy Spirit, of whom it is not said, "He emptied Himself, and took upon Him the form of a servant;" yet the Lord Himself says, "Howbeit, when He the Spirit of Truth is come, He will guide you into all truth. For He shall not speak of Himself, but whatsoever He shall hear that shall He speak; and He will show you things

to come. He shall glorify me; for He shall receive of mine, and shall show it unto you." And except He had immediately gone on to say after this, "All things that the Father hath are mine; therefore said I, that He shall take of mine, and shall show it unto you;"[3] it might, perhaps, have been believed that the Holy Spirit was so born of Christ, as Christ is of the Father. Since He had said of Himself, "My doctrine is not mine, but His that sent me;" but of the Holy Spirit, "For He shall not speak of Himself, but whatsoever he shall hear, that shall He speak;" and, "For He shall receive of mine, and shall show it unto you." But because He has rendered the reason why He said, "He shall receive of mine" (for He says, "All things that the Father hath are mine; therefore said I, that He shall take of mine"); it remains that the Holy Spirit be understood to have of that which is the Father's, as the Son also hath. And how can this be, unless according to that which we have said above, "But when the Comforter is come, whom I will send unto you from the Father, even the Spirit of truth which proceedeth from the Father, He shall testify of me"?[4] He is said, therefore, not to speak of Himself, in that He proceedeth from the Father; and as it does not follow that the Son is less because He said, "The Son can do nothing of Himself, but what He seeth the Father do" (for He has not said this according to the form of a servant, but according to the form of God, as we have already shown, and these words do not set Him forth as less than, but as of the Father), so it is not brought to pass that the Holy Spirit is less, because it is said of Him, "For He shall not speak of Himself, but whatsoever He shall hear, that shall He speak;" for the words belong to Him as *proceeding* from the Father. But whereas both the Son is of the Father, and the Holy Spirit proceeds from the Father, why both are not called sons, and both not said to be begotten, but the former is called the one only-begotten Son, and the latter, *viz.* the Holy Spirit, neither son nor begotten, because if begotten, then certainly a son, we will discuss in another place, if God shall grant, and so far as He shall grant.[5]

CHAP. 4.—THE GLORIFICATION OF THE SON BY THE FATHER DOES NOT PROVE INEQUALITY.

6. But here also let them wake up if they can, who have thought this, too, to be a testimony on their side, to show that the Father

---

[1] John vii. 16.   [2] See above, Book I. c. 12.

[3] John xvi. 13-15.   [4] John xv. 26.
[5] Below, Bk. XV. c. 25.

is greater than the Son, because the Son hath said, " Father, glorify me." Why, the Holy Spirit also glorifies Him. Pray, is the Spirit, too, greater than He? Moreover, if on that account the Holy Spirit glorifies the Son, because He shall receive of that which is the Son's, and shall therefore receive of that which is the Son's because all things that the Father has are the Son's also; it is evident that when the Holy Spirit glorifies the Son, the Father glorifies the Son. Whence it may be perceived that all things that the Father hath are not only of the Son, but also of the Holy Spirit, because the Holy Spirit is able to glorify the Son, whom the Father glorifies. But if he who glorifies is greater than he whom he glorifies, let them allow that those are equal who mutually glorify each other. But it is written, also, that the Son glorifies the Father; for He says, " I have glorified Thee on the earth."[1] Truly let them beware lest the Holy Spirit be thought greater than both, because He glorifies the Son whom the Father glorifies, while it is not written that He Himself is glorified either by the Father or by the Son.

CHAP. 5.—THE SON AND HOLY SPIRIT ARE NOT THEREFORE LESS BECAUSE SENT. THE SON IS SENT ALSO BY HIMSELF. OF THE SENDING OF THE HOLY SPIRIT.

7. But being proved wrong so far, men betake themselves to saying, that he who sends is greater than he who is sent: therefore the Father is greater than the Son, because the Son continually speaks of Himself as being sent by the Father; and the Father is also greater than the Holy Spirit, because Jesus has said of the Spirit, " Whom the Father will send in my name;"[2] and the Holy Spirit is less than both, because both the Father sends Him, as we have said, and the Son, when He says, " But if I depart, I will send Him unto you." I first ask, then, in this inquiry, whence and whither the Son was sent. " I," He says, " came forth from the Father, and am come into the world."[3] Therefore, to be sent, is to come forth forth from the Father, and to come into the world. What, then, is that which the same evangelist says concerning Him, " He was in the world, and the world was made by Him, and the world knew Him not;" and then he adds, " He came unto His own?"[4] Certainly He was sent thither, whither He came; but if He was sent into the world, because He came forth from the Father, then He both came into the

world and was in the world. He was sent therefore thither, where He already was. For consider that, too, which is written in the prophet, that God said, " Do not I fill heaven and earth?"[5] If this is said of the Son (for some will have it understood that the Son Himself spoke either by the prophets or in the prophets), whither was He sent except to the place where He already was? For He who says, " I fill heaven and earth," was everywhere. But if it is said of the Father, where could He be without His own word and without His own wisdom, which "reacheth from one end to another mightily, and sweetly ordereth all things?"[6] But He cannot be anywhere without His own Spirit. Therefore, if God is everywhere, His Spirit also is everywhere. Therefore, the Holy Spirit, too, was sent thither, where He already was. For he, too, who finds no place to which he might go from the presence of God, and who says, " If I ascend up into heaven, Thou art there; if I shall go down into hell, behold, Thou art there;" wishing it to be understood that God is present everywhere, named in the previous verse His Spirit; for He says, " Whither shall I go from Thy Spirit? or whither shall I flee from Thy presence?"[7]

8. For this reason, then, if both the Son and the Holy Spirit are sent thither where they were, we must inquire, how that sending, whether of the Son or of the Holy Spirit, is to be understood; for of the Father alone, we nowhere read that He is sent. Now, of the Son, the apostle writes thus: " But when the fullness of the time was come, God sent forth His Son, made of a woman, made under the law, to redeem them that were under the law."[8] " He sent," he says, " His Son, made of a woman." And by this term, woman,[9] what Catholic does not know that he did not wish to signify the privation of virginity; but, according to a Hebraism, the difference of sex? When, therefore, he says, " God sent His Son, made of a woman," he sufficiently shows that the Son was " sent " in this very way, in that He was " made of a woman." Therefore, in that He was born of God, He was in the world; but in that He was born of Mary, He was sent and came into the world. Moreover, He could not be sent by the Father without the Holy Spirit, not only because the Father, when He sent Him, that is, when He made Him of a woman, is certainly understood not to have so made Him without His own Spirit; but also because it is most plainly and expressly said in the Gospel in answer to the Virgin Mary, when she asked of the angel,

[1] John xvii. 1, 4.   [2] John xiv. 26.
[3] John xvi. 7, 28.   [4] John i. 10, 11.

[5] Jer. xxiii. 24.   [6] Wisd. viii. 1.   [7] Ps. cxxxix. 8, 7.
[8] Gal. iv. 4, 5.   [9] Mulier.

"How shall this be?" "The Holy Ghost shall come upon thee, and the power of the Highest shall overshadow thee."[1] And Matthew says, "She was found with child of the Holy Ghost."[2] Although, too, in the prophet Isaiah, Christ Himself is understood to say of His own future advent, "And now the Lord God and His Spirit hath sent me."[3]

9. Perhaps some one may wish to drive us to say, that the Son is sent also by Himself, because the conception and childbirth of Mary is the working of the Trinity, by whose act of creating all things are created. And how, he will go on to say, has the Father sent Him, if He sent Himself? To whom I answer first, by asking him to tell me, if he can, in what manner the Father hath sanctified Him, if He hath sanctified Himself? For the same Lord says both; "Say ye of Him," He says, "whom the Father hath sanctified and sent into the world, Thou blasphemest, because I said, I am the Son of God;"[4] while in another place He says, "And for their sake I sanctify myself."[5] I ask, also, in what manner the Father delivered Him, if He delivered Himself? For the Apostle Paul says both: "Who," he says, "spared not His own Son, but delivered Him up for us all;"[6] while elsewhere he says of the Saviour Himself, "Who loved me, and delivered Himself for me."[7] He will reply, I suppose, if he has a right sense in these things, Because the will of the Father and the Son is one, and their working indivisible. In like manner, then, let him understand the incarnation and nativity of the Virgin, wherein the Son is understood as sent, to have been wrought by one and the same operation of the Father and of the Son indivisibly; the Holy Spirit certainly not being thence excluded, of whom it is expressly said, "She was found with child by the Holy Ghost." For perhaps our meaning will be more plainly unfolded, if we ask in what manner God sent His Son. He commanded that He should come, and He, complying with the commandment, came. Did He then request, or did He only suggest? But whichever of these it was, certainly it was done by a word, and the Word of God is the Son of God Himself. Wherefore, since the Father sent Him by a word, His being sent was the work of both the Father and His Word; therefore the same Son was sent by the Father and the Son, because the Son Himself is the Word of the Father. For who would embrace so impious an opinion as to think the Father to have uttered a word in time, in order that the eternal Son might thereby be sent and might appear in the flesh in the fullness of time? But assuredly it was in that Word of God itself which was in the beginning with God and was God, namely, in the wisdom itself of God, apart from time, at what time that wisdom must needs appear in the flesh. Therefore, since without any commencement of time, the Word was in the beginning, and the Word was with God, and the Word was God, it was in the Word itself without any time, at what time the Word was to be made flesh and dwell among us.[8] And when this fullness of time had come, "God sent His Son, made of a woman,"[9] that is, made in time, that the Incarnate Word might appear to men; while it was in that Word Himself, apart from time, at what time this was to be done; for the order of times is in the eternal wisdom of God without time. Since, then, that the Son should appear in the flesh was wrought by both the Father and the Son, it is fitly said that He who appeared in that flesh was sent, and that He who did not appear in it, sent Him; because those things which are transacted outwardly before the bodily eyes have their existence from the inward structure (*apparatu*) of the spiritual nature, and on that account are fitly said to be sent. Further, that form of man which He took is the person of the Son, not also of the Father; on which account the invisible Father, together with the Son, who with the Father is invisible, is said to have sent the same Son by making Him visible. But if He became visible in such way as to cease to be invisible with the Father, that is, if the substance of the invisible Word were turned by a change and transition into a visible creature, then the Son would be so understood to be sent by the Father, that He would be found to be only sent; not also, with the Father, sending. But since He so took the form of a servant, as that the unchangeable form of God remained, it is clear that that which became apparent in the Son was done by the Father and the Son not being apparent; that is, that by the invisible Father, with the invisible Son, the same Son Himself was sent so as to be visible. Why, therefore, does He say, "Neither came I of myself?" This, we may now say, is said according to the form of a servant, in the same way as it is said, "I judge no man."[10]

10. If, therefore, He is said to be sent, in so far as He appeared outwardly in the bodily creature, who inwardly in His spiritual nature is always hidden from the eyes of mortals, it is now easy to understand also of the Holy

---

[1] Luke i. 34, 35.   [2] Matt. i. 18.   [3] Isa. xlviii. 16.
[4] John x. 36.   [5] John xvii. 19.   [6] Rom. viii. 32.
[7] Gal. ii. 20.

[8] John i. 1, 2, 14.   [9] Gal. iv. 4.   [10] John viii. 42, 15.

Spirit why He too is said to be sent. For in due time a certain outward appearance of the creature was wrought, wherein the Holy Spirit might be visibly shown; whether when He descended upon the Lord Himself in a bodily shape as a dove, [1] or when, ten days having past since His ascension, on the day of Pentecost a sound came suddenly from heaven as of a rushing mighty wind, and cloven tongues like as of fire were seen upon them, and it sat upon each of them.[2] This operation, visibly exhibited, and presented to mortal eyes, is called the sending of the Holy Spirit; not that His very substance appeared, in which He himself also is invisible and unchangeable, like the Father and the Son, but that the hearts of men, touched by things seen outwardly, might be turned from the manifestation in time of Him as coming to His hidden eternity as ever present.

CHAP. 6.—THE CREATURE IS NOT SO TAKEN BY THE HOLY SPIRIT AS FLESH IS BY THE WORD.

11. It is, then, for this reason nowhere written, that the Father is greater than the Holy Spirit, or that the Holy Spirit is less than God the Father, because the creature in which the Holy Spirit was to appear was not taken in the same way as the Son of man was taken, as the form in which the person of the Word of God Himself should be set forth; not that He might possess the word of God, as other holy and wise men have possessed it, but "above His fellows;"[3] not certainly that He possessed the word more than they, so as to be of more surpassing wisdom than the rest were, but that He was the very Word Himself. For the word in the flesh is one thing, and the Word made flesh is another; i.e. the word in man is one thing, the Word that is man is another. For flesh is put for man, where it is said, "The Word was made flesh;"[4] and again, "And all flesh shall see the salvation of God."[5] For it does not mean flesh without soul and without mind; but "all flesh," is the same as if it were said, every man. The creature, then, in which the Holy Spirit should appear, was not so taken, as that flesh and human form were taken, of the Virgin Mary. For the Spirit did not beatify the dove, or the wind, or the fire, and join them for ever to Himself and to His person in unity and "fashion."[6] Nor, again, is the nature of the Holy Spirit mutable and

changeable; so that these things were not made of the creature, but He himself was turned and changed first into one and then into another, as water is changed into ice. But these things appeared at the seasons at which they ought to have appeared, the creature serving the Creator, and being changed and converted at the command of Him who remains immutably in Himself, in order to signify and manifest Him in such way as it was fit He should be signified and manifested to mortal men. Accordingly, although that dove is called the Spirit;[7] and in speaking of that fire, "There appeared unto them," he says, "cloven tongues, like as of fire, and it sat upon each of them; and they began to speak with other tongues, as the Spirit gave them utterance;"[8] in order to show that the Spirit was manifested by that fire, as by the dove; yet we cannot call the Holy Spirit both God and a dove, or both God and fire, in the same way as we call the Son both God and man; nor as we call the Son the Lamb of God; which not only John the Baptist says, "Behold the Lamb of God,"[9] but also John the Evangelist sees the Lamb slain in the Apocalypse.[10] For that prophetic vision was not shown to bodily eyes through bodily forms, but in the spirit through spiritual images of bodily things. But whosoever saw that dove and that fire, saw them with their eyes. Although it may perhaps be disputed concerning the fire, whether it was seen by the eyes or in the spirit, on account of the form of the sentence. For the text does not say, They saw cloven tongues like fire, but, "There appeared to them." But we are not wont to say with the same meaning, It appeared to me; as we say, I saw. And in those spiritual visions of corporeal images the usual expressions are, both, It appeared to me; and, I saw: but in those things which are shown to the eyes through express corporeal forms, the common expression is not, It appeared to me; but, I saw. There may, therefore, be a question raised respecting that fire, how it was seen; whether within in the spirit as it were outwardly, or really outwardly before the eyes of the flesh. But of that dove, which is said to have descended in a bodily form, no one ever doubted that it was seen by the eyes. Nor, again, as we call the Son a Rock (for it is written, "And that Rock was Christ"[11]), can we so call the Spirit a dove or fire. For that rock was a thing already created, and after the mode of its action was

---

[1] Matt. iii. 16.   [2] Acts ii. 2-4.
[3] Heb. i. 9.   [4] John i. 14.   [5] Luke iii. 6.
[6] [The reference is to σχῆμα, in Phil. ii. 8—the term chosen by St. Paul to describe the "likeness of men," which the second trinitarian person assumed. The variety in the terms by which St. Paul describes the incarnation is very striking. The person incarnated subsists first in a "form of God;" he then takes along with this (still retaining this) a "form of a servant;" which form

of a servant is a "likeness of men;" which likeness of men is a "scheme" (A.V. "fashion") or external form of a man.—W.G. T.S.]
[7] Matt. iii. 16.   [8] Acts ii. 3, 4.
[9] John i. 29.   [10] Apoc. v. 6.   [11] 1 Cor. x. 4.

called by the name of Christ, whom it signified; like the stone placed under Jacob's head, and also anointed, which he took in order to signify the Lord;[1] or as Isaac was Christ, when he carried the wood for the sacrifice of himself.[2] A particular significative action was added to those already existing things; they did not, as that dove and fire, suddenly come into being in order simply so to signify. The dove and the fire, indeed, seem to me more like that flame which appeared to Moses in the bush,[3] or that pillar which the people followed in the wilderness,[4] or the thunders and lightnings which came when the Law was given in the mount.[5] For the corporeal form of these things came into being for the very purpose, that it might signify something, and then pass away.[6]

CHAP. 7.—A DOUBT RAISED ABOUT DIVINE APPEARANCES.

12. The Holy Spirit, then, is also said to be sent, on account of these corporeal forms which came into existence in time, in order to signify and manifest Him, as He must needs be manifested, to human senses; yet He is not said to be less than the Father, as the Son, because He was in the form of a servant, is said to be; because that form of a servant inhered in the unity of the person of the Son, but those corporeal forms appeared for a time, in order to show what was necessary to be shown, and then ceased to be. Why, then, is not the Father also said to be sent, through those corporeal forms, the fire of the bush, and the pillar of cloud or of fire, and the lightnings in the mount, and whatever other things of the kind appeared at that time, when (as we have learned from Scripture testimony) He spake face to face with the fathers, if He Himself was manifested by those modes and forms of the creature, as exhibited and presented corporeally to human sight? But if the Son was manifested by them, why is He said to be sent so long after, when He was made of a woman, as the apostle says, "But when the fullness of time was come, God sent forth His Son, made of a woman,"[7] seeing that He was sent also before, when He appeared to the fathers by those changeable forms of the creature? Or if He cannot

rightly be said to be sent, unless when the Word was made flesh, why is the Holy Spirit said to be sent, of whom no such incarnation was ever wrought? But if by those visible things, which are put before us in the Law and in the prophets, neither the Father nor the Son but the Holy Spirit was manifested, why also is He said to be sent now, when He was sent also before after these modes?

13. In the perplexity of this inquiry, the Lord helping us, we must ask, first, whether the Father, or the Son, or the Holy Spirit; or whether, sometimes the Father, sometimes the Son, sometimes the Holy Spirit; or whether it was without any distinction of persons, in such way as the one and only God is spoken of, that is, that the Trinity itself appeared to the Fathers by those forms of the creature. Next, whichever of these alternatives shall have been found or thought true, whether for this purpose only the creature was fashioned, wherein God, as He judged it suitable at that time, should be shown to human sight; or whether angels, who already existed, were so sent, as to speak in the person of God, taking a corporeal form from the corporeal creature, for the purpose of their ministry, as each had need; or else, according to the power the Creator has given them, changing and converting their own body itself, to which they are not subject, but govern it as subject to themselves, into whatever appearances they would that were suited and apt to their several actions. Lastly, we shall discern that which it was our purpose to ask, *viz.* whether the Son and the Holy Spirit were also sent before; and, if they were so sent, what difference there is between that sending, and the one which we read of in the Gospel; or whether in truth neither of them were sent, except when either the Son was made of the Virgin Mary, or the Holy Spirit appeared in a visible form, whether in the dove or in tongues of fire.

CHAP. 8.—THE ENTIRE TRINITY INVISIBLE.

14. Let us therefore say nothing of those who, with an over carnal mind, have thought the nature of the Word of God, and the Wisdom, which, "remaining in herself, maketh all things new,"[8] whom we call the only Son of God, not only to be changeable, but also to be visible. For these, with more audacity than religion, bring a very dull heart to the inquiry into divine things. For whereas the soul is a spiritual substance, and whereas itself also was made, yet could not be made

---

[1] Gen. xxviii. 18.   [2] Gen. xxii. 6.   [3] Ex. iii. 2.
[4] Ex. xiii. 21, 22.   [5] Ex. xix. 16.
[6] [A theophany, though a harbinger of the incarnation, differs from it, by not effecting a hypostatical or personal union between God and the creature. When the Holy Spirit appeared in the form of a dove, he did not unite himself with it. The dove did not constitute an integral part of the divine person who employed it. Nor did the illuminated vapor in the theophany of the Shekinah. But when the Logos appeared in the form of a man, he united himself with it, so that it became a constituent part of his person. A theophany, as Augustin notices, is temporary and transient. The incarnation is perpetual.—W.G.T.S.]   [7] Gal. iv. 4.

[8] Wisd. vii. 27.

by any other than by Him by whom all things were made, and without whom nothing is made,[1] it, although changeable, is yet not visible; and this they have believed to be the case with the Word Himself and with the Wisdom of God itself, by which the soul was made; whereas this Wisdom is not only invisible, as the soul also is, but likewise unchangeable, which the soul is not. It is in truth the same unchangeableness in it, which is referred to when it was said, "Remaining in herself she maketh all things new." Yet these people, endeavoring, as it were, to prop up their error in its fall by testimonies of the divine Scriptures, adduce the words of the Apostle Paul; and take that, which is said of the one only God, in whom the Trinity itself is understood, to be said only of the Father, and neither of the Son nor of the Holy Spirit: "Now unto the King eternal, immortal, invisible, the only wise God, be honor and glory for ever and ever;"[2] and that other passage, "The blessed and only Potentate, the King of kings, and Lord of lords; who only hath immortality, dwelling in the light which no man can approach unto; whom no man hath seen, nor can see."[3] How these passages are to be understood, I think we have already discoursed sufficiently.[4]

CHAP. 9.—AGAINST THOSE WHO BELIEVED THE FATHER ONLY TO BE IMMORTAL AND INVISIBLE. THE TRUTH TO BE SOUGHT BY PEACEFUL STUDY.

15. But they who will have these texts understood only of the Father, and not of the Son or the Holy Spirit, declare the Son to be visible, not by having taken flesh of the Virgin, but aforetime also in Himself. For He Himself, they say, appeared to the eyes of the Fathers. And if you say to them, In whatever manner, then, the Son is visible in Himself, in that manner also He is mortal in Himself; so that it plainly follows that you would have this saying also understood only of the Father, viz., "Who only hath immortality;" for if the Son is mortal from having taken upon Him our flesh, then allow that it is on account of this flesh that He is also visible: they reply, that it is not on account of this flesh that they say that the Son is mortal; but that, just as He was also before visible, so He was also before mortal. For if they say the Son is mortal from having taken our flesh, then it is not the Father alone without the Son who hath immortality; because His

Word also has immortality, by which all things were made. For He did not therefore lose His immortality, because He took mortal flesh; seeing that it could not happen even to the human soul, that it should die with the body, when the Lord Himself says, "Fear not them which kill the body, but are not able to kill the soul."[5] Or, forsooth, also the Holy Spirit took flesh: concerning whom certainly they will, without doubt, be troubled to say—if the Son is mortal on account of taking our flesh—in what manner they understand that the Father only has immortality without the Son and the Holy Spirit, since, indeed, the Holy Spirit did not take our flesh; and if He has not immortality, then the Son is not mortal on account of taking our flesh; but if the Holy Spirit has immortality, then it is not said only of the Father, "Who only hath immortality." And therefore they think they are able to prove that the Son in Himself was mortal also before the incarnation, because changeableness itself is not unfitly called mortality, according to which the soul also is said to die; not because it is changed and turned into body, or into some substance other than itself, but because, whatever in its own self-same substance is now after another mode than it once was, is discovered to be mortal, in so far as it has ceased to be what it was. Because then, say they, before the Son of God was born of the Virgin Mary, He Himself appeared to our fathers, not in one and the same form only, but in many forms; first in one form, then in another; He is both visible in Himself, because His substance was visible to mortal eyes, when He had not yet taken our flesh, and mortal, inasmuch as He is changeable. And so also the Holy Spirit, who appeared at one time as a dove, and another time as fire. Whence, they say, the following texts do not belong to the Trinity, but singularly and properly to the Father only: "Now unto the King eternal, immortal, and invisible, the only wise God;" and, "Who only hath immortality, dwelling in the light which no man can approach unto; whom no man hath seen, nor can see."

16. Passing by, then, these reasoners, who are unable to know the substance even of the soul, which is invisible, and therefore are very far indeed from knowing that the substance of the one and only God, that is, the Father and the Son and the Holy Spirit, remains ever not only invisible, but also unchangeable, and that hence it possesses true and real immortality; let us, who deny that God, whether the Father, or the Son, or the Holy

---

[1] John i. 3.   [2] 1 Tim. i. 17.   [3] 1 Tim. vi. 15, 16.
[4] [For an example of the manner in which the patristic writers present the doctrine of the divine invisibility, see Irenæus, Adv. Hæress, IV. xx.—W.G.T.S.]

[5] Matt. x. 28.

Spirit, ever appeared to bodily eyes, unless through the corporeal creature made subject to His own power; let us, I say—ready to be corrected, if we are reproved in a fraternal and upright spirit, ready to be so, even if carped at by an enemy, so that he speak the truth—in catholic peace and with peaceful study inquire, whether God indiscriminately appeared to our fathers before Christ came in the flesh, or whether it was any one person of the Trinity, or whether severally, as it were by turns.

CHAP. 10—WHETHER GOD THE TRINITY INDIS-
CRIMINATELY APPEARED TO THE FATHERS, OR
ANY ONE PERSON OF THE TRINITY.　THE AP-
PEARING OF GOD TO ADAM.　OF THE SAME AP-
PEARANCE.　THE VISION TO ABRAHAM.

17. And first, in that which is written in Genesis, *viz.*, that God spake with man whom He had formed out of the dust; if we set apart the figurative meaning, and treat it so as to place faith in the narrative even in the letter, it should appear that God then spake with man in the appearance of a man. This is not indeed expressly laid down in the book, but the general tenor of its reading sounds in this sense, especially in that which is written, that Adam heard the voice of the Lord God, walking in the garden in the cool of the evening, and hid himself among the trees of the garden; and when God said, " Adam, where art thou ?"[1] replied, " I heard Thy voice, and I was afraid because I was naked, and I hid myself from Thy face." For I do not see how such a walking and conversation of God can be understood literally, except He appeared as a man. For it can neither be said that a voice only of God was framed, when God is said to have walked, or that He who was walking in a place was not visible; while Adam, too, says that he hid himself from the face of God. Who then was He ? Whether the Father, or the Son, or the Holy Spirit ? Whether altogether indiscriminately did God the Trinity Himself speak to man in the form of man ? The context, indeed, itself of the Scripture nowhere, it should seem, indicates a change from person to person; but He seems still to speak to the first man, who said, " Let there be light," and, " Let there be a firmament," and so on through each of those days; whom we usually take to be God the Father, making by a word whatever He willed to make. For He made all things by His word, which Word we know, by the right rule of faith, to be His only Son. If, therefore, God the Father spake to the first man, and Himself was walking in the garden in the cool of the evening, and if it was from His face that the sinner hid himself amongst the trees of the garden, why are we not to go on to understand that it was He also who appeared to Abraham and to Moses, and to whom He would, and how He would, through the changeable and visible creature, subjected to Himself, while He Himself remains in Himself and in His own substance, in which He is unchangeable and invisible ? But, possibly, it might be that the Scripture passed over in a hidden way from person to person, and while it had related that the Father said "Let there be light," and the rest which it mentioned Him to have done by the Word, went on to indicate the Son as speaking to the first man; not unfolding this openly, but intimating it to be understood by those who could understand it.

18. Let him, then, who has the strength whereby he can penetrate this secret with his mind's eye, so that to him it appears clearly, either that the Father also is able, or that only the Son and Holy Spirit are able, to appear to human eyes through a visible creature; let him, I say, proceed to examine these things if he can, or even to express and handle them in words; but the thing itself, so far as concerns this testimony of Scripture, where God spake with man, is, in my judgment, not discoverable, because it does not evidently appear even whether Adam usually saw God with the eyes of his body; especially as it is a great question what manner of eyes it was that were opened when they tasted the forbidden fruit;[2] for before they had tasted, these eyes were closed. Yet I would not rashly assert, even if that scripture implies Paradise to have been a material place, that God could not have walked there in any way except in some bodily form. For it might be said, that only words were framed for the man to hear, without seeing any form. Neither, because it is written, "Adam hid himself from the face of God," does it follow forthwith that he usually saw His face. For what if he himself indeed could not see, but feared to be himself seen by Him whose voice he had heard, and had felt His presence as he walked? For Cain, too, said to God, " From Thy face I will hide myself;"[3] yet we are not therefore compelled to admit that he was wont to behold the face of God with his bodily eyes in any visible form, although he had heard the voice of God questioning and speaking with him of his sin. But what

---

[1] Gen. iii. 8-10.　　　[2] Gen. iii. 7.　　　[3] Gen. iv. 14.

manner of speech it was that God then uttered to the outward ears of men, especially in speaking to the first man, it is both difficult to discover, and we have not undertaken to say in this discourse. But if words alone and sounds were wrought, by which to bring about some sensible presence of God to those first men, I do not know why I should not there understand the person of God the Father, seeing that His person is manifested also in that voice, when Jesus appeared in glory on the mount before the three disciples;[1] and in that when the dove descended upon Him at His baptism;[2] and in that where He cried to the Father concerning His own glorification, and it was answered Him, "I have both glorified, and will glorify again."[3] Not that the voice could be wrought without the work of the Son and of the Holy Spirit (since the Trinity works indivisibly), but that such a voice was wrought as to manifest the person of the Father only; just as the Trinity wrought that human form from the Virgin Mary, yet it is the person of the Son alone; for the invisible Trinity wrought the visible person of the Son alone. Neither does anything forbid us, not only to understand those words spoken to Adam as spoken by the Trinity, but also to take them as manifesting the person of that Trinity. For we are compelled to understand of the Father only, that which is said, "This is my beloved Son."[4] For Jesus can neither be believed nor understood to be the Son of the Holy Spirit, or even His own Son. And where the voice uttered, "I have both glorified, and will glorify again," we confess it was only the person of the Father; since it is the answer to that word of the Lord, in which He had said, "Father, glorify thy Son," which He could not say except to God the Father only, and not also to the Holy Spirit, whose Son He was not. But here, where it is written, "And the Lord God said to Adam," no reason can be given why the Trinity itself should not be understood.

19. Likewise, also, in that which is written, "Now the Lord had said unto Abraham, Get thee out of thy country, and from thy kindred, and thy father's house," it is not clear whether a voice alone came to the ears of Abraham, or whether anything also appeared to his eyes. But a little while after, it is somewhat more clearly said, "And the Lord appeared unto Abraham, and said, Unto thy seed will I give this land."[5] But neither there is it expressly said in what form God

appeared to him, or whether the Father, or the Son, or the Holy Spirit appeared to him. Unless, perhaps, they think that it was the Son who appeared to Abraham, because it is not written, God appeared to him, but "the Lord appeared to him." For the Son seems to be called the Lord as though the name was appropriated to Him; as e.g. the apostle says, "For though there be that are called gods, whether in heaven or in earth, (as there be gods many and lords many,) but to us there is but one God, the Father, of whom are all things, and we in Him; and one Lord Jesus Christ, by whom are all things, and we by Him."[6] But since it is found that God the Father also is called Lord in many places,—for instance, "The Lord hath said unto me, Thou art my Son; this day have I begotten Thee;"[7] and again, "The Lord said unto my Lord, Sit Thou at my right hand;"[8] since also the Holy Spirit is found to be called Lord, as where the apostle says, "Now the Lord is that Spirit;" and then, lest any one should think the Son to be signified, and to be called the Spirit on account of His incorporeal substance, has gone on to say, "And where the Spirit of the Lord is, there is liberty;"[9] and no one ever doubted the Spirit of the Lord to be the Holy Spirit: therefore, neither here does it appear plainly whether it was any person of the Trinity that appeared to Abraham, or God Himself the Trinity, of which one God it is said, "Thou shalt fear the Lord thy God, and Him only shalt thou serve."[10] But under the oak at Mamre he saw three men, whom he invited, and hospitably received, and ministered to them as they feasted. Yet Scripture at the beginning of that narrative does not say, three men appeared to him, but, "The Lord appeared to him." And then, setting forth in due order after what manner the Lord appeared to him, it has added the account of the three men, whom Abraham invites to his hospitality in the plural number, and afterwards speaks to them in the singular number as one; and as one He promises him a son by Sara, viz. the one whom the Scripture calls Lord, as in the beginning of the same narrative, "The Lord," it says, "appeared to Abraham." He invites them then, and washes their feet, and leads them forth at their departure, as though they were men; but he speaks as with the Lord God, whether when a son is promised to him, or when the destruction is shown to him that was impending over Sodom.[11]

---

1 Matt. xvii. 5.   2 Matt. iii. 17.   3 John xii. 28.
4 Matt. iii. 17.   5 Gen. xii. 1, 7.

6 1 Cor. viii. 5, 6.   7 Ps. ii. 7;   8 Ps. cx. 1.
9 2 Cor. iii. 17.   10 Deut. vi. 13.   11 Gen. xviii.

CHAP. 11.—OF THE SAME APPEARANCE.

20. That place of Scripture demands neither a slight nor a passing consideration. For if one man had appeared, what else would those at once cry out, who say that the Son was visible also in His own substance before He was born of the Virgin, but that it was Himself? since it is said, they say, of the Father, "To the only invisible God."[1] And yet, I could still go on to demand, in what manner "He was found in fashion as a man," before He had taken our flesh, seeing that his feet were washed, and that He fed upon earthly food? How could that be, when He was still "in the form of God, and thought it not robbery to be equal with God?"[2] For, pray, had He already "emptied Himself, taking upon Him the form of a servant, and made in the likeness of men, and found in fashion as a man?" when we know when it was that He did this through His birth of the Virgin. How, then, before He had done this, did He appear as one man to Abraham? or, was not that form a reality? I could put these questions, if it had been one man that appeared to Abraham, and if that one were believed to be the Son of God. But since three men appeared, and no one of them is said to be greater than the rest either in form, or age, or power, why should we not here understand, as visibly intimated by the visible creature, the equality of the Trinity, and one and the same substance in three persons?[3]

21. For, lest any one should think that one among the three is in this way intimated to have been the greater, and that this one is to be understood to have been the Lord, the Son of God, while the other two were His angels; because, whereas three appeared, Abraham there speaks to one as the Lord: Holy Scripture has not forgotten to anticipate, by a contradiction, such future cogitations and opinions, when a little while after it says that two angels came to Lot, among whom that just man also, who deserved to be freed from the burning of Sodom, speaks to one as to the Lord. For so Scripture goes on to say, "And the Lord went His way, as soon as He left communing with Abraham; and Abraham returned to his place."[4]

CHAP. 12.—THE APPEARANCE TO LOT IS EXAMINED.

"But there came two angels to Sodom at even." Here, what I have begun to set forth must be considered more attentively. Certainly Abraham was speaking with three, and called that one, in the singular number, the Lord. Perhaps, some one may say, he recognized one of the three to be the Lord, but the other two His angels. What, then, does that mean which Scripture goes on to say, "And the Lord went His way, as soon as He had left communing with Abraham; and Abraham returned to his place: and there came two angels to Sodom at even?" Are we to suppose that the one who, among the three, was recognized as the Lord, had departed, and had sent the two angels that were with Him to destroy Sodom? Let us see, then, what follows. "There came," it is said, "two angels to Sodom at even; and Lot sat in the gate of Sodom: and Lot seeing them, rose up to meet them; and he bowed himself with his face toward the ground; and he said, Behold now, my lords, turn in, I pray you, into your servant's house." Here it is clear, both that there were two angels, and that in the plural number they were invited to partake of hospitality, and that they were honorably designated lords, when they perchance were thought to be men.

22. Yet, again, it is objected that except they were known to be angels of God, Lot would not have bowed himself with his face to the ground. Why, then, is both hospitality and food offered to them, as though they wanted such human succor? But whatever may here lie hid, let us now pursue that which we have undertaken. Two appear; both are called angels; they are invited plurally; he speaks as with two plurally, until the departure from Sodom. And then Scripture goes on to say, "And it came to pass, when they had brought them forth abroad, that they said, Escape for thy life; look not behind thee, neither stay thou in all the plain; escape to the mountain, and there thou shalt be saved,[5] lest thou be consumed. And Lot said unto them, Oh! not so, my lord: behold now, thy servant hath found grace in thy sight,"[6] etc. What is meant by his saying to them, "Oh! not so, my lord," if He who was the Lord had already departed, and had sent the angels? Why is it said, "Oh! not so, my lord," and not, "Oh! not so, my lords?" Or if he wished to speak to one of them, why does Scripture say, "But Lot said to them, Oh! not so, my lord: be-

---

[1] 1 Tim. i. 17.   [2] Phil. ii. 6, 7.
[3] [The theophanies of the Pentateuch are trinitarian in their implication. They involve distinctions in God—God sending, and God sent; God speaking of God, and God speaking to God. The trinitarianism of the Old Testament has been lost sight of to some extent in the modern construction of the doctrine. The patristic, mediæval, and reformation theologies worked this vein with thoroughness, and the analysis of Augustin in this reference is worthy of careful study.—W.G.T.S.]
[4] Gen. xviii. 33.

[5] This clause is not in the Hebrew.   [6] Gen. xix. 1-19.

hold now, thy servant hath found grace in thy sight," etc.? Are we here, too, to understand two persons in the plural number, but when the two are addressed as one, then the one Lord God of one substance? But which two persons do we here understand?—of the Father and of the Son, or of the Father and of the Holy Spirit, or of the Son and of the Holy Spirit? The last, perhaps, is the more suitable; for they said of themselves that they were sent, which is that which we say of the Son and of the Holy Spirit. For we find nowhere in the Scriptures that the Father was sent.[1]

CHAP. 13.—THE APPEARANCE IN THE BUSH.

23. But when Moses was sent to lead the children of Israel out of Egypt, it is written that the Lord appeared to him thus: "Now Moses kept the flock of Jethro his father-in-law, the priest of Midian: and he led the flock to the back side of the desert, and came to the mountain of God, even to Horeb. And the Angel of the Lord appeared unto him in a flame of fire, out of the midst of a bush; and he looked, and, behold, the bush burned with fire, and the bush was not consumed. And Moses said, I will now turn aside, and see this great sight, why the bush is not burnt. And when the Lord saw that he turned aside to see, God called unto him out of the midst of the bush, and said, I am the God of thy father, the God of Abraham, the God of Isaac, and the God of Jacob."[2] He is here also first called the Angel of the Lord, and then God. Was an angel, then, the God of Abraham, and the God of Isaac, and the God of Jacob? Therefore He may be rightly understood to be the Saviour Himself, of whom the apostle says, " Whose are the fathers, and of whom as concerning the flesh Christ came, who is over all, God blessed for ever."[3] He, therefore, " who is over all, God blessed for ever," is not unreasonably here understood also to be Himself the God of Abraham, the God of Isaac, and the God of Jacob. But why is He previously called the Angel of the Lord, when

He appeared in a flame of fire out of the bush? Was it because it was one of many angels, who by an economy [or arrangement] bare the person of his Lord? or was something of the creature assumed by Him in order to bring about a visible appearance for the business in hand, and that words might thence be audibly uttered, whereby the presence of the Lord might be shown, in such way as was fitting, to the corporeal senses of man, by means of the creature made subject? For if he was one of the angels, who could easily affirm whether it was the person of the Son which was imposed upon him to announce, or that of the Holy Spirit, or that of God the Father, or altogether of the Trinity itself, who is the one and only God, in order that he might say, " I am the God of Abraham, and the God of Isaac, and the God of Jacob?" For we cannot say that the Son of God is the God of Abraham, and the God of Isaac, and the God of Jacob, and that the Father is not; nor will any one dare to deny that either the Holy Spirit, or the Trinity itself, whom we believe and understand to be the one God, is the God of Abraham, and the God of Isaac, and the God of Jacob. For he who is not God, is not the God of those fathers. Furthermore, if not only the Father is God, as all, even heretics, admit; but also the Son, which, whether they will or not, they are compelled to acknowledge, since the apostle says, " Who is over all, God blessed for ever;" and the Holy Spirit, since the same apostle says, " Therefore glorify God in your body;" when he had said above, " Know ye not that your body is the temple of the Holy Ghost, which is in you, which ye have of God?"[4] and these three are one God, as catholic soundness believes: it is not sufficiently apparent which person of the Trinity that angel bare, if he was one of the rest of the angels, and whether any person, and not rather that of the Trinity itself. But if the creature was assumed for the purpose of the business in hand, whereby both to appear to human eyes, and to sound in human ears, and to be called the Angel of the Lord, and the Lord, and God; then cannot God here be understood to be the Father, but either the Son or the Holy Spirit. Although I cannot call to mind that the Holy Spirit is anywhere else called an angel, which yet may be understood from His work; for it is said of Him, " And He will show you[5] things to come;"[6] and " angel" in Greek is certainly equivalent to " messenger"[7] in Latin: but we read most evidently of the Lord Jesus Christ in the prophet, that He is

---

[1] [It is difficult to determine the details of this theophany, beyond all doubt: namely, whether the " Jehovah" who " went his way as soon as he had left communing with Abraham." (Gen. xviii. 33) joins the "two angels" that " came to Sodom at even" (Gen. xix. 1); or whether one of these "two angels" is Jehovah himself. One or the other supposition must be made; because a person is addressed by Lot as God (Gen. xix. 18-20), and speaks to Lot as God (Gen. xix. 21, 22), and acts as God (Gen. xix. 24). The Masorite marking of the word "lords" in Gen. xix. 2, as " profane," i.e., to be taken in the human sense, would favor the first supposition. The interchange of the singular and plural, in the whole narrative is very striking. " It came to pass, when they had brought them forth abroad, that he said, escape for thy life. And Lot said unto them. Oh not so, my Lord : behold now, thy servant hath found grace in thy sight. And he said unto him, see I have accepted thee; I will not overthrow the city of which thou hast spoken." (Gen. xix. 17-21.)—W.G.T.S.]
[2] Ex. iii. 1-6. [3] Rom. ix. 5.

[4] 1 Cor. vi. 20, 19. [5] Annuntiabit.
[6] John xvi. 13. [7] Nuntius.

called "the Angel of Great Counsel," [1] while both the Holy Spirit and the Son of God is God and Lord of the angels.

CHAP. 14.—OF THE APPEARANCE IN THE PILLAR OF CLOUD AND OF FIRE.

24. Also in the going forth of the children of Israel from Egypt it is written, "And the Lord went before them, by day in a pillar of cloud to lead them the way, and by night in a pillar of fire. He took not away the pillar of the cloud by day, nor the pillar of fire by night, from before the people." [2] Who here, too, would doubt that God appeared to the eyes of mortal men by the corporeal creature made subject to Him, and not by His own substance? But it is not similarly apparent whether the Father, or the Son, or the Holy Spirit, or the Trinity itself, the one God. Nor is this distinguished there either, in my judgment, where it is written, "The glory of the Lord appeared in the cloud, and the Lord spake unto Moses, saying, I have heard the murmurings of the children of Israel," [3] etc.

CHAP. 15.—OF THE APPEARANCE ON SINAI. WHETHER THE TRINITY SPAKE IN THAT APPEARANCE OR SOME ONE PERSON SPECIALLY.

25. But now of the clouds, and voices, and lightnings, and the trumpet, and the smoke on Mount Sinai, when it was said, "And Mount Sinai was altogether on a smoke, because the Lord descended upon it in fire, and the smoke thereof ascended as the smoke of a furnace; and all the people that was in the camp trembled; and when the voice of the trumpet sounded long and waxed louder and louder, Moses spake, and God answered him by a voice." [4] And a little after, when the Law had been given in the ten commandments, it follows in the text, "And all the people saw the thunderings, and the lightnings, and the noise of the trumpet, and the mountain smoking." And a little after, "And [when the people saw it,] they removed and stood afar off, and Moses drew near unto the thick darkness [5] where God was, and the Lord said unto Moses," [6] etc. What shall I say about this, save that no one can be so insane as to believe the smoke, and the fire, and the cloud, and the darkness, and whatever there was of the kind, to be the substance of the word and wisdom of God which is Christ, or of the Holy Spirit? For not even the Arians ever dared to say that they were the substance of God the Father.

All these things, then, were wrought through the creature serving the Creator, and were presented in a suitable economy (*dispensatio*) to human senses; unless, perhaps, because it is said, "And Moses drew near to the cloud where God was," carnal thoughts must needs suppose that the cloud was indeed seen by the people, but that within the cloud Moses with the eyes of the flesh saw the Son of God, whom doting heretics will have to be seen in His own substance. Forsooth, Moses may have seen Him with the eyes of the flesh, if not only the wisdom of God which is Christ, but even that of any man you please and howsoever wise, can be seen with the eyes of the flesh; or if, because it is written of the elders of Israel, that "they saw the place where the God of Israel had stood," and that "there was under His feet as it were a paved work of a sapphire stone, and as it were the body of heaven in his clearness," [7] therefore we are to believe that the word and wisdom of God in His own substance stood within the space of an earthly place, who indeed "reacheth firmly from end to end, and sweetly ordereth all things;" [8] and that the Word of God, by whom all things were made, [9] is in such wise changeable, as now to contract, now to expand Himself; (may the Lord cleanse the hearts of His faithful ones from such thoughts!) But indeed all these visible and sensible things are, as we have often said, exhibited through the creature made subject in order to signify the invisible and intelligible God, not only the Father, but also the Son and the Holy Spirit, "of whom are all things, and through whom are all things, and in whom are all things;" [10] although "the invisible things of God, from the creation of the world, are clearly seen, being understood by the things that are made, even His eternal power and Godhead." [11]

26. But as far as concerns our present undertaking, neither on Mount Sinai do I see how it appears, by all those things which were fearfully displayed to the senses of mortal men, whether God the Trinity spake, or the Father, or the Son, or the Holy Spirit severally. But if it is allowable, without rash assertion, to venture upon a modest and hesitating conjecture from this passage, if it is possible to understand it of one person of the Trinity, why do we not rather understand the Holy Spirit to be spoken of, since the Law itself also, which was given there, is said to have been written upon tables of stone with the

---

[1] Isa. ix. 6. [2] Ex. iii. 21, 22.
[3] Ex. xvi. 10-12. [4] Ex. xix. 18, 19.
[5] *Nebulam*. [6] Ex. xx. 18, 21.

[7] Ex. xxiv. 10. [8] Wisd. viii. 1. [9] John i. 3.
[10] Rom. xi. 36. [11] Rom. i. 20.

finger of God, [1] by which name we know the Holy Spirit to be signified in the Gospel. [2] And fifty days are numbered from the slaying of the lamb and the celebration of the Passover until the day in which these things began to be done in Mount Sinai; just as after the passion of our Lord fifty days are numbered from His resurrection, and then came the Holy Spirit which the Son of God had promised. And in that very coming of His, which we read of in the Acts of the Apostles, there appeared cloven tongues like as of fire, and it sat upon each of them: [3] which agrees with Exodus, where it is written, "And Mount Sinai was altogether on a smoke, because the Lord descended upon it in fire;" and a little after, "And the sight of the glory of the Lord," he says, "was like devouring fire on the top of the mount in the eyes of the children of Israel." [4] Or if these things were therefore wrought because neither the Father nor the Son could be there presented in that mode without the Holy Spirit, by whom the Law itself must needs be written; then we know doubtless that God appeared there, not by His own substance, which remains invisible and unchangeable, but by the appearance above mentioned of the creature; but that some special person of the Trinity appeared, distinguished by a proper mark, as far as my capacity of understanding reaches, we do not see.

CHAP. 16.—IN WHAT MANNER MOSES SAW GOD.

26. There is yet another difficulty which troubles most people, *viz.* that it is written, "And the Lord spake unto Moses face to face, as a man speaketh unto his friend;" whereas a little after, the same Moses says, "Now therefore, I pray Thee, if I have found grace in Thy sight, show me now Thyself plainly, that I may see Thee, that I may find grace in Thy sight, and that I may consider that this nation is Thy people;" and a little after Moses again said to the Lord, "Show me Thy glory." What means this then, that in everything which was done, as above said, God was thought to have appeared by His own substance; whence the Son of God has been believed by these miserable people to be visible not by the creature, but by Himself; and that Moses, entering into the cloud, appeared to have had this very object in entering, that a cloudy darkness indeed might be shown to the eyes of the people, but that Moses within might hear the words of God, as though he beheld His face; and, as it is

said, "And the Lord spake unto Moses face to face, as a man speaketh unto his friend;" and yet, behold, the same Moses says, "If I have found grace in Thy sight, show me Thyself plainly?" Assuredly he knew that he saw corporeally, and he sought the true sight of God spiritually. And that mode of speech accordingly which was wrought in words, was so modified, as if it were of a friend speaking to a friend. Yet who sees God the Father with the eyes of the body? And that Word, which was in the beginning, the Word which was with God, the Word which was God, by which all things were made, [5]—who sees Him with the eyes of the body? And the spirit of wisdom, again, who sees with the eyes of the body? Yet what is, "Show me now Thyself plainly, that I may see Thee," unless, Show me Thy substance? But if Moses had not said this, we must indeed have borne with those foolish people as we could, who think that the substance of God was made visible to his eyes through those things which, as above mentioned, were said or done. But when it is here demonstrated most evidently that this was *not granted* to him, even though he desired it; who will dare to say, that by the like forms which had appeared visibly to him also, not the creature serving God, but that itself which is God, appeared to the eyes of a mortal man?

28. Add, too, that which the Lord afterward said to Moses, "Thou canst not see my face: for there shall no man see my face, and live. And the Lord said, Behold, there is a place by me, and thou' shalt stand upon a rock: and it shall come to pass, while my glory passeth by, that I will put thee into a watch-tower [6] of the rock, and will cover thee with my hand while I pass by: and I will take away my hand, and thou shalt see my back parts; but my face shall not be seen." [7]

CHAP. 17.—HOW THE BACK PARTS OF GOD WERE SEEN. THE FAITH OF THE RESURRECTION OF CHRIST. THE CATHOLIC CHURCH ONLY IS THE PLACE FROM WHENCE THE BACK PARTS OF GOD ARE SEEN. THE BACK PARTS OF GOD WERE SEEN BY THE ISRAELITES. IT IS A RASH OPINION TO THINK THAT GOD THE FATHER ONLY WAS NEVER SEEN BY THE FATHERS.

Not unfitly is it commonly understood to be prefigured from the person of our Lord Jesus Christ, that His "back parts" are to be taken to be His flesh, in which He was

---

1 Ex. xxi. 18.   2 Luke xi. 2c.
3 Acts. ii. 1-4.   4 Ex. xxiv. 17.

5 John i. 1, 3.
6 Clift—A. V. *Spelunca* is one reading in S. Aug., but the Benedictines read *specula* = watch-tower, which the context proves to be certainly right.
7 Ex. xxxiii. 11-23.

born of the Virgin, and died, and rose again; whether they are called back parts[1] on account of the posteriority of mortality, or because it was almost in the end of the world, that is, at a late period,[2] that He deigned to take it: but that His "face" was that form of God, in which He "thought it not robbery to be equal with God,"[3] which no one certainly can see and live; whether because after this life, in which we are absent from the Lord,[4] and where the corruptible body presseth down the soul,[5] we shall see "face to face,"[6] as the apostle says—(for it is said in the Psalms, of this life, "Verily every man living is altogether vanity;"[7] and again, "For in Thy sight shall no man living be justified;"[8] and in this life also, according to John, "It doth not yet appear what we shall be, but we know," he says, "that when He shall appear, we shall be like Him, for we shall see Him as He is,"[9] which he certainly intended to be understood as after this life, when we shall have paid the debt of death, and shall have received the promise of the resurrection);—or whether that even now, in whatever degree we spiritually understand the wisdom of God, by which all things were made, in that same degree we die to carnal affections, so that, considering this world dead to us, we also ourselves die to this world, and say what the apostle says, "The world is crucified unto me, and I unto the world."[10] For it was of this death that he also says, "Wherefore, if ye be dead with Christ, why as though living in the world are ye subject to ordinances?"[11] Not therefore without cause will no one be able to see the "face," that is, the manifestation itself of the wisdom of God, and live. For it is this very appearance, for the contemplation of which every one sighs who strives to love God with all his heart, and with all his soul, and with all his mind; to the contemplation of which, he who loves his neighbor, too, as himself builds up his neighbor also as far as he may; on which two commandments hang all the law and the prophets.[12] And this is signified also in Moses himself. For when he had said, on account of the love of God with which he was specially inflamed, "If I have found grace in thy sight, show me now Thyself plainly, that I may find grace in Thy sight;" he immediately subjoined, on account of the love also of his neighbor, "And that I

may know that this nation is Thy people." It is therefore that "appearance" which hurries away every rational soul with the desire of it, and the more ardently the more pure that soul is; and it is the more pure the more it rises to spiritual things; and it rises the more to spiritual things the more it dies to carnal things. But whilst we are absent from the Lord, and walk by faith, not by sight,[13] we ought to see the "back parts" of Christ, that is His flesh, by that very faith, that is, standing on the solid foundation of faith, which the rock signifies,[14] and beholding it from such a safe watch-tower, namely in the Catholic Church, of which it is said, "And upon this rock I will build my Church."[15] For so much the more certainly we love that face of Christ, which we earnestly desire to see, as we recognize in His back parts how much first Christ loved us.

29. But in the flesh itself, the faith in His resurrection saves and justifies us. For, "If thou shalt believe," he says, "in thine heart, that God hath raised Him from the dead, thou shalt be saved;"[16] and again, "Who was delivered," he says, "for our offenses, and was raised again for our justification."[17] So that the reward of our faith is the resurrection of the body of our Lord.[18] For even His enemies believe that that flesh died on the cross of His passion, but they do not believe it to have risen again. Which we believing most firmly, gaze upon it as from the solidity of a rock: whence we wait with certain hope for the adoption, to wit, the redemption of our body;[19] because we hope for that in the members of Christ, that is, in ourselves, which by a sound faith we acknowledge to be perfect in Him as in our Head. Thence it is that He would not have His back parts seen, unless as He passed by, that His resurrection may be believed. For that which is Pascha in Hebrew, is translated Passover.[20] Whence John the Evangelist also says, "Before the feast of the Passover, when Jesus knew that His hour was come, that He should pass out of this world unto the Father."[21]

30. But they who believe this, but believe it not in the Catholic Church, but in some schism or in heresy, do not see the back parts of the Lord from "the place that is by Him." For what does that mean which the Lord says, "Behold, there is a place by me, and thou

---

[1] *Posteriora.* [2] *Posterius.*
[3] Phil. ii. 6. [4] 2 Cor. v. 6.
[5] Wisd. ix. 15. [6] 1 Cor. xiii. 12.
[7] Ps. xxxix. 5. [8] Ps. cxliii. 2.
[9] 1 John iii. 2. [10] Gal. vi. 14.
[11] Col. ii. 20. *Viventes de hoc mundo decernitis.*
[12] Matt. xxii. 37-40.

[13] 2 Cor. v. 6, 7.
[14] [Augustin here gives the Protestant interpretation of the word "rock," in the passage, "on this rock I will build my church."—W.G.T.S.]
[15] Matt. xvi. 18. [16] Rom. x. 9. [17] Rom. iv. 25.
[18] [The meaning seems to be, that the vivid realization that Christ's body rose from the dead is the reward of a Christian's faith. The unbeliever has no such reward.—W.G.T.S.]
[19] Rom. viii. 23.
[20] *Transitus* = passing by. [21] John xiii. 1.

shalt stand upon a rock?" What earthly place is "by" the Lord, unless that is "by Him" which touches Him spiritually? For what place is not "by" the Lord, who "reacheth from one end to another mightily, and sweetly doth order all things,"[1] and of whom it is said, "Heaven is His throne, and earth is His footstool;" and who said, "Where is the house that ye build unto me, and where is the place of my rest? For has not my hand made all those things?"[2] But manifestly the Catholic Church itself is understood to be "the place by Him," wherein one stands upon a rock, where he healthfully sees the "Pascha Domini," that is, the "Passing by"[3] of the Lord, and His back parts, that is, His body, who believes in His resurrection. "And thou shalt stand," He says, "upon a rock while my glory passeth by." For in reality, immediately after the majesty of the Lord had passed by in the glorification of the Lord, in which He rose again and ascended to the Father, we stood firm upon the rock. And Peter himself then stood firm, so that he preached Him with confidence, whom, before he stood firm, he had thrice from fear denied;[4] although, indeed, already before placed in predestination upon the watch-tower of the rock, but with the hand of the Lord still held over him that he might not see. For he was to see His back parts, and the Lord had not yet "passed by," namely, from death to life; He had not yet been glorified by the resurrection.

31. For as to that, too, which follows in Exodus, "I will cover thee with mine hand while I pass by, and I will take away my hand and thou shalt see my back parts;" many Israelites, of whom Moses was then a figure, believed in the Lord after His resurrection, as if His hand had been taken off from their eyes, and they now saw His back parts. And hence the evangelist also mentions that prophesy of Isaiah, "Make the heart of this people fat, and make their ears heavy, and shut their eyes."[5] Lastly, in the Psalm, that is not unreasonably understood to be said in their person, "For day and night Thy hand was heavy upon me." "By day," perhaps, when He performed manifest miracles, yet was not acknowledged by them; but "by night," when He died in suffering, when they thought still more certainly that, like any one among men, He was cut off and brought to an end. But since, when He had already passed by, so that His back parts were seen, upon the

preaching to them by the Apostle Peter that it behoved Christ to suffer and rise again, they were pricked in their hearts with the grief of repentance,[6] that that might come to pass among the baptized which is said in the beginning of that Psalm, "Blessed are they whose transgressions are forgiven, and whose sins are covered;" therefore, after it had been said, "Thy hand is heavy upon me," the Lord, as it were, passing by, so that now He removed His hand, and His back parts were seen, there follows the voice of one who grieves and confesses and receives remission of sins by faith in the resurrection of the Lord: "My moisture," he says, "is turned into the drought of summer. I acknowledged my sin unto Thee, and mine iniquity have I not hid. I said, I will confess my transgressions unto the Lord, and Thou forgavest the iniquity of my sin."[7] For we ought not to be so wrapped up in the darkness of the flesh, as to think the face indeed of God to be invisible, but His back visible, since both appeared visibly in the form of a servant; but far be it from us to think anything of the kind in the form of God; far be it from us to think that the Word of God and the Wisdom of God has a face on one side, and on the other a back, as a human body has, or is at all changed either in place or time by any appearance or motion.[8]

32. Wherefore, if in those words which were spoken in Exodus, and in all those corporeal appearances, the Lord Jesus Christ was manifested; or if in some cases Christ was manifested, as the consideration of this passage persuades us, in others the Holy Spirit, as that which we have said above admonishes us; at any rate no such result follows, as that God the Father never appeared in any such form to the Fathers. For many such appearances happened in those times, without either the Father, or the Son, or the Holy Spirit being expressly named and designated in them; but yet with some intimations given through certain very probable interpretations, so that it would be too rash to say that God the Father never appeared by any visible forms to the fathers or the prophets. For they gave birth to this opinion who were not able to understand in respect to the unity of the Trinity such texts as, "Now unto the King eternal, immortal, invisible, the only wise God;"[9] and, "Whom no man hath seen, nor

---

[1] Wisd. viii. 1.   [2] Isa. lxvi. 1, 2.
[3] *Transitus.*   [4] Matt. xxvi. 70-74.
[5] Isa. vi. 10; Matt. xiii. 15.

[6] Acts ii. 37, 41.   [7] Ps. xxxii. 4, 5.
[8] [This explanation of the "back parts" of Christ to mean his resurrection, and of "the place that is by him," to mean the church, is an example of the fanciful exegesis into which Augustin, with the fathers generally, sometimes falls. The reasoning, here, unlike that in the preceding chapter, is not from the immediate context, and hence extraneous matter is read into the text. —W. G. T. S.]   [9] 1 Tim. i. 17.

can see."[1] Which texts are understood by a sound faith in that substance itself, the highest, and in the highest degree divine and unchangeable, whereby both the Father and the Son and the Holy Spirit is the one and only God. But those visions were wrought through the changeable creature, made subject to the unchangeable God, and did not manifest God properly as He is, but by intimations such as suited the causes and times of the several circumstances.

CHAP. 18.—THE VISION OF DANIEL.

33. [2] I do not know in what manner these men understand that the Ancient of Days appeared to Daniel, from whom the Son of man, which He deigned to be for our sakes, is understood to have received the kingdom; namely, from Him who says to Him in the Psalms, "Thou art my Son; this day have I begotten Thee; ask of me, and I shall give Thee the heathen for Thine inheritance;"[3] and who has "put all things under His feet."[4] If, however, both the Father giving the kingdom, and the Son receiving it, appeared to Daniel in bodily form, how can those men say that the Father never appeared to the prophets, and, therefore, that He only ought to be understood to be invisible whom no man has seen, nor can see? For Daniel has told us thus: "I beheld," he says, "till the thrones were set,[5] and the Ancient of Days did sit, whose garment was white as snow, and the hair of His head like the pure wool: His throne was like the fiery flame, and His wheels as burning fire; a fiery stream issued and came forth from before Him: thousand thousands ministered unto Him, and ten thousand times ten thousand stood before Him: the judgment was set, and the books were opened," etc. And a little after, "I saw," he says, "in the night visions, and behold, one like the Son of man came with the clouds of heaven, and came to the Ancient of Days, and they brought Him near before Him. And there was given Him dominion, and glory, and a kingdom, that all peoples, nations, and languages should serve Him: His dominion is an everlasting dominion, which shall not pass away, and His kingdom that which shall not be destroyed."[6] Behold the Father giving, and the Son receiving, an eternal kingdom; and both are in

the sight of him who prophesies, in a visible form. It is not, therefore, unsuitably believed that God the Father also was wont to appear in that manner to mortals.

34. Unless, perhaps, some one shall say, that the Father is therefore not visible, because He appeared within the sight of one who was dreaming; but that therefore the Son and the Holy Spirit are visible, because Moses saw all those things being awake; as if, forsooth, Moses saw the Word and the Wisdom of God with fleshly eyes, or that even the human spirit which quickens that flesh can be seen, or even that corporeal thing which is called wind;—how much less can that Spirit of God be seen, who transcends the minds of all men, and of angels, by the ineffable excellence of the divine substance? Or can any one fall headlong into such an error as to dare to say, that the Son and the Holy Spirit are visible also to men who are awake, but that the Father is not visible except to those who dream? How, then, do they understand that of the Father alone, "Whom no man hath seen, nor can see."? When men sleep, are they then not men? Or cannot He, who can fashion the likeness of a body to signify Himself through the visions of dreamers, also fashion that same bodily creature to signify Himself to the eyes of those who are awake? Whereas His own very substance, whereby He Himself is that which He is, cannot be shown by any bodily likeness to one who sleeps, or by any bodily appearance to one who is awake; but this not of the Father only, but also of the Son and of the Holy Spirit. And certainly, as to those who are moved by the visions of waking men to believe that not the Father, but only the Son, or the Holy Spirit, appeared to the corporeal sight of men,—to omit the great extent of the sacred pages, and their manifold interpretation, such that no one of sound reason ought to affirm that the person of the Father was nowhere shown to the eyes of waking men by any corporeal appearance; —but, as I said, to omit this, what do they say of our father Abraham, who was certainly awake and ministering, when, after Scripture had premised, "The Lord appeared unto Abraham," not one, or two, but three men appeared to him; no one of whom is said to have stood prominently above the others, no one more than the others to have shone with greater glory, or to have acted more authoritatively?[7]

35. Wherefore, since in that our threefold division we determined to inquire,[8] first,

---

[1] 1 Tim. vi. 16.
[2] [The original has an awkward anacoluthon in the opening sentence of this chapter, which has been removed by omitting "*quamquam*," and substituting "*autem*" for "*ergo*."—W. G. T. S.]
[3] Ps. ii. 7, 8. [4] Ps. viii. 8.
[5] Cast down—A. V. [6] Dan. vii. 9–14.

[7] Gen. xviii. 1. [8] See above, chap. vii.

whether the Father, or the Son, or the Holy Spirit; or whether sometimes the Father, sometimes the Son, sometimes the Holy Spirit; or whether, without any distinction of persons, as it is said, the one and only God, that is, the Trinity itself, appeared to the fathers through those forms of the creature: now that we have examined, so far as appeared to be sufficient, what places of the Holy Scriptures we could, a modest and cautious consideration of divine mysteries leads, as far as I can judge, to no other conclusion, unless that we may not rashly affirm which person of the Trinity appeared to this or that of the fathers or the prophets in some body or likeness of body, unless when the context attaches to the narrative some probable intimations on the subject. For the nature itself, or substance, or essence, or by whatever other name that very thing, which is God, whatever it be, is to be called, cannot be seen corporeally: but we must believe that by means of the creature made subject to Him, not only the Son, or the Holy Spirit, but also the Father, may have given intimations of Himself to mortal senses by a corporeal form or likeness. And since the case stands thus, that this second book may not extend to an immoderate length, let us consider what remains in those which follow.

BOOK III.

THE QUESTION IS DISCUSSED WITH RESPECT TO THE APPEARANCES OF GOD SPOKEN OF IN THE PREVIOUS BOOK, WHICH WERE MADE UNDER BODILY FORMS, WHETHER ONLY A CREATURE WAS FORMED, FOR THE PURPOSE OF MANIFESTING GOD TO HUMAN SIGHT IN SUCH WAY AS HE AT EACH TIME JUDGED FITTING; OR WHETHER ANGELS, ALREADY EXISTING, WERE SO SENT AS TO SPEAK IN THE PERSON OF GOD; AND THIS, EITHER BY ASSUMING A BODILY APPEARANCE FROM THE BODILY CREATURE, OR BY CHANGING THEIR OWN BODIES INTO WHATEVER FORMS THEY WOULD, SUITABLE TO THE PARTICULAR ACTION, ACCORDING TO THE POWER GIVEN TO THEM BY THE CREATOR; WHILE THE ESSENCE ITSELF OF GOD WAS NEVER SEEN IN ITSELF.

PREFACE. — WHY AUGUSTIN WRITES OF THE TRINITY. WHAT HE CLAIMS FROM READERS. WHAT HAS BEEN SAID IN THE PREVIOUS BOOK.

1. I WOULD have them believe, who are willing to do so, that I had rather bestow labor in reading, than in dictating what others may read. But let those who will not believe this, but are both able and willing to make the trial, grant me whatever answers may be gathered from reading, either to my own inquiries, or to those interrogations of others, which for the character I bear in the service of Christ, and for the zeal with which I burn that our faith may be fortified against the error of carnal and natural men,[1] I must needs bear with; and then let them see how easily I would refrain from this labor, and with how much even of joy I would give my pen a holiday. But if what we have read upon these subjects is either not sufficiently set forth, or is not to be found at all, or at any rate cannot easily be found by us, in the Latin tongue, while we are not so familiar with the Greek tongue as to be found in any way competent to read and understand therein the books that treat of such topics, in which class of writings, to judge by the little which has been translated for us, I do not doubt that everything is contained that we can profit-ably seek;[2] while yet I cannot resist my brethren when they exact of me, by that law by which I am made their servant, that I should minister above all to their praiseworthy studies in Christ by my tongue and by my pen, of which two yoked together in me, Love is the charioteer; and while I myself confess that I have by writing learned many things which I did not know: if this be so, then this my labor ought not to seem superfluous to any idle, or to any very learned reader; while it is needful in no small part, to many who are busy, and to many who are unlearned, and among these last to myself. Supported, then, very greatly, and aided by the writings we have already read of others on this subject, I have undertaken to inquire into and to discuss, whatever it seems to my judgment can be reverently inquired into and discussed, concerning the Trinity, the one supreme and supremely good God; He himself exhorting me to the inquiry, and helping me in the discussion of it; in order that, if there are no other writings of the kind, there may be something for those to have and read who

---

[1] [The English translator renders "*animalium*" by "psychical," to agree with ψυχικός in 1 Cor. ii. 14. The rendering "natural" of the A. V. is more familiar.—W. G. T. S.]

[2] [This is an important passage with reference to Augustin's learning. From it, it would appear that he had not read the Greek Trinitarians in the original, and that only "a little" of these had been translated, at the time when he was composing this treatise. As this was from A.D. 400 to A.D. 416—, the treatises of Athanasius (d. 373), Basil (d. 379), Gregory of Nyssa (d. 400?), and Gregory of Nazianzum (d. 390?) had been composed and were current in the Eastern church. That Augustin thought out this profound scheme of the doctrine of the Trinity by the close study of Scripture alone, and unassisted by the equally profound trinitarianism of the Greek church, is an evidence of the depth and strength of his remarkable intellect.—W. G. T. S.]

are willing and capable; but if any exist already, then it may be so much the easier to find some such writings, the more there are of the kind in existence.

2. Assuredly, as in all my writings I desire not only a pious reader, but also a free corrector, so I especially desire this in the present inquiry, which is so important that I would there were as many inquirers as there are objectors. But as I do not wish my reader to be bound down to me, so I do not wish my corrector to be bound down to himself. Let not the former love me more than the catholic faith, let not the latter love himself more than the catholic verity. As I say to the former, Do not be willing to yield to my writings as to the canonical Scriptures; but in these, when thou hast discovered even what thou didst not previously believe, believe it unhesitatingly; while in those, unless thou hast understood with certainty what thou didst not before hold as certain, be unwilling to hold it fast: so I say to the latter, Do not be willing to amend my writings by thine own opinion or disputation, but from the divine text, or by unanswerable reason. If thou apprehendest anything of truth in them, its being there does not make it mine, but by understanding and loving it, let it be both thine and mine; but if thou convictest anything of falsehood, though it have once been mine, in that I was guilty of the error, yet now by avoiding it let it be neither thine nor mine.

3. Let this third book, then, take its beginning at the point to which the second had reached. For after we had arrived at this, that we desired to show that the Son was not therefore less than the Father, because the Father sent and the Son was sent; nor the Holy Spirit therefore less than both, because we read in the Gospel that He was sent both by the one and by the other; we undertook then to inquire, since the Son was sent thither, where He already was, for He came into the world, and "was in the world;"[1] since also the Holy Spirit was sent thither, where He already was, for "the Spirit of the Lord filleth the world, and that which containeth all things hath knowledge of the voice;"[2] whether the Lord was therefore "sent" because He was born in the flesh so as to be no longer hidden, and, as it were, came forth from the bosom of the Father, and appeared to the eyes of men in the form of a servant; and the Holy Spirit also was therefore "sent," because He too was seen as a dove in a corporeal form,[3] and in cloven tongues, like as of fire;[4] so that, to

be sent, when spoken of them, means to go forth to the sight of mortals in some corporeal form from a spiritual hiding-place; which, because the Father did not, He is said only to have sent, not also to be sent. Our next inquiry was, Why the Father also is not sometimes said to be sent, if He Himself was manifested through those corporeal forms which appeared to the eyes of the ancients. But if the Son was manifested at these times, why should He be said to be "sent" so long after, when the fullness of time was come that He should be born of a woman;[5] since, indeed, He was sent before also, viz., when He appeared corporeally in those forms? Or if He were not rightly said to be "sent," except when the Word was made flesh;[6] why should the Holy Spirit be read of as "sent," of whom such an incarnation never took place? But if neither the Father, nor the Son, but the Holy Spirit was manifested through these ancient appearances; why should He too be said to be "sent" now, when He was also sent before in these various manners? Next we subdivided the subject, that it might be handled most carefully, and we made the question threefold, of which one part was explained in the second book, and two remain, which I shall next proceed to discuss. For we have already inquired and determined, that not only the Father, nor only the Son, nor only the Holy Spirit appeared in those ancient corporeal forms and visions, but either indifferently the Lord God, who is understood to be the Trinity itself, or some one person of the Trinity, whichever the text of the narrative might signify, through intimations supplied by the context.

CHAP. I.—WHAT IS TO BE SAID THEREUPON.

4. Let us, then, continue our inquiry now in order. For under the second head in that division the question occurred, whether the creature was formed for that work only, wherein God, in such way as He then judged it to be fitting, might be manifested to human sight; or whether angels, who already existed, were so sent as to speak in the person of God, assuming a corporeal appearance from the corporeal creature for the purpose of their ministry; or else changing and turning their own body itself, to which they are not subject, but govern it as subject to themselves, into whatever forms they would, that were appropriate and fit for their actions, according to the power given to them by the Creator. And when this part of the question shall have been investigated, so far as God permit, then, last-

ly, we shall have to see to that question with which we started, viz., whether the Son and the Holy Spirit were also " sent " before; and if it be so, then what difference there is between that sending and the one of which we read in the Gospel; or whether neither of them were sent, except when either the Son was made of the Virgin Mary, or when the Holy Spirit appeared in a visible form, whether as a dove or in tongues of fire. [1]

5. I confess, however, that it reaches further than my purpose can carry me to inquire whether the angels, secretly working by the spiritual quality of their body abiding still in them, assume somewhat from the inferior and more bodily elements, which, being fitted to themselves, they may change and turn like a garment into any corporeal appearances they will, and those appearances themselves also real, as real water was changed by our Lord into real wine; [2] or whether they transform their own bodies themselves into that which they would, suitably to the particular act. But it does not signify to the present question which of these it is. And although I be not able to understand these things by actual experience, seeing that I am a man, as the angels do who do these things, and know them better than I know them, viz., how far my body is changeable by the operation of my will; whether it be by my own experience of myself, or by that which I have gathered from others; yet it is not necessary here to say which of these alternatives I am to believe upon the authority of the divine Scriptures, lest I be compelled to prove it, and so my discourse become too long upon a subject which does not concern the present question.

6. Our present inquiry then is, whether the angels were then the agents both in showing those bodily appearances to the eyes of men, and in sounding those words in their ears, when the sensible creature itself, serving the Creator at His beck, was turned for the time into whatever was needful; as it is written in the book of Wisdom, " For the creature that serveth Thee, who art the Maker, increaseth his strength against the unrighteous for their punishment, and abateth his strength for the benefit of such as put their trust in Thee. Therefore, even then was it altered into all fashions, and was obedient to Thy grace, that nourisheth all things according to the desire of them that longed for Thee." [3] For the power of the will of God reaches through the spiritual creature even to visible and sensible effects of the corporeal creature. For where does not the wisdom of the omnipotent God

work that which He wills, which " reacheth from one end to another mightily, and sweetly doth order all things"? [4]

CHAP. 2.—THE WILL OF GOD IS THE HIGHER CAUSE OF ALL CORPOREAL CHANGE. THIS IS SHOWN BY AN EXAMPLE.

7. But there is one kind of natural order in the conversion and changeableness of bodies, which, although itself also serves the bidding of God, yet by reason of its unbroken continuity has ceased to cause wonder; as is the case, for instance, with those things which are changed either in very short, or at any rate not long, intervals of time, in heaven, or earth, or sea; whether it be in rising, or in setting, or in change of appearance from time to time; while there are other things, which, although arising from that same order, yet are less familiar on account of longer intervals of time. And these things, although the many stupidly wonder at them, yet are understood by those who inquire into this present world, and in the progress of generations become so much the less wonderful, as they are the more often repeated and known by more people. Such are the eclipses of the sun and moon, and some kinds of stars, appearing seldom, and earthquakes, and unnatural births of living creatures, and other similar things; of which not one takes place without the will of God; yet, that it is so, is to most people not apparent. And so the vanity of philosophers has found license to assign these things also to other causes, true causes perhaps, but proximate ones, while they are not able to see at all the cause that is higher than all others, that is, the will of God; or again to false causes, and to such as are not even put forward out of any diligent investigation of corporeal things and motions, but from their own guess and error.

8. I will bring forward an example, if I can, that this may be plainer. There is, we know, in the human body, a certain bulk of flesh and an outward form, and an arrangement and distinction of limbs, and a temperament of health; and a soul breathed into it governs this body, and that soul a rational one; which, therefore, although changeable, yet can be partaker of that unchangeable wisdom, so that " it may partake of that which is in and of itself;" [5] as

---

[1] See above, Book ii. chap. vii. n. 13.
[2] John ii. 9.   [3] Wisd. xvi. 24, 25.

[4] Wisd. viii. 1.
[5] [The original is: "ut sit participatio ejus in idipsum." The English translator renders: "So that it may partake thereof in itself." The thought of Augustin is, that the believing soul though mutable partakes of the immutable; and he designates the immutable as the in idipsum: the self-existent. In that striking passage in the Confessions, in which he describes the spiritual and extatic meditations of himself and his mother, as they looked out upon the Mediterranean from the windows at Ostia—a scene well known from Ary Schefer's painting—he denominates God the idipsum: the

it is written in the Psalm concerning all saints, of whom as of living stones is built that Jerusalem which is the mother of us all, eternal in the heavens. For so it is sung, "Jerusalem is builded as a city, that is partaker of that which is in and of itself."[1] For "in and of itself," in that place, is understood of that chiefest and unchangeable good, which is God, and of His own wisdom and will. To whom is sung in another place, "Thou shalt change them, and they shall be changed; but Thou art the same."[2]

CHAP. 3.—OF THE SAME ARGUMENT.

Let us take, then, the case of a wise man, such that his rational soul is already partaker of the unchangeable and eternal truth, so that he consults it about all his actions, nor does anything at all, which he does not by it know ought to be done, in order that by being subject to it and obeying it he may do rightly. Suppose now that this man, upon counsel with the highest reason of the divine righteousness, which he hears with the ear of his heart in secret, and by its bidding, should weary his body by toil in some office of mercy, and should contract an illness; and upon consulting the physicians, were to be told by one that the cause of the disease was overmuch dryness of the body, but by another that it was overmuch moisture; one of the two no doubt would allege the true cause and the other would err, but both would pronounce concerning proximate causes only, that is, corporeal ones. But if the cause of that dryness were to be inquired into, and found to be the self-imposed toil, then we should have come to a yet higher cause, which proceeds from the soul so as to affect the body which the soul governs. Yet neither would this be the first cause, for that doubtless was a higher cause still, and lay in the unchangeable wisdom itself, by serving which in love, and by obeying its ineffable commands, the soul of the wise man had undertaken that self-imposed toil; and so nothing else but the will of God would be found most truly to be the first cause of that illness. But suppose now in that office of pious toil this wise man had employed the help of others to co-operate in the good work, who did not serve God with the same will as himself, but either desired to attain the reward of their own carnal desires, or shunned merely carnal unpleasantnesses;—suppose, too, he had employed beasts of burden, if the

completion of the work required such a provision, which beasts of burden would be certainly irrational animals, and would not therefore move their limbs under their burdens because they at all thought of that good work, but from the natural appetite of their own liking, and for the avoiding of annoyance; —suppose, lastly, he had employed bodily things themselves that lack all sense, but were necessary for that work, as e.g. corn, and wine, and oils, clothes, or money, or a book, or anything of the kind;—certainly, in all these bodily things thus employed in this work, whether animate or inanimate, whatever took place of movement, of wear and tear, of reparation, of destruction, of renewal or of change in one way or another, as places and times affected them; pray, could there be, I say, any other cause of all these visible and changeable facts, except the invisible and unchangeable will of God, using all these, both bad and irrational souls, and lastly bodies, whether such as were inspired and animated by those souls, or such as lacked all sense, by means of that upright soul as the seat of His wisdom, since primarily that good and holy soul itself employed them, which His wisdom had subjected to itself in a pious and religious obedience?

CHAP. 4.—GOD USES ALL CREATURES AS HE WILL, AND MAKES VISIBLE THINGS FOR THE MANIFESTATION OF HIMSELF

9. What, then, we have alleged by way of example of a single wise man, although of one still bearing a mortal body and still seeing only in part, may be allowably extended also to a family, where there is a society of such men, or to a city, or even to the whole world, if the chief rule and government of human affairs were in the hands of the wise, and of those who were piously and perfectly subject to God; but because this is not the case as yet (for it behoves us first to be exercised in this our pilgrimage after mortal fashion, and to be taught with stripes by force of gentleness and patience), let us turn our thoughts to that country itself that is above and heavenly, from which we here are pilgrims. For there the will of God, "who maketh His angels spirits, and His ministers a flaming fire,"[3] presiding among spirits which are joined in perfect peace and friendship, and combined in one will by a kind of spiritual fire of charity, as it were in an elevated and holy and secret seat, as in its own house and in its own temple, thence diffuses itself through all things by certain most per-

---

"self same" (Confessions IX. x). Augustin refers to the same absolute immutability of God, in this place. By faith, man is "a partaker of a divine nature," (2 Pet. i. 4.)—W.G.T.S.]
[1] Ps. cxxii. 3. Vulg.   [2] Ps. cii. 26, 27.   [3] Ps. civ. 4.

fectly ordered movements of the creature; first spiritual, then corporeal; and uses all according to the unchangeable pleasure of its own purpose, whether incorporeal things or things corporeal, whether rational or irrational spirits, whether good by His grace or evil through their own will. But as the more gross and inferior bodies are governed in due order by the more subtle and powerful ones, so all bodies are governed by the living spirit; and the living spirit devoid of reason, by the reasonable living spirit; and the reasonable living spirit that makes default and sins, by the living and reasonable spirit that is pious and just; and that by God Himself, and so the universal creature by its Creator, from whom and through whom and in whom it is also created and established.[1] And so it comes to pass that the will of God is the first and the highest cause of all corporeal appearances and motions. For nothing is done visibly or sensibly, unless either by command or permission from the interior palace, invisible and intelligible, of the supreme Governor, according to the unspeakable justice of rewards and punishments, of favor and retribution, in that far-reaching and boundless commonwealth of the whole creature.

10. If, therefore, the Apostle Paul, although he still bare the burden of the body, which is subject to corruption and presseth down the soul,[2] and although he still saw only in part and in an enigma,[3] wishing to depart and be with Christ,[4] and groaning within himself, waiting for the adoption, to wit, the redemption of his body,[5] yet was able to preach the Lord Jesus Christ significantly, in one way by his tongue, in another by epistle, in another by the sacrament of His body and blood (since, certainly, we do not call either the tongue of the apostle, or the parchments, or the ink, or the significant sounds which his tongue uttered, or the alphabetical signs written on skins, the body and blood of Christ; but that only which we take of the fruits of the earth and consecrate by mystic prayer, and then receive duly to our spiritual health in memory of the passion of our Lord for us: and this, although it is brought by the hands of men to that visible form, yet is not sanctified to become so great a sacrament, except by the spirit of God working invisibly; since God works everything that is done in that work through corporeal movements, by setting in motion primarily the invisible things of His servants, whether the souls of men, or the services of

hidden spirits subject to Himself): what wonder if also in the creature of heaven and earth, of sea and air, God works the sensible and visible things which He wills, in order to signify and manifest Himself in them, as He Himself knows it to be fitting, without any appearing of His very substance itself, whereby He is, which is altogether unchangeable, and more inwardly and secretly exalted than all spirits whom He has created?

CHAP. 5.—WHY MIRACLES ARE NOT USUAL WORKS.

11. For since the divine power administers the whole spiritual and corporeal creature, the waters of the sea are summoned and poured out upon the face of the earth on certain days of every year. But when this was done at the prayer of the holy Elijah; because so continued and long a course of fair weather had gone before, that men were famished; and because at that very hour, in which the servant of God prayed, the air itself had not, by any moist aspect, put forth signs of the coming rain; the divine power was apparent in the great and rapid showers that followed, and by which that miracle was granted and dispensed.[6] In like manner, God works ordinarily through thunders and lightnings: but because these were wrought in an unusual manner on Mount Sinai, and those sounds were not uttered with a confused noise, but so that it appeared by most sure proofs that certain intimations were given by them, they were miracles.[7] Who draws up the sap through the root of the vine to the bunch of grapes, and makes the wine, except God; who, while man plants and waters, Himself giveth the increase?[8] But when, at the command of the Lord, the water was turned into wine with an extraordinary quickness, the divine power was made manifest, by the confession even of the foolish.[9] Who ordinarily clothes the trees with leaves and flowers except God? Yet, when the rod of Aaron the priest blossomed, the Godhead in some way conversed with doubting humanity.[10] Again, the earthy matter certainly serves in common to the production and formation both of all kinds of wood and of the flesh of all animals: and who makes these things, but He who said, Let the earth bring them forth;[11] and who governs and guides by the same word of His, those things which He has created? Yet, when He changed the same matter out of the rod of Moses into the flesh of a serpent, immediately and quickly,

---

[1] Col. i. 16. [2] Wisd. ix. 15. [3] 1 Cor. xiii. 12.
[4] Phil. i. 23. [5] Rom. viii. 23.

[6] 1 Kings xviii. 45. [7] Ex. xix. 6. [8] 1 Cor. iii. 7.
[9] John ii. 9. [10] Num. xvii. 8. [11] Gen. i. 24.

that change, which was unusual, although of a thing which was changeable, was a miracle. [1] But who is it that gives life to every living thing at its birth, unless He who gave life to that serpent also for the moment, as there was need. [2]

CHAP. 6.—DIVERSITY ALONE MAKES A MIRACLE.

And who is it that restored to the corpses their proper souls when the dead rose again, [3] unless He who gives life to the flesh in the mother's womb, in order that they may come into being who yet are to die? But when such things happen in a continuous kind of river of ever-flowing succession, passing from the hidden to the visible, and from the visible to the hidden, by a regular and beaten track, then they are called natural; when, for the admonition of men, they are thrust in by an unusual changeableness, then they are called miracles.

CHAP. 7.—GREAT MIRACLES WROUGHT BY MAGIC ARTS.

12. I see here what may occur to a weak judgment, namely, why such miracles are wrought also by magic arts; for the wise men of Pharaoh likewise made serpents, and did other like things. Yet it is still more a matter of wonder, how it was that the power of those magicians, which was able to make serpents, when it came to very small flies, failed altogether. For the lice, by which third plague the proud people of Egypt were smitten, are very short-lived little flies; yet there certainly the magicians failed, saying, "This is the finger of God." [4] And hence it is given us to understand that not even those angels and powers of the air that transgressed, who have been thrust down into that lowest darkness, as into a peculiar prison, from their habitation in that lofty ethereal purity, through whom magic arts have whatever power they have, can do anything except by power given from above. Now that power is given either to deceive the deceitful, as it was given against the Egyptians, and against the magicians also themselves, in order that in the seducing of those spirits they might seem admirable by whom they were wrought, but to be condemned by the truth of God; or

for the admonishing of the faithful, lest they should desire to do anything of the kind as though it were a great thing, for which reason they have been handed down to us also by the authority of Scripture; or lastly, for the exercising, proving, and manifesting of the patience of the righteous. For it was not by any small power of visible miracles that Job lost all that he had, and both his children and his bodily health itself. [5]

CHAP. 8.—GOD ALONE CREATES THOSE THINGS WHICH ARE CHANGED BY MAGIC ART.

13. Yet it is not on this account to be thought that the matter of visible things is subservient to the bidding of those wicked angels; but rather to that of God, by whom this power is given, just so far as He, who is unchangeable, determines in His lofty and spiritual abode to give it. For water and fire and earth are subservient even to wicked men, who are condemned to the mines, in order that they may do therewith what they will, but only so far as is permitted. Nor, in truth, are those evil angels to be called creators, because by their means the magicians, withstanding the servant of God, made frogs and serpents; for it was not they who created them. But, in truth, some hidden seeds of all things that are born corporeally and visibly, are concealed in the corporeal elements of this world. For those seeds that are visible now to our eyes from fruits and living things, are quite distinct from the hidden seeds of those former seeds; from which, at the bidding of the Creator, the water produced the first swimming creatures and fowl, and the earth the first buds after their kind, and the first living creatures after their kind. [6] For neither at that time were those seeds so drawn forth into products of their several kinds, as that the power of production was exhausted in those products; but oftentimes, suitable combinations of circumstances are wanting, whereby they may be enabled to burst forth and complete their species. For, consider, the very least shoot is a seed; for, if fitly consigned to the earth, it produces a tree. But of this shoot there is a yet more subtle seed in some grain of the same species, and this is visible even to us. But of this grain also there is further still a seed, which, although we are unable to see it with our eyes, yet we can conjecture its existence from our reason; because, except there were some such power in those elements, there would not so frequently be produced from the earth things which had not been sown there; nor

---

[1] Ex. iv. 3.
[2] [One chief reason why a miracle is incredible for the skeptic, is the difficulty of working it. If the miracle were easy of execution for man—who for the skeptic is the measure of power—his disbelief of it would disappear. In reference to this objection, Augustin calls attention to the fact, that so far as difficulty of performance is concerned, the products of nature are as impossible to man as supernatural products. Aaron could no more have made an almond rod blossom and fructuate on an almond tree, than off it. That a miracle is difficult to be wrought is, consequently, no good reason for disbelieving its reality.—W.G.T.S.]
[3] Ezek. xxxvii. 1-10.　　[4] Ex. vii. and viii.

[5] Job i. and ii.　　[6] Gen. i. 20-25.

yet so many animals, without any previous commixture of male and female; whether on the land, or in the water, which yet grow, and by commingling bring forth others, while themselves sprang up without any union of parents. And certainly bees do not conceive the seeds of their young by commixture, but gather them as they lie scattered over the earth with their mouth.[1] For the Creator of these invisible seeds is the Creator of all things Himself; since whatever comes forth to our sight by being born, receives the first beginnings of its course from hidden seeds, and takes the successive increments of its proper size and its distinctive forms from these as it were original rules. As therefore we do not call parents the creators of men, nor farmers the creators of corn,—although it is by the outward application of their actions that the power[2] of God operates within for the creating these things;—so it is not right to think not only the bad but even the good angels to be creators, if, through the subtilty of their perception and body, they know the seeds of things which to us are more hidden, and scatter them secretly through fit temperings of the elements, and so furnish opportunities of producing things, and of accelerating their increase. But neither do the good angels do these things, except as far as God commands, nor do the evil ones do them wrongfully, except as far as He righteously permits. For the malignity of the wicked one makes his own will wrongful; but the power to do so, he receives rightfully, whether for his own punishment, or, in the case of others, for the punishment of the wicked, or for the praise of the good.

14. Accordingly, the Apostle Paul, distinguishing God's creating and forming within, from the operations of the creature which are applied from without, and drawing a similitude from agriculture, says, "I planted, Apollos watered; but God gave the increase."[3] As, therefore, in the case of spiritual life itself, no one except God can work righteousness in our minds, yet men also are able to preach the gospel as an outward means, not only the good in sincerity, but also the evil in pretence;[4] so in the creation of visible things it is God that works from within; but the exterior operations, whether of good or bad, of angels or men, or even of any kind of animal, according to His own absolute power, and to the distribution of faculties, and the several appetites for things pleasant, which He Himself has imparted, are applied by Him to that nature of things wherein He creates all things, in like manner as agriculture is to the soil. Wherefore I can no more call the bad angels, evoked by magic arts, the creators of the frogs and serpents, than I can say that bad men were creators of the corn crop, which I see to have sprung up through their labor.

15. Just as Jacob, again, was not the creator of the colors in the flocks, because he placed the various colored rods for the several mothers, as they drank, to look at in conceiving.[5] Yet neither were the cattle themselves creators of the variety of their own offspring, because the variegated image, impressed through their eyes by the sight of the varied rods, clave to their soul, but could affect the body that was animated by the spirit thus affected only through sympathy with this commingling, so far as to stain with color the tender beginnings of their offspring. For that they are so affected from themselves, whether the soul from the body, or the body from the soul, arises in truth from suitable reasons, which immutably exist in that highest wisdom of God Himself, which no extent of place contains; and which, while it is itself unchangeable, yet quits not one even of those things which are changeable, because there is not one of them that is not created by itself. For it was the unchangeable and invisible reason of the wisdom of God, by which all things are created, which caused not rods, but cattle, to be born from cattle; but that the color of the cattle conceived should be in any degree influenced by the variety of the rods, came to pass through the soul of the pregnant cattle being affected through their eyes from without, and so according to its own measure drawing inwardly within itself the rule of formation, which it received from the innermost power of its own Creator. How great, however, may be the power of the soul in affecting and changing corporeal substance (although certainly it cannot be called the creator of the body, because every cause of changeable and sensible substance, and all its

---

[1] [Augustin is not alone in his belief that the bee is an exception to the dictum; *omne animal ex ovo*. As late as 1744, Thorley, an English "scientist,' said that "the manner in which bees propagate their species is entirely hid from the eyes of all men; and the most strict, diligent, and curious observers and inquisitors have not been able to discover it. It is a secret, and will remain a mystery. Dr. Butler says that they do not copulate as other living creatures do." (Thorley : Melisselogia. Section viii.) The observations of Huber and others have disproved this opinion. Some infer that ignorance of physics proves ignorance of philosophy and theology. The difference between matter and mind is so great, that erroneous opinions in one province are compatible with correct ones in the other. It does not follow that because Augustin had wrong notions about bees, and no knowledge at all of the steam engine and telegraph, his knowledge of God and the soul was inferior to that of a modern materialist.—W.G.T.S.]

[2] [The English translator renders "*virtus*" in its secondary sense of "goodness." Augustin employs it here, in its primary sense of "energy," "force."—W.G.T.S.]

[3] 1 Cor. iii. 6.

[4] Phil. i. 18.   [5] Gen. xxx. 41.

measure and number and weight, by which are brought to pass both its being at all and its being of such and such a nature, arise from the intelligible and unchangeable life, which is above all things, and which reaches even to the most distant and earthly things), is a very copious subject, and one not now necessary. But I thought the act of Jacob about the cattle should be noticed, for this reason, *viz.* in order that it might be perceived that, if the man who thus placed those rods cannot be called the creator of the colors in the lambs and kids; nor yet even the souls themselves of the mothers, which colored the seeds conceived in the flesh by the image of variegated color, conceived through the eyes of the body, so far as nature permitted it; much less can it be said that the creators of the frogs and serpents were the bad angels, through whom the magicians of Pharaoh then made them.

CHAP. 9.—THE ORIGINAL CAUSE OF ALL THINGS IS FROM GOD.

16. For it is one thing to make and administer the creature from the innermost and highest turning-point of causation, which He alone does who is God the Creator; but quite another thing to apply some operation from without in proportion to the strength and faculties assigned to each by Him, so that what is created may come forth into being at this time or at that, and in this or that way. For all these things in the way of original and beginning have already been created in a kind of texture of the elements, but they come forth when they get the opportunity.[1] For as mothers are pregnant with young, so the world itself is pregnant with the causes of things that are born; which are not created in it, except from that highest essence, where nothing either springs up or dies, either begins to be or ceases. But the applying from without of adventitious causes, which, although they are not natural, yet are to be applied according to nature, in order that those things which are contained and hidden in the secret bosom of nature may break forth and be outwardly created in some way by the unfolding of the proper measures and numbers and weights which they have received in secret from Him "who has ordered all things in

measure and number and weight:"[2] this is not only in the power of bad angels, but also of bad men, as I have shown above by the example of agriculture.

17. But lest the somewhat different condition of animals should trouble any one, in that they have the breath of life with the sense of desiring those things that are according to nature, and of avoiding those things that are contrary to it; we must consider also, how many men there are who know from what herbs or flesh, or from what juices or liquids you please, of whatever sort, whether so placed or so buried, or so bruised or so mixed, this or that animal is commonly born; yet who can be so foolish as to dare to call himself the creator of these animals? Is it, therefore, to be wondered at, if just as any, the most worthless of men, can know whence such or such worms and flies are produced; so the evil angels in proportion to the subtlety of their perceptions discern in the more hidden seeds of the elements whence frogs and serpents are produced, and so through certain and known opportune combinations applying these seeds by secret movements, cause them to be created, but do not create them? Only men do not marvel at those things that are usually done by men. But if any one chance to wonder at the quickness of those growths, in that those living beings were so quickly made, let him consider how even this may be brought about by men in proportion to the measure of human capability. For whence is it that the same bodies generate worms more quickly in summer than in winter, or in hotter than in colder places? Only these things are applied by men with so much the more difficulty, in proportion as their earthly and sluggish members are wanting in subtlety of perception, and in rapidity of bodily motion. And hence it arises that in the case of any kind of angels, in proportion as it is easier for them to draw out the proximate causes from the elements, so much the more marvellous is their rapidity in works of this kind.

18. But He only is the creator who is the chief former of these things. Neither can any one be this, unless He with whom primarily rests the measure, number, and weight of all things existing; and He is God the one Creator, by whose unspeakable power it comes to pass, also, that what these angels were able to do if they were permitted, they are therefore not able to do because they are not permitted. For there is no other reason why they who made frogs and serpents were not able to make the most minute flies, unless because

---

[1] [This is the same as the theological distinction between substances and their modifications. "The former," says Howe, "are the proper object of creation strictly taken; the modifications of things are not properly created, in the strictest sense of creation, but are educed and brought forth out of those substantial things that were themselves created, or made out of nothing."—Germs are originated *ex nihilo*, and fall under creation proper; their evolution and development takes place according to the nature and inherent force of the germ, and falls under providence, in distinction from creation. See the writer's Theological Essays, 133-137.—W. G. T. S.]

[2] Wisd. xi. 20.

the greater power of God was present prohibiting them, through the Holy Spirit; which even the magicians themselves confessed, saying, "This is the finger of God."[1] But what they are able to do by nature, yet cannot do, because they are prohibited; and what the very condition of their nature itself does not suffer them to do; it is difficult, nay, impossible, for man to search out, unless through that gift of God which the apostle mentions when he says, "To another the discerning of spirits."[2] For we know that a man can walk, yet that he cannot do so if he is not permitted; but that he cannot fly, even if he be permitted. So those angels, also, are able to do certain things if they are permitted by more powerful angels, according to the supreme commandment of God; but cannot do certain other things, not even if they are permitted by them; because He does not permit from whom they have received such and such a measure of natural powers: who, even by His angels, does not usually permit what He has given them power to be able to do.

19. Excepting, therefore, those corporeal things which are done in the order of nature in a perfectly usual series of times, as *e.g.*, the rising and setting of the stars, the generations and deaths of animals, the innumerable diversities of seeds and buds, the vapors and the clouds, the snow and the rain, the lightnings and the thunder, the thunderbolts and the hail, the winds and the fire, cold and heat, and all like things; excepting also those which in the same order of nature occur rarely, such as eclipses, unusual appearances of stars, and monsters, and earthquakes, and such like;— all these, I say, are to be excepted, of which indeed the first and chief cause is only the will of God; whence also in the Psalm, when some things of this kind had been mentioned, "Fire and hail, snow and vapor, stormy wind," lest any one should think those to be brought about either by chance or only from corporeal causes, or even from such as are spiritual, but exist apart from the will of God, it is added immediately, "fulfilling His word."[3]

CHAP. 10.—IN HOW MANY WAYS THE CREATURE IS TO BE TAKEN BY WAY OF SIGN. THE EUCHARIST.

Excepting, therefore, all these things as I just now said, there are some also of another kind; which, although from the same corporeal substance, are yet brought within reach of our senses in order to announce something from God, and these are properly called miracles and signs; yet is not the person of God Himself assumed in all things which are announced to us by the Lord God. When, however, that person is assumed, it is sometimes made manifest as an angel; sometimes in that form which is not an angel in his own proper being, although it is ordered and ministered by an angel. Again, when it is assumed in that form which is not an angel in his own proper being; sometimes in this case it is a body itself already existing, assumed after some kind of change, in order to make that message manifest; sometimes it is one that comes into being for the purpose, and that being accomplished, is discarded. Just as, also, when men are the messengers, sometimes they speak the words of God in their own person, as when it is premised, "The Lord said," or, "Thus saith the Lord,"[4] or any other such phrase, but sometimes without any such prefix, they take upon themselves the very person of God, as *e.g.*: "I will instruct thee, and teach thee in the way wherein thou shalt go:"[5] so, not only in word, but also in act, the signifying of the person of God is imposed upon the prophet, in order that he may bear that person in the ministering of the prophecy; just as he, for instance, bore that person who divided his garment into twelve parts, and gave ten of them to the servant of King Solomon, to the future king of Israel.[6] Sometimes, also, a thing which was not a prophet in his own proper self, and which existed already among earthly things, was assumed in order to signify this; as Jacob, when he had seen the dream, upon waking up did with the stone, which when asleep he had under his head.[7] Sometimes a thing is made in the same kind, for the mere purpose; so as either to continue a little while in existence, as that brazen serpent was able to do which was lifted up in the wilderness,[8] and as written records are able to do likewise; or so as to pass away after having accomplished its ministry, as the bread made for the purpose is consumed in the receiving of the sacrament.

20. But because these things are known to men, in that they are done by men, they may well meet with reverence as being holy things, but they cannot cause wonder as being miracles. And therefore those things which are done by angels are the more wonderful to us, in that they are more difficult and more unknown; but they are known and easy to them as being their own actions. An angel speaks in the person of God to man, saying, "I am the God of Abraham, and the God of Isaac,

---

[1] Ex. vii. 12, and viii. 7, 18, 19.   [2] 1 Cor. xii. 10.
[3] Ps. cxlviii. 8.
[4] Jer. xxxi. 1, 2.   [5] Ps. xxxii. 8.
[6] 1 Kings xi. 30, 31.   [7] Gen. xxviii. 18.
[8] Num. xxi. 9.

and the God of Jacob;" the Scripture having said just before, "The angel of the Lord appeared to him."[1] And a man also speaks in the person of God, saying, "Hear, O my people, and I will testify unto thee, O Israel: I am the Lord thy God."[2] A rod was taken to serve as a sign, and was changed into a serpent by angelical power;[3] but although that power is wanting to man, yet a stone was taken also by man for a similar sign.[4] There is a wide difference between the deed of the angel and the deed of the man. The former is both to be wondered at and to be understood, the latter only to be understood. That which is understood from both, is perhaps one and the same; but those things from which it is understood, are different. Just as if the name of God were written both in gold and in ink; the former would be the more precious, the latter the more worthless; yet that which is signified in both is one and the same. And although the serpent that came from Moses' rod signified the same thing as Jacob's stone, yet Jacob's stone signified something better than did the serpents of the magicians. For as the anointing of the stone signified Christ in the flesh, in which He was anointed with the oil of gladness above His fellows;[5] so the rod of Moses, turned into a serpent, signified Christ Himself made obedient unto death, even the death of the cross.[6] Whence it is said, "And as Moses lifted up the serpent in the wilderness, even so must the Son of man be lifted up, that whosoever believeth in Him should not perish, but have everlasting life;"[7] just as by gazing on that serpent which was lifted up in the wilderness, they did not perish by the bites of the serpents. For "our old man is crucified with Him, that the body of sin might be destroyed."[8] For by the serpent death is understood, which was wrought by the serpent in paradise,[9] the mode of speech expressing the effect by the efficient. Therefore the rod passed into the serpent, Christ into death; and the serpent again into the rod, whole Christ with His body into the resurrection; which body is the Church;[10] and this shall be in the end of time, signified by the tail, which Moses held, in order that it might return into a rod.[11] But the serpents of the magicians, like those who are dead in the world, unless by believing in Christ they shall have been as it were swallowed up by,[12] and have entered into, His body, will not be able to rise again in Him. Jacob's stone, therefore, as I said, signified something better than did the serpents of the magicians; yet the

deed of the magicians was much more wonderful. But these things in this way are no hindrance to the understanding of the matter; just as if the name of a man were written in gold, and that of God in ink.

21. What man, again, knows how the angels made or took those clouds and fires in order to signify the message they were bearing, even if we supposed that the Lord or the Holy Spirit was manifested in those corporeal forms? Just as infants do not know of that which is placed upon the altar and consumed after the performance of the holy celebration, whence or in what manner it is made, or whence it is taken for religious use. And if they were never to learn from their own experience or that of others, and never to see that species of thing except during the celebration of the sacrament, when it is being offered and given; and if it were told them by the most weighty authority whose body and blood it is; they will believe nothing else, except that the Lord absolutely appeared in this form to the eyes of mortals, and that that liquid actually flowed from the piercing of a side,[13] which resembled this. But it is certainly a useful caution to myself, that I should remember what my own powers are, and admonish my brethren that they also remember what theirs are, lest human infirmity pass on beyond what is safe. For how the angels do these things, or rather, how God does these things by His angels, and how far He wills them to be done even by the bad angels, whether by permitting, or commanding, or compelling, from the hidden seat of His own supreme power; this I can neither penetrate by the sight of the eyes, nor make clear by assurance of reason, nor be carried on to comprehend it by reach of intellect, so as to speak thereupon to all questions that may be asked respecting these matters, as certainly as if I were an angel, or a prophet, or an apostle. "For the thoughts of mortal men are miserable, and our devices are but uncertain. For the corruptible body presseth down the soul, and the earthly tabernacle weigheth down the mind, that museth upon many things. And hardly do we guess aright at things that are upon earth, and with labor do we find the things that are before us; but the things that are in heaven, who hath searched out?" But because it goes on to say, "And Thy counsel who hath known, except Thou give wisdom, and send Thy Holy Spirit from above;"[14] therefore we refrain indeed from searching out the things which are in heaven, under which kind are contained both angelical bodies according to their proper

1 Ex. iii. 6, 2.   2 Ps. lxxxi. 8, 10.   3 Ex. vii. 10.
4 Gen. xxviii. 18.   5 Ps. xlv. 7.   6 Phil. ii. 9.
7 John iii. 14, 15.   8 Rom. vi. 6.   9 Gen. iii.
10 Col. i. 24.   11 Ex. iv. 4.   12 Ex. vii. 12.

13 John xix. 34.   14 Wisd. ix. 14-17.

dignity, and any corporeal action of those bodies; yet, according to the Spirit of God sent to us from above, and to His grace imparted to our minds, I dare to say confidently, that neither God the Father, nor His Word, nor His Spirit, which is the one God, is in any way changeable in regard to that which He is, and whereby He is that which He is; and much less is in this regard visible. Since there are no doubt some things changeable, yet not visible, as are our thoughts, and memories, and wills, and the whole incorporeal creature; but there is nothing that is visible that is not also changeable.

CHAP. II.—THE ESSENCE OF GOD NEVER APPEARED IN ITSELF. DIVINE APPEARANCES TO THE FATHERS WROUGHT BY THE MINISTRY OF ANGELS. AN OBJECTION DRAWN FROM THE MODE OF SPEECH REMOVED. THAT THE APPEARING OF GOD TO ABRAHAM HIMSELF, JUST AS THAT TO MOSES, WAS WROUGHT BY ANGELS. THE SAME THING IS PROVED BY THE LAW BEING GIVEN TO MOSES BY ANGELS. WHAT HAS BEEN SAID IN THIS BOOK, AND WHAT REMAINS TO BE SAID IN THE NEXT.

Wherefore the substance, or, if it is better so to say, the essence of God,[1] wherein we understand, in proportion to our measure, in however small a degree, the Father, the Son, and the Holy Spirit, since it is in no way changeable, can in no way in its proper self be visible.

22. It is manifest, accordingly, that all those appearances to the fathers, when God was presented to them according to His own dispensation, suitable to the times, were wrought through the creature. And if we cannot discern in what manner He wrought them by ministry of angels, yet we say that they were wrought by angels; but not from our own power of discernment, lest we should seem to any one to be wise beyond our measure, whereas we are wise so as to think soberly, as God hath dealt to us the measure of faith;[2] and we believe, and therefore speak.[3] For the authority is extant of the divine Scriptures, from which our reason ought not to turn aside; nor by leaving the solid support of the divine utterance, to fall headlong over the precipice of its own surmisings, in matters wherein neither the perceptions of the body rule, nor the clear reason of the truth shines forth. Now, certainly, it is written most clearly in the Epistle to the Hebrews, when

the dispensation of the New Testament was to be distinguished from the dispensation of the Old, according to the fitness of ages and of times, that not only those visible things, but also the word itself, was wrought by angels. For it is said thus: "But to which of the angels said He at any time, Sit on my right hand, until I make thine enemies thy footstool? Are they not all ministering spirits, sent forth to minister for them who shall be heirs of salvation?"[4] Whence it appears that all those things were not only wrought by angels, but wrought also on our account, that is, on account of the people of God, to whom is promised the inheritance of eternal life. As it is written also to the Corinthians, "Now all these things happened unto them in a figure: and they are written for our admonition, upon whom the ends of the world are come."[5] And then, demonstrating by plain consequence that as at that time the word was spoken by the angels, so now by the Son; "Therefore," he says, "we ought to give the more earnest heed to the things which we have heard, lest at any time we should let them slip. For if the word spoken by angels was steadfast, and every transgression and disobedience received a just recompense of reward; how shall we escape, if we neglect so great salvation?" And then, as though you asked, What salvation?—in order to show that he is now speaking of the New Testament, that is, of the word which was spoken not by angels, but by the Lord, he says, "Which at the first began to be spoken by the Lord, and was confirmed unto us by them that heard Him; God also bearing them witness, both with signs and wonders, and with divers miracles, and gifts of the Holy Ghost, according to His own will."[6]

23. But some one may say, Why then is it written, "The Lord said to Moses;" and not, rather, The angel said to Moses? Because, when the crier proclaims the words of the judge, it is not usually written in the record, so and so the crier said, but so and so the judge. In like manner also, when the holy prophet speaks, although we say, The prophet said, we mean nothing else to be understood than that the Lord said; and if we were to say, The Lord said, we should not put the prophet aside, but only intimate who spake by him. And, indeed, these Scriptures often reveal the angel to be the Lord, of whose speaking it is from time to time said, "the Lord said," as we have shown already. But on account of those who, since the Scripture in that place specifies an angel, will have the Son of God Himself and in

---

[1] ["Substance," from sub stans, is a passive term, denoting latent and potential being. "Essence," from esse, is an active term, denoting energetic being. The schoolmen, as Augustin does here, preferred the latter term to the former, though employing both to designate the divine nature.—W. G. T. S.]
[2] Rom. xii. 3.   [3] 2 Cor. iv. 13.

[4] Heb. i. 13, 14.   [5] 1 Cor. x. 11.   [6] Heb. ii. 1-4.

Himself to be understood, because He is called an angel by the prophet, as announcing the will of His Father and of Himself; I have therefore thought fit to produce a plainer testimony from this epistle, where it is not said by an angel, but "by angels."

24. For Stephen, too, in the Acts of the Apostles, relates these things in that manner in which they are also written in the Old Testament: "Men, brethren, and fathers, hearken," he says; "The God of glory appeared unto our father Abraham, when he was in Mesopotamia."[1] But lest any one should think that the God of glory appeared then to the eyes of any mortal in that which He is in Himself, he goes on to say that an angel appeared to Moses. "Then fled Moses," he says, "at that saying, and was a stranger in the land of Midian, where he begat two sons. And when forty years were expired, there appeared to him in the wilderness of mount Sinai an angel of the Lord in a flame of fire in a bush. When Moses saw it, he wondered at the sight: and as he drew near to behold it, the voice of the Lord came unto him, saying, I am the God of thy fathers, the God of Abraham, and the God of Isaac, and the God of Jacob. Then Moses trembled, and durst not behold. Then said the Lord to him, Put off thy shoes from thy feet,"[2] etc. Here, certainly, he speaks both of angel and of Lord; and of the same as the God of Abraham, and the God of Isaac, and the God of Jacob; as is written in Genesis.

25. Can there be any one who will say that the Lord appeared to Moses by an angel, but to Abraham by Himself? Let us not answer this question from Stephen, but from the book itself, whence Stephen took his narrative. For, pray, because it is written, "And the Lord God said unto Abraham;"[3] and a little after, "And the Lord God appeared unto Abraham;"[4] were these things, for this reason, not done by angels? Whereas it is said in like manner in another place, "And the Lord appeared to him in the plains of Mamre, as he sat in the tent door in the heat of the day;" and yet it is added immediately, "And he lift up his eyes and looked, and, lo, three men stood by him:"[5] of whom we have already spoken. For how will these people, who either will not rise from the words to the meaning, or easily throw themselves down from the meaning to the words,—how, I say, will they be able to explain that God was seen in three men, ex-

cept they confess that they were angels, as that which follows also shows? Because it is not said an angel spoke or appeared to him, will they therefore venture to say that the vision and voice granted to Moses was wrought by an angel because it is so written, but that God appeared and spake in His own substance to Abraham because there is no mention made of an angel? What of the fact, that even in respect to Abraham an angel is not left unmentioned? For when his son was ordered to be offered up as a sacrifice, we read thus: "And it came to pass after these things that God did tempt Abraham, and said unto him, Abraham: and he said, Behold, here I am. And He said, Take now thy son, thine only son Isaac, whom thou lovest, and get thee into the land of Moriah; and offer him there for a burnt-offering upon one of the mountains that I will tell thee of." Certainly God is here mentioned, not an angel. But a little afterwards Scripture hath it thus: "And Abraham stretched forth his hand, and took the knife to slay his son. And the angel of the Lord called unto him out of heaven, and said, Abraham, Abraham: and he said, Here am I. And he said, Lay not thine hand upon the lad, neither do thou anything unto him." What can be answered to this? Will they say that God commanded that Isaac should be slain, and that an angel forbade it? and further, that the father himself, in opposition to the decree of God, who had commanded that he should be slain, obeyed the angel, who had bidden him spare him? Such an interpretation is to be rejected as absurd. Yet not even for it, gross and abject as it is, does Scripture leave any room, for it immediately adds: "For now I know that thou fearest God, seeing thou hast not withheld thy son, thine only son, on account of me."[6] What is "on account of me," except on account of Him who had commanded him to be slain? Was then the God of Abraham the same as the angel, or was it not rather God by an angel? Consider what follows. Here, certainly, already an angel has been most clearly spoken of; yet notice the context: "And Abraham lifted up his eyes, and looked, and behold behind him a ram caught in a thicket by his horns: and Abraham went and took the ram, and offered him up for a burnt-offering in the stead of his son. And Abraham called the name of that place, The Lord saw:[7] as it is said to this day, In the mount the Lord was seen."[8] Just as that

1 Acts vii. 2.
2 Ex. ii. 15 and iii. 7, and Acts vii. 29-33.
3 Gen. xii. 1.   4 Gen. xvii. 1.   5 Gen. xviii. 1, 2.

6 Propter me.   7 Dominus vidit.
8 Dominus visus est.

which a little before God said by an angel, "For now I know that thou fearest God;" not because it was to be understood that God then came to know, but that He brought it to pass that through God Abraham himself came to know what strength of heart he had to obey God, even to the sacrificing of his only son: after that mode of speech in which the effect is signified by the efficient,—as cold is said to be sluggish, because it makes men sluggish; so that He was therefore said to know, because He had made Abraham himself to know, who might well have not discerned the firmness of his own faith, had it not been proved by such a trial. So here, too, Abraham called the name of the place "The Lord saw," that is, caused Himself to be seen. For he goes on immediately to say, "As it is said to this day, In the mount the Lord was seen." Here you see the same angel is called Lord: wherefore, unless because the Lord spake by the angel? But if we pass on to that which follows, the angel altogether speaks as a prophet, and reveals expressly that God is speaking by the angel. "And the angel of the Lord," he says, "called unto Abraham out of heaven the second time, and said, By myself I have sworn, saith the Lord; for because thou hast done this thing, and hast not withheld thy son, thine only son, on account of me,"[1] etc. Certainly these words, viz. that he by whom the Lord speaks should say, "Thus saith the Lord," are commonly used by the prophets also. Does the Son of God say of the Father, "The Lord saith," while He Himself is that Angel of the Father? What then? Do they not see how hard pressed they are about these three men who appeared to Abraham, when it had been said before, "The Lord appeared to him?" Were they not angels because they are called men? Let them read Daniel, saying, "Behold the man Gabriel."[2]

26. But why do we delay any longer to stop their mouths by another most clear and most weighty proof, where not an angel in the singular nor men in the plural are spoken of, but simply angels; by whom not any particular word was wrought, but the Law itself is most distinctly declared to be given; which certainly none of the faithful doubts that God gave to Moses for the control of the children of Israel, or yet, that it was given by angels. So Stephen speaks: "Ye stiff-necked," he says, "and uncircumcised in heart and ears, ye do always resist the Holy Ghost: as your fathers did, so do ye. Which of the prophets have not your fathers persecuted? and they

have slain them which showed before of the coming of the Just One; of whom ye have been now the betrayers and murderers: who have received the Law by the disposition of angels,[3] and have not kept it."[4] What is more evident than this? What more strong than such an authority? The Law, indeed, was given to that people by the disposition of angels; but the advent of our Lord Jesus Christ was by it prepared and pre-announced; and He Himself, as the Word of God, was in some wonderful and unspeakable manner in the angels, by whose disposition the Law itself was given. And hence He said in the Gospel, "For had ye believed Moses, ye would have believed me; for he wrote of me."[5] Therefore then the Lord was speaking by the angels; and the son of God, who was to be the Mediator of God and men, from the seed of Abraham, was preparing His own advent by the angels, that He might find some by whom He would be received, confessing themselves guilty, whom the Law unfulfilled had made transgressors. And hence the apostle also says to the Galatians, "Wherefore then serveth the Law? It was added because of transgressions, till the seed should come to whom the promise was made, which [seed] was ordered[6] through angels in the hand of a mediator;"[7] that is, ordered through angels in His *own* hand. For He was not born in limitation, but in power. But you learn in another place that he does not mean any one of the angels as a mediator, but the Lord Jesus Christ Himself, in so far as He deigned to be made man: "For there is one God," he says, "and one Mediator between God and man, the man Christ Jesus."[8] Hence that passover in the killing of the lamb:[9] hence all those things which are figuratively spoken in the Law, of Christ to come in the flesh, and to suffer, but also to rise again, which Law was given by the disposition of angels; in which angels, were certainly the Father, and the Son, and the Holy Spirit; and in which, sometimes the Father, sometimes the Son, sometimes the Holy Spirit, and sometimes God, without any distinction of person, was figuratively signified by them, although appearing in visible and sensible forms, yet by His own creature, not by His substance, in order to the seeing of which, hearts are cleansed through all those things which are seen by the eyes and heard by the ears.

27. But now, as I think, that which we had undertaken to show in this book has been

---

[1] Gen. xxii.　　　[2] Dan. ix. 21.

[3] *In edictis angelorum.*　　　[4] Acts vii. 51-53.
[5] John v. 46.　　[6] *Dispositum.*　　[7] Gal. iii. 19.
[8] 1 Tim. ii. 5.　　[9] Ex. xii.

sufficiently discussed and demonstrated, according to our capacity; and it has been established, both by probable reason, so far as a man, or rather, so far as I am able, and by strength of authority, so far as the divine declarations from the Holy Scriptures have been made clear, that those words and bodily appearances which were given to these ancient fathers of ours before the incarnation of the Saviour, when God was said to appear, were wrought by angels: whether themselves speaking or doing something in the person of God, as we have shown that the prophets also were wont to do, or assuming from the creature that which they themselves were not, wherein God might be shown in a figure to men; which manner of showing also, Scripture teaches by many examples, that the prophets, too, did not omit. It remains, therefore, now for us to consider,—since both in the Lord as born of a virgin, and in the Holy Spirit descending in a corporeal form like a dove.[1]

[1] Matt. iii. 16.

and in the tongues like as of fire, which appeared with a sound from heaven on the day of Pentecost, after the ascension of the Lord,[2] it was not the Word of God Himself by His own substance, in which He is equal and co-eternal with the Father, nor the Spirit of the Father and of the Son by His own substance, in which He Himself also is equal and co-eternal with both, but assuredly a creature, such as could be formed and exist in these fashions, which appeared to corporeal and mortal senses,—it remains, I say, to consider what difference there is between these manifestations and those which were proper to the Son of God and to the Holy Spirit, although wrought by the visible creature;[3] which subject we shall more conveniently begin in another book.

[2] Acts ii. 1-4.
[3] [The reference here is to the difference between a theophany, and an incarnation; already alluded to, in the note on p. 149.—W. G. T. S.]

BOOK IV.

EXPLAINS FOR WHAT THE SON OF GOD WAS SENT, VIZ. THAT BY CHRIST'S DYING FOR SINNERS, WE WERE TO BE CONVINCED HOW GREAT IS GOD'S LOVE FOR US, AND ALSO WHAT MANNER OF MEN WE ARE WHOM HE LOVED. THAT THE WORD CAME IN THE FLESH, TO THE PURPOSE ALSO OF ENABLING US TO BE SO CLEANSED AS TO CONTEMPLATE AND CLEAVE TO GOD. THAT OUR DOUBLE DEATH WAS ABOLISHED BY HIS DEATH, BEING ONE AND SINGLE. AND HEREUPON IS DISCUSSED, HOW THE SINGLE OF OUR SAVIOUR HARMONIZES TO SALVATION WITH OUR DOUBLE; AND THE PERFECTION IS TREATED AT LENGTH OF THE SENARY NUMBER, TO WHICH THE RATIO ITSELF OF SINGLE TO DOUBLE IS REDUCIBLE. THAT ALL ARE GATHERED TOGETHER FROM MANY INTO ONE BY THE ONE MEDIATOR OF LIFE, VIZ. CHRIST, THROUGH WHOM ALONE IS WROUGHT THE TRUE CLEANSING OF THE SOUL. FURTHER IT IS DEMONSTRATED THAT THE SQN OF GOD, ALTHOUGH MADE LESS BY BEING SENT, ON ACCOUNT OF THE FORM OF A SERVANT WHICH HE TOOK, IS NOT THEREFORE LESS THAN THE FATHER ACCORDING TO THE FORM OF GOD, BECAUSE HE WAS SENT BY HIMSELF: AND THAT THE SAME ACCOUNT IS TO BE GIVEN OF THE SENDING OF THE HOLY SPIRIT.

PREFACE.—THE KNOWLEDGE OF GOD IS TO BE SOUGHT FROM GOD.

1. The knowledge of things terrestrial and celestial is commonly thought much of by men. Yet those doubtless judge better who prefer to that knowledge, the knowledge of themselves; and that mind is more praiseworthy which knows even its own weakness, than that which, without regard to this, searches out, and even comes to know, the ways of the stars, or which holds fast such knowledge already acquired, while ignorant of the way by which itself to enter into its own proper health and strength. But if any one has already become awake towards God, kindled by the warmth of the Holy Spirit, and in the love of God has become vile in his own eyes; and through wishing, yet not having strength to come in unto Him, and through the light He gives, has given heed to himself, and has found himself, and has learned that his own filthiness cannot mingle with His purity; and feels it sweet to weep and to entreat Him, that again and again He will have compassion, until he have put off all his wretchedness; and to pray confidently, as having already received of free gift the pledge of salvation through his only Saviour and Enlightener of man:—such an one, so acting, and so lamenting, knowledge does not puff up, because charity edifieth;[1] for he has preferred knowledge to knowledge, he has preferred to know his own weakness, rather than to know the walls of the world, the foundations of the earth, and the pinnacles of heaven. And by obtaining this knowledge, he has obtained also sorrow;[2] but sorrow for straying away from the desire of reaching his own proper country, and the Creator of it, his own blessed God. And if among men such as these, in the family of Thy Christ, O Lord my God, I groan among Thy poor, give me out of Thy bread to answer men who do not hunger and thirst after righteousness, but are sated and abound.[3] But it is the vain image of those things that has sated them, not Thy truth, which they have repelled and shrunk from, and so fall into their own vanity. I certainly know how many figments the human heart gives birth to. And what is my own heart but a human heart? But I

---

[1] 1 Cor. viii. 1. [2] Eccles. i. 18. [3] Matt. v. 6.

pray the God of my heart, that I may not vomit forth (*eructuem*) into these writings any of these figments for solid truths, but that there may pass into them only what the breath of His truth has breathed into me; cast out though I am from the sight of His eyes,[1] and striving from afar to return by the way which the divinity of His only-begotten Son has made by His humanity. And this truth, changeable though I am, I so far drink in, as far as in it I see nothing changeable: neither in place and time, as is the case with bodies; nor in time alone, and in a certain sense place, as with the thoughts of our own spirits; nor in time alone, and not even in any semblance of place, as with some of the reasonings of our own minds. For the essence of God, whereby He is, has altogether nothing changeable, neither in eternity, nor in truth, nor in will; since there truth is eternal, love eternal; and there love is true, eternity true; and there eternity is loved, and truth is loved.

CHAP. I.—WE ARE MADE PERFECT BY ACKNOWL-
EDGEMENT OF OUR OWN WEAKNESS. THE IN-
CARNATE WORD DISPELS OUR DARKNESS.

2. But since we are exiled from the unchangeable joy, yet neither cut off nor torn away from it so that we should not seek eternity, truth, blessedness, even in those changeable and temporal things (for we wish neither to die, nor to be deceived, nor to be troubled); visions have been sent to us from heaven suitable to our state of pilgrimage, in order to remind us that what we seek is not here, but that from this pilgrimage we must return thither, whence unless we originated we should not here seek these things. And first we have had to be persuaded how much God loved us, lest from despair we should not dare to look up to Him. And we needed to be shown also what manner of men we are whom He loved, lest being proud, as if of our own merits, we should recede the more from Him, and fail the more in our own strength. And hence He so dealt with us, that we might the rather profit by His strength, and that so in the weakness of humility the virtue of charity might be perfected. And this is intimated in the Psalm, where it is said, "Thou, O God, didst send a spontaneous rain, whereby Thou didst make Thine inheritance perfect, when it was weary."[2] For by "spontaneous rain" nothing else is meant than grace, not rendered to merit, but given freely,[3] whence also it is called grace;

for He gave it, not because we were worthy, but because He willed. And knowing this, we shall not trust in ourselves; and this is to be made "weak." But He Himself makes us perfect, who says also to the Apostle Paul, "My grace is sufficient for thee, for my strength is made perfect in weakness."[4] Man, then, was to be persuaded how much God loved us, and what manner of men we were whom He loved; the former, lest we should despair; the latter, lest we should be proud. And this most necessary topic the apostle thus explains: "But God commendeth," he says, "His love towards us, in that, while we were yet sinners, Christ died for us. Much more then, being now justified by His blood, we shall be saved from wrath through Him. For if, when we were enemies, we were reconciled to God by the death of His Son; much more, being reconciled, we shall be saved by His life."[5] Also in another place: "What," he says, "shall we then say to these things? If God be for us, who can be against us? He that spared not His own Son, but delivered Him up for us all, how has He not with Him also freely given us all things?"[6] Now that which is declared to us as already done, was shown also to the ancient righteous as about to be done; that through the same faith they themselves also might be humbled, and so made weak; and might be made weak, and so perfected.

3. Because therefore the Word of God is One, by which all things were made, which is the unchangeable truth, all things are simultaneously therein, potentially and unchangeably; not only those things which are now in this whole creation, but also those which have been and those which shall be. And therein they neither have been, nor shall be, but only *are*; and all things are life, and all things are one; or rather it is one being and one life. For all things were so made by Him, that whatsoever was made in them was not made in Him, but was life in Him. Since," in the beginning," the Word was not made, but "the Word was with God, and the Word was God, and all things were made by Him;" neither had all things been made by Him, unless He had Himself been before all things and not made. But in those things which were made by Him, even body, which is not life, would not have been made by Him, except it had been life in Him before it was made. For "that which was made was already life in Him;" and not life of any kind soever: for the soul also is the life of the body, but this too is made, for it is

changeable; and by what was it made, except by the unchangeable Word of God? For "all things were made by Him; and without Him was not anything made that was made." "What, therefore, was made was already life in Him;" and not any kind of life, but "the life [which] was the light of men;" the light certainly of rational minds, by which men differ from beasts, and therefore are men. Therefore not corporeal light, which is the light of the flesh, whether it shine from heaven, or whether it be lighted by earthly fires; nor that of human flesh only, but also that of beasts, and down even to the minutest of worms. For all these things see that light: but that life was the light of men; nor is it far from any one of us, for in it "we live, and move, and have our being." [1]

CHAP. 2.—HOW WE ARE RENDERED APT FOR THE PERCEPTION OF TRUTH THROUGH THE INCARNATE WORD.

4. But "the light shineth in darkness, and the darkness comprehended it not." Now the "darkness" is the foolish minds of men, made blind by vicious desires and unbelief. And that the Word, by whom all things were made, might care for these and heal them, "The Word was made flesh, and dwelt among us." For our enlightening is the partaking of the Word, namely, of that life which is the light of men. But for this partaking we were utterly unfit, and fell short of it, on account of the uncleanness of sins. Therefore we were to be cleansed. And further, the one cleansing of the unrighteous and of the proud is the blood of the Righteous One, and the humbling of God Himself; [2] that we might be cleansed through Him, made as He was what we are by nature, and what we are not by sin, that we might contemplate God, which by nature we are not. For by nature we are not God: by nature we are men, by sin we are not righteous. Wherefore God, made a righteous man, interceded with God for man the sinner. For the sinner is not congruous to the righteous, but man is congruous to man. By joining therefore to us the likeness of His humanity, He took away the unlikeness of our unrighteousness; and by being made partaker of our mortality, He made us partakers of His divinity. For the death of the sinner springing from the necessity of comdemnation is deservedly abolished by the death of the Righteous One springing from the free choice of His compassion, while His single [death and resurrection] answers

to our double [death and resurrection]. [3] For this congruity, or suitableness, or concord, or consonance, or whatever more appropriate word there may be, whereby one is [united] to two, is of great weight in all compacting, or better, perhaps, co-adaptation, of the creature. For (as it just occurs to me) what I mean is precisely that co-adaptation which the Greeks call ἁρμονία. However this is not the place to set forth the power of that consonance of single to double which is found especially in us, and which is naturally so implanted in us (and by whom, except by Him who created us?), that not even the ignorant can fail to perceive it, whether when singing themselves or hearing others. For by this it is that treble and bass voices are in harmony, so that any one who in his note departs from it, offends extremely, not only trained skill, of which the most part of men are devoid, but the very sense of hearing. To demonstrate this, needs no doubt a long discourse; but any one who knows it, may make it plain to the very ear in a rightly ordered monochord.

CHAP. 3.—THE ONE DEATH AND RESURRECTION OF THE BODY OF CHRIST HARMONIZES WITH OUR DOUBLE DEATH AND RESURRECTION OF BODY AND SOUL, TO THE EFFECT OF SALVATION. IN WHAT WAY THE SINGLE DEATH OF CHRIST IS BESTOWED UPON OUR DOUBLE DEATH.

5. But for our present need we must discuss, so far as God gives us power, in what manner the single of our Lord and Saviour Jesus Christ answers to, and is, so to say, in harmony with our double to the effect of salvation. We certainly, as no Christian doubts, are dead both in soul and body: in soul, because of sin; in body, because of the punishment of sin, and through this also in body because of sin. And to both these parts of ourselves, that is, both to soul and to body, there was need both of a medicine and of resurrection, that what had been changed for the worse might be renewed for the better. Now the death of the soul is ungodliness, and the death of the body is corruptibility, through which comes also a departure of the soul from the body. For as the soul dies when God leaves it, so the body dies when the soul leaves it; whereby the former becomes foolish, the latter lifeless. For the soul is raised up again by repentance, and the renewing of life is begun in the body still mortal by faith, by which men believe on Him who justi-

---

[3] [This singleness and doubleness is explained in chapter 3.—W. G. T. S.]

fies the ungodly;[1] and it is increased and strengthened by good habits from day to day, as the inner man is renewed more and more.[2] But the body, being as it were the outward man, the longer this life lasts is so much the more corrupted, either by age or by disease, or by various afflictions, until it come to that last affliction which all call death. And its resurrection is delayed until the end; when also our justification itself shall be perfected ineffably. For then we shall be like Him, for we shall see Him as He is.[3] But now, so long as the corruptible body presseth down the soul,[4] and human life upon earth is all temptation,[5] in His sight shall no man living be justified,[6] in comparison of the righteousness in which we shall be made equal with the angels, and of the glory which shall be revealed in us. But why mention more proofs respecting the difference between the death of the soul and the death of the body, when the Lord in one sentence of the Gospel has made either death easily distinguishable by any one from the other, where He says, " Let the dead bury their dead "?[7] For burial was the fitting disposal of a dead body. But by those who were to bury it He meant those who were dead in soul by the impiety of unbelief, such, namely, as are awakened when it is said, " Awake thou that sleepest, and arise from the dead, and Christ shall give thee light."[8] And there is a death which the apostle denounces, saying of the widow, " But she that liveth in pleasure is dead while she liveth."[9] Therefore the soul, which was before ungodly and is now godly, is said to have come alive again from the dead and to live, on account of the righteousness of faith. But the body is not only said to be about to die, on account of that departure of the soul which will be; but on account of the great infirmity of flesh and blood it is even said to be now dead, in a certain place in the Scriptures, namely, where the apostle says, that " the body is dead because of sin, but the spirit is life because of righteousness."[10] Now this life is wrought by faith, " since the just shall live by faith,"[11] But what follows? " But if the spirit of Him that raised up Jesus from the dead dwell in you, He that raised up Christ from the dead shall also quicken your mortal bodies by His Spirit which dwelleth in you."[12]

6. Therefore on this double death of ours our Saviour bestowed His own single death; and to cause both our resurrections, He appointed beforehand and set forth in mystery and type His own one resurrection. For He was not a sinner or ungodly, that, as though dead in spirit, He should need to be renewed in the inner man, and to be recalled as it were to the life of righteousness by repentance; but being clothed in mortal flesh, and in that alone dying, in that alone rising again, in that alone did He answer to both for us; since in it was wrought a mystery as regards the inner man, and a type as regards the outer. For it was in a mystery as regards our inner man, so as to signify the death of our soul, that those words were uttered, not only in the Psalm, but also on the cross: " My God, my God, why hast Thou forsaken me?"[13] To which words the apostle agrees, saying, " Knowing this, that our old man is crucified with Him, that the body of sin might be destroyed, that henceforth we should not serve sin;" since by the crucifixion of the inner man are understood the pains of repentance, and a certain wholesome agony of self-control, by which death the death of ungodliness is destroyed, and in which death God has left us. And so the body of sin is destroyed through such a cross, that now we should not yield our members as instruments of unrighteousness unto sin.[14] Because, if even the inner man certainly is renewed day by day,[15] yet undoubtedly it is old before it is renewed. For that is done inwardly of which the same apostle speaks: " Put off the old man, and put on the new;" which he goes on to explain by saying, " Wherefore, putting away lying, speak every man truth. "[16] But where is lying put away, unless inwardly, that he who speaketh the truth from his heart may inhabit the holy hill of God?[17] But the resurrection of the body of the Lord is shown to belong to the mystery of our own inner resurrection, where, after He had risen, He says to the woman, " Touch me not, for I am not yet ascended to my Father;"[18] with which mystery the apostle's words agree, where he says, " If ye then be risen with Christ, seek those things which are above, where Christ sitteth on the right hand of God; set your thoughts[19] on things above."[20] For not to touch Christ, unless when He had ascended to the Father, means not to have thoughts[21] of Christ after a fleshly manner. Again, the death of the flesh of our Lord contains a type of the death of our outer man, since it is by such suffering most of all that He exhorts

---

1 Rom. iv. 5.
3 1 John iii. 1.
5 Job. vii. 1.
7 Matt. viii. 22.
9 1 Tim. v. 6.
Rom. i. 17.

2 2 Cor. iv. 16.
4 Wisd. ix. 15.
6 Ps. cxliii. 2.
8 Eph. v. 14.
10 Rom. viii. 10.
12 Rom. viii. 10, 11.

13 Ps. xxii. 1, and Matt. xxvii. 46.
14 Rom. vi. 6, 13.
16 Eph. iv. 22-25.
18 John xx. 17.
20 Col. iii. 1, 2.

15 2 Cor. iv. 16.
17 Ps. xv. 1, 3.
19 Sapite.
21 Sapere.

His servants that they should not fear those who kill the body, but are not able to kill the soul.[1] Wherefore the apostle says, "That I may fill up that which is behind of the afflictions of Christ in my flesh."[2] And the resurrection of the body of the Lord is found to contain a type of the resurrection of our outward man, because He says to His disciples, "Handle me, and see; for a spirit hath not flesh and bones, as ye see me have."[3] And one of the disciples also, handling His scars, exclaimed, "My Lord and my God!"[4] And whereas the entire integrity of that flesh was apparent, this was shown in that which He had said when exhorting His disciples: "There shall not a hair of your head perish."[5] For how comes it that first is said, "Touch me not, for I am not yet ascended to my Father;"[6] and how comes it that before He ascends to the Father, He actually is touched by the disciples; unless because in the former the mystery of the inner man was intimated, in the latter a type was given of the outer man? Or can any one possibly be so without understanding, and so turned away from the truth, as to dare to say that He was touched by men before He ascended, but by women when He had ascended? It was on account of this type, which went before in the Lord, of our future resurrection in the body, that the apostle says, "Christ the first-fruits; afterward they that are Christ's."[7] For it was the resurrection of the body to which this place refers, on account of which he also says, "Who has changed our vile body, that it may be fashioned like unto His glorious body."[8] The one death therefore of our Saviour brought salvation to our double death, and His one resurrection wrought for us two resurrections; since His body in both cases, that is, both in His death and in His resurrection, was ministered to us by a kind of healing suitableness, both as a mystery of the inner man, and as a type of the outer.

CHAP. 4.—THE RATIO OF THE SINGLE TO THE DOUBLE COMES FROM THE PERFECTION OF THE SENARY NUMBER. THE PERFECTION OF THE SENARY NUMBER IS COMMENDED IN THE SCRIPTURES. THE YEAR ABOUNDS IN THE SENARY NUMBER.

7. Now this ratio of the single to the double arises, no doubt, from the ternary number, since one added to two makes three; but the whole which these make reaches to the senary, for one and two and three make six. And this number is on that account called perfect, because it is completed in its own parts: for it has these three, sixth, third, and half; nor is there any other part found in it, which we can call an aliquot part. The sixth part of it, then, is one; the third part, two; the half, three. But one and two and three complete the same six. And Holy Scripture commends to us the perfection of this number, especially in this, that God finished His works in six days, and on the sixth day man was made in the image of God.[9] And the Son of God came and was made the Son of man, that He might re-create us after the image of God, in the sixth age of the human race. For that is now the present age, whether a thousand years apiece are assigned to each age, or whether we trace out memorable and remarkable epochs or turning-points of time in the divine Scriptures, so that the first age is to be found from Adam until Noah, and the second thence onwards to Abraham, and then next, after the division of Matthew the evangelist, from Abraham to David, from David to the carrying away to Babylon, and from thence to the travail of the Virgin,[10] which three ages joined to those other two make five. Accordingly, the nativity of the Lord began the sixth, which is now going onwards until the hidden end of time. We recognize also in this senary number a kind of figure of time, in that threefold mode of division, by which we compute one portion of time before the Law; a second, under the Law; a third, under grace. In which last time we have received the sacrament of renewal, that we may be renewed also in the end of time, in every part, by the resurrection of the flesh, and so may be made whole from our entire infirmity, not only of soul, but also of body. And thence that woman is understood to be a type of the church, who was made whole and upright by the Lord, after she had been bowed by infirmity through the binding of Satan. For those words of the Psalm lament such hidden enemies: "They bowed down my soul."[11] And this woman had her infirmity eighteen years, which is thrice six. And the months of eighteen years are found in number to be the cube of six, viz. six times six times six. Nearly, too, in the same place in the Gospel is that fig tree, which was convicted also by the third year of its miserable barrenness. But intercession was made for it, that it might be let alone that year, that year, that if it bore fruit, well; if otherwise, it should be cut down.[12] For both three years

---

[1] Matt. x. 28.
[2] Col. i. 24.
[3] Luke xxiv. 39.
[4] John xx. 28.
[5] Luke xxi. 18.
[6] John. xx. 17.
[7] 1 Cor. xv. 23.
[8] Phil. iii. 21.
[9] Gen. i. 27.
[10] Matt. i. 17.
[11] Ps. lvii. 6.
[12] Luke xiii. 6-17.

belong to the same threefold division, and the months of three years make the square of six, which is six times six.

8. A single year also, if the whole twelve months are taken into account, which are made up of thirty days each (for the month that has been kept from of old is that which the revolution of the moon determines), abounds in the number six. For that which six is, in the first order of numbers, which consists of units up to ten, that sixty is in the second order, which consists of tens up to a hundred. Sixty days, then, are a sixth part of the year. Further, if that which stands as the sixth of the second order is multiplied by the sixth of the first order, then we make six times sixty, *i.e.* three hundred and sixty days, which are the whole twelve months. But since, as the revolution of the moon determines the month for men, so the year is marked by the revolution of the sun; and five days and a quarter of a day remain, that the sun may fulfill its course and end the year; for four quarters make one day, which must be intercalated in every fourth year, which they call bissextile, that the order of time may not be disturbed: if we consider, also, these five days and a quarter themselves, the number six prevails in them. First, because, as it is usual to compute the whole from a part, we must not call it five days, but rather six, taking the quarter days for one day. Next, because five days themselves are the sixth part of a month; while the quarter of a day contains six hours. For the entire day, *i.e.* including its night, is twenty-four hours, of which the fourth part, which is a quarter of a day, is found to be six hours. So much in the course of the year does the sixth number prevail.

CHAP. 5.—THE NUMBER SIX IS ALSO COMMENDED IN THE BUILDING UP OF THE BODY OF CHRIST AND OF THE TEMPLE AT JERUSALEM.

9. And not without reason is the number six understood to be put for a year in the building up of the body of the Lord, as a figure of which He said that He would raise up in three days the temple destroyed by the Jews. For they said, "Forty and six years was this temple in building."[1] And six times forty-six makes two hundred and seventy-six. And this number of days completes nine months and six days, which are reckoned, as it were, ten months for the travail of women; not because all come to the sixth day after the ninth month, but because the perfection itself of the body of the Lord

is found to have been brought in so many days to the birth, as the authority of the church maintains upon the tradition of the elders. For He is believed to have been conceived on the 25th of March, upon which day also He suffered; so the womb of the Virgin, in which He was conceived, where no one of mortals was begotten, corresponds to the new grave in which He was buried,[2] wherein was never man laid, neither before nor since. But He was born, according to tradition, upon December the 25th. If, then you reckon from that day to this you find two hundred and seventy-six days which is forty-six times six. And in this number of years the temple was built, because in that number of sixes the body of the Lord was perfected; which being destroyed by the suffering of death, He raised again on the third day. For "He spake this of the temple of His body,"[3] as is declared by the most clear and solid testimony of the Gospel; where He said, "For as Jonas was three days and three nights in the whale's belly, so shall the Son of man be three days and three nights in the heart of the earth."[4]

CHAP. 6.—THE THREE DAYS OF THE RESURRECTION, IN WHICH ALSO THE RATIO OF SINGLE TO DOUBLE IS APPARENT.

10. Scripture again witnesses that the space of those three days themselves was not whole and entire, but the first day is counted as a whole from its last part, and the third day is itself also counted as a whole from its first part; but the intervening day, *i.e.* the second day, was absolutely a whole with its twenty-four hours, twelve of the day and twelve of the night. For He was crucified first by the voices of the Jews in the third hour, when it was the sixth day of the week. Then He hung on the cross itself at the sixth hour, and yielded up His spirit at the ninth hour.[5] But He was buried, "now when the even was come," as the words of the evangelist express it;[6] which means, at the end of the day. Wheresoever then you begin,— even if some other explanation can be given, so as not to contradict the Gospel of John,[7] but to understand that He was suspended on the cross at the third hour,—still you cannot make the first day an entire day. It will be reckoned then an entire day from its last part, as the third from its first part. For the night up to the dawn, when the resurrection of the Lord was made known, belongs to the third day; because God (who commanded

---

[1] John ii. 20.

[2] John xix. 41, 42.   [3] John ii. 19-21.   [4] Matt. xii. 40.
[5] Matt. xxvii. 23-50.   [6] Mark xv. 42-46.   [7] John xix. 14.

the light to shine out of darkness,[1] that through the grace of the New Testament and the partaking of the resurrection of Christ the words might be spoken to us "For ye were sometimes darkness, but now are ye light in the Lord "[2]) intimates to us in some way that the day takes its beginning from the night. For as the first days of all were reckoned from light to night, on account of the future fall of man;[3] so these on account of the restoration of man, are reckoned from darkness to light. From the hour, then, of His death to the dawn of the resurrection are forty hours, counting in also the ninth hour itself. And with this number agrees also His life upon earth of forty days after His resurrection. And this number is most frequently used in Scripture to express the mystery of perfection in the fourfold world. For the number ten has a certain perfection, and that multiplied by four makes forty. But from the evening of the burial to the dawn of the resurrection are thirty-six hours which is six squared. And this is referred to that ratio of the single to the double wherein there is the greatest consonance of co-adaptation. For twelve added to twenty-four suits the ratio of single added to double and makes thirty-six: namely a whole night with a whole day and a whole night, and this not without the mystery which I have noticed above. For not unfitly do we liken the spirit to the day and the body to the night. For the body of the Lord in His death and resurrection was a figure of our spirit and a type of our body. In this way, then, also that ratio of the single to the double is apparent in the thirty-six hours, when twelve are added to twenty-four. As to the reasons, indeed, why these numbers are so put in the Holy Scriptures, other people may trace out other reasons, either such that those which I have given are to be preferred to them, or such as are equally probable with mine, or even more probable than they are; but there is no one surely so foolish or so absurd as to contend that they are so put in the Scriptures for no purpose at all, and that there are no mystical reasons why those numbers are there mentioned. But those reasons which I have here given, I have either gathered from the authority of the church, according to the tradition of our forefathers, or from the testimony of the divine Scriptures, or from the nature itself of numbers and of similitudes. No sober person will decide against reason, no Christian against the Scriptures, no peaceable person against the church.

CHAP. 7.—IN WHAT MANNER WE ARE GATHERED FROM MANY INTO ONE THROUGH ONE MEDIATOR.

11. This mystery, this sacrifice, this priest, this God, before He was sent and came, being made of a woman—of Him, all those things which appeared to our fathers in a sacred and mystical way by angelical miracles, or which were done by the fathers themselves, were similitudes; in order that every creature by its acts might speak in some way of that One who was to be, in whom there was to be salvation in the recovery of all from death. For because by the wickedness of ungodliness we had recoiled and fallen away in discord from the one true and supreme God, and had in many things become vain, being distracted through many things and cleaving fast to many things; it was needful, by the decree and command of God in His mercy, that those same many things should join in proclaiming the One that should come, and that One should come so proclaimed by these many things, and that these many things should join in witnessing that this One had come; and that so, freed from the burden of these many things, we should come to that One, and dead as we were in our souls by many sins, and destined to die in the flesh on account of sin, that we should love that One who, without sin, died in the flesh for us; and by believing in Him now raised again, and by rising again with Him in the spirit through faith, that we should be justified by being made one in the one righteous One; and that we should not despair of our own resurrection in the flesh itself, when we consider that the one Head had gone before us the many members; in whom, being now cleansed through faith, and then renewed by sight, and through Him as mediator reconciled to God, we are to cleave to the One, to feast upon the One, to continue one.

CHAP. 8.—IN WHAT MANNER CHRIST WILLS THAT ALL SHALL BE ONE IN HIMSELF.

12. So the Son of God Himself, the Word of God, Himself also the Mediator between God and men, the Son of man,[4] equal to the Father through the unity of the Godhead, and partaker with us by the taking upon Him of humanity, interceding for us with the Father in that He was man,[5] yet not concealing that He was God, one with the Father, among other things speaks thus: "Neither pray I for these alone," He says, "but for them also which shall believe on me through their word; that they all may be one; as

---

[1] 2 Cor. iv. 6.　　　[2] Eph. v. 8.
[3] Gen. i. 4, 5.

[4] 1 Tim. ii. 5.　　　[5] Rom. viii. 34.

Thou, Father, art in me, and I in Thee, that they also may be one in us: that the world may believe that Thou hast sent me. And the glory which Thou gavest me I have given them; that they may be one, even as we are one."[1]

CHAP. 9.—THE SAME ARGUMENT CONTINUED.

He did not say, I and they are one thing;[2] although, in that He is the head of the church, which is His body,[3] He might have said, I and they are, not one thing,[4] but one person,[5] because the head and the body is one Christ; but in order to show His own Godhead consubstantial with the Father (for which reason He says in another place, "I and my Father are one"[6]), in His own kind, that is, in the consubstantial parity of the same nature, He wills His own to be one,[7] but in Himself; since they could not be so in themselves, separated as they are one from another by divers pleasures and desires and uncleannesses of sin; whence they are cleansed through the Mediator, that they may be one[8] in Him, not only through the same nature in which all become from mortal men equal to the angels, but also through the same will most harmoniously conspiring to the same blessedness, and fused in some way by the fire of charity into one spirit. For to this His words come, "That they may be one, even as we are one;" namely, that as the Father and Son are one, not only in equality of substance, but also in will, so those also may be one, between whom and God the Son is mediator, not only in that they are of the same nature, but also through the same union of love. And then He goes on thus to intimate the truth itself, that He is the Mediator, through whom we are reconciled to God, by saying, "I in them, and Thou in me, that they may be made perfect in one."[9]

CHAP. 10.—AS CHRIST IS THE MEDIATOR OF LIFE, SO THE DEVIL IS THE MEDIATOR OF DEATH.

13. Therein is our true peace and firm bond of union with our Creator, that we should be purified and reconciled through the Mediator of life, as we had been polluted and alienated, and so had departed from Him, through the mediator of death. For as the devil through pride led man through pride to death; so Christ through lowliness led back man through obedience to life.

Since, as the one fell through being lifted up, and cast down [man] also who consented to him; so the other was raised up through being abased, and lifted up [man] also who believed in Him. For because the devil had not himself come thither whither he had led the way (inasmuch as he bare indeed in his ungodliness the death of the spirit, but had not undergone the death of the flesh, because he had not assumed the covering of the flesh), he appeared to man to be a mighty chief among the legions of devils, through whom he exercises his reign of deceits; so puffing up man the more, who is eager for power more than righteousness, through the pride of elation, or through false philosophy; or else entangling him through sacrilegious rites, in which, while casting down headlong by deceit and illusion the minds of the more curious and prouder sort, he holds him captive also to magical trickery; promising too the cleansing of the soul, through those initiations which they call τελεταί, by transforming himself into an angel of light,[10] through divers machinations in signs and prodigies of lying.

CHAP. 11.—MIRACLES WHICH ARE DONE BY DEMONS ARE TO BE SPURNED.

14. For it is easy for the most worthless spirits to do many things by means of aerial bodies, such as to cause wonder to souls which are weighed down by earthly bodies, even though they be of the better inclined. For if earthly bodies themselves, when trained by a certain skill and practice, exhibit to men so great marvels in theâtrical spectacles, that they who never saw such things scarcely believe them when told; why should it be hard for the devil and his angels to make out of corporeal elements, through their own aerial bodies, things at which the flesh marvels; or even by hidden inspirations to contrive fantastic appearances to the deluding of men's senses, whereby to deceive them, whether awake or asleep, or to drive them into frenzy? But just as it may happen that one who is better than they in life and character may gaze at the most worthless of men, either walking on a rope, or doing by various motions of the body many things difficult of belief, and yet he may not at all desire to do such things, nor think those men on that account to be preferred to himself; so the faithful and pious soul, not only if it sees, but even if on account of the frailty of the flesh it shudders at, the miracles of demons, yet will not for that either deplore its own want of power to do such things, or judge

---

1 John xvii. 20-22.   2 Unum.
3 Eph. i. 22, 23.   4 Unum.
5 Unus.   6 John x. 30; unum.
7 Unum.   8 Unum.
9 John xvii. 23.

10 2 Cor. xi. 14.

them on this account to be better than itself; especially since it is in the company of the holy, who, whether they are men or good angels, accomplish, through the power of God, to whom all things are subject, wonders which are far greater and the very reverse of deceptive.

CHAP. 12.—THE DEVIL THE MEDIATOR OF DEATH, CHRIST OF LIFE.

15. In no wise therefore are souls cleansed and reconciled to God by sacrilegious imitations, or curious arts that are impious, or magical incantations; since the false mediator does not translate them to higher things, but rather blocks and cuts off the way thither through the affections, malignant in proportion as they are proud, which he inspires into those of his own company; which are not able to nourish the wings of virtues so as to fly upwards, but rather to heap up the weight of vices so as to press downwards; since the soul will fall down the more heavily, the more it seems to itself to have been carried upwards. Accordingly, as the Magi did when warned of God,[1] whom the star led to adore the low estate of the Lord; so we also ought to return to our country, not by the way by which we came, but by another way which the lowly King has taught, and which the proud king, the adversary of that lowly King, cannot block up. For to us, too, that we may adore the lowly Christ, the "heavens have declared the glory of God, when their sound went into all the earth, and their words to the ends of the world."[2] A way was made for us to death through sin in Adam. For, "By one man sin entered into the world, and death by sin; and so death passed upon all men, in whom all have sinned."[3] Of this way the devil was the mediator, the persuader to sin, and the caster down into death. For he, too, applied his one death to work out our double death. Since he indeed died in the spirit through ungodliness, but certainly did not die in the flesh: yet both persuaded us to ungodliness, and thereby brought it to pass that we deserved to come into the death of the flesh. We desired therefore the one through wicked persuasion, the other followed us by a just condemnation; and therefore it is written, "God made not death,"[4] since He was not Himself the cause of death; but yet death was inflicted on the sinner, through His most just retribution. Just as the judge inflicts punishment on the guilty; yet it is not the justice of the judge, but the desert of the crime, which is the cause of the punishment. Whither, then, the mediator of death caused us to pass, yet did not come himself, that is, to the death of the flesh, there our Lord God introduced for us the medicine of correction, which He deserved not, by a hidden and exceeding mysterious decree of divine and profound justice. In order, therefore, that as by one man came death, so by one man might come also the resurrection of the dead;[5] because men strove more to shun that which they could not shun, viz. the death of the flesh, than the death of the spirit, i.e. punishment more than the desert of punishment (for not to sin is a thing about which either men are not solicitous or are too little solicitous; but not to die, although it be not within reach of attainment, is yet eagerly sought after); the Mediator of life, making it plain that death is not to be feared, which by the condition of humanity cannot now be escaped, but rather ungodliness, which can be guarded against through faith, meets us at the end to which we have come, but not by the way by which we came. For we, indeed, came to death through sin; He through righteousness: and, therefore, as our death is the punishment of sin, so His death was made a sacrifice for sin.

CHAP. 13.—THE DEATH OF CHRIST VOLUNTARY. HOW THE MEDIATOR OF LIFE SUBDUED THE MEDIATOR OF DEATH. HOW THE DEVIL LEADS HIS OWN TO DESPISE THE DEATH OF CHRIST.

16. Wherefore, since the spirit is to be preferred to the body, and the death of the spirit means that God has left it, but the death of the body that the spirit has left it; and since herein lies the punishment in the death of the body, that the spirit leaves the body against its will, because it left God willingly; so that, whereas the spirit left God because it would, it leaves the body although it would not; nor leaves it when it would, unless it has offered violence to itself, whereby the body itself is slain: the spirit of the Mediator showed how it was through no punishment of sin that He came to the death of the flesh, because He did not leave it against His will, but because He willed, when He willed, as He willed. For because He is so commingled [with the flesh] by the Word of God as to be one, He says: "I have power to lay down my life, and I have power to take it again. No man taketh it from me, but I lay down my life that I might take it again."[6] And, as the Gospel tells us, they who were

---

[1] Matt. ii. 12.
[3] Rom. v. 12—in quo.
[2] Ps. xix. 1, 4.
[4] Wisd. i. 13.
[5] 1 Cor. xv. 21, 22.
[6] John x. 17, 18.

present were most astonished at this, that after that [last] word, in which He set forth the figure of our sin, He immediately gave up His spirit. For they who are hung on the cross are commonly tortured by a prolonged death. Whence it was that the legs of the thieves were broken, in order that they might die directly, and be taken down from the cross before the Sabbath. And that He was found to be dead already, caused wonder. And it was this also, at which, as we read, Pilate marvelled, when the body of the Lord was asked of him for burial.[1]

17. Because that deceiver then,—who was a mediator to death for man, and feignedly puts himself forward as to life, under the name of cleansing by sacrilegious rites and sacrifices, by which the proud are led away, —can neither share in our death, nor rise again from his own: he has indeed been able to apply his single death to our double one; but he certainly has not been able to apply a single resurrection, which should be at once a mystery of our renewal, and a type of that waking up which is to be in the end. He then who being alive in the spirit raised again His own flesh that was dead, the true Mediator of life, has cast out him, who is dead in the spirit and the mediator of death, from the spirits of those who believe in Himself, so that he should not reign within, but should assault from without, and yet not prevail. And to him, too, He offered Himself to be tempted, in order that He might be also a mediator to overcome his temptations, not only by succor, but also by example. But when the devil, from the first, although striving through every entrance to creep into His inward parts, was thrust out, having finished all his alluring temptation in the wilderness after the baptism;[2] because, being dead in the spirit, he forced no entrance into Him who was alive in the spirit, he betook himself, through eagerness for the death of man in any way whatsoever, to effecting that death which he could, and was permitted to effect it upon that mortal element which the living Mediator had received from us. And where he could do anything, there in every respect he was conquered; and wherein he received outwardly the power of slaying the Lord in the flesh, therein his inward power, by which he held ourselves, was slain. For it was brought to pass that the bonds of many sins in many deaths were loosed, through the one death of One which no sin had preceded. Which death, though not due, the Lord therefore rendered for us, that the death which

was due might work us no hurt. For He was not stripped of the flesh by obligation of any authority, but He stripped Himself. For doubtless He who was able not to die, if He would not, did die because He would: and so He made a show of principalities and powers, openly triumphing over them in Himself.[3] For whereas by His death the one and most real sacrifice was offered up for us, whatever fault there was, whence principalities and powers held us fast as of right to pay its penalty, He cleansed, abolished, extinguished; and by His own resurrection He also called us whom He predestinated to a new life; and whom He called, them He justified; and whom He justified, them He glorified.[4] And so the devil, in that very death of the flesh, lost man, whom he was possessing as by an absolute right, seduced as he was by his own consent, and over whom he ruled, himself impeded by no corruption of flesh and blood, through that frailty of man's mortal body, whence he was both too poor and too weak; he who was proud in proportion as he was, as it were, both richer and stronger, ruling over him who was, as it were, both clothed in rags and full of troubles. For whither he drove the sinner to fall, himself not following, there by following he compelled the Redeemer to descend. And so the Son of God deigned to become our friend in the fellowship of death, to which because he came not, the enemy thought himself to be better and greater than ourselves. For our Redeemer says, "Greater love hath no man than this, that a man lay down his life for his friends."[5] Wherefore also the devil thought himself superior to the Lord Himself, inasmuch as the Lord in His sufferings yielded to him; for of Him, too, is understood what is read in the Psalm, "For Thou hast made Him a little lower than the angels:"[6] so that He, being Himself put to death, although innocent, by the unjust one acting against us as it were by just right, might by a most just right overcome him, and so might lead captive the captivity wrought through sin,[7] and free us from a captivity that was just on account of sin, by blotting out the handwriting, and redeeming us who were to be justified although sinners, through His own righteous blood unrighteously poured out.

18. Hence also the devil mocks those who are his own until this very day, to whom he presents himself as a false mediator, as though they would be cleansed or rather entangled and drowned by his rites, in that he very

---

[1] Mark xv. 37, 39, 43, 44, and John xix. 30–34.
[2] Matt. iv. 1–11.

[3] Col. ii. 15.   [4] Rom. viii. 30.   [5] John xv. 13.
[6] Ps. viii. 5.   [7] Eph. iv. 8.

easily persuades the proud to ridicule and despise the death of Christ, from which the more he himself is estranged, the more is he believed by them to be the holier and more divine. Yet those who have remained with him are very few, since the nations acknowledge and with pious humility imbibe the price paid for themselves, and in trust upon it abandon their enemy, and gather together to their Redeemer. For the devil does not know how the most excellent wisdom of God makes use of both his snares and his fury to bring about the salvation of His own faithful ones, beginning from the former end, which is the beginning of the spiritual creature, even to the latter end, which is the death of the body, and so "reaching from the one end to the other, mightily and sweetly ordering all things."[1] For wisdom "passeth and goeth through all things by reason of her pureness, and no defiled thing can fall into her."[2] And since the devil has nothing to do with the death of the flesh, whence comes his exceeding pride, a death of another kind is prepared in the eternal fire of hell, by which not only the spirits that have earthly, but also those who have aerial bodies, can be tormented. But proud men, by whom Christ is despised, because He died, wherein He bought us with so great a price,[3] both bring back the former death, and also men, to that miserable condition of nature, which is derived from the first sin, and will be cast down into the latter death with the devil. And they on this account preferred the devil to Christ, because the former cast them into that former death, whither he himself fell not through the difference of his nature, and whither on account of them Christ descended through His great mercy: and yet they do not hesitate to believe themselves better than the devils, and do not cease to assail and denounce them with every sort of malediction, while they know them at any rate to have nothing to do with the suffering of this kind of death, on account of which they despise Christ. Neither will they take into account that the case may possibly be, that the Word of God, remaining in Himself, and in Himself in no way changeable, may yet, through the taking upon Him of a lower nature, be able to suffer somewhat of a lower kind, which the unclean spirit cannot suffer, because he has not an earthly body. And so, whereas they themselves are better than the devils, yet, because they bear a body of flesh, they can so die, as the devils certainly cannot die, who do not bear such a body. They

presume much on the deaths of their own sacrifices, which they do not perceive that they sacrifice to deceitful and proud spirits; or if they have come to perceive it, think their friendship to be of some good to themselves, treacherous and envious although they are, whose purpose is bent upon nothing else except to hinder our return.

CHAP. 14.—CHRIST THE MOST PERFECT VICTIM FOR CLEANSING OUR FAULTS. IN EVERY SACRIFICE FOUR THINGS ARE TO BE CONSIDERED.

19. They do not understand, that not even the proudest of spirits themselves could rejoice in the honor of sacrifices, unless a true sacrifice was due to the one true God, in whose stead they desire to be worshipped: and that this cannot be rightly offered except by a holy and righteous priest; nor unless that which is offered be received from those for whom it is offered; and unless also it be without fault, so that it may be offered for cleansing the faulty. This at least all desire who wish sacrifice to be offered for themselves to God. Who then is so righteous and holy a priest as the only Son of God, who had no need to purge His own sins by sacrifice,[4] neither original sins, nor those which are added by human life? And what could be so fitly chosen by men to be offered for them as human flesh? And what so fit for this immolation as mortal flesh? And what so clean for cleansing the faults of mortal men as the flesh born in and from the womb of a virgin, without any infection of carnal concupiscence? And what could be so acceptably offered and taken, as the flesh of our sacrifice, made the body of our priest? In such wise that, whereas four things are to be considered in every sacrifice,—to whom it is offered, by whom it is offered, what is offered, for whom it is offered,—the same One and true Mediator Himself, reconciling us to God by the sacrifice of peace, might remain one with Him to whom He offered, might make those one in Himself for whom He offered, Himself might be in one both the offerer and the offering.

CHAP. 15.—THEY ARE PROUD WHO THINK THEY ARE ABLE, BY THEIR OWN RIGHTEOUSNESS, TO BE CLEANSED SO AS TO SEE GOD.

20. There are, however, some who think themselves capable of being cleansed by their own righteousness, so as to contemplate God, and to dwell in God; whom their very pride itself stains above all others. For there is no

---

[1] Wisd. viii. 1.　　　[2] Wisd. vii. 24, 25.　　　[3] 1 Cor. vi. 20.　　　[4] Heb. vii.

sin to which the divine law is more opposed, and over which that proudest of spirits, who is a mediator to things below, but a barrier against things above, receives a greater right of mastery: unless either his secret snares be avoided by going another way, or if he rage openly by means of a sinful people (which Amalek, being interpreted, means), and forbid by fighting the passage to the land of promise, he be overcome by the cross of the Lord, which is prefigured by the holding out of the hands of Moses.[1] For these persons promise themselves cleansing by their own righteousness for this reason, because some of them have been able to penetrate with the eye of the mind beyond the whole creature, and to touch, though it be in ever so small a part, the light of the unchangeable truth; a thing which they deride many Christians for being not yet able to do, who, in the meantime, live by faith alone. But of what use is it for the proud man, who on that account is ashamed to embark upon the ship of wood,[2] to behold from afar his country beyond the sea? Or how can it hurt the humble man not to behold it from so great a distance, when he is actually coming to it by that wood upon which the other disdains to be borne?

CHAP. 16.—THE OLD PHILOSOPHERS ARE NOT TO BE CONSULTED CONCERNING THE RESURRECTION AND CONCERNING THINGS TO COME.

21. These people also blame us for believing the resurrection of the flesh, and rather wish us to believe themselves concerning these things. As though, because they have been able to understand the high and unchangeable substance by the things which are made,[3] for this reason they had a claim to be consulted concerning the revolutions of mutable things, or concerning the connected order of the ages. For pray, because they dispute most truly, and persuade us by most certain proofs, that all things temporal are made after a science that is eternal, are they therefore able to see clearly in the matter of this science itself, or to collect from it, how many kinds of animals there are, what are the seeds of each in their beginnings, what measure in their increase, what numbers run through their conceptions, births, ages, settings; what motions in desiring things according to their nature, and in avoiding the contrary? Have they not sought out all these things, not through that unchangeable wisdom, but

through the actual history of places and times, or have trusted the written experience of others? Wherefore it is the less to be wondered at, that they have utterly failed in searching out the succession of more lengthened ages, and in finding any goal of that course, down which, as though down a river, the human race is sailing, and the transition thence of each to its own appropriate end. For these are subjects which historians could not describe, inasmuch as they are far in the future, and have been experienced and related by no one. Nor have those philosophers, who have profited better than others in that high and eternal science, been able to grasp such subjects with the understanding; otherwise they would not be inquiring as they could into past things of the kind, such as are in the province of historians, but rather would foreknow also things future; and those who are able to do this are called by them soothsayers, but by us prophets:

CHAP. 17.—IN HOW MANY WAYS THINGS FUTURE ARE FOREKNOWN. NEITHER PHILOSOPHERS, NOR THOSE WHO WERE DISTINGUISHED AMONG THE ANCIENTS, ARE TO BE CONSULTED CONCERNING THE RESURRECTION OF THE DEAD.

22.—although the name of prophets, too, is not altogether foreign to their writings. But it makes the greatest possible difference, whether things future are conjectured by experience of things past (as physicians also have committed many things to writing in the way of foresight, which they themselves have noted by experience; or as again husbandmen, or sailors, too, foretell many things; for if such predictions are made a long while before, they are thought to be divinations), or whether such things have already started on their road to come to us, and being seen coming far off, are announced in proportion to the acuteness of the sense of those who see them, by doing which the aerial powers are thought to divine (just as if a person from the top of a mountain were to see far off some one coming, and were to announce it beforehand to those who dwelt close by in the plain); or whether they are either foreannounced to certain men, or are heard by them and again transmitted to other men, by means of holy angels, to whom God shows those things by His Word and His Wisdom, wherein both things future and things past consist; or whether the minds of certain men themselves are so far borne upwards by the Holy Spirit, as to behold, not through the angels, but of themselves, the immoveable

---

[1] Ex. xvii. 8-16.
[2] [The wood of the cross is meant. One of the ancient symbols of the church was a ship.—W. G. T. S.
[3] Rom. i. 20.]

causes of things future, in that very highest pinnacle of the universe itself. [And I say, behold,] for the aerial powers, too, *hear* these things, either by message through angels, or through men; and hear only so much as He judges to be fitting, to whom all things are subject. Many things, too, are foretold by a kind of instinct and inward impulse of such as know them not: as Caiaphas did not know what he said, but being the high priest, he prophesied.[1]

23. Therefore, neither concerning the successions of ages, nor concerning the resurrection of the dead, ought we to consult those philosophers, who have understood as much as they could the eternity of the Creator, in whom "we live, and move, and have our being."[2] Since, knowing God through those things which are made, they have not glorified Him as God, neither were thankful; but professing themselves wise, they became fools.[3] And whereas they were not fit to fix the eye of the mind so firmly upon the eternity of the spiritual and unchangeable nature, as to be able to see, in the wisdom itself of the Creator and Governor of the universe, those revolutions of the ages, which in that wisdom were already and were always, but here were about to be so that as yet they were not; or, again, to see therein those changes for the better, not of the souls only, but also of the bodies of men, even to the perfection of their proper measure; whereas then, I say, they were in no way fit to see these things therein, they were not even judged worthy of receiving any announcement of them by the holy angels; whether externally through the senses of the body, or by interior revelations exhibited in the spirit; as these things actually were manifested to our fathers, who were gifted with true piety, and who by foretelling them, obtaining credence either by present signs, or by events close at hand, which turned out as they had foretold, earned authority to be believed respecting things remotely future, even to the end of the world. But the proud and deceitful powers of the air, even if they are found to have said through their soothsayers some things of the fellowship and citizenship of the saints, and of the true Mediator, which they heard from the holy prophets or the angels, did so with the purpose of seducing even the faithful ones of God, if they could, by these alien truths, to revolt to their own proper falsehoods. But God did this by those who knew not what they said, in order that the truth might sound abroad from all sides, to aid the faithful, to be a witness against the ungodly.

CHAP. 18.—THE SON OF GOD BECAME INCARNATE IN ORDER THAT WE BEING CLEANSED BY FAITH MAY BE RAISED TO THE UNCHANGEABLE TRUTH.

24. Since, then, we were not fit to take hold of things eternal, and since the foulness of sins weighed us down, which we had contracted by the love of temporal things, and which were implanted in us as it were naturally, from the root of mortality, it was needful that we should be cleansed. But cleansed we could not be, so as to be tempered together with things eternal, except it were through things temporal, wherewith we were already tempered together and held fast. For health is at the opposite extreme from disease; but the intermediate process of healing does not lead us to perfect health, unless it has some congruity with the disease. Things temporal that are useless merely deceive the sick; things temporal that are useful take up those that need healing, and pass them on healed, to things eternal. And the rational mind, as when cleansed it owes contemplation to things eternal; so, when needing cleansing, owes faith to things temporal. One even of those who were formerly esteemed wise men among the Greeks has said, The truth stands to faith in the same relation in which eternity stands to that which has a beginning. And he is no doubt right in saying so. For what we call temporal, he describes as having had a beginning. And we also ourselves come under this kind, not only in respect to the body, but also in respect to the changeableness of the soul. For that is not properly called eternal which undergoes any degree of change. Therefore, in so far as we are changeable, in so far we stand apart from eternity. But life eternal is promised to us through the truth, from the clear knowledge of which, again, our faith stands as far apart as mortality does from eternity. We then now put faith in things done in time on our account, and by that faith itself we are cleansed; in order that when we have come to sight, as truth follows faith, so eternity may follow upon mortality. And therefore, since our faith will become truth, when we have attained to that which is promised to us who believe: and that which is promised us is eternal life; and the Truth (not that which shall come to be according as our faith shall be, but that truth which is always, because in it is eternity,—the Truth then) has said, "And this is life eternal, that

[1] John xi. 51.   [2] Acts xvii. 28.   [3] Rom. i. 21, 22.

they might know Thee the only true God, and Jesus Christ, whom Thou hast sent:"[1] when our faith by seeing shall come to be truth, then eternity shall possess our now changed mortality.   And until this shall take place, and in order it may take place,—because we adapt the faith of belief to things which have a beginning, as in things eternal we hope for the truth of contemplation, lest the faith of mortal life should be at discord with the truth of eternal life,—the Truth itself, co-eternal with the Father, took a beginning from earth,[2] when the Son of God so came as to become the Son of man, and to take to Himself our faith, that He might thereby lead us on to His own truth, who so undertook our mortality, as not to lose His own eternity. For truth stands to faith in the relation in which eternity stands to that which has a beginning.   Therefore, we must needs so be cleansed, that we may come to have such a beginning as remains eternal, that we may not have one beginning in faith, and another in truth.   Neither could we pass to things eternal from the condition of having a beginning, unless we were transferred, by union of the eternal to ourselves through our own beginning, to His own eternity.   Therefore our faith has, in some measure, now followed thither, whither He in whom we have believed has ascended; born,[3] dead, risen again, taken up.   Of these four things, we knew the first two in ourselves.   For we know that men both have a beginning and die.   But the remaining two, that is, to be raised, and to be taken up, we rightly hope will be in us, because we have believed them done in Him. Since, therefore, in Him that, too, which had a beginning has passed over to eternity, in ourselves also it will so pass over, when faith shall have arrived at truth.   For to those who thus believe, in order that they might remain in the word of faith, and being thence led on to the truth, and through that to eternity, might be freed from death, He speaks thus: "If ye continue in my word, then are ye my disciples indeed."   And as though they would ask, With what fruit?   He proceeds to say, "And ye shall know the truth."   And again, as though they would say, Of what good is truth to mortal men?   "And the truth," He says, "shall make you free."[4]   From what, except from death, from corruption, from changeableness?   Since truth remains immortal, incorrupt, unchangeable.   But true immortality, true incorruptibility, true unchangeableness, is eternity itself.

CHAP. 19.—IN WHAT MANNER THE SON WAS SENT AND PROCLAIMED BEFOREHAND.   HOW IN THE SENDING OF HIS BIRTH IN THE FLESH HE WAS MADE LESS WITHOUT DETRIMENT TO HIS EQUALITY WITH THE FATHER.

25.   Behold, then, why the Son of God was sent; nay, rather behold what it is for the Son of God to be sent.   Whatever things they were which were wrought in time, with a view to produce faith, whereby we might be cleansed so as to contemplate truth, in things that have a beginning, which have been put forth from eternity, and are referred back to eternity: these were either testimonies of this mission, or they were the mission itself of the Son of God.   But some of these testimonies announced Him beforehand as to come, some testified that He had come already.   For that He was made a creature by whom the whole creation was made, must needs find a witness in the whole creation.   For except one were preached by the sending of many [witnesses] one would not be bound to, the sending away of many.   And unless there were such testimonies as should seem to be great to those who are lowly, it would not be believed, that He being great should make men great, who as lowly was sent to the lowly.   For the heaven and the earth and all things in them are incomparably greater works of the Son of God, since all things were made by Him, than the signs and the portents which broke forth in testimony of Him.   But yet men, in order that, being lowly, they might believe these great things to have been wrought by Him, trembled at those lowly things, as if they had been great.

26.   "When, therefore, the fullness of time was come, God sent forth His Son, made of a woman, made under the Law;"[5] to such a degree lowly, that He was "made;" in this way therefore sent, in that He was made. If, therefore, the greater sends the less, we too, acknowledge Him to have been made less; and in so far less, in so far as made; and in so far made, in so far as sent.   For "He sent forth His Son made of a woman." And yet, because all things were made by Him, not only before He was made and sent, but before all things were at all, we confess the same to be equal to the sender, whom we call less, as having been sent.   In what way, then, could He be seen by the fathers, when certain angelical visions were shown to them, before that fullness of time at which it was fitting He should be sent, and so before He was sent, at a time when not yet sent He was seen as He is equal with the Father?   For

---

[1] John xvii. 3.   [2] Ps. lxxxv. 11.
[3] Ortus.   [4] John viii. 31. 32.   [5] Gal. iv. 4.

how does He say to Philip, by whom He was certainly seen as by all the rest, and even by those by whom He was crucified in the flesh, "Have I been so long time with you, and yet hast thou not known me, Philip? he that hath seen me, hath seen the Father also;" unless because He was both seen and yet not seen? He was seen, as He had been made in being sent; He was not seen, as by Him all things were made. Or how does He say this too, "He that hath my commandments, and keepeth them, he it is that loveth me; and he that loveth me shall be loved of my Father, and I will love him, and will manifest myself to him,"[1] at a time when He was manifest before the eyes of men; unless because He was offering that flesh, which the Word was made in the fullness of time, to be accepted by our faith; but was keeping back the Word itself, by whom all things were made, to be contemplated in eternity by the mind when cleansed by faith?

CHAP. 20.—THE SENDER AND THE SENT EQUAL. WHY THE SON IS SAID TO BE SENT BY THE FATHER. OF THE MISSION OF THE HOLY SPIRIT. HOW AND BY WHOM HE WAS SENT. THE FATHER THE BEGINNING OF THE WHOLE GODHEAD.

27. But if the Son is said to be sent by the Father on this account, that the one is the Father, and the other the Son, this does not in any manner hinder us from believing the Son to be equal, and consubstantial, and co-eternal with the Father, and yet to have been sent as Son by the Father. Not because the one is greater, the other less; but because the one is Father, the other Son; the one begetter, the other begotten; the one, He from whom He is who is sent; the other, He who is from Him who sends. For the Son is from the Father, not the Father from the Son. And according to this manner we can now understand that the Son is not only said to have been sent because "the Word was made flesh,"[2] but therefore sent that the Word might be made flesh, and that He might perform through His bodily presence those things which were written; that is, that not only is He understood to have been sent as man, which the Word was made but the Word, too, was sent that it might be made man; because He was not sent in respect to any inequality of power, or substance, or anything that in Him was not equal to the Father; but in respect to this, that the Son is from the Father, not the Father from the Son; for the Son is the Word of the Father, which is also called His wisdom. What wonder, therefore, if He is sent, not because He is unequal with the Father, but because He is "a pure emanation (manatio) issuing from the glory of the Almighty God?" For there, that which issues, and that from which it issues, is of one and the same substance. For it does not issue as water issues from an aperture of earth or of stone, but as light issues from light. For the words, "For she is the brightness of the everlasting light," what else are they than, she is light of everlasting light? For what is the brightness of light, except light itself? and so co-eternal, with the light, from which the light is. But it is preferable to say, "the brightness of light," rather than" the light of light;" lest that which issues should be thought to be darker than that from which it issues. For when one hears of the brightness of light as being light itself, it is more easy to believe that the former shines by means of the latter, than that the latter shines less. But because there was no need of warning men not to think that light to be less, which begat the other (for no heretic ever dared say this, neither is it to be believed that any one will dare to do so), Scripture meets that other thought, whereby that light which issues might seem darker than that from which it issues; and it has removed this surmise by saying, "It is the brightness of that light," namely, of eternal light, and so shows it to be equal. For if it were less, then it would be its darkness, not its brightness; but if it were greater, then it could not issue from it, for it could not surpass that from which it is educed. Therefore, because it issues from it, it is not greater than it is; and because it is not its darkness, but its brightness, it is not less than it is: therefore it is equal. Nor ought this to trouble us, that it is called a pure emanation issuing from the glory of the Almighty God, as if itself were not omnipotent, but an emanation from the Omnipotent; for soon after it is said of it, "And being but one, she can do all things."[3] But who is omnipotent, unless He who can do all things? It is sent, therefore, by Him from whom it issues; for so she is sought after by him who loved and desired her. "Send her," he says, "out of Thy holy heavens, and from the throne of Thy glory, that, being present, she may labor with me;"[4] that is, may teach me to labor [heartily] in order that I may not labor [irksomely]. For her labors are virtues. But she is sent in one way that she may be with man; she has been sent in another way that she herself may be man. For,

---

[1] John xiv. 9, 21.   [2] John i. 3, 18, 14.   [3] Wisd. vii. 25-27.   [4] Wisd. ix. 10.

"entering into holy souls, she maketh them friends of God and prophets;"[1] so she also fills the holy angels, and works all things fitting for such ministries by them.[2] But when the fullness of time was come, she was sent,[3] not to fill angels, nor to be an angel, except in so far as she announced the counsel of the Father, which was her own also; nor, again, to be with men or in men, for this too took place before, both in the fathers and in the prophets; but that the Word itself should be made flesh, that is, should be made man. In which future mystery, when revealed, was to be the salvation of those wise and holy men also, who, before He was born of the Virgin, were born of women; and in which, when done and made known, is the salvation of all who believe, and hope, and love. For this is "the great mystery of godliness, which[4] was manifest in the flesh, justified in the Spirit, seen of angels, preached unto the Gentiles, believed on in the world, received up into glory."[5]

28. Therefore the Word of God is sent by Him, of whom He is the Word; He is sent by Him, from whom He was begotten (genitum); He sends who begot, That is sent which is begotten. And He is then sent to each one, when He is apprehended and perceived by each, in so far as He can be apprehended and perceived, in proportion to the comprehension of the rational soul, either advancing towards God, or already perfect in God. The Son, therefore, is not properly said to have been sent in that He is begotten of the Father; but either in that the Word made flesh appeared to the world, whence He says, "I came forth from the Father, and am come into the world;"[6] or in that from time to time, He is perceived by the mind of each, according to the saying, "Send her, that, being present with me, she may labor with me."[7] What then is born (natum) from eternity is eternal, "for it is the brightness of the everlasting light;" but what is sent from time to time, is that which is apprehended by each. But when the Son of God was made manifest in the flesh, He was sent into this world in the fullness of time, made of a woman. "For after that, in the wisdom of God, the world by wisdom knew not God" (since "the light shineth in darkness, and the darkness comprehended it not"), it "pleased God by the foolishness of preaching to save them that believe ,"[8] and that the

Word should be made flesh, and dwell among us.[9] But when from time to time He comes forth and is perceived by the mind of each, He is said indeed to be sent, but not into this world; for He does not appear sensibly, that is, He does not present Himself to the corporeal senses. For we ourselves, too, are not in this world, in respect to our grasping with the mind as far as we can that which is eternal; and the spirits of all the righteous are not in this world, even of those who are still living in the flesh, in so far as they have discernment in things divine. But the Father is not said to be sent, when from time to time He is apprehended by any one, for He has no one of whom to be, or from whom to proceed; since Wisdom says, "I came out of the mouth of the Most High,"[10] and it is said of the Holy Spirit, "He proceedeth from the Father,"[11] but the Father is from no one.

29. As, therefore, the Father begat, the Son is begotten; so the Father sent, the Son was sent. But in like manner as He who begat and He who was begotten, so both He who sent and He who was sent, are one, since the Father and the Son are one.[12] So also the Holy Spirit is one with them, since these three are one. For as to be born, in respect to the Son, means to be from the Father; so to be sent, in respect to the Son, means to be known to be from the Father. And as to be the gift of God in respect to the Holy Spirit, means to proceed from the Father; so to be sent, is to be known to proceed from the Father. Neither can we say that the Holy Spirit does not also proceed from the Son, for the same Spirit is not without reason said to be the Spirit both of the Father and of the Son.[13] Nor do I see what else He intended to signify, when He breathed on the face of the disciples, and said, "Receive ye the Holy Ghost."[14] For that bodily breathing, proceeding from the body with the feeling of bodily touching, was not the substance of the Holy Spirit, but a declaration by a fitting sign, that the Holy Spirit proceeds not only from the Father, but also from the Son. For the veriest of madmen would not say, that it was one Spirit which He gave when He breathed on them, and another which He sent after His ascension.[15] For the Spirit of God is one, the Spirit of the Father and of the Son, the Holy Spirit, who worketh all in all.[16] But that He was given twice was certainly a significant economy, which we will

---

[1] Wisd. vii. 27.
[2] [The allusion is to the Wisdom of Proverbs, and of the Book of Wisdom, which Augustin regards as canonical, as his frequent citations show.—W. G. T. S.]
[3] Gal. iv. 4.   [4] Quod, scil. sacramentum.
[5] 1 Tim. iii. 16.   [6] John xvi. 28.
[7] Wisd. ix. 10.   [8] 1 Cor. i. 21.

[9] John i. 5, 14.
[10] Ecclus. xxiv. 3.   [11] John xv. 26.   [12] John x. 30.
[13] [Augustin here, as in previous instances, affirms the procession of the Spirit from the Father and Son.—W. G. T. S.]
[14] John xx. 22.   [15] Acts ii. 1-4.
[16] 1 Cor. xii. 6.

discuss in its place, as far as the Lord may grant. That then which the Lord says,— "Whom I will send unto you from the Father,"[1]—shows the Spirit to be both of the Father and of the Son; because, also, when He had said, "Whom the Father will send," He added also, "in my name."[2] Yet He did not say, Whom the Father will send from *me*, as He said, "Whom *I* will send unto you from the Father,"—showing, namely, that the Father is the beginning (*principium*) of the whole divinity, or if it is better so expressed, deity.[3] He, therefore, who proceeds from the Father and from the Son, is referred back to Him from whom the Son was born (*natus*). And that which the evangelist says, "For the Holy Ghost was not yet given, because that Jesus was not yet glorified;"[4] how is this to be understood, unless because the special giving or sending of the Holy Spirit after the glorification of Christ was to be such as it had never been before? For it was not previously none at all, but it had not been such as this. For if the Holy Spirit was not given before, wherewith were the prophets who spoke filled? Whereas the Scripture plainly says, and shows in many places, that they spake by the Holy Spirit. Whereas, also, it is said of John the Baptist, "And he shall be filled with the Holy Ghost, even from his mother's womb." And his father Zacharias is found to have been filled with the Holy Ghost, so as to say such things of him. And Mary, too, was filled with the Holy Ghost, so as to foretell such things of the Lord, whom she was bearing in her womb.[5] And Simeon and Anna were filled with the Holy Spirit, so as to acknowledge the greatness of the little child Christ.[6] How, then, was "the Spirit not yet given, since Jesus was not yet glorified," unless because that giving, or granting, or mission of the Holy Spirit was to have a certain speciality of its own in its very advent, such as never was before? For we read nowhere that men spoke in tongues which they did not know,

through the Holy Spirit coming upon them; as happened then, when it was needful that His coming should be made plain by visible signs, in order to show that the whole world, and all nations constituted with different tongues, should believe in Christ through the gift of the Holy Spirit, to fulfill that which is sung in the Psalm, "There is no speech nor language where their voice is not heard; their sound is gone out through all the earth, and their words to the end of the world."[7]

30. Therefore man was united, and in some sense commingled, with the Word of God, so as to be One Person, when the fullness of time was come, and the Son of God, made of a woman, was sent into this world, that He might be also the Son of man for the sake of the sons of men. And this person angelic nature could prefigure beforehand, so as to pre-announce, but could not appropriate, so as to be that person itself.

CHAP. 21.—OF THE SENSIBLE SHOWING OF THE HOLY SPIRIT, AND OF THE CO-ETERNITY OF THE TRINITY. WHAT HAS BEEN SAID, AND WHAT REMAINS TO BE SAID.

But with respect to the sensible showing of the Holy Spirit, whether by the shape of a dove,[8] or by fiery tongues,[9] when the subjected and subservient creature by temporal motions and forms manifested His substance co-eternal with the Father and the Son, and alike with them unchangeable, while it was not united so as to be one person with Him, as the flesh was which the Word was made;[10] I do not dare to say that nothing of the kind was done aforetime. But I would boldly say, that the Father, Son, and Holy Spirit, of one and the same substance, God the Creator, the Omnipotent Trinity, work indivisibly; but that this cannot be indivisibly manifested by the creature, which is far inferior, and least of all by the bodily creature: just as the Father, Son, and Holy Spirit cannot be named by our words, which certainly are bodily sounds, except in their own proper intervals of time, divided by a distinct separation, which intervals the proper syllables of each word occupy. Since in their proper substance wherein they are, the three are one, the Father, and the Son, and the Holy Spirit, the very same, by no temporal motion, above the whole creature, without any interval of time and place, and at once one and the same from eternity to eternity, as it were eternity itself, which is not without truth

1 John xv. 26. 2 John xiv. 26.
3 [The term "beginning" is employed "relatively, and not according to substance," as Augustin says. The Father is "the beginning of the whole deity," with reference to the personal distinctions of Father, Son, and Spirit—the Son being from the Father, and the Spirit from Father and Son. The trinitarian relations or modes of the essence, "begin" with the first person, not the second or the third. The phrase "whole deity," in the above statement, is put for "trinity," not for "essence." Augustin would not say that the Father is the "beginning (*principium*) of the divine essence considered abstractly, but only of the essence as *trinal*. In this sense, Trinitarian writers denominate the Father "*fons trinitatis*," and sometimes "*fons deitatis*." Turrettin employs this latter phraseology (iii. xxx. i. 8); so does Owen (*Communion with Trinity*, Ch. iii.); and Hooker (*Polity*, v. liv.) But in this case, the guarding clause of Turretin is to be subjoined: "*fons deitatis, si modus subsistendi spectatur*." The phrase "*fons trinitatis*," or "*principium trinitatis*," is less liable to be misconceived, and more accurate than "*fons deitatis*, or "*principium deitatis*."—W. G. T. S.]
4 John vii. 39. 5 Luke i. 15, 41-79. 6 Luke ii. 25-38.
7 Ps. xix. 3, 4. 8 Matt. iii. 16.
9 Acts ii. 3. 10 John i. 14.

and charity. But, in my words, the Father, Son, and Holy Spirit are separated, and cannot be named at once, and occupy their own proper places separately invisible letters. And as, when I name my memory, and intellect, and will, each name refers to each severally, but yet each is uttered by all three; for there is no one of these three names that is not uttered by both my memory and my intellect and my will together [by the soul as a whole]; so the Trinity together wrought both the voice of the Father, and the flesh of the Son, and the dove of the Holy Spirit, while each of these things is referred severally to each person. And by this similitude it is in some degree discernible, that the Trinity, which is inseparable in itself, is manifested separably by the appearance of the visible creature; and that the operation of the Trinity is also inseparable in each severally of those things which are said to pertain properly to the manifesting of either the Father, or the Son, or the Holy Spirit.

31. If then I am asked, in what manner either words or sensible forms and appearances were wrought before the incarnation of the Word of God, which should prefigure it as about to come, I reply that God wrought those things by the angels; and this I have also shown sufficiently, as I think, by testimonies of the Holy Scriptures. And if I am asked how the incarnation itself was brought to pass, I reply that the Word of God itself was made flesh, that is, was made man, yet not turned and changed into that which was made; but so made, that there should be there not only the Word of God and the flesh of man, but also the rational soul of man, and that this whole should both be called God on account of God, and man on account of man. And if this is understood with difficulty, the mind must be purged by faith, by more and more abstaining from sins, and by doing good works, and by praying with the groaning of holy desires; that by profiting through the divine help, it may both understand and love. And if I am asked, how, after the incarnation of the Word, either a voice of the Father was produced, or a corporeal appearance by which the Holy Spirit was manifested: I do not doubt indeed that this was done through the creature; but whether only corporeal and sensible, or whether by the employment also of the spirit rational or intellectual (for this is the term by which some choose to call what

the Greeks name νοερόν), not certainly so as to form one person (for who could possibly say that whatever creature it was by which the voice of the Father sounded, is in such sense God the Father; or whatever creature it was by which the Holy Spirit was manifested in the form of a dove, or in fiery tongues, is in such sense the Holy Spirit, as the Son of God is that man who was made of a virgin?), but only to the ministry of bringing about such intimations as God judged needful; or whether anything else is to be understood: is difficult to discover, and not expedient rashly to affirm. Yet I see not how those things could have been brought to pass without the rational or intellectual creature. But it is not yet the proper place to explain, as the Lord may give me strength, why I so think; for the arguments of heretics must first be discussed and refuted, which they do not produce from the divine books, but from their own reasons, and by which, as they think, they forcibly compel us so to understand the testimonies of the Scriptures which treat of the Father, and the Son, and the Holy Spirit, as they themselves will.

32. But now, as I think, it has been sufficiently shown, that the Son is not therefore less because He is sent by the Father, nor the Holy Spirit less because both the Father sent Him and the Son. For these things are perceived to be laid down in the Scriptures, either on account of the visible creature; or rather on account of commending to our thoughts the emanation [within the Godhead];[1] but not on account of inequality, or imparity, or unlikeness of substance; since, even if God the Father had willed to appear visibly through the subject creature, yet it would be most absurd to say that He was sent either by the Son, whom He begot, or by the Holy Spirit, who proceeds from Him. Let this, therefore, be the limit of the present book. Henceforth in the rest we shall see, the Lord helping, of what sort are those crafty arguments of the heretics, and in what manner they may be confuted.

[1] [The original is: "*propter principii commendationem*," which the English translator renders: "On account of commending to our thoughts the principle [of the Godhead]." The technical use of "principium" is missed. Augustin says that the phrases, "sending the Son," and "sending the Spirit," have reference to the "visible creature" through which in the theophanies each was manifested; but still more, to the fact that the Father is the "beginning of the Son, and the Father and Son are the "beginning" of the Spirit. This fact of a "beginning," or emanation (*manatio*) of one from another, is what is commended to our thoughts.—W. G. T. S.]

BOOK V.

PROCEEDS TO TREAT OF THE ARGUMENTS PUT FORWARD BY THE HERETICS, NOT FROM SCRIPT-
URE, BUT FROM THEIR OWN REASON. THOSE ARE REFUTED, WHO THINK THE SUBSTANCE
OF THE FATHER AND OF THE SON TO BE NOT THE SAME, BECAUSE EVERYTHING PREDICATED
OF GOD IS, IN THEIR OPINION, PREDICATED OF HIM ACCORDING TO SUBSTANCE ; AND THERE-
FORE IT FOLLOWS, THAT TO BEGET AND TO BE BEGOTTEN, OR TO BE BEGOTTEN AND UNBE-
GOTTEN, BEING DIVERSE, ARE DIVERSE SUBSTANCES ; WHEREAS IT IS HERE DEMONSTRATED
THAT NOT EVERYTHING PREDICATED OF GOD IS PREDICATED ACCORDING TO SUBSTANCE, IN
SUCH MANNER AS HE IS CALLED GOOD AND GREAT ACCORDING TO SUBSTANCE, OR ANYTHING
ELSE THAT IS PREDICATED OF HIM IN RESPECT TO HIMSELF ; BUT THAT SOME THINGS ARE
ALSO PREDICATED OF HIM RELATIVELY, I. E. NOT IN RESPECT TO HIMSELF, BUT TO SOME-
THING NOT HIMSELF, AS HE IS CALLED FATHER IN RESPECT TO THE SON, AND LORD IN RE-
SPECT TO THE CREATURE THAT SERVETH HIM ; IN WHICH CASE, IF ANYTHING THUS PREDI-
CATED RELATIVELY, I. E. IN RESPECT TO SOMETHING NOT HIMSELF, IS EVEN PREDICATED AS
HAPPENING IN TIME, AS E. G. "LORD, THOU HAST BECOME OUR REFUGE," YET NOTHING
HAPPENS TO GOD SO AS TO WORK A CHANGE IN HIM, BUT HE HIMSELF REMAINS ABSOLUTELY
UNCHANGEABLE IN HIS OWN NATURE OR ESSENCE.

CHAP. I.—WHAT THE AUTHOR ENTREATS FROM GOD, WHAT FROM THE READER. IN GOD NOTHING IS TO BE THOUGHT CORPOREAL OR CHANGEABLE.

1. Beginning, as I now do henceforward, to speak of subjects which cannot altogether be spoken as they are thought, either by any man, or, at any rate, not by myself; although even our very thought, when we think of God the Trinity, falls (as we feel) very far short of Him of whom we think, nor comprehends Him as He is; but He is seen, as it is written, even by those who are so great as was the Apostle Paul, "through a glass and in an enigma:"[1] first, I pray to our Lord God Himself, of whom we ought always to think, and of whom we are not able to think worthily, in praise of whom blessing is at all times to be rendered,[2] and whom no speech is sufficient to declare, that He will grant me both help for understanding and explaining that which I design, and pardon if in any-thing I offend. For I bear in mind, not only my desire, but also my infirmity. I ask also of my readers to pardon me, where they may perceive me to have had the desire rather than the power to speak, what they either understand better themselves, or fail to un-derstand through the obscurity of my lan-guage, just as I myself pardon them what they cannot understand through their own dullness.

2. And we shall mutually pardon one an-other the more easily, if we know, or at any rate firmly believe and hold, that whatever is said of a nature, unchangeable, invisible and having life absolutely and sufficient to itself, must not be measured after the custom of things visible, and changeable, and mortal, or not self-sufficient. But although we labor, and yet fail, to grasp and know even those things which are within the scope of our cor-poreal senses, or what we are ourselves in the inner man; yet it is with no shamelessness that faithful piety burns after those divine and unspeakable things which are above: piety, I say, not inflated by the arrogance of its own power, but inflamed by the grace of

---

[1] 1 Cor. xiii. 12.   [2] Ps. xxxiv. 1.

13

its Creator and Saviour Himself. For with what understanding can man apprehend God, who does not yet apprehend that very understanding itself of his own, by which he desires to apprehend Him? And if he does already apprehend this, let him carefully consider that there is nothing in his own nature better than it; and let him see whether he can there see any outlines of forms, or brightness of colors, or greatness of space, or distance of parts, or extension of size, or any movements through intervals of place, or any such thing at all. Certainly we find nothing of all this in that, than which we find nothing better in our own nature, that is, in our own intellect, by which we apprehend wisdom according to our capacity. What, therefore, we do not find in that which is our own best, we ought not to seek in Him who is far better than that best of ours; that so we may understand God, if we are able, and as much as we are able, as good without quality, great without quantity, a creator though He lack nothing, ruling but from no position, sustaining all things without "having" them, in His wholeness everywhere, yet without place, eternal without time, making things that are changeable, without change of Himself, and without passion. Whoso thus thinks of God, although he cannot yet find out in all ways what He is, yet piously takes heed, as much as he is able, to think nothing of Him that He is not.

CHAP. 2.—GOD THE ONLY UNCHANGEABLE ESSENCE.

3. He is, however, without doubt, a substance, or, if it be better so to call it, an essence, which the Greeks call οὐσία. For as wisdom is so called from the being wise, and knowledge from knowing; so from being[1] comes that which we call essence. And who is there that IS, more than He who said to His servant Moses, "I am that I am;" and, "Thus shalt thou say unto the children of Israel, He who is hath sent me unto you?"[2] But other things that are called essences or substances admit of accidents, whereby a change, whether great or small, is produced in them. But there can be no accident of this kind in respect to God; and therefore He who is God is the only unchangeable substance or essence, to whom certainly BEING itself, whence comes the name of essence, most especially and most truly belongs. For that which is changed does not retain its own being; and that which can be changed, although it be not actually changed, is able not

to be that which it had been; and hence that which not only is not changed, but also cannot at all be changed, alone falls most truly, without difficulty or hesitation, under the category of BEING.

CHAP. 3.—THE ARGUMENT OF THE ARIANS IS REFUTED, WHICH IS DRAWN FROM THE WORDS BEGOTTEN AND UNBEGOTTEN.

4. Wherefore,—to being now to answer the adversaries of our faith, respecting those things also, which are neither said as they are thought, nor thought as they really are:— among the many things which the Arians are wont to dispute against the Catholic faith, they seem chiefly to set forth this, as their most crafty device, namely, that whatsoever is said or understood of God, is said not according to accident, but according to substance: and therefore, to be unbegotten belongs to the Father according to substance, and to be begotten belongs to the Son according to substance; but to be unbegotten and to be begotten are different; therefore the substance of the Father and that of the Son are different. To whom we reply, If whatever is spoken of God is spoken according to substance, then that which is said, "I and the Father are one,"[3] is spoken according to substance. Therefore there is one substance of the Father and the Son. Or if this is not said according to substance, then something is said of God not according to substance, and therefore we are no longer compelled to understand unbegotten and begotten according to substance. It is also said of the Son, "He thought it not robbery to be equal with God."[4] We ask, equal according to what? For if He is not said to be equal according to substance, then they admit that something may be said of God not according to substance. Let them admit, then, that unbegotten and begotten are not spoken according to substance. And if they do not admit this, on the ground that they will have all things to be spoken of God according to substance, then the Son is equal to the Father according to substance.

CHAP. 4.—THE ACCIDENTAL ALWAYS IMPLIES SOME CHANGE IN THE THING.

5. That which is accidental commonly implies that it can be lost by some change of the thing to which it is an accident. For although some accidents are said to be inseparable, which in Greek are called ἀχώριστα, as the color black is to the feather of a raven;

---

[1] Esse.   [2] Ex. iii. 14.   [3] John x. 30.   [4] Phil. ii. 6.

yet the feather loses that color, not indeed so long as it is a feather, but because the feather is not always. Wherefore the matter itself is changeable; and whenever that animal or that feather ceases to be, and the whole of that body is changed and turned into earth, it loses certainly that color also. Although the kind of accident which is called separable may likewise be lost, not by separation, but by change; as, for instance, blackness is called a separable accident to the hair of men, because hair continuing to be hair can grow white; yet, if carefully considered, it is sufficiently apparent, that it is not as if anything departed by separation away from the head when it grows white, as though blackness departed thence and went somewhere, and whiteness came in its place, but that the quality of color there is turned and changed. Therefore there is nothing accidental in God, because there is nothing changeable or that may be lost. But if you choose to call that also accidental, which, although it may not be lost, yet can be decreased or increased, —as, for instance, the life of the soul: for as long as it is a soul, so long it lives, and because the soul is always, it always lives; but because it lives more when it is wise, and less when it is foolish, here, too, some change comes to pass, not such that life is absent, as wisdom is absent to the foolish, but such that it is less;—nothing of this kind, either, happens to God, because He remains altogether unchangeable.

CHAP. 5.—NOTHING IS SPOKEN OF GOD ACCORDING TO ACCIDENT, BUT ACCORDING TO SUBSTANCE OR ACCORDING TO RELATION.

6. Wherefore nothing in Him is said in respect to accident, since nothing is accidental to Him, and yet all that is said is not said according to substance. For in created and changeable things, that which is not said according to substance, must, by necessary alternative, be said according to accident. For all things are accidents to them, which can be either lost or diminished, whether magnitudes or qualities; and so also is that which is said in relation to something, as friendships, relationships, services, likenesses, equalities, and anything else of the kind; so also positions and conditions, [1] places and times, acts and passions. But in God nothing is said to be according to accident, because in Him nothing is changeable; and yet everything that is said, is not said according to substance. For it is said in relation to something, as the Father in relation to the Son and the Son in relation to the Father, which is not accident; because both the one is always Father, and the other is always Son: yet not "always," meaning from the time when the Son was born [*natus*], so that the Father ceases not to be the Father because the Son never *ceases* to be the Son, but because the Son was *always* born, and never began to be the Son. But if He had begun to be at any time, or were at any time to cease to be, the Son, then He would be called Son according to accident. But if the Father, in that He is called the Father, were so called in relation to Himself, not to the Son; and the Son, in that He is called the Son, were so called in relation to Himself, not to the Father; then both the one would be called Father, and the other Son, according to substance. But because the Father is not called the Father except in that He has a Son, and the Son is not called Son except in that He has a Father, these things are not said according to substance; because each of them is not so called in relation to Himself, but the terms are used reciprocally and in relation each to the other; nor yet according to accident, because both the being called the Father, and the being called the Son, is eternal and unchangeable to them. Wherefore, although to be the Father and to be the Son is different, yet their substance is not different; because they are so called, not according to substance, but according to relation, which relation, however, is not accident, because it is not changeable.

CHAP. 6.—REPLY IS MADE TO THE CAVILS OF THE HERETICS IN RESPECT TO THE SAME WORDS BEGOTTEN AND UNBEGOTTEN.

7. But if they think they can answer this reasoning thus,—that the Father indeed is so called in relation to the Son, and the Son in relation to the Father, but that they are said to be unbegotten and begotten in relation to themselves, not in relation each to the other; for that it is not the same thing to call Him unbegotten as it is to call Him the Father, because there would be nothing to hinder our calling Him unbegotten even if He had not begotten the Son; and if any one beget a son, he is not therefore himself unbegotten, for men, who are begotten by other men, themselves also beget others; and therefore they say the Father is called Father in relation to the Son, and the Son is called Son in relation to the Father, but unbegotten is said in relation to Himself, and begotten in relation to Himself; and therefore, if whatever is said in relation to oneself is said according to sub-

[1] *Habitus.*

stance, while to be unbegotten and to be begotten are different, then the substance is different:—if this is what they say, then they do not understand that they do indeed say something that requires more careful discussion in respect to the term unbegotten, because neither is any one therefore a father because unbegotten, nor therefore unbegotten because he is a father, and on that account he is supposed to be called unbegotten, not in relation to anything else, but in respect to himself; but, on the other hand, with a wonderful blindness, they do not perceive that no one can be said to be begotten except in relation to something. For he is therefore a son because begotten; and because a son, therefore certainly begotten. And as is the relation of son to father, so is the relation of the begotten to the begetter; and as is the relation of father to son, so is the relation of the begetter to the begotten. And therefore any one is understood to be a begetter under one notion, but understood to be unbegotten under another. For though both are said of God the Father, yet the former is said in relation to the begotten, that is to the Son, which, indeed, they do not deny; but that He is called unbegotten, they declare to be said in respect to Himself. They say then, If anything is said to be a father in respect to itself, which cannot be said to be a son in respect to itself, and whatever is said in respect to self is said according to substance; and He is said to be unbegotten in respect to Himself, which the Son cannot be said to be; therefore He is said to be unbegotten according to substance; and because the Son cannot be so said to be, therefore He is not of the same substance. This subtlety is to be answered by compelling them to say themselves according to what it is that the Son is equal to the Father; whether according to that which is said in relation to Himself, or according to that which is said in relation to the Father. For it is not according to that which is said in relation to the Father, since in relation to the Father He is said to be Son, and the Father is not Son, but Father. Since Father and Son are not so called in relation to each other in the same way as friends and neighbors are; for a friend is so called relatively to his friend, and if they love each other equally, then the same friendship is in both; and a neighbor is so called relatively to a neighbor, and because they are equally neighbors to each other (for each is neighbor to the other, in the same degree as the other is neighbor to him), there is the same neighborhood in both. But because the Son is not so called relatively to the Son, but to the Father, it is not according to that which is said in relation to the Father that the Son is equal to the Father; and it remains that He is equal according to that which is said in relation to Himself. But whatever is said in relation to self is said according to substance: it remains therefore that He is equal according to substance; therefore the substance of both is the same. But when the Father is said to be unbegotten, it is not said what He is, but what He is not; and when a relative term is denied, it is not denied according to substance, since the relative itself is not affirmed according to substance.

CHAP. 7.—THE ADDITION OF A NEGATIVE DOES NOT CHANGE THE PREDICAMENT.

8. This is to be made clear by examples. And first we must notice, that by the word begotten is signified the same thing as is signified by the word son. For therefore a son, because begotten, and because a son, therefore certainly begotten. By the word unbegotten, therefore, it is declared that he is not son. But begotten and unbegotten are both of them terms suitably employed; whereas in Latin we can use the word "filius," but the custom of the language does not allow us to speak of "infilius." It makes no difference, however, in the meaning if he is called "non filius;" just as it is precisely the same thing if he is called "non genitus," instead of "ingenitus." For so the terms of both neighbor and friend are used relatively, yet we cannot speak of "invicinus" as we can of "inimicus." Wherefore, in speaking of this thing or that, we must not consider what the usage of our own language either allows or does not allow, but what clearly appears to be the meaning of the things themselves. Let us not therefore any longer call it unbegotten, although it can be so called in Latin; but instead of this let us call it not begotten, which means the same. Is this then anything else than saying that he is not a son? Now the prefixing of that negative particle does not make that to be said according to substance, which, without it, is said relatively; but that only is denied, which, without it, was affirmed, as in the other predicaments. When we say he is a man, we denote substance. He therefore who says he is not a man, enunciates no other kind of predicament, but only denies that. As therefore I affirm according to substance in saying he is a man, so I deny according to substance in saying he is not a man. And when the question is asked, how large he is? and I say he is quadrupedal, that is, four feet in measure,

I affirm according to quantity, and he who says he is not quadrupedal, denies according to quantity. I say he is white, I affirm according to quality; if I say he is not white, I deny according to quality. I say he is near, I affirm according to relation; if I say he is not near, I deny according to relation. I affirm according to position, when I say he lies down; I deny according to position, when I say he does not lie down. I speak according to condition,[1] when I say he is armed; I deny according to condition, when I say he is not armed; and it comes to the same thing as if I should say he is unarmed. I affirm according to time, when I say he is of yesterday; I deny according to time, when I say he is not of yesterday. And when I say he is at Rome, I affirm according to place; and I deny according to place, when I say he is not at Rome. I affirm according to the predicament of action, when I say he smites; but if I say he does not smite, I deny according to action, so as to declare that he does not so act. And when I say he is smitten, I affirm according to the predicament of passion; and I deny according to the same, when I say he is not smitten. And, in a word, there is no kind of predicament according to which we may please to affirm anything, without being proved to deny according to the same predicament, if we prefix the negative particle. And since this is so, if I were to affirm according to substance, in saying son, I should deny according to substance, in saying not son. But because I affirm relatively when I say he is a son, for I refer to the father; therefore I deny relatively if I say he is not a son, for I refer the same negation to the father, in that I wish to declare that he has not a parent. But if to be called son is precisely equivalent to the being called begotten (as we said before), then to be called not begotten is precisely equivalent to the being called not son. But we deny relatively when we say he is not son, therefore we deny relatively when we say he is not begotten. Further, what is unbegotten, unless not begotten? We do not escape, therefore, from the relative predicament, when he is called unbegotten. For as begotten is not said in relation to self, but in that he is *of* a begetter; so when one is called unbegotten, he is not so called in relation to himself, but it is declared that he is not *of* a begetter. Both meanings, however, turn upon the same predicament, which is called that of relation. But that which is asserted relatively does not denote substance, and accordingly, although

begotten and unbegotten are diverse, they do not denote a different substance; because, as son is referred to father, and not son to not father, so it follows inevitably that begotten must be referred to begetter, and not-begotten to not-begetter.[2]

CHAP. 8.—WHATEVER IS SPOKEN OF GOD ACCORDING TO SUBSTANCE, IS SPOKEN OF EACH PERSON SEVERALLY, AND TOGETHER OF THE TRINITY ITSELF. ONE ESSENCE IN GOD, AND THREE, IN GREEK, HYPOSTASES, IN LATIN, PERSONS.

9. Wherefore let us hold this above all, that whatsoever is said of that most eminent and divine loftiness in respect to itself, is said in respect to substance, but that which is said in relation to anything, is not said in respect to substance, but relatively; and that the effect of the same substance in Father and Son and Holy Spirit is, that whatsoever is said of each in respect to themselves, is to be taken of them, not in the plural in sum, but in the singular. For as the Father is God, and the Son is God, and the Holy Spirit is God, which no one doubts to be said in respect to substance, yet we do not say that the very supreme Trinity itself is three Gods, but one God. So the Father is great, the Son great, and the Holy Spirit great; yet not three greats, but one great. For it is not written of the Father alone, as they perversely suppose, but of the Father and the Son and the Holy Spirit, "Thou art great: Thou art God alone."[3] And the Father is good, the Son good, and the Holy Spirit good; yet not three goods, but one good, of whom it is said, "None is good, save one, that is, God." For the Lord Jesus, lest He should be understood as man only by him who said, "Good Master," as addressing a man, does not therefore say, There is none good, save the Father alone; but, "None is good, save one, that is, God."[4] For the Father by Himself is declared by the name of Father; but by the name of God, both Himself and the Son and the Holy Spirit, because the Trinity is one God. But position, and condition, and places, and times,

---

[2] The terms "unbegotten" and "begotten" are interchangeable with the terms Father and Son. This follows from the relation of a substantive to its adjective. In whatever sense a substantive is employed, in the same sense must the adjective formed from it be employed. Consequently, if the first person of the Trinity may be called Father in a sense that implies deity, he may be called Unbegotten in the same sense. And if the second person may be called Son in a sense implying deity, he may be called Begotten in the same sense. The Ancient church often employed the adjective, and spoke of God the Unbegotten and God the Begotten (Justin Martyr, *Apol.* i. 25, 53; ii. 12, 13. Clem. Alex. *Stromata* v. xii.). This phraseology sounds strange to the Modern church, yet the latter really says the same thing when it speaks of God the Father, and God the Son.—W. G. T. S.]

[3] Ps. lxxxvi. 10.　　　　[4] Luke xviii. 18, 19.

are not said to be in God properly, but metaphorically and through similitudes. For He is both said to dwell between the cherubims,[1] which is spoken in respect to position; and to be covered with the deep as with a garment,[2] which is said in respect to condition; and "Thy years shall have no end,"[3] which is said in respect of time; and, "If I ascend up into heaven, Thou art there,"[4] which is said in respect to place. And as respects action (or making), perhaps it may be said most truly of God alone, for God alone makes and Himself is not made. Nor is He liable to passions as far as belongs to that substance whereby He is God. So the Father is omnipotent, the Son omnipotent, and the Holy Spirit is omnipotent; yet not three omnipotents, but one omnipotent:[5] "For of Him are all things, and through Him are all things, and in Him are all things; to whom be glory."[6] Whatever, therefore, is spoken of God in respect to Himself, is both spoken singly of each person, that is, of the Father, and the Son, and the Holy Spirit; and together of the Trinity itself, not plurally but in the singular. For inasmuch as to God it is not one thing to be, and another thing to be great, but to Him it is the same thing to be, as it is to be great; therefore, as we do not say three essences, so we do not say three greatnesses, but one essence and one greatness. I say essence, which in Greek is called οὐσία, and which we call more usually substance.

10. They indeed use also the word hypostasis; but they intend to put a difference, I know not what, between οὐσία and hypostasis: so that most of ourselves who treat these things in the Greek language, are accustomed to say, μίαν οὐσίαν, τρεῖς ὑποστάσεις, or, in Latin, one essence, three substances.[7]

CHAP. 9.—THE THREE PERSONS NOT PROPERLY SO CALLED [IN A HUMAN SENSE].

But because with us the usage has already obtained, that by essence we understand the same thing which is understood by substance; we do not dare to say one essence, three substances, but one essence or substance and three persons: as many writers in Latin, who treat of these things, and are of authority, have said, in that they could not find any other more suitable way by which to enunciate in words that which they understood without words. For, in truth, as the Father is not the Son, and the Son is not the Father, and that Holy Spirit who is also called the gift of God is neither the Father nor the Son, certainly they are three. And so it is said plurally, "I and my Father are one."[8] For He has not said, "is one," as the Sabellians say; but, "are one." Yet, when the question is asked, What three? human language labors altogether under great poverty of speech. The answer, however, is given, three "persons," not that it might be [completely] spoken, but that it might not be left [wholly] unspoken.

CHAP. 10.—THOSE THINGS WHICH BELONG ABSOLUTELY TO GOD AS AN ESSENCE, ARE SPOKEN OF THE TRINITY IN THE SINGULAR, NOT IN THE PLURAL.

11. As, therefore, we do not say three essences, so we do not say three greatnesses, or three who are great. For in things which are great by partaking of greatness, to which it is one thing to *be*, and another to be *great*, as a great house, and a great mountain, and a great mind; in these things, I say, greatness is one thing, and that which is great because of greatness is another, and a great house, certainly, is not absolute greatness itself. But that is absolute greatness by which not only a great house is great, and any great mountain is great, but also by which every other thing whatsoever is great, which is called great; so that greatness itself is one thing, and those things are another which are called great from it. And this greatness certainly is primarily great, and in a much more excellent way than those things which are great by partaking of it. But since God is not great with that greatness which is not Himself, so that God, in being great, is, as it were, partaker of that greatness;—otherwise that will be a greatness greater than God, whereas there is nothing greater than God; therefore, He is great with that greatness by which He Himself *is* that same greatness. And, therefore, as we do not say three essences, so neither do we say three greatnesses; for it is the same thing to God to be, and to be great. For the same reason neither

---

[1] Ps. lxxx. 1. [2] Ps. civ. 6. [3] Ps. cii. 27. [4] Ps. cxxxix. 8.
[5] [This phraseology appears in the analytical statements of the so-called Athanasian creed (cap. 11-16), and affords ground for the opinion that this symbol is a Western one, originating in the school of Augustin.—W. G. T. S.]
[6] Rom. xi. 36.
[7] [It is remarkable that Augustin, understanding thoroughly the distinction between essence and person, should not have known the difference between οὐσία and ὑπόστασις. It would seem as if his only moderate acquaintance with the Greek language would have been more than compensated by his profound trinitarian knowledge.
In respect to the term "*substantia*"—when it was discriminated from "*essentia*," as it is here by Augustin—it corresponds to ὑπόστασις, of which it is the translation. In this case, God is one essence in three substances. But when "*substantia*" was identified with "*essentia*," then to say that God is one essence in three substances would be a self-contradiction. The identification of the two terms led subsequently to the coinage, in the mediæval Latin, of the term "*subsistantia*," to denote ὑπόστασις.—W. G. T. S.]

[8] John x. 30.

do we say three greats, but one who is great; since God is not great by partaking of greatness, but He is great by Himself being great, because He Himself is His own greatness. Let the same be said also of the goodness, and of the eternity, and of the omnipotence of God, and, in short, of all the predicaments which can be predicated of God, as He is spoken of in respect to Himself, not metaphorically and by similitude, but properly, if indeed anything can be spoken of Him properly, by the mouth of man.

CHAP. 11.—WHAT IS SAID RELATIVELY IN THE TRINITY.

12. But whereas, in the same Trinity, some things severally are specially predicated, these are in no way said in reference to themselves in themselves, but either in mutual reference, or in respect to the creature; and, therefore, it is manifest that such things are spoken relatively, not in the way of substance. For the Trinity is called one God, great, good, eternal, omnipotent; and the same God Himself may be called His own deity, His own magnitude, His own goodness, His own eternity, His own omnipotence: but the Trinity cannot in the same way be called the Father, except perhaps metaphorically, in respect to the creature, on account of the adoption of sons. For that which is written, "Hear, O Israel: the Lord our God is one Lord,"[1] ought certainly not to be understood as if the Son were excepted, or the Holy Spirit were excepted; which one Lord our God we rightly call also our Father, as regenerating us by His grace. Neither can the Trinity in any wise be called the Son, but it can be called, in its entirety, the Holy Spirit, according to that which is written, "God is a Spirit;"[2] because both the Father is a spirit and the Son is a spirit, and the Father is holy and the Son is holy. Therefore, since the Father, the Son and the Holy Spirit are one God, and certainly God is holy, and God is a spirit, the Trinity can be called also the Holy Spirit. But yet that Holy Spirit, who is not the Trinity, but is understood as in the Trinity, is spoken of in His proper name of the Holy Spirit relatively, since He is referred both to the Father and to the Son, because the Holy Spirit is the Spirit both of the Father and of the Son. But the relation is not itself apparent in that name, but it is apparent when He is called the gift of God;[3] for He is the gift of the Father and of the Son, because "He proceeds from the Father,"[4] as

the Lord says; and because that which the apostle says, "Now, if any man have not the Spirit of Christ, he is none of His,"[5] he says certainly of the Holy Spirit Himself. When we say, therefore, the gift of the giver, and the giver of the gift, we speak in both cases relatively in reciprocal reference. Therefore the Holy Spirit is a certain unutterable communion of the Father and the Son; and on that account, perhaps, He is so called, because the same name is suitable to both the Father and the Son. For He Himself is called specially that which they are called in common; because both the Father is a spirit and the Son a spirit, both the Father is holy and the Son holy.[6] In order, therefore, that the communion of both may be signified from a name which is suitable to both, the Holy Spirit is called the gift of both. And this Trinity is one God, alone, good, great, eternal, omnipotent; itself its own unity, deity, greatness, goodness, eternity, omnipotence.

CHAP. 12.—IN RELATIVE THINGS THAT ARE RECIPROCAL, NAMES ARE SOMETIMES WANTING.

13. Neither ought it to influence us—since we have said that the Holy Spirit is so called relatively, not the Trinity itself, but He who is in the Trinity—that the designation of Him to whom He is referred, does not seem to answer in turn to His designation. For we cannot, as we say the servant of a master, and the master of a servant, the son of a father and the father of a son, so also say here—because these things are said relatively. For we speak of the Holy Spirit of the Father; but, on the other hand, we do not speak of the Father of the Holy Spirit, lest the Holy Spirit should be understood to be His Son. So also we speak of the Holy Spirit of the Son; but we do not speak of the Son of the

[5] Rom. viii. 9.
[6] [The reason which Augustin here assigns, why the name Holy Spirit is given to the third person—namely, because spirituality is a characteristic of both the Father and Son, from both of whom he proceeds—is not that assigned in the more developed trinitarianism. The explanation in this latter is, that the third person is denominated the Spirit because of the peculiar manner in which the divine essence is *communicated* to him—namely, by *spiration*, or outbreathing: *spiritus quia spiratus.* This is supported by the etymological signification of πνεῦμα, which is breath; and by the symbolical action of Christ in John xx. 22, which suggests the eternal spiration, or out-breathing of the third person. The third trinitarian person is no more spiritual, in the sense of immaterial, than the first and second persons, and if the term "Spirit" is to be taken in this the ordinary signification, the "trinitarian relation," or personal peculiarity, as Augustin remarks, "is not itself apparent in this name;" because it would mention nothing distinctive of the third person, and not belonging to the first and second. But taken technically to denote the spiration or out-breathing by the Father and Son, the trinitarian peculiarity is apparent in the name.
   And the epithet "Holy" is similarly explained. The third person is the *Holy* Spirit, not because he is any more holy than the first and second, but because he is the *source* and *author* of holiness in all created spirits. This is eminently and officially his work. In this way also, the epithet "Holy"—which in its ordinary use would specify nothing peculiar to the third person,—mentions a characteristic that differentiates him from the Father and Son.— W. G. T. S.]

[1] Deut. vi. 4.   [2] John iv. 24.
[3] Acts viii. 20.   [4] John xv. 26.

Holy Spirit, lest the Holy Spirit be understood to be His Father. For it is the case in many relatives, that no designation is to be found by which those things which bear relation to each other may [in name] mutually correspond to each other. For what is more clearly spoken relatively than the word earnest? Since it is referred to that of which it is an earnest, and an earnest is always an earnest of something. Can we, then, as we say, the earnest of the Father and of the Son,[1] say in turn, the Father of the earnest or the Son of the earnest? But, on the other hand, when we say the gift of the Father and of the Son, we cannot indeed say the Father of the gift, or the Son of the gift; but that these may correspond mutually to each other, we say the gift of the giver and the giver of the gift; because here a word in use may be found, there it cannot.

CHAP. 13.—HOW THE WORD BEGINNING (PRINCIPIUM) IS SPOKEN RELATIVELY IN THE TRINITY.

14. The Father is called so, therefore, relatively, and He is also relatively said to be the Beginning, and whatever else there may be of the kind; but He is called the Father in relation to the Son, the Beginning in relation to all things, which are from Him. So the Son is relatively so called; He is called also relatively the Word and the Image. And in all these appellations He is referred to the Father, but the Father is called by none of them. And the Son is also called the Beginning; for when it was said to Him, "Who art Thou?" He replied, "Even the Beginning, who also speak to you."[2] But is He, pray, the Beginning of the Father? For He intended to show Himself to be the Creator when He said that He was the Beginning, as the Father also is the beginning of the creature in that all things are from Him. For creator, too, is spoken relatively to creature, as master to servant. And so, when we say, both that the Father is the Beginning, and that the Son is the Beginning, we do not speak of two beginnings of the creature; since both the Father and the Son together is one beginning in respect to the creature, as one Creator, as one God. But if whatever remains within itself and produces or works anything is a beginning to that thing which it produces or works; then we cannot deny that the Holy Spirit also is rightly called the Beginning, since we do not separate Him from the appellation of Creator: and it is written of Him that He works; and

assuredly, in working, He remains within Himself; for He Himself is not changed and turned into any of the things which He works. And see what it is that He works: "But the manifestation of the Spirit," he says, "is given to every man to profit withal. For to one is given by the Spirit the word of wisdom; to another the word of knowledge by the same Spirit; to another faith by the same Spirit; to another the gifts of healing by the same Spirit; to another the working of miracles; to another prophecy; to another the discerning of spirits; to another divers kinds of tongues; to another the interpretation of tongues: but all these worketh that one and the self-same Spirit, dividing to every man severally as He will;" certainly as God—for who can work such great things but God?—but "it is the same God which worketh all in all."[3] For if we are asked point by point concerning the Holy Spirit, we answer most truly that He is God; and with the Father and the Son together He is one God. Therefore, God is spoken of as one Beginning in respect to the creature, not as two or three beginnings.

CHAP. 14.—THE FATHER AND THE SON THE ONLY BEGINNING (PRINCIPIUM) OF THE HOLY SPIRIT.

15. But in their mutual relation to one another in the Trinity itself, if the begetter is a beginning in relation to that which he begets, the Father is a beginning in relation to the Son, because He begets Him; but whether the Father is also a beginning in relation to the Holy Spirit, since it is said, "He proceeds from the Father," is no small question. Because, if it is so, He will not only be a beginning to that thing which He begets or makes, but also to that which He gives. And here, too, that question comes to light, as it can, which is wont to trouble many, Why the Holy Spirit is not also a son, since He, too, comes forth from the Father, as it is read in the Gospel.[4] For the Spirit came forth, not as born, but as given; and so He is not called a son, because He was neither born, as the Only-begotten, nor made, so that by the grace of God He might be born into adoption, as we are. For that which is born of the Father, is referred to the Father only when called Son, and so the Son is the Son of the Father, and not also our Son; but that which is given is referred both to Him who gave, and to those to whom He gave; and so the Holy Spirit is not only the Spirit of the Father and of the Son who gave Him, but

---

[1] 2 Cor. v. 5, and Eph. i. 14.   [2] John viii. 25.   [3] 1 Cor. xii. 6-11.   [4] John xv. 26.

He is also called ours, who have received Him: as "The salvation of the Lord,"[1] who gives salvation, is said also to be our salvation, who have received it. Therefore, the Spirit is both the Spirit of God who gave Him, and ours who have received Him. Not, indeed, that spirit of ours by which we are, because that is the spirit of a man which is in him; but this Spirit is ours in another mode, *viz.* that in which we also say, "Give us this day our bread."[2] Although certainly we have received that spirit also, which is called the spirit of a man. "For what hast thou," he says, "which thou didst not receive?"[3] But that is one thing, which we have received that we might be; another, that which we have received that we might be holy. Whence it is also written of John, that he "came in the spirit and power of Elias;"[4] and by the spirit of Elias is meant the Holy Spirit, whom Elias received. And the same thing is to be understood of Moses, when the Lord says to him, "And I will take of thy spirit, and will put it upon them;"[5] that is, I will give to them of the Holy Spirit, which I have already given to thee. If, therefore, that also which is given has him for a beginning by whom it is given, since it has received from no other source that which proceeds from him; it must be admitted that the Father and the Son are a Beginning of the Holy Spirit, not two Beginnings; but as the Father and Son are one God, and one Creator, and one Lord relatively to the creature, so are they one Beginning relatively to the Holy Spirit. But the Father, the Son, and the Holy Spirit is one Beginning in respect to the creature, as also one Creator and one God.[6]

CHAP. 15.—WHETHER THE HOLY SPIRIT WAS A GIFT BEFORE AS WELL AS AFTER HE WAS GIVEN.

16. But it is asked further, whether, as the

[1] Ps. iii. 8.   [2] Matt. vi. 11.   [3] 1 Cor. iv. 7.
[4] Luke i. 17.   [5] Num. xi. 17.
[6] [The term "beginning" (*principium*), when referring to the relation of the Trinity, or of any person of the Trinity, to the creature, denotes *creative* energy, whereby a new substance is originated from nothing. This is the reference in chapter 13. But when the term refers to the relations of the persons of the Trinity to each other, it denotes only a *modifying* energy, whereby an existing uncreated substance is communicated by generation and spiration. This is the reference in chapter 14.
When it is said that the Father is the "beginning" of the Son, and the Father and Son are the "beginning" of the Spirit, it is not meant that the substance of the Son is created *ex nihilo* by the Father, and the substance of the Spirit is created by the Father and Son, but only that the Son by eternal generation receives from the Father the one uncreated and undivided substance of the Godhead, and the Spirit by eternal spiration receives the same numerical substance from the Father and Son. The term "beginning" relates not to the essence, but to the personal peculiarity. Sonship originates in fatherhood; but deity is unoriginated. The Son as the second person "begins" from the Father, because the Father communicates the essence to him. His sonship, not his deity or godhood, "begins" from the Father. And the same holds true of the

Son, by being born, has not only this, that He is the Son, but that He is absolutely; and so also the Holy Spirit, by being given, has not only this, that He is given, but that He is absolutely—whether therefore He was, before He was given, but was not yet a *gift*; or whether, for the very reason that God was about to give Him, He was already a gift also before He was given. But if He does not proceed unless when He is given, and assuredly could not proceed before there was one to whom He might be given; how, in that case, was He [absolutely] in His very substance, if He is not unless because He is given? just as the Son, by being born, not only has this, that He is a Son, which is said relatively, but His very substance absolutely, so that He is. Does the Holy Spirit proceed always, and proceed not in time, but from eternity, but because He so proceeded that He was capable of being given, was already a gift even before there was one to whom He might be given? For there is a difference in meaning between a gift and a thing that has been given. For a gift may exist even before it is given; but it cannot be called a thing that has been given unless it has been given.

CHAP. 16.—WHAT IS SAID OF GOD IN TIME, IS SAID RELATIVELY, NOT ACCIDENTALLY.

17. Nor let it trouble us that the Holy Spirit, although He is co-eternal with the Father and the Son, yet is called something which exists in time; as, for instance, this very thing which we have called Him, a thing that has been given. For the Spirit is a gift eternally, but a thing that has been given in time. For if a lord also is not so called unless when he begins to have a slave, that appellation likewise is relative and in time to God; for the creature is not from all eternity, of which He is the Lord. How then shall we make it good that relative terms themselves are not accidental, since nothing happens accidentally to God in time, because He is incapable of change, as we have argued in the beginning of this discussion? Behold! to be the Lord, is not eternal to God; otherwise we should be compelled to say that the creature also is from eternity, since He would not be a lord from all eternity unless the creature also was a servant from all eternity. But as he cannot be a slave who has not a lord, neither can he be a lord who has not a slave. And if there be any one who says that God, indeed, is alone eternal, and that times are

term "beginning" as applied to the Holy Spirit. The "procession" of the Holy Spirit "begins" by spiration from the Father and Son, but not his deity or godhood.—W. G. T. S.]

not eternal on account of their variety and changeableness, but that times nevertheless did not begin to be in time (for there was no time before times began, and therefore it did not happen to God in time that He should be Lord, since He was Lord of the very times themselves, which assuredly did not begin in time): what will he reply respecting man, who was made in time, and of whom assuredly He was not the Lord before he was of whom He was to be Lord? Certainly to be the Lord of man happened to God in time. And that all dispute may seem to be taken away, certainly to be your Lord, or mine, who have only lately begun to be, happened to God in time. Or if this, too, seems uncertain on account of the obscure question respecting the soul, what is to be said of His being the Lord of the people of Israel? since, although the nature of the soul already existed, which that people had (a matter into which we do not now inquire), yet that people existed not as yet, and the time is apparent when it began to exist. Lastly, that He should be Lord of this or that tree, or of this or that corn crop, which only lately began to be, happened in time; since, although the matter itself already existed, yet it is one thing to be Lord of the matter (*materiæ*), another to be Lord of the already created nature (*naturæ*).[1] For man, too, is lord of the wood at one time, and at another he is lord of the chest, although fabricated of that same wood; which he certainly was not at the time when he was already the lord of the wood. How then shall we make it good that nothing is said of God according to accident, except because nothing happens to His nature by which He may be changed, so that those things are relative accidents which happen in connection with some change of the things of which they are spoken. As a friend is so called relatively: for he does not begin to be one, unless when he has begun to love; therefore some change of will takes place, in order that he may be called a friend. And money, when it is called a price, is spoken of relatively, and yet it was not changed when it began to be a price; nor, again, when it is called a pledge, or any other thing of the kind. If, therefore, money can so often be spoken of relatively with no change of itself, so that neither when it begins, nor when it

ceases to be so spoken of, does any change take place in that nature or form of it, whereby it is money; how much more easily ought we to admit, concerning that unchangeable substance of God, that something may be so predicated relatively in respect to the creature, that although it begin to be so predicated in time, yet nothing shall be understood to have happened to the substance itself of God, but only to that creature in respect to which it is predicated? "Lord," it is said, "Thou hast been made our refuge."[2] God, therefore, is said to be our refuge relatively, for He is referred to us, and He then becomes our refuge when we flee to Him; pray does anything come to pass then in His nature, which, before we fled to Him, was not? In us therefore some change does take place; for we were worse before we fled to Him, and we become better by fleeing to Him: but in Him there is no change. So also He begins to be our Father, when we are regenerated through His grace, since He gave us power to become the sons of God.[3] Our substance therefore is changed for the better, when we become His sons; and He at the same time begins to be our Father, but without any change of His own substance. Therefore that which begins to be spoken of God in time, and which was not spoken of Him before, is manifestly spoken of Him relatively; yet not according to any accident of God, so that anything should have happened to Him, but clearly according to some accident of that, in respect to which God begins to be called something relatively. When a righteous man begins to be a friend of God, he himself is changed; but far be it from us to say, that God loves any one in time with as it were a new love, which was not in Him before, with whom things gone by have not passed away and things future have been already done. Therefore He loved all His saints before the foundation of the world, as He predestinated them; but when they are converted and find Him, then they are said to begin to be loved by Him, that what is said may be said in that way in which it can be comprehended by human affections. So also, when He is said to be wroth with the unrighteous, and gentle with the good, they are changed, not He: just as the light is troublesome to weak eyes, pleasant to those that are strong; namely, by their change, not its own.

---

[1] ["Matter" denotes the material as created *ex nihilo;* "nature" the material as formed into individuals. In this reference, Augustin speaks of "the nature of the soul" of the people of Israel as existing while "as yet that people existed not" individually—having in mind their race-existence in Adam.—W. G. T. S.

[2] Ps. xc. 1.　　　　[3] John i. 12.

BOOK VI.

THE QUESTION IS PROPOSED, HOW THE APOSTLE CALLS CHRIST "THE POWER OF GOD, AND THE WISDOM OF GOD." AND AN ARGUMENT IS RAISED, WHETHER THE FATHER IS NOT WISDOM HIMSELF, BUT ONLY THE FATHER OF WISDOM ; OR WHETHER WISDOM BEGAT WISDOM. BUT THE ANSWER TO THIS IS DEFERRED FOR A LITTLE, WHILE THE UNITY AND EQUALITY OF THE FATHER, AND OF THE SON, AND OF THE HOLY GHOST, ARE PROVED ; AND THAT WE OUGHT TO BELIEVE IN A TRINITY, NOT IN A THREEFOLD (TRIPLICEM) GOD. LASTLY, THAT SAYING OF HILARY IS EXPLAINED, ETERNITY IN THE FATHER, APPEARANCE IN THE IMAGE, USE IN THE GIFT.

CHAP. I.—THE SON, ACCORDING TO THE APOSTLE, IS THE POWER AND WISDOM OF THE FATHER. HENCE THE REASONING OF THE CATHOLICS AGAINST THE EARLIER ARIANS. A DIFFICULTY IS RAISED, WHETHER THE FATHER IS NOT WISDOM HIMSELF, BUT ONLY THE FATHER OF WISDOM.

1. Some think themselves hindered from admitting the equality of the Father, Son, and Holy Spirit, because it is written, " Christ, the power of God, and the wisdom of God;" in that, on this ground, there does not appear to be equality; because the Father is not Himself power and wisdom, but the begetter of power and wisdom. And, in truth, the question is usually asked with no common earnestness, in what way God can be called the Father of power and wisdom. For the apostle says, "Christ the power of God, and the wisdom of God."[1] And hence some on our side have reasoned in this way against the Arians, at least against those who at first set themselves up against the Catholic faith. For Arius himself is reported to have said, that if He is a Son, then He was born; if He was born, there was a time when the Son was not: not understanding that even to be born is, to God, from all eternity; so that the Son is co-eternal with the Father, as the brightness which is produced and is spread around by fire is co-eval with it, and would be co-eternal, if fire were eternal. And therefore some of the later Arians have abandoned that opinion, and have confessed that the Son of

God did not begin to be in time. But among the arguments which those on our side used to hold against them who said that there was a time when the Son was not, some were wont to introduce such an argument as this: If the Son of God is the power and wisdom of God, and God was never without power and wisdom, then the Son is co-eternal with God the Father; but the apostle says, "Christ the power of God, and the wisdom of God;" and a man must be senseless to say that God at any time had not power or wisdom; therefore there was no time when the Son was not.

2. Now this argument compels us to say that God the Father is not wise, except by having the wisdom which He begat, not by the Father in Himself being wisdom itself. Further, if it be so, just as the Son also Himself is called God of God, Light of Light, we must consider whether He can be called wisdom of wisdom, if God the Father is not wisdom itself, but only the begetter of wisdom. And if we hold this, why is He not the begetter also of His own greatness, and of His own goodness, and of His own eternity, and of His own omnipotence; so that He is not Himself His own greatness, and His own goodness, and His own eternity, and His own omnipotence; but is great with that greatness which He begat, and good with that goodness, and eternal with that eternity, and omnipotent with that omnipotence, which was born of Him; just as He Himself is not His own wisdom, but is wise with that wisdom which was born of Him? For we need not be afraid of being compelled to say

[1] 1 Cor. i. 24.

7

that there are many sons of God, over and above the adoption of the creature, co-eternal with the Father, if He be the begetter of His own greatness, and goodness, and eternity, and omnipotence. Because it is easy to reply to this cavil, that it does not at all follow, because many things are named, that He should be the Father of many co-eternal *sons;* just as it does not follow that He is the Father of two sons, because Christ is said to be the power of God, and the wisdom of God. For that certainly is the power which is the wisdom, and that is the wisdom which is the power; and in like manner, therefore, of the rest also; so that that is the greatness which is the power, or any other of those things which either have been mentioned above, or may hereafter be mentioned.

CHAP. 2.— WHAT IS SAID OF THE FATHER AND SON TOGETHER, AND WHAT NOT.

3. But if nothing is spoken of the Father as such, except that which is spoken of Him in relation to the Son, that is, that He is His father, or begetter, or beginning; and if also the begetter is by consequence a beginning to that which he begets of himself; but whatever else is spoken of Him is so spoken as *with* the Son, or rather *in* the Son; whether that He is great with that greatness which He begat, or just with that justice which He begat, or good with that goodness which He begat, or powerful with that force or power which He begat, or wise with that wisdom which He begat: yet the Father is not said to be greatness itself, but the begetter of greatness; but the Son, as He is called the Son as such, is not so called *with* the Father but in relation *to* the Father, so is not great in and by himself, but *with* the Father, of whom He is the greatness; and so also is called wise *with* the Father, of whom He Himself is the wisdom; just as the Father is called wise *with* the Son, because He is wise with that wisdom which He begat; therefore the one is not called without the other, whatever they are called in respect to themselves; that is, whatever they are called that manifests their essential nature, both are so called together;—if these things are so, then the Father is not God without the Son, nor the Son God without the Father, but both together are God. And that which is said, " In the beginning was the Word," means that the Word was in the Father, Or if " In the beginning" is intended to mean, Before all things; then in that which follows, "And the Word was with God," the Son alone is understood to be the Word, not the Father and

Son together, as though both were one Word (for He is the Word in the same way as He is the Image, but the Father and Son are not both together the Image, but the Son alone is the Image of the Father: just as He is also the Son of the Father, for both together are not the Son). But in that which is added, "And the Word was with God," there is much reason to understand thus: " The Word," which is the Son alone, "was with God," which is not the Father alone, but God the Father and the Son together.[1] But what wonder is there, if this can be said in the case of some twofold things widely different from each other? For what are so different as soul and body? Yet we can say the soul was with a man, that is, in a man; although the soul is not the body, and man is both soul and body together. So that what follows in the Scripture, "And the Word was God,"[2] may be understood thus: The Word, which is not the Father, was God together with the Father. Are we then to say thus, that the Father is the begetter of His own greatness, that is, the begetter of His own power, or the begetter of His own wisdom; and that the Son is greatness, and power, and wisdom; but that the great, omnipotent, and wise God, is both together? How then God *of* God, Light of Light? For not both together are God of God, but only the Son is of God, that is to say, of the Father; nor are both together Light of Light, but the Son only is of Light, that is, of the Father. Unless, perhaps, it was in order to intimate and inculcate briefly that the Son is co-eternal with the Father, that it is said, God of God, and Light of Light, or anything else of the like kind: as if to say, This which is not the Son without the Father, *of* this which is not the Father without the Son; that is, this Light which is not Light without the Father, *of* that Light, *viz.* the Father, which is not Light without the Son; so that, when it is said, God which is not the Son without the Father, and *of* God which is not the Father without the Son, it may be perfectly understood that the Begetter did not precede that which He begot. And if this be so, then this alone cannot be said of them, namely, this or that of this or that, which they are not both together. Just as the Word cannot be said to be *of* the

---

[1] [The term " God," in the proposition, " the Word was with God," must refer to the Father, not to " the Father and Son together," because the Son could not be said to be " with " himself. St. John says that " the word was God " (θεòς). The absence of the article with θεòς denotes the abstract deity, or the divine nature without reference to the persons in it. He also says that " the Word was with God " (τòν θεòν). The presence of the article in this instance denotes one of the divine persons in the essence: namely, the Father, with whom the Word was from eternity, and upon whose " bosom " he was from eternity. (John i. 18).—W. G. T. S.] [2] John i. 1.

Word, because both are not the Word together, but only the Son; nor image *of* image, since they are not both together the image; nor Son *of* Son, since both together are not the Son, according to that which is said, " I and my Father are one." [1] For "we are one " means, what He is, that am I also; according to essence, not according to relation.

CHAP. 3.—THAT THE UNITY OF THE ESSENCE OF THE FATHER AND THE SON IS TO BE GATHERED FROM THE WORDS, "WE ARE ONE." THE SON IS EQUAL TO THE FATHER BOTH IN WISDOM AND IN ALL OTHER THINGS.

4. And I know not whether the words, "They are one," are ever found in Scripture as spoken of things of which the nature is different. But if there are more things than one of the same nature, and they differ in sentiment, they are not one, and that so far as they differ in sentiment. For if the disciples were already one by the fact of being men, He would not say, " That they may be one, as we are one," [2] when commending them to the Father. But because Paul and Apollos were both alike men, and also of like sentiments, "He that planteth," he says, "and he that watereth are one." [3] When, therefore, anything is so called one, that it is not added in what it is one, and yet more things than one are called one, then the same essence and nature is signified, not differing nor disagreeing. But when it is added in what it is one, it may be meant that something is made one out of things more than one, though they are different in nature. As soul and body are assuredly not one; for what are so different? unless there be added or understood in what they are one, that is, one man, or one animal [person]. Thence the apostle says, " He who is joined to a harlot, is one body;" he does not say, they are one or he is one; but he has added "body," as though it were one body composed by being joined together of two different bodies, masculine and feminine. [4] And, "He that is joined unto the Lord," he says, "is one spirit:" he did not say, he that is joined unto the Lord is one, or they are one; but he added, "spirit" For the spirit of man and the Spirit of God are different in nature; but by being joined they become one spirit of two different spirits, so that the Spirit of God is blessed and perfect without the human spirit, but the spirit of man cannot be blessed without God. Nor is it without cause, I think, that when the Lord said so much in the Gospel according to John, and so often, of unity itself, whether of His own with the Father, or of ours interchangeably with ourselves; He has nowhere said, that we are also one with Himself, but, "that they may be one as we also are one." [5] Therefore the Father and the Son are one, undoubtedly according to unity of substance; and there is one God, and one great, and one wise, as we have argued.

5. Whence then is the Father greater? For if greater, He is greater by greatness; but whereas the Son is His greatness, neither assuredly is the Son greater than He who begat Him, nor is the Father greater than that greatness, whereby He is great; therefore they are equal. For whence is He equal, if not in that which He is, to whom it is not one thing to be, and another to be great? Or if the Father is greater in eternity, the Son is not equal in anything whatsoever. For whence equal? If you say in greatness, that greatness is not equal which is less eternal, and so of all things else. Or is He perhaps equal in power, but not equal in wisdom? But how is that power which is less wise, equal? Or is He equal in wisdom, but not equal in power? But how is that wisdom equal which is less powerful? It remains, therefore, that if He is not equal in anything, He is not equal in all. But Scripture proclaims, that " He thought it not robbery to be equal with God." [6] Therefore any adversary of the truth whatever, provided he feels bound by apostolical authority, must needs confess that the Son is equal with God in each one thing whatsoever. Let him choose that which he will; from it he will be shown, that He is equal in all things which are said of His substance.

CHAP. 4.—THE SAME ARGUMENT CONTINUED.

6. For in like manner the virtues which are in the human mind, although each has its own several and different meaning, yet are in no way mutually separable; so that, for instance, whosoever were equal in courage, are equal also in prudence, and temperance, and justice. For if you say that such and such men are equal in courage, but that one of them is greater in prudence, it follows that the courage of the other is less prudent, and so neither are they equal in courage, since the courage of the former is more prudent. And so you will find it to be the case with the other virtues, if you consider them one by one. For the question is not of the strength of the body, but of the courage of

---

[1] John x. 30.
[3] 1 Cor. iii. 8.
[2] John xvii. 11.
[4] 1 Cor. vi. 16, 17.
[5] John xvii. 11.
[6] Phil. ii. 6.

the mind.   How much more therefore is this the case in that unchangeable and eternal substance, which is incomparably more simple than the human mind is? Since, in the human mind, to be is not the same as to be strong, or prudent, or just, or temperate; for a mind can exist, and yet have none of these virtues. But in God to be is the same as to be strong, or to be just, or to be wise, or whatever is said of that simple multiplicity, or multifold simplicity, whereby to signify His substance. Wherefore, whether we say God of God in such way that this name belongs to each, yet not so that both together are two Gods, but one God; for they are in such way united with each other, as according to the apostle's testimony may take place even in diverse and differing substances; for both the Lord alone is a Spirit, and the spirit of a man alone is assuredly a spirit; yet, if it cleave to the Lord, "it is one spirit:" how much more there, where there is an absolutely inseparable and eternal union, so that He may not seem absurdly to be called as it were the Son of both, when He is called the Son of God, if that which is called God is only said of both together.   Or perhaps it is, that whatever is said of God so as to indicate His substance, is not said except of both together, nay of the Trinity itself together?   Whether therefore it be this or that (which needs a closer inquiry), it is enough for the present to see from what has been said, that the Son is in no respect equal with the Father, if He is found to be unequal in anything which has to do with signifying His substance, as we have already shown. But the apostle has said that He is equal.   Therefore the Son is equal with the Father in all things, and is of one and the same substance.

CHAP. 5.—THE HOLY SPIRIT ALSO IS EQUAL TO THE FATHER AND THE SON IN ALL THINGS.

7. Wherefore also the Holy Spirit consists in the same unity of substance, and in the same equality.   For whether He is the unity of both, or the holiness, or the love, or therefore the unity because the love, and therefore the love because the holiness, it is manifest that He is not one of the two, through whom the two are joined, through whom the Begotten is loved by the Begetter, and loves Him that begat Him, and through whom, not by participation, but by their own essence, neither by the gift of any superior, but by their own, they are "keeping the unity of the Spirit in the bond of peace;"[1] which we are commanded to imitate by grace, both towards

God and towards ourselves.   "On which two commandments hang all the law and the prophets."[2]   So those three are God, one, alone, great, wise, holy, blessed.   But we are blessed from Him, and through Him, and in Him; because we ourselves are one by His gift, and one spirit with Him, because our soul cleaves to Him so as to follow Him. And it is good for us to cleave to God, since He will destroy every man who is estranged from Him.[3]   Therefore the Holy Spirit, whatever it is, is something common both to the Father and Son.   But that communion itself is consubstantial and co-eternal; and if it may fitly be called friendship, let it be so called; but it is more aptly called love.   And this is also a substance, since God is a substance, and "God is love," as it is written.[4] But as He is a substance together with the Father and the Son, so that substance is together with them great, and together with them good, and together with them holy, and whatsoever else is said in reference to substance; since it is not one thing to God to be, and another to be great or to be good, and the rest, as we have shown above. For if love is less great therein [i.e. in God] than wisdom, then wisdom is loved in less degree than according to what it is; love is therefore equal, in order that wisdom may be loved according to its being; but wisdom is equal with the Father, as we have proved above; therefore also the Holy Spirit is equal; and if equal, equal in all things, on account of the absolute simplicity which is in that substance.   And therefore they are not more than three: One who loves Him who is from Himself, and One who loves Him from whom He is, and Love itself.   And if this last is nothing, how is "God love"? If it is not substance, how is God substance?

CHAP. 6. — HOW GOD IS A SUBSTANCE BOTH SIMPLE AND MANIFOLD.

8. But if it is asked how that substance is both simple and manifold: consider, first, why the creature is manifold, but in no way really simple.   And first, all that is body is composed certainly of parts; so that therein one part is greater, another less, and the whole is greater than any part whatever or how great soever.   For the heaven and the earth are parts of the whole bulk of the world; and the earth alone, and the heaven alone, is composed of innumerable parts; and its third part is less than the remainder, and the half of it is less than the whole; and the whole body of the world, which is usually

---

called by its two parts, *viz.* the heaven and the earth, is certainly greater than the heaven alone or the earth alone. And in each several body, size is one thing, color another, shape another; for the same color and the same shape may remain with diminished size; and the same shape and the same size may remain with the color changed ; and the same shape not remaining, yet the thing may be just as great, and of the same color. And whatever other things are predicated together of body can be changed either all together, or the larger part of them without the rest. And hence the nature of body is conclusively proved to be manifold, and in no respect simple. The spiritual creature also, that is, the soul, is indeed the more simple of the two if compared with the body; but if we omit the comparison with the body, it is manifold, and itself also not simple. For it is on this account more simple than the body, because it is not diffused in bulk through extension of place, but in each body, it is both whole in the whole, and whole in each several part of it; and, therefore, when anything takes place in any small particle whatever of the body, such as the soul can feel, although it does not take place in the whole body, yet the whole soul feels it, since the whole soul is not unconscious of it. But, nevertheless, since in the soul also it is one thing to be skillful, another to be indolent, another to be intelligent, another to be of retentive memory; since cupidity is one thing, fear another, joy another, sadness another; and since things innumerable, and in innumerable ways, are to be found in the nature of the soul, some without others, and some more, some less; it is manifest that its nature is not simple, but manifold. For nothing simple is changeable, but every creature is changeable.

CHAP. 7.—GOD IS A TRINITY, BUT NOT TRIPLE (TRIPLEX).

But God is truly called in manifold ways, great, good, wise, blessed, true, and whatsoever other thing seems to be said of Him not unworthily: but His greatness is the same as His wisdom; for He is not great by bulk, but by power; and His goodness is the same as His wisdom and greatness, and His truth the same as all those things; and in Him it is not one thing to be blessed, and another to be great, or wise, or true, or good, or in a word to be Himself.

9. Neither, since He is a Trinity, is He therefore to be thought triple (*triplex*)[1] other-

wise the Father alone, or the Son alone, will be less than the Father and Son together. Although, indeed, it is hard to see how we can say, either the Father alone, or the Son alone; since both the Father is with the Son, and the Son with the Father, always and inseparably: not that both are the Father, or both are the Son; but because they are always one in relation to the other, and neither the one nor the other alone. But because we call even the Trinity itself God alone, although He is always with holy spirits and souls, but say that He only is God, because they are not also God with Him; so we call the Father the Father alone, not because He is separate from the Son, but because they are not both together the Father.

CHAP. 8.—NO ADDITION CAN BE MADE TO THE NATURE OF GOD.

Since, therefore, the Father alone, or the Son alone, or the Holy Spirit alone, is as great as is the Father and the Son and the Holy Spirit together,[2] in no manner is He to be called threefold. Forasmuch as bodies increase by union of themselves. For although he who cleaves to his wife is one body; yet it is a greater body than if it were that of the husband alone, or of the wife alone. But in spiritual things, when the less adheres to the greater, as the creature to the Creator, the former becomes greater than it was, not the latter.[3] For in those things which are not great by bulk, to be greater is to be better. And the spirit of any creature becomes better, when it cleaves to the Creator, than if it did not so cleave; and therefore also greater because better. "He," then, "that is joined unto the Lord is one spirit:"[4] but yet the Lord does not therefore become

---

[1] [The Divine Unity is trinal, not triple. The triple is composed of three different substances. It has parts, and is complex. The trinal is without parts, and is incomplex. It denotes one simple substance in three modes or forms. "We may speak of the trinal, but not of the triple deity." Hollaz, in Hase's *Hutterus*, 172.—W. G. T. S.]

[2] [Each trinitarian person is as great as the Trinity, if reference be had to the essence, but not if reference be had to the persons. Each person has the entire essence, and the Trinity has the entire essence. But each person has the essence with only one personal characteristic; while the Trinity has the essence with all three personal characteristics. No trinitarian person is as comprehensive as the triune Godhead, because he does not possess the two personal characteristics belonging to the other two persons. The Father is God, but he is not God the Son and God the Holy Spirit. —W. G. T. S.]

[3] [The addition of finite numbers, however great, to an infinite number, does not increase the infinite. Similarly, any addition of finite being to the Infinite Being is no increase. God plus the universe is no larger an infinite than God minus the universe. The creation of the universe adds nothing to the infinite being and attributes of God. To add contingent being to necessary being, does not make the latter any more necessary. To add imperfect being to perfect being, does not make the latter more perfect. To add finite knowledge to infinite knowledge, does not produce a greater amount of knowledge. This truth has been overlooked by Hamilton, Mansell, and others, in the argument against the personality of the Infinite, in which the Infinite is confounded with the All, and which assumes that the All is greater than the Infinite —in other words, that God plus the universe is greater than God minus the universe.—W. G. T. S.]

[4] Cor. vi. 17.

greater, although he who is joined to the Lord does so. In God Himself, therefore, when the equal Son, or the Holy Spirit equal to the Father and the Son, is joined to the equal Father, God does not become greater than each of them severally; because that perfectness cannot increase. But whether t be the Father, or the Son, or the Holy Spirit He is perfect, and God the Father the Son and the Holy Spirit is perfect; and therefore He is a Trinity rather than triple.

CHAP. 9.—WHETHER ONE OR THE THREE PERSONS TOGETHER ARE CALLED THE ONLY GOD.

10. And since we are showing how we can say the Father alone, because there is no Father in the Godhead except Himself, we must consider also the opinion which holds that the only true God is not the Father alone, but the Father and the Son and the Holy Spirit. For if any one should ask whether the Father alone is God, how can it be replied that He is not, unless perhaps we were to say that the Father indeed is God, but that He is not God alone, but that the Father, Son, and Holy Spirit are God alone? But then what shall we do with that testimony of the Lord? For He was speaking to the Father, and had named the Father as Him to whom He was speaking, when He says, "And this is life eternal, that they may know Thee the one true God."[1] And this the Arians indeed usually take, as if the Son were not true God. Passing them by, however, we must see whether, when it is said to the Father, "That they may know Thee the one true God," we are forced to understand it as if He wished to intimate that the Father alone is the true God; lest we should not understand any to be God, except the three together, the Father, Son, and Holy Spirit. Are we therefore, from the testimony of the Lord, both to call the Father the one true God, and the Son the one true God, and the Holy Spirit the one true God, and the Father, the Son, and the Holy Spirit together, that is, the Trinity itself together, not three true Gods but one true God? Or because He added, "And Jesus Christ whom Thou hast sent," are we to supply "the one true God;" so that the order of the words is this, "That they may know Thee, and Jesus Christ whom Thou hast sent, the one true God?" Why then did He omit to mention the Holy Spirit? Is it because it follows, that whenever we name One who cleaves to One by a harmony so great that through this harmony both are one, this harmony itself must be understood,

although it is not mentioned? For in that place, too, the apostle seems as it were to pass over the Holy Spirit; and yet there, too, He is understood, where he says, "All are yours, and ye are Christ's, and Christ is God's."[2] And again, "The head of the woman is the man, the head of the man is Christ, and the head of Christ is God."[3] But again, if God is only all three together, how can God be the head of Christ, that is, the Trinity the head of Christ, since Christ is in the Trinity in order that it may be the Trinity? Is that which is the Father with the Son, the head of that which is the Son alone? For the Father with the Son is God, but the Son alone is Christ: especially since it is the Word already made flesh that speaks; and according to this His humiliation also, the Father is greater than He, as He says, "for my Father is greater than I;"[4] so that the very being of God, which is one to Him with the Father, is itself the head of the man who is mediator, which He is alone.[5] For if we rightly call the mind the chief thing of man, that is, as it were the head of the human substance, although the man himself together with the mind is man; why is not the Word with the Father, which together is God, much more suitably and much more the head of Christ, although Christ as man cannot be understood except with the Word which was made flesh? But this, as we have already said, we shall consider somewhat more carefully hereafter. At present the equality and one and the same substance of the Trinity has been demonstrated as briefly as possible, that in whatever way that other question be determined, the more rigorous discussion of which we have deferred, nothing may hinder us from confessing the absolute equality of the Father, Son, and Holy Spirit.

CHAP. X.—OF THE ATTRIBUTES ASSIGNED BY HILARY TO EACH PERSON. THE TRINITY IS REPRESENTED IN THINGS THAT ARE MADE.

11. A certain writer, when he would briefly intimate the special attributes of each of the persons in the Trinity, tells us that "Eternity is in the Father, form in the Image, use in the Gift." And since he was a man of no mean authority in handling the Scriptures, and in the assertion of the faith, for it is Hilary who put this in his book (*On the Trinity*, ii.); I have searched into the hidden meaning of these words as far as I can, that is, of the Father, and the Image, and the Gift, of eternity, and of form, and of use. And I do not think that he intended more by the word eter-

---

[1] John xvii. 3.
[2] 1 Cor. iii. 22, 23.
[3] 1 Cor. xi. 3.
[4] John xiv. 28.
[5] 1 Tim. ii. 5.

nity, than that the Father has not a father from whom He is; but the Son is from the Father, so as to be, and so as to be co-eternal with Him. For if an image perfectly fills the measure of that of which it is the image, then the image is made equal to that of which it is the image, not the latter to its own image. And in respect to this image he has named form, I believe on account of the quality of beauty, where there is at once such great fitness, and prime equality, and prime likeness, differing in nothing, and unequal in no respect, and in no part unlike, but answering exactly to Him whose image it is: where there is prime and absolute life, to whom it is not one thing to live, and another to be, but the same thing to be and to live; and prime and absolute intellect, to whom it is not one thing to live, another to understand, but to understand is to live, and is to be, and all things are one: as though a perfect Word (John i. 1), to which nothing is wanting, and a certain skill of the omnipotent and wise God, full of all living, unchangeable sciences, and all one in it, as itself is one from one, with whom it is one. Therein God knew all things which He made by it; and therefore, while times pass away and succeed, nothing passes away or succeeds to the knowledge of God. For things which are created are not therefore known by God, because they have been made; and not rather have been therefore made, even although changeable, because they are known unchangeably by Him. Therefore that unspeakable conjunction of the Father and His image is not without fruition, without love, without joy. Therefore that love, delight, felicity, or blessedness, if indeed it can be worthily expressed by any human word, is called by him, in short, Use; and is the Holy Spirit in the Trinity, not begotten, but the sweetness of the begetter and of the begotten, filling all creatures according to their capacity with abundant bountifulness and copiousness, that they may keep their proper order and rest satisfied in their proper place.

12. Therefore all these things which are made by divine skill, show in themselves a certain unity, and form, and order; for each of them is both some one thing, as are the several natures of bodies and dispositions of souls; and is fashioned in some form, as are the figures or qualities of bodies, and the various learning or skill of souls; and seeks or preserves a certain order, as are the several weights or combinations of bodies and the loves or delights of souls. When therefore we regard the Creator, who is understood by the things that are made[1] we must needs understand the Trinity of whom there appear traces in the creature, as is fitting. For in that Trinity is the supreme source of all things, and the most perfect beauty, and the most blessed delight. Those three, therefore, both seem to be mutually determined to each other, and are in themselves infinite. But here in corporeal things, one thing alone is not as much as three together, and two are something more than one; but in that highest Trinity one is as much as the three together, nor are two anything more than one. And They are infinite in themselves. So both each are in each, and all in each, and each in all, and all in all, and all are one. Let him who sees this, whether in part, or "through a glass and in an enigma,"[2] rejoice in knowing God; and let him honor Him as God, and give thanks; but let him who does not see it, strive to see it through piety, not to cavil at it through blindness. Since God is one, but yet is a Trinity. Neither are we to take the words, "of whom, and through whom, and to whom are all things," as used indiscriminately [*i.e.*, to denote a unity without distinctions]; nor yet to denote many gods, for "to *Him*, be glory for ever and ever. Amen."[3]

---

[1] Rom. i. 20.   [2] 1 Cor. xiii. 12. Darkly, A.V.
[3] Rom. xi. 36, in A.V.

BOOK VII.

THE QUESTION IS EXPLAINED, WHICH HAD BEEN DEFERRED IN THE PREVIOUS BOOK, VIZ. THAT GOD THE FATHER, WHO BEGAT THE SON, HIS POWER AND WISDOM, IS NOT ONLY THE FATHER OF POWER AND WISDOM, BUT ALSO HIMSELF POWER AND WISDOM ; AND SIMILARLY THE HOLY SPIRIT : YET THAT THERE ARE NOT THREE POWERS OR THREE WISDOMS, BUT ONE POWER AND ONE WISDOM, AS THERE IS ONE GOD AND ONE ESSENCE. INQUIRY IS THEN MADE, WHY THE LATINS SAY ONE ESSENCE, THREE PERSONS, IN GOD ; BUT THE GREEKS, ONE ESSENCE, THREE SUBSTANCES OR HYPOSTASES : AND BOTH MODES OF EXPRESSION ARE SHOWN TO ARISE FROM THE NECESSITIES OF SPEECH, THAT WE MIGHT HAVE AN ANSWER TO GIVE WHEN ASKED, WHAT THREE, WHILE TRULY CONFESSING THAT THERE ARE THREE, VIZ. THE FATHER, AND THE SON, AND THE HOLY SPIRIT.

CHAP. I.—AUGUSTIN RETURNS TO THE QUESTION, WHETHER EACH PERSON OF THE TRINITY BY ITSELF IS WISDOM. WITH WHAT DIFFICULTY, OR IN WHAT WAY, THE PROPOSED QUESTION IS TO BE SOLVED.

1. Let us now inquire more carefully, so far as God grants, into that which a little before we deferred; whether each person also in the Trinity can also by Himself and not with the other two be called God, or great, or wise, or true, or omnipotent, or just, or anything else that can be said of God, not relatively, but absolutely; or whether these things cannot be said except when the Trinity is understood. For the question is raised, —because it is written, " Christ the power of God, and the wisdom of God,"[1]—whether He is so the Father of His own wisdom and His own power, as that He is wise with that wisdom which He begat, and powerful with that power which He begat; and whether, since He is always powerful and wise, He always begat power and wisdom. For if it be so, then, as we have said, why is He not also the Father of His own greatness by which He is great, and of His own goodness by which He is good, and of His own justice by which He is just, and whatever else there is ? Or if all these things are understood, although under more names than one, to be in the same wisdom and power, so that that is greatness which is power, that is goodness which is wisdom, and that again is wisdom which is power, as we have already argued; then let us remember, that when I mention any one of these, I am to be taken as ·if I mentioned all. It is asked, then, whether the Father also by Himself is wise, and is Himself His own wisdom itself; or whether He is wise in the same way as He speaks. For He speaks by the Word which He begat, not by the word which is uttered, and sounds, and passes away, but by the Word which was with God, and the Word was God, and all things were made by Him:[2] by the Word which is equal to Himself, by whom He always and unchangeably utters Himself. For He is not Himself the Word, as He is not the Son nor the image. But in speaking (putting aside those words of God in time which are produced in the creature, for they sound and pass away,—in speaking then) by that co-eternal Word, He is not understood singly, but with that Word itself, without whom certainly He does not speak. Is He then in such way wise as He is one who speaks, so as to be in such way wisdom, as He is the Word, and so that to be the Word is to be wisdom, that is, also to be power, so that power and wisdom and the Word may be

---

[1] 1 Cor. i. 24.

[2] John i. 1, 3.

the same, and be so called relatively as the Son and the image: and that the Father is not singly powerful or wise, but together with the power and wisdom itself which He begat (*genuit*); just as He is not singly one who speaks, but by that Word and together with that Word which He begat; and in like way great by that and together with that greatness, which He begat? And if He is not great by one thing, and God by another, but great by that whereby He is God, because it is not one thing to Him to be great and another to be God; it follows that neither is He God singly, but by that and together with that deity (*deitas*) which He begat; so that the Son is the deity of the Father, as He is the wisdom and power of the Father, and as He is the Word and image of the Father. And because it is not one thing to Him to be, another to be God, the Son is also the essence of the Father, as He is His Word and image. And hence also—except that He is the Father [the Unbegotten]—the Father is not anything unless because He has the Son; so that not only that which is meant by Father (which it is manifest He is not called relatively to Himself but to the Son, and therefore is the Father because He has the Son), but that which He is in respect to His own substance is so called, because He begat His own essence. For as He is great, only with that greatness which He begat, so also He *is*, only with that essence which He begat; because it is not one thing to Him to be, and another to be great. Is He therefore the Father of His own essence, in the same way as He is the Father of His own greatness, as He is the Father of His own power and wisdom? since His greatness is the same as His power, and His essence the same as His greatness.

2. This discussion has arisen from that which is written, that "Christ is the power of God, and the wisdom of God." Wherefore our discourse is compressed into these narrow limits, while we desire to speak things unspeakable; that either we must say that Christ is not the power of God and the wisdom of God, and so shamelessly and impiously resist the apostle; or we must acknowledge that Christ is indeed the power of God and the wisdom of God, but that His Father is not the Father of His own power and wisdom, which is not less impious; for so neither will He be the Father of Christ, because Christ is the power of God and the wisdom of God; or that the Father is not powerful with His own power, or wise with His own wisdom: and who shall dare to say this? Or yet, again, that we must understand,

that in the Father it is one thing to be, another thing to be wise, so that He *is* not by that by which He is wise: a thing usually understood of the soul, which is at some times unwise, at others wise; as being by nature changeable, and not absolutely and perfectly simple. Or, again, that the Father is not anything in respect to His own substance; and that not only that He is the Father, but that He *is*, is said relatively to the Son. How then can the Son be of the same essence as the Father, seeing that the Father, in respect to Himself, is neither His own essence, nor *is* at all in respect to Himself, but even His essence is in. relation to the Son? But, on the contrary, much more is He of one and the same essence, since the Father and Son are one and the same essence; seeing that the Father has His being itself not in respect to Himself, but to the Son, which essence He begat, and by which essence He is whatever He is. Therefore neither [person] *is* in respect to Himself alone; and both exist relatively the one to the other. Or is the Father alone not called Father of himself, but whatever He is called, is called relatively to the Son, but the Son is predicated of in reference to Himself? And if it be so, what is predicated of Him in reference to Himself? Is it His essence itself? But the Son is the essence of the Father, as He is the power and wisdom of the Father, as He is the Word of the Father, and the image of the Father. Or if the Son is called essence in reference to Himself, but the Father is not essence, but the begetter of the essence, and *is* not in respect to Himself, but *is* by that very essence which He begat; as He is great by that greatness which He begat: therefore the Son is also called greatness in respect to Himself; therefore He is also called, in like manner, power, and wisdom, and word, and image. But what can be more absurd than that He should be called image in respect to Himself? Or if image and word are not the very same with power and wisdom, but the former are spoken relatively, and the latter in respect to self, not to another; then we get to this, that the Father is not wise with that wisdom which He begat, because He Himself cannot be spoken relatively to it, and it cannot be spoken relatively to Him. For all things which are said relatively are said reciprocally; therefore it remains that even in essence the Son is spoken of relatively to the Father. But from this is educed a most unexpected sense: that essence itself is not essence, or at least that, when it is called essence, not essence but something relative is intimated. As when we speak of a master, essence is not intimated, but a relative which has reference to a slave; but when we speak of a man, or any such thing which is said in respect to self not to something else, then essence is intimated. Therefore when a man is called a master, man himself is essence, but he is called master relatively; for he is called man in respect to himself, but master in respect to his slave. But in regard to the point from which we started, if essence itself is spoken relatively, essence itself is not essence. Add further, that all essence which is spoken of relatively, is also something, although the relation be taken away; as *e.g.* in the case of a man who is a master, and a man who is a slave, and a horse that is a beast of burden, and money that is a pledge, the man, and the horse, and the money are spoken in respect to themselves, and are substances or essences; but master, and slave, and beast of burden, and pledge, are spoken relatively to something. But if there were not a man, that is, some substance, there would be none who could be called relatively a master; and if there were no horse having a certain essence, there would be nothing that could be called relatively a beast of burden; so if money were not some kind of substance, it could not be called relatively a pledge. Wherefore, if the Father also is not something in respect to Himself, then there is no one at all that can be spoken of relatively to something. For it is not as it is with color. The color of a thing is referred to the thing colored, and color is not spoken at all in reference to substance, but is always of something that is colored; but that thing of which it is the color, even if it is referred to color in respect to its being colored, is yet, in respect to its being a body, spoken of in respect to substance. But in no way may we think, in like manner, that the Father cannot be called anything in respect to His own substance, but that whatever He is called, He is called in relation to the Son; while the same Son is spoken of both in respect to His own substance and in relation to the Father, when He is called great greatness, and powerful power, plainly in respect to Himself, and the greatness and power of the great and powerful Father, by which the Father is great and powerful. It is not so; but both are substance, and both are one substance. And as it is absurd to say that whiteness is not white, so is it absurd to say that wisdom is not wise; and as whiteness is called white in respect to itself, so also wisdom is called wise in respect to itself. But the whiteness of a body is not an essence, since the body

itself is the essence, and that is a quality of it; and hence also a body is said from that quality to be white, to which body to be is not the same thing as to be white. For the form in it is one thing, and the color another; and both are not in themselves, but in a certain bulk, which bulk is neither form nor color, but is formed and colored. True wisdom is both wise, and wise in itself. And since in the case of every soul that becomes wise by partaking of wisdom, if it again becomes foolish, yet wisdom in itself remains; nor when that soul was changed into folly is the wisdom likewise so changed; therefore wisdom is not in him who becomes wise by it, in the same manner as whiteness is in the body which is by it made white. For when the body has been changed into another color, that whiteness will not remain, but will altogether cease to be. But if the Father who begat wisdom is also made wise by it, and to be is not to Him the same as to be wise, then the Son is His quality, not His offspring; and there will no longer be absolute simplicity in the Godhead. But far be it from being so, since in truth in the Godhead is absolutely simple essence, and therefore to be is there the same as to be wise. But if to be is there the same as to be wise, then the Father is not wise by that wisdom which He begat; otherwise He did not beget it, but it begat Him. For what else do we say when we say, that to Him to be is the same as to be wise, unless that He *is* by that whereby He is wise? Wherefore, that which is the cause to Him of being wise, is itself also the cause to Him that He is; and accordingly, if the wisdom which He begat is the cause to Him of being wise, it is also the cause to Him that He is; and this cannot be the case, except either by begetting or by creating Him. But no one ever said in any sense that wisdom is either the begetter or the creator of the Father; for what could be more senseless? Therefore both the Father Himself is wisdom, and the Son is in such way called the wisdom of the Father, as He is called the light of the Father; that is, that in the same manner as light from light, and yet both one light, so we are to understand wisdom of wisdom, and yet both one wisdom; and therefore also one essence, since, in God, to be, is the same as to be wise. For what to be wise is to wisdom, and to be able is to power, and to be eternal is to eternity, and to be just to justice, and to be great to greatness, that being itself is to essence. And since in the Divine simplicity, to be wise is nothing else than to be, therefore wisdom there is the same as essence.

CHAP. 2.—THE FATHER AND THE SON ARE TOGETHER ONE WISDOM, AS ONE ESSENCE, ALTHOUGH NOT TOGETHER ONE WORD.

3. Therefore the Father and the Son together are one essence, and one greatness, and one truth, and one wisdom. But the Father and Son both together are not one Word, because both together are not one Son. For as the Son is referred to the Father, and is not so called in respect to Himself, so also the Word is referred to him whose Word it is, when it is called the Word. Since He is the Son in that He is the Word, and He is the Word in that He is the Son. Inasmuch, therefore, as the Father and the Son together are certainly not one Son, it follows that the Father and the Son together are not the one Word of both. And therefore He is not the Word in that He is wisdom; since He is not called the Word in respect to Himself, but only relatively to Him whose Word He is, as He is called the Son in relation to the Father; but He is wisdom by that whereby He is essence. And therefore, because one essence, one wisdom. But since the Word is also wisdom, yet is not thereby the Word because He is wisdom; for He is understood to be the Word relatively, but wisdom essentially: let us understand, that when He is called the Word, it is meant, wisdom that is *born*, so as to be both the Son and the Image; and that when these two words are used, namely *wisdom (is) born*, in one of the two, namely *born*,[1] both Word, and Image, and Son, are understood, and in all these names essence is not expressed, since they are spoken relatively; but in the other word, namely *wisdom*, since it is spoken also in respect to substance, for wisdom is wise in itself, essence also is expressed, and that being of His which is to be wise. Whence the Father and Son together are one wisdom, because one essence, and singly wisdom of wisdom, as essence of essence. And hence they are not therefore not one essence, because the Father is not the Son, and the Son is not the Father, or because the Father is unbegotten, but the Son is begotten: since by these names only their *relative* attributes are expressed. But both together are one wisdom and one essence; in which to be, is the same as to be wise. And both together are not the Word or the Son, since to be is not the same as to be the Word or the Son, as we have already sufficiently shown that these terms are spoken relatively.

[1] [Augustin sometimes denominates the Son "begotten" (*genitus*), and sometimes "born" (*natus*). Both terms signify that the Son is *of* the Father; God of God, Light of Light, Essence of Essence.—W. G. T. S.]

CHAP. 3.—WHY THE SON CHIEFLY IS INTIMATED IN THE SCRIPTURES BY THE NAME OF WISDOM, WHILE BOTH THE FATHER AND THE HOLY SPIRIT ARE WISDOM. THAT THE HOLY SPIRIT, TOGETHER WITH THE FATHER AND THE SON, IS ONE WISDOM.

4. Why, then, is scarcely anything ever said in the Scriptures of wisdom, unless to show that it is begotten or created of God?—begotten in the case of that Wisdom by which all things are made; but created or made, as in men, when they are converted to that Wisdom which is not created and made but begotten, and are so enlightened; for in these men themselves there comes to be something which may be called their wisdom: even as the Scriptures foretell or narrate, that "the Word was made flesh, and dwelt among us;"[2] for in this way Christ was made wisdom, because He was made man. Is it on this account that wisdom does not speak in these books, nor is anything spoken of it, except to declare that it is born of God, or made by Him (although the Father is Himself wisdom), namely, because wisdom ought to be commended and imitated by us, by the imitation of which we are fashioned [rightly]? For the Father speaks it, that it may be His Word: yet not as a word producing a sound proceeds from the mouth, or is thought before it is pronounced. For this word is completed in certain spaces of time, but that is eternal, and speaks to us by enlightening us, what ought to be spoken to men, both of itself and of the Father. And therefore He says, "No man knoweth the Son, but the Father; neither knoweth any man the Father, save the Son, and he to whomsoever the Son will reveal Him:"[3] since the Father reveals by the Son, that is, by His Word. For if that word which we utter, and which is temporal and transitory, declares both itself, and that of which we speak, how much more the Word of God, by which all things are made? For this Word so declares the Father as He is the Father; because both itself so is, and is that which is the Father, in so far as it is wisdom and essence. For in so far as it is the Word, it is not what the Father is; because the Word is not the Father, and Word is spoken relatively, as is also Son, which assuredly is not the Father. And therefore Christ is the power and wisdom of God, because He Himself, being also power and wisdom, is from the Father, who is power and wisdom; as He is light of the Father, who is light, and the fountain of life with God the Father, who is Himself assuredly the fountain

[2] John i. 14.   [3] Matt. xi. 27.

of life. For "with Thee," He says, "is the fountain of life, and in Thy light shall we see light."[1] Because, "as the Father hath life in Himself, so hath He given to the Son to have life in Himself:"[2] and, "He was the true Light, which lighteth every man that cometh into the world:" and this light, "the Word," was "with God;" but "the Word also was God;"[3] and "God is light, and in Him is no darkness at all:"[4] but a light that is not corporeal, but spiritual; yet not in such way spiritual, that it was wrought by illumination, as it was said to the apostles, "Ye are the light of the world,"[5] but "the light which lighteth every man," that very supreme wisdom itself who is God, of whom we now treat. The Son therefore is Wisdom of wisdom, namely the Father, as He is Light of light, and God of God; so that both the Father singly is light, and the Son singly is light; and the Father singly is God, and the Son singly is God: therefore the Father also singly is wisdom, and the Son singly is wisdom. And as both together are one light and one God, so both are one wisdom. But the Son is "by God made unto us wisdom, and righteousness, and sanctification;"[6] because we turn ourselves to Him in time, that is, from some particular time, that we may remain with Him for ever. And He Himself from a certain time was "the Word made flesh, and dwelt among us."

5. On this account, then, when anything concerning wisdom is declared or narrated in the Scriptures, whether as itself speaking, or where anything is spoken of it, the Son chiefly is intimated to us. And by the example of Him who is the image, let us also not depart from God, since we also are the Image of God: not indeed that which is equal to Him, since we are made so by the Father through the Son, and not born of the Father, as that is. And we are so, because we are enlightened with light; but that is so, because it is the light that enlightens; and which, therefore, being without pattern, is to us a pattern. For He does not imitate any one going before Him, in respect to the Father, from whom He is never separable at all, since He is the very same substance with Him from whom He is. But we by striving imitate Him who abides, and follow Him who stands still, and walking in Him, reach out towards Him; because He is made for us a way in time by His humiliation, which is to us an eternal abiding-place by His divinity. For since to pure intellectual spirits, who have not fallen through pride, He gives an example in the

form of God and as equal with God and as God; so, in order that He might also give Himself as an example of returning to fallen man, who on account of the uncleanness of sins and the punishment of mortality cannot see God, "He emptied Himself;" not by changing His own divinity, but by assuming our changeableness: and "taking upon Him the form of a servant,"[7] "He came to us into this world,"[8] who "was in this world," because "the world was made by Him;"[9] that He might be an example upwards to those who see God, an example downwards to those who admire man, an example to the sound to persevere, an example to the sick to be made whole, an example to those who are to die that they may not fear, an example to the dead that they may rise again, "that in all things He might have the pre-eminence."[10] So that, because man ought not to follow any except God to blessedness, and yet cannot perceive God; by following God made man, he might follow at once Him whom he could perceive, and whom he ought to follow. Let us then love Him and cleave to Him, by charity spread abroad in our hearts, through the Holy Spirit which is given unto us.[11] It is not therefore to be wondered at, if, on account of the example which the Image, which is equal to the Father, gives to us, in order that we may be refashioned after the image of God, Scripture, when it speaks of wisdom, speaks of the Son, whom we follow by living wisely; although the Father also is wisdom, as He is both light and God.

6. The Holy Spirit also, whether we are to call Him that absolute love which joins together Father and Son, and joins us also from beneath, that so that is not unfitly said which is written, "God is love;"[12] how is He not also Himself wisdom, since He is light, because "God is light"? or whether after any other way the essence of the Holy Spirit is to be singly and properly named; then, too, since He is God, He is certainly light; and since He is light, He is certainly wisdom. But that the Holy Spirit is God, Scripture proclaims by the apostle, who says, "Know ye not that ye are the temple of God?" and immediately subjoins, "And the Spirit of God dwelleth in you;"[13] for God dwelleth in His own temple. For the Spirit of God does not dwell in the temple of God as a servant, since he says more plainly in another place, "Know ye not that your body is the temple of the Holy Ghost which is in you, and which ye have of God, and ye are not your own?

---

[1] Ps. xxxvi. 9.   [2] John v. 2.   [3] John i. 9, 1.
[4] 1 John i. 5.   [5] Matt. v. 14.   [6] 1 Cor. i. 30.

[7] Phil. ii. 7.   [8] 1 Tim. i. 15.   [9] John i. 10.
[10] Col. i. 18.   [11] Rom. v. 5.   [12] 1 John iv. 8.
[13] 1 Cor. iii. 16.

For ye are bought with a great price: therefore glorify God in your body."[1] But what is wisdom, except spiritual and unchangeable light? For yonder sun also is light, but it is corporeal; and the spiritual creature also is light, but it is not unchangeable. Therefore the Father is light, the Son is light, and the Holy Spirit is light; but together not three lights, but one light. And so the Father is wisdom, the Son is wisdom, and the Holy Spirit is wisdom, and together not three wisdoms, but one wisdom: and because in the Trinity to be is the same as to be wise, the Father, Son, and Holy Spirit, are one essence. Neither in the Trinity is it one thing to be and another to be God; therefore the Father, Son, and Holy Spirit, are one God.

CHAP. 4.—HOW IT WAS BROUGHT ABOUT THAT THE GREEKS SPEAK OF THREE HYPOSTASES, THE LATINS OF THREE PERSONS. SCRIPTURE NOWHERE SPEAKS OF THREE PERSONS IN ONE GOD.

7. For the sake, then, of speaking of things that cannot be uttered, that we may be able in some way to utter what we are able in no way to utter fully, our Greek friends have spoken of one essence, three substances; but the Latins of one essence or substance, three persons; because, as we have already said,[2] essence usually means nothing else than substance in our language, that is, in Latin. And provided that what is said is understood only in a mystery, such a way of speaking was sufficient, in order that there might be something to say when it was asked what the three are, which the true faith pronounces to be three, when it both declares that the Father is not the Son, and that the Holy Spirit, which is the gift of God, is neither the Father nor the Son. When, then, it is asked what the three are, or who the three are, we betake ourselves to the finding out of some special or general name under which we may embrace these three; and no such name occurs to the mind, because the supereminence of the Godhead surpasses the power of customary speech. For God is more truly thought than He is uttered, and exists more truly than He is thought. For when we say that Jacob was not the same as Abraham, but that Isaac was neither Abraham nor Jacob, certainly we confess that they are three, Abraham, Isaac, and Jacob. But when it is asked what three, we reply three men, calling them in the plural by a specific name; but if we were to say three animals, then by a generic name; for man, as the ancients have defined him, is a rational, mortal animal: or again, as our Scriptures usually speak, three souls, since it is fitting to denominate the whole from the better part, that is, to denominate both body and soul, which is the whole man, from the soul; for so it is said that seventy-five souls went down into Egypt with Jacob, instead of saying so many men.[3] Again, when we say that your horse is not mine, and that a third belonging to some one else is neither mine nor yours, then we confess that there are three; and if any one ask what three, we answer three horses by a specific name, but three animals by a generic one. And yet again, when we say that an ox is not a horse, but that a dog is neither an ox nor a horse, we speak of a three; and if any one questions us what three, we do not speak now by a specific name of three horses, or three oxen, or three dogs, because the three are not contained under the same species, but by a generic name, three animals; or if under a higher genus, three substances, or three creatures, or three natures. But whatsoever things are expressed in the plural number specifically by one name, can also be expressed generically by one name. But all things which are generically called by one name cannot also be called specifically by one name. For three horses, which is a specific name, we also call three animals; but a horse, and an ox, and a dog, we call only three animals or substances, which are generic names, or anything else that can be spoken generically concerning them; but we cannot speak of them as three horses, or oxen, or dogs, which are specific names; for we express those things by one name, although in the plural number, which have that in common that is signified by the name. For Abraham, and Isaac, and Jacob, have in common that which is man; therefore they are called three men: a horse also, and an ox, and a dog, have in common that which is animal; therefore they are called three animals. So three several laurels we also call three trees; but a laurel, and a myrtle, and an olive, we call only three trees, or three substances, or three natures: and so three stones we call also three bodies; but stone, and wood, and iron, we call only three bodies, or by any other higher generic name by which they can be called. Of the Father, therefore, the Son, and the Holy Spirit, seeing that they are three, let us ask what three they are, and what they have in common. For the being the Father is not common to them, so that they should be interchangeably fathers

---

[1] 1 Cor. vi. 19, 20.　　　[2] Bk. v. c. 28.　　　[3] Gen. xlvi. 27, and Deut. x. 22.

= Infinite possible # of gods

to one another: as friends, since they are so called relatively to each other, can be called three friends, because they are so mutually to each other. But this is not the case in the Trinity, since the Father only is there father; and not Father of two, but of the Son only. Neither are they three Sons, since the Father there is not the Son, nor is the Holy Spirit. Neither three Holy Spirits, because the Holy Spirit also, in that proper meaning by which He is also called the gift of God, is neither the Father nor the Son. What three therefore? For if three persons, then that which is meant by person is common to them; therefore this name is either specific or generic to them, according to the manner of speaking. But where there is no difference of nature, there things that are several in number are so expressed generically, that they can also be expressed specifically. For the difference of nature causes, that a laurel, and a myrtle, and an olive, or a horse, and an ox, and a dog, are not called by the specific name, the former of three laurels, or the latter of three oxen, but by the generic name, the former of three trees, and the latter of three animals. But here, where there is no difference of essence, it is necessary that these three should have a specific name, which yet is not to be found. For person is a generic name, insomuch that man also can be so called, although there is so great a difference between man and God.

8. Further, in regard to that very generic (*generalis*) word, if on this account we say three persons, because that which person means is common to them (otherwise they can in no way be so called, just as they are not called three sons, because that which son means is not common to them); why do we not also say three Gods? For certainly, since the Father is a person, and the Son a person, and the Holy Spirit a person, therefore there are three persons: since then the Father is God, and the Son God, and the Holy Spirit God, why not three Gods? Or else, since on account of their ineffable union these three are together one God, why not also one person; so that we could not say three persons, although we call each a person singly, just as we cannot say three Gods, although we call each singly God, whether the Father, or the Son, or the Holy Spirit? Is it because Scripture does not say three Gods? But neither do we find that Scripture anywhere mentions three persons. Or is it because Scripture does not call these three, either three persons or one person (for we read of the person of the Lord, but not of the

Lord as a person), that therefore it was lawful through the mere necessity of speaking and reasoning to say three persons, not because Scripture says it, but because Scripture does not contradict it: whereas, if we were to say three Gods, Scripture would contradict it, which says, "Hear, O Israel; the Lord thy God is one God?"[1] Why then is it not also lawful to say three essences; which, in like manner, as Scripture does not say, so neither does it contradict? For if essence is a specific (*specialis*) name common to three, why are They not to be called three essences, as Abraham, Isaac, and Jacob are called three men, because man is the specific name common to all men? But if essence is not a specific name, but a generic one, since man, and cattle, and tree, and constellation, and angel, are called essences; why are not these called three essences, as three horses are called three animals, and three laurels are called three trees, and three stones three bodies? Or if they are not called three essences, but one essence, on account of the unity of the Trinity, why is it not the case, that on account of the same unity of the Trinity are not to be called three substances or three persons, but one substance and one person? For as the name of essence is common to them, so that each singly is called essence, so the name of either substance or person is common to them. For that which must be understood of persons according to our usage, this is to be understood of substances according to the Greek usage; for they say three substances, one essence, in the same way as we say three persons, one essence or substance.

9. What therefore remains, except that we confess that these terms sprang from the necessity of speaking, when copious reasoning was required against the devices or errors of the heretics? For when human weakness endeavored to utter in speech to the senses of man what it grasps in the secret places of the mind in proportion to its comprehension respecting the Lord God its creator, whether by devout faith, or by any discernment whatsoever; it feared to say three essences, lest any difference should be understood to exist in that absolute equality. Again, it could not say that there were not three somewhats (*tria quædam*), for it was because Sabellius said this that he fell into heresy. For it must be devoutly believed, as most certainly known from the Scriptures, and must be grasped by the mental eye with undoubting perception, that there is both

---

[1] Deut. vi. 4.

Father, and Son, and Holy Spirit; and that the Son is not the same with the Father, nor the Holy Spirit the same with the Father or the Son. It sought then what three it should call them, and answered substances or persons; by which names it did not intend diversity to be meant, but singleness to be denied: that not only unity might be understood therein from the being called one essence, but also Trinity from the being called three substances or persons. For if it is the same thing with God to be (*esse*) as to subsist (*subsistere*), they were not to be called three substances, in such sense as they are not called three essences; just as, because it is the same thing with God to be as to be wise, as we do not say three essences, so neither three wisdoms. For so, because it is the same thing to Him to be God as to be, it is not right to say three essences, as it is not right to say three Gods. But if it is one thing to God to be, another to subsist, as it is one thing to God to be, another to be the Father or the Lord (for that which He is, is spoken in respect to Himself, but He is called Father in relation to the Son, and Lord in relation to the creature which serves Him); therefore He subsists relatively, as He begets relatively, and bears rule relatively: so then substance will be no longer substance, because it will be relative. For as from being, He is called essence, so from subsisting, we speak of substance. But it is absurd that substance should be spoken relatively, for everything subsists in respect to itself; how much more God?[1]

CHAP. 5.—IN GOD, SUBSTANCE IS SPOKEN IMPROPERLY, ESSENCE PROPERLY.

10. If, however, it is fitting that God should be said to subsist—(For this word is rightly applied to those things, in which as subjects those things are, which are said to be in a subject, as color or shape in body. For body subsists, and so is substance; but those things are in the body, which subsists and is their subject, and they are not substances, but are in a substance : and so, if either that color or that shape ceases to be, it does not deprive the body of being a body, because it is not of the being of body, that it should retain this or that shape or color; therefore neither changeable nor simple things are properly called substances.)—If, I say, God subsists so that He can be properly called a sub-

stance, then there is something in Him as it were in a subject, and He is not simple, *i.e.* such that to Him to be is the same as is anything else that is said concerning Him in respect to Himself; as, for instance, great, omnipotent, good, and whatever of this kind is not unfitly said of God. But it is an impiety to say that God subsists, and is a subject in relation to His own goodness, and that this goodness is not a substance or rather essence, and that God Himself is not His own goodness, but that it is in Him as in a subject. And hence it is clear that God is improperly called substance, in order that He may be understood to be, by the more usual name essence, which He is truly and properly called; so that perhaps it is right that God alone should be called essence. For He is truly alone, because He is unchangeable; and declared this to be His own name to His servant Moses, when He says, "I am that I am;" and, "Thus shalt thou say unto the children of Israel: He who is hath sent me unto you."[2] However, whether He be called essence, which He is properly called, or substance, which He is called improperly, He is called both in respect to Himself, not relatively to anything; whence to God to be is the same thing as to subsist; and so the Trinity, if one essence, is also one substance. Perhaps therefore they are more conveniently called three persons than three substances.

CHAP. 6.—WHY WE DO NOT IN THE TRINITY SPEAK OF ONE PERSON, AND THREE ESSENCES. WHAT HE OUGHT TO BELIEVE CONCERNING THE TRINITY WHO DOES NOT RECEIVE WHAT IS SAID ABOVE. MAN IS BOTH AFTER THE IMAGE, AND IS THE IMAGE OF GOD.

11. But lest I should seem to favor ourselves [the Latins], let us make this further inquiry. Although they [the Greeks] also, if they pleased, as they call three substances three hypostases, so might call three persons three "prosopa," yet they preferred that word which, perhaps, was more in accordance with the usage of their language. For the case is the same with the word persons also; for to God it is not one thing to be, another to be a person, but it is absolutely the same thing. For if to be is said in respect to Himself, but person relatively; in this way we should say three persons, the Father, Son, and Holy Spirit; just as we speak of three friends, or three relations, or three neighbors, in that they are so mutually, not that each one of them is so in respect to himself. Wherefore any one of these is the friend of the other two,

---

[1] [Augustin's meaning is, that the term "substance" is not an adequate one whereby to denote a trinitarian distinction, because in order to denote such a distinction it must be employed relatively, while in itself it has an absolute signification. In the next chapter he proceeds to show this.—W. G. T. S.]

[2] Ex. iii. 14.

or the relation, or the neighbor, because these names have a relative signification. What then? Are we to call the Father the person of the Son and of the Holy Spirit, or the Son the person of the Father and of the Holy Spirit, or the Holy Spirit the person of the Father and of the Son? But neither is the word person commonly so used in any case; nor in this Trinity, when we speak of the person of the Father, do we mean anything else than the substance of the Father. Wherefore, as the substance of the Father is the Father Himself, not as He is the Father, but as He is, so also the person of the Father is not anything else than the Father Himself; for He is called a person in respect to Himself, not in respect to the Son, or the Holy Spirit: just as He is called in respect to Himself both God, and great, and good, and just, and anything else of the kind; and just as to Him to be is the same as to be God, or as to be great, or as to be good, so it is the same thing to Him to be, as to be a person. Why, therefore, do we not call these three together one person, as one essence and one God, but say three persons, while we do not say three Gods or three essences; unless it be because we wish some one word to serve for that meaning whereby the Trinity is understood, that we might not be altogether silent, when asked, what three, while we confessed that they are three? For if essence is the genus, and substance or person the species, as some think, then I must omit what I just now said, that they ought to be called three essences, as they are called three substances or persons; as three horses are called three horses, and the same are called three animals, since horse is the species, animal the genus. For in this case the species is not spoken of in the plural, and the genus in the singular, as if we were to say that three horses were one animal; but as they are three horses by the special name, so they are three animals by the generic one. But if they say that the name of substance or person does not signify species, but something singular and individual; so that any one is not so called a substance or person as he is called a man, for man is common to all men, but in the same manner as he is called this or that man, as Abraham, as Isaac, as Jacob, or any one else who, if present, could be pointed out with the finger: so will the same reason reach these too. For as Abraham, Isaac, and Jacob are called three individuals, so are they called three men, and three souls. Why then are both the Father and the Son and the Holy Spirit, if we are to reason about them also according to genus and species and individual, not so called three essences, as they are called

three substances or persons? But this, as I said, I pass over: but I do affirm, that if essence is a genus, then a single essence has no species; just as, because animal is a genus, a single animal has no species. Therefore the Father, Son, and Holy Spirit are not three species of one essence. But if essence is a species, as man is a species, but those are three which we call substances or persons, then they have the same species in common, in such way as Abraham, Isaac, and Jacob have in common the species which is called man; not as man is subdivided into Abraham, Isaac, and Jacob, so can one man also be subdivided into several single men; for this is altogether impossible, since one man is already a single man. Why then is one essence subdivided into three substances or persons? For if essence is a species, as man is, then one essence is as one man is : or do we, as we say that any three human beings of the same sex, of the same constitution of body, of the same mind, are one nature,—for they are three human beings, but one nature,—so also say in the Trinity three substances one essence, or three persons one substance or essence? But this is somehow a parallel case, since the ancients also who spoke Latin, before they had these terms, which have not long come into use, that is, essence or substance, used for them to say nature. We do not therefore use these terms according to genus or species, but as if according to a matter that is common and the same. Just as if three statues were made of the same gold, we should say three statues one gold, yet should neither call the gold genus, and the statues species; nor the gold species, and the statues individuals. For no species goes beyond its own individuals, so as to comprehend anything external to them. For when I define what man is, which is a specific name, every several man that exists is contained in the same individual definition, neither does anything belong to it which is not a man. But when I define gold, not statues alone, if they be gold, but rings also, and anything else that is made of gold, will belong to gold ; and even if nothing were made of it, it would still be called gold; since, even if there were no gold statues, there will not therefore be no statues at all. Likewise no species goes beyond the definition of its genus. For when I define animal, since horse is a species of this genus, every horse is an animal ; but every statue is not gold. So, although in the case of three golden statues we should rightly say three statues, one gold ; yet we do not so say it, as to understand gold to be the genus, and the statues to be species. Therefore neither do we so call the Trinity three persons or substances, one essence and one God, as though three somethings subsisted out of one matter [leaving a remainder, *i. e.*]; although whatever that is, it is unfolded in these three. For there is nothing else of that essence besides the Trinity. Yet we say three persons of the same essence, or three persons one essence ; but we do not say three persons out of the same essence, as though therein essence were one thing, and person another, as we can say three statues out of the same gold; for there it is one thing to be gold, another to be statues. And when we say three men one nature, or three men of the same nature, they also can be called three men out of the same nature, since out of the same nature there can be also three other such men. But in that essence of the Trinity, in no way can any other person whatever exist out of the same essence. Further, in these things, one man is not as much as three men together ; and two men are something more than one man : and in equal statues, three together amount to more of gold than each singly, and one amounts to less of gold than two. But in God it is not so; for the Father, the Son, and the Holy Spirit together is not a greater essence than the Father alone or the Son alone; but these three substances or persons, if they must be so called, together are equal to each singly: which the natural man does not comprehend. For he cannot think except under the conditions of bulk and space, either small or great, since phantasms or as it were images of bodies flit about in his mind.

12. And until he be purged from this uncleanness, let him believe in the Father, Son, and Holy Spirit, one God, alone, great, omnipotent, good, just, merciful, Creator of all things visible and invisible, and whatsoever can be worthily and truly said of Him in proportion to human capacity. And when he is told that the Father only is God, let him not separate from Him the Son or the Holy Spirit ; for together with Him He is the only God, together with whom also He is one God; because, when we are told that the Son also is the only God, we must needs take it without any separation of the Father or the Holy Spirit. And let him so say one essence, as not to think one to be either greater or better than, or in any respect differing from, another. Yet not that the Father Himself is both Son and Holy Spirit, or whatever else each is singly called in relation to either of the others; as Word, which is not said except of the Son, or Gift, which is not said except of the Holy Spirit. And on this account also they admit the plural number, as it is written in the Gos-

pel, "I and my Father are one."[1] He has both said "*one*," [2] and "*we are* [3] one," according to essence, because they are the same God; " we are," according to relation, because the one is Father, the other is Son. Sometimes also the unity of the essence is left unexpressed, and the relatives alone are mentioned in the plural number : " My Father and I will come unto him, and make our abode with him."[4] *We will come*, and *we will make our abode*, is the plural number, since it was said before, " I and my Father," that is, the Son and the Father, which terms are used relatively to one another. Sometimes the meaning is altogether latent, as in Genesis : " Let us make man after our image and likeness."[5] Both *let us make* and *our* is said in the plural, and ought not to be received except as of relatives. For it was not that gods might make, or make after the image and likeness of gods ; but that the Father, and Son, and Holy Spirit might make after the image of Father, and Son, and Holy Spirit, that man might subsist as the image of God. And God is the Trinity. But because that image of God was not made altogether equal to Him, as being not born of Him, but created by Him; in order to signify this, he is in such way the image as that he is " after the image," that is, he is not made equal by parity, but approaches to Him by a sort of likeness. For approach to God is not by intervals of place, but by likeness, and withdrawal from Him is by unlikeness. For there are some who draw this distinction, that they will have the Son to be the image, but man not to be the image, but " after the image." But the apostle refutes them, saying, " For a man indeed ought not to cover his head, forasmuch as he is the image and glory of God."[6] He did not say *after the image*, but *the image*. And this image, since it is elsewhere spoken of as *after the image*, is not as if it were said relatively to the Son, who is the image equal to the Father ; otherwise he would not say *after our image*. For how *our*, when the Son is the image of the Father alone ? But man is said to be " after the image," on account, as we have said, of the inequality of the likeness ; and therefore after *our* image, that man might be the image of the Trinity; [7] not equal to the Trinity as the Son is equal to the Father, but approaching to it, as has been

[1] John x. 30.   [2] *Unum.*   [3] *Sumus.*
[4] John xiv. 23.   [5] Gen. i. 26.   [6] 1 Cor. xi. 7.
[7] [Augustin would find this " image " in the ternaries of nature and the human mind which illustrate the Divine trinality. The remainder of the treatise is mainly devoted to this abstruse subject; and is one of the most metaphysical pieces of composition in patristic literature. The exegetical portion of the work ends substantially with the seventh chapter. The remainder is ontological, yet growing out of, and founded upon the biblical data and results of the first part.—W. G. T. S.]

8

said, by a certain likeness ; just as nearness may in a sense be signified in things distant from each other, not in respect of place, but of a sort of imitation. For it is also said, " Be ye transformed by the renewing of your mind;"[1] to whom he likewise says, " Be ye therefore imitators of God as dear children."[2] For it is said to the new man, " which is renewed to the knowledge of God, after the image of Him that created him."[3] Or if we choose to admit the plural number, in order to meet the needs of argument, even putting aside relative terms, that so we may answer in one term when it is asked what three, and say three substances or three persons; then let no one think of any bulk or interval, or of any distance of howsoever little unlikeness, so that in the Trinity any should be understood to be even a little less than another, in whatsoever way one thing can be less than another : in order that there may be neither a confusion of persons, nor such a distinction as that there should be any inequality. And if this cannot be grasped by the understanding, let it be held by faith, until He shall dawn in the heart who says by the prophet, " If ye will not believe, surely ye shall not understand."[4]

[1] Rom. xii. 2. [2] Eph. v. 1.
[3] Col. iii. 10.

[4] Isa. vii. 9.

BOOK VIII.

EXPLAINS AND PROVES THAT NOT ONLY THE FATHER IS NOT GREATER THAN THE SON, BUT
NEITHER ARE BOTH TOGETHER ANYTHING GREATER THAN THE HOLY SPIRIT, NOR ANY TWO
TOGETHER IN THE SAME TRINITY ANYTHING GREATER THAN ONE, NOR ALL THREE TOGETHER
ANYTHING GREATER THAN EACH SEVERALLY. IT IS THEN SHOWN HOW THE NATURE ITSELF
OF GOD MAY BE UNDERSTOOD FROM OUR UNDERSTANDING OF TRUTH, AND FROM OUR
KNOWLEDGE OF THE SUPREME GOOD, AND FROM THE INNATE LOVE OF RIGHTEOUSNESS,
WHEREBY A RIGHTEOUS SOUL IS LOVED EVEN BY A SOUL THAT IS ITSELF NOT YET RIGHTEOUS.
BUT IT IS URGED ABOVE ALL, THAT THE KNOWLEDGE OF GOD IS TO BE SOUGHT BY LOVE,
WHICH GOD IS SAID TO BE IN THE SCRIPTURES ; AND IN THIS LOVE IS ALSO POINTED OUT
THE EXISTENCE OF SOME TRACE OF A TRINITY.

PREFACE.—THE CONCLUSION OF WHAT HAS BEEN
SAID ABOVE. THE RULE TO BE OBSERVED IN
THE MORE DIFFICULT QUESTIONS OF THE
FAITH.

We have said elsewhere that those things
are predicated specially in the Trinity as belonging severally to each person, which are
predicated relatively the one to the other, as
Father and Son, and the gift of both, the
Holy Spirit; for the Father is not the Trinity,
nor the Son the Trinity, nor the gift the
Trinity: but what whenever each is singly
spoken of in respect to themselves, then
they are not spoken of as three in the plural
number, but one, the Trinity itself, as the
Father God, the Son God, and the Holy
Spirit God; the Father good, the Son good,
and the Holy Spirit good; and the Father
omnipotent, the Son omnipotent, and the
Holy Spirit omnipotent: yet neither three
Gods, nor three goods, nor three omnipotents, but one God, good, omnipotent, the
Trinity itself; and whatsoever else is said of
them not relatively in respect to each other,
but individually in respect to themselves.
For they are thus spoken of according to
essence, since in them to be is the same as to
be great, as to be good, as to be wise, and
whatever else is said of each person individually therein, or of the Trinity itself, in respect

to themselves. And that therefore they are
called three persons, or three substances, not
in order that any difference of essence may be
understood, but that we may be able to answer
by some one word, should any one ask what
three, or what three things ? And that there is
so great an equality in that Trinity, that not
only the Father is not greater than the Son,
as regards divinity, but neither are the Father
and Son together greater than the Holy
Spirit; nor is each individual person, whichever it be of the three, less than the Trinity
itself. This is what we have said; and if it
is handled and repeated frequently, it becomes, no doubt, more familiarly known: yet
some limit, too, must be put to the discussion, and we must supplicate God with most
devout piety, that He will open our understanding, and take away the inclination of
disputing, in order that our minds may discern the essence of the truth, that has neither
bulk nor moveableness. Now, therefore, so
far as the Creator Himself aids us in His
marvellous mercy, let us consider these subjects, into which we will enter more deeply than
we entered into those which preceded, although they are in truth the same; preserving
the while this rule, that what has not yet been
made clear to our intellect, be nevertheless
not loosened from the firmness of our faith.

CHAP. 1.—IT IS SHOWN BY REASON THAT IN GOD THREE ARE NOT ANYTHING GREATER THAN ONE PERSON.

2. For we say that in this Trinity two or three persons are not anything greater than one of them; which carnal perception does not receive, for no other reason except because it perceives as it can the true things which are created, but cannot discern the truth itself by which they are created; for if it could, then the very corporeal light would in no way be more clear than this which we have said. For in respect to the substance of truth, since it alone truly is, nothing is greater, unless because it more truly is.[1] But in respect to whatsoever is intelligible and unchangeable, no one thing is more truly than another, since all alike are unchangeably eternal; and that which therein is called great, is not great from any other source than from that by which it truly is. Wherefore, where magnitude itself is truth, whatsoever has more of magnitude must needs have more of truth; whatsoever therefore has not more of truth, has not also more of magnitude. Further, whatsoever has more of truth is certainly more true, just as that is greater which has more of magnitude; therefore in respect to the substance of truth that is more great which is more true. But the Father and the Son together are not more truly than the Father singly, or the Son singly. Both together, therefore, are not anything greater than each of them singly. And since also the Holy Spirit equally is truly, the Father and Son together are not anything greater than He, since neither are they more truly. The Father also and the Holy Spirit together, since they do not surpass the Son in truth (for they are not more truly), do not surpass Him either in magnitude. And so the Son and the Holy Spirit together are just as great as the Father alone, since they are as truly. So also the Trinity itself is as great as each several person therein. For where truth itself is magnitude, that is not more great which is not more true: since in regard to the essence of truth, to be true is the same as to be, and to be is the same as to be great; therefore to be great is the same as to be true. And in regard to it, therefore, what is equally true must needs also be equally great.

CHAP. 2.—EVERY CORPOREAL CONCEPTION MUST BE REJECTED, IN ORDER THAT IT MAY BE UNDERSTOOD HOW GOD IS TRUTH.

3. But in respect to bodies, it may be the case that this gold and that gold may be equally true [real], but this may be greater than that, since magnitude is not the same thing in this case as truth; and it is one thing for it to be gold, another to be great. So also in the nature of the soul; a soul is not called great in the same respect in which it is called true. For he, too, has a true [real] soul who has not a great soul; since the essence of body and soul is not the essence of the truth [reality] itself; as is the Trinity, one God, alone, great, true, truthful, the truth. Of whom if we endeavor to think, so far as He Himself permits and grants, let us not think of any touch or embrace in local space, as if of three bodies, or of any compactness of conjunction, as fables tell of three-bodied Geryon; but let whatsoever may occur to the mind, that is of such sort as to be greater in three than in each singly, and less in one than in two, be rejected without any doubt; for so everything corporeal is rejected. But also in spiritual things let nothing changeable that may have occurred to the mind be thought of God. For when we aspire from this depth to that height, it is a step towards no small knowledge, if, before we can know what God is, we can already know what He is not. For certainly He is neither earth nor heaven; nor, as it were, earth and heaven; nor any such thing as we see in the heaven; nor any such thing as we do not see, but which perhaps is in heaven. Neither if you were to magnify in the imagination of your thought the light of the sun as much as you are able, either that it may be greater, or that it may be brighter, a thousand times as much, or times without number; neither is this God. Neither as[2] we think of the pure angels as spirits animating celestial bodies, and changing and dealing with them after the will by which they serve God; not even if all, and there are " thousands of thousands," [3] were brought together into one, and became one; neither is any such thing God. Neither if you were to think of the same spirits as without bodies—a thing indeed most difficult for carnal thought to do. Behold and see, if thou canst, O soul pressed down by the corruptible body, and weighed down by earthly thoughts, many and various; behold and see, if thou canst, that God is truth.[4] For it is written that "God is light;"[5] not in such

---

[1] [In this and the following chapter, the meaning of Augustin will be clearer, if the Latin "veritas," "vera," and "vere," are rendered, occasionally, by "reality," "real," and "really." He is endeavoring to prove the equality of the three persons, by the fact that they are equally real (true), and the degree of their reality (truth) is the same. Real being is true being; reality is truth. In common phraseology, truth and reality are synonymous.—W. G. T. S.]

---

[2] Read si for sicut, if for as. Bened. ed.
[3] Apoc. v. 11.   [4] Wisd. ix. 15.   [5] 1 John i. 5.

way as these eyes see, but in such way as the heart sees, when it is said, He is truth [reality]. Ask not what is truth [reality]; for immediately the darkness of corporeal images and the clouds of phantasms will put themselves in the way, and will disturb that calm which at the first twinkling shone forth to thee, when I said truth [reality]. See that thou remainest, if thou canst, in that first twinkling with which thou art dazzled, as it were, by a flash, when it is said to thee, Truth [Reality]. But thou canst not; thou wilt glide back into those usual and earthly things. And what weight, pray, is it that will cause thee so to glide back, unless it be the bird-lime of the stains of appetite thou hast contracted, and the errors of thy wandering from the right path?

CHAP. 3.—HOW GOD MAY BE KNOWN TO BE THE CHIEF GOOD. THE MIND DOES NOT BECOME GOOD UNLESS BY TURNING TO GOD.

4. Behold again, and see if thou canst. Thou certainly dost not love anything except what is good, since good is the earth, with the loftiness of its mountains, and the due measure of its hills, and the level surface of its plains; and good is an estate that is pleasant and fertile; and good is a house that is arranged in due proportions, and is spacious and bright; and good are animal and animate bodies; and good is air that is temperate and salubrious; and good is food that is agreeable and fit for health; and good is health, without pains or lassitude; and good is the countenance of man that is disposed in fit proportions, and is cheerful in look, and bright in color; and good is the mind of a friend, with the sweetness of agreement, and with the confidence of love; and good is a righteous man; and good are riches, since they are readily useful; and good is the heaven, with its sun, and moon, and stars; and good are the angels, by their holy obedience; and good is discourse that sweetly teaches and suitably admonishes the hearer; and good is a poem that is harmonious in its numbers and weighty in its sense. And why add yet more and more? This thing is good and that good, but take away this and that, and regard good itself if thou canst; so wilt thou see God, not good by a good that is other than Himself, but the good of all good. For in all these good things, whether those which I have mentioned, or any else that are to be discerned or thought, we could not say that one was better than another, when we judge truly, unless a conception of the good itself had been impressed upon us, such that according to it we might both approve some things as good, and prefer one good to another. So God is to be loved, not this and that good, but the good itself. For the good that must be sought for the soul is not one above which it is to fly by judging, but to which it is to cleave by loving; and what can this be except God? Not a good mind, or a good angel, or the good heaven, but the good good. For perhaps what I wish to say may be more easily perceived in this way. For when, for instance, a mind is called good, as there are two words, so from these words I understand two things—one whereby it is mind, and another whereby it is good. And itself had no share in making itself a mind, for there was nothing as yet to make itself to be anything; but to make itself to be a good mind, I see, must be brought about by the will: not because that by which it is mind is not itself anything good;—for how else is it already called, and most truly called, better than the body?—but it is not yet called a good mind, for this reason, that the action of the will still is wanted, by which it is to become more excellent; and if it has neglected this, then it is justly blamed, and is rightly called not a good mind. For it then differs from the mind which does perform this; and since the latter is praiseworthy, the former doubtless, which does not perform, it is blameable. But when it does this of set purpose, and becomes a good mind. it yet cannot attain to being so unless it turn itself to something which itself is not. And to what can it turn itself that it may become a good mind, except to the good which it loves, and seeks, and obtains? And if it turns itself back again from this, and becomes not good, then by the very act of turning away from the good, unless that good remain in it from which it turns away, it cannot again turn itself back thither if it should wish to amend.

5. Wherefore there would be no changeable goods, unless there were the unchangeable good. Whenever then thou art told of this good thing and that good thing, which things can also in other respects be called not good, if thou canst put aside those things which are good by the participation of the good, and discern that good itself by the participation of which they are good (for when this or that good thing is spoken of, thou understandest together with them the good itself also): if, then, I say thou canst remove these things, and canst discern the good in itself, then thou wilt have discerned God. And if thou shalt cleave to Him with love, thou shalt be forthwith blessed. But whereas other things are not loved, except because they are good,

be ashamed, in cleaving to them, not to love the good itself whence they are good. That also, which is a mind, only because it is a mind, while it is not yet also good by the turning itself to the unchangeable good, but, as I said, is only a mind; whenever it so pleases us, as that we prefer it even, if we understand aright, to all corporeal light, does not please us in itself, but in that skill by which it was made. For it is thence approved as made, wherein it is seen to have been to be made. This is truth, and simple good: for it is nothing else than the good itself, and for this reason also the chief good. For no good can be diminished or increased, except that which is good from some other good. Therefore the mind turns itself, in order to be good, to that by which it comes to be a mind. Therefore the will is then in harmony with nature, so that the mind may be perfected in good, when that good is loved by the turning of the will to it, whence that other good also comes which is not lost by the turning away of the will from it. For by turning itself from the chief good, the mind loses the being a good mind; but it does not lose the being a mind. And this, too, is a good already, and one better than the body. The will, therefore, loses that which the will obtains. For the mind already was, that could wish to be turned to that from which it was: but that as yet was not, that could wish to be before it was. And herein is our [supreme] good, when we see whether the thing ought to be or to have been, respecting which we comprehend that it ought to be or to have been, and when we see that the thing could not have been unless it ought to have been, of which we also do not comprehend in what manner it ought to have been. This good then is not far from every one of us: for in it we live, and move, and have our being.[1]

CHAP. 4.—GOD MUST FIRST BE KNOWN BY AN UNERRING FAITH, THAT HE MAY BE LOVED.

6. But it is by love that we must stand firm to this and cleave to this, in order that we may enjoy the presence of that by which we are, and in the absence of which we could not be at all. For as "we walk as yet by faith, and not by sight,"[2] we certainly do not yet see God, as the same [apostle] saith, "face to face:"[3] whom however we shall never see, unless now already we love. But who loves what he does not know? For it is possible something may be known and not loved: but I ask whether it is possible that what is not known can be loved; since if it cannot, then

no one loves God before he knows Him. And what is it to know God except to behold Him and steadfastly perceive Him with the mind? For He is not a body to be searched out by carnal eyes. But before also that we have power to behold and to perceive God, as He can be beheld and perceived, which is permitted to the pure in heart; for "blessed are the pure in heart, for they shall see God;"[4] except He is loved by faith, it will not be possible for the heart to be cleansed, in order that it may be apt and meet to see Him. For where are there those three, in order to build up which in the mind the whole apparatus of the divine Scriptures has been raised up, namely Faith, Hope, and Charity,[5] except in a mind believing what it does not yet see, and hoping and loving what it believes? Even He therefore who is not known, but yet is believed, can be loved. But indisputably we must take care, lest the mind believing that which it does not see, feign to itself something which is not, and hope for and love that which is false. For in that case, it will not be charity out of a pure heart, and of a good conscience, and of faith unfeigned, which is the end of the commandment, as the same apostle says.[6]

7. But it must needs be, that, when by reading or hearing of them we believe in any corporeal things which we have not seen, the mind frames for itself something under bodily features and forms, just as it may occur to our thoughts; which either is not true, or even if it be true, which can most rarely happen, yet this is of no benefit to us to believe in by faith, but it is useful for some other purpose, which is intimated by means of it. For who is there that reads or hears what the Apostle Paul has written, or what has been written of him, that does not imagine to himself the countenance both of the apostle himself, and of all those whose names are there mentioned? And whereas, among such a multitude of men to whom these books are known, each imagines in a different way those bodily features and forms, it is assuredly uncertain which it is that imagines them more nearly and more like the reality. Nor, indeed, is our faith busied therein with the bodily countenance of those men; but only that by the grace of God they so lived and so acted as that Scripture witnesses: this it is which it is both useful to believe, and which must not be despaired of, and must be sought. For even the countenance of our Lord Himself in the flesh is variously fancied by the diversity of countless imaginations, which yet was one, whatever it was. Nor in our faith which we have of our

---

[1] Acts xvii. 27, 28.   [2] 2 Cor. v. 7.   [3] 1 Cor. xiii. 12.   [4] Matt. v. 8.   [5] 1 Cor. xiii. 13.   [6] 1 Tim. i. 5.

Lord Jesus Christ, is that wholesome which the mind imagines for itself, perhaps far other than the reality, but that which we think of man according to his kind: for we have a notion of human nature implanted in us, as it were by rule, according to which we know forthwith, that whatever such thing we see is a man or the form of a man.

CHAP. 5.—HOW THE TRINITY MAY BE LOVED THOUGH UNKNOWN.

Our conception is framed according to this notion, when we believe that God was made man for us, as an example of humility, and to show the love of God towards us. For this it is which it is good for us to believe, and to retain firmly and unshakenly in our heart, that the humility by which God was born of a woman, and was led to death through contumelies so great by mortal men, is the chiefest remedy by which the swelling of our pride may be cured, and the profound mystery by which the bond of sin may be loosed. So also, because we know what omnipotence is, we believe concerning the omnipotent God in the power of His miracles and of His resurrection, and we frame conceptions respecting actions of this kind, according to the species and genera of things that are either ingrafted in us by nature, or gathered by experience, that our faith may not be feigned. For neither do we know the countenance of the Virgin Mary; from whom, untouched by a husband, nor tainted in the birth itself, He was wonderfully born. Neither have we seen what were the lineaments of the body of Lazarus; nor yet Bethany; nor the sepulchre, and that stone which He commanded to be removed when He raised Him from the dead; nor the new tomb cut out in the rock, whence He Himself arose; nor the Mount of Olives, from whence He ascended into heaven. And, in short, whoever of us have not seen these things, know not whether they are as we conceive them to be, nay judge them more probably not to be so. For when the aspect either of a place, or a man, or of any other body, which we happened to imagine before we saw it, turns out to be the same when it occurs to our sight as it was when it occurred to our mind, we are moved with no little wonder. So scarcely and hardly ever does it happen. And yet we believe those things most steadfastly, because we imagine them according to a special and general notion, of which we are certain. For we believe our Lord Jesus Christ to be born of a virgin who was called Mary. But what a virgin is, or what it is to be born, and what is a proper name, we do not believe, but

certainly know. And whether that was the countenance of Mary which occurred to the mind in speaking of those things or recollecting them, we neither know at all, nor believe. It is allowable, then, in this case to say without violation of the faith, perhaps she had such or such a countenance, perhaps she had not: but no one could say without violation of the Christian faith, that perhaps Christ was born of a virgin.

8. Wherefore, since we desire to understand the eternity, and equality, and unity of the Trinity, as much as is permitted us, but ought to believe before we understand; and since we must watch carefully, that our faith be not feigned; since we must have the fruition of the same Trinity, that we may live blessedly; but if we have believed anything false of it, our hope would be worthless, and our charity not pure: how then can we love, by believing, that Trinity which we do not know? Is it according to the special or general notion, according to which we love the Apostle Paul? In whose case, even if he was not of that countenance which occurs to us when we think of him (and this we do not know at all), yet we know what a man is. For not to go far away, this *we* are; and it is manifest he, too, was this, and that his soul joined to his body lived after the manner of mortals. Therefore we believe this of him, which we find in ourselves, according to the species or genus under which all human nature alike is comprised. What then do we know, whether specially or generally, of that most excellent Trinity, as if there were many such trinities, some of which we had learned by experience, so that we may believe that Trinity, too, to have been such as they, through the rule of similitude, impressed upon us, whether a special or a general notion; and thus love also that thing which we believe and do not yet know, from the parity of the thing which we do know? But this certainly is not so. Or is it that, as we love in our Lord Jesus Christ, that He rose from the dead, although we never saw any one rise from thence, so we can believe in and love the Trinity which we do not see, and the like of which we never have seen? But we certainly know what it is to die, and what it is to live; because we both live, and from time to time have seen and experienced both dead and dying persons. And what else is it to rise again, except to live again, that is, to return to life from death? When, therefore, we say and believe that there is a Trinity, we know what a Trinity is, because we know what three are; but this is not what we love. For we can easily have this whenever we will, to pass over other things, by just hold-

ing up three fingers. Or do we indeed love, not every trinity, but *the* Trinity, that is God? We love then in the Trinity, that it is God: but we never saw or knew any other God, because God is One; He alone whom we have not yet seen, and whom we love by believing. But the question is, from what likeness or comparison of known things can we believe, in order that we may love God, whom we do not yet know?

CHAP. 6.—HOW THE MAN NOT YET RIGHTEOUS CAN KNOW THE RIGHTEOUS MAN WHOM HE LOVES.

9. Return then with me, and let us consider why we love the apostle. Is it at all on account of his human kind, which we know right well, in that we believe him to have been a man? Assuredly not; for if it were so, he now is not him whom we love, since he is no longer that man, for his soul is separated from his body. But we believe that which we love in him to be still living, for we love his righteous mind. From what general or special rule then, except that we know both what a mind is, and what it is to be righteous? And we say, indeed, not unfitly, that we therefore know what a mind is, because we too have a mind. For neither did we ever see it with our eyes, and gather a special or general notion from the resemblance of more minds than one, which we had seen; but rather, as I have said before, because we too have it. For what is known so intimately, and so perceives itself to be itself, as that by which also all other things are perceived, that is, the mind itself? For we recognize the movements of bodies also, by which we perceive that others live besides ourselves, from the resemblance of ourselves; since we also so move our body in living as we observe those bodies to be moved. For even when a living body is moved, there is no way opened to our eyes to see the mind, a thing which cannot be seen by the eyes; but we perceive something to be contained in that bulk, such as is contained in ourselves, so as to move in like manner our own bulk, which is the life and the soul. Neither is this, as it were, the property of human foresight and reason, since brute animals also perceive that not only they themselves live, but also other brute animals interchangeably, and the one the other, and that we ourselves do so. Neither do they see our souls, save from the movements of the body, and that immediately and most easily by some natural agreement. Therefore we both know the mind of any one from our own, and believe also from our own of him whom we do not know. For not only do we perceive that there is a mind, but we can also know what a mind is, by reflecting upon our own: for we have a mind. But whence do we know what a righteous man is? For we said above that we love the apostle for no other reason except that he is a righteous mind. We know, then, what a righteous man also is, just as we know what a mind is. But what a mind is, as has been said, we know from ourselves, for there is a mind in us. But whence do we know what a righteous man is, if we are not righteous? But if no one but he who is righteous knows what is a righteous man, no one but a righteous man loves a righteous man; for one cannot love him whom one believes to be righteous, for this very reason that one does believe him to be righteous, if one does not know what it is to be righteous; according to that which we have shown above, that no one loves what he believes and does not see, except by some rule of a general or special notion. And if for this reason no one but a righteous man loves a righteous man, how will any one wish to be a righteous man who is not yet so? For no one wishes to be that which he does not love. But, certainly, that he who is not righteous may be so, it is necessary that he should wish to be righteous; and in order that he may wish to be righteous, he loves the righteous man. Therefore, even he who is not yet righteous, loves the righteous man.[1] But he cannot love the righteous man, who is ignorant what a righteous man is. Accordingly, even he who is not yet righteous, knows what a righteous man is. Whence then does he know this? Does he see it with his eyes? Is any corporeal thing righteous, as it is white, or black, or square, or round? Who could say this? Yet with one's eyes one has seen nothing except corporeal things. But there is nothing righteous in a man except the mind; and when a man is called a righteous man, he is called so from the mind, not from the body. For righteousness is in some sort the beauty of the mind, by which men are beautiful; very many too who are misshapen and deformed in body. And as the mind is not seen with the eyes, so neither is its beauty. From whence then does he who is not yet righteous know what a righteous man is, and love the righteous man that he may become righteous? Do certain signs shine forth by the motion of the body, by

---

[1] [The "wish" and "love" which Augustin here attributes to the non-righteous man is not true and spiritual, but selfish. In chapter vii. 10, he speaks of true love as distinct from that kind of desire which is a mere wish. The latter he calls *cupiditas.* "That is to be called love which is true, otherwise it is desire (*cupiditas*): and so those who desire (*cupidi*) are improperly said to love (*diligere*), just as they who love (*diligunt*) are said improperly to desire (*cupere*)."—W. G. T. S.]

which this or that man is manifested to be righteous? But whence does any one know that these are the signs of a righteous mind, when he is wholly ignorant what it is to be righteous? Therefore he does know. But whence do we know what it is to be righteous, even when we are not yet righteous? If we know from without ourselves, we know it by some bodily thing. But this is not a thing of the body. Therefore we know in ourselves what it is to be righteous. For I find this nowhere else when I seek to utter it, except within myself; and if I ask another what it is to be righteous, he seeks within himself what to answer; and whosoever hence can answer truly, he has found within himself what to answer. And when indeed I wish to speak of Carthage, I seek within myself what to speak, and I find within myself a notion or image of Carthage; but I have received this through the body, that is, through the perception of the body, since I have been present in that city in the body, and I saw and perceived it, and retained it in my memory, that I might find within myself a word concerning it, whenever I might wish to speak of it. For its word is the image itself of it in my memory, not that sound of two syllables when Carthage is named, or even when that name itself is thought of silently from time to time, but that which I discern in my mind, when I utter that dissyllable with my voice, or even before I utter it. So also, when I wish to speak of Alexandria, which I never saw, an image of it is present with me. For whereas I had heard from many and had believed that city to be great, in such way as it could be told me, I formed an image of it in my mind as I was able; and this is with me its word when I wish to speak of it, before I utter with my voice the five syllables which make the name that almost every one knows. And yet if I could bring forth that image from my mind to the eyes of men who know Alexandria, certainly all either would say, It is not it; or if they said, It is, I should greatly wonder; and as I gazed at it in my mind, that is, at the image which was as it were its picture, I should yet not know it to be it, but should believe those who retained an image they had seen. But I do not so ask what it is to be righteous, nor do I so find it, nor do I so gaze upon it, when I utter it; neither am I so approved when I am heard, nor do I so approve when I hear; as though I have seen such a thing with my eyes, or learned it by some perception of the body, or heard it from those who had so learned it. For when I say, and say knowingly, that mind is righteous which knowingly and of purpose assigns to every one his due in life and

behavior, I do not think of anything absent, as Carthage, or imagine it as I am able, as Alexandria, whether it be so or not; but I discern something present, and I discern it within myself, though I myself am not that which I discern; and many if they hear will approve it. And whoever hears me and knowingly approves, he too discerns this same thing within himself, even though he himself be not what he discerns. But when a righteous man says this, he discerns and says that which he himself is. And whence also does he discern it, except within himself? But this is not to be wondered at; for whence should he discern himself except within himself? The wonderful thing is, that the mind should see within itself that which it has seen nowhere else, and should see truly, and should see the very true righteous mind, and should itself be a mind, and yet not a righteous mind, which nevertheless it sees within itself. Is there another mind that is righteous in a mind that is not yet righteous? Or if there is not, what does it there see when it sees and says what is a righteous mind, nor sees it anywhere else but in itself, when itself is not a righteous mind? Is that which it sees an inner truth present to the mind which has power to behold it? Yet all have not that power; and they who have power to behold it, are not all also that which they behold, that is, they are not also righteous minds themselves, just as they are able to see and to say what is a righteous mind. And whence will they be able to be so, except by cleaving to that very same form itself which they behold, so that from thence they may be formed and may be righteous minds; not only discerning and saying that the mind is righteous which knowingly and of purpose assigns to every one that which is his due in life and behavior, but so likewise that they themselves may live righteously and be righteous in character, by assigning to every one that which is his due, so as to owe no man anything, but to love one another.[1] And whence can any one cleave to that form but by loving it? Why then do we love another whom we believe to be righteous, and do not love that form itself wherein we see what is a righteous mind, that we also may be able to be righteous? Is it that unless we loved that also, we should not love him at all, whom through it we love; but whilst we are not righteous, we love that form too little to allow of our being able to be righteous? The man therefore who is believed to be righteous, is loved through that form and truth which he who loves discerns and

---

[1] Rom. xiii. 8.

understands within himself; but that very form and truth itself cannot be loved from any other source than itself. For we do not find any other such thing besides itself, so that by believing we might love it when it is unknown, in that we here already know another such thing. For whatsoever of such a kind one may have seen, is itself; and there is not any other such thing, since itself alone is such as itself is. He therefore who loves men, ought to love them either because they are righteous, or that they may become righteous. For so also he ought to love himself, either because he is righteous, or that he may become righteous; for in this way he loves his neighbor as himself without any risk. For he who loves himself otherwise, loves himself wrongfully, since he loves himself to this end that he may be unrighteous; therefore to this end that he may be wicked; and hence it follows next that he does not love himself; for, "He who loveth iniquity,[1] hateth his own soul."[2]

CHAP. 7.—OF TRUE LOVE, BY WHICH WE ARRIVE AT THE KNOWLEDGE OF THE TRINITY. GOD IS TO BE SOUGHT, NOT OUTWARDLY, BY SEEKING TO DO WONDERFUL THINGS WITH THE ANGELS, BUT INWARDLY, BY IMITATING THE PIETY OF GOOD ANGELS.

10. No other thing, then, is chiefly to be regarded in this inquiry, which we make concerning the Trinity and concerning knowing God, except what is true love, nay, rather what is love. For that is to be called love which is true, otherwise it is desire; and so those who desire are said improperly to love, just as they who love are said improperly to desire. But this is true love, that cleaving to the truth we may live righteously, and so may despise all mortal things in comparison with the love of men, whereby we wish them to live righteously. For so we should be prepared also to die profitably for our brethren, as our Lord Jesus Christ taught us by His example. For as there are two commandments on which hang all the Law and the prophets, love of God and love of our neighbor;[3] not without cause the Scripture mostly puts one for both: whether it be of God only, as is that text, "For we know that all things work together for good to them that love God;"[4] and again, "But if any man love God, the same is known of Him;"[5] and that, "Because the love of God is shed abroad in our hearts by the Holy Ghost which is given unto us;"[6] and many other passages; because he who loves God must both needs do what God has commanded, and loves Him just in such proportion as he does so; therefore he must needs also love his neighbor, because God has commanded it: or whether it be that Scripture only mentions the love of our neighbor, as in that text, "Bear ye one another's burdens, and so fulfill the law of Christ;"[7] and again, "For all the law is fulfilled in one word, even in this, Thou shalt love thy neighbor as thyself;"[8] and in the Gospel, "All things whatsoever ye would that men should do to you, do ye even so to them; for this is the Law and the prophets."[9] And many other passages occur in the sacred writings, in which only the love of our neighbor seems to be commanded for perfection, while the love of God is passed over in silence; whereas the Law and the prophets hang on both precepts. But this, too, is because he who loves his neighbor must needs also love above all else love itself. But "God is love; and he that dwelleth in love, dwelleth in God."[10] Therefore he must needs above all else love God.

11. Wherefore they who seek God through those Powers which rule over the world, or parts of the world, are removed and cast away far from Him; not by intervals of space, but by difference of affections: for they endeavor to find a path outwardly, and forsake their own inward things, within which is God. Therefore, even although they may either have heard some holy heavenly Power, or in some way or another may have thought of it, yet they rather covet its deeds at which human weakness marvels, but do not imitate the piety by which divine rest is acquired. For they prefer, through pride, to be able to do that which an angel does, more than, through devotion, to be that which an angel is. For no holy being rejoices in his own power, but in His from whom he has the power which he fitly can have; and he knows it to be more a mark of power to be united to the Omnipotent by a pious will, than to be able, by his own power and will, to do what they may tremble at who are not able to do such things. Therefore the Lord Jesus Christ Himself, in doing such things, in order that He might teach better things to those who marvelled at them, and might turn those who were intent and in doubt about unusual temporal things to eternal and inner things, says, "Come unto me, all ye that labor and are heavy laden, and I will give you rest. Take my yoke upon you." And He does not say, Learn of me, because I raise those

---

1 Violence—A. V.　　　　2 Ps. xi. 6.
3 Matt. xxii. 37-40.　　　4 Rom. viii. 28.
5 1 Cor. viii. 3.　　　　　6 Rom. v. 5.

7 Gal. vi. 2.　　　　　　8 Gal. v. 14.
9 Matt. vii. 12.　　　　　10 1 John iv. 6.

who have been dead four days; but He says, "Learn of me; for I am meek and lowly in heart." For humility, which is most solid, is more powerful and safer than pride, that is most inflated. And so He goes on to say, "And ye shall find rest unto your souls,"[1] for "Love[2] is not puffed up;"[3] and "God is Love;"[4] and "such as be faithful in love shall rest in[5] Him,"[6] called back from the din which is without to silent joys. Behold, "God is Love:" why do we go forth and run to the heights of the heavens and the lowest parts of the earth, seeking Him who is within us, if we wish to be with Him?

CHAP. 8.—THAT HE WHO LOVES HIS BROTHER, LOVES GOD ; BECAUSE HE LOVES LOVE ITSELF, WHICH IS OF GOD, AND IS GOD.

12. Let no one say, I do not know what I love. Let him love his brother, and he will love the same love. For he knows the love with which he loves, more than the brother whom he loves. So now he can know God more than he knows his brother: clearly known more, because more present; known more, because more within him; known more, because more certain. Embrace the love of God, and by love embrace God. That is love itself, which associates together all good angels and all the servants of God by the bond of sanctity, and joins together us and them mutually with ourselves, and joins us subordinately to Himself. In proportion, therefore, as we are healed from the swelling of pride, in such proportion are we more filled with love; and with what is he full, who is full of love, except with God? Well, but you will say, I see love, and, as far as I am able, I gaze upon it with my mind, and I believe the Scripture, saying, that "God is love; and he that dwelleth in love, dwelleth in God;"[7] but when I see love, I do not see in it the Trinity. Nay, but thou dost see the Trinity if thou seest love. But if I can I will put you in mind, that thou mayest see that thou seest it; only let itself be present, that we may be moved by love to something good. Since, when we love love, we love one who loves something, and that on account of this very thing, that he does love something; therefore what does love love, that love itself also may be loved? For that is not love which loves nothing. But if it loves itself it must love something, that it may love itself as love. For as a word indicates something, and indicates also itself, but does not indicate itself to be a word, unless it indicates that it does indicate something; so love also loves indeed itself, but except it love itself as loving something, it loves itself not as love. What therefore does love love, except that which we love with love? But this, to begin from that which is nearest to us, is our brother. And listen how greatly the Apostle John commends brotherly love: "He that loveth his brother abideth in the light, and there is none occasion of stumbling in him."[8] It is manifest that he placed the perfection of righteousness in the love of our brother; for he certainly is perfect in whom "there is no occasion of stumbling." And yet he seems to have passed by the love of God in silence; which he never would have done, unless because he intends God to be understood in brotherly love itself. For in this same epistle, a little further on, he says most plainly thus: "Beloved, let us love one another: for love is of God; and every one that loveth is born of God, and knoweth God. He that loveth not, knoweth not God; for God is love." And this passage declares sufficiently and plainly, that this same brotherly love itself (for that is brotherly love by which we love each other) is set forth by so great authority, not only to be from God, but also to be God. When, therefore, we love our brother from love, we love our brother from God; neither can it be that we do not love above all else that same love by which we love our brother: whence it may be gathered that these two commandments cannot exist unless interchangeably. For since "God is love," he who loves love certainly loves God; but he must needs love love, who loves his brother. And so a little after he says, "For he that loveth not his brother whom he hath seen, how can he love God whom he hath not seen"?[9] because the reason that he does not see God is, that he does not love his brother. For he who does not love his brother, abideth not in love; and he who abideth not in love, abideth not in God, because God is love. Further, he who abideth not in God, abideth not in light; for "God is light, and in Him is no darkness at all."[10] He therefore who abideth not in light, what wonder is it if he does not see light, that is, does not see God, because he is in darkness? But he sees his brother with human sight, with which God cannot be seen. But if he loved with spiritual love him whom he sees with human sight, he would see God, who is love itself, with the inner sight by which He can be seen. Therefore he who does not love his brother whom

---

[1] Matt. xi. 28, 29.　　[2] Charity.--A.V.　　[3] 1 Cor. xiii. 4.
[4] 1 John iv. 8.　　[5] Abide with.--A.V.
[6] Wisd. iii. 9.　　[7] 1 John iv. 16.

[8] 1 John ii. 10.　　[9] 1 John iv. 7, 8, 20.　　[10] 1 John i. 5.

he sees, how can he love God, whom on that account he does not see, because God is love, which he has not who does not love his brother? Neither let that further question disturb us, how much of love we ought to spend upon our brother, and how much upon God: incomparably more upon God than upon ourselves, but upon our brother as much as upon ourselves; and we love ourselves so much the more, the more we love God. Therefore we love God and our neighbor from one and the same love; but we love God for the sake of God, and ourselves and our neighbors for the sake of God.

CHAP. 9. — OUR LOVE OF THE RIGHTEOUS IS KINDLED FROM LOVE ITSELF OF THE UNCHANGEABLE FORM OF RIGHTEOUSNESS.

13. For why is it, pray, that we burn when we hear and read, "Behold, now is the accepted time; behold, now is the day of salvation: giving no offense in anything, that the ministry be not blamed: but in all things approving ourselves as the ministers of God, in much patience, in afflictions, in necessities, in distresses, in stripes, in imprisonments, in tumults, in labors, in watchings, in fastings; by pureness, by knowledge, by long-suffering, by kindness, by the Holy Ghost, by love unfeigned, by the word of truth, by the power of God, by the armor of righteousness on the right hand and on the left, by honor and dishonor, by evil report and good report: as deceivers, and yet true; as unknown, and yet well known; as dying, and, behold, we live; as chastened, and not killed; as sorrowful, yet alway rejoicing; as poor, yet making many rich; as having nothing, and yet possessing all things?"[1] Why is it that we are inflamed with love of the Apostle Paul, when we read these things, unless that we believe him so to have lived? But we do not believe that the ministers of God ought so to live because we have heard it from any one, but because we behold it inwardly within ourselves, or rather above ourselves, in the truth itself. Him, therefore, whom we believe to have so lived, we love for that which we see. And except we loved above all else that form which we discern as always steadfast and unchangeable, we should not for that reason love him, because we hold fast in our belief that his life, when he was living in the flesh, was adapted to, and in harmony with, this form. But some-

how we are stirred up the more to the love of this form itself, through the belief by which we believe some one to have so lived; and to the hope by which we no more at all despair, that we, too, are able so to live; we who are men, from this fact itself, that some men have so lived, so that we both desire this more ardently, and pray for it more confidently. So both the love of that form, according to which they are believed to have lived, makes the life of these men themselves to be loved by us; and their life thus believed stirs up a more burning love towards that same form; so that the more ardently we love God, the more certainly and the more calmly do we see Him, because we behold in God the unchangeable form of righteousness, according to which we judge that man ought to live. Therefore faith avails to the knowledge and to the love of God, not as though of one altogether unknown, or altogether not loved; but so that thereby He may be known more clearly, and loved more steadfastly.

CHAP. 10. — THERE ARE THREE THINGS IN LOVE, AS IT WERE A TRACE OF THE TRINITY.

14. But what is love or charity, which divine Scripture so greatly praises and proclaims, except the love of good? But love is *of* some one that loves, and *with* love something *is* loved. Behold, then, there are three things: he that loves, and that which is loved, and love. What, then, is love, except a certain life which couples or seeks to couple together some two things, namely, him that loves, and that which is loved? And this is so even in outward and carnal loves. But that we may drink in something more pure and clear, let us tread down the flesh and ascend to the mind. What does the mind love in a friend except the mind? There, then, also are three things: he that loves, and that which is loved, and love. It remains to ascend also from hence, and to seek those things which are above, as far as is given to man. But here for a little while let our purpose rest, not that it may think itself to have found already what it seeks; but just as usually the place has first to be found where anything is to be sought, while the thing itself is not yet found, but we have only found already where to look for it; so let it suffice to have said thus much, that we may have, as it were, the hinge of some starting-point, whence to weave the rest of our discourse.

---

[1] 2 Cor. vi. 2-10.

BOOK IX.

THAT A KIND OF TRINITY EXISTS IN MAN, WHO IS THE IMAGE OF GOD, VIZ. THE MIND, AND THE KNOWLEDGE WHEREWITH THE MIND KNOWS ITSELF, AND THE LOVE WHEREWITH IT LOVES BOTH ITSELF AND ITS OWN KNOWLEDGE; AND THESE THREE ARE SHOWN TO BE MUTUALLY EQUAL, AND OF ONE ESSENCE.

CHAP. I. — IN WHAT WAY WE MUST INQUIRE CONCERNING THE TRINITY.

1. WE certainly seek a trinity,—not any trinity, but that Trinity which is God, and the true and supreme and only God. Let my hearers then wait, for we are still seeking. And no one justly finds fault with such a search, if at least he who seeks that which either to know or to utter is most difficult, is steadfast in the faith. But whosoever either sees or teaches better, finds fault quickly and justly with any one who confidently affirms concerning it. "Seek God," he says, "and your heart shall live;"[1] and lest any one should rashly rejoice that he has, as it were, apprehended it, "Seek," he says, "His face evermore."[2] And the apostle: "If any man," he says, "think that he knoweth anything, he knoweth nothing yet as he ought to know. But if any man love God, the same is known of Him."[3] He has not said, has known Him, which is dangerous presumption, but "is known of Him." So also in another place, when he had said, "But now after that ye have known God;" immediately correcting himself, he says, "or rather are known of God."[4] And above all in that other place, "Brethren," he says, "I count not myself to have apprehended: but this one thing I do, forgetting those things which are behind, and reaching forth unto those things which are before, I press in purpose[5] toward the mark, for the prize of the high calling of God in Christ Jesus. Let us therefore, as many as be perfect, be thus minded."[6] Perfection in this life, he tells us, is nothing else than to forget those things which are behind, and to reach forth and press in purpose toward those things which are before. For he that seeks has the safest purpose, [who seeks] until that is taken hold of whither we are tending, and for which we are reaching forth. But that is the right purpose which starts from faith. For a certain faith is in some way the starting-point of knowledge; but a certain knowledge will not be made perfect, except after this life, when we shall see face to face.[7] Let us therefore be thus minded, so as to know that the disposition to seek the truth is more safe than that which presumes things unknown to be known. Let us therefore so seek as if we should find, and so find as if we were about to seek. For "when a man hath done, then he beginneth."[8] Let us doubt without unbelief of things to be believed; let us affirm without rashness of things to be understood: authority must be held fast in the former, truth sought out in the latter. As regards this question, then, let us believe that the Father, and the Son, and the Holy Spirit is one God, the Creator and Ruler of the whole creature; and that the Father is not the Son, nor the Holy Spirit either the Father or the Son, but a trinity of persons mutually inter-related, and a unity of an equal essence. And let us seek to understand this, praying for help from Himself, whom we wish to understand; and as much as He grants, desiring to explain what we understand with so much pious care and anxiety, that even if in any case we say one thing for another, we may at least say nothing unworthy. As, for the sake of example, if we say anything concerning the Father that does not properly belong to the Father, or does belong to the Son, or to the

---

[1] Ps. lxix. 32.
[2] Ps. cv. 4.
[3] 1 Cor. viii. 2.
[4] Gal. iv. 19.
[5] In purpose, *om.* in A.V.
[6] Phil. iii. 13-15.

[7] 1 Cor. xiii. 12.
[8] Ecclus. xviii. 7.

Holy Spirit, or to the Trinity itself; and if anything of the Son which does not properly suit with the Son, or at all events which does suit with the Father, or with the Holy Spirit, or with the Trinity; or if, again, anything concerning the Holy Spirit, which is not fitly a property of the Holy Spirit, yet is not alien from the Father, or from the Son, or from the one God the Trinity itself. Even as now our wish is to see whether the Holy Spirit is properly that love which is most excellent; which if He is not, either the Father is love, or the Son, or the Trinity itself; since we cannot withstand the most certain faith and weighty authority of Scripture, saying, "God is love." [1] And yet we ought not to deviate into profane error, so as to say anything of the Trinity which does not suit the Creator, but rather the creature, or which is feigned outright by mere empty thought.

CHAP. 2. — THE THREE THINGS WHICH ARE FOUND IN LOVE MUST BE CONSIDERED. [2]

2. And this being so, let us direct our attention to those three things which we fancy we have found. We are not yet speaking of heavenly things, nor yet of God the Father, and Son, and Holy Spirit, but of that inadequate image, which yet is an image, that is, man; for our feeble mind perhaps can gaze upon this more familiarly and more easily. Well then, when I, who make this inquiry, love anything, there are three things concerned—myself, and that which I love, and love itself. For I do not love love, except I love a lover; for there is no love where nothing is loved. Therefore there are three things—he who loves, and that which is loved, and love. But what if I love none except myself? Will there not then be two things— that which I love, and love? For he who loves and that which is loved are the same when any one loves himself; just as to love and to be loved, in the same way, is the very same thing when any one loves himself. Since the same thing is said, when it is said, he loves himself, and he is loved by himself. For in that case to love and to be loved are not two different things: just as he who loves and he who is loved are not two different persons. But yet, even so, love and what is loved are still two things. For there is no love when any one loves himself, except when love itself is loved. But it is one thing to love one's self, another to love one's own love. For love is not loved, unless as already loving something; since where nothing is loved there is no love. Therefore there are two things when any one loves himself—love, and that which is loved. For then he that loves and that which is loved are one. Whence it seems that it does not follow that three things are to be understood wherever love is. For let us put aside from the inquiry all the other many things of which a man consists; and in order that we may discover clearly what we are now seeking, as far as in such a subject is possible, let us treat of the mind alone. The mind, then, when it loves itself, discloses two things —mind and love. But what is to love one's self, except to wish to help one's self to the enjoyment of self? And when any one wishes himself to be just as much as he is, then the will is on a par with the mind, and the love is equal to him who loves. And if love is a substance, it is certainly not body, but spirit; and the mind also is not body, but spirit. Yet love and mind are not two spirits, but one spirit; nor yet two essences, but one: and yet here are two things that are one, he that loves and love; or, if you like so to put it, that which is loved and love. And these two, indeed, are mutually said relatively. Since he who loves is referred to love, and love to him who loves. For he who loves, loves with some love, and love is the love of some one who loves. But mind and spirit are not said relatively, but express essence. For mind and spirit do not exist because the mind and spirit of some particular man exists. For if we subtract the body from that which is man, which is so called with the conjunction of body, the mind and spirit remain. But if we subtract him that loves, then there is no love; and if we subtract love, then there is no one that loves. And therefore, in so far as they are mutually referred to one another, they are two; but whereas they are spoken in re-

---

[1] 1 John iv. 16.

[2] [Augustin here begins his discussion of some ternaries that are found in the Finite, that illustrate the trinality of the Infinite. Like all finite analogies, they fail at certain points. In the case chosen—namely, the lover, the loved, and love—the first two are substances, the last is not. The mind is a substance, but its activity in loving is not. In chapter iv. 5, Augustin asserts that "love and knowledge exist substantially, as the mind itself does." But no psychology, ancient or modern, has ever maintained that the agencies of a spiritual entity or substance are themselves spiritual entities or substances. The activities of the human mind in cognizing, loving, etc., are only its energizing, not its substance.

The ambiguity of the Latin contributes to this error. The mind and its loving, and also the mind and its cognizing, are denominated "duo quædam;" the mind, love, and knowledge, are denominated "tria quædam." By bringing the mind and its love and knowledge under the one term "quædam," and then giving the meaning of "substance" to "thing," in "something," the result follows that all three are alike and equally "substantial."

This analogy taken from the mind and its activities illustrates the trinality of the Divine essence, but fails to illustrate the substantiality of the three persons. The three Divine persons are not the Divine essence together with two of its activities (such, e. g., as creation and redemption), but the essence in three modes, or "forms," as St. Paul denominates them in Phil. iii. 6.

If Augustin could prove his assertion that the activities of the human spirit in knowing and loving are strictly "substantial," then this ternary would illustrate not only the trinality of the essence, but the essentiality and objectivity of the persons. The fact which he mentions, that knowledge and love are inseparable from the knowing and loving mind, does not prove their equal substantiality with the mind.—W. G. T. S.]

spect to themselves, each are spirit, and both together also are one spirit; and each are mind, and both together one mind. Where, then, is the trinity? Let us attend as much as we can, and let us invoke the everlasting light, that He may illuminate our darkness, and that we may see in ourselves, as much as we are permitted, the image of God.

CHAP. 3.—THE IMAGE OF THE TRINITY IN THE MIND OF MAN WHO KNOWS HIMSELF AND LOVES HIMSELF. THE MIND KNOWS ITSELF THROUGH ITSELF.

3. For the mind cannot love itself, except also it know itself; for how can it love what it does not know? Or if any body says that the mind, from either general or special knowledge, believes itself of such a character as it has by experience found others to be, and therefore loves itself, he speaks most foolishly. For whence does a mind know another mind, if it does not know itself? For the mind does not know other minds and not know itself, as the eye of the body sees other eyes and does not see itself; for we see bodies through the eyes of the body, because, unless we are looking into a mirror, we cannot refract and reflect the rays into themselves, which shine forth through those eyes, and touch whatever we discern,—a subject, indeed, which is treated of most subtlely and obscurely, until it be clearly demonstrated whether the fact be so, or whether it be not. But whatever is the nature of the power by which we discern through the eyes, certainly, whether it be rays or anything else, we cannot discern with the eyes that power itself; but we inquire into it with the mind, and if possible, understand even this with the mind. As the mind, then, itself gathers the knowledge of corporeal things through the senses of the body, so of incorporeal things through itself. Therefore it knows itself also through itself, since it is incorporeal; for if it does not know itself, it does not love itself.

CHAP. 4. — THE THREE ARE ONE, AND ALSO EQUAL, VIZ. THE MIND ITSELF, AND THE LOVE, AND THE KNOWLEDGE OF IT. THAT THE SAME THREE EXIST SUBSTANTIALLY, AND ARE PREDICATED RELATIVELY. THAT THE SAME THREE ARE INSEPARABLE. THAT THE SAME THREE ARE NOT JOINED AND COMMINGLED LIKE PARTS, BUT THAT THEY ARE OF ONE ESSENCE, AND ARE RELATIVES.

4. But as there are two things (*duo quæ-dam*), the mind and the love of it, when it loves itself; so there are two things, the mind and the knowledge of it, when it knows itself.

Therefore the mind itself, and the love of it, and the knowledge of it, are three things (*tria quædam*), and these three are one; and when they are perfect they are equal. For if one loves himself less than as he is,—as for example, suppose that the mind of a man only loves itself as much as the body of a man ought to be loved, whereas the mind is more than the body,—then it is in fault, and its love is not perfect. Again, if it loves itself more than as it is,—as if, for instance, it loves itself as much as God is to be loved, whereas the mind is incomparably less than God,—here also it is exceedingly in fault, and its love of self is not perfect. But it is in fault more perversely and wrongly still, when it loves the body as much as God is to be loved. Also, if knowledge is less than that thing which is known, and which can be fully known, then knowledge is not perfect; but if it is greater, then the nature which knows is above that which is known, as the knowledge of the body is greater than the body itself, which is known by that knowledge. For knowledge is a kind of life in the reason of the knower, but the body is not life; and any life is greater than any body, not in bulk, but in power. But when the mind knows itself, its own knowledge does not rise above itself, because itself knows, and itself is known. When, therefore, it knows itself entirely, and no other thing with itself, then its knowledge is equal to itself; because its knowledge is not from another nature, since it knows itself. And when it perceives itself entirely, and nothing more, then it is neither less nor greater. We said therefore rightly, that these three things, [mind, love, and knowledge], when they are perfect, are by consequence equal.

5. Similar reasoning suggests to us, if indeed we can any way understand the matter, that these things [*i.e.* love and knowledge] exist in the soul, and that, being as it were involved in it, they are so evolved from it as to be perceived and reckoned up substantially, or, so to say, essentially. Not as though in a subject; as color, or shape, or any other quality or quantity, are in the body. For anything of this [material] kind does not go beyond the subject in which it is; for the color or shape of this particular body cannot be also those of another body. But the mind can also love something besides itself, with that love with which it loves itself. And further, the mind does not know itself only, but also many other things. Wherefore love and knowledge are not contained in the mind as in a subject, but these also exist *substantially, as the mind itself does;* because, even if they are mutually predicated relatively, yet

they exist each severally in their own substance. Nor are they so mutually predicated relatively as color and the colored subject are; so that color is in the colored subject, but has not any proper substance in itself, since colored body is a substance, but color is in a substance; but as two friends are also two men, which are substances, while they are said to be men not relatively, but friends relatively.

6. But, further, although one who loves or one who knows is a substance, and *knowledge is a substance*, and *love is a substance*, but he that loves and love, or, he that knows and knowledge, are spoken of relatively to each other, as are friends: yet mind or spirit are not relatives, as neither are men relatives: nevertheless he that loves and love, or he that knows and knowledge, cannot exist separately from each other, as men can that are friends. Although it would seem that friends, too, can be separated in body, not in mind, in as far as they are friends: nay, it can even happen that a friend may even also begin to hate a friend, and on this account cease to be a friend, while the other does not know it, and still loves him. But if the love with which the mind loves itself ceases to be, then the mind also will at the same time cease to love. Likewise, if the knowledge by which the mind knows itself ceases to be, then the mind will also at the same time cease to know itself. Just as the head of anything that has a head is certainly a head, and they are predicated relatively to each other, although they are also substances: for both a head is a body, and so is that which has a head; and if there be no head, then neither will there be that which has a head. Only these things can be separated from each other by cutting off, those cannot.

7. And even if there are some bodies which cannot be wholly separated and divided, yet they would not be bodies unless they consisted of their own proper parts. A part then is predicated relatively to a whole, since every part is a part of some whole, and a whole is a whole by having all its parts. But since both part and whole are bodies, these things are not only predicated relatively, but exist also substantially. Perhaps, then, the mind is a whole, and the love with which it loves itself, and the knowledge with which it knows itself, are as it were its parts, of which two parts that whole consists. Or are there three equal parts which make up the one whole? But no part embraces the whole, of which it is a part; whereas, when the mind knows itself as a whole, that is,

knows itself perfectly, then the knowledge of it extends through the whole of it; and when it loves itself perfectly, then it loves itself as a whole, and the love of it extends through the whole of it. Is it, then, as one drink is made from wine and water and honey, and each single part extends through the whole, and yet they are three things (for there is no part of the drink which does not contain these three things; for they are not joined as if they were water and oil, but are entirely commingled: and they are all substances, and the whole of that liquor which is composed of the three is one substance),—is it, I say, in some such way as this we are to think these three to be together, mind, love, and knowledge? But water, wine, and honey are not of one substance, although one substance results in the drink made from the commingling of them. And I cannot see how those other three are not of the same substance, since the mind itself loves itself, and itself knows itself; and these three so exist, as that the mind is neither loved nor known by any other thing at all. These three, therefore, must needs be of one and the same essence; and for that reason, if they were confounded together as it were by a commingling, they could not be in any way three, neither could they be mutually referred to each other. Just as if you were to make from one and the same gold three similar rings, although connected with each other, they are mutually referred to each other, because they are similar. For everything similar is similar to something, and there is a trinity of rings, and one gold. But if they are blended with each other, and each mingled with the other through the whole of their own bulk, then that trinity will fall through, and it will not exist at all; and not only will it be called one gold, as it was called in the case of those three rings, but now it will not be called three things of gold at all.

CHAP. 5.—THAT THESE THREE ARE SEVERAL IN THEMSELVES, AND MUTUALLY ALL IN ALL.

8. But in these three, when the mind knows itself and loves itself, there remains a trinity: mind, love, knowledge; and this trinity is not confounded together by any commingling: although they are each severally in themselves and mutually all in all, or each severally in each two, or each two in each. Therefore all are in all. For certainly the mind is in itself, since it is called mind in respect to itself: although it is said to be knowing, or known, or knowable, relatively to its own knowledge; and although also as

loving, and loved, or lovable, it is referred to love, by which it loves itself. And knowledge, although it is referred to the mind that knows or is known, nevertheless is also predicated both as known and knowing in respect to itself: for the knowledge by which the mind knows itself is not unknown to itself. And although love is referred to the mind that loves, whose love it is; nevertheless it is also love in respect to itself, so as to exist also in itself: since love too is loved, yet cannot be loved with anything except with love, that is with itself. So these things are severally in themselves. But so are they in each other; because both the mind that loves is *in* love, and love is *in* the knowledge of him that loves, and knowledge is *in* the mind that knows. And each severally is in like manner in each two, because the mind which knows and loves itself, is in its own love and knowledge: and the love of the mind that loves and knows itself, is in the mind and in its knowledge: and the knowledge of the mind that knows and loves itself is in the mind and in its love, because it loves itself that knows, and knows itself that loves. And hence also each two is in each severally, since the mind which knows and loves itself, is together with its own knowledge in love, and together with its own love in knowledge; and love too itself and knowledge are together in the mind, which loves and knows itself. But in what way all are in all, we have already shown above; since the mind loves itself as a whole, and knows itself as a whole, and knows its own love wholly, and loves its own knowledge wholly, when these three things are perfect in respect to themselves. Therefore these three things are marvellously inseparable from each other, and yet each of them is severally a substance, and all together are one substance or essence, whilst they are mutually predicated relatively.[1]

---

[1] [Augustin here illustrates, by the ternary of mind, love, and knowledge, what the Greek Trinitarians denominate the περιχώρησις of the divine essence. By the figure of a circulation, they describe the eternal inbeing and indwelling of one person in another. This is founded on John xiv. 10, 11; xvii. 21, 23. "Believest thou not that I am in the Father, and the Father in Me? I pray that they all may be one, as thou Father art in Me, and I in Thee." Athanasius (*Oratio*, iii. 21) remarks that Christ here prays that the disciples "may imitate the trinitarian unity of *essence*, in their unity of *affection*. Had it been possible for the disciples to be in the essence of the Father as the Son is, he would have prayed that they all may be "one in *Thee*," instead of "one in Us."

The Platonists, also, employed this figure of circulatory movement, to explain the self-reflecting and self-communing nature of the human mind. "It is not possible for us to know what our souls are, but only by their κινήσεις κυκλικαὶ, their circular and reflex motions and converse with themselves, which only can steal from them their own secrets." J. Smith: *Immortality of the Soul*, Ch. ii.

Augustin's illustration, however, is imperfect, because "the three things" which circulate are *not* "each of them severally a substance." Only one of them, namely, the mind, is a substance. —W. G. T. S.]

9

9. But when the human mind knows itself and loves itself, it does not know and love anything unchangeable: and each individual man declares his own particular mind by one manner of speech, when he considers what takes place in himself; but defines the human mind abstractly by special or general knowledge. And so, when he speaks to me of his own individual mind, as to whether he understands this or that, or does not understand it, or whether he wishes or does not wish this or that, I believe; but when he speaks the truth of the mind of man generally or specially, I recognize and approve. Whence it is manifest, that each sees a thing in himself, in such way that another person may believe what he says of it, yet may not see it; but another [sees a thing] in the truth itself, in such way that another person also can gaze upon it; of which the former undergoes changes at successive times, the latter consists in an unchangeable eternity. For we do not gather a generic or specific knowledge of the human mind by means of resemblance by seeing many minds with the eyes of the body: but we gaze upon indestructible truth, from which to define perfectly, as far as we can, not of what sort is the mind of any one particular man, but of what sort it ought to be upon the eternal plan.

10. Whence also, even in the case of the images of things corporeal which are drawn in through the bodily sense, and in some way infused into the memory, from which also those things which have not been seen are thought under a fancied image, whether otherwise than they really are, or even perchance as they are;—even here too, we are proved either to accept or reject, within ourselves, by other rules which remain altogether unchangeable above our mind, when we approve or reject anything rightly. For both when I recall the walls of Carthage which I have seen, and imagine to myself the walls of Alexandria which I have not seen, and, in preferring this to that among forms which in both cases are imaginary, make that preference upon grounds of reason; the judgment of truth from above is still strong and clear, and rests firmly upon the utterly indestructible rules of its own right; and if it is covered as it were by cloudiness of corporeal images, yet is not wrapt up and confounded in them.

11. But it makes a difference, whether,

under that or in that darkness, I am shut off as it were from the clear heaven; or whether (as usually happens on lofty mountains), enjoying the free air between both, I at once look up above to the calmest light, and down below upon the densest clouds. For whence is the ardor of brotherly love kindled in me, when I hear that some man has borne bitter torments for the excellence and steadfastness of faith? And if that man is shown to me with the finger, I am eager to join myself to him, to become acquainted with him, to bind him to myself in friendship. And accordingly, if opportunity offers, I draw near, I address him, I converse with him, I express my goodwill towards him in what words I can, and wish that in him too in turn should be brought to pass and expressed goodwill towards me; and I endeavor after a spiritual embrace in the way of belief, since I cannot search out so quickly and discern altogether his innermost heart. I love therefore the faithful and courageous man with a pure and genuine love. But if he were to confess to me in the course of conversation, or were through unguardedness to show in any way, that either he believes something unseemly of God, and desires also something carnal in Him, and that he bore these torments on behalf of such an error, or from the desire of money for which he hoped, or from empty greediness of human praise: immediately it follows that the love with which I was borne towards him, displeased, and as it were repelled, and taken away from an unworthy man, remains in that form, after which, believing him such as I did, I had loved him; unless perhaps I have come to love him to this end, that he may become such, while I have found him not to be such in fact. And in that man, too, nothing is changed: although it can be changed, so that he may become that which I had believed him to be already. But in my mind there certainly is something changed, viz., the estimate I had formed of him, which was before of one sort, and now is of another: and the same love, at the bidding from above of unchangeable righteousness, is turned aside from the purpose of enjoying, to the purpose of taking counsel. But the form itself of unshaken and stable truth, wherein I should have enjoyed the fruition of the man, believing him to be good, and wherein likewise I take counsel that he may be good, sheds in an immoveable eternity the same light of incorruptible and most sound reason, both upon the sight of my mind, and upon that cloud of images, which I discern from above, when I think of the same man whom I had seen. Again, when I call back

to my mind some arch, turned beautifully and symmetrically, which, let us say, I saw at Carthage; a certain reality that had been made known to the mind through the eyes, and transferred to the memory, causes the imaginary view. But I behold in my mind yet another thing, according to which that work of art pleases me; and whence also, if it displeased me, I should correct it. We judge therefore of those particular things according to that [form of eternal truth], and discern that form by the intuition of the rational mind. But those things themselves we either touch if present by the bodily sense, or if absent remember their images as fixed in our memory, or picture, in the way of likeness to them, such things as we ourselves also, if we wished and were able, would laboriously build up: figuring in the mind after one fashion the images of bodies, or seeing bodies through the body; but after another, grasping by simple intelligence what is above the eye of the mind, viz., the reasons and the unspeakably beautiful skill of such forms.

CHAP. 7.—WE CONCEIVE AND BEGET THE WORD WITHIN, FROM THE THINGS WE HAVE BEHELD IN THE ETERNAL TRUTH. THE WORD, WHETHER OF THE CREATURE OR OF THE CREATOR, IS CONCEIVED BY LOVE.

12. We behold, then, by the sight of the mind, in that eternal truth from which all things temporal are made, the form according to which we are, and according to which we do anything by true and right reason, either in ourselves, or in things corporeal; and we have the true knowledge of things, thence conceived, as it were as a word within us, and by speaking we beget it from within; nor by being born does it depart from us. And when we speak to others, we apply to the word, remaining within us, the ministry of the voice or of some bodily sign, that by some kind of sensible remembrance some similar thing may be wrought also in the mind of him that hears,—similar, I say, to that which does not depart from the mind of him that speaks. We do nothing, therefore, through the members of the body in our words and actions, by which the behavior of men is either approved or blamed, which we do not anticipate by a word uttered within ourselves. For no one willingly does anything, which he has not first said in his heart.

13. And this word is conceived by love, either of the creature or of the Creator, that is, either of changeable nature or of unchangeable truth.[1]

---

[1] [The inward production of a thought in the finite essence of the human spirit which is expressed outwardly in a spoken word,

CHAP. 8.—IN WHAT DESIRE AND LOVE DIFFER.

[Conceived] therefore, either by desire or by love: not that the creature ought not to be loved; but if that love [of the creature] is referred to the Creator, then it will not be desire (*cupiditas*), but love (*charitas*). For it is desire when the creature is loved for itself. And then it does not help a man through making use of it, but corrupts him in the enjoying it. When, therefore, the creature is either equal to us or inferior, we must use the inferior in order to God, but we must enjoy the equal only in God. For as thou oughtest to enjoy thyself, not in thyself, but in Him who made thee, so also him whom thou lovest as thyself. Let us enjoy, therefore, both ourselves and our brethren in the Lord; and hence let us not dare to yield, and as it were to relax, ourselves to ourselves in the direction downwards. Now a word is born, when, being thought out, it pleases us either to the effect of sinning, or to that of doing right. Therefore love, as it were a mean, conjoins our word and the mind from which it is conceived, and without any confusion binds itself as a third with them, in an incorporeal embrace.

CHAP. 9.—IN THE LOVE OF SPIRITUAL THINGS THE WORD BORN IS THE SAME AS THE WORD CONCEIVED. IT IS OTHERWISE IN THE LOVE OF CARNAL THINGS.

14. But the word conceived and the word born are the very same when the will finds rest in knowledge itself, as is the case in the love of spiritual things. For instance, he who knows righteousness perfectly, and loves it perfectly, is already righteous; even if no necessity exist of working according to it outwardly through the members of the body. But in the love of carnal and temporal things, as in the offspring of animals, the conception of the word is one thing, the bringing forth another. For here what is conceived by desiring is born by attaining. Since it does not suffice to avarice to know and to love gold, except it also have it; nor to know and love to eat, or to lie with any one, unless also one does it; nor to know and love honors and power, unless they actually come to pass. Nay, all these things, even if obtained, do not suffice. "Whosoever drinketh of this water," He says, "shall thirst again."[1] And so also the Psalmist, "He hath conceived pain and brought forth iniquity."[2] And he

speaks of pain or labor as conceived, when those things are conceived which it is not sufficient to know and will, and when the mind burns and grows sick with want, until it arrives at those things, and, as it were, brings them forth. Whence in the Latin language we have the word "parta" used elegantly for both "reperta" and "comperta," which words sound as if derived from bringing forth.[3] Since "lust, when it hath conceived, bringeth forth sin."[4] Wherefore the Lord proclaims, "Come unto me all ye that labor and are heavy laden;"[5] and in another place "Woe unto them that are with child, and to them that give suck, in those days!"[6] And when therefore He referred all either right actions or sins to the bringing forth of the word, "By thy mouth,"[7] He says, "thou shalt be justified, and by thy mouth[8] thou shalt be condemned,"[9] intending thereby not the visible mouth, but that which is within and invisible, of the thought and of the heart.

CHAP. 10.—WHETHER ONLY KNOWLEDGE THAT IS LOVED IS THE WORD OF THE MIND.

15. It is rightly asked then, whether all knowledge is a word, or only knowledge that is loved. For we also know the things which we hate; but what we do not like, cannot be said to be either conceived or brought forth by the mind. For not all things which in anyway touch it, are conceived by it; but some only reach the point of being known, but yet are not spoken as words, as for instance those of which we speak now. For those are called words in one way, which occupy spaces of time by their syllables, whether they are pronounced or only thought; and in another way, all that is known is called a word imprinted on the mind, as long as it can be brought forth from the memory and defined, even though we dislike the thing itself; and in another way still, when we like that which is conceived in the mind. And that which the apostle says, must be taken according to this last kind of word, "No man can say that Jesus is the Lord, but by the Holy Ghost;"[10] since those also say this, but according to another meaning of the term "word," of whom the Lord Himself says, "Not every one that saith unto me, Lord, Lord, shall enter into the kingdom of heaven."[11] Nay, even in the case of things which we hate, when we rightly dislike and rightly censure them, we approve and like the censure bestowed upon them, and it becomes a word. Nor is it the knowledge of vices that displeases us, but the

---

is analogous to the eternal generation of the Eternal Wisdom in the infinite essence of God expressed in the Eternal Word. Both are alike, in that something spiritual issues from something spiritual, without division or diminution of substance. But a thought of the human mind is not an objective thing or substance; while the Eternal Word is.—W. G. T. S.]

[1] John iv. 13.   [2] Ps. vii. 14.

[3] *Partus.*   [4] Jas. i. 15.   [5] Matt. xi. 28.
[6] Matt. xxiv. 19. [7] Words.   [8] Words.—A. V.
[9] Matt. xii. 37. [10] 1 Cor. xii. 3. [11] Matt. vii. 21.

vices themselves. For I like to know and define what intemperance is ; and this is its word. Just as there are known faults in art, and the knowledge of them is rightly approved, when a connoisseur discerns the species or the privation of excellence, as to affirm and deny that it is or that it is not ; yet to be without excellence and to fall away into fault, is worthy of condemnation. And to define intemperance, and to say its word, belongs to the art of morals ; but to be intemperate belongs to that which that art censures. Just as to know and define what a solecism is, belongs to the art of speaking ; but to be guilty of one, is a fault which the same art reprehends. A word, then, which is the point we wish now to discern and intimate, is knowledge together with love. Whenever, then, the mind knows and loves itself, its word is joined to it by love. And since it loves knowledge and knows love, both the word is in love and love is in the word, and both are in him who loves and speaks.[1]

CHAP. 11. — THAT THE IMAGE OR BEGOTTEN WORD OF THE MIND THAT KNOWS ITSELF IS EQUAL TO THE MIND ITSELF.

16. But all knowledge according to species is like the thing which it knows. For there is another knowledge according to privation, according to which we speak a word only when we condemn. And this condemnation of a privation is equivalent to praise of the species, and so is approved. The mind, then, contains some likeness to a known species, whether when liking that species or when disliking its privation. And hence, in so far as we know God, we are like Him, but not like to the point of equality, since we do not know Him to the extent of His own being. And as, when we speak of bodies by means of the bodily sense, there arises in our mind some likeness of them, which is a phantasm of the memory; for the bodies themselves are not at all in the mind, when we think them, but only the likenesses of those bodies ; therefore, when we approve the latter for the former, we err, for the approving of one thing for another is an error ; yet the image of the body in the mind is a thing of a better sort than the species of the body itself, inasmuch as the former is in a better nature, viz. in a living substance, as the mind is : so when we know God, although we are made better than we were be-

fore we knew Him, and above all when the same knowledge being also liked and worthily loved becomes a word, and so that knowledge becomes a kind of likeness of God ; yet that knowledge is of a lower kind, since it is in a lower nature ; for the mind is creature, but God is Creator. And from this it may be inferred, that when the mind knows and approves itself, this same knowledge is in such way its word, as that it is altogether on a par and equal with it, and the same ; because it is neither the knowledge of a lower essence, as of the body, nor of a higher, as of God. And whereas knowledge bears a likeness to that which it knows, that is, of which it is the knowledge ; in this case it has perfect and equal likeness, when the mind itself, which knows, is known. And so it is both image and word ; because it is uttered concerning that mind to which it is equalled in knowing, and that which is begotten is equal to the begetter.

CHAP. 12. — WHY LOVE IS NOT THE OFFSPRING OF THE MIND, AS KNOWLEDGE IS SO. THE SOLUTION OF THE QUESTION. THE MIND WITH THE KNOWLEDGE OF ITSELF AND THE LOVE OF ITSELF IS THE IMAGE OF THE TRINITY.

17. What then is love ? Will it not be an image ? Will it not be a word ? Will it not be begotten ? For why does the mind beget its knowledge when it knows itself, and not beget its love when it loves itself ? For if it is the cause of its own knowing, for the reason that it is knowable, it is also the cause of its own love because it is lovable. It is hard, then, to say why it does not beget both. For there is a further question also respecting the supreme Trinity itself, the omnipotent God the Creator, after whose image man is made, which troubles men, whom the truth of God invites to the faith by human speech ; viz. why the Holy Spirit is not also to be either believed or understood to be begotten by God the Father, so that He also may be called a Son. And this question we are endeavoring in some way to investigate in the human mind, in order that from a lower image, in which our own nature itself as it were answers, upon being questioned, in a way more familiar to ourselves, we may be able to direct a more practised mental vision from the enlightened creature to the unchangeable light ; assuming, however, that the truth itself has persuaded us, that as no Christian doubts the Word of God to be the Son, so that the Holy Spirit is love. Let us return, then, to a more careful questioning and consideration upon this subject of that image which is the creature, that is, of the rational mind ; wherein the knowl-

[1] [The meaning of this obscure chapter seems to be, that only what the mind is pleased with, is the real expression and index of the mind—its true " word." The true nature of the mind is revealed in its sympathies. But this requires some qualification. For in the case of contrary qualities, like right and wrong, beauty and ugliness, the real nature of the mind is seen also in its antipathy as well as in its sympathy; in its hatred of wrong as well as in its love of right. Each alike is a true index of the mind, because each really implies the other.—W. G. T. S.]

edge of some things coming into existence in time, but which did not exist before, and the love of some things which were not loved before, opens to us more clearly what to say: because to speech also itself, which must be disposed in time, that thing is easier of explanation which is comprehended in the order of time.

18. First, therefore, it is clear that a thing may possibly be knowable, that is, such as can be known, and yet that it may be unknown ; but that it is not possible for that to be known which is not knowable. Wherefore it must be clearly held that everything whatsoever that we know begets at the same time in us the knowledge of itself; for knowledge is brought forth from both, from the knower and from the thing known. When, therefore, the mind knows itself, it alone is the parent of its own knowledge ; for it is itself both the thing known and the knower of it. But it was knowable to itself also before it knew itself, only the knowledge of itself was not in itself so long as it did not know itself. In knowing itself, then, it begets a knowledge of itself equal to itself ; since it does not know itself as less than itself is, nor is its knowledge the knowledge of the essence of some one else, not only because itself knows, but also because it knows itself, as we have said above. What then is to be said of love ; why, when the mind loves itself, it should not seem also to have begotten the love of itself? For it was lovable to itself even before it loved itself, since it could love itself ; just as it was knowable to itself even before it knew itself, since it could know itself. For if it were not knowable to itself, it never could have known itself; and so, if it were not lovable to itself, it never could have loved itself. Why therefore may it not be said by loving itself to have begotten its own love, as by knowing itself it has begotten its own knowledge? Is it because it is thereby indeed plainly shown that this is the principle of love, whence it proceeds? for it proceeds from the mind itself, which is lovable to itself before it loves itself, and so is the principle of its own love by which it loves itself : but that this love is not therefore rightly said to be begotten by the mind, as is the knowledge of itself by which the mind knows itself, because in the case of knowledge the thing has been found already, which is what we call brought forth or discovered;[1] and this is commonly preceded by an inquiry such as to find rest when that end is attained. For inquiry is the desire of finding, or, what is the same thing, of

discovering.[2] But those things which are discovered are as it were brought forth, whence they are like offspring; but wherein, except in the case itself of knowledge? For in that case they are as it were uttered and fashioned. For although the things existed already which we found by seeking, yet the knowledge of them did not exist, which knowledge we regard as an offspring that is born. Further, the desire (appetitus) which there is in seeking proceeds from him who seeks, and is in some way in suspense, and does not rest in the end whither it is directed, except that which is sought be found and conjoined with him who seeks. And this desire, that is, inquiry,—although it does not seem to be love, by which that which is known is loved, for in this case we are still striving to know,—yet it is something of the same kind. For it can be called will (voluntas), since every one who seeks wills (vult) to find; and if that is sought which belongs to knowledge, every one who seeks wills to know. But if he wills ardently and earnestly, he is said to study (studere): a word that is most commonly employed in the case of pursuing and obtaining any branches of learning. Therefore, the bringing forth of the mind is preceded by some desire, by which, through seeking and finding what we wish to know, the offspring, viz. knowledge itself, is born. And for this reason, that desire by which knowledge is conceived and brought forth, cannot rightly be called the bringing forth and the offspring; and the same desire which led us to long for the knowing of the thing, becomes the love of the thing when known, while it holds and embraces its accepted offspring, that is, knowledge, and unites it to its begetter. And so there is a kind of image of the Trinity in the mind itself, and the knowledge of it, which is its offspring and its word concerning itself, and love as a third, and these three are one, and one substance.[3] Neither is the offspring less, since the mind knows itself according to the measure of its own being; nor is the love less, since it loves itself according to the measure both of its own knowledge and of its own being.

---

[1] " Partum " or " repertum."

[2] " Reperiendi."

[3] [It is not these three together that constitute the one substance. The mind alone is the substance—the knowledge and the love being only two activities of it. When the mind is not cognizing or loving, it is still an entire mind. As previously remarked in the annotation on IX. ii. this ternary will completely illustrate a trinality of a certain kind, but not that of the Trinity; in which the "tria quædam" are three subsistences, each of which is so substantial as to be the subject of attributes, and to be able to employ them. The human mind is substantial enough to possess and employ the attributes of knowledge and love. We say that the mind knows and loves. But an activity of the mind is not substantial enough to possess and employ the attributes of knowledge and love. We cannot say that the loving loves; or the loving knows; or the knowing loves, etc.—W. G. T. S.]

BOOK X.

IN WHICH THERE IS SHOWN TO BE ANOTHER TRINITY IN THE MIND OF MAN, AND ONE THAT APPEARS MUCH MORE EVIDENTLY, VIZ. IN HIS MEMORY, UNDERSTANDING, AND WILL.

CHAP. I.—THE LOVE OF THE STUDIOUS MIND, THAT IS, OF ONE DESIROUS TO KNOW, IS NOT THE LOVE OF A THING WHICH IT DOES NOT KNOW.

1. LET us now proceed, then, in due order, with a more exact purpose, to explain this same point more thoroughly. And first, since no one can love at all a thing of which he is wholly ignorant, we must carefully consider of what sort is the love of those who are studious, that is, of those who do not already know, but are still desiring to know any branch of learning. Now certainly, in those things whereof the word study is not commonly used, love often arises from hearsay, when the reputation of anything for beauty inflames the mind to the seeing and enjoying it; since the mind knows generically wherein consist the beauties of corporeal things, from having seen them very frequently, and since there exists within a faculty of approving that which outwardly is longed for. And when this happens, the love that is called forth is not of a thing wholly unknown, since its genus is thus known. But when we love a good man whose face we never saw, we love him from the knowledge of his virtues, which virtues we know [abstractly] in the truth itself. But in the case of learning, it is for the most part the authority of others who praise and commend it that kindles our love of it; although nevertheless we could not burn with any zeal at all for the study of it, unless we had already in our mind at least a slight impression of the knowledge of each kind of learning. For who, for instance, would devote any care and labor to the learning of rhetoric, unless he knew before that it was the science of speaking? Sometimes, again, we marvel at the results of learning itself, which we have heard of or experienced; and hence burn to obtain, by learning, the power of attaining these results. Just as if it were said to one who did not know his letters, that there is a kind of learning which enables a man to send words, wrought with the hand in silence, to one who is ever so far absent, for him in turn to whom they are sent to gather these words, not with his ears, but with his eyes; and if the man were to see the thing actually done, is not that man, since he desires to know how he can do this thing, altogether moved to study with a view to the result which he already knows and holds? So it is that the studious zeal of those who learn is kindled: for that of which any one is utterly ignorant, he can in no way love.

2. So also, if any one hear an unknown sign, as, for instance, the sound of some word of which he does not know the signification, he desires to know what it is; that is, he desires to know what thing it is which it is agreed shall be brought to mind by that sound: as if he heard the word *temetum*[1] uttered, and not knowing, should ask what it is. He must then know already that it is a sign, *i.e.* that the word is not an empty sound, but that something is signified by it; for in other respects this trisyllabic word is known to him already, and has already impressed its articulate form upon his mind through the sense of hearing. And then what more is to be required in him, that he may go on to a greater knowledge of that of which all the letters and all the spaces of its several sounds are already known, unless that it shall at the same time have become known to him that it is a sign, and shall have also moved him with the desire of knowing of what it is the sign? The more, then, the thing is known, yet not fully known, the more the mind desires to know concerning it what remains to be known. For if he

---
[1] Wine.

knew it to be only such and such a spoken word, and did not know that it was the sign of something, he would seek nothing further, since the sensible thing is already perceived as far as it can be by the sense. But because he knows it to be not only a spoken word, but also a sign, he wishes to know it perfectly; and no sign is known perfectly, except it be known of what it is the sign. He then who with ardent carefulness seeks to know this, and inflamed by studious zeal perseveres in the search; can such an one be said to be without love? What then does he love? For certainly nothing can be loved unless it is known. For that man does not love those three syllables which he knows already. But if he loves this in them, that he knows them to signify something, this is not the point now in question, for it is not this which he seeks to know. But we are now asking what it is he loves, in that which he is desirous to know, but which certainly he does not yet know; and we are therefore wondering why he loves, since we know most assuredly that nothing can be loved unless it be known. What then does he love, except that he knows and perceives in the reason of things what excellence there is in learning, in which the knowledge of all signs is contained; and what benefit there is in the being skilled in these, since by them human fellowship mutually communicates its own perceptions, lest the assemblies of men should be actually worse than utter solitude, if they were not to mingle their thoughts by conversing together? The soul, then, discerns this fitting and serviceable species, and knows it, and loves it; and he who seeks the meaning of any words of which he is ignorant, studies to render that species perfect in himself as much as he can: for it is one thing to behold it in the light of truth, another to desire it as within his own capacity. For he beholds in the light of truth how great and how good a thing it is to understand and to speak all tongues of all nations, and so to hear no tongue and to be heard by none as from a foreigner. The beauty, then, of this knowledge is already discerned by thought, and the thing being known is loved; and that thing is so regarded, and so stimulates the studious zeal of learners, that they are moved with respect to it, and desire it eagerly in all the labor which they spend upon the attainment of such a capacity, in order that they may also embrace in practice that which they know beforehand by reason. And so every one, the nearer he approaches that capacity in hope, the more fervently desires it with love; for those branches of learning are studied the more eagerly, which men do not despair of being able to attain; for when any one entertains no hope of attaining his end, then he either loves lukewarmly or does not love at all, howsoever he may see the excellence of it. Accordingly, because the knowledge of all languages is almost universally felt to be hopeless, every one studies most to know that of his own nation; but if he feels that he is not sufficient even to comprehend this perfectly, yet no one is so indolent in this knowledge as not to wish to know, when he hears an unknown word, what it is, and to seek and learn it if he can. And while he is seeking it, certainly he has a studious zeal of learning, and seems to love a thing he does not know; but the case is really otherwise. For that species touches the mind, which the mind knows and thinks, wherein the fitness is clearly visible which accrues from the associating of minds with one another, in the hearing and returning of known and spoken words. And this species kindles studious zeal in him who seeks what indeed he knows not, but gazes upon and loves the unknown form to which that pertains. If then, for example, any one were to ask, What is *temetum* (for I had instanced this word already), and it were said to him, What does this matter to you? he will answer, Lest perhaps I hear some one speaking, and understand him not; or perhaps read the word somewhere, and know not what the writer meant. Who, pray, would say to such an inquirer, Do not care about understanding what you hear; do not care about knowing what you read? For almost every rational soul quickly discerns the beauty of that knowledge, through which the thoughts of men are mutually made known by the enunciation of significant words; and it is on account of this fitness thus known, and because known therefore loved, that such an unknown word is studiously sought out. When then he hears and learns that wine was called "temetum" by our forefathers, but that the word is already quite obsolete in our present usage of language, he will think perhaps that he has still need of the word on account of this or that book of those forefathers. But if he holds these also to be superfluous, perhaps he does now come to think the word not worth remembering, since he sees it has nothing to do with that species of learning which he knows with the mind, and gazes upon, and so loves.

3. Wherefore in all cases the love of a studious mind, that is, of one that wishes to know what it does not know, is not the love of that thing which it does not know, but of that which it knows; on account of which it

wishes to know what it does not know. Or if it is so inquisitive as to be carried away, not for any other cause known to it, but by the mere love of knowing things unknown; then such an inquisitive person is, doubtless, distinguishable from an ordinary student, yet does not, any more than he, love things he does not know; nay, on the contrary, he is more fitly said to hate things he knows not, of which he wishes that there should be none, in wishing to know everything. But lest any one should lay before us a more difficult question, by declaring that it is just as impossible for any one to hate what he does not know, as to love what he does not know, we will not withstand what is true; but it must be understood that it is not the same thing to say he loves to know things unknown, as to say he loves things unknown. For it is possible that a man may love to know things unknown; but it is not possible that he should love things unknown. For the word to know is not placed there without meaning; since he who loves to know things unknown, does not love the unknown things themselves, but the knowing of them. And unless he knew what knowing means, no one could say confidently, either that he knew or that he did not know. For not only he who says I know, and says so truly, must needs know what knowing is; but he also who says, I do not know, and says so confidently and truly, and knows that he says so truly, certainly knows what knowing is; for he both distinguishes him who does not know from him who knows, when he looks into himself, and says truly I do not know; and whereas he knows that he says this truly, whence should he know it, if he did not know what knowing is?

CHAP. 2.—NO ONE AT ALL LOVES THINGS UN-KNOWN.

4. No studious person, then, no inquisitive person, loves things he does not know, even while he is urgent with the most vehement desire to know what he does not know. For he either knows already generically what he loves, and longs to know it also in some individual or individuals, which perhaps are praised, but not yet known to him; and he pictures in his mind an imaginary form by which he may be stirred to love. And whence does he picture this, except from those things which he has already known? And yet perhaps he will not love it, if he find that form which was praised to be unlike that other form which was figured and in thought most fully known to his mind. And if he has loved it, he will begin to love it from that time when he

learned it; since a little before, that form which was loved was other than that which the mind that formed it had been wont to exhibit to itself. But if he shall find it similar to that form which report had proclaimed, and to be such that he could truly say I was already loving thee; yet certainly not even then did he love a form he did not know, since he had known it in that likeness. Or else we see somewhat in the species of the eternal reason, and therein love it; and when this is manifested in some image of a temporal thing, and we believe the praises of those who have made trial of it, and so love it, then we do not love anything unknown, according to that which we have already sufficiently discussed above. Or else, again, we love something known, and on account of it seek something unknown; and so it is by no means the love of the thing unknown that possesses us, but the love of the thing known, to which we know the unknown thing belongs, so that we know that too which we seek still as unknown; as a little before I said of an unknown word. Or else, again, every one loves the very knowing itself, as no one can fail to know who desires to know anything. For these reasons they seem to love things unknown who wish to know anything which they do not know, and who, on account of their vehement desire of inquiry, cannot be said to be without love. But how different the case really is, and that nothing at all can be loved which is not known, I think I must have persuaded every one who carefully looks upon truth. But since the examples which we have given belong to those who desire to know something which they themselves are not, we must take thought lest perchance some new notion appear, when the mind desires to know itself.

CHAP. 3.—THAT WHEN THE MIND LOVES ITSELF, IT IS NOT UNKNOWN TO ITSELF.

5. What, then, does the mind love, when it seeks ardently to know itself, whilst it is still unknown to itself? For, behold, the mind seeks to know itself, and is excited thereto by studious zeal. It loves, therefore; but what does it love? Is it itself? But how can this be when it does not yet know itself, and no one can love what he does not know? Is it that report has declared to it its own species, in like way as we commonly hear of people who are absent? Perhaps, then, it does not love itself, but loves that which it imagines of itself, which is perhaps widely different from what itself is: or if the phantasy in the mind is like the mind itself, and

so when it loves this fancied image, it loves itself before it knew itself, because it gazes upon that which is like itself; then it knew other minds from which to picture itself, and so is known to itself generically. Why, then, when it knows other minds, does it not know itself, since nothing can possibly be more present to it than itself? But if, as other eyes are more known to the eyes of the body, than those eyes are to themselves; then let it not seek itself, because it never will find itself. For eyes can never see themselves except in looking-glasses; and it cannot be supposed in any way that anything of that kind can be applied also to the contemplation of incorporeal things, so that the mind should know itself, as it were, in a looking-glass. Or does it see in the reason of eternal truth how beautiful it is to know one's self, and so loves this which it sees, and studies to bring it to pass in itself? because, although it is not known to itself, yet it is known to it how good it is, that it should be known to itself. And this, indeed, is very wonderful, that it does not yet know itself, and yet knows already how excellent a thing it is to know itself. Or does it see some most excellent end, *viz.* its own serenity and blessedness, by some hidden remembrance, which has not abandoned it, although it has gone far onwards, and believes that it cannot attain to that same end unless it know itself? And so while it loves that, it seeks this; and loves that which is known, on account of which it seeks that which is unknown. But why should the remembrance of its own blessedness be able to last, and the remembrance of itself not be able to last as well; that so it should know itself which wishes to attain, as well as know that to which it wishes to attain? Or when it loves to know itself, does it love, not itself, which it does not yet know, but the very act of knowing; and feel the more annoyed that itself is wanting to its own knowledge wherewith it wishes to embrace all things? And it knows what it is to know; and whilst it loves this, which it knows, desires also to know itself. Whereby, then, does it know its own knowing, if it does not know itself? For it knows that it knows other things, but that it does not know itself; for it is from hence that it knows also what knowing is. In what way, then, does that which does not know itself, know itself as knowing anything? For it does not know that some other mind knows, but that itself does so. Therefore it knows itself. Further, when it seeks to know itself, it knows itself now as seeking. Therefore again it knows itself. And hence it cannot altogether not know itself, when certainly it does so far know itself as that it knows itself as not knowing itself. But if it does not know itself not to know itself, then it does not seek to know itself. And therefore, in the very fact that it seeks itself, it is clearly convicted of being more known to itself than unknown. For it knows itself as seeking and as not knowing itself, in that it seeks to know itself.

CHAP. 4.—HOW THE MIND KNOWS ITSELF, NOT IN PART, BUT AS A WHOLE.

6. What then shall we say? Does that which knows itself in part, not know itself in part? But it is absurd to say, that it does not as a whole know what it knows. I do not say, it knows wholly; but what it knows, it as a whole knows. When therefore it knows anything about itself, which it can only know as a whole, it knows itself as a whole. But it does know that itself knows something, while yet except as a whole it cannot know anything. Therefore it knows itself as a whole. Further, what in it is so known to itself, as that it lives? And it cannot at once be a mind, and not live, while it has also something over and above, *viz.*, that it understands: for the souls of beasts also live, but do not understand. As therefore a mind is a whole mind, so it lives as a whole. But it knows that it lives. Therefore it knows itself as a whole. Lastly, when the mind seeks to know itself, it already knows that it is a mind: otherwise it knows not whether it seeks itself, and perhaps seeks one thing while intending to seek another. For it might happen that itself was not a mind, and so, in seeking to know a mind, that it did not seek to know itself. Wherefore since the mind, when it seeks to know what mind is, knows that it seeks itself, certainly it knows that itself is a mind. Furthermore, if it knows this in itself, that it is a mind, and a whole mind, then it knows itself as a whole. But suppose it did not know itself to be a mind, but in seeking itself only knew that it did seek itself. For so, too, it may possibly seek one thing for another, if it does not know this: but that it may not seek one thing for another, without doubt it knows what it seeks. But if it knows what it seeks, and seeks itself, then certainly it knows itself. What therefore more does it seek? But if it knows itself in part, but still seeks itself in part, then it seeks not itself, but part of itself. For when we speak of the mind itself, we speak of it as a whole. Further, because it knows that it is not yet found by itself as a whole, it knows how much the whole is. And so it seeks that

which is wanting, as we are wont to seek to recall to the mind something that has slipped from the mind, but has not altogether gone away from it; since we can recognize it, when it has come back, to be the same thing that we were seeking. But how can mind come into mind, as though it were possible for the mind not to be in the mind? Add to this, that if, having found a part, it does not seek itself as a whole, yet it as a whole seeks itself. Therefore as a whole it is present to itself, and there is nothing left to be sought: for that is wanting which is sought, not the mind which seeks. Since therefore it as a whole seeks itself, nothing of it is wanting. Or if it does not as a whole seek itself, but the part which has been found seeks the part which has not yet been found; then the mind does not seek itself, of which no part seeks itself. For the part which has been found, does not seek itself; nor yet does the part itself which has not yet been found, seek itself; since it is sought by that part which has been already found. Wherefore, since neither the mind as a whole seeks itself, nor does any part of it seek itself, the mind does not seek itself at all.

CHAP. 5.—WHY THE SOUL IS ENJOINED TO KNOW ITSELF. WHENCE COME THE ERRORS OF THE MIND CONCERNING ITS OWN SUBSTANCE.

7. Why therefore is it enjoined upon it, that it should know itself? I suppose, in order that it may consider itself, and live according to its own nature; that is, seek to be regulated according to its own nature, *viz.,* under Him to whom it ought to be subject, and above those things to which it is to be preferred; under Him by whom it ought to be ruled, above those things which it ought to rule. For it does many things through vicious desire, as though in forgetfulness of itself. For it sees some things intrinsically excellent, in that more excellent nature which is God: and whereas it ought to remain steadfast that it may enjoy them, it is turned away from Him, by wishing to appropriate those things to itself, and not to be like to Him by His gift, but to be what He is by its own, and it begins to move and slip gradually down into less and less, which it thinks to be more and more; for it is neither sufficient for itself, nor is anything at all sufficient for it, if it withdraw from Him who is alone sufficient: and so through want and distress it becomes too intent upon its own actions and upon the unquiet delights which it obtains through them: and thus, by the desire of acquiring knowledge from those things that are without, the nature of which it knows and loves, and which it feels can be lost unless held fast with anxious care, it loses its security, and thinks of itself so much the less, in proportion as it feels the more secure that it cannot lose itself. So, whereas it is one thing not to know oneself, and another not to think of oneself (for we do not say of the man that is skilled in much learning, that he is ignorant of grammar, when he is only not thinking of it, because he is thinking at the time of the art of medicine);—whereas, then, I say it is one thing not to know oneself, and another not to think of oneself, such is the strength of love, that the mind draws in with itself those things which it has long thought of with love, and has grown into them by the close adherence of diligent study, even when it returns in some way to think of itself. And because these things are corporeal which it loved externally through the carnal senses; and because it has become entangled with them by a kind of daily familiarity, and yet cannot carry those corporeal things themselves with itself internally as it were into the region of incorporeal nature; therefore it combines certain images of them, and thrusts them thus made from itself into itself. For it gives to the forming of them somewhat of its own substance, yet preserves the while something by which it may judge freely of the species of those images; and this something is more properly the mind, that is, the rational understanding, which is preserved that it may judge. For we see that we have those parts of the soul which are informed by the likenesses of corporeal things, in common also with beasts.

CHAP. 6.—THE OPINION WHICH THE MIND HAS OF ITSELF IS DECEITFUL.

8. But the mind errs, when it so lovingly and intimately connects itself with these images, as even to consider itself to be something of the same kind. For so it is conformed to them to some extent, not by being this, but by thinking it is so: not that it thinks itself to be an image, but outright that very thing itself of which it entertains the image. For there still lives in it the power of distinguishing the corporeal thing which it leaves without, from the image of that corporeal thing which it contains therefrom within itself: except when these images are so projected as if felt without and not thought within, as in the case of people who are asleep, or mad, or in a trance.

CHAP. 7.—THE OPINIONS OF PHILOSOPHERS RE-SPECTING THE SUBSTANCE OF THE SOUL. THE ERROR OF THOSE WHO ARE OF OPINION THAT THE SOUL IS CORPOREAL, DOES NOT ARISE FROM DEFECTIVE KNOWLEDGE OF THE SOUL, BUT FROM THEIR ADDING THERETO SOMETHING FOREIGN TO IT. WHAT IS MEANT BY FINDING.

9. When, therefore, it thinks itself to be something of this kind, it thinks itself to be a corporeal thing; and since it is perfectly conscious of its own superiority, by which it rules the body, it has hence come to pass that the question has been raised what part of the body has the greater power in the body; and the opinion has been held that this is the mind, nay, that it is even the whole soul alto-gether. And some accordingly think it to be the blood, others the brain, others the heart; not as the Scripture says, "I will praise Thee, O Lord, with my whole heart;" and, "Thou shalt love the Lord thy God with all thine heart;"[1] for this word by misapplication or metaphor is transferred from the body to the soul; but they have simply thought it to be that small part itself of the body, which we see when the inward parts are rent asunder. Others, again, have believed the soul to be made up of very minute and individual cor-puscles, which they call atoms, meeting in themselves and cohering. Others have said that its substance is air, others fire. Others have been of opinion that it is no substance at all, since they could not think any sub-stance unless it is body, and they did not find that the soul was body; but it was in their opinion the tempering together itself of our body, or the combining together of the ele-ments, by which that flesh is as it were con-joined. And hence all of these have held the soul to be mortal; since, whether it were body, or some combination of body, certainly it could not in either case continue always with-out death. But they who have held its sub-stance to be some kind of life the reverse of corporeal, since they have found it to be a life that animates and quickens every living body, have by consequence striven also, ac-cording as each was able, to prove it immor-tal, since life cannot be without life.

For as to that fifth kind of body, I know not what, which some have added to the four well-known elements of the world, and have said that the soul was made of this, I do not think we need spend time in discussing it in this place. For either they mean by body

what we mean by it, viz., that of which a part is less than the whole in extension of place, and they are to be reckoned among those who have believed the mind to be corporeal: or if they call either all substance, or all change-able substance, body, whereas they know that not all substance is contained in extension of place by any length and breadth and height, we need not contend with them about a ques-tion of words.

10. Now, in the case of all these opinions, any one who sees that the nature of the mind is at once substance, and yet not corporeal, —that is, that it does not occupy a less ex-tension of place with a less part of itself, and a greater with a greater,—must needs see at the same time that they who are of opinion that it is corporeal,[2] do not err from defect of knowledge concerning mind, but because they associate with it qualities without which they are not able to conceive any nature at all. For if you bid them conceive of existence that is without corporeal phantasms, they hold it merely nothing. And so the mind would not seek itself, as though wanting to itself. For what is so present to knowledge as that which is present to the mind? Or what is so present to the mind as the mind itself? And hence what is called "invention," if we con-sider the origin of the word, what else does it mean, unless that to find out[3] is to "come into" that which is sought? Those things accordingly which come into the mind as it were of themselves, are not usually said to be found out,[4] although they may be said to be known; since we did not endeavor by seeking to come into them, that is, to invent or find them out. And therefore, as the mind itself really seeks those things which are sought by the eyes or by any other sense of the body (for the mind directs even the carnal sense, and then finds out or invents, when that sense comes to the things which are sought); so, too, it finds out or invents other things which it ought to know, not with the medium of corporeal sense, but through itself, when it "comes into" them; and this, whether in the case of the higher substance that is in God, or of the other parts of the soul; just as it does when it judges of bodily images them-selves, for it finds these within, in the soul, impressed through the body.

---

[1] Ps. ix. cxi., and cxxxviii., Deut. vi. 5, and Matt. xxii. 37.

[2] [The distinction between corporeal and incorporeal substance is one that Augustin often insists upon. See Confessions, VII. i-iii. The doctrine that all substance is extended body, and that there is no such entity as spiritual unextended substance, is com-batted by Plato in the Theatetus. For a history of the contest, and an able defence of the substantiality of spirit, see Cudworth's Intellectual System, III. 384 sq. Harrison's Ed.—W. G. T. S.]

[3] Invenire.   [4] Inventa.

CHAP. 8.—HOW THE SOUL INQUIRES INTO IT-
SELF. WHENCE COMES THE ERROR OF THE
SOUL CONCERNING ITSELF.

11. It is then a wonderful question, in what
manner the soul seeks and finds itself; at what
it aims in order to seek, or whither it comes,
that it may come into or find out. For what
is so much in the mind as the mind itself?
But because it is *in* those things which it
thinks of with love, and is wont to be in sensible, that is, in corporeal things with love, it
is unable to be in itself without the images of
those corporeal things. And hence shameful
error arises to block its way, whilst it cannot
separate from itself the images of sensible
things, so as to see itself alone. For they
have marvellously cohered with it by the close
adhesion of love. And herein consists its uncleanness; since, while it strives to think of
itself alone, it fancies itself to be that, without which it cannot think of itself. When,
therefore, it is bidden to become acquainted
with itself, let it not seek itself as though it
were withdrawn from itself; but let it withdraw that which it has added to itself. For
itself lies more deeply within, not only than
those sensible things, which are clearly without, but also than the images of them; which
are indeed in some part of the soul, *viz.*, that
which beasts also have, although these want
understanding, which is proper to the mind.
As therefore the mind is within, it goes forth
in some sort from itself, when it exerts the
affection of love towards these, as it were,
footprints of many acts of attention. And
these footprints are, as it were, imprinted on
the memory, at the time when the corporeal
things which are without are perceived in such
way, that even when those corporeal things
are absent, yet the images of them are at
hand to those who think of them. Therefore
let the mind become acquainted with itself,
and not seek itself as if it were absent; but fix
upon itself the act of [voluntary] attention,
by which it was wandering among other
things, and let it think of itself. So it will
see that at no time did it ever not love itself,
at no time did it ever not know itself; but by
loving another thing together with itself it
has confounded itself with it, and in some
sense has grown one with it. And so, while
it embraces diverse things, as though they
were one, it has come to think those things
to be one which are diverse.

CHAP. 9.—THE MIND KNOWS ITSELF, BY THE
VERY ACT OF UNDERSTANDING THE PRECEPT
TO KNOW ITSELF.

12. Let it not therefore seek to discern

itself as though absent, but take pains to
discern itself as present. Nor let it take
knowledge of itself as if it did not know itself,
but let it distinguish itself from that which it
knows to be another. For how will it take
pains to obey that very precept which is given
it, "Know thyself," if it knows not either
what "know" means or what "thyself"
means? But if it knows both, then it knows
also itself. Since "know thyself" is not so
said to the mind as is "Know the cherubim
and the seraphim;" for they are absent, and
we believe concerning them, and according
to that belief they are declared to be certain
celestial powers. Nor yet again as it is said,
Know the will of that man: for this it is not
within our reach to perceive at all, either by
sense or understanding, unless by corporeal
signs actually set forth; and this in such a
way that we rather believe than understand.
Nor again as it is said to a man, Behold thy
own face; which he can only do in a looking-
glass. For even our own face itself is out of
the reach of our own seeing it; because it is
not there where our look can be directed.
But when it is said to the mind, Know thyself; then it knows itself by that very act by
which it understands the word "thyself;"
and this for no other reason than that it is
present to itself. But if it does not understand what is said, then certainly it does not
do as it is bid to do. And therefore it is
bidden to do that thing which it does do,
when it understands the very precept that
bids it.

CHAP. 10.—EVERY MIND KNOWS CERTAINLY
THREE THINGS CONCERNING ITSELF—THAT IT
UNDERSTANDS, THAT IT IS, AND THAT IT
LIVES.

13. Let it not then add anything to that
which it knows itself to be, when it is bidden
to know itself. For it knows, at any rate,
that this is said to itself; namely, to the self
that is, and that lives, and that understands.
But a dead body also is, and cattle live; but
neither a dead body nor cattle understand.
Therefore it so knows that it so is, and that
it so lives, as an understanding is and lives.
When, therefore, for example's sake, the
mind thinks itself air, it thinks that air understands; it knows, however, that itself understands, but it does not know itself to be air,
but only thinks so. Let it separate that
which it thinks itself; let it discern that which
it knows; let this remain to it, about which
not even have they doubted who have thought
the mind to be this corporeal thing or that.
For certainly every mind does not consider

itself to be air; but some think themselves fire, others the brain, and some one kind of corporeal thing, others another, as I have mentioned before; yet all know that they themselves understand, and are, and live; but they refer understanding to that which they understand, but to be, and to live, to themselves. And no one doubts, either that no one understands who does not live, or that no one lives of whom it is not true that he is; and that therefore by consequence that which understands both is and lives; not as a dead body is which does not live, nor as a soul lives which does not understand, but in some proper and more excellent manner. Further, they know that they will, and they equally know that no one can will who is not and who does not live ; and they also refer that will itself to something which they will with that will. They know also that they remember ; and they know at the same time that nobody could remember, unless he both was and lived; but we refer memory itself also to something, in that we remember those things. Therefore the knowledge and science of many things are contained in two of these three, memory and understanding; but will must be present, that we may enjoy or use them. For we enjoy things known, in which things themselves the will finds delight for their own sake, and so reposes; but we use those things, which we refer to some other thing which we are to enjoy. Neither is the life of man vicious and culpable in any other way, than as wrongly using and wrongly enjoying. But it is no place here to discuss this.

14. But since we treat of the nature of the mind, let us remove from our consideration all knowledge which is received from without, through the senses of the body; and attend more carefully to the position which we have laid down, that all minds know and are certain concerning themselves. For men certainly have doubted whether the power of living, of remembering, of understanding, of willing, of thinking, of knowing, of judging, be of air, or of fire, or of the brain, or of the blood, or of atoms, or besides the usual four elements of a fifth kind of body, I know not what; or whether the combining or tempering together of this our flesh itself has power to accomplish these things. And one has attempted to establish this, and another to establish that. Yet who ever doubts that he himself lives, and remembers, and understands, and wills, and thinks, and knows, and judges? Seeing that even if he doubts, he lives; if he doubts, he remembers why he doubts; if he doubts, he understands that he doubts; if he doubts, he wishes to be certain; if he doubts, he

thinks; if he doubts, he knows that he does not know; if he doubts, he judges that he ought not to assent rashly. Whosoever therefore doubts about anything else, ought not to doubt of all these things; which if they were not, he would not be able to doubt of anything.

15. They who think the mind to be either a body or the combination or tempering of the body, will have all these things to seem to be in a subject, so that the substance is air, or fire, or some other corporeal thing, which they think to be the mind; but that the understanding (*intelligentia*) is *in* this corporeal thing as its quality, so that this corporeal thing is the subject, but the understanding is in the subject: *viz.* that the mind is the subject, which they judge to be a corporeal thing, but the understanding [intelligence], or any other of those things which we have mentioned as certain to us, is in that subject. They also hold nearly the same opinion who deny the mind itself to be body, but think it to be the combination or tempering together of the body; for there is this difference, that the former say that the mind itself is the substance, in which the understanding [intelligence] is, as in a subject; but the latter say that the mind itself is in a subject, *viz.* in the body, of which it is the combination or tempering together. And hence, by consequence, what else can they think, except that the understanding also is in the same body as in a subject?

16. And all these do not perceive that the mind knows itself, even when it seeks for itself, as we have already shown. But nothing is at all rightly said to be known while its substance is not known. And therefore, when the mind knows itself, it knows its own substance; and when it is certain about itself, it is certain about its own substance. But it is certain about itself, as those things which are said above prove convincingly; although it is not at all certain whether itself is air, or fire, or some body, or some function of body. Therefore it is not any of these. And to that whole which is bidden to know itself, belongs this, that it is certain that it is not any of those things of which it is uncertain, and is certain that it is that only, which only it is certain that it is. For it thinks in this way of fire, or air, and whatever else of the body it thinks of. Neither can it in any way be brought to pass that it should so think that which itself is, as it thinks that which itself is not. Since it thinks all these things through an imaginary phantasy, whether fire, or air, or this or that body, or that part or combination and tempering together of the body: nor assuredly is it said to be all those things, but

some one of them. But if it were any one of them, it would think this one in a different manner from the rest, *viz.* not through an imaginary phantasy, as absent things are thought, which either themselves or some of like kind have been touched by the bodily sense; but by some inward, not feigned, but true presence (for nothing is more present to it than itself); just as it thinks that itself lives, and remembers, and understands, and wills. For it knows these things in itself, and does not imagine them as though it had touched them by the sense outside itself, as corporeal things are touched. And if it attaches nothing to itself from the thought of these things, so as to think itself to be something of the kind, then whatsoever remains to it from itself, that alone is itself.

CHAP. 11.—IN MEMORY, UNDERSTANDING [OR INTELLIGENCE], AND WILL, WE HAVE TO NOTE ABILITY, LEARNING, AND USE. MEMORY, UNDERSTANDING, AND WILL ARE ONE ESSENTIALLY, AND THREE RELATIVELY.

17. Putting aside, then, for a little while all other things, of which the mind is certain concerning itself, let us especially consider and discuss these three—memory, understanding, will. For we may commonly discern in these three the character of the abilities of the young also; since the more tenaciously and easily a boy remembers, and the more acutely he understands, and the more ardently he studies, the more praiseworthy is he in point of ability. But when the question is about any one's learning, then we ask not how solidly and easily he remembers, or how shrewdly he understands; but what it is that he remembers, and what it is that he understands. And because the mind is regarded as praiseworthy, not only as being learned, but also as being good, one gives heed, not only to what he remembers and what he understands, but also to what he wills (*velit*); not how ardently he wills, but first what it is he wills, and then how greatly he wills it. For the mind that loves eagerly is then to be praised, when it loves that which ought to be loved eagerly. Since, then, we speak of these three—ability, knowledge, use—the first of these is to be considered under the three heads, of what a man can do in memory, and understanding, and will. The second of them is to be considered in regard to that which any one has in his memory and in his understanding, which he has attained by a studious will. But the third, *viz.* use, lies in the will, which handles those things that are contained in the memory and understanding,

whether it refer them to anything further, or rest satisfied with them as an end. For to use, is to take up something into the power of the will; and to enjoy, is to use with joy, not any longer of hope, but of the actual thing. Accordingly, every one who enjoys, uses; for he takes up something into the power of the will, wherein he also is satisfied as with an end. But not every one who uses, enjoys, if he has sought after that, which he takes up into the power of the will, not on account of the thing itself, but on account of something else.

18. Since, then, these three, memory, understanding, will, are not three lives, but one life; nor three minds, but one mind; it follows certainly that neither are they three substances, but one substance. Since memory, which is called life, and mind, and substance, is so called in respect to itself; but it is called memory, relatively to something. And I should say the same also of understanding and of will, since they are called understanding and will relatively to something; but each in respect to itself is life, and mind, and essence. And hence these three are one, in that they are one life, one mind, one essence; and whatever else they are severally called in respect to themselves, they are called also together, not plurally, but in the singular number. But they are three, in that wherein they are mutually referred to each other; and if they were not equal, and this not only each to each, but also each to all, they certainly could not mutually contain each other; for not only is each contained by each, but also all by each. For I remember that I have memory and understanding, and will; and I understand that I understand, and will, and remember; and I will that I will, and remember, and understand; and I remember together my whole memory, and understanding, and will. For that of my memory which I do not remember, is not in my memory; and nothing is so much in the memory as memory itself. Therefore I remember the whole memory. Also, whatever I understand I know that I understand, and I know that I will whatever I will; but whatever I know I remember. Therefore I remember the whole of my understanding, and the whole of my will. Likewise, when I understand these three things, I understand them together as whole. For there is none of things intelligible which I do not understand, except what I do not know; but what I do not know, I neither remember, nor will. Therefore, whatever of things intelligible I do not understand, it follows also that I neither remember nor will. And whatever of things intelligible I remember and will, it fol-

lows that I understand. My will also embraces my whole understanding and my whole memory, whilst I use the whole that I understand and remember. And, therefore, while all are mutually comprehended by each, and as wholes, each as a whole is equal to each as a whole, and each as a whole at the same time to all as wholes; and these three are one, one life, one mind, one essence.[1]

CHAP. 12.—THE MIND IS AN IMAGE OF THE TRINITY IN ITS OWN MEMORY, AND UNDERSTANDING, AND WILL.

19. Are we, then, now to go upward, with whatever strength of purpose we may, to that

chiefest and highest essence, of which the human mind is an inadequate image, yet an image? Or are these same three things to be yet more distinctly made plain in the soul, by means of those things which we receive from without, through the bodily sense, wherein the knowledge of corporeal things is impressed upon us in time? Since we found the mind itself to be such in its own memory, and understanding, and will, that since it was understood always to know and always to will itself, it was understood also at the same time always to remember itself, always to understand and love itself, although not always to think of itself as *separate* from those things which are not itself; and hence its memory of itself, and understanding of itself, are with difficult discerned in it. For in this case, where these two things are very closely conjoined, and one is not preceded by the other by any time at all, it looks as if they were not two things, but one called by two names; and love itself is not so plainly felt to exist when the sense of need does not disclose it, since what is loved is always at hand. And hence these things may be more lucidly set forth, even to men of duller minds, if such topics are treated of as are brought within reach of the mind in time, and happen to it in time; while it remembers what it did not remember before, and sees what it did not see before, and loves what it did not love before. But this discussion demands now another beginning, by reason of the measure of the present book.

---

[1] [This ternary of memory, understanding, and will, is a better analogue to the Trinity than the preceding one in chapter IX—namely, mind, knowledge, and love. Memory, understanding, and will have equal substantiality, while mind, knowledge, and love have not. The former are three *faculties*, in each of which is the whole mind or spirit. The memory is the whole mind as remembering; the understanding is the whole mind as cognizing; and the will is the whole mind as determining. The one essence of the mind is in each of these three modes, each of which is distinct from the others; and yet there are not three essences or minds. In the other ternary, of mind, knowledge, and love, the last two are not faculties but single *acts* of the mind. A particular act of cognition is not the whole mind in the *general* mode of cognition. This would make it a faculty. A particular act of loving, or of willing, is not the whole mind in the *general* mode of loving, or of willing. This would make the momentary and transient act a permanent faculty. This ternary fails, as we have noticed in a previous annotation (IX. ii. 2), in that only the mind is a substance.

The ternary of memory, understanding, and will is an adequate analogue to the Trinity in respect to equal substantiality. But it fails when the separate *consciousness* of the Trinitarian distinctions is brought into consideration. The three faculties of memory, understanding, and will, are not so objective to each other as to admit of three forms of consciousness, of the use of the personal pronouns, and of the personal actions that are ascribed to the Father, Son, and Holy Spirit. It also fails, in that these three are not *all* the modes of the mind. There are other faculties: *e. g.*, the imagination. The whole essence of the mind is in this also.—W. G. T. S.]

BOOK XI.

A KIND OF IMAGE OF THE TRINITY IS POINTED OUT, EVEN IN THE OUTER MAN ; FIRST OF ALL, IN THOSE THINGS WHICH ARE PERCEIVED FROM WITHOUT, VIZ. IN THE BODILY OBJECT THAT IS SEEN, AND IN THE FORM THAT IS IMPRESSED BY IT UPON THE SIGHT OF THE SEER, AND IN THE PURPOSE OF THE WILL THAT COMBINES THE TWO ; ALTHOUGH THESE THREE ARE NEITHER MUTUALLY EQUAL, NOR OF ONE SUBSTANCE. NEXT, A KIND OF TRINITY, IN THREE SOMEWHATS OF ONE SUBSTANCE, IS OBSERVED TO EXIST IN THE MIND ITSELF, AS IT WERE INTRODUCED THERE FROM THOSE THINGS THAT ARE PERCEIVED FROM WITHOUT ; VIZ. THE IMAGE OF THE BODILY OBJECT WHICH IS IN THE MEMORY, AND THE IMPRESSION FORMED THEREFROM WHEN THE MIND'S EYE OF THE THINKER IS TURNED TO IT, AND THE PURPOSE OF THE WILL COMBINING BOTH. AND THIS LATTER TRINITY IS ALSO SAID TO PERTAIN TO THE OUTER MAN, IN THAT IT IS INTRODUCED INTO THE MIND FROM BODILY OBJECTS, WHICH ARE PERCEIVED FROM WITHOUT.

CHAP. I.—A TRACE OF THE TRINITY ALSO IN THE OUTER MAN.

1. No one doubts that, as the inner man is endued with understanding, so is the outer with bodily sense. Let us try, then, if we can, to discover in this outer man also, some trace, however slight, of the Trinity, not that itself also is in the same manner the image of God. For the opinion of the apostle is evident, which declares the *inner* man to be renewed in the knowledge of God after the image of Him that created him:[1] whereas he says also in another place, " But though our *outer* man perish, yet the inward man is renewed day by day."[2] Let us seek, then, so far as we can, in that which perishes, some image of the Trinity, if not so express, yet perhaps more easy to be discerned. For that outer man also is not called man to no purpose, but because there is in it some likeness of the inner man. And owing to that very order of our condition whereby we are made mortal and fleshly, we handle things visible more easily and more familiarly than things intelligible; since the former are outward, the latter inward; and the former are perceived by the bodily sense, the latter are understood by the mind; and we ourselves, *i.e.* our minds, are not sensible things, that is, bodies, but intelligible things, since we are life. And yet, as I said, we are so familiarly occupied with bodies, and our thought has projected itself outwardly with so wonderful a proclivity towards bodies, that, when it has been withdrawn from the uncertainty of things corporeal, that it may be fixed with a much more certain and stable knowledge in that which is spirit, it flies back to those bodies, and seeks rest there whence it has drawn weakness. And to this its feebleness we must suit our argument; so that, if we would endeavor at any time to distinguish more aptly, and intimate more readily, the inward spiritual thing, we must take examples of likenesses from outward things pertaining to the body. The outer man, then, endued as he is with the bodily sense, is conversant with bodies. And this bodily sense, as is easily observed, is fivefold; seeing, hearing, smelling, tasting, touching. But it is both a good deal of trouble, and is not necessary, that we should inquire of all these five senses about that which we seek. For that which one of them declares to us, holds also good in the rest. Let us use, then, principally the testimony of the eyes. For this bodily

---

[1] Col. iii. 10.　　　[2] 2 Cor. iv. 16.

sense far surpasses the rest; and in proportion to its difference of kind, is nearer to the sight of the mind.

CHAP. 2.—A CERTAIN TRINITY IN THE SIGHT. THAT THERE ARE THREE THINGS IN SIGHT, WHICH DIFFER IN THEIR OWN NATURE. IN WHAT MANNER FROM A VISIBLE THING VISION IS PRODUCED, OR THE IMAGE OF THAT THING WHICH IS SEEN. THE MATTER IS SHOWN MORE CLEARLY BY AN EXAMPLE. HOW THESE THREE COMBINE IN ONE.

2. When, then, we see any corporeal object, these three things, as is most easy to do, are to be considered and distinguished: First, the object itself which we see; whether a stone, or flame, or any other thing that can be seen by the eyes; and this certainly might exist also already before it was seen; next, vision or the act of seeing, which did not exist before we perceived the object itself which is presented to the sense; in the third place, that which keeps the sense of the eye in the object seen, so long as it is seen, *viz.* the attention of the mind. In these three, then, not only is there an evident distinction, but also a diverse nature. For, first, that visible body is of a far different nature from the sense of the eyes, through the incidence of which sense upon it vision arises. And what plainly is vision itself other than perception informed by that thing which is perceived? Although there is no vision if the visible object be withdrawn, nor could there be any vision of the kind at all if there were no body that could be seen; yet the body by which the sense of the eyes is informed, when that body is seen, and the form itself which is imprinted by it upon the sense, which is called vision, are by no means of the same substance. For the body that is seen is, in its own nature, separable; but the sense, which was already in the living subject, even before it saw what it was able to see, when it fell in with something visible,—or the vision which comes to be in the sense from the visible body when now brought into connection with it and seen,—the sense, then, I say, or the vision, that is, the sense informed from without, belongs to the nature of the living subject, which is altogether other than that body which we perceive by seeing, and by which the sense is not so formed as to be sense, but as to be vision. For unless the sense were also in us before the presentation to us of the sensible object, we should not differ from the blind, at times when we are seeing nothing, whether in darkness, or when our eyes are closed. But we differ from them in this, that

there is in us, even when we are not seeing, that whereby we are able to see, which is called the sense; whereas this is not in them, nor are they called blind for any other reason than because they have it not. Further also, that attention of the mind which keeps the sense in that thing which we see, and connects both, not only differs from that visible thing in its nature; in that the one is mind, and the other body; but also from the sense and the vision itself: since this attention is the act of the mind alone; but the sense of the eyes is called a bodily sense, for no other reason than because the eyes themselves also are members of the body; and although an inanimate body does not perceive, yet the soul commingled with the body perceives through a corporeal instrument, and that instrument is called sense. And this sense, too, is cut off and extinguished by suffering on the part of the body, when any one is blinded; while the mind remains the same; and its attention, since the eyes are lost, has not, indeed, the sense of the body which it may join, by seeing, to the body without it, and so fix its look thereupon and see it, yet by the very effort shows that, although the bodily sense be taken away, itself can neither perish nor be diminished. For there remains unimpaired a desire [*appetitus*] of seeing, whether it can be carried into effect or not. These three, then, the body that is seen, and vision itself, and the attention of mind which joins both together, are manifestly distinguishable, not only on account of the properties of each, but also on account of the difference of their natures.

3. And since, in this case, the sensation does not proceed from that body which is seen, but from the body of the living being that perceives, with which the soul is tempered together in some wonderful way of its own; yet vision is produced, that is, the sense itself is informed, by the body which is seen; so that now, not only is there the power of sense, which can exist also unimpaired even in darkness, provided the eyes are sound, but also a sense actually informed, which is called vision. Vision, then, is produced from a thing that is visible; but not from that alone, unless there be present also one who sees. Therefore vision is produced from a thing that is visible, together with one who sees; in such way that, on the part of him who sees, there is the sense of seeing and the intention of looking and gazing at the object; while yet that information of the sense, which is called vision, is imprinted only by the body which is seen, that is, by some visible thing; which being taken away, that form

10

remains no more which was in the sense so long as that which was seen was present: yet the sense itself remains, which existed also before anything was perceived; just as the trace of a thing in water remains so long as the body itself, which is impressed on it, is in the water; but if this has been taken away, there will no longer be any such trace, although the water remains, which existed also before it took the form of that body. And therefore we cannot, indeed, say that a visible thing produces the sense; yet it produces the form, which is, as it were, its own likeness, which comes to be in the sense, when we perceive anything by seeing. But we do not distinguish, through the same sense, the form of the body which we see, from the form which is produced by it in the sense of him who sees; since the union of the two is so close that there is no room for distinguishing them. But we rationally infer that we could not have sensation at all, unless some similitude of the body seen was wrought in our own sense. For when a ring is imprinted on wax, it does not follow that no image is produced, because we cannot discern it unless when it has been separated. But since, after the wax is separated, what was made remains, so that it can be seen; we are on that account easily persuaded that there was already also in the wax a form impressed from the ring before it was separated from it. But if the ring were imprinted upon a fluid, no image at all would appear when it was withdrawn; and yet none the less for this ought the reason to discern that there was in that fluid before the ring was withdrawn a form of the ring produced from the ring, which is to be distinguished from that form which is in the ring, whence that form was produced which ceases to be when the ring is withdrawn, although that in the ring remains, whence the other was produced. And so the [sensuous] perception of the eyes may not be supposed to contain no image of the body, which is seen as long as it is seen, [merely] because when that is withdrawn the image does not remain. And hence it is very difficult to persuade men of duller mind that an image of the visible thing is formed in our sense, when we see it, and that this same form is vision.

4. But if any perhaps attend to what I am about to mention, they will find no such trouble in this inquiry. Commonly, when we have looked for some little time at a light, and then shut our eyes, there seem to play before our eyes certain bright colors variously changing themselves, and shining less and less until they wholly cease; and these we must understand to be the remains of that form which was wrought in the sense, while the shining body was seen, and that these variations take place in them as they slowly and step by step fade away. For the lattices, too, of windows, should we happen to be gazing at them, appear often in these colors; so that it is evident that our sense is affected by such impressions from that thing which is seen. That form therefore existed also while we were seeing, and at that time it was more clear and express. But it was then closely joined with the species of that thing which was being perceived, so that it could not be at all distinguished from it; and this was vision itself. Why, even when the little flame of a lamp is in some way, as it were, doubled by the divergent rays of the eyes, a twofold vision comes to pass, although the thing which is seen is one. For the same rays, as they shoot forth each from its own eye, are affected severally, in that they are not allowed to meet evenly and conjointly, in regarding that corporeal thing, so that one combined view might be formed from both. And so, if we shut one eye, we shall not see two flames, but one as it really is. But why, if we shut the left eye, that appearance ceases to be seen, which was on the right; and if, in turn, we shut the right eye, that drops out of existence which was on the left, is a matter both tedious in itself, and not necessary at all to our present subject to inquire and discuss. For it is enough for the business in hand to consider, that unless some image, precisely like the thing we perceive, were produced in our sense, the appearance of the flame would not be doubled according to the number of the eyes; since a certain way of perceiving has been employed, which could separate the union of rays. Certainly nothing that is really single can be seen as if it were double by one eye, draw it down, or press, or distort it as you please, if the other is shut.

5. The case then being so, let us remember how these three things, although diverse in nature, are tempered together into a kind of unity; that is, the form of the body which is seen, and the image of it impressed on the sense, which is vision or sense informed, and the will of the mind which applies the sense to the sensible thing, and retains the vision itself in it. The first of these, that is, the visible thing itself, does not belong to the nature of the living being, except when we discern our own body. But the second belongs to that nature to this extent, that it is wrought in the body, and through the body in the soul; for it is wrought in the sense, which is neither without the body nor without the soul. But the third is of the soul alone,

because it is the will. Although then the substances of these three are so different, yet they coalesce into such a unity that the two former can scarcely be distinguished, even with the intervention of the reason as judge, namely the form of the body which is seen, and the image of it which is wrought in the sense, that is, vision. And the will so powerfully combines these two, as both to apply the sense, in order to be informed, to that thing which is perceived, and to retain it when informed in that thing. And if it is so vehement that it can be called love, or desire, or lust, it vehemently affects also the rest of the body of the living being; and where a duller and harder matter does not resist, changes it into like shape and color. One may see the little body of a chameleon vary with ready change, according to the colors which it sees. And in the case of other animals, since their grossness of flesh does not easily admit change, the offspring, for the most part, betray the particular fancies of the mothers, whatever it is that they have beheld with special delight. For the more tender, and so to say, the more formable, are the primary seeds, the more effectually and capably they follow the bent of the soul of the mother, and the phantasy that is wrought in it through that body, which it has greedily beheld. Abundant instances might be adduced, but one is sufficient, taken from the most trustworthy books; *viz.* what Jacob did, that the sheep and goats might give birth to offspring of various colors, by placing variegated rods before them in the troughs of water for them to look at as they drank, at the time they had conceived.[1]

CHAP. 3.—THE UNITY OF THE THREE TAKES PLACE IN THOUGHT, VIZ. OF MEMORY, OF INTERNAL VISION, AND OF WILL COMBINING BOTH.

6. The rational soul, however, lives in a degenerate fashion, when it lives according to a trinity of the *outer* man; that is, when it applies to those things which form the bodily sense from without, not a praiseworthy will, by which to refer them to some useful end, but a base desire, by which to cleave to them. Since even if the form of the body, which was corporeally perceived, be withdrawn, its likeness remains in the memory, to which the will may again direct its eye, so as to be formed thence from within, as the sense was formed from without by the presentation of the sensible body. And so that trinity is produced from memory, from internal vision, and from the will which unites both. And when these three things are combined into one, from that

combination[2] itself they are called conception.[3] And in these three there is no longer any diversity of substance. For neither is the sensible body there, which is altogether distinct from the nature of the living being, nor is the bodily sense there informed so as to produce vision, nor does the will itself perform its office of applying the sense, that is to be informed, to the sensible body, and of retaining it in it when informed; but in place of that bodily species which was perceived from without, there comes the memory retaining that species which the soul has imbibed through the bodily sense; and in place of that vision which was outward when the sense was informed through the sensible body, there comes a similar vision within, while the eye of the mind is informed from that which the memory retains, and the corporeal things that are thought of are absent; and the will itself, as before it applied the sense yet to be informed to the corporeal thing presented from without, and united it thereto when informed, so now converts the vision of the recollecting mind to memory, in order that the mental sight may be informed by that which the memory has retained, and so there may be in the conception a like vision. And as it was the reason that distinguished the visible appearance by which the bodily sense was informed, from the similitude of it, which was wrought in the sense when informed in order to produce vision (otherwise they had been so united as to be thought altogether one and the same); so, although that phantasy also, which arises from the mind thinking of the appearance of a body that it has seen, consists of the similitude of the body which the memory retains, together with that which is thence formed in the eye of the mind that recollects; yet it so seems to be one and single, that it can only be discovered to be two by the judgment of reason, by which we understand that which remains in the memory, even when we think it from some other source, to be a different thing from that which is brought into being when we remember, that is, come back again to the memory, and there find the same appearance. And if this were not now there, we should say that we had so forgotten as to be altogether unable to recollect. And if the eye of him who recollects were not informed from that thing which was in the memory, the vision of the thinker could in no way take place; but the conjunction of both, that is, of that which the memory retains, and of that which is thence expressed so as to inform the eye of him who recollects, makes them ap-

---

[1] Gen. xxx. 37-41.

[2] *Coactus.*   [3] *Cogitatio.*

pear as if they were one, because they are exceedingly like. But when the eye of the concipient is turned away thence, and has ceased to look at that which was perceived in the memory, then nothing of the form that was impressed thereon will remain in that eye, and it will be informed by that to which it had again been turned, so as to bring about another conception. Yet that remains which it has left in the memory, to which it may again be turned when we recollect it, and being turned thereto may be informed by it, and become one with that whence it is informed.

CHAP. 4.—HOW THIS UNITY COMES TO PASS.

7. But if that will which moves to and fro, hither and thither, the eye that is to be informed, and unites it when formed, shall have wholly converged to the inward phantasy, and shall have absolutely turned the mind's eye from the presence of the bodies which lie around the senses, and from the very bodily senses themselves, and shall have wholly turned it to that image, which is perceived within; then so exact a likeness of the bodily species expressed from the memory is presented, that not even reason itself is permitted to discern whether the body itself is seen without, or only something of the kind thought of within. For men sometimes either allured or frightened by over-much thinking of visible things, have even suddenly uttered words accordingly, as if in real fact they were engaged in the very midst of such actions or sufferings. And I remember some one telling me that he was wont to perceive in thought, so distinct and as it were solid, a form of a female body, as to be moved, as though it were a reality. Such power has the soul over its own body, and such influence has it in turning and changing the quality of its [corporeal] garment; just as a man may be affected when clothed, to whom his clothing sticks. It is the same kind of affection, too, with which we are beguiled through imaginations in sleep. But it makes a very great difference, whether the senses of the body are lulled to torpor, as in the case of sleepers, or disturbed from their inward structure, as in the case of madmen, or distracted in some other mode, as in that of diviners or prophets; and so from one or other of these causes, the intention of the mind is forced by a kind of necessity upon those images which occur to it, either from memory, or by some other hidden force through certain spiritual commixtures of a similarly spiritual substance: or whether, as sometimes happens to people in health and

awake, that the will occupied by thought turns itself away from the senses, and so informs the eye of the mind by various images of sensible things, as though those sensible things themselves were actually perceived. But these impressions of images not only take place when the will is directed upon such things by desiring them, but also when, in order to avoid and guard against them, the mind is carried away to look upon these very thing so as to *flee* from them. And hence, not only desire, but fear, causes both the bodily eye to be informed by the sensible things themselves, and the mental eye (*acies*) by the images of those sensible things. Accordingly, the more vehement has been either fear or desire, the more distinctly is the eye informed, whether in the case of him who [sensuously] perceives by means of the body that which lies close to him in place, or in the case of him who conceives from the image of the body which is contained in the memory. What then a body in place is to the bodily sense, that, the similitude of a body in memory is to the eye of the mind; and what the vision of one who looks at a thing is to that appearance of the body from which the sense is informed, that, the vision of a concipient is to the image of the body established in the memory, from which the eye of the mind is informed; and what the intention of the will is towards a body seen and the vision to be combined with it, in order that a certain unity of three things may therein take place, although their nature is diverse, that, the same intention of the will is towards combining the image of the body which is in the memory, and the vision of the concipient, that is, the form which the eye of the mind has taken in returning to the memory, in order that here too a certain unity may take place of three things, not now distinguished by diversity of nature, but of one and the same substance; because this whole is within, and the whole is one mind.

CHAP. 5.—THE TRINITY OF THE OUTER MAN, OR OF EXTERNAL VISION, IS NOT AN IMAGE OF GOD. THE LIKENESS OF GOD IS DESIRED EVEN IN SINS. IN EXTERNAL VISION THE FORM OF THE CORPOREAL THING IS AS IT WERE THE PARENT, VISION THE OFFSPRING; BUT THE WILL THAT UNITES THESE SUGGESTS THE HOLY SPIRIT.

8. But as, when [both] the form and species of a body have perished, the will cannot recall to it the sense of perceiving; so, when the image which memory bears is blotted out by forgetfulness, the will will be unable to force

back the eye of the mind by recollection, so as to be formed thereby. But because the mind has great power to imagine not only things forgotten, but also things that it never saw, or experienced, either by increasing, or diminishing, or changing, or compounding, after its pleasure, those which have not dropped out of its remembrance, it often imagines things to be such as either it knows they are not, or does not know that they are. And in this case we have to take care, lest it either speak falsely that it may deceive, or hold an opinion so as to be deceived. And if it avoid these two evils, then imagined phantasms do not hinder it: just as sensible things experienced or retained by memory do not hinder it, if they are neither passionately sought for when pleasant, nor basely shunned when unpleasant. But when the will leaves better things, and greedily wallows in these, then it becomes unclean; and they are so thought of hurtfully, when they are present, and also more hurtfully when they are absent. And he therefore lives badly and degenerately who lives according to the trinity of the *outer* man; because it is the purpose of using things sensible and corporeal, that has begotten also that trinity, which although it imagines within, yet imagines things without. For no one could use those things even well, unless the images of things perceived by the senses were retained in the memory. And unless the will for the greatest part dwells in the higher and interior things, and unless that will itself, which is accommodated either to bodies without, or to the images of them within, refers whatever it receives in them to a better and truer life, and rests in that end by gazing at which it judges that those things ought to be done; what else do we do, but that which the apostle prohibits us from doing, when he says, " Be not conformed to this world "?[1] And therefore that trinity is not an image of God since it is produced in the mind itself through the bodily sense, from the lowest, that is, the corporeal creature, than which the mind is higher. Yet neither is it altogether dissimilar: for what is there that has not a likeness of God, in proportion to its kind and measure, seeing that God made all things very good,[2] and for no other reason except that He Himself is supremely good? In so far, therefore, as anything that is, is good, in so far plainly it has still some likeness of the supreme good, at however, great a distance; and if a natural likeness, then certainly a right and well-ordered one; but if a faulty likeness, then certainly a de-

based and perverse one. For even souls in their very sins strive after nothing else but some kind of likeness of God, in a proud and preposterous, and, so to say, slavish liberty. So neither could our first parents have been persuaded to sin unless it had been said, " Ye shall be as gods." [3] No doubt everything in the creatures which is in any way like God, is not also to be called His image; but that alone than which He Himself alone is higher. For that only is in all points copied from Him, between which and Himself no nature is interposed.

9. Of that vision then; that is, of the form which is wrought in the sense of him who sees; the form of the bodily thing from which it is wrought, is, as it were, the parent. But it is not a true parent; whence neither is that a true offspring; for it is not altogether born therefrom, since something else is applied to the bodily thing in order that it may be formed from it, namely, the sense of him who sees. And for this reason, to love this is to be estranged. [4] Therefore the will which unites both, *viz.* the quasi-parent and the quasi-child, is more spiritual than either of them. For that bodily thing which is discerned, is not spiritual at all. But the vision which comes into existence in the sense, has something spiritual mingled with it, since it cannot come into existence without the soul. But it is not wholly spiritual; since that which is formed is a sense of the body. Therefore the will which unites both is confessedly more spiritual, as I have said; and so it begins to suggest (*insinuare*), as it were, the person of the Spirit in the Trinity. But it belongs more to the sense that is formed, than to the bodily thing whence it is formed. For the sense and will of an animate being belongs to the soul, not to the stone or other bodily thing that is seen. It does not therefore proceed from that bodily thing as from a parent; yet neither does it proceed from that other as it were offspring, namely, the vision and form that is in the sense. For the will existed before the vision came to pass, which will applied the sense that was to be formed to the bodily thing that was to be discerned; but it was not yet satisfied. For how could that which was not yet seen satisfy? And satisfaction means a will that rests content. And, therefore, we can neither call the will the quasi-offspring of vision, since it existed before vision; nor the quasi-parent, since that vision was not formed and expressed

---

[3] Gen. iii. 5.
[4] *Vid. Retract.* Bk. II. c. 15, where Augustin adds that it is possible to love the bodily species to the praise of the Creator, in which case there is no " estrangement."

---

[1] Rom. xii. 2.   [2] Ecclus. xxxix. 16.

from the will, but from the bodily thing that was seen.

CHAP. 6.—OF WHAT KIND WE ARE TO RECKON THE REST (REQUIES), AND END (FINIS), OF THE WILL IN VISION.

10. Perhaps we can rightly call vision the end and rest of the will, only with respect to this one object [namely, the bodily thing that is visible]. For it will not will nothing else merely because it sees something which it is now willing. It is not therefore the whole will itself of the man, of which the end is nothing else than blessedness; but the will provisionally directed to this one object, which has as its end in seeing, nothing but vision, whether it refer the thing seen to any other thing or not. For if it does not refer the vision to anything further, but wills only to see this, there can be no question made about showing that the end of the will is the vision; for it is manifest. But if it does refer it to anything further, then certainly it does will something else, and it will not be now a will merely to see; or if to see, not one to see the particular thing. Just as, if any one wished to see the scar, that from thence he might learn that there had been a wound; or wished to see the window, that through the window he might see the passers-by: all these and other such acts of will have their own proper [proximate] ends, which are referred to that [final] end of the will by which we will to live blessedly, and to attain to that life which is not referred to anything else, but suffices of itself to him who loves it. The will then to see, has as its end vision; and the will to see this particular thing, has as its end the vision of this particular thing. Therefore the will to see the scar, desires its own end, that is, the vision of the scar, and does not reach beyond it; for the will to prove that there had been a wound, is a distinct will, although dependent upon that, of which the end also is to prove that there had been a wound. And the will to see the window, has as its end the vision of the window; for that is another and further will which depends upon it, viz. to see the passers-by through the window, of which also the end is the vision of the passers-by. But all the several wills that are bound to each other, are at once right, if that one is good, to which all are referred; and if that is bad, then all are bad. And so the connected series of right wills is a sort of road which consists as it were of certain steps, whereby to ascend to blessedness; but the entanglement of depraved and distorted wills is a bond by which

he will be bound who thus acts, so as to be cast into outer darkness.[1] Blessed therefore are they who in act and character sing the song of the steps [degrees];[2] and woe to those that draw sin, as it were a long rope.[3] And it is just the same to speak of the will being in repose, which we call its end, if it is still referred to something further, as if we should say that the foot is at rest in walking, when it is placed there, whence yet another foot may be planted in the direction of the man's steps. But if something so satisfies, that the will acquiesces in it with a certain delight; it is nevertheless not yet that to which the man ultimately tends; but this too is referred to something further, so as to be regarded not as the native country of a citizen, but as a place of refreshment, or even of stopping, for a traveller.

CHAP. 7.—THERE IS ANOTHER TRINITY IN THE MEMORY OF HIM WHO THINKS OVER AGAIN WHAT HE HAS SEEN.

11. But yet again, take the case of another trinity, more inward indeed than that which is in things sensible, and in the senses, but which is yet conceived from thence; while now it is no longer the sense of the body that is informed from the body, but the eye of the mind that is informed from the memory, since the species of the body which we perceived from without has inhered in the memory itself. And that species, which is in the memory, we call the quasi-parent of that which is wrought in the phantasy of one who conceives. For it was in the memory also, before we conceived it, just as the body was in place also before we [sensuously] perceived it, in order that vision might take place. But when it is conceived, then from that form which the memory retains, there is copied in the mind's eye (acie) of him who conceives, and by remembrance is formed, that species, which is the quasi-offspring of that which the memory retains. But neither is the one a true parent, nor the other a true offspring. For the mind's vision which is formed from memory when we think anything by recollection, does not proceed from that species which we remember as seen; since we could not indeed have remembered those things, unless we had seen them; yet the mind's eye, which is informed by the recollection, existed also before we saw the body that we remember; and therefore how much more before we committed it to memory? Although therefore the form which is wrought in the mind's eye of him who remembers, is wrought

---

[1] Matt. xxii. 13. [2] Psalms cxx., and following. [3] Isa. v. 18.

from that form which is in the memory; yet the mind's eye itself does not exist from thence, but existed before it. And it follows, that if the one is not a true parent, neither is the other a true offspring. But both that quasi-parent and that quasi-offspring suggest something, whence the inner and truer things may appear more practically and more certainly.

12. Further, it is more difficult to discern clearly, whether the will which connects the vision to the memory is not either the parent or the offspring of some one of them; and the likeness and equality of the same nature and substance cause this difficulty of distinguishing. For it is not possible to do in this case, as with the sense that is formed from without (which is easily discerned from the sensible body, and again the will from both), on account of the difference of nature which is mutually in all three, and of which we have treated sufficiently above. For although this trinity, of which we at present speak, is introduced into the mind from without; yet it is transacted within, and there is no part of it outside of the nature of the mind itself. In what way, then, can it be demonstrated that the will is neither the quasi-parent, nor the quasi-offspring, either of the corporeal likeness which is contained in the memory, or of that which is copied thence in recollecting; when it so unites both in the act of conceiving, as that they appear singly as one, and cannot be discerned except by reason? It is then first to be considered that there cannot be any will to remember, unless we retain in the recesses of the memory either the whole, or some part, of that thing which we wish to remember. For the very will to remember cannot arise in the case of a thing which we have forgotten altogether and absolutely; since we have already remembered that the thing which we wish to remember is, or has been, in our memory. For example, if I wish to remember what I supped on yesterday, either I have already remembered that I did sup, or if not yet this, at least I have remembered something about that time itself, if nothing else; at all events, I have remembered yesterday, and that part of yesterday in which people usually sup, and what supping is. For if I had not remembered anything at all of this kind, I could not wish to remember what I supped on yesterday. Whence we may perceive that the will of remembering proceeds, indeed, from those things which are retained in the memory, with the addition also of those which, by the act of discerning, are copied thence through recollection; that is, from the combination

of something which we have remembered, and of the vision which was thence wrought, when we remembered, in the mind's eye of him who thinks. But the will itself which unites both requires also some other thing, which is, as it were, close at hand, and adjacent to him who remembers. There are, then, as many trinities of this kind as there are remembrances; because there is no one of them wherein there are not these three things, *viz.* that which was stored up in the memory also before it was thought, and that which takes place in the conception when this is discerned, and the will that unites both, and from both and itself as a third, completes one single thing. Or is it rather that we so recognize some one trinity in this kind, as that we are to speak generally, of whatever corporeal species lie hidden in the memory, as of a single unity, and again of the general vision of the mind which remembers and conceives such things, as of a single unity, to the combination of which two there is to be joined as a third the will that combines them, that this whole may be a certain unity made up from three?

CHAP. 8.—DIFFERENT MODES OF CONCEIVING.

But since the eye of the mind cannot look at all things together, in one glance, which the memory retains, these trinities of thought alternate in a series of withdrawals and successions, and so that trinity becomes most innumerably numerous; and yet not infinite, if it pass not beyond the number of things stored up in the memory. For, although we begin to reckon from the earliest perception which any one has of material things through any bodily sense, and even take in also those things which he has forgotten, yet the number would undoubtedly be certain and determined, although innumerable. For we not only call infinite things innumerable, but also those, which, although finite, exceed any one's power of reckoning.

13. But we can hence perceive a little more clearly that what the memory stores up and retains is a different thing from that which is thence copied in the conception of the man who remembers, although, when both are combined together, they appear to be one and the same; because we can only remember just as many species of bodies as we have actually seen, and so great, and such, as we have actually seen; for the mind imbibes them into the memory from the bodily sense; whereas the things seen in conception, although drawn from those things which are in the memory, yet are multiplied

and varied innumerably, and altogether without end. For I remember, no doubt, but one sun, because according to the fact, I have seen but one; but if I please, I conceive of two, or three, or as many as I will; but the vision of my mind, when I conceive of many, is formed from the same memory by which I remember one. And I remember it just as large as I saw it. For if I remember it as larger or smaller than I saw it, then I no longer remember what I saw, and so I do not remember it. But because I remember it, I remember it as large as I saw it; yet I conceive of it as greater or as less according to my will. And I remember it as I saw it; but I conceive of it as running its course as I will, and as standing still where I will, and as coming whence I will, and whither I will. For it is in my power to conceive of it as square, although I remember it as round ; and again, of what color I please, although I have never seen, and therefore do not remember, a green sun; and as the sun, so all other things. But owing to the corporeal and sensible nature of these forms of things, the mind falls into error when it imagines them to exist without, in the same mode in which it conceives them within, either when they have already ceased to exist without, but are still retained in the memory, or when in any other way also, that which we remember is formed in the mind, not by faithful recollection, but after the variations of thought.

14. Yet it very often happens that we believe also a true narrative, told us by others, of things which the narrators have themselves perceived by their senses. And in this case, when we conceive the things narrated to us, as we hear them, the eye of the mind does not seem to be turned back to the memory, in order to bring up visions in our thoughts; for we do not conceive these things from our own recollection, but upon the narration of another; and that trinity does not here seem to come to its completion, which is made when the species lying hid in the memory, and the vision of the man that remembers, are combined by will as a third. For I do not conceive that which lay hid in my memory, but that which I hear, when anything is narrated to me. I am not speaking of the words themselves of the speaker, lest any one should suppose that I have gone off to that other trinity, which is transacted without, in sensible things, or in the senses: but I am conceiving of those species of material things, which the narrator signifies to me by words and sounds; which species certainly I conceive of not by remembering, but by hearing. But if we consider the matter more carefully,

even in this case, the limit of the memory is not overstepped. For I could not even understand the narrator, if I did not remember generically the individual things of which he speaks, even although I then hear them for the first time as connected together in one tale. For he who, for instance, describes to me some mountain stripped of timber, and clothed with olive trees, describes it to me who remembers the species both of mountains, and of timber, and of olive trees; and if I had forgotten these, I should not know at all of what he was speaking, and therefore could not conceive that description. And so it comes to pass, that every one who conceives things corporeal, whether he himself imagine anything, or hear, or read, either a narrative of things past, or a foretelling of things future, has recourse to his memory, and finds there the limit and measure of all the forms at which he gazes in his thought. For no one can conceive at all, either a color or a form of body, which he never saw, or a sound which he never heard, or a flavor which he never tasted, or a scent which he never smelt, or any touch of a corporeal thing which he never felt. But if no one conceives anything corporeal except what he has [sensuously] perceived, because no one remembers anything corporeal except what he has thus perceived, then, as is the limit of perceiving in bodies, so is the limit of thinking in the memory. For the sense receives the species from that body which we perceive, and the memory from the sense; but the mental eye of the concipient, from the memory.

15. Further, as the will applies the sense to the bodily object, so it applies the memory to the sense, and the eye of the mind of the concipient to the memory. But that which harmonizes those things and unites them, itself also disjoins and separates them, that is, the will. But it separates the bodily senses from the bodies that are to be perceived, by movement of the body, either to hinder our perceiving the thing, or that we may cease to perceive it: as when we avert our eyes from that which we are unwilling to see, or shut them; so, again, the ears from sounds, or the nostrils from smells. So also we turn away from tastes, either by shutting the mouth, or by casting the thing out of the mouth. In touch, also, we either remove the bodily thing, that we may not touch what we do not wish, or if we were already touching it, we fling or push it away. Thus the will acts by movement of the body, so that the bodily sense shall not be joined to the sensible things. And it does this according to its

power; for when it endures hardship in so doing, on account of the condition of slavish mortality, then torment is the result, in such wise that nothing remains to the will save endurance. But the will averts the memory from the sense; when, through its being intent on something else, it does not suffer things present to cleave to it. As any one may see, when often we do not seem to ourselves to have heard some one who was speaking to us, because we were thinking of something else. But this is a mistake; for we did hear, but we do not remember, because the words of the speaker presently slipped out of the perception of our ears, through the bidding of the will being diverted elsewhere, by which they are usually fixed in the memory. Therefore, we should say more accurately in such a case, we do not remember, than, we did not hear; for it happens even in reading, and to myself very frequently, that when I have read through a page or an epistle, I do not know what I have read, and I begin it again. For the purpose of the will being fixed on something else, the memory was not so applied to the bodily sense, as the sense itself was applied to the letters. So, too, any one who walks with the will intent on something else, does not know where he has got to; for if he had not seen, he would not have walked thither, or would have felt his way in walking with greater attention, especially if he was passing through a place he did not know; yet, because he walked easily, certainly he saw; but because the memory was not applied to the sense itself in the same way as the sense of the eyes was applied to the places through which he was passing, he could not remember at all even the last thing he saw. Now, to will to turn away the eye of the mind from that which is in the memory, is nothing else but not to think thereupon.

CHAP. 9.—SPECIES IS PRODUCED BY SPECIES IN SUCCESSION.

16. In this arrangement, then, while we begin from the bodily species and arrive finally at the species which comes to be in the intuition (*contuitu*) of the concipient, we find four species born, as it were, step by step one from the other, the second from the first, the third from the second, the fourth from the third: since from the species of the body itself, there arises that which comes to be in the sense of the percipient; and from this, that which comes to be in the memory; and from this, that which comes to be in the mind's eye of the concipient. And the will,

therefore, thrice combines as it were parent with offspring: first the species of the body with that to which it gives birth in the sense of the body; and that again with that which from it comes to be in the memory; and this also, thirdly, with that which is born from it in the intuition of the concipient's mind. But the intermediate combination which is the second, although it is nearer to the first, is yet not so like the first as the third is. For there are two kinds of vision, the one of [sensuous] perception (*sentientis*), the other of conception (*cogitantis*). But in order that the vision of conception may come to be, there is wrought for the purpose, in the memory, from the vision of [sensuous] perception something like it, to which the eye of the mind may turn itself in conceiving, as the glance (*acies*) of the eyes turns itself in [sensuously] perceiving to the bodily object. I have, therefore, chosen to put forward two trinities in this kind: one when the vision of [sensuous] perception is formed from the bodily object, the other when the vision of conception is formed from the memory. But I have refrained from commending an intermediate one; because we do not commonly call it vision, when the form which comes to be in the sense of him who perceives, is entrusted to the memory. Yet in all cases the will does not appear unless as the combiner as it were of parent and offspring; and so, proceed from whence it may, it can be called neither parent nor offspring.[1]

CHAP. 10.—THE IMAGINATION ALSO ADDS EVEN TO THINGS WE HAVE NOT SEEN, THOSE THINGS WHICH WE HAVE SEEN ELSEWHERE.

17. But if we do not remember except what we have [sensuously] perceived, nor conceive except what we remember; why do we often conceive things that are false, when certainly we do not remember falsely those things which we have perceived, unless it be because that will (which I have already taken pains to show as much as I can to be the uniter and the separater of things of this kind) leads the vision of the conceiver that is to be formed, after its own will and pleasure,

---

[1] [Augustin's map of consciousness is as follows: (1). The corporeal species=the external object (outward appearance). (2). The sensible species=the sensation (appearance for the sense). (3). The mental species in its first form=present perception. (4). The mental species in its second form=remembered perception. These three " species " or appearances of the object: namely, corporeal, sensible, and mental, according to him, are combined in one synthesis with the object by the operation of the will. By " will," he does not mean distinct and separate volitions: but the spontaneity of the ego—what Kant denominates the mechanism of the understanding, seen in the spontaneous employment of the categories of thought, as the mind ascends from empirical sensation to rational conception.

The English translator has failed to make clear the sharply defined psychology of these chapters, by loosely rendering "*sentire*," "to perceive," and "*cogitare*" to think.—W.G.T.S.]

through the hidden stores of the memory; and, in order to conceive [imagine] those things which we do not remember, impels it to take one thing from hence, and another from thence, from those which we do remember; and these things combining into one vision make something which is called false, because it either does not exist externally in the nature of corporeal things, or does not seem copied from the memory, in that we do not remember that we ever saw such a thing. For who ever saw a black swan? And therefore no one remembers a black swan; yet who is there that cannot conceive it? For it is easy to apply to that shape which we have come to know by seeing it, a black color, which we have not the less seen in other bodies; and because we have seen both, we remember both. Neither do I remember a bird with four feet, because I never saw one; but I contemplate such a phantasy very easily, by adding to some winged shape such as I have seen, two other feet, such as I have likewise seen.[1] And therefore, in conceiving conjointly, what we remember to have seen singly, we seem not to conceive that which we remember; while we really do this under the law of the memory, whence we take everything which we join together after our own pleasure in manifold and diverse ways. For we do not conceive even the very magnitudes of bodies, which magnitudes we never saw, without help of the memory; for the measure of space to which our gaze commonly reaches through the magnitude of the world, is the measure also to which we enlarge the bulk of bodies, whatever they may be, when we conceive them as great as we can. And reason, indeed, proceeds still beyond, but phantasy does not follow her; as when reason announces the infinity of number also, which no vision of him who conceives according to corporeal things can apprehend. The same reason also teaches that the most minute atoms are infinitely divisible; yet when we have come to those slight and minute particles which we remember to have seen, then we can no longer behold phantasms more slender and more minute, although reason does not cease to continue to divide them. So we conceive no corporeal things, except either those we remember, or from those things which we remember.

CHAP. 11.—NUMBER, WEIGHT, MEASURE.

18. But because those things which are impressed on the memory singly, can be conceived according to number, measure seems to belong to the memory, but number to the vision; because, although the multiplicity of such visions is innumerable, yet a limit not to be transgressed is prescribed for each in the memory. Therefore, measure appears in the memory, number in the vision of things: as there is some measure in visible bodies themselves, to which measure the sense of those who see is most numerously adjusted, and from one visible object is formed the vision of many beholders, so that even a single person sees commonly a single thing under a double appearance, on account of the number of his two eyes, as we have laid down above. Therefore there is some measure in those things whence visions are copied, but in the visions themselves there is number. But the will which unites and regulates these things, and combines them into a certain unity, and does not quietly rest its desire of [sensuously] perceiving or of conceiving, except in those things from whence the visions are formed, resembles weight. And therefore I would just notice by way of anticipation these three things, measure, number, weight, which are to be perceived in all other things also. In the meantime, I have now shown as much as I can, and to whom I can, that the will is the uniter of the visible thing and of the vision; as it were, of parent and of offspring; whether in [sensuous] perception or in conception, and that it cannot be called either parent or offspring. Wherefore time admonishes us to seek for this same trinity in the inner man, and to strive to pass inwards from that animal and carnal and (as he is called) outward man, of whom I have so long spoken. And here we hope to be able to find an image of God according to the Trinity, He Himself helping our efforts, who as things themselves show, and as Holy Scripture also witnesses, has regulated all things in measure, and number, and weight.[2]

---

[1] *Vid. Retract.* II. xv. 2. [Augustin here says that when he wrote the above, he forgot what is said in Leviticus xi. 20, of "fowls that creep, going upon all four, which have legs above their feet to leap withal upon the earth."—W.G.T.S.]

[2] Wisd. xi. 21.

BOOK XII.

COMMENCING WITH A DISTINCTION BETWEEN WISDOM AND KNOWLEDGE, POINTS OUT A KIND OF TRINITY, OF A PECULIAR SORT, IN THAT WHICH IS PROPERLY CALLED KNOWLEDGE, AND WHICH IS THE LOWER OF THE TWO ; AND THIS TRINITY, ALTHOUGH IT CERTAINLY PERTAINS TO THE INNER MAN, IS STILL NOT YET TO BE CALLED OR THOUGHT AN IMAGE OF GOD.

CHAP. I.—OF WHAT KIND ARE THE OUTER AND THE INNER MAN.

1. COME now, and let us see where lies, as it were, the boundary line between the outer and inner man. For whatever we have in the mind common with the beasts, thus much is rightly said to belong to the outer man. For the outer man is not to be considered to be the body only, but with the addition also of a certain peculiar life of the body, whence the structure of the body derives its vigor, and all the senses with which he is equipped for the perception of outward things; and when the images of these outward things already perceived, that have been fixed in the memory, are seen again by recollection, it is still a matter pertaining to the outer man. And in all these things we do not differ from the beasts, except that in shape of body we are not prone, but upright. And we are admonished through this, by Him who made us, not to be like the beasts in that which is our better part—that is, the mind—while we differ from them by the uprightness of the body. Not that we are to throw our mind into those bodily things which are exalted; for to seek rest for the will, even in such things, is to prostrate the mind. But as the body is naturally raised upright to those bodily things which are most elevated, that is, to things celestial; so the mind, which is a spiritual substance, must be raised upright to those things which are most elevated in spiritual things, not by the elation of pride, but by the dutifulness of righteousness.

CHAP. 2.—MAN ALONE OF ANIMATE CREATURES PERCEIVES THE ETERNAL REASONS OF THINGS PERTAINING TO THE BODY.

2. And the beasts, too, are able both to perceive things corporeal from without, through the senses of the body, and to fix them in the memory, and remember them, and in them to seek after things suitable, and shun things inconvenient. But to note these things, and to retain them not only as caught up naturally but also as deliberately committed to memory, and to imprint them again by recollection and conception when now just slipping away into forgetfulness; in order that as conception is formed from that which the memory contains, so also the contents themselves of the memory may be fixed firmly by thought: to combine again imaginary objects of sight, by taking this or that of what the memory remembers, and, as it were, tacking them to one another: to examine after what manner it is that in this kind things like the true are to be distinguished from the true, and this not in things spiritual, but in corporeal things themselves;—these acts, and the like, although performed in reference to things sensible, and those which the mind has deduced through the bodily senses, yet, as they are combined with reason, so are not common to men and beasts. But it is the part of the higher reason to judge of these corporeal things according to incorporeal and eternal reasons; which, unless they were above the human mind, would certainly not be unchangeable; and yet, unless something of our own were subjoined to them, we should not be able to employ them as our measures by which to judge of corporeal things. But we judge of corporeal things from the rule of dimensions and figures, which the mind knows to remain unchangeably.[1]

---

[1] [The distinction drawn here is between that low form of intelligence which exists in the brute, and that high form characteristic of man. In the Kantian nomenclature, the brute has understanding, but unenlightened by reason ; either theoretical or

CHAP. 3.—THE HIGHER REASON WHICH BE-
LONGS TO CONTEMPLATION, AND THE LOWER
WHICH BELONGS TO ACTION, ARE IN ONE
MIND.

3. But that of our own which thus has to
do with the handling of corporeal and temporal things, is indeed rational, in that it is
not common to us with the beasts; but it is
drawn, as it were, out of that rational substance of our mind, by which we depend upon
and cleave to the intelligible and unchangeable truth, and which is deputed to handle
and direct the inferior things. For as among
all the beasts there was not found for the
man a help like unto him, unless one were
taken from himself, and formed to be his
consort: so for that mind, by which we consult
the supernal and inward truth, there is no
like help for such employment as man's
nature requires among things corporeal out
of those parts of the soul which we have in
common with the beasts. And so a certain
part of our reason, not separated so as to
sever unity, but, as it were, diverted so as to
be a help to fellowship, is parted off for the
performing of its proper work. And as the
twain is one flesh in the case of male and
female, so in the mind one nature embraces
our intellect and action, or our counsel and
performance, or our reason and rational appetite, or whatever other more significant
terms there may be by which to express
them; so that, as it was said of the former,
"And they two shall be in one flesh," [1] it
may be said of these, they two are in one
mind.

CHAP. 4. — THE TRINITY AND THE IMAGE OF
GOD IS IN THAT PART OF THE MIND ALONE
WHICH BELONGS TO THE CONTEMPLATION OF
ETERNAL THINGS.

4. When, therefore, we discuss the nature
of the human mind, we discuss a single subject, and do not double it into those two
which I have mentioned, except in respect
to its functions. Therefore, when we seek
the trinity in the mind, we seek it in the
whole mind, without separating the action
of the reason in things temporal from the
contemplation of things eternal, so as to
have further to seek some third thing, by
which a trinity may be completed. But this
trinity must needs be so discovered in the
whole nature of the mind, as that even if

action upon temporal things were to be withdrawn, for which work that help is necessary,
with a view to which some part of the mind is
diverted in order to deal with these inferior
things, yet a trinity would still be found in
the one mind that is no where parted off; and
that when this distribution has been already
made, not only a trinity may be found, but
also an image of God, in that alone which
belongs to the contemplation of eternal
things; while in that other which is diverted
from it in the dealing with temporal things,
although there may be a trinity, yet there
cannot be found an image of God.

CHAP. 5. — THE OPINION WHICH DEVISES AN
IMAGE OF THE TRINITY IN THE MARRIAGE OF
MALE AND FEMALE, AND IN THEIR OFF-
SPRING.

5. Accordingly they do not seem to me to
advance a probable opinion, who lay it down
that a trinity of the image of God in three
persons, so far as regards human nature,
can so be discovered as to be completed in
the marriage of male and female and in their
offspring; in that the man himself, as it were,
indicates the person of the Father, but that
which has so proceeded from him as to be
born, that of the Son; and so the third
person as of the Spirit, is, they say, the
woman, who has so proceeded from the man
as not herself to be either son or daughter, [2]
although it was by her conception that the
offspring was born. For the Lord hath said
of the Holy Spirit that He proceedeth from
the Father, [3] and yet he is not a son. In
this erroneous opinion, then, the only point
probably alleged, and indeed sufficiently
shown according to the faith of the Holy
Scripture, is this,—in the account of the
original creation of the woman,—that what
so comes into existence from some person as
to make another person, cannot in every case
be called a son; since the person of the
woman came into existence from the person
of the man, and yet she is not called his
daughter. All the rest of this opinion is in
truth so absurd, nay indeed so false, that it
is most easy to refute it. For I pass over
such a thing, as to think the Holy Spirit to
be the mother of the Son of God, and the
wife of the Father; since perhaps it may be
answered that these things offend us in carnal things, because we think of bodily conceptions and births. Although these very
things themselves are most chastely thought
of by the pure, to whom all things are pure;
but to the defiled and unbelieving, of whom

---

practical. He has intelligence, but not as modified by the forms
of space and time and the categories of quantity, quality, relation
etc.; and still less as modified and exalted by the ideas of reason—
namely, the mathematical ideas, and the moral ideas of God, freedom, and immortality. The animal has no *rational* intelligence.
He has mere understanding without reason.—W. G. T. S.]

[1] Gen. ii. 24.

[2] Gen. ii. 22.   [3] John xv. 26.

both the mind and conscience are polluted, nothing is pure;[1] so that even Christ, born of a virgin according to the flesh, is a stumbling-block to some of them. But yet in the case of those supreme spiritual things, after the likeness of which those kinds of the inferior creature also are made although most remotely, and where there is nothing that can be injured and nothing corruptible, nothing born in time, nothing formed from that which is formless, or whatever like expressions there may be; yet they ought not to disturb the sober prudence of any one, lest in avoiding empty disgust he run into pernicious error. Let him accustom himself so to find in corporeal things the traces of things spiritual, that when he begins to ascend upwards from thence, under the guidance of reason, in order to attain to the unchangeable truth itself through which these things were made, he may not draw with himself to things above what he despises in things below. For no one ever blushed to choose for himself wisdom as a wife, because the name of wife puts into a man's thoughts the corruptible connection which consists in begetting children; or because in truth wisdom itself is a woman in sex, since it is expressed in both Greek and Latin tongues by a word of the feminine gender.

CHAP. 6. — WHY THIS OPINION IS TO BE REJECTED.

6. We do not therefore reject this opinion, because we fear to think of that holy and inviolable and unchangeable Love, as the spouse of God the Father, existing as it does from Him, but not as an offspring in order to beget the Word by which all things are made; but because divine Scripture evidently shows it to be false. For God said, "Let us make man in our image, after our likeness;" and a little after it is said, "So God created man in the image of God."[2] Certainly, in that it is of the plural number, the word "our" would not be rightly used if man were made in the image of one person, whether of the Father, or of the Son, or of the Holy Spirit; but because he was made in the image of the Trinity, on that account it is said, "After our image." But again, lest we should think that three Gods were to be believed in the Trinity, whereas the same Trinity is one God, it is said, "So God created man in the image of God," instead of saying, "In His own image."

7. For such expressions are customary in the Scriptures; and yet some persons, while maintaining the Catholic faith, do not carefully attend to them, in such wise that they think the words, "God made man in the image of God," to mean that the Father made man after the image of the Son; and they thus desire to assert that the Son also is called God in the divine Scriptures, as if there were not other most true and clear proofs wherein the Son is called not only God, but also the true God. For whilst they aim at explaining another difficulty in this text, they become so entangled that they cannot extricate themselves. For if the Father made man after the image of the Son, so that he is not the image of the Father, but of the Son, then the Son is unlike the Father. But if a pious faith teaches us, as it does, that the Son is like the Father after an equality of essence, then that which is made in the likeness of the Son must needs also be made in the likeness of the Father. Further, if the Father made man not in His own image, but in the image of His Son, why does He not say, "Let us make man after Thy image and likeness," whereas He does say, "our;" unless it be because the image of the Trinity was made in man, that in this way man should be the image of the one true God, because the Trinity itself is the one true God? Such expressions are innumerable in the Scriptures, but it will suffice to have produced these. It is so said in the Psalms, "Salvation belongeth unto the Lord; Thy blessing is upon Thy people;"[3] as if the words were spoken to some one else, not to Him of whom it had been said, "Salvation belongeth unto the Lord." And again, "For by Thee," he says, "I shall be delivered from temptation, and by hoping in my God I shall leap over the wall;"[4] as if he said to some one else, "By Thee I shall be delivered from temptation." And again, "In the heart of the king's enemies; whereby the people fall under Thee;"[5] as if he were to say, in the heart of Thy enemies. For he had said to that King, that is, to our Lord Jesus Christ, "The people fall under Thee," whom he intended by the word King, when he said, "In the heart of the king's enemies." Things of this kind are found more rarely in the New Testament. But yet the apostle says to the Romans, "Concerning His Son who was made to Him of the seed of David according to the flesh, and declared to be the Son of God with power, according to the spirit of holiness, by the resurrection of the dead of Jesus Christ our Lord;"[6] as though he were speaking above of some one

---

[1] Tit. i. 15.   [2] Gen. i. 26, 27.

[3] Ps. iii. 8.   [4] Ps. xviii. 29.
[5] Ps. xlv. 5.   [6] Rom. i. 3, 4.

else. For what is meant by the Son of God declared by the resurrection of the dead of Jesus Christ, except of the same Jesus Christ who was declared to be Son of God with power? And as then in this passage, when we are told, "the Son of God with power of Jesus Christ," or "the Son of God according to the spirit of holiness of Jesus Christ," or "the Son of God by the resurrection of the dead of Jesus Christ," whereas it might have been expressed in the ordinary way, In His own power, or according to the spirit of His own holiness, or by the resurrection of His dead, or of their dead: as, I say, we are not compelled to understand another person, but one and the same, that is, the person of the Son of God our Lord Jesus Christ; so, when we are told that "God made man in the image of God," although it might have been more usual to say, after His own image, yet we are not compelled to understand any other person in the Trinity, but the one and self-same Trinity itself, who is one God, and after whose image man is made.

8. And since the case stands thus, if we are to accept the same image of the Trinity, as not in one, but in three human beings, father and mother and son, then the man was not made after the image of God before a wife was made for him, and before they procreated a son; because there was not yet a trinity. Will any one say there was already a trinity, because, although not yet in their proper form, yet in their original nature, both the woman was already in the side of the man, and the son in the loins of his father? Why then, when Scripture had said, "God made man after the image of God," did it go on to say, "God created him; male and female created He them: and God blessed them"?[1] (Or if it is to be so divided, "And God created man," so that thereupon is to be added, "in the image of God created He him," and then subjoined in the third place, "male and female created He them;" for some have feared to say, He made him male and female, lest something monstrous, as it were, should be understood, as are those whom they call hermaphrodites, although even so both might be understood not falsely in the singular number, on account of that which is said, "Two in one flesh.") Why then, as I began by saying, in regard to the nature of man made after the image of God, does Scripture specify nothing except male and female? Certainly, in order to complete the image of the Trinity, it ought to have added also son, although still placed

in the loins of his father, as the woman was in his side. Or was it perhaps that the woman also had been already made, and that Scripture had combined in a short and comprehensive statement, that of which it was going to explain afterwards more carefully, how it was done; and that therefore a son could not be mentioned, because no son was yet born? As if the Holy Spirit could not have comprehended this, too, in that brief statement, while about to narrate the birth of the son afterwards in its own place; as it narrated afterwards in its own place, that the woman was taken from the side of the man,[2] and yet has not omitted here to name her.

CHAP. 7.—HOW MAN IS THE IMAGE OF GOD. WHETHER THE WOMAN IS NOT ALSO THE IMAGE OF GOD. HOW THE SAYING OF THE APOSTLE, THAT THE MAN IS THE IMAGE OF GOD, BUT THE WOMAN IS THE GLORY OF THE MAN, IS TO BE UNDERSTOOD FIGURATIVELY AND MYSTICALLY.

9. We ought not therefore so to understand that man is made in the image of the supreme Trinity, that is, in the image of God, as that the same image should be understood to be in three human beings; especially when the apostle says that the man is the image of God, and on that account removes the covering from his head, which he warns the woman to use, speaking thus: "For a man indeed ought not to cover his head, forasmuch as he is the image and glory of God; but the woman is the glory of the man." What then shall we say to this? If the woman fills up the image of the trinity after the measure of her own person, why is the man still called that image after she has been taken out of his side? Or if even one person of a human being out of three can be called the image of God, as each person also is God in the supreme Trinity itself, why is the woman also not the image of God? For she is instructed for this very reason to cover her head, which he is forbidden to do because he is the image of God.[3]

10. But we must notice how that which the apostle says, that not the woman but the man is the image of God, is not contrary to that which is written in Genesis, "God created man: in the image of God created He him; male and female created He them: and He blessed them." For this text says that human nature itself, which is complete [only] in both sexes, was made in the image of God; and it does not separate the woman from the image of God which it signifies. For after

---

[1] Gen. i. 27, 28.   [2] Gen. ii. 24, 22.   [3] 1 Cor. xi. 7, 5.

saying that God made man in the image of God, "He created him," it says, "male and female:" or at any rate, punctuating the words otherwise, "male and female created He them." How then did the apostle tell us that the man is the image of God, and therefore he is forbidden to cover his head; but that the woman is not so, and therefore is commanded to cover hers? Unless, forsooth, according to that which I have said already, when I was treating of the nature of the human mind, that the woman together with her own husband is the image of God, so that that whole substance may be one image; but when she is referred separately to her quality of *help-meet*, which regards the woman herself alone, then she is not the image of God; but as regards the man alone, he is the image of God as fully and completely as when the woman too is joined with him in one. As we said of the nature of the human mind, that both in the case when as a whole it contemplates the truth it is the image of God; and in the case when anything is divided from it, and diverted in order to the cognition of temporal things; nevertheless on that side on which it beholds and consults truth, here also it is the image of God, but on that side whereby it is directed to the cognition of the lower things, it is not the image of God. And since it is so much the more formed after the image of God, the more it has extended itself to that which is eternal, and is on that account not to be restrained, so as to withhold and refrain itself from thence; therefore the man ought not to cover his head. But because too great a progression towards inferior things is dangerous to that rational cognition that is conversant with things corporeal and temporal; this ought to have power on its head, which the covering indicates, by which it is signified that it ought to be restrained. For a holy and pious meaning is pleasing to the holy angels.[1] For God sees not after the way of time, neither does anything new take place in His vision and knowledge, when anything is done in time and transitorily, after the way in which such things affect the senses, whether the carnal senses of animals and men, or even the heavenly senses of the angels.

11. For that the Apostle Paul, when speaking outwardly of the sex of male and female, figured the mystery of some more hidden truth, may be understood from this, that when he says in another place that she is a widow indeed who is desolate, without chil-

dren and nephews, and yet that she ought to trust in God, and to continue in prayers night and day,[2] he here indicates, that the woman having been brought into the transgression by being deceived, is brought to salvation by child-bearing; and then he has added, "If they continue in faith, and charity, and holiness, with sobriety."[3] As if it could possibly hurt a good widow, if either she had not sons, or if those whom she had did not choose to continue in good works. But because those things which are called good works are, as it were, the sons of our life, according to that sense of life in which it answers to the question, What is a man's life? that is, How does he act in these temporal things? which life the Greeks do not call ζωή but βίος; and because these good works are chiefly performed in the way of offices of mercy, while works of mercy are of no profit, either to Pagans, or to Jews who do not believe in Christ, or to any heretics or schismatics whatsoever in whom faith and charity and sober holiness are not found: what the apostle meant to signify is plain, and in so far figuratively and mystically, because he was speaking of covering the head of the woman, which will remain mere empty words, unless referred to some hidden sacrament.

12. For, as not only most true reason but also the authority of the apostle himself declares, man was not made in the image of God according to the shape of his body, but according to his rational mind. For the thought is a debased and empty one, which holds God to be circumscribed and limited by the lineaments of bodily members. But further, does not the same blessed apostle say, "Be renewed in the spirit of your mind, and put on the new man, which is created after God;"[4] and in another place more clearly, "Putting off the old man," he says, "with his deeds; put on the new man, which is renewed to the knowledge of God after the image of Him that created him?"[5] If, then, we are renewed in the spirit of our mind, and he is the new man who is renewed to the knowledge of God after the image of Him that created him; no one can doubt, that man was made after the image of Him that created him, not according to the body, nor indiscriminately according to any part of the mind, but according to the rational mind, wherein the knowledge of God can exist And it is according to this renewal, also, that we are made sons of God by the baptism of Christ; and putting on the new man, certainly put on Christ through faith. Who is there, then,

---

[1] 1 Cor. xi. 10.

[2] 1 Tim. v. 5.　　　　[3] 1 Tim. ii. 15.
[4] Eph. iv. 23, 24.　　　　[5] Col. iii. 9, 10.

who will hold women to be alien from this fellowship, whereas they are fellow-heirs of grace with us; and whereas in another place the same apostle says, "For ye are all the children of God by faith in Christ Jesus; for as many as have been baptized into Christ have put on Christ: there is neither Jew nor Greek, there is neither bond nor free, there is neither male nor female; for ye are all one in Christ Jesus?"[1] Pray, have faithful women then lost their bodily sex? But because they are there renewed after the image of God, where there is no sex; man is there made after the image of God, where there is no sex, that is, in the spirit of his mind. Why, then, is the man on that account not bound to cover his head, because he is the image and glory of God, while the woman is bound to do so, because she is the glory of the man; as though the woman were not renewed in the spirit of her mind, which spirit is renewed to the knowledge of God after the image of Him who created him? But because she differs from the man in bodily sex, it was possible rightly to represent under her bodily covering that part of the reason which is diverted to the government of temporal things; so that the image of God may remain on that side of the mind of man on which it cleaves to the beholding or the consulting of the eternal reasons of things; and this, it is clear, not men only, but also women have.

CHAP. 8.—TURNING ASIDE FROM THE IMAGE OF GOD.

13. A common nature, therefore, is recognized in their minds, but in their bodies a division of that one mind itself is figured. As we ascend, then, by certain steps of thought within, along the succession of the parts of the mind, there where something first meets us which is not common to ourselves with the beasts reason begins, so that here the inner man can now be recognized. And if this inner man himself, through that reason to which the administering of things temporal has been delegated, slips on too far by over-much progress into outward things, that which is his head moreover consenting, that is, the (so to call it) masculine part which presides in the watch-tower of counsel not restraining or bridling it: then he waxeth old because of all his enemies,[2] *viz.* the demons with their prince the devil, who are envious of virtue; and that vision of eternal things is withdrawn also from the head himself, eating with his spouse that which was forbidden, so that the light of his eyes is gone from him;[3] and so both

being naked from that enlightenment of truth, and with the eyes of their conscience opened to behold how they were left shameful and unseemly, like the leaves of sweet fruits, but without the fruits themselves, they so weave together good words without the fruit of good works, as while living wickedly to cover over their disgrace as it were by speaking well.[4]

CHAP. 9.—THE SAME ARGUMENT IS CONTINUED.

14. For the soul loving its own power, slips onwards from the whole which is common, to a part, which belongs especially to itself. And that apostatizing pride, which is called "the beginning of sin,"[5] whereas it might have been most excellently governed by the laws of God, if it had followed Him as its ruler in the universal creature, by seeking something more than the whole, and struggling to govern this by a law of its own, is thrust on, since nothing is more than the whole, into caring for a part; and thus by lusting after something more, is made less; whence also covetousness is called "the root of all evil."[6] And it administers that whole, wherein it strives to do something of its own against the laws by which the whole is governed, by its own body, which it possesses only in part; and so being delighted by corporeal forms and motions, because it has not the things themselves within itself, and because it is wrapped up in their images, which it has fixed in the memory, and is foully polluted by fornication of the phantasy, while it refers all its functions to those ends, for which it curiously seeks corporeal and temporal things through the senses of the body, either it affects with swelling arrogance to be more excellent than other souls that are given up to the corporeal senses, or it is plunged into a foul whirlpool of carnal pleasure.

CHAP. 10. — THE LOWEST DEGRADATION IS REACHED BY DEGREES.

15. When the soul then consults either for itself or for others with a good will towards perceiving the inner and higher things, such as are possessed in a chaste embrace, without any narrowness or envy, not individually, but in common by all who love such things; then even if it be deceived in anything, through ignorance of things temporal (for its action in this case is a temporal one), and if it does not hold fast to that mode of acting which it ought, the temptation is but one common to man. And it is a great thing so to pass through this life, on which we travel, as it were, like a road on our return home, that

---

[1] Gal. iii. 26-28.   [2] Ps. vi. 7.   [3] Ps. xxxviii. 10   [4] Gen. iii. 4.   [5] Ecclus. x. 15.   [6] 1 Tim. vi. 10.

no temptation may take us, but what is common to man. [1] For this is a sin without the body, and must not be reckoned fornication, and on that account is very easily pardoned. But when the soul does anything in order to attain those things which are perceived through the body, through lust of proving or of surpassing or of handling them, in order that it may place in them its final good, then whatever it does, it does wickedly, and commits fornication, sinning against its own body: [2] and while snatching from within the deceitful images of corporeal things, and combining them by vain thought, so that nothing seems to it to be divine, unless it be of such a kind as this; by selfish greediness it is made fruitful in errors, and by selfish prodigality it is emptied of strength. Yet it would not leap on at once from the commencement to such shameless and miserable fornication, but, as it is written, " He that contemneth small things, shall fall by little and little." [3]

CHAP. 11.—THE IMAGE OF THE BEAST IN MAN.

16. For as a snake does not creep on with open steps, but advances by the very minutest efforts of its several scales; so the slippery motion of falling away [from what is good] takes possession of the negligent only gradually, and beginning from a perverse desire for the likeness of God, arrives in the end at the likeness of beasts. Hence it is that being naked of their first garment, they earned by mortality coats of skins. [4] For the true honor of man is the image and likeness of God, which is not preserved except it be in relation to Him by whom it is impressed. The less therefore that one loves what is one's own, the more one cleaves to God. But through the desire of making trial of his own power, man by his own bidding falls down to himself as to a sort of intermediate grade. And so, while he wishes to be as God is, that is, under no one, he is thrust on, even from his own middle grade, by way of punishment, to that which is lowest, that is, to those things in which beasts delight: and thus, while his honor is the likeness of God, but his dishonor is the likeness of the beast, " Man being in honor abideth not: he is compared to the beasts that are foolish, and is made like to them." [5] By what path, then, could he pass so great a distance from the highest to the lowest, except through his own intermediate grade? For when he neglects the love of wisdom, which remains always after the same fashion, and lusts after knowledge by experi-

ment upon things temporal and mutable, that knowledge puffeth up, it does not edify: [6] so the mind is overweighed and thrust out, as it were, by its own weight from blessedness; and learns by its own punishment, through that trial of its own intermediateness, what the difference is between the good it has abandoned and the bad to which it has committed itself; and having thrown away and destroyed its strength, it cannot return, unless by the grace of its Maker calling it to repentance, and forgiving its sins. For who will deliver the unhappy soul from the body of this death, unless the grace of God through Jesus Christ our Lord? [7] Of which grace we will discourse in its place, so far as He Himself enables us.

CHAP. 12.—THERE IS A KIND OF HIDDEN WEDLOCK IN THE INNER MAN. UNLAWFUL PLEASURES OF THE THOUGHTS.

17. Let us now complete, so far as the Lord helps us, the discussion which we have undertaken, respecting that part of reason to which knowledge belongs, that is, the cognizance of things temporal and changeable, which is necessary for managing the affairs of this life. For as in the case of that visible wedlock of the two human beings who were made first, the serpent did not eat of the forbidden tree, but only persuaded them to eat of it; and the woman did not eat alone, but gave to her husband, and they eat together; although she alone spoke with the serpent, and she alone was led away by him: [8] so also in the case of that hidden and secret kind of wedlock, which is transacted and discerned in a single human being, the carnal, or as I may say, since it is directed to the senses of the body, the sensuous movement of the soul, which is common to us with beasts, is shut off from the reason of wisdom. For certainly bodily things are perceived by the sense of the body; but spiritual things, which are eternal and unchangeable, are understood by the reason of wisdom. But the reason of knowledge has appetite very near to it: seeing that what is called the science or knowledge of actions reasons concerning the bodily things which are perceived by the bodily sense; if well, in order that it may refer that knowledge to the end of the chief good; but if ill, in order that it may enjoy them as being such good things as those wherein it reposes with a false blessedness. Whenever, then, that carnal or animal sense introduces into this purpose of the mind which is conversant about things temporal and corporeal,

---

[1] 1. Cor. x. 13.   [2] 1 Cor. vi. 18.   [3] Ecclus. xix. 1.
[4] Gen. iii. 21.   [5] Ps. xlix. 12.
[6] 1 Cor. viii. 1.   [7] Rom. vii. 24, 25.   [8] Gen. iii. 1-6.

with a view to the offices of a man's actions, by the living force of reason, some inducement to enjoy itself, that is, to enjoy itself as if it were some private good of its own, not as the public and common, which is the unchangeable, good; then, as it were, the serpent discourses with the woman. And to consent to this allurement, is to eat of the forbidden tree. But if that consent is satisfied by the pleasure of thought alone, but the members are so restrained by the authority of higher counsel that they are not yielded as instruments of unrighteousness unto sin;[1] this, I think, is to be considered as if the woman alone should have eaten the forbidden food. But if, in this consent to use wickedly the things which are perceived through the senses of the body, any sin at all is so determined upon, that if there is the power it is also fulfilled by the body; then that woman must be understood to have given the unlawful food to her husband with her, to be eaten together. For it is not possible for the mind to determine that a sin is not only to be thought of with pleasure, but also to be effectually committed, unless also that intention of the mind yields, and serves the bad action, with which rests the chief power of applying the members to an outward act, or of restraining them from one.

18. And yet, certainly, when the mind is pleased in thought alone with unlawful things, while not indeed determining that they are to be done, but yet holding and pondering gladly things which ought to have been rejected the very moment they touched the mind, it cannot be denied to be a sin, but far less than if it were also determined to accomplished it in outward act. And therefore pardon must be sought for such thoughts too, and the breast must be smitten, and it must be said, "Forgive us our debts;" and what follows must be done, and must be joined in our prayer, "As we also forgive our debtors."[2] For it is not as it was with those two first human beings, of which each one bare his own person; and so, if the woman alone had eaten the forbidden food, she certainly alone would have been smitten with the punishment of death: it cannot, I say, be so said also in the case of a single human being now, that if the thought, remaining alone, be gladly fed with unlawful pleasures, from which it ought to turn away directly, while yet there is no determination that the bad actions are to be done, but only that they are retained with pleasure in remembrance, the woman as it were can be condemned without the man.

Far be it from us to believe this. For here is one person, one human being, and he as a whole will be condemned, unless those things which, as lacking the will to do, and yet having the will to please the mind with them, are perceived to be sins of thought alone, are pardoned through the grace of the Mediator.[3]

19. This reasoning, then, whereby we have sought in the mind of each several human being a certain rational wedlock of contemplation and action, with functions distributed through each severally, yet with the unity of the mind preserved in both; saving meanwhile the truth of that *history* which divine testimony hands down respecting the first two human beings, that is, the man and his wife, from whom the human species is propagated;[4] —this reasoning, I say, must be listened to only thus far, that the apostle may be understood to have intended to signify something to be sought in one individual man, by assigning the image of God to the man only, and not also to the woman, although in the merely different sex of two human beings.

CHAP. 13.—THE OPINION OF THOSE WHO HAVE THOUGHT THAT THE MIND WAS SIGNIFIED BY THE MAN, THE BODILY SENSE BY THE WOMAN.

20. Nor does it escape me, that some who before us were eminent defenders of the Catholic faith and expounders of the word of God, while they looked for these two things in one human being, whose entire soul they perceived to be a sort of excellent paradise, asserted that the man was the mind, but that the woman was the bodily sense. And according to this distribution, by which the man is assumed to be the mind, but the woman the bodily sense, all things seem aptly to agree together if they are handled with due attention: unless that it is written, that in all the beasts and flying things there was not found for man an helpmate like to himself; and then the woman was made out of his side.[5] And on this account I, for my part, have not thought that the bodily sense should be taken for the woman, which we see to be common to ourselves and to the beasts; but I have desired to find something which the beasts had not; and I have rather thought the bodily sense should be understood to be the serpent, whom we read to have been more subtle than all beasts of the field.[6] For in those natural good things which we see are common to our-

---

[1] Rom. vi. 13.   Matt. vi. 12.

[3] [Augustin here teaches that the inward lust is guilt as well as the outward action prompted by it. This is in accordance with Matt. v. 28 ; Acts viii. 21-22 ; Rom. vii. 7 ; James i. 14.—W.G.T.S.]
[4] [Augustin means, that while he has given an allegorical and mystical interpretation to the narrative of the fall, in Genesis, he also holds to its historical sense.—W. G. T. S.]
[5] Gen. ii. 20-22.   [6] Gen. iii. 1.

selves and to the irrational animals, the sense excels by a kind of living power; not the sense of which it is written in the epistle addressed to the Hebrews, where we read, that "strong meat belongeth to them that are of full age, even those who by reason of use have their senses exercised to discern both good and evil;"[1] for these "senses" belong to the rational nature and pertain to the understanding; but that sense which is divided into five parts in the body, through which corporeal species and motion is perceived not only by ourselves, but also by the beasts.

21. But whether that the apostle calls the man the image and glory of God, but the woman the glory of the man,[2] is to be received in this, or that, or in any other way; yet it is clear, that when we live according to God, our mind which is intent on the invisible things of Him ought to be fashioned with proficiency from His eternity, truth, charity; but that something of our own rational purpose, that is, of the same mind, must be directed to the using of changeable and corporeal things, without which this life does not go on; not that we may be conformed to this world,[3] by placing our end in such good things, and by forcing the desire of blessedness towards them, but that whatever we do rationally in the using of temporal things, we may do it with the contemplation of attaining eternal things, passing through the former, but cleaving to the latter.

CHAP. 14.—WHAT IS THE DIFFERENCE BETWEEN WISDOM AND KNOWLEDGE. THE WORSHIP OF GOD IS THE LOVE OF HIM. HOW THE INTELLECTUAL COGNIZANCE OF ETERNAL THINGS COMES TO PASS THROUGH WISDOM.

For knowledge also has its own good measure, if that in it which puffs up, or is wont to puff up, is conquered by love of eternal things, which does not puff up, but, as we know, edifieth.[4] Certainly without knowledge the virtues themselves, by which one lives rightly, cannot be possessed, by which this miserable life may be so governed, that we may attain to that eternal life which is truly blessed.

22. Yet action, by which we use temporal things well, differs from contemplation of eternal things; and the latter is reckoned to wisdom, the former to knowledge. For although that which is wisdom can also be called knowledge, as the apostle too speaks, where he says, "Now I know in part, but then shall I know even as also I am known;"[5] when doubtless he meant his words to be understood of the knowledge of the contemplation of God, which will be the highest reward of the saints; yet where he says, "For to one is given by the Spirit the word of wisdom, to another the word of knowledge by the same Spirit,"[6] certainly he distinguishes without doubt these two things, although he does not there explain the difference, nor in what way one may be discerned from the other. But having examined a great number of passages from the Holy Scriptures, I find it written in the Book of Job, that holy man being the speaker, "Behold, piety, that is wisdom; but to depart from evil is knowledge."[7] In thus distinguishing, it must be understood that wisdom belongs to contemplation, knowledge to action. For in this place he meant by piety the worship of God, which in Greek is called θεοσέβεια. For the sentence in the Greek MSS. has that word. And what is there in eternal things more excellent than God, of whom alone the nature is unchangeable? And what is the worship of Him except the love of Him, by which we now desire to see Him, and we believe and hope that we shall see Him; and in proportion as we make progress, see now through a glass in an enigma, but then in clearness? For this is what the Apostle Paul means by "face to face."[8] This is also what John says, "Beloved, now we are the sons of God, and it doth not yet appear what we shall be; but we know that, when He shall appear, we shall be like Him; for we shall see Him as He is."[9] Discourse about these and the like subjects seems to me to be the discourse itself of wisdom. But to depart from evil, which Job says is knowledge, is without doubt of temporal things. Since it is in reference to time [and this world] that we are in evil, from which we ought to abstain that we may come to those good eternal things. And therefore, whatsoever we do prudently, boldly, temperately, and justly, belongs to that knowledge or discipline wherewith our action is conversant in avoiding evil and desiring good; and so also, whatsoever we gather by the knowledge that comes from inquiry, in the way of examples either to be guarded against or to be imitated, and in the way of necessary proofs respecting any subject, accommodated to our use.

23. When a discourse then relates to these things, I hold it to be a discourse belonging to knowledge, and to be distinguished from a discourse belonging to wisdom, to which those things belong, which neither have been,

---

[1] Heb. v. 14.　　　[2] 1 Cor. xi. 7.
[3] Rom. xii. 2　　　[4] 1 Cor. viii. 1.
[5] 1 Cor. xiii. 12.　　　[6] 1 Cor. xii. 8.　　　[7] Job xxviii. 8.
[8] 1 Cor. xiii. 12.　　　[9] 1 John iii. 2.

nor shall be, but are; and on account of that eternity in which they are, are said to have been, and to be, and to be about to be, without any changeableness of times. For neither have they been in such way as that they should cease to be, nor are they about to be in such way as if they were not now; but they have always had and always will have that very absolute being. And they abide, but not as if fixed in some place as are bodies; but as intelligible things in incorporeal nature, they are so at hand to the glance of the mind, as things visible or tangible in place are to the sense of the body. And not only in the case of sensible things posited in place, there abide also intelligible and incorporeal reasons of them apart from local space; but also of motions that pass by in successive times, apart from any transit in time, there stand also like reasons, themselves certainly intelligible, and not sensible. And to attain to these with the eye of the mind is the lot of few; and when they are attained as much as they can be, he himself who attains to them does not abide in them, but is as it were repelled by the rebounding of the eye itself of the mind, and so there comes to be a transitory thought of a thing not transitory. And yet this transient thought is committed to the memory through the instructions by which the mind is taught; that the mind which is compelled to pass from thence, may be able to return thither again; although, if the thought should not return to the memory and find there what it had committed to it, it would be led thereto like an uninstructed person, as it had been led before, and would find it where it had first found it, that is to say, in that incorporeal truth, whence yet once more it may be as it were written down and fixed in the mind. For the thought of man, for example, does not so abide in that incorporeal and unchangeable reason of a square body, as that reason itself abides: if, to be sure, it could attain to it at all without the phantasy of local space. Or if one were to apprehend the rhythm of any artificial or musical sound, passing through certain intervals of time, as it rested without time in some secret and deep silence, it could at least be thought as long as that song could be heard; yet what the glance of the mind, transient though it was, caught from thence, and, absorbing as it were into a belly, so laid up in the memory, over this it will be able to ruminate in some measure by recollection, and to transfer what it has thus learned into systematic knowledge. But if this has been blotted out by absolute forgetfulness, yet once again,

under the guidance of teaching, one will come to that which had altogether dropped away, and it will be found such as it was.

CHAP. 15. — IN OPPOSITION TO THE REMINISCENCE OF PLATO AND PYTHAGORAS. PYTHAGORAS THE SAMIAN. OF THE DIFFERENCE BETWEEN WISDOM AND KNOWLEDGE, AND OF SEEKING THE TRINITY IN THE KNOWLEDGE OF TEMPORAL THINGS.

24. And hence that noble philosopher Plato endeavored to persuade us that the souls of men lived even before they bare these bodies; and that hence those things which are learnt are rather remembered, as having been known already, than taken into knowledge as things new. For he has told us that a boy, when questioned I know not what respecting geometry, replied as if he were perfectly skilled in that branch of learning. For being questioned step by step and skillfully, he saw what was to be seen, and said that which he saw. [1] But if this had been a recollecting of things previously known, then certainly every one, or almost every one, would not have been able so to answer when questioned. For not every one was a geometrician in the former life, since geometricians are so few among men that scarcely one can be found anywhere. But we ought rather to believe, that the intellectual mind is so formed in its nature as to see those things, which by the disposition of the Creator are subjoined to things intelligible in a natural order, by a sort of incorporeal light of an unique kind; as the eye of the flesh sees things adjacent to itself in this bodily light, of which light it is made to be receptive, and adapted to it. For none the more does this fleshly eye, too, distinguish black things from white without a teacher, because it had already known them before it was created in this flesh. Why, lastly, is it possible only in intelligible things that any one properly questioned should answer according to any branch of learning, although ignorant of it? Why can no one do this with things sensible, except those which he has seen in this his present body, or has believed the information of others who knew them, whether somebody's writings or words? For we must not acquiesce in their story, who assert that the Samian Pythagoras recollected some things of this kind, which he had experienced when he was previously here in another body; and others tell yet of others, that they experienced something of the same

[1] [This fine specimen of the " obstetric method " of Socrates is given in Plato's dialogue, Meno.—W. G. T. S.]

sort in their minds: but it may be conjectured that these were untrue recollections, such as we commonly experience in sleep, when we fancy we remember, as though we had done or seen it, what we never did or saw at all; and that the minds of these persons, even though awake, were affected in this way at the suggestion of malignant and deceitful spirits, whose care it is to confirm or to sow some false belief concerning the changes of souls, in order to deceive men. This, I say, may be conjectured from this, that if they really remembered those things which they had seen here before, while occupying other bodies, the same thing would happen to many, nay to almost all; since they suppose that as the dead from the living, so, without cessation and continually, the living are coming into existence from the dead; as sleepers from those that are awake, and those that are awake from them that sleep.

25. If therefore this is the right distinction between wisdom and knowledge, that the intellectual cognizance of eternal things belongs to wisdom, but the rational cognizance of temporal things to knowledge, it is not difficult to judge which is to be preferred or postponed to which. But if we must employ some other distinction by which to know these two apart, which without doubt the apostle teaches us are different, saying, " To one is given by the Spirit the word of wisdom; to another the word of knowledge, by the same Spirit;" still the difference between those two which we have laid down is a most evident one, in that the intellectual cognizance of eternal things is one thing, the rational cognizance of temporal things another; and no one doubts but that the former is to be preferred to the latter. As then we leave behind those things which belong to the outer man, and desire to ascend within from those things which we have in common with beasts, before we come to the cognizance of things intelligible and supreme, which are eternal, the rational cognizance of temporal things presents itself. Let us then find a trinity in this also, if we can, as we found one in the senses of the body, and in those things which through them entered in the way of images into our soul or spirit; so that instead of corporeal things which we touch by corporeal sense, placed as they are without us, we might have resemblances of bodies impressed within on the memory from which thought might be formed, while the will as a third united them; just as the sight of the eyes was formed from without, which the will applied to the visible thing in order to produce vision, and united both, while itself also added itself thereto as a third. But this subject must not be compressed into this book; so that in that which follows, if God help, it may be suitably examined, and the conclusions to which we come may be unfolded.

BOOK XIII.

THE INQUIRY IS PROSECUTED RESPECTING KNOWLEDGE, IN WHICH, AS DISTINGUISHED FROM WIS-
DOM, AUGUSTIN HAD BEGUN IN THE FORMER BOOK TO LOOK FOR A KIND OF TRINITY. AND
OCCASION IS TAKEN OF COMMENDING CHRISTIAN FAITH, AND OF EXPLAINING HOW THE FAITH
OF BELIEVERS IS ONE AND COMMON. NEXT, THAT ALL DESIRE BLESSEDNESS, YET THAT ALL
HAVE NOT THE FAITH WHEREBY WE ARRIVE AT BLESSEDNESS ; AND THAT THIS FAITH IS DE-
FINED IN CHRIST, WHO IN THE FLESH ROSE FROM THE DEAD ; AND THAT NO ONE IS SET FREE
FROM THE DOMINION OF THE DEVIL THROUGH FORGIVENESS OF SINS, SAVE THROUGH HIM.
IT IS SHOWN ALSO AT LENGTH THAT IT WAS NEEDFUL THAT THE DEVIL SHOULD BE CON-
QUERED BY CHRIST, NOT BY POWER, BUT BY RIGHTEOUSNESS. FINALLY, THAT WHEN THE
WORDS OF THIS FAITH ARE COMMITTED TO MEMORY, THERE IS IN THE MIND A KIND OF
TRINITY, SINCE THERE ARE, FIRST, IN THE MEMORY THE SOUNDS OF THE WORDS, AND THIS
EVEN WHEN THE MAN IS NOT THINKING OF THEM ; AND NEXT, THE MIND'S EYE OF HIS
RECOLLECTION IS FORMED THEREUPON WHEN HE THINKS OF THEM ; AND, LASTLY, THE WILL,
WHEN HE SO THINKS AND REMEMBERS, COMBINES BOTH.

CHAP. I.—THE ATTEMPT IS MADE TO DISTIN-
GUISH OUT OF THE SCRIPTURES THE OFFICES
OF WISDOM AND OF KNOWLEDGE. THAT IN
THE BEGINNING OF JOHN SOME THINGS THAT
ARE SAID BELONG TO WISDOM, SOME TO
KNOWLEDGE. SOME THINGS THERE ARE ONLY
KNOWN BY THE HELP OF FAITH. HOW WE
SEE THE FAITH THAT IS IN US. IN THE
SAME NARRATIVE OF JOHN, SOME THINGS ARE
KNOWN BY THE SENSE OF THE BODY, OTHERS
ONLY BY THE REASON OF THE MIND.

1. IN the book before this, *viz.* the twelfth
of this work, we have done enough to distinguish the office of the rational mind in temporal things, wherein not only our knowing
but our action is concerned, from the more
excellent office of the same mind, which is
employed in contemplating eternal things,
and is limited to knowing alone. But I think
it more convenient that I should insert somewhat out of the Holy Scriptures, by which the
two may more easily be distinguished.

2. John the Evangelist has thus begun his
Gospel: "In the beginning was the Word,
and the Word was with God, and the Word
was God. The same was in the beginning

with God. All things were made by Him;
and without Him was not anything made that
was made. In Him was life; and the life was
the light of men. And the light shineth in
darkness; and the darkness comprehended it
not. There was a man sent from God, whose
name was John. The same came for a witness, to bear witness of the Light, that all
men through Him might believe. He was
not that Light, but was sent to bear witness
of that Light. That was the true Light,
which lighteth every man that cometh into
the world. He was in the world, and the
world was made by Him, and the world knew
Him not. He came unto His own, and His
own received Him not. But as many as received Him, to them gave He power to become the sons of God, even to them that believe on His name: which were born, not of
blood, nor of the will of the flesh, nor of the
will of man, but of God. And the Word was
made flesh, and dwelt among us (and we beheld His glory, the glory as of the only-begotten of the Father), full of grace and
truth."[1] This entire passage, which I have

---

[1] John i. 1–14.

here taken from the Gospel, contains in its earlier portions what is immutable and eternal, the contemplation of which makes us blessed; but in those which follow, eternal things are mentioned in conjunction with temporal things. And hence some things there belong to knowledge, some to wisdom, according to our previous distinction in the twelfth book. For the words,—"In the beginning was the Word, and the Word was with God, and the Word was God. The same was in the beginning with God. All things were made by Him; and without Him was not anything made that was made. In Him was life; and the life was the light of men. And the light shineth in darkness, and the darkness comprehended it not:"—require a contemplative life, and must be discerned by the intellectual mind; and the more any one has profited in this, the wiser without doubt will he become. But on account of the verse, "The light shineth in darkness, and the darkness comprehended it not," faith certainly was necessary, whereby that which was not seen might be believed. For by "darkness" he intended to signify the hearts of mortals turned away from light of this kind, and hardly able to behold it; for which reason he subjoins, "There was a man sent from God, whose name was John. The same came for a witness, to bear witness of the Light, that all men through Him might believe." But here we come to a thing that was done in time, and belongs to knowledge, which is comprised in the cognizance of facts. And we think of the man John under that phantasy which is impressed on our memory from the notion of human nature. And whether men believe or not, they think this in the same manner. For both alike know what man is, the outer part of whom, that is, his body, they have learned through the eyes of the body; but of the inner, that is, the soul, they possess the knowledge in themselves, because they also themselves are men, and through intercourse with men; so that they are able to think what is said, "There was a man, whose name was John," because they know the names also by interchange of speech. But that which is there also, viz. "sent from God," they who hold at all, hold by faith; and they who do not hold it by faith, either hesitate through doubt, or deride it through unbelief. Yet both, if they are not in the number of those over-foolish ones, who say in their heart "There is no God,"[1] when they hear these words, think both things, viz. both what God is, and what it is to be sent from

God; and if they do not do this as the things themselves really are, they do it at any rate as they can.

3. Further, we know from other sources the faith itself which a man sees to be in his own heart, if he believes, or not to be there, if he does not believe: but not as we know bodies, which we see with the bodily eyes, and think of even when absent through the images of themselves which we retain in memory; nor yet as those things which we have not seen, and which we frame howsoever we can in thought from those which we have seen, and commit them to memory, that we may recur to them when we will, in order that therein we may similarly by recollection discern them, or rather discern the images of them, of what sort soever these are which we have fixed there; nor again as a living man, whose soul we do not indeed see, but conjecture from our own, and from corporeal motions gaze also in thought upon the living man, as we have learnt him by sight. Faith is not so seen in the heart in which it is, by him whose it is; but most certain knowledge holds it fast, and conscience proclaims it. Although therefore we are bidden to believe on this account, because we cannot see what we are bidden to believe; nevertheless we see faith itself in ourselves, when that faith is in us; because faith even in absent things is present, and faith in things which are without us is within, and faith in things which are not seen is itself seen, and itself none the less comes into the hearts of men in time; and if any cease to be faithful and become unbelievers, then it perishes from them. And sometimes faith is accommodated even to falsehoods; for we sometimes so speak as to say, I put faith in him, and he deceived me. And this kind of faith, if indeed it too is to be called faith, perishes from the heart without blame, when truth is found and expels it. But faith in things that are true, passes, as one should wish it to pass, into the things themselves. For we must not say that faith perishes, when those things which were believed are seen. For is it indeed still to be called faith, when faith, according to the definition in the Epistle to the Hebrews, is the evidence of things not seen?[2]

4. In the words which follow next, "The same came for a witness, to bear witness of the Light, that all men through him might believe;" the action, as we have said, is one done in time. For to bear witness even to that which is eternal, as is that light that is intelligible, is a thing done in time. And

---

of this it was that John came to bear witness, who "was not that Light, but was sent to bear witness of that Light." For he adds, "That was the true Light that lighteth every man that cometh into the world. He was in the world, and the world was made by Him, and the world knew Him not. He came unto His own, and His own received Him not." Now they who know the Latin language, understand all these words, from those things which they know: and of these, some have become known to us through the senses of the body, as man, as the world itself, of which the greatness is so evident to our sight; as again the sounds of the words themselves, for hearing also is a sense of the body; and some through the reason of the mind, as that which is said, "And His own received Him not;" for this means, that they did not believe in Him; and what belief is, we do not know by any sense of the body, but by the reason of the mind. We have learned, too, not the sounds, but the meanings of the words themselves, partly through the sense of the body, partly through the reason of the mind. Nor have we now heard those words for the first time, but they are words we had heard before. And we were retaining in our memory as things known, and we here recognized, not only the words themselves, but also what they meant. For when the bisyllabic word *mundus* is uttered, then something that is certainly corporeal, for it is a sound, has become known through the body, that is, through the ear. But that which it means also, has become known through the body, that is, through the eyes of the flesh. For so far as the world is known to us at all, it is known through sight. But the quadri-syllabic word *crediderunt* reaches us, so far as its sound, since that is a corporeal thing, through the ear of the flesh; but its meaning is discoverable by no sense of the body, but by the reason of the mind. For unless we knew through the mind what the word *crediderunt* meant, we should not understand what they did not do, of whom it is said, "And His own received Him not." The sound then of the word rings upon the ears of the body from without, and reaches the sense which is called hearing. The species also of man is both known to us in ourselves, and is presented to the senses of the body from without, in other men; to the eyes, when it is seen; to the ears, when it is heard; to the touch, when it is held and touched; and it has, too, its image in our memory, incorporeal indeed, but like the body. Lastly, the wonderful beauty of the world itself is at hand from without, both to our gaze, and to that sense which is called

touch, if we come in contact with any of it: and this also has its image within in our memory, to which we revert, when we think of it either in the enclosure of a room, or again in darkness. But we have already sufficiently spoken in the eleventh book of these images of corporeal things; incorporeal indeed, yet having the likeness of bodies, and belonging to the life of the outer man. But we are treating now of the inner man, and of his knowledge, namely, that knowledge which is of things temporal and changeable; into the purpose and scope of which, when anything is assumed, even of things belonging to the outer man, it must be assumed for this end, that something may thence be taught which may help rational knowledge. And hence the rational use of those things which we have in common with irrational animals belongs to the inner man; neither can it rightly be said that this is common to us with the irrational animals.

CHAP. 2.—FAITH A THING OF THE HEART, NOT OF THE BODY ; HOW IT IS COMMON AND ONE AND THE SAME IN ALL BELIEVERS. THE FAITH OF BELIEVERS IS ONE, NO OTHERWISE THAN THE WILL OF THOSE WHO WILL IS ONE.

5. But faith, of which we are compelled, by reason of the arrangement of our subject, to dispute somewhat more at length in this book: faith I say, which they who have are called the faithful, and they who have not, unbelievers, as were those who did not receive the Son of God coming to His own; although it is wrought in us by hearing, yet does not belong to that sense of the body which is called hearing, since it is not a sound; nor to the eyes of this our flesh, since it is neither color nor bodily form; nor to that which is called touch, since it has nothing of bulk; nor to any sense of the body at all, since it is a thing of the heart, not of the body; nor is it without apart from us, but deeply seated within us; nor does any man see it in another, but each one in himself. Lastly, it is a thing that can both be feigned by pretence, and be thought to be in him in whom it is not. Therefore every one sees his own faith in himself; but does not see, but believes, that it is in another; and believes this the more firmly, the more he knows the fruits of it, which faith is wont to work by love. [1] And therefore this faith is common to all of whom the evangelist subjoins, "But as many as received Him, to them gave He power to become the sons of God, even to them that believe on His name: which were born, not of

[1] Gal. v. 6.

blood, nor of the will of the flesh, nor of the will of man, but of God;'' common I say, not as any form of a bodily object is common, as regards sight, to the eyes of all to whom it is present, for in some way the gaze of all that behold it is informed by the same one form; but as the human countenance can be said to be common to all men; for this is so said, that yet each certainly has his own. We say certainly with perfect truth, that the faith of believers is impressed from one doctrine upon the heart of each several person who believes the same thing. But that which is believed is a different thing from the faith by which it is believed. For the former is in things which are said either to be, or to have been, or to be about to be; but the latter is in the mind of the believer, and is visible to him only whose it is; although not indeed itself, but a faith like it, is also in others. For it is not one in number, but in kind; yet on account of the likeness, and the absence of all difference, we rather call it one than many. For when, too, we see two men exceedingly alike, we wonder, and say that both have one countenance. It is therefore more easily said that the souls were many,—a several soul, of course, for each several person—of whom we read in the Acts of the Apostles, that they were of one soul,[1]—than it is, where the apostle speaks of " one faith,"[2] for any one to venture to say that there are as many faiths as there are faithful. And yet He who says, " O woman, great is thy faith;"[3] and to another, " O thou of little faith, wherefore didst thou doubt?"[4] intimates that each has his own faith. But the like faith of believers is said to be one, in the same way as a like will of those who will is said to be one; since in the case also of those who have the same will, the will of each is visible to himself, but that of the other is not visible, although he wills the same thing; and if it intimate itself by any signs, it is believed rather than seen. But each being conscious of his own mind certainly does not believe, but manifestly sees outright, that this is his own will.

CHAP. 3. — SOME DESIRES BEING THE SAME IN ALL, ARE KNOWN TO EACH. THE POET ENNIUS.

6. There is, indeed, so closely conspiring a harmony in the same nature living and using reason, that although one knows not what the other wills, yet there are some wills of all which are also known to each; and although

each man does not know what any other one man wills, yet in some things he may know what all will. And hence comes that story of the comic actor's witty joke, who promised that he would say in the theatre, in some other play, what all had in their minds, and what all willed; and when a still greater crowd had come together on the day appointed, with great expectation, all being in suspense and silent, is affirmed to have said: You will to buy cheap, and sell dear. And mean actor though he was, yet all in his words recognized what themselves were conscious of, and applauded him with wonderful goodwill, for saying before the eyes of all what was confessedly true, yet what no one looked for. And why was so great expectation raised by his promising that he would say what was the will of all, unless because no man knows the wills of other men? But did not he know that will? Is there any one who does not know it? Yet why, unless because there are some things which not unfitly each conjectures from himself to be in others, through sympathy or agreement either in vice or virtue? But it is one thing to see one's own will; another to conjecture, however certainly, what is another's. For, in human affairs, I am as certain that Rome was built as that Constantinople was, although I have seen Rome with my eyes, but know nothing of the other city, except what I have believed on the testimony of others. And truly that comic actor believed it to be common to all to will to buy cheap and sell dear, either by observing himself or by making experiment also of others. But since such a will is in truth a fault, every one can attain the counter virtue, or run into the mischief of some other fault which is contrary to it, whereby to resist and conquer it. For I myself know a case where a manuscript was offered to a man for purchase, who perceived that the vendor was ignorant of its value, and was therefore asking something very small, and who thereupon gave him, though not expecting it, the just price, which was much more. Suppose even the case of a man possessed with wickedness so great as to sell cheap what his parents left to him, and to buy dear, in order to waste it on his own lusts? Such wanton extravagance, I fancy, is not incredible; and if such men are sought, they may be found, or even fall in one's way although not sought; who, by a wickedness more than that of the theatre, make a mock of the theatrical proposition or declaration, by buying dishonor at a great price, while selling lands at a small one. We have heard, too, of persons that, for the sake of distribution, have bought corn at a higher

---

[1] Acts. iv. 32.   [2] Eph. iv. 5.
[3] Matt. xv. 28.   [4] Matt. xiv. 31.

price, and sold it to their fellow-citizens at a lower one. And note also what the old poet Ennius has said: that "all mortals wish themselves to be praised;" wherein, doubtless, he conjectured what was in others, both by himself, and by those whom he knew by experience; and so seems to have declared what it is that all men will. Lastly, if that comic actor himself, too, had said, You all will to be praised, no one of you wills to be abused; he would have seemed in like manner to have expressed what all will. Yet there are some who hate their own faults, and do not desire to be praised by others for that for which they are displeased with themselves; and who thank the kindness of those who rebuke them, when the purpose of that rebuke is their own amendment. But if he had said, You all will to be blessed, you do not will to be wretched; he would have said something which there is no one that would not recognize in his own will. For whatever else a man may will secretly, he does not withdraw from that will, which is well known to all men, and well known to be in all men.

CHAP. 4.—THE WILL TO POSSESS BLESSEDNESS IS ONE IN ALL, BUT THE VARIETY OF WILLS IS VERY GREAT CONCERNING THAT BLESSEDNESS ITSELF.

7. It is wonderful, however, since the will to obtain and retain blessedness is one in all, whence comes, on the other hand, such a variety and diversity of wills concerning that blessedness itself; not that any one is unwilling to have it, but that all do not know it. For if all knew it, it would not be thought by some to be in goodness of mind; by others, in pleasure of body; by others, in both; and by some in one thing, by others in another. For as men find special delight in this thing or that, so have they placed in it their idea of a blessed life. How, then, do all love so warmly what not all know? Who can love what he does not know?—a subject which I have already discussed in the preceding books.[1] Why, therefore, is blessedness loved by all, when it is not known by all? Is it perhaps that all know what it is itself, but all do not know where it is to be found, and that the dispute arises from this?—as if, forsooth, the business was about some place in this world, where every one ought to will to live who wills to live blessedly; and as if the question where blessedness is were not implied in the question what it is. For certainly, if it is in the pleasure of the body, he is blessed who enjoys the pleasure of the

body; if in goodness of mind, he has it who enjoys this; if in both, he who enjoys both. When, therefore, one says, to live blessedly is to enjoy the pleasure of the body; but another, to live blessedly is to enjoy goodness of mind; is it not, that either both know, or both do not know, what a blessed life is? How, then, do both love it, if no one can love what he does not know? Or is that perhaps false which we have assumed to be most true and most certain, viz. that all men will to live blessedly? For if to live blessedly is, for argument's sake, to live according to goodness of mind, how does he will to live blessedly who does not will this? Should we not say more truly, That man does not will to live blessedly, because he does not wish to live according to goodness, which alone is to live blessedly? Therefore all men do not will to live blessedly; on the contrary, few wish it; if to live blessedly is nothing else but to live according to goodness of mind, which many do not will to do. Shall we, then, hold that to be false of which the Academic Cicero himself did not doubt (although Academics doubt every thing), who, when he wanted in the dialogue Hortensius to find some certain thing, of which no one doubted, from which to start his argument, says, We certainly all will to be blessed? Far be it from me to say this is false. But what then? Are we to say that, although there is no other way of living blessedly than living according to goodness of mind, yet even he who does not will this, wills to live blessedly? This, indeed, seems too absurd. For it is much as if we should say, Even he who does not will to live blessedly, wills to live blessedly. Who could listen to, who could endure, such a contradiction? And yet necessity thrusts us into this strait, if it is both true that all will to live blessedly, and yet all do not will to live in that way in which alone one can live blessedly.

CHAP. 5.—OF THE SAME THING.

8. Or is, perhaps, the deliverance from our difficulties to be found in this, that, since we have said that every one places his idea of a blessed life in that which has most pleased him, as pleasure pleased Epicurus, and goodness Zeno, and something else pleased other people, we say that to live blessedly is nothing else but to live according to one's own pleasure: so that it is not false that all will to live blessedly, because all will that which pleases each? For if this, too, had been proclaimed to the people in the theatre, all would have found it in their own wills. But

---

[1] Bks. viii. c. 4, etc., x. c. 1.

when Cicero, too, had propounded this in opposition to himself, he so refuted it as to make them blush who thought so. For he says: "But, behold! people who are not indeed philosophers, but who yet are prompt to dispute, say that all are blessed, whoever live as they will;" which is what we mean by, as pleases each. But by and by he has subjoined: "But this is indeed false. For to will what is not fitting, is itself most miserable; neither is it so miserable not to obtain what one wills, as to will to obtain what one ought not." Most excellently and altogether most truly does he speak. For who can be so blind in his mind, so alienated from all light of decency, and wrapped up in the darkness of indecency, as to call him blessed, because he lives as he will, who lives wickedly and disgracefully; and with no one restraining him, no one punishing, and no one daring even to blame him, nay more, too, with most people praising him, since, as divine Scripture says, "The wicked is praised in his heart's desire; and he who works iniquity is blessed,"[1] gratifies all his most criminal and flagitious desires; when, doubtless, although even so he would be wretched, yet he would be less wretched, if he could have had nothing of those things which he had wrongly willed? For every one is made wretched by a wicked will also, even though it stop short with will; but more wretched by the power by which the longing of a wicked will is fulfilled. And, therefore, since it is true that all men will to be blessed, and that they seek for this one thing with the most ardent love, and on account of this seek everything which they do seek; nor can any one love that of which he does not know at all what or of what sort it is, nor can be ignorant what that is which he knows that he wills; it follows that all know a blessed life. But all that are blessed have what they will, although not all who have what they will are forewith blessed. But they are forewith wretched, who either have not what they will, or have that which they do not rightly will. Therefore he only is a blessed man, who both has all things which he wills, and wills nothing ill.

CHAP. 6.—WHY, WHEN ALL WILL TO BE BLESSED, THAT IS RATHER CHOSEN BY WHICH ONE WITHDRAWS FROM BEING SO.

9. Since, then, a blessed life consists of these two things, and is known to all, and dear to all; what can we think to be the cause why, when they cannot have both, men choose, out of these two, to have all things that they will, rather than to will all things

well, even although they do not have them? Is it the depravity itself of the human race, in such wise that, while they are not unaware that neither is he blessed who has not what he wills, nor he who has what he wills wrongly, but he who both has whatsoever good things he wills, and wills no evil ones, yet, when both are not granted of those two things in which the blessed life consists, that is rather chosen by which one is withdrawn the more from a blessed life (since he certainly is further from it who obtains things which he wickedly desired, than he who only does not obtain the things which he desired); whereas the good will ought rather to be chosen, and to be preferred, even if it do not obtain the things which it seeks? For he comes near to being a blessed man, who wills well whatsoever he wills, and wills things, which when he obtains, he will be blessed. And certainly not bad things, but good, make men blessed, when they do so make them. And of good things he already has something, and that, too, a something not to be lightly esteemed,—namely, the very good will itself; who longs to rejoice in those good things of which human nature is capable, and not in the performance or the attainment of any evil; and who follows diligently, and attains as much as he can, with a prudent, temperate, courageous, and right mind, such good things as are possible in the present miserable life; so as to be good even in evils, and when all evils have been put an end to, and all good things fulfilled, then to be blessed.

CHAP. 7.—FAITH IS NECESSARY, THAT MAN MAY AT SOME TIME BE BLESSED, WHICH HE WILL ONLY ATTAIN IN THE FUTURE LIFE. THE BLESSEDNESS OF PROUD PHILOSOPHERS RIDICULOUS AND PITIABLE.

10. And on this account, faith, by which men believe in God, is above all things necessary in this mortal life, most full as it is of errors and hardships. For there are no good things whatever, and above all, not those by which any one is made good, or those by which he will become blessed, of which any other source can be found whence they come to man, and are added to man, unless it be from God. But when he who is good and faithful in these miseries shall have come from this life to the blessed life, then will truly come to pass what now is absolutely impossible,—namely, that a man may live as he will.[2] For he will not will to live badly

---

[1] Ps. x. 3.

[2] [The prophet Nathan enunciates the same truth, in his words to David, "Go do all that is in thine heart; for the Lord is with thee." 2 Sam. vii. 3.—W. G. T. S.]

in the midst of that felicity, nor will he will anything that will be wanting, nor will there be wanting anything which he shall have willed. Whatever shall be loved, will be present; nor will that be longed for, which shall not be present. Everything which will be there will be good, and the supreme God will be the supreme good and will be present for those to enjoy who love Him; and what altogether is most blessed, it will be certain that it will be so forever. But now, indeed, philosophers have made for themselves, according to the pleasure of each, their own ideals of a blessed life; that they might be able, as it were by their own power, to do that, which by the common conditions of mortals they were not able to do,—namely, to live as they would. For they felt that no one could be blessed otherwise than by having what he would, and by suffering nothing which he would not. And who would not will, that the life whatsoever it be, with which he is delighted, and which he therefore calls blessed, were so in his own power, that he could have it continually? And yet who is in this condition? Who wills to suffer troubles in order that he may endure them manfully, although he both wills and is able to endure them if he does suffer them? Who would will to live in torments, even although he is able to live laudably by holding fast to righteousness in the midst of them through patience? They who have endured these evils, either in wishing to have or in fearing to lose what they loved, whether wickedly or laudably, have thought of them as transitory. For many have stretched boldly through transitory evils to good things which will last. And these, doubtless, are blessed through hope, even while actually suffering such transitory evils, through which they arrive at good things which will not be transitory. But he who is blessed through hope is not yet blessed: for he expects, through patience, a blessedness which he does not yet grasp. Whereas he, on the other hand, who is tormented without any such hope, without any such reward, let him use as much endurance as he pleases, is not truly blessed, but bravely miserable. For he is not on that account not miserable, because he would be more so if he also bore misery impatiently. Further, even if he does not suffer those things which he would not will to suffer in his own body, not even then is he to be esteemed blessed, inasmuch as he does not live as he wills. For to omit other things, which, while the body remains unhurt, belong to those annoyances of the mind, without which we should will to live, and which are innumerable; he

would will, at any rate, if he were able, so to have his body safe and sound, and so to suffer no inconveniences from it, as to have it within his own control, or even to have it with an imperishableness of the body itself; and because he does not possess this, and hangs in doubt about it, he certainly does not live as he wills. For although he may be ready from fortitude to accept, and bear with an equal mind, whatever adversities may happen to him, yet he had rather they should not happen, and prevents them if he is able; and he is in such way ready for both alternatives, that, as much as is in him, he wishes for the one and shuns the other; and if he have fallen into that which he shuns, he therefore bears it willingly, because that could not happen which he willed. He bears it, therefore, in order that he may not be crushed; but he would not willingly be even burdened. How, then, does he live as he wills? Is it because he is willingly strong to bear what he would not will to be put upon him? Then he only wills what he can, because he cannot have what he wills. And here is the sum-total of the blessedness of proud mortals, I know not whether to be laughed at, or not rather to be pitied, who boast that they live as they will, because they willingly bear patiently what they are unwilling should happen to them. For this, they say, is like Terence's wise saying,—

"Since that cannot be which you will, will that which thou canst." [1]

That this is aptly said, who denies? But it is advice given to the miserable man, that he may not be more miserable. And it is not rightly or truly said to the blessed man, such as all wish themselves to be, That cannot be which you will. For if he is blessed, whatever he wills can be; since he does not will that which cannot be. But such a life is not for this mortal state, neither will it come to pass unless when immortality also shall come to pass. And if this could not be given at all to man, blessedness too would be sought in vain, since it cannot be without immortality.

CHAP. 8.—BLESSEDNESS CANNOT EXIST WITHOUT IMMORTALITY.

11. As, therefore, all men will to be blessed, certainly, if they will truly, they will also to be immortal; for otherwise they could not be blessed. And further, if questioned also concerning immortality, as before concerning blessedness, all reply that they will

---

[1] *Andreia*, Act ii. Scene 1, v. 5, 6.

it. But blessedness of what quality soever, such as is not so, but rather is so called, is sought, nay indeed is feigned in this life, whilst immortality is despaired of, without which true blessedness cannot be. Since he lives blessedly, as we have already said before, and have sufficiently proved and concluded, who lives as he wills, and wills nothing wrongly. But no one wrongly wills immortality, if human nature is by God's gift capable of it; and if it is not capable of it, it is not capable of blessedness. For, that a man may live blessedly, he must needs live. And if life quits him by his dying, how can a blessed life remain with him? And when it quits him, without doubt it either quits him unwilling, or willing, or neither. If unwilling, how is the life blessed which is so within his will as not to be within his power? And whereas no one is blessed who wills something that he does not have, how much less is he blessed who is quitted against his will, not by honor, nor by possessions, nor by any other thing, but by the blessed life itself, since he will have no life at all? And hence, although no feeling is left for his life to be thereby miserable (for the blessed life quits him, because life altogether quits him), yet he is wretched as long as he feels, because he knows that against his will that is being destroyed for the sake of which he loves all else, and which he loves beyond all else. A life therefore cannot both be blessed, and yet quit a man against his will, since no one becomes blessed against his will; and hence how much more does it make a man miserable by quitting him against his will, when it would make him miserable if he had it against his will! But if it quit him with his will, even so how was that a blessed life, which he who had it willed should perish? It remains then for them to say, that neither of these is in the mind of the blessed man; that is, that he is neither unwilling nor willing to be quitted by a blessed life, when through death life quits him altogether; for that he stands firm with an even heart, prepared alike for either alternative. But neither is that a blessed life which is such as to be unworthy of his love whom it makes blessed. For how is that a blessed life which the blessed man does not love? Or how is that loved, of which it is received indifferently, whether it is to flourish or to perish? Unless perhaps the virtues, which we love in this way on account of blessedness alone, venture to persuade us that we do not love blessedness itself. Yet if they did this, we should certainly leave off loving the virtues themselves, when we do not love that on account of which alone we loved them. And further, how will that opinion be true, which has been so tried, and sifted, and thoroughly strained, and is so certain, *viz.* that all men will to be blessed, if they themselves who are already blessed neither will nor do not will to be blessed? Or if they will it, as truth proclaims, as nature constrains, in which indeed the supremely good and unchangeably blessed Creator has implanted that will: if, I say, they will to be blessed who are blessed, certainly they do no will to be not blessed. But if they do not will not to be blessed, without doubt they do not will to be annihilated and perish in regard to their blessedness. But they cannot be blessed except they are alive; therefore they do not will so to perish in regard to their life. Therefore, whoever are either truly blessed or desire to be so, will to be immortal. But he does not live blessedly who has not that which he wills. Therefore it follows that in no way can life be truly blessed unless it be eternal.

CHAP 9.—WE SAY THAT FUTURE BLESSEDNESS IS TRULY ETERNAL, NOT THROUGH HUMAN REASONINGS, BUT BY THE HELP OF FAITH. THE IMMORTALITY OF BLESSEDNESS BECOMES CREDIBLE FROM THE INCARNATION OF THE SON OF GOD.

12. Whether human nature can receive this, which yet it confesses to be desirable, is no small question. But if faith be present, which is in those to whom Jesus has given power to become the sons of God, then there is no question. Assuredly, of those who endeavor to discover it from human reasonings, scarcely a few, and they endued with great abilities, and abounding in leisure, and learned with the most subtle learning, have been able to attain to the investigation of the immortality of the soul alone. And even for the soul they have not found a blessed life that is stable, that is, true; since they have said that it returns to the miseries of this life even after blessedness. And they among them who are ashamed of this opinion, and have thought that the purified soul is to be placed in eternal happiness without a body, hold such opinions concerning the past eternity of the world, as to confute this opinion of theirs concerning the soul: a thing which here it is too long to demonstrate; but it has been, as I think, sufficiently explained by us in the twelfth book of the *City of God.*[1] But that faith promises, not by human reasoning, but by divine authority, that the whole man, who certainly consists of soul

---

[1] C. 20.

and body, shall be immortal, and on this account truly blessed. And so, when it had been said in the Gospel, that Jesus has given "power to become the sons of God to them who received Him;" and what it is to have received Him had been shortly explained by saying, "To them that believe on His name;" and it was further added in what way they are to become sons of God, viz., "Which were born not of blood, nor of the will of the flesh, nor of the will of man, but of God;"— lest that infirmity of men which we all see and bear should despair of attaining so great excellence, it is added in the same place, "And the Word was made flesh, and dwelt among us;"[1] that, on the contrary, men might be convinced of that which seemed incredible. For if He who is by nature the Son of God was made the Son of man through mercy for the sake of the sons of men,—for this is what is meant by "The Word was made flesh, and dwelt among us" men,— how much more credible is it that the sons of men by nature should be made the sons of God by the grace of God, and should dwell in God, in whom alone and from whom alone the blessed can be made partakers of that immortality; of which that we might be convinced, the Son of God was made partaker of our mortality?

CHAP. 10.—THERE WAS NO OTHER MORE SUITABLE WAY OF FREEING MAN FROM THE MISERY OF MORTALITY THAN THE INCARNATION OF THE WORD. THE MERITS WHICH ARE CALLED OURS ARE THE GIFTS OF GOD.

13. Those then who say, What, had God no other way by which He might free men from the misery of this mortality, that He should will the only-begotten Son, God co-eternal with Himself, to become man, by putting on a human soul and flesh, and being made mortal to endure death?—these, I say, it is not enough so to refute, as to assert that that mode by which God deigns to free us through the Mediator of God and men, the man Christ Jesus, is good and suitable to the dignity of God; but we must show also, not indeed that no other mode was possible to God, to whose power all things are equally subject, but that there neither was nor need have been any other mode more appropriate for curing our misery. For what was so necessary for the building up of our hope, and for the freeing the minds of mortals cast down by the condition of mortality itself, from despair of immortality, than that it should be demonstrated to us at how great a price God

rated us, and how greatly He loved us? But what is more manifest and evident in this so great proof hereof, than that the Son of God, unchangeably good, remaining what He was in Himself, and receiving from us and for us what He was not, apart from any loss of His own nature, and deigning to enter into the fellowship of ours, should first, without any evil desert of His own, bear our evils; and so with unobligated munificence should bestow His own gifts upon us, who now believe how much God loves us, and who now hope that of which we used to despair, without any good deserts of our own, nay, with our evil deserts too going before?

14. Since those also which are called our deserts, are His gifts. For, that faith may work by love,[2] "the love of God is shed abroad in our hearts by the Holy Ghost which is given unto us."[3] And He was then given, when Jesus was glorified by the resurrection. For then He promised that He Himself would send Him, and He sent Him;[4] because then, as it was written and foretold of Him, "He ascended up on high, He led captivity captive, and gave gifts unto men."[5] These gifts constitute our deserts, by which we arrive at the chief good of an immortal blessedness. "But God," says the apostle, "commendeth His love towards us, in that, while we were yet sinners, Christ died for us. Much more, then, being now justified by His blood, we shall be saved from wrath through Him." To this he goes on to add, "For if, when we were enemies, we were reconciled to God by the death of His Son; much more, being reconciled, we shall be saved by His life." Those whom he first calls sinners he afterwards calls the enemies of God; and those whom he first speaks of as justified by His blood, he afterwards speaks of as reconciled by the death of the Son of God; and those whom he speaks of first as saved from wrath through Him, he afterwards speaks of as saved by His life. We were not, therefore, before that grace merely anyhow sinners, but in such sins that we were enemies of God. But the same apostle calls us above several times by two appellations, viz. sinners and enemies of God,—one as if the most mild, the other plainly the most harsh,— saying, "For if when we were yet weak, in due time Christ died for the ungodly."[6] Those whom he called weak, the same he called ungodly. Weakness seems something slight; but sometimes it is such as to be called impiety. Yet except it were weakness, it

---

[1] John i. 12–14.

[2] Gal. v. 5.   [3] Rom. v. 4, 5.
[4] John xx, 22, vii. 39, and xv. 26.
[5] Eph. iv. 8 and Ps. lxviii. 18.   [6] Rom. v. 6-10.

would not need a physician, who is in the Hebrew Jesus, in the Greek Σωτήρ, but in our speech Saviour. And this word the Latin language had not previously, but could have, seeing that it could have it when it wanted it. And this foregoing sentence of the apostle, where he says, " For when we were yet weak, in due time He died for the ungodly," coheres with those two following sentences; in the one of which he spoke of sinners, in the other of enemies of God, as though he referred each severally to each, *viz.* sinners to the weak, the enemies of God to the ungodly.

CHAP. 11.—A DIFFICULTY, HOW WE ARE JUSTIFIED IN THE BLOOD OF THE SON OF GOD.

15. But what is meant by " justified in His blood?" What power is there in this blood, I beseech you, that they who believe should be justified in it? And what is meant by "being reconciled by the death of His Son?" Was it indeed so, that when God the Father was wroth with us, He saw the death of His Son for us, and was appeased towards us? Was then His Son already so far appeased towards us, that He even deigned to die for us; while the Father was still so far wroth, that except His Son died for us, He would not be appeased? And what, then, is that which the same teacher of the Gentiles himself says in another place: "What shall we then say to these things? If God be for us, who can be against us? He that spared not His own Son, but delivered Him up for us all; how has He not with Him also freely given us all things?"[1] Pray, unless the Father had been already appeased, would He have delivered up His own Son, not sparing Him for us? Does not this opinion seem to be as it were contrary to that? In the one, the Son dies for us, and the Father is reconciled to us by His death; in the other, as though the Father first loved us, He Himself on our account does not spare the Son, He Himself for us delivers Him up to death. But I see that the Father loved us also before, not only before the Son died for us, but before He created the world; the apostle himself being witness, who says, " According as He hath chosen us in Him before the foundation of the world."[2] Nor was the Son delivered up for us as it were unwillingly, the Father Himself not sparing Him; for it is said also concerning Him, " Who loved me, and delivered up Himself for me."[3] Therefore together both the Father and the Son, and the Spirit of both, work all things equally and harmoniously; yet we are justified in the blood of Christ, and we are reconciled to God

by the death of His Son. And I will explain, as I shall be able, here also, how this was done, as much as may seem sufficient.

CHAP. 12.—ALL, ON ACCOUNT OF THE SIN OF ADAM, WERE DELIVERED INTO THE POWER OF THE DEVIL.

16. By the justice of God in some sense, the human race was delivered into the power of the devil; the sin of the first man passing over originally into all of both sexes in their birth through conjugal union, and the debt of our first parents binding their whole posterity. This delivering up is first signified in Genesis, where, when it had been said to the serpent, " Dust shalt thou eat," it was said to the man, " Dust thou art, and unto dust thou shalt return."[4] In the words, "Unto dust shalt thou return," the death of the body is fore-announced, because he would not have experienced that either, if he had continued to the end upright as he was made; but in that it is said to him whilst still living, " Dust thou art," it is shown that the whole man was changed for the worse. For " Dust thou art" is much the same as, " My spirit shall not always remain in these men, for that they also are flesh."[5] Therefore it was at that time shown, that he was delivered to him, in that it had been said to him, " Dust shalt thou eat." But the apostle declares this more clearly, where he says: " And you who were dead in trespasses and sins, wherein in time past ye walked according to the course of this world, according to the prince of the power of the air, the spirit that now worketh in the children of unfaithfulness; among whom we also had our conversation in times past, in the lusts of our flesh, fulfilling the desires of the flesh and of the mind; and were by nature the children of wrath, even as others."[6] The " children of unfaithfulness" are the unbelievers; and who is not this before he becomes a believer? And therefore all men are originally under the prince of the power of the air, " who worketh in the children of unfaithfulness." And that which I have expressed by " originally " is the same that the apostle expresses when he speaks of themselves who "by nature" were as others; *viz.* by nature as it has been depraved by sin, not as it was created upright from the beginning. But the way in which man was thus delivered into the power of the devil, ought not to be so understood as if God did this, or commanded it to be done; but that He only permitted it, yet that justly. For when He abandoned the sin-

---

[1] Rom. viii. 31, 32.   [2] Eph. i. 4.   [3] Gal. ii. 20.   [4] Gen. iii. 14–19.   [5] Gen. vi. 3. " Strive with man," A. V.
[6] Eph. ii. 1–3.

ner, the author of the sin immediately entered. Yet God did not certainly so abandon His own creature as not to show Himself to him as God creating and quickening, and among penal evils bestowing also many good things upon the evil. For He hath not in anger shut up His tender mercies.[1] Nor did He dismiss man from the law of His own power, when He permitted him to be in the power of the devil; since even the devil himself is not separated from the power of the Omnipotent, as neither from His goodness. For whence do even the evil angels subsist in whatever manner of life they have, except through Him who quickens all things? If, therefore, the commission of sins through the just anger of God subjected man to the devil, doubtless the remission of sins through the merciful reconciliation of God rescues man from the devil.

CHAP. 13.—MAN WAS TO BE RESCUED FROM THE POWER OF THE DEVIL, NOT BY POWER, BUT BY RIGHTEOUSNESS.

17. But the devil was to be overcome, not by the power of God, but by His righteousness. For what is more powerful than the Omnipotent? Or what creature is there of which the power can be compared to the power of the Creator? But since the devil, by the fault of his own perversity, was made a lover of power, and a forsaker and assailant of righteousness,—for thus also men imitate him so much the more in proportion as they set their hearts on power, to the neglect or even hatred of righteousness, and as they either rejoice in the attainment of power, or are inflamed by the lust of it,—it pleased God, that in order to the rescuing of man from the grasp of the devil, the devil should be conquered, not by power, but by righteousness; and that so also men, imitating Christ, should seek to conquer the devil by righteousness, not by power. Not that power is to be shunned as though it were something evil; but the order must be preserved, whereby righteousness is before it. For how great can be the power of mortals? Therefore let mortals cleave to righteousness; power will be given to immortals. And compared to this, the power, how great soever, of those men who are called powerful on earth, is found to be ridiculous weakness, and a pitfall is dug there for the sinner, where the wicked seem to be most powerful. And the righteous man says in his song, "Blessed is the man whom Thou chasteneth, O Lord, and teachest him out of Thy law: that Thou mayest give him rest

from the days of adversity, until the pit be digged for the wicked. For the Lord will not cast off His people, neither will He forsake His inheritance, until righteousness return unto judgment, and all who follow it are upright in heart."[2] At this present time, then, in which the might of the people of God is delayed, "the Lord will not cast off His people, neither will He forsake His inheritance," how bitter and unworthy things soever it may suffer in its humility and weakness; "until the righteousness," which the weakness of the pious now possesses, "shall return to judgment," that is, shall receive the power of judging; which is preserved in the end for the righteous when power in its due order shall have followed after righteousness going before. For power joined to righteousness, or righteousness added to power, constitutes a judicial authority. But righteousness belongs to a good will; whence it was said by the angels when Christ was born: "Glory to God in the highest, and on earth peace to men of good will."[3] But power ought to follow righteousness, not to go before it; and accordingly it is placed in "second," that is, prosperous fortune; and this is called "second,"[4] from "following." For whereas two things make a man blessed, as we have argued above, to will well, and to be able to do what one wills, people ought not to be so perverse, as has been noted in the same discussion, as that a man should choose from the two things which make him blessed, the being able to do what he wills, and should neglect to will what he ought; whereas he ought first to have a good will, but great power afterwards. Further, a good will must be purged from vices, by which if a man is overcome, he is in such wise overcome as that he wills evil; and then how will his will be still good? It is to be wished, then, that power may now be given, but power against vices, to conquer which men do not wish to be powerful, while they wish to be so in order to conquer men; and why is this, unless that, being in truth conquered, they feignedly conquer, and are conquerors not in truth, but in opinion? Let a man will to be prudent, will to be strong, will to be temperate, will to be just; and that he may be able to have these things truly, let him certainly desire power, and seek to be powerful in himself, and (strange though it be) against himself for himself. But all the other things which he wills rightly, and yet is not able to have, as, for instance, immortality and true and full felicity, let him not cease to long for, and let him patiently expect.

CHAP. 14.—THE UNOBLIGATED DEATH OF CHRIST
HAS FREED THOSE WHO WERE LIABLE TO
DEATH.

18. What, then, is the righteousness by
which the devil was conquered? What, except the righteousness of Jesus Christ? And
how was he conquered? Because, when he
found in Him nothing worthy of death, yet he
slew Him. And certainly it is just, that we
whom he held as debtors, should be dismissed
free by believing in Him whom he slew without any debt. In this way it is that we are
said to be justified in the blood of Christ.[1]
For so that innocent blood was shed for the
remission of our sins. Whence He calls Himself in the Psalms, "Free among the dead."[2]
For he only that is dead is free from the debt
of death. Hence also in another psalm He
says, "Then I restored that which I seized
not;"[3] meaning sin by the thing seized, because sin is laid hold of against what is lawful.
Whence also He says, by the mouth of His own
Flesh, as is read in the Gospel: "For the
prince of this world cometh, and hath nothing
in me," that is, no sin; but "that the world
may know," He says, "that I do the commandment of the Father; arise, let us go hence."[4]
And hence He proceeds to His passion, that
He might pay for us debtors that which He
Himself did not owe. Would then the devil
be conquered by this most just right, if Christ
had willed to deal with him by power, not by
righteousness? But He held back what was
possible to Him, in order that He might first
do what was fitting. And hence it was necessary that He should be both man and God.
For unless He had been man, He could not
have been slain; unless He had been God,
men would not have believed that He would
not do what He could, but that He could not
do what He would; nor should we have
thought that righteousness was preferred by
Him to power, but that He lacked power. But
now He suffered for us things belonging to
man, because He was man; but if He had been
unwilling, it would have been in His power to
not so to suffer, because He was also God.
And righteousness was therefore made more
acceptable in humility, because so great power as was in His Divinity, if He had been unwilling, would have been able not to suffer in
humility; and thus by Him who died, being
thus powerful, both righteousness was commended, and power promised, to us, weak
mortals. For He did one of these two things
by dying, the other by rising again. For
what is more righteous, than to come even to

the death of the cross for righteousness? And
what more powerful, than to rise from the
dead, and to ascend into heaven with that
very flesh in which He was slain? And therefore He conquered the devil first by righteousness, and afterwards by power: namely, by
righteousness, because He had no sin, and
was slain by him most unjustly; but by power,
because having been dead He lived again,
never afterwards to die.[5] But He would have
conquered the devil by power, even though
He could not have been slain by him: although it belongs to a greater power to conquer
death itself also by rising again, than to avoid
it by living. But the reason is really a different one, why we are justified in the blood of
Christ, when we are rescued from the power
of the devil through the remission of sins: it
pertains to this, that the devil is conquered
by Christ by righteousness, not by power. For
Christ was crucified, not through immortal
power, but through the weakness which He
took upon Him in mortal flesh; of which
weakness nevertheless the apostle says, "that
the weakness of God is stronger than men."[6]

CHAP. 15 —OF THE SAME SUBJECT.

19. It is not then difficult to see that the
devil was conquered, when he who was slain by
Him rose again. It is something more, and
more profound of comprehension, to see that
the devil was conquered when he thought
himself to have conquered, that is, when
Christ was slain. For then that blood, since
it was His who had no sin at all, was poured
out for the remission of our sins; that, because the devil deservedly held those whom,
as guilty of sin, he bound by the condition of
death, he might deservedly loose them through
Him, whom, as guilty of no sin, the punishment of death undeservedly affected. The
strong man was conquered by this righteousness, and bound with this chain, that his vessels might be spoiled,[7] which with himself and
his angels had been vessels of wrath while
with him, and might be turned into vessels of
mercy.[8] For the Apostle Paul tells us, that
these words of our Lord Jesus Christ Himself
were spoken from heaven to him when he was
first called. For among the other things which
he heard, he speaks also of this as said to him
thus: "For I have appeared unto thee for this
purpose, to make thee a minister and a witness both of these things which thou hast seen
from me, and of those things in the which I
will appear unto thee; delivering thee from
the people, and from the Gentiles, unto whom
now I send thee, to open the eyes of the blind,

---

[1] Rom. v. 9.   [2] Ps. lxxxviii. 5.
[3] Ps. lxix. 4.   [4] John xiv. 30–31.

[5] Rom. vi. 9.   [6] 1 Cor. i. 25.   [7] Mark iii. 27.   [8] Rom. ix. 22, 23.

and to turn them from darkness [to light], and from the power of Satan unto God, that they may receive forgiveness of sins, and inheritance among them which are sanctified, and faith that is in me."[1] And hence the same apostle also, exhorting believers to the giving of thanks to God the Father, says: "Who hath delivered us from the power of darkness, and hath translated us into the kingdom of His dear Son: in whom we have redemption, even the forgiveness of sins."[2] In this redemption, the blood of Christ was given, as it were, as a price for us, by accepting which the devil was not enriched, but bound:[3] that we might be loosened from his bonds, and that he might not with himself involve in the meshes of sins, and so deliver to the destruction of the second and eternal death,[4] any one of those whom Christ, free from all debt, had redeemed by pouring out His own blood unindebtedly; but that they who belong to the grace of Christ, foreknown, and predestinated, and elected before the foundation of the world,[5] should only so far die as Christ Himself died for them, i.e. only by the death of the flesh, not of the spirit.

CHAP. 16.—THE REMAINS OF DEATH AND THE EVIL THINGS OF THE WORLD TURN TO GOOD FOR THE ELECT. HOW FITLY THE DEATH OF CHRIST WAS CHOSEN, THAT WE MIGHT BE JUSTIFIED IN HIS BLOOD. WHAT THE ANGER OF GOD IS.

20. For although the death, too, of the flesh itself came originally from the sin of the first man, yet the good use of it has made most glorious martyrs. And so not only that death itself, but all the evils of this world, and the griefs and labors of men, although they come from the deserts of sins, and especially of original sin, whence life itself too became bound by the bond of death, yet have fitly remained, even when sin is forgiven; that man might have wherewith to contend for truth, and whereby the goodness of the faithful might be exercised; in order that the new man through the new covenant might be made ready among the evils of this world, by bearing wisely the misery which this condemned life deserved, and by rejoicing soberly because it will be

finished, but expecting faithfully and p tiently the blessedness which the future lif being set free, will have for ever. For tl devil being cast forth from his dominion, ar from the hearts of the faithful, in the co demnation and faithlessness of whom he, a though himself also condemned, yet reigne is only so far permitted to be an adversa according to the condition of this mortalit as God knows to be expedient for them: co cerning which the sacred writings spea through the mouth of the apostle: "God faithful, who will not suffer you to be tempte above that ye are able; but will with tl temptation also make a way to escape, th ye may be able to bear it."[6] And those evi which the faithful endure piously, are of pr fit either for the correction of sins, or for tl exercising and proving of righteousness, or manifest the misery of this life, that the li where will be that true and perpetual blesse ness may be desired more ardently, ar sought out more earnestly. But it is on the account that these evils are still kept in b ing, of whom the apostle says: "For we kno that all things work together for good them that love God, to them who are calle to be holy according to His purpose. F whom He did foreknow, He also did prede tinate to be conformed to the image of H Son, that He might be the first-born amor many brethren. Moreover, whom He d predestinate, them He also called; and who He called, them He also justified; and who He justified, them He also glorified." It of these who are predestinated, that not o shall perish with the devil; not one shall r main even to death under the power of tl devil. And then follows what I have alreac cited above:[7] "What shall we then say these things? If God be for us, who can l against us? He that spared not His own So but delivered Him up for us all; how has H not with Him also freely given us all things?'

21. Why then should the death of Chri not have come to pass? Nay, rather, wh should not that death itself have been chose above all else to be brought to pass, to tl passing by of the other innumerable way which He who is omnipotent could have er ployed to free us; that death, I say, where neither was anything diminished or change from His divinity, and so great benefit w conferred upon men, from the humanity whic He took upon Him, that a temporal deat which was not due, was rendered by the ete nal Son of God, who was also the Son of ma whereby He might free them from an etern

---

[1] Acts xxvi. 16-18.   [2] Col. i. 13, 14.
[3] [In this representation of Augustin, the relics of that misconception which appears in the earlier soteriology, particularly that of Irenaeus, are seen: namely, that the death of Christ ransoms the sinner from Satan. Certain texts which teach that redemption delivers from the captivity to sin and Satan, were interpreted to teach deliverance from the *claims* of Satan. Augustin's soteriology is more free from this error than that of Irenaeus, yet not entirely free from it. The doctrine of justification did not obtain its most consistent and complete statement in the Patristic church.—W. G. T. S.]
[4] Apoc. xxi. 8.   [5] 1 Pet. i. 20.   [6] 1 Cor. x. 13.   [7] C. 2.   [8] Rom. viii. 28-32.

death which was due? The devil was holding fast our sins, and through them was fixing us deservedly in death. He discharged them, who had none of His own, and who was led by him to death undeservedly. That blood was of such price, that he who even slew Christ for a time by a death which was not due, can as his due detain no one, who has put on Christ, in the eternal death which was due. Therefore "God commendeth His love towards us, in that, while we were yet sinners, Christ died for us. Much more then, being now justified in His blood, we shall be saved from wrath through Him." Justified, he says, in His blood,—justified plainly, in that we are freed from all sin; and freed from all sin, because the Son of God, who knew no sin, was slain for us. Therefore "we shall be saved from wrath through Him;" from the wrath certainly of God, which is nothing else but just retribution. For the wrath of God is not, as is that of man, a perturbation of the mind; but it is the wrath of Him to whom Holy Scripture says in another place, "But Thou, O Lord, mastering Thy power, judgest with calmness."[1] If, therefore, the just retribution of God has received such a name, what can be the right understanding also of the reconciliation of God, unless that then such wrath comes to an end? Neither were we enemies to God, except as sins are enemies to righteousness; which being forgiven, such enmities come to an end, and they whom He Himself justifies are reconciled to the Just One. And yet certainly He loved them even while still enemies, since "He spared not His own Son, but delivered Him up for us all," when we were still enemies. And therefore the apostle has rightly added: "For if, when we were enemies, we were reconciled to God by the death of His Son," by which that remission of sins was made, "much more, being reconciled, we shall be saved in His life." Saved in life, who were reconciled by death. For who can doubt that He will give His life for His friends, for whom, when enemies, He gave His death? "And not only so," he says, "but we also joy in God, through our Lord Jesus Christ, by whom we have now received the atonement." "Not only," he says, "shall we be saved," but "we also joy;" and not in ourselves, but "in God;" nor through ourselves, "but through our Lord Jesus Christ, by whom we have now received the atonement," as we have argued above. Then the apostle adds, "Wherefore, as by one man sin entered into the world, and death by sin; and so death passed upon all

men, in whom all have sinned;"[2] etc.: in which he disputes at some length concerning the two men; the one the first Adam, through whose sin and death we, his descendants, are bound by, as it were, hereditary evils; and the other the second Adam, who is not only man, but also God, by whose payment for us of what He owed not, we are freed from the debts both of our first father and of ourselves. Further, since on account of that one the devil held all who were begotten through his corrupted carnal concupiscence, it is just that on account of this one he should loose all who are regenerated through His immaculate spiritual grace.

CHAP. 17.—OTHER ADVANTAGES OF THE INCARNATION.

22. There are many other things also in the incarnation of Christ, displeasing as it is to the proud, that are to be observed and thought of advantageously. And one of them is, that it has been demonstrated to man what place he has in the things which God has created; since human nature could so be joined to God, that one person could be made of two substances, and thereby indeed of three—God, soul, and flesh: so that those proud malignant spirits, who interpose themselves as mediators to deceive, although as if to help, do not therefore dare to place themselves above man because they have not flesh; and chiefly because the Son of God deigned to die also in the same flesh, lest they, because they seem to be immortal, should therefore succeed in getting themselves worshipped as gods. Further, that the grace of God might be commended to us in the man Christ without any precedent merits; because not even He Himself obtained by any precedent merits that He should be joined in such great unity with the true God, and should become the Son of God, one Person with Him; but from the time when He began to be man, from that time He is also God; whence it is said, "The Word was made flesh."[3] Then, again, there is this, that the pride of man, which is the chief hindrance against his cleaving to God, can be confuted and healed through such great humility of God. Man learns also how far he has gone away from God; and what it is worth to him as a pain to cure him, when he returns through such a Mediator, who both as God assists men by His divinity, and as man agrees with men by His weakness. For what greater example of obedience could be given to us, who had perished through disobedience,

---

than God the Son obedient to God the Father, even to the death of the cross?[1] Nay, wherein could the reward of obedience itself be better shown, than in the flesh of so great a Mediator, which rose again to eternal life? It belonged also to the justice and goodness of the Creator, that the devil should be conquered by the same rational creature which he rejoiced to have conquered, and by one that came from that same race which, by the corruption of its origin through one, he held altogether.

CHAP. 18.—WHY THE SON OF GOD TOOK MAN UPON HIMSELF FROM THE RACE OF ADAM, AND FROM A VIRGIN.

23. For assuredly God could have taken upon Himself to be man, that in that manhood He might be the Mediator between God and men, from some other source, and not from the race of that Adam who bound the human race by his sin; as He did not create him whom He first created, of the race of some one else. Therefore He was able, either so, or in any other mode that He would, to create yet one other, by whom the conqueror of the first might be conquered. But God judged it better both to take upon Him man through whom to conquer the enemy of the human race, from the race itself that had been conquered; and yet to do this of a virgin, whose conception, not flesh but spirit, not lust but faith, preceded.[2] Nor did that concupiscence of the flesh intervene, by which the rest of men, who derive original sin, are propagated and conceived; but holy virginity became pregnant, not by conjugal intercourse, but by faith,—lust being utterly absent,—so that that which was born from the root of the first man might derive only the origin of race, not also of guilt. For there was born, not a nature corrupted by the contagion of transgression, but the one only remedy of all such corruptions. There was born, I say, a Man having nothing at all, and to have nothing at all, of sin; through whom they were to be born again so as to be freed from sin, who could not be born without sin. For although conjugal chastity makes a right use of the carnal concupiscence which is in our members; yet it is liable to motions not voluntary, by which it shows either that it could not have existed at all in paradise before sin, or if it did, that it was not then such as that sometimes it should resist the will. But now we feel it to be such, that in opposition to the law of the mind, and even if there is no question of begetting, it works in

us the incitement of sexual intercourse; and if in this men yield to it, then it is satisfied by an act of sin; if they do not, then it is bridled by an act of refusal: which two things who could doubt to have been alien from paradise before sin? For neither did the chastity that then was do anything indecorous, nor did the pleasure that then was suffer anything unquiet. It was necessary, therefore, that this carnal concupiscence should be entirely absent, when the offspring of the Virgin was conceived; in whom the author of death was to find nothing worthy of death, and yet was to slay Him in order that he might be conquered by the death of the Author of life: the conqueror of the first Adam, who held fast the human race, conquered by the second Adam, and losing the Christian race, freed out of the human race from human guilt, through Him who was not in the guilt, although He was of the race; that that deceiver might be conquered by that race which he had conquered by guilt. And this was so done, in order that man may not be lifted up, but "that he that glorieth should glory in the Lord."[3] For he who was conquered was only man; and he was therefore conquered, because he lusted proudly to be a god. But He who conquered was both man and God; and therefore He so conquered, being born of a virgin, because God in humility did not, as He governs other saints, so govern that Man, but bare Him [as a Son]. These so great gifts of God, and whatever else there are, which it is too long for us now upon this subject both to inquire and to discuss, could not exist unless the Word had been made flesh.

CHAP. 19.—WHAT IN THE INCARNATE WORD BELONGS TO KNOWLEDGE, WHAT TO WISDOM.

24. And all these things which the Word made flesh did and bare for us in time and place, belong, according to the distinction which we have undertaken to demonstrate, to knowledge, not to wisdom. And as the Word is without time and without place, it is co-eternal with the Father, and in its wholeness everywhere; and if any one can, and as much as he can, speak truly concerning this Word, then his discourse will pertain to wisdom. And hence the Word made flesh, which is Christ Jesus, has the treasures both of wisdom and of knowledge. For the apostle, writing to the Colossians, says: "For I would that ye knew what great conflict I have for you, and for them at Laodicea, and for as many as have not seen my face in the

---

[1] Phil. ii. 8. [2] Luke i. 26-32. [3] 2 Cor. x. 17.

flesh; that their hearts might be comforted, being knit together in love, and unto all riches of the full assurance of understanding, to the acknowledgment of the mystery of God, which is Christ Jesus: in whom are hid all the treasures of wisdom and knowledge."[1] To what extent the apostle knew all those treasures, how much of them he had penetrated, and in them to how great things he had reached, who can know? Yet, for my part, according to that which is written, "But the manifestation of the Spirit is given to every man to profit withal; for to one is given by the Spirit the word of wisdom, to another the word of knowledge by the same Spirit;"[2] if these two are in such way to be distinguished from each other, that wisdom is to be assigned to divine things, knowledge to human, I acknowledge both in Christ, and so with me do all His faithful ones. And when I read, "The Word was made flesh, and dwelt among us," I understand by the Word the true Son of God, I acknowledge in the flesh the true Son of man, and both together joined into one Person of God and man, by an ineffable copiousness of grace. And on account of this, the apostle goes on to say, " And we beheld His glory, the glory as of the Only-begotten of the Father, full of grace and truth."[3] If we refer grace to knowledge, and truth to wisdom, I think we shall not swerve from that distinction between these two things which we have commended. For in those things that have their origin in time, this is the highest grace, that man is joined with God in unity of person; but in things eternal the highest truth is rightly attributed to the Word of God. But that the same is Himself the Only-begotten of the Father, full of grace and truth,—this took place, in order that He Himself in things done for us in time should be the same for whom we are cleansed by the same faith, that we may contemplate Him steadfastly in things eternal. And those distinguished philosophers of the heathen who have been able to understand and discern the invisible things of God by those things which are made, have yet, as is said of them, " held down the truth in iniquity;"[4] because they philosophized without a Mediator, that is, without the man Christ, whom they neither believed to be about to come at the word of the prophets, nor to have come at that of the apostles. For, placed as they were in these lowest things, they could not but seek some media through which they might attain to those lofty things which they had understood; and so they fell upon deceit-

ful spirits, through whom it came to pass, that "they changed the glory of the incorruptible God into an image made like to corruptible man, and to birds, and to four-footed beasts, and creeping things."[5] For in such forms also they set up or worshipped idols. Therefore Christ is our knowledge, and the same Christ is also our wisdom. He Himself implants in us faith concerning temporal things, He Himself shows forth the truth concerning eternal things. Through Him we reach on to Himself: we stretch through knowledge to wisdom; yet we do not withdraw from one and the same Christ, " in whom are hidden all the treasures of wisdom and of knowledge." But now we speak of knowledge, and will hereafter speak of wisdom as much as He Himself shall grant. And let us not so take these two things, as if it were not allowable to speak either of the wisdom which is in human things, or of the knowledge which is in divine. For after a laxer custom of speech, both can be called wisdom, and both knowledge. Yet the apostle could not in any way have written, " To one is given the word of wisdom, to another the word of knowledge," except also these several things had been properly called by the several names, of the distinction between which we are now treating.

CHAP. 20.—WHAT HAS BEEN TREATED OF IN THIS BOOK. HOW WE HAVE REACHED BY STEPS TO A CERTAIN TRINITY, WHICH IS FOUND IN PRACTICAL KNOWLEDGE AND TRUE FAITH.

25. Now, therefore, let us see what this prolix discourse has effected, what it has gathered, whereto it has reached. It belongs to all men to will to be blessed; yet all men have not faith, whereby the heart is cleansed, and so blessedness is reached. And thus it comes to pass, that by means of the faith which not all men will, we have to reach on to the blessedness which every one wills. All see in their own heart that they will to be blessed; and so great is the agreement of human nature on this subject, that the man is not deceived who conjectures this concerning another's mind, out of his own: in short, we know ourselves that all will this. But many despair of being immortal, although no otherwise can any one be that which all will, that is, blessed. Yet they will also to be immortal if they could; but through not believing that they can, they do not so live that they can. Therefore faith is necessary, that we may attain blessedness in all the good things of human nature, that is, of both soul

1 Col. ii. 1-3.   2 1 Cor. xii. 7, 8.
3 John i. 14.   4 Rom. i. 23 ; *detinuerunt*.   5 Rom. i. 18, 20.

and body.   But that same faith requires that this faith be limited in Christ, who rose in the flesh from the dead, not to die any more; and that no one is freed from the dominion of the devil, through the forgiveness of sins, save by Him; and that in the abiding place of the devil, life must needs be at once miserable and never-ending, which ought rather to be called death than life.   All which I have also argued, so far as space permitted, in this book, while I have already said much on the subject in the fourth book of this work as well;[1] but in that place for one purpose, here for another,—namely, there, that I might show why and how Christ was sent in the fullness of time by the Father,[2] on account of those who say that He who sent and He who was sent cannot be equal in nature; but here, in order to distinguish practical knowlege from contemplative wisdom.

26. For we wished to ascend, as it were, by steps, and to seek in the inner man, both in knowledge and in wisdom, a sort of trinity of its own special kind, such as we sought before in the outer man; in order that we may come, with a mind more practised in these lower things, to the contemplation of that Trinity which is God, according to our little measure, if indeed, we can even do this, at least in a riddle and as through a glass.[3]   If, then, any one have committed to memory the words of this faith in their sounds alone, not knowing what they mean, as they commonly who do not know Greek hold in memory Greek words, or similarly Latin ones, or those of any other language of which they are ignorant, has not he a sort of trinity in his mind? because, first, those sounds of words are in his memory, even when he does not think thereupon; and next, the mental vision (*acies*) ·of his act of recollection is formed thence when he conceives of them; and next, the will of him who remembers and thinks unites both.   Yet we should by no means say that the man in so doing busies himself with a trinity of the interior man, but rather of the exterior; because he remembers, and when he wills, contemplates as much as he wills, that alone which belongs to the sense of the body, which is called hearing.   Nor in such an act of thought does he do anything else than deal with images of corporeal things, that is, of sounds.   But if he holds and recollects what those words signify, now indeed something of the inner man is brought into

action; not yet, however, ought he to be said or thought to live according to a trinity of the inner man, if he does not love those things which are there declared, enjoined, promised. For it is possible for him also to hold and conceive these things, supposing them to be false, in order that he may endeavor to disprove them.   Therefore that will, which in this case unites those things which are held in the memory with those things which are thence impressed on the mind's eye in conception, completes, indeed, some kind of trinity, since itself is a third added to two others; but the man does not live according to this, when those things which are conceived are taken to be false, and are not accepted.   But when those things are believed to be true, and those things which therein ought to be loved, are loved, then at last the man does live according to a trinity of the inner man; for every one lives according to that which he loves. But how can things be loved which are not known, but only believed? This question has been already treated of in former books;[4] and we found, that no one loves what he is wholly ignorant of, but that when things not known are said to be loved, they are loved from those things which are known.   And now we so conclude this book, that we admonish the just to live by faith,[5] which faith worketh by love,[6] so that the virtues also themselves, by which one lives prudently, boldly, temperately, and justly, be all referred to the same faith; for not otherwise can they be true virtues.   And yet these in this life are not of so great worth, as that the remission of sins, of some kind or other, is not sometimes necessary here; and this remission comes not to pass, except through Him, who by His own blood conquered the prince of sinners.   Whatsoever ideas are in the mind of the faithful man from this faith, and from such a life, when they are contained in the memory, and are looked at by recollection, and please the will, set forth a kind of trinity of its own sort.[7]   But the image of God, of which by His help we shall afterwards speak, is not yet in that trinity; a thing which will then be more apparent, when it shall have been shown where it is, which the reader may expect in a succeeding book.

---

[1] Cc. 19-21.   [2] Gal. iv. 4.   [3] 1 Cor. xiii. 12.

[4] Bk. viii. cc. 8 seqq., and Bk. x. c. 1, etc.
[5] Rom. i. 1⁷.   [6] Gal. v. 6.
[7] [The ternary is this: 1. The idea of a truth or fact held in the memory. 2. The contemplation of it as thus recollected. 3. The love of it. This last is the "will" that "unites" the first two.—W. G. T. S.]

BOOK XIV.

THE TRUE WISDOM OF MAN IS TREATED OF ; AND IT IS SHOWN THAT THE IMAGE OF GOD, WHICH
MAN IS IN RESPECT TO HIS MIND, IS NOT PLACED PROPERLY IN TRANSITORY THINGS, AS IN
MEMORY, UNDERSTANDING, AND LOVE, WHETHER OF FAITH ITSELF AS EXISTING IN TIME, OR
EVEN OF THE MIND AS BUSIED WITH ITSELF, BUT IN THINGS THAT ARE PERMANENT ; AND
THAT THIS WISDOM IS THEN PERFECTED, WHEN THE MIND IS RENEWED IN THE KNOWLEDGE
OF GOD, ACCORDING TO THE IMAGE OF HIM WHO CREATED MAN AFTER HIS OWN IMAGE, AND
THUS ATTAINS TO WISDOM, WHEREIN THAT WHICH IS CONTEMPLATED IS ETERNAL.

CHAP. I.—WHAT THE WISDOM IS OF WHICH WE ARE HERE TO TREAT. WHENCE THE NAME OF PHILOSOPHER AROSE. WHAT HAS BEEN ALREADY SAID CONCERNING THE DISTINCTION OF KNOWLEDGE AND WISDOM.

1. WE must now discourse concerning wisdom; not the wisdom of God, which without doubt is God, for His only-begotten Son is called the wisdom of God;[1] but we will speak of the wisdom of man, yet of true wisdom, which is according to God, and is His true and chief worship, which is called in Greek by one term, θεοσέβεια. And this term, as we have already observed, when our own countrymen themselves also wished to interpret it by a single term, was by them rendered piety, whereas piety means more commonly what the Greeks call εὐσέβεια. But because θεοσέβεια cannot be translated perfectly by any one word, it is better translated by two, so as to render it rather by "the worship of God." That this is the wisdom of man, as we have already laid down in the twelfth book[2] of this work, is shown by the authority of Holy Scripture, in the book of God's servant Job, where we read that the Wisdom of God said to man, "Behold piety, that is wisdom; and to depart from evil is knowledge;"[3] or, as some have translated the Greek word ἐπιστήμην, "learning,"[4] which certainly takes its name from learning,[4] whence also it may be called knowledge. For everything is learned in order that it may be known. Al-

though the same word, indeed,[5] is employed in a different sense, where any one suffers evils for his sins, that he may be corrected. Whence is that in the Epistle to the Hebrews, "For what son is he to whom the father giveth not discipline?" And this is still more apparent in the same epistle: "Now no chastening[6] for the present seemeth to be joyous, but grievous: nevertheless afterward it yieldeth the peaceable fruit of righteousness unto them which are exercised thereby."[7] Therefore God Himself is the chiefest wisdom; but the worship of God is the wisdom of man, of which we now speak. For "the wisdom of this world is foolishness with God."[8] It is in respect to this wisdom, therefore, which is the worship of God, that Holy Scripture says, "The multitude of the wise is the welfare of the world."[9]

2. But if to dispute of wisdom belongs to wise men, what shall we do? Shall we dare indeed to profess wisdom, lest it should be mere impudence for ourselves to dispute about it? Shall we not be alarmed by the example of Pythagoras?—who dared not profess to be a wise man, but answered that he was a philosopher, i.e., a lover of wisdom; whence arose the name, that became thenceforth so much the popular name, that no matter how great the learning wherein any one excelled, either in his own opinion or that of others, in things pertaining to wisdom, he was still called nothing more than philosopher. Or was it for this reason that no one, even of

---

[1] Ecclus. xxiv. 5 and 1 Cor. i. 24.　　[2] C. 14.
[3] Job. xxviii. 28.　　　　　　　　　　　[4] Disciplina, disco.

[5] Disciplina.　　[6] Disciplina.　　[7] Heb. xii. 7, 11.
[8] 1 Cor. iii. 19.　　[9] Wisd. vi. 26.

such as these, dared to profess himself a wise man,—because they imagined that a wise man was one without sin? But our Scriptures do not say this, which say, "Rebuke a wise man, and he will love thee."[1] For doubtless he who thinks a man ought to be rebuked, judges him to have sin. However, for my part, I dare not profess myself a wise man even in this sense; it is enough for me to assume, what they themselves cannot deny, that to dispute of wisdom belongs also to the philosopher, *i.e.*, the lover of wisdom. For they have not given over so disputing who have professed to be lovers of wisdom rather than wise men.

3. In disputing, then, about wisdom, they have defined it thus: Wisdom is the knowledge of things human and divine. And hence, in the last book, I have not withheld the admission, that the cognizance of both subjects, whether divine or human, may be called both knowledge and wisdom.[2] But according to the distinction made in the apostle's words, "To one is given the word of wisdom, to another the word of knowledge,"[3] this definition is to be divided, so that the knowledge of things divine shall be called wisdom, and that of things human appropriate to itself the name of knowledge; and of the latter I have treated in the thirteenth book, not indeed so as to attribute to this knowledge everything whatever that can be known by man about things human, wherein there is exceeding much of empty vanity and mischievous curiosity, but only those things by which that most wholesome faith, which leads to true blessedness, is begotten, nourished, defended, strengthened; and in this knowledge most of the faithful are not strong, however exceeding strong in the faith itself. For it is one thing to know only what man ought to believe in order to attain to a blessed life, which must needs be an eternal one; but another to know in what way this belief itself may both help the pious, and be defended against the impious, which last the apostle seems to call by the special name of knowledge. And when I was speaking of this knowledge before, my especial business was to commend faith, first briefly distinguishing things eternal from things temporal, and there discoursing of things temporal; but while deferring things eternal to the present book, I showed also that faith respecting things eternal is itself a thing temporal, and dwells in time in the hearts of believers, and yet is necessary in order to attain the things eternal themselves.[4] I argued also, that faith

respecting the things temporal which He that is eternal did and suffered for us as man, which manhood He bare in time and carried on to things eternal, is profitable also for the obtaining of things eternal; and that the virtues themselves, whereby in this temporal and mortal life men live prudently, bravely, temperately, and justly, are not true virtues, unless they are referred to that same faith, temporal though it is, which leads on nevertheless to things eternal.

CHAP. 2.—THERE IS A KIND OF TRINITY IN THE HOLDING, CONTEMPLATING, AND LOVING OF FAITH TEMPORAL, BUT ONE THAT DOES NOT YET ATTAIN TO BEING PROPERLY AN IMAGE OF GOD.

4. Wherefore since, as it is written, "While we are in the body, we are absent from the Lord; for we walk by faith, not by sight;"[5] undoubtedly, so long as the just man lives by faith,[6] howsoever he lives according to the inner man, although he aims at truth and reaches on to things eternal by this same temporal faith, nevertheless in the holding, contemplating, and loving this temporal faith, we have not yet reached such a trinity as is to be called an image of God; lest that should seem to be constituted in things temporal which ought to be so in things eternal. For when the human mind sees its own faith, whereby it believes what it does not see, it does not see a thing eternal. For that will not always exist, which certainly will not then exist, when this pilgrimage, whereby we are absent from God, in such way that we must needs walk by faith, shall be ended, and that sight shall have succeeded it whereby we shall see face to face;[7] just as now, because we believe although we do not see, we shall deserve to see, and shall rejoice at having been brought through faith to sight. For then it will be no longer faith, by which that is believed which is not seen; but sight, by which that is seen which is believed. And then, therefore, although we remember this past mortal life, and call to mind by recollection that we once believed what we did not see, yet that faith will be reckoned among things past and done with, not among things present and always continuing. And hence also that trinity which now consists in the remembering, contemplating, and loving this same faith while present and continuing, will then be found to be done with and past, and not still enduring. And hence it is to be gathered, that if that trinity is indeed an im-

[1] Prov. ix. 8.   [2] Bk. xiii. cc. 1, 19.
[3] 1 Cor. xiii. 12.   [4] Bk. xiii. c. 7.

[5] 2 Cor. v. 6, 7.   [6] Rom. i. 17.   [7] 1 Cor. xiii. 12.

age of God, then this image itself would have to be reckoned, not among things that exist always, but among things transient.

CHAP. 3.—A DIFFICULTY REMOVED, WHICH LIES IN THE WAY OF WHAT HAS JUST BEEN SAID.

But far be it from us to think, that while the nature of the soul is immortal, and from the first beginning of its creation thenceforth never ceases to be, yet that that which is the best thing it has should not endure for ever with its own immortality. Yet what is there in its nature as created, better than that it is made after the image of its Creator?[1] We must find then what may be fittingly called the image of God, not in the holding, contemplating, and loving that faith which will not exist always, but in that which will exist always.

5. Shall we then scrutinize somewhat more carefully and deeply whether the case is really thus? For it may be said that this trinity does not perish even when faith itself shall have passed away; because, as now we both hold it by memory, and discern it by thought, and love it by will; so then also, when we shall both hold in memory, and shall recollect, that we once had it, and shall unite these two by the third, namely will, the same trinity will still continue. Since, if it have left in its passage as it were no trace in us, doubtless we shall not have ought of it even in our memory, whereto to recur when recollecting it as past, and by the third, viz. purpose, coupling both these, to wit, what was in our memory though we were not thinking about it, and what is formed thence by conception. But he who speaks thus, does not perceive, that when we hold, see, and love in ourselves our present faith, we are concerned with a different trinity as now existing, from that trinity which will exist, when we shall contemplate by recollection, not the faith itself, but as it were the imagined trace of it laid up in the memory, and shall unite by the will, as by a third, these two things, viz. that which was in the memory of him who retains, and that which is impressed thence upon the vision of the mind of him who recollects. And that we may understand this, let us take an example from things corporeal, of which we have sufficiently spoken in the eleventh book.[2] For as we ascend from lower to higher things, or pass inward from outer to inner things, we first find a trinity in the bodily object which is seen, and in the vision of the seer, which, when he sees it, is informed thereby, and in the purpose of the will which combines

both. Let us assume a trinity like this, when the faith which is now in ourselves is so established in our memory as the bodily object we spoke of was in place, from which faith is formed the conception in recollection, as from that bodily object was formed the vision of the beholder; and to these two, to complete the trinity, will is to be reckoned as a third, which connects and combines the faith established in the memory, and a sort of effigy of that faith impressed upon the vision of recollection; just as in that trinity of corporeal vision, the form of the bodily object that is seen, and the corresponding form wrought in the vision of the beholder, are combined by the purpose of the will. Suppose, then, that this bodily object which was beheld was dissolved and had perished, and that nothing at all of it remained anywhere, to the vision of which the gaze might have recourse; are we then to say, that because the image of the bodily object thus now past and done with remains in the memory, whence to form the conception in recollecting, and to have the two united by will as a third, therefore it is the same trinity as that former one, when the appearance of the bodily object posited in place was seen? Certainly not, but altogether a different one: for, not to say that that was from without, while this is from within; the former certainly was produced by the appearance of a present bodily object, the latter by the image of that object now past. So, too, in the case of which we are now treating, to illustrate which we have thought good to adduce this example, the faith which is even now in our mind, as that bodily object was in place, while held, looked at, loved, produces a sort of trinity; but that trinity will exist no more, when this faith in the mind, like that bodily object in place, shall no longer exist. But that which will then exist, when we shall remember it to have been, but not now to be, in us, will doubtless be a different one. For that which now is, is wrought by the thing itself, actually present and attached to the mind of one who believes; but that which shall then be, will be wrought by the imagination of a past thing left in the memory of one who recollects.

CHAP. 4.—THE IMAGE OF GOD IS TO BE SOUGHT IN THE IMMORTALITY OF THE RATIONAL SOUL. HOW A TRINITY IS DEMONSTRATED IN THE MIND.

6. Therefore neither is that trinity an image of God, which is not now, nor is that other an image of God, which then will not be; but we must find in the soul of man, i.e.,

---

[1] Gen. i. 27.　　　　[2] Cc. 2 sq.

the rational or intellectual soul, that image of the Creator which is immortally implanted in its immortality. For as the immortality itself of the soul is spoken with a qualification; since the soul too has its proper death, when it lacks a blessed life, which is to be called the true life of the soul; but it is therefore called immortal, because it never ceases to live with some life or other, even when it is most miserable;—so, although reason or intellect is at one time torpid in it, at another appears small, and at another great, yet the human soul is never anything save rational or intellectual; and hence, if it is made after the image of God in respect to this, that it is able to use reason and intellect in order to understand and behold God, then from the moment when that nature so marvellous and so great began to be, whether this image be so worn out as to be almost none at all, or whether it be obscure and defaced, or bright and beautiful, certainly it always is. Further, too, pitying the defaced condition of its dignity, divine Scripture tells us, that "although man walks in an image, yet he disquieteth himself in vain; .he heapeth up riches, and cannot tell who shall gather them."[1] It would not therefore attribute vanity to the image of God, unless it perceived it to have been defaced. Yet it sufficiently shows that such defacing does not extend to the taking away its being an image, by saying, "Although man walks in an image." Wherefore in both ways that sentence can be truly enunciated; in that, as it is said, "Although man walketh in an image, yet he disquieteth himself in vain," so it may be said, "Although man disquieteth himself in vain, yet he walketh in an image." For although the nature of the soul is great, yet it can be corrupted, because it is not the highest; and although it can be corrupted, because it is not the highest, yet because it is capable and can be partaker of the highest nature, it is a great nature. Let us seek, then, in this image of God a certain trinity of a special kind, with the aid of Him who Himself made us after His own image. For no otherwise can we healthfully investigate this subject, or arrive at any result according to the wisdom which is from Him. But if the reader will either hold in remembrance and recollect what we have said of the human soul or mind in former books, and especially in the tenth, or will carefully re-peruse it in the passages wherein it is contained, he will not require here any more lengthy discourse respecting the inquiry into so great a thing.

7. We said, then, among other things in the tenth book, that the mind of man knows itself. For the mind knows nothing so much as that which is close to itself; and nothing is more close to the mind than itself. We adduced also other evidences, as much as seemed sufficient, whereby this might be most certainly proved.

CHAP. 5.—WHETHER THE MIND OF INFANTS KNOWS ITSELF.

What, then, is to be said of the mind of an infant, which is still so small, and buried in such profound ignorance of things, that the mind of a man which knows anything shrinks from the darkness of it? Is that too to be believed to know itself; but that,. as being too intent upon those things which it has begun to perceive through the bodily senses, with the greater delight in proportion to their novelty, it is not able indeed to be ignorant of itself, but is also not able to think of itself? Moreover, how intently it is bent upon sensible things that are without it, may be conjectured from this one fact, that it is so greedy of sensible light, that if any one through carelessness, or ignorance of the possible consequences, place a light at nighttime where an infant is lying down, on that side to which the eyes of the child so lying down can be bent, but its neck cannot be turned, the gaze of that child will be so fixed in that direction, that we have known some to have come to squint by this means, in that the eyes retained that form which habit in some way impressed upon them while tender and soft.[2] In the case, too, of the other bodily senses, the souls of infants, as far as their age permits, so narrow themselves as it were, and are bent upon them, that they either vehemently detest or vehemently desire that only which offends or allures through the flesh, but do not think of their own inward self, nor can be made to do so by admonition; because they do not yet know the signs that express admonition, whereof words are the chief, of which as of other things they are wholly ignorant. And that it is one thing not to know oneself, another not to think of oneself, we have shown already in the same book.[3]

8. But let us pass by the infantine age, since we cannot question it as to what goes on within itself, while we have ourselves pretty well forgotten it. Let it suffice only for us hence to be certain, that when man has come to be able to think of the nature of his own mind, and to find out what is the truth, he

---

[1] Ps. xxxix. 7.

[2] [This occurred in the case of Edward Irving. Oliphant's *Life of Irving.*—W. G. T. S.]   [3] Bk. x. c. 5.

will find it nowhere else but in himself. And he will find, not what he did not know, but that of which he did not think. For what do we know, if we do not know what is in our own mind; when we can know nothing at all of what we do know, unless by the mind?

CHAP. 6.—HOW A KIND OF TRINITY EXISTS IN THE MIND THINKING OF ITSELF. WHAT IS THE PART OF THOUGHT IN THIS TRINITY.

The function of thought, however, is so great, that not even the mind itself can, so to say, place itself in its own sight, except when it thinks of itself; and hence it is so far the case, that nothing is in the sight of the mind, except that which is being thought of, that not even the mind itself, whereby we think whatever we do think, can be in its own sight otherwise than by thinking of itself. But in *what way* it is not in its own sight when it is not thinking of itself, while it can never *be* without itself, as though itself were one thing, and the sight of itself another, it is not in my power to discover. For this is not unreasonably said of the eye of the body; for the eye itself of the body is fixed in its own proper place in the body, but its sight extends to things external to itself, and reaches even to the stars. And the eye is not in its own sight, since it does not look at itself, unless by means of a mirror, as is said above;[1] a thing that certainly does not happen when the mind places itself in its own sight by thinking of itself. Does it then see one part of itself by means of another part of itself, when it looks at itself in thought, as we look at some of our members, which can be in our sight, with other also of our members, *viz.* with our eyes? What can be said or thought more absurd? For by what is the mind removed, except by itself? or where is it placed so as to be in its own sight, except before itself? Therefore it will not be there, where it was, when it was not in its own sight; because it has been put down in one place, after being taken away from another. But if it migrated in order to be beheld, where will it remain in order to behold? Is it as it were doubled, so as to be in this and in that place at the same time, *viz.* both where it can behold, and where it can be beheld; that in itself it may be beholding, and before itself beheld? If we ask the truth, it will tell us nothing of the sort since it is but feigned images of bodily objects of which we conceive when we conceive thus; and that the mind is not such, is very certain to the few minds by

which the truth on such a subject can be inquired. It appears, therefore, that the beholding of the mind is something pertaining to its nature, and is recalled to that nature when it conceives of itself, not as if by moving through space, but by an incorporeal conversion; but when it is not conceiving of itself, it appears that it is not indeed in its own sight, nor is its own perception formed from it, but yet that it knows itself as though it were to itself a remembrance of itself. Like one who is skilled in many branches of learning: the things which he knows are contained in his memory, but nothing thereof is in the sight of his mind except that of which he is conceiving; while all the rest are stored up in a kind of secret knowledge, which is called memory. The trinity, then, which we were setting forth, was constituted in this way: first, we placed in the memory the object by which the perception of the percipient was formed; next, the conformation, or as it were the image which is impressed thereby; lastly, love or will as that which combines the two. When the mind, then, beholds itself in conception, it understands and cognizes itself; it begets, therefore, this its own understanding and cognition. For an incorporeal thing is understood when it is beheld, and is cognized when understood. Yet certainly the mind does not so beget this knowledge of itself, when it beholds itself as understood by conception, as though it had before been unknown to itself; but it was known to itself, in the way in which things are known which are contained in the memory, but of which one is not thinking; since we say that a man knows letters even when he is thinking of something else, and not of letters. And these two, the begetter and the begotten, are coupled together by love, as by a third, which is nothing else than will, seeking or holding fast the enjoyment of something. We held, therefore, that a trinity of the mind is to be intimated also by these three terms, memory, intelligence, will.

9. But since the mind, as we said near the end of the same tenth book, always remembers itself, and always understands and loves itself, although it does not always think of itself as distinguished from those things which are not itself; we must inquire in what way understanding (*intellectus*) belongs to conception, while the notion (*notitia*) of each thing that is in the mind, even when one is not thinking of it, is said to belong only to the memory. For if this is so, then the mind had not these three things: *viz.* the remembrance, the understanding, and the love of itself; but it only remembered itself, and afterwards,

when it began to think of itself, then it understood and loved itself.

CHAP. 7.—THE THING IS MADE PLAIN BY AN EXAMPLE. IN WHAT WAY THE MATTER IS HANDLED IN ORDER TO HELP THE READER.

Wherefore let us consider more carefully that example which we have adduced, wherein it was shown that not knowing a thing is different from not thinking [conceiving] of it; and that it may so happen that a man knows something of which he is not thinking, when he is thinking of something else, not of that. When any one, then, who is skilled in two or more branches of knowledge is thinking of one of them, though he is not thinking of the other or others, yet he knows them. But can we rightly say, This musician certainly knows music, but he does not now understand it, because he is not thinking of it; but he does now understand geometry, for of that he is now thinking? Such an assertion, as far as appears, is absurd. What, again, if we were to say, This musician certainly knows music, but he does not now love it, while he is not now thinking of it; but he does now love geometry, because of that he is now thinking; —is not this similarly absurd? But we say quite correctly, This person whom you perceive disputing about geometry is also a perfect musician, for he both remembers music, and understands, and loves it; but although he both knows and loves it, he is not now thinking of it, since he is thinking of geometry, of which he is disputing. And hence we are warned that we have a kind of knowledge of certain things stored up in the recesses of the mind, and that this, when it is thought of, as it were, steps forth in public, and is placed as if openly in the sight of the mind; for then the mind itself finds that it both remembers, and understands, and loves itself, even although it was not thinking of itself, when it was thinking of something else. But in the case of that of which we have not thought for a long time, and cannot think of it unless reminded; that, if the phrase is allowable, in some wonderful way I know not how, we do not *know* that we know. In short, it is rightly said by him who reminds, to him whom he reminds, You know this, but you do not know that you know it; I will remind you, and you will find that you know what you had thought you did not know. Books, too, lead to the same results, *viz.* those that are written upon subjects which the reader under the guidance of reason finds to be true; not those subjects which he believes to be true on the faith of the narrator, as in the case of history; but

those which he himself also finds to be true, either of himself, or in that truth itself which is the light of the mind. But he who cannot contemplate these things, even when reminded, is too deeply buried in the darkness of ignorance, through great blindness of heart and too wonderfully needs divine help, to be able to attain to true wisdom.

10. For this reason I have wished to adduce some kind of proof, be it what it might, respecting the act of conceiving, such as might serve to show in what way, out of the things contained in the memory, the mind's eye is informed in recollecting, and some such thing is begotten, when a man conceives, as was already in him when, before he conceived, he remembered; because it is easier to distinguish things that take place at successive times, and where the parent precedes the offspring by an interval of time. For if we refer ourselves to the inner memory of the mind by which it remembers itself, and to the inner understanding by which it understands itself, and to the inner will by which it loves itself, where these three always are together, and always have been together since they began to be at all, whether they were being thought of or not; the image of this trinity will indeed appear to pertain even to the memory alone; but because in this case a word cannot be without a thought (for we *think* all that we say, even if it be said by that inner word which belongs to no separate language), this image is rather to be discerned in these three things, *viz.* memory, intelligence, will. And I mean now by intelligence that by which we understand in thought, that is, when our thought is formed by the finding of those things, which had been at hand to the memory but were not being thought of; and I mean that will, or love, or preference, which combines this offspring and parent, and is in some way common to both. Hence it was that I tried also, *viz.* in the eleventh book, to lead on the slowness of readers by means of outward sensible things which are seen by the eyes of the flesh; and that I then proceeded to enter with them upon that power of the inner man whereby he reasons of things temporal, deferring the consideration of that which dominates as the higher power, by which he, contemplates things eternal. And I discussed this in two books, distinguishing the two in the twelfth, the one of them being higher and the other lower, and that the lower ought to be subject to the higher; and in the thirteenth I discussed, with what truth and brevity I could, the office of the lower, in which the wholesome knowledge of things human is contained, in order that we may so

act in this temporal life as to attain that which is eternal; since, indeed, I have cursorily included in a single book a subject so manifold and copious, and one so well known by the many and great arguments of many and great men, while manifesting that a trinity exists also in it, but not yet one that can be called an image of God.

CHAP. 8.—THE TRINITY WHICH IS THE IMAGE OF GOD IS NOW TO BE SOUGHT IN THE NOBLEST PART OF THE MIND.

11. But we have come now to that argument in which we have undertaken to consider the noblest part of the human mind, by which it knows or can know God, in order that we may find in it the image of God. For although the human mind is not of the same nature with God, yet the image of that nature than which none is better, is to be sought and found in us, in that than which our nature also has nothing better. But the mind must first be considered as it is in itself, before it becomes partaker of God; and His image must be found in it. For, as we have said, although worn out and defaced by losing the participation of God, yet the image of God still remains.[1] For it is His image in this very point, that it is capable of Him, and can be partaker of Him; which so great good is only made possible by its being His image. Well, then, the mind remembers, understands, loves itself; if we discern this, we discern a trinity, not yet indeed God, but now at last an image of God. The memory does not receive from without that which it is to hold; nor does the understanding find without that which it is to regard, as the eye of the body does; nor has will joined these two from without, as it joins the form of the bodily object and that which is thence wrought in the vision of the beholder; nor has conception, in being turned to it, found an image of a thing seen without, which has been somehow seized and laid up in the memory, whence the intuition of him that recollects has been formed, will as a third joining the two: as we showed to take place in those trinities which were discovered in things corporeal, or which were somehow drawn within from bodily objects by the bodily sense; of all which we have discoursed in the eleventh book.[2] Nor, again, as it took place, or appeared to do so, when we went on further to discuss that knowledge, which had its place now in the workings of the inner man, and which was to be distinguished from wisdom; of which knowledge the subject-matter was, as it were, ad-

ventitious to the mind, and either was brought thither by historical information,—as deeds and words, which are performed in time and pass away, or which again are established in the nature of things in their own times and places,—or arises in the man himself not being there before, whether on the information of others, or by his own thinking,—as faith, which we commended at length in the thirteenth book, or as the virtues, by which, if they are true, one so lives well in this mortality as to live blessedly in that immortality which God promises. These and other things of the kind have their proper order in time, and in that order we discerned more easily a trinity of memory, sight, and love. For some of such things anticipate the knowledge of learners. For they are knowable also before they are known, and beget in the learner a knowledge of themselves. And they either exist in their own proper places, or have happened in time past; although things that are past do not themselves exist, but only certain signs of them as past, the sight or hearing of which makes it known that they have been and have passed away. And these signs are either situate in the places themselves, as e.g. monuments of the dead or the like; or exist in written books worthy of credit, as is all history that is of weight and approved authority; or are in the minds of those who already know them; since what is already known to them is knowable certainly to others also, whose knowledge it has anticipated, and who are able to know it on the information of those who do know it. And all these things, when they are learned, produce a certain kind of trinity, viz. by their own proper species, which was knowable also before it was known, and by the application to this of the knowledge of the learner, which then begins to exist when he learns them, and by will as a third which combines both; and when they are known, yet another trinity is produced in the recollecting of them, and this now inwardly in the mind itself, from those images which, when they were learned, were impressed upon the memory, and from the informing of the thought when the look has been turned upon these by recollection, and from the will which as a third combines these two. But those things which arise in the mind, not having been there before, as faith and other things of that kind, although they appear to be adventitious, since they are implanted by teaching, yet are not situate without or transacted without, as are those things which are believed; but began to be altogether within in the mind itself. For faith is not that which is believed, but that by which it is believed; and the former is believed, the latter seen. Nevertheless, because it began to be in the mind, which was a mind also before these things began to be in it, it seems to be somewhat adventitious, and will be reckoned among things past, when sight shall have succeeded, and itself shall have ceased to be. And it makes now by its presence, retained as it is, and beheld, and loved, a different trinity from that which it will then make by means of some trace of itself, which in passing it will have left in the memory: as has been already said above.

CHAP. 9.—WHETHER JUSTICE AND THE OTHER VIRTUES CEASE TO EXIST IN THE FUTURE LIFE.

12. There is, however, some question raised, whether the virtues likewise by which one lives well in this present mortality, seeing that they themselves begin also to be in the mind, which was a mind none the less when it existed before without them, cease also to exist at that time when they have brought us to things eternal. For some have thought that they will cease, and in the case of three—prudence, fortitude, temperance—such an assertion seems to have something in it; but justice is immortal, and will rather then be made perfect in us than cease to be. Yet Tullius, the great author of eloquence, when arguing in the dialogue *Hortensius*, says of all four: " If we were allowed, when we migrated from this life, to live forever in the islands of the blessed, as fables tell, what need were there of eloquence when there would be no trials, or what need, indeed, of the very virtues themselves? For we should not need fortitude when nothing of either toil or danger was proposed to us; nor justice, when there was nothing of anybody else's to be coveted; nor temperance, to govern lusts that would not exist; nor, indeed, should we need prudence, when there was no choice offered between good and evil. We should be blessed, therefore, solely by learning and knowing nature, by which alone also the life of the gods is praiseworthy. And hence we may perceive that everything else is a matter of necessity, but this is one of free choice." This great orator, then, when proclaiming the excellence of philosophy, going over again all that he had learned from philosophers, and excellently and pleasantly explaining it, has affirmed all four virtues to be necessary in this life only, which we see to be full of troubles and mistakes; but not one of them when we shall have migrated from this life, if we are permitted to live there where is a blessed life; but that blessed souls are blessed only in learning and knowing, *i.e.*

in the contemplation of nature, than which nothing is better and more lovable. It is that nature which created and appointed all other natures. And if it belongs to justice to be subject to the government of this nature, then justice is certainly immortal; nor will it cease to be in that blessedness, but will be such and so great that it cannot be more perfect or greater. Perhaps, too, the other three virtues —prudence although no longer with any risk of error, and fortitude without the vexation of bearing evils, and temperance without the thwarting of lust—will exist in that blessedness: so that it may be the part of prudence to prefer or equal no good thing to God; and of fortitude, to cleave to Him most steadfastly; and of temperance, to be pleased by no harmful defect. But that which justice is now concerned with in helping the wretched, and prudence in guarding against treachery, and fortitude in bearing troubles patiently, and temperance in controlling evil pleasures, will not exist there, where there will be no evil at all. And hence those acts of the virtues which are necessary to this mortal life, like the faith to which they are to be referred, will be reckoned among things past; and they make now a different trinity, whilst we hold, look at, and love them as present, from that which they will then make, when we shall discover them not to be, but to have been, by certain traces of them which they will have left in passing in the memory; since then, too, there will be a trinity, when that trace, be it of what sort it may, shall be retained in the memory, and truly recognized, and then these two be joined by will as a third.

CHAP. 10.—HOW A TRINITY IS PRODUCED BY THE MIND REMEMBERING, UNDERSTANDING, AND LOVING ITSELF.

13. In the knowledge of all these temporal things which we have mentioned, there are some knowable things which precede the acquisition of the knowledge of them by an interval of time, as in the case of those sensible objects which were already real before they were known, or of all those things that are learned through history; but some things begin to be at the same time with the knowing of them,— just as, if any visible object, which did not exist before at all, were to rise up before our eyes, certainly it does not precede our knowing it; or if there be any sound made where there is some one to hear, no doubt the sound and the hearing that sound begin and end simultaneously. Yet none the less, whether preceding in time or beginning to exist simultaneously, knowable things generate knowl-

edge, and are not generated by knowledge. But when knowledge has come to pass, whenever the things known and laid up in memory are reviewed by recollection, who does not see that the retaining them in the memory is prior in time to the sight of them in recollection, and to the uniting of the two things by will as a third? In the mind, however, it is not so. For the mind is not adventitious to itself, as though there came to itself already existing, that same self not already existing, from somewhere else, or did not indeed come from somewhere else, but that in the mind itself already existing, there was born that same mind not already existing; just as faith, which before was not, arises in the mind which already was. Nor does the mind see itself, as it were, set up in its own memory by recollection subsequently to the knowing of itself, as though it was not there before it knew itself; whereas, doubtless, from the time when it began to be, it has never ceased to remember, to understand, and to love itself, as we have already shown. And hence, when it is turned to itself by thought, there arises a trinity, in which now at length we can discern also a word; since it is formed from thought itself, will uniting both. Here, then, we may recognize, more than we have hitherto done, the image of which we are in search.

CHAP. 11. — WHETHER MEMORY IS ALSO OF THINGS PRESENT.

14. But some one will say, That is not memory by which the mind, which is ever present to itself, is affirmed to remember itself; for memory is of things past, not of things present. For there are some, and among them Cicero, who, in treating of the virtues, have divided prudence into these three—memory, understanding, forethought: to wit, assigning memory to things past, understanding to things present, forethought to things future; which last is certain only in the case of those who are prescient of the future; and this is no gift of men, unless it be granted from above, as to the prophets. And hence the book of Wisdom, speaking of men, "The thoughts of mortals," it says, "are fearful, and our forethought uncertain."[1] But memory of things past, and understanding of things present, are certain: certain, I mean, respecting things incorporeal, which are present; for things corporeal are present to the sight of the corporeal eyes. But let any one who denies that there is any memory of things present, attend to the language used even in

profane literature, where exactness of words was more looked for than truth of things. "Nor did Ulysses suffer such things, nor did the Ithacan forget himself in so great a peril."[2] For when Virgil said that Ulysses did not forget himself, what else did he mean, except that he remembered himself? And since he was present to himself, he could not possibly remember himself, unless memory pertained to things present. And, therefore, as that is called memory in things past which makes it possible to recall and remember them; so in a thing present, as the mind is to itself, that is not unreasonably to be called memory, which makes the mind at hand to itself, so that it can be understood by its own thought, and then both be joined together by love of itself.

CHAP. 12.—THE TRINITY IN THE MIND IS THE IMAGE OF GOD, IN THAT IT REMEMBERS, UNDERSTANDS, AND LOVES GOD, WHICH TO DO IS WISDOM.

15. This trinity, then, of the mind is not therefore the image of God, because the mind remembers itself, and understands and loves itself; but because it can also remember, understand, and love Him by whom it was made. And in so doing it is made wise itself. But if it does not do so, even when it remembers, understands, and loves itself, then it is foolish. Let it then remember its God, after whose image it is made, and let it understand and love Him. Or to say the same thing more briefly, let it worship God, who is not made, by whom because itself was made, it is capable and can be partaker of Him; wherefore it is written, "Behold, the worship of God, that is wisdom."[3] And then it will be wise, not by its own light, but by participation of that supreme Light; and wherein it is eternal, therein shall reign in blessedness. For this wisdom of man is so called, in that it is also of God. For then it is true wisdom; for if it is human, it is vain. Yet not so of God, as is that wherewith God is wise. For He is not wise by partaking of Himself, as the mind is by partaking of God. But as we call it the righteousness of God, not only when we speak of that by which He Himself is righteous, but also of that which He gives to man when He justifies the ungodly, which latter righteousness the apostle commending, says of some, that "not knowing the righteousness of God and going about to establish their own righteousness, they are not subject to the righteousness of God;"[4] so also it may be said of some, that not knowing the wisdom of God

---

[1] Wisd. ix. 14.

[2] Æneid, iii. 628, 629.   [3] Job. xxviii. 28.   [4] Rom. x. 3.

and going about to establish their own wisdom, they are not subject to the wisdom of God.

16. There is, then, a nature not made, which made all other natures, great and small, and is without doubt more excellent than those which it has made, and therefore also than that of which we are speaking; viz. than the rational and intellectual nature, which is the mind of man, made after the image of Him who made it. And that nature, more excellent than the rest, is God. And indeed "He is not far from every one of us," as the apostle says, who adds, "For in Him we live, and are moved, and have our being."[1] And if this were said in respect to the body, it might be understood even of this corporeal world; for in it too in respect to the body, we live, and are moved, and have our being. And therefore it ought to be taken in a more excellent way, and one that is spiritual, not visible, in respect to the mind, which is made after His image For what is there that is not in Him, of whom it is divinely written, "For of Him, and through Him, and in Him, are all things"?[2] If, then, all things are in Him, in whom can any possibly live that do live, or be moved that are moved, except in Him in whom they are? Yet all are not with Him in that way in which it is said to Him, "I am continually with Thee."[3] Nor is He with all in that way in which we say, The Lord be with you. And so it is the especial wretchedness of man not to be with Him, without whom he cannot be. For, beyond a doubt, he is not without Him in whom he is; and yet if he does not remember, and understand, and love Him, he is not with Him. And when any one absolutely forgets a thing, certainly it is impossible even to remind him of it.

CHAP. 13. — HOW ANY ONE CAN FORGET AND REMEMBER GOD.

17. Let us take an instance for the purpose from visible things. Somebody whom you do not recognize, says to you, You know me; and in order to remind you, tells you where, when, and how he became known to you; and if, after the mention of every sign by which you might be recalled to remembrance, you still do not recognize him, then you have so come to forget, as that the whole of that knowledge is altogether blotted out of your mind; and nothing else remains, but that you take his word for it who tells you that you once knew him; or do not even do that, if you do not think the person who speaks to you to be

worthy of credit. But if you do remember him, then no doubt you return to your own memory, and find in it that which had not been altogether blotted out by forgetfulness. Let us return to that which led us to adduce this instance from the intercourse of men. Among other things, the 9th Psalm says, "The wicked shall be turned into hell, and all the nations that forget God;"[4] and again the 22d Psalm, "All the ends of the world shall be reminded, and turned unto the Lord."[5] These nations, then, will not so have forgotten God as to be unable to remember Him when reminded of Him; yet, by forgetting God, as though forgetting their own life, they had been turned into death, i.e. into hell.[6] But when reminded they are turned to the Lord, as though coming to life again by remembering their proper life which they had forgotten. It is read also in the 94th Psalm, "Perceive now, ye who are unwise among the people; and ye fools, when will ye be wise? He that planted the ear, shall He not hear?" etc.[7] For this is spoken to those, who said vain things concerning God through not understanding Him.

CHAP. 14.—THE MIND LOVES GOD IN RIGHTLY LOVING ITSELF ; AND IF IT LOVE NOT GOD, IT MUST BE SAID TO HATE ITSELF. EVEN A WEAK AND ERRING MIND IS ALWAYS STRONG IN REMEMBERING, UNDERSTANDING, AND LOVING ITSELF. LET IT BE TURNED TO GOD, THAT IT MAY BE BLESSED BY REMEMBERING, UNDERSTANDING, AND LOVING HIM.

18. But there are yet more testimonies in the divine Scriptures concerning the love of God. For in it, those other two [namely, memory and understanding] are understood by consequence, inasmuch as no one loves that which he does not remember, or of which he is wholly ignorant. And hence is that well known and primary commandment, "Thou shalt love the Lord thy God."[8] The human mind, then, is so constituted, that at no time does it not remember, and understand, and love itself. But since he who hates any one is anxious to injure him, not undeservedly is the mind of man also said to hate itself when it injures itself. For it wills ill to itself through ignorance, in that it does not think that what it wills is prejudicial to it; but it none the less does will ill to itself, when it wills what would be prejudicial to it. And hence it is written, "He that loveth iniquity, hateth his own soul."[9] He, therefore, who knows how to love himself, loves God; but

---

[1] Acts xvii. 27, 28. [2] Rom. xi. 36. [3] Ps. lxxiii. 23.

[4] Ps. ix. 17. [5] Ps. xxii. 27.
[6] [Augustin here understands "Sheol," to denote the place of retribution for the wicked.—W. G. T. S.]
[7] Ps. xciv. 8, 9. [8] Deut. vi. 5. [9] Ps. xi. 5.

he who does not love God, even if he does love himself,—a thing implanted in him by nature,—yet is not unsuitably said to hate himself, inasmuch as he does that which is adverse to himself, and assails himself as though he were his own enemy. And this is no doubt a terrible delusion, that whereas all will to profit themselves, many do nothing but that which is most pernicious to themselves. When the poet was describing a like disease of dumb animals, " May the gods," says he, " grant better things to the pious, and assign that delusion to enemies. They were rending with bare teeth their own torn limbs." [1] Since it was a disease of the body he was speaking of, why has he called it a delusion, unless because, while nature inclines every animal to take all the care it can of itself, that disease was such that those animals rent those very limbs of theirs which they desired should be safe and sound? But when the mind loves God, and by consequence, as has been said, remembers and understands Him, then it is rightly enjoined also to love its neighbor as itself; for it has now come to love itself rightly and not perversely when it loves God, by pàrtaking of whom that image not only exists, but is also renewed so as to be no longer old, and restored so as to be no longer defaced, and beatified so as to be no longer unhappy. For although it so love itself, that, supposing the alternative to be proposed to it, it would lose all things which it loves less than itself rather than perish; still, by abandoning Him who is above it, in dependence upon whom alone it could guard its own strength, and enjoy Him as its light, to whom it is sung in the Psalm, " I will guard my strength in dependence upon Thee," [2] and again, " Draw near to Him, and be enlightened," [3]—it has been made so weak and so dark, that it has fallen away unhappily from itself too, to those things that are not what itself is, and which are beneath itself, by affections that it cannot conquer, and delusions from which it sees no way to return. And hence, when by God's mercy now penitent, it cries out in the Psalms, " My strength faileth me; as for the light of mine eyes, it also is gone from me." [4]

19. Yet, in the midst of these evils of weakness and delusion, great as they are, it could not lose its natural memory, understanding and love of itself. And therefore what I quoted above [5] can be rightly said, " Although man walketh in an image, surely he is disquieted in vain: he heapeth up treasures, and knoweth not who shall gather them." [6] For why does he heap up treasures, unless because his strength has deserted him, through which he would have God, and so lack nothing? And why cannot he tell for whom he shall gather them, unless because the light of his eyes is taken from him? And so he does not see what the Truth saith, " Thou fool, this night thy soul shall be required of thee. Then whose shall those things be which thou hast provided ? " [7] Yet because even such a man walketh in an image, and the man's mind has remembrance, understanding, and love of itself; if it were made plain to it that it could not have both, while it was permitted to choose one and lose the other, viz. either the treasures it has heaped up, or the mind; who is so utterly without mind, as to prefer to have the treasures rather than the mind? For treasures commonly are able to subvert the mind, but the mind that is not subverted by treasures can live more easily and unencumberedly without any treasures. But who will be able to possess treasures unless it be by means of the mind? For if an infant, born as rich as you please, although lord of everything that is rightfully his, yet possesses nothing if his mind be unconscious, how can any one possibly possess anything whose mind is wholly lost? But why say of treasures, that anybody, if the choice be given him, prefers going without them to going without a mind; when there is no one that prefers, nay, no one that compares them, to those lights of the body, by which not one man only here and there, as in the case of gold, but every man, possesses the very heaven? For every one possesses by the eyes of the body whatever he gladly sees. Who then is there, who, if he could not keep both, but must lose one, would not rather lose his treasures than his eyes? And yet if it were put to him on the same condition, whether he would rather lose eyes than mind, who is there with a mind that does not see that he would rather lose the former than the latter? For a mind without the eyes of the flesh is still human, but the eyes of the flesh without a mind are bestial. And who would not rather be a man, even though blind in fleshly sight, than a beast that can see?

20. I have said thus much, that even those who are slower of understanding, to whose eyes or ears this book may come, might be admonished, however briefly, how greatly even a weak and erring mind loves itself, in wrongly loving and pursuing things beneath itself. Now it could not love itself if it

---

Virg. *Georg.* iii. 513-514.   [2] Ps. lix. 9.
Ps. xxxiv. 5.   [4] Ps. xxxviii. 10.
C. 4.

[6] Ps. xxxix. 6.   [7] Luke xii. 20.

were altogether ignorant of itself, *i. e.* if it did not remember itself, nor understand itself; by which image of God within itself it has such power as to be able to cleave to Him whose image it is. For it is so reckoned in the order, not of place, but of natures, as that there is none above it save Him. When, finally, it shall altogether cleave to Him, then it will be one spirit, as the apostle testifies, saying, "But he who cleaves to the Lord is one spirit."[1] And this by its drawing near to partake of His nature, truth, and blessedness, yet not by His increasing in His own nature, truth and blessedness. In that nature, then, when it happily has cleaved to it, it will live unchangeably, and will see as unchangeable all that it does see. Then, as divine Scripture promises, "His desire will be satisfied with good things,"[2] good things unchangeable, — the very Trinity itself, its own God, whose image it is. And that it may not ever thenceforward suffer wrong, it will be in the hidden place of His presence,[3] filled with so great fullness of Him, that sin thenceforth will never delight it. But now, when it sees itself, it sees something not unchangeable.

CHAP. 15. — ALTHOUGH THE SOUL HOPES FOR BLESSEDNESS, YET IT DOES NOT REMEMBER LOST BLESSEDNESS, BUT REMEMBERS GOD AND THE RULES OF RIGHTEOUSNESS. THE UNCHANGEABLE RULES OF RIGHT LIVING ARE KNOWN EVEN TO THE UNGODLY.

21. And of this certainly it feels no doubt, that it is wretched, and longs to be blessed; nor can it hope for the possibility of this on any other ground than its own changeableness; for if it were not changeable, then, as it could not become wretched after being blessed, so neither could it become blessed after being wretched. And what could have made it wretched under an omnipotent and good God, except its own sin and the righteousness of its Lord? And what will make it blessed, unless its own merit, and its Lord's reward? But its merit, too, is His grace, whose reward will be its blessedness; for it cannot give itself the righteousness it has lost, and so has not. For this it received when man was created, and assuredly lost it by sinning. Therefore it receives righteousness, that on account of this it may deserve to receive blessedness; and hence the apostle truly says to it, when beginning to be proud as it were of its own good, "For what hast thou that thou didst not receive? Now if thou didst receive it, why dost thou glory as if thou

hadst not received it?"[4] But when it rightly remembers its own Lord, having received His Spirit, then, because it is so taught by an inward teaching, it feels wholly that it cannot rise save by His affection freely given, nor has been able to fall save by its own defection freely chosen. Certainly it does not remember its own blessedness; since that has been, but is not, and it has utterly forgotten it, and therefore cannot even be reminded of it.[5] But it believes what the trustworthy Scriptures of its God tell of that blessedness, which were written by His prophet, and tell of the blessedness of Paradise, and hand down to us historical information of that first both good and ill of man. And it remembers the Lord its God; for He always is, nor has been and is not, nor is but has not been; but as He never will not be, so He never was not. And He is whole everywhere. And hence it both lives, and is moved, and is in Him;[6] and so it can remember Him. Not because it recollects the having known Him in Adam or anywhere else before the life of this present body, or when it was first made in order to be implanted in this body; for it remembers nothing at all of all this. Whatever there is of this, it has been blotted out by forgetfulness. But it is reminded, that it may be turned to God, as though to that light by which it was in some way touched, even when turned away from Him. For hence it is that even the ungodly think of eternity, and rightly blame and rightly praise many things in the morals of men. And by what rules do they thus judge, except by those wherein they see how men ought to live, even though they themselves do not so live? And where do they see these rules? For they do not see them in their own [moral] nature; since no doubt these things are to be seen by the mind, and their minds are confessedly changeable, but these rules are seen as unchangeable by him who can see them at all; nor yet in the character of their own mind, since these rules are rules of righteousness, and their minds are confessedly unrighteous. Where indeed are these rules written, wherein even the unrighteous recognizes what is righteous, wherein he discerns that he ought to have what he himself has not? Where, then, are they written, unless in the book of that Light which is called Truth? whence every righteous law is

---

[1] 1 Cor. vi. 17.   [2] Ps. ciii. 5.   [3] Ps. xxxi. 20.

[4] 1 Cor. iv. 7.
[5] [In the case of knowledge that is remembered, there is something latent and potential—as when past acquisitions are recalled by a voluntary act of recollection. The same is true of innate ideas—these also are latent, and brought into consciousness by reflection. But no man can either remember, or elicit, his original holiness and blessedness, because this is not latent and potential, but wholly lost by the fall.—W. G. T. S.]
[6] Acts xvii. 28.

copied and transferred (not by migrating to it, but by being as it were impressed upon it) to the heart of the man that worketh righteousness; as the impression from a ring passes into the wax, yet does not leave the ring. But he who worketh not, and yet sees how he ought to work, he is the man that is turned away from that light, which yet touches him. But he who does not even see how he ought to live, sins indeed with more excuse, because he is not a transgressor of a law that he knows; but even he too is just touched sometimes by the splendor of the everywhere present truth, when upon admonition he confesses.

CHAP. 16.—HOW THE IMAGE OF GOD IS FORMED ANEW IN MAN.

22. But those who, by being reminded, are turned to the Lord from that deformity whereby they were through worldly lusts conformed to this world, are formed anew from the world, when they hearken to the apostle, saying, " Be not conformed to this world, but be ye formed again in the renewing of your mind;"¹ that that image may begin to be formed again by Him by whom it had been formed at first. For that image cannot form itself again, as it could deform itself. He says again elsewhere: " Be ye renewed in the spirit of your mind; and put ye on the new man, which after God is created in righteousness and true holiness."² That which is meant by " created after God," is expressed in another place by "after the image of God."³ But it lost righteousness and true holiness by sinning, through which that image became defaced and tarnished; and this it recovers when it is formed again and renewed. But when he says, "In the spirit of your mind," he does not intend to be understood of two things, as though mind were one, and the spirit of the mind another; but he speaks thus, because all mind is spirit, but all spirit is not mind. For there is a Spirit also that is God,⁴ which cannot be renewed, because it cannot grow old. And we speak also of a spirit in man distinct from the mind, to which spirit belong the images that are formed after the likeness of bodies; and of this the apostle speaks to the Corinthians, where he says, " But if I shall have prayed with a tongue, my spirit prayeth, but my understanding is unfruitful."⁵ For he speaks thus, when that which is said is not understood; since it cannot even be said, unless the images of the corporeal articulate sounds anticipate the oral sound by the thought of the spirit. The soul of man is also called spirit,

whence are the words in the Gospel, " And He bowed His head, and gave up His spirit;"⁶ by which the death of the body, through the spirit's leaving it, is signified. We speak also of the spirit of a beast, as it is expressly written in the book of Solomon called Ecclesiastes; " Who knoweth the spirit of man that goeth upward, and the spirit of the beast that goeth downward to the earth?"⁷ It is written too in Genesis, where it is said that by the deluge all flesh died which " had in it the spirit of life."⁸ We speak also of the spirit, meaning the wind, a thing most manifestly corporeal; whence is that in the Psalms, " Fire and hail, snow and ice, the spirit of the storm."⁹ Since spirit, then, is a word of so many meanings, the apostle intended to express by " the spirit of the mind " that spirit which is called the mind. As the same apostle also, when he says, " In putting off the body of the flesh,"¹⁰ certainly did not intend two things, as though flesh were one, and the body of the flesh another; but because body is the name of many things that have no flesh (for besides the flesh, there are many bodies celestial and bodies terrestrial), he expressed by the body of the flesh that body which is flesh. In like manner, therefore, by the spirit of the mind, that spirit which is mind. Elsewhere, too, he has even more plainly called it an image, while enforcing the same thing in other words. " Do you," he says, " putting off the old man with his deeds, put on the new man, which is renewed in the knowledge of God after the image of Him that created him."¹¹ Where the one passage reads, " Put ye on the new man, which is created after God," the other has, " Put ye on the new man, which is renewed after the image of Him that created him." In the one place he says, " After God;" in the other, " After the image of Him that created him." But instead of saying, as in the former passage," In righteousness and true holiness," he has put in the latter, " In the knowledge of God." This renewal, then, and forming again of the mind, is wrought either after God, or after the image of God. But it is said to be after God, in order that it may not be supposed to be after another creature; and to be after the image of God, in order that this renewing may be understood to take place in that wherein is the image of God, i.e. in the mind. Just as we say, that he who has departed from the body a faithful and righteous man, is dead after the body, not after the spirit. For what do we mean by dead after the body, unless as to

¹ Rom. xii. 2.   ² Eph. iv. 23, 24.   ³ Gen. i. 27.
⁴ John iv. 24.   ⁵ 1 Cor. xiv. 14.
⁶ John xix. 30.   ⁷ Eccles. iii. 21.   ⁸ Gen. vii. 22.
⁹ Ps. cxlviii. 8.   ¹⁰ Col. ii. 11.   ¹¹ Col. iii. 9, 10.

the body or in the body, and not dead as to the soul or in the soul? Or if we want to say he is handsome after the body, or strong after the body, not after the mind; what else is this, than that he is handsome or strong in body, not in mind? And the same is the case with numberless other instances. Let us not therefore so understand the words, "After the image of Him that created him," as though it were a different image after which he is renewed, and not the very same which is itself renewed.

CHAP. 17.—HOW THE IMAGE OF GOD IN THE MIND IS RENEWED UNTIL THE LIKENESS OF GOD IS PERFECTED IN IT IN BLESSEDNESS.

23. Certainly this renewal does not take place in the single moment of conversion itself, as that renewal in baptism takes place in a single moment by the remission of all sins; for not one, be it ever so small, remains unremitted. But as it is one thing to be free from fever, and another to grow strong again from the infirmity which the fever produced; and one thing again to pluck out of the body a weapon thrust into it, and another to heal the wound thereby made by a prosperous cure; so the first cure is to remove the cause of infirmity, and this is wrought by the forgiving of all sins; but the second cure is to heal the infirmity itself, and this takes place gradually by making progress in the renewal of that image: which two things are plainly shown in the Psalm, where we read, "Who forgiveth all thine iniquities," which takes place in baptism; and then follows, "and healeth all thine infirmities;"[1] and this takes place by daily additions, while this image is being renewed.[2] And the apostle has spoken of this most expressly, saying, "And though our outward man perish, yet the inner man is renewed day by day."[3] And "it is renewed in the knowledge of God, i.e. in righteousness and true holiness," according to the testimonies of the apostle cited a little before. He, then, who is day by day renewed by making progress in the knowledge of God, and in righteousness and true holiness, transfers his love from things temporal to things eternal, from things visible to things intelligible, from things carnal to things spiritual;

and diligently perseveres in bridling and lessening his desire for the former, and in binding himself by love to the latter. And he does this in proportion as he is helped by God. For it is the sentence of God Himself, "Without me ye can do nothing."[4] And when the last day of life shall have found any one holding fast faith in the Mediator in such progress and growth as this, he will be welcomed by the holy angels, to be led to God, whom he has worshipped, and to be made perfect by Him; and so will receive in the end of the world an incorruptible body, in order not to punishment, but to glory. For the likeness of God will then be perfected in this image, when the sight of God shall be perfected. And of this the Apostle Paul speaks: "Now we see through a glass, in an enigma, but then face to face."[5] And again: "But we with open face, beholding as in a glass the glory of the Lord, are changed into the same image, from glory to glory, even as by the spirit of the Lord."[6] And this is what happens from day to day in those that make good progress.

CHAP. 18.—WHETHER THE SENTENCE OF JOHN IS TO BE UNDERSTOOD OF OUR FUTURE LIKENESS WITH THE SON OF GOD IN THE IMMORTALITY ITSELF ALSO OF THE BODY.

24. But the Apostle John says, "Beloved, now are we the sons of God; and it doth not yet appear what we shall be: but we know that, when He shall appear, we shall be like Him, for we shall see Him as He is."[7] Hence it appears, that the full likeness of God is to take place in that image of God at that time when it shall receive the full sight of God. And yet this may also possibly seem to be said by the Apostle John of the immortality of the body. For we shall be like to God in this too, but only to the Son, because He only in the Trinity took a body, in which He died and rose again, and which He carried with Him to heaven above. For this, too, is called an image of the Son of God, in which we shall have, as He has, an immortal body, being conformed in this respect not to the image of the Father or of the Holy Spirit, but only of the Son, because of Him alone is it read and received by a sound faith, that "the Word was made flesh."[8] And for this reason the apostle says, "Whom He did foreknow, He also did predestinate to be conformed to the image of His Son, that He might be the first-born among many brethren."[9] "The first-born" certainly "from the dead,"[10] accord-

---

[1] Ps. ciii. 3.
[2] [Justification is instantaneous: sanctification is gradual. Baptism is the sign, not the cause, of the former. "As many of us as were baptized into Jesus Christ, were baptized with reference to (εἰς) his death;" and "are intombed with him by the baptism that has reference to (εἰς) his death." Rom. vi. 3, 4. According to St. Paul, baptism supposes a trust in the atonement of Christ, and is a seal of it. In saying that "the forgiveness of all thine iniquity takes place in baptism," Augustin is liable to be understood as teaching the efficiency of baptism in *producing* forgiveness. This is the weak side of the Post Nicene soteriology. —W. G. T. S.]
[3] 2 Cor. iv. 16.

[4] John xv. 5.　　[5] 1 Cor. xiii. 12.　　[6] 2 Cor. iii. 18.
[7] 1 John iii. 2.　　[8] John i. 14.　　[9] Rom. viii. 29.
[10] Col. i. 18.

ing to the same apostle; by which death His flesh was sown in dishonor, and rose again in glory. According to this image of the Son, to which we are conformed in the body by immortality, we also do that of which the same apostle speaks, " As we have borne the image of the earthy, so shall we also bear the image of the heavenly;"[1] to wit, that we who are mortal after Adam, may hold by a true faith, and a sure and certain hope, that we shall be immortal after Christ. For so can we now bear the same image, not yet in sight, but in faith; not yet in fact, but in hope. For the apostle, when he said this, was speaking of the resurrection of the body.

CHAP. 19. — JOHN IS RATHER TO BE UNDERSTOOD OF OUR PERFECT LIKENESS WITH THE TRINITY IN LIFE ETERNAL. WISDOM IS PERFECTED IN HAPPINESS.

25. But in respect to that image indeed, of which it is said, " Let us make man after our image and likeness,"[2] we believe,—and, after the utmost search we have been able to make, understand,—that man was made after the image of the Trinity, because it is not said, After my, or After thy image. And therefore that place too of the Apostle John must be understood rather according to this image, when he says, " We shall be like Him, for we shall see Him as He is;" because he spoke too of Him of whom he had said, " We are the sons of God."[3] And the immortality of the flesh will be perfected in that moment of the resurrection, of which the Apostle Paul says, " In the twinkling of an eye, at the last trump; and the dead shall be raised incorruptible, and we shall be changed."[4] For in that very twinkling of an eye, before the judgment, the spiritual body shall rise again in power, in incorruption, in glory, which is now sown a natural body in weakness, in corruption, in dishonor. But the image which is renewed in the spirit of the mind in the knowledge of God, not outwardly, but inwardly, from day to day, shall be perfected by that sight itself; which then after the judgment shall be face to face, but now makes progress as through a glass in an enigma.[5] And we must understand it to be said on account of this perfection, that "we shall be like Him, for we shall see Him as He is." For this gift will be given to us at that time, when it shall have been said, " Come, ye blessed of my Father, inherit the kingdom prepared for you."[6] For then will the ungodly be taken away, so that

he shall not see the glory of the Lord,[7] when those on the left hand shall go into eternal punishment, while those on the right go into life eternal.[8] But " this is eternal life," as the Truth tells us; " to know Thee," He says, " the one true God, and Jesus Christ whom Thou hast sent."[9]

26. This contemplative wisdom, which I believe is properly called wisdom as distinct from knowledge in the sacred writings; but wisdom only of man, which yet man has not except from Him, by partaking of whom a rational and intellectual mind can be made truly wise;—this contemplative wisdom, I say, it is that Cicero commends, in the end of the dialogue *Hortensius*, when he says: " While, then, we consider these things night and day, and sharpen our understanding, which is the eye of the mind, taking care that it be not ever dulled, that is, while we live in philosophy; we, I say, in so doing, have great hope that, if, on the one hand, this sentiment and wisdom of ours is mortal and perishable, we shall still, when we have discharged our human offices, have a pleasant setting, and a not painful extinction, and as it were a rest from life: or if, on the other, as ancient philosophers thought,—and those, too, the greatest and far the most celebrated,—we have souls eternal and divine, then must we needs think, that the more these shall have always kept in their own proper course, *i.e.* in reason and in the desire of inquiry, and the less they shall have mixed and entangled themselves in the vices and errors of men, the more easy ascent and return they will have to heaven." And then he says, adding this short sentence, and finishing his discourse by repeating it: " Wherefore, to end my discourse at last, if we wish either for a tranquil extinction, after living in the pursuit of these subjects, or if to migrate without delay from this present home to another in no little measure better, we must bestow all our labor and care upon these pursuits." And here I marvel, that a man of such great ability should promise to men living in philosophy, which makes man blessed by contemplation of truth, " a pleasant setting after the discharge of human offices, if this our sentiment and wisdom is mortal and perishable;" as if that which we did not love, or rather which we fiercely hated, were then to die and come to nothing, so that its setting would be pleasant to us ! But indeed he had not learned this from the philosophers, whom he extols with great praise; but this sentiment is redolent of that New Academy, wherein it pleased him to doubt of even

---

[1] 1 Cor. xv. 43, 49.　　[2] Gen. i. 26.
[3] John iii. 2.　　[4] 1 Cor. xv. 52.
[5] 1 Cor. xiii. 12.　　[6] Matt. xxv. 34.

[7] Isa. xxvi. 10.　　[8] Matt. xxv. 46.　　[9] John xvii. 3.

the plainest things. But from the philosophers that were greatest and far most celebrated, as he himself confesses, he had learned that souls are eternal. For souls that are eternal are not unsuitably stirred up by the exhortation to be found in "their own proper course," when the end of this life shall have come, *i.e.* "in reason and in the desire of inquiry," and to mix and entangle themselves the less in the vices and errors of men, in order that they may have an easier return to God. But that course which consists in the love and investigation of truth does not suffice for the wretched, *i.e.* for all mortals who have only this kind of reason, and are without faith in the Mediator; as I have taken pains to prove, as much as I could, in former books of this work, especially in the fourth and thirteenth.

BOOK XV.

BEGINS BY SETTING FORTH BRIEFLY AND IN SUM THE CONTENTS OF THE PREVIOUS FOURTEEN BOOKS. THE ARGUMENT IS THEN SHOWN TO HAVE REACHED SO FAR AS TO ALLOW OF OUR NOW INQUIRING CONCERNING THE TRINITY, WHICH IS GOD, IN THOSE ETERNAL, INCORPOREAL, AND UNCHANGEABLE THINGS THEMSELVES, IN THE PERFECT CONTEMPLATION OF WHICH A BLESSED LIFE IS PROMISED TO US. BUT THIS TRINITY, AS HE SHOWS, IS HERE SEEN BY US AS BY A MIRROR AND IN AN ENIGMA, IN THAT IT IS SEEN BY MEANS OF THE IMAGE OF GOD, WHICH WE ARE, AS IN A LIKENESS THAT IS OBSCURE AND HARD OF DISCERNMENT. IN LIKE MANNER, IT IS SHOWN, THAT SOME KIND OF CONJECTURE AND EXPLANATION MAY BE GATHERED RESPECTING THE GENERATION OF THE DIVINE WORD, FROM THE WORD OF OUR OWN MIND, BUT ONLY WITH DIFFICULTY, ON ACCOUNT OF THE EXCEEDING DISPARITY WHICH IS DISCERNIBLE BETWEEN THE TWO WORDS; AND, AGAIN, RESPECTING THE PROCESSION OF THE HOLY SPIRIT, FROM THE LOVE THAT IS JOINED THERETO BY THE WILL.

CHAP. I.—GOD IS ABOVE THE MIND.

1. DESIRING to exercise the reader in the things that are made, in order that he may know Him by whom they are made, we have now advanced so far as to His image, which is man, in that wherein he excels the other animals, *i.e.* in reason or intelligence, and whatever else can be said of the rational or intellectual soul that pertains to what is called the mind.[1] For by this name some Latin writers, after their own peculiar mode of speech, distinguish that which excels in man, and is not in the beast, from the soul,[2] which is in the beast as well. If, then, we seek anything that is above this nature, and seek truly, it is God,—namely, a nature not created, but creating. And whether this is the Trinity, it is now our business to demonstrate not only to believers, by authority of divine Scripture, but also to such as understand, by some kind of reason, if we can. And why I say, if we can, the thing itself will show better when we have begun to argue about it in our inquiry.

CHAP. 2.—GOD, ALTHOUGH INCOMPREHENSIBLE, IS EVER TO BE SOUGHT. THE TRACES OF THE TRINITY ARE NOT VAINLY SOUGHT IN THE CREATURE.

2. For God Himself, whom we seek, will, as I hope, help our labors, that they may not be unfruitful, and that we may understand how it is said in the holy Psalm, "Let the heart of them rejoice that seek the Lord. Seek the Lord, and be strengthened: seek His face evermore."[3] For that which is always being sought seems as though it were never found; and how then will the heart of them that seek rejoice, and not rather be made sad, if they cannot find what they seek? For it is not said, The heart shall rejoice of them that find, but of them that seek, the Lord. And yet the prophet Isaiah testifies, that the Lord God can be found when He is sought, when he says: "Seek ye the Lord; and as soon as ye have found Him, call upon Him: and when He has drawn near to you, let the wicked man forsake his ways, and the unrighteous man his thoughts."[4] If, then, when sought, He can be found, why is it said, "Seek ye His face evermore?" Is He perhaps to be sought even when found? For things incomprehensible must so be investigated, as that no one may think he has found nothing, when he has been able to find how incomprehensible that is which he was seeking. Why then does he so seek, if he comprehends that which he seeks to be incomprehensible, unless because he may not give over seeking so long as he makes progress in the inquiry itself into things

---

[1] *Mens* or *animus.*   [2] *Anima.*   [3] Ps. cv. 3, 4.   [4] Isa. lv. 6, 7.

incomprehensible, and becomes ever better and better while seeking so great a good, which is both sought in order to be found, and found in order to be sought? For it is both sought in order that it may be found more sweetly, and found in order that it may be sought more eagerly. The words of Wisdom in the book of Ecclesiasticus may be taken in this meaning: "They who eat me shall still be hungry, and they who drink me shall still be thirsty." [1] For they eat and drink because they find; and they still continue seeking because they are hungry and thirst. Faith seeks, understanding finds; whence the prophet says, "Unless ye believe, ye shall not understand." [2] And yet, again, understanding still seeks Him, whom it finds; for "God looked down upon the sons of men," as it is sung in the holy Psalm, "to see if there were any that would understand, and seek after God." [3] And man, therefore, ought for this purpose to have understanding, that he may seek after God.

3. We shall have tarried then long enough among those things that God has made, in order that by them He Himself may be known that made them. "For the invisible things of Him from the creation of the world are clearly seen, being understood by the things that are made." [4] And hence they are rebuked in the book of Wisdom, "who could not out of the good things that are seen know Him that is: neither by considering the works, did they acknowledge the workmaster; but deemed either fire, or wind, or the swift air, or the circle of the stars, or the violent water, or the lights of heaven, to be the gods which govern the world: with whose beauty if they, being delighted, took them to be gods, let them know how much better the Lord of them is; for the first Author of beauty hath created them. But if they were astonished at their power and virtue, let them understand by them how much mightier He is that made them. For by the greatness and beauty of the creatures proportionably the Maker of them is seen" [5] I have quoted these words from the book of Wisdom for this reason, that no one of the faithful may think me vainly and emptily to have sought first in the creature, step by step through certain trinities, each of their own appropriate kind, until I came at last to the mind of man, traces of that highest Trinity which we seek when we seek God.

CHAP. 3. — A BRIEF RECAPITULATION OF ALL THE PREVIOUS BOOKS.

4. But since the necessities of our discussion and argument have compelled us to say a great many things in the course of fourteen books, which we cannot view at once in one glance, so as to be able to refer them quickly in thought to that which we desire to grasp, I will attempt, by the help of God, to the best of my power, to put briefly together, without arguing, whatever I have established in the several books by argument as known, and to place, as it were, under one mental view, not the way in which we have been convinced of each point, but the points themselves of which we have been convinced; in order that what follows may not be so far separated from that which precedes, as that the perusal of the former shall produce forgetfulness of the latter; or at any rate, if it have produced such forgetfulness, that what has escaped the memory may be speedily recalled by reperusal.

5. In the first book, the unity and equality of that highest Trinity is shown from Holy Scripture. In the second, and third, and fourth, the same: but a careful ·handling of the question respecting the sending of the Son and of the Holy Spirit has resulted in three books; and we have demonstrated, that He who is sent is not therefore less than He who sends because the one sent, the other was sent; since the Trinity, which is in all things equal, being also equally in its own nature unchangeable, and invisible, and everywhere present, works indivisibly. In the fifth,— with a view to those who think that the substance of the Father and of the Son is therefore not the same, because they suppose everything that is predicated of God to be predicated according to substance, and therefore contend that to beget and to be begotten, or to be begotten and unbegotten, as being diverse, are diverse substances,—it is demonstrated that not everything that is predicated of God is predicated according to substance, as He is called good and great according to substance, or anything else that is predicated of Him in respect to Himself, but that some things also are predicated relatively, *i.e.* not in respect to Himself, but in respect to something which is not Himself; as He is called the Father in respect to the Son, or the Lord in respect to the creature that serves Him; and that here, if anything thus relatively predicated, *i.e.* predicated in respect to something that is not Himself, is predicated also as in time, as, *e.g.*, "Lord, Thou hast become our

[1] Ecclus. xxiv. 29.   [2] Isa. vii. 9.
[3] Ps. xiv. 2.   [4] Rom. i. 20.
[5] Wisd. xiii. 1-5.

refuge,"[1] then nothing happens to Him so as to work a change in Him, but He Himself continues altogether unchangeable in His own nature or essence. In the sixth, the question how Christ is called by the mouth of the apostle "the power of God and the wisdom of God,"[2] is so far argued that the more careful handling of that question is deferred, *viz.* whether He from whom Christ is begotten is not wisdom Himself, but only the father of His own wisdom, or whether wisdom begat wisdom. But be it which it may, the equality of the Trinity became apparent in this book also, and that God was not triple, but a Trinity; and that the Father and the Son are not, as it were, a double as opposed to the single Holy Spirit: for therein three are not anything more than one. We considered, too, how to understand the words of Bishop Hilary, " Eternity in the Father, form in the Image, use in the Gift." In the seventh, the question is explained which had been deferred: in what way that God who begat the Son is not only Father of His own power and wisdom, but is Himself also power and wisdom; so, too, the Holy Spirit; and yet that they are not three powers or three wisdoms, but one power and one wisdom, as one God and one essence. It was next inquired, in what way they are called one essence, three persons, or by some Greeks one essence, three substances; and we found that the words were so used through the needs of speech, that there might be one term by which to answer, when it is asked what the three are, whom we truly confess to be three, *viz.* Father, and Son, and Holy Spirit. In the eighth, it is made plain by reason also to those who understand, that not only the Father is not greater than the Son in the substance of truth, but that both together are not anything greater than the Holy Spirit alone, nor that any two at all in the same Trinity are anything greater than one, nor all three together anything greater than each severally. Next, I have pointed out, that by means of the truth, which is beheld by the understanding, and by means of the highest good, from which is all good, and by means of the righteousness for which a righteous mind is loved even by a mind not yet righteous, we might understand, so far as it is possible to understand, that not only incorporeal but also unchangeable nature which is God; and by means, too, of love, which in the Holy Scriptures is called God, [3] by which, first of all, those who have understanding begin also, however feebly, to discern the Trinity, to wit, one that

loves, and that which is loved, and love. In the ninth, the argument advances as far as to the image of God, *viz.* man in respect to his mind; and in this we found a kind of trinity, *i.e.* the mind, and the knowledge whereby the mind knows itself, and the love whereby it loves both itself and its knowledge of itself; and these three are shown to be mutually equal, and of one essence. In the tenth, the same subject is more carefully and subtly handled, and is brought to this point, that we found in the mind a still more manifest trinity of the mind, *viz.* in memory, and understanding, and will. But since it turned out also, that the mind could never be in such a case as not to remember, understand, and love itself, although it did not always think of itself; but that when it did think of itself, it did not in the same act of thought distinguish itself from things corporeal; the argument respecting the Trinity, of which this is an image, was deferred, in order to find a trinity also in the things themselves that are seen with the body, and to exercise the reader's attention more distinctly in that. Accordingly, in the eleventh, we chose the sense of sight, wherein that which should have been there found to hold good might be recognized also in the other four bodily senses, although not expressly mentioned; and so a trinity of the outer man first showed itself in those things which are discerned from without, to wit, from the bodily object which is seen, and from the form which is thence impressed upon the eye of the beholder, and from the purpose of the will combining the two. But these three things, as was patent, were not mutually equal and of one substance. Next, we found yet another trinity in the mind itself, introduced into it, as it were, by the things perceived from without; wherein the same three things, as it appeared, were of one substance: the image of the bodily object which is in the memory, and the form thence impressed when the mind's eye of the thinker is turned to it, and the purpose of the will combining the two. But we found this trinity to pertain to the outer man, on this account, that it was introduced into the mind from bodily objects which are perceived from without. In the twelfth, we thought good to distinguish wisdom from knowledge, and to seek first, as being the lower of the two, a kind of appropriate and special trinity in that which is specially called knowledge; but that although we have got now in this to something pertaining to the inner man, yet it is not yet to be either called or thought an image of God. And this is discussed in the thirteenth book by the commendation of Christian faith. In the

---

[1] Ps. xc. 1.   [2] 1 Cor. i. 24.   [3] 1 John iv. 16.

fourteenth we discuss the true wisdom of man, *viz.* that which is granted him by God's gift in the partaking of that very God Himself, which is distinct from knowledge; and the discussion reached this point, that a trinity is discovered in the image of God, which is man in respect to his mind, which mind is "renewed in the knowledge" of God, "after the image of Him that created" man;[1] "after His own image;"[2] and so obtains wisdom, wherein is the contemplation of things eternal.

CHAP. 4.—WHAT UNIVERSAL NATURE TEACHES US CONCERNING GOD.

6. Let us, then, now seek the Trinity which is God, in the things themselves that are eternal, incorporeal, and unchangeable; in the perfect contemplation of which a blessed life is promised us, which cannot be other than eternal. For not only does the authority of the divine books declare that God is; but the whole nature of the universe itself which surrounds us, and to which we also belong, proclaims that it has a most excellent Creator, who has given to us a mind and natural reason, whereby to see that things living are to be preferred to things that are not living; things that have sense to things that have not; things that have understanding to things that have not; things immortal to things mortal; things powerful to things impotent; things righteous to things unrighteous; things beautiful to things deformed; things good to things evil; things incorruptible to things corruptible; things unchangeable to things changeable; things invisible to things visible; things incorporeal to things corporeal; things blessed to things miserable. And hence, since without doubt we place the Creator above things created, we must needs confess that the Creator both lives in the highest sense, and perceives and understands all things, and that He cannot die, or suffer decay, or be changed; and that He is not a body, but a spirit, of all the most powerful, most righteous, most beautiful, most good, most blessed.

CHAP. 5. — HOW DIFFICULT IT IS TO DEMONSTRATE THE TRINITY BY NATURAL REASON.

7. But all that I have said, and whatever else seems to be worthily said of God after the like fashion of human speech, applies to the whole Trinity, which is one God, and to the several Persons in that Trinity. For who would dare to say either of the one God, which is the Trinity itself, or of the Father,

or Son, or Holy Spirit, either that He is not living, or is without sense or intelligence; or that, in that nature in which they are affirmed to be mutually equal, any one of them is mortal, or corruptible, or changeable, or corporeal? Or is there any one who would deny that any one in the Trinity is most powerful, most righteous, most beautiful, most good, most blessed? If, then, these things, and all others of the kind, can be predicated both of the Trinity itself, and of each several one in that Trinity, where or how shall the Trinity manifest itself? Let us therefore first reduce these numerous predicates to some limited number. For that which is called life in God, is itself His essence and nature. God, therefore, does not live, unless by the life which He is to Himself. And this life is not such as that which is in a tree, wherein is neither understanding nor sense; nor such as is in a beast, for the life of a beast possesses the fivefold sense, but has no understanding. But the life which is God perceives and understands all things, and perceives by mind, not by body, because "God is a spirit."[3] And God does not perceive through a body, as animals do, which have bodies, for He does not consist of soul and body. And hence that single nature perceives as it understands, and understands as it perceives, and its sense and understanding are one and the same. Nor yet so, that at any time He should either cease or begin to be; for He is immortal. And it is not said of Him in vain, that "He only hath immortality."[4] For immortality is true immortality in His case whose nature admits no change. That is also true eternity by which God is unchangeable, without beginning, without end; consequently also incorruptible. It is one and the same thing, therefore, to call God eternal, or immortal, or incorruptible, or unchangeable; and it is likewise one and the same thing to say that He is living, and that He is intelligent, that is, in truth, wise. For He did not receive wisdom whereby to be wise, but He is Himself wisdom. And this is life, and again is power or might, and yet again beauty, whereby He is called powerful and beautiful. For what is more powerful and more beautiful than wisdom, "which reaches from end to end mightily, and sweetly disposes all things"?[5] Or do goodness, again, and righteousness, differ from each other in the nature of God, as they differ in His works, as though they were two diverse qualities of God—goodness one, and righteousness an-

---

[1] Col. iii. 10.   [2] Gen. i. 27.   [3] John iv. 24.   [4] 1 Tim. vi. 16.   [5] Wisd. viii. 1.

other? Certainly not; but that which is righteousness is also itself goodness; and that which is goodness is also itself blessedness. And God is therefore called incorporeal, that He may be believed and understood to be a spirit, not a body.

8. Further, if we say, Eternal, immortal, incorruptible, unchangeable, living, wise, powerful, beautiful, righteous, good, blessed, spirit; only the last of this list as it were seems to signify substance, but the rest to signify qualities of that substance; but it is not so in that ineffable and simple nature. For whatever seems to be predicated therein according to quality, is to be understood according to substance or essence. For far be it from us to predicate spirit of God according to substance, and good according to quality; but both according to substance.[1] And so in like manner of all those we have mentioned, of which we have already spoken at length in the former books. Let us choose, then, one of the first four of those in our enumeration and arrangement, *i.e.* eternal, immortal, incorruptible, unchangeable; since these four, as I have argued already, have one meaning; in order that our aim may not be distracted by a multiplicity of objects. And let it be rather that which was placed first, *viz.* eternal. Let us follow the same course with the four that come next, *viz.* living, wise, powerful, beautiful. And since life of some sort belongs also to the beast, which has not wisdom; while the next two, *viz.* wisdom and might, are so compared to one another in the case of man, as that Scripture says, "Better is he that is wise than he that is strong;"[2] and beauty, again, is commonly attributed to bodily objects also: out of these four that we have chosen, let Wise be the one we take. Although these four are not to be called unequal in speaking of God; for they are four names, but one thing. But of the third and last four,—although it is the same thing in God to be righteous that it is to be good or to be blessed; and the same thing to be a spirit that it is to be righteous, and good, and blessed; yet, because in men there can be a spirit that is not blessed, and there can be one both righteous and good, but not yet blessed; but that which is blessed is doubtless both just, and good, and a spirit,—let

us rather choose that one which cannot exist even in men without the three others, *viz.* blessed.

CHAP. 6.—HOW THERE IS A TRINITY IN THE VERY SIMPLICITY OF GOD. WHETHER AND HOW THE TRINITY THAT IS GOD IS MANIFESTED FROM THE TRINITIES WHICH HAVE BEEN SHOWN TO BE IN MEN.

9. When, then, we say, Eternal, wise, blessed, are these three the Trinity that is called God? We reduce, indeed, those twelve to this small number of three; but perhaps we can go further, and reduce these three also to one of them. For if wisdom and might, or life and wisdom, can be one and the same thing in the nature of God, why cannot eternity and wisdom, or blessedness and wisdom, be one and the same thing in the nature of God? And hence, as it made no difference whether we spoke of these twelve or of those three when we reduced the many to the small number; so does it make no difference whether we speak of those three, or of that one, to the singularity of which we have shown that the other two of the three may be reduced. What fashion, then, of argument, what possible force and might of understanding, what liveliness of reason, what sharp-sightedness of thought, will set forth how (to pass over now the others) this one thing, that God is called wisdom, is a trinity? For God does not receive wisdom from any one as we receive it from Him, but He is Himself His own wisdom; because His wisdom is not one thing, and His essence another, seeing that to Him to be wise is to be. Christ, indeed, is called in the Holy Scriptures, "the power of God, and the wisdom of God."[3] But we have discussed in the seventh book how this is to be understood, so that the Son may not seem to make the Father wise; and our explanation came to this, that the Son is wisdom of wisdom, in the same way as He is light of light, God of God. Nor could we find the Holy Spirit to be in any other way than that He Himself also is wisdom, and altogether one wisdom, as one God, one essence. How, then, do we understand this wisdom, which is God, to be a trinity? I do not say, How do we believe this? For among the faithful this ought to admit no question. But supposing there is any way by which we can see with the understanding what we believe, what is that way?

10. For if we recall where it was in these books that a trinity first began to show itself

---

[1] [In the Infinite Being, qualities are inseparable from essence; in the finite being, they are separable. If man or angel ceases to be good, or wise, or righteous, he does not thereby cease to be man or angel. But if God should lose goodness, wisdom or righteousness, he would no longer be God. This is the meaning of Augustin, when he says that "goodness" as well as "spirit" must be predicated of God, "according to substance"—that is, that qualites in God are *essential* qualities. They are so one with the essence, that they are inseparable.—W. G. T. S.]

[2] Wisd. vi. 1.

[3] 1 Cor. i. 24.

to our understanding, the eighth book is that which occurs to us; since it was there that to the best of our power we tried to raise the aim of the mind to understand that most excellent and unchangeable nature, which our mind is not. And we so contemplated this nature as to think of it as not far from us, and as above us, not in place, but by its own awful and wonderful excellence, and in such wise that it appeared to be with us by its own present light. Yet in this no trinity was yet manifest to us, because in that blaze of light we did not keep the eye of the mind steadfastly bent upon seeking it; only we discerned it in a sense, because there was no bulk wherein we must needs think the magnitude of two or three to be more than that of one. But when we came to treat of love, which in the Holy Scriptures is called God,[1] then a trinity began to dawn upon us a little, i.e. one that loves, and that which is loved, and love. But because that ineffable light beat back our gaze, and it became in some degree plain that the weakness of our mind could not as yet be tempered to it, we turned back in the midst of the course we had begun, and planned according to the (as it were) more familiar consideration of our own mind, according to which man is made after the image of God,[2] in order to relieve our overstrained attention; and thereupon we dwelt from the ninth to the fourteenth book upon the consideration of the creature, which we are, that we might be able to understand and behold the invisible things of God by those things which are made. And now that we have exercised the understanding, as far as was needful, or perhaps more than was needful, in lower things, lo! we wish, but have not strength, to raise ourselves to behold that highest Trinity which is God. For in such manner as we see most undoubted trinities, whether those which are wrought from without by corporeal things, or when these same things are thought of which were perceived from without; or when those things which take their rise in the mind, and do not pertain to the senses of the body, as faith, or as the virtues which comprise the art of living, are discerned by manifest reason, and held fast by knowledge; or when the mind itself, by which we know whatever we truly say that we know, is known to itself, or thinks of itself; or when that mind beholds anything eternal and unchangeable, which itself is not; —in such way, then, I say, as we see in all these instances most undoubted trinities, because they are wrought in ourselves, or are

in ourselves, when we remember, look at, or desire these things;—do we, I say, in such manner also see the Trinity that is God; because there also, by the understanding, we behold both Him as it were speaking, and His Word, i.e. the Father and the Son; and then, proceeding thence, the love common to both, namely, the Holy Spirit? These trinities that pertain to our senses or to our mind, do we rather see than believe them, but rather believe than see that God is a trinity? But if this is so, then doubtless we either do not at all understand and behold the invisible things of God by those things that are made, or if we behold them at all, we do not behold the Trinity in them; and there is therein somewhat to behold, and somewhat also which we ought to believe, even though not beheld. And as the eighth book showed that we behold the unchangeable good which we are not, so the fourteenth reminded us thereof, when we spoke of the wisdom that man has from God. Why, then, do we not recognize the Trinity therein? Does that wisdom which God is said to be, not perceive itself, and not love itself? Who would say this? Or who is there that does not see, that where there is no knowledge, there in no way is there wisdom? Or are we, in truth, to think that the Wisdom which is God knows other things, and does not know itself; or loves other things, and does not love itself? But if this is a foolish and impious thing to say or believe, then behold we have a trinity,—to wit, wisdom, and the knowledge wisdom has of itself, and its love of itself. For so, too, we find a trinity in man also, i.e. mind, and the knowledge wherewith mind knows itself, and the love wherewith it loves itself.

CHAP. 7.—THAT IT IS NOT EASY TO DISCOVER THE TRINITY THAT IS GOD FROM THE TRINITIES WE HAVE SPOKEN OF.

11. But these three are in such way in man, that they are not themselves man. For man, as the ancients defined him, is a rational mortal animal. These things, therefore, are the chief things in man, but are not man themselves. And any one person, i.e. each individual man, has these three things in his mind. But if, again, we were so to define man as to say, Man is a rational substance consisting of mind and body, then without doubt man has a soul that is not body, and a body that is not soul. And hence these three things are not man, but belong to man, or are in man. If, again, we put aside the body, and think of the soul by

---

[1] 1 John iv. 16.　　　[2] Gen. i. 27.

itself, the mind is somewhat belonging to the soul, as though its head, or eye, or countenance; but these things are not to be regarded as bodies. It is not then the soul, but that which is chief in the soul, that is called the mind. But can we say that the Trinity is in such way in God, as to be somewhat belonging to God, and not itself God? And hence each individual man, who is called the image of God, not according to all things that pertain to his nature, but according to his mind alone, is one person, and is an image of the Trinity in his mind. But that Trinity of which he is the image is nothing else in its totality than God, is nothing else in its totality than the Trinity. Nor does anything pertain to the nature of God so as not to pertain to that Trinity; and the Three Persons are of one essence, not as each individual man is one person.

12. There is, again, a wide difference in this point likewise, that whether we speak of the mind in a man, and of its knowledge and love; or of memory, understanding, will,—we remember nothing of the mind except by memory, nor understand anything except by understanding, nor love anything except by will. But in that Trinity, who would dare to say that the Father understands neither Himself, nor the Son, nor the Holy Spirit, except by the Son, or loves them except by the Holy Spirit; and that He remembers only by Himself either Himself, or the Son, or the Holy Spirit; and in the same way that the Son remembers neither Himself nor the Father, except by the Father, nor loves them except by the Holy Spirit; but that by Himself He only understands both the Father and Son and Holy Spirit: and in like manner, that the Holy Spirit by the Father remembers both the Father and the Son and Himself, and by the Son understands both the Father and the Son and Himself; but by Himself only loves both Himself and the Father and the Son;—as though the Father were both His own memory, and that of the Son and of the Holy Spirit; and the Son were the understanding of both Himself, and the Father and the Holy Spirit; but the Holy Spirit were the love both of Himself, and of the Father and of the Son? Who would presume to think or affirm this of that Trinity? For if therein the Son alone understands both for Himself and for the Father and for the Holy Spirit, we have returned to the old absurdity, that the Father is not wise from Himself, but from the Son, and that wisdom has not begotten wisdom, but that the Father is said to be wise by that wisdom which He begat. For where there is no understanding there can be no

wisdom; and hence, if the Father does not understand Himself for Himself, but the Son understands for the Father, assuredly the Son makes the Father wise. But if to God to be is to be wise, and essence is to Him the same as wisdom, then it is not the Son that has His essence from the Father, which is the truth, but rather the Father from the Son, which is a most absurd falsehood. And this absurdity, beyond all doubt, we have discussed, disproved, and rejected, in the seventh book. Therefore God the Father is wise by that wisdom by which He is His own wisdom, and the Son is the wisdom of the Father from the wisdom which is the Father, from whom the Son is begotten; whence it follows that the Father understands also by that understanding by which He is His own understanding (for he could not be wise that did not understand); and that the Son is the understanding of the Father, begotten of the understanding which is the Father. And this same may not be unfitly said of memory also. For how is he wise, that remembers nothing, or does not remember himself? Accordingly, since the Father is wisdom, and the Son is wisdom, therefore, as the Father remembers Himself, so does the Son also remember Himself; and as the Father remembers both Himself and the Son, not by the memory of the Son, but by His own, so does the Son remember both Himself and the Father, not by the memory of the Father, but by His own. Where, again, there is no love, who would say there was any wisdom? And hence we must infer that the Father is in such way His own love, as He is His own understanding and memory. And therefore these three, i.e. memory, understanding, love or will, in that highest and unchangeable essence which is God, are, we see, not the Father and the Son and the Holy Spirit, but the Father alone. And because the Son too is wisdom begotten of wisdom, as neither the Father nor the Holy Spirit understands for Him, but He understands for Himself; so neither does the Father remember for Him, nor the Holy Spirit love for Him, but He remembers and loves for Himself: for He is Himself also His own memory, His own understanding, and His own love. But that He is so comes to Him from the Father, of whom He is born. And because the Holy Spirit also is wisdom proceeding from wisdom, He too has not the Father for a memory, and the Son for an understanding, and Himself for love: for He would not be wisdom if another remembered for Him, and yet another understood for Him, and He only loved for Himself; but Himself has all three things, and has them in such way that they are Himself. But that He is so comes to Him thence, whence He proceeds.

13. What man, then, is there who can comprehend that wisdom by which God knows all things, in such wise that neither what we call things past are past therein, nor what we call things future are therein waited for as coming, as though they were absent, but both past and future with things present are all present; nor yet are things thought severally, so that thought passes from one to another, but all things simultaneously are at hand in one glance;—what man, I say, is there that comprehends that wisdom, and the like prudence, and the like knowledge, since in truth even our own wisdom is beyond our comprehension? For somehow we are able to behold the things that are present to our senses or to our understanding; but the things that are absent, and yet have once been present, we know by memory, if we have not forgotten them. And we conjecture, too, not the past from the future, but the future from the past, yet by an unstable knowledge. For there are some of our thoughts to which, although future, we, as it were, look onward with greater plainness and certainty as being very near; and we do this by the means of memory when we are able to do it, as much as we ever are able, although memory seems to belong not to the future, but to the past. And this may be tried in the case of any words or songs, the due order of which we are rendering by memory; for we certainly should not utter each in succession, unless we foresaw in thought what came next. And yet it is not foresight, but memory, that enables us to foresee it; for up to the very end of the words or the song, nothing is uttered except as foreseen and looked forward to. And yet in doing this, we are not said to speak or sing by foresight, but by memory; and if any one is more than commonly capable of uttering many pieces in this way, he is usually praised, not for his foresight, but for his memory. We know, and are absolutely certain, that all this takes place in our mind or by our mind; but how it takes place, the more attentively we desire to scrutinize, the more do both our very words break down, and our purpose itself fails, when by our understanding, if not our tongue, we would reach to something of clearness. And do such as we are, think, that in so great infirmity of mind we can comprehend whether the foresight of God is the same as His memory and His understanding, who does not regard in thought each several thing, but embraces all that He knows in one eternal and unchangeable and ineffable vision? In this difficulty, then, and strait, we

may well cry out to the living God, "Such knowledge is too wonderful for me: it is high, I cannot attain unto it." [1] For I understand by myself how wonderful and incomprehensible is Thy knowledge, by which Thou madest me, when I cannot even comprehend myself whom Thou hast made! And yet, "while I was musing, the fire burned," [2] so that "I seek Thy face evermore." [3]

CHAP. 8.—HOW THE APOSTLE SAYS THAT GOD IS NOW SEEN BY US THROUGH A GLASS.

14. I know that wisdom is an incorporeal substance, and that it is the light by which those things are seen that are not seen by carnal eyes; and yet a man so great and so spiritual [as Paul] says, "We see now through a glass, in an enigma, but then face to face." [4] If we ask what and of what sort is this "glass," this assuredly occurs to our minds, that in a glass nothing is discerned but an image. We have endeavored, then, so to do; in order that we might see in some way or other by this image which we are, Him by whom we are made, as by a glass. And this is intimated also in the words of the same apostle: "But we with open face, beholding as in a glass the glory of the Lord, are transformed into the same image, from glory to glory, even as by the Spirit of the Lord." [5] "Beholding as in a glass," [6] he has said, i.e. seeing by means of a glass, not looking from a watch-tower: an ambiguity that does not exist in the Greek language, whence the apostolic epistles have been rendered into Latin. For in Greek, a glass,[7] in which the images of things are visible, is wholly distinct in the sound of the word also from a watch-tower,[8] from the height of which we command a more distant view. And it is quite plain that the apostle, in using the word "speculantes" in respect to the glory of the Lord, meant it to come from "speculum," not from "specula." But where he says, "We are transformed into the same image," he assuredly means to speak of the image of God; and by calling it "the same," he means that very image which we see in the glass, because that same image is also the glory of the Lord; as he says elsewhere, "For a man indeed ought not to cover his head, forasmuch as he is the image and glory of God," [9]—a text already discussed in the twelfth book. He means, then, by "We are transformed," that we are changed from one form to another, and that we pass from a form that is obscure to a form

1 Ps. cxxxix. 6.   2 Ps. xxxix. 3.   3 Ps. cv. 4.
4 1 Cor. xiii. 12.   5 2 Cor. iii. 18.   6 Speculantes.
7 Speculum.   8 Specula.   9 1 Cor. xi. 7.

that is bright: since the obscure form, too, is the image of God; and if an image, then assuredly also " glory," in which we are created as men, being better than the other animals. For it is said of human nature in itself, " The man ought not to cover his head, because he is the image and glory of God." And this nature, being the most excellent among things created, is transformed from a form that is defaced into a form that is beautiful, when it is justified by its own Creator from ungodliness. Since even in ungodliness itself, the more the faultiness is to be condemned, the more certainly is the nature to be praised. And therefore he has added, " from glory to glory:" from the glory of creation to the glory of justification. Although these words, " from glory to glory," may be understood also in other ways;—from the glory of faith to the glory of sight, from the glory whereby we are sons of God to the glory whereby we shall be like Him, because " we shall see Him as He is." [1] But in that he has added, " as from the Spirit of the Lord," he declares, that the blessing of so desirable a transformation is conferred upon us by the grace of God.

CHAP. 9.—OF THE TERM " ENIGMA," AND OF TROPICAL MODES OF SPEECH.

15. What has been said relates to the words of the apostle, that " we see now through a glass;" but whereas he has added, " in an enigma," the meaning of this addition is unknown to any who are unacquainted with the books that contain the doctrine of those modes of speech, which the Greeks call Tropes, which Greek word we also use in Latin. For as we more commonly speak of *schemata* than of figures, so we more commonly speak of tropes than of modes. And it is a very difficult and uncommon thing to express the names of the several modes or tropes in Latin, so as to refer its appropriate name to each. And hence some Latin translators, through unwillingness to employ a Greek word, where the apostle says, " Which things are an allegory," [2] have rendered it by a circumlocution—Which things signify one thing by another. But there are several species of this kind of trope that is called allegory, and one of them is that which is called enigma. Now the definition of the generic term must necessarily embrace also all its species; and hence, as every horse is an animal, but not every animal is a horse, so every enigma is an allegory, but every allegory is not an enigma. What then is an allegory, but a trope wherein one thing is understood from another? as in the Epistle to the Thessalonians, " Let us not therefore sleep, as do others; but let us watch and be sober: for they who sleep, sleep in the night; and they who are drunken, are drunken in the night: but let us who are of the day, be sober." [3] But this allegory is not an enigma, for here the meaning is patent to all but the very dull; but an enigma is, to explain it briefly, an obscure allegory, as, *e.g.*, " The horseleech had three daughters," [4] and other like instances. But when the apostle spoke of an allegory, he does not find it in the words, but in the fact; since he has shown that the two Testaments are to be understood by the two sons of Abraham, one by a bondmaid, and the other by a free woman, which was a thing not said, but also done. And before this was explained, it was obscure; and accordingly such an allegory, which is the generic name, could be specifically called an enigma.

16. But because it is not only those that are ignorant of the books that contain the doctrine of tropes, who inquire the apostle's meaning, when he said that we " see now in an enigma, but those, too, who are acquainted with the doctrine, but yet desire to know what that enigma is in which " we now see;" we must find a single meaning for the two phrases, *viz.* for that which says, " we see now through a glass," and for that which adds, " in an enigma." For it makes but one sentence, when the whole is so uttered, " We see now through a glass in an enigma." Accordingly, as far as my judgment goes, as by the word glass he meant to signify an image, so by that of enigma any likeness you will, but yet one obscure, and difficult to see through. While, therefore, any likenesses whatever may be understood as signified by the apostle when he speaks of a glass and an enigma, so that they are adapted to the understanding of God, in such way as He can be understood; yet nothing is better adapted to this purpose than that which is not vainly called His image. Let no one, then, wonder, that we labor to see in any way at all, even in that fashion of seeing which is granted to us in this life, *viz.* through a glass, in an enigma. For we should not hear of an enigma in this place if sight were easy. And this is a yet greater enigma, that we do not see what we cannot but see. For who does not see his own thought? And yet who does see his own thought, I do not say with the eye of the flesh, but with the inner sight itself? Who

---

[1] 1 John iii. 2.   [2] Gal. iv. 24.   [3] 1 Thess. v. 6-8.   [4] Prov. xxx. 15.

does not see it, and who does see it? Since thought is a kind of sight of the mind; whether those things are present which are seen also by the bodily eyes, or perceived by the other senses; or whether they are not present, but their likenesses are discerned by thought; or whether neither of these is the case, but things are thought of that are neither bodily things nor likenesses of bodily things, as the virtues and vices; or as, indeed, thought itself is thought of; or whether it be those things which are the subjects of instruction and of liberal sciences; or whether the higher causes and reasons themselves of all these things in the unchangeable nature are thought of; or whether it be even evil, and vain, and false things that we are thinking of, with either the sense not consenting, or erring in its consent.

CHAP. 10. — CONCERNING THE WORD OF THE MIND, IN WHICH WE SEE THE WORD OF GOD, AS IN A GLASS AND AN ENIGMA.

17. But let us now speak of those things of which we think as known, and have in our knowledge even if we do not think of them; whether they belong to the contemplative knowledge, which, as I have argued, is properly to be called wisdom, or to the active, which is properly to be called knowledge. For both together belong to one mind, and are one image of God. But when we treat of the lower of the two distinctly and separately, then it is not to be called an image of God, although even then, too, some likeness of that Trinity may be found in it; as we showed in the thirteenth book. We speak now, therefore, of the entire knowledge of man altogether, in which whatever is known to us is known; that, at any rate, which is true; otherwise it would not be known. For no one knows what is false, except when he knows it to be false; and if he knows this, then he knows what is true: for it is true that that is false. We treat, therefore, now of those things which we think as known, and which are known to us even if they are not being thought of. But certainly, if we would utter them in words, we can only do so by thinking them. For although there were no words spoken, at any rate, he who thinks speaks in his heart. And hence that passage in the book of Wisdom: "They said within themselves, thinking not aright." [1] For the words, "They said within themselves," are explained by the addition of "thinking." A like passage to this is that in the Gospel,—that certain scribes, when they heard the Lord's words to

the paralytic man, "Be of good cheer, my son, thy sins are forgiven thee," said within themselves, "This man blasphemeth." For how did they "say within themselves," except by thinking? Then follows, "And when Jesus saw their thoughts, He said, Why think ye evil in your thoughts?" [2] So far Matthew. But Luke narrates the same thing thus: "The scribes and Pharisees began to think, saying, Who is this that speaketh blasphemies? Who can forgive sins but God alone? But when Jesus perceived their thoughts, He, answering, said unto them, What think ye in your hearts?" [3] That which in the book of Wisdom is, "They said, thinking," is the same here with, "They thought, saying." For both there and here it is declared, that they spake within themselves, and in their own heart, i.e. spake by thinking. For they "spake within themselves," and it was said to them, "What think ye?" And the Lord Himself says of that rich man whose ground brought forth plentifully, "And he thought within himself, saying." [4]

18. Some thoughts, then, are speeches of the heart, wherein the Lord also shows that there is a mouth, when He says, "Not that which entereth into the mouth defileth a man; but that which proceedeth out of the mouth, that defileth a man." In one sentence He has comprised two diverse mouths of the man, one of the body, one of the heart. For assuredly, that from which they thought the man to be defiled, enters into the mouth of the body; but that from which the Lord said the man was defiled, proceedeth out of the mouth of the heart. So certainly He Himself explained what He had said. For a little after, He says also to His disciples concerning the same thing: "Are ye also yet without understanding? Do ye not understand, that whatsoever entereth in at the mouth goeth into the belly, and is cast out into the draught?" Here He most certainly pointed to the mouth of the body. But in that which follows He plainly speaks of the mouth of the heart, where He says, "But those things which proceed out of the mouth come forth from the heart; and they defile the man. For out of the heart proceed evil thoughts," [5] etc. What is clearer than this explanation? And yet, when we call thoughts speeches of the heart, it does not follow that they are not also acts of sight, arising from the sight of knowledge, when they are true. For when these things are done outwardly by means of the body, then speech and sight are different things; but when we think inwardly, the two

---

1 Wisd. ii. 1.

2 Matt. ix. 2-4.   3 Luke v. 21, 22.
4 Luke xii. 17.   5 Matt. xv. 10-20.

are one,—just as sight and hearing are two things mutually distinct in the bodily senses, but to see and hear are the same thing in the mind; and hence, while speech is not seen but rather heard outwardly, yet the inward speeches, *i.e.* thoughts, are said by the holy Gospel to have been seen, not heard, by the Lord. "They said within themselves, This man blasphemeth," says the Gospel; and then subjoined, "And when Jesus saw their thoughts." Therefore He saw, what they said. For by His own thought He saw their thoughts, which they supposed no one saw but themselves.

19. Whoever, then, is able to understand a word, not only before it is uttered in sound, but also before the images of its sounds are considered in thought,—for this it is which belongs to no tongue, to wit, of those which are called the tongues of nations, of which our Latin tongue is one;—whoever, I say, is able to understand this, is able now to see through this glass and in this enigma some likeness of that Word of whom it is said, "In the beginning was the Word, and the Word was with God, and the Word was God." [1] For of necessity, when we speak what is true, *i.e.* speak what we know, there is born from the knowledge itself which the memory retains, a word that is altogether of the same kind with that knowledge from which it is born. For the thought that is formed by the thing which we know, is the word which we speak in the heart: which word is neither Greek nor Latin, nor of any other tongue. But when it is needful to convey this to the knowledge of those to whom we speak, then some sign is assumed whereby to signify it. And generally a sound, sometimes a nod, is exhibited, the former to the ears, the latter to the eyes, that the word which we bear in our mind may become known also by bodily signs to the bodily senses. For what is to nod or beckon, except to speak in some way to the sight? And Holy Scripture gives its testimony to this; for we read in the Gospel according to John: "Verily, verily, I say unto you, that one of you shall betray me. Then the disciples looked one upon another, doubting of whom He spake. Now there was leaning on Jesus' breast one of His disciples whom Jesus loved. Simon Peter therefore beckons to him, and says to him, Who is it of whom He speaks?" [2] Here he spoke by beckoning what he did not venture to speak by sounds. But whereas we exhibit these and the like bodily signs either to ears or eyes of persons present to whom we speak, letters have been invented that we might be able to converse also with the absent; but these are signs of words, as words themselves are signs in our conversation of those things which we think.

CHAP. 11. — THE LIKENESS OF THE DIVINE WORD, SUCH AS IT IS, IS TO BE SOUGHT, NOT IN OUR OWN OUTER AND SENSIBLE WORD, BUT IN THE INNER AND MENTAL ONE. THERE IS THE GREATEST POSSIBLE UNLIKENESS BETWEEN OUR WORD AND KNOWLEDGE AND THE DIVINE WORD AND KNOWLEDGE.

20. Accordingly, the word that sounds outwardly is the sign of the word that gives light inwardly; which latter has the greater claim to be called a word. For that which is uttered with the mouth of the flesh, is the articulate sound of a word; and is itself also called a word, on account of that to make which outwardly apparent it is itself assumed. For our word is so made in some way into an articulate sound of the body, by assuming that articulate sound by which it may be manifested to men's senses, as the Word of God was made flesh, by assuming that flesh in which itself also might be manifested to men's senses. And as our word becomes an articulate sound, yet is not changed into one; so the Word of God became flesh, but far be it from us to say He was changed into flesh. For both that word of ours became an articulate sound, and that other Word became flesh, by assuming it, not by consuming itself so as to be changed into it. And therefore whoever desires to arrive at any likeness, be it of what sort it may, of the Word of God, however in many respects unlike, must not regard the word of ours that sounds in the ears, either when it is uttered in an articulate sound or when it is silently thought. For the words of all tongues that are uttered in sound are also silently thought, and the mind runs over verses while the bodily mouth is silent. And not only the numbers of syllables, but the tunes also of songs, since they are corporeal, and pertain to that sense of the body which is called hearing, are at hand by certain incorporeal images appropriate to them, to those who think of them, and who silently revolve all these things. But we must pass by this, in order to arrive at that word of man, by the likeness of which, be it of what sort it may, the Word of God may be somehow seen as in an enigma. Not that word which was spoken to this or that prophet, and of which it is said, "Now the word of God grew and multiplied;" [3] and again, "Faith then cometh by hearing, and hearing

---

[1] John i. 1.　　　[2] John xiii. 21-24.　　　[3] Acts vi. 7.

by the word of Christ;"[1] and again, "When ye received the word of God which ye heard of us, ye received it not as the word of men, but, as it is in truth, the word of God"[2] (and there are countless other like sayings in the Scriptures respecting the word of God, which is disseminated in the sounds of many and diverse languages through the hearts and mouths of men; and which is therefore called the word of God, because the doctrine that is delivered is not human, but divine);—but we are now seeking to see, in whatsoever way we can, by means of this likeness, that Word of God of which it is said, "The Word was God;" of which it is said, "All things were made by Him;" of which it is said, "The Word became flesh;" of which it is said, "The Word of God on high is the fountain of wisdom."[3] We must go on, then, to that word of man, to the word of the rational animal, to the word of that image of God, that is not born of God, but made by God; which is neither utterable in sound nor capable of being thought under the likeness of sound, such as must needs be with the word of any tongue; but which precedes all the signs by which it is signified, and is begotten from the knowledge that continues in the mind, when that same knowledge is spoken inwardly according as it really is. For the sight of thinking is exceedingly like the sight of knowledge. For when it is uttered by sound, or by any bodily sign, it is not uttered according as it really is, but as it can be seen or heard by the body. When, therefore, that is in the word which is in the knowledge, then there is a true word, and truth, such as is looked for from man; such that what is in the knowledge is also in the word, and what is not in the knowledge is also not in the word. Here may be recognized, "Yea, yea; nay, nay."[4] And so this likeness of the image that is made, approaches as nearly as is possible to that likeness of the image that is born, by which God the Son is declared to be in all things like in substance to the Father. We must notice in this enigma also another likeness of the word of God; viz. that, as it is said of that Word, "All things were made by Him," where God is declared to have made the universe by His only-begotten Son, so there are no works of man that are not first spoken in his heart: whence it is written, "A word is the beginning of every work."[5] But here also, it is when the word is true, that then it is the beginning of a good work. And a word is true when it is begotten from the knowledge of

working good works, so that there too may be preserved the "yea yea, nay nay;" in order that whatever is in that knowledge by which we are to live, may be also in the word by which we are to work, and whatever is not in the one may not be in the other. Otherwise such a word will be a lie, not truth; and what comes thence will be a sin, and not a good work. There is yet this other likeness of the Word of God in this likeness of our word, that there can be a word of ours with no work following it, but there cannot be any work unless a word precedes; just as the Word of God could have existed though no creature existed, but no creature could exist unless by that Word by which all things are made. And therefore not God the Father, not the Holy Spirit, not the Trinity itself, but the Son only, which is the Word of God, was made flesh; although the Trinity was the maker: in order that we might live rightly through our word following and imitating His example, i.e. by having no lie in either the thought or the work of our word. But this perfection of this image is one to be at some time hereafter. In order to attain this it is that the good master teaches us by Christian faith, and by pious doctrine, that "with face unveiled" from the veil of the law, which is the shadow of things to come, "beholding as in a glass the glory of the Lord," i.e. gazing at it through a glass, "we may be transformed into the same image from glory to glory, as by the Spirit of the Lord;"[6] as we explained above.

21. When, therefore, this image shall have been renewed to perfection by this transformation, then we shall be like God, because we shall see Him, not through a glass, but "as He is;"[7] which the Apostle Paul expresses by "face to face."[8] But now, who can explain how great is the unlikeness also, in this glass, in this enigma, in this likeness such as it is? Yet I will touch upon some points, as I can, by which to indicate it.

CHAP. 12.—THE ACADEMIC PHILOSOPHY.

First, of what sort and how great is the very knowledge itself that a man can attain, be he ever so skillful and learned, by which our thought is formed with truth, when we speak what we know? For to pass by those things that come into the mind from the bodily senses, among which so many are otherwise than they seem to be, that he who is overmuch pressed down by their resemblance to truth, seems sane to himself, but really is not

---

[1] Rom. x. 17.   [2] 1 Thess. ii. 13.   [3] Ecclus. i. 5.
[4] Matt. v. 37.   [5] Ecclus. xxxvii. 20.   [6] 2 Cor. iii. 17.   [7] 1 John iii. 4   [8] 1 Cor. xiii. 12.

sane;—whence it is that the Academic[1] philosophy has so prevailed as to be still more wretchedly insane by doubting all things;—passing by, then, those things that come into the mind by the bodily senses, how large a proportion is left of things which we know in such manner as we know that we live? In regard to this, indeed, we are absolutely without any fear lest perchance we are being deceived by some resemblance of the truth; since it is certain, that he who is deceived, yet lives. And this again is not reckoned among those objects of sight that are presented from without, so that the eye may be deceived in it; in such way as it is when an oar in the water looks bent, and towers seem to move as you sail past them, and a thousand other things that are otherwise than they seem to be: for this is not a thing that is discerned by the eye of the flesh. The knowledge by which we know that we live is the most inward of all knowledge, of which even the Academic cannot insinuate: Perhaps you are asleep, and do not know it, and you see things in your sleep. For who does not know that what people see in dreams is precisely like what they see when awake? But he who is certain of the knowledge of his own life, does not therein say, I know I am awake, but, I know I am alive; therefore, whether he be asleep or awake, he is alive. Nor can he be deceived in that knowledge by dreams; since it belongs to a living man both to sleep and to see in sleep. Nor can the Academic again say, in confutation of this knowledge: Perhaps you are mad, and do not know it: for what madmen see is precisely like what they also see who are sane; but he who is mad is alive. Nor does he answer the Academic by saying, I know I am not mad, but, I know I am alive. Therefore he who says he knows he is alive, can neither be deceived nor lie. Let a thousand kinds, then, of deceitful objects of sight be presented to him who says, I know I am alive; yet he will fear none of them, for he who is deceived yet is alive. But if such things alone pertain to human knowledge, they are very few indeed; unless that they can be so multiplied in each kind, as not only not to be few, but to reach in the result to infinity. For he who says, I know I am alive, says that he knows one single thing. Further, if he says, I know that I know I am alive, now there are two; but that he knows these two is a third thing to know. And so he can add a fourth and a fifth, and innumerable others, if he holds out. But since he

cannot either comprehend an innumerable number by additions of units, or say a thing innumerable times, he comprehends this at least, and with perfect certainty, *viz.* that this is both true and so innumerable that he cannot truly comprehend and say its infinite number. This same thing may be noticed also in the case of a will that is certain. For it would be an impudent answer to make to any one who should say, I will to be happy, that perhaps you are deceived. And if he should say, I know that I will this, and I know that I know it, he can add yet a third to these two, *viz.* that he knows these two; and a fourth, that he knows that he knows these two; and so on *ad infinitum.* Likewise, if any one were to say, I will not to be mistaken; will it not be true, whether he is mistaken or whether he is not, that nevertheless he does will not to be mistaken? Would it not be most impudent to say to him, Perhaps you are deceived? when beyond doubt, whereinsoever he may be deceived, he is nevertheless not deceived in thinking that he wills not to be deceived. And if he says he knows this, he adds any number he choses of things known, and perceives that number to be infinite. For he who says, I will not to be deceived, and I know that I will not to be so, and I know that I know it, is able now to set forth an infinite number here also, however awkward may be the expression of it. And other things too are to be found capable of refuting the Academics, who contend that man can know nothing. But we must restrict ourselves, especially as this is not the subject we have undertaken in the present work. There are three books of ours on that subject,[2] written in the early time of our conversion, which he who can and will read, and who understands them, will doubtless not be much moved by any of the many arguments which they have found out against the discovery of truth. For whereas there are two kinds of knowable things,—one, of those things which the mind perceives by the bodily senses; the other, of those which it perceives by itself,—these philosophers have babbled much against the bodily senses, but have never been able to throw doubt upon those most certain perceptions of things true, which the mind knows by itself, such as is that which I have mentioned, I know that I am alive. But far be it from us to doubt the truth of what we have learned by the bodily senses; since by them we have learned to know the heaven and the earth, and those things in them which are known to us, so far

[1] [Not the Old Academy of Plato and his immediate disciples, who were anti-skeptical; but the ew Academy, to which Augustin has previously referred (XIV. xix. 26). This was skeptical.—W. G. T. S.]

[2] *Libri Tres contra Academicos.*

as He who created both us and them has willed them to be within our knowledge. Far be it from us too to deny, that we know what we have learned by the testimony of others: otherwise we know not that there is an ocean; we know not that the lands and cities exist which most copious report commends to us; we know not that those men were, and their works, which we have learned by reading history; we know not the news that is daily brought us from this quarter or that, and confirmed by consistent and conspiring evidence; lastly, we know not at what place or from whom we have been born: since in all these things we have believed the testimony of others. And if it is most absurd to say this, then we must confess, that not only our own senses, but those of other persons also, have added very much indeed to our knowledge.

22. All these things, then, both those which the human mind knows by itself, and those which it knows by the bodily senses, and those which it has received and knows by the testimony of others, are laid up and retained in the storehouse of the memory; and from these is begotten a word that is true, when we speak what we know, but a word that is before all sound, before all thought of a sound. For the word is then most like to the thing known, from which also its image is begotten, since the sight of thinking arises from the sight of knowledge; when it is a word belonging to no tongue, but is a true word concerning a true thing, having nothing of its own, but wholly derived from that knowledge from which it is born. Nor does it signify when he learned it, who speaks what he knows; for sometimes he says it immediately upon learning it; provided only that the word is true, *i.e.* sprung from things that are known.

CHAP. 13.— STILL FURTHER OF THE DIFFERENCE BETWEEN THE KNOWLEDGE AND WORD OF OUR MIND, AND THE KNOWLEDGE AND WORD OF GOD.

But is it so, that God the Father, from whom is born the Word that is God of God, —is it so, then, that God the Father, in respect to that wisdom which He is to Himself, has learned some things by His bodily senses, and others by Himself? Who could say this, who thinks of God, not as a rational animal, but as One above the rational soul? So far at least as He can be thought of, by those who place Him above all animals and all souls, although they see Him by conjecture through a glass and in an enigma, not yet face to face as He is. Is it that God the Father has learned those very things which

He knows, not by the body, for He has none, but by Himself, from elsewhere from some one? or has stood in need of messengers or witnesses that He might know them? Certainly not; since His own perfection enables Him to know all things that He knows. No doubt He has messengers, *viz.* the angels; but not to announce to Him things that He knows not, for there is nothing He does not know. But their good lies in consulting the truth about their own works. And this it is which is meant by saying that they bring Him word of some things, not that He may learn of them, but they of Him by His word without bodily sound. They bring Him word, too, of that which He wills, being sent by Him to whomever He wills, and hearing all from Him by that word of His, *i.e.* finding in His truth what themselves are to do: what, to whom, and when, they are to bring word. For we too pray to Him, yet do not inform Him what our necessities are. "For your Father knoweth," says His Word, "what things ye have need of, before you ask Him."[1] Nor did He become acquainted with them, so as to know them, at any definite time; but He knew beforehand, without any beginning, all things to come in time, and among them also both what we should ask of Him, and when; and to whom He would either listen or not listen, and on what subjects. And with respect to all His creatures, both spiritual and corporeal, He does not know them because they are, but they are because He knows them. For He was not ignorant of what He was about to create; therefore He created because He knew; He did not know because He created. Nor did He know them when created in any other way than He knew them when still to be created, for nothing accrued to His wisdom from them; but that wisdom remained as it was, while they came into existence as it was fitting and when it was fitting. So, too, it is written in the book of Ecclesiasticus: "All things are known to Him ere ever they were created: so also after they were perfected."[2] "So," he says, not otherwise; so were they known to Him, both ere ever they were created, and after they were perfected. This knowledge, therefore, is far unlike our knowledge. And the knowledge of God is itself also His wisdom, and His wisdom is itself His essence or substance. Because in the marvellous simplicity of that nature, it is not one thing to be wise and another to be, but to be wise is to be; as we have often said already also in the earlier books. But our knowledge is in most things

---

[1] Matt. vi. 8.   [2] Ecclus. xxiii. 20.

capable both of being lost and of being recovered, because to us to be is not the same as to know or to be wise; since it is possible for us to be, even although we know not, neither are wise in that which we have learned from elsewhere. Therefore, as our knowledge is unlike that knowledge of God, so is our word also, which is born from our knowledge, unlike that Word of God which is born from the essence of the Father. And this is as if I should say, born from the Father's knowledge, from the Father's wisdom; or still more exactly, from the Father who is knowledge, from the Father who is wisdom.

CHAP. 14. — THE WORD OF GOD IS IN ALL THINGS EQUAL TO THE FATHER, FROM WHOM IT IS.

23. The Word of God, then, the only-begotten Son of the Father, in all things like and equal to the Father, God of God, Light of Light, Wisdom of Wisdom, Essence of Essence, is altogether that which the Father is, yet is not the Father, because the one is Son, the other is Father. And hence He knows all that the Father knows; but to Him to know, as to be, is from the Father, for to know and to be is there one. And therefore, as to be is not to the Father from the Son, so neither is to know. Accordingly, as though uttering Himself, the Father begat the Word equal to Himself in all things; for He would not have uttered Himself wholly and perfectly, if there were in His Word anything more or less than in Himself. And here that is recognized in the highest sense, "Yea, yea; nay, nay."[1] And therefore this Word is truly truth, since whatever is in that knowledge from which it is born is also in itself, and whatever is not in that knowledge is not in the Word. And this Word can never have anything false, because it is unchangeable, as He is from whom it is. For "the Son can do nothing of Himself, but what He seeth the Father do."[2] Through power He cannot do this; nor is it infirmity, but strength, by which truth cannot be false. Therefore God the Father knows all things in Himself, knows all things in the Son; but in Himself as though Himself, in the Son as though His own Word which Word is spoken concerning all those things that are in Himself. Similarly the Son knows all things, viz. in Himself, as things which are born of those which the Father knows in Himself, and in the Father, as those of which they are born, which the Son Himself knows in Himself. The Father, then, and the Son know mutually; but the one by begetting, the other by being born. And each of them sees simultaneously all things that are in their knowledge, in their wisdom, in their essence: not by parts or singly, as though by alternately looking from this side to that, and from that side to this, and again from this or that object to this or that object, so as not to be able to see some things without at the same time not seeing others; but, as I said, sees all things simultaneously, whereof there is not one that He does not always see.

24. And that word, then, of ours which has neither sound nor thought of sound, but is of that thing in seeing which we speak inwardly, and which therefore belongs to no tongue; and hence is in some sort like, in this enigma, to that Word of God which is also God; since this too is born of our knowledge, in such manner as that also is born of the knowledge of the Father: such a word, I say, of ours, which we find to be in some way like that Word, let us not be slow to consider how unlike also it is, as it may be in our power to utter it.

CHAP. 15. — HOW GREAT IS THE UNLIKENESS BETWEEN OUR WORD AND THE DIVINE WORD. OUR WORD CANNOT BE OR BE CALLED ETERNAL.

Is our word, then, born of our knowledge only? Do we not say many things also that we do not know? And say them not with doubt, but thinking them to be true; while if perchance they are true in respect to the things themselves of which we speak, they are yet not true in respect to our word, because a word is not true unless it is born of a thing that is known. In this sense, then, our word is false, not when we lie, but when we are deceived. And when we doubt, our word is not yet of the thing of which we doubt, but it is a word concerning the doubt itself. For although we do not know whether that is true of which we doubt, yet we do know that we doubt; and hence, when we say we doubt, we say a word that is true, for we say what we know. And what, too, of its being possible for us to lie? And when we do, certainly we both willingly and knowingly have a word that is false, wherein there is a word that is true, viz. that we lie, for this we know. And when we confess that we have lied, we speak that which is true; for we say what we know, for we know that we lied. But that Word which is God, and can do more than we, cannot do this. For it "can do nothing except what it sees the Father do;" and it "speaks not of itself," but it has from the Father all that it

[1] Matt. v. 37.　　　[2] John v. 19.

speaks, since the Father speaks it in a special way; and the great might of that Word is that it cannot lie, because there cannot be there "yea and nay," [1] but "yea yea, nay nay." Well, but that is not even to be called a word, which is not true. I willingly assent, if so it be. What, then, if our word is true, and therefore is rightly called a word? Is it the case that, as we can speak of sight of sight, and knowledge of knowledge, so we can speak of essence of essence, as that Word of God is especially spoken of, and is especially to be spoken of? Why so? Because to us, to be is not the same as to know; since we know many things which in some sense live by memory, and so in some sense die by being forgotten; and so, when those things are no longer in our knowledge, yet we still are; and while our knowledge has slipped away and perished out of our mind, we are still alive.

25. In respect to those things also which are so known that they can never escape the memory, because they are present, and belong to the nature of the mind itself,—as, *e.g.*, the knowing that we are alive (for this continues so long as the mind continues; and because the mind continues always, this also continues always);—I say, in respect to this and to any other like instances, in which we are the rather to contemplate the image of God, it is difficult to make out in what way, although they are always known, yet because they are not always also thought of, an eternal word can be spoken respecting them, when our word is spoken in our thought. For it is eternal to the soul to live; it is eternal to know that it lives. Yet it is not eternal to it to be thinking of its own life, or to be thinking of its own knowledge of its own life; since, in entering upon this or that occupation, it will cease to think of this, although it does not cease from knowing it. And hence it comes to pass, that if there can be in the mind any knowledge that is eternal, while the thought of that knowledge cannot be eternal, and any inner and true word of ours is only said by our thought, then God alone can be understood to have a Word that is eternal, and co-eternal with Himself. Unless, perhaps, we are to say that the very possibility of thought—since that which is known is capable of being truly thought, even at the time when it is not being thought—constitutes a word as perpetual as the knowledge itself is perpetual. But how is that a word which is not yet formed in the vision of the thought? How will it be like the knowledge of which it is born, if it has not the form of that knowl-

edge, and is only now called a word because it can have it? For it is much as if one were to say that a word is to be so called because it can be a word. But what is this that can be a word, and is therefore already held worthy of the name of a word? What, I say, is this thing that is formable, but not yet formed, except a something in our mind, which we toss to and fro by revolving it this way or that, while we think of first one thing and then another, according as they are found by or occur to us? And the true word then comes into being, when, as I said, that which we toss to and fro by revolving it arrives at that which we know, and is formed by that, in taking its entire likeness; so that in what manner each thing is known, in that manner also it is thought, *i.e.* is said in this manner in the heart, without articulate sound, without thought of articulate sound, such as no doubt belongs to some particular tongue. And hence if we even admit, in order not to dispute laboriously about a name, that this something of our mind, which can be formed from our knowledge, is to be already called a word, even before it is so formed, because it is, so to say, already formable, who would not see how great would be the unlikeness between it and that Word of God, which is so in the form of God, as not to have been formable before it was formed, or to have been capable at any time of being formless, but is a simple form, and simply equal to Him from whom it is, and with whom it is wonderfully co-eternal?

CHAP. 16.—OUR WORD IS NEVER TO BE EQUALLED TO THE DIVINE WORD, NOT EVEN WHEN WE SHALL BE LIKE GOD.

Wherefore that Word of God is in such wise so called, as not to be called a thought of God, lest we believe that there is anything in God which can be revolved, so that it at one time receives and at another recovers a form, so as to be a word, and again can lose that form and be revolved in some sense formlessly. Certainly that excellent master of speech knew well the force of words, and had looked into the nature of thought, who said in his poem, "And revolves with himself the varying issues of war," [2] *i.e.* thinks of them. That Son of God, then, is not called the Thought of God, but the Word of God. For our own thought, attaining to what we know, and formed thereby, is our true word. And so the Word of God ought to be understood without any thought on the part of God, so that it be understood as the simple

---

[1] 2 Cor. i. 19.

[2] *Æn.* x. 159, 160.

form itself, but containing nothing formable that can be also unformed. There are, indeed, passages of Holy Scripture that speak of God's thoughts; but this is after the same mode of speech by which the forgetfulness of God is also there spoken of, whereas in strict propriety of language there is in Him certainly no forgetfulness.

26. Wherefore, since we have found now in this enigma so great an unlikeness to God and the Word of God, wherein yet there was found before some likeness, this, too, must be admitted, that even when we shall be like Him, when "we shall see Him as He is"[1] (and certainly he who said this was aware beyond doubt of our present unlikeness), not even then shall we be equal to Him in nature. For that nature which is made is ever less than that which makes. And at that time our word will not indeed be false, because we shall neither lie nor be deceived. Perhaps, too, our thoughts will no longer revolve by passing and repassing from one thing to another, but we shall see all our knowledge at once, and at one glance. Still, when even this shall have come to pass, if indeed it shall come to pass, the creature which was formable will indeed have been formed, so that nothing will be wanting of that form to which it ought to attain; yet nevertheless it will not be to be equalled to that simplicity wherein there is not anything formable, which has been formed or re-formed, but only form; and which being neither formless nor formed, itself is eternal and unchangeable substance.

CHAP. 17.—HOW THE HOLY SPIRIT IS CALLED LOVE, AND WHETHER HE ALONE IS SO CALLED. THAT THE HOLY SPIRIT IS IN THE SCRIPTURES PROPERLY CALLED BY THE NAME OF LOVE.

27. We have sufficiently spoken of the Father and of the Son, so far as was possible for us to see through this glass and in this enigma. We must now treat of the Holy Spirit, so far as by God's gift it is permitted to see Him. And the Holy Spirit, according to the Holy Scriptures, is neither of the Father alone, nor of the Son alone, but of both; and so intimates to us a mutual love, wherewith the Father and the Son reciprocally love one another. But the language of the Word of God, in order to exercise us, has caused those things to be sought into with the greater zeal, which do not lie on the surface, but are to be scrutinized in hidden depths, and to be drawn out from thence. The Scriptures, accordingly, have not said, The Holy Spirit is Love. If they had said so,

they would have done away with no small part of this inquiry. But they have said, "God is love;"[2] so that it is uncertain and remains to be inquired whether God the Father is love, or God the Son, or God the Holy Ghost, or the Trinity itself which is God. For we are not going to say that God is called Love because love itself is a substance worthy of the name of God, but because it is a gift of God, as it is said to God, "Thou art my patience."[3] For this is not said because our patience is God's substance, but in that He Himself gives it to us; as it is elsewhere read, "Since from Him is my patience."[4] For the usage of words itself in Scripture sufficiently refutes this interpretation; for "Thou art my patience" is of the same kind as "Thou, Lord, art my hope,"[5] and "The Lord my God is my mercy,"[6] and many like texts. And it is not said, O Lord my love, or, Thou art my love, or, God my love; but it is said thus, "God is love," as it is said, "God is a Spirit."[7] And he who does not discern this, must ask understanding from the Lord, not an explanation from us; for we cannot say anything more clearly.

28. "God," then, "is love;" but the question is, whether the Father, or the Son, or the Holy Spirit, or the Trinity itself: because the Trinity is not three Gods, but one God. But I have already argued above in this book, that the Trinity, which is God, is not so to be understood from those three things which have been set forth in the trinity of our mind, as that the Father should be the memory of all three, and the Son the understanding of all three, and the Holy Spirit the love of all three; as though the Father should neither understand nor love for Himself, but the Son should understand for Him, and the Holy Spirit love for Him, but He Himself should remember only both for Himself and for them; nor the Son remember nor love for Himself, but the Father should remember for Him, and the Holy Spirit love for Him, but He Himself understand only both for Himself and them; nor likewise that the Holy Spirit should neither remember nor understand for Himself, but the Father should remember for Him, and the Son understand for Him, while He Himself should love only both for Himself and for them; but rather in this way, that both all and each have all three each in His own nature. Nor that these things should differ in them, as in us memory is one thing, understanding another, love or charity another, but should be some one thing that is

---

[1] 1 John iii. 2.

[2] 1 John iv. 16.   [3] Ps. lxxi. 5.
[4] Ps. lxii. 5.   [5] Ps. xci. 9.
[6] Ps. lix. 17.   [7] John iv. 24.

equivalent to all, as wisdom itself; and should be so contained in the nature of each, as that He who has it is that which He has, as being an unchangeable and simple substance. If all this, then, has been understood, and so far as is granted to us to see or conjecture in things so great, has been made patently true, I know not why both the Father and the Son and the Holy Spirit should not be called Love, and all together one love, just as both the Father and the Son and the Holy Spirit is called Wisdom, and all together not three, but one wisdom. For so also both the Father is God, and. the Son God, and the Holy Ghost God, and all three together one God.

29. And yet it is not to no purpose that in this Trinity the Son and none other is called the Word of God, and the Holy Spirit and none other the Gift of God, and God the Father alone is He from whom the Word is born, and from whom the Holy Spirit principally proceeds. And therefore I have added the word principally, because we find that the Holy Spirit proceeds from the Son also. But the Father gave Him this too, not as to one already existing, and not yet having it; but whatever He gave to the only-begotten Word, He gave by begetting Him. Therefore He so begat Him as that the common Gift should proceed from Him also, and the Holy Spirit should be the Spirit of both. This distinction, then, of the inseparable Trinity is not to be merely accepted in passing, but to be carefully considered; for hence it was that the Word of God was specially called also the Wisdom of God, although both Father and Holy Spirit are wisdom. If, then, any one of the three is to be specially called Love, what more fitting than that it should be the Holy Spirit?—namely, that in that simple and highest nature, substance should not be one thing and love another, but that substance itself should be love, and love itself should be substance, whether in the Father, or in the Son, or in the Holy Spirit; and yet that the Holy Spirit should be specially called Love.

30. Just as sometimes all the utterances of the Old Testament together in the Holy Scriptures are signified by the name of the Law. For the apostle, in citing a text from the prophet Isaiah, where he says, "With divers tongues and with divers lips will I speak to this people," yet prefaced it by, "It is written in the Law."[1] And the Lord Himself says, "It is written in their Law, They hated me without a cause,"[2] whereas this is read in the Psalm.[3] And sometimes that which was given by Moses is specially called the Law: as it is

said, "The Law and the Prophets were until John;"[4] and, "On these two commandments hang all the Law and the Prophets."[5] Here, certainly, that is specially called the Law which was from Mount Sinai. And the Psalms, too, are signified under the name of the Prophets; and yet in another place the Saviour Himself says, "All things must needs be fulfilled, which are written in the Law, and the Prophets, and the Psalms concerning me."[6] Here, on the other side, He meant the name of Prophets to be taken as not including the Psalms. Therefore the Law with the Prophets and the Psalms taken together is called the Law universally, and the Law is also specially so called which was given by Moses. Likewise the Prophets are so called in common together with the Psalms, and they are also specially so called exclusive of the Psalms. And many other instances might be adduced to teach us, that many names of things are both put universally, and also specially applied to particular things, were it not that a long discourse is to be avoided in a plain case. I have said so much, lest any one should think that it was therefore unsuitable for us to call the Holy Spirit Love, because both God the Father and God the Son can be called Love.

31. As, then, we call the only Word of God specially by the name of Wisdom, although universally both the Holy Spirit and the Father Himself is wisdom; so the Holy Spirit is specially called by the name of Love, although universally both the Father and the Son are love. But the Word of God, i.e. the only-begotten Son of God, is expressly called the Wisdom of God by the mouth of the apostle, where he says, "Christ the power of God, and the wisdom of God."[7] But where the Holy Spirit is called Love, is to be found by careful scrutiny of the language of John the apostle, who, after saying, "Beloved, let us love one another, for love is of God," has gone on to say, "And every one that loveth is born of God, and knoweth God. He that loveth not, knoweth not God; for God is love." Here, manifestly, he has called that love God, which he said was of God; therefore God of God is love. But because both the Son is born of God the Father, and the Holy Spirit proceeds from God the Father, it is rightly asked which of them we ought here to think is the rather called the love that is God. For the Father only is so God as not to be of God; and hence the love that is so God as to be of God, is either the Son or the Holy Spirit. But when, in what

---

[1] Isa. xxviii, 11 and 1 Cor. xiv. 21.
[2] John xv. 25. [3] Ps. xxxv. 19.
[4] Matt. xi. 13. [5] Matt. xxii. 40.
[6] Luke xxiv. 44. [7] 1 Cor. i. 24.

follows, the apostle had mentioned the love of God, not that by which we love Him, but that by which He "loved us, and sent His Son to be a propitiator for our sins,"[1] and thereupon had exhorted us also to love one another, and that so God would abide in us, —because, namely, he had called God Love; immediately, in his wish to speak yet more expressly on the subject, "Hereby," he says, "know we that we dwell in Him, and He in us, because He hath given us of His Spirit." Therefore the Holy Spirit, of whom He hath given us, makes us to abide in God, and Him in us; and this it is that love does. Therefore He is the God that is love. Lastly, a little after, when he had repeated the same thing, and had said "God is love," he immediately subjoined, "And he who abideth in love, abideth in God, and God abideth in him;" whence he had said above, "Hereby we know that we abide in Him, and He in us, because He hath given us of His Spirit." He therefore is signified, where we read that God is love. Therefore God the Holy Spirit, who proceedeth from the Father, when He has been given to man, inflames him to the love of God and of his neighbor, and is Himself love. For man has not whence to love God, unless from God; and therefore he says a little after, "Let us love Him, because He first loved us."[2] The Apostle Paul, too, says, "The love of God is shed abroad in our hearts by the Holy Ghost, which is given unto us."[3]

CHAP. 18.—NO GIFT OF GOD IS MORE EXCELLENT THAN LOVE.

32. There is no gift of God more excellent than this. It alone distinguishes the sons of the eternal kingdom and the sons of eternal perdition. Other gifts, too, are given by the Holy Spirit; but without love they profit nothing. Unless, therefore, the Holy Spirit is so far imparted to each, as to make him one who loves God and his neighbor, he is not removed from the left hand to the right. Nor is the Spirit specially called the Gift, unless on account of love. And he who has not this love, "though he speak with the tongues of men and angels, is sounding brass and a tinkling cymbal; and though he have the gift of prophecy, and know all mysteries and all knowledge, and though he have all faith, so that he can remove mountains, he is nothing; and though he bestow all his goods to feed the poor, and though he give his body to be burned, it profiteth him nothing."[4] How great a good, then, is that without which

goods so great bring no one to eternal life! But love or charity itself,—for they are two names for one thing,—if he have it that does not speak with tongues, nor has the gift of prophecy, nor knows all mysteries and all knowledge, nor gives all his goods to the poor, either because he has none to give or because some necessity hinders, nor delivers his body to be burned, if no trial of such a suffering overtakes him, brings that man to the kingdom, so that faith itself is only rendered profitable by love, since faith without love can indeed exist, but cannot profit. And therefore also the Apostle Paul says, "In Christ Jesus neither circumcision availeth anything, nor uncircumcision, but faith that worketh by love:"[5] so distinguishing it from that faith by which even "the devils believe and tremble."[6] Love, therefore, which is of God and is God, is specially the Holy Spirit, by whom the love of God is shed abroad in our hearts, by which love the whole Trinity dwells in us. And therefore most rightly is the Holy Spirit, although He is God, called also the gift of God.[7] And by that gift what else can properly be understood except love, which brings to God, and without which any other gift of God whatsoever does not bring to God?

CHAP. 19.—THE HOLY SPIRIT IS CALLED THE GIFT OF GOD IN THE SCRIPTURES. BY THE GIFT OF THE HOLY SPIRIT IS MEANT THE GIFT WHICH IS THE HOLY SPIRIT. THE HOLY SPIRIT IS SPECIALLY CALLED LOVE, ALTHOUGH NOT ONLY THE HOLY SPIRIT IN THE TRINITY IS LOVE.

33. Is this too to be proved, that the Holy Spirit is called in the sacred books the gift of God? If people look for this too, we have in the Gospel according to John the words of our Lord Jesus Christ, who says, "If any one thirst, let him come to me and drink: he that believeth on me, as the Scripture saith, out of his belly shall flow rivers of living water." And the evangelist has gone on further to add, "And this He spake of the Spirit, which they should receive who believe in Him."[8] And hence Paul the apostle also says, "And we have all been made to drink into one Spirit."[9] The question then is, whether that water is called the gift of God which is the Holy Spirit. But as we find here that this water is the Holy Spirit, so we find elsewhere in the Gospel itself that this water is called the gift of God. For when the same Lord was talking with the woman of Samaria at the well, to whom He had said, "Give me

1 John iv. 10.　2 1 John iv. 7-19.　5 Gal. v. 6.　6 Jas. ii. 19.　7 Acts viii. 20.
3 Rom. v. 5.　4 1 Cor. xiii. 1-3.　8 John vii. 37-39.　9 1 Cor. xii. 13.

to drink," and she had answered that the Jews "have no dealings" with the Samaritans, Jesus answered and said unto her, "If thou hadst known the gift of God, and who it is that says to thee, Give me to drink, thou wouldest have asked of Him, and He would have given thee living water. The woman saith unto Him, Sir, thou hast nothing to draw with, and the well is deep: whence then hast thou this living water, etc.? Jesus answered and said unto her, Every one that drinketh of this water shall thirst again; but whoso shall drink of the water that I shall give him, shall never thirst; but the water that I shall give him, shall be in him a fountain of water springing up unto eternal life." [1] Because this living water, then, as the evangelist has explained to us, is the Holy Spirit, without doubt the Spirit is the gift of God, of which the Lord says here, "If thou hadst known the gift of God, and who it is that saith unto thee, Give me to drink, thou wouldest have asked of Him, and He would have given thee living water." For that which is in the one passage, "Out of his belly shall flow rivers of living water," is in the other, "shall be in him a fountain of water springing up unto eternal life."

34. Paul the apostle also says, "To each of us is given grace according to the measure of the gift of Christ;" and then, that he might show that by the gift of Christ he meant the Holy Spirit, he has gone on to add, "Wherefore He saith, He hath ascended up on high, He hath led captivity captive, and hath given gifts to men." [2] And every one knows that the Lord Jesus, when He had ascended into heaven after the resurrection from the dead, gave the Holy Spirit, with whom they who believed were filled, and spake with the tongues of all nations. And let no one object that he says gifts, not gift: for he quoted the text from the Psalm. And in the Psalm it is read thus, "Thou hast ascended up on high, Thou hast led captivity captive, Thou hast received gifts in men." [3] For so it stands in many MSS., especially in the Greek MSS., and so we have it translated from the Hebrew. The apostle therefore said gifts, as the prophet did, not gift. But whereas the prophet said, "Thou hast received gifts in men," the apostle has preferred saying, "He gave gifts to men:" and this in order that the fullest sense may be gathered from both expressions, the one prophetic, the other apostolic; because both possess the authority of a divine utterance. For both are true, as well that He gave to men,

as that He received in men. He gave to men, as the head to His own members: He Himself that gave, received in men, no doubt as in His own members; on account of which, namely, His own members, He cried from heaven, "Saul, Saul, why persecutest thou me?" [4] And of which, namely, His own members, He says, "Since ye have done it to one of the least of these that are mine, ye have done it unto me." [5] Christ Himself, therefore, both gave from heaven and received on earth. And further, both prophet and apostle have said gifts for this reason, because many gifts, which are proper to each, are divided in common to all the members of Christ, by the Gift, which is the Holy Spirit. For each severally has not all, but some have these and some have those; although all have the Gift itself by which that which is proper to each is divided to Him, i.e. the Holy Spirit. For elsewhere also, when he had mentioned many gifts, "All these," he says, "worketh that one and the self-same Spirit, dividing to each severally as He will." [6] And this word is found also in the Epistle to the Hebrews, where it is written, "God also bearing witness both with signs and wonders, and with divers miracles, and gifts [7] of the Holy Ghost." [8] And so here, when he had said, "He ascended up on high, He led captivity captive, He gave gifts to men," he says further, "But that He ascended, what is it but that He also first descended into the lower parts of the earth? He who descended is the same also that ascended up far above all heavens, that He might fill all things. And He gave some apostles, some prophets, and some evangelists, and some pastors and doctors." (This we see is the reason why gifts are spoken of; because, as he says elsewhere, "Are all apostles? are all prophets?" [9] etc.) And here he has added, "For the perfecting of the saints, for the work of the ministry, for the building up of the body of Christ." [10] This is the house which, as the Psalm sings, is built up after the captivity; [11] since the house of Christ, which house is called His Church, is built up of those who have been rescued from the devil, by whom they were held captive. But He Himself led this captivity captive, who conquered the devil. And that he might not draw with him into eternal punishment those who were to become the members of the Holy Head, He bound him first by the bonds of righteousness, and then by those of might. The devil himself, there-

1 John iv. 7-14.　2 Eph. iv. 7, 8.　3 Ps. lxviii. 18.

4 Acts ix. 4.　5 Matt. xxv. 40.
6 1 Cor. xii. 11.　7 Distributionibus.
8 Heb. ii. 4.　9 1 Cor. xii. 29.
10 Eph. iv. 7-12.　11 Ps. cxxvi. 1.

fore, is called captivity, which He led captive who ascended up on high, and gave gifts to men, or received gifts in men.

35. And Peter the apostle, as we read in that canonical book, wherein the Acts of the Apostles are recorded,—when the hearts of the Jews were troubled as he spake of Christ, and they said, "Brethren, what shall we do? tell us,"—said to them, "Repent, and be baptized every one of you in the name of the Lord Jesus Christ, for the remission of sins: and ye shall receive the gift of the Holy Spirit."[1] And we read likewise in the same book, that Simon Magus desired to give money to the apostles, that he might receive power from them, whereby the Holy Spirit might be given by the laying on of his hands. And the same Peter said to him, "Thy money perish with thee: because thou hast thought to purchase for money the gift of God."[2] And in another place of the same book, when Peter was speaking to Cornelius, and to those who were with him, and was announcing and preaching Christ, the Scripture says, "While Peter was still speaking these words, the Holy Spirit fell upon all them that heard the word; and they of the circumcision that believed, as many as came with Peter, were astonished, because that upon the Gentiles also the gift of the Holy Spirit was poured out. For they heard them speak with tongues, and magnify God."[3] And when Peter afterwards was giving an account to the brethren that were at Jerusalem of this act of his, that he had baptized those who were not circumcised, because the Holy Spirit, to cut the knot of the question, had come upon them before they were baptized, and the brethren at Jerusalem were moved when they heard it, he says, after the rest of his words, "And when I began to speak to them, the Holy Spirit fell upon them, as upon us in the beginning. And I remembered the word of the Lord, how He said, that John indeed baptized with water, but ye shall be baptized with the Holy Spirit. If, therefore, He gave a like gift to them, as also to us who believed in the Lord Jesus Christ, who was I, that I could hinder God from giving to them the Holy Spirit?"[4] And there are many other testimonies of the Scriptures, which unanimously attest that the Holy Spirit is the gift of God, in so far as He is given to those who by Him love God. But it is too long a task to collect them all. And what is enough to satisfy those who are not satisfied with those we have alleged?

36. Certainly they must be warned, since they now see that the Holy Spirit is called

the gift of God, that when they hear of "the gift of the Holy Spirit," they should recognize therein that mode of speech which is found in the words, "In the spoiling of the body of the flesh."[5] For as the body of the flesh is nothing else but the flesh, so the gift of the Holy Spirit is nothing else but the Holy Spirit. He is then the gift of God, so far as He is given to those to whom He is given. But in Himself He is God, although He were given to no one, because He was God co-eternal with the Father and the Son before He was given to any one. Nor is He less than they, because they give, and He is given. For He is given as a gift of God in such way that He Himself also gives Himself as being God. For He cannot be said not to be in His own power, of whom it is said, "The Spirit bloweth where it listeth;"[6] and the apostle says, as I have already mentioned above, "All these things worketh that selfsame Spirit, dividing to every man severally as He will." We have not here the creating of Him that is given, and the rule of them that give, but the concord of the given and the givers.

37. Wherefore, if Holy Scripture proclaims that God is love, and that love is of God, and works this in us that we abide in God and He in us, and that hereby we know this, because He has given us of His Spirit, then the Spirit Himself is God, who is love. Next, if there be among the gifts of God none greater than love, and there is no greater gift of God than the Holy Spirit, what follows more naturally than that He is Himself love, who is called both God and of God? And if the love by which the Father loves the Son, and the Son loves the Father, ineffably demonstrates the communion of both, what is more suitable than that He should be specially called love, who is the Spirit common to both? For this is the sounder thing both to believe and to understand, that the Holy Spirit is not alone love in that Trinity, yet is not specially called love to no purpose, for the reasons we have alleged; just as He is not alone in that Trinity either a Spirit or holy, since both the Father is a Spirit, and the Son is a Spirit; and both the Father is holy, and the Son is holy,—as piety doubts not. And yet it is not to no purpose that He is specially called the Holy Spirit; for because He is common to both, He is specially called that which both are in common. Otherwise, if in that Trinity the Holy Spirit alone is love, then doubtless the Son too turns out to be the Son, not of the Father only, but also of the Holy

---

[1] Acts ii. 37, 38.
[2] Acts viii. 18-20.
[3] Acts x. 44, 46.
[4] Acts xi. 15-17.
[5] Col. ii. 11.
[6] John iii. 6.

Spirit. For He is both said and read in countless places to be so,—the only-begotten Son of God the Father; as that what the apostle says of God the Father is true too: "Who hath delivered us from the power of darkness, and hath translated us into the kingdom of the Son of His own love." [1] He did not say, "of His own Son." If He had so said, He would have said it most truly, just as He did say it most truly, because He has often said it ; but He says, "the Son of His own love." Therefore He is the Son also of the Holy Spirit, if there is in that Trinity no love in God except the Holy Spirit. And if this is most absurd, it remains that the Holy Spirit is not alone therein love, but is specially so called for the reasons I have sufficiently set forth; and that the words, "Son of His own love," mean nothing else than His own beloved Son,—the Son, in short, of His own substance. For the love in the Father, which is in His ineffably simple nature, is nothing else than His very nature and substance itself, —as we have already often said, and are not ashamed of often repeating. And hence the "Son of His love," is none other than He who is born of His substance.

CHAP. 20.—AGAINST EUNOMIUS, SAYING THAT THE SON OF GOD IS THE SON, NOT OF HIS NATURE, BUT OF HIS WILL. EPILOGUE TO WHAT HAS BEEN SAID ALREADY.

38. Wherefore the logic of Eunomius, from whom the Eunomian heretics sprang, is ridiculous. For when he could not understand, and would not believe, that the only-begotten Word of God, by which all things were made, is the Son of God by nature,—*i.e.* born of the substance of the Father,—he alleged that He was not the Son of His own nature or substance or essence, but the Son of the will of God; so as to mean to assert that the will by which he begat the Son was something accidental [and optional] to God,—to wit, in that way that we ourselves sometimes will something which before we did not will, as though it was not for these very things that our nature is perceived to be changeable,—a thing which far be it from us to believe of God. For it is written, "Many are the thoughts in the heart of man, but the counsel of the Lord abideth for ever," [2] for no other reason except that we may understand or believe that as God is eternal, so is His counsel for eternity, and therefore unchangeable, as He himself is. And what is said of thoughts can most truly be said also of the will: there are many wills in the heart of man, but the will of the Lord

abideth for ever. Some, again, to escape saying that the only-begotten Word is the Son of the counsel or will of God, have affirmed the same Word to be the counsel or will itself of the Father. But it is better in my judgment to say counsel of counsel, and will of will, as substance of substance, wisdom of wisdom, that we may not be led into that absurdity, which we have refuted already, and say that the Son makes the Father wise or willing, if the Father has not in His own substance either counsel or will. It was certainly a sharp answer that somebody gave to the heretic, who most subtly asked him whether God begat the Son willingly or unwillingly, in order that if he said unwillingly, it would follow most absurdly that God was miserable; but if willingly, he would forthwith infer, as though by an invincible reason, that at which he was aiming, *viz.* that He was the Son, not of His nature, but of His will. But that other, with great wakefulness, demanded of him in turn, whether God the Father was God willingly or unwillingly; in order that if he answered unwillingly, that misery would follow, which to believe of God is sheer madness; and if he said willingly, it would be replied to him, Then He is God too by His own will, not by His nature. What remained, then, except that he should hold his peace, and discern that he was himself bound by his own question in an insoluble bond? But if any person in the Trinity is also to be specially called the will of God, this name, like love, is better suited to the Holy Spirit; for what else is love, except will?

39. I see that my argument in this book respecting the Holy Spirit, according to the Holy Scripture, is quite enough for faithful men who know already that the Holy Spirit is God, and not of another substance, nor less than the Father and the Son,—as we have shown to be true in the former books, according to the same Scriptures. We have reasoned also from the creature which God made, and, as far as we could, have warned those who demand a reason on such subjects to behold and understand His invisible things, so far as they could, by those things which are made,[3] and especially by the rational or intellectual creature which is made after the image of God; through which glass, so to say, they might discern as far as they could, if they could, the Trinity which is God, in our own memory, understanding, will. Which three things, if any one intelligently regards as by nature divinely appointed in his own mind, and remembers by memory, contemplates by

---

[1] Col. i. 13.   [2] Prov. xix. 21.   [3] Rom. i. 20.

understanding, embraces by love, how great a thing that is in the mind, whereby even the eternal and unchangeable nature can be recollected, beheld, desired, doubtless that man finds an image of that highest Trinity. And he ought to refer the whole of his life to the remembering, seeing, loving that highest Trinity, in order that he may recollect, contemplate, be delighted by it. But I have warned him, so far as seemed sufficient, that he must not so compare this image thus wrought by that Trinity, and by his own fault changed for the worse, to that same Trinity as to think it in all points like to it, but rather that he should discern in that likeness, of whatever sort it be, a great unlikeness also.

CHAP. 21.—OF THE LIKENESS OF THE FATHER AND OF THE SON ALLEGED TO BE IN OUR MEMORY AND UNDERSTANDING. OF THE LIKENESS OF THE HOLY SPIRIT IN OUR WILL OR LOVE.

40. I have undoubtedly taken pains so far as I could, not indeed so that the thing might be seen face to face, but that it might be seen by this likeness in an enigma,[1] in how small a degree soever, by conjecture, in our memory and understanding, to intimate God the Father and God the Son: *i.e.* God the begetter, who has in some way spoken by His own co-eternal Word all things that He has in His substance; and God His Word Himself, who Himself has nothing either more or less in substance than is in Him, who, not lyingly but truly, hath begotten the Word; and I have assigned to memory everything that we know, even if we were not thinking of it, but to understanding the formation after a certain special mode of the thought. For we are usually said to understand what, by thinking of it, we have found to be true; and this it is again that we leave in the memory. But that is a still more hidden depth of our memory, wherein we found this also first when we thought of it, and wherein an inner word is begotten such as belongs to no tongue,—as it were, knowledge of knowledge, vision of vision, and understanding which appears in [reflective] thought; of understanding which had indeed existed before in the memory, but was latent there, although, unless the thought itself had also some sort of memory of its own, it would not return to those things which it had left in the memory while it turned to think of other things.

41. But I have shown nothing in this enigma respecting the Holy Spirit such as might appear to be like Him, except our own

will, or love, or affection, which is a stronger will, since our will which we have naturally is variously affected, according as various objects are adjacent or occur to it, by which we are attracted or offended. What, then, is this? Are we to say that our will, when it is right, knows not what to desire, what to avoid? Further, if it knows, doubtless then it has a kind of knowledge of its own, such as cannot be without memory and understanding. Or are we to listen to any one who should say that love knows not what it does, which does not do wrongly? As, then, there are both understanding and love in that primary memory wherein we find provided and stored up that to which we can come in thought, because we find also those two things there, when we find by thinking that we both understand and love anything; which things were there too when we were not thinking of them: and as there are memory and love in that understanding, which is formed by thought, which true word we say inwardly without the tongue of any nation when we say what we know; for the gaze of our thought does not return to anything except by remembering it, and does not care to return unless by loving it: so love, which combines the vision brought about in the memory, and the vision of the thought formed thereby, as if parent and offspring, would not know what to love rightly unless it had a knowledge of what it desired, which it cannot have without memory and understanding.

CHAP. 22.—HOW GREAT THE UNLIKENESS IS BETWEEN THE IMAGE OF THE TRINITY WHICH WE HAVE FOUND IN OURSELVES, AND THE TRINITY ITSELF.

42. But since these are in one person, as man is, some one may say to us, These three things, memory, understanding, and love, are mine, not their own; neither do they do that which they do for themselves, but for me, or rather I do it by them. For it is I who remember by memory, and understand by understanding, and love by love: and when I direct the mind's eye to my memory, and so say in my heart the thing I know, and a true word is begotten of my knowledge, both are mine, both the knowledge certainly and the word. For it is I who know, and it is I who say in my heart the thing I know. And when I come to find in my memory by thinking that I understand and love anything, which understanding and love were there also before I thought thereon, it is my own understanding and my own love that I find in my own memory, whereby it is I that understand,

---

[1] 1 Cor. xiii. 12.

and I that love, not those things themselves. Likewise, when my thought is mindful, and wills to return to those things which it had left in the memory, and to understand and behold them, and say them inwardly, it is my own memory that is mindful, and it is my own, not its will, wherewith it wills. When my very love itself, too, remembers and understands what it ought to desire and what to avoid, it remembers by my, not by its own memory; and understands that which it intelligently loves by my, not by its own, understanding. In brief, by all these three things, it is I that remember, I that understand, I that love, who am neither memory, nor understanding, nor love, but who have them. These things, then, can be said by a single person, which has these three, but is not these three. But in the simplicity of that Highest Nature, which is God, although there is one God, there are three persons, the Father, the Son, and the Holy Spirit.

CHAP. 23.—AUGUSTIN DWELLS STILL FURTHER ON THE DISPARITY BETWEEN THE TRINITY WHICH IS IN MAN, AND THE TRINITY WHICH IS GOD. THE TRINITY IS NOW SEEN THROUGH A GLASS BY THE HELP OF FAITH, THAT IT MAY HEREAFTER BE MORE CLEARLY SEEN IN THE PROMISED SIGHT FACE TO FACE.

43. A thing itself, then, which is a trinity is different from the image of a trinity in some other thing; by reason of which image, at the same time that also in which these three things are is called an image; just as both the panel, and the picture painted on it, are at the same time called an image; but by reason of the picture painted on it, the panel also is called by the name of image. But in that Highest Trinity, which is incomparably above all things, there is so great an indivisibility, that whereas a trinity of men cannot be called one man, in that, there both is said to be and is one God, nor is that Trinity in one God, but it is one God. Nor, again, as that image in the case of man has these three things but is one person, so is it with the Trinity; but therein are three persons, the Father of the Son, and the Son of the Father, and the Spirit of both Father and Son. For although the memory in the case of man, and especially that memory which beasts have not—*viz.* the memory by which things intelligible are so contained as that they have not entered that memory through the bodily senses [1]—has in this image of the Trinity, in

proportion to its own small measure, a likeness of the Father, incomparably unequal, yet of some sort, whatever it be: and likewise the understanding in the case of man, which by the purpose of the thought is formed thereby, when that which is known is said, and there is a word of the heart belonging to no tongue, has in its own great disparity some likeness of the Son; and love in the case of man proceeding from knowledge, and combining memory and understanding, as though common to parent and offspring, whereby it is understood to be neither parent nor offspring, has in that image, some, however exceedingly unequal, likeness of the Holy Spirit: it is nevertheless not the case, that, as in that image of the Trinity, these three are not one man, but belong to one man, so in the Highest Trinity itself, of which this is an image, these three belong to one God, but they are one God, and these are three persons, not one. A thing certainly wonderfully ineffable, or ineffably wonderful, that while this image of the Trinity is one person, but the Highest Trinity itself is three persons, yet that Trinity of three persons is more indivisible than this of one. For that [Trinity], in the nature of the Divinity, or perhaps better Deity, is that which it is, and is mutually and always unchangeably equal: and there was no time when it was not, or when it was otherwise; and there will be no time when it will not be, or when it will be otherwise. But these three that are in the inadequate image, although they are not separate in place, for they are not bodies, yet are now in this life mutually separate in magnitude. For that there are therein no several bulks, does not hinder our seeing that memory is greater than understanding in one man, but the contrary in another; and that in yet another these two are overpassed by the greatness of love; and this whether the two themselves are or are not equal to one another. And so each two by each one, and each one by each two, and each one by each one: the less are surpassed by the greater. And when they have been healed of all infirmity, and are mutually equal, not even then will that thing which by grace will not be changed, be made equal to that which by nature cannot change, because the creature cannot be equalled to the Creator, and when it shall be healed from all infirmity, will be changed.

44. But when the sight shall have come which is promised anew to us face to face, we

---

[1] [The reader will observe that Augustin has employed the term "memory" in a wider sense than in the modern ordinary use. With him, it is the mind as including all that is potential or latent in it. The innate ideas, in this use, are laid up in the "memory," and called into consciousness or "remembered" by reflection. The idea of God, for example, is not in the "memory" when not elicited by reflection. The same is true of the ideas of space and time, etc.—W. G. T. S.]

shall see this not only incorporeal but also absolutely indivisible and truly unchangeable Trinity far more clearly and certainly than we now see its image which we ourselves are: and yet they who see through this glass and in this enigma, as it is permitted in this life to see, are not those who behold in their own mind the things which we have set in order and pressed upon them; but those who see this as if an image, so as to be able to refer what they see, in some way be it what it may, to Him whose image it is, and to see that also by conjecturing, which they see through the image by beholding, since they cannot yet see face to face. For the apostle does not say, We see now a glass, but, We see now through a glass.[1]

CHAP. 24. — THE INFIRMITY OF THE HUMAN MIND.

They, then, who see their own mind, in whatever way that is possible, and in it that Trinity of which I have treated as I could in many ways, and yet do not believe or understand it to be an image of God, see indeed a glass, but do not so far see through the glass Him who is now to be seen through the glass, that they do not even know the glass itself which they see to be a glass, i.e. an image. And if they knew this, perhaps they would feel that He too whose glass this is, should by it be sought, and somehow provisionally be seen, an unfeigned faith purging their hearts,[2] that He who is now seen through a glass may be able to be seen face to face. And if they despise this faith that purifies the heart, what do they accomplish by understanding the most subtle disputes concerning the nature of the human mind, unless that they be condemned also by the witness of their own understanding? And they would certainly not so fail in understanding, and hardly arrive at anything certain, were they not involved in penal darkness, and burdened with the corruptible body that presses down the soul.[3] And for what demerit save that of sin is this evil inflicted on them? Wherefore, being warned by the magnitude of so great an evil, they ought to follow the Lamb that taketh away the sins of the world.[4]

CHAP. 25.—THE QUESTION WHY THE HOLY-SPIRIT IS NOT BEGOTTEN, AND HOW HE PROCEEDS FROM THE FATHER AND THE SON, WILL ONLY BE UNDERSTOOD WHEN WE ARE IN BLISS.

For if any belong to Him, although far duller in intellect than those, yet when they are freed from the body at the end of this life, the envious powers have no right to hold

them. For that Lamb that was slain by them without any debt of sin has conquered them; but not by the might of power before He had done so by the righteousness of blood. And free accordingly from the power of the devil, they are borne up by holy angels, being set free from all evils by the mediator of God and men, the man Christ Jesus.[5] Since by the harmonious testimony of the Divine Scriptures, both Old and New, both those by which Christ was foretold, and those by which He was announced, there is no other name under heaven whereby men must be saved.[6] And when purged from all contagion of corruption, they are placed in peaceful abodes until they take their bodies again, their own, but now incorruptible, to adorn, not to burden them. For this is the will of the best and most wise Creator, that the spirit of a man, when piously subject to God, should have a body happily subject, and that this happiness should last for ever.

45. There we shall see the truth without any difficulty, and shall enjoy it to the full, most clear and most certain. Nor shall we be inquiring into anything by a mind that reasons, but shall discern by a mind that contemplates, why the Holy Spirit is not a Son, although He proceeds from the Father. In that light there will be no place for inquiry: but here, by experience itself it has appeared to me so difficult,—as beyond doubt it will likewise appear to them also who shall carefully and intelligently read what I have written,—that although in the second book[7] I promised that I would speak thereof in another place, yet as often as I have desired to illustrate it by the creaturely image of it which we ourselves are, so often, let my meaning be of what sort it might, did adequate utterance entirely fail me; nay, even in my very meaning I felt that I had attained to endeavor rather than accomplishment. I had indeed found in one person, such as is a man, an image of that Highest Trinity, and had desired, especially in the ninth book, to illustrate and render more intelligible the relation of the Three Persons by that which is subject to time and change. But three things belonging to one person cannot suit those Three Persons, as man's purpose demands; and this we have demonstrated in this fifteenth book.

CHAP. 26.—THE HOLY SPIRIT TWICE GIVEN BY CHRIST. THE PROCESSION OF THE HOLY SPIRIT FROM THE FATHER AND FROM THE SON IS APART FROM TIME, NOR CAN HE BE CALLED THE SON OF BOTH.

Further, in that Highest Trinity which is

---

[1] Cor. xiii. 12. [2] 1 Tim. i. 5.
[3] Wisd. ix. 15. [4] John i. 29.

[5] 1 Tim. ii. 5. [6] Acts iv. 12. C. 3.

God, there are no intervals of time, by which it could be shown, or at least inquired, whether the Son was born of the Father first, and then afterwards the Holy Spirit proceeded from both; since Holy Scripture calls Him the Spirit of both. For it is He of whom the apostle says, " But because ye are sons, God hath sent forth the Spirit of His Son into your hearts:"[1] and it is He of whom the same Son says, " For it is not ye who speak, but the Spirit of your Father who speaketh in you."[2] And it is proved by many other testimonies of the Divine Word, that the Spirit, who is specially called in the Trinity the Holy Spirit, is of the Father and of the Son: of whom likewise the Son Himself says, " Whom I will send unto you from the Father;"[3] and in another place, " Whom the Father will send in my name."[4] And we are so taught that He proceeds from both, because the Son Himself says, He proceeds from the Father. And when He had risen from the dead, and had appeared to His disciples, " He breathed upon them, and said, Receive the Holy Ghost,"[5] so as to show that He proceeded also from Himself. And Itself is that very "power that went out from Him," as we read in the Gospel, " and healed them all."[6]

46. But the reason why, after His resurrection, He both gave the Holy Spirit, first on earth,[7] and afterwards sent Him from heaven,[8] is in my judgment this: that "love is shed abroad in our hearts,"[9] by that Gift itself, whereby we love God and our neighbors, according to those two commandments, " on which hang all the law and the prophets."[10] And Jesus Christ, in order to signify this, gave to them the Holy Spirit, once upon earth, on account of the love of our neighbor, and a second time from heaven, on account of the love of God. And if some other reason may perhaps be given for this double gift of the Holy Spirit, at any rate we ought not to doubt that the same Holy Spirit was given when Jesus breathed upon them, of whom He by and by says, " Go, baptize all nations in the name of the Father, and of the Son, and of the Holy Spirit," where this Trinity is especially commended to us. It is therefore He who was also given from heaven on the day of Pentecost, i.e. ten days after the Lord ascended into heaven. How, therefore, is He not God, who gives the Holy Spirit? Nay, how great a God is He who gives God! For no one of His disciples gave the Holy Spirit, since they prayed that He might come upon those upon whom they laid their hands: they did not give Him themselves. And the Church preserves this custom even now in the case of her rulers. Lastly, Simon Magus also, when he offered the apostles money, does not say, " Give me also this power, that I may give " the Holy Spirit; but, " that on whomsoever I may lay my hands, he may receive the Holy Spirit." Because neither had the Scriptures said before, And Simon, seeing that the apostles gave the Holy Spirit; but it had said," And Simon, seeing that the Holy Spirit was given by the laying on of the apostles' hands."[11] Therefore also the Lord Jesus Christ Himself not only gave the Holy Spirit as God, but also received it as man, and therefore He is said to be full of grace,[12] and of the Holy Spirit.[13] And in the Acts of the Apostles it is more plainly written of Him, " Because God anointed Him with the Holy Spirit."[14] Certainly not with visible oil but with the gift of grace which is signified by the visible ointment wherewith the Church anoints the baptized. And Christ was certainly not then anointed with the Holy Spirit, when He, as a dove, descended upon Him at His baptism.[15] For at that time He deigned to prefigure His body, i.e. His Church, in which especially the baptized receive the Holy Spirit. But He is to be understood to have been then anointed with that mystical and invisible unction, when the Word of God was made flesh,[16] i.e. when human nature, without any precedent merits of good works, was joined to God the Word in the womb of the Virgin, so that with it it became one person. Therefore it is that we confess Him to have been born of the Holy Spirit and of the Virgin Mary. For it is most absurd to believe Him to have received the Holy Spirit when He was near thirty years old: for at that age He was baptized by John;[17] but that He came to baptism as without any sin at all, so not without the Holy Spirit. For if it was written of His servant and forerunner John himself, " He shall be filled with the Holy Spirit, even from his mother's womb,"[18] because, although generated by his father, yet he received the Holy Spirit when formed in the womb; what must be understood and believed of the man Christ, of whose flesh the very conception was not carnal, but spiritual? Both natures, too, as well the human as the divine, are shown in that also that is written of Him, that He received of the Father the promise of the Holy Spirit, and shed forth the Holy Spirit:[19] seeing

---

[1] Gal. iv. 6.　　　　　[2] Matt. x. 20.
[3] John xv. 26.　　　　[4] John xiv. 26.
[5] John xx. 23.　　　　[6] Luke vi. 19.
[7] John xx. 22.　　　　[8] Acts ii. 4.
[9] Rom. v. 5.　　　　　[10] Matt. xxii. 37-40.

[11] Acts viii. 18, 19.　　　[12] John i. 14.
[13] Luke ii. 52 and iv. 1.　[14] Acts x. 38.
[15] Matt. iii. 16.　　　　[16] John i. 14.
[17] Luke iii. 21-23.　　　[18] Luke i. 15.　　[19] Acts ii. 33.

that He received as man, and shed forth as God. And we indeed can receive that gift according to our small measure, but assuredly we cannot shed it forth upon others; but, that this may be done, we invoke over them God, by whom this is accomplished.

47. Are we therefore able to ask whether the Holy Spirit had already proceeded from the Father when the Son was born, or had not yet proceeded, and when He was born, proceeded from both, wherein there is no such thing as distinct times: just as we have been able to ask, in a case where we do find times, that the will proceeds from the human mind first, in order that that may be sought which, when found, may be called offspring; which offspring being already brought forth or born, that will is made perfect, resting in this end, so that what had been its desire when seeking, is its love when enjoying; which love now proceeds from both, *i.e.* from the mind that begets, and from the notion that is begotten, as if from parent and offspring? These things it is absolutely impossible to ask in this case, where nothing is begun in time, so as to be perfected in a time following. Wherefore let him who can understand the generation of the Son from the Father without time, understand also the procession of the Holy Spirit from both without time. And let him who can understand, in that which the Son says, "As the Father hath life in Himself, so hath He given to the Son to have life in Himself,"[1] not that the Father gave life to the Son already existing without life, but that He so begat Him apart from time, that the life which the Father gave to the Son by begetting Him is co-eternal with the life of the Father who gave it:[2] let him, I say, understand, that as the Father has in Himself that the Holy Spirit should proceed from Him, so has He given to the Son that the same Holy Spirit should proceed from Him, and be both apart from time: and that the Holy Spirit is so said to proceed from the Father as that it be understood that His proceeding also from the Son, is a property derived by the Son from the Father. For if the Son has of the Father whatever He has, then certainly He has of the Father, that the Holy Spirit proceeds also from Him. But let no one think of any times therein which imply a sooner and a later; because these things are not there at all. How, then, would it not be most absurd to call Him the Son of both:

when, just as generation from the Father, without any changeableness of nature, gives to the Son essence, without beginning of time; so procession from both, without any changeableness of nature, gives to the Holy Spirit essence without beginning of time? For while we do not say that the Holy Spirit is begotten, yet we do not therefore dare to say that He is unbegotten, lest any one suspect in this word either two Fathers in that Trinity, or two who are not from another. For the Father alone is not from another, and therefore He alone is called unbegotten, not indeed in the Scriptures,[3] but in the usage of disputants, who employ such language as they can on so great a subject. And the Son is born of the Father; and the Holy Spirit proceeds from the Father principally, the Father giving the procession without any interval of time, yet in common from both [Father and Son].[4] But He would be called the Son of the Father and of the Son, if—a thing abhorrent to the feeling of all sound minds—both had *begotten* Him. Therefore the Spirit of both is not begotten of both, but proceeds from both.

CHAP. 27.—WHAT IT IS THAT SUFFICES HERE TO SOLVE THE QUESTION WHY THE SPIRIT IS NOT SAID TO BE BEGOTTEN, AND WHY THE FATHER ALONE IS UNBEGOTTEN. WHAT THEY OUGHT TO DO WHO DO NOT UNDERSTAND THESE THINGS.

48. But because it is most difficult to distinguish generation from procession in that co-eternal, and equal, and incorporeal, and ineffably unchangeable and indivisible Trinity, let it suffice meanwhile to put before those who are not able to be drawn on further, what we said upon this subject in a sermon to be delivered in the ears of Christian people, and after saying wrote it down. For when, among other things, I had taught them by testimonies of the Holy Scriptures that the Holy Spirit proceeds from both, I continue: "If, then, the Holy Spirit proceeds both from the Father and from the Son, why did the Son say, 'He proceedeth from the Father?'"[5] Why, think you, except as He is wont to refer to Him, that also which is His

---

[1] John v. 26.
[2] [Says Turrettin, III. xxix. 21. "The Father does not generate the Son either as previously existing, for in this case there would be no need of generation; nor yet as not yet existing, for in this case the Son would not be eternal; but as *co-existing*, because he is from eternity in the God-head."—W. G. T. S.]

[3] [The term "unbegotten" is not found in Scripture, but it is implied in the terms "begotten" and "only-begotten," which are found. The term "unity" is not applied to God in Scripture, but it is implied in the term "one" which is so applied.—W. G. T. S.]
[4] [The spiration and procession of the Holy Spirit is not by two separate acts, one of the Father, and one of the Son—as perhaps might be inferred from Augustin's remark that "the Holy Spirit proceeds from the Father principally." As Turrettin says: "The Father and Son spirate the Spirit, not as two different essences in each of which resides a spirative energy, but as two personal subsistences of one essence, who concur in one act of spiration." *Institutio* III. xxxi. 6.—W. G. T. S.]
[5] John xv. 26.

15

own, from whom also He Himself is? Whence also is that which He saith, "My doctrine is not mine own, but His that sent me?"[1] If, therefore, it is His doctrine that is here understood, which yet He said was not His own, but His that sent Him, how much more is it there to be understood that the Holy Spirit proceeds also from Himself, where He so says, He proceedeth from the Father, as not to say, He proceedeth not from me? From Him, certainly, from whom the Son had his Divine nature, for He is God of God, He has also, that from Him too proceeds the Holy Spirit; and hence the Holy Spirit has from the Father Himself, that He should proceed from the Son also, as He proceeds from the Father. Here, too, in some way may this also be understood, so far as it can be understood by such as we are, why the Holy Spirit is not said to be born, but rather to proceed;[2] since if He, too, was called a Son, He would certainly be called the Son of both, which is most absurd, since no one is son of two, save of father and mother. But far be it from us to surmise any such thing as this between God the Father and God the Son. Because not even the son of men proceeds at the same time from both father and mother; but when he proceeds from the father into the mother, he does not at that time proceed from the mother; and when he proceeds from the mother into this present light, he does not at that time proceed from the father. But the Holy Spirit does not proceed from the Father into the Son, and from the Son proceed to sanctify the creature, but proceeds at once from both; although the Father has given this to the Son, that He should proceed, as from Himself, so also from Him. For we cannot say that the Holy Spirit is not life, while the Father is life, and the Son is life: and hence as the Father, while He has life in Himself, has given also to the Son to have life in Himself; so has He given also to Him that life should proceed from Him, as it also proceeds from Himself."[3] I have transferred

this from that sermon into this book, but I was speaking to believers, not to unbelievers.

49. But if they are not competent to gaze upon this image, and to see how true these things are which are in their mind, and yet which are not so three as to be three persons, but all three belong to a man who is one person; why do they not believe what they find in the sacred books respecting that highest Trinity which is God, rather than insist on the clearest reason being rendered them, which cannot be comprehended by the human mind, dull and infirm as it is? And to be sure, when they have steadfastly believed the Holy Scriptures as most true witnesses, let them strive, by praying and seeking and living well, that they may understand, i.e. that so far as it can be seen, that may be seen by the mind which is held fast by faith. Who would forbid this? Nay, who would not rather exhort them to it? But if they think they ought to deny that these things are, because they, with their blind minds, cannot discern them, they, too, who are blind from their birth, ought to deny that there is a sun. The light then shineth in darkness; but if the darkness comprehend it not,[4] let them first be illuminated by the gift of God, that they may be believers, and let them begin to be light in comparison with the unbelievers; and when this foundation is first laid, let them be built up to see what they believe, that at some time they may be able to see. For some things are so believed, that they cannot be seen at all. For Christ is not to be seen a second time on the cross; but unless this be believed which has been so done and seen, that it is not now to be hoped for as about to be and to be seen, there is no coming to Christ, such as without end He is to be seen. But as far as relates to the discerning in some way by the understanding that highest, ineffable, incorporeal, and unchangeable nature the sight of the human mind can nowhere better exercise itself, so only that the rule of faith govern it, than in that which man himself has in his own nature better than the other animals, better also than the other parts of his own soul, which is the mind itself, to which has been assigned a certain sight of things invisible, and to which, as though honorably presiding in a higher and inner place, the bodily senses also bring word of all things, that they may be judged, and than which there is no higher, to which it is to be subject, and by which it is to be governed, except God.

50. But among these many things which I have now said, and of which there is nothing

---

[1] John vii. 16.

[2] [Generation and procession are each an emanation of the essence by which it is modified. Neither of them is a creation *ex nihilo*. The school-men attempted to explain the difference between the two emanations, by saying that the generation of the Son is by the mode of the intellect—hence the Son is called Wisdom, or Word (Logos); but the procession of the Spirit is by the mode of the will—hence the Spirit is called Love. Turrettin distinguishes the difference by the following particulars: 1. In respect to the source. Generation is from the Father alone; procession is from Father and Son. 2. In respect to effects. Generation yields not only personality, but resemblance. The Son is the "image" of the Father; but the Spirit is not the image of the Father and Son. Generation is accompanied with the power to communicate the essence; procession is not. 3. In respect to order of relationship. Generation is second, procession is third. In the order of nature, not of time (for both generation and procession are eternal, therefore simultaneous), procession is after generation. *Institutio* III. xxxi. 3.—W. G .T. S.]

[3] Serm. in *Joh. Evang. tract.* 99, n. 8, 9.

[4] John i. 5.

that I dare to profess myself to have said worthy of the ineffableness of that highest Trinity, but rather to confess that the wonderful knowledge of Him is too great for me, and that I cannot attain[1] to it: O thou, my soul, where dost thou feel thyself to be? where dost thou lie? where dost thou stand? until all thy infirmities be healed by Him who has forgiven all thy iniquities.[2] Thou perceivest thyself assuredly to be in that inn whither that Samaritan brought him whom he found with many wounds inflicted by thieves, half-dead.[3] And yet thou hast seen many things that are true, not by those eyes by which colored objects are seen, but by those for which he prayed who said, "Let mine eyes behold the things that are equal."[4] Certainly, then, thou hast seen many things that are true, and hast distinguished them from that light by the light of which thou hast seen them. Lift up thine eyes to the light itself, and fix them upon it if thou canst. For so thou wilt see how the birth of the Word of God differs from the procession of the Gift of God, on account of which the only-begotten Son did not say that the Holy Spirit is begotten of the Father, otherwise He would be His brother, but that He proceeds from Him. Whence, since the Spirit of both is a kind of consubstantial communion of Father and Son, He is not called, far be it from us to say so, the Son of both. But thou canst not fix thy sight there, so as to discern this lucidly and clearly; I know thou canst not. I say the truth, I say to myself, I know what I cannot do; yet that light itself shows to thee these three things in thyself, wherein thou mayest recognize an image of the highest Trinity itself, which thou canst not yet contemplate with steady eye. Itself shows to thee that there is in thee a true word, when it is born of thy knowledge, i.e. when we say what we know: although we neither utter nor think of any articulate word that is significant in any tongue of any nation, but our thought is formed by that which we know; and there is in the mind's eye of the thinker an image resembling that thought which the memory contained, will or love as a third combining these two as parent and offspring. And he who can, sees and discerns that this will proceeds indeed from thought (for no one wills that of which he is absolutely ignorant what or of what sort it is), yet is not an image of the thought: and so that there is insinuated in this intelligible thing a sort of difference between birth and procession, since to behold by thought is not the same as to desire, or

even to enjoy will. Thou, too, hast been able [to discern this], although thou hast not been, neither art, able to unfold with adequate speech what, amidst the clouds of bodily likenesses, which cease not to flit up and down before human thoughts, thou hast scarcely seen. But that light which is not thyself shows thee this too, that these incorporeal likenesses of bodies are different from the truth, which, by rejecting them, we contemplate with the understanding. These, and other things similarly certain, that light hath shown to thine inner eyes. What reason, then, is there why thou canst not see that light itself with steady eye, except certainly infirmity? And what has produced this in thee, except iniquity? Who, then, is it that healeth all thine infirmities, unless it be He that forgiveth all thine iniquities? And therefore I will now at length finish this book by a prayer better than by an argument.

CHAP. 28. — THE CONCLUSION OF THE BOOK WITH A PRAYER, AND AN APOLOGY FOR MULTITUDE OF WORDS.

51. O Lord our God, we believe in Thee, the Father and the Son and the Holy Spirit. For the Truth would not say, Go, baptize all nations in the name of the Father and of the Son and of the Holy Spirit, unless Thou wast a Trinity. Nor wouldest thou, O Lord God, bid us to be baptized in the name of Him who is not the Lord God. Nor would the divine voice have said, Hear, O Israel, the Lord thy God is one God, unless Thou wert so a Trinity as to be one Lord God. And if Thou, O God, wert Thyself the Father, and wert Thyself the Son, Thy Word Jesus Christ, and the Holy Spirit your gift, we should not read in the book of truth, "God sent His Son;"[5] nor wouldest Thou, O Only-begotten, say of the Holy Spirit, "Whom the Father will send in my name;"[6] and, "Whom I will send to you from the Father."[7] Directing my purpose by this rule of faith, so far as I have been able, so far as Thou hast made me to be able, I have sought Thee, and have desired to see with my understanding what I believed; and I have argued and labored much. O Lord my God, my one hope, hearken to me, lest through weariness I be unwilling to seek Thee, "but that I may always ardently seek Thy face."[8] Do Thou give strength to seek, who hast made me find Thee, and hast given the hope of finding Thee more and more. My strength and my infirmity are in Thy sight: preserve the one, and heal the other.

---

[1] Ps. cxxxix. 5.   [2] Ps. ciii. 3.   [5] Gal. iv. 5 and John iii. 17.   [6] John xiv. 26.
[3] Luke x. 30, 34.   [4] Ps. xvii. 2.   [7] John xv. 26.   [8] Ps. cv. 4.

My knowledge and my ignorance are in Thy sight; where Thou hast opened to me, receive me as I enter; where Thou hast closed, open to me as I knock. May I remember Thee, understand Thee, love Thee. Increase these things in me, until Thou renewest me wholly. I know it is written, "In the multitude of speech, thou shalt not escape sin."[1] But O that I might speak only in preaching Thy word, and in praising Thee! Not only should I so flee from sin, but I should earn good desert, however much I so spake. For a man blessed of Thee would not enjoin a sin upon his own true son in the faith, to whom he wrote, "Preach the word: be instant in season, out of season."[2] Are we to say that he has not spoken much, who was not silent about Thy word, O Lord, not only in season, but out of season? But therefore it was not much, because it was only what was necessary. Set me free, O God, from that multitude of speech which I suffer inwardly in my soul, wretched as it is in Thy sight, and flying for refuge to Thy mercy; for I am not silent in thoughts, even when silent in words. And if, indeed, I thought of nothing save what pleased Thee, certainly I would not ask Thee to set me free from such multitude of speech. But many are my thoughts, such as Thou knowest, "thoughts of man, since they are vain."[3] Grant to me not to consent to them; and if ever they delight me, nevertheless to condemn them, and not to dwell in them, as though I slumbered. Nor let them so prevail in me, as that anything in my acts should proceed from them; but at least let my opinions, let my conscience, be safe from them, under Thy protection. When the wise man spake of Thee in his book, which is now called by the special name of Ecclesiasticus, "We speak," he said, "much, and yet come short; and in sum of words, He is all."[4] When, therefore, we shall have come to Thee, these very many things that we speak, and yet come short, will cease; and Thou, as One, wilt remain "all in all."[5] And we shall say one thing without end, in praising Thee in One, ourselves also made one in Thee. O Lord the one God, God the Trinity, whatever I have said in these books that is of Thine, may they acknowledge who are Thine; if anything of my own, may it be pardoned both by Thee and by those who are Thine. Amen.

---

[1] Prov. x. 19.   [2] 2 Tim. iv. 2.   [3] Ps. xciv. 11.   [4] Ecclus. xliii. 29.   [5] 1 Cor. xv. 28.

ST. AUGUSTIN:

THE ENCHIRIDION;

OR

ON FAITH, HOPE, AND LOVE

TRANSLATED BY

PROFESSOR J F. SHAW,

LONDONDERRY.

INTRODUCTORY NOTICE

By the Editor.

St. Augustin speaks of this book in his *Retractations*, l. ii. c. 63, as follows:

"I also wrote a book on *Faith, Hope, and Charity*, at the request of the person to whom I addressed it, that he might have a work of mine which should never be out of his hands, such as the Greeks call an *Enchiridion* (*Hand-Book*). There I think I have pretty carefully treated of the manner in which God is to be worshipped, which knowledge divine Scripture defines to be the true wisdom of man. The book begins: 'I cannot express,'" etc.[1]

The *Enchiridion* is among the latest books of Augustin. It was written after the death of Jerome, which occurred Sept. 30, 420; for he alludes in ch. 87 to Jerome "of blessed memory" (*sanctæ memoriæ Hieronymus presbyter*).

It is addressed to Laurentius, in answer to his questions. This person is otherwise unknown. One MS. calls him a deacon, another a notary of the city of Rome. He was probably a layman.

The author usually calls the book "On Faith, Hope and Love," because he treats the subject under these three heads (comp. I Cor. xiii. 13). He follows under the first head the order of the Apostles' Creed, and refutes, without naming them, the Manichæan, Apollinarian, Arian, and Pelagian heresies. Under the second head he gives a brief exposition of the Lord's Prayer. The third part is a discourse on Christian love.

The original is in the sixth volume of the Benedictine edition. A neat edition of the Latin text, with three other small tracts of Augustin, (*De Catechizandis Rudibus ; De Fide Rerum quæ non creduntur ; De Utilitate Credendi*), is also published in C. Marriott's *S. Aurelius Augustinus*, 4th ed. by H. de Romestin, Oxford and London (Parker and Comp.), 1885 (pp. 150-251.) An English edition of the same tracts by H. de Romestin, Oxford and London, 1885 (pp. 151-251). His English translation is based on that of C. L. Cornish, M.A., which appeared in the Oxford "Library of the Fathers," Oxford 1847 ("Seventeen Short Treatises of St. Aug." pp. 85-158).

The present translation by Professor Shaw was first published in Dr. Dods's series of Augustin's works, Edinburgh, (T. and T. Clark,) 3d ed. 1883. It is more free and idiomatic than that of Cornish. I have in a few cases conformed it more closely to the original.

P. S.

---

[1] "*Scripsi etiam librum 'de Fide, Spe et Charitate' cum a me ad quem scriptus est postulasset ut aliquod opusculum haberet meum de suis manibus nunquam recessurum, quod genus Græci* ENCHIRIDION *vocant. Ubi satis diligenter mihi videor esse complexus quomodo sit colendus Deus quam sapientiam esse hominis utique veram Divina Scriptura definit. Hic liber sic incipit, 'Dici non potest, dilectissime fili Laurenti, quantum tuâ eruditione delecter.'*"

CONTENTS OF THE ENCHIRIDION.

THE ENCHIRIDION,

ADDRESSED TO LAURENTIUS;

BEING A TREATISE ON FAITH, HOPE AND LOVE.

ARGUMENT.

LAURENTIUS HAVING ASKED AUGUSTIN TO FURNISH HIM WITH A HANDBOOK OF CHRISTIAN DOC-
TRINE, CONTAINING IN BRIEF COMPASS ANSWERS TO SEVERAL QUESTIONS WHICH HE HAD
PROPOSED, AUGUSTIN SHOWS HIM THAT THESE QUESTIONS CAN BE FULLY ANSWERED BY ANY
ONE WHO KNOWS THE PROPER OBJECTS OF FAITH, HOPE, AND LOVE. HE THEN PROCEEDS,
IN THE FIRST PART OF THE WORK (CHAP. IX.–CXIII.), TO EXPOUND THE OBJECTS OF FAITH,
TAKING AS HIS TEXT THE APOSTLES' CREED ; AND IN THE COURSE OF THIS EXPOSITION, BE-
SIDES REFUTING DIVERS HERESIES, HE THROWS OUT MANY OBSERVATIONS ON THE CONDUCT
OF LIFE. THE SECOND PART OF THE WORK (CHAP. CXIV.–CXVI.) TREATS OF THE OBJECTS
OF HOPE, AND CONSISTS OF A VERY BRIEF EXPOSITION OF THE SEVERAL PETITIONS IN THE
LORD'S PRAYER. THE THIRD AND CONCLUDING PART (CHAP. CXVII.-CXXII.) TREATS OF THE
OBJECTS OF LOVE, SHOWING THE PRE-EMINENCE OF THIS GRACE IN THE GOSPEL SYSTEM, THAT
IT IS THE END OF THE COMMANDMENT AND THE FULFILLING OF THE LAW, AND THAT GOD
HIMSELF IS LOVE.

CHAP. I.—THE AUTHOR DESIRES THE GIFT OF TRUE WISDOM FOR LAURENTIUS.

I CANNOT express, my beloved son Laurentius, the delight with which I witness your
progress in knowledge, and the earnest desire
I have that you should be a wise man: not one
of those of whom it is said, "Where is the wise ?
where is the scribe? where is the disputer of
this world? hath not God made foolish the
wisdom of this world ?"[1] but one of those of
whom it is said, " The multitude of the wise
is the welfare of the world,"[2] and such as the
apostles wishes those to become, whom he
tells," I would have you wise unto that which
is good, and simple concerning evil."[3] Now,
just as no one can exist of himself, so no one
can be wise of himself, but only by the enlightening influence of Him of whom it is
written," All wisdom cometh from the Lord."[4]

CHAP. 2.—THE FEAR OF GOD IS MAN'S TRUE WISDOM.

The true wisdom of man is piety. You
find this in the book of holy Job. For we read
there what wisdom itself has said to man:
" Behold, the fear of the Lord [*pietas*], that
is wisdom."[5] If you ask further what is
meant in that place by *pietas*, the Greek calls
it more definitely θεοσέβεια, that is, the worship of God. The Greeks sometimes call
piety εὐσέβεια, which signifies right worship,
though this, of course, refers specially to the
worship of God. But when we are defining

---

[1] 1 Cor. i. 20.
[2] Wisd. vi. 24. [Greek text, ver. 25: πλῆθος σοφῶν σωτηρία
κόσμου.—P. S.]   [3] Rom. xvi. 19.

[4] Ecclus. i. 1.   [5] Job xxviii. 28.

in what man's true wisdom consists, the most convenient word to use is that which distinctly expresses the fear of God. And can you, who are anxious that I should treat of great matters in few words, wish for a briefer form of expression? Or perhaps you are anxious that this expression should itself be briefly explained, and that I should unfold in a short discourse the proper mode of worshipping God?

CHAP. 3.—GOD IS TO BE WORSHIPPED THROUGH FAITH, HOPE, AND LOVE.

Now if I should answer, that God is to be worshipped with faith, hope, and love, you will at once say that this answer is too brief, and will ask me briefly to unfold the objects of each of these three graces, viz., what we are to believe, what we are to hope for, and what we are to love. And when I have done this, you will have an answer to all the questions you asked in your letter. If you have kept a copy of your letter, you can easily turn it up and read it over again: if you have not, you will have no difficulty in recalling it when I refresh your memory.

CHAP. 4. — THE QUESTIONS PROPOUNDED BY LAURENTIUS.

You are anxious, you say, that I should write a sort of handbook for you, which you might always keep beside you, containing answers to the questions you put, viz.: what ought to be man's chief end in life ; what he ought, in view of the various heresies, chiefly to avoid; to what extent religion is supported by reason ; what there is in reason that lends no support to faith, when faith stands alone; what is the starting-point, what the goal, of religion; what is the sum of the whole body of doctrine ; what is the sure and proper foundation of the catholic faith. Now, undoubtedly, you will know the answers to all these questions, if you know thoroughly the proper objects of faith, hope, and love. For these must be the chief, nay, the exclusive objects of pursuit in religion. He who speaks against these is either a total stranger to the name of Christ, or is a heretic. These are to be defended by reason, which must have its starting-point either in the bodily senses or in the intuitions of the mind. And what we have neither had experience of through our bodily senses, nor have been able to reach through the intellect, must undoubtedly be believed on the testimony of those witnesses by whom the Scriptures, justly called divine, were written ; and who by divine assistance were enabled, either through bodily sense or

intellectual perception, to see or to foresee the things in question.

CHAP. 5.—BRIEF ANSWERS TO THESE QUESTIONS.

Moreover, when the mind has been imbued with the first elements of that faith which worketh by love,[1] it endeavors by purity of life to attain unto sight, where the pure and perfect in heart know that unspeakable beauty, the full vision of which is supreme happiness. Here surely is an answer to your question as to what is the starting-point, and what the goal : we begin in faith, and are made perfect by sight. This also is the sum of the whole body of doctrine. But the sure and proper foundation of the catholic faith is Christ. "For other foundation," says the apostle, "can no man lay than that is laid, which is Jesus Christ."[2] Nor are we to deny that this is the proper foundation of the catholic faith, because it may be supposed that some heretics hold this in common with us. For if we carefully consider the things that pertain to Christ, we shall find that, among those heretics who call themselves Christians, Christ is present in name only : in deed and in truth He is not among them. But to show this would occupy us too long, for we should require to go over all the heresies which have existed, which do exist, or which could exist, under the Christian name, and to show that this is true in the case of each,—a discussion which would occupy so many volumes as to be all but interminable.

CHAP. 6.—CONTROVERSY OUT OF PLACE IN A HANDBOOK LIKE THE PRESENT.

Now you ask of me a handbook, that is, one that can be carried in the hand, not one to load your shelves. To return, then, to the three graces through which, as I have said, God should be worshipped—faith, hope, and love: to state what are the true and proper objects of each of these is easy. But to defend this true doctrine against the assaults of those who hold an opposite opinion, requires much fuller and more elaborate instruction. And the true way to obtain this instruction is not to have a short treatise put into one's hands, but to have a great zeal kindled in one's heart.

CHAP. 7.—THE CREED AND THE LORD'S PRAYER DEMAND THE EXERCISE OF FAITH, HOPE, AND LOVE.

For you have the Creed and the Lord's Prayer. What can be briefer to hear or to read? What easier to commit to memory?

---

[1] Gal. v. 6.   [2] 1 Cor. iii. 11.

When, as the result of sin, the human race was groaning under a heavy load of misery, and was in urgent need of the divine compassion, one of the prophets, anticipating the time of God's grace, declared : " And it shall come to pass, that whosoever shall call on the name of the Lord shall be delivered."[1] Hence the Lord's Prayer. But the apostle, when, for the purpose of commending this very grace, he had quoted this prophetic testimony, immediately added: " How then shall they call on Him in whom they have not believed ? "[2] Hence the Creed. In these two you have those three graces exemplified: faith believes, hope and love pray. But without faith the two last cannot exist, and therefore we may say that faith also prays. Whence it is written: " How shall they call on Him in whom they have not believed ? "

CHAP. 8.—THE DISTINCTION BETWEEN FAITH AND HOPE, AND THE MUTUAL DEPENDENCE OF FAITH, HOPE, AND LOVE.

Again, can anything be hoped for which is not an object of faith ? It is true that a thing which is not an object of hope may be believed. What true Christian, for example, does not believe in the punishment of the wicked ? And yet such an one does not hope for it. And the man who believes that punishment to be hanging over himself, and who shrinks in horror from the prospect, is more properly said to fear than to hope. And these two states of mind the poet carefully distinguishes, when he says : " Permit the fearful to have hope."[3] Another poet, who is usually much superior to this one, makes a wrong use of the word, when he says : " If I have been able to hope for so great a grief as this."[4] And some grammarians take this case as an example of impropriety of speech, saying, " He said *sperare* [to hope] instead of *timere* [to fear]." Accordingly, faith may have for its object evil as well as good ; for both good and evil are believed, and the faith that believes them is not evil, but good. Faith, moreover, is concerned with the past, the present, and the future, all three. We believe, for example, that Christ died,—an event in the past ; we believe that He is sitting at the right hand of God,—a state of things which is present ; we believe that He will come to judge the quick and the dead,—an event of the future. Again, faith applies both to one's own circumstances and those of others. Every one, for example, believes that his own existence

had a beginning, and was not eternal, and he believes the same both of other men and other things. Many of our beliefs in regard to religious matters, again, have reference not merely to other men, but to angels also. But hope has for its object only what is good, only what is future, and only what affects the man who entertains the hope. For these reasons, then, faith must be distinguished from hope, not merely as a matter of verbal propriety, but because they are essentially different. The fact that we do not see either what we believe or what we hope for, is all that is common to faith and hope. In the Epistle to the Hebrews, for example, faith is defined (and eminent defenders of the catholic faith have used the definition as a standard) "the evidence of things not seen."[5] Although, should any one say that he believes, that is, has grounded his faith, not on words, nor on witnesses, nor on any reasoning whatever, but on the direct evidence of his own senses, he would not be guilty of such an impropriety of speech as to be justly liable to the criticism, "You saw, therefore you did not believe." And hence it does not follow that an object of faith is not an object of sight. But it is better that we should use the word "faith" as the Scriptures have taught us, applying it to those things which are not seen. Concerning hope, again, the apostle says: "Hope that is seen is not hope ; for what a man seeth, why doth he yet hope for ? But if we hope for that we see not, then do we with patience wait for it."[6] When, then, we believe that good is about to come, this is nothing else but to hope for it. Now what shall I say of love ? Without it, faith profits nothing; and in its absence, hope cannot exist. The Apostle James says : "The devils also believe, and tremble."[7]—that is, they, having neither hope nor love, but believing that what we love and hope for is about to come, are in terror. And so the Apostle Paul approves and commends the "faith that worketh by love;"[8] and this certainly cannot exist without hope. Wherefore there is no love without hope, no hope without love, and neither love nor hope without faith.

CHAP. 9.—WHAT WE ARE TO BELIEVE. IN REGARD TO NATURE IT IS NOT NECESSARY FOR THE CHRISTIAN TO KNOW MORE THAN THAT THE GOODNESS OF THE CREATOR IS THE CAUSE OF ALL THINGS.

When, then, the question is asked what we are to believe in regard to religion, it is not necessary to probe into the nature of things,

---

1 Joel. ii. 32.					2 Rom. x. 14.
3 Lucan, *Phars.* ii. 15.			4 Virgil. *Æneid*, iv. 419.

5 Heb. xi. 1.					6 Rom. viii. 24, 25.
7 Jas. ii. 19.					8 Gal. v. 6.

as was done by those whom the Greeks call *physici*; nor need we be in alarm lest the Christian should be ignorant of the force and number of the elements,—the motion, and order, and eclipses of the heavenly bodies; the form of the heavens ; the species and the natures of animals, plants, stones, fountains, rivers, mountains; about chronology and distances ; the signs of coming storms ; and a thousand other things which those philosophers either have found out, or think they have found out. For even these men themselves, endowed though they are with so much genius, burning with zeal, abounding in leisure, tracking some things by the aid of human conjecture, searching into others with the aids of history and experience, have not found out all things; and even their boasted discoveries are oftener mere guesses than certain knowledge. It is enough for the Christian to believe that the only cause of all created things, whether heavenly or earthly, whether visible or invisible, is the goodness of the Creator, the one true God; and that nothing exists but Himself that does not derive its existence from Him ; and that He is the Trinity—to wit, the Father, and the Son begotten of the Father, and the Holy Spirit proceeding from the same Father, but one and the same Spirit of Father and Son.

CHAP. 10.—THE SUPREMELY GOOD CREATOR MADE ALL THINGS GOOD.

By the Trinity, thus supremely and equally and unchangeably good, all things were created; and these are not supremely and equally and unchangeably good, but yet they are good, even taken separately. Taken as a whole, however, they are very good, because their *ensemble* constitutes the universe in all its wonderful order and beauty.

CHAP. 11.—WHAT IS CALLED EVIL IN THE UNIVERSE IS BUT THE ABSENCE OF GOOD.

And in the universe, even that which is called evil, when it is regulated and put in its own place, only enhances our admiration of the good; for we enjoy and value the good more when we compare it with the evil. For the Almighty God, who, as even the heathen acknowledge, has supreme power over all things, being Himself supremely good, would never permit the existence of anything evil among His works, if He were not so omnipotent and good that He can bring good even out of evil. For what is that which we call evil but the absence of good ? In the bodies of animals, disease and wounds mean nothing but the absence of health ; for when a cure is effected, that does not mean that the evils which were present—namely, the diseases and wounds— go away from the body and dwell elsewhere : they altogether cease to exist ; for the wound or disease is not a substance, but a defect in the fleshly substance,—the flesh itself being a substance, and therefore something good, of which those evils—that is, privations of the good which we call health—are accidents. Just in the same way, what are called vices in the soul are nothing but privations of natural good. And when they are cured, they are not transferred elsewhere : when they cease to exist in the healthy soul, they cannot exist anywhere else.

CHAP. 12.—ALL BEINGS WERE MADE GOOD, BUT NOT BEING MADE PERFECTLY GOOD, ARE LIABLE TO CORRUPTION.

All things that exist, therefore, seeing that the Creator of them all is supremely good, are themselves good. But because they are not, like their Creator, supremely and unchangeably good, their good may be diminished and increased. But for good to be diminished is an evil, although, however much it may be diminished, it is necessary, if the being is to continue, that some good should remain to constitute the being. For however small or of whatever kind the being may be, the good which makes it a being cannot be destroyed without destroying the being itself. An uncorrupted nature is justly held in esteem. But if, still further, it be incorruptible, it is undoubtedly considered of still higher value. When it is corrupted, however, its corruption is an evil, because it is deprived of some sort of good. For if it be deprived of no good, it receives no injury; but it does receive injury, therefore it is deprived of good. Therefore, so long as a being is in process of corruption, there is in it some good of which it is being deprived; and if a part of the being should remain which cannot be corrupted, this will certainly be an incorruptible being, and accordingly the process of corruption will result in the manifestation of this great good. But if it do not cease to be corrupted, neither can it cease to possess good of which corruption may deprive it. But if it should be thoroughly and completely consumed by corruption, there will then be no good left, because there will be no being. Wherefore corruption can consume the good only by consuming the being. Every being, therefore, is a good ; a great good, if it can not be corrupted; a little good, if it can : but in any case, only the foolish or ignorant will deny that it is a good. And if it be wholly consumed by corruption, then the corruption itself must cease to exist, as there is no being left in which it can dwell.

CHAP. 13.—THERE CAN BE NO EVIL WHERE THERE IS NO GOOD; AND AN EVIL MAN IS AN EVIL GOOD.

Accordingly, there is nothing of what we call evil, if there be nothing good. But a good which is wholly without evil is a perfect good. A good, on the other hand, which contains evil is a faulty or imperfect good; and there can be no evil where there is no good. From all this we arrive at the curious result: that since every being, so far as it is a being, is good, when we say that a faulty being is an evil being, we just seem to say that what is good is evil, and that nothing but what is good can be evil, seeing that every being is good, and that no evil can exist except in a being. Nothing, then, can be evil except something which is good. And although this, when stated, seems to be a contradiction, yet the strictness of reasoning leaves us no escape from the conclusion. We must, however, beware of incurring the prophetic condemnation: "Woe unto them that call evil good, and good evil: that put darkness for light, and light for darkness: that put bitter for sweet, and sweet for bitter."[1] And yet our Lord says: "An evil man out of the evil treasure of his heart bringeth forth that which is evil."[2] Now, what is an evil man but an evil being? for a man is a being. Now, if a man is a good thing because he is a being, what is an evil man but an evil good? Yet, when we accurately distinguish these two things, we find that it is not because he is a man that he is an evil, or because he is wicked that he is a good; but that he is a good because he is a man, and an evil because he is wicked. Whoever, then, says, "To be a man is an evil," or, "To be wicked is a good," falls under the prophetic denunciation: "Woe unto them that call evil good, and good evil!" For he condemns the work of God, which is the man, and praises the defect of man, which is the wickedness. Therefore every being, even if it be a defective one, in so far as it is a being is good, and in so far as it is defective is evil.

CHAP. 14.—GOOD AND EVIL ARE AN EXCEPTION TO THE RULE THAT CONTRARY ATTRIBUTES CANNOT BE PREDICATED OF THE SAME SUBJECT. EVIL SPRINGS UP IN WHAT IS GOOD, AND CANNOT EXIST EXCEPT IN WHAT IS GOOD.

Accordingly, in the case of these contraries which we call good and evil, the rule of the logicians, that two contraries cannot be predicated at the same time of the same thing, does not hold. No weather is at the same time dark and bright: no food or drink is at the same time sweet and bitter: no body is at the same time and in the same place black and white: none is at the same time and in the same place deformed and beautiful. And this rule is found to hold in regard to many, indeed nearly all, contraries, that they cannot exist at the same time in any one thing. But although no one can doubt that good and evil are contraries, not only can they exist at the same time, but evil cannot exist without good, or in anything that is not good. Good, however, can exist without evil. For a man or an angel can exist without being wicked; but nothing can be wicked except a man or an angel: and so far as he is a man or an angel, he is good; so far as he is wicked, he is an evil. And these two contraries are so far co-existent, that if good did not exist in what is evil, neither could evil exist; because corruption could not have either a place to dwell in, or a source to spring from, if there were nothing that could be corrupted; and nothing can be corrupted except what is good, for corruption is nothing else but the destruction of good. From what is good, then, evils arose, and except in what is good they do not exist; nor was there any other source from which any evil nature could arise. For if there were, then, in so far as this was a being, it was certainly a good: and a being which was incorruptible would be a great good; and even one which was corruptible must be to some extent a good, for only by corrupting what was good in it could corruption do it harm.

CHAP. 15.—THE PRECEDING ARGUMENT IS IN NO WISE INCONSISTENT WITH THE SAYING OF OUR LORD: "A GOOD TREE CANNOT BRING FORTH EVIL FRUIT."

But when we say that evil springs out of good, let it not be thought that this contradicts our Lord's saying: "A good tree cannot bring forth evil fruit."[3] For, as He who is the Truth says, you cannot gather grapes of thorns,[4] because grapes do not grow on thorns. But we see that on good soil both vines and thorns may be grown. And in the same way, just as an evil tree cannot bring forth good fruit, so an evil will cannot produce good works. But from the nature of man, which is good, may spring either a good or an evil will. And certainly there was at first no source from which an evil will could spring, except

1 Isa. v. 20.   2 Luke vi. 45.   3 Matt. vii. 18.   4 Matt. vii. 16.

the nature of angel or of man, which was good. And our Lord Himself clearly shows this in the very same place where He speaks about the tree and its fruit. For He says: " Either make the tree good, and his frùit good; or else make the tree corrupt, and his fruit corrupt," [1]—clearly enough warning us that evil fruits do not grow on a good tree, nor good fruits on an evil tree; but that nevertheless the ground itself, by which He meant those whom He was then addressing, might grow either kind of trees.

CHAP. 16.—IT IS NOT ESSENTIAL TO MAN'S HAPPINESS THAT HE SHOULD KNOW THE CAUSES OF PHYSICAL CONVULSIONS; BUT IT IS, THAT HE SHOULD KNOW THE CAUSES OF GOOD AND EVIL.

Now, in view of these considerations, when we are pleased with that line of Maro, " Happy the man who has attained to the knowledge of the causes of things," [2] we should not suppose that it is necessary to happiness to know the causes of the great physical convulsions, causes which lie hid in the most secret recesses of nature's kingdom, " whence comes the earthquake whose force makes the deep seas to swell and burst their barriers, and again to return upon themselves and settle down." [3] But we ought to know the causes of good and evil as far as man may in this life know them, in order to avoid the mistakes and troubles of which this life is so full. For our aim must always be to reach that state of happiness in which no trouble shall distress us, and no error mislead us. If we must know the causes of physical convulsions, there are none which it concerns us more to know than those which affect our own health. But seeing that, in our ignorance of these, we are fain to resort to physicians, it would seem that we might bear with considerable patience our ignorance of the secrets that lie hid in the earth and heavens.

CHAP. 17.—THE NATURE OF ERROR. ALL ERROR IS NOT HURTFUL, THOUGH IT IS MAN'S DUTY AS FAR AS POSSIBLE TO AVOID IT.

For although we ought with the greatest possible care to avoid error, not only in great but even in little things, and although we cannot err except through ignorance, it does not follow that, if a man is ignorant of a thing, he must forthwith fall into error. That is rather the fate of the man who thinks he knows what he does not know. For he accepts what is false as if it were true, and that is the essence of error. But it is a point of very great importance what the subject is in regard to which a man makes a mistake. For on one and the same subject we rightly prefer an instructed man to an ignorant one, and a man who is not in error to one who is. In the case of different subjects, however,—that is, when one man knows one thing, and another a different thing, and when what the former knows is useful, and what the latter knows is not so useful, or is actually hurtful,—who would not, in regard to the things the latter knows, prefer the ignorance of the former to the knowledge of the latter? For there are points on which ignorance is better than knowledge. And in the same way, it has sometimes been an advantage to depart from the right way,—in travelling, however, not in morals. It has happened to myself to take the wrong road where two ways met, so that I did not pass by the place where an armed band of Donatists lay in wait for me. Yet I arrived at the place whither I was bent, though by a roundabout route; and when I heard of the ambush, I congratulated myself on my mistake, and gave thanks to God for it. Now, who would not rather be the traveller who made a mistake like this, than the highwayman who made no mistake? And hence, perhaps, it is that the prince of poets puts these words into the mouth of a lover in misery: [4] " How I am undone, how I have been carried away by an evil error ! " for there is an error which is good, as it not merely does no harm, but produces some actual advantage. But when we look more closely into the nature of truth, and consider that to err is just to take the false for the true, and the true for the false, or to hold what is certain as uncertain, and what is uncertain as certain, and that error in the soul is hideous and repulsive just in proportion as it appears fair and plausible when we utter it, or assent to it, saying, " Yea, yea; Nay, nay,"—surely this life that we live is wretched indeed, if only on this account, that sometimes, in order to preserve it, it is necessary to fall into error. God forbid that such should be that other life, where truth itself is the life of the soul, where no one deceives, and no one is deceived. But here men deceive and are deceived, and they are more to be pitied when they lead others astray than when they are themselves led astray by putting trust in liars. Yet so much does a rational soul shrink from what is false, and so earnestly does it struggle against error, that even those who love to deceive are most unwilling to be deceived. For the liar does not

---

[1] Matt. xii. 33.
[2] Virgil, *Georgics*, ii. 490.   [3] *Ibid.*

[4] Virgil, *Eclog.* viii. 41.

think that he errs, but that he leads another who trusts him into error. And certainly he does not err in regard to the matter about which he lies, if he himself knows the truth; but he is deceived in this, that he thinks his lie does him no harm, whereas every sin is more hurtful to the sinner than to the sinned against.

CHAP. 18.—IT IS NEVER ALLOWABLE TO TELL A LIE; BUT LIES DIFFER VERY MUCH IN GUILT, ACCORDING TO THE INTENTION AND THE SUBJECT.

But here arises a very difficult and very intricate question, about which I once wrote a large book, finding it necessary to give it an answer. The question is this: whether at any time it can become the duty of a good man to tell a lie? For some go so far as to contend that there are occasions on which it is a good and pious work to commit perjury even, and to say what is false about matters that relate to the worship of God, and about the very nature of God Himself. To me, however, it seems certain that every lie is a sin, though it makes a great difference with what intention and on what subject one lies. For the sin of the man who tells a lie to help another is not so heinous as that of the man who tells a lie to injure another; and the man who by his lying puts a traveller on the wrong road, does not do so much harm as the man who by false or misleading representations distorts the whole course of a life. No one, of course, is to be condemned as a liar who says what is false, believing it to be true, because such an one does not consciously deceive, but rather is himself deceived. And, on the same principle, a man is not to be accused of lying, though he may sometimes be open to the charge of rashness, if through carelessness he takes up what is false and holds it as true; but, on the other hand, the man who says what is true, believing it to be false, is, so far as his own consciousness is concerned, a liar. For in saying what he does not believe, he says what to his own conscience is false, even though it should in fact be true; nor is the man in any sense free from lying who with his mouth speaks the truth without knowing it, but in his heart wills to tell a lie. And, therefore, not looking at the matter spoken of, but solely at the intention of the speaker, the man who unwittingly says what is false, thinking all the time that it is true, is a better man than the one who unwittingly says what is true, but in his conscience intends to deceive. For the former does not think one thing and say another; but the latter, though his statements may be true in fact, has one thought in his heart and another on his lips: and that is the very essence of lying. But when we come to consider truth and falsehood in respect to the subjects spoken of, the point on which one deceives or is deceived becomes a matter of the utmost importance. For although, as far as a man's own conscience is concerned, it is a greater evil to deceive than to be deceived, nevertheless it is a far less evil to tell a lie in regard to matters that do not relate to religion, than to be led into error in regard to matters the knowledge and belief of which are essential to the right worship of God. To illustrate this by example: suppose that one man should say of some one who is dead that he is still alive, knowing this to be untrue; and that another man should, being deceived, believe that Christ shall at the end of some time (make the time as long as you please) die; would it not be incomparably better to lie like the former, than to be deceived like the latter? and would it not be a much less evil to lead some man into the former error, than to be led by any man into the latter?

CHAP. 19.—MEN'S ERRORS VARY VERY MUCH IN THE MAGNITUDE OF THE EVILS THEY PRODUCE; BUT YET EVERY ERROR IS IN ITSELF AN EVIL.

In some things, then, it is a great evil to be deceived; in some it is a small evil; in some no evil at all; and in some it is an actual advantage. It is to his grievous injury that a man is deceived when he does not believe what leads to eternal life, or believes what leads to eternal death. It is a small evil for a man to be deceived, when, by taking falsehood for truth, he brings upon himself temporal annoyances; for the patience of the believer will turn even these to a good use, as when, for example, taking a bad man for a good, he receives injury from him. But one who believes a bad man to be good, and yet suffers no injury, is nothing the worse for being deceived, nor does he fall under the prophetic denunciation: "Woe to those who call evil good!"[1] For we are to understand that this is spoken not about evil men, but about the things that make men evil. Hence the man who calls adultery good, falls justly under that prophetic denunciation. But the man who calls the adulterer good, thinking him to be chaste, and not knowing him to be an adulterer, falls into no error in regard to the nature of good and evil, but only makes a mistake as to the secrets of human conduct. He calls

[1] Isa. v. 20.

the man good on the ground of believing him to be what is undoubtedly good; he calls the adulterer evil, and the pure man good; and he calls this man good, not knowing him to be an adulterer, but believing him to be pure. Further, if by making a mistake one escape death, as I have said above once happened to me, one even derives some advantage from one's mistake. But when I assert that in certain cases a man may be deceived without any injury to himself, or even with some advantage to himself, I do not mean that the mistake in itself is no evil, or is in any sense a good; I refer only to the evil that is avoided, or the advantage that is gained, through making the mistake. For the mistake, considered in itself, is an evil: a great evil if it concern a great matter, a small evil if it concern a small matter, but yet always an evil. For who that is of sound mind can deny that it is an evil to receive what is false as if it were true, and to reject what is true as if it were false, or to hold what is uncertain as certain, and what is certain as uncertain? But it is one thing to think a man good when he is really bad, which is a mistake; it is another thing to suffer no ulterior injury in consequence of the mistake, supposing that the bad man whom we think good inflicts no damage upon us. In the same way, it is one thing to think that we are on the right road when we are not; it is another thing when this mistake of ours, which is an evil, leads to some good, such as saving us from an ambush of wicked men.

CHAP. 20.—EVERY ERROR IS NOT A SIN. AN EXAMINATION OF THE OPINION OF THE ACADEMIC PHILOSOPHERS, THAT TO AVOID ERROR WE SHOULD IN ALL CASES SUSPEND BELIEF.

I am not sure whether mistakes such as the following,—when one forms a good opinion of a bad man, not knowing what sort of man he is; or when, instead of the ordinary perceptions through the bodily senses, other appearances of a similar kind present themselves, which we perceive in the spirit, but think we perceive in the body, or perceive in the body, but think we perceive in the spirit (such a mistake as the Apostle Peter made when the angel suddenly freed him from his chains and imprisonment, and he thought he saw a vision [1]); or when, in the case of sensible objects themselves, we mistake rough for smooth, or bitter for sweet, or think that putrid matter has a good smell; or when we mistake the passing of a carriage for thunder; or mistake one man for another, the two being very much alike, as often happens in the case of twins (hence our great poet calls it "a mistake pleasing to parents"[2]),—whether these, and other mistakes of this kind, ought to be called sins. Nor do I now undertake to solve a very knotty question, which perplexed those very acute thinkers, the Academic philosophers: whether a wise man ought to give his assent to anything, seeing that he may fall into error by assenting to falsehood: for all things, as they assert, are either unknown or uncertain. Now I wrote three volumes shortly after my conversion, to remove out of my way the objections which lie, as it were, on the very threshold of faith. And assuredly it was necessary at the very outset to remove this utter despair of reaching truth, which seems to be strengthened by the arguments of these philosophers. Now in their eyes every error is regarded as a sin, and they think that error can only be avoided by entirely suspending belief. For they say that the man who assents to what is uncertain falls into error; and they strive by the most acute, but most audacious arguments, to show that, even though a man's opinion should by chance be true, yet that there is no certainty of its truth, owing to the impossibility of distinguishing truth from falsehood. But with us, "the just shall live by faith."[3] Now, if assent be taken away, faith goes too; for without assent there can be no belief. And there are truths, whether we know them or not, which must be believed if we would attain to a happy life, that is, to eternal life. But I am not sure whether one ought to argue with men who not only do not know that there is an eternal life before them, but do not know whether they are living at the present moment; nay, say that they do not know what it is impossible they can be ignorant of. For it is impossible that any one should be ignorant that he is alive, seeing that if he be not alive it is impossible for him to be ignorant; for not knowledge merely, but ignorance too, can be an attribute only of the living. But, forsooth, they think that by not acknowledging that they are alive they avoid error, when even their very error proves that they are alive, since one who is not alive cannot err. As, then, it is not only true, but certain, that we are alive, so there are many other things both true and certain; and God forbid that it should ever be called wisdom, and not the height of folly, to refuse assent to these.

CHAP. 21.—ERROR, THOUGH NOT ALWAYS A SIN, IS ALWAYS AN EVIL.

But as to those matters in regard to which

---

[1] Acts xii. 9.   [2] Virgil, Æn. x. 392.   [3] Rom. i. 17.

our belief or disbelief, and indeed their truth or supposed truth or falsity, are of no importance whatever, so far as attaining the kingdom of God is concerned: to make a mistake in such matters is not to be looked on as a sin, or at least as a very small and trifling sin. In short, a mistake in matters of this kind, whatever its nature and magnitude, does not relate to the way of approach to God, which is the faith of Christ that "worketh by love."[1] For the "mistake pleasing to parents" in the case of the twin children was no deviation from this way; nor did the Apostle Peter deviate from this way, when, thinking that he saw a vision, he so mistook one thing for another, that, till the angel who delivered him had departed from him, he did not distinguish the real objects among which he was moving from the visionary objects of a dream;[2] nor did the patriarch Jacob deviate from this way, when he believed that his son, who was really alive, had been slain by a beast.[3] In the case of these and other false impressions of the same kind, we are indeed deceived, but our faith in God remains secure. We go astray, but we do not leave the way that leads us to Him. But yet these errors, though they are not sinful, are to be reckoned among the evils of this life, which is so far made subject to vanity, that we receive what is false as if it were true, reject what is true as if it were false, and cling to what is uncertain as if it were certain. And although they do not trench upon that true and certain faith through which we reach eternal blessedness, yet they have much to do with that misery in which we are now living. And assuredly, if we were now in the enjoyment of the true and perfect happiness that lies before us, we should not be subject to any deception through any sense, whether of body or of mind.

CHAP. 22.—A LIE IS NOT ALLOWABLE, EVEN TO SAVE ANOTHER FROM INJURY.

But every lie must be called a sin, because not only when a man knows the truth, but even when, as a man may be, he is mistaken and deceived, it is his duty to say what he thinks in his heart, whether it be true, or whether he only think it to be true. But every liar says the opposite of what he thinks in his heart, with purpose to deceive. Now it is evident that speech was given to man, not that men might therewith deceive one another, but that one man might make known his thoughts to another. To use speech, then, for

the purpose of deception, and not for its appointed end, is a sin. Nor are we to suppose that there is any lie that is not a sin, because it is sometimes possible, by telling a lie, to do service to another. For it is possible to do this by theft also, as when we steal from a rich man who never feels the loss, to give to a poor man who is sensibly benefited by what he gets. And the same can be said of adultery also, when, for instance, some woman appears likely to die of love unless we consent to her wishes, while if she lived she might purify herself by repentance; but yet no one will assert that on this account such an adultery is not a sin. And if we justly place so high a value upon chastity, what offense have we taken at truth, that, while no prospect of advantage to another will lead us to violate the former by adultery, we should be ready to violate the latter by lying? It cannot be denied that they have attained a very high standard of goodness who never lie except to save a man from injury; but in the case of men who have reached this standard, it is not the deceit, but their good intention, that is justly praised, and sometimes even rewarded. It is quite enough that the deception should be pardoned, without its being made an object of laudation, especially among the heirs of the new covenant, to whom it is said: "Let your communication be, Yea, yea; Nay, nay; for whatsoever is more than these cometh of evil."[4] And it is on account of this evil, which never ceases to creep in while we retain this mortal vesture, that the co-heirs of Christ themselves say, "Forgive us our debts."

CHAP. 23.—SUMMARY OF THE RESULTS OF THE PRECEDING DISCUSSION.

As it is right that we should know the causes of good and evil, so much of them at least as will suffice for the way that leads us to the kingdom, where there will be life without the shadow of death, truth without any alloy of error, and happiness unbroken by any sorrow, I have discussed these subjects with the brevity which my limited space demanded. And I think there cannot now be any doubt, that the only cause of any good that we enjoy is the goodness of God, and that the only cause of evil is the falling away from the unchangeable good of a being made good but changeable, first in the case of an angel, and afterwards in the case of man.

CHAP. 24.—THE SECONDARY CAUSES OF EVIL ARE IGNORANCE AND LUST.

This is the first evil that befell the intelli-

---

[1] Gal. v. 6.   [2] Acts xii. 9-11.
[3] Gen. xxxvii. 33.

[4] Matt. v. 37.   [5] Matt. vi. 12.

gent creation—that is, its first privation of good. Following upon this crept in, and now even in opposition to man's will, *ignorance* of duty, and *lust* after what is hurtful: and these brought in their train *error* and *suffering*, which, when they are felt to be imminent, produce that shrinking of the mind which is called *fear*. Further, when the mind attains the objects of its desire, however hurtful or empty they may be, error prevents it from perceiving their true nature, or its perceptions are overborne by a diseased appetite, and so it is puffed up with a *foolish joy*. From these fountains of evil, which spring out of defect rather than superfluity, flows every form of misery that besets a rational nature.

CHAP. 25.—GOD'S JUDGMENTS UPON FALLEN MEN AND ANGELS. THE DEATH OF THE BODY IS MAN'S PECULIAR PUNISHMENT.

And yet such a nature, in the midst of all its evils, could not lose the craving after happiness. Now the evils I have mentioned are common to all who for their wickedness have been justly condemned by God, whether they be men or angels. But there is one form of punishment peculiar to man—the death of the body. God had threatened him with this punishment of death if he should sin,[1] leaving him indeed to the freedom of his own will, but yet commanding his obedience under pain of death; and He placed him amid the happiness of Eden, as it were in a protected nook of life, with the intention that, if he preserved his righteousness, he should thence ascend to a better place.

CHAP. 26.—THROUGH ADAM'S SIN HIS WHOLE POSTERITY WERE CORRUPTED, AND WERE BORN UNDER THE PENALTY OF DEATH, WHICH HE HAD INCURRED.

Thence, after his sin, he was driven into exile, and by his sin the whole race of which he was the root was corrupted in him, and thereby subjected to the penalty of death. And so it happens that all descended from him, and from the woman who had led him into sin, and was condemned at the same time with him,—being the offspring of carnal lust on which the same punishment of disobedience was visited,—were tainted with the original sin, and were by it drawn through divers errors and sufferings into that last and endless punishment which they suffer in common with the fallen angels, their corrupters and masters, and the partakers of their doom. And thus "by one man sin entered into the world, and death by sin; and so death passed upon all

men, for that all have sinned."[2] By "the world" the apostle, of course, means in this place the whole human race.

CHAP. 27.—THE STATE OF MISERY TO WHICH ADAM'S SIN REDUCED MANKIND, AND THE RESTORATION EFFECTED THROUGH THE MERCY OF GOD.

Thus, then, matters stood. The whole mass of the human race was under condemnation, was lying steeped and wallowing in misery, and was being tossed from one form of evil to another, and, having joined the faction of the fallen angels, was paying the well-merited penalty of that impious rebellion. For whatever the wicked freely do through blind and unbridled lust, and whatever they suffer against their will in the way of open punishment, this all evidently pertains to the just wrath of God. But the goodness of the Creator never fails either to supply life and vital power to the wicked angels (without which their existence would soon come to an end); or, in the case of mankind, who spring from a condemned and corrupt stock, to impart form and life to their seed, to fashion their members, and through the various seasons of their life, and in the different parts of the earth, to quicken their senses, and bestow upon them the nourishment they need. For He judged it better to bring good out of evil, than not to permit any evil to exist. And if He had determined that in the case of men, as in the case of the fallen angels, there should be no restoration to happiness, would it not have been quite just, that the being who rebelled against God, who in the abuse of his freedom spurned and transgressed the command of his Creator when he could so easily have kept it, who defaced in himself the image of his Creator by stubbornly turning away from His light, who by an evil use of his free-will broke away from his wholesome bondage to the Creator's laws,—would it not have been just that such a being should have been wholly and to all eternity deserted by God, and left to suffer the everlasting punishment he had so richly earned? Certainly so God would have done, had He been only just and not also merciful, and had He not designed that His unmerited mercy should shine forth the more brightly in contrast with the unworthiness of its objects.

CHAP. 28.—WHEN THE REBELLIOUS ANGELS WERE CAST OUT, THE REST REMAINED IN THE ENJOYMENT OF ETERNAL HAPPINESS WITH GOD.

Whilst some of the angels, then, in their

---

[1] Gen. ii. 17.   [2] Rom. v. 12.

pride and impiety rebelled against God, and were cast down from their heavenly abode into the lowest darkness, the remaining number dwelt with God in eternal and unchanging purity and happiness. For all were not sprung from one angel who had fallen and been condemned, so that they were not all, like men, involved by one original sin in the bonds of an inherited guilt, and so made subject to the penalty which one had incurred ; but when he, who afterwards became the devil, was with his associates in crime exalted in pride, and by that very exaltation was with them cast down, the rest remained steadfast in piety and obedience to their Lord, and obtained, what before they had not enjoyed, a sure and certain knowledge of their eternal safety, and freedom from the possibility of falling.

CHAP. 29.—THE RESTORED PART OF HUMANITY SHALL, IN ACCORDANCE WITH THE PROMISES OF GOD, SUCCEED TO THE PLACE WHICH THE REBELLIOUS ANGELS LOST.

And so it pleased God, the Creator and Governor of the universe, that, since the whole body of the angels had not fallen into rebellion, the part of them which had fallen should remain in perdition eternally, and that the other part, which had in the rebellion remained steadfastly loyal, should rejoice in the sure and certain knowledge of their eternal happiness; but that, on the other hand, mankind, who constituted the remainder of the intelligent creation, having perished without exception under sin, both original and actual, and the consequent punishments, should be in part restored, and should fill up the gap which the rebellion and fall of the devils had left in the company of the angels. For this is the promise to the saints, that at the resurrection they shall be equal to the angels of God. [1] And thus the Jerusalem which is above, which is the mother of us all, the city of God, shall not be spoiled of any of the number of her citizens, shall perhaps reign over even a more abundant population. We do not know the number either of the saints or of the devils ; but we know that the children of the holy mother who was called barren on earth shall succeed to the place of the fallen angels, and shall dwell for ever in that peaceful abode from which they fell. But the number of the citizens, whether as it now is or as it shall be, is present to the thoughts of the great Creator, who calls those things which are not as though they were,[2] and ordereth all things in measure, and number, and weight.[3]

CHAP. 30.—MEN ARE NOT SAVED BY GOOD WORKS, NOR BY THE FREE DETERMINATION OF THEIR OWN WILL, BUT BY THE GRACE OF GOD THROUGH FAITH.

But this part of the human race to which God has promised pardon and a share in His eternal kingdom, can they be restored through the merit of their own works? God forbid. For what good work can a lost man perform, except so far as he has been delivered from perdition? Can they do anything by the free determination of their own will? Again I say, God forbid. For it was by the evil use of his free-will that man destroyed both it and himself. For, as a man who kills himself must, of course, be alive when he kills himself, but after he has killed himself ceases to live, and cannot restore himself to life; so, when man by his own free-will sinned, then sin being victorious over him, the freedom of his will was lost. " For of whom a man is overcome, of the same is he brought in bondage." [4] This is the judgment of the Apostle Peter. And as it is certainly true, what kind of liberty, I ask, can the bond-slave possess, except when it pleases him to sin? For he is freely in bondage who does with pleasure the will of his master. Accordingly, he who is the servant of sin is free to sin. And hence he will not be free to do right, until, being freed from sin, he shall begin to be the servant of righteousness. And this is true liberty, for he has pleasure in the righteous deed; and it is at the same time a holy bondage, for he is obedient to the will of God. But whence comes this liberty to do right to the man who is in bondage and sold under sin, except he be redeemed by Him who has said, " If the Son shall make you free, ye shall be free indeed?"[5] And before this redemption is wrought in a man, when he is not yet free to do what is right, how can he talk of the freedom of his will and his good works, except he be inflated by that foolish pride of boasting which the apostle restrains when he says, " By grace are ye saved, through faith."[6]

CHAP. 31.—FAITH ITSELF IS THE GIFT OF GOD; AND GOOD WORKS WILL NOT BE WANTING IN THOSE WHO BELIEVE.

And lest men should arrogate to themselves the merit of their own faith at least, not understanding that this too is the gift of God, this same apostle, who says in another place that he had " obtained mercy of the Lord to be faithful,"[7] here also adds: " and that not

---

Luke xx. 36.   [2] Rom. iv. 17.   [3] Wisd. xi. 20.

[4] 2 Pet. ii. 19.   [5] John viii. 36.
[6] Eph. ii. 8.   [7] 1 Cor. vii. 25.

of yourselves; it is the gift of God: not of works, lest any man should boast."[1] And lest it should be thought that good works will be wanting in those who believe, he adds further: "For we are His workmanship, created in Christ Jesus unto good works, which God hath before ordained that we should walk in them."[2] We shall be made truly free, then, when God fashions us, that is, forms and creates us anew, not as men—for He has done that already—but as good men, which His grace is now doing, that we may be a new creation in Christ Jesus, according as it is said: "Create in me a clean heart, O God."[3] For God had already created his heart, so far as the physical structure of the human heart is concerned; but the psalmist prays for the renewal of the life which was still lingering in his heart.

CHAP. 32.—THE FREEDOM OF THE WILL IS ALSO THE GIFT OF GOD, FOR GOD WORKETH IN US BOTH TO WILL AND TO DO.

And further, should any one be inclined to boast, not indeed of his works, but of the freedom of his will, as if the first merit belonged to him, this very liberty of good action being given to him as a reward he had earned, let him listen to this same preacher of grace, when he says: "For it is God which worketh in you, both to will and to do of His own good pleasure;"[4] and in another place: "So, then, it is not of him that willeth, nor of him that runneth, but of God that showeth mercy."[5] Now as, undoubtedly, if a man is of the age to use his reason, he cannot believe, hope, love, unless he will to do so, nor obtain the prize of the high calling of God unless he voluntarily run for it; in what sense is it "not of him that willeth, nor of him that runneth, but of God that showeth mercy," except that, as it is written, "the preparation of the heart is from the Lord?"[6] Otherwise, if it is said, "It is not of him that willeth, nor of him that runneth, but of God that showeth mercy," because it is of both, that is, both of the will of man and of the mercy of God, so that we are to understand the saying, "It is not of him that willeth, nor of him that runneth, but of God that showeth mercy," as if it meant the will of man alone is not sufficient, if the mercy of God go not with it, —then it will follow that the mercy of God alone is not sufficient, if the will of man go not with it; and therefore, if we may rightly say, "it is not of man that willeth, but of God that showeth mercy," because the will of

man by itself is not enough, why may we not also rightly put it in the converse way: "It is not of God that showeth mercy, but of man that willeth," because the mercy of God by itself does not suffice? Surely, if no Christian will dare to say this, "It is not of God that showeth mercy, but of man that willeth," lest he should openly contradict the apostle, it follows that the true interpretation of the saying, "It is not of him that willeth, nor of him that runneth, but of God that showeth mercy," is that the whole work belongs to God, who both makes the will of man righteous, and thus prepares it for assistance, and assists it when it is prepared. For the man's righteousness of will precedes many of God's gifts, but not all; and it must itself be included among those which it does not precede. We read in Holy Scripture, both that God's mercy "shall meet me,"[7] and that His mercy "shall follow me."[8] It goes before the unwilling to make him willing; it follows the willing to make his will effectual. Why are we taught to pray for our enemies,[9] who are plainly unwilling to lead a holy life, unless that God may work willingness in them? And why are we ourselves taught to ask that we may receive,[10] unless that He who has created in us the wish, may Himself satisfy the wish? We pray, then, for our enemies, that the mercy of God may prevent them, as it has prevented us: we pray for ourselves that His mercy may follow us.

CHAP. 33.—MEN, BEING BY NATURE THE CHILDREN OF WRATH, NEEDED A MEDIATOR. IN WHAT SENSE GOD IS SAID TO BE ANGRY.

And so the human race was lying under a just condemnation, and all men were the children of wrath. Of which wrath it is written: "All our days are passed away in Thy wrath; we spend our years as a tale that is told."[11] Of which wrath also Job says: "Man that is born of a woman is of few days, and full of trouble."[12] Of which wrath also the Lord Jesus says: "He that believeth on the Son hath everlasting life: and he that believeth not the Son shall not see life; but the wrath of God abideth on him."[13] He does not say it will come, but it "abideth on him." For every man is born with it; wherefore the apostle says: "We were by nature the children of wrath, even as others."[14] Now, as men were lying under this wrath by reason of their original sin, and as this original sin was the

---

[1] Eph. ii. 8, 9.   [2] Eph. ii. 10.
[3] Ps. li. 10.   [4] Phil. ii. 13.
[5] Rom. ix. 16.   [6] Prov. xvi. 1.

[7] Ps. lix. 10.   [8] Ps. xxiii. 6.
[9] Matt. v. 44.   [10] Matt. vii. 7.
[11] Ps. xc. 9.   [12] Job. xiv. 1.
[13] John iii. 36. These words, attributed by the author to Christ, were really spoken by John the Baptist.
[14] Eph. ii. 3.

more heavy and deadly in proportion to the number and magnitude of the actual sins which were added to it, there was need for a Mediator, that is, for a reconciler, who, by the offering of one sacrifice, of which all the sacrifices of the law and the prophets were types, should take away this wrath. Wherefore the apostle says: "For if, when we were enemies, we were reconciled to God by the death of His Son, much more, being reconciled, we shall be saved by His life."[1] Now when God is said to be angry, we do not attribute to Him such a disturbed feeling as exists in the mind of an angry man; but we call His just displeasure against sin by the name "anger," a word transferred by analogy from human emotions. But our being reconciled to God through a Mediator, and receiving the Holy Spirit, so that we who were enemies are made sons ("For as many as are led by the Spirit of God, they are the sons of God"[2]): this is the grace of God through Jesus Christ our Lord.

CHAP. 34.—THE INEFFABLE MYSTERY OF THE BIRTH OF CHRIST THE MEDIATOR THROUGH THE VIRGIN MARY.

Now of this Mediator it would occupy too much space to say anything at all worthy of Him; and, indeed, to say what is worthy of Him is not in the power of man. For who will explain in consistent words this single statement, that "the Word was made flesh, and dwelt among us,"[3] so that we may believe on the only Son of God the Father Almighty, born of the Holy Ghost and the Virgin Mary? The meaning of the Word being made flesh, is not that the divine nature was changed into flesh, but that the divine nature assumed our flesh. And by "flesh" we are here to understand "man," the part being put for the whole, as when it is said: "By the deeds of the law shall no flesh be justified,"[4] that is, no man. For we must believe that no part was wanting in that human nature which He put on, save that it was a nature wholly free from every taint of sin,—not such a nature as is conceived between the two sexes through carnal lust, which is born in sin, and whose guilt is washed away in regeneration; but such as it behoved a virgin to bring forth, when the mother's faith, not her lust, was the condition of conception. And if her virginity had been marred even in bringing Him forth, He would not have been born of a virgin; and it would be false (which God forbid) that He was born of the Virgin Mary, as is believed and declared by the whole Church, which, in

imitation of His mother, daily brings forth members of His body, and yet remains a virgin. Read, if you please, my letter on the virginity of the holy Mary which I sent to that eminent man, whose name I mention with respect and affection, Volusianus.[5]

CHAP. 35.—JESUS CHRIST, BEING THE ONLY SON OF GOD, IS AT THE SAME TIME MAN.

Wherefore Christ Jesus, the Son of God, is both God and man; God before all worlds; man in our world: God, because the Word of God (for "the Word was God"[6]); and man, because in His one person the Word was joined with a body and a rational soul. Wherefore, so far as He is God, He and the Father are one; so far as He is man, the Father is greater than He. For when He was the only Son of God, not by grace, but by nature, that He might be also full of grace, He became the Son of man; and He Himself unites both natures in His own identity, and both natures constitute one Christ; because, "being in the form of God, He thought it not robbery to be," what He was by nature, "equal with God."[7] But He made Himself of no reputation, and took upon Himself the form of a servant, not losing or lessening the form of God. And, accordingly, He was both made less and remained equal, being both in one, as has been said: but He was one of these as Word, and the other as man. As Word, He is equal with the Father; as man, less than the Father. One Son of God, and at the same time Son of man; one Son of man, and at the same time Son of God; not two Sons of God, God and man, but one Son of God: God without beginning; man with a beginning, our Lord Jesus Christ.

CHAP. 36.—THE GRACE OF GOD IS CLEARLY AND REMARKABLY DISPLAYED IN RAISING THE MAN CHRIST JESUS TO THE DIGNITY OF THE SON OF GOD.

Now here the grace of God is displayed with the greatest power and clearness. For what merit had the human nature in the man Christ earned, that it should in this unparalleled way be taken up into the unity of the person of the only Son of God? What goodness of will, what goodness of desire and intention, what good works, had gone before, which made this man worthy to become one person with God? Had He been a man previously to this, and had He earned this unprecedented reward, that He should be thought worthy to become God? Assuredly

---

[1] Rom. v. 10.　　　[2] Rom. viii. 14.
[3] John i. 14.　　　[4] Rom. iii. 20.

[5] Ep. 137.　　　[6] John i. 1.
[7] Phil. ii. 6.

nay; from the very moment that He began to be man, He was nothing else than the Son of God, the only Son of God, the Word who was made flesh, and therefore He was God; so that just as each individual man unites in one person a body and a rational soul, so Christ in one person unites the Word and man. Now wherefore was this unheard of glory conferred on human nature,—a glory which, as there was no antecedent merit, was of course wholly of grace,—except that here those who looked at the matter soberly and honestly might behold a clear manifestation of the power of God's free grace, and might understand that they are justified from their sins by the same grace which made the man Christ Jesus free from the possibility of sin? And so the angel, when he announced to Christ's mother the coming birth, saluted her thus: "Hail, thou that art full of grace;"[1] and shortly afterwards, "Thou hast found grace with God."[2] Now she was said to be full of grace, and to have found grace with God, because she was to be the mother of her Lord, nay, of the Lord of all flesh. But, speaking of Christ Himself, the evangelist John, after saying, "The Word was made flesh, and dwelt among us," adds, "and we beheld His glory, the glory as of the only-begotten of the Father, full of grace and truth."[3] When he says, "The Word was made flesh," this is "full of grace;" when he says, "the glory of the only-begotten of the Father," this is "full of truth." For the Truth Himself, who was the only-begotten of the Father, not by grace, but by nature, by grace took our humanity upon Him, and so united it with His own person that He Himself became also the Son of man.

CHAP. 37.—THE SAME GRACE IS FURTHER CLEARLY MANIFESTED IN THIS, THAT THE BIRTH OF CHRIST ACCORDING TO THE FLESH IS OF THE HOLY GHOST.

For the same Jesus Christ who is the only-begotten, that is, the only Son of God, our Lord, was born of the Holy Ghost and of the Virgin Mary. And we know that the Holy Spirit is the gift of God, the gift being Himself indeed equal to the Giver. And therefore the Holy Spirit also is God, not inferior to the Father and the Son. The fact, therefore, that the nativity of Christ in His human nature was by the Holy Spirit, is another clear manifestation of grace. For when the Virgin asked the angel how this which he had announced should be, seeing she knew not a man, the angel answered, "The Holy Ghost shall come upon thee, and the power of the Highest shall overshadow thee: therefore also that holy thing which shall be born of thee shall be called the Son of God."[4] And when Joseph was minded to put her away, suspecting her of adultery, as he knew she was not with child by himself, he was told by the angel, "Fear not to take unto thee Mary thy wife; for that which is conceived in her is of the Holy Ghost:"[5] that is, what thou suspectest to be begotten of another man is of the Holy Ghost.

CHAP. 38.—JESUS CHRIST, ACCORDING TO THE FLESH, WAS NOT BORN OF THE HOLY SPIRIT IN SUCH A SENSE THAT THE HOLY SPIRIT IS HIS FATHER.

Nevertheless, are we on this account to say that the Holy Ghost is the father of the man Christ, and that as God the Father begat the Word, so God the Holy Spirit begat the man, and that these two natures constitute the one Christ; and that as the Word He is the Son of God the Father, and as man the Son of God the Holy Spirit, because the Holy Spirit as His father begat Him of the Virgin Mary? Who will dare to say so? Nor is it necessary to show by reasoning how many other absurdities flow from this supposition, when it is itself so absurd that no believer's ears can bear to hear it. Hence, as we confess, "Our Lord Jesus Christ, who of God is God, and as man was born of the Holy Ghost and of the Virgin Mary, having both natures, the divine and the human, is the only Son of God the Father Almighty, from whom proceedeth the Holy Spirit."[6] Now in what sense do we say that Christ was born of the Holy Spirit, if the Holy Spirit did not beget Him? Is it that He made Him, since our Lord Jesus Christ, though as God "all things were made by Him,"[7] yet as man was Himself made; as the apostle says, "who was made of the seed of David according to the flesh?"[8] But as that created thing which the Virgin conceived and brought forth, though it was united only to the person of the Son, was made by the whole Trinity (for the works of the Trinity are not separable), why should the Holy Spirit alone be mentioned as having made it? Or is it that, when one of the Three is mentioned as the author of any work, the whole Trinity is to be understood as working? That is true, and can be proved by examples. But we need not dwell longer on this

---

[1] Luke i. 28 ("Thou that are *highly favored*," A. V.).
[2] Luke i. 30 ("Thou hast found *favor* with God," A. V.).
[3] John i. 14.

[4] Luke i. 35.   [5] Matt. i. 20.
[6] A quotation from a form of the Apostles' Creed anciently in use in the Latin Church.
[7] John i. 3.   [8] Rom. i. 3.

solution. For the puzzle is, in what sense it is said, "born of the Holy Ghost," when He is in no sense the Son of the Holy Ghost? For though God made this world, it would not be right to say that it is the Son of God, or that it was born of God; we would say that it was created, or made, or framed, or ordered by Him, or whatever form of expression we can properly use. Here, then, when we make confession that Christ was born of the Holy Ghost and of the Virgin Mary, it is difficult to explain how it is that He is not the Son of the Holy Ghost and is the Son of the Virgin Mary, when He was born both of Him and of her. It is clear beyond a doubt that He was not born of the Holy Spirit as His father, in the same sense that He was born of the Virgin as His mother.

CHAP. 39.—NOT EVERYTHING THAT IS BORN OF ANOTHER IS TO BE CALLED A SON OF THAT OTHER.

We need not therefore take for granted, that whatever is born of a thing is forthwith to be declared the son of that thing. For, to pass over the fact that a son is born of a man in a different sense from that in which a hair or a louse is born of him, neither of these being a son; to pass over this, I say, as too mean an illustration for a subject of so much importance: it is certain that those who are born of water and of the Holy Spirit cannot with propriety be called sons of the water, though they are called sons of God the Father, and of the Church their mother. In the same way, then, He who was born of the Holy Spirit is the Son of God the Father, not of the Holy Spirit. For what I have said of the hair and the other things is sufficient to show us that not everything which is born of another can be called the son of that of which it is born, just as it does not follow that all who are called a man's sons were born of him, for some sons are adopted. And some men are called sons of hell, not as being born of hell, but as prepared for it, as the sons of the kingdom are prepared for the kingdom.

CHAP. 40.—CHRIST'S BIRTH THROUGH THE HOLY SPIRIT MANIFESTS TO US THE GRACE OF GOD.

And, therefore, as one thing may be born of another, and yet not in such a way as to be its son, and as not every one who is called a son was born of him whose son he is called, it is clear that this arrangement by which Christ was born of the Holy Spirit, but not as His son, and of the Virgin Mary as her son, is intended as a manifestation of the grace of God. For it was by this grace that a man, without any antecedent merit, was at the very commencement of His existence as man, so united in one person with the Word of God, that the very person who was Son of man was at the same time Son of God, and the very person who was Son of God was at the same time Son of man; and in the adoption of His human nature into the divine, the grace itself became in a way so natural to the man, as to leave no room for the entrance of sin. Wherefore this grace is signified by the Holy Spirit; for He, though in His own nature God, may also be called the gift of God. And to explain all this sufficiently, if indeed it could be done at all, would require a very lengthened discussion.

CHAP. 41.—CHRIST, WHO WAS HIMSELF FREE FROM SIN, WAS MADE SIN FOR US, THAT WE MIGHT BE RECONCILED TO GOD.

Begotten and conceived, then, without any indulgence of carnal lust, and therefore bringing with Him no original sin, and by the grace of God joined and united in a wonderful and unspeakable way in one person with the Word, the Only-begotten of the Father, a son by nature, not by grace, and therefore having no sin of His own; nevertheless, on account of the likeness of sinful flesh in which He came, He was called sin, that He might be sacrificed to wash away sin. For, under the Old Covenant, sacrifices for sin were called sins.[1] And He, of whom all these sacrifices were types and shadows, was Himself truly made sin. Hence the apostle, after saying, "We pray you in Christ's stead, be ye reconciled to God," forthwith adds: "for He hath made Him to be sin for us who knew no sin; that we might be made the righteousness of God in Him."[2] He does not say, as some incorrect copies read, "He who knew no sin did sin for us," as if Christ had Himself sinned for our sakes; but he says, "Him who knew no sin," that is, Christ, God, to whom we are to be reconciled, "hath made to be sin for us," that is, hath made Him a sacrifice for our sins, by which we might be reconciled to God. He, then, being made sin, just as we are made righteousness (our righteousness being not our own, but God's, not in ourselves, but in Him); He being made sin, not His own, but ours, not in Himself, but in us, showed, by the likeness of sinful flesh in which He was crucified, that though sin was not in Him, yet that in a certain sense He died to sin, by dying in the flesh which was the likeness of sin; and that although He Himself had never lived the old

---

[1] Hos. iv. 8.   [2] 2 Cor. v. 20, 21.

life of sin, yet by His resurrection He typified our new life springing up out of the old death in sin.

CHAP. 42.—THE SACRAMENT OF BAPTISM INDICATES OUR DEATH WITH CHRIST TO SIN, AND OUR RESURRECTION WITH HIM TO NEWNESS OF LIFE.

And this is the meaning of the great sacrament of baptism which is solemnized among us, that all who attain to this grace should die to sin, as He is said to have died to sin, because He died in the flesh, which is the likeness of sin; and rising from the font regenerate, as He arose alive from the grave, should begin a new life in the Spirit, whatever may be the age of the body?

CHAP. 43.—BAPTISM AND THE GRACE WHICH IT TYPIFIES ARE OPEN TO ALL, BOTH INFANTS AND ADULTS.

For from the infant newly born to the old man bent with age, as there is none shut out from baptism, so there is none who in baptism does not die to sin. But infants die only to original sin; those who are older die also to all the sins which their evil lives have added to the sin which they brought with them.

CHAP. 44.—IN SPEAKING OF SIN, THE SINGULAR NUMBER IS OFTEN PUT FOR THE PLURAL, AND THE PLURAL FOR THE SINGULAR.

But even these latter are frequently said to die to sin, though undoubtedly they die not to one sin, but to all the numerous actual sins they have committed in thought, word, or deed: for the singular number is often put for the plural, as when the poet says, "They fill its belly with the armed soldier,"[1] though in the case here referred to there were many soldiers concerned. And we read in our own Scriptures: "Pray to the Lord, that He take away the serpent from us."[2] He does not say *serpents*, though the people were suffering from many; and so in other cases. When, on the other hand, the original sin is expressed in the plural number, as when we say that infants are baptized for the remission of *sins*, instead of saying for the remission of *sin*, this is the converse figure of speech, by which the plural number is put in place of the singular; as in the Gospel it is said of the death of Herod, "for they are dead which sought the young child's life,"[3] instead of saying, "he is dead." And in Exodus: "They have made them," Moses

says, "gods of gold,"[4] though they had made only one calf, of which they said: "These be thy gods, O Israel, which brought thee up out of the land of Egypt,"[5]—here, too, putting the plural in place of the singular.

CHAP. 45.—IN ADAM'S FIRST SIN, MANY KINDS OF SIN WERE INVOLVED.

However, even in that one sin, which "by one man entered into the world, and so passed upon all men,"[6] and on account of which infants are baptized, a number of distinct sins may be observed, if it be analyzed as it were into its separate elements. For there is in it pride, because man chose to be under his own dominion, rather than under the dominion of God; and blasphemy, because he did not believe God; and murder, for he brought death upon himself; and spiritual fornication, for the purity of the human soul was corrupted by the seducing blandishments of the serpent; and theft, for man turned to his own use the food he had been forbidden to touch; and avarice, for he had a craving for more than should have been sufficient for him; and whatever other sin can be discovered on careful reflection to be involved in this one admitted sin.

CHAP. 46.—IT IS PROBABLE THAT CHILDREN ARE INVOLVED IN THE GUILT NOT ONLY OF THE FIRST PAIR, BUT OF THEIR OWN IMMEDIATE PARENTS.

And it is said, with much appearance of probability, that infants are involved in the guilt of the sins not only of the first pair, but of their own immediate parents. For that divine judgment, "I shall visit the iniquities of the fathers upon the children,"[7] certainly applies to them before they come under the new covenant by regeneration. And it was this new covenant that was prophesied of, when it was said by Ezekiel, that the sons should not bear the iniquity of the fathers, and that it should no longer be a proverb in Israel, "The fathers have eaten sour grapes, and the children's teeth are set on edge."[8] Here lies the necessity that each man should be born again, that he might be freed from the sin in which he was born. For the sins committed afterwards can be cured by penitence, as we see is the case after baptism. And therefore the new birth would not have been appointed only that the first birth was sinful, so sinful that even one who was legitimately born in wedlock says: "I was shapen in iniquities,

1 "Uterumque armato milite complent."—VIRGIL, *Æn.* ii. 20.
2 Num. xxi. 7 ("serpents," A. and R. V.).   3 Matt. ii. 20.
4 Ex. xxxii. 31.
6 Rom. v. 12.
8 Ezek. xviii. 2.
5 Ex. xxxii. 4.
7 Ex. xx. 5; Deut. v. 9.

and in sins did my mother conceive me." [1] He did not say in *iniquity*, or in *sin*, though he might have said so correctly; but he preferred to say "iniquities" and "sins," because in that one sin which passed upon all men, and which was so great that human nature was by it made subject to inevitable death, many sins, as I showed above, may be discriminated; and further, because there are other sins of the immediate parents, which, though they have not the same effect in producing a change of nature, yet subject the children to guilt unless the divine grace and mercy interpose to rescue them.

CHAP. 47.—IT IS DIFFICULT TO DECIDE WHETHER THE SINS OF A MAN'S OTHER PROGENITORS ARE IMPUTED TO HIM.

But about the sins of the other progenitors who intervene between Adam and a man's own parents, a question may very well be raised. Whether every one who is born is involved in all their accumulated evil acts, in all their multiplied original guilt, so that the later he is born, so much the worse is his condition; or whether God threatens to visit the iniquity of the fathers upon the children unto the third and fourth generations, because in His mercy He does not extend His wrath against the sins of the progenitors further than that, lest those who do not obtain the grace of regeneration might be crushed down under too heavy a burden if they were compelled to bear as original guilt all the sins of all their progenitors from the very beginning of the human race, and to pay the penalty due to them; or whether any other solution of this great question may or may not be found in Scripture by a more diligent search and a more careful interpretation, I dare not rashly affirm.

CHAP. 48.—THE GUILT OF THE FIRST SIN IS SO GREAT THAT IT CAN BE WASHED AWAY ONLY IN THE BLOOD OF THE MEDIATOR, JESUS CHRIST.

Nevertheless, that one sin, admitted into a place where such perfect happiness reigned, was of so heinous a character, that in one man the whole human race was originally, and as one may say, radically, condemned; and it cannot be pardoned and blotted out except through the one Mediator between God and men, the man Christ Jesus, who only has had power to be so born as not to need a second birth.

CHAP. 49.—CHRIST WAS NOT REGENERATED IN THE BAPTISM OF JOHN, BUT SUBMITTED TO IT TO GIVE US AN EXAMPLE OF HUMILITY, JUST AS HE SUBMITTED TO DEATH, NOT AS THE PUNISHMENT OF SIN, BUT TO TAKE AWAY THE SIN OF THE WORLD.

Now, those who were baptized in the baptism of John, by whom Christ was Himself baptized,[2] were not regenerated; but they were prepared through the ministry of His forerunner, who cried, "Prepare ye the way of the Lord,"[3] for Him in whom only they could be regenerated. For His baptism is not with water only, as was that of John, but with the Holy Ghost also;[4] so that whoever believes in Christ is regenerated by that Spirit, of whom Christ being generated, He did not need regeneration. Whence that announcement of the Father which was heard after His baptism, "This day have I begotten Thee,"[5] referred not to that one day of time on which He was baptized, but to the one day of an unchangeable eternity, so as to show that this man was one in person with the Only-begotten. For when a day neither begins with the close of yesterday, nor ends with the beginning of to-morrow, it is an eternal to-day. Therefore He asked to be baptized in water by John, not that any iniquity of His might be washed away, but that He might manifest the depth of His humility. For baptism found in Him nothing to wash away, as death found in Him nothing to punish; so that it was in the strictest justice, and not by the mere violence of power, that the devil was crushed and conquered: for, as he had most unjustly put Christ to death, though there was no sin in Him to deserve death, it was most just that through Christ he should lose his hold of those who by sin were justly subject to the bondage in which he held them. Both of these, then, that is, both baptism and death, were submitted to by Him, not through a pitiable necessity, but of His own free pity for us, and as part of an arrangement by which, as one man brought sin into the world, that is, upon the whole human race, so one man was to take away the sin of the world.

CHAP. 50.—CHRIST TOOK AWAY NOT ONLY THE ONE ORIGINAL SIN, BUT ALL THE OTHER SINS THAT HAVE BEEN ADDED TO IT.

With this difference: the first man brought one sin into the world, but this man took away not only that one sin, but all that He found added to it. Hence the apostle says:

---

[1] Ps. li. 5 (The A. V. has the singular, "iniquity" and "sin").

[2] Matt. iii. 13-15. [3] Matt. iii. 3. [4] Matt. iii. 11.
[5] Ps. ii. 7; Heb. i. 5, v. 5. It is by a mistake that Augustin quotes these words as pronounced at our Lord's baptism.

"And not as it was by one that sinned, so is the gift: for the judgment was by one to condemnation, but the free gift is of many offenses unto justification."[1] For it is evident that the one sin which we bring with us by nature would, even if it stood alone, bring us under condemnation; but the free gift justifies man from many offenses: for each man, in addition to the one sin which, in common with all his kind, he brings with him by nature, has committed many sins that are strictly his own.

CHAP. 51.—ALL MEN BORN OF ADAM ARE UNDER CONDEMNATION, AND ONLY IF NEW BORN IN CHRIST ARE FREED FROM CONDEMNATION.

But what he says a little after, "Therefore, as by the offense of one judgment came upon all men to condemnation; even so by the righteousness of one the free gift came upon all men unto justification of life,"[2] shows clearly enough that there is no one born of Adam but is subject to condemnation, and that no one, unless he be new born in Christ, is freed from condemnation.

CHAP. 52.—IN BAPTISM, WHICH IS THE SIMILITUDE OF THE DEATH AND RESURRECTION OF CHRIST, ALL, BOTH INFANTS AND ADULTS, DIE TO SIN THAT THEY MAY WALK IN NEWNESS OF LIFE.

And after he has said as much about the condemnation through one man, and the free gift through one man, as he deemed sufficient for that part of his epistle, the apostle goes on to speak of the great mystery of holy baptism in the cross of Christ, and to clearly explain to us that baptism in Christ is nothing else than a similitude of the death of Christ, and that the death of Christ on the cross is nothing but a similitude of the pardon of sin: so that just as real as is His death, so real is the remission of our sins; and just as real as is His resurrection, so real is our justification. He says: "What shall we say, then? Shall we continue in sin, that grace may abound?"[3] For he had said previously, "But where sin abounded, grace did much more abound."[4] And therefore he proposes to himself the question, whether it would be right to continue in sin for the sake of the consequent abounding grace. But he answers, "God forbid;" and adds, "How shall we, that are dead to sin, live any longer therein?" Then, to show that we are dead to sin, "Know ye not," he says, "that so many of us as were baptized into Jesus Christ, were baptized into His death?" If, then, the fact that we were baptized into the death of Christ proves that we are dead to sin, it follows that even infants who are baptized into Christ die to sin, being baptized into His death. For there is no exception made: "So many of us as were baptized into Jesus Christ, were baptized into His death." And this is said to prove that we are dead to sin. Now, to what sin do infants die in their regeneration but that sin which they bring with them at birth? And therefore to these also applies what follows: "Therefore we are buried with Him by baptism into death; that, like as Christ was raised up from the dead by the glory of the Father, even so we also should walk in newness of life. For if we have been planted together in the likeness of His death, we shall be also in the likeness of His resurrection: knowing this, that our old man is crucified with Him, that the body of sin might be destroyed, that henceforth we should not serve sin. For he that is dead is freed from sin. Now if we be dead with Christ, we believe that we shall also live with Him: knowing that Christ, being raised from the dead, dieth no more; death hath no more dominion over Him. For in that He died, He died unto sin once; but in that He liveth, He liveth unto God. Likewise reckon ye also yourselves to be dead indeed unto sin, but alive unto God through Jesus Christ our Lord." Now he had commenced with proving that we must not continue in sin that grace may abound, and had said: "How shall we that are dead to sin live any longer therein?" And to show that we are dead to sin, he added: "Know ye not, that so many of us as were baptized into Jesus Christ, were baptized into His death?" And so he concludes this whole passage just as he began it. For he has brought in the death of Christ in such a way as to imply that Christ Himself also died to sin. To what sin did He die if not to the flesh, in which there was not sin, but the likeness of sin, and which was therefore called by the name of sin? To those who are baptized into the death of Christ, then,—and this class includes not adults only, but infants as well,—he says: "Likewise reckon ye also yourselves to be dead indeed unto sin, but alive unto God through Jesus Christ our Lord."[5]

CHAP. 53.—CHRIST'S CROSS AND BURIAL, RESURRECTION, ASCENSION, AND SITTING DOWN AT THE RIGHT HAND OF GOD, ARE IMAGES OF THE CHRISTIAN LIFE.

All the events, then, of Christ's crucifixion,

---

[1] Rom. v. 16.   [2] Rom. v. 18.
[3] Rom. vi. 1.   [4] Rom. v. 20.   [5] Rom. vi. 1-11.

of His burial, of His resurrection the third day, of His ascension into heaven, of His sitting down at the right hand of the Father, were so ordered, that the life which the Christian leads here might be modelled upon them, not merely in a mystical sense, but in reality. For in reference to His crucifixion it is said: "They that are Christ's have crucified the flesh, with the affections and lusts."[1] And in reference to His burial: "We are buried with Him by baptism into death."[2] In reference to His resurrection: "That, like as Christ was raised up from the dead by the glory of the Father, even so we also should walk in newness of life."[3] And in reference to His ascension into heaven and sitting down at the right hand of the Father: "If ye then be risen with Christ, seek those things which are above, where Christ sitteth on the right hand of God. Set your affection on things above, not on things on the earth. For ye are dead, and your life is hid with Christ in God."[4]

CHAP. 54.—CHRIST'S SECOND COMING DOES NOT BELONG TO THE PAST, BUT WILL TAKE PLACE AT THE END OF THE WORLD.

But what we believe as to Christ's action in the future, when He shall come from heaven to judge the quick and the dead, has no bearing upon the life which we now lead here; for it forms no part of what He did upon earth, but is part of what He shall do at the end of the world. And it is to this that the apostle refers in what immediately follows the passage quoted above: "When Christ, who is our life, shall appear, then shall ye also appear with Him in glory."[5]

CHAP. 55.—THE EXPRESSION, "CHRIST SHALL JUDGE THE QUICK AND THE DEAD," MAY BE UNDERSTOOD IN EITHER OF TWO SENSES.

Now the expression, "to judge the quick and the dead," may be interpreted in two ways: either we may understand by the "quick" those who at His advent shall not yet have died, but whom He shall find alive in the flesh, and by the "dead" those who have departed from the body, or who shall have departed before His coming; or we may understand the "quick" to mean the righteous, and the "dead" the unrighteous; for the righteous shall be judged as well as others. Now the judgment of God is sometimes taken in a bad sense, as, for example, "They that have done evil unto the resurrection of judgment;"[6] sometimes in a good sense, as,

"Save me, O God, by Thy name, and judge me by Thy strength."[7] This is easily understood when we consider that it is the judgment of God which separates the good from the evil, and sets the good at His right hand, that they may be delivered from evil, and not destroyed with the wicked; and it is for this reason that the Psalmist cried, "Judge me, O God," and then added, as if in explanation, "and distinguish my cause from that of an ungodly nation."[8]

CHAP. 56.—THE HOLY SPIRIT AND THE CHURCH. THE CHURCH IS THE TEMPLE OF GOD.

And now, having spoken of Jesus Christ, the only Son of God, our Lord, with the brevity suitable to a confession of our faith, we go on to say that we believe also in the Holy Ghost,—thus completing the Trinity which constitutes the Godhead. Then we mention the Holy Church. And thus we are made to understand that the intelligent creation, which constitutes the free Jerusalem,[9] ought to be subordinate in the order of speech to the Creator, the Supreme Trinity: for all that is said of the man Christ Jesus has reference, of course, to the unity of the person of the Only-begotten. Therefore the true order of the Creed demanded that the Church should be made subordinate to the Trinity, as the house to Him who dwells in it, the temple to God who occupies it, and the city to its builder. And we are here to understand the whole Church, not that part of it only which wanders as a stranger on the earth, praising the name of God from the rising of the sun to the going down of the same, and singing a new song of deliverance from its old captivity; but that part also which has always from its creation remained steadfast to God in heaven, and has never experienced the misery consequent upon a fall. This part is made up of the holy angels, who enjoy uninterrupted happiness; and (as it is bound to do) it renders assistance to the part which is still wandering among strangers: for these two parts shall be one in the fellowship of eternity, and now they are one in the bonds of love, the whole having been ordained for the worship of the one God. Wherefore, neither the whole Church, nor any part of it, has any desire to be worshipped instead of God, nor to be God to any one who belongs to the temple of God —that temple which is built up of the saints who were created by the uncreated God. And therefore the Holy Spirit, if a creature, could not be the Creator, but would be a part

---

[1] Gal. v. 24. [2] Rom. vi. 4.
[3] Rom. vi. 5. [4] Col. iii. 1-3.
[5] Col. iii. 4. [6] John v. 29 (*damnation*, A. V.)

[7] Ps. liv. 1.
[8] Ps. xliii. 1 ("Plead my cause against an ungodly nation," A. V.) [9] Gal. iv. 26.

of the intelligent creation. He would simply be the highest creature, and therefore would not be mentioned in the Creed before the Church; for He Himself would belong to the Church, to that part of it which is in the heavens. And He would not have a temple, for He Himself would be part of a temple. Now He has a temple, of which the apostle says: "Know ye not that your body is the temple of the Holy Ghost, which is in you, which ye have of God?"[1] Of which body he says in another place: "Know ye not that your bodies are the members of Christ?"[2] How, then, is He not God, seeing that He has a temple? and how can He be less than Christ, whose members are His temple? Nor has He one temple, and God another, seeing that the same apostle says: "Know ye not that ye are the temple of God?"[3] and adds, as proof of this, "and that the Spirit of God dwelleth in you."[4] God, then, dwells in His temple: not the Holy Spirit only, but the Father also, and the Son, who says of His own body, through which He was made Head of the Church upon earth ("that in all things He might have the pre-eminence):"[5] "Destroy this temple, and in three days I will raise it up."[6] The temple of God, then, that is, of the Supreme Trinity as a whole, is the Holy Church, embracing in its full extent both heaven and earth.

CHAP. 57.—THE CONDITION OF THE CHURCH IN HEAVEN.

But of that part of the Church which is in heaven what can we say, except that no wicked one is found in it, and that no one has fallen from it, or shall ever fall from it, since the time that 'God spared not the angels that sinned," as the Apostle Peter writes, "but cast them down to hell, and delivered them into chains of darkness, to be reserved unto judgment?"[7]

CHAP. 58.—WE HAVE NO CERTAIN KNOWLEDGE OF THE ORGANIZATION OF THE ANGELIC SOCIETY.

Now, what the organization is of that supremely happy society in heaven: what the differences of rank are, which explain the fact that while all are called by the general name *angels*, as we read in the Epistle to the Hebrews, " but to which of the angels said God at any time, Sit on my right hand?"[8] (this form of expression being evidently designed to embrace all the angels without exception),

we yet find that there are some called *archangels;* and whether the archangels are the same as those called *hosts*, so that the expression, " Praise ye Him, all His angels: praise ye Him, all His hosts,"[9] is the same as if it had been said, "Praise ye Him, all His angels: praise ye Him, all His archangels;" and what are the various significations of those four names under which the apostle seems to embrace the whole heavenly company without exception, "whether they be thrones, or dominions, or principalities, or powers:"[10]—let those who are able answer these questions, if they can also prove their answers to be true; but as for me, I confess my ignorance. I am not even certain upon this point: whether the sun, and the moon, and all the stars, do not form part of this same society, though many consider them merely luminous bodies, without either sensation or intelligence.

CHAP. 59.—THE BODIES ASSUMED BY ANGELS RAISE A VERY DIFFICULT, AND NOT VERY USEFUL, SUBJECT OF DISCUSSION.

Further, who will tell with what sort of bodies it was that the angels appeared to men, making themselves not only visible, but tangible; and again, how it is that, not through material bodies, but by spiritual power, they present visions not to the bodily eyes, but to the spiritual eyes of the mind, or speak something not into the ear from without, but from within the soul of the man, they themselves being stationed there too, as it is written in the prophet, "And the angel that spake in me said unto me"[11] (he does not say, "that spake *to* me," but "that spake *in* me"); or appear to men in sleep, and make communications through dreams, as we read in the Gospel, "Behold, the angel of the Lord appeared unto him in a dream, saying"?[12] For these methods of communication seem to imply that the angels have not tangible bodies, and make it a very difficult question to solve how the patriarchs washed their feet,[13] and how it was that Jacob wrestled with the angel in a way so unmistakeably material.[14] To ask questions like these, and to make such guesses as we can at the answers, is a useful exercise for the intellect, if the discussion be kept within proper bounds, and if we avoid the error of supposing ourselves to know what we do not know. For what is the necessity for affirming, or denying, or defining with accuracy on these subjects, and others like them, when we may without blame be entirely ignorant of them?

---

[1] 1 Cor. vi. 19. [2] 1 Cor. vi. 15.
[3] 1 Cor. iii. 16. [4] 1 Cor. iii. 16.
[5] Col. i. 18. [6] John ii. 19.
[7] 2 Pet. ii. 4. [8] Heb. i. 13.

[9] Ps. cxlviii. 2, [" host," R. V.]   [10] Col. i. 16.
[11] Zech. i. 9 (" The angel that talked *with* me," A. V.)
[12] Matt. i. 20.   [13] Gen. xviii. 4, xix. 2.   [14] Gen. xxxii. 24, 25.

CHAP. 60.—IT IS MORE NECESSARY TO BE ABLE TO DETECT THE WILES OF SATAN WHEN HE TRANSFORMS HIMSELF INTO AN ANGEL OF LIGHT.

It is more necessary to use all our powers of discrimination and judgment when Satan transforms himself into an angel of light,[1] lest by his wiles he should lead us astray into hurtful courses. For, while he only deceives the bodily senses, and does not pervert the mind from that true and sound judgment which enables a man to lead a life of faith, there is no danger to religion; or if, feigning himself to be good, he does or says the things that befit good angels, and we believe him to be good, the error is not one that is hurtful or dangerous to Christian faith. But when, through these means, which are alien to his nature, he goes on to lead us into courses of his own, then great watchfulness is necessary to detect, and refuse to follow, him. But how many men are fit to evade all his deadly wiles, unless God restrains and watches over them? The very difficulty of the matter, however, is useful in this respect, that it prevents men from trusting in themselves or in one another, and leads all to place their confidence in God alone. And certainly no pious man can doubt that this is most expedient for us.

CHAP. 61.—THE CHURCH ON EARTH HAS BEEN REDEEMED FROM SIN BY THE BLOOD OF A MEDIATOR.

This part of the Church, then, which is made up of the holy angels and the hosts of God, shall become known to us in its true nature, when, at the end of the world, we shall be united with it in the common possession of everlasting happiness. But the other part, which, separated from it, wanders as a stranger on the earth, is better known to us, both because we belong to it, and because it is composed of men, and we too are men. This section of the Church has been redeemed from all sin by the blood of a Mediator who had no sin, and its song is: " If God be for us, who can be against us? He that spared not His own Son, but delivered Him up for us all."[2] Now it was not for the angels that Christ died. Yet what was done for the redemption of man through His death was in a sense done for the angels, because the enmity which sin had put between men and the holy angels is removed, and friendship is restored between them, and by the redemption of man the gaps which the great apostasy left in the angelic host are filled up.

CHAP. 62.—BY THE SACRIFICE OF CHRIST ALL THINGS ARE RESTORED, AND PEACE IS MADE BETWEEN EARTH AND HEAVEN.

And, of course, the holy angels, taught by God, in the eternal contemplation of whose truth their happiness consists, know how great a number of the human race are to supplement their ranks, and fill up the full tale of their citizenship. Wherefore the apostle says, that "all things are gathered together in one in Christ, both which are in heaven and which are on earth."[3] The things which are in heaven are gathered together when what was lost therefrom in the fall of the angels is restored from among men; and the things which are on earth are gathered together, when those who are predestined to eternal life are redeemed from their old corruption. And thus, through that single sacrifice in which the Mediator was offered up, the one sacrifice of which the many victims under the law were types, heavenly things are brought into peace with earthly things, and earthly things with heavenly. Wherefore, as the same apostle says: " For it pleased the Father that in Him should all fullness dwell: and, having made peace through the blood of His cross, by Him to reconcile all things to Himself: by Him, I say, whether they be things in earth, or things in heaven."[4]

CHAP. 63.—THE PEACE OF GOD, WHICH REIGNETH IN HEAVEN, PASSETH ALL UNDERSTANDING.

This peace, as Scripture saith, " passeth all understanding,"[5] and cannot be known by us until we have come into the full possession of it. For in what sense are heavenly things reconciled, except they be reconciled to us, viz. by coming into harmony with us? For in heaven there is unbroken peace, both between all the intelligent creatures that exist there, and between these and their Creator. And this peace, as is said, passeth all understanding; but this, of course, means our understanding, not that of those who always behold the face of their Father. We now, however great may be our human understanding, know but in part, and see through a glass darkly.[6] But when we shall be equal unto the angels of God[7] then we shall see face to face, as they do; and we shall have as great peace towards them as they have towards us, because we shall love them as much as we are loved by them. And so their peace shall be known to us: for our own peace shall be like to theirs, and as great as theirs, nor shall it

---

[1] 2 Cor. xi. 14.   [2] Rom. viii. 31.

[3] Eph. i. 10.   [4] Col. i. 19, 20. [R. V. "summed up."]
[5] Phil. iv. 7.   [6] 1 Cor. xiii. 12.   [7] Luke xx. 36.

then pass our understanding. But the peace of God, the peace which He cherisheth towards us, shall undoubtedly pass not our understanding only, but theirs as well. And this must be so: for every rational creature which is happy derives its happiness from Him; He does not derive His from it. And in this view it is better to interpret "all" in the passage, "The peace of God passeth all understanding," as admitting of no exception even in favor of the understanding of the holy angels: the only exception that can be made is that of God Himself. For, of course, His peace does not pass His own understanding.

CHAP. 64.—PARDON OF SIN EXTENDS OVER THE WHOLE MORTAL LIFE OF THE SAINTS, WHICH, THOUGH FREE FROM CRIME, IS NOT FREE FROM SIN.

But the angels even now are at peace with us when our sins are pardoned. Hence, in the order of the Creed, after the mention of the Holy Church is placed the remission of sins. For it is by this that the Church on earth stands: it is through this that what had been lost, and was found, is saved from being lost again. For, setting aside the grace of baptism, which is given as an antidote to original sin, so that what our birth imposes upon us, our new birth relieves us from (this grace, however, takes away all the actual sins also that have been committed in thought, word, and deed): setting aside, then, this great act of favor, whence commences man's restoration, and in which all our guilt, both original and actual, is washed away, the rest of our life from the time that we have the use of reason provides constant occasion for the remission of sins, however great may be our advance in righteousness. For the sons of God, as long as they live in this body of death, are in conflict with death. And although it is truly said of them, "As many as are led by the Spirit of God, they are the sons of God,"[1] yet they are led by the Spirit of God, and as the sons of God advance towards God under this drawback, that they are led also by their own spirit, weighted as it is by the corruptible body;[2] and that, as the sons of men, under the influence of human affections, they fall back to their old level, and so sin. There is a difference, however. For although every crime is a sin, every sin is not a crime. And so we say that the life of holy men, as long as they remain in this mortal body, may be found without crime; but, as the Apostle John says, "If we say that we have no sin, we deceive ourselves, and the truth is not in us."[3]

CHAP. 65.—GOD PARDONS SINS, BUT ON CONDITION OF PENITENCE, CERTAIN TIMES FOR WHICH HAVE BEEN FIXED BY THE LAW OF THE CHURCH.

But even crimes themselves, however great, may be remitted in the Holy Church; and the mercy of God is never to be despaired of by men who truly repent, each according to the measure of his sin. And in the act of repentance, where a crime has been committed of such a nature as to cut off the sinner from the body of Christ, we are not to take account so much of the measure of time as of the measure of sorrow; for a broken and a contrite heart God doth not despise.[4] But as the grief of one heart is frequently hid from another, and is not made known to others by words or other signs, when it is manifest to Him of whom it is said, "My groaning is not hid from Thee,"[5] those who govern the Church have rightly appointed times of penitence, that the Church in which the sins are remitted may be satisfied; and outside the Church sins are not remitted. For the Church alone has received the pledge of the Holy Spirit, without which there is no remission of sins—such, at least, as brings the pardoned to eternal life.

CHAP. 66.—THE PARDON OF SIN HAS REFERENCE CHIEFLY TO THE FUTURE JUDGMENT.

Now the pardon of sin has reference chiefly to the future judgment. For, as far as this life is concerned, the saying of Scripture holds good: "A heavy yoke is upon the sons of Adam, from the day that they go out of their mother's womb, till the day that they return to the mother of all things."[6] So that we see even infants, after baptism and regeneration, suffering from the infliction of divers evils: and thus we are given to understand, that all that is set forth in the sacraments of salvation refers rather to the hope of future good, than to the retaining or attaining of present blessings. For many sins seem in this world to be overlooked and visited with no punishment, whose punishment is reserved for the future (for it is not in vain that the day when Christ shall come as Judge of quick and dead is peculiarly named the day of judgment); just as, on the other hand, many sins are punished in this life, which nevertheless are pardoned, and shall bring down no punishment in the future life. Accordingly, in reference to certain temporal punishments, which in this life are visited upon sinners, the apostle, addressing those whose sins are

---

[1] Rom. viii. 14.   [2] Wisd. ix. 15.   [3] 1 John i. 8.   [4] Ps. li. 17.   [5] Ps. xxxviii. 9.   [6] Ecclus. xl. 1.

blotted out, and not reserved for the final judgment, says: "For if we would judge ourselves, we should not be judged. But when we are judged, we are chastened of the Lord, that we should not be condemned with the world."[1]

CHAP. 67.—FAITH WITHOUT WORKS IS DEAD, AND CANNOT SAVE A MAN.

It is believed, moreover, by some, that men who do not abandon the name of Christ, and who have been baptized in the Church by His baptism, and who have never been cut off from the Church by any schism or heresy, though they should live in the grossest sin, and never either wash it away in penitence nor redeem it by almsgiving, but persevere in it persistently to the last day of their lives, shall be saved by fire: that is, that although they shall suffer a punishment by fire, lasting for a time proportionate to the magnitude of their crimes and misdeeds, they shall not be punished with everlasting fire. But those who believe this, and yet are Catholics, seem to me to be led astray by a kind of benevolent feeling natural to humanity. For Holy Scripture, when consulted, gives a very different answer. I have written a book on this subject, entitled *Of Faith and Works*, in which, to the best of my ability, God assisting me, I have shown from Scripture, that the faith which saves us is that which the Apostle Paul clearly enough describes when he says: "For in Jesus Christ neither circumcision availeth anything, nor uncircumcision, but faith which worketh by love."[2] But if it worketh evil, and not good, then without doubt, as the Apostle James says, "it is dead, being alone."[3] The same apostle says again, "What doth it profit, my brethren, though a man say he hath faith, and have not works? Can faith save him?"[4] And further, if a wicked man shall be saved by fire on account of his faith alone, and if this is what the blessed Apostle Paul means when he says, "But he himself shall be saved, yet so as by fire;"[5] then faith without works *can* save a man, and what his fellow-apostle James says must be false. And that must be false which Paul himself says in another place: "Be not deceived: neither fornicators, nor idolaters, nor adulterers, nor effeminate, nor abusers of themselves with mankind, nor thieves, nor covetous, nor drunkards, nor revilers, nor extortioners, shall inherit the kingdom of God."[6] For if those who persevere in these wicked courses shall nevertheless be saved on account of their faith in Christ, how can it be true that they shall not inherit the kingdom of God?

CHAP. 68.—THE TRUE SENSE OF THE PASSAGE (I COR. III. 11-15) ABOUT THOSE WHO ARE SAVED, YET SO AS BY FIRE.

But as these most plain and unmistakeable declarations of the apostles cannot be false, that obscure saying about those who build upon the foundation, Christ, not gold, silver, and precious stones, but wood, hay, and stubble (for it is these who, it is said, shall be saved, yet so as by fire, the merit of the foundation saving them[7]), must be so interpreted as not to conflict with the plain statements quoted above. Now wood, hay, and stubble may, without incongruity, be understood to signify such an attachment to worldly things, however lawful these may be in themselves, that they cannot be lost without grief of mind. And though this grief burns, yet if Christ hold the place of foundation in the heart,—that is, if nothing be preferred to Him, and if the man, though burning with grief, is yet more willing to lose the things he loves so much than to lose Christ,—he is saved by fire. If, however, in time of temptation, he prefer to hold by temporal and earthly things rather than by Christ, he has not Christ as his foundation; for he puts earthly things in the first place, and in a building nothing comes before the foundation. Again, the fire of which the apostle speaks in this place must be such a fire as both men are made to pass through, that is, both the man who builds upon the foundation, gold, silver, precious stones, and the man who builds wood, hay, stubble. For he immediately adds: "The fire shall try every man's work, of what sort it is. If any man's work abide which he hath built thereupon, he shall receive a reward. If any man's work shall be burned, he shall suffer loss; but he himself shall be saved, yet so as by fire."[8] The fire then shall prove, not the work of one of them only, but of both. Now the trial of adversity is a kind of fire which is plainly spoken of in another place: "The furnace proveth the potter's vessels: and the furnace of adversity just men."[9] And this fire does in the course of this life act exactly in the way the apostle says. If it come into contact with two believers, one "caring for the things that belong to the Lord, how he may please the Lord,"[10] that is, building upon Christ the foundation, gold, silver, precious stones; the other "caring for the things that are of the

---

[1] I Cor. xi. 31, 32.   [2] Gal. v. 6.
[3] Jas. ii. 17. [See R. V.]   [4] Jas. ii. 14.
[5] I Cor. iii. 15.   [6] I Cor. vi. 9, 10.

[7] I Cor. iii. 11-15. [The "fire" in ver. 15 is not the purgatorial fire in the state between death and resurrection, but, as in ver. 14, the fire of the day of judgment.—P. S.]
[8] I Cor. iii. 13-15.   [9] Ecclus. xxvii. 5, ii. 5.
[10] I Cor. vii. 32.   [11] I Cor. vii. 33. [See R.V.]

world, how he may please his wife,"[11] that is, building upon the same foundation wood, hay, stubble,—the work of the former is not burned, because he has not given his love to things whose loss can cause him grief; but the work of the latter is burned, because things that are enjoyed with desire cannot be lost without pain. But since, by our supposition, even the latter prefers to lose these things rather than to lose Christ, and since he does not desert Christ out of fear of losing them, though he is grieved when he does lose them, he is saved, but it is so as by fire; because the grief for what he loved and has lost burns him. But it does not subvert nor consume him; for he is protected by his immoveable and incorruptible foundation.

CHAP. 69.—IT IS NOT IMPOSSIBLE THAT SOME BELIEVERS MAY PASS THROUGH A PURGATORIAL FIRE IN THE FUTURE LIFE.

And it is not impossible that something of the same kind may take place even after this life. It is a matter that may be inquired into, and either ascertained or left doubtful, whether some believers shall pass through a kind of purgatorial fire, and in proportion as they have loved with more or less devotion the goods that perish, be less or more quickly delivered from it. This cannot, however, be the case of any of those of whom it is said, that they "shall not inherit the kingdom of God,"[1] unless after suitable repentance their sins be forgiven them. When I say "suitable," I mean that they are not to be unfruitful in almsgiving; for Holy Scripture lays so much stress on this virtue, that our Lord tells us beforehand, that He will ascribe no merit to those on His right hand but that they abound in it, and no defect to those on His left hand but their want of it, when He shall say to the former, "Come, ye blessed of my Father, inherit the kingdom," and to the latter, "Depart from me, ye cursed, into everlasting fire."[2]

CHAP. 70.—ALMSGIVING WILL NOT ATONE FOR SIN UNLESS THE LIFE BE CHANGED.

We must beware, however, lest any one should suppose that gross sins, such as are committed by those who shall not inherit the kingdom of God, may be daily perpetrated, and daily atoned for by almsgiving. The life must be changed for the better; and almsgiving must be used to propitiate God for past sins, not to purchase impunity for the commission of such sins in the future. For He has given no man license to sin,[3] although in His mercy

He may blot out sins that are already committed, if we do not neglect to make proper satisfaction.

CHAP. 71.—THE DAILY PRAYER OF THE BELIEVER MAKES SATISFACTION FOR THE TRIVIAL SINS THAT DAILY STAIN HIS LIFE.

Now the daily prayer of the believer makes satisfaction for those daily sins of a momentary and trivial kind which are necessary incidents of this life. For he can say, "Our Father which art in heaven,"[4] seeing that to such a Father he is now born again of water and of the Spirit.[5] And this prayer certainly takes away the very small sins of daily life. It takes away also those which at one time made the life of the believer very wicked, but which, now that he is changed for the better by repentance, he has given up, provided that as truly as he says, "Forgive us our debts" (for there is no want of debts to be forgiven), so truly does he say, "as we forgive our debtors;"[6] that is, provided he does what he says he does: for to forgive a man who asks for pardon, is really to give alms.

CHAP. 72.—THERE ARE MANY KINDS OF ALMS, THE GIVING OF WHICH ASSISTS TO PROCURE PARDON FOR OUR SINS.

And on this principle of interpretation, our Lord's saying, "Give alms of such things as ye have, and, behold, all things are clean unto you,"[7] applies to every useful act that a man does in mercy. Not only, then, the man who gives food to the hungry, drink to the thirsty, clothing to the naked, hospitality to the stranger, shelter to the fugitive, who visits the sick and the imprisoned, ransoms the captive, assists the weak, leads the blind, comforts the sorrowful, heals the sick, puts the wanderer on the right path, gives advice to the perplexed, and supplies the wants of the needy,—not this man only, but the man who pardons the sinner also gives alms; and the man who corrects with blows, or restrains by any kind of discipline one over whom he has power, and who at the same time forgives from the heart the sin by which he was injured, or prays that it may be forgiven, is also a giver of alms, not only in that he forgives, or prays for forgiveness for the sin, but also in that he rebukes and corrects the sinner: for in this, too, he shows mercy. Now much good is bestowed upon unwilling recipients, when their advantage and not their pleasure is consulted; and they themselves

---

[1] 1 Cor. vi. 10.   [2] Matt. xxv. 31-46.   [3] Ecclus. xv. 20.   [4] Matt. vi. 9.   [5] John iii. 5.   [6] Matt. vi. 12.   [7] Luke xi. 41.

frequently prove to be their own enemies, while their true friends are those whom they take for their enemies, and to whom in their blindness they return evil for good. (A Christian, indeed, is not permitted to return evil even for evil.[1]) And thus there are many kinds of alms, by giving of which we assist to procure the pardon of our sins.

CHAP. 73.—THE GREATEST OF ALL ALMS IS TO FORGIVE OUR DEBTORS AND TO LOVE OUR ENEMIES.

But none of those is greater than to forgive from the heart a sin that has been committed against us. For it is a comparatively small thing to wish well to, or even to do good to, a man who has done no evil to you. It is a much higher thing, and is the result of the most exalted goodness, to love your enemy, and always to wish well to, and when you have the opportunity, to do good to, the man who wishes you ill, and, when he can, does you harm. This is to obey the command of God: "Love your enemies, do good to them that hate you, and pray for them which persecute you."[2] But seeing that this is a frame of mind only reached by the perfect sons of God, and that though every believer ought to strive after it, and by prayer to God and earnest struggling with himself endeavor to bring his soul up to this standard, yet a degree of goodness so high can hardly belong to so great a multitude as we believe are heard when they use this petition, "Forgive us our debts, as we forgive our debtors;" in view of all this, it cannot be doubted that the implied undertaking is fulfilled if a man, though he has not yet attained to loving his enemy, yet, when asked by one who has sinned against him to forgive him his sin, does forgive him from his heart. For he certainly desires to be himself forgiven when he prays, "as we forgive our debtors," that is, Forgive us our debts when we beg forgiveness, as we forgive our debtors when they beg forgiveness from us.

CHAP. 74.—GOD DOES NOT PARDON THE SINS OF THOSE WHO DO NOT FROM THE HEART FORGIVE OTHERS.

Now, he who asks forgiveness of the man against whom he has sinned, being moved by his sin to ask forgiveness, cannot be counted an enemy in such a sense that it should be as difficult to love him now as it was when he was engaged in active hostility. And the man who does not from his heart forgive him who repents of his sin, and asks forgiveness,

need not suppose that his own sins are forgiven of God. For the Truth cannot lie. And what reader or hearer of the Gospel can have failed to notice, that the same person who said, "I am the Truth,"[3] taught us also this form of prayer; and in order to impress this particular petition deeply upon our minds, said, "For if ye forgive men their trespasses, your heavenly Father will also forgive you; but if ye forgive not men their trespasses, neither will your Father forgive your trespasses"?[4] The man whom the thunder of this warning does not awaken is not asleep, but dead; and yet so powerful is that voice, that it can awaken even the dead.

CHAP. 75.—THE WICKED AND THE UNBELIEVING ARE NOT MADE CLEAN BY THE GIVING OF ALMS, EXCEPT THEY BE BORN AGAIN.

Assuredly, then, those who live in gross wickedness, and take no care to reform their lives and manners, and yet amid all their crimes and vices do not cease to give frequent alms, in vain take comfort to themselves from the saying of our Lord: "Give alms of such things as ye have; and, behold, all things are clean unto you."[5] For they do not understand how far this saying reaches. But that they may understand this, let them hear what He says. For we read in the Gospel as follows: "And as He spake, a certain Pharisee besought Him to dine with him; and He went in, and sat down to meat. And when the Pharisee saw it, he marvelled that He had not first washed before dinner. And the Lord said unto him, Now do ye Pharisees make clean the outside of the cup and the platter; but your inward part is full of ravening and wickedness. Ye fools, did not he that made that which is without, make that which is within also? But rather give alms of such things as ye have; and, behold, all things are clean unto you."[6] Are we to understand this as meaning that to the Pharisees who have not the faith of Christ all things are clean, if only they give alms in the way these men count almsgiving, even though they have never believed in Christ, nor been born again of water and of the Spirit? But the fact is, that all are unclean who are not made clean by the faith of Christ, according to the expression, "purifying their hearts by faith;"[7] and that the apostle says, "Unto them that are defiled and unbelieving is nothing pure; but even their mind and conscience is defiled."[8] How, then, could all things be clean to the Pharisees, even though they gave

---

1 Rom. xii. 17; Matt. v. 44.   2 Matt. v. 44.

3 John xiv. 6.
5 Luke xi. 41.
7 Acts xv. 9.

4 Matt. vi. 14, 15.
6 Luke xi. 37-41. [See R. V.]
8 Tit. i. 15.

alms, if they were not believers? And how could they be believers if they were not willing to have faith in Christ, and to be born again of His grace? And yet what they heard is true: "Give alms of such things as ye have; and, behold, all things are clean unto you."

CHAP. 76.—TO GIVE ALMS ARIGHT, WE SHOULD BEGIN WITH OURSELVES, AND HAVE PITY UPON OUR OWN SOULS.

For the man who wishes to give alms as he ought, should begin with himself, and give to himself first. For almsgiving is a work of mercy; and most truly is it said, "To have mercy on thy soul is pleasing to God."[1] And for this end are we born again, that we should be pleasing to God, who is justly displeased with that which we brought with us when we were born. This is our first alms, which we give to ourselves when, through the mercy of a pitying God, we find that we are ourselves wretched, and confess the justice of His judgment by which we are made wretched, of which the apostle says, "The judgment was by one to condemnation;"[2] and praise the greatness of His love, of which the same preacher of grace says, "God commendeth His love toward us, in that, while we were yet sinners, Christ died for us:"[3] and thus, judging truly of our own misery, and loving God with the love which He has Himself bestowed, we lead a holy and virtuous life. But the Pharisees, while they gave as alms the tithe of all their fruits, even the most insignificant, passed over judgment and the love of God, and so did not commence their almsgiving at home, and extend their pity to themselves in the first instance. And it is in reference to this order of love that it is said, "Love thy neighbor as thyself."[4] When, then, our Lord had rebuked them because they made themselves clean on the outside, but within were full of ravening and wickedness, He advised them, in the exercise of that charity which each man owes to himself in the first instance, to make clean the inward parts. "But rather," He says, "give alms of such things as ye have; and, behold, all things are clean unto you."[5] Then, to show what it was that He advised, and what they took no pains to do, and to show that He did not overlook or forget their almsgiving, "But woe unto you, Pharisees!"[5] He says; as if He meant to say: I indeed advise you to give alms which shall make all things clean unto you; "but woe unto you! for ye tithe mint, and rue, and all manner of herbs;" as if He meant to say: I know these alms of yours,

and ye need not think that I am now admonishing you in respect of such things; "and pass over judgment and the love of God," an alms by which ye might have been made clean from all inward impurity, so that even the bodies which ye are now washing would have been clean to you. For this is the import of "all things," both inward and outward things, as we read in another place: "Cleanse first that which is within, that the outside may be clean also."[6] But lest He might appear to despise the alms which they were giving out of the fruits of the earth, He says: "These ought ye to have done," referring to judgment and the love of God, "and not to leave the other undone," referring to the giving of the tithes.

CHAP. 77.—IF WE WOULD GIVE ALMS TO OURSELVES, WE MUST FLEE INIQUITY; FOR HE WHO LOVETH INIQUITY HATETH HIS SOUL.

Those, then, who think that they can by giving alms, however profuse, whether in money or in kind, purchase for themselves the privilege of persisting with impunity in their monstrous crimes and hideous vices, need not thus deceive themselves. For not only do they commit these sins, but they love them so much that they would like to go on forever committing them, if only they could do so with impunity. Now, he who loveth iniquity hateth his own soul;[7] and he who hateth his own soul is not merciful but cruel towards it. For in loving it according to the world, he hateth it according to God. But if he desired to give alms to it which should make all things clean unto him, he would hate it according to the world, and love it according to God. Now no one gives alms unless he receive what he gives from one who is not in want of it. Therefore it is said, "His mercy shall meet me."[8]

CHAP. 78.—WHAT SINS ARE TRIVIAL AND WHAT HEINOUS IS A MATTER FOR GOD'S JUDGMENT.

Now, what sins are trivial and what heinous is not a matter to be decided by man's judgment, but by the judgment of God. For it is plain that the apostles themselves have given an indulgence in the case of certain sins: take, for example, what the Apostle Paul says to those who are married: "Defraud ye not one the other, except it be with consent for a time, that ye may give yourselves to fasting and prayer: and come together again, that

---

[1] Ecclus. xxx. 24.
[2] Rom. v. 16.
[3] Rom. v. 8.
[4] Luke x. 27.
[5] Luke xi. 42.
[6] Matt. xxiii. 26.
[7] Ps. xi. 5 ("Him that loveth violence, His (God's) soul hateth," A. V.).
[8] Ps. lix. 10.

Satan tempt you not for your incontinency." [1] Now it is possible that it might not have been considered a sin to have intercourse with a spouse, not with a view to the procreation of children, which is the great blessing of marriage, but for the sake of carnal pleasure, and to save the incontinent from being led by their weakness into the deadly sin of fornication, or adultery, or another form of uncleanness which it is shameful even to name, and into which it is possible that they might be drawn by lust under the temptation of Satan. It is possible, I say, that this might not have been considered a sin, had the apostle not added: " But I speak this by permission, and not of commandment." [2] Who, then, can deny that it is a sin, when confessedly it is only by apostolic authority that permission is granted to those who do it? Another case of the same kind is where he says: " Dare any of you, having a matter against another, go to law before the unjust, and not before the saints?" [3] And shortly afterwards: " If then ye have judgments of things pertaining to this life, set them to judge who are least esteemed in the Church. I speak to your shame. Is it so, that there is not a wise man among you? no, not one that shall be able to judge between his brethren? But brother goeth to law with brother, and that before the unbelievers." [4] Now it might have been supposed in this case that it is not a sin to have a quarrel with another, that the only sin is in wishing to have it adjudicated upon outside the Church, had not the apostle immediately added: " Now therefore there is utterly a fault among you, because ye go to law with one another." [5] And lest any one should excuse himself by saying that he had a just cause, and was suffering wrong, and that he only wished the sentence of the judges to remove his wrong, the apostle immediately anticipates such thoughts and excuses, and says: " Why do ye not rather take wrong? Why do ye not rather suffer yourselves to be defrauded?" Thus bringing us back to our Lord's saying, " If any man will sue thee at the law, and take away thy coat, let him have thy cloak also;" [6] and again, " Of him that taketh away thy goods, ask them not again." [7] Therefore our Lord has forbidden His followers to go to law with other men about worldly affairs. And carrying out this principle, the apostle here declares that to do so is " altogether a fault." But when, notwithstanding, he grants his permission to have such cases between brethren decided in the

Church, other brethren adjudicating, and only sternly forbids them to be carried outside the Church, it is manifest that here again an indulgence is extended to the infirmities of the weak. It is in view, then, of these sins, and others of the same sort, and of others again more trifling still, which consist of offenses in words and thought (as the Apostle James confesses, " In many things we offend all" [8]), that we need to pray every day and often to the Lord, saying, " Forgive us our debts," and to add in truth and sincerity, "as we forgive our debtors."

CHAP. 79.—SINS WHICH APPEAR VERY TRIFLING, ARE SOMETIMES IN REALITY VERY SERIOUS.

Again, there are some sins which would be considered very trifling, if the Scriptures did not show that they are really very serious. For who would suppose that the man who says to his brother, " Thou fool," is in danger of hell-fire, did not He who is the Truth say so? To the wound, however, He immediately applies the cure, giving a rule for reconciliation with one's offended brother: " Therefore, if thou bring thy gift to the altar, and there rememberest that thy brother hath ought against thee; leave there thy gift before the altar, and go thy way: first be reconciled to thy brother, and then come and offer thy gift." [9] Again, who would suppose that it was so great a sin to observe days, and months, and times, and years, as those do who are anxious or unwilling to begin anything on certain days, or in certain months or years, because the vain doctrines of men lead them to think such times lucky or unlucky, had we not the means of estimating the greatness of the evil from the fear expressed by the apostle, who says to such men, " I am afraid of you, lest I have bestowed upon you labor in vain"? [10]

CHAP. 80.—SINS, HOWEVER GREAT AND DETESTABLE, SEEM TRIVIAL WHEN WE ARE ACCUSTOMED TO THEM.

Add to this, that sins, however great and detestable they may be, are looked upon as trivial, or as not sins at all, when men get accustomed to them; and so far does this go, that such sins are not only not concealed, but are boasted of, and published far and wide; and thus, as it is written, " The wicked boasteth of his heart's desire, and blesseth the covetous, whom the Lord abhorreth." [11] Iniquity of this kind is in Scripture called a *cry*. You have an instance in the prophet Isaiah, in the case of the evil vineyard: " He looked

---

1 1 Cor. vii. 5.   2 1 Cor. vii. 6. [" Concession," R. V.]
3 1 Cor. vi. 1.   4 1 Cor. vi. 4-6.   5 1 Cor. vi. 7.
6 Matt. v. 40.   7 Luke vi. 30.

8 Jas. iii. 2. [See R. V.]   9 Matt. v. 22, 23.
10 Gal. iv. 10, 11.   11 Ps. x. 3.

for judgment, but behold oppression; for righteousness, but behold a cry."[1] Whence also the expression in Genesis: "The cry of Sodom and Gomorrah is great,"[2] because in these cities crimes were not only not punished, but were openly committed, as if under the protection of the law. And so in our own times: many forms of sin, though not just the same as those of Sodom and Gomorrah, are now so openly and habitually practised, that not only dare we not excommunicate a layman, we dare not even degrade a clergyman, for the commission of them. So that when, a few years ago, I was expounding the Epistle to the Galatians, in commenting on that very place where the apostle says, " I am afraid of you, lest I have bestowed labor upon you in vain," I was compelled to exclaim, "Woe to the sins of men! for it is only when we are not accustomed to them that we shrink from them: when once we are accustomed to them, though the blood of the Son of God was poured out to wash them away, though they are so great that the kingdom of God is wholly shut against them, constant familiarity leads to the toleration of them all, and habitual toleration leads to the practice of many of them. And grant, O Lord, that we may not come to practise all that we have not the power to hinder." But I shall see whether the extravagance of grief did not betray me into rashness of speech.

CHAP. 81.—THERE ARE TWO CAUSES OF SIN, IGNORANCE AND WEAKNESS ; AND WE NEED DIVINE HELP TO OVERCOME BOTH.

I shall now say this, which I have often said before in other places of my works. There are two causes that lead to sin: either we do not yet know our duty, or we do not perform the duty that we know. The former is the sin of ignorance, the latter of weakness. Now against these it is our duty to struggle; but we shall certainly be beaten in the fight, unless we are helped by God, not only to see our duty, but also, when we clearly see it, to make the love of righteousness stronger in us than the love of earthly things, the eager longing after which, or the fear of losing which, leads us with our eyes open into known sin. In the latter case we are not only sinners, for we are so even when we err through ignorance, but we are also transgressors of the law; for we leave undone what we know we ought to do, and we do what we know we ought not to do. Wherefore not only ought we to pray for pardon when we have sinned,

saying, "Forgive us our debts, as we forgive our debtors;" but we ought to pray for guidance, that we may be kept from sinning, saying, "and lead us not into temptation." And we are to pray to Him of whom the Psalmist says, "The Lord is my light and my salvation:"[3] my light, for He removes my ignorance; my salvation, for He takes away my infirmity.

CHAP. 82.—THE MERCY OF GOD IS NECESSARY TO TRUE REPENTANCE.

Now even penance itself, when by the law of the Church there is sufficient reason for its being gone through, is frequently evaded through infirmity; for shame is the fear of losing pleasure when the good opinion of men gives more pleasure than the righteousness which leads a man to humble himself in penitence. Wherefore the mercy of God is necessary not only when a man repents, but even to lead him to repent. How else explain what the apostle says of certain persons: "if God peradventure will give them repentance"?[4] And before Peter wept bitterly, we are told by the evangelist, "The Lord turned, and looked upon him."[5]

CHAP. 83.—THE MAN WHO DESPISES THE MERCY OF GOD IS GUILTY OF THE SIN AGAINST THE HOLY GHOST.

Now the man who, not believing that sins are remitted in the Church, despises this great gift of God's mercy, and persists to the last day of his life in his obstinacy of heart, is guilty of the unpardonable sin against the Holy Ghost, in whom Christ forgives sins.[6] But this difficult question I have discussed as clearly as I could in a book devoted exclusively to this one point.

CHAP. 84.—THE RESURRECTION OF THE BODY GIVES RISE TO NUMEROUS QUESTIONS.

Now, as to the resurrection of the body, —not a resurrection such as some have had, who came back to life for a time and died again, but a resurrection to eternal life, as the body of Christ Himself rose again,—I do not see how I can discuss the matter briefly, and at the same time give a satisfactory answer to all the questions that are ordinarily raised about it. Yet that the bodies of all men— both those who have been born and those who shall be born, both those who have died and those who shall die—shall be raised again, no Christian ought to have the shadow of a doubt.

---

[1] Isa. v. 7.   [2] Gen. xviii. 20.

[3] Ps. xxvii. 1.   [4] 2 Tim. ii. 25.
[5] Luke xxii. 61.   [6] Matt. xii. 32.

CHAP. 85.—THE CASE OF ABORTIVE CONCEPTIONS.

Hence in the first place arises a question about abortive conceptions, which have indeed been born in the mother's womb, but not so born that they could be born again. For if we shall decide that these are to rise again, we cannot object to any conclusion that may be drawn in regard to those which are fully formed. Now who is there that is not rather disposed to think that unformed abortions perish, like seeds that have never fructified? But who will dare to deny, though he may not dare to affirm, that at the resurrection every defect in the form shall be supplied, and that thus the perfection which time would have brought shall not be wanting, any more than the blemishes which time did bring shall be present: so that the nature shall neither want anything suitable and in harmony with it that length of days would have added, nor be debased by the presence of anything of an opposite kind that length of days has added; but that what is not yet complete shall be completed, just as what has been injured shall be renewed.

CHAP. 86.—IF THEY HAVE EVER LIVED, THEY MUST OF COURSE HAVE DIED, AND THEREFORE SHALL HAVE A SHARE IN THE RESURRECTION OF THE DEAD.

And therefore the following question may be very carefully inquired into and discussed by learned men, though I do not know whether it is in man's power to resolve it: At what time the infant begins to live in the womb: whether life exists in a latent form before it manifests itself in the motions of the living being. To deny that the young who are cut out limb by limb from the womb, lest if they were left there dead the mother should die too, have never been alive, seems too audacious. Now, from the time that a man begins to live, from that time it is possible for him to die. And if he die, wheresoever death may overtake him, I cannot discover on what principle he can be denied an interest in the resurrection of the dead.

CHAP. 87.—THE CASE OF MONSTROUS BIRTHS.

We are not justified in affirming even of monstrosities, which are born and live, however quickly they may die, that they shall not rise again, nor that they shall rise again in their deformity, and not rather with an amended and perfected body. God forbid that the double limbed man who was lately born in the East, of whom an account was brought by most trustworthy brethren who had seen him,—an account which the presbyter Jerome, of blessed memory, left in writing;[1]—God forbid, I say, that we should think that at the resurrection there shall be one man with double limbs, and not two distinct men, as would have been the case had twins been born. And so other births, which, because they have either a superfluity or a defect, or because they are very much deformed, are called *monstrosities*, shall at the resurrection be restored to the normal shape of man; and so each single soul shall possess its own body; and no bodies shall cohere together even though they were born in cohesion, but each separately shall possess all the members which constitute a complete human body.

CHAP. 88.—THE MATERIAL OF THE BODY NEVER PERISHES.

Nor does the earthly material out of which men's mortal bodies are created ever perish; but though it may crumble into dust and ashes, or be dissolved into vapors and exhalations, though it may be transformed into the substance of other bodies, or dispersed into the elements, though it should become food for beasts or men, and be changed into their flesh, it returns in a moment of time to that human soul which animated it at the first, and which caused it to become man, and to live and grow.

CHAP. 89.—BUT THIS MATERIAL MAY BE DIFFERENTLY ARRANGED IN THE RESURRECTION BODY.

And this earthly material, which when the soul leaves it becomes a corpse, shall not at the resurrection be so restored as that the parts into which it is separated, and which under various forms and appearances become parts of other things (though they shall all return to the same body from which they were separated), must necessarily return to the same parts of the body in which they were originally situated. For otherwise, to suppose that the hair recovers all that our frequent clippings and shavings have taken away from it, and the nails all that we have so often pared off, presents to the imagination such a picture of ugliness and deformity, as to make the resurrection of the body all but incredible. But just as if a statue of some soluble metal were either melted by fire, or broken into dust, or reduced to a shapeless mass,

---

[1] Jerome, in his *Epistle to Vitalis:* "Or because in our times a man was born at Lydda with two heads, four hands, one belly, and two feet, does it necessarily follow that all men are so born?"

and a sculptor wished to restore it from the same quantity of metal, it would make no difference to the completeness of the work what part of the statue any given particle of the material was put into, as long as the restored statue contained all the material of the original one; so God, the Artificer of marvellous and unspeakable power, shall with marvellous and unspeakable rapidity restore our body, using up the whole material of which it originally consisted. Nor will it affect the completeness of its restoration whether hairs return to hairs, and nails to nails, or whether the part of these that had perished be changed into flesh, and called to take its place in another part of the body, the great Artist taking careful heed that nothing shall be unbecoming or out of place.

CHAP. 90.—IF THERE BE DIFFERENCES AND IN-EQUALITIES AMONG THE BODIES OF THOSE WHO RISE AGAIN, THERE SHALL BE NOTHING OFFENSIVE OR DISPROPORTIONATE IN ANY.

Nor does it necessarily follow that there shall be differences of stature among those who rise again, because they were of different statures during life; nor is it certain that the lean shall rise again in their former leanness, and the fat in their former fatness. But if it is part of the Creator's design that each should preserve his own peculiarities of feature, and retain a recognizable likeness to his former self, while in regard to other bodily advantages all should be equal, then the material of which each is composed may be so modified that none of it shall be lost, and that any defect may be supplied by Him who can create at His will out of nothing. But if in the bodies of those who rise again there shall be a well-ordered inequality, such as there is in the voices that make up a full harmony, then the material of each man's body shall be so dealt with that it shall form a man fit for the assemblies of the angels, and one who shall bring nothing among them to jar upon their sensibilities. And assuredly nothing that is unseemly shall be there; but whatever shall be there shall be graceful and becoming: for if anything is not seemly, neither shall it be.

CHAP. 91.—THE BODIES OF THE SAINTS SHALL AT THE RESURRECTION BE SPIRITUAL BODIES.

The bodies of the saints, then, shall rise again free from every defect, from every blemish, as from all corruption, weight, and impediment. For their ease of movement shall be as complete as their happiness. Whence their bodies have been called *spiritual*, though

undoubtedly they shall be bodies and not spirits. For just as now the body is called *animate*, though it is a body, and not a soul [*anima*], so then the body shall be called spiritual, though it shall be a body, not a spirit.[1] Hence, as far as regards the corruption which now weighs down the soul, and the vices which urge the flesh to lust against the spirit,[2] it shall not then be flesh, but body; for there are bodies which are called celestial. Wherefore it is said, "Flesh and blood cannot inherit the kingdom of God;" and, as if in explanation of this, "neither doth corruption inherit incorruption."[3] What the apostle first called "flesh and blood," he afterwards calls "corruption;" and what he first called "the kingdom of God," he afterwards calls "incorruption." But as far as regards the substance, even then it shall be flesh. For even after the resurrection the body of Christ was called flesh.[4] The apostle, however, says: "It is sown a natural body; it is raised a spiritual body;"[5] because so perfect shall then be the harmony between flesh and spirit, the spirit keeping alive the subjugated flesh without the need of any nourishment, that no part of our nature shall be in discord with another; but as we shall be free from enemies without, so we shall not have ourselves for enemies within.

CHAP. 92.—THE RESURRECTION OF THE LOST.

But as for those who, out of the mass of perdition caused by the first man's sin, are not redeemed through the one Mediator between God and man, they too shall rise again, each with his own body, but only to be punished with the devil and his angels. Now, whether they shall rise again with all their diseases and deformities of body, bringing with them the diseased and deformed limbs which they possessed here, it would be labor lost to inquire. For we need not weary ourselves speculating about their health or their beauty, which are matters uncertain, when their eternal damnation is a matter of certainty. Nor need we inquire in what sense their body shall be incorruptible, if it be susceptible of pain; or in what sense corruptible, if it be free from the possibility of death. For there is no true life except where there is happiness in life, and no true incorruption except where health is unbroken by any pain. When, however, the unhappy are not permitted to die, then, if I may so speak, death itself dies not; and where pain without intermission afflicts the

---

[1] 1 Cor. xv. 44. [See R. V.]   [2] Wisd. ix. 15; Gal. v. 17.
[3] 1 Cor. xv. 50.   [4] Luke xxiv. 39.
[5] 1 Cor. xv. 44.

soul, and never comes to an end, corruption itself is not completed. This is called in Holy Scripture "the second death."[1]

CHAP. 93.—BOTH THE FIRST AND THE SECOND DEATHS ARE THE CONSEQUENCE OF SIN. PUNISHMENT IS PROPORTIONED TO GUILT.

And neither the first death, which takes place when the soul is compelled to leave the body, nor the second death, which takes place when the soul is not permitted to leave the suffering body, would have been inflicted on man had no one sinned. And, of course, the mildest punishment of all will fall upon those who have added no actual sin, to the original sin they brought with them; and as for the rest who have added such actual sins, the punishment of each will be the more tolerable in the next world, according as his iniquity has been less in this world.

CHAP. 94.—THE SAINTS SHALL KNOW MORE FULLY IN THE NEXT WORLD THE BENEFITS THEY HAVE RECEIVED BY GRACE.

Thus, when reprobate angels and men are left to endure everlasting punishment, the saints shall know more fully the benefits they have received by grace. Then, in contemplation of the actual facts, they shall see more clearly the meaning of the expression in the psalms, " I will sing of mercy and judgment; "[2] for it is only of unmerited mercy that any is redeemed, and only in well-merited judgment that any is condemned.

CHAP. 95.—GOD'S JUDGMENTS SHALL THEN BE EXPLAINED.

Then shall be made clear much that is now dark. For example, when of two infants, whose cases seem in all respects alike, one is by the mercy of God chosen to Himself, and the other is by His justice abandoned (wherein the one who is chosen may recognize what was of justice due to himself, had not mercy intervened); why, of these two, the one should have been chosen rather than the other, is to us an insoluble problem. And again, why miracles were not wrought in the presence of men who would have repented at the working of the miracles, while they were wrought in the presence of others who, it was known, would not repent. For our Lord says most distinctly: " Woe unto thee, Chorazin ! woe unto thee, Bethsaida ! for if the mighty works, which were done in you, had been done in Tyre and Sidon, they would have repented long ago in sackcloth and ashes."[3] And assuredly there was no injustice in God's not willing that they should be saved, though they could have been saved had He so willed it. Then shall be seen in the clearest light of wisdom what with the pious is now a faith, though it is not yet a matter of certain knowledge, how sure, how unchangeable, and how effectual is the will of God; how many things He can do which He does not will to do, though willing nothing which He cannot perform; and how true is the song of the psalmist, " But our God is in the heavens; He hath done whatsoever He hath pleased."[4] And this certainly is not true, if God has ever willed anything that He has not performed; and, still worse, if it was the will of man that hindered the Omnipotent from doing what He pleased. Nothing, therefore, happens but by the will of the Omnipotent, He either permitting it to be done, or Himself doing it.

CHAP. 96.—THE OMNIPOTENT GOD DOES WELL EVEN IN THE PERMISSION OF EVIL.

Nor can we doubt that God does well even in the permission of what is evil. For He permits it only in the justice of His judgment. And surely all that is just is good. Although, therefore, evil, in so far as it is evil, is not a good; yet the fact that evil as well as good exists, is a good. For if it were not a good that evil should exist, its existence would not be permitted by the omnipotent Good, who without doubt can as easily refuse to permit what He does not wish, as bring about what He does wish. And if we do not believe this, the very first sentence of our creed is endangered, wherein we profess to believe in God the Father Almighty. For He is not truly called Almighty if He cannot do whatsoever He pleases, or if the power of His almighty will is hindered by the will of any creature whatsoever.

CHAP. 97.—IN WHAT SENSE DOES THE APOSTLE SAY THAT " GOD WILL HAVE ALL MEN TO BE SAVED," WHEN, AS A MATTER OF FACT, ALL ARE NOT SAVED ?

Hence we must inquire in what sense is said of God what the apostle has mostly truly said: " Who will have all men to be saved."[5] For, as a matter of fact, not all, nor even a majority, are saved: so that it would seem that what God wills is not done, man's will interfering with, and hindering the will of God. When we ask the reason why all men are not saved, the ordinary answer is: " Because men

---

[1] Rev. ii. 2.　　　[2] Ps. ci. 1.　　　[3] Matt. xi. 21.　　[4] Ps. cxv. 3.　　[5] 1 Tim. ii. 4. [See R. V.]

themselves are not willing." This, indeed, cannot be said of infants, for it is not in their power either to will or not to will. But if we could attribute to their will the childish movements they make at baptism, when they make all the resistance they can, we should say that even they are not willing to be saved. Our Lord says plainly, however, in the Gospel, when upbraiding the impious city: "How often would I have gathered thy children together, even as a hen gathereth her chickens under her wings, and ye would not!"[1] as if the will of God had been overcome by the will of men, and when the weakest stood in the way with their want of will, the will of the strongest could not be carried out. And where is that omnipotence which hath done all that it pleased on earth and in heaven, if God willed to gather together the children of Jerusalem, and did not accomplish it? or rather, Jerusalem was not willing that her children should be gathered together? But even though she was unwilling, He gathered together as many of her children as He wished: for He does not will some things and do them, and will others and do them not; but "He hath done all that He pleased in heaven and in earth."

CHAP. 98.—PREDESTINATION TO ETERNAL LIFE IS WHOLLY OF GOD'S FREE GRACE.

And, moreover, who will be so foolish and blasphemous as to say that God cannot change the evil wills of men, whichever, whenever, and wheresoever He chooses, and direct them to what is good? But when He does this, He does it of mercy; when He does it not, it is of justice that He does it not; for "He hath mercy on whom He will have mercy, and whom He will He hardeneth."[2] And when the apostle said this, he was illustrating the grace of God, in connection with which he had just spoken of the twins in the womb of Rebecca, "who being not yet born, neither having done any good or evil, that the purpose of God according to election might stand, not of works, but of Him that calleth, it was said unto her, The elder shall serve the younger."[3] And in reference to this matter he quotes another prophetic testimony: "Jacob have I loved, but Esau have I hated."[4] But perceiving how what he had said might affect those who could not penetrate by their understanding the depth of this grace: "What shall we say then?" he says: "Is there unrighteousness with God? God forbid."[5] For it seems unjust that, in the ab-

sence of any merit or demerit, from good or evil works, God should love the one and hate the other. Now, if the apostle had wished us to understand that there were future good works of the one, and evil works of the other, which of course God foreknew, he would never have said, "not of works," but, "of future works," and in that way would have solved the difficulty, or rather there would then have been no difficulty to solve. As it is, however, after answering, "God forbid;" that is, God forbid that there should be unrighteousness with God; he goes on to prove that there is no unrighteousness in God's doing this, and says: "For He saith to Moses, I will have mercy on whom I will have mercy, and I will have compassion on whom I will have compassion."[6] Now, who but a fool would think that God was unrighteous, either in inflicting penal justice on those who had earned it, or in extending mercy to the unworthy? Then he draws his conclusion: "So then it is not of him that willeth, nor of him that runneth, but of God that showeth mercy."[7] Thus both the twins were born children of wrath, not on account of any works of their own, but because they were bound in the fetters of that original condemnation which came through Adam. But He who said, "I will have mercy on whom I will have mercy," loved Jacob of His undeserved grace, and hated Esau of His deserved judgment. And as this judgment was due to both, the former learnt from the case of the latter that the fact of the same punishment not falling upon himself gave him no room to glory in any merit of his own, but only in the riches of the divine grace; because "it is not of him that willeth, nor of him that runneth, but of God that showeth mercy." And indeeed the whole face, and, if I may use the expression, every lineament of the countenance of Scripture conveys by a very profound analogy this wholesome warning to every one who looks carefully into it, that he who glories should glory in the Lord.[8]

CHAP. 99.—AS GOD'S MERCY IS FREE, SO HIS JUDGMENTS ARE JUST, AND CANNOT BE GAINSAID.

Now after commending the mercy of God, saying, "So it is not of him that willeth, nor of him that runneth, but of God that showeth mercy," that he might commend His justice also (for the man who does not obtain mercy finds, not iniquity, but justice, there being no iniquity with God), he immediately adds:

---

[1] Matt. xxiii. 37.　　[2] Rom. ix. 18.　　[3] Rom. ix. 12.
[4] Rom. ix. 13; Mal. i. 2, 3.　　[5] Rom. ix. 14.

[6] Rom. ix. 15; Ex. xxxiii. 19.　　[7] Rom. ix. 16. [See R. V.]
[8] Comp. 1 Cor. i. 31.

"For the scripture saith unto Pharoah, Even for this same purpose have I raised thee up, that I might show my power in thee, and that my name might be declared throughout all the earth."[1] And then he draws a conclusion that applies to both, that is, both to His mercy and His justice: "Therefore hath He mercy on whom He will have mercy, and whom He will He hardeneth."[2] "He hath mercy" of His great goodness, "He hardeneth" without any injustice; so that neither can he that is pardoned glory in any merit of his own, nor he that is condemned complain of anything but his own demerit. For it is grace alone that separates the redeemed from the lost, all having been involved in one common perdition through their common origin. Now if any one, on hearing this, should say, "Why doth He yet find fault? for who hath resisted His will?"[3] as if a man ought not to be blamed for being bad, because God hath mercy on whom He will have mercy, and whom He will He hardeneth, God forbid that we should be ashamed to answer as we see the apostle answered: "Nay, but, O man, who art thou that repliest against God? Shall the thing formed say to Him that formed it, Why hast Thou made me thus? Hath not the potter power over the clay, of the same lump to make one vessel unto honor, and another unto dishonor?"[4] Now some foolish people think that in this place the apostle had no answer to give; and for want of a reason to render, rebuked the presumption of his interrogator. But there is great weight in this saying: "Nay, but, O man, who art thou?" and in such a matter as this it suggests to a man in a single word the limits of his capacity, and at the same time does in reality convey an important reason. For if a man does not understand these matters, who is he that he should reply against God? And if he does understand them, he finds no further room for reply. For then he perceives that the whole human race was condemned in its rebellious head by a divine judgment so just, that if not a single member of the race had been redeemed, no one could justly have questioned the justice of God; and that it was right that those who are redeemed should be redeemed in such a way as to show, by the greater number who are unredeemed and left in theirj ust condemnation, what the whole race deserved, and whither the deserved judgment of God would lead even the redeemed, did not His undeserved mercy interpose, so that every mouth might be stopped of those who wish to glory in their own merits, and that he that glorieth might glory in the Lord.[5]

CHAP. 100.—THE WILL OF GOD IS NEVER DEFEATED, THOUGH MUCH IS DONE THAT IS CONTRARY TO HIS WILL.

These are the great works of the Lord, sought out according to all His pleasure,[6] and so wisely sought out, that when the intelligent creation, both angelic and human, sinned, doing not His will but their own, He used the very will of the creature which was working in opposition to the Creator's will as an instrument for carrying out His will, the supremely Good thus turning to good account even what is evil, to the condemnation of those whom in His justice He has predestined to punishment, and to the salvation of those whom in His mercy He has predestined to grace. For, as far as relates to their own consciousness, these creatures did what God wished not to be done: but in view of God's omnipotence, they could in no wise effect their purpose. For in the very fact that they acted in opposition to His will, His will concerning them was fulfilled. And hence it is that "the works of the Lord are great, sought out according to all His pleasure," because in a way unspeakably strange and wonderful, even what is done in opposition to His will does not defeat His will. For it would not be done did He not permit it (and of course His permission is not unwilling, but willing); nor would a Good Being permit evil to be done only that in His omnipotence He can turn evil into good.

CHAP. 101. — THE WILL OF GOD, WHICH IS ALWAYS GOOD, IS SOMETIMES FULFILLED THROUGH THE EVIL WILL OF MAN.

Sometimes, however, a man in the goodness of his will desires something that God does not desire, even though God's will is also good, nay, much more fully and more surely good (for His will never can be evil): for example, if a good son is anxious that his father should live, when it is God's good will that he should die. Again, it is possible for a man with evil will to desire what God wills in His goodness: for example, if a bad son wishes his father to die, when this is also the will of God. It is plain that the former wishes what God does not wish, and that the latter wishes what God does wish; and yet the filial love of the former is more in harmony with the good will of God, though its desire is different from God's, than the want of filial

---

[1] Rom. ix. 17 ; Ex. ix. 16.   [2] Rom. ix. 18
[3] Rom. ix. 19.   [4] Rom. ix. 20, 21.

[5] Rom. iii. 19 ; 1 Cor. i. 31.
[6] Ps. cxi. 2 (LXX.) : "The works of the Lord are great, sought out of all them that have pleasure therein." (A. V.)

affection of the latter, though its desire is the same as God's. So necessary is it, in determining whether a man's desire is one to be approved or disapproved, to consider what it is proper for man, and what it is proper for God, to desire, and what is in each case the real motive of the will. For God accomplishes some of His purposes, which of course are all good, through the evil desires of wicked men: for example, it was through the wicked designs of the Jews, working out the good purpose of the Father, that Christ was slain ; and this event was so truly good, that when the Apostle Peter expressed his unwillingness that it should take place, he was designated Satan by Him who had come to be slain. [1] How good seemed the intentions of the pious believers who were unwilling that Paul should go up to Jerusalem lest the evils which Agabus had foretold should there befall him ! [2] And yet it was God's purpose that he should suffer these evils for preaching the faith of Christ, and thereby become a witness for Christ. And this purpose of His, which was good, God did not fulfill through the good counsels of the Christians, but through the evil counsels of the Jews ; so that those who opposed His purpose were more truly His servants than those who were the willing instruments of its accomplishment.

CHAP. 102.—THE WILL OF THE OMNIPOTENT GOD IS NEVER DEFEATED, AND IS NEVER EVIL.

But however strong may be the purposes either of angels or of men, whether of good or bad, whether these purposes fall in with the will of God or run counter to it, the will of the Omnipotent is never defeated; and His will never can be evil; because even when it inflicts evil it is just, and what is just is certainly not evil. The omnipotent God, then, whether in mercy He pitieth whom He will, or in judgment hardeneth whom He will, is never unjust in what He does, never does anything except of His own free-will, and never wills anything that He does not perform.

CHAP. 103.—INTERPRETATIQN OF THE EXPRESSION IN 1 TIM. II. 4: "WHO WILL HAVE ALL MEN TO BE SAVED."

Accordingly, when we hear and read in Scripture that He "will have all men to be saved," [3] although we know well that all men are not saved, we are not on that account to restrict the omnipotence of God, but are rather to understand the Scripture, "Who

will have all men to be saved," as meaning that no man is saved unless God wills his salvation : not that there is no man whose salvation He does not will, but that no man is saved apart from His will; and that, therefore, we should pray Him to will our salvation, because if He will it, it must necessarily be accomplished. And it was of prayer to God that the apostle was speaking when he used this expression. And on the same principle we interpret the expression in the Gospel : "The true light which lighteth every man that cometh into the world :" [4] not that there is no man who is not enlightened, but that no man is enlightened except by Him. Or, it is said, "Who will have all men to be saved;" not that there is no man whose salvation He does not will (for how, then, explain the fact that He was unwilling to work miracles in the presence of some who, He said, would have repented if He had worked them ?), but that we are to understand by "all men," the human race in all its varieties of rank and circumstances,—kings, subjects; noble, plebeian, high, low, learned, and unlearned ; the sound in body, the feeble, the clever, the dull, the foolish, the rich, the poor, and those of middling circumstances ; males, females, infants, boys, youths ; young, middle-aged, and old men ; of every tongue, of every fashion, of all arts, of all professions, with all the innumerable differences of will and conscience, and whatever else there is that makes a distinction among men. For which of all these classes is there out of which God does not will that men should be saved in all nations through His only-begotten Son, our Lord, and therefore does save them ; for the Omnipotent cannot will in vain, whatsoever He may will ? Now the apostle had enjoined that prayers should be made for all men, and had especially added, "For kings, and for all that are in authority," who might be supposed, in the pride and pomp of worldly station, to shrink from the humility of the Christian faith. Then saying, "For this is good and acceptable in the sight of God our Saviour," that is, that prayers should be made for such as these, he immediately adds, as if to remove any ground of despair, "Who will have all men to be saved, and to come unto the knowledge of the truth." [5] God, then, in His great condescension has judged it good to grant to the prayers of the humble the salvation of the exalted ; and assuredly we have many examples of this. Our Lord, too, makes use of the same mode of speech in the Gospel, when He says to the Pharisees : "Ye tithe mint,

---

[1] Matt. xvi. 21-23.   [2] Acts xxi. 10-12.
[3] 1 Tim. ii. 4.   [4] John i. 9.   [5] 1 Tim. ii. 1-4.

and rue, and every herb.'' [1] For the Pharisees did not tithe what belonged to others,
nor all the herbs of all the inhabitants of
other lands. As, then, in this place we must
understand by "every herb," every kind of
herbs, so in the former passage we may understand by "all men," every sort of men.
And we may interpret it in any other way we
please, so long as we are not compelled to
believe that the omnipotent God has willed
anything to be done which was not done : for,
setting aside all ambiguities, if "He hath
done all that He pleased in heaven and in
earth," [2] as the psalmist sings of Him, He
certainly did not will to do anything that He
hath not done.

CHAP. 104.—GOD, FOREKNOWING THE SIN OF
THE FIRST MAN, ORDERED HIS OWN PURPOSES
ACCORDINGLY.

Wherefore, God would have been willing to
preserve even the first man in that state of
salvation in which he was created, and after
he had begotten sons to remove him at a fit
time, without the intervention of death, to a
better place, where he should have been not
only free from sin, but free even from the desire of sinning, if He had foreseen that man
would have the steadfast will to persist in the
state of innocence in which he was created.
But as He foresaw that man would make a
bad use of his free-will, that is, would sin,
God arranged His own designs rather with a
view to do good to man even in his sinful-
ness, that thus the good will of the Omnipotent might not be made void by the evil will
of man, but might be fulfilled in spite of it.

CHAP. 105.—MAN WAS SO CREATED AS TO BE
ABLE TO CHOOSE EITHER GOOD OR EVIL: IN
THE FUTURE LIFE, THE CHOICE OF EVIL WILL
BE IMPOSSIBLE.

Now it was expedient that man should be
at first so created, as to have it in his power
both to will what was right and to will what
was wrong ; not without reward if he willed
the former, and not without punishment if he
willed the latter. But in the future life it
shall not be in his power to will evil; and yet
this will constitute no restriction on the freedom of his will. On the contrary, his will
shall be much freer when it shall be wholly
impossible for him to be the slave of sin.
We should never think of blaming the will, or
saying that it was no will, or that it was not to
be called free, when we so desire happiness,
that not only do we shrink from misery, but

find it utterly impossible to do otherwise.
As, then, the soul even now finds it impossible to desire unhappiness, so in future it
shall be wholly impossible for it to desire sin.
But God's arrangement was not to be broken,
according to which He willed to show how
good is a rational being who is able even to
refrain from sin, and yet how much better is
one who cannot sin at all; just as that was an
inferior sort of immortality, and yet it was
immortality, when it was possible for man to
avoid death, although there is reserved for
the future a more perfect immortality, when
it shall be impossible for man to die.

CHAP. 106.—THE GRACE OF GOD WAS NECES-
SARY TO MAN'S SALVATION BEFORE THE FALL
AS WELL AS AFTER IT.

The former immortality man lost through
the exercise of his free-will ; the latter he
shall obtain through grace, whereas, if he
had not sinned, he should have obtained it by
desert. Even in that case, however, there
could have been no merit without grace; because, although the mere exercise of man's
free-will was sufficient to bring in sin, his free-
will would not have sufficed for his maintenance in righteousness, unless God had as-
sisted it by imparting a portion of His unchangeable goodness. Just as it is in man's
power to die whenever he will (for, not to
speak of other means, any one can put an
end to himself by simple abstinence from
food), but the mere will cannot preserve life
in the absence of food and the other means
of life ; so man in paradise was able of his
mere will, simply by abandoning righteousness, to destroy himself ; but to have maintained a life of righteousness would have been
too much for his will, unless it had been sustained by the Creator's power. After the
fall, however, a more abundant exercise of
God's mercy was required, because the will
itself had to be freed from the bondage in
which it was held by sin and death. And the
will owes its freedom in no degree to itself,
but solely to the grace of God which comes
by faith in Jesus Christ; so that the very will,
through which we accept all the other gifts
of God which lead us on to His eternal gift,
is itself prepared of the Lord, as the Scripture
says. [3]

CHAP. 107.—ETERNAL LIFE, THOUGH THE RE-
WARD OF GOOD WORKS, IS ITSELF THE GIFT
OF GOD.

Wherefore, even eternal life itself, which

---

[1] Luke xi. 42. ["All manner of herbs." A. V.]
[2] Ps. cxv. 3. ["Our God is in the heavens : He hath done
whatsoever He hath pleased." A. V.]

[3] Prov xvi. 1. ["The preparation of the heart in man . . .
is from the Lord." A. V.]

is surely the reward of good works, the apostle calls the gift of God. "For the wages of sin," he says, "is death; but the gift of God is eternal life through Jesus Christ our Lord."[1] Wages (*stipendium*) is paid as a recompense for military service; it is not a gift: wherefore he says, "the *wages* of sin is death," to show that death was not inflicted undeservedly, but as the due recompense of sin. But a gift, unless it is wholly unearned, is not a gift at all.[2] We are to understand, then, that man's good deserts are themselves the gift of God, so that when these obtain the recompense of eternal life, it is simply grace given for grace. Man, therefore, was thus made upright that, though unable to remain in his uprightness without divine help, he could of his own mere will depart from it. And whichever of these courses he had chosen, God's will would have been done, either by him, or concerning him. Therefore, as he chose to do his own will rather than God's, the will of God is fulfilled concerning him; for God, out of one and the same heap of perdition which constitutes the race of man, makes one vessel to honor, another to dishonor; to honor in mercy, to dishonor in judgment;[3] that no one may glory in man, and consequently not in himself.

CHAP. 108.—A MEDIATOR WAS NECESSARY TO RECONCILE US TO GOD; AND UNLESS THIS MEDIATOR HAD BEEN GOD, HE COULD NOT HAVE BEEN OUR REDEEMER.

For we could not be redeemed, even through the one Mediator between God and men, the man Christ Jesus, if He were not also God. Now when Adam was created, he, being a righteous man, had no need of a mediator. But when sin had placed a wide gulf between God and the human race, it was expedient that a Mediator, who alone of the human race was born, lived, and died without sin, should reconcile us to God, and procure even for our bodies a resurrection to eternal life, in order that the pride of man might be exposed and cured through the humility of God; that man might be shown how far he had departed from God, when God became incarnate to bring him back; that an example might be set to disobedient man in the life of obedience of the God-Man; that the fountain of grace might be opened by the Only-begotten taking upon Himself the form of a servant, a form which had no antecedent merit; that an earnest of that resurrection of the body which is promised to the redeemed might be given in the resurrection of the Redeemer; that the devil might be subdued by the same nature which it was his boast to have deceived, and yet man not glorified, lest pride should again spring up; and, in fine, with a view to all the advantages which the thoughtful can perceive and describe, or perceive without being able to describe, as flowing from the transcendent mystery of the person of the Mediator.

CHAP. 109.—THE STATE OF THE SOUL DURING THE INTERVAL BETWEEN DEATH AND THE RESURRECTION.

During the time, moreover, which intervenes between a man's death and the final resurrection, the soul dwells in a hidden retreat, where it enjoys rest or suffers affliction just in proportion to the merit it has earned by the life which it led on earth.

CHAP. 110.—THE BENEFIT TO THE SOULS OF THE DEAD FROM THE SACRAMENTS AND ALMS OF THEIR LIVING FRIENDS.

Nor can it be denied that the souls of the dead are benefited by the piety of their living friends, who offer the sacrifice of the Mediator, or give alms in the church on their behalf. But these services are of advantage only to those who during their lives have earned such merit, that services of this kind can help them. For there is a manner of life which is neither so good as not to require these services after death, nor so bad that such services are of no avail after death; there is, on the other hand, a kind of life so good as not to require them; and again, one so bad that when life is over they render no help. Therefore, it is in this life that all the merit or demerit is acquired, which can either relieve or aggravate a man's sufferings after this life. No one, then, need hope that after he is dead he shall obtain merit with God which he has neglected to secure here. And accordingly it is plain that the services which the church celebrates for the dead are in no way opposed to the apostle's words: "For we must all appear before the judgment-seat of Christ; that every one may receive the things done in his body, according to that he hath done, whether it be good or bad;"[4] for the merit which renders such services as I speak of profitable to a man, is earned while he lives in the body. It is not to every one that these services are profitable. And why are they not profitable to all, except because of the different kinds of lives that men lead in the body? When, then, sacri-

---

fices either of the altar or of alms are offered on behalf of all the baptized dead, they are thank-offerings for the very good, they are propitiatory offerings for the not very bad, and in the case of the very bad, even though they do not assist the dead, they are a species of consolation to the living. And where they are profitable, their benefit consists either in obtaining a full remission of sins, or at least in making the condemnation more tolerable.

CHAP. 111.—AFTER THE RESURRECTION THERE SHALL BE TWO DISTINCT KINGDOMS, ONE OF ETERNAL HAPPINESS, THE OTHER OF ETERNAL MISERY.

After the resurrection, however, when the final, universal judgment has been completed, there shall be two kingdoms, each with its own distinct boundaries, the one Christ's, the other the devil's ; the one consisting of the good, the other of the bad,—both, however, consisting of angels and men. The former shall have no will, the latter no power, to sin, and neither shall have any power to choose death ; but the former shall live truly and happily in eternal life, the latter shall drag a miserable existence in eternal death without the power of dying; for the life and the death shall both be without end. But among the former there shall be degrees of happiness, one being more pre-eminently happy than another ; and among the latter there shall be degrees of misery, one being more endurably miserable than another.

CHAP. 112.—THERE IS NO GROUND IN SCRIPTURE FOR THE OPINION OF THOSE WHO DENY THE ETERNITY OF FUTURE PUNISHMENTS.

It is in vain, then, that some, indeed very many, make moan over the eternal punishment, and perpetual, unintermitted torments of the lost, and say they do not believe it shall be so ; not, indeed, that they directly oppose themselves to Holy Scripture, but, at the suggestion of their own feelings, they soften down everything that seems hard, and give a milder turn to statements which they think are rather designed to terrify than to be received as literally true. For "Hath God," they say, "forgotten to be gracious? hath He in anger shut up His tender mercies?"[1] Now, they read this in one of the holy psalms. But without doubt we are to understand it as spoken of those who are elsewhere called "vessels of mercy,"[2] because even they are freed from misery not on account of any merit of their own, but solely through the pity of God. Or, if the men we speak of insist that this passage applies to all mankind, there is no reason why they should therefore suppose that there will be an end to the punishment of those of whom it is said, "These shall go away into everlasting punishment;" for this shall end in the same manner and at the same time as the happiness of those of whom it is said, "but the righteous unto life eternal.[3] But let them suppose, if the thought gives them pleasure, that the pains of the damned are, at certain intervals, in some degree assuaged. For even in this case the wrath of God, that is, their condemnation (for it is this, and not any disturbed feeling in the mind of God that is called His wrath), abideth upon them;[4] that is, His wrath, though it still remains, does not shut up His tender mercies; though His tender mercies are exhibited, not in putting an end to their eternal punishment, but in mitigating, or in granting them a respite from, their torments; for the psalm does not say, "to put an end to His anger," or, "when His anger is passed by," but "in His anger."[5] Now, if this anger stood alone, or if it existed in the smallest conceivable degree, yet to be lost out of the kingdom of God, to be an exile from the city of God, to be alienated from the life of God, to have no share in that great goodness which God hath laid up for them that fear Him, and hath wrought out for them that trust in Him,[6] would be a punishment so great, that, supposing it to be eternal, no torments that we know of, continued through as many ages as man's imagination can conceive, could be compared with it.

CHAP. 113.—THE DEATH OF THE WICKED SHALL BE ETERNAL IN THE SAME SENSE AS THE LIFE OF THE SAINTS.

This perpetual death of the wicked, then, that is, their alienation from the life of God, shall abide for ever, and shall be common to them all, whatever men, prompted by their human affections, may conjecture as to a variety of punishments, or as to a mitigation or intermission of their woes; just as the eternal life of the saints shall abide for ever, and shall be common to them all, whatever grades of rank and honor there may be among those who shine with an harmonious effulgence.

CHAP. 114.—HAVING DEALT WITH FAITH, WE NOW COME TO SPEAK OF HOPE. EVERYTHING THAT PERTAINS TO HOPE IS EMBRACED IN THE LORD'S PRAYER.

Out of this confession of *faith*, which is

---

1 Ps. lxxvii. 9.   2 Rom. ix. 23.

3 Matt. xxv. 46.   4 John iii. 36.
5 Ps. lxxviii.   6 Ps. xxxi. 19.

briefly comprehended in the Creed, and which, carnally understood, is milk for babes, but, spiritually apprehended and studied, is meat for strong men, springs the good *hope* of believers; and this is accompanied by a holy *love*. But of these matters, all of which are true objects of faith, those only pertain to hope which are embraced in the Lord's Prayer. For, "Cursed is the man that trusteth in man"[1] is the testimony of holy writ; and, consequently, this curse attaches also to the man who trusteth in himself. Therefore, except from God the Lord we ought to ask for nothing either that we hope to do well, or hope to obtain as a reward of our good works.

CHAP. 115.—THE SEVEN PETITIONS OF THE LORD'S PRAYER, ACCORDING TO MATTHEW.

Accordingly, in the Gospel according to Matthew the Lord's Prayer seems to embrace seven petitions, three of which ask for eternal blessings, and the remaining four for temporal; these latter, however, being necessary antecedents to the attainment of the eternal. For when we say, "Hallowed be Thy name: Thy kingdom come: Thy will be done in earth, as it is in heaven"[2] (which some have interpreted, not unfairly, in body as well as in spirit), we ask for blessings that are to be enjoyed for ever; which are indeed begun in this world, and grow in us as we grow in grace, but in their perfect state, which is to be looked for in another life, shall be a possession for evermore. But when we say, "Give us this day our daily bread: and forgive us our debts, as we forgive our debtors: and lead us not into temptation, but deliver us from evil,"[3] who does not see that we ask for blessings that have reference to the wants of this present life? In that eternal life, where we hope to live for ever, the hallowing of God's name, and His kingdom, and His will in our spirit and body, shall be brought to perfection, and shall endure to everlasting. But our *daily* bread is so called because there is here constant need for as much nourishment as the spirit and the flesh demand, whether we understand the expression spiritually, or carnally, or in both senses. It is here too that we need the forgiveness that we ask, for it is here that we commit the sins; here are the temptations which allure or drive us into sin; here, in a word, is the evil from which we desire deliverance: but in that other world there shall be none of these things.

CHAP. 116.—LUKE EXPRESSES THE SUBSTANCE OF THESE SEVEN PETITIONS MORE BRIEFLY IN FIVE.

But the Evangelist Luke in his version of the Lord's prayer embraces not seven, but five petitions: not, of course, that there is any discrepancy between the two evangelists, but that Luke indicates by his very brevity the mode in which the seven petitions of Matthew are to be understood. For God's name is hallowed in the spirit; and God's kingdom shall come in the resurrection of the body. Luke, therefore, intending to show that the third petition is a sort of repetition of the first two, has chosen to indicate that by omitting the third altogether.[4] Then he adds three others: one for daily bread, another for pardon of sin, another for immunity from temptation. And what Matthew puts as the last petition, "but deliver us from evil," Luke has omitted,[4] to show us that it is embraced in the previous petition about temptation. Matthew, indeed, himself says, "*but* deliver," not "*and* deliver," as if to show that the petitions are virtually one: do not this, but this; so that every man is to understand that he is delivered from evil in the very fact of his not being led into temptation.

CHAP. 117.—LOVE, WHICH IS GREATER THAN FAITH AND HOPE, IS SHED ABROAD IN OUR HEARTS BY THE HOLY GHOST.

And now as to *love*, which the apostle declares to be greater than the other two graces, that is, than faith and hope,[5] the greater the measure in which it dwells in a man, the better is the man in whom it dwells. For when there is a question as to whether a man is good, one does not ask what he believes, or what he hopes, but what he loves. For the man who loves aright no doubt believes and hopes aright; whereas the man who has not love believes in vain, even though his beliefs are true; and hopes in vain, even though the objects of his hope are a real part of true happiness; unless, indeed, he believes and hopes for this, that he may obtain by prayer the blessing of love. For, although it is not possible to hope without love, it may yet happen that a man does not love that which is necessary to the attainment of his hope; as, for example, if he hopes for eternal life (and who is there that does not desire this?) and yet does not love righteousness, without which no one can attain to eternal life. Now this is the true faith of Christ which the apos-

---

[1] Jer. xvii. 5.   [2] Matt. vi. 9, 10.   [3] Matt. vi. 11-13.

[4] [These petitions are retained in the A. V., but omitted in the R. V., according to the oldest authorities.—P. S.]
[5] 1 Cor. xiii. 13.

tle speaks of, "which worketh by love;"[1] and if there is anything that it does not yet embrace in its love, asks that it may receive, seeks that it may find, and knocks that it may be opened unto it.[2] For faith obtains through prayer that which the law commands. For without the gift of God, that is, without the Holy Spirit, through whom love is shed abroad in our hearts,[3] the law can command, but it cannot assist; and, moreover, it makes a man a transgressor, for he can no longer excuse himself on the plea of ignorance. Now carnal lust reigns where there is not the love of God.

CHAP. 118.—THE FOUR STAGES OF THE CHRISTAIN'S LIFE, AND THE FOUR CORRESPONDING STAGES OF THE CHURCH'S HISTORY.

When, sunk in the darkest depths of ignorance, man lives according to the flesh, undisturbed by any struggle of reason or conscience, this is his first state. Afterwards, when through the law has come the knowledge of sin, and the Spirit of God has not yet interposed His aid, man, striving to live according to the law, is thwarted in his efforts and falls into conscious sin, and so, being overcome of sin, becomes its slave (" for of whom a man is overcome, of the same is he brought in bondage "[4]); and thus the effect produced by the knowledge of the commandment is this, that sin worketh in man all manner of concupiscence, and he is involved in the additional guilt of willful transgression, and that is fulfilled which is written : " The law entered that the offense might abound."[5] This is man's second state. But if God has regard to him, and inspires him with faith in God's help, and the Spirit of God begins to work in him, then the mightier power of love strives against the power of the flesh; and although there is still in the man's own nature a power that fights against him (for his disease is not completely cured), yet he lives the life of the just by faith, and lives in righteousness so far as he does not yield to evil lust, but conquers it by the love of holiness. This is the third state of a man of good hope; and he who by steadfast piety advances in this course, shall attain at last to peace, that peace which, after this life is over, shall be perfected in the repose of the spirit, and finally in the resurrection of the body. Of these four different stages the first is before the law, the second is under the law, the third is under grace, and the fourth is in full and perfect peace. Thus, too, has the history of God's people been ordered according to His pleasure who disposeth all things in number, and measure, and weight.[6] For the church existed at first before the law; then under the law, which was given by Moses; then under grace, which was first made manifest in the coming of the Mediator. Not, indeed, that this grace was absent previously, but, in harmony with the arrangements of the time, it was veiled and hidden. For none, even of the just men of old, could find salvation apart from the faith of Christ; nor unless He had been known to them could their ministry have been used to convey prophecies concerning Him to us, some more plain, and some more obscure.

CHAP. 119.—THE GRACE OF REGENERATION WASHES AWAY ALL PAST SIN AND ALL ORIGINAL GUILT.

Now in whichever of these four stages (as we may call them) the grace of regeneration finds any particular man, all his past sins are there and then pardoned, and the guilt which he contracted in his birth is removed in his new birth; and so true is it that " the wind bloweth where it listeth,"[7] that some have never known the second stage, that of slavery under the law, but have received the divine assistance as soon as they received the commandment.

CHAP. 120.—DEATH CANNOT INJURE THOSE WHO HAVE RECEIVED THE GRACE OF REGENERATION.

But before a man can receive the commandment, it is necessary that he should live according to the flesh. But if once he has received the grace of regeneration, death shall not injure him, even if he should forthwith depart from this life; " for to this end Christ both died, and rose, and revived, that He might be Lord both of the dead and the living;"[8] nor shall death retain dominion over him for whom Christ freely died.

CHAP. 121.—LOVE IS THE END OF ALL THE COMMANDMENTS, AND GOD HIMSELF IS LOVE.

All the commandments of God, then, are embraced in love, of which the apostle says : " Now the end of the commandment is charity, out of a pure heart, and of a good conscience, and of faith unfeigned."[9] Thus the end of every commandment is charity, that is, every commandment has love for its aim. But whatever is done either through fear of

---

1 Gal. v. 6.   2 Matt. vii. 7.   3 Rom. v. 5.
4 2 Pet. ii. 19.   5 Rom. v. 20.
6 Comp. Wisd. xi. 20.   7 John iii. 8.
8 Rom. xiv. 9.   9 1 Tim. i. 5.

punishment or from some other carnal motive, and has not for its principle that love which the Spirit of God sheds abroad in the heart, is not done as it ought to be done, however it may appear to men. For this love embraces both the love of God and the love of our neighbor, and "on these two commandments hang all the law and the prophets," [1] we may add the Gospel and the apostles. For it is from these that we hear this voice : The end of the commandment is charity, and God is love. [2] Wherefore, all God's commandments, one of which is, "Thou shalt not commit adultery," [3] and all those precepts which are not commandments but special counsels, one of which is, "It is good for a man not to touch a woman," [4] are rightly carried out only when the motive principle of action is the love of God, and the love of our neighbor in God. And this applies both to the present and the future life. We love God now by faith, then we shall love Him through sight. Now we love even our neighbor by faith ; for we who are ourselves mortal know not the hearts of mortal men. But in the future life, the Lord "both will bring to light the hidden things of darkness, and will make manifest the counsels of the hearts, and then shall every man have praise of God;" [5] for every man shall love and praise in his neighbor the virtue which, that it may not be hid, the Lord Himself shall bring to light. Moreover, lust diminishes as love grows, till the latter grows to such a height that it can grow no higher here. For "greater love hath no man than this, that a man lay down his life for his friends." [6] Who then can tell how great love shall be in the future world, when there shall be no lust for it to restrain and conquer? for that will be the perfection of health when there shall be no struggle with death.

CHAP. 122.—CONCLUSION.

But now there must be an end at last to this volume. And it is for yourself to judge whether you should call it a *hand-book*, or should use it as such. I, however, thinking that your zeal in Christ ought not to be despised, and believing and hoping all good of you in dependence on our Redeemer's help, and loving you very much as one of the members of His body, have, to the best of my ability, written this book for you on *Faith, Hope, and Love*. May its value be equal to its length.

[1] Matt. xxii. 40; comp. Rom. v. 5.
[2] 1 Tim. i. 5; 1 John iv. 16.
[3] Comp. Matt. v. 27 and Rom. xiii. 9. [4] 1 Cor. vii. 1. [5] 1 Cor. iv. 5. [6] John xv. 13.

ST. AUGUSTIN:

ON

THE CATECHISING OF THE UNINSTRUCTED

TRANSLATED BY

REV. S. D. F. SALMOND, D.D.,

PROFESSOR OF SYSTEMATIC THEOLOGY, FREE CHURCH COLLEGE, ABERDEEN.

INTRODUCTORY NOTICE.

In the fourteenth chapter of the second book of his *Retractations*, Augustin makes the following statement: "There is also a book of ours on the subject of the *Catechising of the Uninstructed*, [or, *for Instructing the Unlearned, De Catechizandis Rudibus*], that being, indeed, the express title by which it is designated. In this book, where I have said, '*Neither did the angel, who, in company with other spirits who were his satellites, forsook in pride the obedience of God, and became the devil, do any hurt to God, but to himself; for God knoweth how to dispose of souls that leave Him:*' it would be more appropriate to say, '*spirits that leave Him,*' inasmuch as the question dealt with angels. This book commences in these terms: '*You have requested me, brother Deogratias.*'"

The composition so described in the passage cited is reviewed by Augustin in connection with other works which he had in hand about the year 400 A.D., and may therefore be taken to belong to that date. It has been conjectured that the person to whom it is addressed may perhaps be the same with the presbyter Deogratias, to whom, as we read in the epistle which now ranks as the hundred and second, Augustin wrote about the year 406, in reply to some questions of the pagans which were forwarded to him from Carthage.

The Benedictine editors introduce the treatise in the following terms: "At the request of a deacon of Carthage, Augustin undertakes the task of teaching the art of catechising; and in the first place, he gives certain injunctions, to the effect that this kind of duty may be discharged not only in a settled method and an apt order, but also without tediousness, and in a spirit of cheerfulness. Thereafter reducing his injunctions to practical use, he gives an example of what he means by delivering two set discourses, presenting parallels to each other, the one being somewhat lengthened and the other very brief, but both suitable for the instruction of any individual whose desire is to be a Christian."

[This treatise shows what was thought in the age of Saint Augustin to be the most needful instruction in religion. The Latin text: *De Catechizandis Rudibus*, is in the sixth vol. of the Benedictine edition, and in the handy ed. of C. Marriott: *S. Augustini Opuscula quædam*, Oxford and London (Parker & Co.) 4th ed. 1885. An earlier and closer English Version by Rev. C. L. Cornish, M. A., of Exeter College, Oxford, appeared in the Oxford "Library of the Fathers" (1847, pp. 187 sqq.,) under the title *On Instructing the Unlearned*. H. de Romestin reproduces the Oxford translation in the English version of Marriott's ed. of five treatises of St. Augustin, Oxford and London, 1885, pp. 1–71.—P. S.]

CONTENTS OF CATECHISING OF THE UNINSTRUCTED.

THE CATECHISING OF THE UNINSTRUCTED:

IN ONE BOOK.

CHAP. I.—HOW AUGUSTIN WRITES IN ANSWER TO A FAVOR ASKED BY A DEACON OF CARTHAGE.

1. You have requested me, brother Deogratias, to send you in writing something which might be of service to you in the matter of catechising the uninstructed. For you have informed me that in Carthage, where you hold the position of a deacon, persons, who have to be taught the Christian faith from its very rudiments, are frequently brought to you by reason of your enjoying the reputation of possessing a rich gift in catechising, due at once to an intimate acquaintance with the faith, and to an attractive method of discourse;[2] but that you almost always find yourself in a difficulty as to the manner in which a suitable declaration is to be made of the precise doctrine, the belief of which constitutes us Christians: regarding the point at which our statement of the same ought to commence, and the limit to which it should be allowed to proceed: and with respect to the question whether, when our narration is concluded, we ought to make use of any kind of exhortation, or simply specify those precepts in the observance of which the person to whom we are discoursing may know the Christian life and profession to be maintained. [3] At the same time, you have made the confession and complaint that it has often befallen you that in the course of a lengthened and languid address you have become profitless and distasteful even to yourself, not to speak of the learner whom you have been endeavoring to instruct by your utterance, and the other parties who have been present as hearers; and that you have been constrained by these straits to put upon me the constraint of that love which I owe to you, so that I may not feel it a burdensome thing among all my engagements to write you something on this subject.

2. As for myself then, if, in the exercise of those capacities which through the bounty of our Lord I am enabled to present, the same Lord requires me to offer any manner of aid to those whom He has made brethren to me, I feel constrained not only by that love and service which is due from me to you on the terms of familiar friendship, but also by that which I owe universally to my mother the Church, by no means to refuse the task, but rather to take it up with a prompt and devoted willingness. For the more extensively I desire to see the treasure of the Lord [4] distributed, the more does it become my duty, if I ascertain that the stewards, who are my fellow-servants, find any difficulty in laying it out, to do all that lies in my power to the end that they may be able to accomplish easily and expeditiously what they sedulously and earnestly aim at.

CHAP. 2.—HOW IT OFTEN HAPPENS THAT A DISCOURSE WHICH GIVES PLEASURE TO THE HEARER IS DISTASTEFUL TO THE SPEAKER; AND WHAT EXPLANATION IS TO BE OFFERED OF THAT FACT.

3. But as regards the idea thus privately entertained by yourself in such efforts, I

---

[1] [The Oxford Library and H. de Romestin translate the title: *On Instructing the Unlearned.*--P. S.]
[2] Reading *et doctrina fidei et suavitate sermonis*, instead of which, however, *et doctrinam . . . suavitatem, etc.* also occurs, = possessing at once a rich gift in catechising, and an intimate acquaintance with the faith, and an attractive method of discourse, [or, sweetness of language].
[3] Reading *retineri* as in the MSS. Some editions give *retinere* = know how to maintain the Christian life and profession.

[4] *Pecuniam Dominicam.*

would not have you to be disturbed by the consideration that you have often appeared to yourself to be delivering a poor and wearisome discourse. For it may very well be the case that the matter has not so presented itself to the person whom you were trying to instruct, but that what you were uttering seemed to you to be unworthy of the ears of others, simply because it was your own earnest desire that there should be something better to listen to. Indeed with me, too, it is almost always the fact that my speech displeases myself. For I am covetous of something better, the possession of which I frequently enjoy within me before I commence to body it forth in intelligible words :[1] and then when my capacities of expression prove inferior to my inner apprehensions, I grieve over the inability which my tongue has betrayed in answering to my heart. For it is my wish that he who hears me should have the same complete understanding of the subject which I have myself; and I perceive that I fail to speak in a manner calculated to effect that, and that this arises mainly from the circumstance that the intellectual apprehension diffuses itself through the mind with something like a rapid flash, whereas the utterance is slow, and occupies time, and is of a vastly different nature, so that, while this latter is moving on, the intellectual apprehension has already withdrawn itself within its secret abodes. Yet, in consequence of its having stamped certain impressions of itself in a marvellous manner upon the memory, these prints endure with the brief pauses of the syllables ;[2] and as the outcome of these same impressions we form intelligible signs,[3] which get the name of a certain language, either the Latin, or the Greek, or the Hebrew, or some other. And these signs may be objects of thought, or they may also be actually uttered by the voice. On the other hand, however, the impressions themselves are neither Latin, nor Greek, nor Hebrew, nor peculiar to any other race whatsoever, but are made good in the mind just as looks are in the body. For anger is designated by one word in Latin, by another in Greek, and by different terms in other languages, according to their several diversities. But the look of the angry man is neither (peculiarly) Latin nor (peculiarly) Greek. Thus it is that when a person says *Iratus sum*,[4] he is not understood by every nation, but only by the Latins; whereas, if the mood of his mind when it is kindling to wrath comes forth upon the face

and affects the look, all who have the individual within their view understand that he is angry. But, again, it is not in our power to bring out those impressions which the intellectual apprehension stamps upon the memory, and to hold them forth, as it were, to the perception of the hearers by means of the sound of the voice, in any manner parallel to the clear and evident form in which the look appears. For those former are within in the mind, while this latter is without in the body. Wherefore we have to surmise how far the sound of our mouth must be from representing that stroke of the intelligence, seeing that it does not correspond even with the impression produced upon the memory. Now, it is a common occurrence with us that, in the ardent desire to effect what is of profit to our hearer, our aim is to express ourselves to him exactly as our intellectual apprehension is at the time, when, in the very effort, we are failing in the ability to speak; and then, because this does not succeed with us, we are vexed, and we pine in weariness as if we were applying ourselves to vain labors ; and, as the result of this very weariness, our discourse becomes itself more languid and pointless even than it was when it first induced such a sense of tediousness.

4. But ofttimes the earnestness of those who are desirous of hearing me shows me that my utterance is not so frigid as it seems to myself to be. From the delight, too, which they exhibit, I gather that they derive some profit from it. And I occupy myself sedulously with the endeavor not to fail in putting before them a service in which I perceive them to take in such good part what is put before them. Even so, on your side also, the very fact that persons who require to be instructed in the faith are brought so frequently to you, ought to help you to understand that your discourse is not displeasing to others as it is displeasing to yourself; and you ought not to consider yourself unfruitful, simply because you do not succeed in setting forth in such a manner as you desire the things which you discern ; for, perchance, you may be just as little able to discern them in the way you wish. For in this life who sees except as "in an enigma and through a glass "?[5] Neither is love itself of might sufficient to rend the darkness of the flesh, and penetrate into that eternal calm from which even things which pass away derive the light in which they shine. But inasmuch as day by day the good are making advances towards the vision of that day, in-

---

1 *Verbis sonantibus,*—sounding words.
2 *Perdurant illa cum syllabarum morulis.*
3 *Sonantia signa,*—vocal signs.   4 I am angry.   5 1 Cor. xiii. 12.

dependent of the rolling sky,[1] and without the invasion of the night, "which eye hath not seen, nor ear heard, neither hath it entered into the heart of man,"[2] there is no greater reason why our discourse should become valueless in our own estimate, when we are engaged in teaching the uninstructed, than this,—namely, that it is a delight to us to discern in an extraordinary fashion, and a weariness to speak in an ordinary. And in reality we are listened to with much greater satisfaction, indeed, when we ourselves also have pleasure in the same work ; for the thread of our address is affected by the very joy of which we ourselves are sensible, and it proceeds from us with greater ease and with more acceptance. Consequently, as regards those matters which are recommended as articles of belief, the task is not a difficult one to lay down injunctions, with respect to the points at which the narration should be commenced and ended, or with respect to the method in which the narration is to be varied, so that at one time it may be briefer, at another more lengthened, and yet at all times full and perfect ; and, again, with respect to the particular occasions on which it may be right to use the shorter form, and those on which it will be proper to employ the longer. But as to the means by which all is to be done, so that every one may have pleasure in his work when he catechises (for the better he succeeds in this the more attractive will he be),—that is what requires the greatest consideration. And yet we have not far to seek for the precept which will rule in this sphere. For if, in the matter of carnal means, God loves a cheerful giver,[3] how much more so in that of the spiritual? But our security that this cheerfulness may be with us at the seasonable hour, is something dependent upon the mercy of Him who has given us such precepts. Therefore, in accordance with my understanding of what your own wish is, we shall discuss in the first place the subject of the method of narration, then that of the duty of delivering injunction and exhortation, and afterwards that of the attainment of the said cheerfulness, so far as God may furnish us with the ideas.

CHAP. 3.—OF THE FULL NARRATION TO BE EMPLOYED IN CATECHISING.

5. The narration is full when each person is catechised in the first instance from what is written in the text, "In the beginning God created the heaven and the earth,"[4] on to the present times of the Church. This does not imply, however, either that we ought to repeat by memory the entire Pentateuch, and the entire Books of Judges, and Kings, and Esdras,[5] and the entire Gospel and Acts of the Apostles, if we have learned all these word for word ; or that we should put all the matters which are contained in these volumes into our own words, and in that manner unfold and expound them as a whole. For neither does the time admit of that, nor does any necessity demand it. But what we ought to do is, to give a comprehensive statement of all things, summarily and generally, so that certain of the more wonderful facts may be selected which are listened to with superior gratification, and which have been ranked so remarkably among the exact turning-points (of the history);[6] that, instead of exhibiting them to view only in their wrappings, if we may so speak, and then instantly snatching them from our sight, we ought to dwell on them for a certain space, and thus, as it were, unfold them and open them out to vision, and present them to the minds of the hearers as things to be examined and admired. But as for all other details, these should be passed over rapidly, and thus far introduced and woven into the narrative. The effect of pursuing this plan is, that the particular facts which we wish to see specially commended to attention obtain greater prominence in consequence of the others being made to yield to them; while, at the same time, neither does the learner, whose interest we are anxious to stimulate by our statement, come to these subjects with a mind already exhausted, nor is confusion induced upon the memory of the person whom we ought to be instructing by our teaching.

6. In all things, indeed, not only ought our own eye to be kept fixed upon the end of the commandment, which is "charity, out of a pure heart, and a good conscience, and faith unfeigned,"[7] to which we should make all that we utter refer ; but in like manner ought the gaze of the person whom we are instructing by our utterance to be moved[8] toward the same, and guided in that direction. And, in truth, for no other reason were all those things which we read in the Holy Scriptures written, previous to the Lord's advent, but for this,—namely, that His advent might be pressed upon the attention, and that the

---

[1] Sine volumine cæli.
[2] 1 Cor. ii. 9.
[3] 2 Cor. ix. 7.
[4] Gen. i. 1.
[5] In the MSS. we also find the reading Ezræ = Ezra.
[6] In ipsis articulis = " among the very articles," or " connecting links." Reference is made to certain great epochs or articles of time in sections 6 and 39.
[7] 1 Tim. i. 5.
[8] Reading movendus, for which monendus = to be admonished, also occurs in the editions.

Church which was to be, should be intimated beforehand, that is to say, the people of God throughout all nations ; which Church is His body, wherewith also are united and numbered all the saints who lived in this world, even before His advent, and who believed then in His future coming, just as we believe in His past coming. For (to use an illustration) Jacob, at the time when he was being born, first put forth from the womb a hand, with which also he held the foot of the brother who was taking priority of him in the act of birth ; and next indeed the head followed, and thereafter, at last, and as matter of course, the rest of the members:[1] while, nevertheless the head in point of dignity and power has precedence, not only of those members which followed it then, but also of the very hand which anticipated it in the process of the birth, and is really the first, although not in the matter of the time of appearing, at least in the order of nature. And in an analogous manner, the Lord Jesus Christ, previous to His appearing in the flesh, and coming forth in a certain manner out of the womb of His secrecy, before the eyes of men as Man, the Mediator between God and men, [2] "who is over all, God blessed for ever," [3] sent before Him, in the person of the holy patriarchs and prophets, a certain portion of His body, wherewith, as by a hand, He gave token beforetime of His own approaching birth, and also supplanted[4] the people who were prior to Him in their pride, using for that purpose the bonds of the law, as if they were His five fingers. For through five epochs of times[5] there was no cessation in the foretelling and prophesying of His own destined coming; and in a manner consonant with this, he through whom the law was given wrote five books ; and proud men, who were carnally minded, and sought to "establish their own righteousness," [6] were not filled with blessing by the open hand of Christ, but were debarred from such good by the hand compressed and closed; and therefore their feet were tied, and "they fell, while we are risen, and stand upright." [7] But although, as I have said, the Lord Christ did thus send before Him a certain portion of His body, in the person of those holy men who came before Him as regards the time of birth, nevertheless He is Himself the Head of the body, the Church, [8] and all these have been attached to that same body of which He is the head, in virtue of their believing in Him whom they announced prophetically. For they were

not sundered (from that body) in consequence of fulfilling their course before Him, but rather were they made one with the same by reason of their obedience. For although the hand may be put forward away before the head, still it has its connection beneath the head. Wherefore all things which were written aforetime were written in order that we might be taught thereby, [9] and were our figures, and happened in a figure in the case of these men. Moreover they were written for our sakes, upon whom the end of the ages has come.[10]

CHAP. 4.—THAT THE GREAT REASON FOR THE ADVENT OF CHRIST WAS THE COMMENDATION OF LOVE.

7. Moreover, what greater reason is apparent for the advent of the Lord than that God might show His love in us, commending it powerfully, inasmuch as "while we were yet sinners, Christ died for us"? [11] And furthermore, this is with the intent that, inasmuch as charity is "the end of the commandment," [12] and "the fulfilling of the law," [13] we also may love one another and lay down our life for the brethren, even as He laid down His life for us. [14] And with regard to God Himself, its object is that, even if it were an irksome task to love Him, it may now at least cease to be irksome for us to return His love, seeing that "He first loved us," [15] and "spared not His own only Son, but delivered Him up for us all." [16] For their is no mightier invitation to love than to anticipate in loving ; and that soul is over hard which, supposing it unwilling indeed to give love, is unwilling also to give the return of love. But if, even in the case of criminal and sordid loves, we see how those who desire to be loved in return make it their special and absorbing business, by such proofs as are within their power, to render the strength of the love which they themselves bear plain and patent ; if we also perceive how they affect to put forward an appearance of justice in what they thus offer, such as may qualify them in some sort to demand that a response be made in all fairness to them on the part of those souls which they are laboring to beguile ; if, further, their own passion burns more vehemently when they observe that the minds which they are eager to possess are also moved now by the same fire : if thus, I say, it happens at once that the soul which before was torpid is excited so soon as it feels itself to be loved, and that

---

[1] Gen. xxv. 26. [2] 1 Tim. ii. 5. [3] Rom. ix. 5.
[4] Reading *supplantavit*. Some MSS. give *supplantaret* = wherewith also He might supplant, etc.
[5] *Temporum articulos*. [6] Rom. x. 3. [7] Ps. xx. 8.
[8] Col. i. 18.

[9] Rom. xv. 4. [10] 1 Cor. x. 11.
[11] Rom. v. 8, 10. [12] 1 Tim. i. 5.
[13] Rom. xiii. 10. [14] 1 John iii. 16.
[15] 1 John iv. 10, 19. [16] Rom. viii. 32.

the soul which was enkindled already becomes the more inflamed so soon as it is made cognizant of the return of its own love, it is evident that no greater reason is to be found why love should be either originated or enlarged, than what appears in the occasion when one who as yet loves not at all comes to know himself to be the object of love, or when one who is already a lover either hopes that he may yet be loved in turn, or has by this time the evidence of a response to his affection. And if this holds good even in the case of base loves, how much more [1] in (true) friendship? For what else have we carefully to attend to in this question touching the injuring of friendship than to this, namely, not to give our friend cause to suppose either that we do not love him at all, or that we love him less than he loves us? If, indeed, he is led to entertain this belief, he will be cooler in that love in which men enjoy the interchange of intimacies one with another; and if he is not of that weak type of character to which such an offense to affection will serve as a cause of freezing off from love altogether, he yet confines himself to that kind of affection in which he loves, not with the view of enjoyment to himself, but with the idea of studying the good of others. But again it is worth our while to notice how,—although superiors also have the wish to be loved by their inferiors, and are gratified with the zealous attention[2] paid to them by such, and themselves cherish greater affection towards these inferiors the more they become cognizant of that,—with what might of love, nevertheless, the inferior kindles so soon as he learns that he is beloved by his superior. For there have we love in its more grateful aspect, where it does not consume itself[3] in the drought of want, but flows forth in the plenteousness of beneficence. For the former type of love is of misery, the latter of mercy.[4] And furthermore, if the inferior was despairing even of the possibility of his being loved by his superior, he will now be inexpressibly moved to love if the superior has of his own will condescended to show how much he loves this person who could by no means be bold enough to promise himself so great a good. But what is there superior to God in the character of Judge? and what more desperate than man in the character of sinner?—than man, I ask, who had given himself all the more unreservedly up

to the wardship and domination of proud powers which are unable to make him blessed, as he had come more absolutely to despair of the possibility of his being an object of interest to that power which wills not to be exalted in wickedness, but is exalted in goodness.

8. If, therefore, it was mainly for this purpose that Christ came, to wit, that man might learn how much God loves him; and that he might learn this, to the intent that he might be kindled to the love of Him by whom he was first loved, and might also love his neighbor at the command and showing of Him who became our neighbor, in that He loved man when, instead of being a neighbor to Him, he was sojourning far apart : if, again, all divine Scripture, which was written aforetime, was written with the view of presignifying the Lord's advent ; and if whatever has been committed to writing in times subsequent to these, and established by divine authority, is a record of Christ, and admonishes us of love, it is manifest that on those two commandments of love to God and love to our neighbor[5] hang not only all the law and the prophets, which at the time when the Lord spoke to that effect were as yet the only Holy Scripture, but also all those books of the divine literature which have been written[6] at a later period for our health, and consigned to remembrance. Wherefore, in the Old Testament there is a veiling of the New, and in the New Testament there is a revealing of the Old. According to that veiling, carnal men, understanding things in a carnal fashion, have been under the dominion, both then and now, of a penal fear. According to this revealing, on the other hand, spiritual men,— among whom we reckon at once those then who knocked in piety and found even hidden things opened to them, and others now who seek in no spirit of pride, lest even things uncovered should be closed to them,—understanding in a spiritual fashion, have been made free through the love wherewith they have been gifted. Consequently, inasmuch as there is nothing more adverse to love than envy, and as pride is the mother of envy, the same Lord Jesus Christ, God-man, is both a manifestation of divine love towards us, and an example of human humility with us, to the end that our great swelling might be cured by a greater counteracting remedy. For here is great misery, proud man ! But there is greater mercy, a humble God ! Take this love, therefore, as the end that is set before

---

[1] Reading *quanto plus*, for which some MSS. give *plurius*, while in a large number we find *purius* = with how much greater purity should it hold good, etc.
[2] Reading *studioso . . . obsequio*, for which *studiose*, etc., also occurs in the editions = are earnestly gratified with the attention, etc.
[3] *Æstuat* = burn, heave.
[4] *Ex miseria . . . ex misericordia.*

[5] Matt. xxii. 40.
[6] Reading *conscripta*, for which some MSS. have *consecuta* = have followed, and many give *consecrata*, dedicated.

you, to which you are to refer all that you say, and, whatever you narrate, narrate it in such a manner that he to whom you are discoursing on hearing may believe, on believing may hope, on hoping may love.

CHAP. 5.—THAT THE PERSON WHO COMES FOR CATECHETICAL INSTRUCTION IS TO BE EXAMINED WITH RESPECT TO HIS VIEWS, ON DESIRING TO BECOME A CHRISTIAN.

9. Moreover, it is on the gound of that very severity of God, [1] by which the hearts of mortals are agitated with a most wholesome terror, that love is to be built up; so that, rejoicing that he is loved by Him whom he fears, man may have boldness to love Him in return, and yet at the same time be afraid to displease His love toward himself, even should he be able to do so with impunity. For certainly it very rarely happens, nay, I should rather say, never, that any one approaches us with the wish to become a Christian who has not been smitten with some sort of fear of God. For if it is in the expectation of some advantage from men whom he deems himself unlikely to please in any other way, or with the idea of escaping any disadvantage at the hands of men of whose displeasure or hostility he is seriously afraid, that a man wishes to become a Christian, then his wish to become one is not so earnest as his desire to feign one. [2] For faith is not a matter of the body which does obeisance, [3] but of the mind which believes. But unmistakeably it is often the case that the mercy of God comes to be present through the ministry of the catechiser, so that, affected by the discourse, the man now wishes to become in reality that which he had made up his mind only to feign. And so soon as he begins to have this manner of desire, we may judge him then to have made a genuine approach to us. It is true, indeed, that the precise time when a man, whom we perceive to be present with us already in the body, comes to us in reality with his mind, [4] is a thing hidden from us. But, notwithstanding that, we ought to deal with him in such a manner that this wish may be made to arise within him, even should it not be there at present. For no such labor is lost, inasmuch as, if there is any wish at all, it is assuredly strengthened by such action on our part, although we may be ignorant of the time

or the hour at which it began. It is useful certainly, if it can be done, to get from those who know the man some idea beforehand of the state of mind in which he is, or of the causes which have induced him to come with the view of embracing religion. But if there is no other person available from whom we may gather such information, then, indeed, the man himself is to be interrogated, so that from what he says in reply we may draw the beginning of our discourse. Now if he has come with a false heart, desirous only of human advantages or thinking to escape disadvantages, he will certainly speak what is untrue. Nevertheless, the very untruth which he utters should be made the point from which we start. This should not be done, however, with the (open) intention of confuting his falsehood, as if that were a settled matter with you; but, taking it for granted that he has professed to have come with a purpose which is really worthy of approbation (whether that profession be true or false), it should rather be our aim to commend and praise such a purpose as that with which, in his reply, he has declared himself to have come ; so that we may make him feel it a pleasure to be the kind of man actually that he wishes to seem to be. On the other hand, supposing him to have given a declaration of his views other than what ought to be before the mind of one who is to be instructed in the Christian faith, then by reproving him with more than usual kindness and gentleness, as a person uninstructed and ignorant, by pointing out and commending, concisely and in a grave spirit the end of Christian doctrine in its genuine reality, and by doing all this in such a manner as neither to anticipate the times of a narration, which should be given subsequently, nor to venture to impose that kind of statement upon a mind not previously set for it, you may bring him to desire that which, either in mistake or in dissimulation, he has not been desiring up to this stage.

CHAP. 6.—OF THE WAY TO COMMENCE THE CATECHETICAL INSTRUCTION, AND OF THE NARRATION OF FACTS FROM THE HISTORY OF THE WORLD'S CREATION ON TO THE PRESENT TIMES OF THE CHURCH.

10. But if it happens that his answer is to the effect that he has met with some divine warning, or with some divine terror, prompting him to become a Christian, this opens up the way most satisfactorily for a commencement to our discourse, by suggesting the greatness of God's interest in us. His thoughts,

---

[1] De ipsa etiam severitate Dei . . . caritas ædificanda est.
[2] Non fieri vult potius quam fingere.
[3] Or = " signifying assent by its motions," adopting the reading of the best MSS., viz. salutantis corporis. Some editions give salvandi, while certain MSS. have salutis, and others saltantis.
[4] Reading quando veniat animo, for which quo veniat animo also occurs=the mind in which a man comes . . . is a matter hidden from us.

however, ought certainly to be turned away from this line of things, whether miracles or dreams, and directed to the more solid path and the surer oracles of the Scriptures ; so that he may also come to understand how mercifully that warning was administered to him in advance,[1] previous to his giving himself to the Holy Scriptures. And assuredly it ought to be pointed out to him, that the Lord Himself would neither thus have admonished him and urged him on to become a Christian, and to be incorporated into the Church, nor have taught him by such signs or revelations, had it not been His will that, for his greater safety and security, he should enter upon a pathway already prepared in the Holy Scriptures, in which he should not seek after visible miracles, but learn the habit of hoping for things invisible, and in which also he should receive monitions not in sleep but in wakefulness. At this point the narration ought now to be commenced, which should start with the fact that God made all things very good,[2] and which should be continued, as we have said, on to the present times of the Church. This should be done in such a manner as to give, for each of the affairs and events which we relate, causes and reasons by which we may refer them severally to that end of love from which neither the eye of the man who is occupied in doing anything, nor that of the man who is engaged in speaking, ought to be turned away. For if, even in handling the fables of the poets, which are but fictitious creations and things devised for the pleasure[3] of minds whose food is found in trifles, those grammarians who have the reputation and the name of being good do nevertheless endeavor to bring them to bear upon some kind of (assumed) use, although that use itself may be only something vain and grossly bent upon the coarse nutriment of this world :[4] how much more careful does it become us to be, not to let those genuine verities which we narrate, in consequence of any want of a well-considered account of their causes, be accepted either with a gratification which issues in no practical good, or, still less, with a cupidity which may prove hurtful ! At the same time, we are not to set forth these causes in such a manner as to leave the proper course of our narration, and let our heart and our tongue indulge in digressions into the knotty questions of more intricate discussion. But the simple truth of the explanation which we adduce[5]

ought to be like the gold which binds together a row of gems, and yet does not interfere with the choice symmetry of the ornament by any undue intrusion of itself.[6]

CHAP. 7.—OF THE EXPOSITION OF THE RESURRECTION, THE JUDGMENT, AND OTHER SUBJECTS, WHICH SHOULD FOLLOW THIS NARRATION.

11. On the completion of this narration, the hope of the resurrection should be set forth, and, so far as the capacity and strength of the hearer will bear it, and so far also as the measure of time at our disposal will allow, we ought to handle our arguments against the vain scoffings of unbelievers on the subject of the resurrection of the body, as well as on that of the future judgment, with its goodness in relation to the good, its severity in relation to the evil, its truth in relation to all. And after the penalties of the impious have thus been declared with detestation and horror, then the kingdom of the righteous and faithful, and that supernal city and its joy, should form the next themes for our discourse. At this point, moreover, we ought to equip and animate the weakness of man in withstanding temptations and offenses, whether these emerge without or rise within the church itself; without, as in opposition to Gentiles, or Jews, or heretics; within, on the other hand, as in opposition to the chaff of the Lord's threshing-floor. It is not meant, however, that we are to dispute against each several type of perverse men, and that all their wrong opinions are to be refuted by set arrays of argumentations: but, in a manner suitable to a limited allowance of time, we ought to show how all this was foretold, and to point out of what service temptations are in the training of the faithful, and what relief[7] there is in the example of the patience of God, who has resolved to permit them even to the end. But, again, while he is being furnished against these (adversaries), whose perverse multitudes fill the churches so far as bodily presence is concerned, the precepts of a Christian and honorable manner of life should also be briefly and befittingly detailed at the same time, to the intent that he may neither allow himself to be easily led astray in this way, by any who are drunkards, covetous, fraudulent, gamesters, adulterers, fornicators, lovers of public spectacles, wearers of unholy charms, sorcerers, astrologers, or diviners practising

---

[1] *Prærogata sit.*   [2] Gen. i. 31.
[3] Reading *ad voluptatem.* But many MSS. give *ad voluntatem* = according to the inclination, etc.
[4] *Avidam saginæ sæcularis.*
[5] Reading *veritas adhibitæ rationis,* for which we also find

adhibita rationis = the applied truth, etc. ; and *adhibita rationi* = the truth applied to our explanation.
[6] *Non tamen ornamenti seriem ulla immoderatione perturbans.*   [7] *Medicina.*

any sort of vain and wicked arts, and all other parties of a similar character; nor to let himself fancy that any such course may be followed with impunity on his part, simply because he sees many who are called Christians loving these things, and engaging themselves with them, and defending them, and recommending them, and actually persuading others to their use. For as to the end which is appointed for those who persist in such a mode of life, and as to the method in which they are to be borne with in the church itself, out of which they are destined to be separated in the end,—these are subjects in which the learner ought to be instructed by means of the testimonies of the divine books. He should also, however, be informed beforehand that he will find in the church many good Christians, most genuine citizens of the heavenly Jerusalem, if he sets about being such himself. And, finally, he must be sedulously warned against letting his hope rest on man. For it is not a matter that can be easily judged by man, what man is righteous. And even were this a matter which could be easily done, still the object with which the examples of righteous men are set before us is not that we may be justified by them, but that, as we imitate them, we may understand how we ourselves also are justified by their Justifier. For the issue of this will be something which must merit the highest approval,—namely this, that when the person who is hearing us, or rather, who is hearing God by us, has begun to make some progress in moral qualities and in knowledge, and to enter upon the way of Christ with ardor, he will not be so bold as to ascribe the change either to us or to himself; but he will love both himself and us, and whatever other persons he loves as friends, in Him, and for His sake who loved him when he was an enemy, in order that He might justify him and make him a friend. And now that we have advanced thus far, I do not think that you need any preceptor to tell you how you should discuss matters briefly, when either your own time or that of those who are hearing you is occupied; and how, on the other hand, you should discourse at greater length when there is more time at your command. For the very necessity of the case recommends this, apart from the counsel of any adviser.

CHAP. 8.—OF THE METHOD TO BE PURSUED IN CATECHISING THOSE WHO HAVE HAD A LIBERAL EDUCATION.

12. But there is another case which evidently must not be overlooked. I mean the case of one coming to you to receive catchetical instruction who has cultivated the field of liberal studies, who has already made up his mind to be a Christian, and who has betaken himself to you for the express purpose of becoming one. It can scarcely fail to be the fact that a person of this character has already acquired a considerable knowledge of our Scriptures and literature; and, furnished with this, he may have come now simply with the view of being made a partaker in the sacraments. For it is customary with men of this class to inquire carefully into all things, not at the very time when they are made Christians, but previous to that, and thus early also to communicate and reason, with any whom they can reach, on the subject of the feelings of their own minds. Consequently a brief method of procedure should be adopted with these, so as not to inculcate on them, in an odious fashion,[1] things which they know already, but to pass over these with a light and modest touch. Thus we should say how we believe that they are already familiar with this and the other subject, and that we therefore simply reckon up in a cursory manner all those facts which require to be formally urged upon the attention of the uninstructed and unlearned. And we should endeavor so to proceed, that, supposing this man of culture to have been previously acquainted with any one of our themes, he may not hear it now as from a teacher; and that, in the event of his being still ignorant of any of them, he may yet learn the same while we are going over the things with which we understand him to be already familiar. Moreover, it is certainly not without advantage to interrogate the man himself as to the means by which he was induced to desire to be a Christian; so that, if you discover him to have been moved to that decision by books, whether they be the canonical writings or the compositions of literary men worth the studying,[2] you may say something about these at the outset, expressing your approbation of them in a manner which may suit the distinct merits which they severally possess, in respect of canonical authority and of skillfully applied diligence on the part of these expounders;[3] and, in the case of the canonical Scriptures, commending above all the most salutary modesty (of language) displayed alongside their wonderful loftiness (of subject); while, in those other productions you notice, in accordance with the

---

[1] Reading *odiose*, for which several MSS. give *otiose* = idly.
[2] *Utilium tractatorum.*
[3] Reading *exponentium.* Various codices give *ad exponendum* = in expounding.

characteristic faculty of each several writer, a style of a more sonorous and, as it were, more rounded eloquence adapted to minds that are prouder, and, by reason thereof, weaker. We should certainly also elicit from him some account of himself, so that he may give us to understand what writer he chiefly perused, and with what books he was more familiarly conversant, as these were the means of moving him to wish to be associated with the church. And when he has given us this information, then if the said books are known to us, or if we have at least ecclesiastical report as our warrant for taking them to have been written by some catholic man of note, we should joyfully express our approbation. But if, on the other hand, he has fallen upon the productions of some heretic, and in ignorance, it may be, has retained in his mind anything which[1] the true faith condemns, and yet supposes it to be catholic doctrine, then we must set ourselves sedulously to teach him, bringing before him (in its rightful superiority) the authority of the Church universal, and of other most learned men reputed both for their disputations and for their writings in (the cause of) its truth.[2] At the same time, it is to be admitted that even those who have departed this life as genuine catholics, and have left to posterity some Christian writings, in certain passages of their small works, either in consequence of their failing to be understood, or (as the way is with human infirmity) because they lack ability to pierce into the deeper mysteries with the eye of the mind, and in (pursuing) the semblance of what is true, wander from the truth itself, have proved an occasion to the presumptuous and audacious for constructing and generating some heresy. This, however, is not to be wondered at, when, even in the instance of the canonical writings themselves, where all things have been expressed in the soundest manner, we see how it has happened,—not indeed through merely taking certain passages in a sense different from that which the writer had in view or which is consistent with the truth itself, (for if this were all, who would not gladly pardon human infirmity, when it exhibits a readiness to accept correction?), but by persistently defending, with the bitterest vehemence and in impudent arrogance,

opinions which they have taken up in perversity and error,—many have given birth to many pernicious dogmas at the cost of rending the unity of the (Christian) communion. All these subjects we should discuss in modest conference with the individual who makes his approach to the society of the Christian people, not in the character of an uneducated man,[3] as they say, but in that of one who has passed through a finished culture and training in the books of the learned. And in enjoining him to guard against the errors of presumption, we should assume only so much authority as that humility of his, which induced him to come to us, is now felt to admit of. As to other things, moreover, in accordance with the rules of saving doctrine, which require to be narrated or discussed, whether they be matters relating to the faith, or questions bearing on the moral life, or others dealing with temptations, all these should be gone through in the manner which I have indicated, and ought therein to be referred to the more excellent way (already noticed).[4]

CHAP. 9.—OF THE METHOD IN WHICH GRAMMARIANS AND PROFESSIONAL SPEAKERS ARE TO BE DEALT WITH.

13. There are also some who come from the commonest schools of the grammarians and professional speakers, whom you may not venture to reckon either among the uneducated or among those very learned classes whose minds have been exercised in questions of real magnitude. When such persons, therefore, who appear to be superior to the rest of mankind, so far as the art of speaking is concerned, approach you with the view of becoming Christians, it will be your duty in your communications with them, in a higher degree than in your dealings with those other illiterate hearers, to make it plain that they are to be diligently admonished to clothe themselves with Christian humility, and learn not to despise individuals whom they may discover keeping themselves free from vices of conduct more carefully than from faults of language; and also that they ought not to presume so much as to compare with a pure heart the practised tongue which they were accustomed even to put in preference. But above all, such persons should be taught to listen to the divine Scriptures, so that they may neither deem solid eloquence to be mean, merely because it is not inflated, nor suppose that the words or deeds

---

[1] Reading *quod*, with Marriott. But if we accept *quod* with the Benedictine editors, the sense will = and in ignorance it may be that the true faith condemns them, has retained them in his mind.

[2] *Aliorumque doctissimorum hominum et disputationibus et scriptionibus in ejus veritate florentium.* It may also be = bringing before him the authority of the Church universal, as well as both the disputations and the writings of other most learned men well reputed in (the cause of) its truth.

[3] *Idiota.*

[4] 1 Cor. xii. 31. See also above, § 9.

of men, of which we read the accounts in those books, involved and covered as they are in carnal wrappings,[1] are not to be drawn forth and unfolded with a view to an (adequate) understanding of them, but are to be taken merely according to the sound of the letter. And as to this same matter of the utility of the hidden meaning, the existence of which is the reason why they are called also mysteries, the power wielded by these intricacies of enigmatical utterances in the way of sharpening our love for the truth, and shaking off the torpor of weariness, is a thing which the persons in question must have made good to them by actual experience, when some subject which failed to move them when it was placed baldly before them, has its significance elicited by the detailed working out of an allegorical sense. For it is in the highest degree useful to such men to come to know how ideas are to be preferred to words, just as the soul is preferred to the body. And from this, too, it follows that they ought to have the desire to listen to discourses remarkable for their truth, rather than to those which are notable for their eloquence; just as they ought to be anxious to have friends distinguished for their wisdom, rather than those whose chief merit is their beauty. They should also understand that there is no voice for the ears of God save the affection of the soul. For thus they will not act the mocker if they happen to observe any of the prelates and ministers of the Church either calling upon God in language marked by barbarisms and solecisms, or failing in understanding correctly the very words which they are pronouncing, and making confused pauses.[2] It is not meant, of course, that such faults are not to be corrected, so that the people may say "Amen" to something which they plainly understand; but what is intended is, that such things should be piously borne with by those who have come to understand how, as in the forum it is in the sound, so in the church it is in the desire that the grace of speech resides.[3] Therefore that of the forum may sometimes be called good speech, but never gracious speech.[4] Moreover, with respect to the sácrament which they are about to receive, it is enough for the more intelligent simply to hear what the thing signifies. But with those of slower intellect, it will be necessary to adopt a somewhat more detailed explanation, together with the use of similitudes, to prevent them from despising what they see.

CHAP. 10.—OF THE ATTAINMENT OF CHEERFULNESS IN THE DUTY OF CATECHISING, AND OF VARIOUS CAUSES PRODUCING WEARINESS IN THE CATECHUMEN.

14. At this point you perhaps desiderate some example of the kind of discourse intended, so that I may show you by an actual instance how the things which I have recommended are to be done. This indeed I shall do, so far as by God's help I shall be able. But before proceeding to that, it is my duty, in consistency with what I have promised, to speak of the acquisition of the cheerfulness (to which I have alluded). For as regards the matter of the rules in accordance with which your discourse should be set forth, in the case of the catechetical instruction of a person who comes with the express view of being made a Christian, I have already made good, as far as has appeared sufficient, the promise which I made. And surely I am under no obligation at the same time to do myself in this volume that which I enjoin as the right thing to be done. Consequently, if I do that, it will have the value of an overplus. But how can the overplus be superadded by me before I have filled up the measure of what is due? Besides, one thing which I have heard you make the subject of your complaint above all others, is the fact that your discourse seemed to yourself to be poor and spiritless when you were instructing any one in the Christian name. Now this, I know, results not so much from want of matter to say, with which I am well aware you are sufficiently provided and furnished, or from poverty of speech itself, as rather from weariness of mind. And that may spring either from the cause of which I have already spoken, namely, the fact that our intelligence is better pleased and more thoroughly arrested by that which we perceive in silence in the mind, and that we have no inclination to have our attention called off from it to a noise of words coming far short of representing it; or from the circumstance that even when discourse is pleasant, we have more delight in hearing or reading things which have been expressed in a superior manner, and which are set forth without any care or anxiety on our part, than in putting together, with a view to the comprehension of others, words suddenly conceived, and leaving it an uncertain issue, on the one hand, whether such terms occur to us as adequately represent the sense, and on the other, whether they be accepted in such

---

[1] Carnalibus integumentis involuta atque operta.
[2] Or = confusing the sense by false pauses: perturbateque distinguere.
[3] Ut sono in foro, sic voto in ecclesia benedici
[4] Bona dictio, nunquam tamen benedictio.

a manner as to profit; or yet again, from the consideration that, in consequence of their being now thoroughly familiar to ourselves, and no longer necessary to our own advancement, it becomes irksome to us to be recurring very frequently to those matters which are urged upon the uninstructed, and our mind, as being by this time pretty well matured, moves with no manner of pleasure in the circle of subjects so well-worn, and, as it were, so childish. A sense of weariness is also induced upon the speaker when he has a hearer who remains unmoved, either in that he is actually not stirred by any feeling, or in that he does not indicate by any motion of the body that he understands or that he is pleased with what is said.[1] Not that it is a becoming disposition in us to be greedy of the praises of men, but that the things which we minister are of God; and the more we love those to whom we discourse, the more desirous are we that they should be pleased with the matters which are held forth for their salvation: so that if we do not succeed in this, we are pained, and we are weakened, and become broken-spirited in the midst of our course, as if we were wasting our efforts to no purpose. Sometimes, too, when we are drawn off from some matter which we are desirous to go on with, and the transaction of which was a pleasure to us, or appeared to be more than usually needful, and when we are compelled, either by the command of a person whom we are unwilling to offend, or by the importunity of some parties that we find it impossible to get rid of, to instruct any one catechetically, in such circumstances we approach a duty for which great calmness is indispensable with minds already perturbed, and grieving at once that we are not permitted to keep that order which we desire to observe in our actions, and that we cannot possibly be competent for all things; and thus out of very heaviness our discourse as it advances is less of an attraction, because, starting from the arid soil of dejection, it goes on less flowingly. Sometimes, too, sadness has taken possession of our heart in consequence of some offense or other, and at that very time we are addressed thus: "Come, speak with this person; he desires to become a Christian." For they who thus address us do it in ignorance of the hidden trouble which is consuming us within. So it happens that, if they are not the persons to whom it befits us to open up our feelings, we undertake with no sense of pleasure what they desire; and

then, certainly, the discourse will be languid and unenjoyable which is transmitted through the agitated and fuming channel of a heart in that condition. Consequently, seeing there are so many causes serving to cloud the calm serenity of our minds, in accordance with God's will we must seek remedies for them, such as may bring us relief from these feelings of heaviness, and help us to rejoice in fervor of spirit, and to be jocund in the tranquility of a good work. "For God loveth a cheerful giver."[2]

15. Now if the cause of our sadness lies in the circumstance that our hearer does not apprehend what we mean, so that we have to come down in a certain fashion from the elevation of our own conceptions, and are under the necessity of dwelling long in the tedious processes of syllables which come far beneath the standard of our ideas, and have anxiously to consider how that which we ourselves take in with a most rapid draught of mental apprehension is to be given forth by the mouth of flesh in the long and perplexed intricacies of its method of enunciation; and if the great dissimilarity thus felt (between our utterance and our thought) makes it distasteful to us to speak, and a pleasure to us to keep silence, then let us ponder what has been set before us by Him who has "showed us an example that we should follow His steps."[3] For however much our articulate speech may differ from the vivacity of our intelligence, much greater is the difference of the flesh of mortality from the equality of God. And, neverless, "although He was in the same form, He emptied Himself, taking the form of a servant,"—and so on down to the words "the death of the cross."[4] What is the explanation of this but that He made Himself "weak to the weak, in order that He might gain the weak?"[5] Listen to His follower as he expresses himself also in another place to this effect: "For whether we be beside ourselves, it is to God; or whether we be sober, it is for your cause. For the love of Christ constraineth us, because we thus judge that He died for all."[6] And how, indeed, should one be ready to be spent for their souls,[7] if he should find it irksome to him to bend himself to their ears? For this reason, therefore, He became a little child in the midst of us, (and) like a

---

[1] The sentence, "either in that he is actually not stirred . . . by what is said," is omitted in many MSS.

[2] 2 Cor. ix. 7.　　　　　[3] 1 Pet. ii. 21.
[4] Phil. ii. 17. The form in which the quotation is given above, with the omission of the intermediate clauses, is due probably to the copyist, and not to Augustin himself. The words left out are given thus in the Serm. XLVII. on Ezekiel xxxiv.: " Being made in the likeness of men, and being found in the fashion of a man : He humbled Himself, being made obedient unto death, even the death of the cross." [See R. V.]
[5] Cf. 1 Cor. ix. 22.
[6] 2 Cor. v. 13, 14.　　　　[7] Cf. 2 Cor. xii. 15.

5

nurse cherishing her children.[1] For is it a pleasure to lisp shortened and broken words, unless love invites us? And yet men desire to have infants to whom they have to do that kind of service; and it is a sweeter thing to a mother to put small morsels of masticated food into her little son's mouth, than to eat up and devour larger pieces herself. In like manner, accordingly, let not the thought of the hen[2] recede from your heart, who covers her tender brood with her drooping feathers, and with broken voice calls her chirping young ones to her, while they that turn away from her fostering wings in their pride become a prey to birds. For if intelligence brings delights in its purest recesses, it should also be a delight to us to have an intelligent understanding of the manner in which charity, the more complaisantly it descends to the lowest objects, finds its way back, with all the greater vigor to those that are most secret, along the course of a good conscience which witnesses that it has sought nothing from those to whom it has descended except their everlasting salvation.

CHAP. 11.—OF THE REMEDY FOR THE SECOND SOURCE OF WEARINESS.

16. If, however, it is rather our desire to read or hear such things as are already prepared for our use and expressed in a superior style, and if the consequence is that we feel it irksome to put together, at the time and with an uncertain issue, the terms of discourse on our own side, then, provided only that our mind does not wander off from the truth of the facts themselves, it is an easy matter for the hearer, if he is offended by anything in our language, to come to see in that very circumstance how little value should be set, supposing the subject itself to be rightly understood, upon the mere fact that there may have been some imperfection or some inaccuracy in the literal expressions, which were employed indeed simply with the view of securing a correct apprehension of the subject-matter. But if the bent of human infirmity has wandered off from the truth of the facts themselves,—although in the catechetical instruction of the unlearned, where we have to keep by the most beaten track, that cannot occur very readily,—still, lest haply it should turn out that our hearer finds cause of offence even in this direction, we ought not to deem this to have come upon us in any other way than as the issue of God's own wish to put us to the test with respect to our readiness to re-

ceive correction in calmness of mind, so as not to rush headlong, in the course of a still greater error, into the defense of our error. But if, again, no one has told us of it, and if the thing has altogether escaped our own notice, as well as the observation of our hearers, then there is nothing to grieve over, provided only the same thing does not occur a second time. For the most part, however, when we recall what we have said, we ourselves discover something to find fault with, and are ignorant of the manner in which it was received when it was uttered; and so when charity is fervent within us, we are the more vexed if the thing, while really false, has been received with unquestioning acceptance. This being the case, then, whenever an opportunity occurs, as we have been finding fault with ourselves in silence, we ought in like manner to see to it that those persons be also set right on the subject in a considerate method, who have fallen into some sort of error, not by the words of God, but plainly by those used by us. If, on the other hand, there are any who, blinded by insensate spite, rejoice that we have committed a mistake, whisperers as they are, and slanderers, and "hateful to God,"[3] such characters should afford us matter for the exercise of patience with pity, inasmuch as also the "patience of God leadeth them to repentance."[4] For what is more detestable, and what more likely to "treasure up wrath in the day of wrath and revelation of the righteous judgment of God,"[5] than to rejoice, after the evil likeness and pattern of the devil, in the evil of another? At times, too, even when all is correctly and truly spoken, either something which has not been understood, or something which, as being opposed to the idea and wont of an old error, seems harsh in its very novelty, offends and disturbs the hearer. But if this becomes apparent, and if the person shows himself capable of being set right, he should be set right without any delay by the use of abundance of authorities and reasons. On the other hand, if the offense is tacit and hidden, the medicine of God is the effective remedy for it. And if, again, the person starts back and declines to be cured, we should comfort ourselves with that example of our Lord, who, when men were offended at His word, and shrank from it as a hard saying, addressed Himself at the same time to those who had remained, in these terms, "Will ye also go away?"[6] For it ought to be retained as a thoroughly "fixed and immovable" position in our heart, that

---

[1] Cf. 1. Thess. ii. 7.
[2] *Illius gallinæ*,—in reference to Matt. xxiii. 37.

[3] Cf. Rom. i. 30.
[5] Rom. ii. 5.
[4] Rom. ii. 4. [See R. V.]
[6] John vi. 67.

Jerusalem which is in captivity is set free from the Babylon of this world when the times have run their course, and that none belonging to her shall perish : for whoever may perish was not of her. "For the foundation of God standeth sure, having this seal, The Lord knoweth them that are His ; and, let every one that nameth the name of Christ depart from iniquity."[1] If we ponder these things, and call upon the Lord to come into our heart, we shall be less apprehensive of the uncertain issues of our discourse, consequent on the uncertain feelings of our hearers ; and the very endurance of vexations in the cause of a work of mercy will also be something pleasant to us, if we seek not our own glory in the same. For then is a work truly good, when the aim of the doer gets its impetus from charity,[2] and, as if returning to its own place, rests again in charity. Moreover, the reading which delights us, or any listening to an eloquence superior to our own, the effect of which is to make us inclined to set a greater value upon it than upon the discourse which we ourselves have to deliver, and so to lead us to speak with a reluctant or tedious utterance, will come upon us in a happier spirit, and will be found to be more enjoyable after labor. Then, too, with a stronger confidence shall we pray to God to speak to us as we wish, if we cheerfully submit to let Him speak by us as we are able. Thus is it brought about that all things come together for good to them that love God.[3]

CHAP. 12.—OF THE REMEDY FOR THE THIRD
SOURCE OF WEARINESS.

17. Once more, however, we often feel it very wearisome to go over repeatedly matters which are thoroughly familiar, and adapted (rather) to children. If this is the case with us, then we should endeavor to meet them with a brother's, a father's, and a mother's love; and, if we are once united with them thus in heart, to us no less than to them will these things seem new. For so great is the power of a sympathetic disposition of mind, that, as they are affected while we are speaking, and we are affected while they are learning, we have our dwelling in each other; and thus, at one and the same time, they as it were in us speak what they hear, and we in them learn after a certain fashion what we teach. Is it not a common occurrence with

us, that when we show to persons, who have never seen them, certain spacious and beautiful tracts, either in cities or in fields, which we have been in the habit of passing by without any sense of pleasure, simply because we have become so accustomed to the sight of them, we find our own enjoyment renewed in their enjoyment of the novelty of the scene? And this is so much the more our experience in proportion to the intimacy of our friendship with them; because, just as we are in them in virtue of the bond of love, in the same degree do things become new to us which previously were old. But if we ourselves have made any considerable progress in the contemplative study of things, it is not our wish that those whom we love should simply be gratified and astonished as they gaze upon the works of men's hands; but it becomes our wish to lift them to (the contemplation of) the very skill[4] or wisdom of their author, and from this to (see them) rise to the admiration and praise of the all-creating God, with whom[5] is the most fruitful end of love. How much more, then, ought we to be delighted when men come to us with the purpose already formed of obtaining the knowledge of God Himself, with a view to (the knowledge of) whom all things should be learned which are to be learned! And how ought we to feel ourselves renewed in their newness (of experience), so that if our ordinary preaching is somewhat frigid, it may rise to fresh warmth under (the stimulus of) their extraordinary hearing! There is also this additional consideration to help us in the attainment of gladness, namely, that we ponder and bear in mind out of what death of error the man is passing over into the life of faith. And if we walk through streets which are most familiar to us, with a beneficent cheerfulness, when we happen to be pointing out the way to some individual who had been in distress in consequence of missing his direction, how much more should be the alacrity of spirit, and how much greater the joy with which, in the matter of saving doctrine, we ought to traverse again and again even those tracks which, so far as we are ourselves concerned, there is no need to open up any more; seeing that we are leading a miserable soul, and one worn out with the devious courses of this world, through the paths of peace, at the command of Him who made that peace[6] good to us!

---

[1] 2 Tim. ii. 19.   [2] *A caritate jaculatur.*
[3] *Concurrant in bonum.* Rom. viii. 28.

[4] Some editions read *arcem* = stronghold, instead of *artem*.
[5] Or = wherein : *ubi.*
[6] Instead of *eam*, the reading *ea* = those things, also occurs.

CHAP. 13.—OF THE REMEDY FOR THE FOURTH
SOURCE OF WEARINESS.

18. But in good truth it is a serious demand to make upon us, to continue discoursing on to the set limit when we fail to see
our hearer in any degree moved; whether it
be that, under the restraints of the awe of religion, he has not the boldness to signify his
approval by voice or by any movement of his
body, or that he is kept back by the modesty
proper to man,[1] or that he does not understand our sayings, or that he counts them of
no value. Since, then, this must be a matter
of uncertainty to us, as we cannot discern his
mind, it becomes our duty in our discourse
to make trial of all things which may be of
any avail in stirring him up and drawing him
forth as it were from his place of concealment. For that sort of fear which is excessive, and which obstructs the declaration
of his judgment, ought to be dispelled by the
force of kindly exhortation; and by bringing
before him the consideration of our brotherly
affinity, we should temper his reverence for
us; and by questioning him, we should ascertain whether he understands what is addressed
to him; and we should impart to him a sense
of confidence, so that he may give free expression to any objection which suggests
itself to him. We should at the same time ask
him whether he has already listened to such
themes on some previous occasion, and
whether perchance they fail to move him
now in consequence of their being to him like
things well known and commonplace. And
we ought to shape our course in accordance
with his answer, so as either to speak in a
simpler style and with greater detail of explanation, or to refute some antagonistic
opinion, or, instead of attempting any more
diffuse exposition of the subjects which are
known to him, to give a brief summary of
these, and to select some of those matters
which are handled in a mystical manner in
the holy books, and especially in the historical narrative, the unfolding and setting forth
of which may make our addresses more attractive. But if the man is of a very sluggish
disposition, and if he is senseless, and without anything in common with all such sources
of pleasure, then we must simply bear with
him in a compassionate spirit; and, after
briefly going over other points, we ought to
impress upon him, in a manner calculated to
inspire him with awe, the truths which are
most indispensable on the subject of the unity
of the Catholic Church,[2] on that of tempta-

tion, on that of a Christian conversation in
view of the future judgment; and we ought
rather to address ourselves to God for him
than address much to him concerning God.

19. It is likewise a frequent occurrence that
one who at first listened to us with all readiness, becomes exhausted either by the effort
of hearing or by standing, and now no longer
commends what is said, but gapes and yawns,
and even unwillingly exhibits a disposition to
depart. When we observe that, it becomes
our duty to refresh his mind by saying something seasoned with an honest cheerfulness
and adapted to the matter which is being discussed, or something of a very wonderful and
amazing order, or even, it may be, something
of a painful and mournful nature. Whatever
we thus say may be all the better if it affects
himself more immediately, so that the quick
sense of self-concern may keep his attention
on the alert. At the same time, however, it
should not be of the kind to offend his spirit
of reverence by any harshness attaching to
it; but it should be of a nature fitted rather
to conciliate him by the friendliness which it
breathes. Or else, we should relieve him by
accommodating him with a seat, although unquestionably matters will be better ordered if
from the outset, whenever that can be done
with propriety, he sits and listens. And
indeed in certain of the churches beyond the
sea, with a far more considerate regard to the
fitness of things, not only do the prelates sit
when they address the people, but they also
themselves put down seats for the people,
lest any person of enfeebled strength should
become exhausted by standing, and thus have
his mind diverted from the most wholesome
purport (of the discourse), or even be under
the necessity of departing. And yet it is one
thing if it be simply some one out of a great
multitude who withdraws in order to recruit
his strength, he being also already under the
obligations which result from participation in
the sacraments; and it is quite another thing
if the person withdrawing is one (inasmuch
as it is usually the case in these circumstances
that the man is unavoidably urged to that
course by the fear that he should even fall,
overcome by internal weakness) who has to
be initiated in the first sacraments; for a person
in this position is at once restrained by the
sense of shame from stating the reason of his
going, and not permitted to stand through the
force of his weakness. This I speak from
experience. For this was the case with a certain individual, a man from the country, when
I was instructing him catechetically: and from

---

[1] Or = by the reverence which he feels for the man: *humana
verecundia.*
[2] The text gives simply *Catholicæ.* One MS. has *Catholicæ
fidei* = the Catholic faith. But it is most natural to supply
Ecclesiæ.

his instance I have learned that this kind of thing is carefully to be guarded against. For who can endure our arrogance when we fail to make men who are our brethren,[1] or even those who are not yet in that relation to us (for our solicitude then should be all the greater to get them to become our brethren), to be seated in our presence, seeing that even a woman sat as she listened to our Lord Himself, in whose service the angels stand alert?[2] Of course if the address is to be but short, or if the place is not well adapted for sitting, they should listen standing. But that should be the case only when there are many hearers, and when they are not to be formally admitted[3] at the time. For when the audience consists only of one or two, or a few, who have come with the express purpose of being made Christians, there is a risk in speaking to them standing. Nevertheless, supposing that we have once begun in that manner, we ought at least, whenever we observe signs of weariness on the part of the hearer, to offer him the liberty of being seated; nay more, we should urge him by all means to sit down, and we ought to drop some remark calculated at once to refresh him and to banish from his mind any anxiety which may have chanced to break in upon him and draw off his attention. For inasmuch as the reasons why he remains silent and declines to listen cannot be certainly known to us, now that he is seated we may speak to some extent against the incidence of thoughts about worldly affairs, delivering ourselves either in the cheerful spirit to which I have already adverted, or in a serious vein; so that, if these are the particular anxieties which have occupied his mind, they may be made to give way as if indicted by name: while, on the other hand, supposing them not to be the special causes (of the loss of interest), and supposing him to be simply worn out with listening, his attention will be relieved of the pressure of weariness when we address to him some unexpected and extraordinary strain of remark on these subjects, in the mode of which I have spoken, as if they were the particular anxieties,—for indeed we are simply ignorant (of the true causes). But let the remark thus made be short, especially considering that it is thrown in out of order, lest the very medicine even increase the malady of weariness which we desire to relieve; and, at the same time, we should go on rapidly with what remains, and promise and present the prospect of a conclusion nearer than was looked for.

CHAP. 14.—OF THE REMEDY AGAINST THE FIFTH AND SIXTH SOURCES OF WEARINESS.

20. If, again, your spirit has been broken by the necessity of giving up some other employment, on which, as the more requisite, you were now bent; and if the sadness caused by that constraint makes you catechise in no pleasant mood, you ought to ponder the fact that, excepting that we know it to be our duty, in all our dealings with men, to act in a merciful manner, and in the exercise of the sincerest charity,—with this one exception, I say, it is quite uncertain to us what is the more profitable thing for us to do, and what the more opportune thing for us either to pass by for a time or altogether to omit. For inasmuch as we know not how the merits of men, on whose behalf we are acting, stand with God, the question as to what is expedient for them at a certain time is something which, instead of being able to comprehend, we can rather only surmise, without the aid of any (clear) inferences, or (at best) with the slenderest and the most uncertain. Therefore we ought certainly to dispose the matters with which we have to deal according to our intelligence; and then, if we prove able to carry them out in the manner upon which we have resolved, we should rejoice, not indeed that it was our will, but that it was God's will, that they should thus be accomplished. But if anything unavoidable happens, by which the disposition thus proposed by us is interfered with, we should bend ourselves to it readily, lest we be broken; so that the very disposition of affairs which God has preferred to ours may also be made our own. For it is more in accordance with propriety that we should follow His will than that He should follow ours. Besides, as regards this order in the doing of things, which we wish to keep in accordance with our own judgment, surely that course is to be approved of in which objects that are superior have the precedence. Why then are we aggrieved that the precedence over men should be held by the Lord God in His vast superiority to us men, so that in the said love which we entertain for our own order, we should thus (exhibit the disposition to) despise order? For "no one orders for the better" what he has to do, except the man who is rather ready to leave undone what he is prohibited from doing by the divine power, than desirous of doing that which he meditates in his own human cogitations. For "there are many devices in a man's heart; nevertheless, the counsel of the Lord stands for ever."[4]

---

[1] Instead of *viros fratres*, some MSS. read *veros fratres* = our genuine brethren. [2] Luke x. 39. [3] *Initiandi* = initiated.

[4] Prov. xix. 21.

21. But if our mind is agitated by some cause of offense, so as not to be capable of delivering a discourse of a calm and enjoyable strain, our charity towards those for whom Christ died, desiring to redeem them by the price of His own blood from the death of the errors of this world, ought to be so great, that the very circumstance of intelligence being brought us in our sadness, regarding the advent of some person who longs to become a Christian, ought to be enough to cheer us and dissipate that heaviness of spirit, just as the delights of gain are wont to soften the pain of losses. For we are not (fairly) oppressed by the offense of any individual, unless it be that of the man whom we either perceive or believe to be perishing himself, or to be the occasion of the undoing of some weak one. Accordingly, one who comes to us with the view of being formally admitted, in that we cherish the hope of his ability to go forward, should wipe away the sorrow caused by one who fails us. For even if the dread that our proselyte may become the child of hell[1] comes into our thoughts, as, there are many such before our eyes, from whom those offenses arise by which we are distressed, this ought to operate, not in the way of keeping us back, but rather in the way of stimulating us and spurring us on. And in the same measure we ought to admonish him whom we are instructing to be on his guard against imitating those who are Christians only in name and not in very truth, and to take care not to suffer himself to be so moved by their numbers as either to be desirous of following them, or to be reluctant to follow Christ on their account, and either to be unwilling to be in the Church of God, where they are, or to wish to be there in such a character as they bear. And somehow or other, in admonitions of this sort, that address is the more glowing to which a present sense of grief supplies the fuel; so that instead of being duller, we utter with greater fire and vehemence under such feelings things which, in times of greater ease, we would give forth in a colder and less energetic manner. And this should make us rejoice that an opportunity is afforded us under which the emotions of our mind pass not away without yielding some fruit.

22. If, however, grief has taken possession of us on account of something in which we ourselves have erred or sinned, we should bear in mind not only that a "broken spirit is a sacrifice to God,"[2] but also the saying, "Like as water quencheth fire, so alms sin;"[3]

and again, "I will have mercy," saith He, "rather than sacrifice."[4] Therefore, as in the event of our being in peril from fire we would certainly run to the water in order to get the fire extinguished, and we would be grateful if any person were to offer it in the immediate vicinity; so, if some flame of sin has risen from our own stack,[5] and if we are troubled on that account, when an opportunity has been given for a most merciful work, we should rejoice in it, as if a fountain were offered us in order that by it the conflagration which had burst forth might be extinguished. Unless haply we are foolish enough to think that we ought to be readier in running with bread, wherewith we may fill the belly of a hungry man, than with the word of God, wherewith we may instruct the mind of the man who feeds on it.[6] There is this also to consider, namely, that if it would only be of advantage to us to do this thing, and entail no disadvantage to leave it undone, we might despise a remedy offered in an unhappy fashion in the time of peril with a view to the safety, not now of a neighbor, but of ourselves. But when from the mouth of the Lord this so threatening sentence is heard, "Thou wicked and slothful servant, thou oughtest to give my money to the exchangers,"[7] what madness, I pray thee, is it thus, seeing that our sin pains us, to be minded to sin again, by refusing to give the Lord's money to one who desires it and asks it! When these and such like considerations and reflections have succeeded in dispelling the darkness of weary feelings, the bent of mind is rendered apt for the duty of catechising, so that that is received in a pleasant manner which breaks forth vigorously and cheerfully from the rich vein of charity. For these things indeed which are uttered here are spoken, not so much by me to you, as rather to us all by that very "love which is shed abroad in our hearts by the Holy Spirit that is given to us."[8]

CHAP. 15.—OF THE METHOD IN WHICH OUR ADDRESS SHOULD BE ADAPTED TO DIFFERENT CLASSES OF HEARERS.

23. But now, perhaps, you also demand of me as a debt that which, previous to the promise which I made, I was under no obligation to give, namely, that I should not count it burdensome to unfold some sort of example of the discourse intended, and to set it before you for your study, just as if I were my-

---

[1] Matt. xxiii. 15.   [2] Ps. li. 17.   [3] Ecclus. iii. 30.

[4] Hos. vi. 6.   [5] *Fæno* = hay.
[6] Reading *istud edentis;* for which some editions give *studentis* = of one who studies it.
[7] Matt. xxv. 26, 27.   [8] Rom. v. 5.

self engaged in catechising some individual. Before I do that, however, I wish you to keep in mind the fact that the mental effort is of one kind in the case of a person who dictates, with a future reader in his view, and that it is of quite another kind in the case of a person who speaks with a present hearer to whom to direct his attention. And further, it is to be remembered that, in this latter instance in particular, the effort is of one kind when one is admonishing in private, and when there is no other person at hand to pronounce judgment on us; whereas it is of a different order when one is conveying any instruction in public, and when there stands around him an audience of persons holding dissimilar opinions ; and again, that in this exercise of teaching, the effort will be of one sort when only a single individual is being instructed, while all the rest listen, like persons judging or attesting things well known to them, and that it will be different when all those who are present wait for what we have to deliver to them; and once more, that, in this same instance, the effort will be one thing when all are seated, as it were, in private conference with a view to engaging in some discussion, and that it will be quite another thing when the people sit silent and intent on giving their attention to some single speaker who is to address them from a higher position. It will likewise make a considerable difference, even when we are discoursing in that style, whether there are few present or many, whether they are learned or unlearned, or made up of both classes combined; whether they are city-bred or rustics, or both the one and the other together; or whether, again, they are a people composed of all orders of men in due proportion. For it is impossible but that they will affect in different ways the person who has to speak to them and discourse with them, and that the address which is delivered will both bear certain features, as it were, expressive of the feelings of the mind from which it proceeds, and also influence the hearers in different ways, in accordance with that same difference (in the speaker's disposition), while at the same time the hearers themselves will influence one another in different ways by the simple force of their presence with each other. But as we are dealing at present with the matter of the instruction of the unlearned, I am a witness to you, as regards my own experience, that I find myself variously moved, according as I see before me, for the purposes of catechetical instruction, a highly educated man, a dull fellow, a citizen, a foreigner, a rich man, a poor man, a private individual, a man of honors, a person occupy-

ing some position of authority, an individual of this or the other nation, of this or the other age or sex, one proceeding from this or the other sect, from this or the other common error,—and ever in accordance with the difference of my feelings does my discourse itself at once set out, go on, and reach its end. And inasmuch as, although the same charity is due to all, yet the same medicine is not to be administered to all, in like manner charity itself travails with some, is made weak together with others; is at pains to edify some, tremblingly apprehends being an offense to others; bends to some, lifts itself erect to others; is gentle to some, severe to others; to none an enemy, to all a mother. And when one, who has not gone through the kind of experience to which I refer in the same spirit of charity, sees us attaining, in virtue of some gift which has been conferred upon us, and which carries the power of pleasing, a certain repute of an eulogistic nature in the mouth of the multitude, he counts us happy on that account. But may God, into whose cognizance the " groaning of them that are bound enters,''[1] look upon our humility, and our labor, and forgive us all our sins.[2] Wherefore, if anything in us has so far pleased you as to make you desirous of hearing from us some remarks on the subject of the form of discourse which you ought to follow,[3] you should acquire a more thorough understanding of the matter by contemplating us, and listening to us when we are actually engaged with these topics, than by a perusal when we are only dictating them.

CHAP. 16.—A SPECIMEN OF A CATECHETICAL ADDRESS ; AND FIRST, THE CASE OF A CATECHUMEN WITH WORTHY VIEWS.

24. Nevertheless, however that may be, let us here suppose that some one has come to us who desires to be made a Christian, and who belongs indeed to the order of private persons,[4] and yet not to the class of rustics, but to that of the city-bred, such as those whom you cannot fail to come across in numbers in Carthage. Let us also suppose that, on being asked whether the inducement leading him to desire to be a Christian is any advantage looked for in the present life, or the rest which is hoped for after this life, he has answered that his inducement has been the rest that is yet to come. Then perchance such a person might be instructed by us in some such strain of address as the following:

---

[1] Ps. lxxix. 11.   [2] Cf. Ps. xxv. 18.
[3] *Ut aliquam observationem sermonis tui a nobis audire quæreres.*   [4] *Idiotarum.*

"Thanks be to God, my brother; cordially do I wish you joy, and I am glad on your account that, amid all the storms of this world, which are at once so great and so dangerous, you have bethought yourself of some true and certain security. For even in this life men go in quest of rest and security at the cost of heavy labors, but they fail to find such in consequence of their wicked lusts. For their thought is to find rest in things which are unquiet, and which endure not. And these objects, inasmuch as they are withdrawn from them and pass away in the course of time, agitate them by fears and griefs, and suffer them not to enjoy tranquillity. For if it be that a man seeks to find his rest in wealth, he is rendered proud rather than at ease. Do we not see how many have lost their riches on a sudden,—how many, too, have been undone by reason of them, either as they have been coveting to possess them, or as they have been borne down and despoiled of them by others more covetous than themselves? And even should they remain with the man all his life long, and never leave their lover, yet would he himself (have to) leave them at his death. For of what measure is the life of man, even if he lives to old age? Or when men desire for themselves old age, what else do they really desire but long infirmity? So, too, with the honors of this world,—what are they but empty pride and vanity, and peril of ruin? For holy Scripture speaks in this wise: 'All flesh is grass, and the glory of man is as the flower of grass. The grass withereth, the flower thereof falleth away; but the word of the Lord endureth for ever.'[1] Consequently, if any man longs for true rest and true felicity, he ought to lift his hope off things which are mortal and transitory, and fix it on the word of the Lord; so that, cleaving to that which endures for ever, he may himself together with it endure for ever.

25. "There are also other men who neither crave to be rich nor go about seeking the vain pomps of honors, but who nevertheless are minded to find their pleasure and rest in dainty meats, and in fornications, and in those theatres and spectacles which are at their disposal in great cities for nothing. But it fares with these, too, in the same way; or they waste their small means in luxury, and subsequently, under pressure of want, break out into thefts and burglaries, and at times even into highway robberies, and so they are suddenly filled with fears both numerous and great; and men who a little

before were singing in the house of revelry, are now dreaming of the sorrows of the prison. Moreover, in their eager devotion to the public spectacles, they come to resemble demons, as they incite men by their cries to wound each other, and instigate those who have done them no hurt to engage in furious contests with each other, while they seek to please an insane people.. And if they perceive any such to be peaceably disposed, they straightway hate them and persecute them, and raise an outcry, asking that they should be beaten with clubs, as if they had been in collusion to cheat them; and this iniquity they force even the judge, who is the (appointed) avenger of iniquities, to perpetrate. On the other hand, if they observe such men exerting themselves in horrid hostilities against each other, whether they be those who are called sintæ,[2] or theatrical actors and players,[3] or charioteers, or hunters,—those wretched men whom they engage in conflicts and struggles, not only men with men, but even men with beasts,—then the fiercer the fury with which they perceive these unhappy creatures rage against each other, the better they like them, and the greater the enjoyment they have in them; and they favor them when thus excited,[4] and by so favoring them they excite them all the more, the spectators themselves striving more madly with each other, as they espouse the cause of different combatants, than is the case even with those very men whose madness they madly provoke, while at the same time they also long to be spectators of the same in their mad frenzy.[5] How then can that mind keep the soundness of peace which feeds on strifes and contentions? For just as is the food which is received, such is the health which results. In fine, although mad pleasures are no pleasures, nevertheless let these things be taken as they are, and it still remains the case that, whatever their nature may be, and whatever the measure of enjoyment yielded by the boasts of riches, and the inflation of honors, and the spendthrift pleasures of the taverns, and the contests of the theatres, and the impurity of fornications, and the pruriency of the baths, they are all things of which one

---

[1] Isa. xl. 6, 8; 1 Pet. i. 24, 25.

[2] Reading sive sintæ qui appellantur, for which there occur such varieties of reading as these: sint athletæ qui appellantur = those who are called athletes; or sint æqui appellantur: or simply sint qui appellantur = whatever name they bear, whether actors, etc. The term sintæ, borrowed from the Greek Σίνται = devourers, spoilers, may have been a word in common use among the Africans, as the Benedictine editors suggest, for designating some sort of coarse characters.

[3] Thymelici, strictly = the musicians belonging to the thymele, or orchestra.

[4] Reading incitatis favent, for which some MSS. give incitati = excited themselves, they favor them; and others have incitantes = exciting them, they favor them.

[5] Compare a passage in the Confessions, vi. 13.

little fever deprives us, while, even from those who still survive, it takes away the whole false happiness of their life. Then there remains only a void and wounded conscience, destined to apprehend that God as a Judge whom it refused to have as a Father, and destined also to find a severe Lord in Him whom it scorned to seek and love as a tender Father. But thou, inasmuch as thou seekest that true rest which is promised to Christians after this life, wilt taste the same sweet and pleasant rest even here among the bitterest troubles of this life, if thou continuest to love the commandments of Him who hath promised the same. For quickly wilt thou feel that the fruits of righteousness are sweeter than those of unrighteousness, and that a man finds a more genuine and pleasurable joy in the possession of a good conscience in the midst of troubles than in that of an evil conscience in the midst of delights. For thou hast not come to be united to the Church of God with the idea of seeking from it any temporal advantage.

CHAP. 17.—THE SPECIMEN OF CATECHETICAL DISCOURSE CONTINUED, IN REFERENCE SPECIALLY TO THE REPROVAL OF FALSE AIMS ON THE CATECHUMEN'S PART.

26. "For there are some whose reason for desiring to become Christians is either that they may gain the favor of men from whom they look for temporal advantages, or that they are reluctant to offend those whom they fear. But these are reprobate; and although the church bears them for a time, as the threshing-floor bears the chaff until the period of winnowing, yet if they fail to amend and begin to be Christians in sincerity in view of the everlasting rest which is to come, they will be separated from it in the end. And let not such flatter themselves, because it is possible for them to be in the threshing-floor along with the grain of God. For they will not be together with that in the barn, but are destined for the fire, which is their due. There are also others of better hope indeed, but nevertheless in no inferior danger. I mean those who now fear God, and mock not the Christian name, neither enter the church of God with an assumed heart, but still look for their felicity in this life, expecting to have more felicity in earthly things than those enjoy who refuse to worship God. And the consequence of this false anticipation is, that when they see some wicked and impious men strongly established and excelling in this worldly prosperity, while they themselves either possess it in a smaller degree or miss it altogether, they are troubled with the thought that they are serving God without reason, and so they readily fall away from the faith.

27. "But as to the man who has in view that everlasting blessedness and perpetual rest which is promised as the lot destined for the saints after this life, and who desires to become a Christian, in order that he may not pass into eternal fire with the devil, but enter into the eternal kingdom together with Christ,[1] such an one is truly a Christian; (and he will be) on his guard in every temptation, so that he may neither be corrupted by prosperity nor be utterly broken in spirit by adversity, but remain at once modest and temperate when the good things of earth abound with him, and brave and patient when tribulations overtake him. A person of this character will also advance in attainments until he comes to that disposition of mind which will make him love God more than he fears hell; so that even were God to say to him, 'Avail yourself of carnal pleasures for ever, and sin as much as you are able, and you shall neither die nor be sent into hell, but you will only not be with me,' he would be terribly dismayed, and would altogether abstain from sinning, not now (simply) with the purpose of not falling into that of which he was wont to be afraid, but with the wish not to offend Him whom he so greatly loves: in whom alone also there is the rest which eye hath not seen, neither hath ear heard, neither hath it entered into the heart of man (to conceive),—the rest which God hath prepared for them that love Him.[2]

28. "Now, on the subject of this rest Scripture is significant, and refrains not to speak, when it tells us how at the beginning of the world, and at the time when God made heaven and earth and all things which are in them, He worked during six days, and rested on the seventh day.[3] For it was in the power of the Almighty to make all things even in one moment of time. For He had not labored in the view that He might enjoy (a needful) rest, since indeed "He spake, and they were made; He commanded, and they were created;"[4] but that He might signify how, after six ages of this world, in a seventh age, as on the seventh day, He will rest in His saints; inasmuch as these same saints shall rest also in Him after all the good works in which they have served Him,—which He Himself, indeed, works in them, who calls them, and instructs them, and puts away the offenses that are past, and justifies the man who previously

1 Cf. Matt. xxv. 34, 41.   2 1 Cor. ii. 9.
3 Gen. ii. 1-3.   4 Ps. cxlviii. 5.

was ungodly. For as, when by His gift they work that which is good, He is Himself rightly said to work (that in them), so, when they rest in Him, He is rightly said to rest Himself. For, as regards Himself, He seeks no cessation, because He feels no labor. Moreover He made all things by His Word; and His Word is Christ Himself, in whom the angels and all those purest spirits of heaven rest in holy silence. Man, however, in that he fell by sin, has lost the rest which he possessed in His divinity, and receives it again (now) in His humanity; and for this purpose He became man, and was born of a woman, at the seasonable time at which He Himself knew it behoved it so to be fulfilled. And from the flesh assuredly He could not sustain any contamination, being Himself rather destined to purify the flesh. Of His future coming the ancient saints, in the revelation of the Spirit, had knowledge, and prophesied. And thus were they saved by believing that He was to come, even as we are saved by believing that He has come. Hence ought we to love God who has so loved us as to have sent His only Son, in order that He might endue Himself with the lowliness[1] of our mortality, and die both at the hands of sinners and on behalf of sinners. For even in times of old, and in the opening ages, the depth of this mystery ceases not to be prefigured and prophetically announced.

CHAP. 18.—OF WHAT IS TO BE BELIEVED ON THE SUBJECT OF THE CREATION OF MAN AND OTHER OBJECTS.

29. "Whereas, then, the omnipotent God, who is also good and just and merciful, who made all things,—whether they be great or small, whether they be highest or lowest, whether they be things which are seen, such as are the heavens and the earth and the sea, and in the heavens, in particular, the sun and the moon and other luminaries, and in the earth and the sea, again, trees and shrubs and animals each after their kind, and all bodies celestial or terrestrial alike, or whether they be things which are not seen, such as are those spirits whereby bodies are animated and endowed with life,—made also man after His own image, in order that, as He Himself, in virtue of His omnipotence, presides over universal creation, so man, in virtue of that intelligence of his by which he comes to know even his Creator and worships Him, might preside over all the living creatures of earth: Whereas, too, he made the woman to

be an helpmeet for him : not for carnal concupiscence,—since, indeed, they had not corruptible bodies at that period, before the punishment of sin invaded them in the form of mortality,—but for this purpose, that the man might at once have glory of the woman in so far as he went before her to God, and present in himself an example to her for imitation in holiness and piety, even as he himself was to be the glory of God in so far as he followed his wisdom:

30. "Therefore did he place them in a certain locality of perpetual blessedness, which the Scripture designates Paradise: and he gave them a commandment, on condition of not violating which they were to continue for ever in that blessedness of immortality; while, on the other hand, if they transgressed it, they were to sustain the penalties of mortality. Now God knew beforehand that they would transgress it. Nevertheless, in that He is the author and maker of everything good, He chose rather to make them, as He also made the beasts, in order that He might replenish the earth with the good things proper to earth. And certainly man, even sinful man, is better than a beast. And the commandment, which they were not to keep, He yet preferred to give them, in order that they might be without excuse when He should begin to vindicate Himself against them. For whatever man may have done, he finds God worthy to be praised in all His doings: if he shall have acted rightly, he finds Him worthy to be praised for the righteousness of His rewards: if he shall have sinned, he finds Him worthy to be praised for the righteousness of His punishments: if he shall have confessed his sins and returned to an upright life, he finds Him worthy to be praised for the mercy of His pardoning favors. Why, then, should God not make man, although He foreknew that he would sin, when He might crown him if he stood, and set him right if he fell, and help him if he rose, Himself being always and everywhere glorious in goodness, righteousness, and clemency? Above all, why should He not do so, since He also foreknew this, namely, that from the race of that mortality there would spring saints, who should not seek their own, but give glory to their Creator; and who, obtaining deliverance from every corruption by worshipping Him, should be counted worthy to live for ever, and to live in blessedness with the holy angels? For He who gave freedom of will to men, in order that they might worship God not of slavish necessity but with ingenuous inclination, gave it also to the angels; and hence neither did the angel, who, in com-

---

[1] *Humanitate,* = humanity, also occurs instead of *humilitate.*

pany with other spirits who were his satellites, forsook in pride the obedience of God and became the devil, do any hurt to God, but to himself. For God knoweth how to dispose of souls [1] that leave Him, and out of their righteous misery to furnish the inferior sections of His creatures with the most appropriate and befitting laws of His wonderful dispensation. Consequently, neither did the devil in any manner harm God, whether in falling himself, or in seducing man to death; nor did man himself in any degree impair the truth, or power, or blessedness [2] of His Maker, in that, when his partner was seduced by the devil, he of his own deliberate inclination consented unto her in the doing of that which God had forbidden. For by the most righteous laws of God all were condemned, God Himself being glorious in the equity of retribution, while they were shamed through the degradation of punishment: to the end that man, when he turned away from his Creator, should be overcome by the devil and made his subject, and that the devil might be set before man as an enemy to be conquered, when he turned again to his Creator; so that whosoever should consent unto the devil even to the end, might go with him into eternal punishments; whereas those who should humble themselves to God, and by His grace overcome the devil, might be counted worthy of eternal rewards.

CHAP. 19.—OF THE CO-EXISTENCE OF GOOD AND EVIL IN THE CHURCH, AND THEIR FINAL SEPARATION.

31. "Neither ought we to be moved by the consideration that many consent unto the devil, and few follow God; for the grain, too, in comparison with the chaff, has greatly the defect in number. But even as the husbandman knows what to do with the mighty heap of chaff, so the multitude of sinners is nothing to God, who knows what to do with them, so as not to let the administration of His kingdom be disordered and dishonored in any part. Nor is the devil to be supposed to have proved victorious for the mere reason of his drawing away with him more than the few by whom he may be overcome. In this way there are two communities—one of the ungodly, and another of the holy—which are carried down from the beginning of the human race even to the end of the world, which are at present commingled in respect of bodies, but separated in respect of wills, and which, moreover, are destined to be separated also in

respect of bodily presence in the day of judgment. For all men who love pride and temporal power with vain elation and pomp of arrogance, and all spirits who set their affections on such things and seek their own glory in the subjection of men, are bound fast together in one association; nay, even although they frequently fight against each other on account of these things, they are nevertheless precipitated by the like weight of lust into the same abyss, and are united with each other by similarity of manners and merits. And, again, all men and all spirits who humbly seek the glory of God and not their own, and who follow Him in piety, belong to one fellowship. And, notwithstanding this, God is most merciful and patient with ungodly men, and offers them a place for penitence and amendment.

32. "For with respect also to the fact that He destroyed all men in the flood, with the exception of one righteous man together with his house, whom He willed to be saved in the ark, He knew indeed that they would not amend themselves; yet, nevertheless, as the building of the ark went on for the space of a hundred years, the wrath of God which was to come upon them was certainly preached to them: [3] and if they only would have turned to God, He would have spared them, as at a later period He spared the city of Nineveh when it repented, after He had announced to it, by means of a prophet, the destruction that was about to overtake it. [4] Thus, moreover, God acts, granting a space for repentance even to those who He knows will persist in wickedness, in order that He may exercise and instruct our patience by His own example; whereby also we may know how greatly it befits us to bear with the evil in long-suffering, when we know not what manner of men they will prove hereafter, seeing that He, whose cognizance nothing that is yet to be escapes, spares them and suffers them to live. Under the sacramental sign of the flood, however, in which the righteous were rescued by the wood, there was also a fore-announcement of the Church which was to be, which Christ, its King and God, has raised on high, by the mystery of His cross, in safety from the submersion of this world. Moreover, God was not ignorant of the fact that, even of those who had been saved in the ark, there would be born wicked men, who would cover the face of the earth a second time with iniquities. But, nevertheless, He both gave them a pattern of the future judgment, and fore-announced the deliverance of the holy by the

---

[1] Rather "spirits." See the correction made in the *Retractations*, ii. 14, as given above in the Introductory Notice.
[2] The *beatitatem* is omitted by several MSS.

[3] Gen. vi. 7.   [4] Jonah iii.

mystery of the wood. For even after these things wickedness did not cease to sprout forth again through pride, and lusts, and illicit impieties, when men, forsaking their Creator, not only fell to the (standard of the) creature which God made, so as to worship instead of God that which God made, but even bowed their souls to the works of the hands of men and to the contrivances of craftsmen, wherein a more shameful triumph was to be won over them by the devil, and by those evil spirits who rejoice in finding themselves adored and reverenced in such false devices, while they feed[1] their own errors with the errors of men.

33. "But in truth there were not wanting in those times righteous men also of the kind to seek God piously and to overcome the pride of the devil, citizens of that holy community, who were made whole by the humiliation of Christ, which was then only destined to enter, but was revealed to them by the Spirit. From among these, Abraham, a pious and faithful servant of God, was chosen, in order that to him might be shown the sacrament of the Son of God, so that thus, in virtue of the imitation of his faith, all the faithful of all nations might be called his children in the future. Of him was born a people, by whom the one true God who made heaven and earth should be worshipped when all other nations did service to idols and evil spirits. In that people, plainly, the future Church was much more evidently prefigured. For in it there was a carnal multitude that worshipped God with a view to visible benefits. But in it there were also a few who thought of the future rest, and looked longingly for the heavenly fatherland, to whom through prophecy was revealed the coming humiliation of God in the person of our King and Lord Jesus Christ, in order that they might be made whole of all pride and arrogance through that faith. And with respect to these saints who in point of time had precedence of the birth of the Lord, not only their speech, but also their life, and their marriages, and their children, and their doings, constituted a prophecy of this time, at which the Church is being gathered together out of all nations through faith in the passion of Christ. By the instrumentality of those holy patriarchs and prophets this carnal people of Israel, who at a later period were also called Jews, had ministered unto them at once those visible benefits which they eagerly desired of the Lord in a carnal manner, and those chastisements, in the form of bodily punishments, which were intended to ter-

rify them for the time, as was befitting for their obstinacy. And in all these, nevertheless, there were also spiritual mysteries signified, such as were meant to bear upon Christ and the Church; of which Church those saints also were members, although they existed in this life previous to the birth of Christ, the Lord, according to the flesh. For this same Christ, the only-begotten Son of God, the Word of the Father, equal and co-eternal with the Father, by whom all things were made, was Himself also made man for our sakes, in order that of the whole Church, as of His whole body, He might be the Head. But just as when the whole man is in the process of being born, although he may put the hand forth first in the act of birth, yet is that hand joined and compacted together with the whole body under the head, even as also among these same patriarchs some were born[2] with the hand put forth first as a sign of this very thing: so all the saints who lived upon the earth previous to the birth of our Lord Jesus Christ, although they were born antecedently, were nevertheless united under the Head with that universal body of which He is the Head.

CHAP. 20.—OF ISRAEL'S BONDAGE IN EGYPT, THEIR DELIVERANCE, AND THEIR PASSAGE THROUGH THE RED SEA.

34. "That people, then, having been brought down into Egypt, were in bondage to the harshest of kings; and, taught by the most oppressive labors, they sought their deliverer in God; and there was sent to them one belonging to the people themselves, Moses, the holy servant of God, who, in the might of God, terrified the impious nation of the Egyptians in those days by great miracles, and led forth the people of God out of that land through the Red Sea, where the water parted and opened up a way for them as they crossed it, whereas, when the Egyptians pressed on in pursuit, the waves returned to their channel and overwhelmed them, so that they perished. Thus, then, just as the earth through the agency of the flood was cleansed by the waters from the wickedness of the sinners, who in those times were destroyed in that inundation, while the righteous escaped by means of the wood; so the people of God, when they went forth from Egypt, found a way through the waters by which their enemies were devoured. Nor was the sacrament of the wood wanting there. For Moses smote with his rod, in order that that miracle might be effected. Both these

---

[1] Instead of *pascunt* the reading *miscent*,=mix, is also found. [2] Gen. xxv. 26, xxxviii. 27-30.

are signs of holy baptism, by which the faithful pass into the new life, while their sins are done away with like enemies, and perish. But more clearly was the passion of Christ prefigured in the case of that people, when they were commanded to slay and eat the lamb, and to mark their door-posts with its blood, and to celebrate this rite every year, and to designate it the Lord's passover. For surely prophecy speaks with the utmost plainness of the Lord Jesus Christ, when it says that "He was led as a lamb to the slaughter."[1] And with the sign of His passion and cross, thou art this day to be marked on thy forehead, as on the door-post, and all Christians are marked with the same.

35. "Thereafter this people was conducted through the wilderness for forty years. They also received the law written by the finger of God, under which name the Holy Spirit is signified, as it is declared with the utmost plainness in the Gospel. For God is not defined[2] by the form of a body, neither are members and fingers to be thought of as existent in Him in the way in which we see them in ourselves. But, inasmuch as it is through the Holy Spirit that God's gifts are divided to His saints, in order that, although they vary in their capacities, they may nevertheless not lapse from the concord of charity, and inasmuch as it is especially in the fingers that there appears a certain kind of division, while nevertheless there is no separation from unity, this may be the explanation of the phrase. But whether this may be the case, or whatever other reason may be assigned for the Holy Spirit being called the finger of God, we ought not at any rate to think of the form of a human body when we hear this expression used. The people in question, then, received the law written by the finger of God, and that in good sooth on tables of stone, to signify the hardness of their heart in that they were not to fulfill the law. For, as they eagerly sought from the Lord gifts meant for the uses of the body, they were held by carnal fear rather than by spiritual charity. But nothing fulfills the law save charity. Consequently, they were burdened with many visible sacraments, to the intent that they should feel the pressure of the yoke of bondage in the observances of meats, and in the sacrifices of animals, and in other rites innumerable; which things, at the same time, were signs of spiritual matters relating to the Lord Jesus Christ and to the Church; which, furthermore, at that time were both understood by a few holy men to the effect of

yielding the fruit of salvation, and observed by them in accordance with the fitness of the time, while by the multitude of carnal men they were observed only and not understood.

36. "In this manner, then, through many varied signs of things to come, which it would be tedious to enumerate in complete detail, and which we now see in their fulfillment in the Church, that people were brought to the land of promise, in which they were to reign in a temporal and carnal way in accordance with their own longings: which earthly kingdom, nevertheless, sustained the image of a spiritual kingdom. There Jerusalem was founded, that most celebrated city of God, which, while in bondage, served as a sign of the free city, which is called the heavenly Jerusalem[3] which latter term is a Hebrew word, and signifies by interpretation the 'vision of peace.' The citizens thereof are all sanctified men, who have been, who are, and who are yet to be; and all sanctified spirits, even as many as are obedient to God with pious devotion in the exalted regions of heaven, and imitate not the impious pride of the devil and his angels. The King of this city is the Lord Jesus Christ, the Word of God, by whom the highest angels are governed, and at the same time the Word that took unto Himself human nature,[4] in order that by Him men also might be governed, who, in His fellowship, shall reign all together in eternal peace. In the service of prefiguring this King in that earthly kingdom of the people of Israel, King David stood forth preeminent,[5] of whose seed according to the flesh that truest King was to come, to wit, our Lord Jesus Christ, 'who is over all, God blessed for ever.'[6] In that land of promise many things were done, which held good as figures of the Christ who was to come, and of the Church, with which you will have it in your power to acquaint yourself by degrees in the Holy Books.

CHAP. 21.—OF THE BABYLONISH CAPTIVITY, AND THE THINGS SIGNIFIED THEREBY.

37. "Howbeit, after the lapse of some generations, another type was presented, which bears very emphatically on the matter in hand. For that city[7] was brought into captivity, and a large section of the people were carried off into Babylonia. Now, as Jerusalem signifies the city and fellowship of the saints, so Babylonia signifies the city and fellowship of the wicked, seeing that by interpretation it denotes *confusion*. On the sub-

---

[1] Isa. liii. 7.   [2] Or = circumscribed, *definitus.*

[3] Cf. Gal. iv. 26.   [4] Hominem.   [5] 1 Kings xi. 13.
[6] Rom. ix. 5.   [7] Or = community, *civitas.*

ject of these two cities, which have been running their courses, mingling the one with the other, through all the changes of time from the beginning of the human race, and which shall so move on together until the end of the world, when they are destined to be separated at the last judgment, we have spoken already a little ago.[1] That captivity, then, of the city of Jerusalem, and the people thus carried into Babylonia in bondage, were ordained so to proceed by the Lord, by the voice of Jeremiah, a prophet of that time.[2] And there appeared kings[3] of Babylon, under whom they were in slavery, who on occasion of the captivity of this people were so wrought upon by certain miracles that they came to know the one true God who founded universal creation, and worshipped Him, and commanded that He should be worshipped. Moreover the people were ordered both to pray for those by whom they were detained in captivity, and in their peace to hope for peace, to the effect that they should beget children, and build houses, and plant gardens and vineyards.[4] But at the end of seventy years, release from their captivity was promised to them.[5] All this, furthermore, signified in a figure that the Church of Christ in all His saints, who are citizens of the heavenly Jerusalem, would have to do service under the kings of this world. For the doctrine of the apostles speaks also in this wise, that 'every soul should be subject to the higher powers,' and that there ' should be rendered all things to all men, tribute to whom tribute (is due), custom to whom custom,'[6] and all other things in like manner which, without detriment to the worship of our God, we render to the rulers in the constitution of human society: for the Lord Himself also, in order to set before us an example of this sound doctrine, did not deem it unworthy of Him to pay tribute[7] on account of that human individuality[8] wherewith He was invested. Again, Christian servants and good believers are also commanded to serve their temporal masters in equanimity and faithfulness;[9] whom they will hereafter judge, if even on to the end they find them wicked, or with whom they will hereafter reign in equality, if they too shall have been converted to the true God. Still all are enjoined to be subject to the powers that are of man and of earth, even until, at the end of the predetermined time which the seventy years signify, the Church

shall be delivered from the confusion of this world, like as Jerusalem was to be set free from the captivity in Babylonia. By occasion of that captivity, however, the kings of earth too have themselves been led to forsake the idols on account of which they were wont to persecute the Christians, and have come to know, and now worship, the one true God and Christ the Lord; and it is on their behalf that the Apostle Paul enjoins prayer to be made, even although they should persecute the Church. For he speaks in these terms: ' I entreat, therefore, that first of all supplications, adorations,[10] intercessions, and givings of thanks be made for kings, for all men, and all that are in authority, that we may lead a quiet and peaceable life, with all godliness and charity.'[11] Accordingly peace has been given to the Church by these same persons, although it be but of a temporal sort,—a temporal quiet for the work of building houses after a spiritual fashion, and planting gardens and vineyards. For witness your own case, too,—at this very time we are engaged, by means of this discourse, in building you up and planting you. And the like process is going on throughout the whole circle of lands, in virtue of the peace allowed by Christian kings, even as the same apostle thus expresses himself: ' Ye are God's husbandry; ye are God's building.'[12]

38. ''And, indeed, after the lapse of the seventy years of which Jeremiah had mystically prophesied, to the intent of prefiguring the end of times, with a view still to the perfecting of that same figure, no settled peace and liberty were conceded again to the Jews. Thus it was that they were conquered subsequently by the Romans and made tributary. From that period, in truth, at which they received the land of promise and began to have kings, in order to preclude the supposition that the promise of the Christ who was to be their Liberator had met its complete fulfillment in the person of any one of their kings, Christ was prophesied of with greater clearness in a number of prophecies; not only by David himself in the book of Psalms, but also by the rest of the great and holy prophets, even on to the time of their conveyance into captivity in Babylonia; and in that same captivity there were also prophets whose mission was to prophesy of the coming of the Lord Jesus Christ as the Liberator of all. And after the restoration of the temple, when the seventy years had passed, the Jews sus-

---

1 See Chapter XIX. 2 Jer. xxv. 18, xxix. 1.
3 Dan. ii. 47, iii. 29, vi. 26 ; 1 Esdr. ii. 7 ; Bel, 41.
4 Jer. xxix. 4-7. 5 Jer. xxv. 12..
6 Rom. xiii. 1, 7. 7 Matt. xvii. 27.
8 *Pro capite hominis*, literally = on account of that head of man, etc. 9 Eph. vi. 5.

10 Instead of *orationes;* the better authenticated reading is *adorationes*.
11 1 Tim. ii. 1, 2.
12 1 Cor. iii. 9 ; cf. Jer. xxv. 12, xxix. 10.

tained grievous oppressions and sufferings at the hands of the kings of the Gentiles, fitted to make them understand that the Liberator was not yet come, whom they failed to apprehend as one who was to effect for them a spiritual deliverance, and whom they fondly longed for on account of a carnal liberation.

CHAP. 22.—OF THE SIX AGES OF THE WORLD.

39. "Five ages of the world, accordingly, having been now completed (there has entered the sixth). Of these ages the first is from the beginning of the human race, that is, from Adam, who was the first man that was made, down to Noah, who constructed the ark at the time of the flood.[1] Then the second extends from that period on to Abraham, who was called[2] the father indeed of all nations[3] which should follow the example of his faith, but who at the same time in the way of natural descent from his own flesh was the father of the destined people of the Jews; which people, previous to the entrance of the Gentiles into the Christian faith, was the one people among all the nations of all lands that worshipped the one true God: from which people also Christ the Saviour was decreed to come according to the flesh. For these turning-points[4] of those two ages occupy an eminent place in the ancient books. On the other hand, those of the other three ages are also declared in the Gospel,[5] where the descent of the Lord Jesus Christ according to the flesh is likewise mentioned. For the third age extends from Abraham on to David the king; the fourth from David on to that captivity whereby the people of God passed over into Babylonia; and the fifth from that transmigration down to the advent of our Lord Jesus Christ. With His coming the sixth age has entered on its process; so that now the spiritual grace, which in previous times was known to a few patriarchs and prophets, may be made manifest to all nations; to the intent that no man should worship God but freely,[6] fondly desiring of Him not the visible rewards of His services and the happiness of this present life, but that eternal life alone in which he is to enjoy God Himself: in order that in this sixth age the mind of man may be renewed after the image of God, even as on the sixth day man was made after the image of God.[7] For then, too, is the law fulfilled, when all that it has commanded is done, not in the strong desire for things temporal, but in the love of Him who has given

the commandment. Who is there, moreover, who should not be earnestly disposed to give the return of love to a God of supreme righteousness and also of supreme mercy, who has first loved men of the greatest unrighteousness and the loftiest pride, and that, too, so deeply as to have sent in their behalf His only Son, by whom He made all things, and who being made man, not by any change of Himself, but by the assumption of human nature, was designed thus to become capable not only of living with them, but also of dying at once for them and by their hands?

40. "Thus, then, showing forth the New Testament of our everlasting inheritance, wherein man was to be renewed by the grace of God and lead a new life, that is, a spiritual life; and with the view of exhibiting the first one as an old dispensation, wherein a carnal people acting out the old man (with the exception of a few patriarchs and prophets, who had understanding, and some hidden saints), and leading a carnal life, desiderated carnal rewards at the hands of the Lord God, and received in that fashion but the figures of spiritual blessings;—with this intent, I say, the Lord Christ, when made man, despised all earthly good things, in order that He might show us how these things ought to be despised; and He endured all earthly ills which He was inculcating as things needful to be endured; so that neither might our happiness be sought for in the former class, nor our unhappiness be apprehended in the latter. For being born of a mother who, although she conceived without being touched by man and always remained thus untouched, in virginity conceiving, in virginity bringing forth, in virginity dying, had nevertheless been espoused to a handicraftsman, He extinguished all the inflated pride of carnal nobility. Moreover, being born in the city of Bethlehem, which among all the cities of Judæa was so insignificant that even in our own day it is designated a village, He willed not that any one should glory in the exalted position of any city of earth. He, too, whose are all things and by whom all things were created, was made poor, in order that no one, while believing in Him, might venture to boast himself in earthly riches. He refused to be made by men a king, because He displayed the pathway of humility to those unhappy ones whom pride had separated from Him;[8] and yet universal creation attests the fact of His everlasting kingdom. An hungered was He who feeds all men; athirst was He by whom is created whatsoever is drunk, and

---

[1] Gen. vi. 22.
[2] Instead of *dictus est* the MSS. give also *electus est* = was chosen to be.
[3] Gen. xvii. 4.   [4] *articuli* = articles.   [5] Matt. i. 17.
[6] Gratis.   [7] Gen. i. 27.

[8] Reading *ab eo ;* for which some editions give *ab ea* = from that humility.

who in a spiritual manner is the bread of the hungry and the fountain of the thirsty; in journeying on earth, wearied was He who has made Himself the way for us into heaven; as like one dumb and deaf in the presence of His revilers was He by whom the dumb spoke and the deaf heard; bound was He who freed us from the bonds of infirmities; scourged was He who expelled from the bodies of man the scourges of all distresses; crucified was He who put an end to our crucial pains;[1] dead did He become who raised the dead. But He also rose again, no more to die, so that no one should from Him learn so to contemn death as if he were never to live again.

CHAP. 23.—OF THE MISSION OF THE HOLY GHOST FIFTY DAYS AFTER CHRIST'S RESURRECTION.

41. "Thereafter, having confirmed the disciples, and having sojourned with them forty days, He ascended up into heaven, as these same persons were beholding Him. And on the completion of fifty days from His resurrection He sent to them the Holy Spirit (for so He had promised), by whose agency they were to have love shed abroad in their hearts,[2] to the end that they might be able to fulfill the law, not only without the sense of its being burdensome, but even with a joyful mind. This law was given to the Jews in the ten commandments, which they call the Decalogue. And these commandments, again, are reduced to two, namely that we should love God with all our heart, with all our soul, with all our mind; and that we should love our neighbor as ourselves.[3] For that on these two precepts hang all the law and the prophets, the Lord Himself has at once declared in the Gospel and shown in His own example. For thus it was likewise in the instance of the people of Israel, that from the day on which they first celebrated the passover in a form,[4] slaying and eating the sheep, with whose blood their door-posts were marked for the securing of their safety,[5]—from this day, I repeat, the fiftieth day in succession was completed, and then they received the law written by the finger of God,[6] under which phrase we have already stated that the Holy Spirit is signified.[7] And in the same manner, after the passion and resurrection of the Lord, who is the true passover, the Holy Ghost was sent personally to the disciples on the fiftieth day: not now, however, by tables of stone significant of the hardness of their

hearts; but, when they were gathered together in one place at Jerusalem itself, suddenly there came a sound from heaven, as if a violent blast were being borne onwards, and there appeared to them tongues cloven like fire, and they began to speak with tongues, in such a manner that all those who had come to them recognized each his own language[8] (for in that city the Jews were in the habit of assembling from every country wheresoever they had been scattered abroad, and had learned the diverse tongues of diverse nations); and thereafter, preaching Christ with all boldness, they wrought many signs in His name,—so much so, that as Peter was passing by, his shadow touched a certain dead person, and the man rose in life again.[9]

42. "But when the Jews perceived so great signs to be wrought in the name of Him, whom, partly through ill-will and partly in ignorance, they crucified, some of them were provoked to persecute the apostles, who were His preachers; while others, on the contrary, marvelling the more at this very circumstance, that so great miracles were being performed in the name of Him whom they had derided as one overborne and conquered by themselves, repented, and were converted, so that thousands of Jews believed on Him. For these parties were not bent now on craving at the hand of God temporal benefits and an earthly kingdom, neither did they look any more for Christ, the promised king, in a carnal spirit; but they continued in immortal fashion to apprehend and love Him, who in mortal fashion endured on their behalf at their own hands sufferings so heavy, and imparted to them the gift of forgiveness for all their sins, even down to the iniquity of His own blood, and by the example of His own resurrection unfolded immortality as the object which they should hope for and long for at His hands. Accordingly, now mortifying the earthly cravings of the old man, and inflamed with the new experience of the spiritual life, as the Lord had enjoined in the Gospel, they sold all that they had, and laid the price of their possessions at the feet of the apostles, in order that these might distribute to every man according as each had need; and living in Christian love harmoniously with each other, they did not affirm anything to be their own, but they had all things in common, and were one in soul and heart toward God.[10] Afterwards these same persons also themselves suffered persecution

---

[1] There is a play in the words here: *crucifixus est qui cruciatus nostros finivit.*
[2] Cf. Rom. v. 5.
[4] In imagine.
[7] Ex. xxxiv. 28.

[3] Matt. xxii. 37-40.
[5] Ex. xii.
[7] Luke xi. 20.

[8] Acts ii.
[9] The reference evidently is to Acts v. 15, where, however, it is only the people's intention that is noticed, and that only in the instance of the sick, and not of any individual actually dead.
[10] Acts ii. 44, iv. 34.

in their flesh at the hands of the Jews, their carnal fellow-countrymen, and were dispersed abroad, to the end that, in consequence of their dispersion, Christ should be preached more extensively, and that they themselves at the same time should be followers of the patience of their Lord. For He who in meekness had endured them,[1] enjoined them in meekness to endure for His sake.

43. "Among those same persecutors of the saints the Apostle Paul had once also ranked; and he raged with eminent violence against the Christians. But, subsequently, he became a believer and an apostle, and was sent to preach the gospel to the Gentiles, suffering (in that ministry) things more grievous on behalf of the name of Christ than were those which he had done against the name of Christ. Moreover, in establishing churches throughout all the nations where he was sowing the seed of the gospel, he was wont to give earnest injunction that, as these converts (coming as they did from the worship of idols and without experience in the worship of the one God) could not readily serve God in the way of selling and distributing their possessions, they should make offerings for the poor brethren among the saints who were in the churches of Judea which had believed in Christ. In this manner the doctrine of the apostle constituted some to be, as it were, soldiers, and others to be, as it were, provincial tributaries, while it set Christ in the centre of them like the corner-stone (in accordance with what had been announced beforetime by the prophet),[2] in whom both parties, like walls advancing from different sides, that is to say, from Jews and from Gentiles, might be joined together in the affection of kinship. But at a later period heavier and more frequent persecutions arose from the unbelieving Gentiles against the Church of Christ, and day by day was fulfilled that prophetic word which the Lord spake when He said, 'Behold, I send you as sheep in the midst of wolves.'[3]

CHAP. 24.—OF THE CHURCH IN ITS LIKENESS TO A VINE SPROUTING AND SUFFERING PRUNING.

44. "But that vine, which was spreading forth its fruitful shoots throughout the circle of lands, according as had been prophesied with regard to it, and as had been foretold by the Lord Himself, sprouted all the more luxuriantly in proportion as it was watered with richer streams of the blood of martyrs. And as these died in behalf of the truth of the faith in countless numbers throughout all lands, even the persecuting kingdoms themselves desisted, and were converted to the knowledge and worship of Christ, with the neck of their pride broken. Moreover it behoved that this same vine should be pruned in accordance with the Lord's repeated predictions,[4] and that the unfruitful twigs should be cut out of it, by which heresies and schisms were occasioned in various localities, under the name of Christ, on the part of men who sought not His glory but their own; whose oppositions, however, also served more and more to discipline the Church, and to test and illustrate both its doctrine and its patience.

45. "All these things, then, we now perceive to be realized precisely as we read of them in predictions uttered so long before the event. And as the first Christians, inasmuch as they did not see these things literally made good in their own day, were moved by miracles to believe them; so as regards ourselves, inasmuch as all these things have now been brought to pass exactly as we read of them in those books which were written a long time previous to the fulfillment of the things in question, wherein they were all announced as matters yet future, even as they are now seen to be actually present, we are built up unto faith, so that, enduring and persevering in the Lord, we believe without any hesitation in the destined accomplishment even of those things which still remain to be realized. For, indeed, in the same Scriptures, tribulations yet to come are still read of, as well as the final day of judgment itself, when all the citizens of these two states shall receive their bodies again, and rise and give account of their life before the judgment-seat of Christ. For He will come in the glory of His power, who of old condescended to come in the lowliness of humanity; and He will separate all the godly from the ungodly,—not only from those who have utterly refused to believe in Him at all, but also from those who have believed in Him to no purpose and without fruit. To the one class He will give an eternal kingdom together with Himself, while to the other He will award eternal punishment together with the devil. But as no joy yielded by things temporal can be found in any measure comparable to the joy of life eternal which

---

[1] Adopting the Benedictine version, *qui eos mansuetus passus fuerat*, and taking it as a parallel to Acts xiii. 18, Heb. xii. 3. There is, however, great variety of reading here. Thus we find *qui ante eos, etc.* = who had suffered in meekness before them : *qui pro eis, etc.* = who had suffered in their stead : *qui propter eos, etc.* = who had suffered on their account : and *qui per eos, etc.* = who had suffered through them, etc. But the reading in the text appears best authenticated.

[2] Ps. cxviii. 22; Isa. xxviii. 16.   [3] Matt. x. 16.

[4] John xv. 2.

the saints are destined to attain, so no torment of temporal punishments can be compared to the everlasting torments of the unrighteous.

CHAP. 25.—OF CONSTANCY IN THE FAITH OF THE RESURRECTION.

46. "Therefore, brother, confirm yourself in the name and help of Him in whom you believe, so as to withstand the tongues of those who mock at our faith, in whose case the devil speaks seductive words, bent above all on making a mockery of the faith in a resurrection. But, judging from your own history,[1] believe that, seeing you have been, you will also be hereafter, even as you perceive yourself now to be, although previously you were not. For where was this great structure of your body, and where this formation and compacted connection of members a few years ago, before you were born, or even before you were conceived in your mother's womb? Where, I repeat, was then this structure and this stature of your body? Did it not come forth to light from the hidden secrets of this creation, under the invisible formative operations of the Lord God, and did it not rise to its present magnitude and fashion by those fixed measures of increase which come with the successive periods of life?[2] Is it then in any way a difficult thing for God, who also in a moment brings together out of secrecy the masses of the clouds and veils the heavens in an instant of time, to make this quantity of your body again what it was, seeing that He was able to make it what formerly it was not?[3] Consequently, believe with a manful and unshaken spirit that all those things which seem to be withdrawn from the eyes of men as if to perish, are safe and exempt from loss in relation to the omnipotence of God, who will restore them, without any delay or difficulty, when He is so minded,—those of them at least, I should say, that are judged by His justice to merit restoration; in order that men may give account of their deeds in their very bodies in which they have done them; and that in these they may be deemed worthy to receive either the exchange of heavenly incorruption in accordance with the deserts of their piety, or the corruptible condition of body[4] in accordance with the deserts of their wickedness,—and that, too, not a condition such as may be done away with by death, but such as shall furnish material for everlasting pains.

47. "Flee, therefore, by steadfast faith and good manners,—flee, brother, those torments in which neither the torturers fail, nor do the tortured die; to whom it is death without end, to be unable to die in their pains. And be kindled with love and longing for the everlasting life of the saints, in which neither will action be toilsome nor will rest be indolent; in which the praise of God will be without irksomeness and without defect; wherein there will be no weariness in the mind, no exhaustion in the body; wherein, too, there shall be no want, whether on your own part, so that you should crave for relief, or on your neighbor's part, so that you should be in haste to carry relief to him. God will be the whole enjoyment and satisfaction[5] of that holy city, which lives in Him and of Him, in wisdom and beatitude. For as we hope and look for what has been promised by Him, we shall be made equal to the angels of God,[6] and together with them we shall enjoy that Trinity now by sight, wherein at present we walk by faith.[7] For we believe that which we see not, in order that through these very deserts of faith we may be counted worthy also to see that which we believe, and to abide in it; to the intent that these mysteries of the equality of the Father, the Son, and the Holy Spirit, and the unity of this same Trinity, and the manner in which these three subsistences are one God, need no more be uttered by us in words of faith and sounding syllables, but may be drunk in in purest and most burning contemplation in that silence.

48. "These things hold fixed in your heart, and call upon the God in whom you believe, to defend you against the temptations of the devil; and be careful, lest that adversary come stealthily upon you from a strange quarter, who, as a most malevolent solace for his own damnation, seeks others whose companionship he may obtain in that damnation. For he is bold enough not only to tempt Christian people through the instrumentality of those who hate the Christian name, or are pained to see the world taken possession of by that name, and still fondly desire to do service to idols and to the curious rites of evil spirits, but at times he also attempts the same through the agency of such men as we have mentioned a little ago, to wit, persons severed from the unity of the Church, like the twigs which are lopped off when the vine is pruned, who are called heretics or

---

[1] *Sed ex te ipso crede.* It may also = but, on your side, do you believe.

[2] *Certisque ætatum incrementis, etc.*

[3] Reading *sicut non erat;* for which, however, *cum non erat* also occurs = seeing He was able to make it when it was not.

[4] *Corruptibilem corporis conditionem.* But *corruptibilis* also occurs = the condition of a corruptible body.

[5] *Satietas.* Some editions, however, give *societas* = the society.

[6] Luke xx. 36.　　　[7] 2 Cor. v. 7.

schismatics. Howbeit sometimes also he makes the same effort by means of the Jews, seeking to tempt and seduce believers by their instrumentality. Nevertheless, what ought above all things to be guarded against is, that no individual may suffer himself to be tempted and deceived by men who are within the Catholic Church itself, and who are borne by it like the chaff that is sustained against the time of its winnowing. For in being patient toward such persons, God has this end in view, namely, to exercise and confirm the faith and prudence of His elect by means of the perverseness of these others, while at the same time He also takes account of the fact that many of their number make an advance, and are converted to the doing of the good pleasure of God with a great impetus, when led to take pity upon their own souls.[1] For not all treasure up for themselves, through the patience of God, wrath in the day of the wrath of His just judgment;[2] but many are brought by the same patience of the Almighty to the most wholesome pain of repentance.[3] And until that is effected, they are made the means of exercising not only the forbearance, but also the compassion of those who are already holding by the right way. Accordingly, you will have to witness many drunkards, covetous men, deceivers, gamesters, adulterers, fornicators, men who bind upon their persons sacrilegious charms, and others given up to sorcerers and astrologers,[4] and diviners practised in all kinds of impious arts. You will also have to observe how those very crowds which fill the theatres on the festal days of the pagans also fill the churches on the festal days of the Christians. And when you see these things you will be tempted to imitate them. Nay, why should I use the expression, *you will see*, in reference to what you assuredly are acquainted with even already? For you are not ignorant of the fact that many who are called Christians engage in all these evil things which I have briefly mentioned. Neither are you ignorant that at times, perchance, men whom you know to bear the name of Christians are guilty of even more grievous offenses than these. But if you have come with the notion that you may do such things as in a secured position, you are greatly in error; neither will the name of

Christ be of any avail to you when He begins to judge in utmost strictness, who also of old condescended in utmost mercy to come to man's relief. For He Himself has foretold these things, and speaks to this effect in the Gospel: 'Not every one that saith unto me, Lord, Lord, shall enter into the kingdom of heaven; but he that doeth the will of my Father. Many shall say unto me in that day, Lord, Lord, in thy name we have eaten and drunken.'[5] For all, therefore, who persevere in such works the end is damnation. Consequently, when you see many not only doing these things but also defending and recommending them, keep yourself firmly by the law of God, and follow not its willful transgressors. For it is not according to their mind, but according to His[6] truth that you will be judged.

49. "Associate with the good, whom you perceive to be at one with you in loving your King. For there are many such for you to discover, if you also begin to cultivate that character yourself. For if in the public spectacles you wished to be in congenial company, and to attach yourself closely[7] to men who are united with you in a liking for some charioteer, or some hunter, or some player or other, how much more ought you to find pleasure in associating with those who are at one with you in loving that God, with regard to whom no one that loves Him shall ever have cause for the blush of shame, inasmuch as not only is He Himself incapable of being overcome, but He will also render those unconquerable who are affectionately disposed toward Him. At the same time, not even on those same good men, who either anticipate you or accompany you on the way to God, ought you to set your hope, seeing that no more ought you to place it on yourself, however great may be the progress you have made, but on Him who justifies both them and you, and thus makes you what you are. For you are secure in God, because He changes not; but in man no one prudently counts himself secure. But if we ought to love those who are not righteous as yet, with the view that they may be so, how much more warmly ought those to be loved who already are righteous? At the same time, it is one thing to love man, and another thing to set one's hope in man; and the difference is so great, that God enjoins the one and forbids the other. Moreover, if you have to

---

[1] *Ad placendum Deo miserati animas suas, etc.* Instead of *miserati* the reading *miseranti* also occurs = to the doing of the good pleasure of the God who takes pity on their souls. The Benedictine editors suggest that the whole clause is in reference to Ecclesiasticus xxx. 24, (23), which in the Latin runs thus: *miserere animæ tuæ placens Deo.*

[2] Rom. ii. 5.

[3] Cf. Rom. ii. 4.   [4] *Mathematicis.*

[5] Matt. vii. 21, 22.   [6] Or = its (*i.e.* the law's) truth.

[7] Adopting *nam si in spectaculis cum illis esse cupiebas et eis inhærere.* Another, but less weightily supported reading, is, *nam si in spectaculis et vanitatibus insanorum certaminum illis cupiebas inhærere* = for if in the public spectacles and vanities of mad struggles you wish to attach yourself closely to men, etc.

sustain either any insults or any sufferings in the cause of the name of Christ, and neither fall away from the faith nor decline from the good way,[1] you are certain to receive the greater reward; whereas those who give way to the devil in such circumstances, lose even the less reward. But be humble toward God, in order that He may not permit you to be tempted beyond your strength."

CHAP. 26.—OF THE FORMAL ADMISSION OF THE CATECHUMEN, AND OF THE SIGNS THEREIN MADE USE OF.

50. At the conclusion of this address the person is to be asked whether he believes these things and earnestly desires to observe them. And on his replying to that effect, then certainly he is to be solemnly signed and dealt with in accordance with the custom of the Church. On the subject of the sacrament, indeed,[2] which he receives, it is first to be well impressed upon his notice that the signs of divine things are, it is true, things visible, but that the invisible things themselves are also honored in them, and that that species,[3] which is then sanctified by the blessing, is therefore not to be regarded merely in the way in which it is regarded in any common use. And thereafter he ought to be told what is also signified by the form of words to which he has listened, and what in him is seasoned[4] by that (spiritual grace) of which this material substance presents the emblem. Next we should take occasion by that ceremony to admonish him that, if he hears anything even in the Scriptures which may carry a carnal sound, he should, even although he fails to understand it, nevertheless believe that something spiritual is signified thereby, which bears upon holiness of character and the future life. Moreover, in this way he learns briefly that, whatever he may hear in the canonical books of such a kind as to make him unable to refer it to the love of eternity, and of truth, and of sanctity, and to the love of our neighbor, he should believe

that to have been spoken or done with a figurative significance; and that, consequently, he should endeavor to understand it in such a manner as to refer it to that twofold (duty of) love. He should be further admonished, however, not to take the term *neighbor* in a carnal sense, but to understand under it every one who may ever be with him in that holy city, whether there already or not yet apparent. And (he should finally be counselled) not to despair of the amendment of any man whom he perceives to be living under the patience of God for no other reason, as the apostle[5] says, than that he may be brought to repentance.

51. If this discourse, in which I have supposed myself to have been teaching some uninstructed person in my presence, appears to you to be too long, you are at liberty to expound these matters with greater brevity. I do not think, however, that it ought to be longer than this. At the same time, much depends on what the case itself, as it goes on, may render advisable, and what the audience actually present shows itself not only to bear, but also to desire. When, however, rapid despatch is required, notice with what facility the whole matter admits of being explained. Suppose once more that some one comes before us who desires to be a Christian; and accordingly, suppose further that he has been interrogated, and that he has returned the answer which we have taken the former catechumen to have given; for, even should he decline to make this reply, it must at least be said that he ought to have given it;—then all that remains to be said to him should be put together in the following manner:—

52. "Of a truth, brother, that is great and true blessedness which is promised to the saints in a future world. All visible things, on the other hand, pass away, and all the pomp, and pleasure, and solicitude[7] of this world will perish, and (even now) they drag those who love them along with them onward to destruction. The merciful God, willing to deliver men from this destruction, that is to say, from everlasting pains, if they should not prove enemies to themselves, and if they should not withstand the mercy of their Creator, sent His only-begotten Son, that is to say, His Word, equal with Himself, by whom He made all things. And He, while abiding indeed in His divinity, and neither receding from the Father nor being changed in anything, did at the same time, by taking on Himself human nature,[7] and appearing to men in mortal flesh, come unto men; in order that,

---

[1] *Bona via.* Another and well authenticated rendering is, *bona vita* = the good life.

[2] It has been supposed by the Benedictine editors that *sane* may be a misreading for *salis.* Whether that be or be not the case, the *sacramentum* intended here appears to be the *sacramentum salis,* in reference to which Neander (*Church History,* iii. p. 458, Bohn's Translation) states that "in the North African Church the bishop gave to those whom he received as *competentes,* while signing the cross over them as a symbol of consecration, a portion of salt over which a blessing had been pronounced. This was to signify the divine word imparted to the candidates as the true salt for human nature." There is an allusion to the same in the *Confessions* (i. 11), where Augustin says, "Even from my mother's womb who greatly hoped in thee, I was signed with the sign of His cross, and seasoned with His salt."

[3] *Speciem* = kind, in reference to the outward and sensible sign of the *salt.*

[4] Adopting *condiat,* which unquestionably is the reading most accordant with the figure of the sacramental salt here dealt with. Some editions give *condatur* = what is hidden in it, *i.e.* in the said form of words.

[5] Rom. ii. 4.   [6] *Curiositas.*   [7] *Hominem.*

just as death entered among the human race by one man, to wit, the first that was made, that is to say, Adam, because he consented unto his wife when she was seduced by the devil to the effect that they (both) transgressed the commandment of God; even so by one man, Jesus Christ, who is also God, the Son of God, all those who believe in Him might have all their past sins done away with, and enter into eternal life.

CHAP. 27.—OF THE PROPHECIES OF THE OLD TESTAMENT IN THEIR VISIBLE FULFILLMENT IN THE CHURCH.

53. " For all those things, which at present you witness in the Church of God, and which you see to be taking place under the name of Christ throughout the whole world, were predicted long ages ago. And even as we read of them, so also we now see them. And by means of these things we are built up unto faith. Once of old there occurred a flood over the whole earth, the object of which was that sinners might be destroyed. And, nevertheless, those who escaped in the ark exhibited a sacramental sign of the Church that was to be, which at present is floating on the waves of the world, and is delivered from submersion by the wood of the cross of Christ. It was predicted to Abraham, a faithful servant of God, a single man, that of Him it was determined that a people should be born who should worship one God in the midst of all other nations which worshipped idols; and all things which were prophesied of as destined to happen to that people have come to pass exactly as they were foretold. Among that people Christ, the King of all saints and their God, was also prophesied of as destined to come of the seed of that same Abraham according to the flesh, which (flesh) He took unto Himself, in order that all those also who became followers of His faith might be sons of Abraham; and thus it has come to pass: Christ was born of the Virgin Mary, who belonged to that race. It was foretold by the prophets that He would suffer on the cross at the hands of that same people of the Jews, of whose lineage, according to the flesh, He came; and thus it has come to pass. It was foretold that He would rise again: He has risen again; and, in accordance with these same predictions of the prophets, He has ascended into heaven and has sent the Holy Spirit to His disciples. It was foretold not only by the prophets, but also by the Lord Jesus Christ Himself, that His Church would exist throughout the whole world, extended by the martyrdoms and sufferings of the saints; and this was foretold at a time when as yet His name was at once undeclared to the Gentiles, and made a subject of derision where it was known; and, nevertheless, in the power of His miracles, whether those which He wrought by His own hand or those which he effected by means of His servants, as these things are being reported and believed, we already see the fulfillment of that which was predicted, and behold the very kings of the earth, who formerly were wont to persecute the Christians, even now brought into subjection to the name of Christ. It was also foretold that schisms and heresies would arise from His Church, and that under His name they would seek their own glory instead of Christ's, in such places as they might be able to command; and these predictions have been realized.

54. "Will those things, then, which yet remain fail to come to pass? It is manifest that, just as the former class of things which were foretold have come to pass, so will these latter also come to pass. I refer to all the tribulations of the righteous, which yet wait for fulfillment, and to the day of judgment, which will separate all the wicked from the righteous in the resurrection of the dead;— and not only will it thus separate those wicked men who are outside the Church, but also it will set apart for the fire, which is due to such, the chaff of the Church itself, which must be borne with in utmost patience on to the last winnowing. Moreover, they who deride the (doctrine of a) resurrection, because they think that this flesh, inasmuch as it becomes corrupt, cannot rise again, will certainly rise in the same unto punishment, and God will make it plain to such, that He who was able to form these bodies when as yet they were not, is able in a moment to restore them as they were. But all the faithful who are destined to reign with Christ shall rise with the same body in such wise that they may also be counted worthy to be changed into angelic incorruption; so that they may be made equal unto the angels of God, even as the Lord Himself has promised;[1] and that they may praise Him without any failure and without any weariness, ever living in Him and of Him, with such joy and blessedness as can be neither expressed nor conceived by man.

55. "Believe these things, therefore, and be on your guard against temptations (for the devil seeks for others who may be brought to perish along with himself); so that not only may that adversary fail to seduce you by the help of those who are without the Church,

---

[1] Luke xx. 36.

whether they be pagans, or Jews, or heretics; but you yourself also may decline to follow the example of those within the Catholic Church itself whom you see leading an evil life, either indulging in excess in the pleasures of the belly and the throat, or unchaste, or given up to the vain and unlawful observances of curious superstitions, whether they be addicted to (the inanities of) public spectacles, or charms, or divinations of devils,[1] or be living in the pomp and inflated arrogance of covetousness and pride, or be pursuing any sort of life which the law condemns and punishes. But rather connect yourself with the good, whom you will easily find out, if you yourself were once become of that character; so that you may unite with each other in worshipping and loving God for His own sake;[2] for He himself will be our complete reward to the intent that we may enjoy His goodness and beauty[3] in that life. He is to be loved, however, not in the way in which any object that is seen with the eyes is loved, but as wisdom is loved, and truth, and holiness, and righteousness, and charity,[4] and whatever else may be mentioned as of kindred nature; and further, with a love conformable to these things not as they are in men, but as they are in the very fountain of incorruptible and unchangeable wisdom. Whomsoever, therefore, you may observe to be loving these things, attach yourself to them, so that through Christ, who became man in order that He might be the Mediator between God and men, you may be reconciled to God. But as regards the perverse, even if they find their way within the walls of the Church, think not that they will find their way into the kingdom of heaven; for in their own time they will be set apart, if they have not altered to the better. Consequently, follow the example of good men, bear with the wicked, love all; forasmuch as you know not what he will be to-morrow who to-day is evil. Howbeit, love not the unrighteousness of such; but love the persons themselves with the express intent that they may apprehend righteousness; for not only is the love of God enjoined upon us, but also the love of our neighbor, on which two commandments hang all the law and the prophets.[5] And this is fulfilled by no one save the man who has received the (other) gift,[6] the Holy Spirit, who is indeed equal with the Father and with the Son; for this same Trinity is God; and on this God every hope ought to be placed. On man our hope ought not to be placed, of whatsoever character he may be. For He, by whom we are justified, is one thing; and they, together with whom we are justified, are another. Moreover, it is not only by lusts that the devil tempts, but also by the terrors of insults, and pains, and death itself. But whatever a man shall have suffered on behalf of the name of Christ, and for the sake of the hope of eternal life, and shall have endured in constancy, (in accordance therewith) the greater reward shall be given him; whereas, if he shall give way to the devil, he shall be damned along with him. But works of mercy, conjoined with pious humility, meet with this acknowledgment from God, to wit, that He will not suffer His servants to be tempted more than they are able to bear."[7]

---

[1] *Remediorum aut divinationum diabolicarum.* Some editions insert *sacrilegorum* after *remediorum* = sacrilegious charms or divinations of devils.
[2] Gratis.   [3] Cf. Zech. ix. 17.
[4] Many MSS. omit the words: and holiness, and righteousness, and charity.

[5] Matt. xxii. 37, 39.
[6] One edition reads *Dominum*, the Lord, the Holy Spirit, etc., instead of *donum.*
[7] 1 Cor. x. 13.

ST. AUGUSTIN:

TREATISE ON

FAITH AND THE CREED

[DE FIDE ET SYMBOLO.]

TRANSLATED BY

REV. S. D. F. SALMOND, D.D.,

PROFESSOR OF SYSTEMATIC THEOLOGY, FREE CHURCH COLLEGE, ABERDEEN.

INTRODUCTORY NOTICE.

THE occasion and date of the composition of this treatise are indicated in a statement which Augustin makes in the seventeenth chapter of the First Book of his *Retractations*.

From this we learn that, in its original form, it was a discourse which Augustin, when only a presbyter, was requested to deliver in public by the bishops assembled at the Council of Hippo-Regius, and that it was subsequently issued as a book at the desire of friends. The general assembly of the North African Church, which was thus convened at what is now Bona, in the modern territory of Algiers, took place in the year 393 A.D., and was otherwise one of some historical importance, on account of the determined protest which it emitted against the position elsewhere allowed to Patriarchs in the Church, and against the admittance of any more authoritative or magisterial title to the highest ecclesiastical official than that of simply "Bishop of the first Church" (*primæ sedis episcopus*).

The work constitutes an exposition of the several clauses of the so-called Apostles' Creed. The questions concerning the mutual relations of the three Persons in the Godhead are handled with greatest fullness; in connection with which, especially in the use made of the analogies of Being, Knowledge, and Love, and in the cautions thrown in against certain applications of these and other illustrations taken from things of human experience, we come across sentiments which are also repeated in the *City of God*, the books on the *Trinity*, and others of his doctrinal writings.

The passage referred to in the *Retractations* is as follows: "About the same period, in presence of the bishops, who gave me orders to that effect, and who were holding a plenary Council of the whole of Africa at Hippo-Regius, I delivered, as presbyter, a discussion on the subject of *Faith and the Creed*. This disputation, at the very pressing request of some of those who were on terms of more than usual intimacy and affection with us, I threw into the form of a book, in which the themes themselves are made the subjects of discourse, although not in a method involving the adoption of the particular connection of words which is given to the *competentes*[1] to be committed to memory. In this book, when discussing the question of the resurrection of the flesh, I say:[2] 'Rise again the body will, according to the Christian faith, which is incapable of deceiving. And if this appears incredible to any one, [it is because] he looks simply to what the flesh is at present, while he fails to consider of what nature it shall be hereafter. For at that time of angelic change it will no more be flesh and blood, but only body;' and so on, through the other statements which I have made there on the subject of the change of bodies terrestrial into bodies celestial, as the apostle, when he spake from the same point, said, 'Flesh and blood shall not inherit the kingdom of God.'[3] But if any one takes these declarations in a sense leading him to suppose that the earthly body, such as we now have it, is changed in the resurrection into a celestial body, in any such wise as that neither these members nor the substance of the flesh will subsist any

---

[1] *i.e.* the third order of catechumens, embracing those thoroughly prepared for baptism.

[2] Chap. x. § 24.   [3] 1 Cor. xv. 50.

more, undoubtedly he must be set right, by being put in mind of the body of the Lord, who subsequently to His resurrection appeared in the same members, as One who was not only to be seen with the eyes, but also handled with the hands; and made His possession of the flesh likewise surer by the discourse which He spake, saying, 'Handle me, and see; for a spirit hath not flesh and bones, as ye see me have.'[1]   Hence it is certain that the apostle did not deny that the substance of the flesh will exist in the kingdom of God, but that under the name of 'flesh and blood he designated either men who live after the flesh, or the express corruption of the flesh, which assuredly at that period shall subsist no more.   For after he had said, 'Flesh and blood shall not inherit the kingdom of God,' what he proceeds to say next,—namely, 'neither shall corruption inherit incorruption,'—is rightly taken to have been added by way of explaining his previous statement.   And on this subject, which is one on which it is difficult to convince unbelievers, any one who reads my last book, *On the City of God*, will find that I have discoursed with the utmost carefulness of which I am capable.[2]   The performance in question commences thus: 'Since it is written,' etc."

[ADDITIONAL NOTE BY THE AMERICAN EDITOR.]

[Another English edition of this treatise *De Fide et Symbolo* was prepared by the REV. CHARLES A. HEURTLEY, D.D., Margaret Professor of Divinity and Canon of Christ Church, Oxford, and published by Parker & Co., Oxford and London, 1886.

The following text of the Apostles' Creed may be collected from this book of St. Augustin, and was current in North Africa towards the close of the fourth century:

1. I BELIEVE IN GOD THE FATHER ALMIGHTY.   Chs. 2 and 3.
2. (And) IN JESUS CHRIST, THE SON OF GOD, THE ONLY-BEGOTTEN OF THE FATHER, or, HIS ONLY SON, OUR LORD.   Ch. 3.
3. WHO WAS BORN THROUGH THE HOLY SPIRIT OF THE VIRGIN MARY.   Ch. 4 (§ 8.)
4. WHO UNDER PONTIUS PILATE WAS CRUCIFIED AND BURIED.   Ch. 5 (§ 11.)
5. ON THE THIRD DAY HE ROSE AGAIN FROM THE DEAD.   Ch. 5 (§ 12.)
6. HE ASCENDED INTO HEAVEN.   Ch. 6 (§ 13.)
7. HE SITTETH AT THE RIGHT HAND OF THE FATHER.   Ch. 7 (§ 14.)
8. FROM THENCE HE WILL COME AND JUDGE THE LIVING AND THE DEAD.   Ch. 8 (§ 15.)
9. (AND I BELIEVE) IN THE HOLY SPIRIT.   Ch. 9 (§ 16–19.)
10. I BELIEVE THE HOLY CHURCH (CATHOLIC).   Ch. 10 (§ 21.)
11. THE FORGIVENESS OF SIN.   Ch. 10 (§ 23.)
12. THE RESURRECTION OF THE BODY.   Ch. 10 (§ 23, 24.)
13. THE LIFE EVERLASTING.   CH. 10 (§ 24.)]

---

[1] Luke xxiv. 39.   [2] *City of God*, Bk. xxii. Ch. 21.

CONTENTS OF FAITH AND THE CREED

A TREATISE ON FAITH AND THE CREED.

[DE FIDE ET SYMBOLO.]

IN ONE BOOK.

[A DISCOURSE DELIVERED BEFORE A COUNCIL OF THE WHOLE NORTH AFRICAN EPISCOPATE ASSEMBLED AT HIPPO-REGIUS.]

CHAP. I.—OF THE ORIGIN AND OBJECT OF THE COMPOSITION.

1. INASMUCH as it is a position, written and established on the most solid foundation of apostolic teaching, "that the just lives of faith;"[1] and inasmuch also as this faith demands of us the duty at once of heart and tongue,—for an apostle says, "With the heart man believeth unto righteousness, and with the mouth confession is made unto salvation,"[2]—it becomes us to be mindful both of righteousness and of salvation. For, destined as we are to reign hereafter in everlasting righteousness, we certainly cannot secure our salvation from the present evil world, unless at the same time, while laboring for the salvation of our neighbors, we likewise with the mouth make our own profession of the faith which we carry in our heart. And it must be our aim, by pious and careful watchfulness, to provide against the possibility of the said faith sustaining any injury in us, on any side, through the fraudulent artifices [or, cunning fraud] of the heretics.

We have, however, the catholic faith in the Creed, known to the faithful and committed to memory, contained in a form of expression as concise as has been rendered admissible by the circumstances of the case; the purpose of which [compilation] was, that individuals who are but beginners and sucklings among those who have been born again in Christ, and who have not yet been strengthened by most diligent and spiritual handling and understanding of the divine Scriptures, should be furnished with a summary, expressed in few words, of those matters of necessary belief which were subsequently to be explained to them in many words, as they made progress and rose to [the height of] divine doctrine, on the assured and steadfast basis of humility and charity. It is underneath these few words, therefore, which are thus set in order in the Creed, that most heretics have endeavored to conceal their poisons; whom divine mercy has withstood, and still withstands, by the instrumentality of spiritual men, who have been counted worthy not only to accept and believe the catholic faith as expounded in those terms, but also thoroughly to understand and apprehend it by the enlightenment imparted by the Lord. For it is written, "Unless ye believe, ye shall not understand."[3] But the handling of the faith is of service for the protection of the Creed; not, however, to the intent that this should itself be given instead of the Creed, to be committed to memory and repeated by those who are receiving the grace of God, but that it may guard the matters which are retained in the Creed against the insidious assaults of the heretics, by means of catholic authority and a more entrenched defence.

---

[1] Hab. ii. 4; Rom. i. 17; Gal. iii. 11; Heb. x. 38.
[2] Rom. x. 10.

[3] Isa. vii. 9, according to the rendering of the Septuagint.

CHAP. 2.—OF GOD AND HIS EXCLUSIVE ETERNITY.

2. For certain parties have attempted to gain acceptance for the opinion that GOD THE FATHER is not ALMIGHTY: not that they have been bold enough expressly to affirm this, but in their traditions they are convicted of entertaining and crediting such a notion. For when they affirm that there is a nature[1] which God Almighty did not create, but of which at the same time He fashioned this world, which they admit to have been disposed in beauty,[2] they thereby deny that God is almighty, to the effect of not believing that He could have created the world without employing, for the purpose of its construction, another nature, which had been in existence previously, and which He Himself had not made. Thus, forsooth, [they reason] from their carnal familiarity with the sight of craftsmen and house-builders, and artisans of all descriptions, who have no power to make good the effect of their own art unless they get the help of materials already prepared. And so these parties in like manner understand the Maker of the world not to be almighty, if[3] thus He could not fashion the said world without the help of some other nature, not framed by Himself, which He had to use as His materials. Or if indeed they do allow God, the Maker of the world, to be almighty, it becomes matter of course that they must also acknowledge that He made out of nothing the things which He did make. For, granting that He is almighty, there cannot exist anything of which He should not be the Creator. For although He made something out of something, as man out of clay,[4] nevertheless He certainly did not make any object out of aught which He Himself had not made; for the earth from which the clay comes He had made out of nothing. And even if He had made out of some material the heavens and the earth themselves, that is to say, the universe and all things which are in it, according as it is written, "Thou who didst make the world out of matter unseen,"[5] or also "without form," as some copies give it; yet we are under no manner of necessity to believe that this very material of which the universe was made, although it might be "without form," although it might be "unseen," whatever might be the mode of its subsistence, could possibly have subsisted of itself, as if it were co-eternal and co-eval with God. But whatsoever that mode was which it possessed to the effect of subsisting in some manner, whatever that manner might be, and of being capable of taking on the forms of distinct things, this it did not possess except by the hand of Almighty God, by whose goodness it is that everything exists,—not only every object which is already formed, but also every object which is formable. This, moreover, is the difference between the formed and the formable, that the formed has already taken on form, while the formable is capable of taking the same. But the same Being who imparts form to objects, also imparts the capability of being formed. For of Him and in Him is the fairest figure[6] of all things, unchangeable; and therefore He Himself is One, who communicates to everything its possibilities, not only that it be beautiful actually, but also that it be capable of being beautiful. For which reason we do most right to believe that God made all things of nothing. For, even although the world was made of some sort of material, this self-same material itself was made of nothing; so that, in accordance with the most orderly gift of God, there was to enter first the capacity of taking forms, and then that all things should be formed which have been formed. This, however, we have said, in order that no one might suppose that the utterances of the divine Scriptures are contrary the one to the other, in so far as it is written at once that God made all things of nothing, and that the world was made of matter without form.

3. As we believe, therefore, in GOD THE FATHER ALMIGHTY, we ought to uphold the opinion that there is no creature which has not been created by the Almighty. And since He created all things by the Word,[7] which Word is also designated the Truth, and the Power, and the Wisdom of God,[8]—as also under many other appellations the Lord Jesus Christ, who[9] is commended to our faith, is presented likewise to our mental apprehensions, to wit, our Deliverer and Ruler,[10] the Son of God; for that Word, by whose means all things were founded, could not have been begotten by any other than by Him who founded all things by His instrumentality;—

CHAP. 3.—OF THE SON OF GOD, AND HIS PECULIAR DESIGNATION AS THE WORD.

—Since this is the case, I repeat, we be-

---

[1] *Naturam.*
[2] Reading *pulchre ordinatum.* Some editions give *pulchre ornatum* = beautifully adorned.
[3] *Si mundum fabricare non posset.* For *si* some MSS. give *qui* = inasmuch as He could not, etc.
[4] *De limo* = of mud.　　[5] Wisd. xi. 17.

[6] *Speciosissima species* = the seemliest semblance.
[7] John i. 3.　　[8] John xiv. 6; 1 Cor. 1. 24.
[9] For *qui* several MSS. give *quibus* here = under many other appellations is the Lord Jesus Christ introduced to our mental apprehensions, by which He is commended to our faith.
[10] For *Rector* we also find *Creator* = Creator.

lieve also in JESUS CHRIST, THE SON OF GOD, THE ONLY-BEGOTTEN OF THE FATHER, that is to say, HIS ONLY SON, OUR LORD. This Word, however, we ought not to apprehend merely in the sense in which we think of our own words, which are given forth by the voice and the mouth, and strike the air and pass on, and subsist no longer than their sound continues. For that Word remains unchangeably: for of this very Word was it spoken when of Wisdom it was said, " Remaining in herself, she maketh all things new." [1] Moreover, the reason of His being named the Word of the Father, is that the Father is made known by Him. Accordingly, just as it is our intention, when we speak truth, that by means of our words our mind should be made known to him who hears us, and that whatever we carry in secrecy in our heart may be set forth by means of signs of this sort for the intelligent understanding of another individual; so this Wisdom that God the Father begat is most appropriately named His Word, inasmuch as the most hidden Father is made known to worthy minds by the same. [2]

4. Now there is a very great difference between our mind and those words of ours, by which we endeavor to set forth the said mind. We indeed do not beget intelligible words, [3] but we form them; and in the forming of them the body is the underlying material. Between mind and body, however, there is the greatest difference. But God, when He begat the Word, begat that which He is Himself. Neither out of nothing, nor of any material already made and founded, did He then beget; but He begat of Himself that which He is Himself. For we too aim at this when we speak, (as we shall see) if we carefully consider the inclination [4] of our will; not when we lie, but when we speak the truth. For to what else do we direct our efforts then, but to bring our own very mind, if it can be done at all, in upon the mind of the hearer, with the view of its being apprehended and thoroughly discerned by him; so that we may indeed abide in our very selves, and make no retreat from ourselves, and yet at the same time put forth a sign of such a nature as that by it a knowledge of us [5] may

be effected in another individual; that thus, so far as the faculty is granted us, another mind may be, as it were, put forth by the mind, whereby it may disclose itself? This we do, making the attempt [6] both by words, and by the simple sound of the voice, and by the countenance, and by the gestures of the body,—by so many contrivances, in sooth, desiring to make patent that which is within; inasmuch as we are not able to put forth aught of this nature [in itself completely]: and thus it is that the mind of the speaker cannot become perfectly known; thus also it results that a place is open for falsehoods. God the Father, on the other hand, who possessed both the will and the power to declare Himself with the utmost truth to minds designed to obtain knowledge of Him, with the purpose of thus declaring Himself begat this [Word] which He Himself is who did beget; which [Person] is likewise called His Power and Wisdom, [7] inasmuch as it is by Him that He has wrought all things, and in order disposed them; of whom these words are for this reason spoken: " She (Wisdom) reacheth from one end to another mightily, and sweetly doth she order all things." [8]

CHAP. 4.—OF THE SON OF GOD AS NEITHER MADE BY THE 'FATHER NOR LESS THAN THE FATHER, AND OF HIS INCARNATION.

5. Wherefore THE ONLY-BEGOTTEN SON OF GOD was neither made by the Father; for, according to the word of an evangelist, " all things were made by Him:" [9] nor begotten instantaneously; [10] since God, who is eternally [11] wise, has with Himself His eternal Wisdom: nor unequal with the Father, that is to say, in anything less than He; for an apostle also speaks in this wise, " Who, although He was constituted in the form of God, thought it not robbery to be equal with God." [12] By this catholic faith, therefore, those are excluded, on the one hand, who affirm that the Son is the same [Person] as the Father; for [it is clear that] this Word could not possibly be *with* God, were it not with God *the Father*, and [it is just as evident that] He who is *alone* is *equal* to no one. And, on the other hand, those are equally excluded who affirm that the Son is a creature, although not such an one as the rest of the creatures are. For

---

[1] Wisd. vii. 27.
[2] Adopting the Benedictine version, *per ipsam innotescit dignis animis secretissimus Pater.* There is, however, great variety of reading here. Some MSS. give *ignis* for *dignis* = the most hidden fire of the Father is made known to minds. Others give *signis* = the most hidden Father is made known by signs to minds. Others have *innotescit animus secretissimus Patris*, or *innotescit signis secretissimus Pater* = the most hidden mind of the Father is made known by the same, or = the most hidden Father is made known by the same in signs.
[3] *Sonantia verba* = sounding, vocal words.
[4] *Appetitum.*
[5] *Nostra notitia* = our knowledge.

[6] Reading *conantes et verbis*, etc. Three good MSS. give *conante fetu verbi* = as the offspring of the word makes the attempt. The Benedictine editors suggest *conantes fetu verbi* = making the attempt by the offspring of the word.
[7] 1 Cor. i. 24. [8] Wisd. viii. 1. [9] John i. 3.
[10] According to the literal meaning of the phrase *ex tempore*. It may, however, here be used as = under conditions of time, or in time.
[11] Reading *sempiterne;* for which *sempiternus* = the eternal wise God, is also given. [12] Phil. ii. 6.

however great they declare the creature to be, if it is a creature, it has been fashioned and made.[1] For the terms *fashion* and *create*[2] mean one and the same thing; although in the usage of the Latin tongue the phrase *create* is employed at times instead of what would be the strictly accurate word, *beget*. But the Greek language makes a distinction. For we call that *creatura* (creature) which they call κτίσμα or κτίσις; and when we desire to speak without ambiguity, we use not the word *creare* (create), but the word *condere* (fashion, found). Consequently, if the Son is a creature, however great that may be, He has been made. But we believe in Him by whom *all* things (*omnia*) were made, not in Him by whom the *rest* of things (*cetera*) were made. For here again we cannot take this term *all things* in any other sense than as meaning whatsoever things have been made.

6. But as "the Word was made flesh, and dwelt among us,"[3] the same Wisdom which was begotten of God condescended also to be created among men.[4] There is a reference to this in the word, "The Lord created me in the beginning of His ways."[5] For the beginning of His ways is the Head of the Church, which is Christ[6] endued with human nature (*homine indutus*), by whom it was purposed that there should be given to us a pattern of living, that is, a sure[7] way by which we might reach God. For by no other path was it possible for us to return but by humility, who fell by pride, according as it was said to our first creation, "Taste, and ye shall be as gods."[8] Of this humility, therefore, that is to say, of the way by which it was needful for us to return, our Restorer Himself has deemed it meet to exhibit an example in His own person, "who thought it not robbery to be equal with God, but emptied Himself, taking the form of a servant;"[9] in order that He might be created Man in the beginning of His ways, the Word by whom all things were made. Wherefore, in so far as He is the Only-begotten, He has no brethren; but in so far as He is the First-begotten, He has deemed it worthy of Him to give the name of brethren to all those who, subsequently to and by means of His pre-eminence,[10] are born again into the grace of

God through the adoption of sons, according to the truth commended to us by apostolic teaching.[11] Thus, then, the Son according to nature (*naturalis filius*) was born of the very substance of the Father, the only one so born, subsisting as that which the Father is,[12] God of God, Light of Light. We, on the other hand, are not the light by nature, but are enlightened by that Light, so that we may be able to shine in wisdom. For, as one says, "that was the true Light, which lighteth every man that cometh into the world."[13] Therefore we add to the faith of things eternal likewise the temporal dispensation[14] of our Lord, which He deemed it worthy of Him to bear for us and to minister in behalf of our salvation. For in so far as He is the only-begotten Son of God, it cannot be said of Him that *He was* and that *He shall be*, but only that *He is;* because, on the one hand, that which *was, now is* not; and, on the other, that which *shall be, as yet is* not. He, then, is unchangeable, independent of the condition of times and variation. And it is my opinion that this is the very consideration to which was due the circumstance that He introduced to the apprehension of His servant Moses the kind of name [which He then adopted]. For when he asked of Him by whom he should say that he was sent, in the event of the people to whom he was being sent despising him, he received his answer when He spake in this wise: "I AM THAT I AM." Thereafter, too, He added this: "Thus shalt thou say unto the children of Israel, HE THAT IS (*Qui est*) has sent me unto you."[15]

7. From this, I trust, it is now made patent to spiritual minds that there cannot possibly exist any nature contrary to God. For if He *is*,—and this is a word which can be spoken with propriety only of God (for that which truly *is* remains unchangeably; inasmuch as that which is changed has been something which now it is not, and shall be something which as yet it is not),—it follows that God has nothing contrary to Himself. For if the question were put to us, What is contrary to white? we would reply, black; if the question were, What is contrary to hot? we would reply, cold; if the question were, What is contrary to quick? we would reply, slow; and

---

[1] *Condita et facta est.*
[2] *Condere* and *creare.*   [3] John i. 14.
[4] Adopting in *hominibus creavi.* One important MS. gives *in omnibus* = amongst all.
[5] Prov. viii. 22, with *creavit me* instead of the *possessed me* of the English version.
[6] Various editions give *principium et caput Ecclesiæ est Christus*=the beginning of His ways and the Head of the Church is Christ.   [7] For *via certa* others give *via recta* = a right way.
[8] Gen. iii. 5.   [9] Phil. ii. 6, 7.
[10] *Per ejus primatum* = by means of His standing as the First-

born. We follow the Benedictine reading, *qui post ejus et per ejus primatum in Dei gratiam renascuntur.* But there is another, although less authoritative, version, viz. *qui post ejus primitias in Dei gratia nascimur* = all of us who, subsequently to His first-fruits, are born in the grace of God.
[11] Luke viii. 21; Rom. viii. 15–17; Gal. iv. 5; Eph. i. 5; Heb. ii. 11.
[12] *Id existens quod Pater est*, etc. Another version is, *idem existens quod Pater Deus* = subsisting as the same that God the Father is.   [13] John i. 9.
[14] The term *dispensatio* occurs very frequently as the equivalent of the Greek οἰκονομία = economy, designating the Incarnation.   [15] Ex. iii. 14.

all similar interrogations we would answer in like manner. When, however, it is asked, What is contrary to *that which is?* the right reply to give is, *that which is not.*

8. But whereas, in a temporal dispensation, as I have said, with a view to our salvation and restoration, and with the goodness of God acting therein, our changeable nature has been assumed by that unchangeable Wisdom of God, we add the faith in temporal things which have been done with salutary effect on our behalf, believing in that Son of God who was born through the Holy Ghost of the Virgin Mary. For by the gift of God, that is, by the Holy Spirit, there was granted to us so great humility on the part of so great a God, that He deemed it worthy of Him to assume the entire nature of man (*totum hominem*) in the womb of the Virgin, inhabiting the material body so that it sustained no detriment (*integrum*), and leaving it[1] without detriment. This temporal dispensation is in many ways craftily assailed by the heretics. But if any one shall have grasped the catholic faith, so as to believe that the entire nature of man was assumed by the Word of God, that is to say, body, soul, and spirit, he has sufficient defense against those parties. For surely, since that assumption was effected in behalf of our salvation, one must be on his guard lest, as he believes that there is something belonging to our nature which sustains no relation to that assumption, this something may fail also to sustain any relation to the salvation.[2] And seeing that, with the exception of the form of the members, which has been imparted to the varieties of living objects with differences adapted to their different kinds, man is in nothing separated from the cattle but in [the possession of] a rational spirit (*rationali spiritu*), which is also named mind (*mens*), how is that faith sound, according to which the belief is maintained, that the Wisdom of God assumed that part of us which we hold in common with the cattle, while He did not assume that which is brightly illumined by the light of wisdom, and which is man's peculiar gift?

9. Moreover, those parties[3] also are to be abhorred who deny that our Lord Jesus Christ had in Mary a mother upon earth; while that dispensation has honored both sexes, at once the male and the female, and has made it plain that not only that sex which He assumed pertains to God's care, but also that sex by which He did assume this other, in that He bore [the nature of] the man (*virum gerendo*), [and] in that He was born of the woman. Neither is there anything to compel us to a denial of the mother of the Lord, in the circumstance that this word was spoken by Him: "Woman, what have I to do with thee? Mine hour is not yet come."[4] But He rather admonishes us to understand that, in respect of His being God, there was no mother for Him, the part of whose personal majesty (*cujus majestatis personam*) He was preparing to show forth in the turning of water into wine. But as regards His being crucified, He was crucified in respect of his being man; and that was the *hour* which had not come as yet, at the time when this word was spoken, "What have I to do with thee? Mine hour is not yet come;" that is, the hour at which I shall recognize thee. For at that period, when He was crucified as man, He recognized His human mother (*hominem matrem*), and committed her most humanely (*humanissime*) to the care of the best beloved disciple.[5] Nor, again, should we be moved by the fact that, when the presence of His mother and His brethren was announced to Him, He replied, "Who is my mother, or who my brethren?" etc.[6] But rather let it teach us, that when parents hinder our ministry wherein we minister the word of God to our brethren, they ought not to be recognized by us. For if, on the ground of His having said, "Who is my mother?" every one should conclude that He had no mother on earth, then each should as matter of course be also compelled to deny that the apostles had fathers on earth; since He gave them an injunction in these terms: "Call no man your father upon the earth; for one is your Father, which is in heaven."[7]

10. Neither should the thought of the woman's womb impair this faith in us, to the effect that there should appear to be any necessity for rejecting such a generation of our Lord for the mere reason that worthless men consider it unworthy (*sordidi sordidam putant*). For most true are these sayings of an apostle, both that "the foolishness of God is wiser than men,"[8] and that "to the pure all things are pure."[9] Those,[10] therefore, who entertain this opinion ought to ponder the fact that the rays of this sun, which indeed they do not praise as a creature of God, but adore as God, are diffused all the world over, through the noisomenesses of sewers and every kind of horrible thing, and that

---

1 *Deserens.* With less point, *deferens* has been suggested = bearing it, or delivering it.
2 Or it may = *he* should fail to have any relation to the salvation.   3 Referring to the Manicheans.

4 John ii. 4.   5 John xix. 26, 27.
6 Matt. xii. 48.   7 Matt. xxiii. 9.
8 1 Cor. i. 25.   9 Tit. i. 15.
10 In reference to the Manicheans.

they operate in these according to their nature, and yet never become debased by any defilement thence contracted, albeit that the visible light is by nature in closer conjunction with visible pollutions. How much less, therefore, could the Word of God, who is neither corporeal nor visible, sustain defilement from the female body, wherein He assumed human flesh together with soul and spirit, through the incoming of which the majesty of the Word dwells in a less immediate conjunction with the frailty of a human body![1] Hence it is manifest that the Word of God could in no way have been defiled by a human body, by which even the human soul is not defiled. For not when it rules the body and quickens it, but only when it lusts after the mortal good things thereof, is the soul defiled by the body. But if these persons were to desire to avoid the defilements of the soul, they would dread rather these falsehoods and profanities.

CHAP. 5.—OF CHRIST'S PASSION, BURIAL, AND RESURRECTION.

11. But little [comparatively] was the humiliation (*humilitas*) of our Lord on our behalf in His being born: it was also added that He deemed it meet to die in behalf of mortal men. For "He humbled Himself, being made subject even unto death, yea, the death of the cross:"[2] lest any one of us, even were he able to have no fear of death [in general], should yet shudder at some particular sort of death which men reckon most shameful. Therefore do we believe in Him WHO UNDER PONTIUS PILATE WAS CRUCIFIED AND BURIED. For it was requisite that the name of the judge should be added, with a view to the cognizance of the times. Moreover, when that burial is made an object of belief, there enters also the recollection of the new tomb,[3] which was meant to present a testimony to Him in His destiny to rise again to newness of life, even as the Virgin's womb did the same to Him in His appointment to be born. For just as in that sepulchre no other dead person was buried,[4] whether before or after Him; so neither in that womb, whether before or after, was anything mortal conceived.

12. We believe also, that ON THE THIRD DAY HE ROSE AGAIN FROM THE DEAD, the first-begotten for brethren destined to come after Him, whom He has called into the adoption of the sons of God,[5] whom [also] He has deemed it meet to make His own joint-partners and joint-heirs.[6]

CHAP. 6.—OF CHRIST'S ASCENSION INTO HEAVEN.

13. We believe that HE ASCENDED INTO HEAVEN, which place of blessedness He has likewise promised unto us, saying, "They shall be as the angels in the heavens,"[7] in that city which is the mother of us all,[8] the Jerusalem eternal in the heavens. But it is wont to give offense to certain parties, either impious Gentiles or heretics, that we should believe in the assumption of an earthly body into heaven. The Gentiles, however, for the most part, set themselves diligently to ply us with the arguments of the philosophers, to the effect of affirming that there cannot possibly be anything earthly in heaven. For they know not our Scriptures, neither do they understand how it has been said, "It is sown an animal body, it is raised a spiritual body."[9] For thus it has not been expressed, as if body were turned into spirit and became spirit; inasmuch as at present, too, our body, which is called animal (*animale*), has not been turned into soul and become soul (*anima*). But by a spiritual body is meant one which has been made subject to spirit in such wise[10] that it is adapted to a heavenly habitation, all frailty and every earthly blemish having been changed and converted into heavenly purity and stability. This is the change concerning which the apostle likewise speaks thus: "We shall all rise, but we shall not all be changed."[11] And that this change is made not unto the worse, but unto the better, the same [apostle] teaches, when he says, "And we shall be changed."[12] But the question as to where and in what manner the Lord's body is in heaven, is one which it would be altogether over-curious and superfluous to prosecute. Only we must believe that it is in heaven. For it pertains not to our frailty to investigate the secret things of heaven, but it does pertain to our faith to hold elevated and honorable sentiments on the subject of the dignity of the Lord's body.

CHAP. 7.—OF CHRIST'S SESSION AT THE FATHER'S RIGHT HAND.

14. We believe also that HE SITTETH AT THE RIGHT HAND OF THE FATHER. This, however, is

---

[1] The Benedictine text gives, *quibus intervenientibus habitat majestas Verbi ab humani corporis fragilitate secretius.* Another well-supported version is, *ad humani corporis fragilitatem*, etc. = more retired in relation to the frailty of the human body.   [2] Phil. ii. 8.
[3] For *monumenti* some editions give *testamenti* = testament.
[4] John xix. 41.

[5] Eph. i. 5.   [6] Rom. viii. 17.
[7] Matt. xxii. 30.   [8] Gal. iv. 26.
[9] 1 Cor. xv. 44.
[10] Adopting the Benedictine reading, *quod ita spiritui subditum est.* But several MSS. give *quia ita coaptandum est* = it is understood to be a spiritual body, in that it is to be so adapted as to suit a heavenly habitation.
[11] 1 Cor. xv. 51, according to the Vulgate's transposition of the negative.   [12] 1 Cor. xv. 52.

not to lead us to suppose that God the Father is, as it were, circumscribed by a human form, so that, when we think of Him, a right side or a left should suggest itself to the mind. Nor, again, when it is thus said in express terms that the Father sitteth, are we to fancy that this is done with bended knees; lest we should fall into that profanity, in [dealing with] which an apostle execrates those who "changed the glory of the incorruptible God into the likeness of corruptible man." [1] For it is unlawful for a Christian to set up any such image for God in a temple; much more nefarious is it, [therefore], to set it up in the heart, in which truly is the temple of God, provided it be purged of earthly lust and error. This expression, " at the right hand," therefore, we must understand to signify a position in supremest blessedness, where righteousness and peace and joy are; just as the kids are set on the left hand, [2] that is to say, in misery, by reason of unrighteousness, labors, and torments. [3] And in accordance with this, when it is said that God " sitteth," the expression indicates not a posture of the members, but a judicial power, which that Majesty never fails to possess, as He is always awarding deserts as men deserve them (*digna dignis tribuendo*); although at the last judgment the unquestionable brightness of the only-begotten Son of God, the Judge of the living and the dead, is destined yet to be [4] a thing much more manifest among men.

CHAP. 8.—OF CHRIST'S COMING TO JUDGMENT.

15. We believe also, that at the most seasonable time HE WILL COME FROM THENCE, AND WILL JUDGE THE QUICK AND THE DEAD: whether by these terms are signified the righteous and sinners, or whether it be the case that those persons are here called the *quick*, whom at that period He shall find, previous to [their] death,[5] upon the earth, while the *dead* denote those who shall rise again at His advent. This temporal dispensation not only *is*, as holds good of that generation which respects His being God, but also *hath been* and *shall be*. For our Lord *hath been* upon the earth, and at present He *is* in heaven, and [hereafter] He *shall be* in His brightness as the Judge of the quick and the dead. For He shall yet come, even so as He has ascended, according

to the authority which is contained in the Acts of the Apostles.[6] It is in accordance with this temporal dispensation, therefore, that He speaks in the Apocalypse, where it is written in this wise: " These things saith He, who is, and who was, and who is to come." [7]

CHAP. 9.—OF THE HOLY SPIRIT AND THE MYSTERY OF THE TRINITY.

16. The divine generation, therefore, of our Lord, and his human dispensation, having both been thus systematically disposed and commended to faith,[8] there is added to our Confession, with a view to the perfecting of the faith which we have regarding God, [the doctrine of] THE HOLY SPIRIT, who is not of a nature inferior [9] to the Father and the Son, but, so to say, consubstantial and co-eternal: for this Trinity is one God, not to the effect that the Father is the same [Person] as the Son and the Holy Spirit, but to the effect that the Father is the Father, and the Son is the Son, and the Holy Spirit is the Holy Spirit; and this Trinity is one God, according as it is written, " Hear, O Israel, the Lord your God is one God." [10] At the same time, if we be interrogated on the subject of each separately, and if the question be put to us, " Is the Father God?" we shall reply, " He is God." If it be asked whether the Son is God, we shall answer to the same effect. Nor, if this kind of inquiry be addressed to us with respect to the Holy Spirit, ought we to affirm in reply that He is anything else than God; being earnestly on our guard, [however], against an acceptance of this merely in the sense in which it is applied to men, when it is said, " Ye are gods." [11] For of all those who have been made and fashioned of the Father, through the Son, by the gift of the Holy Spirit, none are gods according to nature. For it is this same Trinity that is signified when an apostle says, " For of Him, and in Him, and through Him, are all things." [12] Consequently, although, when we are interrogated on the subject of each [of these Persons] severally, we reply that that particular one regarding whom the question is asked, whether it be the Father, or the Son, or the Holy Spirit, is God, no one, notwithstanding this, should suppose that three Gods are worshipped by us.

---

[1] Rom. i. 23.   [2] Matt. xxv. 33.
[3] Reading *propter iniquitates, labores atque cruciatus.* Several MSS. give *propter iniquitatis labores*, etc. = by reason of the labors and torments of unrighteousness.
[4] Reading *futura sit;* for which *fulsura sit* also occurs = is destined to shine much more manifestly, etc.
[5] The text gives simply *ante mortem.* Some editions insert *nostram* = previous to our death.

[6] Acts i. 11.   [7] Rev. i. 8.
[8] Instead of *fideique commendata et divina generatione*, etc., another, but weakly supported, version is, *fide atque commendata divina*, etc., which makes the sense = The faith, therefore, having been systematically disposed, and our Lord's divine generation and human dispensation having been commended to the understanding, etc.
[9] *Non minore natura quam Pater.* The Benedictine editors suggest *minor* for *minore* = not inferior in nature, etc.
[10] Deut. vi. 4.   [11] Ps. lxxxii. 6.   [12] Rom. xi. 36.

17. Neither is it strange that these things are said in reference to an ineffable Nature, when even in those objects which we discern with the bodily eyes, and judge of by the bodily sense, something similar holds good. For take the instance of an interrogation on the subject of a fountain, and consider how we are unable then to affirm that the said fountain is itself the river; and how, when we are asked about the river, we are as little able to call it the fountain; and, again, how we are equally unable to designate the draught, which comes of the fountain or the river, either river or fountain. Nevertheless, in the case of this trinity we use the name *water* [for the whole]; and when the question is put regarding each of these separately, we reply in each several instance that the thing is *water*. For if I inquire whether it is water in the fountain, the reply is given that it is water; and if we ask whether it is water in the river, no different response is returned; and in the case of the said draught, no other answer can possibly be made: and yet, for all this, we do not speak of these things as three waters, but as one water. At the same time, of course, care must be taken that no one should conceive of the ineffable substance of that Majesty merely as he might think of this visible and material[1] fountain, or river, or draught. For in the case of these latter, that water which is at present in the fountain goes forth into the river, and does not abide in itself; and when it passes from the river or from the fountain into the draught, it does not continue permanently there where it is taken from. Therefore it is possible here that the same water may be in view at one time under the appellation of the fountain, and at another under that of the river, and at a third under that of the draught. But in the case of that Trinity, we have affirmed it to be impossible that the Father should be sometime the Son, and sometime the Holy Spirit: just as, in a tree, the root is nothing else than the root, and the trunk (*robur*) is nothing else than the trunk, and we cannot call the branches anything else than branches; for, what is called the root cannot be called trunk and branches; and the wood which belongs to the root cannot by any sort of transference be now in the root, and again in the trunk, and yet again in the branches, but only in the root; since this rule of designation stands fast, so that the root is wood, and the trunk is wood, and the branches are wood, while nevertheless it is not three woods that are thus spoken of, but only one.

Or, if these objects have some sort of dissimilarity, so that on account of their difference in strength they may be spoken of, without any absurdity, as three woods; at least all parties admit the force of the former example,—namely, that if three cups be filled out of one fountain, they may certainly be called three cups, but cannot be spoken of as three waters, but only as one all together. Yet, at the same time, when asked concerning the several cups, one by one, we may answer that in each of them by itself there is water; although in this case no such transference takes place as we were speaking of as occurring from the fountain into the river. But these examples in things material (*corporalia exempla*) have been adduced not in virtue of their likeness to that divine Nature, but in reference to the oneness which subsists even in things visible, so that it may be understood to be quite a possibility for three objects of some sort, not only severally, but also all together, to obtain one single name; and that in this way no one may wonder and think it absurd that we should call the Father God, the Son God, the Holy Spirit God, and that nevertheless we should say that there are not three Gods in that Trinity, but one God and one substance.[2]

18. And, indeed, on this subject of the Father and the Son, learned and spiritual[3] men have conducted discussions in many books, in which, so far as men could do with men, they have endeavored to introduce an intelligible account as to how the Father was not one personally with the Son, and yet the two were one substantially;[4] and as to what the Father was individually (*proprie*), and what the Son: to wit, that the former was the Begetter, the latter the Begotten; the former not of the Son, the latter of the Father: the former the Beginning of the latter, whence also He is called the Head of Christ,[5] although Christ likewise is the Beginning,[6] but not of the Father; the latter, moreover, the Image[7] of the former, although in no respect dissimilar, and although absolutely and without difference equal (*omnino et indifferenter æqualis*). These questions are handled with greater breadth by those who, in less narrow limits than ours are at present, seek to set

---

[1] *Corporeum* = corporeal.

[2] Many MSS., however, insert *colamus* after *Deum* in the closing sentence, *sed unum Deum unamque substantiam.* The sense then will be = and that nevertheless we should worship in that Trinity not three Gods, but one God and one substance.
[3] *Spiritales*, for which *religiosi* = religious, is also sometimes given.
[4] *Non unus esset Pater et Filius, sed unum essent* = how the Father and the Son were not one in person, but were one in essence.
[5] 1 Cor. xi. 3.
[6] In reference probably to John viii. 25, where the Vulgate gives *principium qui et loquor vobis* as the literal equivalent for the Greek τὴν ἀρχὴν ὅ,τι καὶ λαλῶ ὑμῖν.   [7] Col. i. 15.

forth the profession of the Christian faith in its totality. Accordingly, in so far as He is the Son, of the Father received He it that He *is*, while that other [the Father] received not this of the Son; and in so far as He, in unutterable mercy, in a temporal dispensation took upon Himself the [nature of] man (*hominem*),—to wit, the changeable creature that was thereby to be changed into something better,—many statements concerning Him are discovered in the Scriptures, which are so expressed as to have given occasion to error in the impious intellects of heretics, with whom the desire to teach takes precedence of that to understand, so that they have supposed Him to be neither equal with the Father nor of the same substance. Such statements [are meant] as the following: "For the Father is greater than I;"[1] and, "The head of the woman is the man, the Head of the man is Christ, and the Head of Christ is God;"[2] and, "Then shall He Himself be subject unto Him that put all things under Him;"[3] and, "I go to my Father and your Father, my God and your God"[4] together with some others of like tenor. Now all these have had a place given them, [certainly] not with the object of signifying an inequality of nature and substance; for to take them so would be to falsify a different class of statements, such as, "I and my Father are one" (*unum*);[5] and, "He that hath seen me hath seen my Father also;"[6] and, "The Word was God,"[7] for He was not made, inasmuch as "all things were made by Him;"[8] and, "He thought it not robbery to be equal with God:"[9] together with all the other passages of a similar order. But these statements have had a place given them, partly with a view to that administration of His assumption of human nature (*administrationem suscepti hominis*), in accordance with which it is said that "He emptied Himself:" not that that Wisdom was changed, since it is absolutely unchangeable; but that it was His will to make Himself known in such humble fashion to men. Partly then, I repeat, it is with a view to this administration that those things have been thus written which the heretics make the ground of their false allegations; and partly it was with a view to the consideration that the Son owes to the Father that which He *is*,[10]—thereby also certainly owing this in particular to the Father, to wit, that He is equal to the same Father, or that He is His Peer (*eidem Patri æqualis aut par*

est), whereas the Father owes whatsoever He is to no one.

19. With respect to the HOLY SPIRIT, however, there has not been as yet, on the part of learned and distinguished investigators of the Scriptures, a discussion of the subject full enough or careful enough to make it possible for us to obtain an intelligent conception of what also constitutes His special individuality (*proprium*): in virtue of which special individuality it comes to be the case that we cannot call Him either the Son or the Father, but only the Holy Spirit; excepting that they predicate Him to be the Gift of God, so that we may believe God not to give a gift inferior to Himself. At the same time they hold by this position, namely, to predicate the Holy Spirit neither as begotten, like the Son, of the Father; for Christ is the only one [so begotten]: nor as [begotten] of the Son, like a Grandson of the Supreme Father: while they do not affirm Him to owe that which He is to no one, but [admit Him to owe it] to the Father, of whom are all things; lest we should establish two Beginnings without beginning (*ne duo constituamus principia isne principio*), which would be an assertion at once most false and most absurd, and one proper not to the catholic faith, but to the error of certain heretics.[11] Some, however, have gone so far as to believe that the communion of the Father and the Son, and (so to speak) their Godhead (*deitatem*), which the Greeks designate θεότης, is the Holy Spirit; so that, inasmuch as the Father is God and the Son God, the Godhead itself, in which they are united with each other,—to wit, the former by begetting the Son, and the latter by cleaving to the Father,[12]—should [thereby] be constituted equal with Him by whom He is begotten. This Godhead, then, which they wish to be understood likewise as the love and charity subsisting between these two [Persons], the one toward the other, they affirm to have received the name of the Holy Spirit. And this opinion of theirs they support by many proofs drawn from the Scriptures; among which we might instance either the passage which says, "For the love of God is shed abroad in our hearts by the Holy Ghost, who has been given unto us,"[13] or many other proofs texts of a similar tenor: while they ground their position also upon the express fact that it is through the Holy Spirit that we are reconciled unto God; whence also, when He is called the Gift of God, they will have it that sufficient indication is of-

---

[1] John xiv. 28. [2] 1 Cor. xi. 3. [3] 1 Cor. xv. 28.
[4] John xx. 17. [5] John x. 30. [6] John xiv. 9.
[7] John i. 1. [8] John i. 3.
[9] Phil. ii. 9. [See R. V.]
[10] Or it may be = that the Son owes it to the Father that He *is*.

[11] In reference, again, to Manichean errorists.
[12] *Patri cohærendo* = by close connection with the Father.
[13] Rom. v. 5.

fered of the love of God and the Holy Spirit being identical. For we are not reconciled unto Him except through that love in virtue of which we are also called sons:[1] as we are no more "under fear, like servants,"[2] because "love, when it is made perfect, casteth out fear;"[3] and [as] "we have received the spirit of liberty, wherein we cry, Abba, Father."[4] And inasmuch as, being reconciled and called back into friendship through love, we shall be able to become acquainted with all the secret things of God, for this reason it is said of the Holy Spirit that "He shall lead you into all truth."[5] For the same reason also, that confidence in preaching the truth, with which the apostles were filled at His advent,[6] is rightly ascribed to love; because diffidence also is assigned to fear, which the perfecting of love excludes. Thus, likewise, the same is called the Gift of God,[7] because no one enjoys that which he knows, unless he also love it. To enjoy the Wisdom of God, however, implies nothing else than to cleave to the same in love (ei dilectione cohærere). Neither does any one abide in that which he apprehends, but by love; and accordingly the Holy Spirit is called the Spirit of sanctity (Spiritus Sanctus), inasmuch as all things that are sanctioned (sanciuntur)[8] are sanctioned with a view to their permanence, and there is no doubt that the term sanctity (sanctitatem) is derived from sanction (a sanciendo). Above all, however, that testimony is employed by the upholders of this opinion, where it is thus written, "That which is born of the flesh is flesh, and that which is born of the Spirit is spirit;"[9] "for God is a Spirit."[10] For here He speaks of our regeneration,[11] which is not, according to Adam, of the flesh, but, according to Christ, of the Holy Spirit. Wherefore, if in this passage mention is made of the Holy Spirit, when it is said, "For God is a Spirit," they maintain that we must take note that it is not said, "for the Spirit is God,"[12] but, "for God is a Spirit;" so that the very Godhead of the Father and the Son is in this passage called God, and that is the Holy Spirit. To this is added another testimony which the Apostle John offers, when he says, "For God is love."[13]

For here, in like manner, what he says is not, "Love is God,"[14] but, "God is love;" so that the very Godhead is taken to be love. And with respect to the circumstance that, in that enumeration of mutually connected objects which is given when it is said, "All things are yours, and ye are Christ's, and Christ is God's,"[15] as also, "The head of the woman is the man, the Head of the man is Christ, and the Head of Christ is God,"[16] there is no mention of the Holy Spirit; this they affirm to be but an application of the principle that, in general, the connection itself is not wont to be enumerated among the things which are connected with each other. Whence, also, those who read with closer attention appear to recognize the express Trinity likewise in that passage in which it is said, "For of Him, and through Him, and in Him, are all things."[17] "Of Him," as if it meant, of that One who owes it to no one that He is; "through Him," as if the idea were, through a Mediator; "in Him," as if it were, in that One who holds together, that is, unites by connecting.

20. Those parties oppose this opinion who think that the said communion, which we call either Godhead, or Love, or Charity, is not a substance. Moreover, they require the Holy Spirit to be set forth to them according to substance; neither do they take it to have been otherwise impossible for the expression "God is Love" to have been used, unless love were a substance. In this, indeed, they are influenced by the wont of things of a bodily nature. For if two bodies are connected with each other in such wise as to be placed in juxtaposition one with the other, the connection itself is not a body: inasmuch as when these bodies which had been connected are separated, no such connection certainly is found [any more]; while, at the same time, it is not understood to have departed, as it were, and migrated, as is the case with those bodies themselves. But men like these should make their heart pure, so far as they can, in order that they may have power to see that in the substance of God there is not anything of such a nature as would imply that therein substance is one thing, and that which is accident to substance (aliud quod accidat substantiæ) another thing, and not substance; whereas whatsoever can be taken to be therein is substance. These things, however, can easily be spoken and believed; but seen, so as to reveal how they are in themselves, they absolutely cannot be, except by the pure heart. For which reason,

---

[1] 1 John iii. 1. The word Dei=of God, is sometimes added here.
[2] Rom. viii. 15.   [3] 1 John iv. 18.   [4] Rom. viii. 15.
[5] John xvi. 13.   [6] Acts ii. 4.   [7] Eph. iii. 7, 8.
[8] Instead of sanciuntur, which is the reading of the MSS., some editions give sanctificantur — all things that are sanctified are sanctioned, etc.
[9] John iii. 6.   [10] John iv. 24.
[11] Reading, with the MSS. and the Benedictine editors, Hic enim regenerationem nostram dicit. Some editions give Hoc for Hic, and dicunt for dicit = for they say that this expresses our regeneration.
[12] Quoniam Spiritus Deus est. But various editions and MSS. give Dei for Deus = for the Spirit is of God.
[13] 1 John iv. 16.
[14] Here again, instead of dilectio Deus est, we also find dilectio Dei est = love is of God.

[15] 1 Cor. iii. 22, 23.   [16] 1 Cor. xi. 3.   [17] Rom. xi. 36.

whether the opinion in question be true, or something else be the case, the faith ought to be maintained unshaken, so that we should call the Father God, the Son God, the Holy Spirit God, and yet not affirm three Gods, but hold the said Trinity to be one God; and again, not affirm these [Persons] to be different in nature, but hold them to be of the same substance; and further uphold it, not as if the Father were sometime the Son, and sometime the Holy Spirit, but in such wise that the Father is always the Father, and the Son always the Son, and the Holy Spirit always the Holy Spirit. Neither should we make any affirmation on the subject of things unseen rashly, as if we had knowledge, but [only modestly] as believing. For these things cannot be seen except by the heart made pure; and [even] he who in this life sees them "in part," as it has been said, and "in an enigma," [1] cannot secure it that the person to whom he speaks shall also see them, if he is hampered by impurities of heart. "Blessed," however, "are they of a pure heart, for they shall see God." [2] This is the faith on the subject of God our Maker and Renewer.

21. But inasmuch as love is enjoined upon us, not only toward God, when it was said, "Thou shalt love the Lord thy God with all thy heart, and with all thy soul, and with all thy mind;" [3] but also toward our neighbor, for "thou shalt love," saith He, "thy neighbor as thyself;" [4] and inasmuch, moreover, as the faith in question is less fruitful, if it does not comprehend a congregation and society of men, wherein brotherly charity may operate;—

CHAP. 10.—OF THE CATHOLIC CHURCH, THE RE-
MISSION OF SINS, AND THE RESURRECTION OF
THE FLESH.

—Inasmuch, I repeat, as this is the case, we believe also in THE HOLY CHURCH, [intending thereby] assuredly the CATHOLIC. For both heretics and schismatics style their congregations churches. But heretics, in holding false opinions regarding God, do injury to the faith itself; while schismatics, on the other hand, in wicked separations break off from brotherly charity, although they may believe just what we believe. Wherefore neither do the heretics belong to the Church catholic, which loves God; nor do the schismatics form a part of the same, inasmuch as it loves the neighbor, and consequently readily forgives the neighbor's sins, because it prays that forgiveness may be extended to itself

by Him who has reconciled us to Himself, doing away with all past things, and calling us to a new life. And until we reach the perfection of this new life, we cannot be without sins. Nevertheless it is a matter of consequence of what sort those sins may be.

22. Neither ought we only to treat of the difference between sins, but we ought most thoroughly to believe that those things in which we sin are in no way forgiven us, if we show ourselves severely unyielding in the matter of forgiving the sins of others. [5] Thus, then, we believe also in THE REMISSION OF SINS.

23. And inasmuch as there are three things of which man consists,—namely, spirit, soul, and body,—which again are spoken of as two, because frequently the soul is named along with the spirit; for a certain rational portion of the same, of which beasts are devoid, is called spirit: the principal part in us is the spirit; next, the life whereby we are united with the body is called the soul; finally, the body itself, as it is visible, is the last part in us. This "whole creation" (*creatura*), however, "groaneth and travaileth until now." [6] Nevertheless, He has given it the first-fruits of the Spirit, in that it has believed God, and is now of a good will. [7] This spirit is also called the mind, regarding which an apostle speaks thus: "With the mind I serve the law of God." [8] Which apostle likewise expresses himself thus in another passage: "For God is my witness, whom I serve in my spirit." [9] Moreover, the soul, when as yet it lusts after carnal good things, is called the flesh. For a certain part thereof resists[10] the Spirit, not in virtue of nature, but in virtue of the custom of sins; whence it is said, "With the mind I serve the law of God, but with the flesh the law of sin." And this custom has been turned into a nature, according to mortal generation, by the sin of the first man. Consequently it is also written in this wise, "And we were sometime by nature the children of wrath," [11] that is, of vengeance, through which it has come to pass that we serve the law of sin. The nature of the soul, however, is perfect when it is made subject to its own spirit, and when it follows that spirit as the same follows God. Therefore "the animal man [12] receiveth not the things which are of the Spirit of God." [13] But the soul is not so speedily subdued to the spirit

[1] 1 Cor. xiii. 12.   [2] Matt. v. 8.   [3] Deut. vi. 5.
[4] Luke x. 27.

[5] Matt. vi. 15.   [6] Rom. viii. 22.
[7] Reading *spiritus*. Taking *spiritus*, the sense might be = Nevertheless, the spirit hath imparted the first-fruits, in that it has believed God, and is now of a good will.
[8] Rom. vii. 25.   [9] Rom. i. 9.
[10] Instead of *caro nominatur. Pars enim ejus quædam resistit*, etc., some good MSS. read *caro nominatur et resistit*, etc. = is called the flesh, and resists, etc.
[11] Eph. ii. 3.
[12] *Animalis homo*, literally = the *soulish* man.   [13] 1 Cor. ii. 14.

unto good action, as is the spirit to God unto true faith and goodwill; but sometimes its impetus, whereby it moves downwards into things carnal and temporal, is more tardily bridled. But inasmuch as this same soul is also made pure, and receives the stability of its own nature, under the dominance of the spirit, which is the head for it, which head of the said soul has again its own head in Christ, we ought not to despair of the restoration of the body also to its own proper nature. But this certainly will not be effected so speedily as is the case with the soul; just as the soul, too, is not restored so speedily as the spirit. Yet it will take place in the appropriate season, at the last trump, when "the dead shall rise uncorrupted, and we shall be changed."[1] And accordingly we believe also in THE RESURRECTION OF THE FLESH, to wit, not merely that that soul, which at present by reason of carnal affections is called the flesh, is restored; but that it shall' be so likewise with this visible flesh, which is the flesh according to nature, the name of which has been received by the soul, not in virtue of nature, but in reference to carnal affections: this visible flesh, then, I say, which is the flesh properly so called, must without doubt be believed to be destined to rise again. For the Apostle Paul appears to point to this, as it were, with his finger, when he says, "This corruptible must put on incorruption."[2] For when he says *this*, he, as it were, directs his finger toward it. Now it is that which is visible that admits of being pointed out with the finger; since the soul might also have been called corruptible, for it is itself corrupted by vices of manners. And when it is read, "and this mortal [must] put on immortality," the same visible flesh is signified, inasmuch as at it ever and anon the finger is thus as it were pointed. For the soul also may thus in like manner be called mortal, even as it is designated corruptible in reference to vices of manners. For assuredly it is "the death of the soul to apostatize from God;"[3] which is its first sin in Paradise, as it is contained in the sacred writings.

24. Rise again, therefore, the body will, according to the Christian faith, which is incapable of deceiving. And if this appears incredible to any one, [it is because] he looks simply to what the flesh is at present, while he fails to consider of what nature it shall be hereafter. For at that time of angelic change it will no more be flesh and blood, but only

body.[4] For when the apostle speaks of the flesh, he says, "There is one flesh of cattle, another of birds, another of fishes, another of creeping things: there are also both celestial bodies and terrestrial bodies."[5] Now what he has said here is not "celestial flesh," but "both celestial bodies and terrestrial bodies." For all flesh is also body; but every body is not also flesh. In the first instance, [for example, this holds good] in the case of those terrestrial bodies, inasmuch as wood is body, but not flesh. In the case of man, again, or in that of cattle, we have both body and flesh. In the case of celestial bodies, on the other hand, there is no flesh, but only those simple and lucent bodies which the apostle designates spiritual, while some call them ethereal. And consequently, when he says, "Flesh and blood shall not inherit the kingdom of God,"[6] that does not contradict the resurrection of the flesh; but the sentence predicates what will be the nature of that hereafter which at present is flesh and blood. And if any one refuses to believe that the flesh is capable of being changed into the sort of nature thus indicated, he must be led on, step by step, to this faith. For if you inquire of him whether earth is capable of being changed into water, the nearness of the thing will make it not seem incredible to him. Again, if you inquire whether water is capable of being changed into air, he replies that this also is not absurd, for the elements are near each other. And if, on the subject of the air, it is asked whether that can be changed into an ethereal, that is, a celestial body, the simple fact of the nearness at once convinces him of the possibility of the thing. But if, then, he concedes that through such gradations it is quite a possible thing that earth should be changed into an ethereal body, why does he refuse to believe, when that will of God, too, enters in addition, whereby a human body had power to walk upon the waters, that the same change is capable of being effected with the utmost rapidity, precisely in accordance with the saying, "in the twinkling of an eye,"[7] and without any such gradations, even as, according to common wont, smoke is changed into flame with marvellous quickness? For our flesh assuredly is of earth. But philosophers, on the ground of whose arguments opposition is for the most part offered to the resurrection of the flesh, so far as in these they assert that no terrene body can possibly exist in heaven, yet concede that any kind of body may be converted and

---

[1] 1 Cor. xv. 52.   [2] 1 Cor. xv. 53.
[3] The text gives, *Mors quippe animæ est apostatare a Deo.* The reference, perhaps, is to Ecclus. x. 12, where the Vulgate has, *initium superbiæ hominis, apostatare a Deo.*

[4] Augustin refers to this statement in the passage quoted from the *Retractations* in the Introductory Notice above.
[5] 1 Cor. xv. 39, 40.   [6] 1 Cor. xv. 50.   [7] 1 Cor. xv. 52.

changed into every [other] sort of body. And when this resurrection of the body has taken place, being set free then from the condition of time, we shall fully enjoy ETERNAL LIFE in ineffable love and steadfastness, without corruption.[1] For "then shall be brought to pass the saying which is written, Death is swallowed up in victory. Where is, O death, thy sting? Where is, O death, thy contention?"[2]

25. This is the faith which in few words is given in the Creed to Christian novices, to be held by them. And these few words are known to the faithful, to the end that in believing they may be made subject to God; that being made subject, they may rightly live; that in rightly living, they may make the heart pure; that with the heart made pure, they may understand that which they believe.

---

[1] Instead of *a temporis conditione liberati, æterna vita ineffabili caritate atque stabilitate sine corruptione perfruemur*, several MSS. read, *corpus a temporis conditione liberatum æterna vita ineffabili caritate perfruetur* = the body, set free from the condition of time, shall fully enjoy eternal life in ineffable love.

[2] 1 Cor. xv. 54, 55.

ST. AUGUSTIN:

CONCERNING

FAITH OF THINGS NOT SEEN

[DE FIDE RERUM QUÆ NON VIDENTUR.]

TRANSLATED BY

REV. C. L. CORNISH, M.A.

CONCERNING

FAITH OF THINGS NOT SEEN.

[DE FIDE RERUM QUÆ NON VIDENTUR.]

This tract was thought spurious by some, but is known to be St. Augustin's by his mention of it in Ep. ccxxxi. *ad Darium Comitem.* It seems to have been written after 399, from what is said about Idols, § 10; for in that year Honorius enacted laws against them.—*From Bened. Ed.*

The reader of Butler's Analogy will recognise many similar turns of thought.

1. THERE are those who think that the Christian religion is what we should smile at, rather than hold fast, for this reason, that, in it, not what may be seen, is shown, but men are commanded faith of things which are not seen. We therefore, that we may refute these, who seem to themselves through prudence to be unwilling to believe what they cannot see, although we are not able to show unto human sight those divine things which we believe, yet do show unto human minds that even those things which are not seen are to be believed. And first they are to be admonished, (whom folly hath so made subject to their carnal eyes, as that, whatsoever they see not through them, they think not that they are to believe,) how many things they not only believe but also know, which cannot be seen by such eyes. Which things being without number in our mind itself, (the nature of which mind is incapable of being seen,) not to mention others, the very faith whereby we believe, or the thought whereby we know that we either believe any thing, or believe not, being as it is altogether alien from the sight of those eyes; what so naked, so clear, what so certain is there to the inner eyes of our minds? How then are we not to believe what we see not with the eyes of the body, whereas, either that we believe, or that we

believe not, in a case where we cannot apply the eyes of the body, we without any doubt see?

2. But, say they, those things which are in the mind, in that we can by the mind itself discern them, we have no need to know through the eyes of the body; but those things, which you say unto us that we should believe, you neither point to without, that through the eyes of the body we may know them; nor are they within, in our own mind, that by exercising thought we may see them. And these things they so say, as though any one would be bidden to believe, if that, which is believed, he could already see set before him. Therefore certainly ought we to believe certain temporal things also, which we see not, that we may merit[1] to see eternal things also, which we believe. But, whosoever thou art who wilt not believe save what thou seest, lo, bodies that are present thou seest with the eyes of the body, wills and thoughts of thine own that are present, because they are in thine own mind, thou seest by the mind itself; tell me, I pray thee, thy friend's will towards thee by what eyes seest thou? For no will can be seen by the eyes of the body. What? see you in your own mind this also

---

[1] *Mereamur.*

22

which is going on in the mind of another? But if you see it not, how do you repay in turn the good will of your friend, if what you cannot see, you believe not? Will you haply say that you see the will of another through his works? Therefore you will see acts, and hear words, but, concerning your friend's will, that which cannot be seen and heard you will believe. For that will is not color or figure, so as to be thrown upon the eyes; or sound or strain, so as to glide into the ears; nor indeed is it your own, so as to be perceived by the motion[1] of your own heart. It remains therefore that, being neither seen, nor heard, nor beheld within thyself, it be believed, that thy life be not left deserted without any friendship, or affection bestowed upon thee be not repaid by thee in return. Where then is that which thou saidest, that thou oughtest not to believe, save what thou sawest either outwardly in the body, or inwardly in the heart? Lo, out of thine own heart, thou believest an heart not thine own; and lendest thy faith, where thou dost not direct the glance of thy body or of thy mind. Thy friend's face thou discernest by thy own body, thy own faith thou discernest by thine own mind; but thy friend's faith is not loved by thee, unless there be in thee in return that faith, whereby thou mayest believe that which in him thou seest not. Although a man may also deceive by feigning good will, and hiding malice: or, if he have no thought to do harm, yet by expecting some benefit from thee, feigns, because he has not, love.

3. But you say, that you therefore believe your friend, whose heart you cannot see, because you have proved him in your trials, and have come to know of what manner of spirit he was towards you in your dangers, wherein he deserted you not. Seemeth it therefore to you that we must wish for our own affliction, that our friend's love towards us may be proved? And shall no man be happy in most sure friends, unless he shall be unhappy through adversity? so that, forsooth, he enjoy not the tried love of the other, unless he be racked by pain and fear of his own? And how in the having of true friends can that happiness be wished for, and not rather feared, which nothing save unhappiness can put to the proof? And yet it is true that a friend may be had also in prosperity, but proved more surely in adversity. But assuredly in order to prove him, neither would you commit yourself to dangers of your own, unless you believed; and thus, when you commit yourself in order to prove, you believe before you prove. For surely, if we ought not to believe things not seen,[2] since indeed we believe the hearts of our friends, and that, not yet surely proved; and, after we shall have proved them good by our own ills, even then we believe rather than see their good will towards us: except that so great is faith, that, not unsuitably, we judge that we see, with certain eyes of it, that which we believe, whereas we ought therefore to believe, because we cannot see.

4. If this faith be taken away from human affairs, who but must observe how great disorder in them, and how fearful confusion must follow? For who will be loved by any with mutual affection, (being that the loving[3] itself is invisible,) if what I see not, I ought not to believe? Therefore will the whole of friendship perish, in that it consists not save of mutual love. For what of it will it be able to receive from any, if nothing of it shall be believed to be shown? Further, friendship perishing, there will be preserved in the mind the bonds neither of marriages, nor of kindreds and relations; because in these also there is assuredly a friendly union of sentiment. Spouse therefore will not be able to love spouse in turn, inasmuch as each believes not the other's love, because the love itself cannot be seen. Nor will they long to have sons, who they believe not will make them a return. And if these be born and grow up, much less will the parents themselves love their own children, whose love towards themselves in those children's hearts they will not see, it being invisible; if it be not praiseworthy faith, but blameable rashness, to believe those things which are not seen. Why should I now speak of the other connections, of brothers, sisters, sons-in-law, and fathers-in-law, and of them who are joined together by any kindred or affinity, if love is uncertain, and the will suspected, that of parents by sons, and that of sons by parents, whilst due benevolence is not rendered; because neither is it thought to be due, that which is not seen in another not being thought to exist. Further, if this caution be not a mark of ability,[4] but be hateful, wherein we believe not that we are loved, because we see not the love of them who love, and repay not them, unto whom we think not that we owe a return; to that degree are human affairs thrown into disorder, if what we see not we believe not, as to be altogether and utterly overthrown, if we believe no wills of men,

---

[1] *Affectione.*

[2] The text seems corrupt. A MS. in Brasenose Library reads, " *si non vis rebus credere.*" If we read "*Si non vis rebus non visis credere,*" the sense will be, "For certainly if you will not have us believe things unseen, we ought not (to believe this), since" etc.
[3] *Dilectio.*   [4] *Ingeniosa.*

which assuredly we cannot see. I omit to mention in how many things they, who find fault with us because we believe what we see not, believe report or history; or concerning places where they have not themselves been; and say not, we believe not, because we have not seen. Since if they say this, they are obliged to confess that their own parents are not surely known to them: because on this point also they have believed the accounts of others telling of it, who yet are unable to show it, because it is a thing already past; retaining themselves no sense of that time, and yet yielding assent without any doubting to others speaking of that time: and unless this be done, there must of necessity be incurred a faithless impiety towards parents, whilst we are, as it were, showing a rashness of belief in those things which we cannot see. Since therefore, if we believe not those things which we cannot see, human society itself, through concord perishing, will not stand; how much more is faith to be applied to divine things, although they be not seen; failing the application of which, it is not the friendship of some men or other, but the very chiefest bond of piety[1] that is violated, so as for the chiefest misery to follow.

5. But you will say, the good will of a friend towards me, although I cannot see it, yet can I trace it out by many proofs; but you, what things you will us to believe not being seen, you have no proofs whereby to show them. In the mean time it is no slight thing, that you confess that by reason of the clearness of certain proofs, some things, even such as are not seen, ought to be believed: for even thus it is agreed, that not all things which are not seen, are not to be believed; and that saying, "that we ought not to believe things which we see not," falls to the ground, cast away, and refuted. But they are much deceived, who think that we believe in Christ without any proofs concerning Christ. For what are there clearer proofs than those things, which we now see to have been foretold and fulfilled? Wherefore do ye, who think that there are no proofs why ye ought to believe concerning Christ those things which ye have not seen, give heed to what things ye see. The Church herself addresses you out of the mouth of a mother's love: "I, whom ye view with wonder throughout the whole world, bearing fruit and increasing, was not once such as ye now behold me." But, "In thy Seed shall all nations be blessed."[2] When God blessed Abraham, He gave the promise of me; for throughout all nations in

the blessing of Christ am I shed abroad. That Christ is the Seed of Abraham, the order of successive generations bears witness. Shortly to sum up which, Abraham begat Isaac, Isaac begat Jacob, Jacob begat twelve sons, of whom sprung the people Israel. For Jacob himself was called Israel. Among these twelve sons he begat Judah, whence the Jews have their name, of whom was born the Virgin Mary, who bore Christ. And, lo, in Christ, that is, in the seed of Abraham, that all the nations are blessed, ye see and are amazed: and do ye still fear to believe in Him, in Whom ye ought rather to have feared not to believe? What? doubt ye, or refuse ye to believe, the travail of a Virgin, whereas ye ought rather to believe that it was fitting that so God should be born Man. For this also receive ye to have been foretold by the Prophet;[3] "Behold, a Virgin shall conceive in the womb, and shall bring forth a Son, and they shall call His Name Emmanuel, which is, being interpreted, God with us." Ye will not therefore doubt of a Virgin bringing forth, if ye be willing to believe of a God being born; leaving not the governance of the world, and coming unto men in the flesh; unto His Mother bringing fruitfulness, not taking away maidenhood. For thus behoved it that He should be born as Man, albeit[4] He was ever[5] God, by which birth He might become a God unto us. Hence again the Prophet says concerning Him, "Thy Throne, O God, is for ever and ever; a sceptre of right, the sceptre of Thy Kingdom. Thou hast loved righteousness, and hated iniquity; therefore God, Thy God, hath anointed Thee with the oil of gladness above Thy fellows."[6] This anointing is spiritual, wherewith God anointed God, the Father, that is, the Son: whence called from the "Chrism," that is, from the anointing, we know Him as Christ. I am the Church, concerning whom it is said unto Him in the same Psalm, and what was future foretold as already done; "There stood at Thy right hand the Queen, in a vesture of gold, in raiment of divers colors;" that is, in the mystery of wisdom, "adorned with divers tongues." There it said unto me, "Hearken, O daughter, and see, and incline thine ear, and forget thy own people and thy father's house: for the King hath desired thy beauty: seeing that He is the Lord thy God: and the daughters of Tyre shall worship Him with gifts, thy face shall all the rich of the people entreat. All the glory of that King's daughter is within, in fringes of gold, with raiment of divers colors. There shall be brought unto the

---

[1] "Religio," (toward parents). [2] Gen. xxii. 18.

[3] Is. vii. 14; Matt. i. 23.
[4] MSS. "si"—"if." [5] Semper. [6] Ps. xlv. 6-17.

King the maidens after her; her companions shall be brought unto Thee. They shall be brought with joy and gladness, they shall be brought into the Temple of the King. Instead of thy fathers, there are born unto thee sons, thou shalt set them as princes over the whole earth. They shall be mindful of thy name, even from generation to generation. Therefore shall the people confess unto thee for ever, and for ever and ever.

6. If this Queen ye see not, now rich also with royal progeny. If she see not that fulfilled which she heard to have been promised, she, unto whom it was said, "Hear, O daughter, and see." If she hath not left the ancient rites of the world, she, unto whom it was said, "Forget thy own people and thy Father's house." If she confesses not every where Christ the Lord, she, unto whom it was said, "The King hath desired thy beauty, for He is the Lord thy God." If she sees not the cities of the nations pour forth prayers and offer gifts unto Christ, concerning Whom it was said unto her, "There shall worship Him the daughters of Tyre with gifts." If the pride also of the rich is not laid aside, and they do not entreat help of the Church, unto whom it was said, "Thy face shall all the rich of the people entreat." If He acknowledges not the King's daughter, unto Whom she was bidden to say, "Our Father, Who art in Heaven;"[1] and in her saints in the inner man she is not renewed from day to day, concerning whom it was said, "All the glory of that King's daughter is within:" although she strike upon the eyes of them also that are without with the blaze[2] of the fame of her preachers, in diversity of tongues, as "in fringes of gold, and raiment of divers colors." If there be not, now that His fame is spread abroad in every place by His good odor,[3] virgins also brought unto Christ to be consecrated, of Whom it is said, and to Whom it is said, "There shall be brought unto the King the virgins after her, her companions shall be brought unto Thee." And that they might not seem to be brought like captives, into some, as it were, prison, he says, "They shall be brought in joy and gladness, they shall be brought into the King's temple." If she brings not forth sons, that of them she may have, as it were, fathers, whom she may appoint unto herself every where as rulers, she, unto whom it is said, "Instead of thy fathers there are born unto thee sons, thou shalt set them as princes over the whole earth:" unto whose prayers their mother both

preferred and made subject, commends herself, "They shall be mindful of thy name, even from generation to generation." If, by reason of the preaching of those same fathers, wherein they have without ceasing made mention of her name, there are not so great multitudes in her gathered together, and without end in their own tongues unto her confess the praise of grace, unto whom it is said, "Therefore shall the people confess unto thee for ever, and for ever and ever." If these things are not so shown to be clear, as that the eyes of enemies find not in what direction to turn aside, where the same clearness strikes them not, so as by it to be obliged to confess what is evident: you perhaps assert with reason, that no proofs are shown to you, by seeing which you may believe those things also which you see not. But if those things, which you see, both have been foretold long before, and are so clearly fulfilled; if the truth itself makes itself clear to you, by effects[4] going before and following after, O remnant of unbelief, that ye may believe the things which you see not, blush at those things which ye see.

7. "Give heed unto me," the Church says unto you; give heed unto me, whom ye see, although to see ye be unwilling. For the faithful, who were in those times in the land of Judæa, were present at, and learnt as present, Christ's wonderful birth of a virgin, and His passion, resurrection, ascension; all His divine words and deeds. These things ye have not seen, and therefore ye refuse to believe. Therefore behold these things, fix your eyes on these things, these things which ye see reflect on, which are not told you as things past, nor foretold you as things future, but are shown you as things present. What? seemeth it to you a vain or a light thing, and think you it to be none, or a little, divine miracle, that in the name of One Crucified the whole human race runs? Ye saw not what was foretold and fulfilled concerning the human birth of Christ, "Behold, a Virgin shall conceive in the womb, and shall bear a Son;"[5] but you see the Word of God which was foretold and fulfilled unto Abraham, "In thy seed shall all nations be blessed."[6] Ye saw not what was foretold concerning the wonderful works of Christ, "Come ye, and see the works of the Lord, what wonders He hath set upon the earth:"[7] but ye see that which was foretold, "The Lord said unto Me, My Son art Thou, I have this day begotten Thee; demand of Me and I will give

---

[1] Matt. vi. 9; [2] 2 Cor. iv. 16.
[2] *Ben. conj.* "*fulgente*," for "*fulgentes*."
[3] Song of Sol. i. 3.

[4] The Prophecy might be called an "effect" as well as its fulfillment; or read "*verbis*," for "*vobis*," "clear by words going before and effects following after." For further illustration see St. Aug. on Ps. 45.
[5] Is. vii. 14.   [6] Gen. xxii. 18.   [7] Ps. xlvi. 8.

Thee nations as Thy inheritance, and as Thy possession the bounds of the earth."[1] Ye saw not that which was foretold and fulfilled concerning the Passion of Christ, "They pierced My hands and My feet, they numbered all My bones; but they themselves regarded and beheld Me; they divided among them My garments, and upon My vesture they cast the lot;"[2] but ye see that which was in the same Psalm foretold, and now is clearly fulfilled; "All the ends of the earth shall remember and be turned unto the Lord, and all the kindreds of the nations shall worship in His sight; for the kingdom is the Lord's, and He shall rule over the nations."[3] Ye saw not what was foretold and fulfilled concerning the Resurrection of Christ, the Psalm speaking, in His Person, first concerning His betrayer and persecutors: "They went forth out of doors, and spake together: against Me whispered all My enemies, against Me thought they evil for Me;" they set in order an unrighteous word against Me.[4] Where, to show that they availed nothing by slaying Him Who was about to rise again, He adds and says; "What? will not He, that sleeps, add this, that He rise again?" And a little after, when He had foretold, by means of the same prophecy, concerning His betrayer himself, that which is written in the Gospel also, "He that did eat of My bread, enlarged his heel upon Me,"[5] that is, trampled Me under foot: He straightway added, "But do Thou, O Lord, have mercy upon Me, and raise Thou Me up again, and I shall repay them." This was fulfilled, Christ slept and awoke, that is, rose again: Who through the same prophecy in another Psalm says, "I slept and took my rest; and I rose again, for the Lord will uphold Me."[6] But this ye saw not, but ye see His Church, concerning whom it is written in like manner, and fulfilled, "O Lord My God, the nations shall come unto Thee from the extremity of the earth and shall say, Truly our fathers worshipped lying images, and there is not in them any profit."[7] This certainly, whether ye will or no, ye behold; even although ye yet believe, that there either is, or was, in those idols some profit; yet certainly unnumbered peoples of the nations, after having left, or cast away, or broken in pieces such like vanities, ye have heard say, "Truly our fathers worshipped lying images, and there is not in them any profit; shall a man make gods, and, lo, they are no gods?"[8] Nor think that it was foretold that the nations should come unto some

one place of God, in that it was said, "Unto Thee shall the nations come from the extremity of the earth." Understand, if you can, that unto the God of the Christians, Who is the Supreme and True God, the peoples of the nations come, not by walking but by believing. For the same thing was by another prophet thus foretold, "The Lord," saith he, "shall prevail against them, and shall utterly destroy all the gods of the nations of the earth: and all the isles of the nations shall worship Him, each man from his place."[9] Whereas the one says, "Unto Thee all nations shall come;" this the other says, "They shall worship Him, each man from his place." Therefore they shall come unto Him, not departing from their own place, because believing in Him they shall find Him in their hearts. Ye saw not what was foretold and fulfilled concerning the ascension of Christ; "Be Thou exalted above the Heavens, O God;"[10] but ye see what follows immediately after, "And above all the earth Thy Glory." Those things concerning Christ already done and past, all of them ye have not seen; but these things present in His Church ye deny not that ye see. Both things we point out to you as foretold; but the fulfillment of both we are therefore unable to point out for you to see, because we cannot bring back into sight things past.

8. But as the wills of friends, which are not seen, are believed through tokens which are seen; thus the Church, which is now seen, is, of all things which are not seen, but which are shown forth in those writings wherein itself also is foretold, an index of the past, and a herald of the future. Because both things past, which cannot now be seen, and things present which cannot be seen all of them, at the time at which they were foretold, no one of these could then be seen. Therefore, since they have begun to come to pass as they were foretold, from those things which have come to pass unto those which are coming to pass, those things which were foretold concerning Christ and the Church have run on in an ordered series: unto which series these pertain concerning the day of Judgment, concerning the resurrection of the dead, concerning the eternal damnation of the ungodly with the devil, and concerning the eternal recompense of the godly with Christ, things which, foretold in like manner, are yet to come. Why therefore should we not believe the first and the last things which we see not, when we have, as witnesses of both, the things between, which we see, and in the books of the Prophets either hear or read both

---

[1] Ps. ii. 7, 8; Heb. i. 5 ; v. 5; Acts. xiii. 33.
[2] Ps. xxii. 16, 17, 18; John xix. 23, 24.
[3] Ps. xxii. 27, 28. [4] Ps. xli. 6-8. [5] Ps. xli. 9, 10.
[6] Ps. iv. 8. [7] Jer. xvi. 19. [8] Jer. xvi. 19, 20. [9] Zeph. ii. 11. [10] Ps. cviii. 5.

the first things, and the things between, and the last things, foretold before they came to pass? Unless haply unbelieving men judge those things to have been written by Christians, in order that those things which they already believed might have greater weight of authority, if they should be thought to have been promised before they came.

9. If they suspect this, let them examine carefully the copies[1] of our enemies the Jews. There let them read those things of which we have made mention, foretold concerning Christ in Whom we believe, and the Church whom we discern from the toilsome beginning of faith even unto the eternal blessedness of the kingdom. But, whilst they read, let them not wonder that they, whose are the books, understand not by reason of the darkness of enmity. For that they would not understand was foretold beforehand by the same Prophets; which it behoved should be fulfilled in like manner as the rest, and that by the secret and just judgment of God a due punishment should be rendered to their deserts. He indeed, Whom they crucified, and unto Whom they gave gall and vinegar, although when hanging upon the Tree, by reason of those whom He had been about to lead forth from darkness into light, He said unto the Father, "Forgive them, for they know not what they do;"[2] yet by reason of those whom through more hidden causes He had been about to desert, by the Prophet so long before foretold, "They gave Me gall for My meat, and in My thirst they gave Me vinegar to drink; let their table become a snare before them, and a recompense, and a stumbling-block: let their eyes be darkened that they see not, and ever bow Thou down their back."[3] Thus, having with them the clearest testimonies of our cause, they walk round about with eyes darkened, that by their means those testimonies may be proved, wherein they themselves are disapproved. Therefore was it brought to pass, that they should not be so blotted out, as that this same sect should altogether exist not: but it was scattered abroad upon the earth, in order that, carrying with it the prophecies of the grace conferred upon us, more surely to convince unbelievers, it might every where profit us. And this very thing which I assert, receive ye after what manner it was prophesied of: "Slay them not," saith He, "lest at any time they forget Thy law, but scatter them abroad in Thy might."[4] Therefore they were not slain, in that they forgot not those things which were read and heard among

them. For if they were altogether to forget, albeit they understand not, the Holy Scriptures, they would be slain in the Jewish ritual itself; because, when the Jews should know nothing of the Law and of the Prophets, they would be unable to profit us. Therefore they were not slain, but scattered abroad; in order that, although they should not have in faith, whence they might be saved; yet they should retain in their memory, whence we might be helped; in their books our supporters, in their hearts our enemies, in their copies our witnesses.

10. Although, even if there went before no testimonies concerning Christ and the Church, whom ought it not to move unto belief, that the Divine brightness hath on a sudden shone on the human race, when we see, (the false gods now abandoned, and their images every where broken in pieces, their temples overthrown or changed into other uses, and so many vain rites plucked out by the roots from the most inveterate usage of men,) the One True God invoked by all? And that this hath been brought to pass by One Man, by men mocked, seized, bound, scourged, smitten with the palms of the hand, reviled, crucified, slain: His disciples, (whom He chose common men,[5] and unlearned, and fishermen, and publicans, that by their means His teaching might be set forth,) proclaiming His Resurrection, His Ascension, which they asserted that they had seen, and being filled with the Holy Ghost, sounded forth this Gospel, in all tongues which they had not learned. And of them who heard them, part believed, part, believing not, fiercely withstood them who preached. Thus while they were faithful even unto death for the truth, strove not by returning evil, but by enduring, overcame not by killing, but by dying; thus was the world changed unto this religion, thus unto this Gospel were the hearts of mortals turned, of men and women, of small and great, of learned and unlearned, of wise and foolish, of mighty and weak, of noble and ignoble, of high and low, and throughout all nations the Church shed abroad so increased, that even against the Catholic faith itself there arises not any perverse sect, any kind of error, which is found so to oppose itself to Christian truth, as that it affect not and go not about to glory in the name of Christ: which very error would not be suffered to spring up throughout the earth, were it not that the very gainsaying exercised an wholesome discipline. How[6] would The Crucified have availed so greatly, had He not been God

---

[1] Codices. [2] Luke xxiii. 34.
[3] Ps. lxix. 21-23. [4] Ps. lix. 11.

[5] Idiotas. [6] Lit. "when."

that took upon Him Man, even if He had through the Prophet foretold no such things to come? But when now this so great mystery of godliness hath had its prophets and heralds going before, by whose divine voices it was afore proclaimed; and when it hath come in such manner as it was afore proclaimed, who is there so mad as to assert that the Apostles lied concerning Christ, of Whom they preached that He was come in such manner as the Prophets foretold afore that He should come, which Prophets were not silent as to true things to come concerning the Apostles themselves? For concerning these they had said, " There is neither speech nor language, whereof their voices are not heard; their sound went out into all the earth, and their words unto the ends of the world." [1] And this at any rate we see fulfilled in the world, although we have not yet seen Christ in the flesh. Who therefore, unless blinded by amazing madness, or hard and steeled by amazing obstinacy, would be unwilling to put faith in the sacred Scriptures, which have foretold the faith of the whole world?

11. But you, beloved, who possess this faith, or who have begun now newly to have it, let it be nourished and increase in you. For as things temporal have come, so long before foretold, so will things eternal also come, which are promised. Nor let them deceive you, either the vain heathen, or the false Jews, or the deceitful heretics, or also within the Catholic (Church) itself evil Christians, enemies by so much the more hurtful, as they are the more within us. For, lest on this subject also the weak should be troubled, divine prophecy hath not been silent, where in the Song of Songs the Bridegroom speaking unto the Bride, that is, Christ the Lord unto the Church, saith, "As a lily in the midst of thorns, so is my best Beloved [2] in the midst of the daughters." [3] He said not, in the midst of them that are without; but, " in the midst of daughters. Whoso hath ears to hear, let him hear:" [4] and whilst the net which is cast into the sea, [5] and gathers together all kinds of fishes, as saith the holy Gospel, is being drawn unto the shore, that is, unto the end of the world, let him separate himself from the evil fishes, in heart, not in body; by changing evil habits, not by breaking sacred nets; lest they who now seem being approved to be mingled with the reprobate, find, not life, but punishment everlasting, [6] when they shall begin on the shore to be separated.

---

[1] Ps. xix. 3, 4.

[2] *Proxima.*   [3] Song of Sol. ii. 2.
[4] Matt. xiii. 9.   [5] Matt. xiii. 47-50.
[6] Some MSS. " that they &c. may find not punishment, but life."

ST. AUGUSTIN:

ON

THE PROFIT OF BELIEVING

[DE UTILITATE CREDENDI.]

TRANSLATED BY

REV. C. L. CORNISH. M.A.

ON

THE PROFIT OF BELIEVING.

[DE UTILITATE CREDENDI.]

Retract. i. cap. 14. Moreover now at Hippo-Regius as Presbyter I wrote a book *on the Profit of Believing*, to a friend of mine who had been taken in by the Manichees, and whom I knew to be still held in that error, and to deride the Catholic school of Faith, in that men were bid believe, but not taught what was truth by a most certain method. In this book I said, &c. * * *. This book begins thus, "*Si mihi Honorate, unum atque idem videretur esse.*"

St. Augustin enumerates his book *on the Profit of Believing* first amongst those he wrote as Presbyter, to which order he was raised at Hippo about the beginning of the year 391. The person for whom he wrote had been led into error by himself, and appears to have been recovered from it, at least if he is the same who wrote to St. Augustin from Carthage about 412, proposing several questions, and to whom St. Augustin wrote his 140th Epistle. Cassiodorus calls him a Presbyter, though at that time he was not baptized. In Ep. 83, St. Augustin speaks of the death of another Honoratus, a Presbyter. Towards the end of his life he also wrote his 228th Epistle to a Bishop of Thabenna of the same name.—(*Bened. Ed.*)

The remarks in the *Retractations* are given in notes to the passages where they occur.

1. If, Honoratus, a heretic, and a man trusting heretics seemed to me one and the same, I should judge it my duty to remain silent both in tongue and pen in this matter. But now, whereas there is a very great difference between these two: forasmuch as he, in my opinion, is an heretic, who, for the sake of some temporal advantage, and chiefly for the sake of his own glory and pre-eminence, either gives birth to, or follows, false and new opinions; but he, who trusts men of this kind, is a man deceived by a certain imagination of truth and piety. This being the case, I have not thought it my duty to be silent towards you, as to my opinions on the finding and retaining of truth: with great love of which, as you know, we have burned from our very earliest youth: but it is a thing far removed from the minds of vain men, who, having too far advanced and fallen into these corporeal things, think that there is nothing else than what they perceive by those five well-known reporters of the body; and what impressions[1] and images they have received from these, they carry over with themselves, even when they essay to withdraw from the senses; and by the deadly and most deceitful rule of these think that they measure most rightly the unspeakable recesses of truth. Nothing is more easy, my dearest friend, than for one not only to say, but also to think, that he hath found out the truth; but how difficult it is in reality, you will perceive, I trust, from this letter of mine. And that this may profit you, or at any rate may in no way harm you, and also all, into whose hands it shall chance to come,

---

[1] *Plagas.*

I have both prayed, and do pray, unto God; and I hope that it will be so, forasmuch as[1] I am fully conscious that I have undertaken to write it, in a pious and friendly spirit, not as aiming at vain reputation, or trifling display.

2. It is then my purpose to prove to you, if I can, that the Manichees profanely and rashly inveigh against those, who, following the authority of the Catholic Faith, before that they are able to gaze upon that Truth, which the pure mind beholds, are by believing forearmed, and prepared for God Who is about to give them light. For you know, Honoratus, that for no other reason we fell in with such men, than because they used to say, that, apart from all terror of authority, by pure and simple reason, they would lead within to God, and set free from all error those who were willing to be their hearers. For what else constrained me, during nearly nine years, spurning the religion which had been set in me from a child by my parents, to be a follower and diligent hearer of those men,[2] save that they said that we are alarmed by superstition, and are commanded to have faith before reason, but that they urge no one to have faith, without having first discussed and made clear the truth? Who would not be enticed by such promises, especially the mind of a young man desirous of the truth, and further a proud and talkative mind by discussions of certain learned men in the school? such as they then found me, disdainful forsooth as of old wives' fables, and desirous to grasp and drink in, what they promised, the open and pure Truth? But what reason, on the other hand, recalled me, not to be altogether joined to them, so that I continued in that rank which they call of Hearers, so that I resigned not the hope and business of this world; save that I noticed that they also are rather eloquent and full in refutation of others, than abide firm and sure in proof of what is their own. But of myself what shall I say, who was already a Catholic Christian? teats which now, after very long thirst, I almost exhausted and dry, have returned to with all greediness, and with deeper weeping and groaning have shaken together and wrung them out more deeply, that so there might flow what might be enough to refresh me affected as I was, and to bring back hope of life and safety. What then shall I say of myself? You, not yet a Christian, who, through encouragement from me, execrating them greatly as you did, were hardly led to believe that you ought to listen to them and make trial of them, by what else,

I pray you, were you delighted, call to mind, I entreat you, save by a certain great presumption and promise of reasons? But because they disputed long and much with very great copiousness and vehemence concerning the errors of unlearned men, a thing which I learned too late at length to be most easy for any moderately educated man; if even of their own they implanted in us any thing, we thought that we were obliged to retain it, insomuch as there fell not in our way other things, wherein to acquiesce. So they did in our case what crafty fowlers are wont to do, who set branches smeared with bird-lime beside water to deceive thirsty birds. For they fill up and cover anyhow the other waters which are around, or fright them from them by alarming devices, that they may fall into their snares, not through choice, but want.

3. But why do I not make answer to myself, that these fair and clever similes, and charges of this nature may be poured forth against all who are teachers of any thing by any adversary, with abundance of wit and sarcasm? But I thought that I ought to insert something of this kind in my letter, in order to admonish them to give over such proceedings; so that, as he[3] says, apart from trifles of common-places, matter may contend with matter, cause with cause, reason with reason. Wherefore let them give over that saying, which they have in their mouths as though of necessity, when any one, who hath been for some long time a hearer, hath left them; "The Light hath made a passage through him." For you see, you who are my chief care, (for I am not over anxious about them,) how empty this is, and most easy for any one to find fault with. Therefore I leave this for your own wisdom to consider. For I have no fear that you will think me possessed by indwelling Light, when I was entangled in the life of this world, having a darkened hope, of beauty of wife, of pomp of riches, of emptiness of honors, and of all other hurtful and deadly pleasures. For all these, as is not unknown to you, I ceased not to desire and hope for, at the time when I was their attentive hearer. And I do not lay this to the charge of their teaching; for I also confess that they also carefully advise to shun these. But now to say that I am deserted by light, when I have turned myself from all these shadows of things, and have determined to be content with that diet merely which is necessary for health of body; but that I was enlightened and shining, at a time when I loved these things, and was wrapped up in

---

[1] Si.   [2] Confess. b. i. c. 11; b. v. c. 14.   [3] Cicero.

them, is the part of a man, to use the mildest expression, wanting in a keen insight into matters, on which he loves to speak at length. But, if you please, let us come to the cause in hand.

4. For you well know that the Manichees move the unlearned by finding fault with the Catholic Faith, and chiefly by rending in pieces and tearing the Old Testament: and they are utterly ignorant, how far[1] these things are to be taken, and how drawn out they descend with profit into the veins and marrows of souls as yet as it were but able to cry.[2] And because there are in them certain things which are some slight offense to minds ignorant and careless of themselves, (and there are very many such,) they admit of being accused in a popular way: but defended in a popular way they cannot be, by any great number of persons, by reason of the mysteries that are contained in them. But the few, who know how to do this, do not love public and much talked of controversies and disputes:[3] and on this account are very little known, save to such as are most earnest in seeking them out. Concerning then this rashness of the Manichees, whereby they find fault with the Old Testament and the Catholic Faith, listen, I entreat you, to the considerations which move me. But I desire and hope that you will receive them in the same spirit in which I say them. For God, unto Whom are known the secrets of my conscience, knows, that in this discourse I am doing nothing of evil craft; but, as I think it should be received, for the sake of proving the truth, for which one thing we have now long ago determined to live; and with incredible anxiety, lest it may have been most easy for me to err with you, but most difficult, to use no harder term, to hold the right way with you. But I venture[4] to anticipate that, in this hope, wherein I hope that you will hold with us the way of wisdom, He will not fail me, unto Whom I have been consecrated; Whom day and night I endeavor to gaze upon: and since, by reason of my sins, and by reason of past habit, having the eye of the mind wounded by strokes of feeble opinions, I know that I am without strength, I often entreat with tears, and as, after long blindness and darkness the eyes being hardly opened, and as yet, by frequent throbbing and turning away, refusing the light which yet they long after: specially if one endeavor to show to them the very sun; so it has now befallen me, who do not deny that there is a certain unspeakable and singular good of the soul,

which the mind sees; and who with tears and groaning confess that I am not yet worthy of it. He will not then fail me, if I feign nothing, if I am led by duty, if I love truth, if I esteem friendship, if I fear much lest you be deceived.

5. All that Scripture therefore, which is called the Old Testament, is handed down fourfold to them who desire to know it, according to history, according to ætiology, according to analogy, according to allegory. Do not think me silly for using Greek words. In the first place, because I have so received, nor do I dare to make known to you otherwise than I have received. Next you yourself perceive, that we have not in use terms for such things: and had I translated and made such, I should have been indeed more silly: but, were I to use circumlocution, I should be less free in treating: this only I pray you to believe, that in whatever way I err, I am not inflated or swollen in any thing that I do. Thus (for example) it is handed down according to history, when there is taught what hath been written, or what hath been done; what not done, but only written as though it had been done. According to ætiology, when it is shown for what cause any thing hath been done or said. According to analogy, when it is shown that the two Testaments, the Old and the New, are not contrary the one to the other. According to allegory, when it is taught that certain things which have been written are not to be taken in the letter, but are to be understood in a figure.

6. All these ways our Lord Jesus Christ and His Apostles used. For when it had been objected that His disciples had plucked the ears of corn on the sabbath-day, the instance was taken from history; "Have ye not read," saith He, "what David did when he was an hungered, and they that were with him; how he entered into the house of God, and did eat the shewbread, which was not lawful for him to eat, neither for them that were with him, but only for the priests?"[5] But the instance pertains to ætiology, that, when Christ had forbidden a wife to be put away, save for the cause of fornication, and they, who asked Him, had alleged that Moses had granted permission after a writing of divorcement had been given, This, saith He, "Moses did because of the hardness of your heart."[6] For here a reason was given, why that had been well allowed by Moses for a time; that this command of Christ might seem to show that now the times were other. But it were long to explain the changes of these times, and

1 *Quatenus.*   2 *Vagientium.*
3 *Famigerula.*   4 *Præsumo.*   5 Matt. xii. 3. 4.   6 Mat. xix. 8.

their order arranged and settled by a certain marvellous appointment of Divine Providence.

7. And further, analogy, whereby the agreement of both Testaments is plainly seen, why shall I say that all have made use of, to whose authority they yield; whereas it is in their power to consider with themselves, how many things they are wont to say have been inserted in the divine Scriptures by certain, I know not who, corrupters of truth? Which speech of theirs I always thought to be most weak, even at the time that I was their hearer: nor I alone, but you also, (for I well remember,) and all of us, who essayed to exercise a little more care in forming a judgment than the crowd of hearers. But now, after that many things have been expounded and made clear to me, which used chiefly to move me: those, I mean, wherein their discourse for the most part boasts itself, and expatiates the more freely, the more safely it can do so as having no opponent; it seems to me that there is no assertion of theirs more shameless, or (to use a milder phrase) more careless and weak, than that the divine Scriptures have been corrupted; whereas there are no copies in existence, in a matter of so recent date, whereby they can prove it. For were they to assert, that they thought not that they ought thoroughly to receive them, because they had been written by persons, who they thought had not written the truth; any how their refusal[1] would be more right, or their error more natural.[2] For this is what they have done in the case of the Book which is inscribed the Acts of the Apostles. And this device of theirs, when I consider with myself, I cannot enough wonder at. For it is not the want of wisdom in the men that I complain of in this matter, but the want of ordinary understanding.[3] For that book hath so great matters, which are like what they receive, that it seems to me great folly to refuse to receive this book also, and if any thing offend them there to call it false and inserted. Or, if such language is shameless, as it is why in the Epistles of Paul, why in the four books of the Gospel, do they think that they[4] are of any avail, in which I am not sure but that there are in proportion many more things, than could be in that book, which they will have believed to have been interpolated by falsifiers. But fosooth this is what I believe to be the case, and I ask of you to consider it with me with as calm and serene a judgment as possible. For you know that, essaying to bring the person of their founder

Manichæus into the number of the Apostles, they say that the Holy Spirit, Whom the Lord promised His disciples that He would send, hath come to us through him. Therefore, were they to receive those Acts of the Apostles, in which the coming of the Holy Spirit is plainly set forth,[5] they could not find how to say that it was interpolated. For they will have it that there were some, I know not who, falsifiers of the divine Books before the times of Manichæus himself; and that they were falsified by persons who wished to combine the Law of the Jews with the Gospel. But this they cannot say concerning the Holy Spirit, unless haply they assert that those persons divined, and set in their books what should be brought forward against Manichæus, who should at some future time arise, and say that the Holy Spirit had been sent through him. But concerning the Holy Spirit we will speak somewhat more plainly in another place. Now let us return to my purpose.

8. For that both history of the Old Testament, and ætiology, and analogy are found in the New Testament, has been, as I think, sufficiently proved: it remains to show this of allegory. Our Redeemer Himself in the Gospel uses allegory out of the Old Testament. "This generation," saith He, "seeketh a sign, and there shall not be given it save the sign of Jonas the prophet. For as Jonas was three days and three nights in the whale's belly, so also shall the Son of Man be three days and three nights in the heart of the earth."[6] For why should I speak of the Apostle Paul, who in his first Epistle to the Corinthians shows that even the very history of the Exodus was an allegory of the future Christian People. "But I would not that ye should be ignorant, brethren, how that all our fathers were under the cloud, and all passed through the sea, and were all baptized into Moses, in the cloud, and in the sea, and did all eat the same spiritual meat, and did all drink the same spiritual drink; for they drank of the spiritual Rock that followed with them; and that Rock was Christ. But in the more part of them God was not well pleased: for they were overthrown in the wilderness. But these things were figures of us,[7] that we be not lustful of evil things, as they also lusted. Neither let us worship idols, as certain of them; as it is written, The people sat down to eat and drink, and rose up to play. Neither let us commit fornication, as certain of them committed, and fell in one day three and twenty thousand men. Neither let us tempt

---

[1] *Tergiversatio.*   [2] *Humanior.*
[3] *Cor mediocre.*   [4] *Ea.*

[5] Acts ii. 2, 3, 4.   [6] Matt. xii. 39, 40.
[7] *Figuræ nostra* τύποι ἡμῶν Gr. *in figura facta sunt nostri.* Vulg.

Christ, as certain of them tempted, and perished of serpents. Neither murmur we, as certain of them murmured, and perished of the destroyer. But all these things happened unto them in a figure.[1] But they were written for our admonition, upon whom the ends of the world have come."[2] There is also in the Apostle a certain allegory, which indeed greatly relates to the cause in hand, for this reason that they themselves are wont to bring it forward, and make a display of it in disputing. For the same Paul says to the Galatians, "For it is written, that Abraham had two sons, one of a bond-maid, and one of a free woman. But he who was of the bond-maid was born after the flesh: but he who was of the free woman, by promise: which things were spoken by way of allegory.[3] For these are the two Testaments, one of Mount Sinai gendering unto bondage, which is Agar: for Sinai is a mount in Arabia, which bordereth[4] upon that Jerusalem which now is, and is in bondage with her children. But that Jerusalem which is above is free, which is the mother of us all."[5]

9. Here therefore these men too evil, while they essay to make void the Law, force us to approve these Scriptures. For they mark what is said, that they who are under the Law are in bondage, and they keep flying above the rest that last saying, "Ye are made empty[6] of Christ, as many of you as are justified in the Law; ye have fallen from Grace."[7] We grant that all these things are true, and we say that the Law is not necessary, save for them unto whom bondage is yet profitable: and that the Law was on this account profitably enacted, in that men, who could not be recalled from sins by reason, needed to be restrained by such a Law, that is to say, by the threats and terrors of those punishments which can be seen by fools: from which when the Grace of Christ sets us free, it condemns not that Law, but invites us at length to yield obedience to its love, not to be slaves to the fear of the Law. Itself is Grace, that is free gift,[8] which they understand not to have come to them from God, who still desire to be under the bonds of the Law. Whom Paul deservedly rebukes as unbelievers, because they do not believe that now through our Lord Jesus they have been set free from that bondage, under which they were placed for a certain time by the most just appointment of God. Hence is that saying of the same Apostle, "For the Law was our schoolmaster in Christ."[9] He. therefore gave to men a

schoolmaster to fear, Who after gave a Master to love. And yet in these precepts and commands of the Law, which now it is not allowed Christians to use, such as either the Sabbath, or Circumcision, or Sacrifices, and if there be any thing of this kind, so great mysteries are contained, as that every pious person may understand, there is nothing more deadly than that whatever is there be understood to the letter, that is, to the word:[10] and nothing more healthful than that it be unveiled in the Spirit. Hence it is: "The letter killeth, but the Spirit quickeneth."[11] Hence it is, "That same veil remaineth in the reading of the Old Testament, which veil is not taken away; since it is made void in Christ."[12] For there is made void in Christ, not the Old Testament, but its veil: that so through Christ that may be understood, and, as it were, laid bare, which without Christ is obscure and covered. Forasmuch as the same Apostle straightway adds, "But when thou shalt have passed over to Christ, the veil shall be taken away."[13] For he saith not, the Law shall be taken away, or, the Old Testament. Not therefore through the Grace of the Lord, as though useless things were there hidden, have they been taken away; but rather the covering whereby useful things were covered. In this manner all they are dealt with, who earnestly and piously, not disorderly and shamelessly, seek the sense of those Scriptures, and they are carefully shown both the order of events, and the causes of deeds and words, and so great agreement of the Old Testament with the New, that there is left no jot[14] that agrees not; and so great secrets of figures, that all the things that are drawn forth by interpretation force them to confess that they are wretched, who will to condemn these before they learn them.

10. But, passing over in the mean while the depth of knowledge, to deal with you as I think I ought to deal with my intimate friend; that is, as I have myself power, not as I have wondered at the power of very learned men; there are three kinds of error, whereby men err, when they read anything. I will speak of them one by one. The first kind is, wherein that which is false is thought true, whereas the writer thought otherwise. A second kind, although not so extensive, yet not less hurtful, when that, which is false, is

---

[1] τύποι   [2] 1 Cor. x. 1-11. (See R.R.)   [3] ἀλληγορούμενα Gr.
[4] Confinis.   [5] Gal. iv. 22-26.   [6] Ventilant.
[7] Gal. v. 4.   [8] Beneficium.   [9] Gal. iii. 24. in Christo.

[10] Ad verbum.
[11] Vid. Retr. l. i. c. 14. n. l. "In this book I said, 'in which &c. but I have otherwise explained those words of the Apostle Paul, and as far a I can see, or rather as is apparent from the plain state of the case, much more suitably, in the book entitled De Spiritu et Literâ, though this sense too is not to be utterly rejected." 2 Cor. iii. 6.
[12] 2 Cor. iii. 14. quoniam, ὅτι Gr. "which veil," Eng. T.
[13] 2 Cor. iii. 16.   [14] Apex.

thought true, yet the thought is the same as that of the writer. A third kind, when from the writing of another some truth is understood, whereas the writer understood it not. In which kind there is no little profit, rather, if you consider carefully, the whole entire fruit of reading. An instance of the first kind is, as if any one, for example, should say and believe that Rhadamanthus hears and judges the causes of the dead in the realms below, because he hath so read in the strain of Maro.[1] For this one errs in two ways: both in that he believes a thing not to be believed, and also in that he, whom he reads, is not to be thought to have believed it. The second kind may be thus noticed: if one, because Lucretius writes that the soul is formed of atoms, and that after death it is dissolved into the same atoms and perishes, were to think this to be true and what he ought to believe. For this one also is not less wretched, if, in a matter of so great moment, he hath persuaded himself of that which is false, as certain; although Lucretius, by whose books he hath been deceived, held this opinion. For what doth it profit this one to be assured of the meaning of the author, whereas he hath chosen him to himself not so as through him to escape error, but so as with him to err. An instance suited to the third kind is, if one, after having read in the books of Epicurus some place wherein he praises continence, were to assert that he had made the chief good to consist in virtue, and that therefore he is not to be blamed. For how is this man injured by the error of Epicurus, what though Epicurus believe that bodily pleasure is the chief good of man: whereas he hath not surrendered up himself to so base and hurtful an opinion, and is pleased with Epicurus for no other reason, than that he thinks him not to have held sentiments which ought not to be holden. This error is not only natural to man,[2] but often also most worthy of a man. For what, if word were brought to me, concerning some one whom I loved, that, when now he was of bearded age, he had said, in the hearing of many, that he was so pleased with boyhood and childhood, as even to swear that he wished to live after the same fashion, and that that was so proved to me, as that I should be shameless to deny it: I should not, should I, seem worthy of blame, if I thought that, in saying this, he wished to show, that he was pleased with the innocence, and with the temper of mind alien from those desires in which the race of man is wrapped up, and from this circumstance should love him yet more and more, than I used to love him before; although perhaps he had been foolish enough to love in the age of children a certain freedom in play and food, and an idle ease? For suppose that he had died after this report had reached me, and that I had been unable to make any inquiry of him, so as for him to open his meaning; would there be any one so shameless as to be angry with me, for praising the man's purpose and wish, through those very words which I had heard? What, that even a just judge of matters would not hesitate perhaps to praise my sentiment and wish, in that both I was pleased with innocence, and, as man of man, in a matter of doubt, preferred to think well, when it was in my power also to think ill?

11. And, this being so, hear also just so many conditions and differences of the same Scriptures. For it must be that just so many meet us. For either any one hath written profitably, and is not profitably understood by some one: or both take place unprofitably: or the reader understands profitably, whereas he, who is read, hath written contrariwise. Of these the first I blame not, the last I regard not. For neither can I blame the man, who without any fault of his own hath been ill understood; nor can I be distressed at any one being read, who hath failed to see the truth, when I see that the readers are no way injured. There is then one kind most approved, and as it were most cleansed, when both the things written are well, and are taken in a good sense by the readers. And yet that also is still further divided into two: for it doth not altogether shut out error. For it generally comes to pass, that, when a writer hath held a good sense, the reader also holds a good sense; still other than he, and often better, often worse, yet profitably. But when both we hold the same sense as he whom we read, and that is every way suited to right conduct of life, there is the fullest possible measure of truth, and there is no place opened for error from any other quarter. And this kind is altogether very rare, when what we read is matter of extreme obscurity: nor can it, in my opinion, be clearly known, but only believed. For by what proofs shall I so gather the will of a man who is absent or dead, as that I can swear to it: when, even if he were questioned being present, there might be many things, which, if he were no ill man, he would most carefully hide? But I think that it hath nothing to do towards learning the matter of fact, of what character the writer was; yet is he most fairly believed good, whose writings have benefited the human race and posterity.

Virg. Æn. vi. 566-569.   Humanus.

12. Wherefore I would that they would tell me, in what kind they place the, supposed, error of the Catholic Church. If in the first, it is altogether a grave charge; but it needs not a far-fetched defense: for it is enough to deny that we so understand, as the persons, who inveigh against us, suppose. If in the second, the charge is not less grave; but they shall be refuted by the same saying. If in the third, it is no charge at all. Proceed, and next consider the Scriptures themselves. For what objection do they raise against the books of (what is called) the Old Testament? Is it that they are good, but are understood by us in an ill sense? But they themselves do not receive them. Or is it that they are neither good, nor are well understood? But our defense above is enough to drive them from this position. Or is it this that they will say, although they are understood by you in a good sense, yet they are evil? What is this other than to acquit living adversaries, with whom they have to do, and to accuse men long ago dead, with whom they have no strife? I indeed believe that both those men profitably delivered to memory all things, and that they were great and divine. And that that Law was published, and framed by the command and will of God: and of this, although I have but very slight knowledge of books of that kind, yet I can easily persuade any, if there apply to me a mind fair and no way obstinate: and this I will do, when you shall grant to me your ears and mind well disposed: this however when it shall be in my power: but now is it not enough for me, however that matter may stand, not to have been deceived?

13. I call to witness, Honoratus, my conscience, and God Who hath His dwelling in pure souls, that I account nothing more prudent, chaste, and religious, than are all those Scriptures, which under the name of the Old Testament the Catholic Church retains. You wonder at this, I am aware. For I cannot hide that we were far otherwise persuaded. But there is indeed nothing more full of rashness, (which at that time, being boys, we had in us,) than in the case of each several book, to desert expounders, who profess that they hold them, and that they can deliver them to their scholars, and to seek their meaning from those, who, I know not from what cause compelling, have proclaimed a most bitter war against the framers and authors of them. For who ever thought that the hidden and dark books of Aristotle were to be expounded to him by one who was the enemy of Aristotle; to speak of these systems of teaching, wherein a reader may perhaps err without sacrilege? Who, in fine, willed to read or

learn the geometrical writings of Archimedes, under Epicurus as a master; against which Epicurus used to argue with great obstinacy, so far as I judge, understanding them not at all? What are those Scriptures of the law most plain, against which, as though set forth in public, these men make their attack in vain and to no purpose? And they seem to me to be like that weak woman, whom these same men are wont to mock at, who enraged at the sun being extolled to her, and recommended as an object of worship by a certain female Manichee, being as she was simpleminded and of a religious spirit, leaped up in haste, and often striking with her foot that spot on which the sun through the window cast light, began to cry out, Lo, I trample on the sun and your God: altogether after a foolish and womanish manner; Who denies it? But do not those men seem to you to be such, who, in matters which they understand not, either wherefore, or altogether of what kind they are, although like to matters cast in the way,[1] yet to such as understand them exact[2] and divine, rending them with great onset of speech and reproaches, think that they are effecting something, because the unlearned applaud them? Believe me, whatever there is in these Scriptures, it is lofty and divine: there is in them altogether truth, and a system of teaching most suited to refresh and renew minds: and clearly so ordered in measure, as that there is no one but may draw thence, what is enough for himself, if only he approach to draw with devotion and piety, as true religion demands. To prove this to you, needs many reasons and a longer discourse. For first I must so treat with you as that you may not hate the authors themselves; next, so as that you may love them: and this I must treat in any other way, rather than by expounding their meanings and words. For this reason, because in case we hated Virgil, nay, rather in case we loved him not, before understanding him, by the commendation of our forefathers, we should never be satisfied on those questions about him without number, by which grammarians are wont to be disquieted and troubled; nor should we listen willingly to one who solved these at the same time praising him; but should favor that one who by means of these essayed to show that he had erred and doated. But now, whereas many essay to open these, and each in a different way according to his capacity, we applaud these in preference, through whose exposition the poet is found better, who is believed, even by those who do not

---

23

understand him, not only in nothing to have offended, but also to have sung nothing but what was worthy of praise. So that in some minute question, we are rather angry with the master who fails, and has not what to answer, than think him silent through any fault in Maro. And now, if, in order to defend himself, he should wish to assert a fault in so great an author, hardly will his scholars remain with him, even after they have paid his fee. How great matter were it, that we should shew like good will towards them, of whom it hath been confirmed by so long time of old that the Holy Spirit spake by them? But, forsooth, we youths of the greatest understanding, and marvellous searchers out of reasons, without having at least unrolled these writings, without having sought teachers, without having somewhat chided our own dullness, lastly, without having yielded our heart even in a measure[1] to those who have willed that writings of this kind be so long read, kept, and handled through the whole world; have thought that nothing in them is to be believed, moved by the speech of those who are unfriendly and hostile to them, with whom, under a false promise of reason, we should be compelled to believe and cherish thousands of fables.

14. But now I will proceed with what I have begun, if I can, and I will so treat with you, as not in the mean while to lay open the Catholic Faith, but, in order that they may search out its great mysteries, to show to those who have a care for their souls, hope of divine fruit, and of the discerning of truth. No one doubts of him who seeks true religion, either that he already believes that there is an immortal soul for that religion to profit, or that he also wishes to find that very thing in this same religion. Therefore all religion is for the sake of the soul; for howsoever the nature of the body may be, it causes no care or anxiety, especially after death, to him, whose soul possesses that whereby it is blessed. For the sake of the soul, therefore, either alone or chiefly, hath true religion, if there be any such, been appointed. But this soul, (I will consider for what reason, and I confess the matter to be most obscure,) yet errs, and is foolish, as we see, until it attain to and perceive wisdom, and perhaps this very [wisdom] is true religion. I am not, am I, sending you to fables? I am not, am I, forcing you to believe rashly? I say that our soul entangled and sunk in error and folly seeks the way of truth, if there be any such. If this be not your case, pardon me, I pray,

and share with me your wisdom; but if you recognize in yourself what I say, let us, I entreat, together seek the truth.

15. Put the case that we have not as yet heard a teacher of any religion. Lo we have undertaken a new matter and business. We must seek, I suppose, them who profess this matter, if it have any existence. Suppose that we have found different persons holding different opinions, and through their difference of opinions seeking to draw persons each one to himself: but that, in the mean while, there are certain pre-eminent from being much spoken of, and from having possession of nearly all peoples. Whether these hold the truth, is a great question: but ought we not to make full trial of them first, in order that, so long as we err, being as we are men, we may seem to err with the human race itself?

16. But it will be said, the truth is with some few; therefore you already know what it is, if you know with whom it is. Said I not a little above, that we were in search of it as unlearned men? But if from the very force of truth you conjecture that few possess it, but know not who they are; what if it is thus, that there are so few who know the truth, as that they hold the multitude by their authority, whence the small number may set itself free, and, as it were, strain itself[2] forth into those secrets? Do we not see how few attain the highest eloquence, whereas through the whole world the schools of rhetoricians are resounding with troops of young men? What, do they, as many as desire to turn out good orators, alarmed at the multitude of the unlearned, think that they are to bestow their labor on the orations of Cæcilius, or Erucius, rather than those of Tullius? All aim at these, which are confirmed by authority of our forefathers. Crowds of unlearned persons essay to learn the same, which by the few learned are received as to be learned: yet very few attain, yet fewer practise, the very fewest possible become famous. What, if true religion be some such thing? What if a multitude of unlearned persons attend the Churches, and yet that be no proof, that therefore no one is made perfect by these mysteries? And yet, if they who studied eloquence were as few as the few who are eloquent, our parents would never believe that we ought to be committed to such masters. Whereas, then, we have been called to these studies by a multitude, which is numerous in that portion of it which is made up of the unlearned, so as to become enamored of that which few can attain unto; why are we unwill-

---

[1] *Mediocri corde.*

[2] *Eliquare.*

ing to be in the same case in religion, which perhaps we despise with great danger to our soul? For if the truest and purest worship of God, although it be found with a few, be yet found with those, with whom a multitude, albeit wrapped up in lusts, and removed far from purity of understanding, agrees; (and who can doubt that this may happen?) I ask, if one were to charge us with rashness and folly, that we seek not diligently with them who teach it, that, which we are greatly anxious to discover, what can we answer? [Shall we say,] I was deterred by numbers? Why from the pursuit of liberal arts, which hardly bring any profit to this present life; why from search after money? Why from attaining unto honor; why, in fine, from gaining and keeping good health; lastly, why from the very aim at a happy life; whereas all are engaged in these, few excel; were you deterred by no numbers?

17. "But they seemed there to make absurd statements." On whose assertion? Forsooth on that of enemies, for whatever cause, for whatever reason, for this is not now the question, still enemies. Upon reading, I found it so of myself. Is it so? Without having received any instruction in poetry, you would not dare to essay to read Terentianus Maurus without a master: Asper, Cornutus, Donatus, and others without number are needed, that any poet whatever may be understood, whose strains seem to court even the applause of the theatre; do you in the case of those books, which, however they may be, yet by the confession of well-nigh the whole human race are commonly reported to be sacred and full of divine things, rush upon them without a guide, and dare to deliver an opinion on them without a teacher; and, if there meet you any matters, which seem absurd, do not accuse rather your own dullness, and mind decayed by the corruption of this world, such as is that of all that are foolish, than those [books] which haply cannot be understood by such persons! You should seek some one at once pious and learned, or who by consent of many was said to be such, that you might be both bettered by his advice, and instructed by his learning. Was he not easy to find? He should be searched out with pains. Was there no one in the country in which you lived? What cause could more profitably force to travel? Was he quite hidden, or did he not exist on the continent[1]? One should cross the sea. If across the sea he was not found in any place near to us, you should proceed even as far as those lands, in which the things related in those books are

said to have taken place. What, Honoratus, have we done of this kind? And yet a religion perhaps the most holy, (for as yet I am speaking as though it were matter of doubt,) the opinion whereof hath by this time taken possession of the whole world, we wretched boys condemned at our own discretion and sentence. What if those things which in those same Scriptures seem to offend some unlearned persons, were so set there for this purpose, that when things were read of such as are abhorrent from the feeling of ordinary men, not to say of wise and holy men, we might with much more earnestness seek the hidden meaning. Perceive you not how the Catamite of the Bucolics,[2] for whom the rough shepherd gushed forth into tears, men essay to interpret, and affirm that the boy Alexis, on whom Plato also is said to have composed a love strain, hath some great meaning or other, but escapes the judgment of the unlearned; whereas without any sacrilege a poet however rich may seem to have published wanton songs?

18. But in truth was there either decree of any law, or power of gainsayers, or vile character of persons consecrated, or shameful report, or newness of institution, or hidden profession, to recall us from, and forbid us, the search? There is nothing of these. All laws divine and human allow us to seek the Catholic Faith; but to hold and exercise it is allowed us at any rate by human law, even if so long as we are in error there be a doubt concerning divine law; no enemy alarms our weakness, (although truth and the salvation of the soul, in case being diligently sought it be not found where it may with most safety, ought to be sought at any risk); the degrees of all ranks and powers most devotedly minister to this divine worship; the name of religion is most honorable and most famous. What, I pray, hinders to search out and discuss with pious and careful enquiry, whether there be here that which it must needs be few know and guard in entire purity, although the goodwill and affection of all nations conspire in its favor?

19. The case standing thus, suppose, as I said, that we are now for the first time seeking unto what religion we shall deliver up our souls, for it to cleanse and renew them; without doubt we must begin with the Catholic Church. For by this time there are more Christians, than if the Jews and idolaters be added together. But of these same Christians, whereas there are several heresies, and all wish to appear Catholics, and call all others besides themselves heretics, there is one

---

[1] Continenti.   [2] Virg. Ecl. ii.

Church, as all allow: if you consider the whole world, more full filled in number; but, as they who know affirm, more pure also in truth than all the rest. But the question of truth is another; but, what is enough for such as are in search, there is one Catholic, to which different heresies give different names, whereas they themselves are called each by names of their own, which they dare not deny. From which may be understood, by judgment of umpires who are hindered by no favor, to which is to be assigned the name Catholic, which all covet. But, that no one may suppose that it is to be made matter of over garrulous or unnecessary discussion, this is at any rate one, in which human laws themselves also are in a certain way Christian. I do not wish any prejudgment to be formed from this fact, but I account it a most favorable commencement for enquiry. For we are not to fear lest the true worship of God, resting on no strength of its own, seem to need to be supported by them whom it ought to support: but, at any rate, it is perfect happiness, if the truth may be there found, where it is most safe both to search for it and to hold it: in case it cannot, then at length, at whatever risk, we must go and search some other where.

20. Having then laid down these principles, which, as I think, are so just that I ought to win this cause before you, let who will be my adversary, I will set forth to you, as I am able, what way I followed, when I was searching after true religion in that spirit, in which I have now set forth that it ought to be sought. For upon leaving you and crossing the sea, now delaying and hesitating, what I ought to hold, what to let go; which delay rose upon me every day the more, from the time that I was a hearer of that man,[1] whose coming was promised to us, as you know, as if from heaven, to explain all things which moved us, and found him, with the exception of a certain eloquence, such as the rest; being now settled in Italy, I reasoned and deliberated greatly with myself, not whether I should continue in that sect, into which I was sorry that I had fallen, but in what way I was to find the truth, my sighs through love of which are known to no one better than to yourself. Often it seemed to me that it could not be found, and huge waves of my thoughts would roll toward deciding in favor of the Academics. Often again, with what power I had, looking into the human soul, with so much life, with so much intelligence, with so much clearness, I thought that the truth lay not

hid, save that in it the way of search lay hid, and that this same way must be taken from some divine authority. It remained to enquire what was that authority, where in so great dissensions each promised that he would deliver it. Thus there met me a wood, out of which there was no way, which I was very loath to be involved in: and amid these things, without any rest, my mind was agitated through desire of finding the truth. However, I continued to unsew myself more and more from those whom now I had proposed to leave. But there remained nothing else, in so great dangers, than with words full of tears and sorrow to entreat the Divine Providence to help me. And this I was content to do: and now certain disputations of the Bishop of Milan[2] had almost moved me to desire, not without some hope, to enquire into many things concerning the Old Testament itself, which, as you know, we used to view as accursed, having been ill commended to us. And I had decided to be a Catechumen in the Church, unto which I had been delivered by my parents, until such time as I should either find what I wished, or should persuade myself that it needed not to be sought. Therefore had there been one who could teach me, he would find me at a very critical moment most fervently disposed and very apt to learn. If you see that you too have been long affected in this way, therefore, and with a like care for thy soul, and if now you seem to yourself to have been tossed to and fro enough, and wish to put an end to labors of this kind, follow the pathway of Catholic teaching, which hath flowed down from Christ Himself through the Apostles even unto us, and will hereafter flow down to posterity.

21. This, you will say, is ridiculous, whereas all profess to hold and teach this: all heretics make this profession, I cannot deny it; but so, as that they promise to those whom they entice, that they will give them a reason concerning matters the most obscure: and on this account chiefly charge the Catholic [Church], that they who come to her are enjoined to believe; but they make it their boast, that they impose not a yoke of believing, but open a fount of teaching. You answer, What could be said, that should pertain more to their praise? It is not so. For this they do, without being endued with any strength, but in order to conciliate to themselves a crowd by the name of reason: on the promise of which the human soul naturally is pleased, and, without considering its own

---

[1] i. e. Faustus. v. Conf. b. v. c. vi. § 10.

[2] i. e. S. Ambrose. v. Conf. b. v. c. xiii. xiv. § 23, 24, 25.

strength and state of health, by seeking the food of the sound, which is ill entrusted save to such as are in health, rushes upon the poisons of them who deceive. For true religion, unless those things be believed, which each one after, if he shall conduct himself well and shall be worthy, attains unto and understands, and altogether without a certain weighty power of authority, can in no way be rightly entered upon.

22. But perhaps you seek to have some reason given you on this very point, such as may persuade you, that you ought not to be taught by reason before faith. Which may easily be done, if only you make yourself a fair hearer. But, in order that it may be done suitably, I wish you as it were to answer my questions; and, first, to tell me, why you think that one ought not to believe. Because, you say, credulity, from which men are called credulous, in itself, seems to me to be a certain fault: otherwise we should not use to cast this as a term of reproach. For if a suspicious man is in fault, in that he suspects things not ascertained; how much more a credulous man, who herein differs from a suspicious man, that the one allows some doubt, the other none, in matters which he knows not. In the mean while I accept this opinion and distinction. But you know that we are not wont to call a person even curious without some reproach; but we call him studious even with praise. Wherefore observe, if you please, what seems to you to be the difference between these two. This surely, you answer, that, although both be led by great desire to know, yet the curious man seeks after things that no way pertain to him, but the studious man, on the contrary, seeks after what pertain to him. But, because we deny not that a man's wife and children, and their health, pertain unto him; if any one, being settled abroad, were to be careful to ask all comers, how his wife and children are and fare, he is surely led by great desire to know, and yet we call not this man studious, who both exceedingly wishes to know, and that (in) matters which very greatly pertain unto him. Wherefore you now understand that the definition of a studious person falters in this point, that every studious person wishes to know what pertain to himself, and yet not every one, who makes this his business, is to be called studious; but he who with all earnestness seeks those things which pertain unto the liberal culture and adornment of the mind. Yet we rightly call him one who studies,[1] especially if we add what he studies

to hear. For we may call him even studious of his own (family) if he love only his own (family), we do not however, without some addition, think him worthy of the common name of the studious. But one who was desirous to hear how his family were I should not call studious of hearing, unless taking pleasure in the good report, he should wish to hear it again and again: but one who studied, even if only once. Now return to the curious person, and tell me, if any one should be willing to listen to some tale, such as would no way profit him, that is, of matters that pertain not to him: and that not in an offensive way and frequently, but very seldom and with great moderation, either at a feast, or in some company, or meeting of any kind; would he seem to you curious? I think not: but at any rate he would certainly seem to have a care for that matter, to which he was willing to listen. Wherefore the definition of a curious person also must be corrected by the same rule as that of a studious person. Consider therefore whether the former statements also do not need to be corrected. For why should not both he, who at some time suspects something, be unworthy the name of a suspicious person; and he who at some time believes something, of a credulous person? Thus as there is very great difference between one who studies any matter, and the absolutely studious; and again between him who hath a care and the curious; so is there between him who believes and the credulous.

23. But you will say, consider now whether we ought to believe in religion. For, although we grant that it is one thing to believe, another to be credulous, it does not follow that it is no fault to believe in matters of religion. For what if it be a fault both to believe and to be credulous, as (it is) both to be drunk and to be a drunkard? Now he who thinks this certain, it seems to me can have no friend; for, if it is base to believe any thing, either he acts basely who believes a friend, or in nothing believing a friend I see not how he can call either him or himself a friend. Here perhaps you may say, I grant that we must believe something at some time; now make plain, how in the case of religion it be not base to believe before one knows. I will do so, if I can. Wherefore I ask of you, which you esteem the graver fault, to deliver religion to one unworthy, or to believe what is said by them who deliver it. If you understand not whom I call unworthy, I call him, who approaches with feigned breast. You grant, as I suppose, that it is more blameable to unfold unto such an one whatever holy secrets there are, than to believe religious

men affirming any thing on the matter of religion itself. For it would be unbecoming you to make any other answer. Wherefore now suppose him present, who is about to deliver to you a religion, in what way shall you assure him, that you approach with a true mind, and that, so far as this matter is concerned, there is in you no fraud or feigning? You will say, your own good conscience that you are no way feigning, asserting this with words as strong as you can, but yet with words. For you cannot lay open man to man the hiding places of your soul, so that you may be thoroughly known. But if he shall say, Lo, I believe you, but is it not more fair that you also believe me, when, if I hold any truth, you are about to receive, I about to give, a benefit? what will you answer, save that you must believe?

24. But you say, Were it not better that you should give me a reason, that, wherever that shall lead me, I may follow without any rashness? Perhaps it were: but, it being so great a matter, that you are by reason to come to the knowledge of God, do you think that all are qualified to understand the reasons, by which the human soul is led to know God, or many, or few? Few I think, you say. Do you believe that you are in the number of these? It is not for me, you say, to answer this. Therefore you think it is for him to believe you in this also: and this indeed he does: only do you remember, that he hath already twice believed you saying things uncertain; that you are unwilling to believe him even once admonishing you in a religious spirit. But suppose that it is so, and that you approach with a true mind to receive religion, and that you are one of few men in such sense as to be able to take in the reasons by which the Divine Power [1] is brought into certain knowledge; what? do you think that other men, who are not endued with so serene a disposition, are to be denied religion? or do you think that they are to be led gradually by certain steps unto those highest inner recesses? You see clearly which is the more religious. For you cannot think that any one whatever in a case where he desires so great a thing, ought by any means to be abandoned or rejected. But do you not think, that, unless he do first believe that he shall attain unto that which he purposes; and do yield his mind as a suppliant; and, submitting to certain great and necessary precepts, do by a certain course of life thoroughly cleanse it, that he will not otherwise attain the things that are purely true? Certainly you think

so. What, then, is the case of those, (of whom I already believe you to be one,) who are able most easily to receive divine secrets by sure reason, will it, I ask, be to them any hindrance at all, if they so come as they who at the first believe? I think not. But yet, you say, what need to delay them? Because although they will in no way harm themselves by what is done, yet they will harm the rest by the precedent. For there is hardly one who has a just notion of his own power: but he who has a less notion must be roused; he who has a greater notion must be checked: that neither the one be broken by despair, nor the other carried headlong by rashness. And this is easily done, if even they, who are able to fly, (that they be not alluring the occasion of any into danger,) are forced for a short time to walk where the rest also may walk with safety. This is the forethought of true religion: this the command of God: this what hath been handed down from our blessed forefathers, this what hath been preserved even unto us: to wish to distrust and overthrow this, is nothing else than to seek a sacrilegious way unto true religion. And whoso do this, not even if what they wish be granted to them are they able to arrive at the point at which they aim. For whatever kind of excellent genius they have, unless God be present, they creep on the ground. But He is then present, if they, who are aiming at God, have a regard for their fellow men. Than which step there can be found nothing more sure Heavenward. I for my part cannot resist this reasoning, for how can I say that we are to believe nothing without certain knowledge? whereas both there can be no friendship at all, unless there be believed something which cannot be proved by some reason, and often stewards, who are slaves, are trusted by their masters without any fault on their part. But in religion what can there be more unfair than that the ministers [2] of God believe us when we promise an unfeigned mind, and we are unwilling to believe them when they enjoin us any thing. Lastly, what way can there be more healthful, than for a man to become fitted to receive the truth by believing those things, which have been appointed by God to serve for the previous culture and treatment of the mind? Or, if you be already altogether fitted, rather to make some little circuit where it is safest to tread, than both to cause yourself danger, and to be a precedent for rashness to other men?

25. Wherefore it now remains to consider, in what manner we ought not to follow these,

---

[1] *Vis divina.*

[2] *Antistites.*

who profess that they will lead by reason. For how we may without fault follow those who bid us to believe, hath been already said: but unto these who make promises of reason certain think that they come, not only without blame, but also with some praise: but it is not so. For there are two (classes of) persons, praiseworthy in religion; one of those who have already found, whom also we must needs judge most blessed; another of those who are seeking with all earnestness and in the right way. The first, therefore, are already in very possession, the other on the way, yet on that way whereby they are most sure to arrive.[1] There are three other kinds of men altogether to be disapproved of and detested. One is of those who hold an opinion,[2] that is, of those who think that they know what they know not. Another is of those who are indeed aware that they know not, but do not so seek as to be able to find. A third is of those who neither think that they know, nor wish to seek. There are also three things, as it were bordering upon one another, in the minds of men well worth distinguishing; understanding, belief, opinion. And, if these be considered by themselves, the first is always without fault, the second sometimes with fault, the third never without fault. For the understanding of matters great, and honorable, and even divine, is most blessed.[3] But the understanding of things unnecessary is no injury; but perhaps the learning was an injury, in that it took up the time of necessary matters. But on the matters themselves that are injurious, it is not the understanding, but the doing or suffering them, that is wretched. For not, in case any understand how an enemy may be slain without danger to himself, is he guilty from the mere understanding, not the wish; and, if the wish be absent, what can be called more innocent? But belief is then worthy of blame, when either any thing is believed of God which is unworthy of Him, or any thing is over easily believed of man. But in all other matters if any believe aught, provided he understand that he knows it not, there is no fault. For I believe that very wicked conspirators were formerly put to death by the virtue of Cicero; but this I not only know not, but also I know for certain that I can by no means know. But opinion is on two accounts very base; in that both he who hath persuaded himself that he already knows, cannot learn; provided only it may be learnt; and in itself rashness is a sign of a mind not well disposed. For even if any suppose that he know what I said of Cicero, (although it be no hindrance to him from learning, in that the matter itself is incapable of being grasped by any knowledge;) yet, (in that he understands not that there is a great difference, whether any thing be grasped by sure reason of mind, which we call understanding, or whether for practical purposes it be entrusted to common fame or writing, for posterity to believe it,) he assuredly errs, and no error is without what is base. What then we understand, we owe to reason; what we believe, to authority; what we have an opinion on, to error.[4] But every one who understands also believes, and also every one who has an opinion believes; not every one who believes understands, no one who has an opinion understands. Therefore if these three things be referred unto the five kinds of men, which we mentioned a little above; that is, two kinds to be approved, which we set first, and three that remain faulty; we find that the first kind, that of the blessed, believe the truth itself; but the second kind, that of such as are earnest after, and lovers of, the truth, believe authority. In which kinds, of the two, the act of belief is praiseworthy. But in the first of the faulty

---

[1] cf. *Retract.* b. i. ch. xiv. 2. " I also said, 'For there are two &c.' In these words of mine if ' those who have already found" whom we have said to be ' now in possession,' are in such sort understood to be ' most happy,' as that they are so not in this life, but in that we hope for, and aim at by the path of faith, the meaning is free from error: for they are to be judged to have found that which is to be sought, who are now there, whither we by seeking and believing, that is by keeping the path of faith, do seek to come. But if they are thought to be or to have been such in this life, that seems to me not to be true: not that in this life no truth at all can be found that can be discerned by the mind, not believed on faith; but because it is but so much, what there is of it, as not to make men ' most blessed.' For neither is that which the Apostle says, *We see now through a glass in a riddle* and *now I know in part* (1 Cor. xiii. 12), incapable of being discerned by the mind. It is discerned, clearly, but does not yet make us most blessed. For that makes men most blessed which he saith, *but then face to face,* and, *then I shall know even as I am known.* They that have found this, they are to be said to stand in possession of bliss, to which leads that path of faith which we keep, and whither we desire to arrive at by believing. But who are those most blessed, who are already in that possession whither this path leads, is a great question. And for the holy Angels indeed, there is no question but they be there. But of holy men already departed, whether so much may yet be said of them as that they stand already in that possession, is fairly made a question. For they are already freed from the corruptible body that weigheth down the soul (Wisd. 9.), but they still wait for the redemption of their body (Rom. 8.), and their flesh resteth in hope, nor is yet glorified in the incorruption that is to come. (Ps. 16.) But whether for all that they are none the less qualified to contemplate the truth with the eyes of the heart, as it is said, *Face to face,* there is not space to discuss here."

[2] *Opinantium.*

[3] cf. *Retract.* b. i. ch. 14. 2. " Also what I said, ' for to know great and noble and even divine things,' we should refer to the same blessedness. For in this life whatsoever there be of it known amounts not to perfect bliss, because that part of it which remains unknown is far more without all comparison."

[4] cf. *Retract.* b. i. ch. xiv. 3. " And what I said, ' that there is a great difference whether anything be grasped by sure reason of mind, which we call knowing, or whether for practical purposes it be entrusted to common fame or writing, for posterity to believe it, and presently after, 'what therefore we know, we owe to reason; what we believe to authority;' is not to be so taken as that in conversation we should fear to say we ' know' what we believe of suitable witnesses. For when we speak strictly we are said to know that only which by the mind's own firm reason we comprehend. But when we speak in words more suited to common use, as also Divine Scripture speaketh, we should not hesitate to say we know both what we have perceived with our bodily senses, and what we believe of trustworthy witnesses, whilst however between one and the other we are aware what difference exists."

kinds, that is, of those who have an opinion that they know what they know not, there is an altogether faulty credulity. The other two kinds that are to be disapproved believe nothing, both they who seek the truth despairing of finding it, and they who seek it not at all. And this only in matters which pertain unto any system of teaching. For in the other business of life, I am utterly ignorant by what means a man can believe nothing. Although in the case of those also, they who say that in practical matters they follow probabilities, would seem rather to be unable to know than unable to believe. For who believes not what he approves?[1] or how is what they follow probable, if it be not approved? Wherefore there may be two kinds of such as oppose the truth: one of those who assail knowledge alone, not faith; the other of those who condemn both: and yet again, I am ignorant whether these can be found in matters of human life. These things have been said, in order that we might understand, that, in retaining faith, even of those things which as yet we comprehend not, we are set free from the rashness of such as have an opinion. For they, who say that we are to believe nothing but what we know, are on their guard against that one name " opining,"[2] which must be confessed to be base and very wretched, but, if they consider carefully that there is a very great difference, whether one think that he knows, or moved by some authority believe that which he understands not that he knows not, surely he will escape the charge of error, and inhumanity, and pride.

26. For I ask, if what is not known must not be believed, in what way may children do service to their parents, and love with mutual affection those whom they believe not to be their parents? For it cannot, by any means, be known by reason. But the authority of the mother comes in, that it be believed of the father; but of the mother it is usually not the mother that is believed, but midwives, nurses, servants. For she, from whom a son may be stolen and another put in his place, may she not being deceived deceive? Yet we believe, and believe without any doubt, what we confess we cannot know. For who but must see, that unless it be so, filial affection, the most sacred bond of the human race, is violated by extreme pride of wickedness? For what madman even would think him to be blamed who discharged the duties that were due to those whom he believed to be his parents, although they were not so? Who, on the other hand, would not judge him to

deserve banishment, who failed to love those who were perhaps his true parents, through fear lest he should love pretended. Many things may be alleged, whereby to show that nothing at all of human society remains safe, if we shall determine to believe nothing, which we cannot grasp by full apprehension.[3]

27. But now hear, what I trust I shall by this time more easily persuade you of. In a matter of religion, that is, of the worship and knowledge of God, they are less to be followed, who forbid us to believe, making most ready professions of reason. For no one doubts that all men are either fools or wise.[4] But now I call wise, not clever and gifted men, but those, in whom there is, so much as may be in man, the knowledge of man himself and of God most surely received, and a life and manners suitable to that knowledge; but all others, whatever be their skill or want of skill, whatever their manner of life, whether to be approved or disapproved, I would account in the number of fools. And, this being so, who of moderate understanding but will clearly see, that it is more useful and more healthful for fools to obey the precepts of the wise, than to live by their own judgment? For everything that is done, if it be not rightly done, is a sin, nor can that any how be rightly done which proceeds not from right reason. Further, right reason is very virtue. But to whom of men is virtue at hand, save to the mind of the wise? Therefore the wise man alone sins not. Therefore every fool sins, save in those actions, in which he hath obeyed a wise man: for all such actions proceed from right reason, and, so to say, the fool is not to be accounted master of his own action, he being, as it were, the instrument and that which ministers[5] to the wise man. Wherefore, if it be better for all men not to sin than to sin; assuredly all fools would live better, if they could be slaves of the wise. And, if no one doubts that this is better in lesser matters, as in buying and selling, and cultivating the ground, in taking

---

[3] *Tenere perceptum.*
[4] cf. *Retract.* b. i. ch. 14. 4. " Also what I said, ' No one doubts that all men are either fools or wise,' may seem contrary to what is read in my third book *On Free Will*, (c. 24.) 'as though human nature admitted of no middle state between folly and wisdom.' But that is said when the question was about the first man, whether he was made wise, or foolish, or neither : since we could in no wise call him foolish, who was made without fault, since folly is a great fault ; and how we could call him wise, who was capable of being led astray, did not appear. So for shortness I thought well to say, ' as though human nature admitted of no middle state between folly and wisdom.' I also had infants in view, whom though we confess to bear with them original sin, yet we cannot properly call them folly or foolish, not as yet using free will either well or ill. But now I said that men were either wise or foolish, meaning those to be understood who are already using reason, by which they are distinguished from cattle, so as to be men ; as we say that ' all men wish to be happy. For can we in so true and manifest a statement be in fear of being supposed to mean infants, who have not yet the power of so wishing?"
[5] *Ministerium.*

---

[1] *Probat.*   [2] *Opinationis.*

a wife, in undertaking and bringing[1] up children, lastly, in the management of household property, much more in religion. For both human matters are more easy to distinguish between, than divine; and in all matters of greater sacredness and excellence, the greater obedience and service we owe them, the more wicked and the more dangerous is it to sin. Therefore you see henceforth[2] that nothing else is left us, so long as we are fools, if our heart be set on an excellent and religious life, but to seek wise men, by obeying whom we may be enabled both to lessen the great feeling of the rule of folly, whilst it is in us, and at the last to escape from it.

28. Here again arises a very difficult question. For in what way shall we fools be able to find a wise man, whereas this name, although hardly any one dare openly, yet most men lay claim to indirectly: so disagreeing one with another in the very matters, in the knowledge of which wisdom consists, as that it must needs be that either none of them, or but some certain one be wise? But when the fool enquires, who is that wise man? I do not at all see, in what way he can be distinguished and perceived. For by no signs whatever can one recognize any thing, unless he shall have known that thing, whereof these are signs. But the fool is ignorant of wisdom. For not, as, in the case of gold and silver and other things of that kind, it is allowed both to know them when you see them, and not to have them, thus may wisdom be seen by the mind's eye of him who hath it not. For whatever things we come into contact with by bodily sense, are presented to us from without; and therefore we may perceive by the eyes what belong to others, when we ourselves possess not any of them or of that kind. But what is perceived by the understanding is within in the mind, and to have it is nothing else than to see. But the fool is void of wisdom, therefore he knows not wisdom. For he could not see it with the eyes: but he cannot see it and not have it, nor have it and be a fool. Therefore he knoweth it not, and, so long as he knoweth it not, he cannot recognize it in another place. No one, so long as he is a fool, can by most sure knowledge find out a wise man, by obeying whom he may be set free from so great evil of folly.

29. Therefore this so vast difficulty, since our enquiry is about religion, God alone can remedy: nor indeed, unless we believe both that He is, and that He helps men's minds, ought we even to enquire after true religion itself. For what I ask do we with so great

endeavor desire to search out? What do we wish to attain unto? Whither do we long to arrive? Is it at that which we believe not exists or pertains to us? Nothing is more perverse than such a state of mind. Then, when you would not dare to ask of me a kindness, or at any rate would be shameless in daring, come you to demand the discovery of religion, when you think that God neither exists, nor, if He exist, hath any care for us? What, if it be so great a matter, as that it cannot be found out, unless it be sought carefully and with all our might? What, if the very extreme difficulty of discovery be an exercise for the mind of the inquirer, in order to receive what shall be discovered? For what more pleasant and familiar to our eyes than this light? And yet men are unable after long darkness to bear and endure it. What more suited to the body exhausted by sickness than meat and drink? And yet we see that persons who are recovering are restrained and checked, lest they dare to commit themselves to the fullness of persons in health, and so bring to pass by means of their very food their return to that disease which used to reject it. I speak of persons who are recovering. What, the very sick, do we not urge them to take something? Wherein assuredly they would not with so great discomfort obey us, if they believed not that they would recover from that disease. When then will you give yourself up to a search very full of pains and labor? When will you have the heart to impose upon yourself so great care and trouble as the matter deserves, when you believe not in the existence of that which you are in search of? Rightly therefore hath it been ordained by the majesty of the Catholic system of teaching, that they who approach unto religion be before all things persuaded to have faith.

30. Wherefore that heretic, (inasmuch as our discourse is of those who wish to be called Christians,) I ask you, what reason he alleges to me? What is there whereby for him to call me back from believing, as if from rashness? If he bid me believe nothing; I believe not that this very true religion hath any existence in human affairs; and what I believe not to exist, I seek not. But He, as I suppose, will show it to me seeking it: for so it is written, " He that seeketh shall find."[3] Therefore I should not come unto him, who forbids me to believe, unless I believed something. Is there any greater madness, than that I should displease him by faith alone, which is founded on no knowledge, which faith alone led me to him?

---

[1] Or "begetting,"—suscipiendis.
[2] Ben. ed.—a modo. Mss. admodum.

[3] Matt. vii. 8.

31. What, that all heretics exhort us to believe in Christ? Can they possibly be more opposed to themselves? And in this matter they are to be pressed in a twofold way. In the first place we must ask of them, where is the reason which they used to promise, where the reproof of rashness, where the assumption of knowledge? For, if it be disgraceful to believe any without reason, what do you wait for, what are you busied about, that I believe some one without reason, in order that I may the more easily be led by your reason? What, will your reason raise any firm superstructure on the foundation of rashness? I speak after their manner, whom we displease by believing. For I not only judge it most healthful to believe before reason, when you are not qualified to receive reason, and by the very act of faith thoroughly to cultivate the mind to receive the seeds of truth, but altogether a thing of such sort as that without it health cannot return to sick souls. And, in that this seems to them matter for mockery and full of rashness, surely they are shameless in making it their business that we believe in Christ. Next, I confess that I have already believed in Christ, and have convinced myself that what He hath said is true, although it be supported by no reason; is this, heretic, what you will teach me in the first place? Suffer me to consider a little with myself, (since I have not seen Christ Himself, as He willed to appear unto men, Who is said to have been seen by them, even by common eyes,) who they are that I have believed concerning Him, in order that I may approach you already furnished beforehand with such a faith. I see that there are none that I have believed, save the confirmed opinion and widely extended report of peoples and nations: and that the mysteries of the Church Catholic have in all times and places had possession of these peoples. Why therefore shall I not of these, in preference to others, inquire with all care, what Christ commanded, by whose authority I have been moved already to believe that Christ hath commanded something that is profitable? Are you likely to be a better expounder to me of what He said, Whose past or present existence I should not believe, if by you I were to be recommended to believe thus? This therefore I have believed, as I said, trusting to report strengthened by numbers, agreement, antiquity. But you, who are both so few, and so turbulent, and so new, no one doubts that ye bring forward nothing worthy of authority. What then is that so great madness? Believe them, that you are to believe in Christ, and learn from us what He

said. Why, I pray you? For were they t fail and to be unable to teach me any thing with much greater ease could I persuade my self, that I am not to believe in Christ, than that I am to learn any thing concerning Him, save from those through whom I had believed in Him. O vast confidence, or rather absurdity! I teach you what Christ, in Whom you believe, commanded. What, in case I believed not in Him? You could not, could you, teach me any thing concerning Him? But, says he, it behoves you to believe. You do not mean, do you, that I am (to believe) you when you commend Him to my faith? No, saith he, for we lead by reason them who believe in Him. Why then should I believe in Him? Because report hath been grounded. Whether is it through you, or through others? Through others, saith he. Shall I then believe them, in order that you may teach me? Perhaps I ought to do so, were it not that they gave me this chief charge, that I should not approach you at all; for they say that you have deadly doctrines. You will answer, They lie. How then shall I believe them concerning Christ, Whom they have not seen, (and) not believe them concerning you, whom they are unwilling to see? Believe the Scriptures, saith he. But every writing,[1] if it be brought forward new and unheard of, or be commended by few, with no reason to confirm it, it is not it that is believed, but they who bring it forward. Wherefore, for those Scriptures, if you are they who bring them forward, you so few and unknown, I am not pleased to believe them. At the same time also you are acting contrary to your promise, in enforcing faith rather than giving a reason. You will recall me again to numbers and (common) report. Curb, I pray you, your obstinacy, and that untamed lust, I know not what, of spreading your name: and advise me rather to seek the chief men of this multitude, and to seek with all care and pains rather to learn something concerning these writings from these men, but for whose existence, I should not know that I had to learn at all. But do you return into your dens, and lay not any snares under the name of truth, which you endeavor to take from those, to whom you yourself grant authority.

32. But if they say that we are not even to believe in Christ, unless undoubted reason shall be given us, they are not Christians. For this is what certain pagans say against us, foolishly indeed, yet not contrary to, or inconsistent with, themselves. But who can endure that these profess to belong to Christ,

---

[1] Scripturæ.

who contend that they are to believe nothing, unless they shall bring forward to fools most open reason concerning God? But we see that He Himself, so far as that history, which they themselves believe, teaches, willed nothing before, or more strongly than, that He should be believed in: whereas they, with whom He had to do, were not yet qualified to receive the secret things of God. For, for what other purpose are so great and so many miracles, He Himself also saying, that they are done for no other cause, than that He may be believed in? He used to lead fools by faith, you lead by reason. He used to cry out, that He should be believed in, ye cry out against it. He used to praise such as believe in Him, ye blame them. But unless either He should change water into wine, [1] to omit other (miracles), if men would follow Him, doing no such, but (only) teaching; either we must make no account of that saying, " Believe ye God, believe also Me;" [2] or we must charge him with rashness, who willed not that He should come into his house, believing that the disease of his servant would depart at His mere command. [3] Therefore He bringing to us a medicine such as should heal our utterly corrupt manners, by miracles procured to Himself authority, [4] by authority obtained Himself belief, by belief drew together a multitude, by a multitude possessed antiquity, by antiquity strengthened religion: so that not only the utterly foolish novelty of heretics dealing deceitfully, but also the inveterate error of the nations opposing with violence, should be unable on any side to rend it asunder.

33. Wherefore, although I am not able to teach, yet I cease not to advise, that, (whereas many wish to appear wise, and it is no easy matter to discern whether they be fools,) with all earnestness, and with all prayers, and lastly with groans, or even, if so it may be, with tears, you entreat of God to set you free from the evil of error; if your heart be set on a happy life. And this will take place the more easily, if you obey with a willing mind His commands, which He hath willed should be confirmed by so great authority of the Catholic Church. For whereas the wise man is so joined to God in mind, as that there is nothing set between to separate; for God is Truth; and no one is by any means wise, unless his mind come into contact with the Truth; we cannot deny that between the folly of man, and the most pure Truth of God, the wisdom of man is set, as something in the middle. For the wise man, so far as

it is given unto him, imitates God; but for a man who is a fool, there is nothing nearer to him, than a man who is wise, for him to imitate with profit: and since, as has been said, it is not easy to understand this one by reason, it behoved that certain miracles be brought near to the very eyes, which fools use with much greater readiness than the mind, that, men being moved by authority, their life and habits might first be cleansed, and they thus rendered capable of receiving reason. Whereas, therefore, it needed both that man be imitated, and that our hope be not set in man, what could be done on the part of God more full of kindness and grace, than that the very pure, eternal, unchangeable Wisdom of God, unto Whom it behoves us to cleave, should deign to take upon Him (the nature of) man? That not only He might do what should invite us to follow God, but also might suffer what used to deter us from following God. For, whereas no one can attain unto the most sure and chief good, unless he shall fully and perfectly love it; which will by no means take place, so long as the evils of the body and of fortune are dreaded; He by being born after a miraculous manner and working caused Himself to be loved; and by dying and rising again shut out fear. And, further, in all other matters, which it were long to go through, He shewed Himself such, as that we might perceive unto what the clemency of God could be reached forth, and unto what the weakness of man be lifted up.

34. This is, believe me, a most wholesome authority, this a lifting up first of our mind from dwelling on the earth, this a turning from the love of this world unto the True God. It is authority alone which moves fools to hasten unto wisdom. So long as we cannot understand pure (truths), it is indeed wretched to be deceived by authority, but surely more wretched not to be moved. For, if the Providence of God preside not over human affairs, we have no need to busy ourselves about religion. But if both the outward form of all things, which we must believe assuredly flows from some fountain of truest beauty, and some, I know not what, inward conscience exhorts, as it were, in public and in private, all the better order of minds to seek God, and to serve God; we must not give up all hope that the same God Himself hath appointed some authority, whereon, resting as on a sure step, we may be lifted up unto God. But this, setting aside reason, which (as we have often said) it is very hard for fools to understand pure, moves us two ways; in part by miracles, in part by

---

[1] John ii. 7-9.   [2] John xiv. 1.   [3] Matt. viii. 8, 9.   [4] *Meruit.*

multitude of followers: no one of these is necessary to the wise man; who denies it? But this is now the business in hand, that we may be able to be wise, that is, to cleave to the truth; which the filthy soul is utterly unable to do: but the filth of the soul, to say shortly what I mean, is the love of any things whatsoever save God and the soul: from which filth the more any one is cleansed, the more easily he sees the truth. Therefore to wish to see the truth, in order to purge your soul, when as it is purged for the very purpose that you may see, is surely perverse and preposterous. Therefore to man unable to see the truth, authority is at hand, in order that he may be made fitted for it, and may allow himself to be cleansed; and, as I said a little above, no one doubts that this prevails, in part by miracles, in part by multitude. But I call that a miracle, whatever appears that is difficult or unusual above the hope or power of them who wonder. Of which kind there is nothing more suited for the people, and in general for foolish men, than what is brought near to the senses. But these, again, are divided into two kinds; for there are certain, which cause only wonder, but certain others procure also great favor and good-will. For, if one were to see a man flying, inasmuch as that matter brings no advantage to the spectator, beside the spectacle itself, he only wonders. But if any affected with grievous and hopeless disease were to recover straightway, upon being bidden, his affection for him who heals, will go beyond even his wonder at his healing. Such were done at that time at which God in True Man appeared unto men, as much as was enough. The sick were healed, the lepers were cleansed; walking was restored to the lame, sight to the blind, hearing to the deaf. The men of that time saw water turned into wine, five thousand filled with five loaves, seas passed on foot, dead rising again: thus certain provided for the good of the body by more open benefit, certain again for the good of the soul by more hidden sign, and all for the good of men by their witness to Majesty: thus, at that time, was the divine authority moving towards Itself the wandering souls of mortal men. Why, say you, do not those things take place now? because they would not move, unless they were wonderful, and, if they were usual, they would not be wonderful.[1] For the interchanges of day and night,

and the settled order of things in Heaven, the revolution of years divided into four parts, the fall and return of leaves to trees, the boundless power of seeds, the beauty of light, the varieties of colors, sounds, tastes, and scents, let there be some one who shall see and perceive them for the first time, and yet such an one as we may converse with; he is stupified and overwhelmed with miracles: but we contemn all these, not because they are easy to understand, (for what more obscure than the causes of these?) but surely because they constantly meet our senses. Therefore they were done at a very suitable time, in order that, by these a multitude of believers having been gathered together and spread abroad, authority might be turned with effect upon habits.

35. But any habits whatever have so great power to hold possession of men's minds, that even what in them are evil, which usually takes place through excess of lusts, we can sooner disapprove of and hate, than desert or change. Do you think that little hath been done for the benefit of man, that not some few very learned men maintain by argument, but also an unlearned crowd of males and females in so many and different nations both believe and set forth, that we are to worship as God nothing of earth, nothing of fire, nothing, lastly, which comes into contact with the senses of the body, but that we are to seek to approach Him by the understanding only? that abstinence is extended even unto the slenderest food of bread and water, and fastings not only for the day,[2] but also continued through several days together; that chastity is carried even unto the contempt of marriage and family; that patience even unto the setting light by crosses and flames; that liberality even unto the distribution of estates unto the poor; that, lastly, the contempt of this whole world even unto the desire of death? Few do these things, yet fewer do them well and wisely: but whole nations approve, nations hear, nations favor, nations, lastly, love. Nations accuse their own weakness that they cannot do these things, and that not without the mind being carried forward unto God, nor without certain sparks of virtue. This hath been brought to pass by the Divine Providence, through the prophecies of the Prophets, through the manhood and teaching of Christ, through the journeys of the Apostles, through the insults, crosses, blood, of the Martyrs, through the praiseworthy life of the Saints, and, in all these,

---

[1] cf. *Retract.* b. i. c. 14. 5. "In another place, where I had made mention of the miracles, which our Lord Jesus did, while He was here in the Flesh, I added, saying, 'Why, say you, do not those things take place now?' and I answered, 'Because they would not move unless they were wonderful, and if they were usual they would not be wonderful.' But this I said because not so great miracles, nor all take place now, not because there are none wrought even now."

[2] *Quotidiana*, i. e. each day till evening.

according as times were seasonable, through miracles worthy of so great matters and virtues. When therefore we see so great help of God, so great progress and fruit, shall we doubt to hide ourselves in the bosom of that Church, which even unto the confession of the human race from [the] apostolic chair[1] through successions of Bishops,[2] (heretics in vain lurking around her and being condemned, partly by the judgment of the very people, partly by the weight of councils, partly also by the majesty of miracles,) hath held the summit of authority. To be unwilling to grant to her the first place,[3] is either surely the height of impiety, or is headlong arrogance. For, if there be no sure way unto wisdom and health of souls, unless where faith prepare them for reason, what else is it to be ungrateful for the Divine help and aid, than to wish to resist authority furnished with so great labor?[4] And if every system of teaching, however mean and easy, requires, in order to its being received, a teacher or master, what more full of rash pride, than, in the case of books of divine mysteries,[5] both to be unwilling to learn from such as interpret them, and to wish to condemn them unlearned?

36. Wherefore, if either our reasoning or our discourse hath in any way moved you, and if you have, as I believe, a true care for yourself, I would you would listen to me, and with pious faith, lively hope, and simple charity, entrust yourself to good teachers of Catholic Christianity; and cease not to pray unto God Himself, by Whose goodness alone we were created, and suffer punishment by His justice, and are set free by His mercy. Thus there will be wanting to you neither precepts and treatises of most learned and truly Christian men, nor books, nor calm thoughts themselves, whereby you may easily find what you are seeking. For do you abandon utterly those wordy and wretched men, (for what other milder name can I use?) who, whilst they seek to excess whence is evil, find nothing but evil. And on this question they often rouse their hearers to inquire; but after that they have been roused, they teach them such lessons as that it were preferable even to sleep for ever, than thus to be awake. For in place of lethargic they make them frantic, between which diseases, both being usually fatal, there is still this difference, that lethargic persons die without doing violence

to others; but the frantic person many who are sound, and specially they who wish to help him, have reason to fear. For neither is God the author of evil, nor hath it ever repented Him that He hath done aught, nor is He troubled by storm of any passion of soul, nor is a small part of earth His Kingdom: He neither approves nor commands any sins or wickedness, He never lies. For these and such like used to move us, when they used them to make great and threatening assaults, and charged this as being the system of teaching of the Old Testament, which is most false. Thus then I allow that they do right in censuring these. What then have I learnt? What think you, save that, when these are censured, the Catholic system of teaching is not censured. Thus what I had learnt among them that is true, I hold, what is false that I had thought I reject. But the Catholic Church hath taught me many other things also, which those men of bloodless bodies, but coarse minds, cannot aspire unto; that is to say, that God is not corporeal, that no part of Him can be perceived by corporeal eyes, that nothing of His Substance or Nature can any way suffer violence or change, or is compounded or formed; and if you grant me these, (for we may not think otherwise concerning God,) all their devices are overthrown. But how it is, that neither God begot or created evil, nor yet is there, or hath there been ever, any nature and substance, which God either begot not or created not, and yet that He setteth us free from evil, is proved by reasons so necessary, that it cannot at all be matter of doubt; especially to you and such as you; that is, if to a good disposition there be added piety and a certain peace of mind, without which nothing at all can be understood concerning so great matters. And here there is no rumor concerning smoke, and I know not what Persian vain fable, unto which it is enough to lend an ear, and soul not subtile, but absolutely childish. Far altogether, far otherwise is the truth, than as the Manichees dote. But since this discourse of ours hath gone much further than I thought, here let us end the book; in which I wish you to remember, that I have not yet begun to refute the Manichees, and that I have not yet assailed that nonsense; and that neither have I unfolded any thing great concerning the Catholic Church itself, but that I have only wished to root out of you, if I could, a false notion concerning true Christians that was maliciously or ignorantly suggested to us, and to arouse you to learn certain great and divine things. Wherefore let this volume be as it is; but when your soul becomes more

---

[1] He clearly means the Apostolic office and presidency in general. For illustration, see St. Cyprian on the Unity of the Church, §. 3 and 4. vid. Oxf. Tr. p. 134. and note.
[2] The plural "*successiones*." Compare Con. Faustus, b. xiii. § 13, xxxii. §, 19, xxxiii. § 6, 9.
[3] *Primas*.   [4] al. *strength*.   [5] *Sacramentorum*.

calmed, I shall perhaps be more ready in
what remains.[1]

---

[1] cf. *Retr.* b. i. ch. 14. 6. " But in the end of the book I say,
' But since this discourse of ours, &c.'   This I did not say in such
sort as though I had not hitherto written anything against the
Manichæans, or had not committed to writing anything at all
about Catholic doctrine, when so many volumes before published
were witnesses that I had not been silent on either subject ; but in
this book written to him I had not yet begun to refute the Manichæans, and had not yet attacked those follies, nor had I as yet
opened anything great concerning the Catholic Church itself ; because I hoped that after that beginning made, I should write to
that same person what I had not yet here written."

ST. AUGUSTIN:

ON

THE CREED:

A SERMON TO THE CATECHUMENS

[DE SYMBOLO AD CATECHUMENOS.]

TRANSLATED BY THE

REV. C. L. CORNISH, M.A.,

OF EXETER COLLEGE, OXFORD.

ON THE CREED:

A SERMON TO THE CATECHUMENS.

[DE SYMBOLO AD CATECHUMENOS.]

1. RECEIVE, my children, the Rule of Faith, which is called the Symbol (or Creed [1]). And when ye have received it, write it in your heart, and be daily saying it to yourselves; before ye sleep, before ye go forth, arm you with your Creed. The Creed no man writes so as it may be able to be read: but for rehearsal of it, lest haply forgetfulness obliterate what care hath delivered, let your memory be your record-roll:[2] what ye are about to hear, that are ye to believe; and what ye shall have believed, that are about to give back with your tongue. For the Apostle says, "With the heart man believeth unto righteousness, and with the mouth confession is made unto salvation."[3] For this is the Creed which ye are to rehearse and to repeat in answer. These words which ye have heard are in the Divine Scriptures scattered up and down: but thence gathered and reduced into one, that the memory of slow persons might not be distressed; that every person may be able to say, able to hold, what he believes. For have ye now merely heard that God is Almighty? But ye begin to have him for your father, when ye have been born by the church as your Mother.

2. Of this, then, ye have now received, have meditated, and having meditated have held, that ye should say, "I believe in God the Father Almighty." God is Almighty, and yet, though Almighty, He cannot die, cannot be deceived, cannot lie; and, as the Apostle says, "cannot deny Himself."[4] How many things that He cannot do, and yet is Almighty! yea therefore is Almighty, because He cannot do these things. For if He could die, He were not Almighty; if to lie, if to be deceived, if to do unjustly, were possible for Him, He were not Almighty: because if this

were in Him, He should not be worthy to be Almighty. To our Almighty Father, it is quite impossible to sin. He does whatsoever He will: that is Omnipotence. He does whatsoever He rightly will, whatsoever He justly will: but whatsoever is evil to do, He wills not. There is no resisting one who is Almighty, that He should not do what He will. It was He Who made heaven and earth, the sea, and all that in them is, invisible and visible. Invisible such as are in heaven, thrones, dominions, principalities, powers, archangels, angels: all, if we shall live aright, our fellow-citizens. He made in heaven the things visible; the sun, the moon, the stars. With its terrestrial animals He adorned the earth, filled the air with things that fly, the land with them that walk and creep, the sea with them that swim: all He filled with their own proper creatures. He made also man after His own image and likeness, in the mind: for in that is the image of God. This is the reason why the mind cannot be comprehended even by itself, because in it is the image of God. To this end were we made, that over the other creatures we should bear rule: but through sin in the first man we fell, and are all come into an inheritance of death. We were brought low, became mortal, were filled with fears, with errors: this by desert of sin: with which desert and guilt is every man born.[5] This is the reason why, as ye have seen to-day, as ye know, even little children undergo exsufflation, exorcism; to drive away from them the power of the devil their enemy, which deceived man that it might possess mankind. It is not then the creature of God that in infants undergoes exorcism or exsufflation: but he under whom are all that are born with sin; for he is the first[6] of sinners. And for this cause by reason of one

---

[1] Symbolum.
[3] Rom. x. 10.

[2] 2 Codex.
[4] 2 Tim. ii. 13.

[5] Gen. i-iii.

[6] Princeps.

who fell and brought all into death, there was sent One without sin, Who should bring unto life, by delivering them from sin, all that believe on Him.

3. For this reason we believe also in His Son, that is to say, God the Father Almighty's, "His Only Son, our Lord." When thou hearest of the Only Son of God, acknowledge Him God. For it could not be that God's Only Son should not be God. What He is, the same did He beget, though He is not that Person Whom He begot. If He be truly Son, He is that which the Father is; if He be not that which the Father is, He is not truly Son. Observe mortal and earthly creatures: what each is, that it engendereth. Man begets not an ox, sheep begets not dog, nor dog sheep. Whatever it be that begetteth, that which it is, it begetteth. Hold ye therefore boldly, firmly, faithfully, that the Begotten of God the Father is what Himself is, Almighty. These mortal creatures engender by corruption. Does God so beget? He that is begotten mortal generates that which himself is; the Immortal generates what He is: corruptible begets corruptible, Incorruptible begets Incorruptible: the corruptible begets corruptibly, Incorruptible, Incorruptibly: yea, so begetteth what Itself is, that One begets One, and therefore Only. Ye know, that when I pronounced to you the Creed, so I said, and so ye are bounden to believe; that we "believe in God the Father Almighty, and in Jesus Christ His Only Son." Here too, when thou believest that He is the Only, believe Him Almighty: for it is not to be thought that God the Father does what He will, and God the Son does not what He will. One Will of Father and Son, because one Nature. For it is impossible for the will of the Son to be any whit parted from the Father's will. God and God; both one God: Almighty and Almighty; both One Almighty.

4. We do not bring in two Gods as some do, who say, "God the Father and God the Son, but greater God the Father and lesser God the Son." They both are what? Two Gods? Thou blushest to speak it, blush to believe it. Lord God the Father, thou sayest, and Lord God the Son: and the Son Himself saith, "No man can serve two Lords."[1] In His family shall we be in such wise, that, like as in a great house where there is the father of a family and he hath a son, so we should say, the greater Lord, the lesser Lord? Shrink from such a thought. If ye make to yourselves such-like in your heart, ye set up idols in the "one soul" Utterly re-

pel it. First believe, then understand. Now to whom God gives that when he has believed he soon understands; that is God's gift, not human frailness. Still, if ye do not yet understand, believe: One God the Father, God Christ the Son of God. Both are what? One God. And how are both said to be One God? How? Dost thou marvel? In the Acts of the Apostles, "There was," it says, "in the believers, one soul and one heart."[2] There were many souls, faith had made them one. So many thousands of souls were there; they loved each other, and many are one: they loved God in the fire of charity, and from being many they are come to the oneness of beauty. If all those many souls the dearness of love[3] made one soul, what must be the dearness of love in God, where is no diversity, but entire equality! If on earth and among men there could be so great charity as of so many souls to make one soul, where Father from Son, Son from Father, hath been ever inseparable, could They both be other than One God? Only, those souls might be called both many souls and one soul; but God, in Whom is ineffable and highest conjunction, may be called One God, not two Gods.

5. The Father doeth what He will, and what He will doeth the Son. Do not imagine an Almighty Father and a not Almighty Son: it is error, blot it out within you, let it not cleave in your memory, let it not be drunk into your faith, and if haply any of you shall have drunk it in, let him vomit it up. Almighty is the Father, Almighty the Son. If Almighty begat not Almighty, He begat not very Son. For what say we, brethren, if the Father being greater begat a Son less than He? What said I, begat? Man engenders, being greater, a son being less: it is true: but that is because the one grows old, the other grows up, and by very growing attains to the form of his father. The Son of God, if He groweth not because neither can God wax old, was begotten perfect. And being begotten perfect, if He groweth not, and remained not less, He is equal. For that ye may know Almighty begotten of Almighty, hear Him Who is Truth. That which of Itself Truth saith, is true. What saith Truth? What saith the Son, Who is Truth? "Whatsoever things the Father doeth, these also the Son likewise doeth."[4] The Son is Almighty, in doing all things that He willeth to do. For if the Father doeth some things which the Son doeth not, the Son said falsely, "Whatsoever things the Father doeth, these also the Son doeth likewise." But because the Son spake

---

[1] Matt. vi. 24.   [2] Acts iv. 32.   [3] *Charitas.*   [4] John v. 19.

truly, believe it: "Whatsoever things the Father doeth, these also the Son doeth likewise," and ye have believed in the Son that He is Almighty. Which word although ye said not in the Creed, yet this is it that ye expressed when ye believed in the Only Son, Himself God. Hath the Father aught that the Son hath not? This Arian heretic blasphemers say, not I. But what say I? If the Father aught that the Son hath not, the Son lieth in saying, "All things that the Father hath, are Mine."[1] Many and innumerable are the testimonies by which it is proved that the Son is Very Son of God the Father, and the Father God hath His Very-begotten Son God, and Father and Son is One God.

6. But this Only Son of God, the Father Almighty, let us see what He did for us, what He suffered for us. "Born of the Holy Ghost and of the Virgin Mary." He, so great God, equal with the Father, born of the Holy Ghost and of the Virgin Mary, born lowly, that thereby He might heal the proud. Man exalted himself and fell; God humbled Himself and raised him up. Christ's lowliness, what is it? God hath stretched out an hand to man laid low. We fell, He descended: we lay low, He stooped. Let us lay hold and rise, that we fall not into punishment. So then His stooping to us is this, "Born of the Holy Ghost and of the Virgin Mary." His very Nativity too as man, it is lowly, and it is lofty. Whence lowly? That as man He was born of men. Whence lofty? That He was born of a virgin. A virgin conceived, a virgin bore, and after the birth was a virgin still.

7. What next? "Suffered under Pontius Pilate." He was in office as governor and was the judge, this same Pontius Pilate, what time as Christ suffered. In the name of the judge there is a mark of the times, when He suffered under Pontius Pilate: when He suffered, "was crucified, dead, and buried." Who? what? for whom? Who? God's Only Son, our Lord. What? Crucified, dead, and buried. For whom? for ungodly and sinners. Great condescension, great grace! "What shall I render unto the Lord for all that He hath bestowed on me?"[2]

8. He was begotten before all times, before all worlds. "Begotten before." Before what, He in Whom is no before? Do not in the least imagine any time before that Nativity of Christ whereby He was begotten of the Father; of that Nativity I am speaking by which He is Son of God Almighty, His Only Son our Lord; of that am I first speaking. Do not imagine in this Nativity a beginning of time; do not imagine any space of eternity in which the Father was and the Son was not. Since when the Father was, since then the Son. And what is that "since," where is no beginning? Therefore ever Father without beginning, ever Son without beginning. And how, thou wilt say, was He begotten, if He have no beginning? Of eternal, coeternal. At no time was the Father, and the Son not, and yet Son of Father was begotten. Whence is any manner of similitude to be had? We are among things of earth, we are in the visible creature. Let the earth give me a similitude: it gives none. Let the element of the waters give me some similitude: it hath not whereof to give. Some animal give me a similitude: neither can this do it. An animal indeed engenders, both what engenders and what is engendered: but first is the father, and then is born the son. Let us find the coeval and imagine it coeternal. If we shall be able to find a father coeval with his son, and son coeval with his father, let us believe God the Father coeval with His Son, and God the Son coeternal with His Father. On earth we can find some coeval, we cannot find any coeternal. Let us stretch[3] the coeval and imagine it coeternal. Some one, it may be, will put you on the stretch,[4] by saying, "When is it possible for a father to be found coeval with his son, or son coeval with his father? That the father may beget he goes before in age; that the son may be begotten, he comes after in age: but this father coeval with son, or son with father, how can it be?" Imagine to yourselves fire as father, its shining as son; see, we have found the coevals. From the instant that the fire begins to be, that instant it begets the shining: neither fire before shining, nor shining after fire. And if we ask, which begets which? the fire the shining, or the shining the fire? Immediately ye conceive by natural sense, by the innate wit of your minds ye all cry out, The fire the shining, not the shining the fire. Lo, here you have a father beginning; lo, a son at the same time, neither going before nor coming after. Lo, here then is a father beginning, lo, a son at the same time beginning. If I have shown you a father beginning, and a son at the same time beginning, believe the Father not beginning, and with Him the Son not beginning either; the one eternal, the other coeternal. If ye get on with your learning, ye understand: take

---

[1] John xvi. 15.   [2] Ps. cxvi. 12.   [3] *Intendamus.*   [4] *Intentos.*

pains to get on. The being born, ye have; but also the growing, ye ought to have; because no man begins with being perfect. As for the Son of God, indeed, He could be born perfect, because He was begotten without time, coeternal with the Father, long before all things, not in age, but in eternity. He then was begotten coeternal, of which generation the Prophet said, " His generation who shall declare?"[1] begotten of the Father without time, He was born of the Virgin in the fullness of times. This nativity had times going before it. In opportunity of time, when He would, when He knew, then was He born: for He was not born without His will. None of us is born because he will, and none of us dies when he will: He, when He would, was born; when He would, He died: how He would, He was born of a Virgin: how He would, He died; on the cross. Whatever He would, He did: because He was in such wise Man that, unseen,[2] He was God; God assuming, Man assumed;[3] One Christ, God and Man.

9. Of His cross what shall I speak, what say? This extremest kind of death He chose, that not any kind of death might make His Martyrs afraid. The doctrine He shewed in His life as Man, the example of patience He demonstrated in His Cross. There, you have the work, that He was crucified; example of the work, the Cross; reward of the work, Resurrection. He shewed us in the Cross what we ought to endure, He shewed in the Resurrection what we have to hope. Just like a consummate task-master in the matches of the arena, He said, Do, and bear; do the work and receive the prize; strive in the match and thou shalt be crowned. What is the work? Obedience. What the prize? Resurrection without death. Why did I add, "without death?" Because Lazarus rose, and died: Christ rose again, " dieth no more, death will no longer have dominion over Him."[4]

10. Scripture saith, " Ye have heard of the patience of Job, and have seen the end of the Lord."[5] When we read what great trials Job endured, it makes one shudder, it makes one shrink, it makes one quake. And what did he receive? The double of what he had lost. Let not a man therefore with an eye to temporal rewards be willing to have patience, and say to himself, " Let me endure loss, God will give me back sons twice as many; Job received double of all, and begat as many sons as he had buried." Then is this not the double? Yes, precisely the double, because the former sons still lived. Let none say, " Let me bear evils, and God will repay me as He repaid Job:" that it be now no longer patience but avarice. For if it was not patience which that Saint had, nor a brave enduring of all that came upon him; the testimony which the Lord gave, whence should he have it? " Hast thou observed," saith the Lord, " my servant Job? For there is not like him any on the earth, a man without fault,[6] a true worshipper of God." What a testimony, my brethren, did this holy man deserve of the Lord! And yet him a bad woman sought by her persuasion to deceive, she too representing that serpent, who, like as in Paradise he deceived the man whom God first made, so likewise here by suggesting blasphemy thought to be able to deceive a man who pleased God. What things he suffered, my brethren! Who can have so much to suffer in his estate, his house, his sons, his flesh, yea in his very wife who was left to be his tempter! But even her who was left, the devil would have taken away long ago, but that he kept her to be his helper: because by Eve he had mastered the first man, therefore had he kept an Eve. What things, then, he suffered! He lost all that he had; his house fell; would that were all! it crushed his sons also. And, to see that patience had great place in him, hear what he answered; " The Lord gave, the Lord hath taken away; as it pleased the Lord, so hath it been done;[7] blessed be the name of the Lord."[8] He hath taken what He gave, is He lost Who gave? He hath taken what He gave. As if he should say, He hath taken away all, let Him take all, send me away naked, and let me keep Him. What shall I lack if I have God? or what is the good of all else to me, if I have not God? Then it came to his flesh, he was stricken with a wound from head to foot; he was one running sore, one mass of crawling worms: and showed himself immovable in his God, stood fixed. The woman wanted, devil's helper as she was not husband's comforter, to put him up to blaspheme God. " How long," said she, " dost thou suffer" so and so; " speak some word against the Lord,[9] and die."[10] So then, because he had been brought low, he was to be exalted. And this the Lord did, in order to show it to men; as for His servant, He kept greater things for him in heaven. So then Job who was brought low, He exalted; the devil who was lifted up, He brought low:

[1] Is. liii. 8. [See R. V.]   [2] *Ut lateret Deus.*
[3] *Susceptor susceptus.*   [4] Rom. vi. 9.   [5] James v. 11.
[6] *Querela.*   [7] Lat. from LXX.   [8] Job i. 21.
[9] Lat. from LXX.   [10] Job ii. 9.

for "He putteth down one and setteth up another."[1] But let not any man, my beloved brethren, when he suffers any such-like tribulations, look for a reward here: for instance, if he suffer any losses, let him not peradventure say, "The Lord gave, the Lord hath taken away; as it pleased the Lord, so is it done: blessed be the name of the Lord;" only with the mind to receive twice as much again. Let patience praise God, not avarice. If what thou hast lost thou seekest to receive back twofold, and therefore praisest God, it is of covetousness thou praisest, not of love. Do not imagine this to be the example of that holy man; thou deceivest thyself. When Job was enduring all, he was not hoping for to have twice as much again. Both in his first confession when he bore up under his losses, and bore out to the grave the dead bodies of his sons, and in the second when he was now suffering torments of sores in his flesh, ye may observe what I am saying. Of his former confession the words run thus: "The Lord gave, and the Lord hath taken away: as it pleased the Lord, so is it done: blessed be the name of the Lord."[2] He might have said, "The Lord gave, and the Lord hath taken away; He that took away can once more give; can bring back more than He took." He said not this, but, "As it pleased the Lord," said he, "so is it done:" because it pleases Him, let it please me: let not that which hath pleased the good Lord misplease His submissive servant; what pleased the Physician, not misplease the sick man. Hear his other confession: "Thou hast spoken," said he to his wife, "like one of the foolish women. If we have received good at the hand of the Lord, why shall we not bear evil?"[3] He did not add, what, if he had said it, would have been true. "The Lord is able both to bring back my flesh into its former condition, and that which He hath taken away from us, to make manifold more:" lest he should seem to have endured in hope of this. This was not what he said, not what he hoped. But, that we might be taught, did the Lord that for him, not hoping for it, by which we should be taught, that God was with him: because if He had not also restored to him those things, there was the crown indeed, but hidden, and we could not see it. And therefore what says the divine Scripture in exhorting to patience and hope of things future, not reward of things present? "Ye have heard of the patience of Job, and have seen the end of the Lord." Why is it, "the patience of Job," and not, Ye have seen the

end of Job himself? Thou wouldest open thy mouth for the "twice as much;" wouldest say, "Thanks be to God; let me bear up: I receive twice as much again, like Job." "Patience of Job, end of the Lord." The patience of Job we know, and the end of the Lord we know.[4] What end of the Lord? "My God, my God, why hast Thou forsaken Me?" They are the words of the Lord hanging on the cross. He did as it were leave Him for present felicity, not leave Him for eternal immortality. In this is "the end of the Lord." The Jews hold Him, the Jews insult, the Jews bind Him, crown Him with thorns, dishonor Him with spitting, scourge Him, overwhelm Him with revilings, hang Him upon the tree, pierce Him with a spear, last of all bury Him. He was as it were left: but by whom? By those insulting ones. Therefore thou shalt but to this end have patience, that thou mayest rise again and not die, that is, never die, even as Christ. For so we read, "Christ rising from the dead henceforth dieth not."[5]

11. "He ascended into heaven:" believe. "He sitteth at the right hand of the Father:" believe. By sitting, understand dwelling: as [in Latin] we say of any person, "In that country he dwelt (*sedit*) three years." The Scripture also has that expression, that such an one dwelt (*sedisse*) in a city for such a time.[6] Not meaning that he sat and never rose up? On this account the dwellings of men are called seats (*sedes*).[7] Where people are seated (in this sense), are they always sitting? Is there no rising, no walking, no lying down? And yet they are called seats (*sedes*). In this way, then, believe an inhabiting of Christ on the right hand of God the Father: He is there. And let not your heart say to you, What is He doing? Do not want to seek what is not permitted to find: He is there; it suffices you. He is blessed, and from blessedness which is called the right hand of the Father, of very blessedness the name is, right hand of the Father. For if we shall take it carnally, then because He sitteth on the right hand of the Father, the Father will be on His left hand. Is it consistent with piety so to put Them together, the Son on the right, the Father on the left? There it is all right-hand, because no misery is there.

12. "Thence He shall come to judge the quick and dead." The quick, who shall be alive and remain; the dead, who shall have gone before. It may also be understood thus:

---

[1] Ps. lxxv. 7.   [2] Job i. xxi.   [3] Job ii. 10.

[4] Ps. xxii. 1.
[5] Rom. vi. 9.   The Article of the descent into Hell appears not to have been included in this Creed.
[6] 1 Kings ii. 38. LXX.   [7] Cf. Serm. 214, n. 8. Ben.

The living, the just; the dead, the unjust. For He judges both, rendering unto each his own. To the just He will say in the judgment, "Come, ye blessed of My Father, receive the kingdom prepared for you from the beginning of the world." [1] For this prepare yourselves, for these things hope, for this live, and so live, for this believe, for this be baptized, that it may be said to you, "Come ye blessed of My Father, receive the kingdom prepared for you from the foundation of the world." To them on the left hand, what? "Go into everlasting fire prepared for the devil and his angels." [2] Thus will they be judged by Christ, the quick and the dead. We have spoken of Christ's first nativity, which is without time; spoken of the other in the fullness of time, Christ's nativity of the Virgin; spoken of the passion of Christ; spoken of the coming of Christ to judgment. The whole is spoken, that was to be spoken of Christ, God's Only Son, our Lord. But not yet is the Trinity perfect.

13. It follows in the Creed, "And in the Holy Ghost." This Trinity, one God, one nature, one substance, one power; highest equality, no division, no diversity, perpetual dearness of love.[3] Would ye know the Holy Ghost, that He is God? Be baptized, and ye will be His temple. The Apostle says, "Know ye not that your bodies are the temple within you of the Holy Ghost, Whom ye have of God?" [4] A temple is for God: thus also Solomon, king and prophet, was bidden to build a temple for God. If he had built a temple for the sun or moon or some star or some angel, would not God condemn him? Because therefore he built a temple for God, he showed that he worshipped God. And of what did he build? Of wood and stone, because God deigned to make unto Himself by His servant an house on earth, where He might be asked, where He might be had in mind. Of which blessed Stephen says, "Solomon built Him an house; howbeit the Most High dwelleth not in temples made by hand." [5] If then our bodies are the temple of the Holy Ghost, what manner of God is it that built a temple for the Holy Ghost? But it was God. For if our bodies be a temple of the Holy Ghost, the same built this temple for the Holy Ghost, that built our bodies. Listen to the Apostle saying, "God hath tempered the body, giving unto that which lacked the greater honor;" [6] when he was speaking of the different members that there should be no schisms in the body. God

created our body. The grass, God created; our body Who created? How do we prove that the grass is God's creating? He that clothes, the same creates. Read the Gospel, "If then the grass of the field," saith it, "which to-day is, and to-morrow is cast into the oven, God so clotheth." [7] He, then, creates Who clothes. And the Apostle: "Thou fool, that which thou sowest is not quickened except it die; and that which thou sowest, thou sowest not that body that shall be, but a bare grain, as perchance of wheat, or of some other corn; but God giveth it a body as He would, and to each one of seeds its proper body." [8] If then it be God that builds our bodies, God that builds our members, and our bodies are the temple of the Holy Ghost, doubt not that the Holy Ghost is God. And do not add as it were a third God; because Father and Son and Holy Ghost is One God. So believe ye.

14. It follows after commendation of the Trinity, "The Holy Church." God is pointed out, and His temple. "For the temple of God is holy," says the Apostle, "which (temple) are ye." [9] This same is the holy Church, the one Church, the true Church, the catholic Church, fighting against all heresies: fight, it can: be fought down, it cannot. As for heresies, they went all out of it, like as unprofitable branches pruned from the vine: but itself abideth in its root, in its Vine, in its charity. "The gates of hell shall not prevail against it." [10]

15. "Forgiveness of sins." Ye have [this article of] the Creed perfectly in you when ye receive Baptism. Let none say, "I have done this or that sin: perchance that is not forgiven me." What hast thou done? How great a sin hast thou done? Name any heinous thing thou hast committed, heavy, horrible, which thou shudderest even to think of: have done what thou wilt: hast thou killed Christ? There is not than that deed any worse, because also than Christ there is nothing better. What a dreadful thing is it to kill Christ! Yet the Jews killed Him, and many afterwards believed on Him and drank His blood: they are forgiven the sin which they committed. When ye have been baptized, hold fast a good life in the commandments of God, that ye may guard your Baptism even unto the end. I do not tell you that ye will live here without sin; but they are venial, without which this life is not. For the sake of all sins was Baptism provided; for the sake of light sins, without which we cannot be, was prayer provided. [11] What hath

---

[1] Matt. xxv. 34.   [2] Matt. xxv. 41.
[3] *Charitas.*   [4] 1 Cor. vi. 19.
[5] Acts vii. 47, 48.   [6] 1 Cor. xii. 24.

[7] Matt. vi. 30.   [8] 1 Cor. xv. 36–38.   [9] 1 Cor. iii. 17.
[10] Matt. xvi. 18. [See R.V.]   [11] *Inventus.*

the Prayer? "Forgive us our debts, as we also forgive our debtors."[1] Once for all we have washing in Baptism, every day we have washing in prayer. Only, do not commit those things for which ye must needs be separated from Christ's body: which be far from you! For those whom ye have seen doing penance,[2] have committed heinous things, either adulteries or some enormous crimes: for these they do penance. Because if theirs had been light sins, to blot out these daily prayer would suffice.

16. In three ways then are sins remitted in the Church; by Baptism, by prayer, by the greater humility of penance; yet God doth not remit sins but to the baptized. The very sins which He remits first, He remits not but to the baptized. When? when they are baptized. The sins which are after remitted upon prayer, upon penance, to whom He remits, it is to the baptized that He remitteth. For how can they say, "Our Father," who are not yet born sons? The Catechumens, so long as they be such, have upon them all their sins. If Catechumens, how much more Pagans? how much more heretics? But to heretics we do not change their baptism. Why? because they have baptism in the same way as a deserter has the soldier's mark:[3] just so these also have Baptism; they have it, but to be condemned thereby, not crowned. And yet if the deserter himself, being amended, begin to do duty as a soldier, does any man dare to change his mark?

17. We believe also "the resurrection of the flesh," which went before in Christ: that the body too may have hope of that which went before in its Head. The Head of the Church, Christ: the Church, the body of Christ. Our Head is risen, ascended into heaven: where the Head, there also the members. In what way the resurrection of the flesh? Lest any should chance to think it like as Lazarus's resurrection, that thou mayest know it to be not so, it is added, "Into life everlasting." God regenerate you! God preserve and keep you! God bring you safe unto Himself, Who is the Life Everlasting. Amen.

---

[1] Matt. vi. 12. [See R.V.] [2] "*Agere pœnitentiam.*" [3] "*Characterem.*"

ST. AUGUSTIN:

ON CONTINENCE

[DE CONTINENTIA.]

TRANSLATED BY

REV. C. L. CORNISH, M.A.,

OF EXETER COLLEGE, OXFORD.

ON CONTINENCE.

[DE CONTINENTIA.]

St. Augustin speaks of his work *On Continence* in *Ep.* 231, *Ad Darium Comitem.* [See vol. I. of this edition, p. 584.—P. S.] Possidius, *Ind.* c. 10, mentions it, and it is cited in the *Collectanea* of Bede or Florus, and by Eugypius. Erasmus is therefore wrong in ascribing it to Hugo on the ground of the style, which is not unlike that of the earlier discourses. It is evidently a discourse, and probably for that reason unnoticed in the *Retractations.* The Manichæan heresy is impugned after the manner of his early works.—(*Abridged from Benedictine ed.* vol. vi.)

1. It is difficult to treat of the virtue of the soul, which is called Continence, in a manner fully suitable and worthy; but He, whose great gift this virtue is, will help our littleness under the burden of so great a weight. For He, who bestows it upon His faithful ones when they are continent, Himself gives discourse of it to His ministers when they speak. Lastly, of so great a matter purposing to speak what Himself shall grant, in the first place we say and prove that Continence is the gift of God.[1] We have it written in the Book of Wisdom, that no one can be continent, unless God grant it. But the Lord, concerning that greater and more glorious Continence itself, whereby there is continence from the marriage bond, says, "Not all can receive this saying, but they to whom it is given."[2] And since marriage chastity also itself cannot be guarded, unless there be Continence from unlawful intercourse, the Apostle declared both to be the gift of God, when He spake of both lives, that is, both that of marriage and that without marriage, saying, "I would that all men were so as myself; but each· hath his own gift from

God; one in this manner, another in that manner."[3]

2. And lest it should seem that necessary Continence was to be hoped for from the Lord only in respect of the lust of the lower parts of the flesh, it is also sung in the Psalm; "Set, O Lord, a watch to my mouth, and a door of Continence around my lips."[4] But in this witness of the divine speech, if we understand "mouth" as we ought to understand it, we perceive how great a gift of God Continence there set is. Forsooth it is little to contain the mouth of the body, lest any thing burst forth thence, which is not for the better, through the sound of the voice. For there is, within, the mouth of the heart, where he, who spake these words, and wrote them for us to speak, desired of the Lord that the watch and door of Continence should be set for him. For many things we say not with the mouth of the body, and cry aloud with the heart: but there goes forth from the mouth of the body no word of any thing, whereof there is silence in the heart. Therefore what flows not forth thence, sounds not abroad: but what flows forth thence, if it be

---

[1] Wis. viii. 21.   [2] Matt. xix. 11.   [3] 1 Cor. vii. 7.   [4] Ps. cxli. 3.

evil, although it move not the tongue, defiles the soul. Therefore Continence must be set there, where the conscience even of them who are silent speaks. For it is brought to pass by means of the door of Continence, that there go not forth thence that, which, even when the lips of the flesh are closed, pollutes the life of him that hath the thought.

3. Lastly, to show more plainly the inner mouth, which by these words he meant, after having said, "Set a watch, O Lord, to my mouth, and a door of Continence around my lips," he added straightway, "Cause not my heart to fall aside into evil words."[1] The falling aside of the heart, what is it but the consent? For he hath not yet spoken, whosoever in his heart hath with no falling aside of the heart consented unto suggestions that meet him of each several thing that is seen. But, if he hath consented, he hath already spoken in his heart, although he hath not uttered sound by the mouth; although he hath not done with hand or any part whatever of the body, yet hath he done what in his thought he hath already determined that he is to do: guilty by the divine laws, although hidden to human senses; the word having been spoken in the heart, no deed having been committed through the body. But in no case would he have moved the limb without, in a deed, the beginning of which deed had not gone before within in word. For it is no lie that is written, that "the beginning of every work is a word."[2] Forsooth men do many things with mouth closed, tongue quiet, voice bridled; but yet they do nothing by work of the body, which they have not before spoken in the heart. And through this since there are many sins in inward sayings which are not in outward deeds, whereas there are none in outward deeds, which do not go before in inward sayings, there will be purity of innocence from both, if the door of Continence be set around the inward lips.

4. For which cause our Lord Himself also with His own mouth saith, "Cleanse what are within, and what are without will be clean."[3] And, also, in another place, when He was refuting the foolish speeches of the Jews, in that they spake evil against His disciples, eating with unwashen hands; "Not what entereth into the mouth," said He, "defileth the man: but what cometh forth out of the mouth, that defileth the man."[4] Which sentence, if the whole of it be taken of the mouth of the body, is absurd. For neither doth vomit defile him, whom food defileth not. Forsooth food entereth into the mouth,

vomit proceedeth forth out of the mouth. But without doubt the former words relate to the mouth of the flesh, where He says, "Not what entereth into the mouth defileth the man," but the latter words to the mouth of the heart, where He saith, "But what proceedeth forth out of the mouth, this defileth the man."[5] Lastly, when the Apostle Peter sought of Him an explanation of this as of a parable, He answered, "Are ye also yet without understanding? understand ye not, that whatsoever entereth into the mouth, goeth into the belly, and is cast out into the draught?" Here surely we perceive the mouth of the flesh, into which the food enters. But in what He next adds, in order that we might recognize the mouth of the heart, the slowness of our heart would not follow, did not the Truth deign to walk even with the slow. For He saith, "But what things go forth from the mouth, go out of the heart;" as though He should say, When you hear it said "from the mouth," understand "from the heart." I say both, but I set forth one by the other. The inner man hath an inner mouth, and this the inner ear discerns: what things go forth from this mouth, go out of the heart, and they defile the man. Then having left the term mouth, which may be understood also of the body, He shows more openly what He is saying. "For from the heart go out," saith He, "evil thoughts, murders, adulteries, fornications, thefts, false witness, blasphemies; these are what defile the man." There is surely no one of those evils, which can be committed also by the members of the body, but that the evil thoughts go before and defile the man, although something hinder the sinful and wicked deeds of the body from following. For if, because power is not given, the hand is free from the murder of a man, is the heart of the murderer forsooth therefore clean from sin? Or if she be chaste, whom one unchaste wishes to commit adultery with, hath he on that account failed to commit adultery with her in his heart? Or if the harlot be not found in the brothel, doth he, who seeks her, on that account fail to commit fornication in his heart? Or if time and place be wanting to one who wishes to hurt his neighbor by a lie, hath he on that account failed already to speak false witness with his inner mouth? Or if any one fearing men, dare not utter aloud blasphemy with tongue of flesh, is he on this account guiltless of this crime, who saith in his heart, "There is no God."[6] Thus all the other evil deeds of

---

[1] Ps. cxli. 4. [See R.V.]   [2] Ecclus. xxxvii. 16. LXX.
[3] Matt. xxiii. 26.   [4] Matt. xv. 11.   [5] Matt. xv. 17-20.   [6] Ps. xiv. 1.

men, which no motion of the body performs, of which no sense of the body is conscious, have their own secret criminals, who are also polluted by consent alone in thought, that is, by evil words of the inner mouth. Into which he (the Psalmist) fearing lest his heart should fall aside, asks of the Lord that the door of Continence be set around the lips of this mouth, to contain the heart, that it fall not aside into evil words: but contain it, by not suffering thought to proceed to consent: for thus, according to the precept of the Apostle, sin reigneth not in our mortal body, nor do we yield our members as weapons of unrighteousness unto sin.[1] From fulfilling which precept they are surely far removed, who on this account turn not their members to sin, because no power is allowed them; and if this be present, straightway by the motions of their members, as of weapons, they show, who reigneth in them within. Wherefore, so far as is in themselves, they yield their members weapons of unrighteousness unto sin; because this is what they wish, which for this reason they yield' not, because they are not able.

5. And on this account that, which, the parts that beget being bridled by modesty, is most chiefly and properly to be called Continence, is violated by no transgression, if the higher Continence, concerning which we have been some time speaking, be preserved in the heart. For this reason the Lord, after He had said, "For from the heart go forth evil thoughts," then went on to add what it is that belongs to evil thoughts, "murders, adulteries," and the rest. He spake not of all; but, having named certain by way of instance, He taught that we are to understand others also. Of which there is no one that can take place, unless an evil thought have gone before, whereby that is prepared within, which is done without, and going forth out of the mouth of the heart already defiles the man, although, through no power being granted, it be not done without by means of the members of the body. When therefore a door of Continence hath been set in the mouth of the heart, whence go out all that defile the man, if nothing such be permitted to go out thence, there followeth a purity, wherein now the conscience may rejoice; although there be not as yet that perfection, wherein Continence shall not strive with vice. But now, so long as "the flesh lusteth against the spirit, and the spirit against the flesh,"[2] it is enough for us not to consent unto the evils which we feel in us. But, when

that consent takes place, then there goeth out of the mouth of the heart what defileth the man. But when through Continence consent is withheld, the evil of the lust of the flesh, against which the lust of the spirit fights, is not suffered to harm.

6. But it is one thing to fight well, which now is, when the strife[3] of death is resisted; another thing not to have an adversary, which will then be, when death, "the last enemy,"[4] shall be destroyed. For Continence also itself, when it curbs and restrains lusts, at once both seeks the good unto the immortality of which we aim, and rejects the evil with which in this mortality we contend. Of the one it is forsooth the lover and beholder, but of the other both the enemy and witness: both seeking what becomes, and fleeing what misbecomes. Assuredly Continence would not labor in curbing lusts, if we had no wishes contrary to what is becoming, if there were no opposition on the part of evil lust unto our good will. The Apostle cries aloud, "I know," saith he, "that there dwelleth not in me, that is in my flesh, good. For to will lieth near to me, but to accomplish good I find not."[5] For now good can be done, so far as that there be no assent given unto evil lust: but good will be accomplished, when the evil lust itself shall come to an end. And also the same teacher of the Gentiles cries aloud, "I take pleasure together with the law of God after the inner man: but I see another law in my members, warring against the law of my mind."[6]

7. This conflict none experience in themselves, save such as war on the side of the virtues, and war down the vices: nor doth any thing storm the evil of lust, save the good of Continence. But there are, who, being utterly ignorant of the law of God, account not evil lusts among their enemies, and through wretched blindness being slaves to them, over and above think themselves also blessed, by satisfying them rather than taming them. But whoso through the Law have come to know them, ("For through the Law is the knowledge of sin,"[7] and, "Lust," saith he, "I knew not, unless the Law should say, Thou shalt not lust after,"[8]) and yet are overcome by their assault, because they live under the Law, whereby what is good is commanded, but not also given: they live not under Grace, which gives through the Holy Spirit what is commanded through the Law: unto these the Law therefore entered, that in them the offense might abound. The prohibition in-

---

[1] Rom. vi. 12, 13.   Gal. v. 17.

[3] (Reading νεῖκος.)   [4] 1 Cor. xv. 55; ib. 26.   [5] Rom. vii. 18.
[6] Rom. vii. 22, 23.   [7] Rom. iii. 20.
[8] Rom. vii. 7. [See R.V.]

creased the lust, and made it unconquered:[1] that there might be transgression also, which without the Law was not, although there was sin, "For where there is not Law, neither is there transgression."[2] Thus the Law, Grace not helping, forbidding sin, became over and above the strength of sin; whence the Apostle saith, "The Law is the strength of sin."[3] Nor is it to be wondered at, that man's weakness even from the good Law added strength to evil, whilst it trusts to fulfill the Law itself of its own strength. Forsooth being ignorant of the righteousness of God,[4] which He gives unto the weak, and wishing to establish his own, of which the weak is void, he was not made subject to the righteousness of God, reprobate and proud. But if the Law, as a schoolmaster, lead unto Grace one made an offender, as though for this purpose more grievously wounded, that he may desire a Physician; against the baneful sweetness, whereby lust prevailed, the Lord gives a sweetness that worketh good, that by it Continence may the more delight, and "our land giveth her fruit,"[5] whereby the soldier is fed, who by the help of the Lord wars down sin.

8. Such soldiers the Apostolic trumpet enkindles for battle with that sound, "Therefore let not," saith he, "sin reign in your mortal body to obey its lusts; nor yield your members weapons of unrighteousness unto sin; but yield yourselves unto God, as living in place of dead, and your members weapons of righteousness unto God. For sin shall not rule over you. For ye are not under the law, but under Grace."[6] And in another place, "Therefore," saith he, "brethren, we are debtors, not to the flesh, to live after the flesh. For if ye shall live after the flesh, ye shall die; but if by the Spirit ye shall mortify the deeds of the flesh, ye shall live. For as many as are led by the Spirit of God, these are sons of God."[7] This therefore is the business in hand, so long as this our mortal life under Grace lasts, that sin, that is the lust of sin, (for this he in this place calls by the name of sin,) reign not in this our mortal body. But it is then shown to reign, if obedience be yielded to its desires. There is therefore in us lust of sin, which must not be suffered to reign; there are its desires, which we must not obey, lest obeying it reign over us. Wherefore let not lust usurp our members, but let Continence claim them for herself; that they be weapons of righteousness unto God, that they be not weapons of

unrighteousness unto sin; for thus sin shall not rule over us. For we are not under the Law, which indeed commandeth what is good yet giveth it not: but we are under Grace, which, making us to love that which the Law commands, is able to rule over the free.

9. And also, when he exhorts us, that we live not after the flesh, lest we die, but that by the Spirit we mortify the deeds of the flesh, that we may live; surely the trumpet which sounds, shows the war in which we are engaged, and enkindles us to contend keenly, and to do our enemies to death,[8] that we be not done to death by them. But who those enemies are, it hath set forth plainly enough. For those are they, whom it willed should be done to death by us, that is to say, the works of the flesh. For so it saith, "But if by the Spirit ye shall mortify the deeds of the flesh, ye shall live." And in order that we may know what these are, let us hear the same in like manner writing unto the Galatians, and saying, "But the works of the flesh are manifest, which are, fornications, uncleannesses, luxuries, idolatry, witchcrafts, hatreds, contentions, emulations, wraths, strifes, heresies, envyings, drunkennesses, revellings, and such like; of which I foretell to you, as I have foretold, that they who do such things shall not possess the kingdom of God."[9] For the very war there also was he showing, that he should speak of these, and unto the death-doing of these enemies was he calling up the soldiers of Christ by the same heavenly and spiritual trumpet. For he had said above, "But I say, walk in the Spirit, and perform ye not the lusts of the flesh. For the flesh lusteth against the Spirit, and the Spirit against the flesh. For these are opposed one to the other, that ye do not what ye would. But if ye are led by the Spirit, ye are not under the Law."[10] Therefore being set under Grace, he would have them have that conflict against the works of the flesh. And in order to point out these works of the flesh, he added what I have mentioned above. "But the works of the flesh are manifest, which are, fornications," and the rest, whether what he mentioned, or whether what he admonished were to be understood, chiefly as he added, "and such like." Lastly, in this battle, against what is in a manner the carnal army leading forth as it were another spiritual line, "But the fruit of the Spirit is," saith he, "charity, joy, peace, long-suffering, kindness, goodness, faith, gentleness, continence; against such there is no law."[11] He saith not "against

---

[1] Rom. v. 20. [2] Rom. iv. 15. [3] 1 Cor. xv. 56.
[4] Rom. x. 3. [5] Ps. lxxxv. 12. [6] Rom. vi. 12, 13, 14.
[7] Rom. viii. 12, 13, 14.

[8] *Mortificare.* [9] Gal. v. 19-21.
[10] Gal. v. 16-18. [See R. V.] [11] Gal. v. 22, 23.

these," lest they should be thought to be alone: although even were he to say this, we ought to understand all, whatever goods of the same kind we could think of: but he saith, "against such," that is to say, both these and whatsoever are such like. However, in that among the goods of which he made mention, he set Continence in the last[1] place, (concerning which we have now undertaken to treat, and on account of which we have already said much,) he willed that it should in an especial manner cleave to our minds. Forsooth this same is of great avail in this case, wherein the Spirit lusteth against the flesh; forasmuch as in a certain way it crucifies the lusts of the flesh. Whence, after the Apostle had thus spoken, he added straightway, "But they who are Jesus Christ's have crucified their own flesh, with the passions and lusts."[2] This is the acting of Continence: thus the works of the flesh are done to death. But they do to death those, whom falling away from Continence lust draweth into consent to do such works.

10. But in order that we fall not away from Continence, we ought to watch specially against those snares of the suggestions of the devil, that we presume not of our own strength. For, "Cursed is every one that setteth his hope in man."[3] And who is he, but man? We cannot therefore truly say that he setteth not his hope in man, who setteth it in himself. For this also, to "live after man," what is it but to "live after the flesh?" Whoso therefore is tempted by such a suggestion, let him hear, and, if he have any Christian feeling, let him tremble. Let him hear, I say, "If ye shall live after the flesh, ye shall die."

11. But some one will say to me that it is one thing to live after man, another thing to live after the flesh; because man forsooth is a rational creature, and there is in him a rational soul, whereby he differs from the beast: but the flesh is the lowest and earthly part of man, and thus to live after it is faulty: and for this reason, he who lives after man, assuredly lives not after the flesh, but rather after that part of man, whereby he is man, that is, after the spirit of the mind whereby he excels the beasts. But this discussion is perhaps of some force in the schools of philosophers: but we, in order to understand the Apostle of Christ, ought to observe in what manner the Christian books are used to speak; at any rate it is the belief of all of us, to whom to live is Christ, that Man was taken

unto Himself by the Word of God, not surely without a rational soul, as certain heretics will have it; and yet we read, "The Word was made flesh."[4] What is to be here understood by "flesh," but Man? "And all flesh shall see the salvation of God."[5] What can be understood, but all men? "Unto Thee shall all flesh come."[6] What is it, but all men? "Thou hast given unto Him power over all flesh."[7] What is it, but all men? "Of the works of the Law shall no flesh be justified."[8] What is it, but no man shall be justified? And this the same Apostle in another place confessing more plainly saith, "Man shall not be justified of the works of the Law."[9] The Corinthians also he rebukes, saying, "Are ye not carnal, and walk after man?"[10] After he had called them carnal, he saith not, ye walk after the flesh, but after man, forasmuch as by this also what would he have understood, but after the flesh? For surely if to walk, that is, to live, after the flesh deserved blame, but after man deserved praise, he would not say by way of rebuke, "ye walk after man." Let man recognize the reproach; let him change his purpose, let him shun destruction. Hear thou man: walk not thou after man, but after Him Who made man. Fall not thou away from Him Who made thee, even unto thyself. For a man said, who yet lived not after man, "Not that we are sufficient to think any thing from ourselves, as though of ourselves: but our sufficiency is of God."[11] Consider if he lived after man, who spake these things with truth. Therefore the Apostle, admonishing man not to live after man, restores man to God. But whoso liveth not after man, but after God, assuredly liveth not even after himself, because himself also is a man. But he is therefore said also to live after the flesh, when he so lives; because also when the flesh alone hath been named, man is understood, as we have already shown: just as when the soul alone hath been named, man is understood: whence it is said, "Let every soul be subject unto the higher powers,"[12] that is, every man; and, "Seventy-five souls went down into Egypt with Jacob,"[13] that is, seventy-five men. Therefore live thou not after thyself, O man: thou hadst thence perished, but thou wast sought. Live not then, I say, after thyself, O man; thou hadst thence perished, but thou wast found. Accuse not thou the nature of the flesh, when you hear it said, "If ye shall live after the flesh, ye shall die."[14] For thus

---

[1] Vulg. adds, "*patientia, modestia, castitas.*"
[2] Gal. v. 24. [3] Jer. xvii. 5.

[4] John i. 14. [5] Luke iii. 6. [6] Ps. lxv. 2.
[7] John xvii. 2. [8] Rom. iii. 20. [9] Gal. ii. 16.
[10] 1 Cor. iii. 3. [11] Cor. iii. 5. [12] Rom. xiii. 1.
[13] Gen. xlvi. 27. [14] Rom. viii. 13.

could it be said, and most truly could it, If ye shall live after yourselves ye shall die. For the devil hath not flesh, and yet, because he would live after himself, "he abode not in the truth."[1] What wonder therefore, if, living after himself, "when he speaketh a lie, he speaketh of his own," which the Truth spake truly of him.

12. When, therefore, you hear it said, "Sin shall not reign over you;"[2] have not thou confidence of thyself, that sin reign not over thee, but of Him, unto Whom a certain Saint saith in prayer, "Direct my paths after Thy Word, and let no iniquity have dominion over me."[3] For lest haply, after that we had heard, "sin shall not reign over you," we should lift up ourselves, and lay this to our own strength, straightway the Apostle saw this, and added, "For ye are not under the Law, but under Grace." Therefore, Grace causeth that sin reign not over you. Do not thou, therefore, have confidence of thyself, lest it thence reign much more over thee. And, when we hear it said, "If by the Spirit ye shall mortify the deeds of the flesh, ye shall live,"[4] let us not lay this so great good unto our own spirit, as though of itself it can do this. For, in order that we should not entertain that carnal sense, the spirit being dead rather than that which putteth others to death, straightway he added, "For as many as are led by the Spirit of God, these are sons of God."[5] Therefore that by our spirit we may mortify the works of the flesh, we are led by the Spirit of God, Who gives Continence, whereby to curb, tame, overcome lust.

13. In this so great conflict, wherein man under Grace lives, and when, being aided, he fights well, rejoices in the Lord with trembling, there yet are not wanting even to valiant warriors, and mortifiers however unconquered of the works of the flesh, some wounds of sins, for the healing of which they may say daily, "Forgive us our debts:"[6] against the same vices, and against the devil the prince and king of vices, striving with much greater watchfulness and keenness by the very prayer, that his deadly suggestions avail not aught, whereby he further urges the sinner to excuse rather than accuse his own sins; and thus those wounds not only be not healed, but also, although they were not deadly, yet may be pressed home to grievous and fatal harm. And here therefore there is need of a more cautious Continence, whereby to restrain the proud appetite of man; whereby he is self-pleased, and unwilling to be found worthy of blame, and disdains, when he sins, to be convicted that he himself has sinned; not with healthful humility taking upon him to accuse himself, but rather with fatal arrogance seeking to find an excuse. In order to restrain this pride, he, whose words I have already set down above, and, as I could, commended, sought Continence from the Lord. For, after that he had said, "Set, O Lord, a watch to my mouth, and a door of Continence around my lips. Make not my heart to fall aside unto evil words;"[7] explaining more clearly whereof he spake this, he saith, "to make excuses in sins." For what more evil than these words, whereby the evil man denies that he is evil, although convicted of an evil work, which he cannot deny. And since he cannot hide the deed, or say that it is well done, and still sees that it is clear that it was done by him, he seeks to refer to another what he hath done, as though he could remove thence what he hath deserved. Being unwilling that himself be guilty, he rather adds to his guilt, and by excusing, not accusing, his own sins, he knows not that he is putting from him, not punishment, but pardon. For before human judges, forasmuch as they may be deceived, it seems to profit somewhat for the time, to cleanse as it were what hath been done amiss by any deceit whatever; but before God, Who cannot be deceived, we are to use, not a deceitful defense, but a true confession of sins.

14. And some indeed, who are used to excuse their own sins, complain that they are driven to sin by fate, as though the stars had decreed this, and heaven had first sinned by decreeing such, in order that man should after sin by committing such, and thus had rather impute their sin to fortune: who think that all things are driven to and fro by chance accidents, and yet contend that this their wisdom and assertion is not of chance rashness, but of ascertained reason. What madness then is it, to lay to reason their discussions, and to make their actions subject to accidents! Others refer to the devil the whole of what they do ill: and will not have even a share with him, whereas they may suspect whether he by hidden suggestions hath persuaded them to evil, and on the other hand cannot doubt that they have consented to those suggestions, from whatever source they have come. There are also they who extend their defense of self unto an accusation of God, wretched by the divine judgment, but blasphemers by their own madness. For

1 John viii. 44.   2 Rom. vi. 14.
3 Ps. cxix. 133.   4 Rom. viii. 13.
5 Rom. viii. 14.   6 Matt. vi. 12.

7 Ps. cxli. 3, 4.

against Him they bring in from a contrary principle a substance of evil rebelling, which He could not have resisted, had He not blended with that same that was rebelling a portion of His own Substance and Nature, for it to contaminate and corrupt; and they say that they then sin when the nature of evil prevails over the nature of God. This is that most unclean madness of the Manichæans, whose devilish devices the undoubted truth most easily overthrows; which confesses that the nature of God is incapable of contamination and corruption. But what wicked contamination and corruption do they not deserve to have believed of them, by whom God, Who is good in the very highest degree, and in a way that admits not of comparison, is believed to be capable of contamination and corruption?

15. And there are also they who in excuse of their sins so accuse God, as to say that sins are pleasing to Him. For, if they were displeasing, say they, surely by His most Almighty power He would by no means suffer them to take place. As though indeed God suffered sins to be unpunished, even in the case of those whom by remission of sins He frees from eternal punishment! No one forsooth receives pardon of more grievous punishment due, unless he hath suffered some punishment, be it what it may, although far less than what was due: and the fullness of mercy is so conveyed, as that the justice also of discipline is not abandoned. For also sin, which seems unavenged, hath its own attendant punishment, so that there is no one but by reason of what he hath done either suffers pain from bitterness, or suffers not through blindness. As therefore you say, Why doth He permit those things, if they are displeasing? so I say, Why doth He punish them, if they are pleasing? And thus, as I confess that those things would not take place at all, unless they were permitted by the Almighty, so confess thou that what are punished by the Just One ought not to be done; in order that, by not doing what He punishes, we may deserve to learn of Him, why He permits to exist what He punishes. For, as it is written, " solid food is for the perfect," [1] wherein they who have made good progress already understand, that it pertained rather unto the Almighty power of God, to allow the existence of evils coming from the free choice of the will So great forsooth is His Almighty goodness, as that even of evil He can make good, either by pardoning, or by healing, or by fitting and turning unto the profit of the

pious, or even by most justly taking vengeance. For all these are good, and most worthy a good and Almighty God: and yet they are not made save of evils. What therefore better, what more Almighty, than He, Who, whereas He maketh no evil, even of evils maketh well? They who have done ill cry unto Him, " Forgive us our debts;" [2] He hears, He pardons. Their own evils have hurt the sinners; He helps and heals their sicknesses. The enemies of His people rage; of their rage He makes martyrs. Lastly, also, He condemns those, whom He judges worthy of condemnation; although they suffer their own evils, yet He doeth what is good. For what is just cannot but be good, and assuredly as sin is unjust, so the punishment of sin is just.

16. But God wanted not power to make man such as that he should not be able to sin: but He chose rather to make him such, as that it should lie in his power [3] to sin, if he would; not to sin, if he would not; forbidding the one, enjoining the other; that it might be to him first a good desert not to sin, and after a just reward not to be able to sin. For such also at the last will He makes His Saints, as to be without all power to sin. Such forsooth even now hath He His angels, whom in Him we so love, as to have no fear for any of them, lest by sinning he become a devil. And this we presume not of any just man in this mortal life. But we trust that all will be 'such in that immortal life. For Almighty God Who worketh good even of our evils, what good will He give, when He shall have set us free from all evils? Much may be said more fully and more subtilely on the good use of evil; but this is not what we have undertaken in our present discourse, and we must avoid in it excess of length.

17. Now therefore let us return to that, wherefore we have said what we have. We have need of Continence, and we know it to be a divine gift, that our heart fall not away unto evil words, to make excuses in sins. But what sin is there but that we have need of Continence, to restrain it from being committed, since it is this very Continence which, in case it have been committed, restrains it from being defended by wicked pride? Universally therefore we have need of Continence, in order to turn away from evil. But to do good seems to pertain to another virtue, that is, to righteousness.[4] This the sacred Psalm admonishes us, where we read, " Turn away from evil, and do good." But with what end we do this, it adds bye and bye, saying,

---

"Seek peace, and ensue it."[1] For we shall then have perfect peace, when, our nature cleaving inseparably to its Creator, we shall have nothing of ourselves opposed to ourselves. This our Saviour also Himself would have us to understand, so far as seems to me, when He said, "Let your loins be girt, and your lamps burning."[2] What is it, to gird the loins? To restrain lusts, which is the work of continence. But to have lamps burning is to shine and glow with good works, which is the work of righteousness. Nor was He here silent with what end we do these things, adding and saying, "And you like unto men waiting for their Lord, when He cometh from the marriage."[3] But, when He shall have come, He will reward us, who have kept ourselves from those things which lust, and have done those things which charity hath bidden us: that we may reign in His perfect and eternal peace, without any strife of evil, and with the highest delight of good.

18. All we therefore, who believe in the Living and True God, Whose Nature, being in the highest sense good and incapable of change, neither doth any evil, nor suffers any evil, from Whom is every good, even that which admits of decrease, and Who admits not at all of decrease in His own Good, Which is Himself, when we hear the Apostle saying, "Walk in the Spirit, and perform ye not the lusts of the flesh. For the flesh lusteth against the Spirit, and the Spirit against the flesh: For these are opposed one to another, that ye do not what ye would."[4] Far be it from us to believe, what the madness of the Manichees believes, that there are here shown two natures or principles contrary one to another at strife, the one nature of good, the other of evil. Altogether these two are both good; both the Spirit is a good, and the flesh a good: and man, who is composed of both, one ruling, the other obeying, is assuredly a good, but a good capable of change, which yet could not be made save by a Good incapable of change, by Whom was created every good, whether small or great; but how small soever, yet made by What is Great; and how great soever, yet no way to be compared with the greatness of the Maker. But in this nature of man, that is good, and well formed and ordered by One That is Good, there is now war, since there is not yet health. Let the sickness be healed, there is peace. But that sickness fault hath deserved, not nature hath had. And this fault indeed through the laver of regeneration the grace of God hath already remitted unto the faithful; but under

the hands of the same Physician nature as yet striveth with its sickness. But in such a conflict victory will be entire soundness; and that, soundness not for a time, but for ever: wherein not only this sickness is to come to an end, but also none to arise after it. Wherefore the just man addresseth his soul and saith, "Bless the Lord, O my soul, and forget not all His returns: Who becometh propitious to all thy iniquities, Who healeth all thy sicknesses."[5] He becometh propitious to our iniquities, when He pardons sins: He heals sicknesses when He restrains evil desires. He becometh propitious unto iniquities by the grant of forgiveness: He heals sicknesses, by the grant of continence. The one was done in Baptism to persons confessing; the other is done in the strife to persons contending; wherein through His help we are to overcome our disease. Even now the one is done, when we are heard, saying, "Forgive us our debts;"[6] but the other, when we are heard, saying, "Lead us not into temptation. For every one is tempted," saith the Apostle James, "being drawn away and enticed by his own lust."[7] And against this fault there is sought the help of medicine from Him, Who can heal all such sicknesses, not by the removal of a nature that is alien from us, but in the renewal of our own nature. Whence also the above-mentioned Apostle saith not, "Every one is tempted" by lust, but added, "by his own:" that he who hears this may understand, how he ought to cry, "I said, Lord, have mercy upon me, heal my soul, for I have sinned against Thee."[8] For it would not have needed healing, had it not corrupted[9] itself by sinning, so that its own flesh should lust against it, that is, itself should be opposed to itself, on that side, wherein in the flesh it was made sick.

19. For the flesh lusts after nothing save through the soul, but the flesh is said to lust against the spirit, when the soul with fleshly lust wrestles against the spirit. This whole are we: and the flesh itself, which on the departure of the soul dies, the lowest part of us is not put away as what we are to flee from, but is laid aside as what we are to receive again, and, after having received it, never again to leave. But "there is sown an animal body, there shall rise again a spiritual body."[10] Then from that time the flesh will not lust after any thing against the spirit, when as itself also shall be called spiritual, forasmuch as not only without any opposition, but also without any need of bodily aliment,

---

[1] Ps. xxxiv. 14.　　[2] Luke xii. 35.　　[3] Luke xii. 36.
[4] Gal. v. 16, 17.

[5] Ps. ciii. 2, 3.　　　[6] Matt. vi. 12, 13.
[7] James i. 14.　　　　[8] Ps. xli. 4.
[9] *Vitiasset.*　　　　　[10] 1 Cor. xv. 44.

it shall be for ever made subject unto the spirit, to be quickened by Christ. Therefore these two things, which are now opposed the one to the other within us, since we exist in both, let us pray and endeavor that they may agree. For we ought not to think the one of them an enemy, but the fault, whereby the flesh lusteth against the spirit: and this, when healed, will itself cease to exist, and either substance will be safe, and no strife between either. Let us hear the Apostle; "I know," saith he, "that there dwelleth not in me, that is, in my flesh, any good."[1] This certainly he saith; that the fault of the flesh, in a good thing, is not good; and, when this shall have ceased to exist, it will be flesh, but it will not be now corrupted or faulty[2] flesh. And yet that this pertains to our nature the same teacher shows, by saying, first, "I know that there dwelleth not in me," in order to expound which, he added, "that is, in my flesh, any good." Therefore he saith that his flesh is himself. It is not then itself that is our enemy: and when its faults are resisted, itself is loved, because itself is cared for; "For no one ever hated his own flesh,"[3] as the Apostle himself saith. And in another place he saith, "So then I myself with the mind serve the Law of God, but with the flesh the Law of sin." Let them hear that have ears. "So then I myself;" I with the mind, I with the flesh, but "with the mind I serve the Law of God, but with the flesh the law of sin."[4] How "with the flesh the law of sin?" was it at all by consenting unto fleshly lust? Far be it! but by having there motions of desires which he would not have, and yet had. But, by not consenting to them, with the mind he served the Law of God, and kept his members from becoming weapons of sins.

20. There are therefore in us evil desires, by consenting not unto which we live not ill: there are in us lusts of sins, by obeying not which we perfect not evil, but by having them do not as yet perfect good. The Apostle shows both, that neither is good here perfected, where evil is so lusted after, nor evil here perfected, whereas such lust is not obeyed. The one forsooth he shows, where he says, "To will is present with me, but to perfect good is not;"[5] the other, where he says, "Walk in the Spirit, and perfect not the lusts of the flesh."[6] For neither in the former place doth he say that to do good is not with him, but "to perfect," nor here doth he say, Have not "lusts of the flesh," but "perfect

not." Therefore there take place in us evil lusts, when that pleases which is not lawful; but they are not perfected, when evil lusts are restrained by the mind serving the Law of God. And good takes place, when that, which wrongly pleases, takes not place through the good delight prevailing. But the perfection of good is not fulfilled, so long as by the flesh serving the law of sin, evil lust entices, and, although it be restrained, is yet moved. For there would be no need for it to be restrained, were it not moved. There will be at some time also the perfection of good, when the destruction of evil: the one will be highest, the other will be no more. And if we think that this is to be hoped for in this mortal state, we are deceived. For it shall be then, when death shall not be; and it shall be there, where shall be life eternal. For in that world,[7] and in that kingdom, there shall be highest good, no evil: when there shall be, and where there shall be, highest love of wisdom, no labor of continence. Therefore the flesh is not evil, if it be void of evil, that is, of fault, whereby man was rendered faulty, not made ill, but himself making. For on either part, that is, both soul and body, being made good by the good God, himself made the evil, whereby he was made evil. From the guilt of which evil being already also set free through forgiveness,[8] that he may not think what he hath done to be light, he yet wars with his own fault through continence. But far be it that there be any faults in such as reign in that peace which shall be hereafter; since in this state of war there are lessened daily in such as make progress, not sins only, but the very lusts also, with which, by not consenting, we strive, and by consenting unto which we sin.

21. That, therefore, the flesh lusteth against the Spirit, that there dwelleth not in our flesh good, that the law in our members is opposed to the law of the mind, is not a mingling of two natures caused of contrary principles, but a division of one against itself caused through desert of sin. We were not so in Adam, before that nature, having listened to and followed its deceiver, had despised and offended its Creator: that is, not the former life of man created, but the latter punishment of man condemned. From which condemnation when set free by Grace, through Jesus Christ, being free they contend with their punishment, having received not as yet full salvation, but already a pledge of salvation: but when not set free, they are both guilty by reason of sins, and involved in punishments. But after this life for the guilty

---

[1] Rom. vii. 18.   [2] *Vitiata vel vitiosa.*
[3] Eph. v 29.   [4] Rom. vii. 25.
[5] Rom. vii. 18.   [6] Gal. v. 16.

[7] *Sæculo.*   [8] *Indulgentiam.*

there will remain for ever punishment for their crime: for the free there will no more remain for ever either crime or punishment: but the good substances, spirit and flesh, will continue for ever, which God, Who is good, and incapable of change, created good although capable of change. But they will continue having been changed for the better, never from this time to be changed for the worse: all evil being utterly destroyed, both what man hath unjustly done, and what he hath justly suffered. And, these two kinds of evil perishing utterly, whereof the one is of iniquity going before, the other of unhappiness following after, the will of man will be upright without any depravity. There it will be clear and plain to all, what now many of the faithful believe, few understand, that evil is not a substance: but that, as a wound in a body, so in a substance, which hath made itself faulty, it hath begun to exist, when the disease hath commenced, and ceaseth to exist in it, when the healing hath been perfected. Therefore, all evil having arisen from us, and having been destroyed in us, our good also having been increased and perfected unto the height of most happy incorruption and immortality, of what kind shall either of our substances be? forasmuch as now, in this corruption and mortality, when as yet "the corruptible body weigheth down the soul;"[1] and, what the Apostle saith, "the body is dead by reason of sin;"[2] yet the same himself beareth such witness unto our flesh, that is, to our lowest and earthly part, as to say, what I made mention of a little above, "No one ever hated his own flesh."[3] And to add straightway, "but nourisheth and cherisheth it, as also Christ the Church."

22. I say not, therefore, with what error, but with what utter madness, do the Manichees attribute our flesh to some, I know not what, fabled "race of darkness,"[4] which they will have hath had its own nature without any beginning ever evil: whereas the true teacher exhorts men to love their own wives by the pattern of their own flesh, and exhorts them unto this very thing by the pattern also of Christ and the Church. Lastly, we must call to mind the whole place itself of the Epistle of the Apostle, relating greatly unto the matter in hand. "Husbands," saith he, "love your wives, as Christ also loved the Church, and delivered Himself up for it, that He might sanctify it, cleansing it by the laver of the water in the word: that He might set forth unto Himself a glorious Church, not having

spot, or wrinkle, or any such thing, but that it may be holy and unspotted. So," saith he, "husbands also ought to love their own wives, as their own bodies. Whoso loveth his own wife, loveth himself."[5] Then he added, what we have already made mention of, "For no man ever hated his own flesh, but nourisheth it, and cherisheth it; as also Christ the Church."[6] What saith the madness of most impure impiety in answer to these things? What say ye in answer to these things, ye Manichees; ye who wish to bring in upon us, as if out of the Epistles of the Apostles, two natures without beginning, one of good, the other of evil: and will not listen to the Epistles of the Apostles, that they may correct you from that sacrilegious perverseness? As ye read, "The flesh lusteth against the spirit,"[7] and, "There dwelleth not in my flesh any good;"[8] so read ye, "No one ever hated his own flesh, but nourisheth and cherisheth it, as also Christ the Church."[9] As ye read, "I see another law in my members, opposed to the law of my mind;"[10] so read ye, "As Christ loved the Church, so also ought men to love their own wives, as their own bodies." Be not ye crafty in the former witnesses of Holy Scripture, and deaf in this latter, and ye shall be correct in both. For, if ye receive the latter as right is, ye will endeavor to understand the former also as truth is.

23. The Apostle has made known to us certain three unions, Christ and the Church, husband and wife, spirit and flesh. Of these the former consult for the good of the latter, the latter wait upon the former. All the things are good, when, in them, certain set over by way of pre-eminence, certain made subject in a becoming manner, observe the beauty of order. Husband and wife receive command and pattern how they ought to be one with another. The command is, "Let wives be subject unto their own husbands, as unto the Lord; because the husband is the head of the wife;"[11] and, "Husbands, love your wives." But there is given a pattern, unto wives from the Church, unto husbands from Christ: "As the Church," saith he, "is subject unto Christ, so also wives unto their own husbands in all things." In like manner also, having given command to husbands to love their own wives, he added a pattern, "As Christ loved the Church." But husbands he exhorted to it from a lower matter also, that is, from their own body: not only from a higher, that is, from their Lord.

---

1 Wisd. ix. 15.   2 Rom. viii. 10.   3 Eph. v. 29.
4 See *De Ag. Christ.* § 4.

5 Eph. v. 25-28.   6 Eph v. 29.   7 Gal. v. 17.
8 Rom. vii. 18.   9 Eph. v. 29.   10 Rom. vii. 23.
11 Eph. v. 22-28.

For he not only saith, "Husbands, love your wives, as Christ also loved the Church," which is from an higher: but he said also, "Husbands ought to love their own wives, as their own bodies," which is from a lower: because both higher and lower are all good. And yet the woman received not pattern from the body, or flesh, to be so subject to the husband as the flesh to the spirit; but either the Apostle would have understood by consequence, what he omitted to state: or haply because the flesh lusteth against the spirit in the mortal and sick estate of this life, therefore he would not set the woman a pattern of subjection from it. But the men he would for this reason, because, although the spirit lusteth against the flesh, even in this it consults for the good of the flesh: not like as the flesh lusting against the spirit, by such opposition consulteth neither for the good of the spirit, nor for its own. Yet the good spirit would not consult for its good, whether by nourishing and cherishing its nature by forethought, or by resisting its faults by continence, were it not that each substance showeth God to be the Creator of each, even by the seemliness of this its order. What is it, therefore, that with true madness ye both boast yourselves to be Christians, and with so great perverseness contend against the Christian Scriptures, with eyes closed, or rather put out, asserting both that Christ hath appeared unto mortals in false flesh, and that the Church in the soul pertains to Christ, in the body to the devil, and that the male and female sex are works of the devil, not of God, and that the flesh is joined unto the spirit, as an evil substance unto a good substance?

24. If what we have made mention of out of the Apostolic Epistles seem to you to fall short of an answer, hear yet others, if ye have ears. What saith the utterly mad Manichæan of the Flesh of Christ? That it was not true, but false. What saith the blessed Apostle to this? "Remember that Christ Jesus rose again from the dead of the seed of David, according to my Gospel."[1] And Christ Jesus Himself saith, "Handle and see, that a spirit hath not flesh and bones, as ye see me to have."[2] How is there truth in their doctrine, which asserts that in the Flesh of Christ there was falsehood? How was there in Christ no evil, in Whom was so great a lie? Because forsooth to men over-clean true flesh is an evil, and false flesh instead of true is not an evil: it is an evil, true flesh of one born of the seed of David, and it is no evil, false tongue of one saying, "Handle, and

see, that a spirit hath not flesh and bones, as ye see me to have." Of the Church what saith the deceiver of men with deadly error? That on the side of souls it pertains unto Christ, on the side of bodies unto the devil? What to this saith the Teacher of the Gentiles in faith and truth? "Know ye not," saith he, "that your bodies are members of Christ?"[3] Of the sex of male and female what saith the son of perdition? That either sex is not of God, but of the devil. What to this saith the Vessel of Election? "As," saith he, "the woman from out the man, so also the man through the woman: but all things of God."[4] Of the flesh what saith the unclean spirit through the Manichæan? That it is an evil substance, and not the creation of God, but of an enemy. What to this saith the Holy Spirit through Paul? "For as the body is one," saith he, "and hath many members, but all the members of the body, being many, are one body: so also is Christ."[5] And a little after; "God hath set," saith he, "the members, each one of them in the body, as He willed."[6] Also a little after; "God," saith he, "hath tempered the body, giving greater honor unto that to which it was wanting, that there should be no schisms in the body, but that the members have the self-same care one for another: and whether one member suffer, all the members suffer with it: or one member be glorified, all the members rejoice with it."[7] How is the flesh evil, when the souls themselves are admonished to imitate the peace of its members? How is it the creation of the enemy, when the souls themselves, which rule the bodies, take pattern from the members of the body, not to have schisms of enmities among themselves, in order that, what God hath granted unto the body by nature, this themselves also may love to have by grace? With good cause, writing to the Romans, "I beseech you," saith he, "brethren, by the mercy of God, that ye present your bodies a sacrifice, living, holy, pleasing to God."[8] Without reason we contend that darkness is not light, nor light darkness, if we present a sacrifice, living, holy, pleasing to God, of the bodies of the "nation of darkness."

25. But, say they, how is the flesh by a certain likeness compared unto the Church? What! doth the Church lust against Christ? whereas the same Apostle said, "The Church is subject unto Christ."[9] Clearly the Church is subject unto Christ; because the spirit therefore lusteth against the flesh, that on every side the Church may be made subject

---

. [1] 2 Tim. ii. 8.   [2] Luke xxiv. 39.

[3] 1 Cor. vi. 15.   [4] 1 Cor. xi. 12.   [5] 1 Cor. xii. 12.
[6] 1 Cor. xii. 18.   [7] 1 Cor. xii. 24, 25, 26.
[8] Rom. xii. 1.   [9] Eph. v. 24.

to Christ; but the flesh lusteth against the spirit, because not as yet hath the Church received that peace which was promised perfect. And for this reason the Church is made subject unto Christ for the pledge of salvation, and the flesh lusteth against the spirit from the weakness of sickness. For neither were those other than members of the Church, unto whom he thus spake, "Walk in the spirit, and fulfill not the lusts of the flesh. For the flesh lusteth against the spirit, and the spirit against the flesh; for these are opposed the one to the other; that ye do not what we would."[1] These things were assuredly spoken unto the Church, which if it were not made subject unto Christ, the spirit would not in it lust against the flesh through continence. By reason of which they were indeed able not to perfect the lusts of the flesh, but through the flesh lusting against the Spirit they were not able to do the things which they would, that is, not even to have the very lusts of the flesh. Lastly, why should we not confess that in spiritual men the Church is subject unto Christ, but in carnal men yet lusteth against Christ? Did not they lust against Christ unto whom it was said, "Is Christ divided?"[2] and, "I could not speak unto you as unto spiritual, but as unto carnal. I have given unto you milk to drink as unto babes in Christ, not meat, for ye were not as yet able; but not even now are ye able: for ye are still carnal. For whereas there is among you emulation, and strife, are ye not carnal?"[3] Against whom doth emulation and strife lust, but against Christ? For these lusts of the flesh Christ healeth in His own, but loveth in none. Whence the holy Church, so long as it hath such members, is not yet without spot or wrinkle. To these are added those other sins also, for which the daily cry of the whole Church is, "Forgive us our debts:"[4] and, that we should not think spiritual persons exempt from these, not any one soever of carnal persons, nor any one soever of spiritual persons themselves, but he, who lay on the breast of the Lord,[5] and whom He loved before others, saith, "If we shall say that we have not sin, we deceive ourselves, and the truth is not in us."[6] But in every sin, more in what is greater, less in what is less, there is an act of lust against righteousness. And of Christ it is written: "Who was made unto us by God, Wisdom, and Righteousness, and Sanctification, and Redemption."[7] In every sin therefore without doubt there is an act of lust against Christ. But when He, Who

"healeth all our sicknesses,"[8] shall have led His Church unto the promised healing of sickness, then in none of its members shall there be any, even the very least spot or wrinkle. Then in no way shall the flesh lust against the spirit, and therefore there shall be no cause why the spirit also lust against the flesh. Then all this conflict shall come to an end, then there shall be the highest concord of both substances; then to such a degree shall no one there be carnal, that even the flesh itself shall be spiritual. What therefore each one living after Christ doth with his flesh, whereas he both lusts against its evil lust, which he restrains, hereafter to be healed, which he holds, not yet healed; and yet nourisheth and cherisheth its good nature, since "no one ever hated his own flesh,"[9] this also Christ doth with the Church, so far as it is lawful to compare lesser with greater matters. For He both represses it with rebukes, that it burst not being puffed up with impunity; and raises it up with consolations, that it sink not being weighed down with infirmity. Hence is that of the Apostle, "For if we would judge ourselves, we should not be judged; but when we are judged, we are rebuked of the Lord, that we be not condemned with this world."[10] And that in the Psalm, "After the multitude of my griefs in my heart, Thy consolations have gladdened my soul."[11] We are therefore then to hope for perfect soundness of our flesh without any opposition, when there shall be sure security of the Church of Christ without any fear.

26. Thus much will suffice to have treated on behalf of true Continence against the Manichees deceitfully continent, lest the fruitful and glorious labor of Continence, when it restrains and curbs the lowest part of us, that is, the body, from immoderate and unlawful pleasures, be believed not healthfully to chasten, but hostilely to persecute. Forsooth the body is indeed different from the nature of the soul, yet is it not alien from the nature of man: for the soul is not made up of body, but yet man is made up of soul and body: and assuredly, whom God frees, He frees the whole man. Whence our Saviour Himself also took upon Him the whole man, having deigned to free in us all that He made. They who hold contrary to this truth, what doth it profit them to restrain lusts? if, that is, they restrain any. What in them can be made clean through Continence, whose such Continence is unclean? and which ought not to be called Continence. Forsooth to hold

---

[1] Gal. v. 16, 17.　　[2] 1 Cor. i. 13.　　[3] 1 Cor. iii. 1, 2, 3.
[4] Matt. vi. 12.　　[5] John xiii. 23.　　[6] 1 John i. 8.
[7] 1 Cor. i. 30.

[8] Ps. ciii. 3.　　　　[9] Eph. v. 29.
[10] 1 Cor. xi. 31, 3　　[11] Ps. xciv. 19.

what they hold is the poison of the devil; but Continence is the gift of God. But as not every one who suffers any thing, or with the greatest endurance suffers any pain whatever, possesses that virtue, which in like manner is the gift of God, and is called Patience; for many endure many torments, in order not to betray either such as are wickedly privy with them in their crimes, or themselves; many in order to satiate glowing lusts, and to obtain, or not to abandon those things, whereunto they are bound by chain of evil love; many on behalf of different and destructive errors, whereby they are strongly held: of all of whom far be it from us to say that they have true patience: thus not every one, who contains in any thing, or who marvellously retrains even the very lusts of the flesh, or mind, is to be said to possess that continence, of the profit and beauty of which we are treating. For certain, what may seem marvellous to say, through incontinence contain themselves: as if a woman were to contain herself from her husband, because she hath sworn this to an adulterer. Certain through injustice, as if spouse yield not to spouse the due of sexual intercourse, because he or she is already able to overcome such appetite of the body. Also certain contain deceived by false faith, and hoping what is vain, and following after what is vain: among whom are all heretics, and whosoever under the name of religion are deceived by any error: whose continence would be true, if their faith also were true: but, whereas that is not to be called faith, on this account, because it is false; without doubt that also is unworthy the name of continence. For what? are we prepared to call continence, which we must truly say is the gift of God, sin? Far be from our hearts so hateful madness. But the blessed Apostle saith "Every thing that is not of faith is sin." [1] What therefore hath not faith, is not to be called continence.

27. There are also they who, in doing open service to evil demons, contain from pleasures of the body, that, through their means, they may satisfy unlawful pleasures, the violence and glow whereof they contain not. Whence also, (to name one case, and pass over the rest in silence by reason of the length of the discourse,) certain come not near even unto their own wives, whilst, as though clean, they essay through magic arts to gain access unto the wives of others. O marvellous continence, nay rather, singular wickedness and uncleanness! For, if it were true continence, the lust of the flesh ought rather to contain from adultery, than, in order to commit adultery, from marriage. Forsooth marriage continence is wont to ease this lust of the flesh, and to check its curb but thus far, that neither in marriage itself it run riot by immoderate license, but that a measure be observed, either such as is due to the weakness of the spouse, unto whom the Apostle enjoins not this, as of command, but yields it as of permission; [2] or such as is suited for the begetting of sons, which was formerly the one alone occasion of sexual intercourse to both holy fathers and mothers. But continence doing this, that is, moderating, and in a certain way limiting in married persons the lust of the flesh, and ordering in a certain way within fixed limits its unquiet and inordinate motion, uses well the evil of man, whom it makes and wills to make perfect good: as God uses even evil men, for their sake whom He perfects in goodness.

28. Far be it therefore that we say of continence, of which Scripture saith. "And this very thing was wisdom, to know whose gift it was," [3] that even they possess it, who, by containing, either serve errors, or overcome any lesser desires for this purpose, that they may fulfill others, by the greatness of which they are overcome. But that continence which is true, coming from above, wills not to repress some evils by other evils, but to heal all evils by goods. And, briefly to comprehend its mode of action, it is the place of continence to keep watch to restrain and heal all delights whatsoever of lust, which are opposed to the delight of wisdom. Whence without doubt they set it within too narrow bounds, who limit it to restraining the lusts of the body alone: certainly they speak better, who say that it pertains to Continence to rule in general lust or desire. Which desire is set down as a fault, nor is it only of the body, but also of the soul. For, if the desire of the body be in fornications and drunkennesses; have enmities, strifes, emulations, lastly, hatreds, their exercise in the pleasure of the body, and not rather in the motion and troubled states of the soul? Yet the Apostle called all these "works of the flesh," whether what pertained to the soul, or what pertained properly to the flesh, calling forsooth the man himself by the name of the flesh. [4] Forsooth they are the works of man, whatsoever are not called works of God; forasmuch as man, who does these, lives after himself, not after God, so far as he does these. But there are other works of man, which are rather to be called works of God. "For it is God," [5] saith the Apostle, "Who

[1] Rom. xiv. 23.

[2] 1 Cor. vii. 6.
[4] Gal. v. 19, 20, 21.

[3] Wisd. viii. 21.
[5] Phil. ii. 13.

worketh in you both to will and to do, according to His good pleasure." Whence also is that, " For as many as are led by the spirit of God, these are sons of God."[1]

29. Thus the spirit of man, cleaving unto the Spirit of God, lusts against the flesh, that is, against itself: but for itself, in order that those motions, whether in the flesh or in the soul, after man, not after God, which as yet exist through the sickness man hath gotten, may be restrained by continence, that so health may be gotten; and man, not living after man, may now be able to say, " But I live, now not I, but there liveth in me Christ."[2] For where not I, there more happily I: and, when any evil motion after man arises, unto which he, who with the mind serves the Law of God, consents not, let him say that also, " Now it is not I that do this."[3] To such forsooth are said those words, which we, as partners and sharers with them, ought to listen to.[4] " If ye have risen together with Christ, seek the things that are above, where Christ is sitting at the Right Hand of God: mind[5] the things that are above, not what are upon earth. For ye are dead, and your life is hid with Christ in God: when Christ your life shall have appeared, then ye also shall appear with Him in glory." Let us understand unto whom he is speaking, yea, rather, let us listen with more attention. For what more plain than this? what more clear? He is certainly speaking unto those, who had risen again with Christ, not yet surely in the flesh, but in the mind: whom he calls dead, and on this account the more living: for " your life," saith he, "is hid with Christ in God." Of such dead the speech is: " But I live, now not I, but there liveth in me Christ." They therefore, whose life was hidden in God, are admonished and exhorted to mortify their members, which are upon the earth. For this follows, " Mortify, therefore, your members, which are upon the earth." And, lest any through excess of dullness should think that such are to mortify the members of the body that are seen, straightway opening what it is he saith, "Fornication," saith he, "uncleanness, passion, evil lust, and covetousness, which is idolatry."[6] But is it so to be believed, that they, who were already dead, and their life hidden with Christ in God, were still committing fornication, were still living in unclean habits and works, were still slaves to passions of evil lust and covetousness? What madman would thus think of such? What, therefore, would he that they mortify, save the motions themselves still living in a certain

intrusion[7] of their own, without the consent of our mind, without the action of the members of the body? And how are they mortified by the work of continence, save when we consent not to them with the mind, nor are the members of the body yielded to them as weapons; and, what is greater, and to be looked to with yet greater watchfulness of continence, our very thought itself, although in a certain way it be touched by their suggestion, and as it were, whisper, yet turns away from these, that it receive not delight from them, and turns to more delightful thoughts of things above: on this account naming them in discourse, that men abide not in them, but flee from them. And this is brought to pass, if we listen effectually, with His help, Who, through His Apostle gives this command, " Seek things that are above, where Christ is sitting at the Right Hand of God. Mind the things that are above, not what are on earth."[8]

30. But, after that he had made mention of these evils, he added and said, " On account of which cometh the wrath of God on the sons of unbelief."[9] Surely it was a wholesome alarm that believers might not think that they could be saved on account of their faith alone, even although they should live in these evils: the Apostle James with most clear speech crying out against that notion, and saying, " If any say that he have faith, and have not works, shall his faith be able to save him?"[10] Whence also here the Teacher of the Gentiles said, that on account of these evils the wrath of God cometh on the sons of unbelief. But when he saith, " Wherein ye also walked sometime, when ye were living therein;"[11] he shows sufficiently that now they were not living therein. Forsooth unto these they had died, that their life might be hidden in God with Christ. When then they were now not living in them, they were now bidden to mortify such. Forsooth, themselves not living in the same, the things were living, as I have already shown a little above, and were called their members, that is to say, those faults which dwelt in their members; by a way of speech, that which is contained through that which contains; as it is said, The whole Forum talks of it, when men talk who are in the Forum. In this very way of speech it is sung in the Psalm, " Let all the earth worship Thee:"[12] that is, all men who are in the earth.

31. " But now do ye also," saith he, " put down all;"[13] and he makes mention of several

---

[1] Rom. viii. 14. 　[2] Gal. ii. 20. 　[3] Rom. vii. 17.
[4] Col. iii. 1-4. 　[5] *Sapite.* 　[6] Col. iii. 5.

[7] *Interpellatione.* 　[8] Col. iii. 1, 2. 　[9] Col. iii. 6.
[10] James ii. 14. 　[11] Col. iii. 7.
[12] Ps. lxvi. 4. 　[13] Col. iii. 8.

more evils of that sort. But what is it, that it is not enough for him to say, "Do ye put down all," but that he added the conjunction and said, "ye also?" save that lest they should not think that they did those evils and lived in them with impunity on this account, because their faith set them free from wrath, which cometh upon the sons of unbelief, doing these things, and living in them without faith. Do ye also, saith he, put down those evils, on account of which cometh the wrath of God on the children of unbelief; nor promise yourselves impunity of them on account of merit of faith. But he would not say, "put ye down," unto those who had already laid down so far as that they consented not to such faults, nor were yielding their members to them as weapons of sin, save that the life of Saints stands in this past deed, and is still engaged in this work, so long as we are mortal. For, so long as the Spirit lusteth against the flesh, this business proceeds with great earnestness, resistance is offered unto evil delights, unclean lusts, carnal and shameful motions, by the sweetness of holiness, by the love of chastity, by spiritual vigor, and by the beauty of continence; thus they are laid down by them who are dead to them, and who live not in them by consenting. Thus, I say, they are put down, whilst they are weighed down by continued continence, that they rise not again. Whosoever, as though secure, shall cease from this laying aside of them, straightway they will assault the Citadel of the mind, and will themselves put it down thence, and will reduce it into slavery to them, captive after a base and unseemly fashion. Then sin will reign in the mortal body of man to obey its desires; then will it yield its members weapons of unrighteousness unto sin:[1] and the last state of that man shall be worse than the former.[2] For it is much more tolerable not to have begun a contest of this kind, than after one hath begun to have left the conflict, and to have become in place of a good warrior, or even in place of a conqueror, a captive. Whence the Lord saith not, whoso shall begin, but "Whoso shall persevere unto the end, he shall be saved."[3]

32. But whether keenly contending, that we be not overcome, or overcoming divers times, or even with unhoped and unlooked for ease, let us give the glory unto Him Who giveth continence unto us. Let us remember that a certain just man said, "I shall never be moved:" and that it was showed him how rashly he had said this, attributing as though to his own strength, what was given to him from above. But this we have learnt from his own confession: for soon after he added, "Lord, in Thy will Thou hast given strength to my beauty; but Thou hast turned away Thy Face, and I was troubled."[4] Through a remedial Providence he was for a short time deserted by his Ruler, in order that he might not himself through deadly pride desert his Ruler. Therefore, whether here, where we engage with our faults in order to subdue and make them less, or there, as it shall be in the end, where we shall be void of every enemy, because of all infection,[5] it is for our health that we are thus dealt with, in order that, "whoso glorieth, he may glory in the Lord."[6]

---

[1] Rom. vi. 12, 13.   [2] Matt. xii. 45.   [3] Matt. x. 22.
[4] Ps. xxx. 6, 7.   [5] "Peste."   [6] 1 Cor. i. 31.

ST. AUGUSTIN:

ON

THE GOOD OF MARRIAGE

[DE BONO CONJUGALI.]

TRANSLATED BY

REV. C. L. CORNISH, M.A.,

OF EXETER COLLEGE, OXFORD.

ON THE GOOD OF MARRIAGE.

[DE BONO CONJUGALI.]

THIS treatise, and the following, were written against somewhat that still remained of the heresy of Jovinian. S. Aug. mentions this error in b. ii. c. 23, *de Nuptiis et Conc.* "Jovinianus," he says, "who a few years since tried to found a new heresy, said that the Catholics favored the Manichæans, because in opposition to him they preferred holy Virginity to Marriage. And in his book on *Heresies*, c. 82. "That heresy took its rise from one Jovinianus, a Monk, in our own time, when we were yet young." And he adds that it was soon overborne and extinguished, say about A.D. 390, having been condemned first at Rome, then at Milan. There are letters of Pope Siricius on the subject to the Church of Milan, and the answer sent him by the Synod of Milan, at which St. Ambrose presided. Jerome had refuted Jovinian, but was said to have attempted the defense of the excellency of the virgin state, at the expense of condemning marriage. That Augustin might not be subject to any such complaint or calumny, before speaking of the superiority of Virginity, he thought it well to write on the Good of Marriage.

This work we learn to have been finished about the year 401, not only from the order of his *Retractations*, but also from his books on Genesis after the Letter, begun about that year. For in b. ix. on Genesis, c. 7, where he commends the Good of Marriage, he says: "Now this is threefold, faithfulness, offspring, and the Sacrament. For faithfulness, it is observed, that there be no lying with other man or woman, out of the bond of wedlock: for the offspring, that it be lovingly welcomed, kindly nourished, religiously brought up: for the Sacrament, that marriage be not severed, and that man or woman divorced be not joined to another even for the sake of offspring. This is as it were the rule of Marriage, by which rule either fruitfulness is made seemly, or the perverseness of incontinence is brought to order. Upon which since we have sufficiently discoursed in that book, which we lately published, *on the Good of Marriage*, where we have also distinguished the Widow's continence and the Virgin's excellency, according to the worthiness of their degrees, our pen is not to be now longer occupied." This very work is referred to in Book I. on the *Deserts and Remission of Sins*, c. 29.—*Bened. Ed*.

NOTICE.

The Editors are, of course, aware of the danger there is in reading a treatise like the following in a spirit of idle curiosity, and they beg any reader who has not well assured himself that his aim is right and holy to abstain from perusing it. At the same time it must not be forgotten, that something far other than a mere shrinking from subjects offensive to modern delicacy is needed, in order to purify the thoughts with respect to the holy estate of Matrimony. The mind that will but seriously attend to it in that light, will certainly be strengthened against evil suggestions by seeing in the whole subject a field of Christian duty.

It seemed further requisite to bring forward a work calculated to remove the imputation so falsely cast on the holy Fathers, that they regarded Matrimony as unholy, and almost agreed with the Manichean view of it, as a defilement and degradation to the Christian. They did, it is true, prefer Virginity to Marriage, but, as St. Augustin expressly states, as the " better of two good things," not as though one were good, and the other evil.

In estimating the work and the writer, the age in which it was written must be kept in view, and what that age required must not be imputed as a fault to him or to his religion. And perhaps what was written for another age may serve the more safely towards our improvement and guidance from the very circumstance that the style and manner of antiquity has become a kind of veil, which takes off somewhat from the strength and vividness of first impressions, and leaves the mind more at liberty to use what is laid before it as it will, than a more modern way of speaking would be likely to do. Let that liberty be used rightly and conscientiously, and the effect of reading will be good.—*Eds. of the Oxford Library.*

ON THE GOOD OF MARRIAGE.

[DE BONO CONJUGALI.]

1. FORASMUCH as each man is a part of the human race, and human nature is something social, and hath for a great and natural good, the power also of friendship; on this account God willed to create all men out of one, in order that they might be held in their society not only by likeness of kind, but also by bond of kindred. Therefore the first natural bond of human society is man and wife. Nor did God create these each by himself, and join them together as alien by birth: but He created the one out of the other, setting a sign also of the power of the union in the side, whence she was drawn, was formed.[1] For they are joined one to another side by side, who walk together, and look together whither they walk. Then follows the connexion of fellowship in children, which is the one alone worthy fruit, not of the union of male and female, but of the sexual intercourse. For it were possible that there should exist in either sex, even without such intercourse, a certain friendly and true union of the one ruling, and the other obeying.

2. Nor is it now necessary that we enquire, and put forth a definite opinion on that question, whence could exist the progeny of the first men, whom God had blessed, saying, " Increase, and be ye multiplied, and fill the earth; "[2] if they had not sinned, whereas their bodies by sinning deserved the condition of death, and there can be no sexual intercourse save of mortal bodies. For there have existed several and different opinions on this matter; and if we must examine, which of them be rather agreeable to the truth of Divine Scriptures, there is matter for a lengthened discussion.[3] Whether, therefore, without intercourse, in some other way, had they not sinned, they would have had sons, from the gift of the Almighty Creator, Who was able to create themselves also without parents, Who was able to form the Flesh of Christ in a virgin womb, and (to speak even to unbelievers themselves) Who was able to bestow on bees a progeny without sexual intercourse; or whether many things there were spoken by way of mystery and figure, and we are to understand in another sense what is written, " Fill the earth, and rule over it; " that is, that it should come to pass by fullness and perfection of life and power, so that the very increase and multiplication, whereby it is said, " Increase, and be ye multiplied," be understood to be by advance of mind, and abundance of virtue, as it is set in the Psalm, " Thou shall multiply me in my soul by virtue; "[4] and that succession of progeny was not given unto man, save after that, by reason of sin, there was to be hereafter departure in death: or whether the body was not made spiritual in the case of these men, but at the first animal, in order that by merit of obedience it might after become spiritual, to lay hold of immortality, not after death, which by the malice of the devil enterèd into the world, and was made the punishment of sin; but after that change, which the Apostle signifies, when he says, " Then we living, who remain, together with them, shall be caught up in the clouds, to meet Christ, into the air,"[5] that we may understand both that those bodies of the first pair were mortal, in the first forming, and yet that they would not have died, had they not sinned, as God had threatened: even as if He should threaten a wound, in that the body was capable of wounds; which yet would not have happened, unless what He had forbidden were done. Thus, therefore, even through sexual intercourse there might take place generations of such bodies, as up to a certain point should have increase, and

---

[1] Gen. ii. 21, 22.   [2] Gen. i. 28.   [3] See *De Civ. Dei*, b. xiv.   Ps. cxxxviii. 3, LXX.   [5] 1 Thess. iv. 17.

yet should not pass into old age; or even into old age, and yet not into death; until the earth were filled with that multiplication of the blessing. For if to the garments of the Israelites [1] God granted their proper state without any wearing away during forty years, how much more would He grant unto the bodies of such as obeyed His command a certain most happy temperament of sure state, until they should be changed for the better, not by death of the man, whereby the body is abandoned by the soul, but by a blessed change from mortality to immortality, from an animal to a spiritual quality. Of these opinions which be true, or whether some other or others yet may be formed out of these words, were a long matter to enquire and discuss.

3. This we now say, that, according to this condition of being born and dying, which we know, and in which we have been created, the marriage of male and female is some good; the compact whereof divine Scripture so commends, as that neither is it allowed one put away by her husband to marry, so long as her husband lives: nor is it allowed one put away by his wife to marry another, unless she who have separated from him be dead. Therefore, concerning the good of marriage, which the Lord also confirmed in the Gospel, not only in that He forbade to put away a wife,[2] save because of fornication, but also in that He came by invitation to a marriage,[3] there is good ground to inquire for what reason it be a good. And this seems not to me to be merely on account of the begetting of children, but also on account of the natural society itself in a difference of sex. Otherwise it would not any longer be called marriage in the case of old persons, especially if either they had lost sons, or had given birth to none. But now in good, although aged, marriage, albeit there hath withered away the glow of full age between male and female, yet there lives in full vigor the order of charity between husband and wife: because, the better they are, the earlier they have begun by mutual consent to contain from sexual intercourse with each other: not that it should be matter of necessity afterwards not to have power to do what they would, but that it should be matter of praise to have been unwilling at the first, to do what they had power to do. If therefore there be kept good faith of honor, and of services mutually due from either sex, although the members of either be languishing and almost corpse-like, yet of souls duly joined together, the

chastity [3] continues, the purer by how much it is the more proved, the safer, by how much it is the calmer. Marriages have this good also, that carnal or youthful incontinence, although it be faulty, is brought unto an honest use in the begetting of children, in order that out of the evil of lust the marriage union may bring to pass some good. Next, in that the lust of the flesh is repressed, and rages in a way more modestly, being tempered by parental affection. For there is interposed a certain gravity of glowing pleasure, when in that wherein husband and wife cleave to one another, they have in mind that they be father and mother.

4. There is this further, that in that very debt which married persons pay one to another, even if they demand it with somewhat too great intemperance and incontinence, yet they owe faith alike one to another. Unto which faith the Apostle allows so great right, as to call it "power," saying, "The woman hath not power of her own body, but the man; again in like manner also the man hath not power of his own body, but the woman."[5] But the violation of this faith is called adultery, when either by instigation of one's own lust, or by consent of lust of another, there is sexual intercourse on either side with another against the marriage compact: and thus faith is broken, which, even in things that are of the body, and mean, is a great good of the soul: and therefore it is certain that it ought to be preferred even to the health of the body, wherein even this life of ours is contained. For, although a little chaff in comparison of much gold is almost nothing; yet faith, when it is kept pure in a matter of chaff, as in gold, is not therefore less because it is kept in a lesser matter. But when faith is employed to commit sin, it were strange that we should have to call it faith; however of what kind soever it be, if also the deed be done against it, it is the worse done; save when it is on this account abandoned, that there may be a return unto true and lawful faith, that is, that sin may be amended, by correction of perverseness of the will. As if any, being unable alone to rob a man, should find a partner in his iniquity, and make an agreement with him to do it together, and to divide the spoil; and, after the crime hath been committed, should take off the whole to himself alone. That other grieves and complains that faith hath not been kept with him, but in his very complaint he ought to consider, that he himself rather ought to have kept faith with human society in a good life,

---

not to make unjust spoil of a man, if he feels with how great injustice it hath failed to be kept with himself in a fellowship of sin. Forsooth the former, being faithless in both instances, must assuredly be judged the more wicked. But, if he had been displeased at what they had done ill, and had been on this account unwilling to divide the spoil with his partner in crime, in order that it might be restored to the man, from whom it had been taken, not even a faithless man would call him faithless. Thus a woman, if, having broken her marriage faith, she keep faith with her adulterer, is certainly evil: but, if not even with her adulterer, worse. Further, if she repent her of her sin, and returning to marriage chastity, renounce all adulterous compacts and resolutions, I count it strange if even the adulterer himself will think her one who breaks faith.

5. Also the question is wont to be asked, when a male and female, neither the one the husband, nor the other the wife, of any other, come together, not for the begetting of children, but, by reason of incontinence, for the mere sexual intercourse, there being between them this faith, that neither he do it with any other woman, nor she with any other man, whether it is to be called marriage.[1] And perhaps this may, not without reason, be called marriage,[2] if it shall be the resolution[3] of both parties until the death of one, and if the begetting of children, although they came not together for that cause, yet they shun not, so as either to be unwilling to have children born to them, or even by some evil work to use means that they be not born. But, if either both, or one, of these be wanting, I find not how we can call it marriage. For, if a man should take unto him any one for a time, until he find another worthy either of his honors, or of his means, to marry as his compeer; in his soul itself he is an adulterer, and that not with her whom he is desirous of finding, but with her, with whom he so lies, as not to have with her the partnership of a husband. Whence she also herself, knowing and willing this, certainly acts unchastely in having intercourse with him, with whom she has not the compact of a wife. However, if she keep to him faith of bed, and after he shall have married, have no thought of marriage herself, and prepare to contain herself altogether from any such work, perhaps I should not dare lightly to call her an adulteress; but who shall say that she sins not, when he is aware that she has intercourse with a man, not being his wife? But further, if

from that intercourse, so far as pertains to herself, she has no wish but for sons, and suffers unwilling whatever she suffers beyond the cause of begetting; there are many matrons to whom she is to be preferred; who, although they are not adulteresses, yet force their husbands, for the most part also wishing to exercise continence, to pay the due of the flesh, not through desire of children, but through glow of lust making an intemperate use of their very right; in whose marriages, however, this very thing, that they are married, is a good. For for this purpose are they married, that the lust being brought under a lawful bond, should not float at large without form and loose; having of itself weakness of flesh that cannot be curbed, but of marriage fellowship of faith that cannot be dissolved; of itself encroachment of immoderate intercourse, of marriage a way of chastely begetting. For, although it be shameful to wish to use a husband for purposes of lust, yet it is honorable to be unwilling to have intercourse save with an husband, and not to give birth to children save from a husband. There are also men incontinent to that degree, that they spare not their wives even when pregnant. Therefore whatever that is immodest, shameless, base, married persons do one with another, is the sin of the persons, not the fault of marriage.

6. Further, in the very case of the more immoderate requirement of the due of the flesh, which the Apostle enjoins not on them by way of command, but allows to them by way of leave, that they have intercourse also beside the cause of begetting children; although evil habits impel them to such intercourse, yet marriage guards them from adultery or fornication. For neither is that committed because of marriage, but is pardoned because of marriage. Therefore married persons owe one another not only the faith of their sexual intercourse itself, for the begetting of children, which is the first fellowship of the human kind in this mortal state; but also, in a way, a mutual service of sustaining[4] one another's weakness, in order to shun unlawful intercourse: so that, although perpetual continence be pleasing to one of them, he may not, save with consent of the other. For thus far also, "The wife hath not power of her own body, but the man: in like manner also the man hath not power of his own body, but the woman."[5] That that also, which, not for the begetting of children, but for weakness and incontinence, either he seeks of marriage, or she of her husband,

---

[1] *Nuptiæ.*   [2] *Connubium.*   [3] *Placuerit.*   [4] *Excipiendæ.*   [5] 1 Cor. vii. 4.

they deny not the one or the other; lest by this they fall into damnable seductions, through temptation of Satan, by reason of incontinence either of both, or of whichever of them. For intercourse of marriage for the sake of begetting hath not fault; but for the satisfying of lust, but yet with husband or wife, by reason of the faith of the bed, it hath venial fault: but adultery or fornication hath deadly fault, and, through this, continence from all intercourse is indeed better even than the intercourse of marriage itself, which takes place for the sake of begetting. But because that Continence is of larger desert, but to pay the due of marriage is no crime, but to demand it beyond the necessity of begetting is a venial fault, but to commit fornication or adultery is a crime to be punished; charity of the married ought to beware, lest, whilst it seek for itself occasion of larger honor, it do that for its partner which cause condemnation. "For whosoever putteth away his wife, except for the cause of fornication, maketh her to commit adultery."[1] To such a degree is that marriage compact entered upon a matter of a certain sacrament, that it is not made void even by separation itself, since, so long as her husband lives, even by whom she hath been left, she commits adultery, in case she be married to another: and he who hath left her, is the cause of this evil.

7. But I marvel, if, as it is allowed to put away a wife who is an adulteress, so it be allowed, having put her away, to marry another. For holy Scripture causes a hard knot in this matter, in that the Apostle says, that, by commandment of the Lord, the wife ought not to depart from her husband, but, in case she shall have departed, to remain unmarried, or to be reconciled to her husband;[2] whereas surely she ought not to depart and remain unmarried, save from an husband that is an adulterer, lest by withdrawing from him, who is not an adulterer, she cause him to commit adultery. But perhaps she may justly be reconciled to her husband, either he being to be borne with, if she cannot contain herself, or being now corrected. But I see not how the man can have permission to marry another, in case he have left an adulteress, when a woman has not to be married to another, in case she have left an adulterer. And, this being the case, so strong is that bond of fellowship in married persons, that, although it be tied for the sake f begetting children, not even for the sake of begetting children is it loosed. For it is in a man's power to put away a wife that is. barren, and marry one of whom to have children. And yet it is not allowed; and now indeed in our times, and after the usage of Rome, neither to marry in addition, so as to have more than one wife living: and, surely, in case of an adulteress or adulterer being left, it would be possible that more men should be born, if either the woman were married to another, or the man should marry another. And yet, if this be not lawful, as the Divine Rule seems to prescribe, who is there but it must make him attentive to learn, what is the meaning of this so great strength of the marriage bond? Which I by no means think could have been of so great avail, were it not that there were taken a certain sacrament of some greater matter from out this weak mortal state of men, so that, men deserting it, and seeking to dissolve it, it should remain unshaken for their punishment. Seeing that the compact of marriage is not done away by divorce intervening; so that they continue wedded persons one to another, even after separation; and commit adultery with those, with whom they shall be joined, even after their own divorce, either the woman with a man, or the man with a woman. And yet, save in the City of our God, in His Holy Mount, the case is not such with the wife.[3] But, that the laws of the Gentiles are otherwise, who is there that knows not; where, by the interposition of divorce, without any offense of which man takes cognizance, both the woman is married to whom she will, and the man marries whom he will. And something like this custom, on account of the hardness of the Israelites, Moses seems to have allowed, concerning a bill of divorcement.[4] In which matter there appears rather a rebuke, than an approval, of divorce.[5]

8. "Honorable," therefore, "is marriage in all, and the bed undefiled."[6] And this we do not so call a good, as that it is a good in comparison of fornication: otherwise there will be two evils, of which the second is worse: or fornication will also be a good, because adultery is worse: for it is worse to violate the marriage of another, than to cleave unto an harlot: and adultery will be a good, because incest is worse; for it is worse to lie with a mother than with the wife of another: and, until we arrive at those things, which, as the Apostle saith, "it is a shame even to speak of,"[7] all will be good in comparison of what are worse. But who can doubt that this is false? Therefore marriage and forni-

---

[1] Matt. v. 32. [2] I Cor. vii. 10, 11.

[3] Ps. xlviii. 1. [4] Deut. xxiv. 1. [5] Matt. xix. 8.
[6] Heb. xiii. 4. [See R. V.] [7] Eph. v. 12.

cation are not two evils, whereof the second is worse: but marriage and continence are two goods, whereof the second is better, even as this temporal health and sickness are not two evils, whereof the second is worse; but that health and immortality are two goods, whereof the second is better. Also knowledge and vanity are not two evils, whereof vanity is the worse: but knowledge and charity are two goods, whereof charity is the better. For " knowledge shall be destroyed," [1] saith the Apostle: and yet it is necessary for this time: but "charity shall never fail." Thus also this mortal begetting, on account of which marriage takes place, shall be destroyed: but freedom from all sexual intercourse is both angelic exercise [2] here, and continueth for ever. But as the repasts of the Just are better than the fasts of the sacrilegious, so the marriage of the faithful is to be set before the virginity of the impious. However neither in that case is repast preferred to fasting, but righteousness to sacrilege; nor in this, marriage to virginity, but faith to impiety. For for this end the righteous, when need is, take their repast, that, as good masters, they may give to their slaves, i.e., their bodies, what is just and fair: but for this end the sacrilegious fast, that they may serve devils. Thus for this end the faithful are married, that they may be chastely joined unto husbands, but for this end the impious are virgins, that they may commit fornication away from the true God. As, therefore, that was good, which Martha was doing, being engaged in the ministering unto the Saints, but that better, which Mary, her sister, sitting at the feet of the Lord, and hearing His word; thus we praise the good of Susanna [3] in married chastity, but yet we set before her the good of the widow Anna, [4] and, much more, of the Virgin Mary. [5] It was good that they were doing, who of their substance were ministering necessaries unto Christ and His disciples: but better, who left all their substance, that they might be freer to follow the same Lord. But in both these cases of good, whether what these, or whether what Martha and Mary were doing, the better could not be done, unless the other had been passed over or left. Whence we are to understand, that we are not, on this account, to think marriage an evil, because, unless there be abstinence from it, widowed chastity, or virgin purity, cannot be had. For neither on this account was what Martha was doing evil, because, unless her sister abstained from it, she could not do what was better:

nor on this account is it evil to receive a just man or a prophet into one's house, because he, who wills to follow Christ unto perfection, ought not even to have a house, in order to do what is better.

9. Truly we must consider, that God gives us some goods, which are to be sought for their own sake, such as wisdom, health, friendship: but others, which are necessary for the sake of somewhat, such as learning, meat, drink, sleep, marriage, sexual intercourse. For of these certain are necessary for the sake of wisdom, as learning: certain for the sake of health, as meat and drink and sleep: certain for the sake of friendship, as marriage or sexual intercourse: for hence subsists the propagation of the human kind, wherein friendly fellowship is a great good. These goods, therefore, which are necessary for the sake of something else, whoso useth not for this purpose, wherefore they were instituted, sins; in some cases venially, in other cases damnably. But whoso useth them for this purpose, wherefore they were given doeth well. Therefore, to whomsoever they are not necessary, if he use them not, he doeth better. Wherefore, these goods, when we have need, we do well to wish; but we do better not to wish than to wish: because ourselves are in a better state, when we account them not necessary. And on this account it is good to marry, because it is good to beget children, to be a mother of a family: but it is better not to marry, [6] because it is better not to stand in need of this work, in order to human fellowship itself. For such is the state of the human race now, that (others, who contain not, not only being taken up with marriage, but many also waxing wanton through unlawful concubinages, the Good Creator working what is good out of their evils) there fails not numerous progeny, and abundant succession, out of which to procure holy friendships. Whence we gather, that, in the first times of the human race, chiefly for the propagation of the People of God, through whom the Prince and Saviour of all people should both be prophesied of, and be born, it was the duty of the Saints to use this good of marriage, not as to be sought for its own sake, but necessary for the sake of something else: but now, whereas, in order to enter upon holy and pure fellowship, there is on all sides from out all nations an overflowing fullness of spiritual kindred, even they who wish to contract marriage only for the sake of children, are to be admonished, that they use rather the larger good of continence.

[1] 1 Cor. xiii. 8.   [2] *Meditatio.*
[3] Hist. of Susanna, 22, 23. [4] Luke ii. 37. [5] Luke i. 27, 28.   [6] 1 Tim. v. 14.

10. But I am aware of some that murmur: What, say they, if all men should abstain from all sexual intercourse, whence will the human race exist? Would that all would this, only in "charity out of a pure heart, and good conscience, and faith unfeigned;"[1] much more speedily would the City of God be filled, and the end of the world hastened. For what else doth the Apostle, as is manifest, exhort to, when he saith, speaking on this head, "I would that all were as myself;"[2] or in that passage, "But this I say, brethren, the time is short: it remains that both they who have wives, be as though not having: and they who weep, as though not weeping: and they who rejoice, as though not rejoicing: and they who buy, as though not buying: and they who use this world as though they use it not. For the form of this world passeth by. I would have you without care." Then he adds, "Whoso is without a wife, thinks of the things of the Lord, how to please the Lord: but whoso is joined in marriage, thinks of the things of the world, how to please his wife: and a woman that is unmarried and a virgin is different: she that is unmarried is anxious about the things of the Lord, to be holy both in body and spirit: but she that is married, is anxious about the things of the world, how to please her husband."[3] Whence it seems to me, that at this time, those only, who contain not, ought to marry, according to that sentence of the same Apostle, "But if they contain not, let them be married: for it is better to be married than to burn."[4]

11. And yet not to these themselves is marriage a sin; which, if it were chosen in comparison of fornication, would be a less sin than fornication, and yet would be a sin. But now what shall we say against the most plain speech of the Apostle, saying, "Let her do what she will; she sinneth not, if she be married;"[5] and, "If thou shalt have taken a wife, thou hast not sinned: and, if a virgin shall have been married, she sinneth not."[6] Hence surely it is not lawful now to doubt that marriage is no sin. Therefore the Apostle alloweth not marriage as matter "of pardon:"[7] for who can doubt that it is extremely absurd to say, that they have not sinned, unto whom "pardon" is granted. But he allows, as matter of "pardon," that sexual intercourse, which takes place through incontinence, not alone for the begetting of children, and, at times, not at all for the begetting of children; and it is not that marriage forces this to take place, but

that it procures pardon for it; provided however it be not so in excess as to hinder what ought to be set aside as seasons of prayer, nor be changed into that use which is against nature, on which the Apostle could not be silent, when speaking of the excessive corruptions of unclean and impious men. For necessary sexual intercourse for begetting is free from blame, and itself is alone worthy of marriage. But that which goes beyond this necessity, no longer follows reason, but lust.[8] And yet it pertains to the character of marriage, not to exact this, but to yield it to the partner, lest by fornication the other sin damnably. But, if both are set under such lust, they do what is plainly not matter of marriage. However, if in their intercourse they love what is honest more than what is dishonest, that is, what is matter of marriage more than what is not matter of marriage, this is allowed to them on the authority of the Apostle as matter of pardon: and for this fault, they have in their marriage, not what sets them on to commit it, but what entreats pardon for it, if they turn not away from them the mercy of God, either by not abstaining on certain days, that they may be free to pray, and through this abstinence, as through fasting, may commend their prayers; or by changing the natural use into that which is against nature, which is more damnable when it is done in the case of husband or wife.

12. For, whereas that natural use, when it pass beyond the compact of marriage, that is, beyond the necessity of begetting, is pardonable in the case of a wife, damnable in the case of an harlot; that which is against nature is execrable when done in the case of an harlot, but more execrable in the case of a wife. Of so great power is the ordinance of the Creator, and the order of Creation, that, in matters allowed us to use, even when the due measure is exceeded, it is far more tolerable, than, in what are not allowed, either a single, or rare excess. And, therefore, in a matter allowed, want of moderation, in a husband or wife, is to be borne with, in order that lust break not forth into a matter that is not allowed. Hence is it also that he sins far less, who is ever so unceasing in approaches to his wife, than he who approaches ever so seldom to commit fornication. But, when the man shall wish to use the member of the wife not allowed for this purpose, the wife is more shameful, if she suffer it to take place in her own case, than if in the case of another woman. Therefore the ornament of marriage is chastity of begetting, and faith of yielding

---

[1] 1 Tim. i. 5.   [2] 1 Cor. vii. 7.   [3] Ver. 29-34.
[4] 1 Cor. vii. 9.   [5] 1 Cor. vii. 36.   [6] Ver. 28.
[7] Veniam.

[8] Rom. i. 26, 27.

the due of the flesh: this is the work of marriage, this the Apostle defends from every charge, in saying, "Both if thou shalt have taken a wife, thou hast not sinned: and if a virgin shall have been married, she sinneth not:" and, "Let her do what she will: she sinneth not if she be married." [1] But an advance beyond moderation in demanding the due of either sex, for the reasons which I have stated above, is allowed to married persons as matter of pardon.

13. What therefore he says, "She, that is unmarried, thinketh of the things of the Lord, that she may be holy both in body and spirit;" we are not to take in such sense, as to think that a chaste Christian wife is not holy in body. Forsooth unto all the faithful it was said, "Know ye not that your bodies are a temple of the Holy Ghost within you, Whom ye have from God?" [2] Therefore the bodies also of the married are holy, so long as they keep faith to one another and to God. And that this sanctity of either of them, even an unbelieving partner does not stand in the way of, but rather that the sanctity of the wife profits the unbelieving husband, and the sanctity of the husband profits the unbelieving wife, the same Apostle is witness, saying, "For the unbelieving husband is sanctified in the wife, and the unbelieving wife is sanctified in a brother." [3] Wherefore that was said according to the greater sanctity of the unmarried than of the married, unto which there is also due a greater reward, according as, the one being a good, the other is a greater good: inasmuch as also she has this thought only, how to please the Lord. For it is not that a female who believes, keeping married chastity, thinks not how to please the Lord; but assuredly less so, in that she thinks of the things of the world, how to please her husband. For this is what he would say of them, that they may, in a certain way, find themselves obliged by marriage to think of the things of the world, how to please their husbands.

14. And not without just cause a doubt is raised, whether he said this of all married women, or of such as so many are, as that nearly all may be thought so to be. For neither doth that, which he saith of unmarried women, "She, that is unmarried, thinkest of the things of the Lord, to be holy both in body and spirit:" [4] pertain unto all unmarried women: whereas there are certain widows who are dead, who live in delights. However, so far as regards a certain distinction and, as it were, character of their own, of the

unmarried and married; as she deserves the excess of hatred, who containing from marriage, [5] that is, from a thing allowed, does not contain from offenses, either of luxury, or pride, or curiosity and prating; so the married woman is seldom met with, who, in the very obedience of married life, hath no thought save how to please God, by adorning herself, not with plaited hair, or gold and pearls and costly attire, [6] but as becometh women making profession of piety, through a good conversation. Such marriages, forsooth, the Apostle Peter also describes by giving commandment. "In like manner," saith he, "wives obeying their own husbands; in order that, even if any obey not the word, they may be gained without discourse through the conversation of the wives, seeing your fear and chaste conversation: that they be not they that are adorned without with crispings of hair, or clothed with gold or with fair raiment; but that hidden man of your heart, in that unbroken continuance of a quiet and modest spirit, which before the Lord also is rich. For thus certain holy women, who hoped in the Lord, used to adorn themselves, obeying their own husbands: as Sarah obeyed Abraham, calling him Lord: whose daughters ye are become, when ye do well, and fear not with any vain fear. Husbands in like manner living at peace and in chastity with your wives, both give ye honor as to the weaker and subject vessel, as with co-heirs of grace, and see that your prayers be not hindered." [7] Is it indeed that such marriages have no thought of the things of the Lord, how to please the Lord? But they are very rare: who denies this? And, being, as they are, rare, nearly all the persons who are such, were not joined together in order to be such, but being already joined together became such.

15. For what Christian men of our time being free from the marriage bond, having power to contain from all sexual intercourse, seeing it to be now "a time," as it is written, "not of embracing, but of abstaining from embrace," [8] would not choose rather to keep virginal or widowed continence, than (now that there is no obligation from duty to human society) to endure tribulation of the flesh, without which marriages cannot be (to pass over in silence other things from which the Apostle spares.) But when through desire reigning they shall have been joined together, if they shall after overcome it, because it is not lawful to loose, in such wise as it was lawful not to tie, the marriage bond, they be-

---

[1] 1 Cor. vii. 28, 36.   [2] 1 Cor. vi. 19.   [5] 1 Tim. v. 6.   [6] 1 Tim. ii. 9, 10.
[3] 1 Cor. vii. 14.   [4] 1 Cor. vii. 34.   [7] 1 Peter iii. 1-7.   [8] Eccles. iii.5.

come such as the form of marriage makes profession of, so as that either by mutual consent they ascend unto a higher degree of holiness, or, if both are not such, the one who is such will not be one to exact but to yield the due, observing in all things a chaste and religious concord. But in those times, wherein as yet the mystery of our salvation was veiled in prophetic sacraments, even they who were such before marriage, yet contracted marriage through the duty of begetting children, not overcome by lust, but led by piety, unto whom if there were given such choice, as in the revelation of the New Testament there hath been given, the Lord saying "Whoso can receive, let him receive;"[1] no one doubts that they would have been ready to receive it even with joy, who reads with careful attention what use they made of their wives, at a time when also it was allowed one man to have several, whom he had with more chastity, than any now has his one wife, of these, unto whom we see what the Apostle allows by way of leave.[2] For they had them in the work of begetting children, not "in the disease of desire, as the nations which know not God."[3] And this is so great a thing, that many at this day more easily abstain from all sexual intercourse their whole life through, than, if they are joined in marriage, observe the measure of not coming together except for the sake of children. Forsooth we have many brethren and partners in the heavenly inheritance of both sexes that are continent, whether they be such as have made trial of marriage, or such as are entirely free from all such intercourse: forsooth they are without number: yet, in our familiar discourses with them, whom have we heard, whether of those who are, or of those who have been, married, declaring to us that he has never had sexual intercourse with his wife, save with the hope of conception? What, therefore, the Apostles command the married, this is proper to marriage, but what they allow by way of pardon, or what hinders prayers, this marriage compels not, but bears with.

16. Therefore if haply, (which whether it can take place, I know not; and rather think it cannot take place; but yet, if haply), having taken unto himself a concubine for a time, a man shall have sought sons only from this same intercourse; neither thus is that union to be preferred to the marriage even of those women, who do this, that is matter of pardon.[4] For we must consider what belongs to marriage, not what belongs to such women as marry and use marriage with less moderation than they ought. For neither if each one so use lands entered upon unjustly and wrongly, as out of their fruits to give large alms, doth he therefore justify rapine: nor if another brood over, through avarice, an estate to which he has succeeded, or which he hath justly gained, are we on this account to blame the rule of civil law, whereby he is made a lawful owner. Nor will the wrongfulness of a tyrannical rebellion deserve praise, if the tyrant treat his subjects with royal clemency: nor will the order of royal power deserve blame, if a king rage with tyrannical cruelty. For it is one thing to wish to use well unjust power, and it is another thing to use unjustly just power. Thus neither do concubines taken for a time, if they be such in order to sons, make their concubinage lawful; nor do married women, if they live wantonly with their husbands, attach any charge to the order of marriage.

17. That marriage can take place of persons first ill joined, an honest decree following after, is manifest. But a marriage once for all entered upon in the City of our God, where, even from the first union of the two, the man and the woman, marriage bears a certain sacramental character, can no way be dissolved but by the death of one of them. For the bond of marriage remains, although a family, for the sake of which it was entered upon, do not follow through manifest barrenness; so that, when now married persons know that they shall not have children, yet it is not lawful for them to separate even for the very sake of children, and to join themselves unto others. And if they shall so do, they commit adultery with those unto whom they join themselves, but themselves remain husbands and wives. Clearly with the good will of the wife to take another woman, that from her may be born sons common to both, by the sexual intercourse and seed of the one, but by the right and power of the other, was lawful among the ancient fathers: whether it be lawful now also, I would not hastily pronounce. For there is not now necessity of begetting children, as there then was, when, even when wives bare children, it was allowed, in order to a more numerous posterity, to marry other wives in addition, which now is certainly not lawful. For the difference that separates times causes the due season to have so great force unto the justice and doing or not doing any thing, that now a man does better, if he marry not even one wife, unless he be unable to contain. But then they married even several without any blame, even

1 Matt. xix. 12.   2 1 Cor. vii. 6.
3 1 Thess. iv. 5.   4 Veniale.

those who could much more easily contain, were it not that piety at that time had another demand upon them. For, as the wise and just man, [1] who now desires to be dissolved and to be with Christ, and takes more pleasure in this, the best, now not from desire of living here, but from duty of being useful [2], takes food that he may remain in the flesh, which is necessary for the sake of others; so to have intercourse with females in right of marriage, was to holy men at that time a matter of duty not of lust.

18. For what food is unto the conservation of the man, this sexual intercourse is unto the conservation of the race: and both are not without carnal delight: which yet being modified, and by restraint of temperance reduced unto the use after nature, cannot be lust. [3] But what unlawful food is in the supporting of life, this sexual intercourse of fornication or adultery is in the seeking of a family. And what unlawful food is in luxury of belly and throat, this unlawful intercourse is in lust that seeks not a family. And what the excessive appetite of some is in lawful food, this that intercourse that is matter of pardon is in husband and wife. As therefore it is better to die of hunger than to eat things offered unto idols: so it is better to die without children, than to seek a family from unlawful intercourse. But from whatever source men be born, if they follow not the vices of their parents, and worship God aright, they shall be honest and safe. For the seed of man, from out what kind of man soever, is the creation of God, and it shall fare ill with those who use it ill, yet shall not itself at any time be evil. But as the good sons of adulterers are no defense of adulteries, so the evil sons of married persons are no charge against marriage. Wherefore as the Fathers of the time of the New Testament taking food from the duty of conservation, although they took it with natural delight of the flesh, were yet in no way compared with the delight of those who fed on what had been offered in sacrifice, or of those who, although the food was lawful, yet took it to excess: so the Fathers of the time of the Old Testament from the duty of conservation used sexual intercourse; and yet that their natural delight, by no means relaxed unto unreasonable and unlawful lust, is not to be compared either with the vileness of fornications, or with the intemperance of married persons. Forsooth through the same vein [4]

of charity, now after the spirit, then after the flesh, it was a duty to beget sons for the sake of that mother Jerusalem: but it was nought save the difference of times which made the works of the fathers different. But thus it was necessary that even Prophets, not living after the flesh, should come together after the flesh; even as it was necessary that Apostles also, not living after the flesh, should eat food after the flesh.

19. Therefore as many women as there are now, unto whom it is said, "if they contain not, let them be married, [5]" are not to be compared to the holy women then, even when they married. Marriage itself indeed in all nations is for the same cause of begetting sons, and of what character soever these may be afterward, yet was marriage for this purpose instituted, that they may be born in due and honest order. But men, who contain not, as it were ascend unto marriage by a step of honesty: but they, who without doubt would contain, if the purpose of that time had allowed this, in a certain measure descended unto marriage by a step of piety. And, on this account, although the marriages of both, so far as they are marriages, in that they are for the sake of begetting, are equally good, yet these men when married are not to be compared with those men as married. For these have, what is allowed them by the way of leave, on account of the honesty of marriage, although it pertain not to marriage; that is, the advance which goes beyond the necessity of begetting, which they had not. But neither can these, if haply there be now any found, who neither seek, nor desire, in marriage any thing, save that wherefore marriage was instituted, be made equal to those men. For in these the very desire of sons is carnal, but in those it was spiritual, in that it was suited to the sacrament of that time. Forsooth now no one who is made perfect in piety seeks to have sons, save after a spiritual sense; but then it was the work of piety itself to beget sons even after a carnal sense: in that the begetting of that people was fraught with tidings of things to come, and pertained unto the prophetic dispensation.

20. And on this account, not, so as it was allowed one man to have even several wives, was it allowed one female to have several husbands, not even for the sake of a family, in case it should happen that the woman could bear, the man could not beget. For by a secret law of nature things that stand chief love to be singular; but what are subject are set under, not only one under one,

---

[1] Phil. i. 23. [2] *Consulendi.*
[3] *Retract.* b. ii. c. xxii. 2. "it was meant that the good and right use of lust is not lust, for as it is evil will to use good things, so is it good will to use evil things." [4] "*Vena.*"

[5] 1 Cor. vii. 9.

but, if the system of nature or society allow, even several under one, not without becoming beauty. For neither hath one slave so several masters, in the way that several slaves have one master. Thus we read not that any of the holy women served two or more living husbands: but we read that many females served one husband, when the social state[1] of that nation allowed it, and the purpose of the time persuaded to it: for neither is it contrary to the nature of marriage. For several females can conceive from one man: but one female cannot from several, (such is the power of things principal:) as many souls are rightly made subject unto one God. And on this account there is no True God of souls, save One: but one soul by means of many false gods may commit fornication, but not be made fruitful.

21. But since out of many souls there shall be hereafter one City of such as have one soul and one heart[2] towards God; which perfection of our unity shall be hereafter, after this sojourn in a strange land, wherein the thoughts of all shall neither be hidden one from another, nor shall be in any matter opposed one to another; on this account the Sacrament of marriage of our time hath been so reduced to one man and one wife, as that it is not lawful to ordain any as a steward of the Church, save the husband of one wife.[3] And this they have understood more acutely who have been of opinion, that neither is he to be ordained,[4] who as a catechumen or as a heathen[5] had a second wife. For it is a matter of sacrament, not of sin. For in baptism all sins are put away. But he who said, "If thou shalt have taken a wife, thou hast not sinned; and if a virgin shall have been married, she sinneth not:"[6] and, "Let her do what she will, she sinneth not, if she be married," hath made it plain enough that marriage is no sin. But on account of the sanctity of the Sacrament, as a female, although it be as a catechumen that she hath suffered violence, cannot after Baptism be consecrated among the virgins of God: so there was no absurdity in supposing of him who had exceeded the number of one wife, not that he had committed any sin, but that he had lost a certain prescript rule[7] of a sacrament necessary not unto desert of good life, but unto the seal of ecclesiastic ordination; and thus, as the many wives of the old Fathers signified our future Churches out of all nations made subject unto one husband, Christ: so our chief-priest,[8] the husband of one wife, signifies unity out of all nations, made subject unto one husband, Christ: which shall then be perfected, when He shall have unveiled the hidden things of darkness,[9] and shall have made manifest the thoughts of the heart, that then each may have praise from God. But now there are manifest, there are hidden, dissensions, even where charity is safe between those, who shall be hereafter one, and in one; which shall then certainly have no existence. As therefore the Sacrament of marriage with several of that time signified the multitude that should be hereafter made subject unto God in all nations of the earth, so the Sacrament of marriage with one of our times signifies the unity of us all made subject to God, which shall be hereafter in one Heavenly City. Therefore as to serve two or more, so to pass over from a living husband into marriage with another, was neither lawful then, nor is it lawful now, nor will it ever be lawful. Forsooth to apostatise from the One God, and to go into adulterous superstition of another, is ever an evil. Therefore not even for the sake of a more numerous family did our Saints do, what the Roman Cato is said to have done,[10] to give up his wife, during his own life, to fill even another's house with sons. Forsooth in the marriage of one woman the sanctity of the Sacrament is of more avail than the fruitfulness of the womb.

22. If, therefore, even they who are united in marriage only for the purpose of begetting, for which purpose marriage was instituted, are not compared with the Fathers, seeking their very sons in a way far other than do these; forasmuch as Abraham, being bidden to slay his son, fearless and devoted, spared not his only son, whom from out of great despair he had received[11] save that he laid down his hand, when He forbade him, at Whose command he had lifted it up; it remains that we consider, whether at least continent persons among us are to be compared to those Fathers who were married; unless haply now these are to be preferred to them, to whom we have not yet found persons to compare. For there was a greater good in their marriage, than is the proper good of marriage: to which without doubt the good of Continence is to be preferred: because they sought not sons from marriage by such duty as these are led by, from a certain sense of mortal nature requiring succession against decease. And, whoso denies this to be good he knows not

---

[1] Societas. [2] Acts iv. 32. [3] 1 Tim. iii. 2. [4] Tit. i. 6.
[5] Thus Ambrose, Verellæ, and ancient Jerome, Ep. ad Ocean. and harshly against Ep. to Ch. of general custom, speaks strongly this interpretation, and says, b. i. near the end, that Ruffinus had found fault with him for this. Ben.
[6] 1 Cor. vii. 28, 36. [7] Normam.

[8] Antistes.
[10] Cato minor, cf. Plutarch. p. 771.
[9] 1 Cor. iv. 5.
[11] Gen. xxii. 12.

God, the Creator of all things good, from things heavenly even unto things earthly, from things immortal even unto things mortal. But neither are beasts altogether without this sense of begetting, and chiefly birds, whose care of building nests meets us at once, and a certain likeness to marriages, in order to beget and nurture together. But those men, with mind far holier, surpassed this affection of mortal nature, the chastity whereof in its own kind, there being added thereto the worship of God, as some have understood, is set forth as bearing first thirty-fold; who sought sons of their marriage for the sake of Christ; in order to distinguish His race after the flesh from all nations : even as God was pleased to order, that this above the rest should avail to prophesy of Him, in that it was foretold of what race also, and of what nation, He should hereafter come in the flesh. Therefore it was a far greater good than the chaste marriages of believers among us, which father Abraham knew in his own thigh, under which he bade his servant to put his hand, that he might take an oath concerning the wife, whom his son was to marry. For putting his hand under the thigh of a man, and swearing by the God of Heaven,[1] what else did he signify, than that in that Flesh, which derived its origin from that thigh, the God of Heaven would come? Therefore marriage is a good, wherein married persons are so much the better, in proportion as they fear God with greater chastity and faithfulness, specially if the sons, whom they desire after the flesh, they also bring up after the spirit.

23. Nor, in that the Law orders a man to be purified even after intercourse with a wife, doth it show it to be sin: unless it be that which is allowed by way of pardon, which also, being in excess, hinders prayers. But, as the Law sets[2] many things in sacraments and shadows of things to come; a certain as it were material formless state of the seed, which having received form will hereafter produce the body of man, is set to signify a life formless, and untaught: from which formless state, forasmuch as it behoves that man be cleansed by form and teaching of learning; as a sign of this, that purification was ordered after the emission of seed. For neither in sleep also doth it take place through sin. And yet there also a purification was commanded. Or, if any think this also to be sin, thinking that it comes not to pass save from some lust of this kind, which without doubt is false; what? are the ordinary menses also of women sins? And yet from these the same

old Law commanded that they should be cleansed by expiation; for no other cause, save the material formless state itself, in that which, when conception hath taken place, is added as it were to build up the body, and for this reason, when it flows without form, the Law would have signified by it a soul without form of discipline, flowing and loose in an unseemly manner. And that this ought to receive form, it signifies, when it commands such flow of the body to be purified. Lastly, what? to die, is that also a sin? or, to bury a dead person, is it not also a good work of humanity? and yet a purification was commanded even on occasion of this also; because also a dead body, life abandoning it, is not sin, but signifies the sin of a soul abandoned by righteousness.[3]

24. Marriage, I say, is a good, and may be, by sound reason, defended against all calumnies. But with the marriage of the holy fathers, I inquire not what marriage, but what continence, is on a level: or rather not marriage with marriage; for it is an equal gift in all cases given to the mortal nature of men; but men who use marriage, forasmuch as I find not, to compare with other men who used marriage in a far other spirit, we must inquire what continent persons admit of being compared with those married persons. Unless, haply, Abraham could not contain from marriage, for the sake of the kingdom of heaven, he who, for the sake of the kingdom of heaven, could fearless sacrifice his only pledge of offspring, for whose sake marriage was dear!

25. Forsooth continence is a virtue, not of the body, but of the soul. But the virtues of the soul are sometimes shown in work, sometimes lie hid in habit, as the virtue of martyrdom shone forth and appeared by enduring sufferings; but how many are there of the same virtue of mind, unto whom trial is wanting, whereby what is within, in the sight of God, may go forth also into the sight of men, and not to men begin to exist, but only become known? For there was already in Job patience, which God knew, and to which He bore witness: but it became known unto men by test of trial:[4] and what lay hid within was not produced, but shown, by the things that were brought on him from without. Timothy also certainly had the virtue of abstaining from wine,[5] which Paul took not from him, by advising him to use a moderate portion of wine, "for the sake of his stomach and his often infirmities," otherwise he taught him a deadly lesson, that for the sake of the health

---

[1] Gen. xxiv. 2-4.   [2] *Infirmitas.*   [3] Numb. xix. 11.   [4] Job i. 8.   [5] 1 Tim. v. 23.

of the body there should be a loss of virtue in the soul: but because what he advised could take place with safety to that virtue, the profit of drinking was so left free to the body, as that the habit of continence continued in the soul. For it is the habit itself, whereby any thing is done, when there is need;[1] but when it is not done, it can be done, only there is no need. This habit, in the matter of that continence which is from sexual intercourse, they have not, unto whom it is said, "If they contain not, let them be married."[2] But this they have, unto whom it is said, "Whoso can receive, let him receive."[3] Thus have perfect souls used earthly goods, that are necessary for something else, through this habit of continence, so as, by it, not to be bound by them, and so as by it, to have power also not to use them, in case there were no need. Nor doth any use them well, save who hath power also not to use them. Many indeed with more ease practise abstinence, so as not to use, than practise temperance, so as to use well. But no one can wisely use them, save who can also continently not use them. From this habit Paul also said, "I know both to abound, and to suffer want."[4] Forsooth to suffer want is the part of any men soever; but to know to suffer want is the part of great men. So, also, to abound, who cannot? but to know also to abound, is not, save of those, whom abundance corrupts not.

26. But, in order that it may be more clearly understood, how there may be virtue in habit, although it be not in work, I speak of an example, about which no Catholic Christian can doubt. For that our Lord Jesus Christ in truth of flesh hungered and thirsted, ate and drank, no one doubts of such as out of the Gospel are believers. What, then, was there not in Him the virtue of continence from meat and drink, as great as in John Baptist? "For John came neither eating nor drinking; and they said, He hath a devil; the Son of Man came both eating and drinking; and they said, "Lo, a glutton and wine-bibber, a friend of publicans and sinners."[5] What, are not such things said also against them of His household, our fathers, from another kind of using of things earthy, so far as pertains to sexual intercourse; "Lo, men lustful and unclean, lovers of women and lewdness?" And yet as in Him that was not true, although it were true that He abstained not, even as John, from eating and drinking, for Himself saith most plainly and truly, "John came, not eating, nor drinking; the Son of Man came eating and drinking:" so neither is this true in these Fathers; although there hath come now the Apostle of Christ, not wedded, nor begetting, so that the heathen say of him, He was a magician; but there came then the Prophet of Christ, marrying and begetting sons, so that the Manichees say of him, He was a man fond of women: "And wisdom," saith He, "hath been justified of her children."[6] What the Lord there added, after He had thus spoken of John and of Himself; "But wisdom," saith He, "hath been justified of her children." Who see that the virtue of continence ought to exist even in the habit of the soul, but to be shown forth in deed, according to opportunity of things and times; even as the virtue of patience of holy martyrs appeared in deed; but of the rest equally holy was in habit. Wherefore, even as there is not unequal desert of patience in Peter, who suffered, and in John, who suffered not; so there is not unequal desert of continence in John who made no trial of marriage,[7] and in Abraham, who begat sons. For both the celibate of the one, and the marriage estate of the other, did service as soldiers to Christ, as times were allotted; but John had continence in work also, but Abraham in habit alone.

27. Therefore at that time, when the Law also, following upon the days of the Patriarchs,[8] pronounced accursed, whoso raised not up seed in Israel, even he, who could, put it not forth, but yet possessed it. But from the period that the fullness of time hath come,[9] that it should be said, "Whoso can receive, let him receive,"[10] from that period even unto this present, and from henceforth even unto the end, whoso hath, worketh: whoso shall be unwilling to work, let him not falsely say, that he hath. And through this means, they, who corrupt good manners by evil communications,[11] with empty and vain craft, say to a Christian man exercising continence, and refusing marriage, What then, are you better than Abraham? But let him not, upon hearing this, be troubled; neither let him dare to say, "Better," nor let him fall away from his purpose: for the one he saith not truly, the other he doth not rightly. But let him say, I indeed am not better than Abraham, but the chastity of the unmarried is better than the chastity of marriage; whereof Abraham had one in use, both in habit. For he lived chastely in the marriage state: but it was in his power to be chaste without marriage, but at that time it behoved not. But I with more ease use not marriage,

---

[1] Or "work."   [2] 1 Cor. vii. 9.   [3] Matt. xix. 12.
[4] Phil. iv. 12.   [5] Matt. xi. 18-19.

[6] Matt. xi. 19.   [7] S. Jerome agt. Jovinianus.   [8] Deut. xxv. 5, 10.
[9] Gal. iv. 4.   [10] Matt. xix. 12.   [11] 1 Cor. xv. 33.

which Abraham used, than so use marriage as Abraham used it: and therefore I am better than those, who through incontinence of mind cannot do what I do; not than those, who, on account of difference of time, did not do what I do. For what I now do, they would have done better, if it had been to be done at that time; but what they did, I should not so do, although it were now to be done. Or, if he feels and knows himself to be such, as that, (the virtue of continence being preserved and continued in the habit of his mind, in case he had descended unto the use of marriage from some duty of religion,) he should be such an husband, and such a father, as Abraham was; let him dare to make plain answer to that captious questioner, and to say, I am not indeed better than Abraham, only in this kind of continence, of which he was not void, although it appeared not: but I am such, not having other than he, but doing other. Let him say this plainly: forasmuch as, even if he shall wish to glory, he will not be a fool, for he saith the truth. But if he spare, lest any think of him above what he sees him,[1] or hears any thing of him; let him remove from his own person the knot of the question, and let him answer, not concerning the man, but concerning the thing itself, and let him say, Whoso hath so great power is such as Abraham. But it may happen that the virtue of continence is less in his mind, who uses not marriage, which Abraham used: but yet it is greater than in his mind, who on this account held chastity of marriage, in that he could not a greater. Thus also let the unmarried woman, whose thoughts are of the things of the Lord, that she may be holy both in body and spirit,[2] when she shall have heard that shameless questioner saying, What, then, are you better than Sara? answer, I am better, but than those, who are void of the virtue of continence, which I believe not of Sara: she therefore together with this virtue did what was suited to that time, from which I am free, that in my body also may appear, what she kept in her mind.

28. Therefore, if we compare the things themselves, we may no way doubt that the chastity of continence is better than marriage chastity, whilst yet both are good: but when we compare the persons, he is better, who hath a greater good than another. Further, he who hath a greater of the same kind, hath also that which is less; but he, who only hath what is less, assuredly hath not that which is greater. For in sixty, thirty also are con-

tained, not sixty also in thirty. But not to work from out that which he hath, stands in the allotment of duties, not in the want of virtues: forasmuch as neither is he without the good of mercy, who finds not wretched persons such as he may mercifully assist.

29. And there is this further, that men are not rightly compared with men in regard of some one good. For it may come to pass, that one hath not what another hath, but hath another thing, which must be esteemed of more value. The good of obedience is better than of continence. For marriage is in no place condemned by authority of our Scriptures, but disobedience is in no place acquitted. If therefore there be set before us a virgin about to continue so, but yet disobedient, and a married woman who could not continue a virgin, but yet obedient, which shall we call better? shall it be (the one) less praiseworthy, than if she were a virgin, or (the other) worthy of blame, even as she is a virgin? So, if you compare a drunken virgin with a sober married woman, who can doubt to pass the same sentence? Forsooth marriage and virginity are two goods, whereof the one is greater; but sobriety and drunkenness, even as obedience and stubbornness, are, the one good, and the other evil. But it is better to have all goods even in a less degree, than great good with great evil: forasmuch as in the goods of the body also it is better to have the stature of Zacchæus with sound health, than that of Goliah with fever.

30. The right question plainly is, not whether a virgin every way disobedient is to be compared to an obedient married woman, but a less obedient to a more obedient: forasmuch as that also of marriage is chastity, and therefore a good, but less than virginal. Therefore if the one, by so much less in the good of obedience, as she is greater in the good of chastity, be compared with the other, which of them is to be preferred that person judges, who in the first place comparing chastity itself and obedience, sees that obedience is in a certain way the mother of all virtues. And therefore, for this reason, there may be obedience without virginity, because virginity is of counsel, not of precept. But I call that obedience, whereby precepts are complied with. And, therefore, there may be obedience to precepts without virginity, but not without chastity. For it pertains unto chastity, not to commit fornication, not to commit adultery, to be defiled by no unlawful intercourse: and whoso observe not these, do contrary to the precepts of God, and on this account are banished from the virtue of obedience. But there may be vir-

---

[1] 2 Cor. xii. 6.   [2] 1 Cor. vii. 34.

ginity without obedience, on this account, because it is possible for a woman, having received the counsel of virginity, and having guarded virginity, to slight precepts: even as we have known many sacred virgins, talkative, curious, drunken, litigious, covetous, proud: all which are contrary to precepts, and slay one, even as Eve herself, by the crime of disobedience. Wherefore not only is the obedient to be preferred to the disobedient, but a more obedient married woman to a less obedient virgin.

31. From this obedience that Father, who was not without a wife, was prepared to be without an only son,[1] and that slain by himself. For I shall not without due cause call him an only son, concerning whom he heard the Lord say, " In Isaac shall there be called for thee a seed.[2] " Therefore how much sooner would he hear it, that he should be even without a wife, if this he were bidden? Wherefore it is not without reason that we often consider, that some of both sexes, containing from all sexual intercourse, are negligent in obeying precepts, after having with so great warmth caught at the not making use of things that are allowed. Whence who doubts that we do not rightly compare unto the excellence of those holy fathers and mothers begetting sons, the men and women of our time, although free from all intercourse, yet in virtue of obedience inferior: even if there had been wanting to those men in habit of mind also, what is plain in the deed of the latter. Therefore let these follow the Lamb, boys singing the new song, as it is written in the Apocalypse, " who have not defiled themselves with women:"[3] for no other reason than that they have continued virgins. Nor let them on this account think themselves better than the first holy fathers, who used marriage, so to speak, after the fashion of marriage. Forsooth the use of it is such, as that, if in it there hath taken place through carnal intercourse aught which exceeds necessity of begetting, although in a way that deserves pardon, there is pollution. For what doth pardon expiate, if that advance cause no pollution whatever? From which pollution it were strange if boys following the Lamb were free, unless they continued virgins.

32. Therefore the good of marriage throughout all nations and all men stands in the occasion of begetting, and faith of chastity: but, so far as pertains unto the People of God, also in the sanctity of the Sacrament, by reason of which it is unlawful for one who leaves her husband, even when she has been put away, to be married to another, so long as her husband lives, no not even for the sake of bearing children: and, whereas this is the alone cause, wherefore marriage takes place, not even where that very thing, wherefore it takes place, follows not, is the marriage bond loosed, save by the death of the husband or wife. In like manner as if there take place an ordination of clergy in order to form a congregation of people, although the congregation of people follow not, yet there remains in the ordained persons the Sacrament of Ordination; and if, for any fault, any be removed from his office, he will not be without the Sacrament of the Lord once for all set upon him, albeit continuing unto condemnation. Therefore that marriage takes place for the sake of begetting children, the Apostle is a witness thus, " I will," says he, " that the younger women be married." And, as though it were said to him, For what purpose? straightway he added, " to have children, to be mothers of families." But unto the faith of chastity pertains that saying, " The wife hath not power of her own body, but the husband: likewise also the husband hath not power of his own body, but the wife."[4] But unto the sanctity of the Sacrament that saying, " The wife not to depart from her husband, but, in case she shall have departed, to remain unmarried, or to be reconciled to her husband: and let not the husband put away his wife."[5] All these are goods, on account of which marriage is a good; offspring, faith, sacrament. But now, at this time, not to seek offspring after the flesh, and by this means to maintain a certain perpetual freedom from every such work, and to be made subject after a spiritual manner unto one Husband Christ, is assuredly better and holier; provided, that is, men so use that freedom, as it is written, so as to have their thoughts of the things of the Lord, how to please the Lord; that is, that Continence[6] at all times do take thought, that obedience fall not short in any matter: and this virtue, as the root-virtue, and (as it is wont to be called) the womb, and clearly universal, the holy fathers of old exercised in deed; but that Continence they possessed in habit of mind. Who assuredly, through that obedience, whereby they were just and holy, and ever prepared unto every good work, even if they were bidden to abstain from all sexual intercourse, would perform it. For how much more easily could they, at the

<hr/>

[1] *Retract*. b. ii. c. 22. 2. " I do not quite approve this; as one should rather believe that he believed his son would presently be restored to him by resurrection, as we read in the Epistle to the Hebrews."
[2] Gen. xxi. 12.   [3] Rev. xiv. 4.

[4] 1 Cor. vii. 4.   [5] 1 Cor. vii. 10, 11.   [6] 1 Cor. vii. 32.

bidding or exhortation of God, not use sexual intercourse, who, as an act of obedience, could slay the child, for the begetting of which alone they used the ministry of sexual intercourse?

33. And, the case being thus, enough and more than enough answer has been made to the heretics, whether they be Manichees, or whosoever other that bring false charges against the Fathers of the Old Testament, on the subject of their having several wives, thinking this a proof whereby to convict them of incontinence: provided, that is, that they perceive, that that is no sin, which is committed neither against nature, in that they used those women not for wantonness, but for the begetting of children: nor against custom, forasmuch as such things were usually done at those times: nor against command, forasmuch as they were forbidden by no law. But such as used women unlawfully, either the divine sentence in those Scriptures convicts them, or the reading sets them forth for us to condemn and shun, not to approve or imitate.

34. But those of ours who have wives we advise, with all our power, that they dare not to judge of those holy fathers after their own weakness, comparing, as the Apostle says, themselves with themselves;[1] and therefore, not understanding how great strength the soul hath, doing service unto righteousness against lusts, that it acquiesce not in carnal motions of this sort, or suffer them to glide on or advance unto sexual intercourse beyond the necessity of begetting children, so far as the order of nature, so far as the use of custom, so far as the decrees of laws prescribe. Forsooth it is on this account that men have this suspicion concerning those fathers, in that they themselves have either chosen marriage through incontinence, or use their wives with intemperance. But however let such as are continent, either men, who, on the death of their wives, or, women, who, on the death of their husbands, or both, who, with mutual consent, have vowed continence unto God, know that to them indeed there is due a greater recom-

pense than marriage chastity demands; but, (as regards) the marriages of the holy Fathers, who were joined after the manner of prophecy, who neither in sexual intercourse sought aught save children, nor in children themselves aught save what should set forward Christ coming hereafter in the flesh, not only let them not despise them in comparison of their own purpose, but let them without any doubting prefer them even to their own purpose.

35. Boys also and virgins dedicating unto God actual chastity we do before all things admonish, that they be aware that they must guard their life meanwhile upon earth with so great humility, by how much the more what they have vowed is heavenly. Forsooth it is written, "How great soever thou art, by so much humble thyself in all things."[2] Therefore it is our part to say something of their greatness, it is their part to have thought of great humility. Therefore, except certain, those holy fathers and mothers who were married, than whom these although they be not married are not better, for this reason, that, if they were married, they would not be equal, let them not doubt that they surpass all the rest of this time, either married, or after trial made of marriage, exercising continence; not so far as Anna surpasses Susanna; but so far as Mary surpasses both. I am speaking of what pertains unto the holy chastity itself of the flesh; for who knows not, what other deserts Mary hath? Therefore let them add to this so high purpose conduct suitable, that they may have an assured security of the surpassing reward; knowing of a truth, that, unto themselves and unto all the faithful, beloved and chosen members of Christ, coming many from the East, and from the West, although shining with light of glory that differeth one from another, according to their deserts, there is this great gift bestowed in common, to sit down in the kingdom of God with Abraham, and Isaac, and Jacob,[3] who not for the sake of this world, but for the sake of Christ, were husbands, for the sake of Christ were fathers.

---

[1] 2 Cor. x. 12.

[2] Ecclus. iii. 18.   [3] Matt. viii. 11.

bidding or exhortation of God, not use sev...
intercourse, who, as an act of obed...
could slay the child, for the be...
which alone they used the minis...
intercourse?

33. And, the case being t...
more than enough answer t...
the heretics, whether th...
or whosoever other that...
against the Fathers of...
the subject of their own...
thinking this a proof...
of incontinence; pr...
perceive, that that...
mitted neither ag...
used those wom...
for the begettin...
custom, forasm...
ally done at tho...
mand, forasmuc...
no law. But so...
either the divin...
convicts them, ...
for us to cond...
or imitate.

34. But th...
advise, with...
not to judge...
own weakne...
says, themselves...
fore, not un...
the soul...
ness again...
carnal and...
glide or...
beyon...
so far.
use...
pr...
ti

ST. AUGUSTIN:

OF HOLY VIRGINITY

[DE VIRGINITATE.]

TRANSLATED BY

REV. C. I CORNISH, M.A.,

OF EXETER COLLEGE, OXFORD.

OF HOLY VIRGINITY.

[DE VIRGINITATE.]

Retr. ii. 23. "After I had written 'on the Good of Marriage,' it was expected that I should write on Holy Virginity; and I did not delay to do so: and that it is God's gift, and how great a gift, and with what humility to be guarded, so far as I was able I set forth in one volume. This book begins," &c.

1. WE lately put forth a book "of the Good of Marriage," in which also we admonished and admonish the virgins of Christ, not, on account of that greater gift which they have received, to despise, in comparison of themselves, the fathers and mothers of the People of God; and not to think those men,[1] (whom the Apostle sets forth as the olive, that the engrafted wild olive be not proud,) who did service to Christ about to come hereafter, even by the begetting of sons, on this account of less desert, because by divine right continence is preferred to wedded life, and pious virginity to marriage. Forsooth in them were being prepared and brought forth future things, which now we see fulfilled in a marvellous and effectual manner, whose married life also was prophetic: whence, not after the wonted custom of human wishes and joys, but by the very deep counsel of God, in certain of them fruitfulness obtained to be honored, in certain also barrenness to be made fruitful. But at this time, towards them unto whom it is said, "if they contain not, let them be married,"[2] we must use not consolation, but exhortation. But them, unto whom it is said, "Whoso can receive, let him receive,"[3] we must exhort, that

they be not alarmed; and alarm that they be not lifted up. Wherefore virginity is not only to be set forth, that it may be loved, but also to be admonished, that it be not puffed up.

2. This we have undertaken in our present discourse: may Christ help us, the Son of a virgin, and the Spouse of virgins, born after the flesh of a virgin womb, and wedded after the Spirit in virgin marriage. Whereas, therefore, the whole Church itself is a virgin espoused unto one Husband Christ,[4] as the Apostle saith, of how great honor are its members worthy, who guard this even in the flesh itself, which the whole Church guards in the faith? which imitates the mother of her husband, and her Lord. For the Church also is both a mother and a virgin. For whose virgin purity consult we for, if she is not a virgin? or whose children address we, if she is not a mother? Mary bare the Head of This Body after the flesh, the Church bears the members of that Body after the Spirit. In both virginity hinders not fruitfulness: in both fruitfulness takes not away virginity. Wherefore, whereas the whole Church is holy both in body and spirit, and yet the whole is not virgin in body but in spirit; how much

---

[1] Rom. xi. 17, 18.   [2] 1 Cor. vii. 9.   [3] Mat. xix. 12.   [4] 2 Cor. xi. 2.

more holy is it in these members, wherein it is virgin both in body and spirit?

3. It is written in the Gospel, of the mother and brethren of Christ, that is, His kindred after the flesh, that, when word had been brought to Him, and they were standing without, because they could not come to Him by reason of the crowd, He made answer, "Who is My mother? or who are My brethren? and stretching forth His Hand over His disciples, He saith, These are My brethren: and whosoever shall have done the will of My Father, that man is to Me brother, and mother, and sister."[1] What else teaching us, than to prefer to kindred after the flesh, our descent after the Spirit: and that men are not blessed for this reason, that they are united by nearness of flesh unto just and holy men, but that, by obeying and following, they cleave unto their doctrine and conduct. Therefore Mary is more blessed in receiving the faith of Christ, than in conceiving the flesh of Christ. For to a certain one who said, "Blessed is the womb, which bare Thee,"[2] He Himself made answer, "Yea, rather, blessed are they who hear the Word of God, and keep it." Lastly, to His brethren, that is, His kindred after the flesh, who believed not in Him, what profit was there in that being of kin? Thus also her nearness as a Mother would have been of no profit to Mary, had she not borne Christ in her heart after a more blessed manner than in her flesh.

4. Her virginity also itself was on this account more pleasing and accepted, in that it was not that Christ being conceived in her, rescued it beforehand from a husband who would violate it, Himself to preserve it; but, before He was conceived, chose it, already dedicated to God, as that from which to be born. This is shown by the words which Mary spake in answer to the Angel announcing to her her conception; "How," saith she, "shall this be, seeing I know not a man?"[3] Which assuredly she would not say, unless she had before vowed herself unto God as a virgin. But, because the habits of the Israelites as yet refused this, she was espoused to a just man, who would not take from her by violence, but rather guard against violent persons, what she had already vowed. Although, even if she had said this only, "How shall this take place?" and had not added, "seeing I know not a man," certainly she would not have asked, how, being a female, she should give birth to her promised Son, if she had married with purpose of sexual intercourse. She might have been bidden also to

continue a virgin, that in her by fitting miracle the Son of God should receive the form of a servant, but, being to be a pattern to holy virgins, lest it should be thought that she alone needed to be a virgin, who had obtained to conceive a child even without sexual intercourse, she dedicated her virginity to God, when as yet she knew not what she should conceive, in order that the imitation of a heavenly life in an earthly and mortal body should take place of vow, not of command; through love of choosing, not through necessity of doing service. Thus Christ by being born of a virgin, who, before she knew Who was to be born of her, had determined to continue a virgin, chose rather to approve, than to command, holy virginity. And thus, even in the female herself, in whom He took the form of a servant, He willed that virginity should be free.

5. There is, therefore, no reason why the virgins of God be sad, because themselves also cannot, keeping their virginity, be mothers of the flesh. For Him alone could virginity give birth to with fitting propriety, Who in His Birth could have no peer. However, That Birth of the Holy Virgin is the ornament of all holy virgins; and themselves together with Mary are mothers of Christ, if they do the will of His Father. For Mary also is on this account the Mother of Christ in a way more full of praise and blessing, according to His sentence mentioned above. "Whosoever doeth the will of my Father Who is in heaven, that one is to Me brother, and sister, and mother." All these degrees of nearness of kin to Himself, He shows forth in a spiritual manner, in the People whom He hath redeemed: as brothers and sisters He hath holy men and holy women, forasmuch as they all are co-heirs in the heavenly inheritance. His mother is the whole Church, because she herself assuredly gives birth to His members, that is, His faithful ones. Also His mother is every pious soul, doing the will of His Father with most fruitful charity, in them of whom it travaileth, until Himself[4] be formed in them. Mary, therefore, doing the will of God, after the flesh is only the mother of Christ, but after the Spirit she is both His sister and mother.

6. And on this account, that one female, not only in the Spirit, but also in the flesh, is both a mother and a virgin. And a mother indeed in the Spirit, not of our Head, Which is the Saviour Himself, of Whom rather she was born after the Spirit: forasmuch as all, who

1 Matt. xii. 46–50.   2 Luke xi. 27, 28.   3 Luke i. 34.   4 Gal. iv. 19.

have believed in Him, among whom is herself also, are rightly called "children of the Bridegroom:"[1] but clearly the mother of His members, which are we: in that she wrought together by charity, that faithful ones should be born in the Church, who are members of That Head: but in the flesh, the mother of the Head Himself. For it behoved that our Head, on account of a notable miracle, should be born after the flesh of a virgin, that He might thereby signify that His members would be born after the Spirit, of the Church a virgin: therefore Mary alone both in Spirit and in flesh is a mother and a virgin: both the mother of Christ, and a virgin of Christ; but the Church, in the Saints who shall possess the kingdom of God, in the Spirit indeed is altogether the mother of Christ, altogether a virgin of Christ: but in the flesh not altogether, but in certain a virgin of Christ, in certain a mother, but not of Christ. Forsooth both faithful women who are married, and virgins dedicated to God, by holy manners, and charity out of a pure heart,[2] and good conscience, and faith unfeigned, because they do the will of the Father, are after a spiritual sense mothers of Christ. But they who in married life give birth to (children) after the flesh, give birth not to Christ, but to Adam, and therefore run, that their offspring having been dyed[3] in His Sacraments, may become members of Christ, forasmuch as they know what they have given birth to.

7. I have said this, lest haply married fruitfulness dare to vie with virgin chastity, and to set forth Mary herself, and to say unto the virgins of God, She had in her flesh two things worthy of honor, virginity and fruitfulness; inasmuch as she both continued a virgin, and bore: this happiness, since we could not both have the whole, we have divided, that ye be virgins, we be mothers: for what is wanting to you in children, let your virginity, that hath been preserved, be a consolation: for us, let the gain of children make up for our lost virginity. This speech of faithful women married, unto holy virgins, would any how be to be endured, if they gave birth to Christians in the flesh; that in this alone, save virginity, the fruitfulness of Mary in the flesh should be more excellent, that she gave birth to the Head Himself of these members, but they to the members of That Head: but now, although by this speech there vie such as on this one account wed and have intercourse with husbands, that they may have sons, and have no other thought of their sons, than to gain them for Christ, and do this so soon as they

can: yet are not Christians born of their flesh, but made so afterwards: the Church giving them birth, through this, that in a spiritual manner she is the mother of the members of Christ, of Whom also after a spiritual manner she is the virgin. And unto this holy birth mothers also who have not borne in the flesh Christians, are workers together, that they may become what they know that they could not give birth to in the flesh: yet are they workers together through this, wherein themselves also are virgins and mothers[4] of Christ, that is to say, in "faith which worketh through love."[5]

8. Therefore no fruitfulness of the flesh can be compared to holy virginity even of the flesh. For neither is itself also honored because it is virginity, but because it hath been dedicated to God, and, although it be kept in the flesh, yet is it kept by religion and devotion of the Spirit. And by this means even virginity of body is spiritual, which continence of piety vows and keeps. For, even as no one makes an immodest use of the body, unless the sin have been before conceived in the spirit, so no one keeps modesty in the body, unless chastity have been before implanted in the spirit. But, further, if modesty of married life, although it be guarded in the flesh, is yet attributed to the soul, not to the flesh, under the rule and guidance of which, the flesh itself hath no intercourse with any beside its own proper estate of marriage; how much more, and with how much greater honor, are we to reckon among the goods of the soul that continence, whereby the virgin purity of the flesh is vowed, consecrated, and kept, for the Creator Himself of the soul and flesh.

9. Wherefore neither are we to believe that their fruitfulness of the flesh, who at this time seek in marriage nothing else save children, to make over unto Christ, can be set against the loss of virginity. Forsooth, in former times, unto Christ about to come after the flesh, the race itself of the flesh was needful, in a certain large and prophetic nation: but now, when from out every race of men, and from out all nations, members of Christ may be gathered unto the People of God, and City of the kingdom of heaven, whoso can receive sacred virginity, let him receive it; and let her only, who contains not, be married.[6] For what, if any rich woman were to expend much money on this good work, and to buy, from out different nations,

---

[4] It has been proposed to omit "que," making the sense,"wherein the virgins themselves also are mothers of Christ," but the sense is good as it stands.

[1] Matt. ix. 15. [See R. V.] [2] 1 Tim. i. 5. [3] *Imbuti.* [5] Gal. v. 6. [6] Matt. xix. 12; 1 Cor. vii. 9.

slaves to make Christians, will she not provide for the giving birth to members of Christ in a manner more rich, and more numerous, than by any, how great soever, fruitfulness of the womb? And yet she will not therefore dare to compare her money to the offering[1] of holy virginity. But if for the sake of making such as shall be born Christians, fruitfulness of the flesh shall with just reason be set against the loss of chastity, this matter will be more fruitful, if virginity be lost at a great price of money, whereby many more children may be purchased to be made Christians, than could be born from the womb, however fruitful, of a single person. But, if it be extreme folly to say this, let the faithful women that are married possess their own good, of which we have treated, so far as seemed fit, in another volume; and let them more highly honor, even as they are most rightly used to do, in the sacred virgins, their better good, of which we are treating in our present discourse.

10. For not even herein ought such as are married to compare themselves with the deserts of the continent, in that of them virgins are born: for this is not a good of marriage, but of nature: which was so ordered of God, as that of every sexual intercourse whatever of the two sexes of human kind, whether in due order and honest, or base and unlawful, there is born no female save a virgin, yet is none born a sacred virgin: so it is brought to pass that a virgin is born even of fornication, but a sacred virgin not even of marriage.

11. Nor do we ourselves set forth this in virgins, that they are virgins; but that they are virgins dedicated unto God by pious continence. For it is not at a venture that I may say, a married woman seems to me happier than a virgin about to be married: for the one hath what the other as yet desires, especially if she be not yet even the betrothed of any one. The one studies to please one, unto whom she hath been given; the other many, in doubt unto whom she is to be given: by this one thing she guards modesty of thought from the crowd, that she is seeking, not an adulterer, but a husband, in the crowd. Therefore that virgin is with good reason set before a married woman, who neither sets herself forth for the multitude to love, whereas she seeks from out the multitude the love of one; nor, having now found him, orders herself[2] for one, taking thought of the things of the world, "how to please her husband;"[3] but hath so loved "Him of fair beauty above the sons of men,"[4] as that, because she could not, even as Mary, conceive Him in her flesh, she hath kept her flesh also virgin for Him conceived in her heart. This kind of virgins no fruitfulness of the body hath given birth to: this is no progeny of flesh and blood. If of these the mother be sought for, it is the Church. None bears sacred virgins save a sacred virgin, she who hath been espoused to be presented chaste unto one Husband, Christ.[5] Of her, not altogether in body, but altogether in spirit virgin, are born holy virgins both in body and in spirit.

12. Let marriages possess their own good, not that they beget sons, but that honestly, that lawfully, that modestly, that in a spirit of fellowship they beget them, and educate them, after they have been begotten, with coöperation, with wholesome teaching, and earnest purpose: in that they keep the faith of the couch one with another; in that they violate not the sacrament of wedlock. All these, however, are offices of human duty: but virginal chastity and freedom through pious continence from all sexual intercourse is the portion of Angels, and a practice,[6] in corruptible flesh, of perpetual incorruption. To this let all fruitfulness of the flesh yield, all chastity of married life; the one is not in (man's) power, the other is not in eternity; free choice hath not fruitfulness of the flesh, heaven hath not chastity of married life. Assuredly they will have something great beyond others in that common immortality, who have something already not of the flesh in the flesh.

13. Whence they are marvellously void of wisdom, who think that the good of this continence is not necessary for the sake of the kingdom of heaven, but for the sake of the present world: in that, forsooth, married persons are strained different ways by earthly cares more and more straitened, from which trouble virgins and continent persons are free: as though on this account only it were better not to be married, that the straits of this present time may be escaped, not that it is of any profit unto a future life. And, that they may not seem to have put forth this vain opinion from out the vanity of their own heart, they take the Apostle to witness, where he saith, "But concerning virgins I have not command of the Lord, but I give counsel, as having obtained mercy from God to be faithful. Therefore I think that this is good on account of the present necessity, because it is good for a man so to be."[7] Lo, say

---

1 *Muneri.*   2 *Componit.*   3 1 Cor. vii. 34.   4 Ps. xlv. 2.   5 2 Cor. xi. 2.

6 *Meditatio.*   7 1 Cor. vii. 25, 26.

they, where the Apostle shows "that this is good on account of the present necessity," not on account of the future eternity. As though the Apostle would have regard for the present necessity, otherwise than as providing and consulting for the future; whereas all his dealing[1] calls not save unto life eternal.

14. It is, therefore, the present necessity that we are to avoid, but yet such as is a hindrance to somewhat of the good things to come; by which necessity the married life is forced to have thought of the things of the world, how to please, the husband the wife, or the wife the husband. Not that these separate from the kingdom of God, as there are sins, which are restrained by command, not by counsel, on this account, because it is matter of condemnation not to obey the Lord when He commands: but that, which, within the kingdom of God itself, might be more largely possessed, if there were larger thoughts how they were to please God, will assuredly be less, when as this very thing is less thought of by necessity of marriage. Therefore he says, "Concerning virgins I have not command of the Lord."[2] For whosoever obeys not a command, is guilty and liable for punishment. Wherefore, because it is not sin to marry a wife or to be married, (but if it were a sin, it would be forbidden by a "Command,") on this account there is no "Command" of the Lord concerning virgins. But since, after we have shunned or had forgiveness of sins, we must approach eternal life, wherein is a certain or more excellent glory, to be assigned not unto all who shall live for ever, but unto certain there; in order to obtain which it is not enough to have been set free from sins, unless there be vowed unto Him, Who setteth us free, something, which it is no matter of fault not to have vowed, but matter of praise to have vowed and performed; he saith, "I give counsel, as having obtained mercy from God that I should be faithful." For neither ought I to grudge faithful counsel, who not by my own merits, but by the mercy of God, am faithful. "I think therefore that this is good, by reason of the present necessity."[3] This, saith he, on which I have not command of the Lord, but give counsel, that is concerning virgins, I think to be good by reason of the present necessity. For I know what the necessity of the present time, unto which marriages serve, compels, that the things of God be less thought of than is enough for the obtaining that glory, which shall not be of

all, although they abide in eternal life and salvation: "For star differeth from star in brightness; so also the Resurrection of the dead.[4] It is," therefore, "good for a man so to be."

15. After that the same Apostle adds, and says, "Thou art bound to a wife, seek not loosening: thou art loosed from a wife, seek not a wife."[5] Of these two, that, which he set first, pertains unto command, against which it is not lawful to do. For it is not lawful to put away a wife, save because of fornication,[6] as the Lord Himself saith in the Gospel. But that, which he added, "Thou art loosed from a wife, seek not a wife," is a sentence of counsel, not of command; therefore it is lawful to do, but it is better not to do. Lastly, he added straightway, "Both if thou shalt have taken a wife, thou hast not sinned; and, if a virgin shall have been married, she sinneth not."[7] But, after saying of his, "Thou art bound to a wife, seek not loosening," he added not, did he, "And if thou shalt have loosed, thou hast not sinned?" For he had already said above, "But to these, who are in marriage, I command, not I, but the Lord, that the wife depart not from her husband: but, if she shall have departed, that she remain unmarried, or be reconciled unto her own husband;" for it may come to pass that she depart, not through any fault of her own, but of her husband. Then he saith, "And let not the man put away his wife," which, nevertheless, he set down of command of the Lord: nor did he then add, And, if he shall have put her away, he sinneth not. For this is a command, not to obey which is sin: not a counsel, which if you shall be unwilling to use, you will obtain less good, not do any ill. On this account, after he had said, "Thou art loosed from a wife, seek not a wife;" because he was not giving command, in order that there be not evil done, but was giving counsel, in order that there be done what is better: straightway he added, "Both, if thou shalt have taken a wife, thou hast not sinned; and, if a virgin shall have been married, she sinneth not."

16. Yet he added, "But such shall have tribulation of the flesh, but I spare you:"[8] in this manner exhorting unto virginity, and continual continence, so as some little to alarm also from marriage, with all modesty, not as from a matter evil and unlawful, but as from one burdensome and troublesome. For it is one thing to incur dishonor of the flesh, and another to have tribulation of the flesh: the

---

[1] *Dispensatio.*   [2] 1 Cor. vii. 25   [3] 1 Cor. vii. 26.

[4] 1 Cor. xv. 41, 42.   [5] 1 Cor. vii. 27.   [6] Matt. xix. 9.
[7] 1 Cor. vii. 10, 11.   [8] 1 Cor. vii 28.

one is matter of crime to do, the other of labor to suffer, which for the most part men refuse not even for the most honorable duties. But for the having of marriage, now at this time, wherein there is no service done unto Christ about to come through descent of flesh by the begetting of the family itself, to take upon one to bear that tribulation of the flesh, which the Apostle foretells to such as shall be married, would be extremely foolish, did not incontinent persons fear, lest, through the temptation of Satan, they should fall into damnable sins. But whereas he says that he spares them, who he saith will have tribulation of the flesh, there suggests itself to me in the mean while no sounder interpretation, than that he was unwilling to open, and unfold in words, this self-same tribulation of the flesh, which he fore-announced to those who choose marriage, in suspicions of jealousy of married life, in the begetting and nurture of children, in fears and sorrows of childlessness. For how very few, after they have bound themselves with the bonds of marriage, are not drawn and driven to and fro by these feelings? And this we ought not to exaggerate, lest we spare not the very persons, who the Apostle thought were to be spared.

17. Only by this, which I have briefly set down, the reader ought to be set on his guard against those, who, in this that is written, "but such shall have tribulation of the flesh, but I spare you," falsely charge marriage, as indirectly condemned by this sentence; as though he were unwilling to utter the condemnation itself, when he saith, "But I spare you;" so that, forsooth, when he spares them, he spared not his own soul, as saying falsely, "And, if thou shalt have taken a wife, thou hast not sinned; and if a virgin shall have been married, she sinneth not." And this, whoso believe or would have believed concerning holy Scripture, they, as it were, prepare for themselves a way for liberty of lying, or for defense of their own perverse opinion, in whatever case they hold other sentiments than what sound doctrine demands. For if there shall be alleged any plain statement from the divine books, whereby to refute their errors, this they have at hand as a shield, whereby defending themselves as it were against the truth, they lay themselves bare to be wounded by the devil: to say that the author of the book did not speak the truth in this instance, at one time in order to spare the weak, at another in order to alarm despisers: just as a case shall come to hand, wherein to defend their own perverse opinion: and thus, whilst they had rather defend than amend their own opinions, they essay to break the authority of holy Scripture, whereby alone all proud and hard necks are broken.

18. Wherefore I admonish both men and women who follow after perpetual continence and holy virginity, that they so set their own good before marriage, as that they judge not marriage an evil: and that they understand that it was in no way of deceit, but of plain truth that it was said by the Apostle, "Whoso gives in marriage does well; and whoso gives not in marriage, does better; and, if thou shalt have taken a wife, thou hast not sinned; and, if a virgin shall have been married, she sinneth not;"[1] and a little after, "But she will be more blessed, if she shall have continued so, according to my judgment." And, that the judgment should not be thought human, he adds, "But I think I also have the Spirit of God." This is the doctrine of the Lord, this of the Apostles, this true, this sound, so to choose greater gifts, as that the lesser be not condemned. The truth of God, in the Scripture of God, is better than virginity of man in the mind or flesh of any. Let what is chaste be so loved, as that what is true be not denied. For what evil thought may they not have even concerning their own flesh, who believe that the tongue of the Apostle, in that very place, wherein he was commending virginity of body, was not virgin from corruption of lying. In the first place, therefore, and chiefly, let such as choose the good of virginity, hold most firmly that the holy Scriptures have in nothing spoken lies; and, thus, that that also is true which is said, "And if thou shalt have taken a wife, thou hast not sinned; and, if a virgin shall have been married, she sinneth not." And let them not think that the so great good of virgin chastity is made less, if marriage shall not be an evil. Yea rather, let her hence feel confident, rather, that there is prepared for her a palm of greater glory, who feared not to be condemned, in case she were married, but desired to receive a more honorable crown, in that she was not married. Whoso therefore shall be willing to abide without marriage, let them not flee from marriage as a pitfall of sin; but let them surmount it as a hill of the lesser good, in order that they may rest in the mountain of the greater, continence. It is on this condition, forsooth, that this hill is dwelt on; that one leave it not when he will. For, "a woman is bound, so long as her husband liveth."[2] However unto widowed continence one ascends from it as from a step: but for the sake of virgin continence, one must either turn aside from it by not consenting to suitors, or overleap it by anticipating suitors.

---

[1] Cor. vii. 38, 28. 40. [2] 1 Cor. vii. 39.

19. But lest any should think that of two works, the good and the better, the rewards will be equal, on this account it was necessary to treat against those, who have so interpreted that saying of the Apostle, "But I think that this is good by reason of the present necessity,"[1] as to say that virginity is of use not in order to the kingdom of heaven, but in order to this present time: as though in that eternal life, they, who had chosen this better part, would have nothing more than the rest of men. And in this discussion when we came to that saying of the same Apostle, "But such shall have tribulation of the flesh, but I spare you;"[2] we fell in with other disputants, who so far from making marriage equal to perpetual virginity, altogether condemned it. For whereas both are errors, either to equal marriage to holy virginity, or to condemn it: by fleeing from one another to excess, these two errors come into open collision, in that they have been unwilling to hold the mean of truth: whereby, both by sure reason and authority of holy Scriptures, we both discover that marriage is not a sin, and yet equal it not to the good either of virginal or even of widowed chastity. Some forsooth by aiming at virginity have thought marriage hateful even as adultery: but others, by defending marriage, would have the excellence of perpetual continence to deserve nothing more than married chastity; as though either the good of Susanna be the lowering of Mary: or the greater good of Mary ought to be the condemnation of Susanna.

20. Far be it, therefore, that the Apostle so said, unto such as are married or are about to marry, "But I spare you," as if he were unwilling to say what punishment is due to the married in another life. Far be it that she, whom Daniel set free from temporal judgment, be cast by Paul into hell! Far be it that her husband's bed be unto her punishment before the judgment seat of Christ, keeping faith to which she chose, under false charge of adultery, to meet either danger, or death! To what effect that speech, "It is better for me to fall into your hands, than to sin in the sight of God:"[3] if God had been about, not to set her free because she kept married chastity, but to condemn her because she had married? And now so often as married chastity is by truth of holy Scripture justified against such as bring calumnies and charges against marriage, so often is Susanna by the Holy Spirit defended against false witnesses, so often is she set free from a false charge, and with much greater ado. For then

against one married woman, now against all; then of hidden and untrue adultery, now of true and open marriage, an accusation is laid. Then one woman, upon what the unjust elders said, now all husbands and wives, upon what the Apostle would not say, are accused. It was, forsooth, your condemnation, say they, that he was silent on, when he said, "But I spare you." Who (saith) this? Surely he, who had said above; "And, if thou shalt have taken a wife, thou hast not sinned; and, if a virgin shall have been married, she sinneth not."[4] Why, therefore, wherein he hath been silent through modesty, suspect ye a charge against marriage; and wherein he hath spoken openly, recognize ye not a defense of marriage? What, doth he condemn by his silence them whom he acquitted by his words? Is it not now a milder charge, to charge Susanna, not with marriage, but with adultery itself, than to charge the doctrine of the Apostle with falsehood? What in so great peril could we do, were it not as sure and plain that chaste marriage ought not to be condemned, as it is sure and plain that holy Scripture cannot lie?

21. Here some one will say, What has this to do with holy virginity, or perpetual continence, the setting forth of which was undertaken in this discourse? To whom I make answer in the first place, what I mentioned above, that the glory of that greater good is greater from the fact that, in order to obtain it, the good of married life is surmounted, not the sin of marriage shunned. Otherwise it would be enough for perpetual continence, not to be specially praised, but only not to be blamed: if it were maintained on this account, because it was a crime to wed. In the next place, because it is not by human judgment, but by authority of Divine Scripture, that men must be exhorted unto so excellent a gift, we must plead not in a common-place manner, or merely by the way, that divine Scripture itself seem not to any one in any matter to have lied. For they discourage rather than exhort holy virgins, who compel them to continue so by passing sentence on marriage. For whence can they feel sure that that is true, which is written, "And he, who gives her not in marriage, does better:"[5] if they think that false, which yet is written close above, "Both he, who gives his virgin, does well?" But, if they shall without all doubt have believed Scripture speaking of the good of marriage, confirmed by the same most true authority of the divine oracle, they will hasten beyond unto their own better part with glow-

---

[1] 1 Cor. vii. 26. [2] 1 Cor. vii. 28. Hist. of Sus. 23. [4] 1 Cor. vii. 28. [5] 1 Cor. vii. 38.

ing and confident eagerness. Wherefore we have already spoken enough for the business which we have taken in hand, and, so far as we could, have shown, that neither that saying of the Apostle, "But I think that this is good by reason of the present necessity,"[1] is so to be understood, as though in this life holy virgins are better than faithful women married, but are equal in the kingdom of heaven, and in a future life: nor that other, where he saith of such as wed, "But such shall have tribulation of the flesh, but I spare you;"[2] is to be so understood, as though he chose rather to be silent on, than to speak of, the sin and condemnation of marriage. Forsooth two errors, contrary the one to the other, have, through not understanding them, taken hold of each one of these two sentences. For that concerning the present necessity they interpret in their own favor, who contend to equal such as wed to such as wed not: but this, where it is said, "But I spare you," they who presume to condemn such as wed. But we, according to the faith and sound doctrine of holy Scriptures, both say that marriage is no sin, and yet set its good not only below virginal, but also below widowed continence; and say that the present necessity of married persons is an hindrance to their desert, not indeed unto life eternal, but unto an excellent glory and honor, which is reserved for perpetual continence: and that at this time marriage is not expedient save for such as contain not; and that on the tribulation of the flesh, which cometh from the affection of the flesh, without which marriages of incontinent persons cannot be, the Apostle neither wished to be silent, as forewarning what was true, nor to unfold more fully, as sparing man's weakness.

22. And now by plainest witnesses of divine Scriptures, such as according to the small measure of our memory we shall be able to remember, let it more clearly appear, that, not on account of the present life of this world, but on account of that future life which is promised in the kingdom of heaven, we are to choose perpetual continence. But who but must observe this in that which the same Apostle says a little after, "Whoso is without a wife has thought of the things of the Lord, how to please the Lord: but whoso is joined in marriage has thought of the things of the world, how to please his wife. And a woman unmarried and a virgin is divided;[3] she that is unmarried is careful about the things of the Lord, to be holy both in body and spirit: but she that is married is

careful about the things of the world, how to please her husband."[4] Certainly he saith not, hath thought of the things of a state without care in this world, to pass her time without weightier troubles; nor doth he say that a woman unmarried and a virgin is divided, that is, distinguished, and separated from her who is married, for this end, that the unmarried woman be without care in this life, in order to avoid temporal troubles, which the married woman is not free from: but, "She hath thought," saith he, "of the things of the Lord, how to please the Lord; and is careful about the things of the Lord, to be holy both in body and spirit." Unless to such a degree, perchance, each be foolishly contentious, as to essay to assert, that it is not on account of the kingdom of heaven, but on account of this present world, that we wish to "please the Lord," or that it is on account of this present life, not on account of life eternal, that they are "holy both in body and spirit." To believe this, what else is it, than to be more miserable than all men? For so the Apostle saith, "If in this life only we are hoping in Christ, we are more miserable than all men."[5] What? is he who breaks his bread to the hungry, if he do it only on account of this life, a fool; and shall he be prudent, who chastens his own body even unto continence, whereby he hath no intercourse even in marriage, if it shall profit him nought in the kingdom of heaven?

23. Lastly, let us hear the Lord Himself delivering most plain judgment on this matter. For, upon His speaking after a divine and fearful manner concerning husband and wife not separating, save on account of fornication, His disciples said to Him, "If the case be such with a wife, it is not good to marry."[6] To whom He saith, "Not all receive this saying. For there are eunuchs who were so born: but there are others who were made by men: and there are eunuchs, who made themselves eunuchs for the sake of the kingdom of heaven: whoso can receive, let him receive." What could be said more true, what more clear? Christ saith, the Truth saith, the Power and Wisdom of God saith, that they, who of pious purpose have contained from marrying a wife, make themselves eunuchs for the sake of the kingdom of heaven: and against this, human vanity with impious rashness contends, that they, who do so, shun only the present necessity of the troubles of married life, but in the kingdom of heaven have no more than others.

24. But concerning what eunuchs speaketh

---

[1] 1 Cor. vii 26,   [2] 1 Cor. vii. 28.   [3] cf. de Bon. Conj. 10.   [4] 1 Cor. vii. 32, 33, 34.   [6] Matt. xix. 10, 11, 12.   [5] 1 Cor. xv. 19.

God by the prophet Isaiah, unto whom He saith that He will give in His house and in His wall a place by name, much better than of sons and daughters,[1] save concerning these, who make themselves eunuchs for the sake of the kingdom of heaven? For for these, whose bodily organ is without strength, so that they cannot beget, (such as are the eunuchs of rich men and of kings,) it is surely enough, when they become Christians, and keep the commands of God, yet have this purpose, that, if they could, they would have wives, to be made equal to the rest of the faithful in the house of God, who are married, who bring up in the fear of God a family which they have lawfully and chastely gotten, teaching their sons to set their hope on God; but not to receive a *better* place than of sons and daughters. For it is not of virtue of the soul, but of necessity of the flesh, that they marry not wives. Let who will contend that the Prophet foretold this of those eunuchs who have suffered mutilation of body; that even also helps the cause which we have undertaken. For God hath not preferred these eunuchs to such as have no place in His house, but assuredly to those who keep the desert of married life in begetting sons. For, when He saith, "I will give unto them a place much better;" He shows that one is also given unto the married, but much inferior. Therefore, to allow that in the house of God there will be the eunuchs after the flesh spoken of above, who were not in the People of Israel: because we see that these also themselves, whereas they become not Jews, yet become Christians: and that the Prophet spake not of them, who through purpose of continence seeking not marriage, make themselves eunuchs for the sake of the kingdom of heaven: is any one so madly opposed to the truth as to believe that eunuchs made so in the flesh have a better place than married persons in the house of God, and to contend that persons being of pious purpose continent, chastening the body even unto contempt of marriage, making themselves eunuchs, not in the body, but in the very root of concupiscence, practising an heavenly and angelic life in an earthly mortal state, are on a level with the deserts of the married; and, being a Christian, to gainsay Christ when He praises those who have made themselves eunuchs, not for the sake of this world, but for the sake of the kingdom of heaven, affirming that this is of use for the present life, not for a future? What else remains for these, save to assert that the kingdom of

heaven itself pertains unto this temporal life, wherein we now are? For why should not blind presumption advance even to this madness? And what more full of phrensy than this assertion? For, although at times the Church, even that which is at this time, is called the kingdom of heaven; certainly it is so called for this end, because it is being gathered together for a future and eternal life. Although, therefore, it have the promise of the present, and of a future life, yet in all its good works it looks not to "the things that are seen, but to what are not seen. For what are seen are temporal; but what are not seen, are eternal."[2]

25. Nor indeed hath the Holy Spirit failed to speak what should be of open and unshaken avail against these men, most shamelessly and madly obstinate, and should repel their assault, as of wild beasts, from His sheep-fold, by defences that may not be stormed. For, after He had said concerning eunuchs, "I will give unto them in My house and in My wall a named place, much better than of sons and daughters;"[3] lest any too carnal should think that there was any thing temporal to be hoped for in these words, straightway He added, "An eternal name I will give unto them, nor shall it ever fail:" as though He should say, Why dost thou draw back, impious blindness? Why dost thou draw back? Why dost thou pour the clouds of thy perverseness over the clear (sky) of truth? Why in so great light of Scriptures dost thou seek after darkness from out which to lay snares? Why dost thou promise temporal advantage only to holy persons exercising continence? "An eternal name I will give unto them:" why, where persons keep from all sexual intercourse, and also in the very fact that they abstain from these, have thought of the things of the Lord, how to please the Lord, do you essay to refer them unto earthly advantage? "An eternal name I will give unto them." Why contend you that the kingdom of heaven, for the sake of which holy eunuchs have made themselves eunuchs, is to be understood in this life only? "An eternal name I will give unto them." And if haply in this place you endeavor to take the word itself eternal in the sense of lasting for a long time, I add, I heap up, I tread in, "nor shall it ever fail." What more seek you? What more say you? This eternal name, whatever it be, unto the eunuchs of God, which assuredly signifies a certain peculiar and excellent glory, shall not be in common with many, although set in the same

---

[1] Is. lvi. 4, 5. [See R.V.]

[2] 2 Cor. iv. 18; 1 Tim. iv. 8. [3] Is. lvi. 4, 5. [See R.V.]

kingdom, and in the same house. For on this account also, perhaps, it is called a *name*, that it distinguishes those, to whom it is given, from the rest.

26. What then, say they, is the meaning of that penny, which is given in payment to all alike when the work of the vineyard is ended? whether it be to those who have labored from the first hour, or to those who have labored one hour?[1] What assuredly doth it signify, but something, which all shall have in common, such as is life eternal itself, the kingdom of heaven itself, where shall be all, whom God hath predestinated, called, justified, glorified? " For it behoveth that this corruptible put on incorruption, and this mortal put on immortality."[2] This is that penny, wages for all. Yet "star differeth from star in glory; so also the resurrection of the dead."[3] These are the different merits of the Saints. For, if by that penny the heaven were signified, have not all the stars in common to be in the heaven? And yet, " There is one glory of the sun, another glory of the moon, another of the stars." If that penny were taken for health of body, have not all the members, when we are well, health in common; and, should this health continue even unto death, is it not in all alike and equally? And yet, "God hath set the members, each one of them, in the body, as He would;"[4] that neither the whole be an eye, nor the whole hearing, nor the whole smelling: and, whatever else there is, it hath its own property, although it have health equally with all. Thus because life eternal itself shall be alike to all, an equal penny was assigned to all; but, because in that life eternal itself the lights of merits shall shine with a distinction, there are " many mansions " in the house of the Father:[5] and, by this means, in the penny not unlike, one lives not longer than another; but in the many mansions, one is honored with greater brightness than another.

27. Therefore go on, Saints of God, boys and girls, males and females, unmarried men and women; go on and persevere unto the end. Praise more sweetly the Lord, Whom ye think on more richly: hope more happily in Him, Whom ye serve more instantly: love more ardently Him, whom ye please more attentively. With loins girded, and lamps burning, wait for the Lord, when He cometh from the marriage.[6] Ye shall bring unto the marriage of the Lamb a new song, which ye shall sing on your harps. Not surely such as the whole earth singeth, unto which it is said, " Sing unto the Lord a new song; sing unto the Lord, the whole earth "[7]: but such as no one shall be able to utter but you. For thus there saw you in the Apocalypse a certain one[8] beloved above others by the Lamb, who had been wont to lie on His breast, and who used to drink in, and burst[9] forth, the Word of God above wonders of heaven. He saw you twelve times twelve thousand of holy harpers, of undefiled virginity in body, of inviolate truth in heart; and he wrote of you, that ye follow the Lamb whithersoever He shall go. Where think we that This Lamb goeth, where no one either dares or is able to follow save you? Where think we that He goeth? Into what glades and meadows? Where, I think, the grass are joys; not vain joys of this world, lying madnesses; nor joys such as shall be in the kingdom of God itself, for the rest that are not virgins; but distinct from the portion of joys of all the rest. Joy of the virgins of Christ, of Christ, in Christ, with Christ, after Christ, through Christ, for Christ. The joys peculiar to the virgins of Christ, are not the same as of such as are not virgins, although of Christ. For there are to different persons different joys, but to none such. Go (enter) into these, follow the Lamb, because the Flesh of the Lamb also is assuredly virgin. For this He retained in Himself when grown up, which He took not away from His Mother by His conception and birth. Follow Him, as ye deserve,[10] in virginity of heart and flesh, wheresoever He shall have gone. For what is it to follow, but to imitate? Because " Christ hath suffered for us,"[11] leaving us an example, as saith the Apostle Peter, "that we should follow His steps." Him each one follows in that, wherein he imitates Him: not so far forth as He is the only Son of God, by Whom all things were made; but so far forth as, the Son of Man, He set forth in Himself, what behoved for us to imitate. And many things in Him are set forth for all to imitate: but virginity of the flesh not for all; for they have not what to do in order to be virgins, in whom it hath been already brought to pass that they be not virgins.

28. Therefore let the rest of the faithful, who have lost virginity, follow the Lamb, not whithersoever He shall have gone, but so far as ever they shall have been able. But they are able every where, save when He walks in the grace of virginity. " Blessed are the poor in spirit;"[12] imitate Him, Who, "whereas "He was rich, was made poor for your sakes."[13] "Blessed are the meek;" imitate Him, Who said, " Learn of Me, for I am meek and lowly

---

[1] Matt. xx. 9, 10.   [2] 1 Cor. xv. 53.   [3] 1 Cor. xv. 41, 42.
[4] 1 Cor. xii. 18.   [5] John xiv. 2.   [6] Luke xii. 35, 36.

[7] Ps. xcvi. 1.   [8] Rev. xiv. 1-5.
[9] " *Eructuabat.*" cf. Ps. xlv. 1. Vulg.   [10] *Merito.*
[11] 1 Peter ii. 21.   [12] Matt. v. 3-10.   [13] 2 Cor. viii. 9.

of heart."[1] "Blessed are they that mourn;" imitate Him, Who "wept over" Jerusalem.[2] "Blessed are they, who hunger and thirst after righteousness:" imitate Him, Who said, "My meat is to do the will of Him Who sent Me."[3] "Blessed are the merciful;" imitate Him, Who came to the help of him who was wounded by robbers, and who lay in the way half-dead and despaired of.[4] "Blessed are the pure in heart;" imitate Him, "Who did no sin, neither was guile found in His mouth."[5] "Blessed are the peace-makers;" imitate Him, Who said on behalf of His persecutors, "Father, forgive them, for they know not what they do."[6] "Blessed are they, who suffer persecution for righteousness sake;" imitate Him, Who "suffered for you, leaving you an example, that ye follow His steps."[7] These things, whoso imitate, in these they follow the Lamb. But surely even married persons may go in those steps, although not setting their foot perfectly in the same print,[8] yet walking in the same paths.

29. But, lo, That Lamb goeth by a Virgin road, how shall they go after Him, who have lost what there is no way for them to recover? Do ye, therefore, do ye go after Him, His virgins; do ye thither also go after Him, in that on this one account whithersoever He shall have gone, ye follow Him: for unto any other gift whatsoever of holiness, whereby to follow Him, we can exhort married persons, save this which they have lost beyond power of recovery. Do ye, therefore, follow Him, by holding with perseverance what ye have vowed with ardor. Go when ye can, that the good of virginity perish not from you, unto which ye can do nothing, in order that it may return. The rest of the multitude of the faithful will see you, which cannot unto this follow the Lamb; it will see you, it will not envy you: and by rejoicing together with you, what it hath not in itself, it will have in you. For that new song also, which is your own, it will not be able to utter; but it will not be unable to hear, and to be delighted with your so excellent good: but ye, who shall both utter and hear, in that what ye shall say, this ye shall hear of yourselves, will exult with greater happiness, and reign with greater joy. But they will have no sorrow on account of your greater joy, to whom this shall be wanting. Forsooth That Lamb, Whom ye shall follow whithersoever He shall have gone, will not desert those who cannot follow Him, where you can. Almighty is the Lamb, of Whom we speak. He both will go

before you, and will not depart from them, when God shall be all in all.[9] And they, who shall have less, shall not turn away in dislike from you: for, where there is no envying, difference exists with concord. Take to you,[10] then, have trust, be strong, continue, ye who vow and pay unto the Lord your God vows of perpetual continence, not for the sake of this present world, but for the sake of the kingdom of Heaven.

30. Ye also who have not yet made this vow, who are able to receive it, receive it.[11] Run with perseverance, that ye may obtain.[12] Take ye each his sacrifices, and enter ye into the courts[13] of the Lord, not of necessity, having power over your own will.[14] For not as, "Thou shalt not commit adultery, Thou shalt not kill,"[15] can it so be said, Thou shalt not wed. The former are demanded, the latter are offered. If the latter are done, they are praised: unless the former are done, they are condemned. In the former the Lord commands us what is due; but in the latter, if ye shall have spent any thing more, on His return He will repay you.[16] Think of (whatever that be) within His wall "a place named, much better than of sons and of daughters."[17] Think of "an eternal name" there.[18] Who unfolds of what kind that name shall be? Yet, whatever it shall be, it shall be eternal. By believing and hoping and loving this, ye have been able, not to shun marriage, as forbidden, but to fly past it, as allowed.

31. Whence the greatness of this service,[19] unto the undertaking of which we have according to our strength exhorted, the more excellent and divine it is, the more doth it warn our anxiety, to say something not only concerning most glorious chastity, but also concerning safest humility. When then such as make profession of perpetual chastity, comparing themselves with married persons, shall have discovered that, according to the Scriptures, the others are below both in work and wages, both in vow and reward, let what is written straightway come into their mind, "By how much thou art great, by so much humble thyself in all things: and thou shalt find favor before God."[20] The measure of humility for each hath been given from the measure of his greatness itself: unto which pride is full of danger, which layeth the greater wait against persons the greater they be. On this followeth envying, as a daughter in her train; forsooth pride straight-

[1] Matt. xi. 29.   [2] Luke xix. 41.   [3] John iv. 34.
[4] Luke x. 30-35.   [5] 1 Peter ii. 22.   [6] Luke xxiii. 34.
[7] 1 Peter ii. 21.   [8] *Forma.*

[9] 1 Cor. xv. 28.   [10] "*Præsumite.*"   [11] Matt. xix. 12.
[12] 1 Cor. ix. 24.   [13] Ps. xcvi. 8.   [14] 1 Cor. vii. 37.
[15] Ex. xx. 14, 13.   [16] "*Supererogaveritis.*"
[17] Luke x. 35. See § 48.   [18] Is. lvi. 5.
[19] *Muneris.*   [20] Ecclus. iii. 18.

way giveth birth to her, nor is she ever without such a daughter and companion. By which two evils, that is, pride and envying, is the devil (a devil). Therefore it is against pride, the mother of envying, that the whole Christian discipline chiefly wars. For this teaches humility, whereby both to gain and to keep charity; of which after that it had been said, "Charity envieth not;"[1] as though we were asking the reason, how it comes to pass that it envieth not, he straightway added, "is not puffed up;" as though he should say, on this account it hath not envying, in that neither hath it pride. Therefore the Teacher of humility, Christ, first "emptied Himself, taking the form of a servant, made in the likeness of men, and found in fashion as a man, He humbled Himself, made obedient even unto death, even the death of the Cross."[2] But His teaching itself, how carefully it suggests humility, and how earnest and instant it is in commanding this, who can easily unfold, and bring together all witnesses for proof of this matter? This let him essay to do, or do, whosoever shall wish to write a separate treatise on humility; but of this present work the end proposed is different, and it hath been undertaken on a matter so great, as that it hath chiefly to guard against pride.

32. Wherefore a few witnesses, which the Lord deigns to suggest to my mind, I proceed to mention, from out the teaching of Christ concerning humility, such as perhaps may be enough for my purpose. His discourse, the first which He delivered to His disciples at greater length, began from this. "Blessed are the poor in spirit, for theirs is the Kingdom of Heaven."[3] And these without all controversy we take to be humble. The faith of that Centurion He on this account chiefly praised, and said that He had not found in Israel so great faith, because he believed with so great humility as to say, "I am not worthy that thou shouldest enter under my roof."[4] Whence also Matthew for no other reason said that he "came" unto Jesus, (whereas Luke most plainly signifies that he came not unto Him himself, but sent his friends,) save that by his most faithful humility he himself came unto Him more than they whom he sent. Whence also is that of the Prophet, "The Lord is very high, and hath respect unto things that are lowly: but what are very high He noteth afar off;"[5] assuredly as not coming unto Him. Whence also He saith to that woman of Canaan, "O woman, great is thy faith; be it done unto

thee as thou wilt;"[6] whom above He had called a dog, and had made answer that the bread of the sons was not to be cast to her. And this she taking with humility had said, "Even so, Lord; for the dogs also eat of the crumbs which fall from their masters' table." And thus what by continual crying she obtained not, by humble confession she earned.[7] Hence also those two are set forth praying in the Temple, the one a Pharisee, and the other a Publican, for the sake of those who seem to themselves just and despise the rest of men, and the confession of sins is set before the reckoning up of merits. And assuredly the Pharisee was rendering thanks unto God by reason of those things wherein he was greatly self-satisfied. "I render thanks to Thee," saith he, "that I am not even as the rest of men, unjust, extortioners, adulterers, even as also this publican. I fast twice in the week, I give tithes of all things whatsoever I possess. But the Publican was standing afar off, not daring to lift up his eyes to Heaven, but beating his breast, saying, God be merciful unto me a sinner." But there follows the divine judgment, "Verily I say unto you, the Publican went down from the Temple justified more than that Pharisee."[8] Then the cause is shown, why this is just; "Forasmuch as he who exalteth himself shall be humbled, and whoso humbleth himself shall be exalted." Therefore it may come to pass, that each one both shun real evils, and reflect on real goods in himself, and render thanks for these unto "the Father of lights, from Whom cometh down every best gift, and every perfect gift,"[9] and yet be rejected by reason of the sin of haughtiness, if through pride, even in his thought alone, which is before God, he insult other sinners, and specially when confessing their sins in prayer, unto whom is due not upbraiding with arrogance, but pity without despair. What is it that, when His disciples were questioning among themselves, who of them should be greater, He set a little child before their eyes, saying, "Unless ye shall be as this child, ye shall not enter into the Kingdom of Heaven?"[10] Did He not chiefly commend humility, and set in it the desert of greatness? Or when unto the sons of Zebedee desiring to be at His side in lofty seats He so made answer,[11] as that they should rather think of having to drink the Cup of His Passion, wherein He humbled Himself even unto death, even the death of the Cross,[12] than with proud desire demand to be preferred to the rest; what

1 1 Cor. xiii. 4. [See R. V.]   2 Phil. ii. 7, 8. [See R. V.]
3 Matt. v. 3.   4 Matt. viii. 5-10; Luke vii. 6, 7.
5 Ps. cxxxviii. 6.

6 Matt. xv. 22-28.   7 Promeruit.   8 Luke xviii. 11-14.
9 James i. 17.   10 Matt. xviii. 1-3.   11 Matt. xx. 21, 22.
12 Phil. ii. 8.

did He show, save, that He would be a bestower of exaltation upon them, who should first follow Him as a teacher of humility? And now, in that, when about to go forth unto His Passion, He washed the feet of His disciples, and most openly taught them to do for their fellow-disciples and fellow-servants this, which He their Lord and Master had done for them; how greatly did He commend humility?[1] And in order to commend this He chose also that time, wherein they were looking on Him, as immediately about to die, with great longing ; assuredly about to retain in their memory this especially, which their Master, Whom they were to imitate, had pointed out to them as the last thing. But He did this at that time, which surely He could have done on other days also before, wherein He had been conversant with them; at which time if it were done, this same would indeed be delivered, but certainly would not be so received.

33. Whereas, then, all Christians have to guard humility, forasmuch as it is from Christ that they are called Christians, Whose Gospel no one considers with care, but that he discovers Him to be a Teacher of humility; specially is it becoming that they be followers and keepers of this virtue, who excel the rest of men in any great good, in order that they may have a great care of that, which I set down in the beginning, " By how much thou art great, by so much humble thyself in all things, and thou shalt find grace before God."[2] Wherefore, because perpetual Continence and specially virginity, is a great good in the Saints of God, they must with all watchfulness beware, that it be not corrupted with pride.

34. Paul the Apostle censures evil unmarried women, curious and prating, and says that this fault comes of idleness. " But at the same time," saith he, " being idle they learn to go about to houses: but not only idle, but curious also and prating, speaking what they ought not."[3] Of these he had said above, " But younger widows avoid; for when they have past their time in delights, they wish to wed in Christ; having condemnation, in that they have made void their first faith:" that is, have not continued in that, which they had vowed at the first. And yet he saith not, they marry, but "they wish to marry." For many of them are recalled from marrying, not by love of a noble purpose, but by fear of open shame, which also itself comes of pride, whereby persons fear to displease men more than God. These, there-

fore, who wish to marry, and do not marry on this account, because they cannot with impunity, who would do better to marry than to be burned, that is, than to be laid waste in their very conscience by the hidden flame of lust, who repent of their profession, and who feel their confession irksome; unless they correct and set right their heart, and by the fear of God again overcome their lust, must be accounted among the dead; whether they pass their time in delights, whence the Apostle says, " But she who passes her time in delights, living, is dead;"[4] or whether in labors and fastings, which are useless where there is no correction of the heart, and serve rather for display than amendment. I do not, for my part, impose on such a great regard for humility, in whom pride itself is confounded, and bloodstained by wound of conscience. Nor on such as are drunken, or covetous, or who are lying in any other kind whatever of damnable disease, at the same time that they have profession of bodily continence, and through perverse manners are at variance with their own name, do I impose this great anxiety about pious humility: unless haply in these evils they shall dare even to make a display of themselves, unto whom it is not enough, that the punishments of these are deferred. Nor am I treating of these, in whom there is a certain aim of pleasing, either by more elegant dress than the necessity of so great profession demands, or by remarkable manner of binding the head, whether by bosses of hair swelling forth, or by coverings so yielding, that the fine net-work below appears: unto these we must give precepts, not as yet concerning humility, but concerning chastity itself, or virgin modesty. Give me one who makes profession of perpetual continence, and who is free from these, and all such faults and spots of conduct; for this one I fear pride, for this so great good I am in alarm from the swelling of arrogance. The more there is in any one on account of which to be self-pleased, the more I fear, lest, by pleasing self, he please not Him, Who " resisteth the proud, but unto the humble giveth grace."[5]

35. Certainly we are to contemplate in Christ Himself, the chief instruction and pattern of virginal purity. What further precept then concerning humility shall I give to the continent, than what He saith to all, " Learn of Me, in that I am meek and lowly of heart?"[6] when He had made mention above of His greatness, and, wishing to show this very thing, how great He was, and how

---

[1] John xiii. 1-17.　　[2] Ecclus. iii. 18.
[3] 1 Tim. v. 11, 12, 13.　[See R. V.]　　[4] 1 Tim. v. 6.　　[5] James iv. 6.　　[6] Matt. xi. 29.

little He had been made for our sakes, saith, "I confess to Thee, O Father, Lord of heaven and earth, in that Thou hast hidden these things from the wise and prudent, and hast revealed them unto little children. Even so, O Father, in that so it hath been pleasing before Thee. All things have been delivered unto Me of My Father: and no one knoweth the Son, save the Father; and no one knoweth the Father, save the Son, and he to whom the Son shall have willed to reveal Him. Come unto Me, all ye who labor and are burdened, and I will refresh you. Take My yoke upon you, and learn of Me, in that I am meek and lowly of heart."[1] He, He, unto Whom the Father hath delivered all things, and Whom no one knoweth but the Father, and Who alone, (and he, unto whom He shall have willed to reveal Him), knoweth the Father, saith not, "Learn of Me" to make the world, or to raise the dead, but, "in that I am meek and lowly of heart." O saving teaching? O Teacher and Lord of mortals, unto whom death was pledged and passed on in the cup of pride, He would not teach what Himself was not, He would not bid what Himself did not. I see Thee, O good Jesu, with the eyes of faith, which Thou hast opened for me, as in an assembly of the human race, crying out and saying, "Come unto Me, and learn of Me." What, I beseech Thee, through Whom all things were made, O Son of God, and the Same Who was made among all things, O Son of Man: to learn what of Thee, come we to Thee? "For that I am meek," saith He, "and lowly of heart." Is it to this that all the treasures of wisdom and knowledge hidden in Thee[2] are brought, that we learn this of Thee as a great thing, that Thou art "meek and lowly of heart?" Is it so great a thing to be little, that it could not at all be learned unless it were brought to pass by Thee, Who art so great? So indeed it is. For by no other way is there found out rest for the soul, save when the unquiet swelling hath been dispersed, whereby it was great unto itself, when it was not sound unto Thee.

36. Let them hear Thee, and let them come to Thee, and let them learn of Thee to be meek and lowly, who seek Thy Mercy and Truth, by living unto Thee, unto Thee, not unto themselves. Let him hear this, laboring and laden, who is weighed down by his burthen, so as not to dare to lift up his eyes to heaven, that sinner beating his breast, and drawing near from afar.[3] Let him hear, the centurion, not worthy that Thou shouldest enter under his roof.[4] Let him hear, Zaccheus, chief of publicans, restoring fourfold the gains of damnable sins.[5] Let her hear, the woman in the city a sinner, by so much the more full of tears at Thy feet, the more alien she had been from Thy steps.[6] Let them hear, the harlots and publicans, who enter into the kingdom of heaven before the Scribes and Pharisees.[7] Let them hear, every kind of such ones, feastings with whom were cast in Thy teeth as a charge, forsooth, as though by whole persons who sought not a physician, whereas Thou camest not to call the righteous, but sinners to repentance.[8] All these, when they are converted unto Thee, easily grow meek, and are humbled before Thee, mindful of their own most unrighteous life, and of Thy most indulgent mercy, in that, "where sin hath abounded, grace hath abounded more."[9]

37. But regard the troops of virgins, holy boys and girls: this kind hath been trained up in Thy Church: there for Thee it hath been budding from its mother's breasts; for Thy Name it hath loosed its tongue to speak, Thy Name, as through the milk of its infancy, it hath had poured in and hath sucked, no one of this number can say, "I, who before was a blasphemer, and persecutor, and injurious, but I obtained mercy, in that I did it being ignorant, in unbelief."[10] Yea more, that, which Thou commandedst not, but only didst set forth, for such as would, to seize, saying, "Whoso can receive, let him receive;" they have seized, they have vowed, and, for the sake of the kingdom of heaven, not for that Thou threatenedst, but for that Thou exhortedst, they have made themselves eunuchs.[11] To these cry out, let these hear Thee, in that Thou art "meek and lowly of heart." Let these, by how much they are great, by so much humble themselves in all things, that they may find grace before Thee. They are just: but they are not, are they, such as Thou, justifying the ungodly? They are chaste: but them in sins their mothers nurtured in their wombs.[12] They are holy, but Thou art also Holy of Holies. They are virgins, but they are not also born of virgins. They are wholly chaste both in spirit and in flesh: but they are not the Word made flesh.[13] And yet let them learn, not from those unto whom Thou forgivest sins, but from Thee Thyself, The Lamb of God Who takest away the sins of the world,[14] in that Thou art "meek and lowly of heart."

---

[1] Matt. xi. 25-29.   [2] Col. ii. 3.   [3] Luke xviii. 13

[4] Matt. viii. 8.   [5] Luke xix. 2-8.   [6] Luke vii. 37, 38.
[7] Matt. xxi. 31.   [8] Matt. ix. 11-13. [See R.V.]
[9] Rom. v. 20.   [10] 1 Tim. i. 13.   [11] Matt. xix. 12.
[12] Ps. li. 5.   [13] John i. 14.   [14] John i. 29.

38. I send thee not, soul that art religiously chaste, that hast not given the reins to fleshly appetite even so far as to allowed marriage, that hast not indulged thy body about to depart even to the begetting one to succeed thee, that hast sustained aloft thy earthly members, afloat to acccustom them to heaven; I send thee not, in order that thou mayest learn humility, unto publicans and sinners, who yet enter into the kingdom of heaven before the proud: I send thee not to these: for they, who have been set free from the gulf of uncleanness, are unworthy that undefiled virginity be sent to them to take pattern from. I send thee unto the King of Heaven, unto Him, by Whom men were created, and Who was created among men for the sake of men; unto Him, Who is fair of beauty above the sons of men,[1] and despised by the sons of men on behalf of the sons of men: unto Him, Who, ruling the immortal angels, disdained not to do service unto mortals. Him, at any rate, not unrighteousness, but charity, made humble; "Charity, which rivalleth not, is not puffed up, seeketh not her own;"[2] forasmuch as "Christ also pleased not Himself, but, as it is written of Him, The reproaches of such as reproached Thee have fallen upon Me.[3] Go then, come unto Him, and learn, in that He is "meek and lowly of heart." Thou shalt not go unto him, who dared not by reason of the burden of unrighteousness to lift up his eyes to heaven, but unto Him, Who by the weight of charity came down from heaven.[4] Thou shalt not go unto her, who watered with tears the feet of her Lord, seeking forgiveness of heavy sins; but thou shalt go unto Him, Who, granting forgiveness of all sins, washed the feet of His own disciples.[5] I know the dignity of thy virginity; I propose not to thee to imitate the Publican humbly accusing his own faults; but I fear for the Pharisee proudly boasting of his own merits.[6] I say not, Be thou such as she, of whom it was said, "There are forgiven unto her many sins, in that she hath loved much;"[7] but I fear lest, as thinking that thou hast little forgiven to thee, thou love little.

39. I fear, I say, greatly for thee, lest, when thou boastest that thou wilt follow the Lamb wheresoever He shall have gone, thou be unable by reason of swelling pride to follow Him through strait ways. It is good for thee, O virgin soul, that thus, as thou art a virgin, thus altogether keeping in thy heart that thou hast been born again, keeping in thy flesh that thou hast been born, thou yet conceive of the fear of the Lord, and give birth to the spirit of salvation.[8] "Fear," indeed, "there is not in charity, but perfect charity," as it is written, "casteth out fear:"[9] but fear of men, not of God: fear of temporal evils, not of the Divine Judgment at the last. "Be not thou high-minded, but fear."[10] Love thou the goodness of God; fear thou His severity: neither suffers thee to be proud. For by loving you fear, lest you grievously offend One Who is loved and loves. For what more grievous offense, than that by pride thou displease Him, Who for thy sake hath been displeasing to the proud? And where ought there to be more that "chaste fear abiding for ever and ever,"[11] than in thee, who hast no thought of the things of this world, how to please a wedded partner; but of the things of the Lord, how to please the Lord?[12] That other fear is not in charity, but this chaste fear quitteth not charity. If you love not, fear lest you perish; if you love, fear lest you displease. That fear charity casteth out, with this it runneth within. The Apostle Paul also says, "For we have not received the spirit of bondage again to fear; but we have received the spirit of adoption of sons, wherein we cry, Abba, Father."[13] I believe that he speaks of that fear, which had been given in the Old Testament, lest the temporal goods should be lost, which God had promised unto those not yet sons under grace, but as yet slaves under the law. There is also the fear of eternal fire, to serve God in order to avoid which is assuredly not yet of perfect charity. For the desire of the reward is one thing, the fear of punishment another. They are different sayings, "Whither shall I go away from Thy Spirit, and from Thy face whither shall I flee?"[14] and, "One thing I have sought of the Lord, this I will seek after; that I may dwell in the house of the Lord through all the days of my life, that I may consider the delight of the Lord, that I be protected in His temple:"[15] and, "Turn not away Thy face from me:"[16] and, "My soul longeth and fainteth unto the courts of the Lord.[17] Those sayings let him have had, who dared not to lift up his eyes to heaven; and she who was watering with tears His feet, in order to obtain pardon for her grievous sins; but these do thou have, who art careful about the things of the Lord, to be holy both in body and spirit. With those sayings there companies fear which hath torment, which

---

[1] Ps. xlv. 2.   [2] 1 Cor. xiii. 4, 5.   [3] Rom. xv. 3.
[4] John vi. 38.   [5] John xiii. 5.   [6] Luke xviii. 10-14.
[7] Luke vii. 38, 47.

[8] Is. xxvi. 18. see LXX.   [9] 1 John, iv. 18. [See R.V.]
[10] Rom. xi. 20.   [11] Ps. xix. 9.   [12] 1 Cor. vii. 32.
[13] Rom. viii. 15.   [14] Ps. cxxxix. 7.   [15] Ps. xxvii. 4.
[16] Ps. xxvii. 9.   [17] Ps. lxxxiv. 2.

perfect charity casteth forth; but with these sayings there companies chaste fear of the Lord, that abideth for ever and ever. And to both kinds it must be said, "Be not thou high-minded, but fear;"[1] that man neither of defense of his sins, nor of presumption of righteousness set himself up. For Paul also himself, who saith, "For ye have not received the spirit of bondage again to fear;"[2] yet, fear being a companion of charity, saith, "With fear and much trembling was I towards you:"[3] and that saying, which I have mentioned, that the engrafted wild olive tree be not proud against the broken branches of the olive tree, himself made use of, saying, "Be not thou high-minded, but fear;" himself admonishing all the members of Christ in general, saith, "With fear and trembling work out your own salvation; for it is God Who worketh in you both to will and to do, according to His good pleasure;"[4] that it seem not to pertain unto the Old Testament what is written, "Serve the Lord in fear, and rejoice unto Him with trembling."[5]

40. And what members of the holy body, which is the Church, ought more to take care, that upon them the holy Spirit may rest, than such as profess virginal holiness? But how doth He rest, where He findeth not His own place? what else than an humbled heart, to fill, not to leap back from; to raise up, not to weigh down? whereas it hath been most plainly said, "On whom shall rest My Spirit? On him that is humble and quiet, and trembles at My words."[6] Already thou livest righteously, already thou livest piously, thou livest chastely, holily, with virginal purity; as yet, however, thou livest here, and art thou not humbled at hearing, "What, is not human life upon earth a trial?[7] Doth it not drive thee back from over-confident arrogance, "Woe unto the world because of offenses?"[8] Dost thou not tremble, lest thou be accounted among the many, whose "love waxeth cold, because that iniquity abounds?"[9] Dost thou not smite thy breast, when thou hearest, "Wherefore, whoso thinketh that he standeth, let him see to it lest he fall?"[10] Amid these divine warnings and human dangers, do we yet find it so hard to persuade holy virgins to humility?

41. Or are we indeed to believe that it is for any other reason, that God suffers to be mixed up with the number of your profession, many, both men and women, about to fall, than that by the fall of these your fear may be increased, whereby to repress pride; which God so hates, as that against this one thing The Highest humbled Himself? Unless haply, in truth, thou shalt therefore fear less, and be more puffed up, so as to love little Him, Who hath loved thee so much, as to give up Himself for thee,[11] because He hath forgiven thee little, living, forsooth from childhood, religiously, piously, with pious chastity, with inviolate virginity. As though in truth you ought not to love with much greater glow of affection Him, Who, whatsoever things He hath forgiven unto sinners upon their being turned to Him, suffered you not to fall into them. Or indeed that Pharisee,[12] who therefore loved little, because he thought that little was forgiven him, was it for any other reason that he was blinded by this error, than because being ignorant of the righteousness of God, and seeking to establish his own, he had not been made subject unto the righteousness of God?[13] But you, an elect race, and among the elect more elect, virgin choirs that follow the Lamb, even you "by grace have been saved through faith; and this not of yourselves, but it is the gift of God: not of works, lest haply any be elated. For we are His workmanship, created in Jesus Christ in good works, which God hath prepared, that in them we may walk."[14] What therefore, by how much the more ye are adorned by His gifts, shall ye by so much the less love Him? May He Himself turn away so dreadful madness! Wherefore forasmuch as the Truth has spoken the truth, that he, unto whom little is forgiven, loveth little; do ye, in order that ye may love with full glow of affection Him, Whom ye are free to love, being loosened from ties of marriage, account as altogether forgiven unto you, whatever of evil, by His governance, ye have not committed. For "your eyes ever unto the Lord, forasmuch as He shall pluck out of the net your feet,[15] and, "Except the Lord shall have kept the city, in vain hath he watched who keepeth it."[16] And speaking of Continence itself the Apostle says, "But I would that all men were as I myself; but each one hath his own proper gift from God; one in this way, and another in that way."[17] Who therefore bestoweth these gifts? Who distributeth his own proper gifts unto each as He will?[18] Forsooth God, with Whom there is not unrighteousness,[19] and by this means with what equity He makes some in this way, and others in that way, for man to know is either impossible or altogether hard: but that with

1 Rom. xi. 20.　　　2 Rom. viii. 15.　　　3 1 Cor. ii. 3.
4 Phil. ii. 12, 13. [See R. V.]　5 Ps. ii. 11.　　6 Is. lxvi. 2.
7 Job. vii. 1. LXX.　8 Matt. xviii. 7. [See R. V.]
9 Matt. xxiv. 12.　　10 1 Cor. x. 12.

11 Gal. ii. 20.　　　12 Luke vii. 36-47.　　13 Rom. x. 3.
14 Eph. ii. 8-10. [See R. V.]　15 Ps. xxv. 15.　16 Ps. cxxvii. 1.
17 1 Cor. vii. 7.　　18 1 Cor. xii. 11.　　19 Rom. ix. 16.

equity He maketh, it is not lawful to doubt. "What," therefore, "hast thou, which thou hast not received?"[1] And by what perversity dost thou less love Him, of Whom thou hast received more?

42. Wherefore let this be the first thought for the putting on of humility, that God's virgin think not that it is of herself that she is such, and not rather that this best "gift cometh down from above from the Father of Lights, with Whom is no change nor shadow of motion."[2] For thus she will not think that little hath been forgiven her, so as for her to love little, and, being ignorant of the righteousness of God, and wishing to establish her own, not to be made subject to the righteousness of God. In which fault was that Simon, who was surpassed by the woman, unto whom many sins were forgiven, because she loved much. But she will have more cautious and true thoughts, that we are so to account all sins as though forgiven, from which God keeps us that we commit them not. Witnesses are those expressions of pious prayers in holy Scriptures, whereby it is shown, that those very things, which are commanded by God, are not done save by His Gift and help, Who commands. For there is a falsehood in the asking for them, if we could do them without the help of His grace. What is there so generally and chiefly charged, as obedience whereby the Commandments of God are kept? And yet we find this wished for. "Thou," saith he, "hast charged, that Thy commandments be greatly kept." Then it follows, "O that my ways were directed to keep Thy righteousnesses: then shall I not be confounded, whilst I look unto all Thy commandments."[3] That which he had set down above that God had commanded, that he wished might of himself be fulfilled. This is done assuredly, that there be not sin; but, if there hath been sin, the command is that one repent; lest by defense and excuse of sin he perish through pride, who hath done it, whilst he is unwilling that what he hath done perish through repentance. This also is asked of God, so that it may be understood that it is not done, save by His grant from Whom it is asked. "Set," saith he, "O Lord, a watch to my mouth, and a door of continence around my lips: let not my heart turn away unto evil words, to make excuses in sins, with men that work unrighteousness."[4] If, therefore, both obedience, whereby we keep His commandments, and repentance whereby we excuse not our sins, are wished for and asked, it is plain that, when it is done, it is by His

gift that it is possessed, by His help that it is fulfilled, yet more openly is it said by reason of obedience, "By the Lord the steps of a man are directed, and He shall will His way:"[5] and of repentance the Apostle says, "if haply God may grant unto them repentance."[6]

43. Concerning continence also itself hath it not been most openly said, "And when I knew that no one can be continent unless God give it, this also itself was a part of wisdom, to know whose gift it was?"[7] But perhaps continence is the gift of God, but wisdom man bestows upon himself, whereby to understand, that that gift is, not his own, but of God. Yea, "The Lord maketh wise the blind:"[8] and, "The testimony of the Lord is faithful, it giveth wisdom unto little ones:"[9] and, "If any one want wisdom, let him ask of God, Who giveth unto all liberally, and upbraideth not, and it shall be given to him."[10] But it becometh virgins to be wise, that their lamps be not extinguished.[11] How "wise," save "not having high thoughts, but consenting unto the lowly."[12] For Wisdom Itself hath said unto man, "Lo, piety is wisdom!"[13] If therefore thou hast nothing, which thou hast not received, "Be not highminded, but fear."[14] And love not thou little, as though Him by Whom little hath been forgiven to thee; but, rather, love Him much, by Whom much hath been given to thee. For if he loves, unto whom it hath been given not to repay: how much more ought he to love, unto whom it hath been given to possess. For both, whosoever continues chaste from the beginning, is ruled by Him; and whosoever is made chaste instead of unchaste, is corrected by Him; and whosoever is unchaste even unto the end, is abandoned by Him. But this He can do by secret counsel, by unrighteous He cannot: and perhaps it is for this end that it lies hid, that there may be more fear, and less pride.

44. Next let not man, now that he knoweth that by the grace of God he is what he is, fall into another snare of pride, so as by lifting up himself for the very grace of God to despise the rest. By which fault that other Pharisee both gave thanks unto God for the goods which he had, and yet vaunted himself above the Publican confessing his sins. What therefore should a virgin do, what should she think, that she vaunt not herself above those, men or women, who have not this so great gift? For she ought not to feign humility,

---

[1] 1 Cor. iv. 7. [2] James i. 17. [See R. V.] [3] Ps. cxix. 4-6. [4] Ps. cxli. 3, 4.

[5] Ps. xxxvii. 23. [6] 2 Tim. ii. 25. [7] Wisd. viii. 21. [8] Ps. cxlvi. 8. [9] Ps. xix. 7. [10] James i. 5. [11] Matt. xxv. 4. [12] Rom. xii. 16. [13] Job xxviii. 28. LXX. [14] Rom. xi. 20.

but to set it forth: for the feigning of humility is greater pride. Wherefore Scripture wishing to show that humility ought to be true, after having said, "By how much thou art great, by so much humble thyself in all things," added soon after, "And thou shalt find grace before God:"[1] assuredly where one could not humble one's self deceitfully.

45. Wherefore what shall we say? is there any thought which a virgin of God may truly have, by reason of which she dare not to set herself before a faithful woman, not only a widow, but even married? I say not a reprobate virgin; for who knows not that an obedient woman is to be set before a disobedient virgin? But where both are obedient unto the commands of God, shall she so tremble to prefer holy virginity even to chaste marriage, and continence to wedded life, the fruit an hundred-fold to go before the thirty-fold? Nay, let her not doubt to prefer this thing to that thing; yet let not this or that virgin, obeying and fearing God, dare to set herself before this or that woman, obeying and fearing God; otherwise she will not be humble, and "God resisteth the proud!"[2] What, therefore, shall she have in her thoughts? Forsooth the hidden gifts of God, which nought save the questioning of trial makes known to each, even in himself. For, to pass over the rest, whence doth a virgin know, although careful of the things of the Lord, how to please the Lord,[3] but that haply, by reason of some weakness of mind unknown to herself, she be not as yet ripe for martyrdom, whereas that woman, whom she rejoiced to set herself before, may already be able to drink the Cup of the Lord's humiliation,[4] which He set before His disciples, to drink first, when enamored of high place? Whence, I say, doth she know but that she herself be not as yet Thecla, that other be already Crispina.[5] Certainly, unless there be present trial, there takes place no proof of this gift.

46. But this is so great, that certain understand it to be the fruit an hundred-fold.[6] For the authority of the Church bears a very conspicuous witness, in which it is known to the faithful in what place the Martyrs, in what place the holy nuns deceased, are rehearsed at the Sacraments of the Altar.[7] But what the meaning is of that difference of fruitfulness, let them see to it, who understand these things better than we; whether the virginal life be in fruit an hundred-fold, in sixty-fold the widowed, in thirty-fold the married; or whether the hundred-fold fruitfulness be ascribed unto martyrdom, the sixty-fold unto continence, the thirty-fold unto marriage; or whether virginity, by the addition of martyrdom, fill up the hundred-fold, but when alone be in sixty-fold, but married persons bearing thirty-fold arrive at sixty-fold, in case they shall be martyrs: or whether, what seems to me more probable, forasmuch as the gifts of Divine grace are many, and one is greater and better than another, whence the Apostle says, "But emulate ye the better gifts;"[8] we are to understand that they are more in number than to allow of being distributed under those different kinds. In the first place, that we set not widowed continence either as bearing no fruit, or set it but level with the desert of married charity, or equal it unto virgin glory; or think that the Crown of Martyrdom, either established in habit of mind, although proof of trial be wanting, or in actual making trial of suffering, be added unto either one of those these chastities, without any increase of fruitfulness. Next, when we set it down that many men and women so keep virginal chastity, as that yet they do not the things which the Lord saith, "If thou willest to be perfect, go, sell all that thou hast, and give unto the poor, and thou shalt have treasure in Heaven: and come, follow me;"[9] and dare not unite themselves to those dwelling together, among whom no one saith that any thing is his own, but all things are unto them common;[10] do we think that there is no addition of fruitfulness unto the virgins of God, when they do this? or that the virgins of God are without any fruit, although they do not this? Therefore there are many gifts, and some brighter and higher than others, each than each. And at times one is fruitful in fewer gifts, but better; another in lower gifts, but more. And in what manner they be either made equal one to another, or distinguished one from another, in receiving eternal honors, who of men would dare to pronounce? whereas yet it is plain both that those differences are many, and that the better are profitable not for the present time, but for eternity. But I judge that the Lord willed to make mention of three differences

---

[1] Ecclus. iii. 18.　　[2] James iv. 6.
[3] 1 Cor. vii. 32.　　[4] Matt. xx. 22.
[5] A married woman, who was beheaded in the persecution under Diocletian and Maximian at Thebeste in Africa. See Ser. 354, ad Continentes, n. 5. where he says, "bethink you that in the time of persecution not only Agnes the Virgin was crowned, but likewise Crispina, the wife; and perchance, as there is no doubt, some of the continent then failed, and many of the wedded fought and conquered." Ben. ed.
[6] St. Jerome mentions this interpretation; but b. 1. agt. Jovinian, and on Matt. 13, takes that which assigns the hundred-fold to virginity. Ben. ed.

[7] Ser. 159, he says, "Martyrs are in such place rehearsed at the Altar of God as that prayer is not made for them; but for the other deceased that are mentioned prayer is made." Ben. ed.
[8] 1 Cor. xii. 31.　[9] Matt. xix. 21.　[10] Acts ii. 44, 4, 32.

of fruitfulness, the rest He left to such as understand.[1] For also another Evangelist hath made mention only of the hundred-fold:[2] we are not, therefore, are we, to think that he either rejected, or knew not of, the other two, but rather that he left them to be understood?

47. But, as I had begun to say, whether the fruit an hundred-fold be virginity dedicated to God, or whether we are to understand that interval of fruitfulness in some other way, either such as we have made mention of, or such as we have not made mention of; yet no one, as I suppose, will have dared to prefer virginity to martyrdom, and no one will have doubted that this latter gift is hidden, if trial to test it be wanting. A virgin, therefore, hath a subject for thought, such as may be of profit to her for the keeping of humility, that she violate not that charity, which is above all gifts, without which assuredly whatever other gifts she shall have had, whether few or many, whether great or small, she is nothing. She hath, I say, a subject for thought, that she be not puffed up, that she rival not; forsooth that she so make profession that the virginal good is much greater and better than the married good, as that yet she know not whether this or that married woman be not already able to suffer for Christ, but herself as yet unable, and she herein spared, that her weakness is not put to the question by trial. "For God," saith the Apostle, "is faithful, Who will not suffer you to be tried above what ye are able; but will make with the trial a way out, that ye may be able to bear it."[3] Perhaps, therefore, those men or women keeping a way of married life praiseworthy in its kind, are already able, against an enemy forcing to unrighteousness, to contend even by tearing in pieces of bowels, and shedding of blood; but these men or women, continent from childhood, and making themselves eunuchs for the sake of the Kingdom of Heaven, still are not as yet able to endure such, either for righteousness, or for chastity itself. For it is one thing, for truth and an holy purpose, not to consent unto one who would persuade and flatter, but another thing not to yield even to one who tortures and strikes. These lie hid in the powers and strength of souls, by trial they are unfolded, by actual essay they come forth. In order, therefore, that each be not puffed up by reason of that, which he sees clearly that he can do, let him humbly consider that he knows not that there is perchance something more excellent which he cannot do, but that some, who neither have

nor profess that of which he is lawfully self-conscious, are able to do this, which he himself cannot do. Thus will be kept, not by feigned but by true humility, "In honor preventing one another,"[4] and, "esteeming each the other higher than himself."[5]

48. What now shall I say concerning the very carefulness and watchfulness against sin? "Who shall boast that he hath a chaste heart? or who shall boast that he is clean from sin?"[6] Holy virginity is indeed inviolate from the mother's womb; but "no one," saith he, "is clean in Thy sight, not even the infant whose life is of one day upon the earth."[7] There is kept also in faith inviolate a certain virginal chastity, whereby the Church is joined as a chaste virgin unto One Husband: but That One Husband hath taught, not only the faithful who are virgin in mind and body, but all Christians altogether, from spiritual even unto carnal, from Apostles even unto the last penitents, as though from the height of heaven even unto the bounds of it,[8] to pray, and in the prayer itself hath admonished them to say, "And forgive us our debts, even as we also forgive our debtors:"[9] where, by this which we seek, He shews what also we should remember that we are. For neither on behalf of those debts, which for our whole past life we trust have been forgiven unto us in Baptism through His peace, hath He charged us to pray, saying, "And forgive us our debts, even as we also forgive our debtors:" otherwise this were a prayer which Catechumens rather ought to pray up to the time of Baptism; but whereas it is what baptized persons pray, rulers and people, pastors and flocks; it is sufficiently shown that in this life, the whole of which is a trial, no one ought to boast himself as though free from all sins.[10]

49. Wherefore also the virgins of God without blame indeed, "follow the Lamb whithersoever He shall have gone," both the cleansing of sins being perfected, and virginity being kept, which, were it lost, could not return: but, because that same Apocalypse itself, wherein such unto one such were revealed, in this also praises them, that "in their mouth there was not found a lie:"[11] let them remember in this also to be true, that they dare not say that they have not sin. Forsooth the same John, who saw that, hath said this, "If we shall have said that we have not sin, we deceive our own selves, and the truth is not in us; but if we shall have confessed our faults, He is faithful and just,

[1] Matt. xiii. 8.   [2] Luke viii. 8.   [3] 1 Cor. x. 13.

[4] Rom. xii. 10. [See R.V.]   [5] Phil. ii. 3.   [6] Prov. xx. 9.
[7] Job xxv. 4.   [8] Matt. xxiv. 31. [See R.V.]
[9] Matt. vi. 12.   [10] Job vii. 1.   [11] Rev. xiv. 4, 5.

so as to forgive us our sins, and to cleanse us from all unrighteousness. But if we shall have said that we have not sinned, we shall make Him a liar, and His word shall not be in us."[1] This surely is not said unto these or those, but unto all Christians, wherein virgins also ought to recognize themselves. For thus they shall be without a lie, such as in the Apocalypse they appeared. And by this means so long as there is not as yet perfection in heavenly height, confession in lowliness maketh them without blame.

50. But, again, lest by occasion of this sentence, any one should sin with deadly security, and should allow himself to be carried away, as though his sins were soon by easy confession to be blotted out, he straightway added, " My little children, these things have I written unto you, that ye sin not; and, if one shall have sinned, we have an Advocate with the Father, Jesus Christ the righteous, and Himself is a propitiation of our sins."[2] Let no one therefore depart from sin as though about to return to it, nor bind himself as it were by compact of alliance of this kind with unrighteousness, so as to take delight rather to confess it than to shun it. But, forasmuch as even upon such as are busy and on the watch not to sin, there creep by stealth, in a certain way, from human weakness, sins, however small, however few, yet not none; these same themselves become great and grievous, in case pride shall have added to them increase and weight: but by the Priest, Whom we have in the heavens, if by pious humility they be destroyed, they are with all ease cleansed.

51. But I contend not with those, who assert that a man can in this life live without any sin: I contend not, I gainsay not. For perhaps we take measure of the great from out our own misery, and, comparing ourselves with ourselves, understand not.[3] One thing I know, that those great ones, such as we are not, such as we have not as yet made proof of, by how much they are great, by so much humble themselves in all things, that they may find grace before God. For, let them be how great soever they will, " there is no servant greater than his Lord, nor disciple greater than his master."[4] And assuredly He is the Lord, Who saith, "All things have been delivered unto Me of My Father;"[5] and He is the Master, Who saith, " Come unto Me, all ye who labor, and learn of Me;" and yet what learn we? " In that I am meek," saith He, " and lowly of heart."

52. Here some one will say, This is now not to write of virginity, but of humility. As though truly it were any kind of virginity, and not that which is after God, which we had undertaken to set forth. And this good, by how much I see it to be great, by so much I fear for it, lest it be lost, the thief pride. Therefore there is none that guardeth the virginal good, save God Himself Who gave it: and God is Charity.[6] The Guardian therefore of virginity is Charity: but the place of this Guardian is humility. There forsooth He dwelleth, Who said, that on the lowly and quiet, and that trembleth at His words, His Spirit resteth.[7] What, therefore, have I done foreign from my purpose, if wishing the good, which I have praised, to be more securely guarded, I have taken care also to prepare a place for the Guardian? For I speak with confidence, nor have I any fear lest they be angry with me, whom I admonish with care to fear for themselves together with me. More easily do follow the Lamb, although not whithersoever He shall have gone, yet so far as they shall have had power, married persons who are humble, than virgins who are proud. For how doth one follow Him, unto Whom one wills not to approach? or how doth one approach Him, unto Whom one comes not to learn, " in that I am meek and lowly of heart?" Wherefore those the Lamb leadeth following whithersoever He shall have gone, in whom first Himself shall have found where to lay His Head. For also a certain proud and crafty person had said to Him, " Lord, I will follow Thee whithersoever Thou shalt have gone;"[8] to whom He made answer, " Foxes have dens, and fowls of heaven nests: but the Son of Man hath not where to lay His Head." By the term of foxes He reproved wily craftiness, and by the name of birds puffed-up arrogance, wherein He found not pious humility to rest in. And by this no where at all did he follow the Lord, who had promised that he would follow Him, not unto a certain point of progress, but altogether whithersoever He should have gone.

53. Wherefore this do ye, virgins of God, this do ye: follow ye the Lamb, whithersoever He shall have gone. But first come unto Him, Whom ye are to follow, and learn, in that He is meek and lowly of heart. Come ye in lowly wise unto the Lowly, if ye love: and depart not from Him, lest ye fall. For whoso fears to depart from Him asks and says, " Let there not come to me foot of pride."[9] Go on in the way of loftiness with the foot of lowliness; Himself lifteth up such

---

1 1 John i. 8–10. [SeeR.V.]   2 1 John ii. 1, 2.   3 2 Cor. x. 12.
4 John xiii. 16.   5 Matt. xi. 27, 28.

6 1 John iv. 8.   7 Is. lxvi. 2.
8 Matt. viii. 19, 20.   9 Ps. xxxvi. 11.

as follow in lowly wise, Who thought it not a trouble to come down unto such as lay low. Commit ye His gifts unto Him to keep, "guard ye your strength unto Him."[1] Whatever of evil through His guardianship ye commit not, account as forgiven unto you by Him: lest, thinking that you have little forgiven unto you, ye love little, and with ruinous boasting despise the publicans beating their breasts. Concerning that strength of yours which hath been tried beware, that ye be not puffed up, because ye have been able to bear something: but concerning that which hath been untried, pray, that ye be not tempted above that ye are able to bear. Think that some are superior to you in secret, than whom ye are openly better. When the good things of others, haply unknown to you, are kindly believed by you, your own that are known to you are not lessened by comparison, but strengthened by love: and what haply as yet are wanting, are by so much the more easily given, by how much they are the more humbly desired. Let such among your number as persevere afford to you an example: but let such as fall increase your fear. Love the one that ye may imitate it; mourn over the other, that ye be not puffed up. Do not ye establish your own righteousness; submit yourselves unto God Who justifies you. Pardon the sins of others, pray for your own: future sins shun by watching, past sins blot out by confessing.

54. Lo, already ye are such, as that in the rest of your conduct also ye correspond with the virginity which ye have professed and kept. Lo, already not only do ye abstain from murders, devilish sacrifices and abominations, thefts, rapines, frauds, perjuries, drunkennesses, and all luxury and avarice, hatreds, emulations, impieties, cruelties; but even those things, which either are, or are thought, lighter, are not found nor arise among you: not bold face, not wandering eyes, not unbridled tongue, not petulant laugh, not scurrilous jest, not unbecoming mien, not swelling or loose gait; already ye render not evil for evil, nor curse for curse;[2] already, lastly, ye fulfill that measure of love, that ye lay down your lives for your brethren.[3] Lo, already ye are such, because also such ye ought to be. These, being added to virginity, set forth an angelic life unto men, and the ways of heaven unto the earth. But, by how much ye are great, whosoever of you are so great, " by so much humble yourselves in all things, that ye may find grace before God," that He resist you not as proud, that He humble you not as lifting up yourselves, that He lead you not

through straits as being puffed up: although anxiety be unnecessary, that, where Charity glows, humility be not wanting.

55. If, therefore, ye despise marriages of sons of men, from which to beget sons of men, love ye with your whole heart Him, Who is fair of form above the sons of men; ye have leisure; your heart is free from marriage bonds. Gaze on the Beauty of your Lover: think of Him equal to the Father, made subject also to His Mother: ruling even in the heavens, and serving upon the earth: creating all things, created among all things. That very thing, which in Him the proud mock at, gaze on, how fair it is: with inward eyes gaze on the wounds of Him hanging, the scars of Him rising again, the blood of Him dying, the price of him that believes, the gain of Him that redeems. Consider of how great value these are, weigh them in the scales of Charity; and whatever of love ye had to expend upon your marriages, pay back to Him.

56. It is well that He seeks your beauty within, where He hath given unto you power to become daughters of God:[4] He seeks not of you a fair flesh, but fair conduct, whereby to bridle also the flesh. He is not one unto Whom any one can lie concerning you, and make him rage through jealousy. See with how great security ye love Him, Whom ye fear not to offend by false suspicions. Husband and wife love each other, in that they see each other: and what they see not, that they fear between themselves: nor have they sure delight in what is visible, while in what is concealed they usually suspect what is not. Ye in Him, Whom ye see not with the eyes, and behold by faith, neither have what is real to blame, nor fear lest haply ye offend Him by what is false. If therefore ye should owe great love to husbands, Him, for Whose sake ye would not have husbands, how greatly ought ye to love? Let Him be fixed in your whole heart, Who for you was fixed on the Cross: let Him possess in your soul all that, whatever it be, that ye would not have occupied by marriage. It is not lawful for you to love little Him, for Whose sake ye have not loved even what were lawful. So loving Him Who is meek and lowly of heart, I have no fear for you of pride.

57. Thus, after our small measure, we have spoken enough both of sanctity, whereby ye are properly called " sanctimoniales," and of humility, whereby whatever great name ye bear is kept. But more worthily let those Three Children, unto whom He, Whom they loved with full glow of heart, afforded refresh-

---

[1] Ps. lix. 9. [See R.V.] [2] 1 Pet. iii. 9. [See R.V.] [3] 1 John iii. 16. [4] John i. 12.

ing in the fire, admonish you concerning this our little work, much more shortly indeed in number of words, but much more greatly in weight of authority, in the Hymn wherein God is honored by them. For joining humility unto holiness in such as praise God, they have most plainly taught, that each, by how much he make any more holy profession, by so much do beware that he be not deceived by pride.

Wherefore do ye also praise Him, Who grants unto you, that in the midst of the flames of this world, although ye be not joined in marriage, yet ye be not burned: and praying also for us, " Bless ye the Lord, ye holy and humble men of heart; utter an hymn, and exalt Him above all forever." [1]

[1] Song of Three Children 65.

ST. AUGUSTIN:

ON

THE GOOD OF WIDOWHOOD

[DE BONO VIDUITATIS.]

TRANSLATED BY

REV. C. L. CORNISH, M.A.,

OF EXETER COLLEGE, OXFORD.

ON

THE GOOD OF WIDOWHOOD

[DE BONO VIDUITATIS.]

This work is not mentioned in the *Retractations*, probably because it is a letter, and as such it is reckoned by Possidius, cap. 7. It is also marked as St. Augustin's by its references to his other works, *De Bono Conjugali*, etc. cap. 15. Ep. to Proba, cap. 23. The date is marked by the recent consecration of Demetrias, which was in 413. The admonition for which he is thanked by Juliana, Ep. 188, may be that against Pelagianism.

An objection has been raised from its disagreement with the fourth Council of Carthage, an. 398. can. 104, which excommunicates widows who marry again after consecration, and pronounces them guilty of adultery, whereas in cap. 10 and 11, the opinion that such marriages are no marriages, and that they ought to return to continence, is refuted. The two, however, are not wholly irreconcileable, as there may be a guilt similar to that of adultery incurred, and it may be visited with a censure in the form of excommunication, and yet the marriage may remain valid. The 16th Canon of Chalcedon imposes such a penalty, with power to the Bishop to relax it.—*Abridged from the Benedictine Edition.*

AUGUSTIN the Bishop, servant of Christ, and of the servants of Christ, unto the religious handmaiden of God, Juliana, in the Lord of lords health.

Not any longer to be in debt of my promise to your request and love in Christ, I have seized the occasion as I could, amid other my very pressing engagements, to write to you somewhat concerning the profession of holy widowhood, forasmuch as, when I was present, you laded me with entreaty, and, when I had not been able to deny you this, you often by letters demanded my promise. And in this work of ours, when you shall find in reading that some things pertain not at all unto your own person, or unto the person of you, who are living together in Christ, nor are strictly necessary to give counsel unto your life, it will be your duty not on this account to judge them superfluous. Forsooth this letter, although it be addressed to you, was not to be written for you alone; but certainly it was a matter for us not to neglect, that it should profit others also through your means. Whatsoever, therefore, you shall find here, such as either hath been at no time necessary for you, or is not so now, and which yet you shall perceive to be necessary for others, grieve not either to possess or to lend to read; that your charity also may be the profit of others.

2. Whereas, therefore, in every question, which relates to life and conduct, not only teaching, but exhortation also is necessary;

in order that by teaching we may know what is to be done, and by exhortation may be incited not to think it irksome to do what we already know is to be done; what more can I teach you, than what we read in the Apostle? For holy Scripture setteth a rule to our teaching, that we dare not "be wise more than it behoveth to be wise;"[1] but be wise, as himself saith, "unto soberness, according as unto each God hath allotted the measure of faith."[2] Be it not therefore for me to teach you any other thing, save to expound to you the words of the Teacher, and to treat of them as the Lord shall have given to me.

3. Therefore (thus) saith the Apostle, the teacher of the Gentiles, the vessel of election, "But I say unto the unmarried and the widows, that it is good for them, if they shall have so continued, even as I also."[3] These words are to be so understood, as that we think not that widows ought not to be called unmarried, in that they seem to have made trial of marriage: for by the name of unmarried women he means those, who are not now bound by marriage, whether they have been, or whether they have not been so. And this in another place he opens, where he says, "Divided is a woman unmarried and a virgin."[4] Assuredly when he adds a virgin also, what would he have understood by an unmarried woman, but a widow? Whence also, in what follows, under the one term "unmarried" he embraces both professions, saying, "She who is unmarried is careful of the things of the Lord, how to please the Lord: but she who is married is careful of the things of the world, how to please her husband."[5] Certainly by the unmarried he would have understood, not only her who hath never married, but her also, who, being by widowhood set free from the bond of marriage, hath ceased to be married; for on this account also he calleth not married, save her, who hath an husband; not her also, who hath had, and hath not. Wherefore every widow is unmarried; but, because not every unmarried woman is a widow, for there are virgins also; therefore he hath here set both, where he says, "But I say unto the unmarried and the widows;" as if he should say, What I say unto the unmarried, I say not unto them alone, who are virgins, but unto them also who are widows; "that it is good for them, if they shall have so continued, even as also I."[6]

4. Lo, there is your good compared to that good, which the Apostle calls his own, if faith be present: yea, rather, because faith is present. Short is this teaching, yet not on this account to be despised, because it is short; but on this account to be retained the more easily and the more dearly, in that in shortness it is not cheap. For it is not every kind of good soever, which the Apostle would here set forth, which he hath unambiguously placed above the faith of married women. But how great good the faith of married women, that is, of Christian and religious women joined in marriage, hath, may be understood from this, that, when he was giving charge for the avoiding of fornication, wherein assuredly he was addressing married persons also, he saith, "Know ye not that your bodies are the members of Christ?"[7] So great then is the good of faithful marriage, that even the very members are (members) of Christ. But, forasmuch as the good of widowed continence is better than this good, the purpose of this profession is, not that a catholic widow be any thing more than a member of Christ, but that she have a better place, than a married woman, among the members of Christ. Forsooth the same Apostle says, "For, as in one body we have many members, but all members have not the same course of action; so being many we are one body in Christ, and each members one of another: having gifts diverse according unto the grace, which hath been given unto us."[8]

5. Wherefore also when he was advising married persons not to defraud one another of the due of carnal intercourse; lest, by this means, the one of them, (the due of marriage being denied to him,) being through his own incontinence tempted of Satan, should fall away into fornication, he saith, "But this I say of leave, not of command; but I would that all men were as I myself; but each one hath his own proper gift from God; but one in this way, and another in that."[9] You see that wedded chastity also, and the marriage faith of the Christian bed, is a "gift," and this of God; so that, when as carnal lust exceeds somewhat the measure of sensual intercourse, beyond what is necessary for the begetting of children, this evil is not of marriage, but venial by reason of the good of marriage. For not concerning marriage, which is contracted for the begetting of children, and the faith of wedded chastity, and the sacrament (indissoluble, so long as both live) of matrimony, all which are good; but concerning that immoderate use of the flesh, which is recognized in the weakness of married persons, and is pardoned by the intervention of the good of marriage, the Apostle saith, "I

---

[1] So V. [2] Rom. xii. 3. [3] τοῖς, ταῖς: 1 Cor. vii. 8.
[4] ἡ γυνὴ καὶ ἡ παρθένος. [5] 1 Cor. vii. 34. [6] 1 Cor. vii. 8. [7] 1 Cor. vi. 15. [8] Rom. xii. 4-6. [9] 1 Cor. vii. 6, 7.

speak of leave, not of command." Also, when he says, "The woman is bound, so long as her husband lives: but, in case her husband shall have died, she is set free: let her be married to whom she will, only in the Lord: but she shall be more blessed, if she shall have so continued, according to my counsel;"[1] he shows sufficiently that a faithful woman is blessed in the Lord, even when she marries a second time after the death of her husband, but that a widow is more blessed in the same Lord; that is, to speak not only in the words, but by instances also, of the Scriptures, that Ruth is blessed, but that Anna is more blessed.

6. Wherefore this in the first place you ought to know, that by the good, which you have chosen, second marriages are not condemned, but are set in lower honor. For, even as the good of holy virginity, which thy daughter hath chosen, doth not condemn thy one marriage; so neither doth thy widowhood the second marriage of any. For hence, specially, the heresies of the Cataphryges and of the Novatians swelled, which Tertullian also, inflated with cheeks full of sound not of wisdom, whilst with railing tooth he attacks[2] second marriages, as though unlawful, which the Apostle with sober mind allows[3] to be altogether lawful. From this soundness of doctrine let no man's reasoning, be he unlearned, or be he learned, move thee; nor do thou so extol thy own good, as to charge as evil that of another's which is not evil; but do thou rejoice so much the more of thy own good, the more thou seest, that, by it, not only are evils shunned, but some goods too surpassed. For adultery and fornication are evils. But from these unlawful things she is very far removed, who hath bound herself by liberty of vow, and, not by command of law, but by counsel of charity, hath brought to pass that even things lawful should not be lawful to her. And marriage chastity is a good, but widowed continence is a better good. Therefore this better good is honored by the submission of that other, not that other condemned by the praise of this that is better.

7. But whereas the Apostle, when commending the fruit of unmarried men and women, in that they have thought of the things of the Lord, how to please God, added and saith, "But this I say for your profit, not to cast a snare on you"[4] that is, not to force you; "but in order to that which is honorable;" we ought not, because he saith that the good of the unmarried is honorable,

therefore to think that the bond of marriage is base; otherwise we shall condemn first marriages also, which neither Cataphryges, nor Novatians, nor their most learned upholder Tertullian dared to call base. But as, when he says, "But I say unto the unmarried and widows, that it is good for them if they shall have so continued;"[5] assuredly he set down "good" for "better," since every thing, which, when compared with a good, is called better, this also without doubt is a good; for what else is it that it is so called better, save that it is more good? and yet we do not on this account suppose him by consequence to have thought that it was an evil, in case they married, in that he said, "it is good for them, if they shall have so continued;" so also, when he says, "but in order to that which is honest," he hath not shown that marriage is base, but that which was honester than (another thing also) honest, he hath commended by the name of honest in general. Because what is honester, save what is more honest? But what is more honest is certainly honest. Forsooth he plainly showed that this is better than that other that is good, where he says, "Whoso giveth to marry, doeth well; but whoso giveth not to marry, doeth better."[6] And this more blessed than that other that is blessed, where he saith, "But she shall be more blessed, if she shall have so continued."[7] As, therefore, there is than good a better, and than blessed a more blessed, so is there than honest an honester, which he chose to call honest. For far be it that that be base, of which the Apostle Peter speaking saith, "Husbands, unto your wives, as unto the weaker and subject vessel, give honor, as unto co-heirs of grace;" and addressing the wives, he exhorts them, by the pattern of Sarah, to be subject unto their husbands; "For so," saith he, "certain holy women, who hoped in God, adorned themselves, obeying their own husbands; even as Sarah obeyed Abraham, calling him lord, whose daughters ye are made, well-doing, and not fearing any disturbance."[8]

8. Whence, also, what the Apostle Paul said of the unmarried woman, "that she may be holy both in body and spirit;"[9] we are not so to understand, as though a faithful woman being married and chaste, and according to the Scriptures subject unto her husband, be not holy in body, but only in spirit. For it cannot come to pass, that when the spirit is sanctified, the body also be not holy, of which the sanctified spirit maketh use: but, that we seem not to any to argue rather than

---

[1] 1 Cor. vii. 39, 40. [2] "Concidit."
[3] "Concedit." [4] 1 Cor. vii. 35.

[5] 1 Cor. vii. 8. [6] 1 Cor. vii. 38. [7] ver. 40.
[8] 1 Pet. iii. 5-7. [See R.V.] [9] 1 Cor. vii. 34.

to prove this by divine saying; since the Apostle Peter, making mention of Sarah, saith only "holy women," and saith not, "and in body;" let us consider that saying of the same Paul, where forbidding fornication he saith, "Know ye not, that your bodies are members of Christ? Taking, therefore, members of Christ, shall I make them members of an harlot? Far be it."[1] Therefore let any one dare to say that the members of Christ are not holy; or let him not dare to separate from the members of Christ the bodies of the faithful that are married. Whence, also, a little after he saith, "Your body is the temple within you of the Holy Spirit, Whom ye have from God; and ye are not your own; for ye have been bought with a great price."[2] He saith that the body of the faithful is both members of Christ, and the temple of the Holy Spirit, wherein assuredly the faithful of both sexes are understood. There therefore are married women, there unmarried women also; but distinct in their deserts, and as members preferred to members, whilst yet neither are separated from the body. Whereas, therefore, he saith, speaking of an unmarried woman, "that she may be holy both in body and spirit," he would have understood a fuller sanctification both in body and in spirit, and hath not deprived the body of married women of all sanctification.

9. Learn, therefore, that thy good, yea, rather, remember what thou hast learned, that thy good is more praised, because there is another good than which this is better, than if this could not on any other condition be a good, unless that were an evil, or altogether were not. The eyes have great honor in the body, but they would have less, if they were alone, and there were not other members of less honor. In heaven itself the sun by its light surpasses, not chides, the moon; and star from star differs in glory,[3] not is at variance through pride. Therefore, "God made all things, and, lo, very good;"[4] not only "good," but also "very;" for no other reason, than because "all." For of each several work throughout it was also said, "God saw that it is good." But, when "all" were named, "very" was added; and it was said, "God saw all things which He made, and, lo, very good." For certain several things were better than other several, but all together better than any several. Therefore, may the sound doctrine of Christ make thee in His Body sound through His Grace, that, what thou hast better than others in

body and spirit, the self-same thy spirit, which ruleth the body, may neither extol with insolence, nor distinguish with lack of knowledge.

10. Nor, because I called Ruth blessed, Anna more blessed, in that the former married twice, the latter, being soon widowed of her one husband, so lived long, do you straightway also think that you are better than Ruth. Forsooth different in the times of the Prophets was the dispensation of holy females, whom obedience, not lust, forced to marry, for the propagation of the people of God,[5] that in them Prophets of Christ might be sent beforehand; whereas the People itself also, by those things which in figure happened among them, whether in the case of those who knew, or in the case of those who knew not those things, was nothing else than a Prophet of Christ, of whom should be born the Flesh also of Christ. In order therefore for the propagation of that people, he was accounted accursed by sentence of the Law, whoso raised not up seed in Israel.[6] Whence also holy women were kindled, not by lust of sensual intercourse, but by piety of bearing; so that we most rightly believe of them that they would not have sought sensual intercourse, in case a family could have come by any other means. And to the husbands was allowed the use of several wives living; and that the cause of this was not lust of the flesh, but forethought of begetting, is shown by the fact, that, as it was lawful for holy men to have several wives living, it was not likewise lawful for holy women to have intercourse with several husbands living; in that they would be by so much the baser, by how much the more they sought what would not add to their fruitfulness. Wherefore holy Ruth, not having seed such as at that time was necessary in Israel, on the death of her husband sought another of whom to have it. Therefore than this one twice married, Anna once married a widow was on this account more blessed, in that she attained also to be a prophetess of Christ; concerning whom we are to believe, that, although she had no sons, (which indeed Scripture by keeping silence hath left uncertain,) yet, had she by that Spirit foreseen that Christ would immediately come of a virgin, by Which she was enabled to recognize Him even as a child: whence, with good reason, even without sons, (that is, assuming she had none,) she refused a second marriage: in that she knew that now was the time wherein Christ were better served, not by duty of bearing, but by zeal of containing: not by fruitfulness of married womb, but by chastity

---

[1] 1 Cor. vi. 15. [See R.V.]   [2] 1 Cor. vi. 19, 20. [3] 1 Cor. xv. 41.   [4] Gen. i. 31.   [5] 1 Cor. x. 11.   [6] Deut. xxv. 5-10.

of widowed conduct. But if Ruth also was aware that by her flesh was propagated a seed, whereof Christ should hereafter have flesh, and by marrying set forth her ministering to this knowledge, I dare not any longer say that the widowhood of Anna was more blessed than her fruitfulness.

11. But thou who both hast sons, and livest in that end of the world, wherein now is the time not of casting stones, but of gathering; not of embracing, but of abstaining from embracing;[1] when the Apostle cries out, "But this I say, brethren, the time is short; it remains, that both they who have wives be as not having;"[2] assuredly if thou hadst sought a second marriage, it would have been no obedience of prophecy or law, no carnal desire even of family, but a mark of incontinence alone. For you would have done what the Apostle says, after he had said, "It is good for them, if they shall have so continued, even as I;"[3] forsooth he straightway added, "But if they contain not themselves, let them marry; for I had rather that they marry than be burned." For this he said, in order that the evil of unbridled desire might not be carried headlong into criminal baseness, being taken up by the honest estate of marriage. But thanks be to the Lord, in that thou hast given birth to what thou wouldest not be, and the virginity of thy child hath compensated for the loss of thy virginity. For Christian doctrine, having diligent question made of it, makes answer, that a first marriage also now at this time is to be despised, unless incontinence stand in the way. For he, who said, "If they contain not themselves, let them marry," could have said, "If they have not sons, let them marry," if, when now after the Resurrection and Preaching of Christ, there is unto all nations so great and abundant supply of sons to be spiritually begotten, it were any such duty to beget sons after the flesh, as it was in the first times. And, whereas in another place he saith, "But I will that the younger marry, bear children, be mothers of families,"[4] he commends with apostolic sobriety and authority the good of marriage, but doth not impose the duty of bearing, as though in order to obey the law, even on those who "receive" the good of continence. Lastly, why he had said this, he unfolds, when he adds and says, "To give no occasion of speaking evil to the adversary; for already certain have turned back after Satan:" that by these words of his we may understand, that those, whom he would have marry, could have done better to contain than marry; but

better to marry than to go back after Satan, that is, to fall away from that excellent purpose of virginal or widowed chastity, by looking back to things that are behind, and perish. Wherefore, such as contain not themselves, let them marry before they make profession of continence, before they vow unto God, what, if they pay not, they are justly condemned. Forsooth in another place he saith of such, "For when they have lived in delights in Christ, they wish to marry: having condemnation, in that they have made of none effect their first faith;"[5] that is, they have turned aside their will from the purpose of continence unto marriage. Forsooth they have made of none effect the faith, whereby they formerly vowed what they were unwilling by perseverance to fulfill. Therefore the good of marriage is indeed ever a good: but in the people of God it was at one time an act of obedience unto the law; now it is a remedy for weakness, but in certain a solace of human nature. Forsooth to be engaged in the begetting of children, not after the fashion of dogs by promiscuous use of females, but by honest order of marriage, is not an affection such as we are to blame in a man; yet this affection itself the Christian mind, having thoughts of heavenly things, in a more praiseworthy manner surpasses and overcomes.

12. But since, as the Lord saith, "Not all receive this word;"[6] therefore let her who can receive it, receive it; and let her, who containeth not, marry; let her, who hath not begun, deliberate; let her, who hath undertaken it, persevere; let there be no occasion given unto the adversary, let there be no oblation withdrawn from Christ. Forsooth in the marriage bond if chastity be preserved, condemnation is not feared; but in widowed and virginal continence, the excellence of a greater gift[7] is sought for: and, when this has been sought, and chosen, and by debt of vow offered, from this time not only to enter upon marriage, but, although one be not married, to wish to marry is matter of condemnation. For, in order to show this, the Apostle saith not, "When they shall have lived in delights, in Christ" they marry;[8] but "they wish to marry; having," saith he, "condemnation, in that they have made of none effect their first faith," although not by marrying, yet by wishing; not that the marriages even of such are judged matter of condemnation; but there is condemned a wrong done to purpose, there is condemned a broken faith of vow, there is condemned not a relief by lower good, but a fall from higher good:

---

[1] Eccl. iii. 5.
[3] 1 Cor. vii. 8, 9.
[2] 1 Cor. vii. 29. [See R.V.]
[4] 1 Tim v. 14, 15.
[5] 1 Tim. v. 11, 12. [See R.V.]
[7] *Muneris.*
[6] Matt. xix. 11.
[8] 1 Tim. v. 11, 12.

lastly, such are condemned, not because they have entered upon marriage faith afterwards, but because they have made of none effect the first faith of continence. And in order to suggest this in few words, the Apostle would not say, that they have condemnation, who after purpose of greater sanctity marry, (not because they are not condemned, but lest in them marriage itself should be thought to be condemned:) but, after he had said, " they wish to marry," he straightway added, " having condemnation." And he stated the reason, " in that they have made of none effect their former faith," in order that it may appear that it is the will which fell away from its purpose, which is condemned, whether marriage follow, or fail to follow.

13. Wherefore they who say that the marriages of such are not marriages, but rather adulteries, seem not to me to consider with sufficient acuteness and care what they say; forsooth they are misled by a semblance of truth. For, whereas they, who of Christian sanctity marry not, are said to choose the marriage of Christ, hence certain argue saying, If she, who during the life of her husband is married to another, be an adulteress, even as the Lord Himself hath laid down in the Gospel; therefore, during the life of Christ, over Whom death hath no more dominion,[1] if she who had chosen His marriage, be married to a man, she is an adulteress. They, who say this, are moved indeed with acuteness, but fail to observe, how great absurdity in fact follows on this reasoning. For whereas it is praiseworthy that, even during the life of her husband, by his consent, a female vow continence unto Christ, now, according to the reasoning of these persons, no one ought to do this, lest she make Christ Himself, what is impious to imagine, an adulterer, by being married to Him during the life of her husband. Next, whereas first marriages are of better desert than second, far be it that this be the thought of holy widows, that Christ seem unto them as a second husband. For Himself they used heretofore also to have, (when they were subject and did faithful service to their own husbands,) not after the flesh, but after the Spirit a Husband; unto Whom the Church herself, of which they are members, is the wife; who by soundness of faith, of hope, of charity, not in the virgins alone, but in widows also, and faithful married women, is altogether a virgin. Forsooth unto the universal Church, of which they all are members, the Apostle saith, " I joined you unto one husband a chaste virgin to present

unto Christ." [2] But He knoweth how to make fruitful, without marring of chastity, a wife a virgin, Whom even in the flesh itself His Mother could without violation of chastity conceive. But there is brought to pass by means of this ill-considered notion, (whereby they think that the marriages of women who have fallen away from this holy purpose, in case they shall have married, are no marriages,) no small evil, that wives be separated from their husbands, as though they were adulteresses, not wives; and wishing to restore to continence the women thus separated, they make their husbands real adulterers, in that during the life of their wives they have married others.

14. Wherefore I cannot indeed say, of females who have fallen away from a better purpose, in case they shall have married, that they are adulteries, not marriages; but I plainly would not hesitate to say, that departures and fallings away from a holier chastity, which is vowed unto the Lord, are worse than adulteries. For if, what may no way be doubted, it pertains unto an offense against Christ, when a member of Him keepeth not faith to her husband; how much graver offense is it against Him, when unto Himself faith is not kept, in a matter which He requires when offered, Who had not required that it should be offered. For when each fails to render that which, not by force of command, but by advice of counsel, he vowed, by so much the more doth he increase the unrighteousness of the wrong done to his vow, by how much the less necessity he had to vow. These matters I for this reason treat of, that you may not think either that second marriages are criminal, or that any marriages whatsoever, being marriages, are an evil. Therefore let this be your mind, not that you condemn them, but that you despise them. Therefore the good of widowed chastity is becoming after a brighter fashion, in that in order to make vow and profession of it, females may despise what is both pleasing and lawful. But after profession of vow made they must continue to rein in, and overcome, what is pleasing, because it is no longer lawful.

15. Men are wont to move a question concerning a third or fourth marriage, and even more numerous marriages than this. On which to make answer strictly, I dare neither to condemn any marriage, nor to take from these the shame of their great number. But, lest the brevity of this my answer may chance to displease any, I am prepared to listen to my reprover

---

[1] Rom. vi. 9.

[2] 2 Cor. xi. 2. [See R.V.]

treating more fully. For perhaps he alleges some reason, why second marriages be not condemned, but third be condemned. For I, as in the beginning of this discourse I gave warning, dare not to be more wise than it behoveth to be wise.[1] For who am I, that I should think that that must be defined which I see that the Apostle hath not defined? For he saith, "A woman is bound, so long as her husband liveth."[2] He said not, her first; or, second; or, third; or, fourth;[3] but, "A woman," saith he, "is bound, so long as her husband liveth; but if her husband shall be dead, she is set free; let her be married to whom she will, only in the Lord: but she shall be more blessed, if she shall have so continued." I know not what can be added to, or taken from, this sentence, so far as relates to this matter. Next I hear Himself also, the Master and Lord of the Apostles and of us, answering the Sadducees, when they had proposed to Him a woman not once-married, or twice-married, but, if it can be said, seven-married,[4] whose wife she should be in the resurrection? For rebuking them, He saith, "Ye do err, not knowing the Scriptures, nor the power of God. For in the resurrection they shall neither be married, nor marry wives;[5] for they shall not begin to die, but shall be equal to the Angels of God."[6] Therefore He made mention of their resurrection, who shall rise again unto life, not who shall rise again unto punishment. Therefore He might have said, Ye do err, knowing not the Scriptures, nor the power of God: for in that resurrection it will not be possible that there be those that were wives of many; and then added, that neither doth any there marry. But neither, as we see, did He in this sentence show any sign of condemning her who was the wife of so many husbands. Wherefore neither dare I, contrary to the feeling of natural shame, say, that, when her husbands are dead, a woman marry as often as she will; nor dare I, out of my own heart, beside the authority of holy Scripture, condemn any number of marriages whatever. But, what I say to a widow, who hath had one husband, this I say to every widow; you will be more blessed, if you shall have so continued.

16. For that also is no foolish question which is wont to be proposed, that whoso can may say, which widow is to be preferred in desert; whether one who hath had one husband, who, after having lived a considerable time with her husband, being left a widow with sons born to her and alive, hath made

profession of continence; or she who as a young woman having lost two husbands within two years, having no children left alive to console her, hath vowed to God continence, and in it hath grown old with most enduring sanctity. Herein let them exercise themselves, if they can, by discussing, and by showing some proof to us, who weigh the merits of widows by number of husbands, not by the strength itself of continence. For, if they shall have said, that she who hath had one husband is to be preferred to her who hath had two; unless they shall have alleged some special reason or authority, they will assuredly be found to set before excellence of soul, not greater excellence of soul, but good fortune of the flesh. Forsooth it pertained unto good fortune of the flesh, both to live a long time with her husband, and to conceive sons. But, if they prefer her not on this account, that she had sons; at any rate the very fact that she lived a long time with her husband, what else was it than good fortune of the flesh? Further, the desert of Anna herself is herein chiefly commended, in that, after she had so soon buried her husband, through her protracted life she long contended with the flesh, and overcame. For so it is written, "And there was Anna, a prophetess, the daughter of Phanuel, of the tribe of Aser; she was far advanced in many days; and had lived with her husband seven years from her virginity; and she was a widow even unto eighty-four years, who used not to depart from the Temple, by fastings and prayers serving day and night."[7] You see how the holy widow is not only commended in this, that she had had one husband, but also, that she had lived few years with a husband from her virginity, and had with so great service of piety continued her office of widowed chastity even unto so great age.

17. Let us therefore set before our eyes three widows, each having one of the things, the whole of which were in her: let us suppose one who had had one husband, in whose case is wanting both so great length of widowhood, in that she hath lived long with her husband, and so great zeal of piety, in that she doth not so serve with fasts and prayers: a second, who after the very short life of her former husband, had quickly lost a second also, and is now long time a widow, but yet herself also doth not so set herself to the most religious service of fasts and prayers: a third, who not only hath had two husbands, but also hath lived long with each of them singly, or with one of them, and being left a

[1] Rom. xii. 3. [2] 1 Cor. vii. 39, 40. [3] Al. "or any number." [4] *Septiviram.* [5] Matt. xxii. 29, 30. [6] Luke xx. 35, 36. [7] Luke ii. 36, 37.

widow at a later period of life, wherein indeed, in case she had wished to marry, she might also conceive sons, hath taken upon her widowed continence; but is more intent on God, more careful to do always the things that please Him, day and night, like Anna, serving by prayers and fasts. If a question be raised, which of these is to be preferred in deserts, who but must see that in this contest the palm must be given to the greater and more glowing piety? So also if three others be set, in each of whom are two of those three, but one of the three in each wanting, who can doubt that they will be the better, who shall have in a more excellent manner in their two goods pious humility, in order that there may be lofty piety?

18. No one indeed of these six widows could come up to your standard. For you, in case that you shall have maintained this vow even unto old age, mayest have all the three things wherein the desert of Anna excelled. For both thou hast had one husband, and he lived not long with thee in the flesh; and, by this means, in case that thou shalt show forth obedience to the words of the Apostle, saying, "But she who is a widow indeed and desolate, hath hoped in the Lord, and persevereth in prayers night and day,"[1] and with sober watchfulness shalt shun what follows, "But she who passes her time in delights, living is dead," all those three goods, which were Anna's, shall be thine also. But you have sons also, which haply she had not. And yet you are not on this account to be praised, that you have them, but that you are zealous to nurture and educate them piously. For that they were born to thee, was of fruitfulness; that they are alive, is of good fortune; that they be so brought up, is of your will and disposal.[2] In the former let men congratulate you, in this let them imitate you. Anna, through prophetic knowledge, recognized Christ with His virgin Mother; thee the grace of the Gospel hath made the mother of a virgin of Christ. Therefore that holy virgin,[3] whom herself willing and seeking it ye have offered unto Christ, hath added something of virginal desert also unto the widowed deserts of her grandmother and mother. For ye who have her, fail not to have something thence; and in her ye are, what in yourselves ye are not. For that holy virginity should be taken from you at your marriage, was on this account brought to pass, in order that she should be born of you.

19. These discussions, therefore, concerning the different deserts of married women, and of different widows, I would not in this work enter upon, if, what I am writing unto you, I were writing only for you. But, since there are in this kind of discourse certain very difficult questions, it was my wish to say something more than what properly relates to you, by reason of certain, who seem not to themselves learned, unless they essay, not by passing judgment to discuss, but by rending to cut in pieces the labors of others: in the next place, that you yourself also may not only keep what you have vowed, and make advance in that good; but also know more carefully and more surely, that this same good of yours is not distinguished from the evil of marriage, but is set before the good of marriage. For let not such, as condemn the marriage of widowed females, although they exercise their continence in abstaining from many things, which you make use of, on this account lead you astray, to think what they think, although you cannot do what they do. For no one would be a madman, although he see that the strength of a madman is greater than of men in their sound senses. Chiefly, therefore, let sound doctrine both adorn and guard goodness of purpose. Forsooth it is from this cause that catholic females, even after that they have been married more than once, are by just judgment preferred, not only to the widows who have had one husband, but also to the virgins of heretics. There are indeed on these three matters, of marriage, widowhood, and virginity, many winding recesses of questions, many perplexities; and in order by discussion to enter deeply into and solve these, there is required both greater care, and a fuller discourse; that either we may have a right mind in all those things, or, if in any matter we be otherwise minded, this also God may reveal unto us. However, what there also the Apostle saith next after, "Whereunto we have arrived, in that let us walk."[4] But we have arrived, in what relates to this matter on which we are speaking, so far as to set continence before marriage, but holy virginity even before widowed continence; and not to condemn any marriages, which yet are not adulteries but marriages, by praise of any purpose whatever of our own or of our friends. Many other things on these matters we have said in a Book concerning the Good of Marriage, and in another Book concerning Holy Virginity, and in a Book which we composed with as great pains as we could against Faustus the Manichee; since, by most biting reproaches in his writ-

---

[1] 1 Tim. v. 5, 6. [2] *Potestatis.*
[3] Demetrias, whose grandmother was Proba Faltonia, her mother, Juliana. See S. Aug. Ep. 130. and 150. Vol. I. pp. 459, 503, sqq.
[4] Phil. iii. 15, 16.

ings of the chaste marriages of Patriarchs and Prophets, he had turned aside the minds of certain unlearned persons from soundness of faith.

20. Wherefore, forasmuch as in the beginning of this little work I had proposed certain two necessary matters, and had undertaken to follow them out; one which related to doctrine, the other to exhortation; and I have not failed in the former part, to the best of my power, according to the business which I had undertaken; let us come to exhortation, in order that the good which is known wisely, may be pursued ardently. And in this matter I give you this advice first, that, how great soever love of pious continence you feel to be in you, you ascribe it to the favor of God, and give Him thanks, Who of His Holy Spirit hath freely given unto you so much, as that, His love being shed abroad in your heart, the love of a better good should take away from you the permission of a lawful matter. For it was His gift to you that you should not wish to marry, when it was lawful, in order that now it should not be lawful, even if you wished; and that by this means the wish not to do it might be the more settled, lest what were now unlawful be done, which was not done even when lawful; and that, a widow of Christ, you should so far attain as to see your daughter also a virgin of Christ; for whilst you are praying as Anna, she hath become what Mary was. These by how much the more you know them to be gifts of God, by so much the more are you by the same gifts blessed; yea, rather, you are not so otherwise than as you know from Whom you have what you have. For listen to what the Apostle said on this matter, "But we have received not the spirit of this world, but the Spirit Which is of God, that we may know what things have been given to us by God."[1] Forsooth many have many gifts of God, and by not knowing from Whom they have them, come to boast themselves with impious vanity. But there is no one blessed with the gifts of God, who is ungrateful to the Giver. Forasmuch as, also, whereas in the course of the sacred Mysteries we are bidden to "lift up our hearts," it is by His help that we are able, by Whose bidding we are admonished; and therefore it follows, that, of this so great good of the heart lifted up, we give not the glory to ourselves as of our own strength, but render thanks unto our Lord God. For of this we are straightway admonished, that "this is meet," "this is right." You remember whence these words

are taken, you recognize by what sanction, and by how great holiness they are commended within. Therefore hold and have what you have received, and return thanks to the Giver. For, although it be yours to receive and have, yet you have that, which you have received; forasmuch as to one waxing proud, and impiously glorying of that which he had, as though he had it of himself, the Truth saith by the Apostle, "But what hast thou, which thou hast not received? But, if thou hast received, why boastest thou, as if thou hadst not received?"[3]

21. These things I am compelled to admonish by reason of certain little discourses of some men, that are to be shunned and avoided, which have begun to steal through the ears unto the minds of many, being (as must be said with tears) hostile to the grace of Christ, which go to persuade that we count not as necessary for us prayer unto the Lord, that we enter not into temptation. For they so essay to defend the free will of man, as that by it alone, even without help of the grace of God, we are able to fulfill what is commanded us of God. And thus it follows, that the Lord in vain said, "Watch and pray, lest ye enter into temptation;"[4] and in vain daily in the Lord's Prayer itself we say, "Lead us not into temptation."[5] For if it is of our own power alone that we be not overcome by temptation, why do we pray that we enter not, nor be led into it? Rather let us do what is of our own free will, and most absolute power; and let us mock at the Apostle, saying, "God is faithful, Who will not suffer you to be tempted above what ye are able;"[6] and let us oppose him, and say, Why seek I of the Lord, what He hath set in my own power? But far be it, that he be so minded, who is sound minded. Wherefore let us seek that He may give, what He bids us that we have. For to this end He bids us have this, which as yet we have not, to admonish as what to seek; and that when we shall have found the power to do what He hath bidden, we may understand, of this also, whence we have received it; lest, being puffed and lifted up by the spirit of this world, we know not what things have been given unto us of God. Wherefore the free choice of the human will we by no means destroy, when the Grace of God, by which the free choice itself is helped, we deny not with ungrateful pride, but rather set forth with grateful piety. For it is ours to will: but the will itself is both admonished

---

[1] 1 Cor. ii. 12.
29

[2] "*Intus qua sanctione*," al. "*inter quas actiones*," "amongst what actions;" there are other various readings besides.
[3] 1 Cor. iv. 7.   [4] Matt. xxvi. 41.
[5] Matt. vi. 13.   [6] 1 Cor. x. 13.

that it may arise, and healed, that it may have power;[1] and enlarged, that it may receive; and filled, that it may have. For were not we to will, certainly neither should we receive the things that are given, nor should we have. For who would have continence, (among the rest of the gifts of God to speak of this rather, of which I am speaking to you,) who, I say, would have continence, unless willing? forasmuch as also no one would receive unless willing. But if you ask, Whose gift it is, that it can be by our will received and had? listen to Scripture; yea, rather, because thou knowest, recollect what thou hast read, "Whereas I knew," saith he, "that no one can be continent, unless God give it, and this itself was of wisdom, to know whose gift it was."[2] Great are these two gifts, wisdom and continence; wisdom, forsooth, whereby we are formed in the knowledge of God; but continence, whereby we are not conformed unto this world. But God bids us that we be both wise and continent, without which goods we cannot be just and perfect. But let us pray that He give what He bids, by helping and inspiring, Who hath admonished us what to will by commanding and calling. Whatsoever of this He hath given, let us pray that He preserve; but what Hé hath not given as yet, let us pray that He supply; yet let us pray and give thanks for what we have received; and for what we have not yet received, from the very fact that we are not ungrateful for what we have received, let us trust that we shall receive it. For He, Who hath given power unto the faithful who are married to contain from adulteries and fornications, Himself hath given unto holy virgins and widows to contain from all sexual intercourse; in the case of which virtue now the term inviolate chastity[3] or continence is properly used. Or is it haply that from Him indeed we have received continence, but from ourselves have wisdom? What then is it that the Apostle James saith, "But if any of you lack wisdom, let him ask of God, Who giveth unto all liberally, and upbraideth not, and it shall be given unto him."[4] But on this question, already in other little works of ours, so far as the Lord hath helped us, we have said many things; and at other times, so far as through Him we shall be able, when opportunity is given, we will speak.

22. Now it has been my wish on this account to say something on this subject, by reason of certain of our brethren most friendly and dear to us, and without willful guilt indeed entangled in this error, but yet entangled;

who think, that, when they exhort any to righteousness and piety, their exhortation will not have force, unless the whole of that, wherein they would work upon man that man should work, they set in the power of man, not helped by the grace of God, but put forth by the alone choice of the free will; as though there can be free will to perform a good work, unless set free by the gift of God! And they mark not that this very thing themselves also have by the gift of God, that with such power they exhort, as to excite the dull wills of men to enter upon a good life, to enkindle the cold, to correct such as are in error, to convert such as are turned aside, to pacify such as are opposed. For thus they are able to succeed in persuading what they would persuade to, or if they work not these things in the wills of men, what is their work? wherefore speak they? Let them leave them rather to their own choice. But if in them they work these things, what? I pray, doth man, in the will of man, work so great things by speaking, and doth God work nothing there by helping? Yea rather, with how great soever power of discourse man may prevail, as that by skill of discussion, and sweetness of speech, he in the will of man implant truth, nourish charity, by teaching remove error, by exhortation remove sloth, "Neither he who planteth is any thing, nor he who watereth, but God Who giveth the increase."[5] For in vain would the workman use all means without, unless the Creator should work secretly within. I hope therefore that this letter of mine by the worthy deed[6] of your Excellence will soon come into the hands of such also; on this account I thought that I ought to say something on this subject. Next that both you yourself, and whatsoever other widows shall read this, or hear it read, may know that you make more advance unto the love and profession of the good of continence by your own prayers than by our exhortations; forasmuch as if it be any help to you that our addresses also are supplied to you, the whole must be assigned to His grace, "in Whose Hand," as it is written, "are both we and our discourses."[7]

23. If, therefore, you had not as yet vowed unto God widowed continence, we would assuredly exhort you to vow it; but, in that you have already vowed it, we exhort you to persevere. And yet I see that I must so speak as to lead those also who had as yet thought of marriage to love it and to seize on it. Therefore let us give ear unto the Apostle, "She who is unmarried," saith he, "is

---

[1] Or "be sound."　　　　[2] Wisd. viii. 21.
[3] "Integritas."　　　　[4] James i. 5.

[5] 1 Cor. iii. 7.　　　　[6] Merito.　　　　[7] Wisdom vii. 16.

careful about the things of the Lord, to be holy both in body and spirit; but she who is married is careful about the things of the world, how to please her husband."[1] He saith not, is careful about the things of the world, so as not to be holy; but certainly that that marriage holiness[2] is less, in regard of that portion of cares, which hath thought of the pleasure of the world. Whatever, therefore, of earnest purpose of mind would be expended also on these things whereby she would have to please a husband, the unmarried Christian woman ought in a certain way to gather and bring together unto that earnest purpose whereby she is to please the Lord. And consider, Whom she pleases, who pleases the Lord; and assuredly she is by so much the more blessed by how much the more she pleases Him; but by how much the more her thoughts are of the things of the world, by so much the less does she please Him. Therefore do ye with all earnest purpose please Him, Who is "fair of form above the sons of men."[3] For that ye please Him, it is by His grace which is "shed abroad on His lips." Please ye Him in that portion of thought also, which would be occupied by the world, in order to please a husband. Please ye Him, Who displeased the world, in order that such as please Him might be set free from the world. For This One, fair of form above the sons of men, men saw on the Cross of the Passion; "and He had not form or beauty, but His face cast down, and His posture unseemly."[4] Yet from this unseemliness of your Redeemer flowed the price of your beauty, but of a beauty within, for "all the beauty of the King's daughter is within."[5] By this beauty please ye Him, this beauty order ye with studious care and anxious thought. He loves not dyes of deceits; the Truth delighteth in things that are true, and He, if you recognize what you have read, is called the Truth. "I am," saith He, "the Way, and the Truth, and the Life."[6] Run ye to Him through Him, please ye Him of Him; live ye with Him, in Him, of Him. With true affections and holiest chastity love ye to be loved by such a Husband.

24. Let the inner ear of the virgin also, thy holy child, hear these things. I shall see[7] how far she goes before you in the Kingdom of That King: it is another question. Yet ye have found, mother and daughter, Him, Whom by beauty of chastity ye ought to please together, having despised, she all,

you second, marriage. Certainly if there were husbands whom ye had to please, by this time, perhaps, you would feel ashamed to adorn yourself together with your daughter; now let it not shame you, to set yourselves to do what may adorn you both together; because it is not matter of blame, but of glory, that ye be loved both together by That One. But white and red, feigned and laid on with paints, ye would not use, even if ye had husbands; not thinking that they were fit persons for you to deceive, or yourselves such as ought to deceive; now therefore That King, Who had longed for the beauty of His Only Spouse, of Whom ye are members, do ye with all truth together please, together cleave unto; she with virginal chastity, you with widowed continence, both with spiritual beauty. In which beauty also her grandmother, and your mother-in-law, who by this time surely hath grown old, is beautiful together with you. Forsooth whilst charity carries the vigor of this beauty into things that are before, length of years causeth not in it a wrinkle. You have with you a holy aged woman, both in your house and in Christ, whom to consult concerning perseverance; how you are to fight with this or that temptation, what you are to do, that it may be the more easily overcome; what safeguard you are to take, that it may not easily again lay wait; and if there be any thing of this sort, she teaches you, who is now by time fixed, by love a well-wisher, by natural affection full of cares, by age secure. Do you specially, do you in such things consult her, who hath made trial of what you have made trial of. For your child sings that song,[8] which in the Apocalypse none save virgins can sing. But for both of you she prays more carefully than for herself, but she is more full of care for her granddaughter, for whom there remains a longer space of years to overcome temptations; but you she sees nearer to her own age, and mother of a daughter of such an age, as that, had you seen her married, (which now is not lawful, and far be it from her,) I think you would have blushed to bear children together with her. How much then is it that now remains to you of a dangerous age, who are on this account not called a grandmother, in order that together with your daughter you may be fruitful in offspring of holy thoughts and works? Therefore not without reason is the grandmother more full of care for her, for whom you also the mother; because both what she hath vowed is greater, and the whole of what she hath just now begun remains to

[1] 1 Cor. vii. 34.
[2] Most mss. "but certainly that divine holiness."
[3] Ps. xlv. 2.   [4] Is. liii. 2. [See R.V.]
Ps. lxv. 13. [See R.V.]   [6] John xiv. 6.   [7] One ms "to see."   [8] Rev. xiv. 3, 4. [See R.V.]

her. May the Lord hear her prayers, that ye may holily follow her good deserts, who in youth gave birth to the flesh of your husband,[1] in old age travaileth with the heart of your daughter. Therefore do ye all, alike and with one accord, by conduct please, by prayers press upon, That One Husband of One Wife, in Whose Body by One Spirit ye are living.

25. The past day returns not hereafter, and after yesterday proceeds to-day, and after to-day will proceed to-morrow; and, lo, all times and the things of time pass away, that there may come the promise that shall abide; and "whoso shall have persevered even unto the end, this one shall be saved."[2] If the world is now perishing, the married woman, for whom beareth she? Or in heart about to bear, and in flesh not about to bear, why doth she marry? But if the world is still about to last, why is not He more loved, by Whom the world was made? If already enticements of this life are failing, there is not any thing for a Christian soul with desire to seek after; but if they shall yet remain, there is what with holiness he may despise. For the one of these two there is no hope of lust, in the other greater glory of charity. How many or how long are the very years, in which the flower of carnal age seems to flourish? Some females having thoughts of marriage, and with ardor wishing it, whilst they are being despised or put off, on a sudden have grown old, so as that now they would feel shame, rather than desire, to marry. But many having married, their husbands having set out into distant countries very soon after their union, have grown aged expecting their return, and, as though soon left widows, at times have not even attained so as at least as old women to receive their old men on their return. If therefore, when betrothed bridegrooms despised or delayed, or when husbands were abroad, carnal desire could be restrained from commission of fornication or adultery, why cannot it be restrained from commission of sacrilege? If it hath been repressed, when being deferred it was glowing, why is it not put down, when having been cut off it had grown cold? For they in greater measure endure glowing of desire, who despair not of the pleasure of the same desire. But whoso of unmarried persons vow chastity to God, withdraw that very hope, which is the fuel of love. Hence with more ease is desire bridled, which is kindled by no expectation; and yet, unless against this prayer be made, in order to overcome it, itself as unlawful is the more ardently wished for.

26. Therefore let spiritual delights succeed to the place of carnal delights in holy chastity; reading, prayer, psalm, good thought, frequency in good works, hope of the world to come, and a heart upward; and for all these giving of thanks unto the Father of lights, from Whom, without any doubt, every good gift, and every perfect gift, as Scripture bears witness, cometh down.[3] For when, in stead of the delights of married women, which they have in the flesh of their husbands, the use of other carnal delights is taken, as it were to solace them, why should I speak of the evils which follow, when the Apostle hath said in short, that the widow, who lives in delights, living is dead.[4] But far be it from you, that ye be taken with lust of riches instead of lust of marriage, or that in your hearts money succeed to the place of love of a husband. For looking into men's conversation, we have often found by experience, that in certain persons, when wantonness hath been restrained, avarice hath increased. For, as, in the senses themselves of the body, they who see not hear more keenly, and discern many things by touch, nor have such as have the use of their eyes so great life in their touch; and in this instance it is understood that, when the exertion of the power of attention[5] hath been restrained in one approach, that is, of the eyes, it puts itself forth into other senses, more ready with keenness to distinguish, as though it essayed to supply from the one what was denied in the other; thus also often carnal lust, being restrained from pleasure of sensual intercourse, with greater strength reaches itself forth to desire money, and when turned away from the one, turns itself with more glow of passion to the other. But in you let the love of riches grow cold together with the love of marriage, and let a pious use of what property you possess be directed to spiritual delights, that your liberality wax warm rather in helping such as are in want than in enriching covetous persons. Forsooth into the heavenly treasury are sent not gifts to the covetous, but alms to the needy, which above measure help the prayers of widows. Fastings, also, and watchings, so far as they disturb not health, if they be spent in praying, singing psalms, reading, and meditating in the Law of God, even the very things which seem laborious are turned into spiritual delights. For no way burdensome are the labors of such as love, but even of themselves delight, as of such as hunt, fowl, fish, gather grapes, traffic, delight themselves with some game. It matters therefore what

---

[1] Olibrius, see S. Jerome to Demetr. *Ben. ed.*   [2] Matt. x. 22.   [3] James i. 17.   [4] 1 Tim. v. 6.   [5] *Intentione.*

be loved. For, in the case of what is loved, either there is no labor, or the labor also is loved. And consider how it should be matter for shame and grief, if there be pleasure in labor, to take a wild beast, to fill cask and purse,[1] to cast a ball, and there be no pleasure in labors to win God !

27. Indeed in all spiritual delights, which unmarried women enjoy, their holy conversation ought also to be with caution; lest haply, though their life be not evil through naughtiness, their report be evil through negligence. Nor are they to be listened to, whether they be holy men or women, when (upon occasion of their neglect in some matter being blamed, through which it comes to pass that they fall into evil suspicion, from which they know that their life is far removed) they say that it is enough for them their conscience before God, despising what men think of them, not only imprudently[2] but also cruelly; when they slay the souls of others; whether of such as blaspheme the way of God, who following their suspicion are displeased at what is the chaste life of the Saints, as though it were shameful, or of such also as make excuse, and imitate, not what they see, but what they think. Wherefore whosoever guards his life from charges of shameful and evil deeds, does good to himself; but whosoever guards his character too, is merciful also towards others. For unto ourselves our own life is necessary, unto others our character; and certainly even what we mercifully minister unto others, for their health, abounds also to our own profit. Whence not in vain the Apostle, "We provide good things," saith he, "not only before God, but also before men;"[3] also he saith, "Please ye all men through all things; even as I also please all men through all things, not seeking what is of profit unto myself, but what unto many, that they may be saved."[4] Also in a certain exhortation he says, "For the rest, brethren, whatsoever things are true, whatsoever things are holy, whatsoever things are just, whatsoever things are pure, whatsoever things are most dear, whatsoever things are of good report; if any virtue, if any praise, these things think on, which ye have both learned, and received, and heard, and seen in me."[5] You see how among many things, unto which by exhortation he admonished them, he neglected not to set, "whatsoever things are of good report;" and in two words included all things, where he saith, "if any virtue, if any praise." For unto virtue pertain the good things of which

He made mention above; but good report unto praise. I think that the Apostle took not the praise of men for any great thing, saying in another place, "But to me it is the least thing, that I be judged of you, or of day of man;"[6] and in another place, "If I were pleasing men, I should not be a servant of Christ;"[7] and again, "For our glory is this, the testimony of our conscience."[8] But of these two, that is, of a good life, and a good report, or as is said more shortly, of virtue and praise, the one for his own sake he most wisely kept, the other for the sake of others he most mercifully provided. But, forasmuch as human caution, how great soever, cannot on every side avoid most malevolent suspicions, when for our good report we shall have done whatever we rightly can, if any, either by falsely pretending evil things of us, or from believing evil of us, endeavor to stain our fair fame, let there be present the solace of conscience, and clearly also the joy, in that our reward is great in Heaven, even when men say many evil things of us,[9] and we yet live godly and righteously. For that reward is as the pay of such as serve as soldiers, through the arms of righteousness, not only on the right hand, but on the left also; that is to say, through glory and mean estate, through ill report and good report.[10]

28. Go on therefore in your course, and run with perseverance, in order that ye may obtain; and by pattern of life, and discourse of exhortation, carry away with you into this same your course, whomsoever ye shall have had power. Let there not bend you from this earnest purpose, whereby ye excite many to follow, the complaint of vain persons, who say, How shall the human race subsist, if all shall have been continent? As though it were for any other reason that this world is delayed, save that the predestined number of the Saints be fulfilled, and were this the sooner fulfilled, assuredly the end of the world would not be put off. Nor let it stay you from your earnest purpose of persuading others to the same good ye have, if it be said to you, Whereas marriage also is good, how shall there be all goods in the Body of Christ, both the greater, forsooth, and the lesser, if all through praise and love of continence imitate? In the first place, because with the endeavor that all be continent, there will still be but few, for "not all receive this word." But forasmuch as it is written, "Whoso can receive, let him receive;"[11] then do they receive who can, when silence is not kept even toward those who cannot. Next, neither ought we

---

[1] *Cupa et sacculus.*
[2] al. *"impudenter,"* "with lack of modesty."
[3] 2 Cor. viii. 21. [See R.V.]   [4] 1 Cor. x. 33.   [5] Phil. iv. 8, 9.

[6] 1 Cor. iv. 3.   [7] Gal. i. 10.   [8] 2 Cor. i. 12.
[9] Matt. v. 11, 12.   [10] 2 Cor. vi. 7, 8.   [11] Matt. xix. 11, 12.

to fear lest haply all receive it, and some one of lesser goods, that is, married life, be wanting in the body of Christ. For if all shall have heard, and all shall have received, we ought to understand that this very thing was predestinated, that married goods already suffice in the number of those members which so many have passed out of this life. For neither now, if all shall have been continent, will they give the honor of the continent to those who have already borne into the garners of the Lord the fruit thirty-fold, if that be understood of married good. Therefore all these goods will have there their place, although from this time no woman wish to be married, no man wish to marry a wife. Therefore without anxiety urge on whom ye can, to become what ye are; and pray with watchfulness and fervor, that by the help of the Right Hand of the Most High, and by the abundance of the most merciful grace of the Lord, ye may both persevere in that which ye are, and may make advances unto that which ye shall be.

29. Next I entreat you, by Him, from Whom ye have both received this gift, and hope for the rewards of this gift, that ye be mindful to set me also in your prayers with all your household Church. Forsooth it hath come to pass in most proper order, that I should write unto your Mother now aged a letter[1] concerning prayer; unto her, forsooth, it chiefly pertains by praying to contend on your behalf, who is less full of care for herself than for you; and that for you rather than for her I should compose this little work concerning widowed continence; because unto you it remaineth to overcome, what her age hath already overcome. But the holy virgin your child, if she desire aught concerning her profession from our labors, she hath a large book on Holy Virginity to read. Concerning the reading of which I had also admonished you, forasmuch as it contains many things necessary unto either chastity, that is, virginal and widowed, which things on this account I have here partly touched on lightly, partly altogether passed over, because I there discussed them more fully.

May you persevere in the grace of Christ.

---

[1] Ep. 150, *ad Probam.* Vol. I. p. 503.

ST. AUGUSTIN:

ON LYING

[DE MENDACIO.]

TRANSLATED BY

REV. H. BROWNE, M.A.,

OF CORPUS CHRISTI COLLEGE, CAMBRIDGE, LATE PRINCIPAL OF THE DIOCESAN
COLLEGE, CHICHESTER.

ON LYING.

[DE MENDACIO.]

This book appears from its place in the *Retractations* to have been written about A. D. 395, as it is the last work named in the first book, which contains those which he wrote before he was Bishop. Some editions represent it as addressed to Consentius, but not the MSS. The latter are probably right, as his other work on the subject was written in answer to the inquiries of Consentius on the case of the Priscillianists many years later.—*Bened. Ed.*

Retractations, Book I. last Chapter.

" I have also written a Book on Lying, which though it takes some pains to understand, contains much that is useful for the exercise of the mind, and more that is profitable to morals, in inculcating the love of speaking the truth. This also I was minded to remove from my works, because it seemed to me obscure, and intricate, and altogether troublesome ; for which reason I had not sent it abroad. And when I had afterwards written another book, under this title, *Against Lying*, much more had I determined and ordered that the former should cease to exist ; which however was not done. Therefore in this retractation of my works, as I have found this still in being, I have ordered that it should remain ; chiefly because therein are to be found some necessary things which in the other are not. Why the other has for its title, *Against Lying*, but this, *Of Lying*, the reason is this, that throughout the one is an open assault upon lying, whereas great part of this is taken up with the discussion of the question for and against. Both, however, are directed to the same object. This book begins thus : " *Magna quæstio est de Mendacio.*"

1. THERE is a great question about Lying, which often arises in the midst of our every day business, and gives us much trouble, that we may not either rashly call that a lie which is not such, or decide that it is sometimes right to tell a lie, that is, a kind of honest, well-meant, charitable lie. This question we will painfully discuss by seeking with them that seek : whether to any good purpose, we need not take upon ourselves to affirm, for the attentive reader will sufficiently gather from the course of the discussion. It is, indeed, very full of dark corners, and hath many cavern-like windings, whereby it oft eludes the eagerness of the seeker; so that at one moment what was found seems to slip out of one's hands, and anon comes to light again, and then is once more lost to sight. At last, however, the chase will bear down more surely, and will overtake our sentence. Wherein if there is any error, yet as Truth is that which setteth free from all error, and

Falsehood that which entangleth in all error, one never errs more safely, methinks, than when one errs by too much loving the truth, and too much rejecting of falsehood. For they who find great fault say it is too much, whereas peradventure Truth would say after all, it is not yet enough. But whoso readest, thou wilt do well to find no fault until thou have read the whole; so wilt thou have less fault to find. Eloquence thou must not look for: we have been intent upon things, and upon dispatch in putting out of hand a matter which nearly concerns our every day life, and therefore have had small pains, or almost none, to bestow upon words.

2. Setting aside, therefore, jokes, which have never been accounted lies, seeing they bear with them in the tone of voice, and in the very mood of the joker a most evident indication that he means no deceit, although the thing he utters be not true: touching which kind of discourse, whether it be meet to be used by perfect minds, is another question which we have not at this time taken in hand to clear; but setting jokes apart, the first point to be attended to, is, that a person should not be thought to lie, who lieth not.

3. For which purpose we must see what a lie is. For not every one who says a false thing lies, if he believes or opines that to be true which he says. Now between believing and opining there is this difference, that sometimes he who believes feels that he does not know that which he believes, (although he may know himself to be ignorant of a thing, and yet have no doubt at all concerning it, if he most firmly believes it:) whereas he who opines, thinks he knows that which he does not know. Now whoever utters that which he holds in his mind either as belief or as opinion, even though it be false, he lies not. For this he owes to the faith of his utterance, that he thereby produce that which he holds in his mind, and has in that way in which he produces it. Not that he is without fault, although he lie not, if either he believes what he ought not to believe, or thinks he knows what he knows not, even though it should be true: for he accounts an unknown thing for a known. Wherefore, that man lies, who has one thing in his mind and utters another in words, or by signs of whatever kind. Whence also the heart of him who lies is said to be double; that is, there is a double thought: the one, of that thing which he either knows or thinks to be true and does not produce; the other, of that thing which he produces instead thereof, knowing or thinking it to be false. Whence it comes to pass, that he may say a false thing and yet not lie, if he thinks it to be so as he says although it be not so; and, that he may say a true thing, and yet lie, if he thinks it to be false and utters it for true, although in reality it be so as he utters it. For from the sense of his own mind, not from the verity or falsity of the things themselves, is he to be judged to lie or not to lie. Therefore he who utters a false thing for a true, which however he opines to be true, may be called erring and rash: but he is not rightly said to lie; because he has not a double heart when he utters it, neither does he wish to deceive, but is deceived. But the fault of him who lies, is, the desire of deceiving in the uttering of his mind; whether he do deceive, in that he is believed when uttering the false thing; or whether he do not deceive, either in that he is not believed, or in that he utters a true thing with will to deceive, which he does not think to be true: wherein being believed, he does not deceive though it was his will to deceive: except that he deceives in so far as he is thought to know or think as he utters.

4. But it may be a very nice question whether in the absence of all will to deceive, lying is altogether absent. Thus, put the case that a person shall speak a false thing, which he esteems to be false, on the ground that he thinks he is not believed, to the intent, that in that way falsifying his faith he may deter the person to whom he speaks, which person he perceives does not choose to believe him. For here is a person who tells a lie with studied purpose of not deceiving, if to tell a lie is to utter any thing otherwise than you know or think it to be. But if it be no lie, unless when something is uttered with wish to deceive, that person lies not, who says a false thing, knowing or thinking it to be false, but says it on purpose that the person to whom he speaks by not believing him may not be deceived, because the speaker either knows or thinks the other will not believe him. Whence if it appear to be possible that a person should say a false thing on purpose that he to whom it is said may not be deceived, on the other hand there is this opposite case, the case of a person saying the truth on purpose that he may deceive. For if a man determines to say a true thing because he perceives he is not believed, that man speaks truth on purpose that he may deceive: for he knows or thinks that what is said may be accounted false, just because it is spoken by him. Wherefore in saying a true thing on purpose that it may be thought false, he says a true thing on purpose to deceive. So that it may be inquired, which rather lies: he who says a false thing that he

may not deceive, or he who says a true thing that he may deceive? the one knowing or thinking that he says a false thing, and the other knowing or thinking that he says a true thing? For we have already said that the person who does not know the thing to be false which he utters, does not lie if he thinks it to be true; and that that person rather lies who utters even a true thing when he thinks it false: because it is by the sense of their mind that they are to be judged. Concerning these persons therefore, whom we have set forth, there is no small question. The one, who knows or thinks he says a false thing, and says it on purpose that he may not deceive: as, if he knows a certain road to be beset by robbers, and fearing lest some person for whose safety he is anxious should go by that road, which person he knows does not trust him, should tell him that that road has no robbers, on purpose that he may not go by it, as he will think there are robbers there precisely because the other has told him there are none, and he is resolved not to believe him, accounting him a liar. The other, who knowing or thinking that to be true which he says, says it on purpose that he may deceive: for instance, if he tells a person who does not believe him, that there are robbers in that road where he really knows them to be, that he to whom he tells it may the rather go by that road and so fall among robbers, because he thinks that to be false which the other told him. Which then of these lies? the one who has chosen to say a false thing that he may not deceive? or the other who has chosen to say a true thing that he may deceive? that one, who in saying a false thing aimed that he to whom he spake should follow the truth? or this one, who in saying a true thing aimed that he to whom he spake should follow a falsehood? Or haply have both lied? the one, because he wished to say a false thing: the other, because he wished to deceive? Or rather, has neither lied? not the one, because he had the will not to deceive: not the other, because he had the will to speak the truth? For the question is not now which of them sinned, but which of them lied: as indeed it is presently seen that the latter sinned, because by speaking a truth he brought it about that a person should fall among robbers, and that the former has not sinned, or éven has done good, because by speaking a false thing he has been the means of a person's avoiding destruction. But then these instances may be turned the other way, so that the one should be supposed to wish some

more grievous suffering to the person whom he wishes not to be deceived; for there are many cases of persons who through knowing certain things to be true, have brought destruction upon themselves, if the things were such as ought to have continued unknown to them: and the other may be supposed to wish some convenience to result to the person whom he wishes to be deceived; for there have been instances of persons who would have destroyed themselves had they known some evil that had really befallen those who were dear to them, and through deeming it false have spared themselves: and so to be deceived has been a benefit to them, as to others it has been a hurt to know the truth. The question therefore is not with what purpose of doing a kindness or a hurt, either the one said a false thing that he might not deceive, or the other a true thing that he might deceive: but, setting apart the convenience or inconvenience of the persons spoken to, in so far as relates to the very truth and falsehood, the question is, whether both of them or neither has lied. For if a lie is an utterance with will of uttering a false thing, that man has rather lied who willed to say a false thing, and said what he willed, albeit he said it of set purpose not to deceive. But if a lie is any utterance whatever with will to deceive, then not the former has lied, but the latter, who even in speaking truth willed to deceive. And if a lie is an utterance with will of any falsity, both have lied; because both the former willed his utterance to be false, and the latter willed a false thing to be believed concerning his utterance which was true. Further, if a lie is an utterance of a person wishing to utter a false thing that he may deceive, neither has lied; because both the former in saying a false thing had the will to make a true thing believed, and the latter to say a true thing in order that he might make a false thing believed. We shall be clear then of all rashness and all lying, if, what we know to be true or right to be believed, we utter when need is, and wish to make that thing believed which we utter. If, however, either thinking that to be true which is false, or accounting as known that which is to us unknown, or believing what we ought not to believe, or uttering it when need is not, we yet have no other aim than to make that believed which we utter; we do not stand clear indeed of the error of temerity, but we do stand clear of all lying. For there is no need to be afraid of any of those definitions, when the mind has a good conscience, that it utters that which to be true it either knows, or opines, or believes, and that it has no wish to make any thing believed but that which it utters.

5. But whether a lie be at some times useful, is a much greater and more concerning question. Whether, as above, it be a lie, when a person has no will to deceive, or even makes it his business that the person to whom he says a thing shall not be deceived, although he did wish the thing itself which he uttered to be false, but this on purpose that he might cause a truth to be believed; whether, again, it be a lie when a person willingly utters even a truth for the purpose of deceiving; this may be doubted. But none doubts that it is a lie when a person willingly utters a falsehood for the purpose of deceiving: wherefore a false utterance put forth with will to deceive is manifestly a lie. But whether this alone be a lie, is another question. Meanwhile, taking this kind of lie, in which all agree, let us inquire, whether it be sometimes useful to utter a falsehood with will to deceive. They who think it is, advance testimonies to their opinion, by alleging the case of Sarah,[1] who, when she had laughed, denied to the Angels that she laughed: of Jacob questioned by his father, and answering that he was the elder son Esau:[2] likewise that of the Egyptian midwives, who to save the Hebrew infants from being slain at their birth, told a lie, and that with God's approbation and reward:[3] and many such like instances they pick out, of lies told by persons whom you would not dare to blame, and so must own that it may sometimes be not only not blameworthy, but even praiseworthy to tell a lie. They add also a case with which to urge not only those who are devoted to the Divine Books, but all men and common sense, saying, Suppose a man should take refuge with thee, who by thy lie might be saved from death, wouldest thou not tell it? If a sick man should ask a question which it is not expedient that he should know, and might be more grievously afflicted even by thy returning him no answer, wilt thou venture either to tell the truth to the destruction of the man's life, or rather to hold thy peace, than by a virtuous and merciful lie to be serviceable to his weak health? By these and such like arguments they think they most plentifully prove, that if occasion of doing good require, we may sometimes tell a lie.

6. On the other hand, those who say that we must never lie, plead much more strongly, using first the Divine authority, because in the very Decalogue it is written " Thou shalt not bear false witness; "[4] under which general term it comprises all lying: for whoso utters any thing bears witness to his own mind. But lest any should contend that not every lie is to be called false witness, what will he say to that which is written, " The mouth that lieth slayeth the soul: "[5] and lest any should suppose that this may be understood with the exception of some liars, let him read in another place, " Thou wilt destroy all that speak leasing. "[6] Whence with His own lips the Lord saith, " Let your communication be yea, yea; nay, nay; for whatsoever is more than these cometh of evil."[7] Hence the Apostle also in giving precept for the putting off of the old man, under which name all sins are understood, says straightway, " Wherefore putting away lying, speak ye truth."[8]

7. Neither do they confess that they are awed by those citations from the Old Testament which are alleged as examples of lies: for there, every incident may possibly be taken figuratively, although it really did take place: and when a thing is either done or said figuratively, it is no lie. For every utterance is to be referred to that which it utters. But when any thing is either done or said figuratively, it utters that which it signifies to those for whose understanding it was put forth. Whence we may believe in regard of those persons of the prophetical times who are set forth as authoritative, that in all that is written of them they acted and spoke prophetically; and no less, that there is a prophetical meaning in all those incidents of their lives which by the same prophetic Spirit have been accounted worthy of being recorded in writing. As to the midwives, indeed, they cannot say that these women did through the prophetic Spirit, with purpose of signifying a future truth, tell Pharaoh one thing instead of another, (albeit that Spirit did signify something, without their knowing what was doing in their persons:) but, they say that these women were according to their degree approved and rewarded of God. For if a person who is used to tell lies for harm's sake comes to tell them for the sake of doing good, that person has made great progress. But it is one thing that is set forth as laudable in itself, another that in comparison with a worse is preferred. It is one sort of gratulation that we express when a man is in sound health, another when a sick man is getting better. In the Scripture, even Sodom is said to be

[1] Gen. xviii. 15.   [2] Gen. xxvii. 19.   [3] Exod. i. 19, 20.
[4] Exod. xx. 16.
[5] Wisdom i. 11. *Os quod mentitur.* "The mouth that belieth," E. V., στόμα καταψευδόμενον.
[6] Psalm v. 6.   [7] Matt. v. 37. [See R.V.]   [8] Eph. iv. 25.

justified in comparison with the crimes of the people Israel. And to this rule they apply all the instances of lying which are produced from the Old Books, and are found not reprehended, or cannot be reprehended: either they are approved on the score of a progress towards improvement and hope of better things, or in virtue of some hidden signification they are not altogether lies.

8. For this reason, from the books of the New Testament, except the figurative presignifications used by our Lord, if thou consider the life and manners of the Saints, their actions and sayings, nothing of the kind can be produced which should provoke to imitation of lying. For the simulation of Peter and Barnabas is not only recorded, but also reproved and corrected.[1] For it was not, as some suppose,[2] out of the same simulation that even Paul the Apostle either circumcised Timothy, or himself celebrated certain ceremonies[3] according to the Jewish rite; but he did so, out of that liberty of his mind whereby he preached that neither are the Gentiles the better for circumcision, nor the Jews the worse. Wherefore he judged that neither the former should be tied to the custom of the Jews, nor the Jews deterred from the custom of their fathers. Whence are those words of his: "Is any man called being circumcised? let him not become uncircumcised. Is any called in uncircumcision? let him not be circumcised. Circumcision is nothing, and uncircumcision is nothing, but the keeping of the commandments of God. Let every man abide in the same calling wherein he was called."[4] How can a man become uncircumcised after circumcision? but let him not do so, saith he: let him not so live as if he had become uncircumcised, that is, as if he had covered again with flesh the part that was bared, and ceased to be a Jew; as in another place he saith, "Thy circumcision is become uncircumcision."[5] And this the Apostle said, not as though he would compel either those to remain in uncircumcision, or the Jews in the custom of their fathers: but that neither these nor those should be forced to the other custom; and, each should have power of abiding in his own custom, not necessity of so doing. For neither if the Jew should wish, where it would disturb no man, to recede from Jewish observances, would he be prohibited by the Apostle, since the object of his counselling to abide therein was that Jews might not by being troubled about superfluous things be hindered from coming to those things which are necessary to salvation. Neither would it be prohibited by him, if any of the Gentiles should wish to be circumcised for the purpose of showing that he does not detest the same as noxious, but holds it indifferently, as a seal,[6] the usefulness of which had already passed away with time; for it did not follow that, if there were now no salvation to be had from it, there was destruction to be dreaded therefrom. And for this reason, Timothy, having been called in uncircumcision, yet because his mother was a Jewess and he was bound, in order to gain his kindred, to show them that he had not learnt in the Christian discipline to abominate the sacraments of the old Law, was circumcised by the Apostle;[7] that in this way they might prove to the Jews, that the reason why the Gentiles do not receive them, is not that they are evil and were perniciously observed by the Fathers, but because they are no longer necessary to salvation after the advent of that so great Sacrament, which through so long times the whole of that ancient Scripture in its prophetical prefigurations did travail in birth withal. For he would circumcise Titus also, when the Jews urged this,[8] but that false brethren, privily brought in, wished it to be done to the intent they might have it to disseminate concerning Paul himself as a token that he had given place to the truth of their preaching, who said that the hope of Gospel salvation is in circumcision of the flesh and observances of that kind, and that without these Christ profiteth no man: whereas on the contrary Christ would nothing profit them, who should be circumcised because they thought that in it was salvation; whence that saying, "Behold, I Paul say unto you, that if ye be circumcised, Christ shall profit you nothing.[9] Out of this liberty, therefore, did Paul keep the observances of his fathers, but with this one precaution and express declaration, that people should not suppose that without these was no Christian salvation. Peter, however, by his making as though salvation consisted in Judaism, was compelling the Gentiles to judaize; as is shown by Paul's words, where he says, "Why compellest thou the Gentiles to live as do the Jews?"[10] For they would be under no compulsion unless they saw that he observed them in such manner as if beside them could be no salvation. Peter's simulation therefore is not to be compared to Paul's liberty. And while we ought to love Peter for that he willingly received correction, we must not bolster up lying even by the authority of Paul, who

---

[1] Gal. ii. 12-21.
[2] S. Jerome Ep. inter Augustinianas, 75, n. 9-11.
[3] *Sacramenta*.   [4] 1 Cor. vii. 18-20.   [5] Rom. ii. 25.

[6] *Signaculum*.   [7] Acts xvi. 1-3.   [8] Gal. ii. 3, 4.
[9] Gal. v. 2.   [10] Gal. ii. 14.

both recalled Peter to the right path in the presence of them all, lest the Gentiles through him should be compelled to judaize; and bare witness to his own preaching, that whereas he was accounted hostile to the traditions of the fathers in that he would not impose them on the Gentiles, he did not despise to celebrate them himself according to the custom of his fathers, and therein sufficiently showed that this has remained in them at the coming of Christ; that neither to the Jews they are pernicious, nor to the Gentiles necessary, nor henceforth to any of mankind means of salvation.[1]

9. But if no authority for lying can be alleged, neither from the ancient Books, be it because that is not a lie which is received to have been done or said in a figurative sense, or be it because good men are not challenged to imitate that which in bad men, beginning to amend, is praised in comparison with the worse; nor yet from the books of the New Testament, because Peter's correction rather than his simulation, even as his tears rather than his denial, is what we must imitate: then, as to those examples which are fetched from common life, they assert much more confidently that there is no trust to be given to these. For first they teach, that a lie is iniquity, by many proofs of holy writ, especially by that which is written, "Thou, Lord, hatest all workers of iniquity, thou shalt destroy them that speak leasing."[2] For either as the Scripture is wont, in the following clause it expounds the former; so that, as iniquity is a term of a wider meaning, leasing is named as the particular sort of iniquity intended: or if they think there is any difference between the two, leasing is by so much worse than iniquity as "thou wilt destroy" is heavier than "thou hatest." For it may be that God hates a person to that degree more mildly, as not to destroy him, but whom He destroys He hates the more exceedingly, by how much He punisheth more severely. Now He hateth all who work iniquity: but all who speak leasing He also destroyeth. Which thing being fixed, who of them which assert this will be moved by those examples, when it is said, suppose a man should seek shelter with thee who by thy lie may be saved from death? For that death which men are foolishly afraid of, who are not afraid to sin, kills not the soul but the body, as the Lord teacheth in the Gospel; whence He charges us not to fear that death:[3] but the mouth which lies kills not the body but the soul. For in these words it is most plainly written, "The mouth that lieth slayeth the soul."[4] How then can it be said without the greatest perverseness, that to the end one man may have life of the body, it is another man's duty to incur death of the soul? The love of our neighbor hath its bounds in each man's love of himself. "Thou shall love," saith He, "thy neighbor as thyself."[5] How can a man be said to love as himself that man, for whom that he may secure a temporal life, himself loseth life eternal? Since if for his temporal life he lose but his own temporal life, that is not to love as himself, but more than himself: which exceeds the rule of sound doctrine. Much less then is he by telling a lie to lose his own eternal for another's temporal life. His own temporal life, of course, for his neighbor's eternal life a Christian man will not hesitate to lose: for this example has gone before, that the Lord died for us. To this point He also saith, "This is my commandment, that ye love one another as I have loved you. Greater love hath no man than this, that a man lay down his life for his friends."[6] For none is so foolish as to say that the Lord did other than consult for the eternal salvation of men, whether in doing what He hath charged us to do, or in charging us to do what Himself hath done. Since then by lying eternal life is lost, never for any man's temporal life must a lie be told. And as to those who take it ill and are indignant that one should refuse to tell a lie, and thereby slay his own soul in order that another may grow old in the flesh; what if by our committing theft, what if by committing adultery, a person might be delivered from death: are we therefore to steal, to commit whoredom? They cannot prevail with themselves in a case of this kind: namely, if a person should bring a halter and demand that one should yield to his carnal lust, declaring that he will hang himself unless his request be granted: they cannot prevail with themselves to comply for the sake of, as they say, saving a life. If this is absurd and wicked, why should a man corrupt his own soul with a lie in order that another may live in the body, when, if he were to give his body to be corrupted with such an object, he would in the judgment of all men be held guilty of nefarious turpitude? Therefore the only point to be attended to in this question is, whether a lie be iniquity. And since this is asserted by the texts above rehearsed, we must see that to ask, whether a man ought to tell a lie for the safety of another, is just the same as asking whether for another's safety a

---

[1] Salutares.　[2] Ps. v. 5, 6. [See R.V.]　[3] Matt. x. 28.

[4] Wisd. i. 11; "believeth," E.V.　[5] Levit. xix. 18; Matt. xxii. 39.
[6] John xv. 12, 13.

man ought to commit iniquity. But if the salvation of the soul rejects this, seeing it cannot be secured but by equity, and would have us prefer it not only to another's, but even to our own temporal safety: what remains, say they, that should make us doubt that a lie ought not to be told under any circumstances whatsoever? For it cannot be said that there is aught among temporal goods greater or dearer than the safety and life of the body. Wherefore if not even that is to be preferred to truth, what can be put in our way for the sake of which they who think it is sometimes right to lie, can urge that a lie ought to be told?

10. As concerning purity of body; here indeed a very honorable regard seems to come in the way, and to demand a lie in its behalf; to wit, that if the assault of the ravisher may be escaped by means of a lie, it is indubitably right to tell it: but to this it may easily be answered, that there is no purity of body except as it depends on integrity of mind; this being broken, the other must needs fall, even though it seem intact; and for this reason it is not to be reckoned among temporal things, as a thing that might be taken away from people against their will. By no means therefore must the mind corrupt itself by a lie for the sake of its body, which it knows remaineth incorrupt if from the mind itself incorruptness depart not. For that which by violence, with no lust foregoing, the body suffereth, is rather to be called deforcement than corruption. Or if all deforcement is corruption, then not every corruption hath turpitude, but only that which lust hath procured, or to which lust hath consented. Now by how much the mind is more excellent than the body, so much the more heinous is the wickedness if that be corrupted. There, then, purity can be preserved, because there none but a voluntary corruption can have place. For assuredly if the ravisher assault the body, and there is no escaping him either by contrary force, or by any contrivance or lie, we must needs allow that purity cannot be violated by another's lust. Wherefore, since no man doubts that the mind is better than the body, to integrity of body we ought to prefer integrity of mind, which can be preserved for ever. Now who will say that the mind of him who tells a lie hath its integrity? Indeed lust itself is rightly defined, An appetite of the mind by which to eternal goods any temporal goods whatever are preferred. Therefore no man can prove that it is at any time right to tell a lie, unless he be able to show that any eternal good can be obtained by a lie. But since

each man departs from eternity just in so far as he departs from truth, it is most absurd to say, that by departing therefrom it is possible for any man to attain to any good. Else if there be any eternal good which truth compriseth not, it will not be a true good, therefore neither will it be good, because it will be false. But as the mind to the body, so must also truth be preferred to the mind itself, so that the mind should desire it not only more than the body, but even more than its own self. So will the mind be more entire and chaste, when it shall enjoy the immutability of truth rather than its own mutability. Now if Lot,[1] being so righteous a man that he was meet [2] to entertain even Angels, offered his daughters to the lust of the Sodomites, to the intent, that the bodies of women rather than of men might be corrupted by them; how much more diligently and constantly ought the mind's chasteness in the truth to be preserved, seeing it is more truly preferable to its body, than the body of a man to the body of a woman?

11. But if any man supposes that the reason why it is right for a person to tell a lie for another is, that he may live the while, or not be offended in those things which he much loveth, to the end he may attain unto eternal truth by being taught: that man doth not understand, in the first place, that there is no flagitious thing which he may not upon the same ground be compelled to commit, as has been above demonstrated; and in the next place, that the authority of the doctrine itself is cut off and altogether undone if those whom we essay to bring thereunto, are by our lie made to think that it is somewhiles right to lie. For seeing the doctrine which bringeth salvation consisteth partly in things to be believed, partly in things to be understood; and there is no attaining unto those things which are to be understood, unless first those things are believed, which are to be believed; how can there be any believing one who thinks it is sometimes right to lie, lest haply he lie at the moment when he teacheth us to believe? For how can it be known whether he have at that moment some cause, as he thinks, for a well-meant [3] lie, deeming that by a false story a man may be frightened and kept from lust, and in this way account that by telling a lie he is doing good even in spiritual things? Which kind of lie once admitted and approved, all discipline of faith is subverted altogether; and this being subverted, neither is there any attaining to understanding, for the receiving of which that discipline nurtur-

---

[1] Gen. xix. 8.   [2] "*Ut mereretur.*"   [3] *Officiosi.*

eth the babes: and so all the doctrine of truth is done away, giving place to most licentious falsehood, if a lie, even well-meant, may from any quarter have place opened for it to enter in. For either whoso tells a lie prefers temporal advantages, his own or another's, to truth; than which what can be more perverse? or when by aid of a lie he wishes to make a person fit for gaining the truth, he bars the approach to truth, for by wishing when he lies to be accommodating,[1] it comes to pass that when he speaks the truth, he cannot be depended upon. Wherefore, either we must not believe good men, or we must believe those whom we think obliged sometimes to tell a lie, or we must not believe that good men sometimes tell lies: of these three the first is pernicious, the second foolish; it remains therefore that good men should never tell lies.

12. Thus has the question been on both sides considered and treated; and still it is not easy to pass sentence: but we must further lend diligent hearing to those who say, that no deed is so evil, but that in avoidance of a worse it ought to be done; moreover that the deeds of men include not only what they do, but whatever they consent to be done unto them. Wherefore, if cause have arisen that a Christian man should choose to burn incense to idols, that he might not consent to bodily defilement which the persecutor threatened him withal, unless he should do so, they think they have a right to ask why he should not also tell a lie to escape so foul a disgrace. For the consent itself to endure violation of the person rather than to burn incense to idols, this, they say, is not a passive thing, but a deed; which rather than do, he chose to burn incense. How much more readily then would he have chosen a lie, if by a lie he might ward off from a holy body so shocking a disgrace?

13. In which proposition these points may well deserve to be questioned: whether such consent is to be accounted as a deed: or whether that is to be called consent which hath not approbation: or whether it be approbation, when it is said, "It is expedient to suffer this rather than do that;" and whether the person spoken of did right to burn incense rather than suffer violation of his body; and whether it would be right rather to tell a lie, if that was the alternative proposed, than to burn incense? But if such consent is to be accounted as a deed, then are they murderers who have chosen rather to be put to death than bear false witness, yea, what is worse, they are murderers

of themselves. For why, at this rate, should it not be said that they have slain themselves, because they chose that this should be done to them that they might not do what they were urged to do? Or, if it be accounted a worse thing to slay another than himself, what if these terms were offered to a Martyr, that, upon his refusing to bear false witness of Christ and to sacrifice to demons, then, before his eyes, not some other man, but his own father should be put to death; his father entreating him that he would not by his persevering permit that to be done? Is it not manifest, that, upon his remaining steadfast in his purpose of most faithful testimony, they alone would be the murderers who should slay his father, and not he a parricide into the bargain? As therefore, in this case, the man would be no party to this so heinous deed, for choosing, rather than violate his faith by false testimony, that his own father should be put to death by others, (yea, though that father were a sacrilegious person whose soul would be snatched away to punishment;) so the like consent, in the former case, would not make him a party to that so foul disgrace, if he refused to do evil himself, let others do what they might in consequence of his not doing it. For what do such persecutors say, but, "Do evil that we may not?" If the case were so, that our doing evil would make them not to have done it, even then it would not be our duty by doing wickedness ourselves to vote them harmless; but as in fact they are already doing it when they say nothing of the kind,[2] why are they to have us to keep them company in wickedness rather than be vile and noisome by themselves? For that is not to be called consent; seeing that we do not approve what they do, always wishing that they would not, and, as much as in us lies, hindering them that they should not do it, and, when it is done, not only not committing it with them, but with all possible detestation condemning the same.

14. "How," sayest thou, "is it not his doing as well as theirs, when they would not do this, if he would do that?" Why, at this rate we go housebreaking with house-breakers, because if we did not shut the door, they would not break it open: and we go and murder with highwaymen, if it chance we know that they are going to do it, because if we killed them out of hand, they would not kill others. Or, if a person confess to us that he is going to commit a parricide, we commit it along with him, if, being able, we do not slay him before he can do the deed when we can-

---

[1] Aptus.

[2] Al. when they say such things.

not in some other way prevent or thwart him. For it may be said, word for word as before, " Thou hast done it as well as he; for he had not done this, hadst thou done that." With my good will, neither ill should be done; but only the one was in my power, and I could take care that this should not be done; the other rested with another, and when by my good advice I could not quench the purpose, I was not bound by my evil deed to thwart the doing. It is therefore no approving of a sinner, that one refuses to sin for him; and neither the one nor the other is liked by him who would that neither were done; but in that which pertains to him, he hath the power to do it or not, and with that he perpetrateth it not; in that which pertains to another, he hath only the will to wish it or not, and with that he condemneth. And therefore, on their offering those terms, and saying, " If thou burn not incense, this shalt thou suffer;" if he should answer, " For me, I choose neither, I detest both, I consent unto you in none of these things:" in uttering these and the like words, which certainly, because they would be true, would afford them no consent, no approbation of his, let him suffer at their hands what he might, to his account would be set down the receipt of wrongs, to theirs the commission of sins. "Ought he then," it may be asked, "to suffer his person to be violated rather than burn incense?" If the question be what he ought, he ought to do neither. For should I say that he ought to do any of these things, I shall approve this or that, whereas I reprobate both. But if the question be, which of these he ought in preference to avoid, not being able to avoid both but able to avoid one or other: I will answer, " His own sin, rather than another's; and rather a lighter sin being his own, than a heavier being another's." For, reserving the point for more diligent inquiry, and granting in the mean while that violation of the person is worse than burning incense, yet the latter is his own, the former another's deed, although he had it done to him; now, whose the deed, his the sin. For though murder is a greater sin than stealing, yet it is worse to steal than to suffer murder. Therefore, if it were proposed to any man that, if he would not steal he should be killed, that is, murder should be committed upon him; being he could not avoid both, he would prefer to avoid that which would be his own sin, rather than that which would be another's. Nor would the latter become his act for being committed upon him, and because he might avoid it if he would commit a sin of his own.

15. The whole stress, then, of this question comes to this; whether it be true universally that no sin of another, committed upon thee, is to be imputed to thee, if, being able to avoid it by a lighter sin of thine own, thou do it not; or whether there be an exception of all bodily defilement. No man says that a person is defiled by being murdered, or cast into prison, or bound in chains, or scourged, or afflicted with other tortures and pains, or proscribed and made to suffer most grievous losses even to utter nakedness, or stripped of honors, and subjected to great disgrace by reproaches of whatsoever kind; whatever of all these a man may have unjustly suffered, no man is so senseless as to say that he is thereby defiled. But if he have filth poured all over him, or poured into his mouth, or crammed into him, or if he be carnally used like a woman; then almost all men regard him with a feeling of horror, and they call him defiled and unclean. One must conclude then that the sins of others, be they what they may, those always excepted which defile him on whom they are committed, a man must not seek to avoid by sin of his own, either for himself or for any other, but rather he must put up with them, and suffer bravely; and if by no sins of his own he ought to avoid them, therefore not by a lie: but those which by being committed upon a man do make him unclean, these we are bound to avoid even by sinning ourselves; and for this reason those things are not to be called sins, which are done for the purpose of avoiding that uncleanness. For whatever is done, in consideration that the not doing it were just cause of blame, that thing is not sin. Upon the same principle, neither is that to be called uncleanness when there is no way of avoiding it; for even in that extremity he who suffers it has what he may do aright, namely, patiently bear what he cannot avoid. Now no man while acting aright can be defiled by any corporal contagion. For the unclean in the sight of God is every one who is unrighteous; clean therefore is every one who is righteous; if not in the sight of men, yet in the sight of God, Who judges without error. Nay, even in the act of suffering that defilement with power given of avoiding it, it is not by the mere contact that the man is defiled; but by the sin of refusing to avoid it when he might. For that would be no sin, whatever might be done for the avoiding of it. Whoever therefore, for the avoiding of it, shall tell a lie, sinneth not.

16. Or, are some lies, also, to be excepted, so that it were better to suffer this than to commit those? If so, then not every thing

that is done in order to the avoiding of that defilement ceases to be sin; seeing there are some lies to commit which is worse than to suffer that foul violence. For, suppose quest be making after a person that his body may be deflowered, and that it be possible to screen him by a lie; who dares to say that even in such a case a lie ought not be told? But, if the lie by which he may be concealed be one which may hurt the fair fame of another, by bringing upon him a false accusation of that very uncleanness, to suffer which the other is sought after; as, if it should be said to the inquirer, "Go to such an one," (naming some chaste man who is a stranger to vices of this kind,) "and he will procure for you one whom you will find a more willing subject, for he knows and loves such;" and thereby the person might be diverted from him whom he sought: I know not whether one man's fair fame ought to be violated by a lie, in order that another's body may not be violated by lust to which he is a stranger. And in general, it is never right to tell a lie for any man, such as may hurt another, even if the hurt be slighter than would be the hurt to him unless such a lie were told. Because neither must another man's bread be taken from him against his will, though he be in good health, and it is to feed one who is weak; nor must an innocent man, against his will, be beaten with rods, that another may not be killed. Of course, if they are willing, let it be done, because they are not hurt if they be willing that so it should be: but whether, even with his own consent, a man's fair fame ought to be hurt with a false charge of foul lusts, in order that lust may be averted from another's body, is a great question. And I know not whether it be easy to find in what way it can be just that a man's fair fame, even with his consent, should be stained with a false charge of lust, any more than a man's body should be polluted by the lust itself against his will.

17. But yet if the option were proposed to the man who chose to burn incense to idols rather than yield his body to abominable lust, that, if he wished to avoid that, he should violate the fame of Christ by some lie; he would be most mad to do it. I say more: that he would be mad, if, to avoid another man's lust, and not to have that done upon his person which he would suffer with no lust of his own, he should falsify Christ's Gospel with false praises of Christ ; more eschewing that another man should corrupt his body, than himself to corrupt the doctrine of sanctification of souls and bodies. Wherefore, from the doctrine of religion, and from those utterances universally, which are uttered on behalf of the doctrine of religion, in the teaching and learning of the same, all lies must be utterly kept aloof. Nor can any cause whatever be found, one should think, why a lie should be told in matters of this kind, when in this doctrine it is not right to tell a lie for the very purpose of bringing a person to it the more easily. For, once break or but slightly diminish the authority of truth, and all things will remain doubtful: which unless they be believed true, cannot be held as certain. It is lawful then either to him that discourses, disputes, and preaches of things eternal, or to him that narrates or speaks of things temporal pertaining to edification of religion and piety, to conceal at fitting time whatever seems fit to be concealed: but to tell a lie is never lawful, therefore neither to conceal by telling a lie.

18. This being from the very first and most firmly established, touching other lies the question proceeds more securely. But by consequence we must also see that all lies must be kept aloof which hurt any man unjustly: because no man is to have a wrong, albeit a lighter one is done to him, that another may have a heavier kept from him. Nor are those lies to be allowed, which, though they hurt not another, yet do nobody any good, and are hurtful to the persons themselves who gratuitously tell them. Indeed, these are the persons who are properly to be called liars. For there is a difference between lying and being a liar. A man may tell a lie unwillingly; but a liar loves to lie, and inhabits in his mind in the delight of lying. Next to such are those to be placed who by a lie wish to please men, not that they may do wrong or bring reproach upon any man; for we have already before put away that kind; but that they may be pleasant in conversation. These, differ from the class .in which we have placed liars in this respect, that liars delight in lying, rejoicing in deceit for its own sake: but these lust to please by agreeable talk, and yet would rather please by saying things that were true, but when they do not easily find true things to say that are pleasant to the hearers, they choose rather to tell lies than to hold their tongues. Yet it is difficult for these sometimes to undertake a story which is the whole of it false; but most commonly they interweave falsehood with truth, where they are at a loss for something sweet. Now these two sorts of lies do no harm to those who believe them, because they are not deceived concerning any matter of religion and truth, or concerning any profit or advantage of their own. It

suffices them, to judge the thing possible which is told, and to have faith in a man of whom they ought not rashly to think that he is telling a lie. For where is the harm of believing that such an one's father or grandfather was a good man, when he was not? or that he has served with the army even in Persia, though he never set foot out of Rome? But to the persons who tell these lies, they do much harm: to the former sort, because they so desert truth as to rejoice in deceit: to the latter, because they want to please people better than the truth.

19. These sorts of lies having been without any hesitation condemned, next follows a sort, as it were by steps rising to something better, which is commonly attributed to well-meaning and good people, when the person who lies not only does no harm to another, but even benefits somebody. Now it is on this sort of lies that the whole dispute turns, whether that person does harm to himself, who benefits another in such sort as to act contrary to the truth. Or, if that alone may be called truth which illustrateth the very minds of men with an intimate and incommutable light, at least he acts contrary to some true thing, because although the bodily senses are deceived, yet he acts contrary to a true thing who says that a thing is so or not so, whereof neither his mind nor senses nor his opinion or belief giveth him any report. Whether therefore he does not hurt himself in so profiting another, or in that compensation not hurt himself in which he profiteth the other, is a great question. If it be so, it should follow that he ought to profit himself by a lie which damages no man. But these things hang together, and if you concede that point, it necessarily draws in its train some very embarrassing consequences. For should it be asked, what harm it does to a person rolling in superfluous wealth, if from countless thousands of bushels of wheat he lose one bushel, which bushel may be profitable as necessary food to the person stealing it; it will follow that theft also may be committed without blame, and false witness borne without sin. Than which, what can be mentioned more perverse? Or truly, if another had stolen the bushel, and thou sawest it done, and wert questioned, wouldest thou tell a lie with honesty for the poor man, and if thou do it for thine own poverty wilt thou be blamed? As if it were thy duty to love another more than thyself. Both then are disgraceful, and must be avoided.

20. But haply some may think that there is an exception to be added; that there be some honest lies which not only hurt no man, but profit some man, excepting those by which crimes are screened and defended: so that the reason why the aforesaid lie is disgraceful, is that, although it hurt no man, and profit the poor, it screens a theft; but if it should in such sort hurt nobody and profit somebody as not to screen and defend any sin, it would not be morally wrong. As, put the case that some one should in thy sight hide his money that he might not lose it by theft or violence, and thereupon being questioned thou shouldest tell a lie; thou wouldest hurt no man, and wouldest serve him who had need that his money were hidden, and wouldest not have covered a sin by telling a lie. For it is no sin if a man hide his property which he fears to lose. But, if we therefore sin not in telling a lie, for that, while covering no man's sin, we hurt nobody and do good to somebody, what are we about as concerning the sin itself of a lie? For where it is laid down, "Thou shalt not steal," there is also this, "Thou shalt not bear false witness."[1] Since then each is severally prohibited, why is false witness culpable if it cover a theft or any other sin, but if without any screening of sin it be done by itself, then not culpable, whereas stealing is culpable in and by itself, and so other sins? Or is it so that to hide a sin is not lawful; to do it, lawful?

21. If this be absurd, what shall we say? Is it so, that there is no "false witness," but when one tells a lie either to invent a crime against some man, or to hide some man's crime, or in any way to oppress any man in judgment? For a witness seems to be necessary to the judge for cognizance of the cause. But if the Scripture named a "witness" only so far as that goes, the Apostle would not say, "Yea, and we are found false witnesses of God; because we have testified of God that He raised up Christ: whom He raised not up."[2] For so he shows that it is false witness to tell a lie, yea, in falsely praising a person.

Or peradventure, doth the person who lies then utter false witness when he either invents or hides any man's sin, or hurts any man in whatever way? For, if a lie spoken against a man's temporal life is detestable, how much more one against eternal life? as is every lie, if it take place in doctrine of religion. And it is for this reason that the Apostle calls it false witness, if a man tell a lie about Christ, yea, one which may seem to pertain to His praise. Now if it be a lie that neither inventeth or hideth any man's sin, nor is an-

---

[1] Exodus xx. 15, 16   [2] 1 Cor. xv. 15.

swered to a question of the judge, and hurteth no man, and profits some man, are we to say that it is neither false witness, nor a reprehensible lie?

22. What then, if a homicide seek refuge with a Christian, or if he see where the homicide have taken refuge, and be questioned of this matter by him who seeks, in order to bring to punishment a man, the slayer of man? Is he to tell a lie? For how does he not hide a sin by lying, when he for whom he lies has been guilty of a heinous sin? Or is it because he is not questioned concerning his sin, but about the place where he is concealed? So then to lie in order to hide a person's sin is evil; but to lie in order to hide the sinner is not evil? "Yea, surely:" says some one: "for a man sins not in avoiding punishment, but in doing something worthy of punishment. Moreover, it pertaineth to Christian discipline neither to despair of any man's amendment, nor to bar against any man the way of repentance." What if thou be led to the judge, and then questioned concerning the very place where the other is in hiding? Art thou prepared to say, either, "He is not there," when thou knowest him to be there; or, "I know not, and have not seen," what thou knowest and hast seen? Art thou then prepared to bear false witness, and to slay thy soul that a manslayer may not be slain? Or, up to the presence of the judge wilt thou lie, but when the judge questions thee, then speak truth that thou be not a false witness? So then thou art going to slay a man thyself by betraying him. Surely the betrayer too is one whom the divine Scripture detesteth. Or haply is he no betrayer, who in answer to the judge's interrogation gives true information; but would be a betrayer, if, unasked, he should delate a man to his destruction? Put the case with respect to a just and innocent man, that thou know where he is in hiding, and be questioned by the judge; which man, however, has been ordered to be taken to execution by a higher power, so that he who interrogates is charged with the execution of the law, not the author of the sentence? Will it be no false witness that thou shalt lie for an innocent man, because the interrogator is not a judge, but only charged with the execution? What if the author of the law interrogate thee, or any unjust judge, making quest of an innocent man to bring him to punishment? What wilt thou do? wilt thou be false witness, or betrayer? Or will he be a betrayer, who to a just judge shall ultroneously delate a lurking homicide; and he not so, who to an unjust judge, interrogating him of the hiding-place of an innocent man whom he seeks to slay, shall inform against the person who has thrown himself upon his honor? Or between the crime of false witness and that of betrayal, wilt thou remain doubtful and unable to make up thy mind? Or by holding thy peace or professing that thou wilt not tell, wilt thou make up thy mind to avoid both? Then why not do this before thou come to the judge, that thou mayest shun the lie also? For, having kept clear of a lie, thou wilt escape all false witness; whether every lie be false witness, or not every: but by keeping clear of all false witness in thy sense of the word, thou wilt not escape all lying. How much braver then, how much more excellent, to say, "I will neither betray nor lie?"

23. This did a former Bishop of the Church of Thagasta, Firmus by name, and even more firm in will. For, when he was asked by command of the emperor, through officers sent by him, for a man who was taking refuge with him, and whom he kept in hiding with all possible care, he made answer to their questions, that he could neither tell a lie, nor betray a man; and when he had suffered so many torments of body, (for as yet emperors were not Christian,) he stood firm in his purpose. Thereupon being brought before the emperor, his conduct appeared so admirable, that he without any difficulty obtained a pardon for the man whom he was trying to save. What conduct could be more brave and constant? But peradventure some more timid person may say, "I can be prepared to bear any torments, or even to submit to death, that I may not sin; but, since it is no sin to tell a lie such that you neither hurt any man, nor bear false witness, and benefit some man, it is foolish and a great sin, voluntarily and to no purpose to submit to torments, and, when one's health and life may haply be useful, to fling them away for nothing to people in a rage." Of whom I ask; Why he fears that which is written, "Thou shalt not bear false witness,"[1] and fears not that which is said unto God, "Thou wilt destroy all them that speak leasing?"[2] Says he, "It is not written, Every lie: but I understand it as if it were written, Thou wilt destroy all that speak false witness." But neither there is it said, All false witness. "Yes, but it is set there," saith he, "where the other things are set down which are in every sort evil." What, is this the case with what is set down there, "Thou shalt not kill?"[3] If this be in every sort evil, how shall one clear of this crime even just men, who, upon a law given, have

---

[1] Exod. xx. 16. [2] Ps. v. 6. [3] Exod. xx. 13.

killed many? " But," it is rejoined, " that man doth not himself kill, who is the minister of some just command." These men's fear, then, I do accept, that I still think that laudable man who would neither lie, nor betray a man, did both better understand that which is written, and what he understood did bravely put in practice.

25. But one sometimes comes to a case of this kind, that we are not interrogated where the person is who is sought, nor forced to betray him, if he is hidden in such manner that he cannot easily be found unless betrayed: but we are asked, whether he be in such a place or not. If we know him to be there, by holding our peace we betray him, or even by saying that we will in no wise tell whether he be there or not: for from this the questioner gathers that he is there, as, if he were not, nothing else would be answered by him who would not lie nor betray a man, but only, that he is not there. So, by our either holding our peace, or saying such words, a man is betrayed, and he who seeks him hath but to enter in, if he have the power, and find him: whereas he might have been turned aside from finding him by our telling a lie. Wherefore if thou know not where he is, there is no cause for hiding the truth, but thou must confess that thou knowest not. But, if thou know where he is, whether he be in the place which is named in the question or elsewhere; thou must not say, when it is asked whether he be there or not, " I will not tell thee what thou askest," but thou must say, " I know where he is, but I will never show." For if, touching one place in particular thou answer not and profess that thou wilt not betray, it is just as if thou shouldest point to that same place with thy finger: for a sure suspicion is thereby excited. But if at the first thou confess that thou know where he is, but will not tell, haply the inquisitor may be diverted from that place, and begin now to ply thee that the place where he is may be betrayed. For which good faith and humanity whatever thou shalt bravely bear, is judged to be not only not culpable, but even laudable; save only these things which if a man suffer he is said to suffer not bravely, but immodestly and foully. For this is the last description of lie, concerning which we must treat more diligently.

25. For first to be eschewed is that capital lie and far to be fled from, which is done in doctrine of religion; to which lie a man ought by no consideration to be induced. The second, that he should hurt some man unjustly: which is such that it profits no man and hurts some man. The third, which so profits one as to hurt another, but not in corporal defilement. The fourth, that which is done through only lust of lying and deceiving, which is an unmixed lie. The fifth, what is done with desire of pleasing by agreeableness in talk. All these being utterly eschewed and rejected, there follows a sixth sort which at once hurts nobody and helps somebody; as when, if a person's money is to be unjustly taken from him, one who knows where the money is, should say that he does not know, by whomsoever the question be put. The seventh, which hurts none and profits some: except if a judge interrogate: as when, not wishing to betray a man who is sought for to be put to death, one should lie; not only a just and innocent, but also a culprit; because it belongs to Christian discipline neither to despair of any man's amendment, nor to bar the way of repentance against any. Of which two sorts, which are wont to be attended with great controversy, we have sufficiently treated, and have shown what was our judgment; that by taking the consequences, which are honorably and bravely borne, these kinds also should be eschewed by brave and faithful and truthful men and women. The eighth sort of lie is that which hurts no man, and does good in the preserving somebody from corporal defilement, at least that defilement which we have mentioned above. For even to eat with unwashen hands the Jews thought defilement. Or if a person think this also a defilement, yet not such that a lie ought to be told to avoid it. But if the lie be such as to do an injury to any man, even though it screen a man from that uncleanness which all men abhor and detest; whether a lie of this kind may be told provided the injury done by the lie be such as consists not in that sort of uncleanness with which we are now concerned, is another question: for here the question is no longer about lying, but it is asked whether an injury ought to be done to any man, even otherwise than by a lie, that the said defilement may be warded off from another. Which I should by no means think: though the case proposed be the slightest wrongs, as that which I mentioned above, about a single measure of wheat; and though it be very embarrassing whether it be our duty not to do even such an injury to any man, if thereby another may be defended or screened from a lustful outrage upon his person. But, as I said, this is another question: at present let us go on with what we have taken in hand: whether a lie ought to be told, if even the inevitable condition be proposed that we either do this, or suffer the deed of lust or

some execrable pollution; even though by lying we do no man harm.

26. Touching which matter, there will be some place open for consideration, if first the divine authorities which forbid a lie be diligently discussed: for if these give no place, we vainly seek a loophole; for we are bound to keep in every way the command of God, and the will of God in all that through keeping His command we may suffer, it is our duty with an even mind to follow: but if by some relaxation any outlet be allowed, in such a case we are not to decline a lie. The reason why the Divine Scriptures contain not only God's commands, but the life and character of the just, is this: that, if haply it be hidden in what way we are to take that which is enjoined, by the actions of the just it may be understood. With the exception, therefore, of those actions which one may refer to an allegorical significance, although none doubts that they really took place, as is the case with almost all the occurrences in the books of the Old Testament. For who can venture to affirm of any thing there, that it does not pertain to a figurative foretelling? Seeing the Apostle, speaking of the sons of Abraham, of whom of course it is most easily said that they were born and did live in the natural order of propagating the people, (for not monsters and prodigies were born, to lead the mind to some presignification,) nevertheless asserteth that they signify the two Testaments;[1] and saith of that marvellous benefit which God bestowed upon His people Israel to rescue them out of the bondage in which they in Egypt were oppressed, and of the punishment which avenged their sin on their journey, that these things befell them in a figure:[2] what actions wilt thou find, from which thou mayest set aside that rule, and take upon thee to affirm that they are not to be reduced to some figure? Excepting therefore these, the things which in the New Testament are done by the Saints, where there is a most evident commending of manners to our imitation, may avail as examples for the understanding of the Scriptures, which things are digested in the commands.

27. As, when we read in the Gospel, "Thou hast received a blow in the face, make ready the other cheek."[3] Now as an example of patience can none be found than that of the Lord Himself more potent and excellent; but He, when smitten on the cheek, said not, Behold here is the other cheek, but He said, "If I have spoken ill, bear witness of the evil; but if well, why smitest thou

Me?"[4] Where He shows that the preparation of the other cheek is to be done in the heart. Which also the Apostle Paul knew. for he, too, when he was smitten on the face before the high priest, did not say, Smite the other cheek: but, "God," saith he, "shall smite thee, thou whited wall: and sittest thou to judge me according to law, and contrary to law commandest me to be smitten?"[5] with most deep insight beholding that the priesthood of the Jews was already become such, that in name it outwardly was clean and fair, but within was foul with muddy lusts; which priesthood he saw in spirit to be ready to pass away through vengeance of the Lord, when he spake those words: but yet he had his heart ready not only to receive other blows on the cheek, but also to suffer for the truth any torments whatever, with love of them from whom he should suffer the same.

28. It is also written, "But I say unto you, Swear not at all." But the Apostle himself has used oaths in his Epistles.[6] And so he shows how that is to be taken which is said, "I say unto you, Swear not at all:" that is, lest by swearing one come to a facility in swearing, from facility to a custom, and so from a custom there be a downfall into perjury. And therefore he is not found to have sworn except in writing, where there is more wary forethought, and no precipitate tongue withal. And this indeed came of evil, as it is said, "Whatever is more than these is of evil:"[7] not however from evil of his own, but from the evil of infirmity which was in them, in whom he even in this way endeavored to work faith. For that he used an oath in speaking, while not writing, I know not that any Scripture has related concerning him. And yet the Lord says, "Swear not at all:" for He hath not granted license thereof to persons writing. Howbeit, because to pronounce Paul guilty of violating the commandment, especially in Epistles written and sent forth for the spiritual life and salvation of the nations, were an impiety, we must understand that word which is set down, "At all," to be set down for this purpose, that as much as in thee lies, thou affect not, love not, nor as though it were for a good thing, with any delight desire, an oath.

29. As that, "Take no thought for the morrow," and, "Take therefore no thought what ye shall eat, or what ye shall drink, or what ye shall put on."[8] Now when we see that the Lord Himself had a bag in which was put what was given,[9] that it might be

[1] Gal. iv. 22–24. [2] 1 Cor. x. 1–11. [3] Matt. v. 39.

[4] John xviii. 22, 23. [5] Acts xxiii. 3.
[6] Rom. ix. 1; Phil. i. 8; Gal. i. 20. [7] Matt. v. 34 37.
[8] Matt. vi. 34, 31. [9] John xii. 6. [See R.V.]

kept for necessary uses as the time should require; and that the Apostles themselves made much provision for the indigence of the brethren, not only for the morrow, but even for the more protracted time of impending dearth, as we read in the Acts of the Apostles;[1] it is sufficiently clear that these precepts are so to be understood, that we are to do nothing of our work as matter of necessity, through love of obtaining temporal things, or fear of want.

30. Moreover, it was said to the Apostles that they should take nothing with them for their journey, but should live by the Gospel.[2] And in a certain place too the Lord Himself signified why He said this, when He added, "The laborer is worthy of his hire:"[3] where He sufficiently shows that this is permitted, not ordered; lest haply he who should do this, namely, that in this work of preaching the word he should take aught for the uses of this life from them to whom he preached, should think he was doing any thing unlawful. And yet that it may more laudably not be done is sufficiently proved in the Apostle Paul: who, while he said, "Let him that is taught in the word, communicate unto him that teacheth in all things,"[4] and showed in many places that this is wholesomely done by them to whom he preached the word, "Nevertheless," saith he, "I have not used this power."[5] The Lord, therefore, when He spake those words, gave power, not bound men by a command. So in general, what in words we are not able to understand, in the actions of the Saints we gather how it is meet to be taken, which would easily be drawn to the other side, unless it were recalled by an example.

31. Thus then what is written, "The mouth that lieth, slayeth the soul;"[6] of what mouth it speaketh, is the question. For in general when the Scripture speaks of the mouth, it signifies the very seat of our conception[7] in the heart, where is approved and decreed whatever also by the voice, when we speak the truth, is uttered: so that he lieth with the heart who approveth a lie; yet that man may possibly not lie with the heart, who uttereth other than is in his mind, in such sort that he knows it to be for the sake of avoiding a greater evil that he admitteth an evil, disapproving withal both the one and the other. And they who assert this, say that thus also is to be understood that which is written, "He that speaketh the truth in his heart:"[8] because always in the heart truth must be spoken; but not always in the mouth of the body, if any cause of avoiding a greater evil require that other than is in the mind be uttered with the voice. And that there is indeed a mouth of the heart, may be understood even from this, that where there is speech, there a mouth is with no absurdity understood: nor would it be right to say, "Who speaketh in his heart," unless it were right to understand that there is also a mouth in the heart. Though in that very place where it is written, "The mouth that lieth, slayeth the soul," if the context of the lesson be considered, it may peradventure be taken for no other than the mouth of the heart. For there is an obscure response there, where it is hidden from men, to whom the mouth of the heart, unless the mouth of the body sound therewith, is not audible. But that mouth, the Scripture in that place saith, doth reach to the hearing of the Spirit of the Lord, Who hath filled the whole earth; at the same time mentioning lips and voice and tongue in that place; yet all these the sense permitteth not to be taken, but concerning the heart, because it saith of the Lord, that what is spoken is not hidden from Him: now that which is spoken with that sound which reacheth to our ears, is not hidden from men either. Thus, namely, is it written: "The Spirit of wisdom is loving, and will not acquit an evil-speaker of his lips: for of his reins God is witness, and of his heart a true searcher, and of his tongue a hearer. For the Spirit of the Lord hath filled the whole earth, and that which containeth all things hath knowledge of the voice. Therefore he that speaketh unrighteous things cannot be hid: but neither shall the judgment when it punisheth pass by him. For in the thoughts of the ungodly shall there be interrogation; and the hearing of his words shall come from the Lord, to the punishment of his iniquities.[9] For the ear of jealousy heareth all things, and the tumult of murmurings will not be hid. Therefore keep yourselves from murmuring, which profiteth nothing, and from backbiting refrain your tongue: because an obscure response will not go into the void.[10] But the mouth that lieth, slayeth the soul."[11] It seems then to threaten them who think that to be obscure and secret, which they agitate and turn over in their heart. And this, it would show, is so clear to the ears of God, that it even calls it "tumult."

32. Manifestly also in the Gospel we find

---

[1] Acts xi. 28–30. [2] Luke ix. 3; x. 4, 7. [3] Matt. x. 10.
[4] Gal. vi. 6. [5] 1 Cor. ix. 12. [See R.V.] [6] Wisd. i. 11.
[7] *Conceptaculum.* [8] Ps. xv. 2.

[9] *A Domino,* "unto the Lord." E. V.
[10] *Obscurum responsum in vacuum non ibit,* "There is no word so secret that shall go for nought." E. V.
[11] Wisd. i. 6–11.

the mouth of the heart: so that in one place the Lord is found to have mentioned the mouth both of the body and of the heart, where he saith, "Are ye also yet without understanding? Do ye not yet understand, that whatsoever entereth in at the mouth, goeth into the belly, and is cast out into the draught? but those things which proceed out of the mouth come forth from the heart, and they defile the man. For out of the heart proceed evil thoughts, murders, adulteries, fornications, thefts, false witness, blasphemies: these are the things which defile a man."[1] Here if thou understand but one mouth, that of the body, how wilt thou understand, "Those things which proceed out of the mouth, come forth from the heart;" since spitting also and vomiting proceed out of the mouth? Unless peradventure a man is but then defiled when he eateth aught unclean, but is defiled when he vomits it up. But if this be most absurd, it remains that we understand the mouth of the heart to have been expounded by the Lord, when He saith, "The things which proceed out of the mouth, come forth from the heart." For being that theft also can be, and often is, perpetrated with silence of the bodily voice and mouth; one must be out of his mind so to understand it as then to account a person to be contaminated by the sin of theft, when he confesses or makes it known, but when he commits it and holds his peace, then to think him undefiled. But, in truth, if we refer what is said to the mouth of the heart, no sin whatever can be committed tacitly: for it is not committed unless it proceed from that mouth which is within.

33. But, like as it is asked of what mouth the Scripture saith, "The mouth that lieth, slayeth the soul," so it may be asked, of what lie. For it seems to speak of that lie in particular, which consists in detraction. It says, "Keep yourselves from murmuring, which profiteth nothing, and from detraction refrain your tongue." Now this detraction takes place through malevolence, when any man not only with mouth and voice of the body doth utter what he forgeth against any, but even without speaking wisheth him to be thought such; which is in truth to detract with the mouth of the heart; which thing, it saith, cannot be obscure and hidden from God.

34. For what is written in another place, "Wish not to use every lie;"[2] they say is not of force for this, that a person is not to

use any lie. Therefore, when one man shall say, that according to this testimony of Scripture we must to that degree hold every sort and kind of lie in detestation, that even if a man wish to lie, yea, though he lie not, the very wish is to be condemned; and to this sense interpreteth, that it is not said, Do not use every lie, but, "Do not wish to use every lie;" that one must not dare not only to tell, but not even to wish to tell, any lie whatever: saith another man, "Nay, in that it saith, Do not wish to use every lie, it willeth that from the mouth of the heart we exterminate and estrange lying: so that while from some lies we must abstain with the mouth of the body, as are those chiefly which pertain to doctrine of religion; from some, we are not to abstain with the mouth of the body, if reason of avoiding a greater evil require; but with the mouth of the heart we must abstain utterly from every lie." Where it behoveth to be understood what is said, "Do not wish:" namely, the will itself is taken as it were the mouth of the heart, so that it concerneth not the mouth of the heart when in shunning a greater evil we lie unwillingly. There is also a third sense in which thou mayest so take this word, "not every," that, except some lies, it giveth thee leave to lie. Like as if he should say, wish not to believe every man: he would not mean to advise that none should be believed; but that not all, some however, should be believed. And that which follows, "For assiduity thereof will not profit for good," sounds as if, not lying, but assiduous lying, that is, the custom and love of lying, should seem to be that which he would prohibit. To which that person will assuredly slide down,[3] who either shall think that every lie may be boldly used (for so he will shun not that even which is committed in the doctrine of piety and religion; than which what more abominably wicked thing canst thou easily find, not among all lies, but among all sins?) or to some lie (no matter how easy, how harmless,) shall accommodate the inclination of the will; so as to lie, not unwillingly for the sake of escaping a greater evil, but willingly and with liking. So, seeing there be three things which may be understood in this sentence, either "Every lie, not only tell thou not, but do not even wish to tell:" or, "Do not wish, but even unwillingly tell a lie when aught worse is to be avoided:" or, "Not every," to wit, that except some lies, the rest are admitted: one of these is found to make for those who hold that one is never to lie, two for those who think that sometimes

---

[1] Matt. xv. 16-20.
[2] Ecclus. vii. 13. μὴ θέλε ψεύδεσθαι πᾶν ψεῦδος, *noli velle mentiri omne mendacium.* " Use not to make any manner of lie," E. V. " Every " is used for " any."

[3] *Abutendum.*

one may tell a lie. But yet what follows, "For assiduity thereof will not profit to good," I know not whether it can countenance the first sentence of these three; except haply so, that while it is a precept for the perfect not only not to lie, but not even to wish; assiduity of lying is not permitted even to beginners. As if, namely, on laying down the rule at no time whatever not merely to lie but so much as to have a wish to lie, and this being gainsaid by examples, in regard that there are some lies which have been even approved by great authority, it should be rejoined that those indeed are lies of beginners, which have, in regard of this life, some kind of duty of mercy; and yet to that degree is every lie evil, and by perfect and spiritual minds in every way to be eschewed, that not even beginners are permitted to have assiduous custom thereof. For we have already spoken concerning the Egyptian midwives, that it is in respect of the promise of growth and proficiency to better things that they while lying are spoken of with approval: because it is some step towards loving the true and eternal saving of the soul, when a person doth mercifully for the saving of any man's albeit mortal life even tell a lie.

35. Moreover what is written, "Thou wilt destroy all that speak leasing:"[1] one saith that no lie is here excepted, but all condemned. Another saith: Yea verily: but they who speak leasing from the heart, as we disputed above; for that man speaketh truth in his heart, who hateth the necessity of lying, which he understands as a penalty of the mortal life. Another saith: All indeed will God destroy who speak leasing, but not all leasing: for there is some leasing which the Prophet was at that time insinuating, in which none is spared; that is, if refusing to confess each one his sins, he defend them rather, and will not do penance,[2] so that not content to work iniquity, he must needs wish to be thought just, and succumb not to the medicine of confession: as the very distinction of the words may seem to intimate no other, "Thou hatest all that work iniquity;"[3] but wilt not destroy them if upon repenting they speak the truth in confession, that by doing that truth they may come to the light; as is said in the Gospel according to John, "But he that doeth truth cometh unto the light.[4] Thou wilt destroy all who" not only work what Thou hatest, but also "speak leasing;"[5] in holding out before them false righteousness, and not confessing their sins in penitence.

36. For, concerning false witness, which is set down in the ten commands of the Law, it can indeed in no wise be contended that love of truth may at heart be preserved, and false witness brought forth to him unto whom the witness is borne. For, when it is said to God only, then it is only in the heart that the truth is to be embraced: but when it is said to man, then must we with the mouth also of the body bring forth truth, because man is not an inspector of the heart. But then, touching the witness itself, it is not unreasonably asked, to whom one is a witness? For not to whomsoever we speak unto are we witnesses, but to them to whom it is expedient and due that they by our means should come to know or believe the truth; as is a judge, that he may not err in judging; or he who is taught in doctrine of religion, that he may not err in faith, or by very authority of the teacher waver in doubt. But when the person who interrogates thee or wishes to know aught from thee seeks that which concerneth him not, or which is not expedient for him to know, he craveth not a witness, but a betrayer. Therefore if to him thou tell a lie, from false witness peradventure thou wilt be clear, but from a lie assuredly not. So then with this salvo, that to bear false witness is never lawful, the question is, whether it be lawful sometimes to tell a lie. Or if it be false witness to lie at all, it is to be seen whether it admit of compensation, to wit, that it be said for the sake of avoiding a greater sin: as that which is written, "Honor father and mother,"[6] under stress of a preferable duty is disregarded; whence the paying of the last honors of sepulture to a father, is forbidden to that man who by the Lord Himself is called to preach the kingdom of God.

37. Likewise, touching that which is written, "A son which receiveth the word shall be far from destruction: but receiving, he receiveth it for himself, and no falsehood proceedeth out of his mouth:"[7] some one may say, that what is here set down, "A son which receiveth the word," is to be taken for no other than the word of God, which is truth. Therefore, "A son receiving the truth shall be far from destruction," refers to that which is written, "Thou wilt destroy all that speak leasing." But when it follows, "Receiving he receiveth for himself," what other doth this insinuate than what the Apostle saith, "But let every man prove his own work, and then he shall have glorying in him-

---

[1] Ps. v. 6.   [2] *Agere pœnitentiam.*   [3] Ps. v. 5.
[4] John iii. 21.   [5] Ps. v. 6, 7.

[6] Exod. xx. 12.
[7] Prov. xxix. 27. Lat. Not in the Hebrew, but LXX. xxiv. 23.
λόγον φυλασσόμενος υἱὸς ἀπωλείας ἐκτὸς ἔσται δεχόμενος δὲ ἐδέξατο
αὐτόν. Μηδὲν ψεῦδος ἀπὸ γλώσσης βασιλέως λεγέσθω, καὶ οὐδὲν
ψεῦδος ἀπὸ γλώσσης αὐτοῦ οὐ μὴ ἐξέλθῃ.

self and not in another?"[1] For he that receiveth the word, that is, truth, not for himself, but for men-pleasing, keepeth it not when he sees they can be pleased by a lie. But whoso receiveth it for himself, no falsehood proceedeth out of his mouth: because even when the way to please men is to lie, that man lieth not, who receiving the truth not thereby to please them but to please God, hath received it for himself. Therefore there is no reason why it should be said here, He will destroy all who speak leasing, but not all leasing: because all lies, universally, are cut off in this saying, "And no falsehood proceedeth out of his mouth." But another saith, it is to be so taken as the Apostle Paul took our Lord's saying, "But I say unto you, Swear not at all."[2] For here also all swearing is cut off; but from the mouth of the heart, that it should never be done with approbation of the will, but through necessity of the weakness of another; that is, "from the evil" of another, when it shows that he cannot otherwise be got to believe what is said, unless faith be wrought by an oath; or, from that "evil" of our own, that while as yet involved in the skins of this mortality we are not able to show our heart: which thing were we able to do, of swearing there were no need. Though moreover in this whole sentence, if the saying, "A son receiving the word shall be far from destruction," be said of none other than that Truth,[3] by Whom all things were made, which remaineth ever incommutable; then, because the doctrine of Religion strives to bring men to the contemplation of this Truth, it may seem that the saying, "And no falsehood proceedeth out of his mouth," is said to this purpose, that he speaketh no falsehood that pertaineth to doctrine. Which sort of lie is upon no compensation whatever to be gone into, and is utterly and before all to be eschewed. Or if the saying, "No falsehood," is absurdly taken if it be not referred to every lie, the saying, "From his mouth," should, as was argued above, be taken to mean the mouth of the heart, in the opinion of him who accounts that sometimes one may tell a lie.

38. Certain it is, albeit all this disputation go from side to side, some asserting that it is never right to lie, and to this effect reciting divine testimonies: others gainsaying, and even in the midst of the very words of the divine testimonies seeking place for a lie; yet no man can say, that he finds this either in example or in word of the Scriptures, that

any lie should seem a thing to be loved, or not had in hatred; howbeit sometimes by telling a lie thou must do that thou hatest, that what is more greatly to be detested may be avoided. But then here it is that people err; they put the precious beneath the vile. For when thou hast granted that some evil is to be admitted, that another and more grievous may not be admitted; not by the rule of truth, but by his own cupidity and custom doth each measure the evil, accounting that to be the more grievous, which himself more greatly dreads, not which is in reality more greatly to be fled from. All this fault is engendered by perversity of loving. For being there are two lives of ours; the one eternal, which is promised of God; the other temporal, in which we now are: when a man shall have begun to love this temporal more than that eternal, for the sake of this which he loveth he thinks all things right to be done; and there are not any, in his estimation, more grievous sins than those which do injury to this life, and either take away from it any commodity unjustly and unlawfully, or by inflicting of death take it utterly away. And so thieves, and robbers, and ruffians, and torturers, and slayers, are more hated of them than lascivious, drunken, luxurious men, if these molest no man. For they do not understand or at all care, that these do wrong to God; not indeed to any inconvenience of Him, but to their own pernicious hurt; seeing they corrupt His gifts bestowed upon them, even His temporal gifts, and by their very corruptions turn away from eternal gifts: above all, if they have already begun to be the Temple of God; which to all Christians the Apostle saith thus: "Know ye not that ye are the temple of God, and that the Spirit of God dwelleth in you? Whoso shall corrupt God's temple, God will corrupt him. For the temple of God is holy: which temple are ye."[4]

39. And all these sins, truly, whether such whereby an injury is done to men in the comforts of this life, or whereby men corrupt themselves and hurt none against his will: all these sins, then, even though they seem to mean well by this temporal life to the procuring of any delight or profit, (for no man commits any of these things with any other purpose and end;) yet in regard of that life which is forever and ever, they do entangle and in all ways hinder. But there are some of these that hinder the doers only, others likewise those on whom they are done. For as to the things which people keep safe for the sake of utility to this life, when these are

---

[1] Gal. vi. 4.   [2] Matt. v. 34.
[3] Or "of Him who is Truth itself."

[4] 1 Cor. iii. 16, 17.

taken away by injurious persons, they alone sin and are hindered from eternal life who do this, not they to whom they do it. Therefore, even if a person consent to the taking of them from him, either that he may not do some evil, or that he may not in these very things suffer some greater inconvenience; not only does he not sin, but in the one case he acts bravely and laudably, in the other usefully and unblameably. But as to those things which are kept for the sake of sanctity and religion, when injurious persons wish to violate these, it is right, if the condition be proposed and the means given, to redeem them even by sins of lesser moment, yet not by wrongs to other men. And then do these things thenceforth cease to be sins, which are undertaken in order to the avoidance of greater sins. For as in things useful, for instance in pecuniary or any other corporal commodity, that is not called a loss which is parted with in order to a greater gain; so in things holy, that is not called sin which is admitted lest a worse be admitted. Or if that is called loss, which one foregoes that he may not forego more; let this also be called sin, while however the necessity of undertaking it in order to the eschewing of a greater is no more to be doubted, than that, in order to avoid a greater loss, it is right to suffer a smaller one.

40. Now the things which are to be kept safe for sanctity's sake are these: pudicity of body, and chastity of soul,[1] and verity of doctrine. Pudicity of body, without consent and permission of the soul, doth no man violate. For, whatever against our will and without our empowering the same is by greater force done upon our body, is no lewdness. Howbeit, of permitting there may be some reason, but of consenting, none. For we consent, when we approve and wish: but we permit even not willing, because of some greater turpitude to be eschewed. Consent, truly, to corporal lewdness violates also chastity of mind. For the mind's[2] chastity consists in a good will and sincere love, which is not corrupted, unless when we love and desire that which Truth teaches ought not to be loved and desired. We have therefore to guard the sincerity of love toward God and our neighbor; for in this is chastity of mind sanctified: and we must endeavor with all the strength in our power, and with pious supplication, that, when the pudicity of our body is sought to be violated, not even that outermost sense of the soul,[3] which is entangled with the flesh, may be touched with any delight; but if it cannot this, at least the mind and thought[4] in not consenting may have its chastity preserved entire. Now what we have to guard in chastity of mind,[5] is, as pertaining to the love of our neighbor, innocence and benevolence; as pertaining to the love of God, piety. Innocence is that we hurt no man; benevolence, that we also do good to whom we can; piety, that we worship God. But as for verity of doctrine, of religion and piety, that is not violated unless by a lie; whereas the highest and inmost Verity Itself, Whose that doctrine is, can in no wise be violated: which Truth to attain unto, and in It on every wise to remain, and to It thoroughly to cleave, will not be permitted, but when this corruptible shall have put on incorruption, and this mortal shall have put on immortality. But, because all piety in this life is practice by which we tend to that life, which practice hath a guidance afforded unto it from that doctrine, which in human words and signs[6] of corporal sacraments doth insinuate and intimate Truth herself: for this cause this also, which by lying is possible to be corrupted, is most of all to be kept incorrupt; that so, if aught in that chastity of mind be violated, it may have that wherefrom it may be repaired. For once corrupt authority of doctrine, and there can be none either course or recourse to chastity of mind.

41. There resulteth then from all these this sentence, that a lie which doth not violate the doctrine of piety, nor piety itself, nor innocence, nor benevolence, may on behalf of pudicity of body be admitted. And yet if any man should propose to himself so to love truth, not only that which consists in contemplation, but also in uttering the true thing, which each in its own kind of things is true, and no otherwise to bring forth with the mouth of the body his thought than in the mind it is conceived and beheld; so that he should prize the beauty of truth-telling honesty, not only above gold and silver and jewels and pleasant lands, but above this temporal life itself altogether and every good thing of the body, I know not whether any could wisely say that that man errs. And if he should prefer this and prize it more than all that himself hath of such things; rightly also would he prefer it to the temporal things of other men, whom by his innocence and benevolence he was bound to keep and to help. For he would love perfect faith, not only of believing aright those things which by an excellent authority and worthy of faith should to himself be spoken, but also of faith-

---

[1] *Animæ.*   [2] *Animi.*   [4] *Animæ.*   [4] *Mentis.*   [5] *Animi.*   [6] *Signaculis.*

fully uttering what himself should judge right to be spoken, and should speak. For faith hath its name in the Latin tongue, from that the thing is done which is said:[1] and thus it is manifest that one doth not exhibit when telling a lie. And even if this faith be less violated, when one lies in such sort that he is believed to no inconvenience and no pernicious hurt, with added intention moreover of guarding either one's life or corporal purity; yet violated it is, and a thing is violated which ought to be kept safe in chastity and sanctity of mind. Whence we are constrained, not by opinion of men, which for the most part is in error, but by truth itself, truth which is eminent above all, and alone is most invincible, to prefer even to purity of body, perfect faith. For chastity of mind is, love well ordered, which does not place the greater below the smaller. Now it is less, whatever in the body than whatever in the mind can be violated. For assuredly when for corporal chasteness a man tells a lie, he sees indeed that his body is threatened with corruption, not from his own, but from another's lust, but is cautious lest by permitting at least, he be a party. That permission, however, where is it but in the mind? So then, even corporal chasteness cannot be corrupted but in the mind; which not consenting nor permitting, it can by no means be rightly said that corporal chasteness is violated whatever in the body be perpetrated by another's lust. Whence it is gathered, that much more must the chastity of the mind be preserved in the mind, in the which is the guardianship of the pudicity of the body. Wherefore, what in us lies, both the one and the other must by holy manners and conversation be walled and hedged round, lest from another quarter it be violated. But when both cannot be, which is to be slighted in comparison of which, who doth not see? when he seeth which to which is to be preferred, the mind to the body, or the body to the mind; and which is more to be shunned among sins, the permitting of another's deed, or the committing of the deed thyself.

42. It clearly appears then, all being discussed, that those testimonies of Scripture have none other meaning than that we must never at all tell a lie: seeing that not any examples of lies, worthy of imitation, are found in the manners and actions of the Saints, as regards those Scriptures which are referred to no figurative signification, such as is the history in the Acts of the Apostles. For all those sayings of our Lord in the Gospel, which to more ignorant minds seem lies, are figurative significations. And as to what the Apostle says: "I am made all things to all men, that I might gain all;"[2] the right understanding is, that he did this not by lying, but by sympathy; so that he dealt with them in liberating them with so great charity, as if he were himself in that evil from which he wished to make them whole. There must therefore be no lying in the doctrine of piety: it is a heinous wickedness, and the first sort of detestable lie. There must be no lying of the second sort; because no man must have a wrong done to him. There must be no lying of the third sort; because we are not to consult any man's good to the injury of another. There must be no lying of the fourth sort, that is, for the lust of lying, which of itself is vicious. There must be no lying of the fifth sort, because not even the truth itself is to be uttered with the aim of men-pleasing, how much less a lie, which of itself, as a lie, is a foul thing? There must be no lying of the sixth sort; for it is not right that even the truth of testimony be corrupted for any man's temporal convenience and safety. But unto eternal salvation none is to be led by aid of a lie. For not by the ill manners of them that convert him is he to be converted to good manners: because if it is meet to be done towards him, himself also ought when converted to do it toward others; and so is he converted not to good, but to ill manners, seeing that is held out to be imitated by him when converted, which was done unto him in converting him. Neither in the seventh sort must there be any lying; for it is meet that not any man's commodity or temporal welfare be preferred to the perfecting of faith. Not even if any man is so ill moved by our right deeds as to become worse in his mind, and far more remote from piety, are right deeds therefore to be foregone: since what we are chiefly to hold is that whereunto we ought to call and invite them whom as our own selves we love; and with most courageous mind we must drink in that apostolic sentence: "To some we are a savor of life unto life, to others a savor of death unto death; and who is sufficient for these things?"[3] Nor in the eighth sort must there be lying: because both among good things chastity of mind is greater than pudicity of body; and among evil things, that which ourselves do, than that which we suffer to be done. In these eight kinds, however, a man sins less when he tells a lie, in proportion as he emerges to the eighth: more, in proportion as he di-

---

[1] "Fides, quia fit quod dicitur."　　　[2] 1 Cor. ix. 22.　　　[3] 2 Cor. ii. 16.

verges to the first. But whoso shall think there is any sort of lie that is not sin, will deceive himself foully, while he deems himself honest as a deceiver of other men.

43. So great blindness, moreover, hath occupied men's minds, that to them it is too little if we pronounce some lies not to be sins; but they must needs pronounce it to be sin in some things if we refuse to lie: and to such a pass have they been brought by defending lying, that even that first kind which is of all the most abominably wicked they pronounce to have been used by the Apostle Paul. For in the Epistle to the Galatians, written as it was, like the rest, for doctrine of religion and piety, they say that he has told a lie, in the passage where he says concerning Peter and Barnabas, "When I saw that they walked not uprightly according to the truth of the Gospel."[1] For, while they wish to defend Peter from error, and from that pravity of way into which he had fallen; the very way of religion in which is salvation for all men, they by breaking and mincing the authority of the Scriptures do endeavor themselves to overthrow. In which they do not see that it is not only lying, but perjury that they lay to the charge of the Apostle in the very doctrine of piety, that is, in an Epistle in which he preaches the Gospel; seeing that he there saith, before he relates that matter, "What I write unto you, behold, before God, I lie not."[2] But it is time that we set bounds to this disputation: in the consideration and treatment whereof altogether there is nothing more meet to be, before all else, borne in mind and made our prayer, than that which the same Apostle saith: "God is faithful, Who will not suffer you to be tempted above that ye are able to bear, but will with the temptation make also a way to escape, that ye may be able to bear it."[3]

---

[1] Gal. ii. 14.

[2] Gal. i. 20.

[3] 1 Cor. x. 13.

ST. AUGUSTIN:

TO

CONSENTIUS: AGAINST LYING

[CONTRA MENDACIUM.]

TRANSLATED BY THE

REV. H. BROWNE, M.A.,

OF CORPUS CHRISTI COLLEGE, CAMBRIDGE, LATE PRINCIPAL OF THE DIOCESAN
COLLEGE, CHICHESTER.

TO CONSENTIUS: AGAINST LYING.

[CONTRA MENDACIUM.]

From the Retractations, Book II. Chap. 60.

"Then[1] also I wrote a Book against Lying, the occasion of which work was this. In order to discover the Priscillianist heretics, who think it right to conceal their heresy not only by denial and lies, but even by perjury, it seemed to certain Catholics that they ought to pretend themselves Priscillianists, in order that they might penetrate their lurking places. In prohibition of which thing, I composed this book. It begins : *Multa mihi legenda misisti.*"

1. A great deal for me to read hast thou sent, my dearest brother Consentius: a great deal for me to read: to the which while I am preparing an answer, and am drawn off first by one, then by another, more urgent occupation, the year has measured out its course, and has thrust me into such straits, that I must answer in what sort I may, lest the time for sailing being now favorable, and the bearer desirous to return, I should too long detain him. Having therefore unrolled and read through all that Leonas, servant of God, brought me from thee, both soon after I received it, and afterwards when about to dictate this reply, and having weighed it with all the consideration in my power, I am greatly delighted with thy eloquence, and memory of the holy Scripture, and cleverness of wit, and the resentment with which thou bitest negligent Catholics, and the zeal with which thou gnashest against even latent heretics. But I am not persuaded that it is right to unearth them out of their hiding places by our telling lies. For to what end do we take such pains in tracking them out and running them down, but that having taken them and brought them forth into open day, we may either teach them the truth, or at least having convicted them by the truth, may not allow them to hurt others? to this end, therefore, that their lie may be blotted out, or shunned, and God's truth increased. How then by a lie shall I rightly be able to prosecute lies? Or is it by robbery that robberies, and by sacrilege that sacrileges, and by adultery that adulteries, are to be prosecuted? "But if the truth of God shall abound by my lie," are we too to say, "Let us do evil that good may come?"[2] A thing which thou seest how the Apostle detesteth. For what else is, "Let us lie, that we may bring heretic liars to the truth," but, "Let us do evil that good may come?" Or, is a lie sometimes good, or sometimes a lie not evil? Why then is it written, "Thou hatest, Lord, all that work iniquity; Thou wilt destroy all that speak leasing."[3] For he hath not excepted some, or said indefinitely, "Thou wilt destroy them that speak leasing;" so as to permit some, not all, to be understood: but it is an universal sentence that he hath passed, saying, "Thou wilt destroy all who speak leasing." Or, be·

---

1 i. e. A.D. 420, the work mentioned just before belonging to the early part of that year. Consentius is thought to be the writer of ep. 119, to Augustin, and ep. 120, and 205, are addressed to him. This is the work referred to in the Enchiridion, ch. 18, p. 243.

2 Rom. iii. 7, 8.
3 Psalm v. 6, 7. [See R.V.] "Thou wilt destroy them that speak a lie," Heb. πάντας τοὺς λαλοῦντας τὸ ψεῦδος, LXX.

cause it is not said, Thou wilt destroy all who speak all leasing, or, who speak any leasing whatsoever; is it therefore to be thought that there is place allowed for some lie; to wit, that there should be some leasing, and them who speak it, God should not destroy, but destroy them all which speak unjust leasing, not what lie soever, because there is found also a just lie, which as such ought to be matter of praise, not of crime?

2. Perceivest thou not how much this reasoning aideth the very persons whom as great game we make ado to catch by our lies? For, as thyself hast shown, this is the sentiment of the Priscillianists to prove which, they apply testimonies from the Scriptures exhorting their followers to lie, as though by the examples of Patriarchs, Prophets, Apostles, Angels; not hesitating to add even the Lord Christ Himself; and deeming that they cannot otherwise prove their falsehood truthful, unless they pronounce Truth to be a liar. It must be refuted, this; not imitated: nor ought we to be partners with the Priscillianists in that evil in which they are convicted to be worse than other heretics. For they alone, or at least they in the greatest degree, are found to make a dogma of lying for the purpose of hiding their truth, as they call it: and this so great evil therefore to esteem just, because they say that in the heart must be held that which is true, but with the mouth to utter unto aliens a false thing, is no sin; and that this is written, "Who speaketh the truth in his heart:"[1] as though this were enough for righteousness, even though a person do with his mouth speak a lie, when not his neighbor but a stranger is he that heareth it. On this account they think the Apostle Paul, when he had said, "Putting away lying, speak ye truth," to have immediately added, "Every man with his neighbor, for we are members one of another."[2] Meaning, that with them who are not our neighbors in society of the truth, nor, so to say, our co-members,[3] it is lawful and right to speak a lie.

3. Which sentence dishonoreth the holy Martyrs, nay rather taketh away holy martyrdoms altogether. For they would do more justly and wisely, according to these men, not to confess to their persecutors that they were Christians, and by confessing make them murderers: but rather by telling a lie, and denying what they were, should both themselves keep safe the convenience of the flesh and purpose of the heart, and not allow those to accomplish the wickedness which they had

conceived in their mind. For they were not their neighbors in the Christian faith, that with them it should be their duty to speak the truth in their mouth which they spake in their heart; but moreover enemies of Truth itself. For if Jehu (whom it seems they do prudently to single out unto themselves to look unto as an example of lying) falsely gave himself out for a servant of Baal, that he might slay Baal's servants: how much more justly, according to their perversity, might, in time of persecution, the servants of Christ falsely give themselves out for servants of demons, that the servants of demons might not slay servants of Christ; and sacrifice to idols that men might not be killed, if Jehu sacrificed to Baal that he might kill men? For what harm would it do them, according to the egregious doctrine of these speakers of lies, if they should lyingly pretend a worship of the Devil in the body, when the worship of God was preserved in the heart? But not so have the Martyrs understood the Apostle, the true, the holy Martyrs. They saw and held that which is written, "With the heart man believeth unto righteousness, and with the mouth confession is made unto salvation;"[4] and, "In their mouth was found no lie:"[5] and so they departed irreproachable, to that place where to be tempted by liars any further they will not fear; because they will not have liars any more in their heavenly assemblies, either for strangers or neighbors. As for that Jehu, by an impious lie and a sacrilegious sacrifice making inquisition for impious and sacrilegious men for to kill them, they would not imitate him, no, not though the Scripture had said nothing concerning him, what manner of man he was. But, seeing it is written that he had not his heart right with God;[6] what profited it him, that for some obedience which, concerning the utter destruction of the house of Ahab, he exhibited for the lust of his own domination, he received some amount of transitory wages in a temporal kingdom? Let, rather, the truth-telling sentence of the Martyrs be thine to defend: to this I exhort thee, my brother, that thou mayst be against liars, not a teacher of lying, but an asserter of truth. For, I pray thee, attend diligently to what I say, that thou mayest find how needful to be shunned is that which, with laudable zeal indeed towards impious men, that they may be caught and corrected, or avoided, but yet too incautiously, is thought fit to be taught.

4. Of lies are many sorts, which indeed

---

[1] Ps. xv. 2.   [2] Eph. iv. 25.   [3] *Commembres.*

[4] Rom. x. 10.
[5] Rev. xiv. 5. ψεῦδος, Griesbach; δόλος, text rec.; *guile,* E. V.
[6] 2 Kings x. 31.

all, universally, we ought to hate. For there is no lie that is not contrary to truth. For, as light and darkness, piety and impiety, justice and iniquity, sin and right-doing, health and weakness, life and death, so are truth and a lie contrary the one to the other. Whence by how much we love the former, by so much ought we to hate the latter. Yet in truth there be some lies which to believe does no harm: although even by such sort of lie to wish to deceive, is hurtful to him that tells it, not to him that believes it. As though, if that brother, the servant of God, Fronto, in the information which he gave thee, should (though far be the thought!) say some things falsely; he would have hurt himself assuredly, not thee, although thou, without iniquity of thine, hadst believed all, upon his telling it. Because, whether those things did so take place or not so, yet they have not any thing, which if a person believe to have been so, though it were not so, he by the rule of truth and doctrine of eternal salvation should be judged worthy of blame. Whereas, if a person tell a lie which if any believe he will be an heretic against the doctrine of Christ, by so much is he who tells the lie more hurtful, by how much he that believes it is more miserable. See then, what manner of thing it is, if against the doctrine of Christ we shall tell a lie which whoso believes shall perish, in order that we may catch the enemies of the same doctrine, to the end we may bring them to the truth, while we recede from it; nay rather, when we catch liars by lying, teach worse lies. For it is one thing what they say when they lie, another when they are deceived. For, when they teach their heresy, they speak the things in which they are deceived; but when they say that they think what they do not think, or that they do not think what they do think, they say the things in which they lie. In that any believeth them, what though he do not find them out, himself perisheth not. For it is no receding from the catholic rule, if, when a heretic lyingly professes the catholic doctrines, one believes him to be a catholic: and therefore it is not pernicious to him; because he is mistaken in the mind of a man, of which, when latent, he cannot judge, not in the faith of God which it is his duty to keep safe planted within him. Moreover, when they teach their heresy, whoso shall believe them, in thinking it truth, will be partaker, as of their error, so of their damnation. So it comes to pass, that when they fable their nefarious dogmas in which they are with deadly error deceived, then whoso believeth them is lost: whereas when we preach catholic dogmas, in which we hold the right faith, then if he shall believe, that man is found, whoso was lost. But when, they being Priscillianists, do, in order that they may not betray their venom, lyingly give themselves out to be of us; whoever of us believes them, even while they escape detection, himself perseveres a Catholic: we on the other hand, if, in order to attain to the discovery of them, we falsely give ourselves out for Priscillianists, because we shall praise their dogmas as though they were our own, whoso shall believe the same, will either be confirmed among them, or will be transferred to them in the meantime straightway: but what the coming hour may bring forth, whether they shall be afterwards set free therefrom by us when speaking true things, who were deceived by us when speaking false; and whether they will be willing to hear one teaching whom they have thus experienced telling a lie, who can know for certain? who can be ignorant that this is uncertain? Whence it is gathered, that it is more pernicious, or to speak more mildly, that it is more perilous for Catholics to lie that they may catch heretics, than for heretics to lie that they may not be found out by Catholics. Because, whoso believes Catholics when they tell a lie to tempt people, is either made or confirmed a heretic: but whoso believes heretics when they tell a lie to conceal themselves, doth not cease to be a Catholic. But that this may become more plain, let us propose some cases by way of example, and from those writings in preference which thou hast sent me to read.

5. Well then, let us set before our eyes a cunning spy as he makes up to the person whom he has already perceived to be a Priscillianist; he begins with Dictinius the bishop, and lyingly bepraises either his life, if he knew him, or his fame, if he knew him not; this is more tolerable thus far, because Dictinius is accounted to have been a Catholic, and to have been corrected of that error. Then, passing on to Priscillian, (for this comes next in the art of lying,) he shall make reverend mention of him, of an impious and detestable person, condemned for his nefarious wickedness and crimes! In which reverend mention, if haply the person for whom this sort of net is spread, had not been a firm Priscillianist, by this preaching of him, he will be confirmed. But when the spy shall go on to discourse of the other matters, and saying that he pities them whom the author of darkness hath involved in such darkness of error, that they acknowledge not the honor of their own soul, and the brightness of their divine ancestry: then speaking of Dictinius's Book, which is called "the Pound," because it

treats, first and last, of a dozen questions, being as the ounces which go to the pound, shall extol it with such praise, as to protest that such a " Pound " (in which awful blasphemies are contained) is more precious than many thousands of pounds of gold; truly, this astuteness of him who tells the lie slays the soul of him who believes it, or, that being slain already, doth in the same death sink, and hold it down. But, thou wilt say, " afterwards it shall be set at liberty." What if it come not to pass, either upon something intervening that prevents what was begun from being completed, or through obstinacy of an heretical mind denying the same things over again, although of some it had already begun to make confession? especially because, if he shall find out that he has been tampered with by a stranger, he will just the more boldy study to conceal his sentiments by a lie, when he shall have learned much more certainly that this is to be done without blame, even by the example of the very person who tampered with him. This, truly, in a man who thinks it right to hide the truth by telling a lie, with what face can we blame, and dare to condemn what we teach?

6. It remains, then, that what the Priscillianists think,. according to the nefarious falsity of their heresy, of God, of the soul, of the body, and the rest, we hesitate not with truthful pity to condemn; but what they think of the right of telling a lie to hide the truth is to be to us and them (which God forbid !) a common dogma. This is so great an evil, that even though this attempt of ours, whereby we desire by means of a lie to catch them and change them, should so prosper that we do catch and change them, there is no gain that can compensate the damage of making ourselves wrong with them in order to set them right. For through this lie shall both we be in that respect perverse, and they but half corrected; seeing that their thinking it right to tell a lie on behalf of the truth is a fault which we do not correct in them, because we have learned and do teach the same thing, and lay it down that it is fit to be done, in order that we may be able to attain to the amending of them. Whom yet we amend not, for their fault, with which they think right to hide the truth, we take not away, rather we make ourselves faulty when by such a fault we seek them; nor do we find how we can believe them, when converted, to whom, while perverted, we have lied; lest haply what was done to them that they might be caught, they do to us when caught; not only because to do it hath been their wont, but because in us also, to whom they come, they find the same.

7. And, what is more miserable, even they, already made as it were our own, cannot find how they may believe us. For if they suspect that even in the catholic doctrines themselves we speak lyingly, that we may conceal I know not what other thing which we think true; of course to one suspecting the like thou shalt say, I did this then only to catch thee: but what wilt thou answer when he says, Whence then do I know whether thou art not doing it even now, lest thou be caught by me? Or indeed, can any man be made to believe that a man does not lie not to be caught, who lies to catch? Seest thou whither this evil tends? that is, that not only we to them, and they to us, but every brother to every brother shall not undeservedly become suspected? And so while that which is aimed at by means of the lie, is that faith may be taught, the thing which is brought about is, rather, that there shall be no having faith in any man. For if we speak even against God when we tell a lie, what so great evil will people be able to discover in any lie, that, as though it were a most wretched thing, we should be bound in every way to eschew it?

8. But now observe how more tolerable in comparison with us is the lying of the Priscillianists, when they know that they speak deceitfully: whom by our own lying we think right to deliver from those false things in which they by erring are deceived. A Priscillianist saith, that the soul is a part of God, and of the same nature and substance with Him. This is a great and detestable blasphemy. For it follows that the nature of God may be taken captive, deceived, cheated, disturbed, and defiled, condemned and tortured. But if that man also saith this, who from so great an evil desires to deliver a man by a lie, let us see what is the difference between the one blasphemer and the other. " Very much," sayest thou: " for this the Priscillianist saith, also believing it so: but the catholic not so believing, though so speaking." The one, then, blasphemes without knowing, the other with knowledge: the one against science, the other against conscience; the one hath the blindness of thinking false things, but in them hath at least the will of saying true things; the other in secret seeth truth, and willingly speaketh false. " But the one," thou wilt say, " teacheth this, that he may make men partakers of his error and madness: the latter saith it, that from that error and madness he may deliver men." Now I have already shown above how hurtful is this very

thing which people believe will do good: but meanwhile if we weigh in these two the present evils, (for the future good which a catholic seeks from correcting a heretic is uncertain,) who sins worse? he who deceives a man without knowing it, or he who blasphemes God, knowing it? Assuredly which is the worse, that man understands, who with solicitous piety preferreth God to man. Add to this, that, if God may be blasphemed in order that we may bring men to praise Him, without doubt we do by our example and doctrine invite men not only to praise, but also to blaspheme God: because they whom through blasphemies against God we plot to bring to the praises of God, verily, if we do bring them, will learn not only to praise, but also to blaspheme. These be the benefits we confer on them whom, by blaspheming not ignorantly but with knowledge, we deliver from heretics! And whereas the Apostle delivered men to Satan himself that they might learn not to blaspheme,[1] we endeavor to rescue men from Satan, that they may learn to blaspheme not with ignorance, but with knowledge. And upon ourselves, their masters, we bring this so great bane, that, for the sake of catching heretics, we first become, which is certain, blasphemers of God, in order that we may for the sake of delivering them, which is uncertain, be able to be teachers of His truth.

9. When therefore we teach ours to blaspheme God that the Priscillianists may believe them theirs, let us see what evil themselves say when they therefore lie that we may believe them ours. They anathematize Priscillian, and detest him according to our mind; they say that the soul is a creature of God, not a part; they execrate the Priscillianists' false martyrdoms; the catholic bishops by whom that heresy has been stripped, attacked, prostrated, they extol with great praises, and so forth. Behold, themselves speak truth when they lie: not that the very thing which is a lie can be true at the same time; but when in one thing they lie, in another they speak truth: for when, in saying they are of us, they lie, of the catholic faith they speak truth. And therefore they, that they may not be found out for Priscillianists, speak in lying manner the truth: but we, that we may find them out, not only speak lyingly, that we may be believed to belong to them; but we also speak false things which we know to belong to their error. Therefore as for them, when they wish to be thought of us, it is both false in part, and true in part, what they say; for it is false that they are of us, but true

that the soul is not a part of God: but as for us, when we wish to be thought to belong to them, it is false, both the one and the other that we say, both that we are Priscillianists, and that the soul is a part of God. They, then, praise God, not blaspheme, when they conceal themselves; and when they do not so, but utter their own sentiments, they know not that they blaspheme. So that if they be converted to the catholic faith, they console themselves, because they can say what the Apostle said: who when among other things he had said, "I was before a blasphemer; but," saith he, "I obtained mercy, because I did it ignorantly."[2] We on the contrary, in order that they may open themselves to us, if we utter this as if it were a just lie for deceiving and catching them, do assuredly both say that we belong to the blaspheming Priscillianists, and that they may believe us, do without excuse of ignorance blaspheme. For a catholic, who by blaspheming wishes to be thought a heretic, cannot say, "I did it ignorantly."

10. Ever, my brother, in such cases, it behoves with fear to recollect, "Whoso shall deny Me before men, I will deny him before My Father which is in heaven."[3] Or truly is it no denying of Christ before men, to deny Him before Priscillianists, that when they hide themselves, one may by a blasphemous lie strip them and catch them? But who doubts, I pray thee, that Christ is denied, when so as He is in truth, we say that He is not; and so as the Priscillianist believes Him, we say that He is?

11. "But, hidden wolves," thou wilt say, "clad in sheep's clothing, and privily and grievously wasting the Lord's flock, can we no otherwise find out." Whence then have the Priscillianists become known, ere this way of hunting for them with lies was excogitated? Whence was their very author, more cunning doubtless, and therefore more covert, got at in his bed? Whence so many and so great persons made manifest and condemned, and the others innumerable partly corrected, partly as if corrected, and in the Church's compassion gathered into her fold? For many ways giveth the Lord, when He hath compassion, whereby we may come to the discovery of them: two of which are more happy than others; namely, that either they whom they have wished to seduce, or they whom they had already seduced, shall, when they repent and are converted, point them out. Which is more easily effected, if their nefarious error, not by lying tricks, but by truthful

---

[1] 1 Tim. i. 20.   [2] 1 Tim. i. 13.   [3] Matt. x. 33.

reasonings be overthrown. In the writing of which it behoves thee to bestow thy pains, since God hath bestowed the gift that thou canst do this: which wholesome writings whereby their insane perversity is destroyed, becoming more and more known, and being by catholics, whether prelates who speak in the congregations, or any studious men full of zeal for God, every where diffused, these will be holy nets in which they may be caught truthfully, not with lies hunted after. For so being taken, either, of their own accord, they will confess what they have been, and others whom they know to be of the evil fellowship they will either kindly[1] correct, or mercifully betray. Or else, if they shall be ashamed to confess what with long-continued simulation they have concealed, by the hidden hand of God healing them shall they be made whole.

12. "But," thou wilt say, "we more easily penetrate their concealment if we pretend to be ourselves what they are." If this were lawful or expedient, Christ might have instructed His sheep that they should come clad in wolves' clothing to the wolves, and by the cheat of this artifice discover them: which He hath not said, no, not when He foretold that He would send them forth in the midst of wolves.[2] But thou wilt say: "They needed not at that time to have inquisition made for them, being most manifest wolves; but their bite and savageness were to be endured." What, when foretelling later times, He said that ravening wolves would come in sheep's clothing? Was there not room there to give this advice and say, And do ye, that ye may find them out, assume wolves' clothing, but within be ye sheep still? Not this saith He: but when He had said, "Many will come to you in sheep's clothing, but within are ravening wolves;"[3] He went on to say, not, By your lies, but, "By their fruits ye shall know them." By truth must we beware of, by truth must we take, by truth must we kill, lies. Be it far from us, that the blasphemies of the ignorant we by wittingly blaspheming should overcome: far from us, that the evils of deceitful men we by imitating should guard against. For how shall we guard against them if in order to guard against them we shall have them? For if in order that he may be caught who blasphemes unwittingly, I shall blaspheme wittingly, worse is the thing I do than that which I catch. If in order that he may be found who denies Christ unwittingly, I shall deny Him wittingly, to his undoing will he follow me whom I shall so find, since in order that I may find him out, I first am undone.

13. Or haply is it so, that he who plots in this way to find out Priscillianists, denies not Christ, forasmuch as with his mouth he utters what with his heart he believes not? As if truly (which I also said a little above) when it was said, "With the heart man believeth unto righteousness," it was added to no purpose, "with the mouth confession is made unto salvation?"[4] Is it not so that almost all who have denied Christ before the persecutors, held in their heart what they believed of Him? And yet, by not confessing with the mouth unto salvation, they perished, save they which through penitence have lived again? Who can be so vain,[5] as to think that the Apostle Peter had that in his heart which he had on his lips when he denied Christ? Surely in that denial he held the truth within and uttered the lie without. Why then did he wash away with tears the denial which he uttered with his mouth, if that sufficed for salvation that with the heart he believed? Why, speaking the truth in his heart, did he punish with so bitter weeping the lie which he brought forth with his mouth, unless because he saw it to be a great and deadly evil, that while with his heart he believed unto righteousness, with his mouth he made not confession unto salvation?

14. Wherefore, that which is written, "Who speaketh the truth in his heart,"[6] is not so to be taken, as if, truth being retained in the heart, in the mouth one may speak a lie. But the reason why it is said, is, because it is possible that a man may speak with his mouth a truth which profiteth him nothing, if he hold it not in his heart, that is, if what he speaketh, himself believe not; as the heretics, and, above all, these same Priscillianists do, when they do, not indeed believe the catholic faith, but yet speak it, that they may be believed to be of us. They speak therefore the truth in their mouth, not in their heart. On this account were they to be distinguished from him of whom it is written, "He that speaketh truth in his heart." Now this truth the catholic as in his heart he speaketh, because so he believeth, so also in his mouth ought he, that so he may preach it; but against it, neither in heart nor in mouth have falsehood, that both with the heart he may believe unto righteousness, and with the mouth may make confession unto salvation. For also in that psalm, after it had been said, "Who speaketh truth in his heart," presently this is added, "Who hath used no deceit in his tongue."[7]

1 "Concorditer"—"Misericorditer."
2 Matt. x. 16.   3 Matt. vii. 15, 16.

4 Rom. x. 10.   5 Evanescat.
6 Ps. xv. 2.   7 Ps. xv. 2.

15. And as for that saying of the Apostle, " Putting away lying, speak every man truth with his neighbor, for we°are members one of another,"¹ far be it that we should so understand it, as though he had permitted to speak a lie with those who are not yet with us members of the body of Christ. But the reason why it is said, is, because each one of us ought to account every man to be that which he wishes him to become, although he be not yet become such; as the Lord showed the alien Samaritan to be neighbor to him unto whom he showed mercy."² A neighbor then, and not an alien, is that man to be accounted, with whom our concern is that he remain not an alien; and if, on the score of his not being yet made partaker of our Faith and Sacrament, there be some truths that must be concealed from him, yet is that no reason why false things should be told him.

16. For there were even in the Apostles' times some who preached the truth not in truth, that is, not with truthful mind: of whom the Apostle saith that they preached Christ not chastely, but of envy and strife. And on this account even at that time some were tolerated while preaching truth not with a chaste mind: yet not any have been praised as preaching falsehood with a chaste mind. Lastly, he saith of those, " Whether in pretence or in truth Christ be preached: "³ but in no wise would he say, In order that Christ may after be preached, let Him be first denied.

17. Wherefore, though there be indeed many ways in which latent heretics may be sought out, without vituperating the catholic faith or praising heretical impiety, yet if there were no other way at all of drawing out heretical impiety from its caverns, but that the catholic tongue should deviate from the straight path of truth; more tolerable were it that that should be hid, than that this should be precipitated; more tolerable that the foxes should lurk in their pits unseen, than for the sake of catching them the huntsmen should fall into the pit of blasphemy; more tolerable that the perfidy of Priscillianists should be covered with the veil of truth, than that the faith of catholics, lest it should of lying Priscillianists be praised, should of believing catholics be denied. For if lies, not of whatsoever kind, but blasphemous lies, are therefore just because they are committed with intent to detect hidden heretics; it will be possible at that rate, if they be committed with the same intention, that there should be chaste adulteries. For put the case that of a number of lewd Priscillianists, some woman should cast her eye upon a catholic Joseph, and promise him that she will betray their hidden retreats if she obtain from him that he lie with her, and it be certain that if he consent unto her she will make good her promise: shall we judge that it ought to be done? Or shall we understand that by no means must such a price be paid in purchase of that kind of merchandise? Why then do we not rout out heretics, in order to their being caught, by the flesh committing lasciviousness in adultery, and yet think right to rout them out by a mouth committing fornication in blasphemy? For either it will be lawful to defend both the one and the other with equal reason, that these things be therefore said to be not unjust, because they were done with intention of finding out the unjust: or if sound doctrine willeth not even for the sake of finding out heretics that we should have to do with unchaste women, albeit only in body, not in mind, assuredly not even for the sake of finding out heretics willeth it that by us, albeit only in voice not in mind, either unclean heresy were preached, or the chaste Catholic Church blasphemed. Because even the very sovereignty of the mind, to which every inferior motion of the man ought to be obedient, will not lack deserved opprobrium, when a thing is done that ought not to be done, whether by member or by word. Although even when it is done by word, it is done by member: because the tongue is a member, by which the word is made; nor is any deed of ours by any member brought to the birth unless it is first conceived in the heart; or rather being by our inwardly thinking upon and consenting unto it already brought to the birth, it is brought forth abroad in our doing of it, by a member. It is therefore no excusing the mind from the deed, when any thing is said to be done not after the purpose of the mind,⁴ which yet were not done, unless the mind decreed it to be done.

18. It does indeed make very much difference, for what cause, with what end, with what intention a thing be done: but those things which are clearly sins, are upon no plea of a good cause, with no seeming good end, no alleged good intention, to be done. Those works, namely, of men, which are not in themselves sins, are now good, now evil, according as their causes are good or evil; as, to give food to a poor man is a good work, if it be done because of pity, with right faith; as to lie with a wife, when it is done for the

sake of generation, if it be done with faith to beget subjects for regeneration. These and the like works according to their causes are good or evil, because the self-same, if they have evil causes, are turned into sins: as, if for boasting sake a poor man is fed; or for lasciviousness a man lies with his wife; or children are begotten, not that they may be nurtured for God, but for the devil. When, however, the works in themselves are evil, such as thefts, fornications, blasphemies, or other such; who is there that will say, that upon good causes they may be done, so as either to be no sins, or, what is more absurd, just sins? Who is there that would say, That we may have to give to the poor, let us commit thefts upon the rich: or, Let us sell false witness, especially if innocent men are not hurt thereby, but rather guilty men are rescued from the judges who would condemn them? For two good things are done by selling of this lie, that money may be taken wherewith a poor man may be fed, and a judge deceived that a man be not punished. Even in the matter of wills, if we can, why not suppress the true, and forge false wills, that inheritances or legacies may not come to unworthy persons, who do no good with them; but rather to those by whom the hungry are fed, the naked clothed, strangers entertained, captives redeemed, Churches builded? For why should not those evil things be done for the sake of these good things, if, for the sake of these good things, those are not evil at all? Nay, further, if lewd and rich women are likely to enrich moreover their lovers and paramours, why should not even these parts and arts be undertaken by a man of merciful heart, to use them for so good a cause as that he may have whence to bestow upon the needy; and not hear the Apostle saying, " Let him that stole steal no more, but rather let him labor, working with his hands that which is good, that he may have to give to him that needeth?"[1] If indeed not only theft itself, but also false witness and adultery and every evil work will be not evil but good, if it be done for the sake of being the means of doing good. Who can say these things, except one who endeavors to subvert human affairs and all manners and laws? For of what most heinous deed, what most foul crime, what most impious sacrilege, may it not be said that it is possible for it to be done rightly and justly; and not only with impunity, but even gloriously, that in perpetrating thereof not only no punishments should be feared, but there should be

hope even of rewards: if once we shall concede in all evil works of men, that not what is done, but wherefore done, must be the question; and this, to the end that whatever are found to have been done for good causes, not even they should be judged to be evil? But if justice deservedly punisheth a thief, albeit he shall say and shew that he therefore withdrew superfluities from a rich that he might afford necessaries to a poor man; if deservedly she punisheth a forger, albeit he prove that he therefore corrupted another's will, that he might be heir, who should thence make large alms, not he who should make none; if deservedly she punisheth an adulterer, yea, though he shall demonstrate that of mercy he did commit adultery, that through her with whom he did it he might deliver a man from death; lastly, to draw nearer to the matter in question, if deservedly she punisheth him who hath with that intent mixed in adulterous embrace with some woman, privy to the turpitude of the Priscillianists, that he might enter into their concealments; I pray thee, when the Apostle saith, " Neither yield ye your members instruments of unrighteousness unto sin;"[2] and therefore neither hands, nor members of generation, nor other members, can it be right to yield unto flagitious deeds with intent that we may be able to find out Priscillianists; what hath our tongue, what our whole mouth, what the organ of the voice, offended us, that we should yield these as instruments to sin, and to so great a sin, in which, that we may apprehend and rescue Priscillianists from blaspheming in ignorance, we, without excuse of ignorance, are to blaspheme our God?

19. Some man will say, " So then any thief whatever is to be accounted equal with that thief who steals with will of mercy?" Who would say this? But of these two it does not follow that any is good, because one is worse. He is worse who steals through coveting, than he who steals through pity: but if all theft be sin, from all theft we must abstain. For who can say that people may sin, even though one sin be damnable, another venial? but now we are asking, if a man shall do this or that, who will not sin or will sin? not, who will sin more heavily or lightly. For even thefts themselves are more lightly punished by law than crimes of lust: they are, however, both sins, albeit the one lighter, the other heavier; so that a theft which is committed of concupiscence is held to be lighter than an act of lust which is committed for

---

[1] Eph. iv. 28.

[2] Rom. vi. 13.

doing a good turn. Namely, in their own kind these become lighter than other sins of the same kind, which appear to be committed with a good intention; when yet the same compared with sins of another kind lighter in respect of the kind itself, are found to be heavier. It is a heavier sin to commit theft of avarice, than of mercy; and likewise it is a heavier sin to perpetrate lewdness of luxury, than of mercy; and yet is it a heavier sin to commit adultery of mercy, than to commit theft of avarice. Nor is it our concern now, what is lighter or what heavier, but what are sins or are not. For no man can say that it was a duty for a sin to be done, where it is clearly a sin; but we say that it is a duty, if the sin were done so or so, to forgive or not to forgive.

20. But, what must be confessed, to human minds certain compensative sins do cause such embarrassment, that they are even thought meet to be praised, and rather to be called right deeds. For who can doubt it to be a great sin, if a father prostitute his own daughters to the fornications of the impious? And yet hath there arisen a case in which a just man thought it his duty to do this, when the Sodomites with nefarious onset of lust were rushing upon his guests. For he said, " I have two daughters which have not known man; I will bring them out to you, and do ye to them as is good in your eyes: only unto these men do ye no wrong, for that they have come under covering of my roof." [1] What shall we say here? Do we not so abhor the wickedness which the Sodomites were attempting to do to the guests of the just man, that, whatever were done so this were not done, he should deem right to be done? Very much also moveth us the person of the doer, which by merit of righteousness was obtaining deliverance from Sodom, to say that, since it is a less evil for women to suffer lewdness than for men, it even pertained to the righteousness of that just man, that to his daughters he chose this rather to be done, than to his guests; not only willing this in his mind, but also offering it in word, and, if they should assent, ready to fulfill it in deed. But then, if we shall open this way to sins, that we are to commit less sins, in order that others may not commit greater; by a broad boundary, nay rather, with no boundary at all, but with a tearing up and removing of all bounds, in infinite space, will all sins enter in and reign. For, when it shall be defined, that a man is to sin less, that another may not sin more; then, of

course, by our committing thefts shall other men's committing of lewdness be guarded against, and incest by lewdness; and if any impiety shall seem even worse than incest, even incest shall be pronounced meet to be done by us, if in such wise it can be wrought that that impiety be not committed by others: and in each several kind of sins, both thefts for thefts, and lewdness for lewdness, and incest for incest, shall be accounted meet to be done: our own sins for other men's, not only less for greater, but even if it come to the very highest and worst, fewer for more; if the stress of affairs so turns, that otherwise other men would not abstain from sin unless by our sinning, somewhat less indeed, but still sinning; so that in every case where an enemy who shall have power of this sort shall say, " Unless thou be wicked, I will be more wicked, or unless thou do this wickedness, I will do more such," we must seem to admit wickedness in ourselves, if we wish to refrain (others) from wickedness. To be wise in this sort, what is it but to lose one's wits, or rather, to be downright mad? Mine own iniquity, not another's, whether perpetrated upon me or upon others, is that from which I must beware of damnation. For " the soul that sinneth, it shall die. [2]

21. If then to sin, that others may not commit a worse sin, either against us or against any, without doubt we ought not; it is to be considered in that which Lot did, whether it be an example which we ought to imitate, or rather one which we ought to avoid. For it seems meet to be more looked into and noted, that, when so horrible an evil from the most flagitious impiety of the Sodomites was impending over his guests, which he wished to ward off and was not able, to such a degree may even that just man's mind have been disturbed, that he was willing to do that which, not man's fear with its misty tempest, but God's Law in its tranquil serenity, if it be consulted by us, will cry aloud, must not be done, and will command rather that we be so cautious not to sin ourselves, that we sin not through fear of any sins whatever of other men. For that just man, by fearing other men's sins, which cannot defile except such as consent thereto, was so perturbed that he did not attend to his own sin, in that he was willing to subject his daughters to the lusts of impious men. These things, when we read in holy Scriptures, we must not, for that we believe them done, therefore believe them meet to be done; lest we violate precepts while we indis-

---

[1] Gen. xix. 8.

[2] Ezek. xviii. 4.

criminately follow precedents. Or, truly, because David swore to put Nabal to death, and, upon more considerate clemency, did it not, [1] shall we therefore say that he is to be imitated, so that we may swear to do a thing which afterwards we may see to be not meet to be done? But as fear perturbed the one, so that he was willing to prostitute his daughters, so did anger the other, that he swore rashly. In short, if it were allowed us to inquire of them both, by asking them to tell us why they did these things, the one might answer, "Fearfulness and trembling came upon me, and darkness covered me;" [2] the other too might say, "Mine eye was troubled through wrath: [3]" so that we should not marvel either that the one in the darkness of fear, or the other with troubled eye, saw not what was meet to have been seen, that they might not do what was not meet to have been done.

22. And to holy David indeed it might more justly be said, that he ought not to have been angry; no, not with one however ungrateful and rendering evil for good; yet if, as man, anger did steal over him, he ought not to have let it so prevail, that he should swear to do a thing which either by giving way to his rage he should do, or by breaking his oath leave undone. But to the other, set as he was amid the libidinous frenzy of the Sodomites, who would dare to say, "Although thy guests in thine own house, whither to enter in thou by most violent humanity hast compelled them, be laid hold upon by lewd men, and being deforced be carnally known as women, fear thou not a whit, care for it not a whit, have no dread, no horror, no trembling?" What man, even a companion of those wretches, would dare to say this to the pious host? But assuredly it would be most rightly said, "Do what thou canst, that the thing be not done which thou deservedly fearest: but let not this fear of thine drive thee to do a thing which if thy daughters be willing that it be done unto them, they will through thee do wickedness with the Sodomites, if unwilling, will through thee from the Sodomites suffer violence. Commit not thou a great crime of thine own, while thou dreadest a greater crime of other men; for be the difference as great as thou wilt between thine own and that of others, this will be thine own, that other men's." Unless perchance in defending this man one should so crowd himself into a corner, as to say, "Since to receive a wrong is better than to do one, and those

guests were not about to do but to suffer a wrong, that just man chose that his daughters should suffer wrong rather than his guests, acting upon his rights as his daughters' lord; and he knew that it would be no sin in them, if the thing were done, because they would but bear them which did the sin, not consenting unto them, and so without sin of their own. In fine, they did not offer themselves (albeit better females than males) to be carnally known instead of those guests, lest they should be rendered guilty, not by the suffering of others' lust, but by consenting of their own will: nor yet did their father permit it to be done unto himself, when they essayed to do it, because he would not betray his guests to them, (albeit there had been less of evil, if it were done to one man than to two;) but as much as he could he resisted, lest himself also should be defiled by any assent of his own, though even if the frenzy of others' lust had prevailed by strength of body, it would not have defiled him so long as he consented not. Now as the daughters sinned not, neither did he sin in their persons, because he was not making them to sin, if they should be deforced against their will, but only to bear them that did the sin. Just as if he should offer his slaves to be beaten by ruffians, that his guests might not suffer the wrong of beating." Of which matter I shall not dispute, because it would take long to argue, whether even a master may justly use his right of power over his slave, so as to cause an unoffending slave to be smitten, that his unoffending friend may not be beaten in his house by violent bad men. But certainly, as concerning David, it is no wise right to say that he ought to have sworn to do a thing which afterwards he would perceive that he ought not to do. Whence it is clear that we ought not to take all that we read to have been done by holy or just men, and transfer the same to morals, but hence too we must learn how widely that saying of the Apostle extends, and even to what persons it reaches: "Brethren, if a man be overtaken in a fault, ye which are spiritual restore such an one in the spirit of meekness, considering thyself also, lest thou be tempted." [4] The being overtaken in a fault happens, either while one does not see at the time what is right to be done, or while, seeing it, one is overcome; that is, that a sin is done, either for that the truth is hidden, or for that infirmity compelleth.

23. But in all our doings, even good men are very greatly embarrassed in the matter

---

[1] 1 Sam. xxv. 22-35.   [2] Ps. lv. 5.
[3] Ps. vi. 7, *turbatus est præ ira*, as in LXX. "Mine eye is consumed because of grief." E. V.

[4] Gal. vi. 1.

of compensative sins; so that these are not esteemed to be sins, if they have such causes for the which they be done, and in the which it may seem to be rather sin, if they be left undone. And chiefly as concerning lies hath it come to this pass in the opinion of men, that those lies are not accounted sins, nay rather are believed to be rightly done, when one tells a lie for the benefit of him for whom it is expedient to be deceived, or lest a person should hurt others, who seems likely to hurt unless he be got rid of by lies. In defense of these kinds of lies, very many examples from holy Scripture are accounted to lend their support. It is not, however, the same thing to hide the truth as it is to utter a lie. For although every one who lies wishes to hide what is true, yet not every one who wishes to hide what is true, tells a lie. For in general we hide truths not by telling a lie, but by holding our peace. For the Lord lied not when He said, "I have many things to say unto you, but ye cannot bear them now." [1] He held His peace from true things, not spake false things; for the hearing of which truths He judged them to be less fit. But if He had not indicated this same to them, that is, that they were not able to bear the things which He was unwilling to speak, He would indeed hide nevertheless somewhat of truth, but that this may be rightly done we should peradventure not know, or not have so great an example to confirm us. Whence, they who assert that it is sometimes meet to lie, do not conveniently mention that Abraham did this concerning Sarah, whom he said to be his sister. For he did not say, She is not my wife, but he said, "She is my sister;" [2] because she was in truth so near akin, that she might without a lie be called a sister. Which also afterwards he confirmed, after she had been given back by him who had taken her, answering him and saying, "And indeed she is my sister, by father, not by mother;" that is, by the father's kindred, not the mother's. Somewhat therefore of truth he left untold, not told aught of falsehood, when he left wife untold, and told of sister. This also did his son Isaac: for him too we know to have gotten a wife near of kin. [3] It is not then a lie, when by silence a true thing is kept back, but when by speech a false thing is put forward.

24. Touching Jacob, however, that which he did at his mother's bidding, so as to seem to deceive his father, if with diligence and in faith it be attended to, is no lie, but a mystery. The which if we shall call lies, all parables also, and figures designed for the

signifying of any things soever, which are not to be taken according to their proper meaning, but in them is one thing to be understood from another, shall be said to be lies: which be far from us altogether. For he who thinks this, may also in regard of tropical expressions of which there are so many, bring in upon all of them this calumny; so that even metaphor, as it is called, that is, the usurped transferring of any word from its proper object to an object not proper, may at this rate be called a lie. For when he speaks of waving corn-fields, of vines putting forth gems, [4] of the bloom of youth, of snowy hairs; without doubt the waves, the gems, the bloom, the snow, for that we find them not in those objects to which we have from other transferred these words, shall by these persons be accounted lies. And Christ a Rock, and the stony heart of the Jews; also, Christ a Lion, and the devil a lion, and innumerable such like, shall be said to be lies. [5] Nay, this tropical expression reaches even to what is called antiphrasis, as when a thing is said to abound which does not exist, a thing said to be sweet which is sour; "*lucus quod non luceat, Parcæ quod non parcant.*" Of which kind is that in holy Scripture, "If he will not bless [6] Thee to Thy face;" which the devil saith to the Lord concerning holy Job, and the meaning is "curse." By which word also the feigned crime of Naboth is named by his calumniators; for it is said that he "blessed [7] the king," that is, cursed. All these modes of speaking shall be accounted lies, if figurative speech or action shall be set down as lying. But if it be no lie, when things which signify one thing by another are referred to the understanding of a truth, assuredly not only that which Jacob did or said to his father that he might be blessed, but that too which Joseph spoke as if in mockery of his brothers, [8] and David's feigning of madness, [9] must be judged to be no lies, but prophetical speeches and actions, to be referred to the understanding of those things which are true; which are covered as it were with a garb of figure on purpose to exercise the sense of the pious inquirer, and that they may not become cheap by lying bare and on the surface. Though even the things which we have learned from other places, where they are spoken openly and manifestly, these, when they are brought out from their hidden retreats, do, by our (in some sort) discovering of them, become re-

---

[1] John xvi. 12. [2] Gen. xx. 2, 12. [3] Gen. xxvi. 7, and xxiv.

[4] "*Gemmare.*"
[5] 1 Cor. x. 4; Ezek. xxxvi. 26; Rev. v. 5; 1 Pet. v. 8.
[6] Job ii. 5, *benedixerit:* as LXX. εὐλογήσει: E. V. "curse."
[7] 1 Kings xxi. 10, 13. LXX. εὐλόγηκας: E. V. "didst blaspheme."
[8] Gen. xlii. [9] 1 Sam. xxi. 13.

newed, and by renewal sweet. Nor is it that they are begrudged to the learners, in that they are in these ways obscured; but are presented in a more winning manner, that being as it were withdrawn, they may be desired more ardently, and being desired may with more pleasure be found. Yet true things, not false, are spoken; because true things, not false, are signified, whether by word or by deed; the things that are signified namely, those are the things spoken. They are accounted lies only because people do not understand that the true things which are signified are the things said, but believe that false things are the things said. To make this plainer by examples, attend to this very thing that Jacob did. With skins of the kids, no doubt, he did cover his limbs; if we seek the immediate cause, we shall account him to have lied; for he did this, that he might be thought to be the man he was not: but if this deed be referred to that for the signifying of which it was really done, by skins of the kids are signified sins; by him who covered himself therewith, He who bare not His own, but others' sins. The truthful signification, therefore, can in no wise be rightly called a lie. And as in deed, so also in word. Namely, when his father said to him, "Who art thou, my son?"[1] he answered, "I am Esau, thy first-born." This, if it be referred to those two twins, will seem a lie; but if to that for the signifying of which those deeds and words are written, He is here to be understood, in His body, which is His Church, Who, speaking of this thing, saith, "When ye shall see Abraham, and Isaac, and Jacob, and all the prophets in the kingdom of God, and yourselves cast out. And they shall come from the east and from the west and from the north and from the south, and shall sit down in the kingdom of God; and, behold, there are last which shall be first, and there are first which shall be last."[2] For so in a certain sort the younger brother did bear off the primacy of the elder brother, and transfer it to himself. Since then things so true, and so truthfully, be signified, what is there here that ought to be accounted to have been done or said lyingly? For when the things which are signified are not in truth things which are not, but which are, whether past or present or future, without doubt it is a true signification, and no lie. But it takes too long in the matter of this prophetical signification by stripping off the shell to search out all,[3] wherein truth hath the palm, because as by being signified they

were fore-announced, so by ensuing have they become clear.

25. Nor have I undertaken that in the present discourse, as it more pertains to thee, who hast laid open the hiding-places of the Priscillianists, so far as relates to their false and perverse dogmas; that they may not seem to have been in such sort investigated as if they were meet to be taught, not to be argued against. Make it therefore more thy work that they be beaten down and laid low, as thou hast made it, that they should be betrayed and laid open; lest while we wish to get at the discovery of men practising falsehood, we allow the falsehoods themselves, as if insuperable, to stand their ground; when we ought rather even in the hearts of latent heretics to destroy falsehoods, than by sparing falsehoods to find out the deceivers who practise falsehood. Moreover, among those dogmas of theirs which are to be subverted, is this which they dogmatize, namely, that in order to hide religion religious people ought to lie, to that degree that not only concerning other matters, not pertaining to doctrine of religion, but concerning religion itself, it is meet to lie, that it may not become exposed to aliens; to wit, that one may deny Christ, in order that one may in the midst of His enemies be in secret a Christian. This impious and nefarious dogma do thou likewise, I beseech thee, overthrow; to bolster up which they in their argumentations do gather from the Scriptures testimonies to make it appear that lies are not only to be pardoned and tolerated, but even honored. To thee therefore it pertains, in refuting that detestable sect, to show that those testimonies of Scripture are so to be received, that either thou shalt teach those to be no lies which are accounted to be such, if they be understood in that manner in which they ought to be understood; or, that those are not to be imitated which be manifestly lies; or in any wise at last, that concerning those matters at least which pertain to doctrine of religion, it is in no wise meet to tell a lie. For thus are they truly from the very foundation overthrown, while that is overthrown wherein they lurk: that in that very matter they be judged least fit for us to follow, most fit to be shunned, in that they, for the hiding of their heresy, do profess themselves liars. This it is in them that must from the very first be assaulted, this which is, as it were, their fitting bulwark must with blows of Truth be battered and cast down. Nor must we afford them another lurking-place, which they had not, wherein they may take refuge, to wit, that being perhaps betrayed of them whom they have es-

---

[1] Gen. xxvii. 16-19.   [2] Luke xiii. 28-30.
[3] *Enucleate cuncta rimari.*

sayed to seduce but could not, they should say, "We only wanted to try them, because prudent Catholics have taught that to find out heretics it is right to do this." But it is necessary with somewhat more earnest bespeaking of thy favor to say why this seems to me a tripartite method of disputing against those who want to apply the divine Scriptures as advocates of their lies; to wit, by showing that some which are there accounted to be lies, are not what they are accounted, if rightly understood; next, that if there be there any manifest lies, they are not meet to be imitated; thirdly, contrary to all opinions of all persons who think it pertains to the duty of a good man sometimes to lie, that it must in every way be held that in doctrine of religion there must in no wise a lie be told. For these are the three things to follow up which I shortly before recommended, and in some sort enjoined thee.

26. To show then that some things in the Scriptures which are thought to be lies are not what they are thought, if they be rightly understood, let it not seem to thee to tell little against them, that it is not from Apostolic but from Prophetical books that they find as it were precedents of lying. For all those which they mention by name, in which each lied, are read in those books in which not only words but many deeds of a figurative meaning are recorded, because it was also in a figurative sense that they were done. But in figures that which is spoken as a seeming lie, being well understood, is found to be a truth. The Apostles, however, in their Epistles spoke in another sort, and in another sort are written the Acts of the Apostles, to wit, because now the New Testament was revealed, which was veiled in those prophetic figures. In short, in all those Apostolic Epistles, and in that large book in which their acts are narrated with canonical truth, we do not find any person lying, such that from him a precedent can be set forth by these men for license of lying. For that simulation of Peter and Barnabas with which they were compelling the Gentiles to Judaize, was deservedly reprehended and set right, both that it might not do harm at the time, and that it might not weigh with posterity as a thing to be imitated. For when the Apostle Paul saw that they walked not uprightly according to the truth of the Gospel, he said to Peter in the presence of them all, "If thou, being a Jew, livest as the Gentiles; and not as do the Jews, how compellest thou the Gentiles to Judaize?"[1] But in that which

himself did, to the intent that by retaining and acting upon certain observances of the law after the Jewish custom he might show that he was no enemy to the Law and to the Prophets, far be it from us to believe that he did so as a liar. As indeed concerning this matter his sentence is sufficiently well known, whereby it was settled that neither Jews who then believed in Christ were to be prohibited from the traditions of their fathers, nor Gentiles when they became Christians to be compelled thereunto: in order that those sacred rites[2] which were well known to have been of God enjoined, should not be shunned as sacrileges; nor yet accounted so necessary, now that the New Testament was revealed, as though without them whoso should be converted unto God, could not be saved. For there were some who thought so and preached, albeit after Christ's Gospel received; and to these had feignedly consented both Peter and Barnabas, and so were compelling the Gentiles to Judaize. For it was a compelling, to preach them to be so necessary as if, even after the Gospel received, without them were no salvation in Christ. This the error of certain did suppose, this Peter's fear did feign, this Paul's liberty did beat down. What therefore he saith, "I am made all things to all, that I might gain all,"[3] that did he, by suffering with others, not by lying. For each becomes as though he were that person whom he would fain succor, when he succoreth with the same pity wherewith he would wish himself to be succored, if himself were set in the same misery. Therefore he becomes as though he were that person, not for that he deceives him, but for that he thinks himself as him. Whence is that of the Apostle, which I have before rehearsed, "Brethren, if a man be overtaken in a fault, ye which are spiritual restore such an one in the spirit of meekness, considering thyself lest thou also be tempted."[4] For if, because he said, "To the Jews became I as a Jew, and to them which were under the law as under the law,"[5] he is therefore to be accounted to have in a lying manner taken up the sacraments of the old law, he ought in the same manner to have taken up, in a lying way, the idolatry of the Gentiles, because he hath said that to them which were without law he became as without law; which thing in any wise he did not. For he did not any where sacrifice to idols or adore those figments and not rather freely as a martyr of Christ show that they were to be detested and eschewed. From no apostolic acts or speeches, there-

---

[1] Gal. ii. 13, 14.

[2] "Sacramenta."

[3] 1 Cor. ix. 22. [See R.V.]

[4] Gal. vi. 1.

[5] 1 Cor. ix. 20.

fore, do these men allege things meet for imitation as examples of lying. From prophetical deeds or words, then, the reason why they seem to themselves to have what they may allege, is only for that they take figures prenunciative to be lies, because they are sometimes like unto lies. But when they are referred to those things for the signifying of which they were so done or said, they are found to be significations full of truth, and therefore in no wise to be lies. A lie, namely, is a false signification with will of deceiving. But that is no false signification, where, although one thing is signified by another, yet the thing signified is a true thing, if it be rightly understood.

27. There are some things of this sort even of our Saviour in the Gospel, because the Lord of the Prophets deigned to be Himself also a Prophet. Such are those where, concerning the woman which had an issue of blood, He said, "Who touched Me?"[1] and of Lazarus. "Where have ye laid him?"[2] He asked, namely, as if not knowing that which in any wise He knew. And He did on this account feign that He knew not, that He might signify somewhat else by that His seeming ignorance: and since this signification was truthful, it was assuredly not a lie. For those were signified, whether by her which had the issue, or by him which had been four days dead, whom even He Who knew all things did in a certain sort know not. For both she bore the type of the people of the Gentiles, whereof the prophecy had gone before, "A people whom I have not known hath served Me:"[3] and Lazarus, removed from the living, did as it were in that place lie in significative similitude where He lay, Whose voice that is, "I am cast out of the sight of thine eyes."[4] And with that intent, as though it were not known by Christ, both who she was, and where he was laid, by His words of interrogating a figure was enacted, and by truthful signification all lying left apart.

28. Hence is also that which thou hast mentioned that they speak of, that the Lord Jesus, after He was risen, walked in the way with two disciples; and upon their drawing near to the village whither they were going, He made as though He would have gone farther: where the Evangelist, saying, "But He Himself feigned that He would go further,"[5] hath put that very word in which liars too greatly delight, that they may with impunity lie: as if every thing that is feigned

is a lie, whereas in a truthful way, for the sake of signifying one thing by another, so many things use to be feigned. If then there had been no other thing that Jesus signified, in that He feigned to be going further, with reason might it be judged to be a lie: but then if it be rightly understood and referred to that which He willed to signify, it is a mystery. Else will all things be lies which, on account of a certain similitude of things to be signified, although they never were done, are related to have been done. Of which sort is that concerning the two sons of one man, the elder who tarried with his father, and the younger who went into a far country, which is narrated so much at length.[6] In which sort of fiction, men have put even human deeds or words to irrational animals and things without sense, that by this sort of feigned narrations but true significations, they might in more winning manner intimate the things which they wished. Nor is it only in authors of secular letters, as in Horace,[7] that mouse speaks to mouse, and weasel to fox, that through a fictitious narration a true signification may be referred to the matter in hand; whence the like fables of Æsop being referred to the same end, there is no man so untaught as to think they ought to be called lies: but in Holy Writ also, as in the book of Judges, the trees seek them a king, and speak to the olive, to the fig and to the vine and to the bramble.[8] Which, in any wise, is all feigned, with intent that one may get to the thing which is intended, by a feigned narration indeed, yet not a lying one, but with a truthful signification. This I have said on account of that which is written concerning Jesus, "And Hmself feigned to be going further:" lest any from this word, like the Priscillianists, wishing to have license of lying, should contend that beside others even Christ did lie. But whoso would understand what He by feigning that did prefigure, let him attend to that which He by acting did effect. For when afterwards He did go further, above all heavens, yet deserted He not His disciples. In order to signify this which in the future He did as God, at the present He feigned to do that as Man. And therefore was a veritable signification caused in that feigning to go before, because in this departure the verity of that signification did follow after. Let him therefore contend that Christ did lie by feigning, who denieth that He fulfilled by doing that which He signified.

29. Because, therefore, lying heretics find not in the books of the New Testament any

[1] Luke viii. 45. [2] John xi. 34. [3] Ps. xviii. 44—"*Servivit.*"
[4] Ps. xxxi. 22. [5] Luke xxiv. 28—"*Finxit.*"
[6] Luke xv. 11–32. [7] Serm. ii. 6; Epist. i. 7. [8] Judg. ix. 8–15.

precedents of lying which are meet to be imitated, they esteem themselves to be most copious in their disputation wherein they opine that it is right to lie, when from the old prophetical books, because it doth not appear therein, save to the few who understand, to what must be referred the significative sayings and doings which as such be true, they seem to themselves to find out and allege many that be lies. But desiring to have, wherewith they may defend themselves, precedents of deceit seemingly meet to be imitated, they deceive themselves, and "their iniquity lieth unto itself.[1] Those persons, however, of whom it is not there to be believed that they wished to prophesy, if in doing or saying they feigned aught with will of deceiving, however it may be that from the very things also which they did or said somewhat prophetical may be shapen out, being by His omnipotence afore deposited therein as a seed and pre-disposed, Who knoweth how to turn to good account even the ill-deeds of men, yet as far as regards the persons themselves, without doubt they lied. But they ought not to be esteemed meet for imitation simply for that they are found in those books which are deservedly called holy and divine: for those books contain the record of both the ill deeds and the good deeds of men; the one to be eschewed, the other to be followed after: and some are so put, that upon them is also sentence passed; some, with no judgment there expressed, are left permitted for us to judge of: because it was meet that we should not only be nourished by that which is plain, but exercised by that which is obscure.

30. But why do these persons think they may imitate Tamar telling a lie, and not think they may imitate Judah committing fornication?[2] For there they have read both, and nought of these hath that Scripture either blamed or praised, but has merely narrated both, and to our judgment dismissed both: but it is marvellous if it hath permitted aught of these to be imitated with impunity. For, that Tamar not through lust of playing the harlot, but through wish of conceiving seed, did tell the lie, we know. But fornication also, howbeit Judah's was not such, yet some man's may be such whereby to procure that a man may be delivered, just as her lie was in order that a man might be conceived; is it right then to commit fornication on this account, if on that account it is thought that it was right to lie? Not therefore concerning lying only,

but concerning all works of men in which there arise as it were compensative sins, must we consider what sentence we ought to pass; lest we open a way not only to small sins whatsoever, but even to all wickednesses, and there remain no outrageous, flagitious, sacrilegious deed, in which there may not arise a cause upon which it may rightly seem a thing meet to be done, and so universal probity of life be by that opinion subverted.

31. But he who says that some lies are just, must be judged to say no other than that some sins are just, and therefore some things are just which are unjust: than which what can be more absurd? For whence is a thing a sin, but for that it is contrary to justice? Be it said then that some sins are great, some small, because it is true; and let us not listen to the Stoics who maintain all to be equal: but to say that some sins are unjust, some just, what else is it than to say that there be some unjust, some just iniquities? When the Apostle John saith, "Every man who doeth sin, doeth also iniquity, and sin is iniquity."[3] It is impossible therefore that a sin should be just, unless when we put the name of sin upon another thing in which one doth not sin, but either doeth or suffereth aught for sin. Namely, both sacrifices for sins are named "sins," and the punishments of sins are sometimes called sins. These doubtless can be understood to be just sins, when just sacrifices are spoken of, or just punishments. But those things which are done against God's law cannot be just. It is said unto God, "Thy law is truth:"[4] and consequently, what is against truth cannot be just. Now who can doubt that every lie is against truth? Therefore there can be no just lie. Again, what man doth not see clearly that every thing which is just is of the truth? And John crieth out, "No lie is of the truth."[5] No lie therefore is just. Wherefore, when from holy Scriptures are proposed to us examples of lying, either they are not lies, but are thought to be so while they are not understood; or, if lies they be, they are not meet to be imitated, because they cannot be just.

32. But, as for that which is written, that God did good to the Hebrew midwives, and to Rahab the harlot of Jericho,[6] this was not because they lied, but because they were merciful to God's people. That therefore which was rewarded in them was, not their deceit, but their benevolence; benignity of mind, not iniquity of lying.[7] For, as it would not be marvellous and absurd if God on ac-

[1] Ps. 26 (Heb. xxvii), 12. "*Mentitur eorum iniquitas sibi.*" LXX. ἐψεύσατο ἡ ἀδικία ἑαυτῇ. Heb. and E. V. "And such as breathe out cruelty."
[2] Gen. xxxviii. 14-18.

[3] 1 John iii. 4. [See R.V.]   [4] Ps. cxix. 142.   [5] 1 John. ii. 21.
[6] Exod. i. 17-20 ; Josh. ii., and vi. 25.   [7] *Mentis, mentientis.*

count of good works after done by them should be willing to forgive some evil works at another time before committed, so it is not to be marvelled at that God beholding at one time, in one cause, both these, that is, the thing done of mercy and the thing done of deceit, did both reward the good, and for the sake of this good forgive that evil. For if sins which are done of carnal concupiscence, not of mercy, are for the sake of after works of mercy remitted,[1] why are not those through merit of mercy remitted which of mercy itself are committed? For more grievous is a sin which with purpose of hurting, than that which with purpose of helping, is wrought. And consequently if that is blotted out by a work of 'mercy thereafter following, why is this, which is less heinous, not blotted out by the mercy itself of the man, both going before that he may sin, and going along with him while he sins? So indeed it may seem: but in truth it is one thing to say, "I ought not to have sinned, but I will do works of mercy whereby I may blot out the sin which I did before;" and another to say, "I ought to sin, because I cannot else show mercy." It is, I say, one thing to say, "Because we have already sinned, let us do good," and another to say, "Let us sin, that we may do good." There it is said, "Let us do good, because we have done evil;" but here, "Let us do evil that good may come."[2] And, consequently, there we have to drain off the sink of sin, here to beware of a doctrine which teacheth to sin.

33. It remains then that we understand as concerning those women, whether in Egypt or in Jericho, that for their humanity and mercy they received a reward, in any wise temporal, which indeed itself, while they wist not of it, should by prophetical signification prefigure somewhat eternal. But whether it be ever right, even for the saving of a man's life, to tell a lie, as it is a question in resolving which even the most learned do weary themselves, it did vastly surpass the capacity of those poor women, set in the midst of those nations, and accustomed to those manners. Therefore their ignorance in this as well as in those other things of which they were alike unknowing, but which are to be known by the children not of this world but of that which is to come, the patience of God did bear withal: Who yet, for their human kindness which they had shown to His servants, rendered unto them rewards of an earthly sort, albeit signifying somewhat of an heavenly. And Rahab, indeed, delivered out of Jericho, made transition into the people

of God, where, being proficient, she might attain to eternal and immortal prizes which are not to be sought by any lie. Yet at that time when she did for the Israelite spies that good, and, for her condition of life, laudable work, she was not as yet such that it should be required of her, "In your mouth let Yea be yea, Nay nay."[3] But as for those midwives, albeit Hebrewesses, if they savored only after the flesh, what or how great is the good they got of their temporal reward in that they made them houses, unless by making proficiency they attained unto that house of which is sung unto God, "Blessed are they that dwell in thine house; for ever and ever they will praise thee?"[4] It must be confessed, however, that it approacheth much unto righteousness, and though not yet in reality, yet even now in respect of hopefulness and disposition that mind is to be praised, which never lies except with intention and will to do good to some man, but to hurt no man. But as for us, when we ask whether it be the part of a good man sometimes to lie, we ask not concerning a person pertaining to Egypt, or to Jericho, or to Babylon, or still to Jerusalem itself, the earthly, which is in bondage with her children;[5] but concerning a citizen of that city which is above and free, our mother, eternal in the heavens. And to our asking it is answered, "No lie is of the truth."[6] The sons of that city, are sons of the Truth. That city's sons are they of whom it is written, "In their mouth was found no lie:"[7] son of that city is he of whom is also written, "A son receiving the word shall be far from destruction: but receiving, he hath received that for himself, and nothing false proceedeth out of his mouth."[8] These sons of Jerusalem on high, and of the holy city eternal, if ever, as they be men, a lie of what kind soever doth worm itself into them, they ask humbly for pardon, not therefrom seek moreover glory.

34. But some man will say, Would then those midwives and Rahab have done better if they had shown no mercy, by refusing to lie? Nay verily, those Hebrew women, if they were such as that sort of persons of whom we ask whether they ought ever to tell a lie, would both eschew to say aught false, and would most frankly refuse that foul service of killing the babes. But, thou wilt say, themselves would die. Yea, but see what follows. They would die with an heavenly habitation for their incomparably more ample reward than those houses which they made them on earth could be: they would die, to

---

[1] *Dimittuntur.*   Rom. iii. 8.

3 Matt. v. 37.   4 5 Ps. lxxxiv. 4.   5 Gal. iv, 25, 26.
6 1 John ii. 21.   7 Rev. xiv. 5.
8 Prov. xxix. 27. Lat. (not in Hebrew).

be in eternal felicity, after enduring of death for most innocent truth. What of her in Jericho? Could she do this? Would she not, if she did not by telling a lie deceive the inquiring citizens, by speaking truth betray the lurking guests? Or could she say [1] to their questionings, I know where they are; but I fear God, I will not betray them? She could indeed say this, were she already a true Israelitess in whom was no guile: [2] which thing she was about to be, when through the mercy of God passing over into the city of God. But they, hearing this (thou wilt say), would slay her, would search the house. But did it follow that they would also find them, whom she had diligently concealed? For in the foresight of this, that most cautious woman had placed them where they would have been able to remain undiscovered if she, telling a lie, should not be believed. So both she, if after all she had been slain by her countrymen for the work of mercy, would have ended this life, which must needs come to an end, by a death precious in the sight of the Lord,[3] and towards them her benefit had not been in vain. But, thou wilt say, "What if the men who sought them, in their thorough-going search, had come to the place where she had concealed them?" In this fashion it may be said: What if a most vile and base woman, not only telling, but swearing a lie, had not got them to believe her? Of course even so would the things have been like to come to pass, through fear of which she lied. And where do we put the will and power of God? or haply was He not able to keep both her, neither telling a lie to her own townsmen, nor betraying men of God, and them, being His, safe from all harm? For by Whom also after the woman's lie they were guarded, by Him could they, even if she had not lied, have in any wise been guarded. Unless perchance we have forgotten that this did come to pass in Sodom, where males burning towards males with hideous lust could not so much as find the door of the house in which were the men they sought; when that just man, in a case altogether most similar, would not tell a lie for his guests, whom he knew not to be Angels, and feared lest they should suffer a violence worse than death. And doubtless, he might have given the seekers the like answer as that woman gave in Jericho. For it was in precisely the like manner that they sought by interrogating. But that just person was not willing that for the bodies of his guests his soul should be spotted by his own

telling of a lie, for which bodies he was willing that the bodies of his daughters by iniquity of others' lust should be deforced.[4] Let then a man do even for the temporal safety of men what he can; but when it comes to that point that to consult for such saving of them except by sinning is not in his power, thenceforth let him esteem himself not to have what he may do, when he shall perceive that only to be left him which he may not rightly do. Therefore, touching Rahab in Jericho, because she entertained strangers, men of God, because in entertaining of them she put herself in peril, because she believed on their God, because she diligently hid them where she could, because she gave them most faithful counsel of returning by another way, let her be praised as meet to be imitated even by the citizens of Jerusalem on high. But in that she lied, although somewhat therein as prophetical be intelligently expounded, yet not as meet to be imitated is it wisely propounded: albeit that God hath those good things memorably honored, this evil thing mercifully overlooked.

35. Since these things are so, because it were too long to treat thoroughly of all that in that " Pound "[5] of Dictinius are set down as precedents of lying, meet to be imitated, it seemeth to me that this is the rule to which not only these, but whatever such there be, must be reduced. Namely, either what is believed to be a lie must be shown not to be such; whether it be where a truth is left untold, and yet no falsehood told; or where a true signification willeth one thing to be understood of another, which kind of figurative either sayings or doings abounds in the prophetical writings. Or, those which are convicted to be lies, must be proved to be not meet to be imitated: and if any (as other sins) should stealthily creep in upon us, we are not to attribute righteousness to them, but to ask pardon for them. So indeed it seems to me, and to this sentence the things above disputed do compel me.

36. But for that we are men and among men do live, and I confess that I am not yet in the number of them whom compensative sins embarrass not, it oft befalleth me in human affairs to be overcome by human feeling, nor am I able to resist when it is said to me, " Lo, here is a sick man in peril of his life with a grievous disease, whose strength will no more be able to bear it, if the death of his only and most dear son be announced to him; he asks of thee whether his son liveth, and thou knowest that he is departed this

---

[1] MSS. and edd. "*An posset ;*" but Ben. ed. propose "*an non posset,*" "Could she not?"
[2] John i. 47.   [3] Ps. cxvi. 15.   [4] Gen. xix. 5-11.   [5] Or "Balance."

life; what wilt thou reply, when, whatever thou shalt say beside one of these three; either, He is dead; or, He liveth; or, I know not; he believes no other than that he is dead; which thing he perceives thee to be afraid to tell, and unwilling to tell a lie?" It comes to the same thing, if thou altogether hold thy peace. But of those three, two are false, He liveth, and, I know not; and they cannot be said by thee but by telling a lie. Whereas if thou shalt say that one thing which is true, that is, that he is dead, and the man be so perturbed that death follow, people will cry out that thou hast killed him. And who can bear men casting up to him what a mischief it is to shun a lie that might save life, and to choose truth which murders a man? I am moved by these objections exceedingly, but it were marvellous whether also wisely. For, when I shall set before the eyes of my heart (such as they be) the intellectual[1] beauty of Him out of Whose mouth nothing false proceedeth, albeit where truth in her radiance doth more and more brighten upon me, there my weak and throbbing sense is beaten back: yet I am with love of that surpassing comeliness so set on fire, that I despise all human regards which would thence recall me. But it is much that this affection persevere to that degree, that in temptation it lack not its effect. Nor doth it move me, while contemplating that luminous Good in which is no darkness of a lie, that, when we refuse to lie, and men through hearing of a truth do die, truth is called a murderer. For, if a lewd woman crave of thee the gratification of her lust, and, when thou consentest not, she perturbed with the fierceness of her love should die, will chastity also be a murderer? Or, truly, because we read, "We are a sweet savor of Christ in every place, both in them which are saved and in them which perish;"[2] to the one, indeed, a savor of life unto life, to others a savor of death unto death; shall we pronounce even the savor of Christ to be a murderer? But, for that we, being men, are in questions and contradictions of this sort for the most part overcome or wearied out by our feeling as men, for that very reason hath the Apostle also presently subjoined, "And who is sufficient for these things?"

37. Add to this, (and here is cause to cry out more piteously,) that, if once we grant it to have been right for the saving of that sick man's life to tell him the lie, that his son was alive, then, by little and little and by minute degrees, the evil so grows upon us, and by slight accesses to such a heap of wicked lies does it, in its almost imperceptible encroachments, at last come, that no place can ever be any where found on which this huge mischief, by smallest additions rising into boundless strength, might be resisted. Wherefore, most providently is it written, "He that despiseth small things shall fall by little and little."[3] Nay more: for these persons who are so enamored of this life, that they hesitate not to prefer it to truth, that a man may not die, say rather, that a man who must some time die may die somewhat later, would have us not only to lie, but even to swear falsely; to wit, that, lest the vain health of man should somewhat more quickly pass away, we should take the name of the Lord our God in vain! And there are among them learned men who even fix rules, and set bounds when it is a duty, when not a duty, to commit perjury! O, where are ye, fountains of tears? And what shall we do? whither go? where hide us from the ire of truth, if we not only neglect to shun lies, but dare moreover to teach perjuries? For look they well to it, who uphold and defend lying, what kind, or what kinds, of lying they shall delight to justify: at least in the worship of God let them grant that there must be no lying; at least let them keep themselves from perjuries and blasphemies; at least there, where God's name, where God as witness, where God's oath[4] is interposed, where God's religion is the matter of discourse or colloquy, let none lie, none praise, none teach and enjoin, none justify a lie: of the other kinds of lies let him choose him out that which he accounteth to be the mildest and most innocent kind of lying, he who will have it to be right to lie. This I know, that even he who teaches that it is meet to tell lies, wishes to be thought to teach a truth. For if it be false which he teaches, who would care to give heed to false doctrine, in which both he deceives that teaches and he is deceived that learns? But if, in order that he may be able to find some disciple, he upholds that he teaches a truth when he teaches that it is meet to lie, how will that lie be of the truth, when the Apostle John reclaimeth, "No lie is of the truth?"[5] It is therefore not true, that it is sometimes right to lie; and that which is not true to no man is at all to be persuaded.

38. But infirmity pleadeth its part, and with favor of the crowds proclaims itself to have a cause invincible. Where it contradicts, and says, "What way is there among men, who without doubt by being deceived

1 *Intelligibilem.*   2 2 Cor. ii. 15, 16. [See R.V.]   3 Ecclus. xix. 1.   4 "*Sacramentum.*"   5 1 John ii. 21.

are turned aside from a deadly harm to others or themselves, to succor men in peril, if our affection as men may not incline us to lie?" If it will hear me patiently, this crowd of mortality, crowd of infirmity, I will say somewhat in answer on the behalf of truth. Surely at the least pious, true, holy chastity is not otherwise than of the truth: and whoso acts against it, acts against truth. Why then, if otherwise it be not possible to succor men in peril, do I not also commit whoredom, which is therefore contrary to truth, for that it is contrary to chastity, and yet, to succor men in peril, do speak a lie which most openly is contrary to truth itself? Wherein hath chastity so highly deserved at our hands, and truth offended us? When all chastity is of the truth, and not the body's but the mind's chastity is truth, yea, in the mind dwelleth even the body's chastity. Lastly, as I shortly before said, and say again, whoever for the recommending and defending of any lie speaks against me, what speaks he, if he speaks not truth? Now if he is therefore to be heard because he speaks truth, how wishes he to make me, by speaking truth, a liar? How does lying take unto itself truth as its patroness? Or, is it for her own adversary that she conquers, that by herself she may be conquered? Who can bear this absurdity? In no wise therefore may we say, that they who assert that it is sometimes right to lie, in asserting that are truthful; lest, what is most absurd and foolish to believe, truth should teach us to be liars. For what sort of thing is it, that no man learns of chastity that we may commit adultery; that we may offend God none learns of piety; that we may do any man harm, none learns of kindness; and that we may tell lies, we are to learn of truth! But then if this thing truth teaches not, it is not true; if not true, it is not meet to be learned; if not meet to be learned, never therefore is it meet to tell a lie.

39. But, some man will say, "Strong meat is for them that are perfect."[1] For in many things a relaxation by way of indulgence is allowed to infirmity, although in her utmost sincerity the things be nowise pleasing to truth. Let him say this, whoever dreads not the consequences which are to be dreaded, if once there shall be in any way any lies permitted. In nowise, however, must they be permitted to climb up to such a height as to reach to perjuries and blasphemies: nor must any plea whatever be held out, for which it should be right that perjury should be committed, or, what is more execrable, that God

should be blasphemed. For it does not follow that because the blaspheming is only in pretence and a lie, therefore He is not blasphemed. For at this rate it might be said that perjury is not committed, because it is by a lie that it is committed: for who can be by truth a perjurer? So also by truth can no man be a blasphemer. Doubtless it is a milder kind of false swearing, when a person does not know that thing to be false and believes it to be true, which he swears: like as also Saul blasphemed more excusably, because he did it ignorantly.[2] But the reason why it is worse to blaspheme than to perjure one's self, is, that in false swearing God is taken to witness a false thing, but in blaspheming false things are spoken of God Himself. Now by so much is a man more inexcusable, whether perjurer or blasphemer, by how much the more, while asserting the things wherein they perjure or blaspheme, they know or believe them to be false. Whoever therefore says that for an imperilled man's temporal safety or life a lie may be told, doth too much himself swerve from the path of eternal safety and life, if he says that on that behalf one may even swear by God, or even blaspheme God.

40. But sometimes a peril to eternal salvation itself is put forth against us;[3] which peril, they cry out, we by telling a lie, if otherwise it cannot be, must ward off. As, for instance, if a person who is to be baptized be in the power of impious and infidel men, and cannot be got at that he may be washed with the laver of regeneration, but by deceiving his keepers with a lie. From this most invidious cry, by which we are compelled, not for a man's wealth or honors in this world which are fleeting by, not for the life itself of this present time, but for the eternal salvation of a human being, to tell a lie, whither shall I betake me for refuge but unto thee, O truth? And by thee is put forth before me,[4] Chastity. For why, if those keepers may be enticed to admit us to baptize the man, by our committing lewdness, do we refuse to do things contrary to chastity, and yet, if by a lie they may be deceived, consent to do things contrary to truth? when without doubt no man would faithfully think chastity amiable, but because it is enjoined of truth? So then, to get at a man to baptize him, let the keepers be deceived by lying, if truth bid it. But how can truth bid in order that a man may be baptized, that we should tell a lie, if chastity biddeth not, in order that a man be baptized, that we should commit whoredom? Now

why doth chastity not bid this, but because this truth teacheth not? If then, save what truth teacheth, we ought not to do, when truth teacheth not even for the sake of baptizing a man to do what is contrary to chastity, how shall she teach us to do for the sake of baptizing a man what is contrary to herself, the truth? But like as eyes not strong enough to look upon the sun yet do gladly look upon the objects which are by the sun enlightened, so, souls which have already strength to delight in the beauty of chastity are yet not straightway able to consider in her very self that truth whence chastity hath her light, insomuch that when it cometh to the doing of somewhat that is adverse to truth, they should so start back in horror as they do start back in horror if aught be proposed to be done that is adverse to chastity. But that son, who, receiving the word shall be far from perdition, and nothing false cometh forth of his mouth,[1] accounts it as much debarred from him if, to the succoring of his fellow man he be urged to pass through a lie, as if it were through the deed of lewdness. And the Father heareth and granteth his prayer that he may avail without a lie to succor whom the Father Himself, Whose judgments are unsearchable, willeth to be succored. Such a son therefore so keeps watch against a lie, as he doth against sin. For indeed sometimes the name of lie is put for the name of sin: whence is that saying, "All men are liars."[2] For it is so said, as if it were said, "All men are sinners." And that: "But if the truth of God hath abounded through my lie."[3] And therefore, when he lies as a man he sins as a man, and will be held by that sentence in which it is said, "All men are liars;" and, "If we say that we have no sin, we deceive ourselves, and the truth is not in us."[4] But when nothing false cometh forth of his mouth, according to that grace will it so be, of which is said: "He that is born of God, sinneth not."[5] For were this nativity by itself alone in us, no man would sin: and when it shall be alone, no man will sin. But now, we as yet drag on that which we were born corruptible: although, according to that which we are new-born, if we walk aright, from day to day we are renewed inwardly.[6] But when this corruptible shall have put on incorruption, life will swallow it up wholly, and not a sting of death will remain.[7] Now this sting of death is sin.

41. Either then we are to eschew lies by right doing, or to confess them by repenting: but not, while they unhappily abound in our living, to make them more by teaching also.

But let him who thinks this, choose out whereby he may help his fellow man being in peril, to what safety he will, what kinds soever of lies; provided yet even of such men we obtain our demand, that upon no cause must we be carried on to false-swearing and to blaspheming. These wickednesses at least let us judge either greater than deeds of lewdness, or certainly not smaller. For indeed it is worth thinking of, that very often men, where they suspect them of adultery, challenge their wives to an oath: which surely they would not do, unless they believed that even they who were not afraid to perpetrate adultery, might be afraid of perjury. Because in fact also some lewd women who were not afraid by unlawful embraces to deceive their husbands, have been afraid to call God deceitfully to witness unto those same husbands whom they had deceived. What cause then can there be, that a chaste and religious person should be unwilling by adultery to help a man to baptism, yet be willing to help him by perjury, which even adulterers are wont to dread? And then, if it be shocking to do this by perjuring one's self, how much rather by blaspheming? Far be it then from a Christian to deny and blaspheme Christ, that he may make another man a Christian; and by losing himself seek to find one, whom, if he teach him such things, he may cause to be lost when found. The book then which is called " the Pound," thou must in this method refute and destroy; namely, that head of it in which they dogmatize that for the purpose of concealing religion a lie may be told, this thou shalt understand must be the first to be amputated; in such manner, that their testimonies by which they labor to advance the Holy Books as patrons of their lies, thou must demonstrate partly not to be lies, partly, even those which are such, to be not meet to be imitated: and if infirmity usurps to herself thus much, that somewhat shall be venially permitted unto her which truth approve not, yet that thou unshakenly hold and defend, that in divine religion it is at no time whatever right to tell a lie. And, as for concealed heretics, that, as we are not to find out concealed adulterers by committing of adulteries, nor murderers by committing of murders, nor practisers of black arts[8] by practising of black arts, so neither must we seek to find out liars by telling lies or blasphemers by blaspheming: according to the reasonings which we have in this volume so copiously set forth, that unto the goal of the same, which we fixed to be in this place, we have with difficulty come at last.

---

[1] Prov. xxix. 27. Lat.   [2] Ps. cxvi. 11. [See R. V.]
[3] Rom. iii. 7.   [4] 1 John i. 8.   [5] 1 John iii. 9.
[6] 2 Cor. iv. 16.   [7] 1 Cor. xv. 53-56. [See R.V.]

[8] Maleficos.

ST. AUGUSTIN:

OF

THE WORK OF MONKS

[DE OPERE MONACHORUM.]

TRANSLATED BY

REV. H. BROWNE, M.A.,

OF CORPUS CHRISTI COLLEGE, CAMBRIDGE; LATE PRINCIPAL OF THE DIOCESAN
COLLEGE, CHICHESTER.

OF THE WORK OF MONKS.

[DE OPERE MONACHORUM.]

From the Retractations, ii. 21.

To write the Book *on the Work of Monks*, the need whicn compelled me was this. When at Carthage there had begun to be monasteries, some maintained themselves by their own hands, obeying the Apostle ; but others wished so to live on the oblations of the faithful, that doing no work whence they might either have or supply the necessaries of life, they thought and boasted that they did rather fulfill the precept of the Gospel, where the Lord saith, *Behold the fowls of heaven, and the lilies of the field*, (Matt. vi. 26). Whence also among laics of inferior purpose, but yet fervent in zeal, there had begun to arise tumultuous contests, whereby the Church was troubled, some defending the one, others the other part. Add to this, that some of them who were for not working, wore their hair long. Whence contentions between those who reprehended and those who justified the practice, were, according to their party affections, increased. On these accounts the venerable old Aurelius, Bishop of the Church of the same city, desired me to write somewhat of this matter ; and I did so. This Book begins, " Jussioni tuæ, sancte frater Aureli."

This work is placed in the *Retractations* next after that "On the Good of Marriage," which belongs to the year 401.

1. THY bidding, holy brother Aurelius, it was meet that I should comply withal, with so much the more devotion, by how much the more it became clear unto me Who, out of thee, did speak that bidding. For our Lord Jesus Christ, dwelling in thine inner part, and inspiring into thee a solicitude of fatherly and brotherly charity, whether our sons and brothers the monks, who neglect to obey blessed Paul the Apostle, when he saith, " If any will not work, neither let him eat," [1] are to have that license permitted unto them; He, assuming unto His work thy will and tongue, hath commanded me out ôf thee, that I should hereof write somewhat unto thee. May He therefore Himself be present with me also, that I may obey in such sort that from His gift, in the very usefulness of fruitful labor, I may understand that I am indeed obeying Him.

2. First then, it is to be seen, what is said by persons of that profession, who will not work: then, if we shall find that they think not aright, what is meet to be said for their correction? " It is not," say they, " of this corporal work in which either husbandmen or handicraftsmen labor, that the Apostle gave precept, when he said, ' If any will not work, neither let him eat.' " For he could not be contrary to the Gospel, where the Lord Him-

---

[1] 2 Thess. iii. 10. [See R.V.]

self saith, " Therefore I say unto you, be not solicitous for your life, what ye shall eat, neither for your body, what ye shall put on. Is not the life more than meat, and the body than raiment? Consider the fowls of heaven, that they sow not, nor reap, nor gather into barns; and your heavenly Father feedeth them. Are not ye rather of more worth than they? But who of you by taking thought can add to his stature one cubit? And concerning raiment, why are ye solicitous? Consider the lilies of the field, how they grow; they labor not, neither spin; but I say unto you, that not even Solomon in all his glory was arrayed like one of these. But if the grass of the field, which to-day is, and to-morrow is cast into the oven, God so clotheth; how much more you, (O ye) of little faith! Be not therefore solicitous, saying, What shall we eat, or what shall we drink, or wherewithal shall we be clad? for all these things do the Gentiles seek. And your heavenly Father knoweth that ye need all these. But seek ye first the kingdom of God, and His righteousness, and all these shall be added unto you. Be not therefore solicitous for the morrow: for the morrow will be solicitous for itself. Sufficient unto the day is the evil thereof."[1] Lo, say they, where the Lord biddeth us be without care concerning our food and clothing: how then could the Apostle think contrary to the Lord, that he should instruct us that we ought to be in such sort solicitous, what we shall eat, or what we shall drink, or wherewithal we shall be clothed, that he should even burden us with the arts, cares, labors of handicraftsmen? Wherefore in that he saith, " If any will not work, neither let him eat;" works spiritual, say they, are what we must understand: of which he saith in another place, " To each one according as the Lord hath given: I have planted, Apollos hath watered; but God gave the increase."[2] And a little after, " Each one shall receive his reward according to his own labor. We are God's fellow-workers; God's husbandry, God's building are ye: according to the grace which is given unto me, as a wise masterbuilder I have laid the foundation." As therefore the Apostle worketh in planting, watering, building, and foundation-laying, in that way whoso will not work, let him not eat. For what profiteth in eating spiritually to be fed with the word of God, if he do not thence work others' edification? As that slothful servant, what did it profit to receive a talent and to hide it, and not work for the Lord's gain? Was it that it

should be taken from him at last, and himself cast into outer darkness? So, say they, do we also. We read with the brethren, who come to us fatigued from the turmoil of the world, that with us, in the word of God, and in prayers, psalms, hymns, and spiritual songs, they may find rest. We speak to them, console, exhort, building up in them whatever unto their life, according to their degree, we perceive to be lacking. Such works if we wrought not, with peril should we receive of the Lord our spiritual sustenance itself. For this is it the Apostle said, " If any one will not work, neither let him eat." Thus do these men deem themselves to comply with the apostolic and evangelic sentence, when both the Gospel they believe to have given precept concerning the not caring for the corporal and temporal indigence of this life, and the Apostle concerning spiritual work and food to have said, " If any will not work, neither let him eat."

3. Nor do they attend to this, that if another should say, that the Lord indeed, speaking in parables and in similitudes concerning spiritual food and clothing, did warn that not on these accounts should His servants be solicitous; (as He saith, " When they shall drag you to judgment-seats, take no thought what ye shall speak. For it will be given you in that hour what ye shall speak: but it is not ye that speak, but the Spirit of your Father that speaketh in you."[3] For the discourse of spiritual wisdom is that for which He would not that they should take thought, promising that it should be given unto them, nothing solicitous thereof;) but the Apostle now, in manner Apostolical, more openly discoursing and more properly, than figuratively speaking, as is the case with much, indeed wellnigh all, in his Apostolic Epistles, said it properly of corporal work and food, " If any will not work, neither let him eat:" by those would their sentence be rendered doubtful, unless, considering the other words of the Lord, they should find somewhat whereby they might prove it to have been of not caring for corporal food and raiment that He spake when He said, " Be not solicitous what ye shall eat, or what ye shall drink, or wherewithal ye shall be clothed." As, if they should observe what He saith, " For all these things do the Gentiles seek;" for there He shows that it was of very corporal and temporal things that He spake. So then, were this the only thing that the Apostle has said on this subject, " If any will not work, neither let him eat;" these words might be drawn over to another mean-

---

ing: but since in many other places of his Epistles, what is his mind on this point, he most openly teaches, they superfluously essay to raise a mist before themselves and others, that what that charity adviseth they may not only refuse to do, but even to understand it themselves, or let it be understood by others; not fearing that which is written, "He would not understand that he might do good." [1]

4. First then we ought to demonstrate that the blessed Apostle Paul willed the servants of God to work corporal works which should have as their end a great spiritual reward, for this purpose that they should need food and clothing of no man, but with their own hands should procure these for themselves: then, to show that those evangelical precepts from which some cherish not only their sloth but even arrogance, are not contrary to the Apostolical precept and example. Let us see then whence the Apostle came to this, that he should say, "If any will not work, neither let him eat," and what he thereupon joineth on, that from the very context [2] of this lesson may appear his declared sentence. "We command you, brethren, in the name of our Lord Jesus Christ, that ye withdraw yourselves from every brother that walketh unquietly, and not according to the tradition which they have received [3] of us. For yourselves know how ye ought to imitate us; for we were not unquiet among you, neither ate we bread of any man for nought, but in labor and travail night and day working that we might not burden any of you: not for that we have not power, but that we might give ourselves as a pattern to you in which ye should imitate us. For also when we were with you, we gave you this charge, that if any will not work, let him not eat. For we have heard that certain among you walk unquietly, working not at all, but being busy-bodies. Now them that are such we charge and beseech in our Lord Jesus Christ, that with silence they work, and eat their own bread." [4] What can be said to these things, since, that none might thereafter have license to interpret this according to his wish, not according to charity, he by his own example hath taught what by precept he hath enjoined? To him, namely, as to an Apostle, a preacher of the Gospel, a soldier of Christ, a planter of the vineyard, a shepherd of the flock, had the Lord appointed that he should live by the Gospel; and yet himself exacted not the pay which was his due, that he might make himself a pattern to them which desired what was not their due; as he saith to the Corinthians, "Who goeth a war-

fare at any time at his own charges? Who planteth a vineyard, and of its fruit eateth not? Who feedeth a flock, and of the milk of the flock partaketh not?" [5] Therefore, what was due to him, he would not receive, that by his example they might be checked, who, although not so ordained in the Church, did deem the like to be due to themselves. For what is it that he saith, "Neither ate we bread of any man for naught, but in labor and travail night and day working that we might not burden any of you; not for that we have not power, but that we might give ourselves as a pattern to you wherein ye should follow us?" Let them, therefore, hear to whom he hath given this precept, that is, they which have not this power which he had, to wit, that while only spiritually working they should eat bread by corporal labor not earned: [6] and as he says, "We charge and beseech in Christ that with silence they work and eat their own bread," let them not dispute against the most manifest words of the Apostle, because this also pertaineth to that "silence" with which they ought to work and eat their own bread.

5. I would, however, proceed to a more searching [7] and diligent consideration and handling of these words, had I not other places of his Epistles much more manifest, by comparing which, both these are made more clearly manifest, and if these were not in existence, those others would suffice. To the Corinthians, namely, writing of this same thing, he saith thus, "Am I not free? am I not an Apostle? [8] Have I not seen Christ Jesus our Lord? Are not ye my work in the Lord? If to others I am not an Apostle, to you assuredly I am. For the seal of mine Apostleship are ye in the Lord. My defense to them which interrogate me is this. Have we not power to eat and to drink? Have we not power to lead about a woman who is a sister, [9] as also the other Apostles, and the brethren of the Lord, and Cephas?" See how first he shows what is lawful to him, and therefore lawful for that he is an Apostle. For with that he began, "Am I not free? am I not an Apostle?" and proves himself to be an Apostle, saying, "Have I not seen Christ Jesus our Lord? Are not ye my work in the Lord?" Which being proved, he shows that to be lawful to him which was so to the other Apostles; that is, that he should not work with his hands, but live by the Gospel, as the Lord appointed, which in what follows he has most

---

[1] Ps. xxxvi. 3, (35, 4,) "noluit intelligere ut bene ageret."   [2] "Circumstantia."   [3] "Acceperunt."   [4] 2 Thess. iii. 6-12.

[5] 1 Cor. ix. 1-7.   [6] Gratuitum.   [7] Enucleatius.
[8] So Griesbach and Lachmann. But text recept. "Am I not an Apostle? am I not free?"
[9] "Sororem mulierem."

openly demonstrated; for to this end did also faithful women which had earthly substance go with them, and minister unto them of their substance, that they might lack none of those things which pertain to the necessaries of this life. Which thing blessed Paul demonstrates to be lawful indeed unto himself, as also the other Apostles did it, but that he had not chosen to use this power he afterwards mentions. This thing some not understanding, have interpreted not "a woman which is a sister," when he said, "Have we not power to lead about a sister a woman;" but, "a sister a wife." They were misled by the ambiguity of the Greek word, because both "wife" and "woman" is expressed in Greek by the same word. Though indeed the Apostle has so put this that they ought not to have made this mistake; for that he neither says "a woman" merely, but "a sister woman;" nor "to take" (as in marriage), but "to take about" (as on a journey). Howbeit other interpreters have not been misled by this ambiguity, and they have interpreted "woman" not "wife."

6. Which thing whoso thinks cannot have been done by the Apostles, that with them women of holy conversation should go about wheresoever they preached the Gospel, that of their substance they might minister to their necessities, let him hear the Gospel, and learn how in this they did after the example of the Lord Himself. Our Lord, namely, according to the wont of His pity, sympathizing with the weak, albeit Angels might minister unto Him, had both a bag in which should be put the money which was bestowed doubtless by good and believing persons, as necessary for their living, (which bag He gave in charge to Judas, that even thieves, if we could not keep clear of such, we might learn to tolerate in the Church. He, namely, as is written of him, "stole[1] what was put therein:") and He willed that women should follow Him for the preparing and ministering what was necessary, showing what was due to evangelists and ministers of God as soldiers, from the people of God as the provincials; so that if any should not choose to use that which is due unto him, as Paul the Apostle did not choose, he might bestow the more upon the Church, by not exacting the pay which was due to him, but by earning his daily living of his own labors. For it had been said to the inn-keeper to whom that wounded man was brought, "Whatever thou layest out more, at my coming again I will repay thee."[2] The Apostle Paul, then, did "lay out more,"[3] in

that he, as himself witnesseth, did at his own charges go a warfare. In the Gospel, namely, it is written, "Thereafter also Himself was making a journey through cities and villages preaching and evangelizing of the kingdom of God; and the twelve with Him, and certain women which had been healed of evil spirits and infirmities: Mary who is called Magdalene, out of whom seven devils had gone forth, and Joanna wife of Chuza Herod's steward, and Susanna, and many others, who ministered unto Him of their substance."[4] This example of the Lord the Apostles did imitate, to receive the meat which was due unto them; of which the same Lord most openly speaketh: "As ye go," saith He, "preach, saying, The kingdom of heaven is at hand. Heal the sick, raise the dead, cleanse lepers, cast out devils. Freely have ye received, freely give. Possess not gold nor silver nor money in your purses, neither scrip on your journey, neither two coats, neither shoes, neither staff: for the workman is worthy of his meat."[5] Lo, where the Lord appointeth the very thing which the Apostle doth mention. For to this end He told them not to carry all those things, namely, that where need should be, they might receive them of them unto whom they preached the kingdom of God.

7. But lest any should fancy that this was granted only to the twelve, see also what Luke relateth: "After these things," saith he, "the Lord chose also other seventy and two, and sent them by two and two before His face into every city and place whither He was about to come. And He said unto them, The harvest indeed is plentiful, but the laborers few: ask ye therefore the Lord of the harvest, that He would send forth laborers into His harvest. Go your ways: behold, I send you as lambs in the midst of wolves. Carry neither purse nor scrip nor shoes, and salute no man by the way. Into whatsoever house ye shall enter, first say, Peace be to this house. And if the son of peace be there, your peace shall rest upon him: if not, it shall return to you. And in the same house remain, eating and drinking such things as are with them: for the workman is worthy of his hire."[6] Here it appears that these things were not commanded, but permitted, that whoso should choose to use, might use that which was lawful unto him by the Lord's appointment; but if any should not choose to use it, he would not do contrary to a thing commanded, but would be yielding up his own right, by demeaning himself more merci-

---

[1] "Auferebat."   [2] Luke x. 35.
[3] 1 Cor. ix. 7-15 ; and 2 Cor. xi. 7.

[4] Luke viii. 1-3. [See R.V.]   [5] Matt. x. 7-10.   [6] Luke x. 1-7.

fully and laboriously in the Gospel in the which he would not accept even the hire which was his due. Otherwise the Apostle did contrary to a command of the Lord: for, after he had shown it to be lawful unto him, he hath straightway subjoined, "But yet have I not used this power."

8. But let us return to the order of our discourse, and the whole of the passage itself of the Epistle let us diligently consider. "Have we not," saith he, "leave[1] to eat and to drink? have we not leave to lead about a woman, a sister?" What leave meant he, but what the Lord gave unto them whom He sent to preach the kingdom of heaven, saying, "Those things which are (given) of them, eat ye;[2] for the workman is worthy of his hire;" and proposing Himself as an example of the same power, to Whom most faithful women did of their means minister such necessaries? But the Apostle Paul hath done more, from his fellow-Apostles alleging a proof of this license permitted of the Lord. For not as finding fault hath he subjoined, "As do also the other Apostles, and the brethren of the Lord, and Cephas;" but that hence he might show that this which he would not accept was a thing which, that it was lawful for him to accept was proved by the wont of the rest also his fellow-soldiers. "Or I only and Barnabas, have we not power to forbear working?" Lo, he hath taken away all doubt even from the slowest hearts, that they may understand of what working he speaks. For to what end saith he, "Or I only and Barnabas, have we not power to forbear working?" but for that all evangelists and ministers of God's word had power received of the Lord, not to work with their hands, but to live by the Gospel, working only spiritual works in preaching of the kingdom of heaven and edifying of the peace of the Church? For no man can say that it is of that very spiritual working that the Apostle said, "Or I only and Barnabas, have we not power to forbear working?" For this power to forbear working all those had: let him say then, who essays to deprave and pervert precepts Apostolical; let him say, if he dares, that all evangelists received of the Lord power to forbear preaching the Gospel. But if this is most absurd and mad to say, why will they not understand what is plain to all, that they did indeed receive power not to work, but works bodily, whereby to get a living, because "the workman is worthy of his hire," as the Gospel speaks. It is not therefore that Paul and Barnabas only had not power to forbear working; but that all alike had this power, of which these availed not themselves in "laying out more" upon the Church; so as in those places where they preached the Gospel they judged to be meet for the weak. And for this reason, that he might not seem to have found fault with his fellow-Apostles, he goes on to say: "Who goeth a warfare at any time at his own charges? Who feedeth a flock, and of the milk of the flock partaketh not? Speak I these things as a man? Saith not the Law the same? For in the law of Moses it is written, Thou shalt not muzzle the ox that treadeth out the corn. Doth God care for oxen? Or saith he it for our sake altogether? For our sakes truly is it written, because he that plougheth ought to plough in hope, and he that thresheth in hope of partaking of the fruits."[3] By these words the Apostle Paul sufficiently indicates, that it was no usurping unto themselves of aught beyond their due on the part of his fellow-Apostles, that they wrought not bodily, whence they might have the things which to this life are necessary, but as the Lord ordained, should, living by the Gospel, eat bread gratuitously given of them unto whom they were preaching a gratuitous grace. Their charges, namely, they did like soldiers receive, and of the fruit of the vineyard by them planted, they did, as need was, freely gather; and of the milk of the flock which they fed, they drank; and of the threshing-floor on which they threshed, they took their meat.

9. But he speaks more openly in the rest which he subjoins, and altogether removes all causes of doubting. "If we unto you," saith he, "have sown spiritual things, is it a great matter if we shall reap your carnal things?" What are the spiritual things which he sowed, but the word and mystery of the sacrament of the kingdom of heaven? And what the carnal things which he saith he had a right to reap, but these temporal things which are indulged to the life and indigency of the flesh? These however being due to him he declares that he had not sought nor accepted, lest he should cause any impediment to the Gospel of Christ. What work remaineth for us to understand him to have wrought, whereby he should get his living, but bodily work, with his own bodily and visible hands? For if from spiritual work he sought food and clothing, that is, to receive these of them whom he was edifying in the Gospel, he could not, as he does, go on to say, "If others be partakers of this power over you, are not we rather? Nevertheless,

---

[1] *Licentiam.*   [2] Luke x. 7. *"Ea quæ ab ipsis sunt.'*   [3] 1 Cor. ix. 7-10. [See R.V.]

we have not used this power, but tolerate all things that we may not cause any hindrance to the Gospel of Christ."[1] What power doth he say he had not used, but that which he had over them, received of the Lord, the power to reap their carnal things, in order to the sustenance of this life which is lived in the flesh? Of which power were others also partakers, who did not at the first announce the Gospel to them, but came thereafter to their Church preaching the self-same. Therefore, when he had said, "If we have sown unto you spiritual things, is it a great matter if we shall reap your carnal things?" he subjoined, "If others be partakers of this power over you, are not we rather?" And when he had demonstrated what power they had: "Nevertheless we have not used," saith he, "this power; but we put up with all things, lest we should cause any impediment to the Gospel of Christ." Let therefore these persons say in what way from spiritual work the Apostle had carnal food, when himself openly says that he had not used this power. But if from spiritual work he had not carnal food, it remains that from bodily work he had it, and thereof saith, "Neither did we eat any man's bread for nought; but wrought with labor and travail night and day, that we might not be chargeable to any of you: not because we have not power, but to make ourselves an example unto you to follow us.[2] All things," saith he, "we suffer, lest we cause any hindrance to the Gospel of Christ."

10. And he comes back again, and in all ways, over and over again, enforceth what he hath the right to do, yet doeth not. "Do ye not know," saith he, "that they which work in the temple, eat of the things which are in the temple? they which serve the altar, have their share with the altar? So hath the Lord ordained for them which preach the Gospel, to live of the Gospel. But I have used none of these things."[3] What more open than this? what more clear? I fear lest haply, while I discourse wishing to expound this, that become obscure which in itself is bright and clear. For they who understand not these words, or feign not to understand, do much less understand mine, or profess to understand: unless perchance they do therefore quickly understand ours, because it is allowed them to deride them being understood; but concerning the Apostle's words this same is not allowed. For this reason, where they cannot interpret them otherwise according to their own sentence, be it ever so clear and manifest, they answer that it is ob-

scure and uncertain, because wrong and perverse they dare not call it. Cries the man of God, "The Lord hath ordained for them which preach the Gospel, of this Gospel to live; but I have used none of these things;" and flesh and blood essayeth to make crooked what is straight; what open, to shut; what serene, to cloud over. "It was," saith it, "spiritual work that he was doing, and thereof did he live." If it be so, of the Gospel did he live: why then doth he say, "The Lord hath ordained for them which preach the Gospel, of the Gospel to live; but I have used none of these things?" Or if this very word, "to live," which is here used, they will needs also interpret in respect of spiritual life, then had the Apostle no hope towards God, in that he did not live by the Gospel, because he hath said, "I have used none of these things." Wherefore, that he should have certain hope of life eternal, the Apostle did of the Gospel in any wise spiritually live. What therefore he saith, "But I have used none of these things," doth without doubt make to be understood of this life which is in the flesh, that which he hath said of the Lord's ordaining to them which preach the Gospel, that of the Gospel they should live; that is, this life which hath need of food and clothing, they by the Gospel shall sustain; as above he said of his fellow-apostles; of whom the Lord Himself saith, "The workman is worthy of his meat;" and, "The workman is worthy of his hire." This meat, then, and this hire of the sustenance of this life, due to evangelists, this of them to whom he evangelized the Apostle accepted not, saying a true thing, "I have used none of these things."

11. And he goes on, and adjoins, lest perchance any should imagine that he only therefore received not, because they had not given: "But I have not written these things that they may be so done unto me: good is it for me rather to die than that any make void my glory."[4] What glory, unless that which he wished to have with God, while in Christ suffering with the weak? As he is presently about to say most openly; "For if I shall have preached the Gospel, there is not to me any glory: for necessity is laid upon me;"[5] that is, of sustaining this life. "For woe will be to me," he saith, "if I preach not the Gospel:" that is, to my own will shall I forbear to preach the Gospel, because I shall be tormented with hunger, and shall not have whereof to live. For he goes on, and says; "For if willingly I do this, I have a reward." By his doing it

---

[1] 1 Cor. ix. 12.   [2] 2 Thess. iii. 8, 9.   [3] 1 Cor. ix. 13-15.   [4] 1 Cor. ix. 15.   [5] 1 Cor. ix. 16. [See R.V.]

willingly, he means, if he do it uncompelled by any necessity of supporting this present life; and for this he hath reward, to wit, with God, of glory everlasting. "But if unwilling," saith he, "a dispensation is entrusted unto me:"[1] that is, if being unwilling, I am by necessity of passing through this present life, compelled to preach the Gospel, "a dispensation is entrusted unto me;" to wit, that by my dispensation as a steward, because Christ, because the truth, is that which I preach, howsoever because of occasion, howsoever seeking mine own, howsoever by necessity of earthly emolument compelled so to do, other men do profit, but I have not that glorious and everlasting reward with God. "What then," saith he, "shall be my reward?" He saith it as asking a question: therefore the pronunciation must be suspended, until he give the answer. Which the more easily to understand, let, as it were, us put the question to him, "What, then, will be thy reward, O Apostle, when that earthly reward due to good evangelists, not for its sake evangelizing, but yet taking it as the consequence and offered to them by the Lord's appointment, thou acceptest not? What shall be thy reward then?" See what he replies: "That, preaching the Gospel, I may make the Gospel of Christ without charge;" that is, that the Gospel may not be to believers expensive, lest they account that for this end is the Gospel to be preached to them, that its preachers should seem as it were to sell it. And yet he comes back again and again, that he may show what, by warrant of the Lord, he hath a right unto, yet doeth not: "that I abuse not," saith he, "my power in the Gospel."[2]

12. But now, that as bearing with the infirmity of men he did this, let us hear what follows: "For though I be free from all men, yet have I made myself servant unto all, that I might gain the more. To them that are under the law, I became as under the law, that I might gain them that are under the law; to them that are without law, as without law, (being not without law to God, but under the law to Christ,) that I might gain them that are without law."[3] Which thing he did, not with craftiness of simulation, but with mercy of compassion with others; that is, not as if to feign himself a Jew, as some have thought, in that he observed at Jerusalem the things prescribed by the old law.[4] For he did this in accordance with his free and openly declared sentence, in which he says, "Is any called being circumcised? let him not become

uncircumcised." That is, let him not so live, as though he had become uncircumcised, and covered that which he had laid bare: as in another place he saith, "Thy circumcision is become uncircumcision."[5] It was in accordance then with this his sentence, in which he saith, "Is any called being circumcised? let him not become uncircumcised. Is any called in uncircumcision? let him not be circumcised;'[6] that he did those things, in which, by persons not understanding and not enough attending, he has been accounted to have feigned. For he was a Jew, and was called being circumcised; therefore he would not become uncircumcised; that is, would not so live as if he had not been circumcised. For this he now had in his power to do. And "under" the law, indeed, he was not as they who servilely wrought it; but yet "in" the law of God and of Christ. For that law was not one, and the law of God another, as accursed Manicheans are wont to say. Otherwise, if when he did those things he is to be accounted to have feigned, then he feigned himself also a pagan, and sacrificed to idols, because he says that he became to those without law, as without law. By whom, doubtless, he would have us to understand no other than Gentiles whom we call Pagans. It is one thing therefore to be under the law, another in the law, another without law. "Under the law," the carnal Jews; "in the law," spiritual men, both Jews and Christians; (whence the former kept that custom of their fathers, but did not impose unwonted burdens upon the believing Gentiles; and therefore they also were circumcised;) but "without law," are the Gentiles which have not yet believed, to whom yet the Apostle testifieth himself to have become like, through sympathy of a merciful heart, not simulation of a changeable exterior; that is, that he might in that way succor carnal Jew or Pagan, in which way himself, if he were that, would have wished to be succored: bearing, to wit, their infirmity, in likeness of compassion, not deceiving in fiction of lying; as he straightway goes on, and says, "I became to the weak as weak, that I might gain the weak."[7] For it was from this point that he was speaking, in saying all those other things. As then, that he became to the weak as weak, was no lie; so all those other things above rehearsed. For what doth he mean his weakness towards the weak to have been, but that of suffering with them, insomuch that, lest he should appear to be a seller of the Gospel, and by falling into an ill suspicion with ig-

[1] 1 Cor. ix. 17.   [2] 1 Cor. ix. 18.   [3] 1 Cor. ix. 19-21.
[4] S. Jerome in Ep. inter Augustinianas, 75, n. 9-11.

[5] Rom. ii. 25.   [6] 1 Cor. vii. 18.   [7] 1 Cor. ix. 22.

norant men, should hinder the course of God's word, he would not accept what by warrant of the Lord was his due? Which if he were willing to accept, he would not in any wise lie, because it was truly due to him; and for that he would not, he did not in any wise lie. For he did not say, it was not due; but he showed it to be due, and that being due he had not used it, and professed that he would not at all use it, in that very thing becoming weak; namely, in that he would not use his power; being, to wit, with so merciful affection endued, that he thought in what way he should wish to be dealt withal, if himself also were made so weak, that possibly, if he should see them by whom the Gospel was preached to him, accepting their charges, he might think it a bringing of wares to market, and hold them in suspicion accordingly.

13. Of this weakness of his, he saith in another place, "We made ourselves small among you, even as a nurse cherisheth her children." [1] For in that passage the context indicates this: "For neither at any time," saith he, "used we flattering words, as ye know, nor an occasion of covetousness; God is witness: nor of men sought we glory, neither of you, nor yet of others when we might have been burdensome to you as the Apostles of Christ: but we made ourselves small among you, even as a nurse cherisheth her children." What therefore he saith to the Corinthians, that he had power of his apostleship, as also the other Apostles, which power he testifieth that he had not used; this also he saith in that place to the Thessalonians, "When we might have been burdensome to you as Christ's Apostles:" according to that the Lord saith, "The workman is worthy of his hire." For that of this he speaks, is indicated by that which he above set down, "Neither for occasion of covetousness, God is witness." By reason, namely, of this which by right of the Lord's appointment was due to good evangelists, who not for its sake do evangelize but seek the kingdom of God, so that all these things should be added unto them, others were taking advantage thereof, of whom he also saith, "For they that are such serve not God, but their own belly." [2] From whom the Apostle wished so to cut off this occasion, that even what was justly due to him, he would forego. For this himself doth openly show in the second to the Corinthians, speaking of other Churches supplying his necessities. For he had come, as it appears, to so great indigence, that from distant Churches were sent supplies for his necessities, while yet from them among whom he was, he accepted nothing of that kind. "Have I committed a sin," saith he, "in humbling myself that ye might be exalted, because I have preached to you the Gospel of God freely? Other Churches I despoiled, taking wages of them to minister unto you: and when I was present with you and wanted, to no man was I burdensome. For that which was lacking to me the brethren which came from Macedonia supplied, and in all things I have kept myself from being burdensome to you, and will keep myself. It is the truth of Christ in me, that this glory shall not be infringed in me in the regions of Achaia. Wherefore? because I love you not? God knoweth. But what I do, I also mean to do, that I may cut off occasion from them which seek occasion, that wherein they glory they may be found as also we." [3] Of this occasion, therefore, which he here saith that he cuts off, he would have that understood which he saith in the former place, "Neither for occasion of covetousness, God is witness." And what he here saith, "In humbling myself that ye might be exalted:" this in the first to the same Corinthians, "I became to the weak as weak;" this to the Thessalonians, "I became small among you, as a nurse cherisheth her children." [4] Now then observe what follows: "So," saith he, "being affectionately desirous of you, we are minded to impart unto you not alone the Gospel of God, but our own souls also; because ye are become most dear to us. For ye remember, brethren, our labor and toil, night and day working, that we might not burden any of you." For this he said above, "When we might be burdensome to you, as Christ's Apostles." Because, then, the weak were in peril, lest, agitated by false suspicions, they should hate an, as it were, venal Gospel, for this cause, trembling for them as with a father's and a mother's bowels of compassion, did he this thing. So too in the Acts of the Apostles he speaks the same thing, when, sending from Miletus to Ephesus, he had called thence the presbyters of the Church, to whom, among much else, "Silver," saith he, "and gold, or apparel of no man have I coveted; yourselves know, that to my necessities and theirs who were with me these hands have ministered. In all things have I shown you that so laboring it behoveth to help the weak, mindful also of the words of the Lord Jesus, for that He said, More blessed is it rather to give than to receive." [5]

14. Here peradventure some man may

1 "*Parvuli.*" 1 Thess. ii. 5-7. [See R.V.]   2 Rom. xvi. 18.   3 2 Cor. xi. 7-12. [See R.V.]   4 1 Thess. ii. 7-9.   5 Acts xx. 33-35.

say, "If it was bodily work that the Apostle wrought, whereby to sustain this life, what was that same work, and when did he find time for it, both to work and to preach the Gospel?" To whom I answer: Suppose I do not know; nevertheless that he did bodily work, and thereby lived in the flesh, and did not use the power which the Lord had given to the Apostles, that preaching the Gospel he should live by the Gospel, those things above-said do without all doubt bear witness. For it is not either in one place or briefly said, that it should be possible for any most astute arguer with all his tergiversation to traduce and pervert it to another meaning. Since then so great an authority, with so mighty and so frequent blows mauling the gainsayers, doth break in pieces their contrariness, why ask they of me either what sort of work he did, or when he did it? One thing I know, that he neither did steal, nor was a housebreaker or highwayman, nor chariot-driver or hunter or player, nor given to filthy lucre: but innocently and honestly wrought things which are fitted for the uses of men; such as are the works of carpenters, builders, shoemakers, peasants, and such like. For honesty itself reprehends not what their pride doth reprehend, who love to be called, but love not to be, honest. The Apostle then would not disdain either to take in hand any work of peasants, or to be employed in the labor of craftsmen. For he who saith, "Be ye without offense to Jews and to Greeks and to the Church of God,"[1] before what men he could possibly stand abashed, I know not. If they shall say, the Jews; the Patriarchs fed cattle: if the Greeks, whom we call also Pagans; they have had philosophers, held in high honor, who were shoemakers: if the Church of God; that just man, elect to the testimony of a conjugal and ever-during virginity, to whom was betrothed the Virgin Mary who bore Christ, was a carpenter.[2] Whatever therefore of these with innocence and without fraud men do work, is good. For the Apostle himself takes precaution of this, that no man through necessity of sustaining life should turn aside to evil works. "Let him that stole," saith he, "steal no more; but rather let him labor good with his hands, that he may have to impart to him that needeth."[3] This then is enough to know, that also in the very work of the body the Apostle did work that which is good.

15. But when he might use to work, that is, in what spaces of time, that he might not be hindered from preaching the Gospel, who

can make out? Though, truly, that he wrought at hours of both day and night himself hath not left untold.[4] Yet these men truly, who as though very full of business and occupation inquire about the time of working, what do they? Have they from Jerusalem round about even to Illyricum filled the lands with the Gospel?[5] or whatever of barbarian nations hath remained yet to be gone unto, and to be filled of the peace of the Church, have they undertaken? We know them into a certain holy society most leisurely gathered together. A marvellous thing did the Apostle, that in very deed amid his so great care of all the Churches, both planted and to be planted, to his care and labor appertaining, he did also with his hands work: yet on that account, when he was with the Corinthians, and wanted, was burdensome to no man of those among whom he was, but altogether that which was lacking to him the brethren which came from Macedonia supplied.[6]

16. For he himself also, with an eye to the like necessities of saints, who, although they obey his precepts, "that with silence they work and eat their own bread," may yet from many causes stand in need of somewhat by way of supplement to the like sustenance, therefore, after he had thus said, teaching and premonishing, "Now them which are such we command and beseech in our Lord Jesus Christ, that with silence they work and eat their own bread;"[7] yet, lest they which had whereof they might supply the needs of the servants of God, should hence take occasion to wax lazy, providing against this he hath straightway added, "But ye, brethren, become not weak in showing beneficence."[8] And when he was writing to Titus, saying, "Zenas the lawyer and Apollos do thou diligently send forward, that nothing may be wanting to them;"[9] that he might show from what quarter nothing ought to be wanting to them, he straightway subjoined, "But let ours also learn to maintain good works[10] for necessary use, that they be not unfruitful." In the case of Timothy also,[11] whom he calls his own most true[12] son, because he knew him weak of body, (as he shows, in advising him not to drink water, but to use a little wine for his stomach's sake and his often infirmities,) lest then haply, because in bodily work he could not labor, he being unwilling to stand in need of daily food at their hands, unto

[1] 1 Cor. x. 32. [2] Matt. xiii. 55. [3] Eph. iv. 28.

[4] 1 Thess. ii. 9; 2 Thess. iii. 8. [5] Rom. xv. 19.
[6] 2 Cor. xi. 9. [7] 2 Thess. iii. 12, 13.
[8] *Infirmari benefacientes.* [9] Tit. iii. 13, 14.
[10] *Bonis operibus præsse,* καλῶν ἔργων προΐστασθαι. E. V. in margin, "profess honest trades."
[11] 1 Tim. i. 2. [12] "*Germanissimum.*" 1 Tim. v. 23.

whom he ministered the Gospel, should seek some business in which the stress of his mind would become entangled; (for it is one thing to labor in body, with the mind free, as does a handicraftsman, if he be not fraudulent and avaricious and greedy of his own private gain; but another thing, to occupy the mind itself with cares of collecting money without the body's labor, as do either dealers, or bailiffs, or undertakers, for these with care of the mind conduct their business, not with their hands do work, and in that regard occupy their mind itself with solicitude of getting;) lest then Timothy should fall upon such like ways, because from weakness of body he could not work with his hands, he thus exhorts, admonishes, and comforts him: "Labor," saith he, "as a good soldier of Jesus Christ. No man, going a warfare for God, entangleth himself with secular business; that he may please Him to whom he hath proved himself.[1] For he that striveth for masteries, is not crowned except he strive lawfully."[2] Hereupon, lest the other should be put to straits, saying, "Dig I cannot, to beg I am ashamed,"[3] he adjoined, "The husbandman that laboreth must be first partaker of the fruits:" according to that which he had said to the Corinthians, "Who goeth a warfare any time at his own charges? Who planteth a vineyard, and eateth not of the fruit thereof? Who feedeth a flock, and partaketh not of the milk of the flock?"[4] Thus did he make to be without care a chaste evangelist, not to that end working as an evangelist that he might sell the Gospel, but yet not having strength to supply unto himself with his own hands the necessities of this life; for that he should understand whatever being necessary for himself he was taking of them whom as provincials he as a soldier was serving, and whom as a vineyard he was culturing, or as a flock was feeding, to be not matter of mendicity, but of power.

17. On account then of these either occupations of the servants of God, or bodily infirmities, which cannot be altogether wanting, not only doth the Apostle permit the needs of saints to be supplied by good believers, but also most wholesomely exhorteth. For, setting apart that power, which he saith himself had not used, which yet that the faithful must serve unto, he enjoins, saying, "Let him that is catechised in the word, communicate unto him that doth catechise him, in all good things:"[5] setting apart, then, this power, which that the preachers of the word have over them to whom they preach,

he often testifieth; speaking, moreover, of the saints who had sold all that they had and distributed the same, and were dwelling at Jerusalem in an holy communion of life, not saying that any thing was their own, to whom all things were in common, and their soul and heart one in the Lord: that these by the Churches of the Gentiles should have what they needed bestowed upon them, he chargeth and exhorteth. Thence is also that to the Romans: "Now therefore I will go unto Jerusalem, to minister unto the saints. For it hath pleased Macedonia and Achaia to make a certain contribution for the poor of the saints which are at Jerusalem. For it hath pleased them; and their debtors they are. For if in their spiritual things the Gentiles have communicated, they ought also in carnal things to minister unto them."[7] This is like that which he says to the Corinthians: "If we have sown unto you spiritual things, is it a great thing if we reap your carnal things?" Also to the Corinthians in the second Epistle: "Moreover, brethren, we do you to wit of the grace of God bestowed on the Churches of Macedonia; how that in a great trial of affliction the abundance of their joy and their deep poverty abounded in the riches of their liberality; for to their power, I bear record, yea, and beyond their power, they were willing of themselves; with many prayers beseeching of us the grace and the fellowship of the ministering to the saints: and not as we hoped, but first they gave their own selves to the Lord, and unto us by the will of God, insomuch, that we desired Titus, that as he had begun, so he would also finish in you the same grace also. But as ye abound in every thing, in faith, and utterance, and knowledge, and in all diligence, and in your love to us, see that ye abound in this grace also. I speak not by commandment, but by occasion of the forwardness of others, and to prove the exceeding dearness of your love. For ye know the grace of our Lord Jesus Christ, that, though He was rich, yet for your sakes He became poor, that ye through His poverty might be made rich. And herein I give advice: for this is expedient for you, who have begun before, not only to do, but also to be willing a year ago; now therefore perfect it in the doing; that as there is a readiness to will, so of performance also out of that which each hath. For if there be first a ready mind, it is acceptable according to that a man hath, not according to that he hath not. Not, namely, that others may have ease, and ye straits· but by an equality, that

---

[1] *Cui se probavit.*　[2] 2 Tim. ii. 3-6.　[3] Luke xvi. 3. [See R.V.]
[5] 1 Cor. ix. 7.　[8] Gal. vi. 6.　　　　　　[6] Acts ii. 44; iv. 32.　[7] Rom. xv. 25-27.　[8] 1 Cor. ix. 11.

now at this time your abundance may be a supply for their want, that their abundance also may become a supply for your want: that there may be equality, as it is written, He that had gathered much had nothing over; and he that had gathered little had no lack. But thanks be to God, which put the same earnest care for you into the heart of Titus: for indeed he accepted the exhortation; but being more forward, of his own accord he went forth unto you. And we have sent with him the brother, whose praise is in the Gospel throughout all the Churches; and not that only, but he was also ordained of the Churches as a companion of our travail, with this grace which is administered by us to the glory of the Lord, and our ready mind: avoiding this, that no man should blame us in this abundance which is administered by us. For we provide for honest things, not only in the sight of the Lord, but also in the sight of men.''[1] In these words appeareth how much[2] the Apostle willed it not only to be the care of the holy congregations[3] to minister necessaries to the holy servants of God, giving counsel in this, because this was profitable more to the persons themselves who did this, than to them towards whom they did it, (for to those another thing was profitable, that is, that they should make of this service of their brethren towards them an holy use, and not with an eye to this serve God, nor take these things but to supply necessity, not to feed laziness:) but likewise his own care the blessed Apostle saith to be so great in this ministration which was now in transmitting through Titus, that a companion of his journey was on this account, he tells us, ordained by the Churches, a man of God well reported of, "whose praise," says he, "is in the Gospel throughout all the Churches." And to this end, he says, was the same ordained to be his companion, that he might avoid men's reprehensions, lest, without witness of saints associated with him in this ministry, he should be thought by weak and impious men to receive for himself and turn aside into his own bosom, what he was receiving for supplying the necessities of the saints, by him to be brought and distributed to the needy.

18. And a little after he saith, "For as touching the ministering to the saints, it is superfluous for me to write to you. For I know the forwardness of your mind, for which I boast of you to them of Macedonia, that Achaia was ready a year ago; and your zeal hath provoked very many. Yet have we sent the brethren, lest our boasting of you should be in vain in this behalf; that, as I said, ye may be ready: lest haply if they of Macedonia come with me, and find you unprepared, we (that we say not, ye) should be ashamed in this substance. Therefore I thought it necessary to exhort the brethren, that they would go before unto you, and make up beforehand this your long promised benediction, that the same might be ready, as benediction, and not as covetousness. But this I say, He which soweth sparingly shall reap also sparingly; and he which soweth in benediction shall reap also in benediction. Every man according as he hath purposed in his heart, not grudgingly, or of necessity: for God loveth a cheerful giver. And God is able to make all grace abound in you; that ye, always having all sufficiency in all things, may abound to every good work: as it is written, He hath dispersed abroad; he hath given to the poor: his righteousness remaineth for ever. But He that ministereth seed to the sower will both minister bread for your food, and multiply your seed sown, and increase the growing fruits of your righteousness; that ye may be enriched in every thing to all bountifulness, which causeth through us thanksgiving to God: for the administration of this service not only supplieth the want of the saints, but makes them also to abound by thanksgiving unto God of many, while by the proof of this ministration they glorify God for the obedience of your confession unto the Gospel of Christ, and for your liberal distribution unto them, and unto all men; and in the praying for you of them which long after you for the excellent grace of God in you. Thanks be unto God for His unspeakable gift."[4] In what richness of holy gladness must the Apostle have been steeped, while he speaks of the mutual supply of the need of Christ's soldiers and His other subjects,[5] on the one part of carnal things to those, on the other of spiritual things to these, to exclaim as he does, and as it were in repletion of holy joys to burst out[6] with, "Thanks be to God for His unspeakable gift!"

19. As therefore the Apostle, nay rather the Spirit of God possessing and filling and actuating his heart, ceased not to exhort the faithful who had such substance, that nothing should be lacking to the necessities of the servants of God, who wished to hold a more lofty degree of sanctity in the Church, in cutting off all ties of secular hope, and dedicating a mind at liberty to their godly service

---

[1] 2 Cor. viii. 1-21.
[2] Read perhaps "*quantam;*" "how great the Apostle willed to be the care."
[3] *Plebium.*

[4] 2 Cor. ix.   [5] *Provincialium.*   [6] "*Eructuare.*"

of warfare: likewise ought themselves also to obey his precepts, in sympathizing with the weak, and unshackled by love of private wealth, to labor with their hands for the common good, and submit to their superiors without a murmur; that there may be made up for them out of the oblations of good believers that which, while they labor and do some work whereby they may get their living, yet still by reason of bodily infirmities of some, and by reason of ecclesiastical occupations or erudition of the doctrine which bringeth salvation, they shall account to be lacking.

20. For what these men are about, who will not do bodily work, to what thing they give up their time, I should like to know. "To prayers," say they, "and psalms, and reading, and the word of God." A holy life, unquestionably, and in sweetness of Christ worthy of praise; but then, if from these we are not to be called off, neither must we eat, nor our daily viands themselves be prepared, that they may be put before us and taken. Now if to find time for these things the servants of God at certain intervals of times by very infirmity are of necessity compelled, why do we not make account of some portions of times to be allotted also to the observance of Apostolical precepts? For one single prayer of one who obeyeth is sooner heard than ten thousand of a despiser. As for divine songs, however, they can easily, even while working with their hands, say them, and like as rowers with a boat-song,[1] so with godly melody cheer up their very toil. Or are we ignorant how it is with all workmen, to what vanities, and for the most part even filthinesses, of theatrical fables they give their hearts and tongues, while their hands recede not from their work? What then hinders a servant of God while working with his hands to meditate in the law of the Lord, and sing unto the Name of the Lord Most High?[2] provided, of course, that to learn what he may by memory rehearse, he have times set apart. For to this end also those good works of the faithful ought not to be lacking, for resource of making up what is necessary, that the hours which are so taken up in storing of the mind that those bodily works cannot be carried on, may not oppress with want. But they which say that they give up their time to reading, do they not there find that which the Apostle enjoineth? Then what perversity is this, to refuse to be ruled by his reading while he wishes to give up his time thereto; and that he may spend more time in reading what is good, therefore to refuse to do what is read? For who knows not

that each doth the more quickly profit when he reads good things, the quicker he is in doing what he reads?

21. Moreover, if discourse must be bestowed upon any, and this so take up the speaker that he have not time to work with his hands, are all in the monastery able to hold discourse unto brethren which come unto them from another kind of life, whether it be to expound the divine lessons, or concerning any questions which may be put, to reason in an wholesome manner? Then since not all have the ability, why upon this pretext do all want to have nothing else to do? Although even if all were able, they ought to do it by turns; not only that the rest might not be taken up from necessary works, but also because it sufficeth that to many hearers there be one speaker. To come now to the Apostle; how could he find time to work with his hands, unless for the bestowing of the word of God he had certain set times? And indeed God hath not willed this either to be hidden from us. For both of what craft he was a workman, and at what times he was taken up with dispensing the Gospel, holy Scripture has not left untold. Namely, when the day of his departure caused him to be in haste, being at Troas, even on the first day of the week when the brethren were assembled to break bread, such was his earnestness, and so necessary the disputation, that his discourse was prolonged even until midnight,[3] as though it had slipped from their minds that on that day it was not a fast:[4] but when he was making longer stay in any place and disputing daily, who can doubt that he had certain hours set apart for this office? For at Athens, because he had there found most studious inquirers of things, it is thus written of him: "He disputed therefore with the Jews in the synagogue, and with the Gentile inhabitants[5] in the market every day to those who were there."[6] Not, namely, in the synagogue every day, for there it was his custom to discourse on the sabbath; but "in the market," saith he, "every day;" by reason, doubtless, of the studiousness of the Athenians. For so it follows: "Certain however of the Epicurean and Stoic philosophers conferred with him." And a little after, it says: "Now the Athenians and strangers which were there spent their time in nothing else

---

[1] Celeumate.   [2] Ps. i. 2; xiii. 6

[3] Acts xx. 7.
[4] S. Augustin therefore assumes that the Christians of the Apostolic age did not break their fast before receiving the Eucharist. See St. Chrys. on *Stat. Hom.* ix. § 2. Τт. p. 159, and note g.
[5] Τοῖς Ἰουδαίοις καὶ τοῖς σεβομένοις καὶ ἐν τῇ ἀγορᾷ κατὰ πᾶσαν ἡμέραν πρὸς τοὺς παρατυγχάνοντας. For καὶ τοῖς σεβομένοις Aug. has *et Gentibus incolis:* for which some MSS. have *Gentibus in viculis.*
[6] Acts xvii. 17, 18, 21.

but either to tell or to hear some new thing." Let us suppose him all those days that he was at Athens not to have worked: on this account, indeed, was his need supplied from Macedonia, as he says in the second to the Corinthians:[1] though in fact he could work both at other hours and of nights, because he was so strong in both mind and body. But when he had gone from Athens, let us see what says the Scripture: "He disputed," saith it, " in the synagogue every sabbath;"[2] this at Corinth. In Troas, however, where through necessity of his departure being close at hand, his discourse was protracted until midnight, it was the first day of the week, which is called the Lord's Day: whence we understand that he was not with Jews but with Christians; when also the narrator himself saith they were gathered together to break bread. And indeed this same is the best management, that all things be distributed to their times and be done in order, lest becoming ravelled in perplexing entanglements, they throw our human mind into confusion.

22. There also is said at what work the Apostle wrought. "After these things," it says, " he departed from Athens and came to Corinth; and having found a certain Jew, by name Aquila, of Pontus by birth, lately come from Italy, and Priscilla his wife, because that Claudius had ordered all Jews to depart from Rome, he came unto them, and because he was of the same craft he abode with them, doing work: for they were tentmakers."[3] This if they shall essay to interpret allegorically, they show what proficients they be in ecclesiastical learning, on which they glory that they bestow all their time. And, at the least, touching those sayings above recited, " Or I only and Barnabas, have we not power to forbear working?" and, " We have not used this power;"[4] and, " When we might be burdensome to you, as Apostles of Christ,"[5] and, " Night and day working that we might not burden any of you;"[6] and, " The Lord hath ordained for them which preach the Gospel, of the Gospel to live; but I have used none of these things:"[7] and the rest of this kind, let them either expound otherwise, or if by most clear shining light of truth they be put to it, let them understand and obey; or if to obey they be either unwilling or unable, at least let them own them which be willing, to be better, and them which be also able, to be happier men than they. For it is one thing to plead infirmity of body, either truly alleged, or falsely pretended: but another so to be deceived and so to deceive, that it shall even be thought a proof of righteousness obtaining more mightily in servants of God, if laziness have gotten power to reign among a set of ignorant men. He, namely, who shows a true infirmity of body, must be humanely dealt withal; he who pretends a false one, and cannot be convicted, must be left unto God: yet neither of them fixeth a pernicious rule; because a good servant of God both serves his manifestly infirm brother; and, when the other deceives, if he believes him because he does not think him a bad man, he does not imitate him that he may be bad; and if he believe him not; he thinks him deceitful, and does, nevertheless, not imitate him. But when a man says, "This is true righteousness, that by doing no bodily work we imitate the birds of the air, because he who shall do any such work, goes against the Gospel :" whoso being infirm in mind hears and believes this, that person, not for that he so bestows all his time, but for that he so erreth, must be mourned over.

23. Hence arises another question; for peradventure one may say, " What then ? did the other Apostles, and the brethren of the Lord, and Cephas, sin, in that they did not work ? Or did they occasion an hindrance to the Gospel, because blessed Paul saith that he had not used this power on purpose that he might not cause any hindrance to the Gospel of Christ ? For if they sinned because they wrought not, then had they not received power not to work, but to live instead by the Gospel. But if they had received this power, by ordinance of the Lord, that they which preach the Gospel should live by the Gospel; and by His saying, " The workman is worthy of his meat;" which power Paul, laying out somewhat more,[8] would not use; then truly they sinned not. If they sinned not, they caused no hindrance. For it is not to be thought no sin to hinder the Gospel.[9] If this be so, " to us also," say they, "it is free either to use or not to use this power."

24. This question I should briefly solve, if I should say, because I should also justly say, that we must believe the Apostle. For he himself knew why in the Churches of the Gentiles it was not meet that a venal Gospel were carried about; not finding fault with his fellow-apostles, but distinguishing his own ministry; because they, without doubt by admonition of the Holy Ghost, had so distributed among them the provinces of evangelizing, that Paul and Barnabas should go

---

[1] 2 Cor. xi. 9.   [2] Acts xviii. 4.   [3] Acts xviii. 1–3.
[4] 1 Cor. ix. 6–12.   [5] 1 Thess. ii. 6.   [6] 2 Thess. iii. 8.
[7] 1 Cor. ix. 14, 15.

[8] *Amplius aliquid erogans.*   [1] 1 Cor. ix. 12.

unto the Gentiles, and they unto the Circumcision.[1] But that he gave this precept to them who had not the like power, those many things already said do make manifest. But these brethren of ours rashly arrogate unto themselves, so far as I can judge, that they have this kind of power. For if they be evangelists, I confess, they have it: if ministers of the altar, dispensers of sacraments, of course it is no arrogating to themselves, but a plain vindicating of a right.

25. If at the least they once had in this world wherewithal they might easily without handiwork sustain this life, which property, when they were converted unto God, they disparted to the needy, then must we both believe their infirmity, and bear with it. For usually such persons, having been, not better brought up, as many think, but what is the truth, more languidly brought up, are not able to bear the labor of bodily works. Such peradventure were many in Jerusalem. For it is also written, that they sold their houses and lands, and laid the prices of them at the Apostles' feet, that distribution might be made to every one as he had need.[2] Because they were found, being near, and were useful to the Gentiles, who, being afar off,[3] were thence called from the worship of idols, as it is said, "Out of Zion shall go forth the law, and the word of the Lord from Jerusalem,"[4] therefore hath the Apostle called the Christians of the Gentiles their debtors: "their debtors," saith he, "they are:" and hath added the reason why, "For if in their spiritual things the Gentiles have communicated, they ought also in carnal things to minister unto them."[5] But now there come into this profession of the service of God, both persons from the condition of slaves, or also freedmen, or persons on this account freed by their masters or about to be freed, likewise from the life of peasants, and from the exercise and plebeian labor of handicraftsmen, persons whose bringing up doubtless has been all the better for them, the harder it has been: whom not to admit, is a heavy sin. For many of that sort have turned out truly great men and meet to be imitated. For on this account also "hath God chosen the weak things of the world to confound the things which are mighty, and the foolish things of the world hath He chosen to confound them who are wise; and ignoble things of the world, and things which are not, as though they were, that the things that are may be brought to nought: that no flesh may glory before God."[6] This pious and holy thought, accordingly,

causeth that even such be admitted as bring no proof of a change of life for the better. For it doth not appear whether they come of purpose for the service of God, or whether running away empty from a poor and laborious life they want to be fed and clothed; yea, moreover, to be honored by them of whom they were wont to be despised and trampled on. Such persons therefore because they cannot excuse themselves from working by pleading infirmity of body, seeing they are convicted by the custom of their past life, do therefore shelter themselves under the screen of an ill scholarship, that from the Gospel badly understood they should essay to pervert precepts apostolical: truly "fowls of the air," but in lifting themselves on high through pride; and "grass of the field," but in being carnally minded.

26. That, namely, befalleth them which in undisciplined younger widows, the same Apostle saith must be avoided: "And withal they learn to be idle; and not only idle, but also busy bodies and full of words, speaking what they ought not."[7] This very thing said he concerning evil women, which we also in evil men do mourn and bewail, who against him, the very man in whose Epistles we read these things, do, being idle and full of words, speak what they ought not. And if there be any among them who did with that purpose come to the holy warfare,[8] that they may please Him to whom they have proved themselves, these, when they be so vigorous in strength of body, and soundness of health, that they are able not only to be taught, but also, agreeably unto the Apostle, to work, do, by receiving of these men's idle and corrupt discourses, which they are unable, by reason of their unskilled rawness, to judge of, become changed by pestiferous contagion into the same noisomeness: not only not imitating the obedience of saints which quietly work, and of other monasteries[9] which in most wholesome discipline do live after the apostolic rule; but also insulting better men than themselves, preaching up laziness as the keeper of the Gospel, accusing mercy as the prevaricator therefrom. For a much more merciful work is it to the souls of the weak, to consult for the fair fame of the servants of God, than it is to the bodies of men, to break bread to the hungry. Wherefore I would to God that these, which want to let their hands lie idle, would altogether let their tongues lie idle too. For they would not make so many willing to imitate them, if the examples they set were not merely lazy ones, but mute withal.

---

[1] Acts xiii. 2; Gal. ii. 9. [2] Acts ii. 45; iv. 34. [3] Acts ii. 39.
[4] Is. ii. 3. [5] Rom. xv. 27. [6] 1 Cor. i. 27-29.
[7] 1 Tim. v. 13. [8] 2 Tim. ii. 4. [See R.V.]
[9] Cassian. de Inst. x. 22.

27. As it is, however, they, against the Apostle of Christ, recite a Gospel of Christ. For so marvellous are the works of the sluggards, hindered that they want to have that very thing by Gospel, which the Apostle enjoined and did on purpose that the Gospel itself should not be hindered. And yet, if from the very words of the Gospel we should compel them to live agreeably with their way of understanding it, they will be the first to endeavor to persuade us how they are not to be understood so as they do understand them. For certainly, they say that they therefore ought not to work, for that the birds of the air neither sow nor reap, of which the Lord hath given us a similitude that we should take no thought about such necessaries. Then why do they not attend to that which follows? For it is not only said, that "they sow not, neither reap;"[1] but there is added, "nor gather in apothecas." Now "apothecæ" may be called either "barns," or word for word, "repositories." Then why do these persons want to have idle hands and full repositories? Why do they lay by and keep what they receive of the labors of others, that thereof may be every day somewhat forthcoming? Why, in short, do they grind and cook? For the birds do not this. Or, if they find some whom they may persuade to this work also, namely, to bring unto them day by day viands ready made; at least their water they either fetch them from springs, or from cisterns and wells draw and set it by: this the fowls do not. But if so please them, let it be the study of good believers and most devoted subjects of the Eternal King, to carry their service to His most valiant soldiers even to that length, that they shall not be forced even to fill a vessel of water for themselves, if now-a-days people have surpassed even them which at that time were at Jerusalem, in a new grade of righteousness, stepping out beyond them. To them, namely, by reason of famine being imminent, and foretold by the Prophets which were at that time,[2] good believers sent out of Greece supplies of corn; of which I suppose they made them bread, or at least procured to be made; which thing the birds do not. But if now-a-days these persons, as I began to say, have surpassed these in some grade of righteousness, and do altogether in things pertaining to the maintenance of this life, as do the birds; let them show us men doing such service unto birds as they wish to be done unto them, except indeed birds caught and caged because they are not trusted, lest if they fly they come not back: and yet these would rather enjoy liberty and receive from the fields what is enough, than take their food by men laid before them and made ready.

28. Here then shall these persons be in their turn in another more sublime degree of righteousness outdone, by them who shall so order themselves, that every day they shall betake them into the fields as unto pasture, and at what time they shall find it, pick up their meal, and having allayed their hunger, return. But plainly, on account of the keepers of the fields, how good were it, if the Lord should deign to bestow wings also, that the servants of God being found in other men's fields should not be taken up as thieves, but as starlings be scared off. As things are, however, such an one will do all he can to be like a bird, which the fowler shall not be able to catch. But, lo, let all men allow this to the servants of God, that when they will they should go forth into their fields, and thence depart fearless and refreshed: as it was ordered to the people Israel by the law, that none should lay hands on a thief in his fields, unless he wanted to carry any thing away with him from thence;[3] for if he laid hands on nothing but what he had eaten, they would let him go away free and unpunished. Whence also when the disciples of the Lord plucked the ears of corn, the Jews calumniated them on the score of the sabbath[4] rather than of theft. But how is one to manage about those times of year, at which food that can be taken on the spot is not found in the fields? Whoso shall attempt to take home with him any thing which by cooking he may prepare for himself, he shall, according to these persons' understanding of it, be accosted from the Gospel with, "Put it down; for this the birds do not."

29. But let us grant this also, that there be found in the fields the whole year round either of tree or of herbs or of any manner of roots, that which may be taken as food uncooked; or, at any rate, let so great exercise of body be used, that the things which require cooking, may be taken even raw without hurt, and people may even in winter weather, no matter how rough, go forth to their fodder; and so it shall be the case that nothing be taken away to be prepared, nothing laid up for the morrow. Yet will not those men be able to keep these rules, who for many days separating themselves from sight of men, and allowing none access to them, do shut themselves up, living in great earnestness of prayers. For these do use to shut up with themselves store of aliments,

---

[1] Matt. vi. 26.   [2] Acts xi. 28-30.   [3] Deut. xxiii. 24, 25.   [4] Matt. xii. 1, 2.

such indeed as are most easily and cheaply had, yet still a store which may suffice for those days during which they purpose that no man shall see them; which thing the birds do not. Now touching these men's exercising of themselves in so marvellous continency, seeing that they have leisure for the doing of these things, and not in proud elation but in merciful sanctity do propose themselves for men's imitation, I not only do not blame it, but know not how to praise it as much as it deserves. And yet what are we to say of such men, according to these persons' understanding of the evangelical words? Or haply the holier they be, the more unlike are they to the fowls? because unless they lay by for themselves food for many days, to shut themselves up as they do they will not have strength? Howbeit, to them as well as us is it said, "Take therefore no thought for the morrow."[1]

30. Wherefore, that I may briefly embrace the whole matter, let these persons, who from perverse understanding of the Gospel labor to pervert apostolical precepts, either take no thought for the morrow, even as the birds of the air; or let them obey the Apostle, as dear children: yea rather, let them do both, because both accord. For things contrary to his Lord, Paul the servant of Jesus Christ would never advise.[2] This then we say openly to these persons; If the birds of the air ye in such wise understand in the Gospel, that ye will not by working with your hands procure food and clothing; then neither must ye put any thing by for the morrow, like as the birds of the air do put nothing by. But if to put somewhat by for the morrow, is possibly not against the Gospel where it is said, "Behold the birds of the air, for they neither sow nor reap nor gather into stores;"[3] then is it possibly not against the Gospel nor against similitude of the birds of the air, to maintain this life of the flesh by labor of corporal working.

31. For if they be urged from the Gospel that they should put nothing by for the morrow, they most rightly answer, "Why then had the Lord Himself a bag in which to put by the money which was collected?[4] Why so long time beforehand, on occasion of impending famine, were supplies of corn sent to the holy fathers?[5] Why did Apostles in such wise provide things necessary for the indigence of saints lest there should be lack thereafter, that most blessed Paul should thus write to the Corinthians in his Epistle: "Now

concerning the collection for the saints, as I have given order to the Churches of Galatia, even so do ye. Upon the first day of the week let every one of you lay by him in store, as God hath prospered him, that the gatherings be not then first made when I come. And when I come, whomsoever ye shall approve by your letters, them will I send to bring your liberality unto Jerusalem. And if it be meet that I go also, they shall go with me?"[6] These and much else they most copiously and most truly bring forward. To whom we answer: Ye see then, albeit the Lord said, "Take no thought for the morrow," yet ye are not by these words constrained to reserve nothing for the morrow: then why do ye say that by the same words ye are constrained to do nothing? Why are the birds of the air not a pattern unto you for reserving nothing, and ye will have them to be a pattern for working nothing?

32. Some man will say: "What then does it profit a servant of God, that, having left the former doings which he had in the world he is converted unto the spiritual life and warfare, if it still behove him to do business as of a common workman?" As if truly it could be easily unfolded in words, how greatly profiteth what the Lord, in answer to that rich man who was seeking counsel of laying hold on eternal life, told him to do if he would fain be perfect: sell that he had, distribute all to the indigence of the poor, and follow Him?[7] Or who with so unimpeded course hath followed the Lord, as he who saith, "Not in vain have I run, nor in vain labored?"[8] who yet both enjoined these works, and did them. This unto us, being by so great authority taught and informed, ought to suffice for a pattern of relinquishing our old resources, and of working with our hands. But we too, aided by the Lord Himself, are able perchance in some sort to apprehend what it doth still profit the servants of God to have left their former businesses, while they do yet thus work. For if a person from being rich is converted to this mode of life, and is hindered by no infirmity of body, are we so without taste of the savor of Christ, as not to understand what an healing it is to the swelling of the old pride, when, having pared off the superfluities by which erewhile the mind was deadly inflamed, he refuses not, for the procuring of that little which is still naturally necessary for this present life, even a common workman's lowly toil? If however he be from a poor estate converted unto this manner of life, let him not account himself

---

[1] Matt. vi. 34. [2] Rom. i. 1. [3] Matt. vi. 26.
[4] John xii. 6. [5] Acts xi. 28-30.
[6] 1 Cor. xvi. 1-4. [7] Matt. xix. 21. [8] Phil. ii. 16.

to be doing that which he was doing aforetime, if foregoing the love of even increasing his ever so small matter of private substance, and now no more seeking his own but the things which be Jesu Christ's, [1] he hath translated himself into the charity of a life in common, to live in fellowship of them who have one soul and one heart to Godward, so that no man saith that any thing is his own, but they have all things common.[2] For if in this earthly commonwealth its chief men in the old times did, as their own men of letters are wont in their most glowing phrase to tell of them, to that degree prefer the common weal of the whole people of their city and country to their own private affairs, that one of them,[3] for subduing of Africa honored with a triumph, would have had nothing to give to his daughter on her marriage, unless by decree of the senate she had been dowered from the public treasury: of what mind ought he to be towards his commonwealth, who is a citizen of that eternal City, the heavenly Jerusalem, but that even what with labor of his own hands he earns, he should have in common with his brother, and if the same lack any thing, supply it from the common store; saying with him whose precept and example he hath followed, "As having nothing, and possessing all things?"[4]

33. Wherefore even they which having relinquished or distributed their former, whether ample or in any sort opulent, means, have chosen with pious and wholesome humility to be numbered among the poor of Christ; if they be so strong in body and free from ecclesiastical occupations, (albeit, bringing as they do so great a proof of their purpose, and conferring from their former havings, either very much, or not a little, upon the indigence of the same society, the common fund itself and brotherly charity owes them in return a sustenance of their life,) yet if they too work with their hands, that they may take away all excuse from lazy brethren who come from a more humble condition in life, and therefore one more used to toil; therein they act far more mercifully than when they divided all their goods to the needy. If indeed they be unwilling to do this, who can venture to compel them? Yet then there ought to be found for them works in the monastery, which if more free from bodily exercise, require to be looked unto with vigilant administration, that not even they may eat their bread for nought, because it is now become the common property. Nor is it to be regarded in what mon-

asteries, or in what place, any man may have bestowed his former having upon his indigent brethren. For all Christians make one commonwealth. And for that cause whoso shall have, no matter in what place, expended upon Christians the things they needed, in what place soever he also receiveth what himself hath need of, from Christ's goods [5] he doth receive it. Because in what place soever himself has given to such, who but Christ received it? But, as for them who before they entered this holy society got their living by labor of the body, of which sort are the more part of them which come into monasteries, because of mankind also the more part are such; if they will not work, neither let them eat. For not to that end are the rich, in this Christian warfare, brought low unto piety, that the poor may be lifted up unto pride. As indeed it is by no means seemly that in that mode of life where senators become men of toil, there common workmen should become men of leisure; and whereunto there come, relinquishing their dainties, men who had been masters of houses and lands, there common peasants should be dainty.

34. But then the Lord saith, "Be not solicitous for your life what ye shall eat, nor for the body, what ye shall put on." Rightly: because He had said above, "Ye cannot serve God and mammon." For he who preaches the Gospel with an eye to this, that he may have whereof he may eat and whereof be clothed, accounts that he at the same time both serves God, because he preaches the Gospel; and mammon, because he preaches with an eye to these necessaries: which thing the Lord saith to be impossible. And hereby he who doth for the sake of these things preach the Gospel is convicted that he serves not God but mammon; however God may use him, he knows not how, to other men's advancement. For to this sentence doth He subjoin, saying "Therefore I say unto you, Be not solicitous for your life what ye shall eat, nor for your body what ye shall put on:" not that they should not procure these things, as much as is enough for necessity, by what means they honestly may; but that they should not look to these things, and for the sake of these do whatever in preaching of the Gospel they are bidden to do. The intention, namely, for which a thing is done, He calls the eye: of which a little above He was speaking with purpose to come down to this, and saying, "The light of thy body is thine eye: if thine eye be single, thy whole body shall be full of light; but if thine eye

---

be evil, thy whole body shall be full of darkness;" that is, such will be thy deeds as shall be thine intention for which thou doest them. For indeed that He might come to this, He had before given precept concerning alms, saying, "Lay not up for yourselves treasures on earth where rust and moth doth corrupt, and where thieves break through and steal. But lay up for yourselves treasure in heaven, where neither moth nor rust doth corrupt, and where thieves do not break through nor steal. For where thy treasure shall be, there will thy heart be also.[1]" Thereupon He subjoined, "The light of thy body is thine eye:" that they, to wit, which do alms, do them not with that intention that they should either wish to please men, or seek to have repayment on earth of the alms they do. Whence the Apostle, giving charge to Timothy for warning of rich men, "Let them," says he "readily give, communicate, treasure up for themselves a good foundation for the time to come, that they may lay hold on the true life."[2] Since then the Lord hath to the future life directed the eye of them which do alms, and to an heavenly reward, in order that the deeds themselves may be full of light when the eye shall be simple, (for of that last retribution is meant that which He says in another place, "He that receiveth you receiveth Me, and he that receiveth Me receiveth Him that sent Me. He that receiveth a prophet in the name of a prophet shall receive a prophet's reward; and he that receiveth a righteous man in the name of a righteous man shall receive a righteous man's reward. And whosoever shall give to drink unto one of these little ones a cup of cold water only in the name of a disciple, verily I say unto you, his reward shall not be lost,"[3]) lest haply after he had reproved the eye[4] of them which bestow things needful upon the indigent both prophets and just men and disciples of the Lord, the eye of the persons to whom these things were done should become depraved, so that for the sake of receiving these things they should wish to serve Christ as His soldiers: "No man," saith He, "can serve two masters." And a little after: "Ye cannot," saith He, "serve God and mammon."[5] And straightway He hath added, "Therefore I say unto you, be not solicitous for your life what ye shall eat, nor for the body what ye shall put on."

35. And that which follows concerning birds of the air and lilies of the field, He saith to this end, that no man may think that God careth not for the needs of His servants; when His most wise Providence reacheth unto these in creating and governing those. For it must not be deemed that it is not He that feeds and clothes them also which work with their hands. But lest they turn aside the Christian service of warfare unto their purpose of getting these things, the Lord in this premonisheth His servants that in this ministry which is due to His Sacrament, we should take thought, not for these, but for His kingdom and righteousness: and all these things shall be added unto us, whether working by our hands, or whether by infirmity of body hindered from working, or whether bound by such occupation of our very warfare that we are able to do nothing else. For neither does it follow that because the Lord hath said, "Call upon Me in the day of tribulation and I will deliver thee, and thou shalt glorify Me,"[6] therefore the Apostle ought not to have fled, and to be let down by the wall in a basket that he might escape the hands of a pursuer,[7] but should rather have waited to be taken, that, like the three children from the midst of the fires, the Lord might deliver him. Or for this reason ought not the Lord either to have said this, "If they shall persecute you in one city, flee ye to another,"[8] namely, because He hath said, "If ye shall ask of the Father any thing in My name, He will give it you."[9] As then whoever to Christ's disciples when fleeing from persecution should cast up this sort of question, why they did not rather stand, and by calling upon God obtain through His marvellous works in such wise deliverance, as Daniel from the lions, as Peter from his chains, they would answer that they ought not to tempt God, but He would then and then only do the like for them, if it should please Him, when they had nothing that they could do; but when He put flight in their power, although they were thereby delivered, yet were they not delivered but by Him: so likewise to servants of God having time and strength after the example and precept of the Apostle to get their living by their own hands, if any from the Gospel shall raise a question concerning the birds of the air, which sow not nor reap nor gather into stores, and concerning lilies of the field that they toil not neither do they spin; they will easily answer, "If we also, by reason of any either infirmity or occupation cannot work, He will so feed and clothe us, as He doth the birds and the lilies, which do no work of this kind:

---

[1] Matt. vi. 19–22.　[2] 1 Tim. vi. 18, 19.　[3] Matt. x. 40–42.
[4] *Correpto oculo*.　[5] Matt. vi. 24, 25, 34.

[6] Ps. l. 15.　[7] Acts ix. 25 ; 2 Cor. xi. 33.
[8] Matt. x. 23.　[9] John xvi. 23.

but when we are able, we ought not to tempt our God; because this very ability of ours, we have it by His gift, and in living by it, we live by His bounty Who hath bounteously bestowed upon us that we should have this ability. And therefore concerning these necessary things we are not solicitous; because when we are able to do these things, He by Whom mankind are fed and clothed doth feed and clothe us: but when we are not able to do these things, He feeds and clothes us by Whom the birds are fed and the lilies clothed, because we are more worth than they. Wherefore in this our warfare, neither for the morrow take we thought: because not for the sake of these temporal things, whereunto pertaineth To-morrow, but for the sake of those eternal things, where it is evermore To-day, have we proved ourselves unto Him, that, entangled in no secular business, we may please Him.[1]

36. Since these things are so, suffer me awhile, holy brother, (for the Lord giveth me through thee great boldness,) to address these same our sons and brethren whom I know with what love thou together with us dost travail in birth withal, until the Apostolic discipline be formed in them. O servants of God, soldiers of Christ, is it thus ye dissemble the plottings of our most crafty foe, who fearing your good fame, that so goodly odor of Christ, lest good souls should say, "We will run after the odor of thine ointments,"[2] and so should escape his snares, and in every way desiring to obscure it with his own stenches, hath dispersed on every side so many hypocrites under the garb of monks, strolling about the provinces, no where sent, no where fixed, no where standing, no where sitting. Some hawking about limbs of martyrs, if indeed of martyrs; others magnifying their fringes and phylacteries;[3] others with a lying story, how they have heard say that their parents or kinsmen are alive in this or that country, and therefore be they on their way to them: and all asking, all exacting, either the costs of their lucrative want, or the price of their pretended sanctity. And in the meanwhile wheresoever they be found out in their evil deeds, or in whatever way they become notorious, under the general name of monks, your purpose is blasphemed, a purpose so good, so holy, that in Christ's name we desire it, as through other lands so through all Africa, to grow and flourish. Then are ye not inflamed with godly jealousy? Does not your heart wax hot within

you, and in your meditation a fire kindle,[4] that these men's evil works ye should pursue with good works, that ye should cut off from them occasion of a foul trafficking, by which your estimation is hurt, and a stumbling-block put before the weak? Have mercy then and have compassion, and show to mankind that ye are not seeking in ease a ready subsistence, but through the strait and narrow way of this purpose, are seeking the kingdom of God. Ye have the same cause which the Apostle had, to cut off occasion from them which seek occasion, that they who by their stinks are suffocated, by your good odor may be refreshed.

37. We are not binding heavy burdens and laying them upon your shoulders, while we with a finger will not touch them. Seek out, and acknowledge the labor of our occupations, and in some of us the infirmities of our bodies also, and in the Churches which we serve, that custom now grown up, that they do not suffer us to have time ourselves for those works to which we exhort you. For though we might say, "Who goeth a warfare any time at his own charges? Who planteth a vineyard, and eateth not of the fruit thereof? Who feedeth a flock, and partaketh not of the milk of the flock?"[5] yet I call our Lord Jesus, in Whose name I fearlessly say these things, for a witness upon my soul, that so far as it concerns mine own convenience, I would much rather every day at certain hours, as much as is appointed by rule in well-governed monasteries, do some work with my hands, and have the remaining hours free for reading and praying, or some work pertaining to Divine Letters,[6] than have to bear these most annoying perplexities of other men's causes about secular matters, which we must either by adjudication bring to an end, or by intervention cut short. Which troubles the same Apostle hath fastened us withal, (not by his own sentence, but by His who spake through him,) while yet we do not read that he had to put up with them himself: indeed his was not the sort of work to admit of it, while running to and fro in his Apostleship. Nor hath he said, "If then ye have secular law-suits, bring them before us;" or, "Appoint us to judge them;" but, "Them which are contemptible in the Church, these," saith he, "put ye in place. To your abashment I say it: is it so that there is not among you any wise man who can judge between his brother, but brother goeth to law with brother, and that before

---

[1] 2 Tim. ii. 4. [2] Cant. i. 3, 4.
[3] Reg. S. Ben. c. l. Cass. Coll. xviii. 7.

[4] Ps. xxxix. 3. [See R.V.] [5] 1 Cor. ix. 7.
[6] Reg. S. Ben. c. xlviii.

infidels?"[1] So then wise believers and saints, having their stated abode in the different places, not those who were running hither and hither on the business of the Gospel, were the persons whom he willed to be charged with examination of such affairs. Whence it is no where written of him that he on any occasion gave up his time to such matters; from which we are not able to excuse ourselves, even though we be contemptible; because he willed even such to be put in place, in case there were lack of wise men, rather than have the affairs of Christians to be brought into the public courts. Which labor, however, we not without consolation of the Lord take upon us, for hope of eternal life, that we may bring forth fruit with patience. For we are servants unto His Church, and most of all to the weaker members, whatsoever members we in the same body may chance to be. I pass by other innumerable ecclesiastical cares, which perchance no man credits but he who hath experienced the same. Therefore we do not bind heavy burdens and place them on your shoulders, while we ourselves touch them not so much as with a finger; since indeed if with safety to our office we might, (He seeth it, Who tries our hearts!) we would rather do these things which we exhort you to do, than the things which we ourselves are forced to do. True it is, to all both us and you, while according to our degree and office we labor, both the way is strait in labor and toil; and yet, while we rejoice in hope, His yoke is easy and His burden light, Who hath called us unto rest, Who passed forth before us from the vale of tears, where not Himself either was without pressure of griefs. If ye be our brethren, if our sons, if we be your fellow-servants, or rather in Christ your servants, hear what we admonish, acknowledge what we enjoin, take what we dispense. But if we be Pharisees, binding heavy burdens and laying them on your shoulders;[2] yet do ye the things we say, even though ye disapprove the things we do. But to us it is a very small thing that we be judged by you,[3] or of any human assize.[4] Of how near and dear[5] charity is our care on your behalf, let Him look into it Who hath given what we may offer to be looked into by His eyes. In fine: think what ye will of us: Paul the Apostle enjoins and beseeches you in the Lord, that with silence, that is, quietly and obediently ordered, ye do work and eat your own bread.[6] Of him, as I suppose, ye be-

lieve no evil, and He who by him doth speak, on Him have ye believed.

38. These things, my brother Aurelius, most dear unto me, and in the bowels of Christ to be venerated, so far as He hath bestowed on me the ability Who through thee commanded me to do it, touching work of Monks, I have not delayed to write; making this my chief care, lest good brethren obeying apostolic precepts, should by lazy and disobedient be called even prevaricators from the Gospel: that they which work not, may at the least account them which do work to be better than themselves without doubt. But who can bear that contumacious persons resisting most wholesome admonitions of the Apostle, should, not as weaker brethren be borne withal, but even be preached up as holier men; insomuch that monasteries founded on sounder doctrine should be by this double enticement corrupted, the dissolute license of vacation from labor, and the false name of sanctity? Let it be known then to the rest, our brethren and sons, who are accustomed to favor such men, and through ignorance to defend this kind of presumption, that they need themselves most chiefly to be corrected, in order that those may be corrected, nor that they become "weary in well-doing."[7] Truly, in that they do promptly and with alacrity minister unto the servants of God the things they need, not only we blame them not, but we most cordially embrace them: only let them not with perverse mercy more hurt these men's future life, than to their present life they render aid.

39. For there is less sin, if people do not praise the sinner in the desires of his soul, and speak good of him who practiseth iniquities.[8] Now what is more an iniquity than to wish to be obeyed by inferiors, and to refuse to obey superiors? The Apostle, I mean, not us: insomuch that they even let their hair grow long: a matter, of which he would have no disputing at all, saying, "If any chooseth to be contentious, we have no such custom, neither the Church of God.[9] Now this I command;"[10] which gives us to understand that it is not cleverness of reasoning that we are to look for, but authority of one giving command to attend unto. For whereunto, I pray thee, pertaineth this also, that people so openly against the Apostle's precepts wear long hair? Is it that there must be in such sort vacation, that not even the barbers are to work? Or, because they say that they

---

[7] 2 Thess. iii. 13.　　[8] Ps. x. 3 [ix. 24].　　[9] 1 Cor. xi. 16, 17.
[10] E. V. follows text rec. τοῦτο δὲ παραγγελλων οὐκ ἐπαινῶ, but good MSS. and Versions besides the Ital. and Vulg. have τοῦτο δὲ παραγγελλω οὐκ ἐπαινῶν, hoc autem præcipio non laudans.

[1] 1 Cor. vi. 4–6.　　[2] Matt. xxiii. 3.　　[3] 1 Cor. iv. 3.
[4] Ab humano die.　　[5] Germana.　　[6] 2 Thess. iii. 12.

imitate the Gospel birds, do they fear to be, as it were, plucked, lest they be not able to fly? I shrink from saying more against this fault, out of respect for certain long-haired brethren, in whom, except this, we find much, and well-nigh every thing, to venerate. But the more we love them in Christ, the more solicitously do we admonish them. Nor are we afraid indeed, lest their humility reject our admonition; seeing that we also desire to be admonished by such as they, wherever we chance to stumble or to go aside. This then we admonish so holy men, not to be moved by foolish quibblings of vain persons, and imitate in this perversity them whom in all else they are far from resembling. For those persons, hawking about a venal hypocrisy, fear lest shorn sanctity be held cheaper than long-haired; because forsooth he who sees them shall call to mind those ancients whom we read of, Samuel and the rest who did not cut off their hair.[1] And they do not consider what is the difference between that prophetic veil, and this unveiling which is in the Gospel, of which the Apostle saith, "When thou shalt go over[2] unto Christ, the veil shall be taken away."[3] That, namely, which was signified in the veil interposed between the face of Moses and the beholding of the people Israel,[4] that same was also signified in those times by the long hair of the Saints. For the same Apostle saith, that long hair is also instead of a veil: by whose authority these men are hard pressed. Seeing he saith openly, "If a man wear long hair, it is a disgrace to him." "The very disgrace," say they, "we take upon us, for desert of our sins:" holding out a screen of simulated humility, to the end that under cover of it they may carry on their trade of self-importance.[5] Just as if the Apostle were teaching pride when he says, "Every man praying or prophesying with veiled head shameth his head;"[6] and, "A man ought not to veil his head, forsomuch as he is the image and glory of God."[7] Consequently he who says, "Ought not," knows not perchance how to teach humility! However, if this same disgrace in time of the Gospel, which was a thing of a holy meaning[8] in time of Prophecy, be by these people courted as matter of humility, then let them be shorn, and veil their head with haircloth. Only then there will be none of that attracting of people's eyes in which they trade,[9] because Samson was veiled not with haircloth, but with his long hair.

40. And then that further device of theirs, (if words can express it), how painfully ridiculous is it, which they have invented for defense of their long locks! "A man," say they, "the Apostle hath forbidden to have long hair: but then they who have made themselves eunuchs for the kingdom of God are no longer men." O dotage unparalleled! Well may the person who says this arm himself against Holy Scripture's most manifest proclamations, with counsel of outrageous impiety, and persevere in a tortuous path, and essay to bring in a pestiferous doctrine that not "Blessed is the man who hath not walked in the counsel of the ungodly, and in the way of sinners hath not stood, and in the chair of noisome wickedness[10] hath not sat."[11] For if he would meditate in God's law day and night, there he should find the Apostle Paul himself, who assuredly professing highest chastity saith, "I would that all men were even as I:" and yet shows himself a man, not only in so being, but also in so speaking. For he saith, "When I was a child, I spake as a child, I understood as a child, I thought as a child; when I became a man, I put away childish things."[12] But why should I mention the Apostle, when concerning our Lord and Saviour Himself they know not what they think who say these things. For of Whom but Him is it said, "Until we come all to unity of faith and to knowledge of the Son of God, to the Perfect Man, to the measure of the age of the fullness of Christ; that we be no longer babes, tossed and carried about with every wind of doctrine, in sleight of men, in cunning craftiness for machination of error."[13] With which sleight these persons deceive ignorant people, with which cunning craftiness and machinations of the enemy both they themselves are whirled round, and in their whirling essay to make the minds of the weak which cohere unto them so (in a manner) to spin round with them, that they also may not know where they are. For they have heard or read that which is written, "Whosoever of you have been baptized in Christ, have put on Christ: where is no Jew nor Greek; no bond nor free; no male nor female."[14] And they do not understand that it is in reference to concupiscence of carnal sex[15] that this is said, because in the inner man, wherein we are renewed in newness of our mind, no sex of this kind exists. Then let them not deny themselves to be men, just because in respect of their masculine sex they work not. For wedded Christians also who

[1] Numb. vi. 5
[2] *Cum transieris.* Gr. ἡνίκα δ' ἂν ἐπιστρέψῃ, sc. ὁ 'Ισραὴλ Chrys. Theod. or τὶς Origen.   [3] 2 Cor. iii. 16.
[4] Exod. xxxiv. 33.   [5] *Venalem typhum.*   [6] 1 Cor. xi. 4.
[7] 1 Cor. xi. 14.   [8] *Sacramentum.*   [9] *Species illa venalis.*
[10] *Pestilentiæ.*   [11] Ps. i. 1.
[12] 1 Cor. xiii. 11. [See R.V.]   [13] Eph. iv. 13, 14.
[14] Gal. iii. 27, 28. [See R.V.]   [15] 2 Cor. iv. 16.

do this work, are of course not Christians on the score of that which they have in common with the rest who are not Christians and with the very cattle. For that is one thing that is either to infirmity conceded or to mortal propagation paid as a debt, but another that which for the laying hold of incorrupt and eternal life is by faithful profession signified. That then which concerning not veiling of the head is enjoined to men, in the body indeed it is set forth in a figure, but that it is enacted in the mind, wherein is the image and glory of God, the words themselves do indicate: "A man indeed," it saith, "ought not to veil his head, forsomuch as he is the image and glory of God." For where this image is, he doth himself declare, where he saith, "Lie not one to another; but stripping off the old man with his deeds, put ye on the new, which is renewed to the acknowledging of God, according to the image of Him who created him."[1] Who can doubt that this renewing takes place in the mind? But and if any doubt, let him hear a more open sentence. For, giving the same admonition, he thus saith in another place: "As is the truth in Jesus, that ye put off concerning the former conversation the old man, him which is corrupt according to the lust of deception; but be ye renewed in the spirit of your mind, and put on the new man, him which after God is created."[2] What then? Have women not this renewal of mind in which is the image of God? Who would say this? But in the sex of their body they do not signify this; therefore they are bidden to be veiled. The part, namely, which they signify in the very fact of their being women, is that which may be called the concupiscential part, over which the mind[3] bears rule, itself also subjected to its God, when life is most rightly and orderly conducted. What, therefore, in a single individual human being is the mind and the concupiscence, (that ruling, this ruled; that lord, this subject,) the same in two human beings, man and woman, is in regard of the sex of the body exhibited in a figure. Of which sacred import[4] the Apostle speaks when he says, that the man ought not to be veiled, the women ought. For the mind doth the more gloriously advance to higher things, the

more diligently the concupiscence is curbed from lower things; until the whole man together with even this now mortal and frail body in the last resurrection be clothed with incorruption and immortality, and death be swallowed up in victory.[5]

41. Wherefore, they which will not do right things, let them give over at least to teach wrong things. Howbeit they be others whom in this speech we reprove: but as for those who by this one fault, of letting their hair contrary to apostolic precept grow long, offend and trouble the Church, because when some being unwilling to think of them any thing amiss are forced to twist the manifest words of the Apostle into a wrong meaning, others choose to defend the sound understanding of the Scriptures rather than fawn upon any men, there arise between the weaker and the stronger brethren most bitter and perilous contentions: which things perchance if they knew, these would correct without hesitation this also, in whom we admire and love all else. Those then we not reprove, but ask and solemnly beseech by the Godhead and the Manhood of Christ and by the charity of the Holy Ghost, that they no more put this stumbling-block before the weak for whom Christ died, and aggravate the grief and torment of our heart when we bethink us how much more readily evil men can imitate this evil thing for deceiving of mankind, when they see this in them whom on the score of other so great good we with deserved offices of Christian love do honor. If however, after this admonition, or rather this solemn entreaty of ours, they shall think fit to persevere in the same, we shall do nothing else but only grieve and mourn. This let them know; it is enough. If they be servants of God, they have pity. If they have not pity, I will not say any thing worse. All these things, therefore, in the which peradventure I have been more loquacious than the occupations both of thee and of me could wish, if thou approve the same, make thou to be known to our brethren and sons, on whose behalf thou hast deigned to put this burden upon me: but if aught seem to thee meet to be withdrawn or amended, by reply of your Blessedness I shall know the same.

---

[1] Col. iii. 9, 10.   [2] Eph. iv. 21-24. [See R.V.]
[3] *Mens.*   [4] *Sacramentum.*

[5] 1 Cor. xv. 54.

ST. AUGUSTIN:

ON PATIENCE

[DE PATIENTIA.]

TRANSLATED BY THE

REV. H. BROWNE, M.A.

OF CORPUS CHRISTI COLLEGE, CAMBRIDGE, LATE PRINCIPAL OF THE DIOCESAN
COLLEGE, CHICHESTER.

ON PATIENCE

[DE PATIENTIA.]

Erasmus infers from the style and language of this piece, that it is not S. Augustin's, putting it in the same category with the treatises *On Continence, On substance of Charity, On Faith of things invisible*. The Benedictine editors acknowledge that it has peculiarities of style which are calculated to move suspicion; (especially the studied assonances and rhyming endings, e. g. "*cautior fuit iste in doloribus quam ille in nemoribus . . . consensit ille oblectamentis, non cessit ille tormentis*," chap. 12.); yet they feel themselves bound to retain it among the genuine works by Augustin's own testimony, who mentions both this piece and that *On Continence* in his Epistle to Darius, 231. chap. 7. [Vol. I. 584.] That it is not named in the *Retractations* is accounted for by the circumstance that it appears to have been delivered as a sermon, see chap. 1. and 3, and Augustin did not live to fulfill his intention of composing a further book of retractations on review of his popular discourses and letters. *Ep.* 224. chap. 2. In point of matter and doctrine this treatise has nothing contrary to or not in harmony with S. Augustin's known doctrine and sentiments.

1. THAT virtue of the mind which is called Patience, is so great a gift of God, that even in Him who bestoweth the same upon us, that, whereby He waiteth for evil men that they may amend, is set forth by the name of Patience, [or long-suffering.] So, although in God there can be no suffering,[1] and "patience" hath its name *a patiendo*, from suffering, yet a patient God we not only faithfully believe, but also wholesomely confess. But the patience of God, of what kind and how great it is, His, Whom we say to be impassible,[2] yet not impatient, nay even most patient, in words to unfold this who can be able? Ineffable is therefore that patience, as is His jealousy, as His wrath, and whatever there is like to these. For if we conceive of these as they be in us, in Him are there none. We, namely, can feel none of these without molestation: but be it far from us to surmise that the impassible nature of God is liable to any molestation. But like as He is jealous without any darkening of spirit,[3] wroth without any perturbation, pitiful without any pain, repenteth Him without any wrongness in Him to be set right; so is He patient without aught of passion. Now therefore as concerning human patience, which we are able to conceive and beholden to have, of what sort it is, I will, as God granteth and the brevity of the present discourse alloweth, essay to set forth.

2. The patience of man, which is right and laudable and worthy of the name of virtue, is understood to be that by which we tolerate evil things with an even mind, that we may not with a mind uneven desert good things, through which we may arrive at better. Wherefore the impatient, while they will not suffer ills, effect not a deliverance from ills, but only the suffering of heavier ills. Whereas the patient who choose rather by not committing to bear, than by not bearing

---

[1] *Pati.*   [2] *Nihil patientem.*   [3] *Livore.*

to commit, evil, both make lighter what through patience they suffer, and also escape worse ills in which through impatience they would be sunk. But those good things which are great and eternal they lose not, while to the evils which be temporal and brief they yield not: because "the sufferings of this present time are not worthy to be compared," as the Apostle says, "with the future glory that shall be revealed in us."[1] And again he says, "This our temporal and light tribulation doth in inconceivable manner work for us an eternal weight of glory."[2]

3. Look we then, beloved, what hardships in labors and sorrows men endure, for things which they viciously love, and by how much they think to be made by them more happy, by so much more unhappily covet. How much for false riches, how much for vain honors, how much for affections of games and shows, is of exceeding peril and trouble most patiently borne! We see men hankering after money, glory, lasciviousness, how, that they may arrive at their desires, and having gotten not lose them, they endure sun, rain, icy cold, waves, and most stormy tempests, the roughnesses and uncertainties of wars, the strokes of huge blows, and dreadful wounds, not of inevitable necessity but of culpable will. But these madnesses are thought, in a manner, permitted. Thus avarice, ambition, luxury, and the delights of all sorts of games and shows, unless for them some wicked deed be committed or outrage which is prohibited by human laws, are accounted to pertain to innocence: nay moreover, the man who without wrong to any shall, whether for getting or increasing of money, whether for obtaining or keeping of honors, whether in contending in the match, or in hunting, or in exhibiting with applause some theatrical spectacle, have borne great labors and pains, it is not enough that through popular vanity he is checked by no reproofs, but he is moreover extolled with praises: "Because," as it is written, "the sinner is praised in the desires of his soul."[3] For the force of desires makes endurance of labors and pains: and no man save for that which he enjoyeth, freely takes on him to bear that which annoyeth. But these lusts, as I said, for the fulfilling of which they which are on fire with them most patiently endure much hardship and bitterness, are accounted to be permitted, and allowed by laws.

4. Nay more; for is it not so that even for open wickednesses, not to punish but to perpetrate them, men put up with many most

grievous troubles? Do not authors of secular letters tell of a certain right noble parricide of his country, that hunger, thirst, cold, all these he was able to endure, and his body was patient of lack of food and warmth and sleep to a degree surpassing belief?[5] Why speak of highway robbers, all of whom while they lie in wait for travellers endure whole nights without sleep, and that they may catch, as they pass by, men who have no thought of harm, will, no matter how foul the weather, plant in one spot their mind and body, which are full of thoughts of harm? Nay it is said that some of them are wont to torture one another by turns, to that degree that this practice and training against pains is not a whit short of pains. For, not so much perchance are they excruciated by the Judge, that through smart of pain the truth may be got at, as they are by their own comrades, that through patience of pain truth may not be betrayed. And yet in all these the patience is rather to be wondered at than praised: nay neither wondered at nor praised, seeing it is no patience; but we must wonder at the hardness, deny the patience: for there is nothing in this rightly to be praised, nothing usefully to be imitated; and thou wilt rightly judge the mind to be all the more worthy of greater punishment, the more it yields up to vices the instruments of virtues. Patience is companion of wisdom, not handmaid of concupiscence: patience is the friend of a good conscience, not the foe of innocence.

5. When therefore thou shalt see any man suffer aught patiently, do not straightway praise it as patience; for this is only shown by the cause of suffering. When it is a good cause, then is it true patience: when that is not polluted by lust, then is this distinguished from falsity. But when that is placed in crime, then is this much misplaced in name. For not just as all who know are partakers of knowledge, just so are all who suffer partakers of patience: but they which rightly use the suffering, these in verity of patience are praised, these with the prize of patience are crowned.

6. But yet, seeing that for lusts' sake, or even wickednesses, seeing, in a word, that for this temporal life and weal men do wonderfully bear the brunt of many horrible sufferings, they much admonish us how great things ought to be borne for the sake of a good life, that it may also hereafter be eternal life, and without any bound of time, without waste or loss of any advantage, in true felicity secure. The Lord saith, "In your patience ye shall

---

[1] Rom. viii. 18.   [2] 2 Cor. iv. 17.   [3] Ps. x. 3.   [4] *Sallust Catilin,* c. v.

possess your souls:"[1] He saith not, your farms, your praises, your luxuries; but, "your souls." If then the soul endures so great sufferings that it may possess that whereby it may be lost, how great ought it to bear that it may not be lost? And then, to mention a thing not culpable, if it bear so great sufferings for saving of the flesh under the hands of chirurgeons cutting or burning the same, how great ought it to bear for saving of itself under the fury of any soever enemies? Seeing that leeches, that the body may not die, do by pains consult for the body's good; but enemies by threatening the body with pains and death, would urge us on to the slaying of soul and body in hell.

7. Though indeed the welfare even of the body is then more providently consulted for, if its temporal life and welfare be disregarded for righteousness' sake, and its pain or death most patiently for righteousness' sake endured. Since it is of the body's redemption which is to be in the end, that the Apostle speaks, where he says, "Even we ourselves groan within ourselves, waiting the adoption of sons, the redemption of our body."[2] Then he subjoins, "For in hope are we saved. But hope which is seen is not hope: for what a man seeth, why doth he also hope for? But if what we see not we hope for, we do by patience wait for it." When therefore any ills do torture us indeed, yet not extort from us ill works, not only is the soul possessed through patience; but even when through patience the body itself for a time is afflicted or lost, it is unto eternal stability and salvation resumed, and hath through grief and death an inviolable health and happy immortality laid up for itself. Whence the Lord Jesus exhorting his Martyrs to patience, hath promised of the very body a future perfect entireness, without loss, I say not of any limb, but of a single hair. "Verily I say unto you," saith He, "a hair of your head shall not perish."[3] That so, because, as the Apostle says, "no man ever hated his own flesh,"[4] a faithful man may more by patience than by impatience take vigilant care for the state of his flesh, and find amends for its present losses, how great soever they may be, in the inestimable gain of future incorruption.

8. But although patience be a virtue of the mind, yet partly the mind exercises it in the mind itself, partly in the body. In itself it exercises patience, when, the body remaining unhurt and untouched, the mind is goaded by any adversities or filthinesses of things or words, to do or to say something that is not expedient or not becoming, and patiently bears all evils that it may not itself commit any evil in work or word. By this patience we bear, even while we be sound in body, that in the midst of the offenses of this world our blessedness is deferred: of which is said what I cited a little before, "If what we see not we hope for, we do by patience wait for it." By this patience, holy David bore the revilings of a railer,[5] and, when he might easily have avenged himself, not only did it not, but even refrained another who was vexed and moved for him; and more put forth his kingly power by prohibiting than by exercising vengeance. Nor at that time was his body afflicted with any disease or wound, but there was an acknowledging of a time of humility, and a bearing of the will of God, for the sake of which there was a drinking of the bitterness of contumely with most patient mind. This patience the Lord taught, when, the servants being moved at the mixing in of the tares and wishing to gather them up, He said that the householder answered, "Leave both to grow until the harvest."[6] That, namely, must be patience put up with, which must not be in haste put away. Of this patience Himself afforded and showed an example, when, before the passion of His Body, He so bore with His disciple Judas, that ere He pointed him out as the traitor, He endured him as a thief;[7] and before experience of bonds and cross and death, did, to those lips so full of guile, not deny the kiss of peace.[8] All these, and whatever else there be, which it were tedious to rehearse, belong to that manner of patience, by which the mind doth, not its own sins but any evils soever from without, patiently endure in itself, while the body remains altogether unhurt. But the other manner of patience is that by which the same mind bears any troubles and grievances whatsoever in the sufferings of the body; not as do foolish or wicked men for the sake of getting vain things or perpetrating crimes; but as is defined by the Lord, "for righteousness' sake."[9] In both kinds, the holy Martyrs contended. For both with scornful reproofs of the ungodly were they filled, where, the body remaining intact, the mind hath its own (as it were) blows and wounds, and bears these unbroken: and in their bodies they were bound, imprisoned, vexed with hunger and thirst, tortured, gashed, torn asunder, burned, butchered; and with piety immovable submitted unto

---

1 Luke xxi. 19. 2 Rom. viii. 23-25.
3 Luke xxi. 18. 4 Eph. v. 29.
5 2 Sam. xvi. 5-12. 6 Matt. xiii. 30. 7 John xii. 6; xiii. 29.
8 Matt. xxvi. 49. 9 Matt. v. 10.

God their mind, while they were suffering in the flesh all that exquisite cruelty could devise in its mind.

9. It is indeed a greater fight of patience, when it is not a visible enemy that by persecution and rage would urge us into crime, which enemy may openly and in broad day be by not consenting overcome; but the devil himself, (he who doth likewise by means of the children of infidelity, as by his vessels, persecute the children of light) doth by himself hiddenly attack us, by his rage putting us on to do or say something against God. As such had holy Job experience of him, by both temptations vexed, but in both through steadfast strength of patience and arms of piety unconquered. For first, his body being left unhurt, he lost all that he had, in order that the mind, before excruciation of the flesh, might through withdrawal of the things which men are wont to prize highly, be broken, and he might say something against God upon loss of the things for the sake of which he was thought to worship Him. He was smitten also with sudden bereavement of all his sons, so that whom he had begotten one by one he should lose all at once, as though their numerousness had been not for the adorning of his felicity, but for the increasing of his calamity. But where, having endured these things, he remained immovable in his God, he cleaved to His will, Whom it was not possible to lose but by his own will; and in place of the things he had lost he held Him who took them away, in Whom he should find what should never be lost. For He that took them away was not that enemy who had will of hurting, but He who had given to that enemy the power of hurting. The enemy next attacked also the body, and now not those things which were in the man from without, but the man himself, in whatever part he could, he smote. From the head to the feet were burning pains, were crawling worms, were running sores; still in the rotting body the mind remained entire, and horrid as were the tortures of the consuming flesh, with inviolate piety and uncorrupted patience it endured them all. There stood the wife, and instead of giving her husband any help, was suggesting blasphemy against God. For we are not to think that the devil, in leaving her when he took away the sons, went to work as one unskilled in mischief: rather, how necessary she was to the tempter, he had already learned in Eve. But now he had not found a second Adam whom he might take by means of a woman. More cautious was Job in his hours of sadness, than Adam in his bowers of gladness, the one was overcome

in the midst of pleasant things, the other overcame in the midst of pains; the one consented to that which seemed delightsome, this other quailed not in torments most affrightsome. There stood his friends too, not to console him in his evils, but to suspect evil in him. For while he suffered so great sorrows, they believed him not innocent, nor did their tongue forbear to say that which his conscience had not to say; that so amid ruthless tortures of the body, his mind also might be beaten with truthless reproaches. But he, bearing in his flesh his own pains, in his heart others' errors, reproved his wife for her folly, taught his friends wisdom, preserved patience in each and all.

10. To this man let them[1] look who put themselves to death when they are sought for to have life put upon them; and by bereaving themselves of the present, deny and refuse also that which is to come. Why, if people were driving them to deny Christ or to do any thing contrary to righteousness, like true Martyrs, they ought rather to bear all patiently than to dare death impatiently. If it could be right to do this for the sake of running away from evils, holy Job would have killed himself, that being in so great evils, in his estate, in his sons, in his limbs, through the devil's cruelty, he might escape them all. But he did it not. Far be it from him, a wise man, to commit upon himself what not even that unwise woman suggested. And if she had suggested it, she would with good reason here also have had that answer which she had when suggesting blasphemy; "Thou hast spoken as one of the foolish women. If we have received good at the hand of the Lord, shall we not bear evil?"[2] Seeing even he also would have lost patience, if either by blasphemy as she had suggested, or by killing himself which not even she had dared to speak of, he should die, and be among them of whom it is written, "Woe unto them that have lost patience!"[3] and rather increase than escape pains, if after the death of his body he should be hurried off to punishment either of blasphemers, or of murderers, or of them which are worse even than parricides. For if a parricide be on that account more wicked than any homicide, because he kills not merely a man but a near relative; and among parricides too, the nearer the person killed, the greater criminal he is judged to be: without doubt worse still is he who kills himself, because there is none nearer to a man than himself. What then do these miserable persons mean, who, though both here they

---

[1] Donatists.   [2] Job ii. 10.   [3] Ecclus. ii. 14.

have inflicted pain upon themselves, and hereafter not only for their impiety towards God but for the very cruelty which they have exercised upon themselves will deservedly suffer pains of His inflicting, do yet seek moreover the glories of Martyrs? since, even if for the true testimony of Christ they suffered persecution, and killed themselves, that they might not suffer any thing from their persecutors, it would be rightly said to them, " Woe unto them which have lost patience !" For how hath patience her just reward, if even an impatient suffering receives the crown? or how shall that man be judged innocent, to whom is said, " Thou shalt love thy neighbor as thyself,"[1] if he commit murder upon himself which he is forbidden to commit upon his neighbor?

11. Let then the Saints hear from holy Scripture the precepts of patience: " My son, when thou comest to the service of God, stand thou in righteousness and fear, and prepare thy soul for temptation: bring thine heart low, and bear up; that in the last end thy life may increase. All that shall come upon thee receive thou, and in pain bear up, and in thy humility have patience. For in the fire gold and silver is proved, but acceptable men in the furnace[2] of humiliation."[3] And in another place we read: " My son, faint not thou in the discipline of the Lord, neither be wearied when thou art chidden of Him. For whom the Lord loveth He chasteneth, and scourgeth every son whom He receiveth."[4] What is here set down, " son whom He receiveth," the same in the above mentioned testimony is, " acceptable men." For this is just, that we who from our first felicity of Paradise for contumacious appetence of things to enjoy were dismissed, through humble patience of things that annoy may be received back: driven away for doing evil, brought back by suffering evil: there against righteousness doing ill, here for righteousness' sake patient of ills.

12. But concerning true patience, worthy of the name of this virtue, whence it is to be had, must now be inquired. For there are some[5] who attribute it to the strength of the human will, not which it hath by Divine assistance, but which it hath of free-will. Now this error is a proud one: for it is the error of them which abound, of whom it is said in the Psalm, "A scornful reproof to them which abound, and a despising to the proud."[7] It is not therefore that " patience of the poor " which " perisheth not forever."[8] For these

poor receive it from that Rich One, to Whom is said, " My God art Thou, because my goods Thou needest not:"[8] of Whom is " every good gift, and every perfect gift;"[9] to Whom crieth the needy and the poor, and in asking, seeking, knocking, saith, " My God, deliver me from the hand of the sinner, and from the hand of the lawless and unjust: because Thou art my patience, O Lord, my hope from my youth up."[10] But these which abound, and disdain to be in want before God, lest they receive of Him true patience, they which glory in their own false patience, seek to " confound the counsel of the poor, because the Lord is his hope."[11] Nor do they regard, seeing they are men, and attribute so much to their own, that is, to the human will, that they run into that which is written, " Cursed is every one who putteth his hope in man."[12] Whence even if it chance them that they do bear up under any hardships or difficulties, either that they may not displease men, or that they may not suffer worse, or in self-pleasing and love of their own presumption, do with most proud will bear up under these same, it is meet that concerning patience this be said unto them, which concerning wisdom the blessed Apostle James saith, " This wisdom cometh not from above, but is earthly, animal, devilish."[13] For why may there not be a false patience of the proud, as there is a false wisdom of the proud? But from Whom cometh true wisdom, from Him cometh also true patience. For to Him singeth that poor in spirit, " Unto God is my soul subjected, because from Him is my patience."[14]

13. But they answer and speak, saying, " If the will of man without any aid of God by strength of free choice[15] bears so many grievous and horrible distresses, whether in mind or body, that it may enjoy the delight of this mortal life and of sins, why may it not be that in the same manner the self-same will of man by the same strength of free-choice, not thereunto looking to be aided of God, but unto itself by natural possibility sufficing, doth, in all of labor or sorrow that is put upon it, for righteousness and eternal life's sake most patiently sustain the same? Or is it so, say they, that the will of the unjust is sufficient, without aid of God, for them, yea even to exercise themselves in undergoing torture for iniquity, and before they be tortured by others; sufficient the will of them which love the respiting of this life that, without aid of God, they should in the midst of

[1] Matt. xix. 19.   [2] Receptibiles.   [3] Ecclus. ii. 1-5.
[4] Prov. iii. 11, 12.   [5] Pelagians.   [6] Ps. cxxiii. 4.
[7] Ps. ix. 18.

[8] Ps. xvi. 2.   [9] James i. 17.   [10] Ps. lxxi. 4, 5.
[11] Ps. xiv. 6.   [12] Jer. xvii. 5.   [13] James iii. 15.
[14] Ps. lxii. 5.   [15] Liberi arbitrii.

most atrocious and protracted torments persevere in a lie, lest confessing their misdeeds
they be ordered to be put to death; and not
sufficient the will of the just, unless strength
be put into them from above, that whatever
be their pains, they should, either for beauty's
sake of very righteousness or for love of eternal life, bear the same?"

14. They which say these things, do not
understand that as well each one of the wicked
is in that measure for endurance of any ills
more hard, in what measure the lust of the
world is mightier in him; as also that each
one of the just is in that measure for endurance of any ills more brave, in what measure
in him the love of God is mightier. But lust
of the world hath its beginning from choice
of the will, its progress from enjoyableness of
pleasure, its confirmation from the chain of
custom, whereas "the love of God is shed
abroad in our hearts,"[1] not verily from ourselves, but "by the Holy Spirit which is given
unto us." And therefore from Him cometh
the patience of the just, by Whom is shed
abroad their love (of Him). Which love (of
charity) the Apostle praising and setting off,
among its other good qualities, saith, that it
"beareth all things."[2]   "Charity," saith he,
"is magnanimous."[3] And a little after he
saith, "endureth all things." The greater
then is in saints the charity (or love) of God,
the more do they endure all things for Him
whom they love, and the greater in sinners
the lust of the world, the more do they endure all things for that which they lust after.
And consequently from that same source
cometh true patience of the righteous, from
which there is in them the love of God; and
from that same source the false patience of
the unrighteous, from which is in them the
lust of the world. With regard to which the
Apostle John saith; "Love not the world,
neither the things that be in the world. If
any man love the world, the love of the
Father is not in him: because all that is in
the world, is lust of the flesh, and lust of the
eyes, and pride of life;[4] which is not of the
Father, but is of the world."[5] This concupiscence, then, which is not of the Father, but
is of the world, in what measure it shall in
any man be more vehement and ardent, in
that measure becometh each more patient of
all troubles and sorrows for that which he
lusteth after. Therefore, as we said above,
this is not the patience which descendeth
from above, but the patience of the godly is
from above, coming down from the Father of
lights. And so that is earthly, this heavenly;

that animal, this spiritual; that devilish, this
Godlike.[6] Because concupiscence, whereof it
cometh that persons sinning suffer all things
stubbornly, is of the world; but charity,
whereof cometh that persons living aright
suffer all things bravely, is of God. And
therefore to that false patience it is possible
that, without aid of God, the human will may
suffice; harder, in proportion as it is more
eager of lust, and bearing ills with the more
endurance the worse itself becometh: while to
this, which is true patience, the human will,
unless aided and inflamed from above, doth
not suffice, for the very reason that the Holy
Spirit is the fire thereof; by Whom unless it
be kindled to love that impassible Good, it is
not able to bear the ill which it suffereth.

15. For, as the Divine utterances testify,
"God is love, and he that dwelleth in love
dwelleth in God, and God dwelleth in him."[7]
Whoso therefore contends that love of God
may be had without aid of God, what else
does he contend, but that God may be had
without God? Now what Christian would say
this, which no madman would venture to say?
Therefore in the Apostle, true, pious, faithful
patience, saith exultingly, and by the mouth
of the Saints; "Who shall separate us from
the love of Christ? shall tribulation, or distress, or persecution, or famine, or nakedness, or peril, or sword? As it is written,
For Thy sake we are killed all the day long;
we are accounted as sheep for the slaughter.
Nay, in all these things we are more than
conquerors through Him that loved us:" not
through ourselves, but, "through Him that
loved us."[8] And then he goes on and adds;
"For I am persuaded, that neither death,
nor life, nor angels, nor principalities, nor
powers, nor things present, nor things to
come, nor height, nor depth, nor any other
creature, shall be able to separate us from the
love of God, which is in Christ Jesus our
Lord." This is that "love of God" which
"is shed abroad in our hearts by the Holy
Spirit which is given unto us." But the concupiscence of the bad, by reason of which
there is in them a false patience, "is not of
the Father,"[9] as saith the Apostle John, but
is of the world.

16. Here some man shall say; "If the
concupiscence of the bad, whereby it comes
that they bear all evils for that which they
lust after, be of the world, how is it said to be
of their will?" As if, truly, they were not
themselves also of the world, when they love
the world, forsaking Him by Whom the world
was made. For "they serve the creature

---

[1] Rom. v. 5.   [2] 1 Cor. xiii. 4, 7.   [3] *Magnanima.*   [6] *Deifica.*   [7] 1 John iv. 16.
[4] *Ambitio sæculi.*   [5] 1 John ii. 15, 16.   [8] Rom. viii. 35–39.   [9] 1 John ii. 16.

more than the Creator, Who is blessed for ever." [1] Whether then by the word "world," the Apostle John signifies lovers of the world, the will, as it is of themselves, is therefore of the world: or whether under the name of the world he comprises heaven and earth, and all that is therein, that is the creature universally, it is plain that the will of the creature, not being that of the Creator, is of the world. For which cause to such the Lord saith, "Ye are from beneath, I am from above: ye are of this world, I am not of this world." [2] And to the Apostle He saith, "If ye were of the world, the world would love his own." But lest they should arrogate more unto themselves than their measure craved, and when He said that they were not of the world, should imagine this to be of nature, not of grace, therefore He saith, "But because ye are not of the world, but I have chosen you out of the world, therefore the world hateth you." It follows, that they once were of the world: for, that they might not be of the world, they were chosen out of the world.

17. Now this election the Apostle demonstrating to be, not of merits going before in good works, but election of grace, saith thus: "And in this time a remnant by election of grace is saved. But if by grace, then is it no more of works, otherwise grace is no more grace." [3] This is election of grace; that is, election in which through the grace of God men are elected: this, I say, is election of grace which goes before all good merits of men. For if it be to any good merits that it is given, then is it no more gratuitously given, but is paid as a debt, and consequently is not truly called grace; where "reward," as the same Apostle saith, "is not imputed as grace, but as debt." [4] Whereas if, that it may be true grace, that is, gratuitous, it find nothing in man to which it is due of merit, (which thing is well understood in that saying, "Thou wilt save them for nothing," [5]) then assuredly itself gives the merits, not to merits is given. Consequently it goes before even faith, from which it is that all good works begin. "For the just," as is written, "shall live by faith." [6] But, moreover, grace not only assists the just, but also justifies the ungodly. And therefore even when it does aid the just and seems to be rendered to his merits, not even then does it cease to be grace, because that which it aids it did itself bestow. With a view therefore to this grace, which precedes all good merits of man, not only was Christ put to death by

the ungodly, but "died for the ungodly." [7] And ere that He died, He elected the Apostles, not of course then just, but to be justified: to whom He saith, "I have chosen you out of the world." For to whom He said, "Ye are not of the world," and then, lest they should account themselves never to have been of the world, presently added, "But I have chosen you out of the world;" assuredly that they should not be of the world was by His own election of them conferred upon them. Wherefore, if it had been through their own righteousness, not through His grace, that they were elected, they would not have been chosen out of the world, because they would already not be of the world if already they were just. And again, if the reason why they were elected was, that they were already just, they had already first chosen the Lord. For who can be righteous but by choosing righteousness? "But the end of the law is Christ, for righteousness is to every one that believeth. [8] Who is made unto us wisdom of God, and righteousness, and sanctification, and redemption: that, as it is written, He that glorieth, let him glory in the Lord." [9] He then is Himself our righteousness.

18. Whence also the just of old, before the Incarnation of the Word, in this faith of Christ, and in this true righteousness, (which thing Christ is unto us,) were justified; believing this to come which we believe come: and they themselves by grace were saved through faith, not of themselves, but by the gift of God, not of works, lest haply they should be lifted up. [10] For their good works did not come before God's mercy, but followed it. For to them was it said, and by them written, long ere Christ was come in the flesh, "I will have mercy on whom I will have mercy, and I will show compassion on whom I will have compassion." [11] From which words of God the Apostle Paul, should so long after say; "It is not therefore of him that willeth, nor of him that runneth, but of God that showeth mercy." It is also their own voice, long ere Christ was come in the flesh, "My God, His mercy shall prevent me." [12] How indeed could they be aliens from the faith of Christ, by whose charity even Christ was fore-announced unto us; without the faith of Whom, not any of mortals either hath been, or is, or ever shall be able to be, righteous? If then, being already just, the Apostles were elected by Christ, they would have first chosen Him, that just men might be chosen, because without Him they

---

[1] Rom. i. 25. [2] John viii. 23.
[3] Rom. xi. 5, 6. [4] Rom. iv. 4.
[5] Psalm lvi. 7, Lat. and LXX. ὑπὲρ τοῦ μηθενὸς σώσεις αὐτούς.
But Heb. and E. V. "shall they escape by iniquity?"
[6] Habak. ii. 4.

[7] Rom. v. 6. [8] Rom. x. 4. [9] 1 Cor. i. 30, 31. [10] Eph. ii. 8, 9.
[11] Ex. xxxiii. 19 ; Rom. ix. 15, 16. [12] Ps. lix. 10.

could not be just. But it was not so: as Himself saith to them, " Not ye have chosen Me, but I have chosen you." Of which the Apostle John speaks, " Not that we loved God, but that He loved us."[1]

19. Since the case is so, what is man, while in this life he uses his own proper will, ere he choose and love God, but unrighteous and ungodly? " What," I say, " is man," a creature going astray from the Creator, unless his Creator " be mindful of him,"[2] and choose[3] him freely, and love[4] him freely? Because he is himself not able to choose or love, unless being first chosen and loved he be healed, because by choosing blindness he perceiveth not, and by loving laziness is soon wearied. But perchance some man may say: In what manner is it that God first chooses and loves unjust men, that He may justify them, when it is written, " Thou hatest, Lord, all that work iniquity?"[5] In what way, think we, but in a wonderful and ineffable manner? And yet even we are able to conceive, that the good Physician both hates and loves the sick man: hates him, because he is sick; loves him, that he may drive away his sickness.

20. Let thus much have been said with regard to charity, without which in us there cannot be true patience, because in good men it is the love of God which endureth all things, as in bad men the lust of the world. But this love is in us by the Holy Spirit which was given us. Whence, of Whom cometh in us love, of Him cometh patience. But the lust of the world, when it patiently bears the burdens of any manner of calamity, boasts of the strength of its own will, like as of the stupor of disease, not robustness of health. This boasting is insane: it is not the language of patience, but of dotage. A will like this in that degree seems more patient of bitter ills, in which it is more greedy of temporal good things, because more empty of eternal.

21. But if it be goaded on and inflamed with deceitful visions and unclean incentives by the devilish spirit, associated and conspiring therewith in malignant agreement, this spirit makes the will of the man either frantic with error, or burning with appetite of some worldly delight; and hence, it seems to show a marvellous endurance of intolerable evils: but yet it does not follow from this that an evil will without instigation of another and unclean spirit, like as a good will without aid of the Holy Spirit, cannot exist. For that there may be an evil will even without any spirit either seducing or inciting, is sufficiently clear in the instance of the devil himself, who is found to have become a devil, not through some other devil, but of his own proper will. An evil will therefore, whether it be hurried on by lust, whether called back by fear, whether expanded by gladness, whether contracted by sadness, and in all these perturbations of mind enduring and making light of whatever are to others, or at another time, more grievous, this evil will may, without another spirit to goad it on, seduce itself, and in lapsing by defection from the higher to the lower, the more pleasant it shall account that thing to be which it seeks to get or fears to lose, or rejoices to have gotten, or grieves to have lost, the more tolerably for its sake bear what is less for it to suffer than that is to be enjoyed. For whatever that thing be, it is of the creature, of which one knows the pleasure. Because in some sort, the creature loved approaches itself to the creature loving in fond contact and connection, to the giving experience of its sweetness.

22. But the pleasure of the Creator, of which is written, "And from the river of Thy pleasure wilt Thou give them to drink,"[6] is of far other kind, for it is not, like us, a creature. Unless then its love be given to us from thence, there is no source whence it may be in us. And consequently, a good will, by which we love God, cannot be in man, save in whom God also worketh to will. This good will therefore, that is, a will faithfully subjected to God,[7] a will set on fire by sanctity of that ardor which is above, a will which loves God and his neighbor for God's sake; whether through love, of which the Apostle Peter makes answer, "Lord, Thou knowest that I love Thee;"[8] whether through fear, of which says the Apostle Paul, "In fear and trembling work out your own salvation;"[9] whether through joy, of which he says, "In hope rejoicing, in tribulation patient;"[10] whether through sorrow, with which he says he had great grief for his brethren;[11] in whatever way it endure what bitterness and hardships soever, it is the love of God which "endureth all things,"[12] and which is not shed abroad in our hearts but by the Holy Spirit given unto us.[13] Whereof piety makes no manner of doubt, but, as the charity of them which holily love, so the patience of them which piously endure, is the gift of God. For it cannot be that the divine Scripture deceiveth or is deceived, which not only in the Old Books hath testimonies of this thing, when it is said unto God, " My Patience art Thou," and, " From Him is my

---

[1] 1 John iv. 10.   [2] Ps. viii. 4.   *Eligere.*
[4] *Diligere.*   [5] Ps. v. 5.

[6] Ps. xxxvi. 9.   [7] Phil. ii. 13.   [8] John xxi. 15.
[9] Phil. ii. 12.   [10] Rom. xii. 12.   [11] Rom. ix. 2.
[12] 1 Cor. xiii. 7.   [13] Rom. v. 5.

patience;"[1] and where another prophet saith, that we receive the spirit of fortitude;[2] but also in the Apostolic writings we read, "Because unto you is given on behalf of Christ, not only to believe on Him, but to suffer for Him."[3] Therefore let not that make the mind to be as of its own merit uplifted, wherewith he is told that he is of Another's mercy gifted.

23. But if moreover any not having charity, which pertaineth to the unity of spirit and the bond of peace whereby the Catholic Church is gathered and knit together, being involved in any schism, doth, that he may not deny Christ, suffer tribulations, straits, hunger, nakedness, persecution, perils, prisons, bonds, torments, swords, or flames, or wild beasts, or the very cross, through fear of hell and everlasting fire; in nowise is all this to be blamed, nay rather this also is a patience meet to be praised. For we cannot say that it would have been better for him that by denying Christ he should suffer none of these things, which he did suffer by confessing Him: but we must account that it will perhaps be more tolerable for him in the judgment, than if by denying Christ he should avoid all those things: so that what the Apostle saith, "If I shall give my body to be burned, but have not charity, it profiteth me nothing,"[4] should be understood to profit nothing for obtaining the kingdom of heaven, but not for having more tolerable punishment to undergo in the last judgment.

24. [5] But it may well be asked, whether this patience likewise be the gift of God, or to be attributed to strength of the human will, by which patience, one who is separated from the Church doth, not for the error which separated him but for the truth of the Sacrament or Word which hath remained with him, for fear of pains eternal suffer pains temporal. For we must take heed lest haply, if we affirm that patience to be the gift of God, they in whom it is should be thought to belong also to the kingdom of God; but if we deny it to be the gift of God, we should be compelled to allow that without aid and gift of God there can be in the will of man somewhat of good. Because it is not to be denied that it is a good thing that a man believe he shall undergo pain of eternal punishment if he shall deny Christ, and for that faith endure and make light of any manner of punishment of man's inflicting.

25. So then, as we are not to deny that this is the gift of God, we are thus to understand that there be some gifts of God possessed by the sons of that Jerusalem which is above,[6] and free, and mother of us all, (for these are in some sort the hereditary possessions in which we are "heirs of God and joint-heirs with Christ:") but some other which may be received even by the sons of concubines to whom carnal Jews and schismatics or heretics are compared. For though it be written, "Cast out the bondmaid and her son, for the son of the bondmaid shall not be heir with my son Isaac:"[7] and though God said to Abraham, "In Isaac shall thy seed be called:" which the Apostle hath so interpreted as to say, "That is, not they which be sons of the flesh, these be the sons of God; but the sons of the promise are counted for the seed;"[8] that we might understand the seed of Abraham in regard of Christ to pertain by reason of Christ to the sons of God, who are Christ's body and members, that is to say, the Church of God, one, true, very-begotten, catholic, holding the godly faith; not the faith which works through elation or fear, but "which worketh by love;"[9] nevertheless, even the sons of the concubines, when Abraham sent them away from his son Isaac, he did not omit to bestow upon them some gifts, that they might not be left in every way empty, but not that they should be held as heirs. For so we read: "And Abraham gave all his estate unto Isaac; and to the sons of his concubines gave Abraham gifts, and sent them away from his son Isaac."[10] If then we be sons of Jerusalem the free, let us understand that other be the gifts of them which are put out of the inheritance, other the gifts of them which be heirs. For these be the heirs, to whom is said, "Ye have not received the spirit of bondage again to fear, but ye have received the spirit of adoption of sons, whereby we cry, Abba, Father."[11]

26. Cry we therefore with the spirit of charity, and until we come to the inheritance in which we are alway to remain, let us be, through love which becometh the free-born, not through fear which becometh bondmen, patient of suffering. Cry we, so long as we are poor, until we be with that inheritance made rich. Seeing how great earnest thereof we have received, in that Christ to make us rich made Himself poor; Who being exalted unto the riches which are above, there was sent One Who should breathe into our hearts holy longings, the Holy Spirit. Of these poor, as yet believing, not yet beholding; as yet hoping, not yet enjoying; as yet sighing in desire, not yet reigning in felicity; as yet hungering

---

[1] Ps. lxxi. 5 ; and lxii. 5.
[2] Is. xi. 2.
[3] Phil. i. 29.
[4] 1 Cor. xiii. 3.
[5] See on *Profit of Believing*, c. 1, p. 347.

[6] Gal. iv. 26.
[7] Gal. iv. 30; and Gen. xxi. 10.
[8] Gen. xxi 12; and Rom. ix. 7, 8.
[9] Gal. v. 6
[10] Gen. xxv. 5, 6.
[11] Rom. viii. 15.

and thirsting, not yet satisfied: of these poor, then, "the patience shall not perish for ever:" [1] not that there will be patience there also, where aught to endure shall not be; but "will not perish," meaning that it will not be unfruitful. But its fruit it will have for ever, therefore it "shall not perish for ever." For he who labors in vain, when his hope fails for which he labored, says with good cause, "I have lost so much labor:" but he who comes to the promise of his labor says, congratulating himself, I have not lost my labor.

Labor then is said not to perish (or be lost), not because it lasts perpetually, but because it is not spent in vain. So also the patience of the poor of Christ (who yet are to be made rich as heirs of Christ) shall not perish for ever: not because there also we shall be commanded patiently to bear, but because for that which we have here patiently borne, we shall enjoy eternal bliss. He will put no end to everlasting felicity, Who giveth temporal patience unto the will: because both the one and the other is of Him bestowed as a gift upon charity, Whose gift that charity is also.

[1] Ps. ix. 18.

ST. AUGUSTIN:

ON CARE

TO BE HAD FOR THE DEAD

[DE CURA PRO MORTUIS.]

TRANSLATED BY

REV. H. BROWNE. M.A.,

OF CORPUS CHRISTI COLLEGE, CAMBRIDGE, LATE PRINCIPAL OF THE DIOCESAN
COLLEGE, CHICHESTER.

ON CARE TO BE HAD FOR THE DEAD.

[DE CURA PRO MORTUIS.]

From the Retractations, Book ii. Chap. 64.

The book, *On care to be had for the dead*, I wrote, having been asked by letter whether it profits any person after death that his body shall be buried at the memorial of any Saint.[1] The book begins thus : *Long time unto your Holiness, my venerable fellow-bishop Paulinus.*

1. LONG time, my venerable fellow-bishop Paulinus, have I been thy Holiness's debtor for an answer; even since thou wrotest to me by them of the household[2] of our most religious daughter Flora, asking of me whether it profit any man after death that his body is buried at the memorial of some Saint. This, namely, had the said widow begged of thee for her son deceased in those parts, and thou hadst written her an answer, consoling her, and announcing to her concerning the body of the faithful young man Cynegius, that the thing which she with motherly and pious affection desired was done, to wit, by placing it in the basilica of most blessed Felix the Confessor. Upon which occasion it came to pass, that by the same bearers of thy letter thou didst write also to me, raising the like question, and craving that I would answer what I thought of this matter, at the same time not forbearing to say what are thine own sentiments. For thou sayest that to thy thinking these be no empty motions of religious and faithful minds, which take this care for their deceased friends. Thou addest, moreover, that it can-

not be void of effect[3] that the whole Church is wont to supplicate for the departed: so that hence it may be further conjectured that it doth profit a person after death, if by the faith of his friends for the interment of his body such a spot be provided wherein may be apparent the aid, likewise in this way sought, of the Saints.

2. But this being the case, how to this opinion that should not be contrary which the Apostle says, " For we shall all stand before the judgment-seat of Christ, that each may receive according to the things he hath done by the body,[4] whether good or bad;"[5] this, thou signifiest, thou dost not well see. For this apostolic sentence doth before death admonish to be done, that which may profit after death; not then, first, when there is to be now a receiving of that which a person shall have done before death. True, but this question is thus solved, namely, that there is a certain kind of life by which is acquired, while one lives in this body, that it should be possible for these things to be of some help to the departed; and, consequently, it is " according to the things done by the body," that they are aided by the things which shall, after they have left the body, be religiously done on their behalf. For there are whom these things aid nothing at all, namely, when

---

[1] The date may be conjectured from the order of the *Retractations*, where this book is mentioned next after the *Enchiridion aa Laurentium*, which was not finished earlier than A. D. 421. The first two paragraphs of this treatise will be found quoted by Augustin in his Book *On Eight Questions of Dulcitius*, Quæst. ii. 2, 3. *Ben. ed.* Paulinus, to whom it was addressed, was Bishop of Nolæ, and took great pains to honor the memory of St. Felix, who is mentioned in the beginning of it. Several poems of his on the subject are extant.

[2] *Homines.*

[3] *Vacare.*   [4] *Per corpus.*   [5] 2 Cor. v. 10.

they are done either for persons whose merits are so evil, that neither by such things are they worthy to be aided; or for persons whose merits are so good, that of such things they have no need as aids. Of the kind of life, therefore, which each hath led by the body, doth it come, that these things profit or profit not, whatever are piously done on his behalf when he has left the body. For touching merit whereby these things profit, if none have been gotten in this life, it is in vain sought after this life. So it comes to pass as well that not unmeaningly [1] doth the Church, or care of friends, bestow upon the departed whatever of religion it shall be able; as also that, nevertheless, each receiveth " according to the things which he hath done by the body, whether it be good or bad," the Lord rendering unto each according to his works. For, that this which is bestowed should be capable of profiting him after the body, this was acquired in that life which he hath led in the body.

3. Possibly thy inquiry is satisfied by this my brief reply. But what other considerations move me, to which I think meet to answer, do thou for a short space attend. In the books of the Maccabees we read of sacrifice offered for the dead.[2] Howbeit, even if it were no where at all read in the Old Scriptures, not small is the authority, which in this usage is clear, of the whole Church, namely, that in the prayers of the priest which are offered to the Lord God at His altar, the commendation of the dead hath also its place. But then, whether there be some profit accruing unto the soul of the dead from the place of its body, requires a more careful inquiry. And first, whether it make any difference in causing or increasing of misery after this life to the spirits of men if their bodies be not buried, this must be looked into, not in the light of opinion however commonly received, but rather of the holy writ of our religion. For we are not to credit that, as is read in Maro, the unburied are prohibited from navigating and crossing the infernal stream: because forsooth

> " To none is giv'n to pass the hideous banks
> And waters hoarse, ere in their meet abode
> The bones have sunk to rest." [3]

Who can incline a Christian heart to these poetical and fabulous figments, when the Lord Jesus, to the intent that under the hands of their enemies, who should have their bodies in their power, Christians might lie down without a fear, asserts that not a hair of their head shall perish, exhorting that they should not fear them which when they have killed the body have nothing more that they can do?[4] Of which in the first book "On the City of God," I have methinks enough spoken, to break the teeth in their mouths who, in imputing to Christian times the barbarous devastation, especially that which Rome has lately suffered, do cast up to us this also, that Christ did not there come to the succor of His own. To whom when it is answered that the souls of the faithful were, according to the merits of their faith, by Him taken into protection, they insult over us with talking of their corpses left unburied. All this matter, then, concerning burial I have in such words as these expounded.

4. " But " (say I) " in such a slaughter-heap of dead bodies, could they not even be buried? not this, either, doth pious faith too greatly dread, holding that which is foretold that not even consuming beasts will be an hindrance to the rising again of bodies of which not a hair of the head shall perish.[5] Nor in any wise would Truth say, " Fear not them which kill the body, but cannot kill the soul;" if it could at all hinder the life to come whatever enemies might choose to do with the bodies of the slain. Unless haply any is so absurd as to contend that they ought not to be feared before death, lest they kill the body, but ought to be feared after death, lest, having killed the body, they suffer it not to be buried. Is that then false which Christ says, " Who kill the body, and afterwards have no more that they can do," if they have so great things that they can do on dead bodies? Far be the thought, that that should be false which Truth hath said. For the thing said is, that they do somewhat when they kill, because in the body there is feeling while it is in killing, but afterward they have nothing more that they can do because there is no feeling in the body when killed. Many bodies, then, of Christians the earth hath not covered: but none of them hath any separated from heaven and earth, the whole of which He filleth with presence of Himself, Who knoweth whence to resuscitate that which He created. It is said indeed in the Psalm, " The dead bodies of thy servants have they given for meat unto the fowls of the heaven, the flesh of thy saints unto the beasts of the earth: they have shed their blood like water round about Jerusalem, and there was no man to bury them:"[6] but more to heighten the cruelty of them who did these things, not to the

---

[1] *Inaniter.* [2] 2 Mac. xii. 43. [3] *Æneid* vi. 327, 328.

[4] Matt. x. 28.
[5] Luke xxi. 18 ; xii. 4-7; Matt. x. 28-30.
[6] Ps. lxxix. 2, 3.

infelicity of them who suffered them. For, however, in sight of men these things may seem hard and dire, yet "precious in the sight of the Lord is the death of His saints."[1] So, then, all these things, care of funeral, bestowal in sepulture, pomp of obsequies, are more for comfort of the living, than for help to the dead. If it at all profit the ungodly to have costly sepulture, it shall harm the godly to have vile sepulture or none. Right handsome obsequies in sight of men did that rich man who was clad in purple receive of the crowd of his housefolk; but far more handsome did that poor man who was full of sores obtain of the ministry of Angels; who bore him not out into a marble tomb, but into Abraham's bosom bore him on high.[2] All this they laugh at, against whom we have undertaken to defend the City of God: but for all that their own philosophers, even, held care of sepulture in contempt; and often whole armies, while dying for their earthly country, cared not where they should after lie, or to what beasts they should become meat; and the poets had leave to say of this matter with applause

> "though all unurn'd he lie,
> His cov'ring is the overarching sky."[3]

How much less ought they to make a vaunting about unburied bodies of Christians, to whom the flesh itself with all its members, re-fashioned, not only from the earth, but even from the other elements, yea, from their most secret windings, whereinto these evanished corpses have retired, is assured to be in an instant of time rendered back and made entire as at the first, according to His promise?

5. Yet it follows not that the bodies of the departed are to be despised and flung aside, and above all of just and faithful men, which bodies as organs and vessels to all good works their spirit hath holily used. For if a father's garment and ring, and whatever such like, is the more dear to those whom they leave behind, the greater their affection is towards their parents, in no wise are the bodies themselves to be spurned, which truly we wear in more familiar and close conjunction than any of our putting on. For these pertain not to ornament or aid which is applied from without, but to the very nature of man. Whence also the funerals of the just men of old were with dutiful piety cared for, and their obsequies celebrated, and sepulture provided:[4] and themselves while living did touching

burial or even translation of their bodies give charge to their sons. Tobias also, to have by burying of the dead obtained favor with God, is by witness of an Angel commended.[5] The Lord Himself also, about to rise on the third day, both preaches, and commends to be preached, the good work of a religious woman, that she poured out a precious ointment over His limbs, and did it for His burial:[6] and they are with praise commemorated in the Gospel, who having received His Body from the cross did carefully and with reverend honor see it wound and laid in the sepulchre.[7] These authorities however do not put us upon thinking that there is in dead bodies any feeling; but rather, that the Providence of God (Who is moreover pleased with such offices of piety) doth charge itself with the bodies also of the dead, this they betoken, to the intent our faith of resurrection might be stayed up thereby. Where also is wholesomely learned, how great may be the reward for alms which we do unto the living and feeling, if not even that be lost before God, whatever of duty and of diligence is paid to the lifeless members of men. There are indeed also other things, which in speaking of the bestowal or removal of their bodies the holy Patriarchs willed to be understood as spoken by the prophetic Spirit: but this is not the place to treat thoroughly of these things, seeing that sufficeth which we have said. But if the lack of those things which are necessary for sustentation of the living, as food and clothing, however heavy affliction attend the lacking, do not break in good men the manly courage of bearing and enduring, nor eradicate piety from the mind, but by exercising make it more fruitful; how much more doth lack of those things which are wont to be applied for care of funerals and bestowal of bodies of the departed, not make them wretched, now that in the hidden abodes of the pious they are at rest! And therefore, when these things have to dead bodies of Christians in that devastation of the great City or of other towns also been lacking, there is neither fault of the living, who could not afford these things, nor pain of the dead who could not feel the same.[8] This is my opinion concerning the ground and reason of sepulture. Which I have therefore from another book of mine transferred to this, because it was easier to rehearse this, than to express the same matter in another way.

6. If this be true, doubtless also the providing for the interment of bodies a place at

---

[1] Ps. cxvi. 15.　　　　[2] Luke xvi. 19-22.
[3] Lucan vii. 819, speaking of the slain in the battle of Pharsalia, whose bodies Cæsar forbad to burn or inter.
[4] Gen. xxiii.; xxv. 9, 10; xlvii. 30.

[5] Tobit ii. 7; xii. 12.　　[6] Matt. xxvi. 7-13.　　[7] John xix. 38, 39.
[8] *On the City of God*, book i. chap. xii. 13. Vol. ii. p. 10.

the Memorials of Saints, is a mark of a good human affection towards the remains of one's friends: since if there be religion in the burying, there cannot but be religion in taking thought where the burying shall be.   But while it is desirable there should be such like solaces of survivors, for the showing forth of their pious mind towards their beloved, I do not see what helps they be to the dead save in this way: that upon recollection of the place in which are deposited the bodies of those whom they love, they should by prayer commend them to those same Saints, who have as patrons taken them into their charge to aid them before the Lord.   Which indeed they would be still able to do, even though they were not able to inter them in such places.   But then the only reason why the name Memorials or Monuments is given to those sepulchres of the dead which become specially distinguished, is that they recall to memory, and by putting in mind cause us to think of, them who by death are withdrawn from the eyes of the living, that they may not by forgetfulness be also withdrawn from men's hearts.   For both the term Memorial [1] most plainly shews this, and Monument is so named from monishing, that is, putting in mind.   For which reason the Greeks also call that μνημεῖον which we call a Memorial or Monument: because in their tongue the memory itself, by which we remember, is called μνήμη.   When therefore the mind recollects where the body of a very dear friend lies buried, and thereupon there occurs to the thoughts a place rendered venerable by the name of a Martyr, to that same Martyr doth it commend the soul in affection of heartfelt recollection [2] and prayer.   And when this affection is exhibited to the departed by faithful men who were most dear to them, there is no doubt that it profits them who while living in the body merited that such things should profit them after this life.   But even if some necessity should through absence of all facility not allow bodies to be interred, or in such places interred, yet should there be no pretermitting of supplications for the spirits of the dead: which supplications, that they should be made for all in Christian and catholic fellowship departed, even without mentioning of their names, under a general commemoration, the Church hath charged herself withal; to the intent that they which lack, for these offices, parents or sons or whatever kindred or friends, may have the same afforded unto them by the one pious mother which is common to all.   But

if there were lack of these supplications, which are made with right faith and piety for the dead, I account that it should not a whit profit their spirits, howsoever in holy places the lifeless bodies should be deposited.

7. When therefore the faithful mother of a faithful son departed desired to have his body deposited in the basilica of a Martyr, forasmuch as she believed that his soul would be aided by the merits of the Martyr, the very believing of this was a sort of supplication, and this profited, if aught profited. And in that she recurs in her thoughts to this same sepulchre, and in her prayers more and more commends her son, the spirit of the departed is aided, not by the place of its dead body, but by that which springs from memory of the place, the living affection of the mother.   For at once the thought, who is commended and to whom, doth touch, and that with no unprofitable emotion, the religious mind of her who prays.   For also in prayer to God,[3] men do with the members of their bodies that which becometh suppliants, when they bend their knees, when they stretch forth their hands, or even prostrate themselves on the ground, and whatever else they visibly do, albeit their invisible will and heart's intention be known unto God, and He needs not these tokens that any man's mind should be opened unto Him: only hereby one more excites himself to pray and groan more humbly and more fervently.   And I know not how it is, that, while these motions of the body cannot be made but by a motion of the mind preceding, yet by the same being outwardly in visible sort made, that inward invisible one which made them is increased: and thereby the heart's affection which preceded that they might be made, groweth because they are made.   But still if any be in that way held, or even bound, that he is not able to do these things with his limbs, it does not follow that the inner man does not pray, and before the eyes of God in its most secret chamber, where it hath compunction, cast itself on the ground.   So likewise, while it makes very much difference, where a person deposits the body of his dead, while he supplicates for his spirit unto God, because both the affection preceding chose a spot which was holy, and after the body is there deposited the recalling to mind of that holy spot renews and increases the affection which had preceded; yet, though he may not be able in that place which his religious mind did choose to lay in the ground him whom he loves, in no wise ought he to cease from

---

[1] *Memoria.*   [2] *Recordationis.*   [3] *Orantes.*

necessary supplications in commending of the same. For wheresoever the flesh of the departed may lie or not lie, the spirit requires rest and must get it: for the spirit in its departing from thence took with it the consciousness without which it could make no odds how one exists, whether in a good estate or a bad: and it does not look for aiding of its life from that flesh to which it did itself afford the life which it withdrew in its departing, and is to render back in its returning; since not flesh to spirit, but spirit unto flesh procureth merit even of very resurrection, whether it be unto punishment or unto glory that it is to come to life again.

8. We read in the Ecclesiastical History which Eusebius wrote in Greek, and Ruffinus turned into the Latin tongue, of Martyr's bodies in Gaul exposed to dogs, and how the leavings of those dogs and bones of the dead were, even to uttermost consumption, by fire burned up; and the ashes of the same scattered on the river Rhone, lest any thing should be left for any sort whatever of memorial.[1] Which thing must be believed to have been to no other end divinely permitted, but that Christians should learn in confessing Christ, while they despise this life, much more to despise sepulture. For this thing, which with savage rage was done to the bodies of Martyrs, if it could any whit hurt them, to impair the blessed resting of their most victorious spirits, would assuredly not have been suffered to be done. In very deed therefore it was declared, that the Lord in saying, "Fear not them which kill the body, and afterward have no more that they can do,"[2] did not mean that He would not permit them to do any thing to the bodies of His followers when dead; but that whatever they might be permitted to do, nothing should be done that could lessen the Christian felicity of the departed, nothing thereof reach to their consciousness while yet living after death; nothing avail to the detriment, no, not even of the bodies themselves, to diminish aught of their integrity when they should rise again.

9. And yet, by reason of that affection of the human heart, whereby "no man ever hateth his own flesh,"[3] if men have reason to know that after their death their bodies will lack any thing which in each man's nation or country the wonted order of sepulture demandeth, it makes them sorrowful as men; and that which after death reacheth not unto them,

they do before death fear for their bodies: so that we find in the Books of Kings, God by one prophet threatening another prophet who had transgressed His word, that his carcase should not be brought into the sepulchre of his fathers. Which the Scripture hath on this wise: "Thus saith the Lord, Because thou hast been disobedient to the mouth of the Lord, and hast not kept the charge which the Lord thy God commanded thee, and hast returned and eaten bread and drunk water in the place in which He commanded thee not to eat bread, nor drink water, thy carcase shall not be brought into the sepulchre of thy fathers."[4] Now if in considering what account is to be made of this punishment, we go by the Gospel, where we have learned that after the slaying of the body there is no cause to fear lest the lifeless members should suffer any thing, it is not even to be called a punishment. But if we consider a man's human affection towards his own flesh, it was possible for him to be frightened or saddened, while living, by that of which he would have no sense when dead: and this was a punishment, because the mind was pained by that thing about to happen to its body, howsoever when it did happen it would feel no pain. To this intent, namely, it pleased the Lord to punish His servant, who not of his own contumacy had spurned to fulfill His command, but by deceit of another's falsehood thought himself to be obeying when he obeyed not. For it is not to be thought that he was killed by the teeth of the beast as one whose soul should be thence snatched away to the torments of hell: seeing that over his very body the same lion which had killed it did keep watch, while moreover the beast on which he rode was left unhurt, and along with that fierce beast did with intrepid presence stand there beside his master's corpse. By which marvellous sign it appeareth, that the man of God was, say rather, checked temporally even unto death, than punished after death. Of which matter, the Apostle when on account of certain offenses he had mentioned the sicknesses and deaths of many, says, "For if we would judge ourselves, we should not be judged of the Lord. But when we are judged we are chastened of the Lord, that we may not be condemned with the world."[5] That Prophet, truly, the very man who had beguiled him, did with much respect bury in his own tomb, and took order for his own burying beside his bones: in hope that thereby his own bones might be spared, when, according to the prophecy of that man

---

[1] Eusebius, H. E. book v. chap. i. relates, that the bodies of these martyrs of Lyons lay exposed in the open air for six days successively, and were then burned and cast into the Rhone. —Ben. ed.

[2] Matt. x. 28; Luke xii. 4.   [3] Eph. v. 29.

[4] 1 Kings xiii. 21, 22.   [5] 1 Cor. xi. 31, 32.   [See R. V.]

of God, Josiah king of Judah did in that land disinter the bones of many dead, and with the same bones defile the sacrilegious altars which had been set up for the graven images. For he spared that tomb in which lay the prophet who more than three hundred years before predicted those things, and for his sake neither was the sepulture of him who had seduced him violated. By that affection, namely, which causes that no man ever hateth his own flesh, this man had taken forethought for his carcase, who had slain with a lie his own soul. By reason then of this, the natural love which every man hath for his own flesh, it was both to the one a punishment to learn that he should not be in the sepulchre of his fathers, and to the other a care to take order beforehand that his own bones should be spared, if he should lie beside him whose sepulchre no man should violate.

10. This affection the Martyrs of Christ contending for the truth did overcome: and it is no marvel that they despised that whereof they should, when death was overpast, have no feeling, when they could not by those tortures, which while alive they did feel, be overcome. God was able, no doubt, (even as He permitted not the lion when it had slain the Prophet, to touch his body further, and of a slayer made it to be a keeper): He was able, I say, to have kept the slain bodies of His own from the dogs to which they had been flung; He was able in innumerable ways to have deterred the rage of the men themselves, that to burn the carcases, to scatter the ashes, they should not dare: but it was fit that this experience also should not be lacking to manifold variety of temptations, lest the fortitude of confession which would not for the saving of the life of the body give way to the savageness of persecution, should be tremblingly anxious for the honor of a sepulchre: in a word, lest faith of resurrection should dread the consuming of the body. It was fit then, that even these things should be permitted, in order that, even after these examples of so great horror, the Martyrs, fervent in confession of Christ, should become witnesses of this truth also, in which they had learned that they by whom their bodies should be slain had after that no more that they could do.[1] Because, whatever they should do to dead bodies, they would after all do nothing, seeing that in flesh devoid of all life, neither was it possible for him to feel aught who had thence departed, nor for Him to lose aught thereof, Who created the same. But while these things were doing to the bodies of the slain, albeit the Martyrs, not frightened by them, did with great fortitude suffer, yet among the brethren was there exceeding sorrow, because there was given them no means of paying the last honors to the remains of the Saints, neither secretly to withdraw any part thereof, (as the same history testifies,) did the watchings of cruel sentinels permit. So, while those which had been slain, in the tearing asunder of their limbs, in the burning up of their bones, in the dispersion of their ashes, could feel no misery; yet these who had nothing of them that they could bury, did suffer torture of exceeding grief in pitying them; because what those did in no sort feel, these in some sort did feel for them, and where was henceforth for those no more suffering, yet these did in woful compassion suffer for them.

11. In regard to that woful compassion which I have mentioned, are those praised, and by king David blessed, who to the dry bones of Saul and Jonathan afforded mercy of sepulture.[2] But yet what mercy is that, which is afforded to them that have feeling of nothing? Or haply is this to be challenged back to that conceit of an infernal river which men unburied were not able to pass over? Far be this from the faith of Christians: else hath it gone most ill with so great a multitude of Martyrs, for whom there could be no burying of their bodies, and Truth did cheat them when It said, "Fear not them which kill the body, and after that have no more that they can do,"[3] if these have been able to do to them so great evils, by which they were hindered to pass over to the places which they longed for. But, because this without all doubt is most false, and it neither any whit hurts the faithful to have their bodies denied sepulture, nor any whit the giving of sepulture unto infidels advantageth them; why then are those who buried Saul and his son said to have done mercy, and for this are blessed by that godly king, but because it is a good affection with which the hearts of the pitiful are touched, when they grieve for that in the dead bodies of other men, which, by that affection through which no man ever hateth his own flesh, they would not have done after their own death to their own bodies; and what they would have done by them when they shall have no more feeling, that they take care to do by others now having no feeling while themselves have yet feeling?

12. Stories are told of certain appearances or visions,[4] which may seem to bring into

---

[1] Matt. x. 28.

[2] 2 Sam. ii. 5.   [3] Luke xii. 4.   [4] *Visa.*

this discussion a question which should not be slighted. It is said, namely, that dead men have at times either in dreams or in some other way appeared to the living who knew not where their bodies lay unburied, and have pointed out to them the place, and admonished that the sepulture which was lacking should be afforded them. These things if we shall answer to be false, we shall be thought impudently to contradict the writings of certain faithful men, and the senses of them who assure us that such things have happened to themselves. But it is to be answered, that it does not follow that we are to account the dead to have sense of these things, because they appear in dreams to say or indicate or ask this. For living men do also appear ofttimes to the living as they sleep, while they themselves know not that they do appear; and they are told by them, what they dreamed, namely, that in their dream the speakers saw them doing or saying something. Then if it ·may be that a person in a dream should see me indicating to him something that has happened or even foretelling something about to happen, while I am perfectly unwitting of the thing and altogether regardless not only what he dreams, but whether he is awake while I am asleep, or he asleep while I am awake, or whether at one and the same time we are both awake or asleep, at what time he has the dream in which he sees me: what marvel if the dead be unconscious and insensible of these things, and, for all that, are seen by the living in their dreams, and say something which those on awaking find to be true? By angelical operations, then, I should think it is effected, whether permitted from above, or commanded, that they seem in dreams to say something about burying of their bodies, when they whose the bodies are are utterly unconscious of it. Now this is sometimes serviceably done; whether for some sort of solace to the survivors, to whom pertain those dead whose likenesses[1] appear to them as they dream; or whether that by these admonitions the human race may be made to have regard to humanity of sepulture, which, allow that it be no help to the departed, yet is there culpable irreligiousness in slighting of it. Sometimes however, by fallacious visions,[2] men are cast into great errors, who deserve to suffer this. As, if one should see in a dream, what Æneas by poetic falsity is told to have seen in the world beneath: and there should appear to him the likeness of some unburied man, which should speak such

words as Palinurus is said to have spoken to him; and when he awakes, he should find the body in that place where he heard say while dreaming, that it lay unburied, and was admonished and asked to bury it when found; and because he finds this to be true, should believe that the dead are buried on purpose that their souls may pass to places from which he dreamed that the souls of men unburied are by an infernal law prohibited: does he not, in believing all this, exceedingly swerve from the path of truth?

13. Such, however, is human infirmity, that when in a dream a person shall see a dead man, he thinks it is the soul that he sees: but when he shall in like manner dream of a living man, he has no doubt that it is not a soul nor a body, but the likeness of a man that has appeared to him: just as if it were not possible in regard of dead men, in the same sort unconscious of it, that it should not be their souls, but their likenesses that appear to the sleepers. Of a surety, when we were at Milan, we heard tell of a certain person of whom was demanded payment of a debt, with production of his deceased father's acknowledgment,[3] which debt unknown to the son the father had paid, whereupon the man began to be very sorrowful, and to marvel that his father while dying did not tell him what he owed when he also made his will. Then in this exceeding anxiousness of his, his said father appeared to him in a dream, and made known to him where was the counter[4] acknowledgment by which that acknowledgment was cancelled. Which when the young man had found and showed, he not only rebutted the wrongful claim of a false debt, but also got back his father's note[5] of hand which the father had not got back when the money was paid. Here then the soul of a man is supposed to have had care for his son, and to have come to him in his sleep, that, teaching him what he did not know, he might relieve him of a great trouble. But about the very same time as we heard this, it chanced at Carthage that the rhetorician Eulogius, who had been my disciple in that art, being (as he himself, after our return to Africa, told us the story) in course of lecturing to his disciples on Cicero's rhetorical books, as he looked over the portion of reading which he was to deliver on the following day, fell upon a certain passage, and not being able to understand it, was scarce able to sleep for the trouble of his mind: in which night, as he dreamed, I expounded to him that which he did not understand; nay,

---

[1] *Imagines.*   [2] *Visis.*   [3] *Cautio.*   [4] *Recautum.*   [5] *Chirographum.*

35

not I, but my likeness, while I was unconscious of the thing, and far away beyond the sea, it might be, doing, or it might be dreaming, some other thing, and not in the least caring for his cares. In what way these things come about, I know not: but in what way soever they come, why do we not believe it comes in the same way for a person in a dream to see a dead man, as it comes that he sees a living man? both, no doubt, neither knowing nor caring who, or where, or when, dreams of their images.

14. Like dreams, moreover, are also some visions of persons awake, who have had their senses troubled, such as phrenetic persons, or those who are mad in any way: for they too talk to themselves just as though they were speaking to people verily present, and as well with absent as with present, whose images they perceive, whether persons living or dead. But just as they which live, are unconscious that they are seen of them and talk with them; for indeed they are not really themselves present, or themselves make speeches, but through troubled senses, these persons are wrought upon by such-like imaginary visions; just so they also who have departed this life, to persons thus affected appear as present, while they be absent, and whether any man sees them in regard of their image,[1] are themselves utterly unconscious.

15. Similar to this is also that condition when persons, with their senses more profoundedly in abeyance than is the case in sleep, are occupied with the like visions. For to them also appear images of quick and dead; but then, when they return to their senses, whatever dead they say they have seen are thought to have been verily with them: and they who hear these things pay no heed to the circumstance that there were seen in like manner the images of certain living persons, absent and unconscious. A certain man by name Curma, of the municipal town of Tullium, which is hard by Hippo, a poor member of the Curia,[2] scarcely competent to serve the office of a duumvir[3] of that place, and a mere rustic, being ill, and all his senses entranced, lay all but dead for several days: a very slight breathing in his nostrils, which on applying the hand was just felt, and barely betokened that he lived, was all that kept him from being buried for dead. Not a limb did he stir, nothing did he take in the way of sustenance, neither in the eyes nor in any other bodily sense was he sensible of any annoyance that impinged upon them. Yet he was seeing many things like as in

a dream, which, when at last after a great many days he woke up, he told that he had seen. And first, presently after he opened his eyes, Let some one go, said he, to the house of Curma the smith, and see what is doing there. And when some one had gone thither, the smith was found to have died in that moment that the other had come back to his senses, and, it might almost be said, revived from death. Then, as those who stood by eagerly listened, he told them how the other had been ordered to be had up, when he himself was dismissed; and that he had heard it said in that place from which he had returned, that it was not Curma of the Curia, but Curma the smith who had been ordered to be fetched to that place of the dead. Well, in these dream-like visions of his, among those deceased persons whom he saw handled according to the diversity of their merits, he recognized also some whom he had known when alive. That they were the very persons themselves I might perchance have believed, had he not in the course of this seeming dream of his seen also some who are alive even to this present time, namely, some clerks of his district, by whose presbyter there he was told to be baptized at Hippo by me, which thing he said had also taken place. So then he had seen a presbyter, clerks, myself, persons, to wit, not yet dead, in this vision in which he afterwards also saw dead persons. Why may he not be thought to have seen these last in the same way as he saw us? that is, both the one sort, and the other, absent and unconscious, and consequently not the persons themselves, but similitudes of them just as of the places? He saw, namely, both a plot of ground where was that presbyter with the clerks, and Hippo where he was by me seemingly baptized: in which spots assuredly he was not, when he seemed to himself to be there. For what was at that time going on there, he knew not: which, without doubt, he would have known if he had verily been there. The sights beheld, therefore, were those which are not presented in the things themselves as they are, but shadowed forth in a sort of images of the things. In fine, after much that he saw, he narrated how he had, moreover, been led into Paradise, and how it was there said to him, when he was thence dismissed to return to his own family, "Go, be baptized, if thou wilt be in this place of the blessed." Thereupon, being admonished to be baptized by me, he said it was done already. He who was talking with him replied, "Go, be truly baptized; for that thou didst but see in the vision." After this he re-

---

[1] *Imaginaliter.*   [2] *Curialis.*   [3] *Duumviralitius.*

covered, went his way to Hippo. Easter was now approaching, he gave his name among the other Competents, alike with very many unknown to us; nor did he care to make known the vision to me or to any of our people. He was baptized, at the close of the holy days he returned to his own place. After the space of two years or more, I learned the whole matter; first, through a certain friend of mine and his at my own table, while we were talking about some such matters: then I took it up, and made the man in his own person tell me the story, in the presence of some honest townsmen of his attesting the same, both concerning his marvellous illness, how he lay all but dead for many days, and about that other Curma the smith, what I have mentioned above, and about all these matters; which, while he was telling me, they recalled to mind, and assured me, that they had also at that time heard them from his lips. Wherefore, just as he saw his own baptism, and myself, and Hippo, and the basilica, and the baptistery, not in the very realities, but in a sort of similitudes of the things; and so likewise certain other living persons, without consciousness on the part of the same living persons: then why not just so those dead persons also, without consciousness on the part of the same dead persons?

16. Why should we not believe these to be angelic operations through dispensation of the providence of God, Who maketh good use of both good things and evil, according to the unsearchable depth of His judgments? whether thereby the minds of mortals be instructed, or whether deceived; whether consoled, or whether terrified: according as unto each one there is to be either a showing of mercy, or a taking of vengeance, by Him to Whom, not without a meaning, the Church doth sing "of mercy and of judgment."[1] Let each, as it shall please him, take what I say. If the souls of the dead took part in the affairs of the living, and if it were their very selves that, when we see them, speak to us in sleep; to say nothing of others, there is my own self, whom my pious mother would no night fail to visit, that mother who by land and sea followed me that she might live with me. Far be the thought that she should, by a life more happy, have been made cruel, to that degree that when any thing vexes my heart she should not even console in his sadness the son whom she loved with an only love, whom she never wished to see mournful. But assuredly that which the sacred Psalm sings in our ears, is true; "Because my father and my mother have forsaken me, but the Lord hath taken me up."[2] Then if our parents have forsaken us, how take they part in our cares and affairs? But if parents do not, who else are there of the dead who should know what we are doing, or what we suffer? Isaiah the Prophet says, "For Thou art our Father: because Abraham hath not known us, and Israel is not cognizant of us."[3] If so great Patriarchs were ignorant what was doing towards the People of them begotten, they to whom, believing God, the People itself to spring from their stock was promised; how are the dead mixed up with affairs and doings of the living, either for cognizance or help? How say we that those were favored who deceased ere the evils came which followed hard upon the decease, if also after death they feel whatever things befall in the calamitousness of human life? Or haply do we err in saying this, and in accounting them to be quietly at rest whom the unquiet life of the living makes solicitous? What then is that which to the most godly king Josias God promised as a great benefit, that he should first die, that he might not see the evils which He threatened should come to that place and People? Which words of god are these: "Thus saith the Lord God of Israel: concerning My words which thou hast heard, and didst fear before My face when thou didst hear what I have spoken concerning this place and them which dwell therein, that it should be forsaken and under a curse; and hast rent thy garments, and wept before Me, and I have heard thee, saith the Lord of Sabaoth: not so; behold, I will add thee unto thy fathers, and thou shalt be added unto them in peace; and thine eyes shall not see all the evils which I am bringing upon this place and upon them that dwell therein."[4] He, frightened by God's comminations, had wept, and rent his garments, and is made, by hastening on of his death, to be without care of all future evils, because he should so rest in peace, that all those things he should not see. There then are the spirits of the departed, where they see not whatever things are doing, or events happening, in this life to men. Then how do they see their own graves, or their own bodies, whether they lie cast away, or buried? How do they take part in the misery of the living, when they are either suffering their own evils, if they have contracted such merits; or do rest in peace, as was promised to this Josiah, where they undergo no evils, either by suffering themselves, or by compassionate suffering with others, freed from all evils which by suffer-

ing themselves or with others while they lived here they did undergo?

17. Some man may say: "If there be not in the dead any care for the living, how is it that the rich man, who was tormented in hell, asked father Abraham to send Lazarus to his five brothers not as yet dead, and to take course with them, that they should not come themselves also into the same place of torments?"[1] But does it follow, that because the rich man said this, he knew what his brethren were doing, or what they were suffering at that time? Just in that same way had he care for the living, albeit what they were doing he wist not at all, as we have care for the dead, albeit what they do we confessedly wot not. For if we cared not for the dead, we should not, as we do, supplicate God on their behalf. In fine, Abraham did not send Lazarus, and also answered, that they have here Moses and the Prophets, whom they ought to hear that they might not come to those torments. Where again it occurs to ask, how it was that what was doing here, father Abraham himself wist not, while he knew that Moses and the Prophets are here, that is, their books, by obeying which men should escape the torments of hell: and knew, in short, that rich man to have lived in delights, but the poor man Lazarus to have lived in labors and sorrows? For this also he says to him; "Son, remember that thou in thy lifetime hast received good things, but Lazarus evil things." He knew then these things which had taken place of course among the living, not among the dead. True, but it may be that, not while the things were doing in their lifetime, but after their death, he learned these things, by information of Lazarus: that it be not false which the Prophet saith, "Abraham hath not known us."[2]

18. So then we must confess that the dead indeed do not know what is doing here, but while it is in doing here: afterwards, however, they hear it from those who from hence go to them at their death; not indeed every thing, but what things those are allowed to make known who are suffered also to remember these things; and which it is meet for those to hear, whom they inform of the same. It may be also, that from the Angels, who are present in the things which are doing here, the dead do hear somewhat, which for each one of them to hear He judgeth right to Whom all things are subject. For were there not Angels, who could be present in places both of quick and dead, the Lord Jesus had not said, "It came to pass

also that the poor man died, and was carried by the angels into Abraham's bosom."[3] Therefore, now here, now there, were they able to be, who from hence bore thither whom God willed. It may be also, that the spirits of the dead do learn some things which are doing here, what things it is necessary that they should know, and what persons it is necessary should know the same, not only things past or present, but even future, by the Spirit of God revealing them: like as not all men, but the Prophets while they lived here did know, nor even they all things, but only what things to be revealed to them the providence of God judged meet. Moreover, that some from the dead are sent to the living, as, on the other hand, Paul from the living was rapt into Paradise, divine Scripture doth testify.[4] For Samuel the Prophet, appearing to Saul when living, predicted even what should befall the king:[5] although some think it was not Samuel himself, that could have been by magical arts evoked, but that some spirit, meet for so evil works, did figure his semblance:[6] though the book Ecclesiasticus, which Jesus, son of Sirach, is reputed to have written, and which on account of some resemblance of style is pronounced to be Solomon's,[7] contains in the praise of the Fathers, that Samuel even when dead did prophesy. But if this book be spoken against from the canon of the Hebrews,[8] (because it is not contained therein,) what shall we say of Moses, whom certainly we read both in Deuteronomy to have died,[9] and in the Gospel to have, together with Elias who died not, appeared unto the living?[10]

19. Hence too is solved that question, how is it that the Martyrs, by the very benefits which are given to them that pray, indicate that they take an interest in the affairs of men, if the dead know not what the quick are doing. For not only by effects of benefits, but in the very beholding of men, it is certain,[11] that the Confessor Felix (whose denizenship among you thou piously lovest) appeared when the barbarians were attacking Nola, as we have heard not by uncertain rumors, but by sure witnesses. But such things are of God exhibited, far otherwise than as the usual order hath itself, unto each kind of creatures apportioned. For it does not follow because water was, when it pleased the Lord, in a moment changed into wine, that we are not to regard the worth and efficacy of water in

---

[1] Luke xvi. 24-29.   [2] Is. lxiii. 16.

[3] Luke xvi. 22.   [4] 2 Cor. xii. 4.   [5] 1 Sam. xxviii. 11-19.
[6] *Quæst. ad Simplicianum, lib.* ii. *qu.* 4.
[7] *Retract.* ii. 4, and "*On Christian Doctrine*," book ii. chap. viii., vol. ii. p. 539. *Ben. ed.*
[8] Ecclus. xlvi. 20.   [9] Deut. xxxiv. 5.
[10] Matt. xvii. 3.   [11] *Inquilinatum.*

the proper order of the elements, as distinct from the rarity, or rather singularity, of that divine work: nor because Lazarus rose again, therefore that every dead man rises when he will; or that a lifeless man is raised up by a living, in the same way as a sleeping man by one who is awake. Other be the limits of human things, other the signs of divine virtues: other they be that are naturally, other that be miraculously done: albeit both unto nature God is present that it may be, and unto miracles nature is not lacking. We are not to think then, that to be interested in the affairs of the living is in the power of any departed who please, only because to some men's healing or help the Martyrs be present: but rather we are to understand that it must needs be by a Divine power that the Martyrs are interested in affairs of the living, from the very fact that for the departed to be by their proper nature interested in affairs of the living is impossible.

20. Howbeit it is a question which surpasses the strength of my understanding, after what manner the Martyrs aid them who by them, it is certain, are helped; whether themselves by themselves be present at the same time in so different places, and by so great distance lying apart one from another, either where their Memorials are, or beside their Memorials, wheresoever they are felt to be present: or whether, while they themselves, in a place congruous with their merits, are removed from all converse with mortals, and yet do in a general sort pray for the needs of their suppliants, (like as we pray for the dead, to whom however we are not present, nor know where they be or what they be doing,) God Almighty, Who is every where present, neither bounded in [1] with us nor remote from us, hearing and granting the Martyrs' prayers, doth by angelic ministries every where diffused afford to men those solaces, to whom in the misery of this life He seeth meet to afford the same, and, touching His Martyrs, doth where He will, when He will, how He will, and chiefest through their Memorials, because this He knoweth to be expedient for us unto edifying of the faith of Christ for Whose confession they suffered, by marvellous and ineffable power and goodness cause their merits to be had in honor. A matter is this, too high that I should have power to attain unto it, too abstruse that I should be able to search it out; and therefore which of these two be the case, or whether perchance both one and the other be the case, that sometimes these things be done by very

presence of the Martyrs, sometimes by Angels taking upon them the person of the Martyrs, I dare not define; rather would I seek this at them who know it. For it is not to be thought that no man knows these things: (not indeed he who thinks he knows, and knows not,) for there be gifts of God, Who bestows on these some one, on those some other, according to the Apostle who says, that "to each one is given the manifestation of the Spirit to profit withal; to one [2] indeed," saith he, "is given by the Spirit discourse of wisdom; to another[2] discourse of science according to the same Spirit; while to another [3] faith in the same Spirit; to another [3] the gift of healings in one Spirit; to one [2] workings of miracles; to one[2] prophecy; to one [2] discerning of spirits; to one[2] kinds of tongues; to one[2] interpretation of discourses. But all these worketh one and the same spirit, dividing to every man severally as He will." [4] Of all these spiritual gifts, which the Apostle hath rehearsed, to whomsoever is given discerning of spirits, the same knoweth these things as they are meet to be known.

21. Such, we may believe, was that John the Monk, whom the elder Theodosius, the Emperor, consulted concerning the issue of the civil war: seeing he had also the gift of prophecy. For that not each several person has a several one of those gifts, but that one man may have more gifts than one, I make no question. This John, then, when once a certain most religious woman desired to see him, and to obtain this did through her husband make vehement entreaty, refused indeed this request because he had never allowed this to women, but "Go," said he, "tell thy wife, she shall see me this night, but in her sleep." And so it came to pass: and he gave her advice, whatever was meet to be given to a wedded believing woman. And she, on her awaking, made known to her husband that she had seen a man of God, such as he knew him to be, and what she had been told by him. The person who learned this from them, reported it to me, a grave man and a noble, and most worthy to be believed. But if I myself had seen that holy monk, because (it is said) he was most patient in hearing questions and most wise in answering, I would have sought of him, as touching our question, whether he himself came to that woman in sleep, that is to say, his spirit in the form of his body, just as we dream that we see ourselves in the form of our own body; or whether, while he himself was doing something else, or, if asleep, was dreaming of

---

[1] *Concretus*

[2] *Alii*, ἄλλῳ. [3] *Alteri*, ἑτέρῳ. [4] 1 Cor. xii. 7–10.

something else, it was either by an Angel or in some other way that such vision took place in the woman's dream; and that it would so be, as he promised, he himself foreknew by the Spirit of prophecy revealing the same. For if he was himself present to her in her dream, of course it was by miraculous grace that he was enabled so to do, not by nature; and by God's gift, not by faculty of his own. But if, while he was doing some other thing or sleeping and occupied with other sights, the woman saw him in her sleep, then doubtless some such thing took place, as that is which we read in the Acts of the Apostles, where the Lord Jesus speaks to Ananias concerning Saul,[1] and informs him that Saul has seen Ananias coming unto him, while Ananias himself wist not of it. The man of God would make answer to me of these things as the case might be, and then about the Martyrs I should go on to ask of him, whether they be themselves present in dreams, or in whatever other way to those who see them, in what shape they will; and above all when the demons in men confess themselves tormented by the Martyrs, and ask them to spare them; or whether these things be wrought through angelic powers, to the honor and commendation of the Saints for men's profit, while those are in supreme rest, and wholly free for other far better sights, apart from us, and praying for us. For it chanced at Milan at (the tomb of) the holy Martyrs Protasius and Gervasius, that Ambrose the bishop, at that time living, being expressly named, in like manner as were the dead whose names they were rehearsing, the demons confessed him and besought him to spare them, he being the while otherwise engaged, and when this was taking place, altogether unwitting of it. Or whether indeed these things are wrought, somewhiles by very presence of the Martyrs, otherwhiles by that of Angels; and whether it be possible, or by what tokens possible, for us to discriminate these two cases; or whether to perceive and to judge of these things none be able, but he which hath that gift through God's Spirit, " dividing unto every man severally as He will:"[2] the same John, methinks, would discourse to me of all these matters, as I should wish; that either by his teaching I might learn, and what I should be told should know to be true and certain; or I should believe what I knew not, upon his telling me what things he knew. But if peradventure he should make answer out of holy Scripture, and say, "Things higher than thou, seek thou not; and things stronger than thou,

search thou not; but what the Lord hath commanded thee, of those things bethink thee alway:"[3] this also I should thankfully accept. For it is no small gain if, when any things are obscure and uncertain to us, and we not able to comprehend them, it be at any rate clear and certain that we are not to seek them; and what thing each one wishes to learn, accounting it to be profitable that he should know it, he should learn that it is no harm that he know it not.

22. Which things being so, let us not think that to the dead for whom we have a care, any thing reaches save what by sacrifices either of the altar, or of prayers, or of alms, we solemnly supplicate: although not to all for whom they are done be they profitable, but to them only by whom while they live it is obtained that they should be profitable. But forasmuch as we discern not who these be, it is meet to do them for all regenerate persons, that none of them may be passed by to whom these benefits may and ought to reach. For better it is that these things shall be superfluously done to them whom they neither hinder nor help, than lacking to them whom they help. More diligently however doth each man these things for his own near and dear friends, in order that they may be likewise done unto him by his. But as for the burying of the body, whatever is bestowed on that, is no aid of salvation, but an office of humanity, according to that affection by which "no man ever hateth his own flesh."[4] Whence it is fitting that he take[5] what care he is able for the flesh of his neighbor, when he is gone that bare[6] it. And if they do these things who believe not the resurrection of the flesh, how much more are they beholden to do the same who do believe; that so, an office of this kind bestowed upon a body, dead but yet to rise again and to remain to eternity, may also be in some sort a testimony of the same faith? But, that a person is buried at the memorials of the Martyrs, this, I think, so far profits the departed, that while commending him also to the Martyrs' patronage, the affection of supplication on his behalf is increased.

23. Here, to the things thou hast thought meet to inquire of me, thou hast such reply as I have been able to render: which if it be more than enough prolix, thou must excuse this, for it was done through love of holding longer talk with thee. For this book, then, how thy charity shall receive it, let me, I pray thee, know by a second letter: though doubt-

---

[1] Acts ix. 12. [2] 1 Cor. xii. 11.

[3] Ecclus. iii. 22. [4] Eph. v. 29.
[5] *Gerat.* [6] *Gerebat.*

less it will be more welcome for its bearer's sake, to wit our brother and fellow-presbyter Candidianus, whom, having been by thy letter made acquainted with him, I have welcomed with all my heart, and am loath to let him depart. For greatly in the charity of Christ hath he by his presence consoled us, and, to say truth, it was at his instance that I have done thy bidding. For with so great businesses is my heart distraught, that had not he by ever and anon putting me in mind not suffered me to forget it, assuredly to thy questioning reply of mind had not been forthcoming.

INDEXES

ON THE TRINITY

INDEX OF SUBJECTS.

ON THE TRINITY

INDEX OF TEXTS.

FIFTEEN

DOCTRINAL AND MORAL TREATISES

INDEX OF SUBJECTS.

FIFTEEN

DOCTRINAL AND MORAL TREATISES

INDEX OF TEXTS